Becoming a
Sexual Person

BECOMING A

Sexual Person

SECOND EDITION

Robert T. Francoeur

Fairleigh Dickinson University

MACMILLAN PUBLISHING COMPANY
New York
COLLIER MACMILLAN CANADA
Toronto

6—16—11

Editor: Robert Miller
Development Editor: Sharon Balbos
Production Supervisor: Linda Greenberg
Production Manager: Nick Sklitsis
Text and Cover Designer: Patrice Fodero
Cover Illustration: Timothy Foley
Photo Researcher: John Schultz
Photo Editor: Chris Migdol

This book was set in Palatino by Waldman Graphics, Inc., and printed and bound by Von Hoffmann Press, Inc.
The cover was printed by The Lehigh Press, Inc.

Macmillan Publishing Company
866 Third Avenue, New York, New York 10022

Collier Macmillan Canada, Inc.
1200 Eglinton Avenue East
Suite 200
Don Mills, Ontario M3C 3N1

LIBRARY OF CONGRESS CATALOGING-IN-PUBLICATION DATA

Francoeur, Robert T.
    Becoming a sexual person / Robert T. Francoeur. —2nd ed.
        p.   cm.
    Includes bibliographical references and index.
    ISBN 0-02-339220-7
    1. Sex instruction.   2. Sex customs—United States.   I. Title.
HQ56.F66   1991
306.7—dc20   90-36472
                CIP

Printing: 1 2 3 4 5 6 7   Year: 1 2 3 4 5 6 7

About the Author

Robert T. Francoeur has drawn on his diverse background in writing this text-book. After undergraduate work in philosophy and the liberal arts, he earned a master of science degree in genetics and embryology and a master of arts degree in theology. He taught high school biology and physics for four years before earning a doctorate in experimental embryology.

He pursued his interest in human evolution, becoming an internationally recognized expert on the evolutionary synthesis of Teilhard de Chardin. In 1970, after writing three books on human evolution, Francoeur published *Utopian Motherhood*. One of the first books to deal with the revolutionary advances in reproductive technologies and their social impact, *Utopian Motherhood* went through three editions. This led to three studies of male/female roles, marriage, and the family: *Eve's New Rib* (1972), *Hot and Cool Sex: Cultures in Conflict* (1974), and *The Future of Sexual Relations* (1974).

Francoeur has edited three editions of *Taking Sides: Clashing Views on Controversial Issues in Human Sexuality;* contributed chapters to over 60 anthologies, texts, and handbooks in English, Italian, and Spanish; and written more than 50 professional papers. Francoeur has published over 120 articles in popular magazines and is a frequent guest on television and radio shows across the United States. He is also editor-in-chief for the authoritative *A Descriptive Dictionary and Atlas of Sexology* (1990), which provides a substantial basis for the key terms defined in the glossary of this second edition of *Becoming a Sexual Person*.

In 1971, Francoeur introduced a two-semester human sexuality course at Fairleigh Dickinson University in Madison, New Jersey. As a full professor in

Fairleigh Dickinson's Department of Biological and Allied Health Sciences, he teaches human sexuality, human embryology, biomedical ethics, human genetics, and two humanities core courses. A distinguished visiting professor at a dozen universities in his career, he currently teaches in the graduate Human Sexuality Program at New York University.

Francoeur is past president of the Society for the Scientific Study of Sex (SSSS), Eastern Region, and a fellow of the same society; a past officer in the American Association of Sex Educators, Counselors, and Therapists; and a charter member of both the World Future Society and the American College of Sexologists. In 1978, he received the Annual Award of the Educational Foundation for Human Sexuality.

He has lectured on many aspects of human sexuality at over 270 colleges and universities in the United States and abroad. He has presented over 100 papers and workshops at meetings of the Society for the Scientific Study of Sex, the World Congress of Sexology, the National Council on Family Relations, the Groves Conference on Marriage and the Family, the World Future Society, the World Congress of Sociology, the American Association for the Advancement of Science, and many other professional groups.

Other books authored or edited by Robert T. Francoeur are *The World of Teilhard de Chardin* (1961); *Perspectives in Evolution* (1965); *Evolving World Converging Man* (1970); *Regeneration in Lower Vertebrates and Invertebrates* (1970); and *Biomedical Ethics: A Guide to Decision Making* (1983).

Dedicated to Anna, Nicole, and Danielle Francoeur, who
suffered patiently during the long gestation of this second
edition, and to the living memory of
David L. McManus, 1927–1981,
my first publisher and dear friend, a rare spirit and a truly
outrageous human. Often enough he threw the gauntlet to
his friends, daring us to let our humanness come to
flower. Much of the wholeness of this book is due to his
challenges and strong support over 25 years. I sincerely
hope the readers of this book are fortunate enough to
know and love a person as *outrageously* human as David L.

Preface

When the first edition of *Becoming a Sexual Person* appeared in 1982, the *SIECUS (Sex Information and Education Council of the United States) Report* compared it with two dozen college sexuality textbooks then on the market. *Becoming a Sexual Person* ranked with two other texts at the very top of this detailed analysis and rating.

To improve on the high rating and outstanding quality of the first edition, I made an unprecedented decision to recruit **70 special consultants** to work with me to update, simplify, and balance the treatment of complex and controversial issues. The outstanding readability, nonsexist approach, cross-cultural perspectives, and range of viewpoints that characterized the first edition have been enhanced with advice from the special consultants.

Although I am a biologist by professional training, *Becoming a Sexual Person* continues and expands on the balanced, interdisciplinary approach that was highly praised in the first edition. My graduate studies in biology and the humanities and my strong interest in the social sciences have always inclined me to take an interdisciplinary approach in my research and writing. The approach I take here can best be described as a **bio-psycho-socio-cultural approach.** With the help of the special consultants, colleagues who come from all different disciplines, the balance, nuances, and range of perspective are much richer in this second edition.

New in This Edition

- **A more flexible and easy to use organization of chapters.** Feedback from users of the first edition suggested reorganizing the topics into 24 chapters instead of the original 15 chapters. Instructors can arrange the sequence of topics easily to suit their particular interests and needs.

- **A more dynamic and balanced organization of chapters.**   Three chapters in Part One open the text with perspectives on American sexual customs, sexual customs in four other major cultures, and sexual values and moral development. The ten chapters in Part Two deal with personal, developmental, and health issues. Part Three contains eight chapters on the interpersonal context, including sexual attraction, intimacy, love, gender orientations, lifestyles, aging, disabilities, gender conflicts, unconventional sex, and sexual dysfunctions. Part Four focuses on the social context: sex and the law, sexual coercion, prostitution, and pornography.

- **Newly expanded and updated art,** including **full, four-color illustrations and photographs** in chapters on anatomy (Chapter 6) and sexually transmitted diseases (STDs) (Chapter 12).   Many new charts, tables, and figures are included. Cartoons have been added to help make the material more accessible.

- **Enhanced strengths.**   The *SIECUS Report* rated the first edition ''exceptional'' in eight areas: sexual anatomy, sexual responses, contraception, intimacy, relationships, sexual assault, sexually transmitted diseases, and sexual dysfunctions. These strengths have been enhanced with simpler and clearer diagrams, new summary tables, new integrating perspectives, and improved balance.

  The 19 topics given a ''thorough'' rating in the first edition have also been improved by critical updating, more concise and clearer summaries, and a more effective, student-conscious use of tables, surveys, and statistics.

  I have targeted other topics for improvement. **Abraham Risk, M.D.,** director of obstetrics and gynecology at a leading teaching hospital, and **Lori B. Andrews, J.D.,** author of *New Conceptions: A Consumer's Guide to the Newest Infertility Treatments,* helped with the treatment of infertility. The chapter and sections on sexual coercion, date rape, and incest were rewritten with advice from **Peter Anderson,** who has researched women who assault males, and **Andrea Parrot, Sharon E. King,** and **Margaretta Dwyer,** who work with the survivors of sexual assault, date rape, and incest.

- **A chapter has been added on body image, masturbation, and sexual fantasies.**   **Paul A. Fleming, M.D.,** editor of *Sex over 40* newsletter, **Sandra S. Cole,** noted specialist on sexuality and disabilities, and **Pamela S. Boyle,** president of the Coalition for Sexuality and Disabilities, were consulted for **a new chapter on sexuality, aging, and health.** The treatment of sex education has been much enhanced with the advice of **Floyd M. Martinson,** research professor of sociology, Gustavus Adolphus College, and an international expert on childhood sexuality; **Peggy Brick,** director of education for Planned Parenthood of Greater Northern New Jersey and coauthor of *Positive Images: A New Approach to Contraceptive Education;* **Michael Perry,** editor of Volume 7, *Childhood and Adolescent Sexology* in the *Handbook of Sexology;* and **Ann Welbourne-Moglia,** former executive director of the Sex Information and Education Council of the United States.

- **Expanded coverage of gender development and orientations.** Extensive revisions and new perspectives were made in the chapters on gender development and gender and erotic orientations. These chapters have many interconnections and also present a number of complex, sensitive, and controversial issues. I was challenged in having 11 special consultants for these two chapters. The consultants included **John Money,** director of the Psychohormonal Research Unit at Johns Hopkins Medical School and internationally acknowledged expert on gender development; **Eli Coleman,** associate professor in the Human Sexuality Program at the University of Minnesota Medical School and editor of the *Journal of Psychology and Human Sexuality;* **James D. Weinrich,** assistant research psychobiologist at the University of California (San Diego) and author of *Sexual Landscapes: Why We Are What We Are, Why We Love Whom We Love;* **Nancy J. Barbara,** a psychotherapist working with lesbian and gay persons; **Robert O. Hawkins, Jr.,** coauthor of *Counseling Lesbian Women and Gay Men: A Life-Issues Approach;* **Timothy Perper,** a behavioral biologist and author of *Sex Signals: The Biology of Love;* and **Fritz Klein, M.D.,** author of *The Bisexual Option* and coauthor of *Bisexualities: Theory and Research.* Any one familiar with the expertise and diverse viewpoints of these consultants will quickly recognize the demands I faced in writing these two chapters in a balanced and nuanced manner.

- **Revised chapter on American sexual customs.** This much praised and unique opening chapter has been restructured and rewritten to make it easier for the students to focus on key trends. Eight threads or aspects of changing American sexual attitudes and behavior between colonial times and the present have been isolated: religious influences, courtship patterns, medical advances, shifting sex ratios, the impact of war and slavery, legal trends, sex research, and the media and arts. A decade-by-decade description of changing sexual customs is provided for the pre-counterculture of the 1950s, the counterculture decades of the 1960s and 1970s, and the post-counterculture of the 1980s. The implications of these past trends for the future are also explored.

- **Extensively revised treatment of sexual customs in other cultures.** This chapter has been completely rewritten to focus on four cultures today's college students are most likely to encounter: the sexual attitudes and values of the Islamic world, India, China, and the Latino world. In researching and writing this chapter, I called on 12 special consultants who have a first-hand familiarity with these cultures.

- **A full chapter devoted to abortion** includes timely and practical information on current controversies, such as fetal personhood, fetal viability, and the rights of minors, the poor, and people in the Third World.

- **A full chapter on AIDS.** This new and unique chapter has been added with the assistance of **Roger Cooper, M.D.,** medical training officer for the Centers for Disease Control, and director of the STD/AIDS Clinic, St. Michael's Hospital, Newark, New Jersey: **William Yarber, H.S.D.,** author of *AIDS: What Young Adults Should Know* and former advisor on school AIDS education for the Centers for Disease Control and the World Health Organization; and **Norman A. Scherzer,** an AIDS expert at Essex County College and Rutgers, The State University of New Jersey (Newark).

Special Features

- I have already referred to the most unique and outstanding feature of this second edition: the **70 special consultants** who reviewed and critiqued specific chapters or sections of chapters. The generous contributions of these colleagues give this second edition a balance, authority, and standard of excellence no other sexuality text can match.

  I must admit that at times I almost regretted recruiting so many experts to examine not the whole text but to focus only on those areas and topics on which they have special expertise. In return for limiting the focus of the special consultants, I received line-by-line, word-for-word reviews and detailed, constructive criticisms. Often we debated how a particular controversial issue could be best summarized, what terms we should use, and what should be included or deleted. At times our discussions were heated, but they generated many new insights and more understandable ways of presenting the material. Negotiations sometimes were delicate, but the reader of this second edition now has the benefit of detailed input from 70 experts.

  The names of these special consultants are listed on the opening page of the chapter(s) that they so carefully reviewed. A more complete identification of the special consultants appears in the acknowledgments section of this preface and in the *Instructor's Manual*.

Other important features include:

- **Chapter openings** that focus the students' attention with art, a concise chapter outline, and a list of special consultants.
- **Key terms** highlighted in boldface in the text, listed at the end of each chapter, and concisely, clearly defined in the end-of-text glossary.
- **Highlight boxes** that stimulate student discussion and provide grist for class discussions.
- **A friendly, accessible style of writing** that students will find easy to understand and enjoyable to read.
- **Numerous in-text questions** posed to students throughout the book to encourage critical thinking and classroom discussion. This text has been written with the hope that the students will become actively involved with the material.
- **End-of-chapter student aids** include briefly stated key concepts, key terms, summary questions, and interesting, annotated suggested readings.
- **A glossary with authoritative, clear, concise definitions** based on the author's work as editor-in-chief for *A Descriptive Dictionary and Atlas of Sexology*.
- **An appendix of resources and hot lines** with listings for abortion, AIDS, disabilities, gender conflicts, gender orientation, sexual abuse, and sexually transmitted diseases.

Supplemental Materials

The supplements package for this edition of *Becoming a Sexual Person* has been extensively updated and revised for today's students. The *Instructor's Manual, Test Bank,* and student *Study Guide* were written by the author. This is a distinct advantage over manuals and guides written by someone other than the author of the text.

- The *Instructor's Manual* contains guides to each chapter, with a detailed outline, lecture notes, key terms with their definitions, class activities, and resources. Anatomical diagrams from the text are included (with and without labels) for use in class as guides for student review and in tests.

- **Four-color and two-color transparency acetates,** which include key diagrams and figures from the text, are available for instructors adopting this book.

- The **Test Bank** with over 2000 questions is available to instructors in both a printed version and **on Macintosh and IBM computer discs.**

- The student *Study Guide* contains outlines for the student to do his or her own sexual self-analysis or history, a chapter-by-chapter study guide, and ten exercises to share with a partner. Each chapter guide contains sample test questions for review and study.

Acknowledgments

Any good textbook is the result of a talented and effective team effort. This is particularly true of a textbook on human sexuality because of the unique interdisciplinary nature of sexology.

On the production and publishing side at Macmillan, I was most fortunate to have the finest team of editors and support staff I have worked with in publishing some twenty books. I want to particularly acknowledge the contributions of my editor, Robert Miller, and my development editor, Sharon Balbos; my production supervisor, Linda Greenberg; the photo researchers Chris Migdol and John Schultz; and the book and cover designer, Patrice Fodero.

A special thanks is due the numerous colleagues who reviewed the first edition and/or the manuscript for the second edition as it approached its final form: M. Betsy Bergen, Kansas State University; Kathryn Norcross Black, Purdue University; Sandra L. Caron, University of Maine; Patricia Barthalow Koch, The Pennsylvania State University; Jean Levitan, William Paterson State College; Phil Marty, University of Arkansas; Ronald Moglia, New York University; Barbara A. Rienzo, University of Gainesville; Norman A. Scherzer, Essex County College; Ann Welbourne-Moglia, New York University; and William L. Yarber, Indiana University, Bloomington.

I am indebted to three special colleagues and dear friends: Linda L. Hendrixson for her many creative suggestions for new material; Norman A. Scherzer for his critical review of the precision and clarity of biological details; and George P. Sellmer for his copyediting expertise. I also am grateful to Sita Venkateswar for her additional perspectives and insights on women in India, and to Danielle Francoeur for her preliminary computer drafts of the figures in Chapter 4.

Finally, I am pleased to thank my special consultants for their generosity in sharing so much of themselves and their expertise with me. I owe an incalculable debt to the following:

Peter Anderson, Ph.D., an assistant professor in the Department of Human Performance and Health Promotion at the University of New Orleans. His doctoral dissertation for the Human Sexuality Program at New York University dealt with female sexual assault on males. *(Chapter 23, Sexual Coercion)*

Lori B. Andrews, J.D., research fellow in medical law for the American Bar Foundation; senior scholar at the University of Chicago Center for Clinical Medical Ethics; and author of *New Conceptions: A Consumer's Guide to the Newest Infertility Treatments* (1985) and *Between Strangers: Surrogate Mothers, Expectant Fathers, and Brave New Babies* (1989). *(Chapter 22, Sex and the Law)*

Paula E. Ardehali, Ph.D., cultural anthropologist and linguist, was born and educated in Great Britain. She spent 11 years in Iran where she taught linguistics at the National University. She is currently an adjunct professor of anthropology at Rutgers, The State University of New Jersey, and at Fairleigh Dickinson University, Madison, New Jersey. *(Chapter 2, Sexual Customs in Other Cultures)*

Nancy J. Barbara, M.A., sexologist and psychotherapist working with lesbian and gay persons, as well as the deaf. She also teaches sexuality at the College of Social and Behavioral Sciences at the University of Southern Florida (Tampa). *(Chapter 16, Gender and Erotic Orientations)*

Joan E. Blank, M.A., M.P.H., editor-in-chief of Down There Press, and author of *The Playbook for Women about Sex* and *Good Vibrations: A Complete Guide to Vibrators*. She has been a sex counselor at the University of California San Francisco Medical Center and is currently manager of Good Vibrations, an erotic boutique in San Francisco. *(Chapter 14, Sexual Desire and Love Play)*

Anne Bolin, Ph.D., cultural anthropologist and assistant professor in the Department of Sociology at Elon College in North Carolina, is the author of the award-winning book *In Search of Eve: Transsexual Rites of Passage*. *(Chapter 15, Intimacy and Love)*

Pamela S. Boyle, M.S., ACSC, president and member of the board for the Coalition for Sexuality and Disabilities, Inc., New York City, has written extensively on issues related to sexuality and persons with disabilities. *(Chapter 18, Sexuality, Aging, and Health)*

Peggy Brick, M.Ed., director of education, Planned Parenthood of Greater Northern New Jersey, and author of *Positive Images: A New Approach to Contraceptive Education*. *(Chapter 5, Sexuality in Childhood and Adolescence; Chapter 9, Contraception: Shared Responsibilities)*

Bonnie Bullough, Ph.D., R.N., dean of nursing, State University of New York at Buffalo, and coauthor of several works on the history and sociology of sexual behavior, including *Sin, Sickness, and Sanity: A History of Sexual Attitudes* (1977) and *Women and Prostitution: A Social History* (1987). *(Chapter 24, Prostitution and Pornography)*

Vern L. Bullough, Ph.D., R.N., dean of natural and social sciences, State University College of New York (Buffalo), State University of New York Distinguished Professor, and author or coauthor of several works on the history and sociology of sexual behavior, including *Sin, Sickness, and Sanity: A History of Sexual Attitudes* (1977) and *Women and Prostitution: A Social History* (1987). *(Chapter 1, American Sexual Customs; Chapter 24, Prostitution and Pornography)*

Antonio W. Burr, Ph.D., clinical psychologist and columnist for *El Diario-La Prensa* in New York City. Dr. Burr was born in Chile where he worked as a psychologist and program coordinator for an adolescent and young adult program. *(Chapter 2, Sexual Customs in Other Cultures)*

Wayne Carpenter, Ph.D., completed his doctoral research in the Department of Child and Family Studies at Syracuse University under the direction of Dr. Eleanor Macklin, who pioneered the study of American cohabitation patterns. His 12-year retrospective study of cohabiting and noncohabiting college students is in press. Dr. Anderson is a counselor at Western New England College in Springfield, Massachusetts. *(Chapter 17, Lifestyles of Singles and Couples)*

Sandra S. Cole, Ph.D., has published and lectured widely on sexuality, disabilities, and rehabilitation. She has coauthored three books on the subject, most notably *Sexual Options for Paraplegics and Quadriplegics* (1975). After 10 years in the Program in Human Sexuality at the University of Minnesota Medical School, (Minneapolis), Dr. Cole moved to the University of Michigan Medical School in 1981, where she continues her teaching and research in the Sexuality Training Center, the Department of Preventative Medicine and Rehabilitation. *(Chapter 18, Sexuality, Aging, and Health)*

Eli Coleman, Ph.D., associate professor, Program in Human Sexuality, Department of Family Practice and Community Health, Medical School, University of Minnesota (Minneapolis), and editor of the *Journal of Psychology and Human Sexuality* and *Psychotherapy with Homosexual Men and Women: Integrated Identity Approaches for Clinical Practice* (1987). *(Chapter 4, Our Gender Development Before Birth)*

Roger Cooper, M.D., medical training officer, Centers for Disease Control, and director, STD/AIDS Clinic, St. Michael's Hospital, Newark. *(Chapter 12, Reducing Your Risk for Sexual Diseases; Chapter 13, AIDS: Health and Social Issues)*

Martha Cornog, M.A., M.S., a linguist and librarian, has served as secretary of the Society for the Scientific Study of Sex and as editorial assistant for the *Journal of Sex Research*. Currently employed at the American College of Physicians, she is completing a book on libraries, erotica, and pornography. *(Chapter 15, Intimacy and Love)*

Diane De Mauro, Ph.D., manager of education programs and computer systems for the Sex Information and Education Council of the United States (SIECUS). Dr. De Mauro has worked extensively with the Latino community in Chile and New York City. In the early 1980s, she wrote a biweekly column on female sexuality, gynecology, and health care, and ran sexuality workshops in Santiago, Chile. *(Chapter 2, Sexual Customs in Other Cultures)*

Sylvia D. Diehl, M.D., medical director, Planned Parenthood of Greater Northern New Jersey, and staff physician, Student Health Services, Fairleigh Dickinson University, Madison, New Jersey. *(Chapter 9, Contraception: Shared Responsibilities; Chapter 10, Abortion: Our Shared Responsibilities)*

Margaretta Dwyer, R.S.M., M.A., licensed psychologist and instructor in the Program in Human Sexuality, Department of Family Practice and Community Health, University of Minnesota Medical School, works with sex offenders and their victims. *(Chapter 20, Unconventional Sexual Expressions; Chapter 22, Sex and the Law; Chapter 23, Sexual Coercion)*

Hussein Elkholy, Ph.D., born and raised in Egypt, maintains strong political and family ties in his native country and travels there frequently. He is professor of physics at Fairleigh Dickinson University, Madison, New Jersey. *(Chapter 2, Sexual Customs in Other Cultures)*

Paul A. Fleming, M.D., D.H.S., director, The Fleming Center, Raleigh, North Carolina, and editor, *Sex over Forty Newsletter.* *(Chapter 6, Our Sexual Anatomy; Chapter 8, Pregnancy and Birth; Chapter 10, Abortion: Our Shared Responsibilities; Chapter 18, Sexuality, Aging, and Health)*

Suzanne G. Frayser, Ph.D., social anthropologist and founding member and officer of the Society for Cross-Cultural Research, author of *Varieties of Sexual Experience: An Anthropological Perspective on Human Sexuality* (1985), and coauthor of *Studies in Human Sexuality: A Selected Guide* (1987). Dr. Frayser teaches at the University College, University of Denver, Colorado. *(Chapter 2, Sexual Customs in Other Cultures)*

Richard A. Friend, Ph.D., assistant professor, Human Sexuality Education Program, Graduate School of Education, University of Pennsylvania. He has published on social issues of gender orientation in the *Journal of Homosexuality, Holistic Nursing Practice,* and other journals. *(Chapter 16, Gender and Erotic Orientations)*

Depaul Genska, O.F.M., board member of Genesis House, an outreach facility in Chicago for prostitutes who want a new life. Fr. Genska has worked with prostitutes since 1972; he is also a professor at the Catholic Theological Union in Chicago. *(Chapter 24, Prostitution and Pornography)*

Mrudulla Gnanadesikan, Ph.D., born and raised in India, is currently a professor of Information Systems and Sciences at Fairleigh Dickinson University, Madison, New Jersey. *(Chapter 2, Sexual Customs in Other Cultures)*

Kalman Goldstein, Ph.D., professor of American cultural history, Fairleigh Dickinson University, Teaneck, New Jersey, and a specialist in American pop culture. *(Chapter 1, American Sexual Customs)*

Deborah Eve Grayson, M.S., R.P.T., licensed mental health counselor, registered poetry therapist, creative arts specialist, and sex therapist in private practice in Fort Lauderdale, Florida. Her 1987 book *Parents and Other Strangers: A Creative Guide to Better Relationships* was a *Psychology Today* book-of-the-month selection. Her latest book, *Breath Marks in the Wind*, a book of erotic poetry illustrated by Linda F. Shotz, was created to promote healthy sexual attitudes. *(Chapter 14, Sexual Desire and Love Play)*

Paul Hanson, founding member and current board member of The Renaissance Education Association, Inc., an organization that provides support and information services to transvestites and transsexuals. *(Chapter 19, Gender Conflicts)*

Robert O. Hawkins, Jr., Ph.D., associate dean, School of Allied Health Professions, Health Sciences Center, State University of New York at Stony Brook, and coauthor of *Counseling Lesbian Women and Gay Men: A Life-Issues Approach.* He is board-certified by the American College of Sexologists and is a certified sex educator and counselor (American Association of Sex Educators, Counselors and Therapists). *(Chapter 4, Our Gender Development Before Birth; Chapter 16, Gender and Erotic Orientations)*

Linda L. Hendrixson, M.A., Ph.D. (cand.), health educator and adjunct professor of health and human sexuality, Upsala College, Montclair State College, and Fairleigh Dickinson University. *(Chapter 6, Our Sexual Anatomy; Chapter 9, Contraception: Shared Responsibilities; Chapter 11, Your Sexual Health)*

Sergio Jaime, M.D., clinical psychiatrist in Guadalajara, Jalisco, Mexico, and graduate of the Institute for the Advanced Study of Human Sexuality, San Francisco. *(Chapter 2, Sexual Customs in Other Cultures)*

Mario Kamenetzky, native of Argentina, has published widely in Argentinian, French, and American journals on the human implications of technology. For many years a science and technology advisor for the World Bank, he has observed sexual attitudes and customs in many Third World cultures, and is especially familiar with Latin American cultures. *(Chapter 2, Sexual Customs in Other Cultures)*

Sophia Kamenetzky, M.D., specialist in Third World population programs and a native of Argentina, is a graduate of the Institute for the Advanced Study of Human Sexuality and has worked at The Johns Hopkins University. *(Chapter 2, Sexual Customs in Other Cultures)*

Arno Karlen, researcher on lifestyles in America and author of *Sexuality and Homosexuality* and *Threesomes: Studies in Sex, Power, and Intimacy*; coauthor of *Sexual Decisions*, a college text; and coeditor of *Sex Education in Medicine*. *(Chapter 17, Lifestyles of Singles and Couples)*

Sharon E. King, M.S.Ed., R.C.H., C.A.S., graduate of the Human Sexuality Program at the University of Pennsylvania, and abuse, incest, and sexual assault counselor at The Starting Point, Collingswood, New Jersey. *(Chapter 20, Unconventional Sexual Expressions; Chapter 23, Sexual Coercion)*

Fritz Klein, M.D., director, Institute for Sexual Behavior in San Diego; author of *The Bisexual Option*; and coauthor of *Bisexualities: Theory and Research*. *(Chapter 16, Gender and Erotic Orientations)*

Sandra R. Leiblum, Ph.D., professor of clinical psychiatry, and co-director of the Sexual Counseling Service, University of Medicine and Dentistry of New Jersey, Robert Wood Johnson Medical School; and coeditor of *Sexual Desire Disorders* (1988) and *Principles and Practice of Sex Therapy* (2nd ed. 1989). *(Chapter 21, Sexual Problems and Therapies)*

Teresa Donati Marciano, Ph.D., professor of sociology at Fairleigh Dickinson University, Teaneck, New Jersey; active member of the Groves Conference on Marriage and the Family; author of numerous papers on alternate lifestyles; and member of a 1987 task force that examined sexual morality and lifestyles for the Episcopal Church of Northern New Jersey. *(Chapter 17, Lifestyles of Singles and Couples)*

Floyd M. Martinson, Ph.D., research professor of sociology, Gustavus Adolphus College, St. Peter, Minnesota; an international expert on childhood and adolescent sexuality and the author of many papers on the subject. *(Chapter 5, Sexuality in Childhood and Adolescence)*

Robert L. McGinley, Ph.D., founder and director of both The Lifestyles Organization and the North American Swing Club Association. *(Chapter 17, Lifestyles of Singles and Couples)*

Ronald Moglia, Ed.D., professor and director of the Human Sexuality Program, New York University, and specialist in children and sexuality education. *(Chapter 5, Sexuality in Childhood and Adolescence)*

John Money, Ph.D., director, Psychohormonal Research Unit, Johns Hopkins Medical School; internationally acknowledged expert on gender development; and author of such classics as *Gay, Straight, and Inbetween: Sexology of Erotic Orientation; Lovemaps: Clinical Concepts of Sexual/Erotic Health and Pathology, Paraphilia, and Gender Transposition in Childhood, Adolescence and Maturity; Venuses Penuses; The Destroying Angel; Love and Love Sickness: The Science of Sex, Gender Difference, and Pairbonding;* and *Man and Woman, Boy and Girl: The Differentiation and Dimorphism of Gender Identity from Conception to Maturity*. *(Chapter 4, Our Gender Development Before Birth)*

Nelwyn B. Moore, Ph.D., professor of family and child development, Department of Home Economics, Southwest Texas State University, San Marcos, Texas. *(Chapter 5, Sexuality in Childhood and Adolescence)*

Douglas E. Mould, Ph.D., clinical psychologist in private practice in Wichita, Kansas, and author of a major comparative study of research on the effects of violent erotica, abstracted in the *Journal of Sex Research* (1988). *(Chapter 24, Prostitution and Pornography)*

Javad Namazi, Ph.D., a native of Iran, is currently assistant professor of mathematics at Fairleigh Dickinson University, Madison, New Jersey. *(Chapter 2, Sexual Customs in Other Cultures)*

Jaya Natarajan, Ph.D., a native of India, taught college for several years in India before accepting a position as deputy chair and assistant professor in the Department of Information Systems and Sciences at Fairleigh Dickinson University, Madison, New Jersey. *(Chapter 2, Sexual Customs in Other Cultures)*

Berta Numata, R.N.C., Ob/Gyn Nurse Practitioner, has 30 years of practical experience with contraception and adolescent sexuality at Planned Parenthood of Greater Northern New Jersey. *(Chapter 9, Contraception: Shared Responsibilities; Chapter 10, Abortion: Our Shared Responsibilities; Chapter 11, Your Sexual Health; Chapter 12, Reducing Your Risk for Sexual Diseases)*

Andrea Parrot, Ph.D., assistant professor, Human Services Studies, Cornell University, is nationally known for her research and workshops on sexual assaults and rape prevention. *(Chapter 23, Sexual Coercion)*

Roger E. Peo, Ph.D., has a private practice in New York working with persons with gender dysphorias and unconventional sexual preferences. *(Chapter 19, Gender Conflicts; Chapter 20, Unconventional Sexual Expressions)*

Timothy Perper, Ph.D., behavioral biologist, expert in the ethological and ethnographic study of courtship and the North American singles scene, and author of *Sex Signals: The Biology of Love* (1985). His research on courtship and flirtation has received extensive media coverage nationwide. *(Chapter 4, Our Gender Development Before Birth; Chapter 14, Sexual Desire and Love Play; Chapter 15, Intimacy and Love)*

Michael Perry, Ph.D., editor of Volume 7, *Childhood and Adolescent Sexology* in the *Handbook of Sexology*, and a sexual therapist in private practice in Sherman Oaks, California. *(Chapter 5, Sexuality in Childhood and Adolescence)*

Carol A. Pollis, Ph.D., sociologist and dean of humanities, social sciences, and general education, University of Wisconsin at Green Bay; and researcher on the impacts of feminism on sexual science and on the consumers of pornography. *(Chapter 24, Prostitution and Pornography)*

James W. Prescott, Ph.D., developmental neuropsychologist internationally known for his neurological and cross-cultural studies of the effects of nurturance and somatosensory affectional deprivation on adult social skills and intimacy. After 20 years at the Institute for Child and Human Development at the National Institutes of Health, he continues his studies of environmental factors that impact on the individual's biological and behavioral health as president of Bio Behavioral Systems in San Diego, California. *(Chapter 15, Intimacy and Love)*

Newton Richards, health education specialist, New Jersey Department of Health, and coauthor of *Foundations for Decision Making: A VD Teaching Guide*, published by the American Council for Healthful Living. *(Chapter 12, Reducing Your Risk for Sexual Diseases)*

Abraham Risk, M.D., director of obstetrics and gynecology, Morristown Memorial Hospital, Morristown, New Jersey. *(Chapter 8, Pregnancy and Birth)*

JoAnn Roberts, Ph.D., founder and director of The Rennaisance Education Association, Inc., an organization that provides support and information services to transvestites and transsexuals. *(Chapter 19, Gender Conflicts)*

Fang Fu Ruan, M.D., associate professor of medical history at Beijing Medical University, the People's Republic of China; head of the Department of Oriental Sexology at The Institute for the Advanced Study of Human Sexuality (San Francisco); and editor of *The Handbook of Sex Knowledge* (Beijing, People's Republic of China). *(Chapter 2, Sexual Customs in Other Cultures)*

Mary Jane St. Peter, R.N., director, Student Health Services, Fairleigh Dickinson University, Madison, New Jersey; former assistant supervisor, Department of Gynecology at St. Francis Hospital, Hartford, Connecticut; and coordinator of maternal/child health at Morristown Memorial Hospital, Morristown, New Jersey. *(Chapter 9, Contraception: Shared Responsibilities; Chapter 10, Abortion: Our Shared Responsibilities)*

Leah Cahan Schaefer, Ed.D., charter member of the Harry Benjamin International Gender Dysphoria Association, past president of the Society for the Scientific Study of Sex, and author of *Women and Sex* (1974). She has a private practice in psychotherapy and gender dysphoria in New York City. *(Chapter 19, Gender Conflicts)*

Norman A. Scherzer, Ph.D., professor of human anatomy and physiology, Department of Biological Sciences and Allied Health, Essex County College; and Visiting Professor, Department of Biology, Rutgers, The State University of New Jersey (Newark). *(Chapter 6, Our Sexual Anatomy; Chapter 7, Our Sexual Responses; Chapter 11, Your Sexual Health; Chapter 13, AIDS: Health and Social Issues; Chapter 20, Unconventional Sexual Expressions)*

Joseph W. Scott, Ph.D., professor of American ethnic studies, University of Washington (Seattle), and author of several studies of sexual customs and lifestyles among black Americans. *(Chapter 17, Lifestyles of Singles and Couples)*

Julian W. Slowinski, Psy.D., marital and sex therapist, Pennsylvania Hospital, and faculty member, University of Pennsylvania School of Medicine, Department of Psychiatry. *(Chapter 3, Sexual Values and Moral Development; Chapter 21, Sexual Problems and Therapies)*

William R. Stayton, M. Div., Th.D., assistant professor, Psychiatry and Human Behavior, Jefferson Medical College; and adjunct professor, Human Sexuality Program, University of Pennsylvania Graduate School of Education and LaSalle University. His pastoral experience has been in Massachusetts. *(Chapter 3, Sexual Values and Moral Development; Chapter 20, Unconventional Sexual Expressions)*

Anne Tripp, M.S., former executive director of the American Council for Healthful Living. *(Chapter 12, Reducing Your Risk for Sexual Diseases)*

James D. Weinrich, Ph.D., assistant research psychobiologist, Department of Psychiatry, University of California (San Diego), and author of *Sexual Landscapes: Why We Are What We Are, Why We Love Whom We Love*. *(Chapter 4, Our Gender Development Before Birth)*

David L. Weis, Ph.D., associate professor of human development and family studies, Department of Applied Human Ecology, Bowling Green State University, Bowling Green, Ohio, and author of numerous research articles in the areas of extramarital sexuality and intimate lifestyles. *(Chapter 15, Intimacy and Love; Chapter 17, Lifestyles of Singles and Couples)*

Ann Welbourne-Moglia, Ph.D., former executive director of the Sex Information and Education Council of the United States (SIECUS), and currently in private practice as a sexuality education consultant. *(Chapter 5, Sexuality in Childhood and Adolescence)*

Connie Christine Wheeler, M.S., Ph.D. (cand.), charter member of the Harry Benjamin International Gender Dysphoria Association; editor (with Robert Gemme) of *Progress in Sexology*; and coauthor (with Wardell Pomeroy and Carol Flax) of *Taking a Sex History*. *(Chapter 19, Gender Conflicts)*

Beverly Whipple, Ph.D., R.N., associate professor of nursing, Rutgers, The State University of New Jersey (Newark), and coauthor of *The G Spot and Other Recent Discoveries in Human Sexuality* (1982) and *Safe Encounters* (1989). *(Chapter 6, Our Sexual Anatomy; Chapter 7, Our Sexual Responses; Chapter 11, Your Sexual Health)*

William Yarber, H.S.D., professor, Department of Applied Health Science, Indiana University, Bloomington; author of *AIDS: What Young Adults Should Know* (1987); and former advisor on school AIDS education for the Centers for Disease Control and the World Health Organization. *(Chapter 13, AIDS: Health and Social Issues)*

Brief Contents

Part One: Our Cultural Heritage   1

  1. American Sexual Customs   3
  2. Sexual Customs in Other Cultures   29
  3. Sexual Values and Moral Development   51

Part Two: The Personal Context   69

  4. Our Gender Development Before Birth   71
  5. Sexuality in Childhood and Adolescence   105
  6. Our Sexual Anatomy   141
  7. Our Sexual Responses   169
  8. Pregnancy and Birth   203
  9. Contraception: Shared Responsibilities   239
  10. Abortion: Our Shared Responsibilities   279
  11. Your Sexual Health   301
  12. Reducing Your Risk for Sexual Diseases   327
  13. AIDS: Health and Social Issues   353

Part Three: The Interpersonal Context   375

  14. Sexual Desire and Love Play   377
  15. Intimacy and Love   405

16.   Gender and Erotic Orientations   431
17.   Lifestyles of Singles and Couples   463
18.   Sexuality, Aging, and Health   497
19.   Gender Conflicts   515
20.   Unconventional Sexual Expressions   527
21.   Sexual Problems and Therapies   549

Part Four: The Social Context   *579*

22.   Sex and the Law   581
23.   Sexual Coercion   597
24.   Prostitution and Pornography   623

Appendix: Resources and Hot Lines   *651*

Glossary   *654*

Bibliography   *B-1*

Index   *I-1*

Detailed Contents

Part One: Our Cultural Heritage   1

Chapter 1   American Sexual Customs   3

The Fabric of Human Sexuality   4
Historical Threads and Trends   4
  Religious Influences   4
  Courtship Patterns   8
Highlight Box 1.1. One Founding Father's View of Sex   9
  Medical Advances   10
  Shifting Sex Ratios   11
  The Impact of War and Slavery   13
  Legal Trends   14
  Sex Research   15
Highlight Box 1.2. Sex Education in the 1930s and 1940s   16
  The Media and the Arts   18
The Pre-Counterculture of the 1950s   18
  Playboy   19
  The Media and Rock Music   19
The Counterculture in the 1960s   21
  Civil Rights for Women and Homosexuals   21
  A Sexual Revolution   21

The Counterculture in the 1970s   22
  Liberal Trends   22
Highlight Box 1.3. Economics and Women's
Hemlines 1921–1977   23
  Conservative Trends   24
The 1980s: A Post-Counterculture   24
  Liberal Trends   24
  Neoconservativism   25
Looking Ahead   25

Chapter 2   Sexual Customs in Other Cultures   29

The Cross-Cultural Perspective   30
Sexual Customs in the Islamic World   30
  The Islamic View of Sex   30
  A Shame Culture   31
  Women in Islam   32
  Marriage   33
  Homosexuality   34
  Islam and the Western World   34
Sexual Customs in the Hindu World   35
  The Hindu View of Sex   35
  Hindu Women   36
  Marriage   37
Highlight Box 2.1. Arranged Marriages in India   37
  Homosexuality   38
  Hinduism and the Western World   38
Sexual Customs in the People's Republic of China   39
  The Chinese View of Sex   39
  Marriage   41
  Homosexuality   42
  China and the Western World   42
Sexual Customs in the Latino Cultures   43
  The Latino View of Sex   43
  Four Basic Sexual Values   45
  The Latino Experience Today   46
The Complexities of Sexual Customs   46

Chapter 3   Sexual Values and Moral Development   51

Values, Morals, and Ethics   52
  Formal and Informal Values   52
Religion and Sexual Values   53
  Guilt or Shame   54
  Natural or Unnatural Sex   54
  Two Different Worldviews   54
Highlight Box 3.1. A Spectrum of Ethical Systems   55

Highlight Box 3.2. A Sampling of Fixed
and Process Perspectives 59
   A Humanist View 60
How We Develop Our Values 61
   Social Development and Values 61
   Piaget's Model of Moral Development 61
   Kohlberg's Developmental Model 62
   Gilligan's View of Moral Development 64
Sexual Values in the Future 64
Highlight Box 3.3. Gender and Morals 65

Part Two: The Personal Context **69**

Chapter 4   Our Gender Development Before Birth 71

Gender and Sex 72
The Gates of Psychosexual Development 74
The First Two Months of Gender Development 75
   Nature's Basic Plan 75
   Gate 1: Chromosomal/Genetic Gender 77
   Gate 2: Gonadal Gender 79
   Gate 3: Prenatal Hormonal Gender 79
The Fetal Period of Psychosexual Development 82
   Gate 4: Our Internal Sexual Anatomy 84
   Gate 5: Our External Sexual Anatomy 86
   Gate 6: Neurological Tendencies 86
Psychosexual Development After Birth 92
   Gate 7: Gender Assignment 92
   Gate 8: Gender Scripting 92
   Gate 9: Gender Roles 93
   Gate 10: Gender Identity 94
   Gate 11: Gender Orientations 95
   Gate 12: Pubertal Gender Development 95
Variations 96
   Chromosomal Variations at Gate 1 96
   Genetic Variations at Gate 1 97
   A Postnatal Variation 99
An Integrating Framework 100

Chapter 5   Sexuality in Childhood and Adolescence 105

Childhood Sexuality 106
   The Limits of What We Know 106
   Sexuality in Infants and Children 106
Puberty 114
   Puberty and Adolescence in the Western World 114
   The Hormones That Control Puberty 114

Female Cycles   117
Some Medical Complications   120
Adjusting to the Changes of Puberty   123
Adolescent Sexuality   124
Making Decisions About Sex   124
Legal Rights of Children and Adolescents   125
Sexuality Education   126
Highlight Box 5.1. Sex Education in Norway   128
Theories of Child and Adolescent Development   130
Sigmund Freud   130
Erik Erikson   132
Jean Piaget and Lawrence Kohlberg   134
John Gagnon and William Simon   134
The Future of Childhood and Adolescent Sexuality   136

Chapter 6   Our Sexual Anatomy   141

The Evolution of Privacy   143
Female Anatomy   143
External Structures   144
Internal Structures   150
The Female Breast   153
A Sexual Fantasyland   154
Male Anatomy   155
Penis Myths and Realities   155
Highlight Box 6.1. The Size of a Man   156
Male Anatomy   158
Circumcision   163
Male Circumcision   163
Female Circumcision   164

Chapter 7   Our Sexual Responses   169

The Varieties of Human Sexual Responses   170
The Desire Phase (1)   173
The Excitement/Plateau Phase (2)   174
Two Arousal Processes   174
Excitement   174
Plateau   179
The Orgasm Phase (3)   182
Orgasmic Variations in Women   184
Orgasmic Variations in Men   188
Highlight Box 7.1. One Male's Experience
with Being Multiorgasmic   190
Exercising the Pubococcygeal Muscles   191
The Resolution Stage (4)   191
An Integrated Psychophysiological Model   193
Cautions About Sexual Response Models   194

The Control of Sexual Responses 194
Two Types of Control 194
Reflexogenic Responses 195
Intermediate Controls 198
The Conscious Levels of Sexual Response 199

Chapter 8 Pregnancy and Birth 203

Part One: Conception and Pregnancy 204
Coitus and Conception 204
Fertilization 204
Ectopic Pregnancy 206
Twins 208
Pregnancy Signs and Tests 208
The Embryonic Period 210
Embryonic Development 210
The Placental System 210
Fetal Development 211
The Second Trimester 212
The Third Trimester 213
Prenatal Care 214
Problems During Pregnancy 215

Part Two: Childbirth and Options in Delivery 221
Vaginal Delivery 221
The Stages of Labor 221
Options in Vaginal Delivery 223
Cesarean Section Delivery 226
Breast Feeding 228
Custom-Made Pregnancies 229
Infertility and Possible Treatments 229
Artificial Insemination and Frozen Sperm 230
Test Tube Fertilization and Embryo Transfer 231
The Surrogate Mother Controversy 233

Chapter 9 Contraception: Shared Responsibilities 239

The Struggle to Control Human Reproduction 240
Highlight Box 9.1. Four Hundred Years
of Contraceptive Progress 242
Deciding to Use a Contraceptive 243
Erotophiles and Erotophobes 244
Why Contraceptives Aren't Used 244
Sharing the Responsibility 247
Contraceptive Effectiveness 247
Contraceptive Choices 249
1. Outercourse 250
2. Barrier and Spermicidal Contraceptives 250
3. Hormonal Contraceptives 261

4. *Natural Contraception*   263
5. *Surgical Methods*   265
Choosing a Contraceptive You Will Use   268
Unreliable Contraceptive Methods   268
Teenage Pregnancies and Contraceptives   269
The Ambivalence of Americans   272
School-Based Health Clinics   272
A Fuller Picture   272
Highlight Box 9.2. Clashing Views on School-Based
Health Clinics   273
The Costs of Accidental Pregnancies   273
Contraception in the 1990s   274
Coping with a New Reality   275

Chapter 10   Abortion: Our Shared Responsibilities   279

A History of Abortion   280
Religious Views   280
Who Has Abortions?   281
Legal Aspects   282
Abortion Controversies   283
The Antiabortion and Prochoice Movements   283
A Human Life Amendment or Statute   285
When Does Human Life Begin?   285
Highlight Box 10.1. The Turning Point of Viability   286
The Rights of Minors and Their Parents   287
The Rights of the Poor   287
The Rights of People in the Third World   288
Abortion and Sex Selection   288
Making Decisions About Pregnancy   289
The Single Parent Option and Adoption   289
The Abortion Choice   290
Abortion Options   293
Postcoital Hormonal Contraception   293
Medical Procedures   295
Medical and Emotional Aftercare   297
A National Dilemma   298

Chapter 11   Your Sexual Health   301

Self-Image and Sexual Health for Women   302
Vulval and Vaginal Self-Examinations   302
The Bimanual Pelvic Examination   304
Sexually Related Disorders of the Female Pelvis   307
Breast Self-Examination   312
Sexually Related Disorders of the Breast   315
Some Health Problems Men and Women Share   317

Self-Image and Sexual Health for Men   318
  Self-Health Examinations   *318*
  Prostate and Rectal Examinations   *319*
  Sexually Related Diseases   *320*
Choosing the Best Doctor for Your Sexual Health   322

Chapter 12   Reducing Your Risk for Sexual Diseases   327

The STD Scene   328
  Who Gets Them?   *328*
  Why We Haven't Controlled Them   *330*
  Where Did They Come From?   *331*
  Reducing Your Risk   *332*
  STDs as a Weapon   *334*
A Summary of Sexually Transmitted Diseases   335
  Sexual Diseases Caused by Bacteria   *335*
  Sexual Diseases Caused by Fungi or Yeasts   *340*
  Sexual Diseases Caused by Parasites   *341*
  Sexual Diseases Caused by Viruses   *344*
Getting Help   347
  Where to Go   *347*
  What to Expect   *348*
A Look to the Future   349

Chapter 13   AIDS: Health and Social Issues   353

Plagues, Past and Present   354
HIV and What It Does   355
  The Viruses That Cause AIDS   *355*
  How the Virus Is Spread   *356*
  HIV and the Immune System   *358*
  The Consequences   *361*
Highlight Box 13.1. When Fear Takes Charge   362
Testing for HIV   362
  Two Tests   *362*
  When Should You Be Tested?   *363*
High Risk Behaviors and Risk Reduction   364
  Risky Behaviors   *364*
  HIV Prevention and Risk Reduction   *365*
Highlight Box 13.2. Conflicting Public Policies   368
Personal and Social Issues   371
  Educating the Young   *371*
  Public Health Issues   *371*
  Who Pays?   *372*
  The Global Consequences   *373*
What You Can Do to Help   373

Part Three: The Interpersonal Context   **375**

Chapter 14   Sexual Desire and Love Play   377

Sexual Desire   378
The Nature of Sexual Desire   378
The Enemies of Desire   380
Highlight Box 14.1. A Sex Appeal Survey   382
Aphrodisiacs   385
Solo Sexual Pleasures   386
The Erotic Mind   386
Sex for One   390
Sharing Sexual Pleasures   393
Erotic Touches   393
Highlight Box 14.2. Kissing   395
Intercourse Positions   396
Highlight Box 14.3 Two Poems   398
Oral Sex   398
Love Play and Gender   401

Chapter 15   Intimacy and Love   405

The Evolution of Love   406
Making Contact   410
A Different Past   410
The Dating Scene Today   410
Developing Intimacy Skills   412
Intimacy, Nurturance, and Violence   412
Partner Choice   416
Two Models of Mate Selection   416
Lovemaps   417
The Dance of Intimacy   419
Intimacy and Love   422
Four Types of Intimacy   422
Conflicting Gender Experiences of Intimacy   423
Highlight Box 15.1. Ten Rules for Avoiding Intimacy   424
Jealousy   425
The Paradoxes of True Intimacy   427

Chapter 16   Gender and Erotic Orientations   431

Gender and Erotic Orientations   432
A Question of Labels   432
A Historical Perspective   434
Research Perspectives   435
Highlight Box 16.1. Measuring the Complexities
of Gender Orientations   439

What Is Normal Sexual Behavior? 440
  The Personal View 440
  Other Perspectives and Views 440
Gender Orientation Research 444
  Biological Theories 445
  Psychoanalytic Theories 445
  Social Learning Theories 446
  Biobehavioral Interactions 447
Variations on a Theme 448
  Lesbians and Gay Men 448
  Gay Teens 449
  Gay Politicians and Clergy 450
  Bisexualities 451
Adjusting to a "Different" Orientation 451
  Social Issues 451
Highlight Box 16.2. Gay and Lesbian Teachers 452
  Family Issues 454
  Legal Issues 455
  Coming Out 456
Are We Born with a Panerotic Potential? 457

Chapter 17   Lifestyles of Singles and Couples 463

Today's Relationships 464
  A Changing Society 464
  A New Ecosystem 464
Singles 468
  The Singles Population 468
  Deciding Whether to Be Sexually Active 469
Highlight Box 17.1. American Singles Speak Out 471
  Creative Singlehood 474
Couples 474
  Monogamy and Its Evolution 474
  Variations on a Theme 480
Single Again 489
  The Divorced and Widowed 489
How to Define a Family 491
Highlight Box 17.2. Face-Off: Recognizing
"Domestic Partners" 491
Shifting Sex Ratios and Sexual Values 493

Chapter 18   Sexuality, Aging, and Health 497

Sexuality in the Middle and Later Years 498
  Love, Sex, and Aging 498
Highlight Box 18.1. Sex and the Older Person 500
  Social Dimensions 502
  Health Issues 503

Sexuality and Persons with Disabilities   506
The Double Social Taboo of Sex and Disability   *506*
The Impact of Disabilities   *507*
Chronic Illness and Sexuality   *508*
A More Humane Perspective   511

Chapter 19   Gender Conflicts   515

Gender Discomfort   516
Gender Role Transpositions   516
Transvestism   *517*
Highlight Box 19.1. Six Myths of Transvestism   518
Transgenderism and Transsexualism   *520*
Highlight Box 19.2. Billy Tipton   521
Support Groups and Therapies   *522*
The Gender Rainbow   524

Chapter 20   Unconventional Sexual Expressions   527

Normal and Unconventional Sexual Behaviors   528
Four Patterns of Response   *528*
How Normal Lovemaps Are Vandalized   *530*
Pedophilia   *531*
Other Paraphilias   *534*
Highlight Box 20.1. The Irresistible Urge
of an Exhibitionist   536
Highlight Box 20.2. An S & M Couple   539
The Controversy over Sexual Addiction   543
When the Unconventional Is a Problem   544

Chapter 21   Sexual Problems and Therapies   549

Sexual Health   550
Sexual Unfolding   *550*
Sexual Skills   *550*
Sexual Adequacy   552
Definition   *552*
Work or Play?   *552*
Sexual Communications   *553*
Highlight Box 21.1. What Is the Goal of Sex?   554
When the Sexual Becomes Problematic   555
Sexual Difficulties and Problems   555
What Causes a Sexual Problem or Difficulty?   557
Highlight Box 21.2. The Carousel Dynamics   558
Some Biological Factors   *559*
Some Psychological Causes   *559*
Highlight Box 21.3. Sex as a Status Symbol   561
Some Social or Interpersonal Causes   *562*

Sex Therapies 563
The PLISSIT Model 563
Combined Therapies 567
Sex Therapy for Gay Persons 568
What to Look for in a Therapist 569
Types of Sexual Difficulties 570
Desire Phase Difficulties 570
Highlight Box 21.4. How Common Are Sexual Problems
and Difficulties? 571
Sexual Arousal Difficulties 572
Orgasm Difficulties 573
Highlight Box 21.5. The Stop-Go Exercise 574
Other Sexual Difficulties 575
Dealing with the Unavoidable 576

Part Four: The Social Context 579

Chapter 22　Sex and the Law 581

American Sex Laws 582
How Our Laws Regulate Sex 582
Why Do We Have Laws Regulating Sexual Behavior? 583
Protecting Marriage 585
Protecting Public Morality and Health 588
Protecting Against Sexual Assaults 589
Protecting Minors 590
The Reform of Sex Laws 592
Rape Penalties 592
Privacy and Minorities 593
Highlight Box 22.1. Should Congress Censor Art? 593
Victimless Crimes 594
The Trend Toward Consenting Adult Laws 594

Chapter 23　Sexual Coercion 597

Rape 598
Rape in History 598
What Constitutes Rape? 599
What Motivates Rapists? 601
Types of Rape 602
Reducing the Risk of Sexual Assault 608
Highlight Box 23.1. What Men Can Do
to Help Stop Rape 609
A Developmental-Descriptive Profile of the Rapist 610
Resisting a Rape Attempt 611
Incest 612
Sexual Abuse Within the Family 612
Coping During and After a Sexual Assault 614

During an Assault Attempt   614
Reporting Rape or Incest   615
The Trauma of Rape and Abuse   615
Sexual Harassment   616
Sexual Harassment from 1964 to the Present   616
Two Definitions   617
What Constitutes Sexual Harassment?   618
Dealing with Sexual Harassment   618
Highlight Box 23.2. Myths and Facts about Sexual
Harassment   619

Chapter 24   Prostitution and Pornography   623

Part One: Prostitution   624
Prostitution in America   624
The Varieties of Prostitution   625
Female Prostitution   626
Teenage Prostitution   629
Male Prostitution   629
Commercial Exhibitionism/Voyeurism   630
The Customers Who Buy Sex   631
The Economics of Prostitution   631
The Criminal Element   631
The Costs and Politics of Enforcement   632
Three Ways of Handling Prostitution   633
Licensing   633
Criminalization   633
Decriminalization   634
A Declining Future?   635

Part Two: Pornography, Erotica, and Obscenity   635
Defining Obscenity in Legal Terms   635
Pornography's Impact on Individuals and Society   636
Some Models of Pornography   636
Three Federal Studies   638
Erotica Versus Pornography   639
Some Types of Pornography   640
Pornography, Sexism, and Violence   642
The Censorship Question   642
Highlight Box 24.1. Public Attitudes on Pornography
and Censorship   643

Appendix: Resources and Hot Lines   651

Glossary   654

Bibliography   B-1

Index   I-1

Part One

Our Cultural Heritage

1. American Sexual Customs
2. Sexual Customs in Other Cultures
3. Sexual Values and Moral Development

*T*he Fabric of Human
  Sexuality
*H*istorical Threads
  and Trends
  Religious Influences
  Courtship Patterns
  Medical Advances
  Shifting Sex Ratios
  *The Impact of War
  and Slavery*
  Legal Trends
  Sex Research
  The Media and the Arts
*T*he Pre-Counterculture
  of the 1950s
  Playboy
  *The Media and Rock
  Music*
*T*he Counterculture
  in the 1960s
  *Civil Rights for Women
  and Homosexuals*
  A Sexual Revolution
*T*he Counterculture
  in the 1970s
  Liberal Trends
  Conservative Trends
*T*he 1980s: A Post-
  Counterculture
  Liberal Trends
  Neoconservativism
*L*ooking Ahead

Chapter 1

*A*merican Sexual Customs

Special Consultants

Vern L. Bullough, Ph.D., R.N., dean of Natural and Social Sciences, State University College of New York (Buffalo), State University of New York Distinguished Professor, and author of several works on the history and sociology of sexual behavior.

Kalman Goldstein, Ph.D., professor, American Cultural History, Fairleigh Dickinson University.

Sex is a word that easily catches our attention, but it is also a word with many meanings. For all of us it represents a very personal experience, an experience we share with all other humans. This book conveys that fact by examining the many aspects of our human sexuality.

The Fabric of Human Sexuality

Even the most basic description of human **sexuality** must include these four major aspects: (1) who we are because of our male or female sexual anatomy, (2) the identity we develop as gendered—masculine or feminine—persons, (3) the roles and behaviors we adopt because they are appropriate to our sexual anatomy and gender identity, and (4) the gender of the persons we are sexually attracted to and/or fall in love with. However, these four elements evolve as part of a constantly changing fabric woven out of a variety of biological, psychological, social, and cultural threads. Thus we view human sexuality as a **bio-psycho-socio-cultural phenomenon**.

In our development as sexual persons the biological threads include our genetic makeup, the development and functioning of our sexual anatomy and reproductive systems, and the sex hormones which mold the neural pathways of our brains. We all share this foundation. However, because these biological aspects are defined and elaborated on by our psychological development as a gendered person, we can also speak of sex as a psychological phenomenon. We learn about expressing our sexuality from our relatives and society, so our sexuality can further be described as a social phenomenon. On a fourth level, threads reach out to us from the recent and distant history of our Western European-American cultures, and from other cultures, to add further details to our sexuality as we experience it. Hence our view of sexuality as a bio-psycho-socio-cultural fabric is composed of many interrelated threads.

In Part One we devote three chapters to the social and cultural aspects of our human sexuality. This first chapter focuses on American culture, tracing the impact of religion, courtship patterns, developments in medicine, shifting sex ratios, wars, legal trends, sex research, and the media and the arts on the ways in which we see ourselves and relate with others.

In Chapter 2 we move beyond American culture to examine the sexual customs in the Muslim Near East, in the Hindu traditions of India, in China, and in Latino cultures. Here we see how different societal and cultural forces have yielded an array of sexual values and behaviors that illustrate the variety, complexity, and richness of human sexuality.

Chapter 3 explores the impact of religious beliefs on sexual values and lifestyles in America. We examine the ties between religious morality and sexuality to help you understand the origins of our attitudes, both positive and negative, about our sexuality. Keep in mind that changes in individual threads may change the whole design of the way we experience our sexuality.

Historical Threads and Trends

Religious Influences

American sexual attitudes and customs have often been described as puritanical or Victorian. More recently these attitudes have undergone a profound change toward more liberal values. To understand American sexual customs we need to appreciate the religious influences that helped mold our current values.

The Puritans

The Protestant **Puritans** who landed in New England in 1620 were mostly merchants and tradesmen who came with their families to establish a "holy commonwealth" in which the Bible would direct every aspect of life. For the God-fearing, hard-working Puritans, sex was associated with the sin of Adam and Eve. Women were honored, although as the daughters of Eve they were viewed as weak, seductive, and in need of a strict moral code.

The Puritans frowned on celibacy and discriminated against bachelors. Unmarried men were expected to live with a family and were subject to its rules. Widowers and widows quickly remarried to provide for the care of their children, often within six weeks. Contrary to popular opinion, the Puritans emphasized the pleasures of marital sex; they just didn't acknowledge them in public (Smith 1978:68).

The Puritans broke with the near-universal European view of marriage as an indissoluble religious union. Puritan marriage was a civil contract and could be terminated by civil authorities. In the early 1600s civil divorces were granted in all the New England colonies, starting a trend that led to our current liberalized and no-fault divorce laws.

The 1800s: Turmoil and Conflicting Values

America in the 1800s was a pattern of conflicting trends and values. A frontier mentality inspired some Americans to experiment with communal living, equality for women, celibacy, group marriage, eugenic parenthood, polygamy, and free love. Yet the dominant conservative trend was reinforced by three major financial depressions, the "Second Great Awakening of Protestantism" in 1831, and the Civil War. This tension between conservative and liberal attitudes toward sexuality has remained a major characteristic of American culture up to the present (Figure 1.1).

Figure 1.1. *At the height of the Victorian era, American companies discovered sex appeal as a way of selling their products. This whiskey label from 1892, like many other such advertisements, slipped by the Comstock law despite its use of female nudity as a sales pitch.*

The Victorian Era

In the 1800s, **Victorian** morality, named for England's Queen Victoria (1837–1901), provided a pattern of male/female relations and family values that met the overwhelming cultural and functional needs of the late Industrial Revolution. To increase the efficiency of manufacturing, men had to be free of family responsibilities to work in centralized factories 12 or more hours a day, and 6 or 7 days a week. This new male role created its counterpart in the middle-class urban wife who no longer contributed directly to the family income as she once did on the farm. All her time was devoted to child care and providing her husband with a safe refuge from the harsh world (D'Emilio & Freedman 1988: 55–169).

The antisexual Victorian values are evident in the writings of Sylvester Graham, a prominent New York preacher, who warned of the dangers of "excessive" sexual activity. Graham claimed that young men were too frail to engage in sex before age 30. Married couples who had sex more than once every three years risked

> languor, lassitude, muscular relaxation, general debility and heaviness, depression of spirits, loss of appetite, indigestion, faintness and sinking at the pit of the stomach, increased susceptibilities of the skin and lungs to all atmospheric changes, feebleness of circulation, chilliness, headache, melancholy, hypochondria, hysterics, feebleness of all the senses, impaired vision, loss of sight, weakness of the lungs, nervous cough, pulmonary consumption, disorders of the liver and kidneys, urinary difficulties, disorders of the genital organs, spinal diseases, weakness of the brain, loss of memory, epilepsy, insanity, apoplexy, abortions, premature births, and extreme feebleness, morbid predispositions, and early death of offspring.
>
> *(Money 1985a:17–26, 61–67)*

Insanity and early death from "an overexcited and convulsed heart" would inevitably follow "excessive indulgence."

Sylvester Graham had a simple way of preventing such excesses, based on his theory that any food that stimulated the digestive tract would also arouse the sexual organs. Graham's remedy was to rid the diet of all meat, animal products (eggs, milk, and cheese), and all spicy foods. As a substitute, he recommended bland but nutritious graham bread and graham crackers! At a Seventh-Day Adventist health resort in Battle Creek, Michigan, Dr. John Kellogg and his brother invented cornflakes to reduce the monotony of eating graham products at every meal (Bullough 1987a:232–258; Gardella 1985:39–67; Money 1985a:17-28, 83–97).

Victorian antisexual views were reinforced by a new medical belief that the loss of seminal fluid in masturbation and intercourse drained a man's body of vital fluids (Figure 1.2) (D'Emilio & Freedman 1988:68–69; Money 1985a:50–55). Because masturbation was associated with insanity, parents were determined to protect their children. Ointments could make the genitals painful to touch. Special bed cradles were designed to lift the blankets from the genital area so children would not rub against them when sleeping on their backs. A variety of harnesses that protected the genital area from being touched were patented. The female harness usually had a wire-type mesh so the girl could urinate but never touch herself. Surgeons inserted a ring in the foreskin of the penis so a

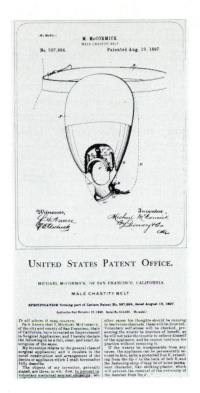

Figure 1.2. *The McCormick "Male Chastity Belt,"
granted a U.S. patent in 1897, was designed first,* to
prevent involuntary nocturnal seminal emissions;
second, to control waking thoughts; *and third,* to prevent self-abuse. *Typical of "surgical appliances" used
in the Victorian era to prevent masturbation by males,
this chastity belt could be* permanently secured *to a
male irresponsible enough to want to remove it.*

boy could urinate without touching his penis. Circumcision was encouraged to
eliminate retracting the foreskin to wash the glans of the penis. Spiked penile
rings, secured in the back with a lock for which the parent had the only key,
discouraged any erection. In severe cases, the clitoris could be removed by
surgery or the nerves of the penis destroyed (Bullough & Bullough 1977:55–73;
Bullough 1987b).

Sexual Pioneers and Marriage Experiments

While the middle class abided by antisexual Victorian advice, the upper class
in the 1800s appears to have enjoyed an active sexual life and the pleasure of
orgasms (Degler 1980). Another equally small group of Americans rejected the
Victorian value system. Encouraged by Jean-Jacques Rousseau's belief that
man's troubles stem from a sick, deformed society, religious and economic
communes sprang up from New England to the Rocky Mountains. Members
advocated "utopian free love," group marriage and polygamy, sexual freedom
for women, the intellectual equality of men and women, and women's right to
vote and obtain divorces.

At the other end of the spectrum, New England Shakers and midwestern
communes experimented with Christian communism based on **celibacy**, total
abstinence from all sexual relations. The Mormons, a Christian sect founded in
1830 in upstate New York, allowed their members to practice **polygyny** and
have several wives. Enforcement of an 1862 federal law prohibiting this custom
was delayed by the Civil War. In 1890, with over a thousand Mormons in jail,
church leaders finally officially abandoned polygyny. Many Mormons, however, have continued to practice polygyny up to the present time. Despite its

association with sexual promiscuity, Mormon polygyny was hardly permissive. The women engaged in marital sex solely for reproduction, and each wife decided when her husband would share her bed (D'Emilio & Freedman 1988:112–120; Murstein 1974:350–362; Smith 1978:92–93).

Members of the utopian Oneida Community (1831–1881) believed that **monogamy** was the ultimate selfishness because it promoted sexual and emotional exclusiveness between two people. All the members of God's community, they believed, should love one another equally. In this **group marriage** arrangement, members of the community were discouraged from limiting themselves to one sexual partner (D'Emilio & Freedman 1988:112–120).

Although they allowed and even encouraged open sexual relations, Oneida members were concerned about producing more children than they could support. They practiced male continence in which any couple might engage in sexual intercourse as long as the male refrained from ejaculation. Only those carefully selected for their ideal biological makeup were allowed to reproduce. The children were raised by other members whose psychological temperaments made them excellent nurturers. They called this practice stirpiculture (family culture) (Murstein 1974:340–350; Parker 1935; Robertson 1970; Smith 1978: 89–92).

Victoria Woodhull, a prominent feminist and one of the first women stockbrokers in New York, championed the **"free love" movement**. She publicized the adulterous behavior of socially prominent men, arguing that women should have the same right to sexual liberation and divorce. She also advocated that women take responsibility for their own health and understand the functioning of their own bodies instead of accepting the Victorian view that women should be passive, nonpassionate, and asexual creatures.

Although they never numbered more than a few thousand, the utopian socialists and the advocates of free love and women's equality had an influence on sex in America far greater than their numbers would indicate (D'Emilio & Freedman 1988:160–166; Murstein 1974:368–379; Smith 1978:94–95). The Puritan and Victorian views of sex and the marital experiments of the 1800s are the source of many of the tensions that exist today between fundamentalists and liberal religious views of premarital sex, sexually nonexclusive marriages, contraception, abortion, and homosexuality.

Courtship Patterns

For the colonists and later immigrants, the month-long 3,000-mile voyage to the New World weakened kinship ties. Instead of marriages arranged by parents, single men in the colonies arranged with ship captains to bring them suitable brides from Europe for which they paid in trade or tobacco. In the southern colonies, white women married by age 13 or 14; in New England, before age 20.

Courtship and marriage in the 1700s rarely included love as we think of it, for they were practical matters that had more to do with survival and raising children for farm work than with romance. Although passion and sex were frowned on, a clearly double moral standard allowed men to indulge in lusty pleasures with female servants, slaves, Indians, and others who did not have social status.

The lack of privacy in the small log cabin or sod house directly affected courtship values and behavior. With living quarters often limited to one or two

HIGHLIGHT BOX 1.1.
ONE FOUNDING FATHER'S
VIEW OF SEX

This classic 1876 Currier & Ives lithograph of Benjamin Franklin flying his famous kite in a June 1752 thunderstorm is evidence of the open lifestyles that existed among the emerging upper class of colonial America. The boy is Franklin's first son William, who was born out of wedlock by a lower-class woman and then adopted by Frankin and his wife Deborah Reed. William remained a loyalist during the Revolution and was appointed Royal Governor of the New Jersey Colony by King George. During his 44-year marriage, Franklin had several long-term extramarital affairs, some during his 17 consecutive years abroad spent apart from his wife.

In *Poor Richard's Almanack*, Franklin gave spicy, sexy, and frank advice in such features as "Bachelor's Folly," "Game for Kisses," "On Choosing a Mistress," "Conjugal Debate," and "The Speach of Miss Molly Baker" who had five offspring out of wedlock. In the "Old Mistresse's Apologue," Franklin recommended marriage to a lusty young friend: "But if you cannot take this Counsel and persist in thinking a Commerce with the Sex inevitable, then I repeat my former Advice, that in all your Amours you should prefer old Women to younger ones . . ." because they are more worldly, more experienced with sex, less likely to become pregnant, more discreet, less likely to make you feel guilty over debauching a virgin, and are "so grateful"!

How would Franklin's lifestyle be viewed in American politics today?

rooms, children were aware of their parents' lovemaking (D'Emilio & Freedman 1988:15–53). For the pioneers this situation created a natural acceptance of the body and sexual behavior that often conflicted with strong religious restrictions on indulgence in any sexual behavior that was not marital and procreative. Typical of the realities of Puritan life are the records of a Connecticut church where a third of the people joining the church between 1761 and 1775 confessed to premarital sex (Calhoun 1945:58–59).

Courtship in rural areas produced an interesting custom of premarital sex known as **bundling**. On the scattered farms, young men would stay overnight when they went courting a young lady rather than return home in the dark. When everyone retired at sundown, the young man and woman usually shared the same bed. The young woman might be enclosed in a large bag with a tightly secured drawstring or separated from her suitor by a bundling board. This nod to Puritan ethics had its practical side, as Washington Irving noted:

> To this sagacious custom, therefore do I chiefly attribute the unparalleled increase of the Yankee race; for it is a certain fact, well authenticated by court record and parish registers, that, wherever the practice of bundling prevailed, there was an amazing number of sturdy brats annually born unto the State, without the license, the law, or the benefit of clergy.
>
> *(Knickerbocker's History of New York:* 189)

Bundling allowed a couple to make sure they could conceive and produce the children they would need to help out with the farm work. Once a pregnancy was assured, marriage followed (Murstein 1974:317–318; Smith 1978:57-58; Turner 1955).

By the time of the American Revolution, the larger houses of the emerging urban middle class allowed for privacy and such amenities as sitting rooms. Turkish-style sofas became fashionable as a more proper site for courtship than the bundling bed (Smith 1978:57–58). The privacy of the nuclear family became a new and important value. Larger homes nourished Victorian ethics, with the private bedrooms and bath area clearly separated from social rooms shared with friends. Children in these families enjoyed an extended childhood marked by sexual innocence. Public elementary and secondary schools appeared. With the economic productivity of upper- and middle-class children replaced by an extended dependence on the parents, the functional family shrank from 10 or more children to around 6. Today adolescence extends into the mid-twenties.

Mobility has also altered courtship. Mass-produced bicycles in the late 1800s, automobiles in the 1920s, the privacy of the movie theater and dance halls (the 1930s through the 1950s), and the freedom of coed college life liberated young people from the supervision of parents and allowed them to seek a partner for marriage on their own terms.

Medical Advances

Medical discoveries have also had a major impact on our sexual behavior, especially the development and social acceptance of more effective and easier-to-use contraceptives. Contraceptives had been around for centuries, but Charles Goodyear's discovery of vulcanized rubber in 1839 led to mass-produced rubber condoms and diaphragms that gave men and women some control over their reproductive functions. In 1864 antiseptics checked the outbreak of puerperal fever, an often fatal infection occurring during childbirth. This discovery greatly reduced both infant and maternal deaths. The labor needs of the Industrial Revolution encouraged large families, and abortion was hard to come by because it was condemned by the emerging medical establishment.

In the early 1900s, Margaret Sanger (1883–1966), a young nurse, was fired with a crusader's zeal by the overcrowded slums of New York City. She was determined to do something about the many unwanted pregnancies and the high rate of infant and maternal death among immigrants. Sanger argued that *birth control,* a term she introduced, was every woman's right. Her efforts to provide the poor with then-illegal contraceptive information and devices was fought by police and religious leaders who argued that these innovations would increase immoral behavior and eliminate the unwanted pregnancy as a divine punishment for illicit sex. Despite police harassment, Sanger opened her first birth control clinic in New York City in 1916. Ultimately, her efforts led to the International Planned Parenthood/World Population organization which now plays a major role in the struggle to control population growth (D'Emilio & Freedman 1988:243-254; Haeberle 1978:473–477).

In 1920 Kimberly Clark Company had a surplus of cellulose wadding that had been used as bandaging material during World War I. When a company manager learned that army nurses had adapted the absorbent material to use as menstrual pads instead of the clean rags that had been customary, the disposable sanitary napkin was invented. This seemingly innocuous product helped change sexual customs by giving women greater freedom (Bullough 1980).

During World War II, the discovery of penicillin provided an effective cure for several sexually transmitted diseases and greatly reduced the risks of premarital and extramarital sex (Figure 1.3).

Without a doubt the most influential of all medical discoveries affecting sexual customs has been the oral contraceptive—the Pill. Anthropologist Ashley Montagu ranks the discovery of the Pill in 1954 and its release for public use in the early 1960s among the half-dozen major innovations in more than two million years of human history. He puts the Pill on a par with the discovery of fire, the creation and use of tools, and the development of agriculture, hunting, urban life, scientific medicine, and nuclear power (Montagu 1969). For the first time in human history women and men could engage in sexual intercourse without worrying about pregnancy. Equally important, unlike other contraceptives, the Pill is taken every day without any direct connection with the decision to have intercourse (D'Emilio & Freedman 1988:250–252). Although the Pill probably contributed to an increase in premarital and extramarital sex, it did not result in the hedonist promiscuity some critics forecast. Nor did it bring the reduction in unwanted pregnancies its advocates hoped for, mainly because sex education was practically nonexistent and discussion of contraception for teenagers carried a strong social taboo.

Other recent medical developments, such as test tube babies and the appearance of herpes and AIDS, are discussed later in our chronology of the 1950s to the present.

Shifting Sex Ratios

The Western frontier and the 1849 Gold Rush openly challenged the proprieties of Victorian morality. On the frontier, women often played a leading role inconceivable to their Victorian counterparts back east. The harsh and demanding

Figure 1.3. *Typical of the ambivalence of the Victorian era are the advertisements that ran in popular newspapers and magazines. These advertisements appeared in the May 28, 1892, National Police Gazette.*

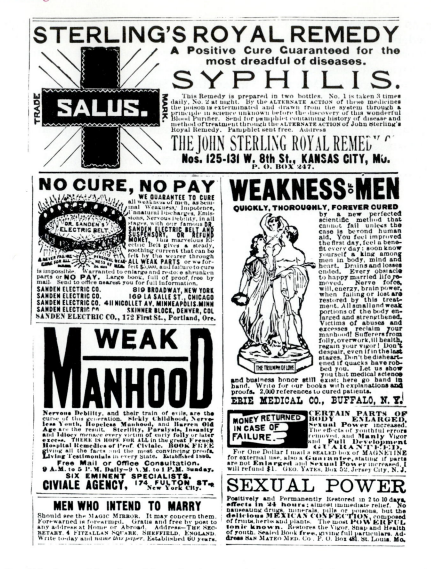

frontier life forced husbands and wives to break out of the Victorian roles of male as the breadwinner and female as the domestic. Equal status was a functional necessity.

At the same time, rapid growth brought a major imbalance of the sexes and a definite shortage of women. In 1850 men in California outnumbered women 12 to 1; Colorado had 16 men for every woman! Thousands of women were imported from Latin America, Asia, and the South Pacific to cater to the sexual needs of the men who rode the cattle trails or searched for gold. In the more settled Midwest, there were roughly equal numbers of both sexes. On the East Coast, women began to outnumber men as the men headed west. This surplus, especially among the poor and recent immigrants, forced many young women to turn to prostitution to supplement their meager incomes (Bullough & Bullough 1987:211–231; D'Emilio & Freedman 1988:188–215; Guttentag & Secord 1983:113–150). Toward the end of the 1800s, the sex ratios across the country began to even out: White middle-class women moved west in significant numbers when the transcontinental railroads provided safe transport (Smith 1978: 99–176).

In more recent years, the baby boom (1945 through the mid-1960s) produced a new imbalance, with women of marriageable age outnumbering single available men. In the 1970s and 1980s, this shortage of men left women freer to seek careers and to meet their sexual needs outside marriage. In the 1990s, the sex ratio is shifting to a shortage of women with perhaps a reversal in some of our recent sexual values (see Chapter 17).

The Impact of War and Slavery

Wars always produce social turmoil. The aftermath of the Civil War made a number of changes in the fabric of American sexual customs. It opened up opportunities for many middle-class women to move into the business world as they replaced men leaving to fight the war. Many women learned to nurse the wounded. Ten years later the nation had 15 schools to train women in the new profession of nursing. By 1900 432 nursing schools had opened. Another postwar opportunity for female employment developed when male clerks refused to use the new "automatic writer" machines mass-produced by Remington (Figure 1.4). Although men were the first operators for the newly invented telephones, complaints from customers about their bursts of profanity over malfunctioning equipment soon led to their being replaced by the more mannered women of the time. The growing affluence of the middle and upper class also led to the opening of colleges for women (D'Emilio & Freedman 1988: 172–201).

After the Civil War, industrialization created a new social environment. Many, perhaps the majority, of workers in the textile factories on the East Coast

Figure 1.4. *This turn-of-the-century woman in a Madison, Wisconsin, law office was referred to as a "typewriter." It was years before such typewriters were called secretaries, but office work was a new career possibility for women after the Civil War. As opportunities for financial independence increased, the stage was set for drastic changes in male/female relationships.*

were women, mostly young and single. Although they worked 12 to 15 hours a day in the mills for low wages, many preferred this livelihood because it gave them more freedom than they would have as domestic servants (Bullough & Bullough 1987:216).

World War I also brought changes in male/female relations. The wartime economy required that women leave behind their Victorian proprieties and work in factories, thereby opening new opportunities for financial and social independence. Soldiers returning from Europe often brought home more liberal views about sex and a new knowledge about contraceptives and the prevention of venereal diseases. Between 1910 and 1920, the divorce rate doubled. Premarital sex became more common, with perhaps a third of the brides going to the altar as sexually experienced women. Extramarital sex also increased.

We can trace laws prohibiting sexual relations and marriage between whites and Orientals or blacks back to early British colonists who opposed marriage with the Indians or blacks. The African slave trade, which started in Virginia in 1619, complicated interracial sex and marriage. On the brutal voyage from Africa to the West Indies and on the southern plantations, many slave owners were quick to take sexual advantage of black female slaves they thought of as "breeding stock." In almost every colony, interracial sexual relations were outlawed, despite the prevalence of sexual exploitation by white males (Ferm 1971:54; Murstein 1974:300–303; Smith 1978:26–30).

In the South, slavery profoundly altered marriage for both whites and blacks. Most of the middle- and upper-class young southern white men had their first sexual experiences with black women. Many of them found the casual sexual relationships and the variety so pleasing that they hesitated to marry and even avoided marriage with white women. When they did marry, many did not give up their easy access to black women who were considered "children of nature." White wives and black husbands had no choice but to accept this situation. For the black woman of light color, the position of the master's concubine was easier than fieldwork (Murstein 1974:307).

World War II brought the issue of interracial relationships to a head. Thousands of American soldiers returned home with Oriental or European brides, although at the time more than half of the states had laws forbidding interracial sex and marriages. These illegal unions openly challenged many state laws, the last of which was declared unconstitutional by a U.S. Supreme Court decision in 1967.

Legal Trends

When the Founding Fathers declared that "all men are created equal" and did not include women, they set the stage for an ongoing fight over the legal rights of women. In 1848 the first women's rights convention was held in Seneca Falls, New York. The suffragists pressed hard for their rights to enter colleges and professional careers, to retain custody of their children in divorce, and to own property as married women in their own names. Until these and other rights were recognized, women could not possibly express their sexuality in any way on a par with men. When a 1920 amendment to the Constitution gave women the vote, other major legal changes followed, including the 1964 Civil Rights Act and various guidelines from the Equal Employment Opportunities Commission prohibiting discrimination based on gender.

After the Civil War, the reformer Anthony Comstock (1844–1915) became known as "the nation's censor." In 1873 he engineered the passage of a broadly worded federal law allowing the confiscation of any book, painting, photograph, or other material designed, adapted, or intended to explain human sexual functions, prevent conception, or produce abortion. Known as the **Comstock Prohibition**, this law remained in effect for the next hundred years. It was used in the 1920s to prevent import of Englishwoman Marie Stopes's books, *Married Love* and *Wise Parenthood,* because they discussed women's sexual desire and advocated the use of contraceptives. In 1963 the U.S. Supreme Court declared unconstitutional a Connecticut law forbidding sale of contraceptives to married women. A similar Massachusetts law banning contraceptive sales to single women was declared unconstitutional in 1972 (D'Emilio & Freedman 1988:146–164; Money 1985a:108–114).

For decades the Comstock law was also used to control sexually explicit material. If a prosecutor could prove that the morals of an innocent child might be corrupted by exposure to a book or movie, it was deemed legally obscene. A single page or even a single sentence was enough to have a book banned. However, in 1957, the U.S. Supreme Court created a new, broader definition of **obscenity** using the following three criteria: The dominant theme of the whole work, not just a part of it, must appeal to depraved sexual interests; the material must be offensive to the average community member, not merely to the most susceptible member; and finally, the material must have no redeeming social value. The court's 1957 Roth decision resulted in a change in mores that continues to influence what we see in films and on television, what ads we see, and what books and magazines we can read.

In the early 1970s, a White House Commission on Pornography and Obscenity found no real harm in pornographic films, pictures, and literature, much to the dismay of President Nixon and the U.S. Congress. This debate continues today, long after the 1986 Meese Commission Report declared a nationwide war on pornography.

Sex Research

Sigmund Freud

Sigmund Freud (1856–1939) shocked Victorian society by emphasizing the centrality of sex in every aspect of human development. He challenged the Victorian belief that children and women were sexually innocent. He argued that our infantile sexual experiences shape our adult life and behavior.

Although Freud stressed the biological and psychoanalytic explanations of female sexuality, he failed to consider the role of social expectations in creating the image of the delicate Victorian lady. He also claimed that female orgasm achieved by "narcissistic" masturbation was immature whereas an orgasm resulting from penile intercourse was psychologically mature (Murstein 1974: 288–297).

In a curious way, Freud's theories served to reinforce some Victorian sexual standards, even while they opened the door for radically new views. What made Freud so influential in American sexual traditions was not so much what he said, but his creation of the psychoanalytic movement which claimed sex as its own territory (Haeberle 1978:465).

Havelock Ellis

Havelock Ellis (1859–1939), an English physician, went far beyond his Victorian contemporaries in suggesting that sex could and should be enjoyable and that lovemaking should be sensual and pleasurable. He claimed there was no single pattern of normal sex. "Whatever gives satisfaction and relief to both parties is good and right," he wrote in 1896. On masturbation, Ellis disagreed with the Victorian belief that it caused illness, insanity, and depravity. Masturbation was a natural outlet for sexual energy and an absolute necessity in a society that allowed no sexual expression for children and teenagers. Ellis was also a strong advocate of sex education starting in early childhood and believed that homosexual orientation was congenital and could not be considered a freely chosen "vice" (Highlight Box 1.2).

HIGHLIGHT BOX 1.2. SEX EDUCATION IN THE 1930s AND 1940s

Despite the efforts of Havelock Ellis, Margaret Sanger, and other pioneers of sex education, parents seldom discussed sex with their children in the 1930s and 1940s. Teenage boys could learn about sex from *Tijuana bibles.* Rumor suggested that these eight-page booklets were smuggled in from Tijuana, Mexico, although they were actually printed on the cheapest pa-per in Brooklyn. Selling for a penny, they were passed furtively from one curious teenager to another. The bibles, which fitted perfectly into a wallet, illustrated every type of sexual behavior from intercourse to oral and anal sex, group sex, and bestiality, using all the famous cartoon characters of the day, even Snow White and the Seven Dwarfs.

Robert L. Dickinson

The industrial demands for labor during World War I and the social changes of the exuberant Roaring Twenties also contributed to more liberal sexual attitudes and behavior, but the Great Depression of the 1930s witnessed a temporary return to Victorian morality. R. L. Dickinson, a noted gynecologist of that era, documented the impact of a revitalized conservatism on marital sex when he reported that:

> The characteristic coitus of American middle-class couples is brief and physiologically male, the female remaining passive and isolated. Once or twice a week there takes place, without preliminaries, an intromission lasting up to five minutes, at the end of which the husband has an orgasm and the wife does not. Both man and woman know that the woman has no animating desire. She submits without welcome to the embrace, it may occur without [her sexual] excitement and she expects it to terminate without [her] orgasm.

> *(Cited by Brecher 1969:154)*

Alfred Kinsey

In 1938 Alfred Kinsey, a biology professor at the University of Indiana, set out to remedy the lack of knowledge about American sexual behavior. Recruiting a few colleagues, he worked throughout World War II interviewing 5,300 men and compiling detailed sexual case histories. In 1948, as America was confronting new roles and tensions in male/female relations brought on by the war, the "Kinsey report," *Sexual Behavior in the Human Male*, showed that American men were much more sexually active than most were willing to admit. Among Kinsey's main findings were these:

- 95% of all males were sexually active by age 15.
- The average single male had three to four orgasms a week.
- About 70% of men had relations with prostitutes by age 35.
- 37% of males had some homosexual experience by age 21.
- Half of the married males had had extramarital relations by age 40.

Kinsey's study clearly showed that the sexual behavior of the American male did not match the values openly endorsed by society. Kinsey, in fact, concluded that his figures on adultery were probably understated, since infidelity was not easily admitted in the 1940s (Pomeroy 1972).

In 1953 Kinsey's research team added to our knowledge with their book *Sexual Behavior in the Human Female*:

- 30% of unmarried females were not virgins by age 23.
- The average American wife experienced 233 orgasms before marriage, and frequently became nonorgasmic after marriage. (Compare this statistic with Dickinson's observations in the 1930s on the top of this page.)
- One in 4 girls had some sexual contact before age of 12: 52% with strangers, 32% with friends, 9% with uncles, 4% with fathers, and 3% with brothers.

Kinsey's second report also revealed that the female orgasm, even in married women, was usually achieved by masturbation. This revelation, coupled with the birth control pill, began to free sex from the procreation-only category and legitimize oral-genital sex and noncoital sex as acceptable sexual outlets.

Masters and Johnson

In the 1960s the research of William H. Masters, M.D., and Virginia E. Johnson focused public attention on the scientific study of physiology and psychology of the human sexual response. For 12 years, Masters and Johnson interviewed and observed individuals experiencing orgasm through masturbation and/or intercourse. Their research gave us our first detailed scientific information about the stages of human sexual response, what happens to our bodies during sexual arousal and orgasm.

The work of Masters and Johnson opened the door for television talk-show hosts and magazine articles to discuss sexual dysfunctions such as a man's inability to have an erection or a woman's lack of orgasm. Their work also led to a wide range of behavioral therapies for such problems. Within a few years sexual therapists were as popular and legitimate as psychotherapists.

The Media and the Arts

Although social commentators often debate whether the media and the arts—music, dance, paintings, photography, film, and television—merely reflect social changes or actually help promote such changes, the truth probably is a combination of both. Thus the impact of the media and the arts is worth examining in any discussion of the evolution of American sexual customs.

As with any time of postwar prosperity and peace, the Roaring Twenties was a decade of social change and new freedoms, characterized by short skirts and short hair for women. Young people danced both cheek to cheek and the wild Charleston (Figure 1.5). Scott Joplin's syncopated ragtime rhythms found their way on phonograph disks from the bordellos of New Orleans into American middle-class living rooms. In the silent films, Rudolph Valentino was an irresistible sex idol. Vamps such as Clara Bow, the ''It Girl,'' and Theda Bara replaced the petticoated Victorian ladies as popular icons (D'Emilio & Freedman 1988:256–260; Ehrenberg 1981).

The Pre-Counterculture of the 1950s

Our overview of eight threads in the fabric of American sexual customs has revealed an accelerating movement away from restrictive attitudes. This momentum picked up speed in the 1950s and burst into a full-blown sexual revolution in the 1960s. In the explosion, a counterculture emerged to challenge the social stability and sexual values of the past.

Many factors contributed to the emerging counterculture, including sex research, the birth control pill, and new developments in the media. Another key was the emergence of teenagers as a distinct consumer group with their own rock music and a powerful sense of their own sexuality.

Figure 1.5. *While the U.S. Federation of Women's Clubs rose in wrath to condemn the new body-clutching, cheek-to-cheek dancing popularized by Vernon and Irene Castle, it spread across the country as the bunny hug, the turkey trot, and, most scandalous of all, the tango and hesitation waltz.*

Playboy

In 1953 *Playboy* magazine, emphasizing female nudity and sex, became the best selling man's magazine. Its publisher, Hugh Hefner, was as surprised as the rest of the country when *Playboy* made pornography a mainstream phenomenon. In 1978 he admitted, "When I conceived this magazine a quarter of a century ago, I had no notion that it would become one of the most important, imitated, influential, and yet controversial publishing ventures of all time. . . . *Playboy* was intended as a response to the repressive antisexual, antipleasure values of our Puritan heritage." Its philosophy, however, was and still is very much in keeping with a patriarchal tradition that views women as sexual objects for men's pleasure and overemphasizes idealized female physical beauty. At the same time, this publicity of the unabashedly erotic has been a major influence on films, magazines, and advertising in the last half of the twentieth century.

The Media and Rock Music

Early television programs tended to present the traditional American family without reference to sex. Innocuous as it was in its early days, however, television soon took on a major role in publicizing and thus reinforcing changes in our sexual values and behavior. In less than forty years, television moved from programs like "Leave It to Beaver," "I Love Lucy," and "The Honeymooners" to "General Hospital," "Dynasty," and "Thirtysomething."

Developing alongside the benign treatment of sex on television in the 1950s was a new phenomenon. Teenagers began to emerge as a social group, conscious of their own identity. They watched Dick Clark's "All American Bandstand" not just to hear the Top Ten but to find out the latest trends in teen clothes, magazines, and accessories. Television and advertisers quickly responded to the teenagers' buying power and their budding sexuality. Instead of the sweet ballads of earlier generations, teens in the 1950s listened to their own rock music including songs by Elvis Presley, the early king of rock, who was described by one critic as an

> Adonis-faced hoodlum in a vulgar, flashy suit of phosphorescent threads, a pretty boy slick plateau of hair half-falling over his bedroom eyes, bestial sideburns dribbling down his cheeks, and a phallic guitar jutting out from his body like a mini howitzer (Figure 1.6).

In giving birth to rock and roll, Elvis gave free expression to the adolescent sexual and aggressive energies coming to the surface in the post-World War II baby boom. Out of this experience has come today's sexually explicit music and MTV (D'Emilio & Freedman 1988:302–305; Ehrenreich et al. 1987).

Figure 1.6. *When Elvis emerged from the backwoods of Tennessee to become the king and troubadour of rock music, the older generation roundly condemned his obscene gyrations. In 1956 Ed Sullivan paid Presley a king's ransom of $100,000 to sing his famous "You Ain't Nothing But a Hound Dog" for the Sunday night television audience. At the last moment, Sullivan decided that the cameras must avoid showing those famous movements, which to us appear quite tame.*

The 1950s were also marked by increasing affluence and travel, new signs of sexual freedom in the growing popularity of motels as convenient places for trysts, panty raids on college campuses, and a lasting hallmark of what would become the sexual revolution in the 1960s—the bikini swimsuit.

The Counterculture in the 1960s

As the 1960s began it soon became apparent that traditional American culture was being shaken on all sides by what soon became known as the counterculture (D'Emilio & Freedman 1988:306-308).

Civil Rights for Women and Homosexuals

The social environment can often shape our sexual behavior. Thus the racial integration of schools and colleges in the 1960s, the civil rights marches, and a basic atmosphere of rebellion and ensuing change resulted in a similar desire for change in the sexual arena. Women began to demand not only their civil rights, but also their sexual rights.

Betty Friedan's 1963 book, *The Feminine Mystique*, spotlighted the inequalities and restrictions that prevailed in American male/female relations and marriage. Her impassioned bestseller helped galvanize the feminist movement and focused the consciousness and passion of many on women's rights. As women fought to gain equality, an Equal Rights Amendment to the U.S. Constitution was proposed, although this effort eventually failed to gain ratification in 1982 (D'Emilio & Freedman 1988:308–318).

On the legal front, antiquated laws regulating sexual behavior dating back to the 1800s were overturned. In 1961 Illinois became the first state to adopt a criminal code based on **consenting adult laws** which removed the long-standing penalties for private consensual sex, fornication, adultery, and homosexual relations. Other states then began to update a variety of laws regulating sexual behavior and marital relations. Eventually this effort led to changes that protect the rights of the victims of rape and spouse abuse.

The 1960s began with the start of the women's liberation movement and closed with the birth of the gay liberation movement. In June 1969 when the New York City police raided the Stonewall Bar, a favorite leisure spot for gay men in Greenwich Village, the patrons fought back. This highly publicized event was followed by political efforts to achieve recognition of the civil, legal, and social rights of gays and lesbians.

A Sexual Revolution

In the aftermath of the Pill, an extended adolescence and new freedoms for teenagers, sex was treated more casually in the 1960s. Public discussion of sexuality became much more acceptable, thanks to Masters and Johnson's research. So-called flower children for whom sex was liberated from all commitment and responsibility symbolized the new sexual openness in the tribal love rock and frontal nudity of *Hair* on Broadway. Today, nudity on television or in movies is almost commonplace. In August 1968 400,000 American youths gathered at a farm in Bethel, New York, for an open-air rock festival that gave the name of the nearby town of Woodstock to a whole generation (Figure 1.7) (Morrison & Morrison 1987:197–221).

Figure 1.7. *The so-called establishment and adult generation discreetly retreated when 400,000 young people descended on the small rural town of Bethel, New York, in August 1968 to establish the Woodstock Nation while they listened to rock music. Nudity, marijuana, hard drugs, and open displays of sexuality were part of the happening.*

The Counterculture in the 1970s

By the 1970s it was evident that America was in the midst of a revolution in sexual attitudes and behavior. Divorce rates had risen by about 10% a year in the 1960s. The frequency of premarital and extramarital intercourse had increased significantly. These permissive trends in sexual mores continued through most of the 1970s, along with an even greater openness about sexual matters. A backlash also emerged, however, as a new conservatism and economic hard times challenged many of these social changes (Highlight Box 1.3).

Liberal Trends

In the 1970s, the efforts of women to achieve equality with men had a major impact on male/female relations, courtship, marriage, sexual mores, and our views of sexuality. Pressure from women's groups was a major factor in two U.S. Supreme Court decisions. In 1972 the court declared unconstitutional all laws prohibiting the sale of contraceptives to unmarried persons. In its 1973 Roe v. Wade decision, the court recognized a woman's right to the privacy of her body and declared state laws prohibiting abortion unconstitutional. The separation of sexual intercourse and reproduction received an added psychological boost when the world's first test-tube baby was born on July 25, 1978, in England. At the same time the National Organization of Non-Parents (NON)

HIGHLIGHT BOX 1.3.
ECONOMICS AND WOMEN'S
HEMLINES 1921–1977

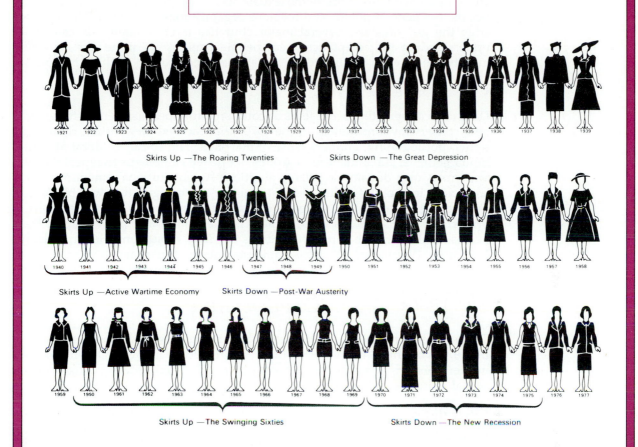

Skirts Up —The Roaring Twenties   Skirts Down —The Great Depression

Skirts Up —Active Wartime Economy   Skirts Down —Post-War Austerity

Skirts Up —The Swinging Sixties   Skirts Down —The New Recession

The history of women's hemlines documents a correlation between skirt length and the economics of 60 years. Short skirts turn up when the Gross National Product is up and long skirts return when times are austere.

and Zero Population Growth (ZPG) were publicizing a growing concern about world overpopulation.

The equality of men and women was promoted by the 1972 bestseller *Open Marriage*. The authors, Nena and George O'Neil, advocated an equal partnership between husband and wife as two friends. Sexual exclusivity was not essential in a happy, healthy marriage. At the same time, the number of single men and women increased as more young people delayed marriage. Singles and married couples turned for advice about their sex lives to bestsellers like

Alex Comfort's *The Joy of Sex* and *The Sensuous Man*. Alternate lifestyles, open marriages, swinging, and mate swapping were popular topics on television.

In the decade after the 1969 Stonewall Bar riot, gay and lesbian groups expanded their work in the political arena against discrimination in housing and employment. As more homosexuals acknowledged their orientation, politicians, the general public, and religious organizations were forced to acknowledge the gay lifestyle. Several major churches issued statements calling for understanding and acceptance of gay people as members of the Christian community. Some even began ordaining gay men and women to the ministry.

Conservative Trends

Difficult economic times and fears of counterculture permissiveness triggered a new conservative movement in the 1970s that focused on abortion rights, gay rights, pornography, and a defense of marriage. The so-called Moral Majority, fundamentalist and antiabortion groups, launched campaigns to repeal the 1973 Supreme Court decision legalizing abortion. A constitutional amendment was advocated to prohibit all abortions. Local gay rights legislation was blocked or repealed. Antipornography groups organized marches and demonstrations to protest sex shops, peep shows, X-rated movies, and other pornographic businesses. Bestsellers like Marabel Morgan's *The Total Woman* and Helen Andelin's *Fascinating Womanhood* defended traditional views of marriage.

The 1980s: A Post-Counterculture

The turmoil of the 1960s counterculture and the conservative-liberal tensions of the 1970s continued into a post-counterculture decade in the 1980s with increasing tensions triggered by two decades of rapid, often radical changes in our sexual attitudes and behaviors.

Liberal Trends

Despite a slowing of the pace of change in the 1980s, new liberal trends appeared, no doubt the result of the more open atmosphere fostered by an increasing candor about sexual issues.

Bisexual and homosexual issues made headline news. Such public figures as tennis star Martina Navratilova, and Congressmen Barney Frank (D-Massachusetts), Gerry E. Studds (D-Massachusetts), and Robert E. Bauman (R-Maryland) discussed their homosexual lifestyles. Restrictions on homosexuals in the military and civilian employment were challenged in the courts with limited success. Some courts recognized the rights of the "domestic partners" in gay and lesbian unions.

Popular music and movies reflected the increased candor about sexual issues. Songs such as Marvin Gaye's 1982 "Sexual Healing," "Let's Get It On," and "Midnight Love," Madonna's 1986 "Papa, Don't Preach" about a pregnant teenager, Poison's heavy metal "Talk Dirty to Me," and George Michael's 1987 hit "I Want Your Sex" made it to the top of the charts. Soft- and hard-core pornography became common entertainment with the advent of cable TV and X-rated and soft-core videocassettes for home VCRs.

More than any other factor, herpes and AIDS created an urgent need for greater candor about sexuality. We had hardly recovered from the panic of 1981 when an estimated 2 million Americans were reported infected with the herpes virus when AIDS surfaced in the summer of 1983. Gay communities led in mobilizing the nation's awareness of safer sex practices. The deaths of Rock Hudson, Liberace, fashion designer Perry Ellis, Broadway director Michael Bennett, and a U.S. Congressman, along with thousands memorialized in the AIDS quilt displayed across the nation, forced Americans to face the issue of sexuality with greater candor. By the late 1980s, U.S. Surgeon General C. Everett Koop was advocating sex education programs, including discussion of AIDS, safer sex practices, and condoms, as early as the third grade. Efforts to cope with AIDS prevention in the schools and on national television forced us to deal far more openly with discussions of sexually active youth, homosexuality, bisexuality, condoms, and oral and anal sex.

Neoconservatism

A new form of conservatism, led by the New Right and the Moral Majority, was also very visible in the 1980s. With Ronald Reagan at the nation's helm from 1980 to 1988, conservatism had a popular and powerful hero and leader with strong views on traditional values and roles. Conservative views on abortion, women's rights, gay rights, and other issues clashed with liberal laws passed in the 1960s and 1970s. Early in the decade, the proposed Equal Rights Amendment was defeated. A constitutional amendment to prohibit abortion was repeatedly proposed to eliminate the 1.5 million abortions performed in the United States every year. Threats of boycotts kept American pharmaceutical companies from marketing the RU 486 abortion pill. Laws were passed to prevent the use of public money to fund abortions for poor women or to support the population control efforts of international agencies like Planned Parenthood and the United Nations. The 1989 U.S. Supreme Court ruling on Webster v. Reproductive Health Services of Missouri allowed states to prohibit use of any state funds, facilities, or property for abortion services, raising the possibility that future Supreme Court decisions might dismantle the 1973 Roe decision legalizing abortion.

Looking Ahead

The changes in sexual values and lifestyles in recent years have set the stage for the sexual issues that will be most visible in the 1990s. As you can no doubt guess, abortion rights, especially for minors, gay and lesbian rights, and policies on AIDS will continue to cause controversy. Other issues may arise unexpectedly, as AIDS did ten years ago.

The legality of abortion and restrictions on the use of public funds or facilities for the procedure will be decided in state legislatures and courts across the nation. Debates will continue to be heated as church authorities grapple with the role of homosexuals in their communities. Many will continue to oppose any accommodation to or acceptance of gay and lesbian lifestyles. Others will defend such lifestyles as God-given and acceptable. In the 1990s, some will work to expand education programs that promote contraceptive use and safer sex practices to reduce the numbers of teenage and unwanted pregnancies and to slow the spread of AIDS. Others will denounce these programs as promoting promiscuity, and will endorse only programs that stress monogamy and sexual abstinence.

It is interesting to speculate on how our sexual attitudes and behaviors may shift as we approach the 21st century. Will the 1990s be a decade of great change? As in the past, social, political, economic, medical, and other developments will interact to influence our sexual attitudes and behaviors. Since these factors are always in flux, the likelihood is that sexual lifestyles, behaviors, and values also will continue to change.

The trends evident in our past will continue to affect the course of the present and future. This chapter should have helped you understand and evaluate the effects of social and historical forces on the ways we experience our sexuality. You may now recognize how particular events have influenced the sexual development of your grandparents, your parents, and yourself.

Key Concepts

1. Human sexuality is expressed as a bio-psycho-socio-cultural phenomenon that includes our sexual anatomy, our gender identity, and the roles and behaviors we adopt to express it, and the gender of the persons we fall in love with or are attracted to.

2. Studying the history of American sexual customs enables us to realize that the terms *normal* and *traditional* have to be used very carefully.

3. American sexual customs have been marked by a continual tension between conservative and liberal forces, although the overall trend has been away from structured and uniform values and lifestyles toward a more flexible and pluralistic value system.

4. Critical factors promoting changes in a conservative direction have included economic depressions, war, the perceived survival or identity needs of an ethnic or socioeconomic group within a culture, the needs of a particular economic or technological system for support from a particular pattern of male/female relationships, and the psychological threat of change which pushes people to use political or religious arguments to buttress their traditional values and lifestyles.

5. Factors promoting changes in a liberal direction have included the introduction of new sex roles and attitudes from other cultures during wartime, advances in technology which create new sex role opportunities, economic prosperity that allows people leisure and security to explore different sexual values and lifestyles, medical advances, pioneering advances in the arts, media, and sex research, and the flexible, more fluid social fabric of frontier times.

6. Religious beliefs, legal changes, and shifting sex ratios can either promote changes in sexual attitudes and behavior, or restrict people by narrowly defining what is sexually acceptable.

Key Terms

bio-psycho-socio-cultural
  phenomenon (4)
bundling (10)
celibacy (7)
Comstock Prohibition (15)
consenting adult laws (21)
"free love" movement (8)

group marriage (8)
monogamy (8)
obscenity (15)
polygyny (7)
Puritan (5)
sexuality (4)
Victorian (6)

Summary Questions

1. What specific factors have fostered changing attitudes toward premarital and extramarital sex from colonial times to the present?

2. Discuss the role of six or more developments in medicine or the law in triggering changes in male/female roles and relationships.

3. Outline changes in male/female roles and expectations, in marriage patterns, and in sexual attitudes that occurred in the aftermath of the Civil War, World War I, and World War II.

4. Identify five or more technological inventions, not including medical advances, that have liberalized courtship, male/female relations, and opened new opportunities for women.

5. How do changes in music and dance in the 20th century reflect and/or reinforce changing sexual attitudes and behaviors?

Suggested Readings

Bailey, B. L. (1988). *From Front Porch to Back Seat: Courtship in Twentieth-Century America*. Baltimore: Johns Hopkins University Press. Insights into the privatization of courtship.

D'Emilio, J., & E. B. Freedman. (1988). *Intimate Matters: A History of Sexuality in America*. New York: Harper & Row. A readable history of sex in America stressing the role of economics.

Ehrenreich, B., E. Hess, & G. Jacobs. (1987). *Remaking Love: The Feminization of Sex*. New York: Doubleday. A feminist overview of changing sexual attitudes.

Gardella, P. (1985). *Innocent Ecstasy: How Christianity Gave America an Ethic of Sexual Pleasure*. New York: Oxford University Press. A revisionist interpretation of the positive role played by religion in changing sexual attitudes.

Gordon, L., & A. Gordon. (1987). *American Chronicle: Six Decades in American Life 1920–1980*. New York: Atheneum. Comprehensive lists of developments and events, but with no analysis.

Morrison, J., & R. K. Morrison. (1987). *From Camelot to Kent State*. Brief, powerful personal recollections of persons who participated in Woodstock, the feminist movement, and other social movements of the 1970s.

The Cross-Cultural
Perspective
Sexual Customs in the
Islamic World
The Islamic View of Sex
A Shame Culture
Women in Islam
Marriage
Homosexuality
Islam and the Western
World
Sexual Customs in the
Hindu World
The Hindu View of Sex
Hindu Women
Marriage
Homosexuality
Hinduism and the
Western World
Sexual Customs in the
People's Republic
of China
The Chinese View of Sex
Marriage
Homosexuality
China and the Western
World
Sexual Customs in the
Latino Cultures
The Latino View of Sex
Four Basic Sexual
Values
The Latino Experience
Today
The Complexities of
Sexual Customs

Chapter 2

Sexual Customs in Other Cultures

Special Consultants

For Islamic traditions, *Paula E. Ardehali, Ph.D.*, cultural anthropologist, has taught in Iran. *Hussein Elkholy, Ph.D.*, is a native of Egypt, and *Javad Namazi, Ph.D.*, is a native of Iran.

For Hindu traditions and India, *Mrudulla Gnanadesikan, Ph.D.*, and *Jaya Natarajan, Ph.D.*, were born and raised in India and teach at Fairleigh Dickinson University.

For the People's Republic of China, *Fang Fu Ruan, M.D.*, medical anthropologist, Beijing Medical University, the People's Republic of China.

For the Latino cultures, *Diane De Mauro, Ph.D.*, Latin American specialist, SIECUS; *Antonio W. Burr, Ph.D.*, clinical psychologist and Latin American sexuality educator; *Sophia Kamenetzky, M.D.*, Latin American population specialist; *Mario Kamenetzky*, former advisor for the World Bank; and *Sergio Jaime, M.D.*, clinical psychiatrist, Guadalajara, Mexico.

For the chapter context: *Suzanne G. Frayser, Ph.D.*, author of *Varieties of Sexual Experience: An Anthropological Perspective on Human Sexuality* (1985), and coauthor of *Studies in Human Sexuality: A Selected Guide* (1987).

Male and female relations and sexual values and lifestyles are always an integral part of a culture's whole fabric. The American sexual customs we examined in Chapter 1 are rooted in thousands of years of European cultural history, in the Jewish and Christian value systems, and in the cultural experiences of America. One out of every 5 people today is the product of this Western Judaeo-Christian culture. We examine the sexual mores of this tradition in Chapter 3. Here we focus on the 80% of the world's people who are not products of an American or European religious or cultural tradition.

As a student on today's college campus and as an American in this multi-cultural nation, you have undoubtedly been confronted with cultural and sexual values that are unfamiliar to you. These encounters are understandable, since 1 out of every 10 students in American colleges is foreign born. To broaden your knowledge and to give you some perspective on other sexual lifestyles, we devote this chapter to the sexual customs in four major religious and cultural traditions. We begin with Islamic and Hindu views of sex. We also look at the traditions of mainland China, with their Confucian and Taoist heritage and recent Communist influences. Finally we return to the West and provide some insights into the sexual values of the Latin American world.

The Cross-Cultural Perspective

Exploring the sexual patterns in other cultures enables us to gain a perspective on our own sexuality. It is natural to view other cultures with an ethnocentric bias or to use our own values as the standard for judging others. We actively avoid that approach here by looking at other cultures for the richness and variety of ways in which humans have learned to express their sexuality within different social contexts. Just as American sexual attitudes and customs developed in response to our changing social environment over the years, so the sexual attitudes and customs of other cultures have also evolved diverse patterns. Customs of courtship, marriage patterns, and sexual behavior change in response to economic, political, religious, and other forces.

After reading this chapter, it will be difficult for you to maintain the assumption that there is only one acceptable pattern of male/female relations, sexual patterns, or customs. You will see that each society has rules governing sexual behavior and that there is no universal agreement on what is considered normal.

Sexual Customs in the Islamic World

Worldwide today, there are over 800 million Muslims, or followers of the 7th-century prophet Mohammed. Half of all the people in the Middle East, Turkey, Saudi Arabia, Iraq, Iran, Pakistan, Afghanistan, Indonesia, and Malaysia, as well as many in northern Africa, live in accordance with Islamic traditions (Fellows 1979; Ludwig 1989:174–244).

The Islamic View of Sex

Like Judaism and Christianity, the Islamic culture was born in the land of the eastern Mediterranean. Unlike the Christian tradition, Islam was not molded by the Greek and Stoic philosophers who gave Christianity a negative view of

Figure 2.1. *The Muslim religion never demanded the suppression of sexual interests and pleasure as the price of eternal salvation. Thus, Islamic literature and art are often very sensual, even erotic.*

the body with its emotions and passions. In Islam, there is no concept of a primeval human couple committing an original sin. Nor is there an Islamic equivalent of an innocent Adam and Eve being expelled from a Garden of Eden for disobeying God and being punished with a life of hardship and denial. Consequently, Islam does not have a tradition of asceticism or redemption by avoidance of passions and sensual pleasures. Instead, the Islamic faith celebrates sensuality and sexuality. Muslims do not believe in denying the pleasures of sex to gain entry to heaven. However, the Islamic culture is quite patriarchal and male-oriented. The paradise of Islam is a garden of sensual delights where men are waited on by bright-eyed beautiful virgins and where both partners enjoy sexual delights (Figure 2.1). This celebration of sexuality is evident in Islamic sexual anecdotes and romances such as the classic "Thousand and One (Arabian) Nights" and the "Perfumed Garden for the Soul's Delectation" (Tannahill 1980:229–255).

Because Islam is a dominant influence in cultures from Africa to the Far East, it is difficult to make universal statements about the relations of Muslim men and women, their attitudes toward sex, and their marriage patterns. Local ethnic, social, and historical factors affect the ways in which the Islamic faith is interpreted and applied. These influences determine how strict and traditional or how flexible and open the interpretation of Islam is in any given place. Nonetheless, we can make some generalizations about sexual trends in today's Islamic world.

A Shame Culture

According to anthropologist Margaret Mead, a culture may control sexual behavior in one of two ways: with internal guilt or with the social pressure of shame. In **guilt cultures**, which prevail in Europe and North America, internal constraints based on a sense of personal guilt are used to keep people on the straight and narrow. Guilt cultures stress the personal fear of committing a sin or doing something inherently bad and then being punished with eternal fires of hell and damnation. Most Islamic cultures are what Margaret Mead calls shame cultures. A **shame culture** uses external constraints and family pressures to prevent people from violating social mores.

In shame cultures, sexual activity is not considered sinful, as it is in a guilt culture because sex is accepted as the inevitable outcome of any male/female social encounter. But shame cultures are quick to control sexual expression and protect the honor of males and their families. Among the rural Pahktun of Pakistan, for example, a husband is permitted to kill or cut off the nose of his wife if she is seen in the company of another man. Because the relationship is perceived to be sexual, the husband is obligated to avenge the shame his wife has brought on him and his family. In shame cultures, it is the family's responsibility to ensure that a woman is not left alone with an unrelated male. The honor of the woman, her mate, and both families is at stake. Girls, consequently, are taught not to pay any attention to the seductive talk of males in order to avoid shaming themselves and their families. Men in this patriarchal tradition, however, are allowed to do everything in their power to be alone with a woman and seduce her. If successful, the man can abandon the woman if he likes because she has lost her honor (Ardehali 1990).

Women in Islam

In less traditional Islamic countries, Muslim women work outside the home and dress in Western attire. But in Pakistan, Saudi Arabia, and other more conservative Muslim cultures, the practice of **purdah**, the institution of female seclusion, is an important custom (Figure 2.2). Purdah requires that Muslim women never be seen by a man who is not a close relative. These women wear a veil, known in Iran as a *chador*, that covers most of the face and the entire body. Worn in public, the chador protects a woman from being viewed by strangers. In the Muslim view, women are considered to be very sexual and sensual. The chador keeps them anonymous and reduces the risk of their being approached by men.

In traditional Islamic countries, the chador is a symbol of the way women are viewed:

> In these tribal or feudal societies, women are viewed as properties of men. As properties, women may attract, or be attracted to strangers, and so must be controlled. The slightest contact of a woman with a nonrelative male is regarded as an invasion of property. By keeping a woman in seclusion, a man secures his property. It is no accident that in some traditional societies men use the word "house" when referring to their wives.
>
> *(Namazi 1990)*

To the casual observer, Iran appears to be among the strictest adherents of purdah. Women caught in public without the chador are severely punished by the Revolutionary Guard. A man and woman walking side by side on the street may be stopped and asked for proof of marriage or immediate family relationship. Imprisonment and torture are the cost of violating purdah. Yet in most Iranian homes in urban areas, women have a freedom they do not have in other Islamic nations. Although Shiite fundamentalists have succeeded in restoring

Figure 2.2. *Although the Muslim women of Morocco are becoming more emancipated as their culture comes into contact with the Western world, most of them still wear the veil in public. Here housewives shop in the souks of Marrakesh. Notice the hint of stylish Western dress under their chadors, the modern sandals and high heels, and the completely Western dress of the young boys.*

many archaic laws, including the death penalty by stoning for women suspected of adultery, actual adherence to these ancient codes is not very common (Namazi 1990).

Westerners tend to view purdah and the chador as a way of repressing or denying the sexuality of women. In reality, the Islamic tradition is a candid recognition of the sexual potential of women. For centuries while the Western world denied the existence of a female orgasm, the Islamic world celebrated female sexuality. But, as you have seen, purdah is also a product of a male-dominated society in which women are viewed as property. This is reflected in a system of **patrilineage** in which the male bloodline and kinship are all-important, and all relationships traced through the female line are ignored.

Marriage

Islamic marriages are usually arranged by the parents. As you might expect in a shame culture, the family is intimately involved in all aspects of the **arranged marriage**. For instance, the families of both the bride and groom are concerned about the proper consummation of the marriage. It is not uncommon for a close female relative of the bride and a close female relative of the groom to sleep outside the bridal chamber and later collect the physical evidence of virginity and consummation. In earlier times, the mother of the bride might actually assist the groom in the consummation in order to document the bride's virginity and maintain her family's honor.

Although the Qur'an—the sacred Muslim writings—allows every Muslim man to take four wives, polygamy is not widely practiced because tradition stipulates that the husband treat all his wives equally. Most Islamic men find such a requirement to be impossible to meet. However, a variation on polygamy can be seen in the custom of temporary marriage, or marriage of pleasure. This practice, known as **mut'a**, allows a couple to spend a few hours, days, or even a few months together, based on mutual agreement. Traditionally, mut'a companions are favored by men who spend considerable time away from their homes and families. In the West, the woman in such a temporary marriage would be considered a mistress or prostitute. However, in a male-dominated society where women have few options and family and personal reputation is a concern, the mut'a offers a way to adapt to the realities of life. In Iran, for example, thousands of women were left without financial support by the Iran-Iraq war, but manage to get along by arranging these temporary marriages (Bullough & Bullough 1987: 75–76; Elkholy 1990; Namazi 1990; Parrinder 1980: 158).

Homosexuality

Generally speaking, Islamic attitudes toward sexual variation are more relaxed than those found in the West. There is no mention of punishments for homosexual behavior in the Qur'an, and early religious writings contain only mildly negative attitudes toward homosexuality. Thus most Islamic societies treat homosexuality with indifference, if not admiration. Less traditional and secular Islamic societies are tolerant of homosexual activity, particularly if it remains private. It is, however, severely punished in fundamentalist Islamic societies such as Iran and Pakistan. Much of the application of Islamic doctrines on homosexuality and other sexual matters depends on the prevailing ethnic influence, be this Arabic, Indic, Pakistani, Malaysian, Indonesian, Philippine, Egyptian, or black African (Boswell 1980:194–196; Haeberle 1978:325).

Islam and the Western World

Whereas the Western world has gone through major social changes and a few sexual revolutions in recent centuries, the Islamic nations did not experience similar upheavals until lately. In many such countries, social behavior and cultural patterns have remained relatively stable for centuries. Despite rapid economic and industrial changes, strict Islamic traditions are widely accepted by both men and women in Saudi Arabia where tribal or feudal social structure persist. In spite of the Islamic Revolution, Iran remains one of the more westernized of Islamic countries, along with Egypt and the secular Muslim state of Turkey. However, even the most westernized Islamic country is significantly different from any Western country in its value systems, which naturally affect what is socially acceptable in male/female relations and sexual behavior.

Although most Westerners associate the Islamic faith with the Arab world, many Muslims are not ethnic Arabs, and many Arabic people are not Muslim, but belong to Christian or other religious traditions. The largest concentration of Arab-Americans is in the metropolitan area of Detroit, Michigan. Of the 150,000 to 180,000 Arab-Americans in that area, over a third are Muslim. The variations in sexual customs, male/female relations, and patterns of marriage among Americans of Arabic origin or the Islamic faith easily match the wide range of ethnic, national, and political realities from which these people came. Immigrants from Turkey or Saudi Arabia have different sexual customs and face different problems adapting to life in the United States than Muslim immigrants from Lebanon, Jordan, the United Arab Emirates, Nigeria, or Pakistan.

Among Muslims in the United States, assimilation is the rule, as it is for most immigrant groups. The shift is invariably toward the dominant Western thinking. The chador is left behind. Young women go to college and seek careers. Their Muslim husbands often adapt, as most American husbands do today, to sharing household chores and child rearing. The family tradition remains strong, and the patrilineal tradition also continues, but strict observance is softened in the new environment. As with all immigrants, some values are lost while others retained. The tradition of arranged marriages is challenged by ideas of romance and love. Many Muslim men continue to have a ritual washing after they have sex and before they leave the house. Many Islamic and Christian women, particularly from Egypt, still keep their pubic area completely free of any hair because they believe it increases the pleasures of sexual intercourse for both partners.

Sexual Customs in the Hindu World

In few traditions are sex and religion more closely linked than in the beliefs of Hinduism, the religion of 83% of the 800 million people in India. Hinduism is native to the Indian subcontinent and includes a wide range of often seemingly contradictory variations, including a belief in reincarnation and a pantheon of gods and goddesses who symbolize the many attributes of the indescribable supreme being. Shakti, the consort of Shiva, the Lord over Death, for instance, is referred to as Parvati, the embodiment of sensuality and the delights of Tantric sexuality, and as Kali, the dark, awesome goddess of the transcendent powers of sex (Fellows 1979:67–124; Ludwig 1989:245–301; Tannahill 1980:199–228).

The Hindu View of Sex

Hinduism in India has blended an important ascetic tradition of celibate monks with an equally strong religious celebration of sexual pleasure in all its forms as a path to the divine. Sexual abstinence is favored at certain stages in the life cycle. But, unlike the sin and guilt-based sexual asceticism characteristic of the Judeao-Christian tradition, Hindu sexual asceticism complements other Hindu traditions that celebrate sexual pleasure. Most Hindus, even the ascetics, view sex as something to be enjoyed in moderation, without repression or overindulgence. Sacred writings, devotional poetry, and annual festivals celebrate married love, the fidelity of women, and the religious power of sexual union.

The paradox of asceticism and sexual pleasure is inherent in Shiva, who is at once the Hindu god of sex and of asceticism. The *lingam*, a stone symbol of the penis, is Shiva's symbol of sexual energy concentrated by asceticism. The lingam and the *yoni*, stone sculptures of the vagina, are regularly part of Hindu and Tantric religious ceremonies.

This erotic tradition also produced the 2nd century B.C. *Kama Sutra* and *Kama Shastra*, the best known of the world's sex manuals. These books were allegedly written by the gods to urge all women and men to be serious students of the erotic arts in preparation for marriage. The thousand-year-old intensely erotic and spiritual sculptures of the so-called "love temples" of Khajuraho and Konarak in northern India celebrate all forms of sexual behavior except adultery and rape.

Tantric religious traditions, found in both Hinduism and Buddhism, worship divinities whose main concern is sexual and cosmic energy (Figure 2.3). Over the centuries, the ecstatic, and at times orgiastic, cults inspired by Tantric visions of cosmic sexuality have been attacked by more ascetic Hindus and the British

Figure 2.3. *This small Tibetan bronze of the god Vajrasattva and his goddess consort is typical of the statues Tibetans keep in their home shrines. Hindu gods and goddesses are frequently shown as a couple, in sexual embrace or* yab-yum. *(From the author's collection.)*

colonial government. Tantric yoga, which has become popular in the United States, stresses a physiology in which a great vein runs from the lowest part of the spine where serpent power, the kundalini, rests, to the highest and most powerful psychic center, the mind, symbolized by the lotus. By arousing the serpent power and channeling its energy upward, a person can learn to be open to the universe and transcendent. In Tantra, the greatest source of energy in the universe is sexual and ritual intercourse; orgasm is a cosmic experience (Parrinder 1980:41–76; Tannahill 1980:309–314).

Between the 1500s and mid-1800s, Muslim invaders attempted to suppress many of the Hindu erotic traditions. English colonialists followed and again tried unsuccessfully to suppress the ancient erotic traditions. Although many threads of the early traditions persist today, the only form of sexual behavior not frowned upon is marital sex.

Hindu Women

Indian children are pampered as much as possible, often until age 6 or 7. Before puberty, a natural approach to sexuality and nudity prevails, especially in rural areas. Daughters and sons are carefully prepared for their future domestic roles as mothers and fathers. Women are considered to be much more skilled than males in love and sexual pleasures. At puberty, most boys and girls are segregated. In some regions of India, pubescent girls are not even allowed to enter a house where a single young man is present. Essentially, tradition dictates that women be subservient to their husbands.

Premarital sex is frowned on, but commonly occurs among college students. There is much more freedom and mobility for women in the cities and suburbs where a unique combination of new affluence, Western values, and traditional Hindu, Buddhist, and Sikh religious values occurs. The urban/suburban environment has also given birth to a fascinating mix of traditional and new sex roles among the affluent middle class. Also interesting to note, in 1966, Indira Gandhi became prime minister of India, at a time when few Western nations would have accepted a woman head of state. And yet, India remains a very male-dominated society.

Marriage

Like Islamic marriages, those in Hindu India are arranged by parents. Family concerns take precedence over the interests of young couples because Indian parents strongly believe that a marriage will be good only if the bride and groom come from similar backgrounds. The impetus for these arranged marriages is respect for the wisdom of one's elders. To assure that their offspring marry within their own community or caste, many Indian parents use the classified advertisement sections of newspapers to make contact and arrange marriages for their children (Highlight Box 2.1).

HIGHLIGHT BOX 2.1. ARRANGED MARRIAGES IN INDIA

Matrimonial advertisements, placed by Indian parents, commonly describe the age, educational background, status, and caste of their sons and daughters. A word or two of physical description might be included, "wheatish complexion" or "fair-skinned," along with mention that a young lady is "homely," meaning she is a skilled homemaker. The parents might indicate that they are willing to negotiate a dowry, although this custom is now officially illegal.

Despite the emergence of romantic love, most marriages in India are still arranged. Only about 5% of college students in India meet without the arrangement being made by their parents or family. Indian students do get to know each other by going out in groups. Dating is frowned on unless the couple has some understanding about marriage. Even in the larger cities like Delhi and Bombay, young people who date and fall in love usually would not want their parents to find out until they are ready to marry. Because of family expectations, many such young people date or marry without their parents' knowledge or approval. A minority of parents are willing to accept the loved-based marriage of their child, after the fact.

MATRIMONIALS
Parents invite correspondence from a tall, handsome, professional, or educated businessman for their 27-year-old, 5'-5", very handsome, fair complexion, homely daughter with green card and M.B.B.S. from a prestigious institution in India.

Physician father Brahmin invites correspondence from presentable, charming, and homely Gujarati girls for his son U.S. citizen, 29, 5'-8", 145, vegetarian, M.S. (computer eng.). Send biodata with recent photographs (returnable).

Although the custom of arranged marriages has a practical value in preserving family traditions and values, it encounters some opposition as young Indian men and women learn of Western styles of romance and love. Urban middle-class Indians are most affected. Most Indian men and women attending college in the United States are careful not to compromise their prospects back home by letting their family know they have dated a foreigner. American women who date Indian men are often surprised to find that the young man fully expects his parents to pick his bride when the time comes.

The centuries-old marital tradition of the dowry has recently become troublesome among some young married couples. Since females historically could not inherit property, parents would give their daughters money and property, a **dowry**, when they married. Young men came to depend on a good-sized dowry to start them off in a comfortable middle-class life. Although dowries were made illegal in the 1970s, the law has created serious problems for brides whose parents refuse to give a sizable gift—the equivalent of the traditional dowry—to the groom. In such cases, some new husbands and their families conspire to drive the young bride to suicide, or if this tactic fails, to even murder her. In this way, a young man might marry several times and eventually accumulate enough in illegal dowries to live comfortably.

Effective enforcement of the antidowry law and protection of brides from abuse are difficult, despite the efforts of women's rights groups and special courts set up by the government. Many believe the only hope for permanent improvement lies in changing social attitudes, including the promotion of marriages based on love instead of a contrived arrangement.

Nevertheless, dowries remain important for many Indian women today. Even though they can now inherit and no longer depend on the dowry for financial security, Indian women still consider the dowry their right. In the mobile social strata of the cities, the size of a woman's dowry definitely affects her social status.

Homosexuality

Although early Hindu and Tantric traditions included homosexual relations in their celebration of sexuality, such activity is generally frowned on in modern India because of Western influences. However, the Hindu culture allows some flexibility in gender roles. Indian culture, in fact, has three genders: male, female, and the *hijras*, the "sexless ones" or "not men." **Hijras** are male homosexuals who adopt a full-time female role. As teenage boys they leave their families to live with other hijras in the larger cities (Figure 2.4). Eventually, they may undergo castration to finalize their status as a member of this third gender which is part cult and part caste. It is not unusual for hijras to entertain at weddings and other festivals (Money 1986:106–107; Nanda 1984; Weinrich 1987:96).

Hinduism and the Western World

Western influences have had a major impact on the sexual values and lifestyles of Indians and Hindus and on those who immigrate to Western countries. A Hindu family leaving India in search of better opportunities in the United States or Europe experiences a shift from the security of a close traditional extended family to the isolation of a nuclear family. It also must confront totally foreign

Figure 2.4. *In the culture of India, the hijras or "sexless ones" form a third gender in the society. Hijras may have their testes removed to symbolize their social and religious status. These hijras are participating in an annual three-week convention of song, dance, and prayer.*

values in a country with a vastly different view of sexuality, marriage, male/female relations, and lifestyles. In the meeting of Hindu and Western values, it becomes obvious that, despite Western influences, the Hindu tradition of India is often more positive about sex than most other world religions.

Sexual Customs in the People's Republic of China

One out of every 4 people today, approximately 1 billion people, live in the People's Republic of China. Increased communications between China and the West have brought Chinese sexual customs into public view after several decades of secrecy.

The Chinese View of Sex

Unlike the Christian West where sexual values and practices have been molded by a continuity within the Judaeo-Christian tradition, Chinese sexual customs have deep roots in three traditional and distinct philosophical and religious sources. For centuries, the teachings of Confucius have directed the proprieties and customs of public life. Taoism, a mystical philosophy based on the teachings of Lao-tzu, regulates private life, the bedroom, and the spiritual quest. Buddhism, as the adopted public religion, also plays a role in Chinese culture (Butterfield 1980; Fellows 1979:199–242; Ludwig 1989:302–349, 377–460; Murstein 1974:467–485; Shon & Ja 1982; Tannahill 1980:164–198).

Confucianism and Taoism teach a duality of the yin and yang that differs from the body/soul opposition underlying much of western Christian thought where there is a very clear split between the body and soul, or spirit, and between male and female. For Christians, salvation and redemption is achieved by subjection of the body and its passions to reason and the spiritual soul. In the Taoist tradition, the vital energies of **yin** and **yang**, variously described as heaven and earth, dark and light, weak and strong, receptive and penetrating, or male and female, are complementary rather than opposing aspects of nature. All reality is composed of yin and yang. The challenge of life is to achieve a dynamic balance between the two principles.

Since both yin and yang coexist in every man and woman, in different proportions, everyone can cultivate, balance, and unite their cosmic energies. In sexual play yin and yang are aroused and can be channeled from the lower levels to the heart and head. This can be achieved in masturbation, and also in both heterosexual and homosexual relations. Heterosexual intercourse has two main purposes: procreation and strengthening of the male through his absorption of yin from the female partner. Even though the male loses some of his limited supply of yang in ejaculation, the female partner has an inexhaustible source of yin on which he can draw, especially if he does not ejaculate during intercourse. Yin and yang are released in orgasm, passing between the partners. The mutual exchange of yin and yang essences is believed to produce perfect harmony, increase vigor, and bring long life (Chia & Chia 1986; Chia & Winn 1984; Parrinder 1980:77–102) (Figure 2.5).

For their first 4,000 years, under Confucian and Taoist influences, the Chinese enjoyed a very open and liberal sexual expression. Sensuality and sexuality were celebrated in a rich erotic art. Homosexuality was accepted, with many of the emperors openly homosexual or bisexual. Because women were viewed as more skilled than men in sexual pleasuring and because the society was patriarchal, concubinage was popular (Ruan & Tsai 1988).

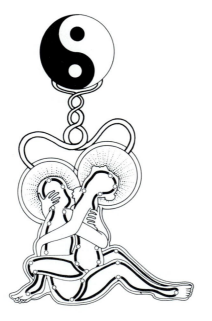

Figure 2.5. *This drawing is typical of the Taoist view of sexual intercourse as a way of channeling all the animal and spiritual energies from the lower centers of the body through the heart to the lotus, or brain. By channeling and exchanging sexual energies in ritual intercourse, a couple can experience the original cosmic unity of yin and yang energies symbolized by the black and white intertwined fish enclosed in a circle. Similar classic drawings may substitute an image of a god and goddess in yab-yum.*

However, a tendency toward sexual repression started slowly, about a thousand years ago, during the Sung Dynasty (A.D. 960–1279). This new trend had little noticeable effect on the prevailing positive attitude toward sexuality until after Sun Yat-Sen's republicans deposed the last Manchu Emperor, Pu-Yi, in 1911. War always brings a repression of sexuality and pleasure and the civil war that wracked China for 40 years set the stage for the active suppression of sexuality that began in 1949, when Mao Tse-tung led his Communist forces to power and urged the people to put all their energy into the revolution. Although Confucian and Taoist traditions have not been totally eliminated, the Communist revolution has been very effective in censoring these earlier traditions and replacing them with sexual repression. The Communists denounced the homosexuality and bisexuality of emperors and the sexual permissiveness of both imperial China and Western nations. "Hand lewdness," or masturbation, was also severely denounced because it allegedly weakens the nerves, has a bad effect on work and concentration, and eventually leads to intense nervous disorders (Mace 1960:334–359).

Marriage

Prior to the Communist revolution, all marriages were arranged by parents. Today, only about 10% of marriages fit into this category. Friends, marriage introduction bureaus, personal ads, and matchmakers have taken over the role once played by parents for the vast majority of Chinese youth.

Politics largely dictates sexual morality in China. Government guidelines, published in 1966 and 1976, advised young women not to marry until age 25 and men until at least age 28. When the number of single people over age 30 increased significantly, a worried government revised the marriage law in 1980 and reduced the minimum age for marriage to 22 for men and 20 for women.

Control of a rapidly growing population is a major government concern affecting every aspect of courtship and marriage in China, which expects to have 1.3 billion people by the year 2000. This growth rate is double what economic experts say is optimal as China struggles to increase its industrial base and modernize.

For years, the government has provided free contraceptives and abortions to control population growth and limit families to a single child. Couples who have only one or no children are given bonuses, priority in housing, and medical and educational advantages. Those expecting a second child forfeit 20% of their salaries unless the wife has an abortion. If the second child is born, the parents are taxed an additional 15% of their salaries until the child turns 7. Penalties for a third child are even more severe. In a country accustomed to large extended families, with many relatives sharing the child-rearing tasks, the family with a single child is a new reality.

Despite the need for population control, the government was confronted with mounting evidence that when parents are limited to one child, 80% of couples want a boy and will arrange an "accidental death" for a firstborn female because they depend on their male children for support in their old age. In some areas female infanticide has resulted in a ratio of 5 boys to 1 girl. In 1988 the government announced that families in rural areas would be allowed two children (Bullough & Ruan 1988).

China's unique policies on sex, marriage, and population growth raise perplexing questions about the conflict between the rights of individuals to have as many children as they want and the prerogative of the state to control its population growth in order to improve the standard of living and economic future of the country.

Homosexuality

The Communist government condemns homosexuality. When caught, homosexuals are severely punished and are sent to reform camps for rehabilitation. Electric shock treatments are standard policy. The government prohibits any public discussion or publication on homosexual issues. These rules were bent slightly in 1985 when an article on the history of homosexuality in China by a professor at Beijing Medical University was published in a medical journal. The author argued that since gays pose no threat to the welfare of society and certainly promote the effort to control China's population, they should not be singled out for prejudice and punishment. The treatment of homosexuals became a public issue when this article was reprinted in *Duzhe Wenzhai* ("Reader's Digest"), the largest monthly in mainland China (Ruan & Chong 1987; Ruan & Tsai 1988).

China and the Western World

Increasing contact with the West has resulted in some tentative revisions of official Chinese sexual morality and in actual behavior. A government booklet, *Sexual Knowledge,* was revised in 1980 to cope with changing mores and Western influences. It contains clear drawings and descriptions of male and female sexual organs, but does not discuss intercourse. Newlywed couples are told to expect sex "very, very frequently" at first, meaning once or twice a week. After the honeymoon, sex is recommended two or three times a month at most. The guide adds, "The best time to have sex is at night, before sleeping. People should rest after sex in order to repair their strength" (Butterfield 1980).

Although premarital sex is still very much frowned upon, along with kissing or holding hands in public, these activities are becoming more common. In one survey, almost 40% of all university students admitted having had premarital sex (Elliott & Gries 1988). Two other surveys in large cities and one in a rural area revealed 60% to 80% of single girls had had premarital sex. And although living together without being married is considered counterrevolutionary, it does occur with increasing frequency (Li et al. 1987; Liu 1987; Yi 1980).

At the same time, discussion of sexual matters has become more open. Magazines now carry articles and letters from men who are frustrated by wives who know nothing about sex except what they learn in a one-hour state-sponsored premarital instruction course. Women are more and more vocal about their frustration with husbands who place their pleasure first and ignore the woman's needs. Articles on adultery are increasing, and the divorce rate has jumped 11% annually for several years (Clark 1982; Elliott & Gries 1988, Ruan 1990).

The full story of the changing sexual attitudes and behavior patterns in the People's Republic of China is just starting to emerge and be examined. But what we know adds to our understanding of how, as always, sexual relations are very much an integral part of the whole social fabric in any culture or time. How the Chinese government adapts to the pressures for democracy and the increasing influence of Western cultures will determine the direction of change in Chinese sexual customs in the years ahead.

Sexual Customs in the Latino Cultures

In Central and South America and in the Caribbean, a unique combination of pre-Columbian native Indian, Roman Catholic, African, Spanish, and Portuguese influences has produced a distinctive Latino culture and heritage. This variation in Western culture is shared by close to half a billion people.

The Latino View of Sex

Just as the Islamic, Hindu, and Chinese cultures have been forced to adapt a heritage of eroticism and sexual liberation to accommodate the mores and social forces of other cultures, so the Latino culture is the product of assimilation. Long before the arrival of Columbus and the conquistadors, the Aztecs, Mayans, pre-Incas, and Inca cultures had strong, positive attitudes about sexuality. Pre-Inca Moche pottery is extremely erotic, with ornamental pieces exalting every form of sexual behavior (Figure 2.6). After the Spanish and Portuguese conquest in the 1500s, the indigenous populations were forced to adopt the images and symbols of Christianity. The people, however, continued to worship their own deities under the guise of the Christian God, the Virgin Mary, and the saints. The imposition of Catholicism brought an active repression of the sexual instinct, rigid gender roles, a strong homophobia, and strict taboos on any public display of sexual behavior. As a result, sexuality in the Latino world is overshadowed by the cloud of the forbidden and original sin. Sex education is very limited, and children and adolescents learn to associate fear and guilt with sexual behavior (Tannahill 1980:289–308).

It would be a mistake to generalize about all Latino cultures, since important variations do exist. For instance, Brazilians tend to allow expressions of sexuality and eroticism that are quite unacceptable in other areas of the Latino world,

Figure 2.6. *The erotic sensibility of the Mochica, a pre-Inca culture that flourished between* A.D. *600 and 800 is well expressed in the pottery vessels they buried with their dead. The storage vessels shown here are typical of the Mochica's open eroticism and easy familiarity with sexual behavior. The grin on the leopard's face and the somewhat lecherous expression of the priest raise a question in the viewer's mind, suggesting that something is amiss. When you turn the vessel over, you find that the leopard is having anal intercourse with the priest. (From the author's collection.)*

Figure 2.7. *Annual festivals like the Mardi Gras in Louisiana and Carnival in Brazil provide a social "safety valve" in what sociologist Victor Turner calls an "anti-structure" ritual that allows people to indulge in behaviors normally suppressed by society. "Behind the mask of Mardi Gras," the saying goes, "there is no shame."*

especially in public. This variation can be traced to the blend of Roman Catholic and native Indian values with a strong African influence in Brazil. The Portuguese who conquered the country brought thousands of black slaves, many of whom were especially comfortable with the sexual and erotic. Like other Latinos, however, Brazilians have taboos and restrictions on public sexual behavior. They draw an important distinction between public and private behaviors that preserves traditional Indian and African values. As the saying goes, "Within four walls, beneath the sheets, and behind the mask of *carnival,* everything can happen!" "Everything," or *tudo,* refers to the world of erotic experiences and pleasure (Figure 2.7). The Brazilian phrase *fazendo tudo,* "doing everything," means every man and woman has an obligation to experience and enjoy every form of sexual pleasure and excitement, or more precisely those practices which the *public* world most strictly prohibits. These activities, however, must all be done in *private* (Moitoza 1982; Parker 1984, 1987:163–165).

In contrast with European and American sexual values which frown on sexual rehearsal play among children and adolescents, the Brazilian culture expects young boys and girls to experiment with sexual pleasure and prepare for marriage within certain limits and in private.

In the game *troca-troca*—literally "exchange-exchange"— pubescent and adolescent boys take turns, each inserting his penis in the other's anus. In addition, the early sexual interactions of adolescent boys and girls draw on a wide range of nonvaginal sexual practices, in particular on anal intercourse, in order to avoid both unwanted pregnancy and rupture of the hymen, still an important sign of a young woman's sexual purity.

(Parker 1987:164)

The cultural values and sexual attitudes of black Africa have also created a more liberal approach to sexuality in the Caribbean, Cuba, Puerto Rico, and Haiti than occurs in Mexico and those areas of Latin America with a Spanish heritage.

Four Basic Sexual Values

Male/female relationships in the Latino cultures revolve around four basic sexual values—*machismo, etiqueta, marianismo,* and *pronatalism*—that dictate sharply drawn lines for men's and women's sexual behavior.

A common pejorative implication of the terms macho and **machismo** refers to a chauvinistic, tyrannical male. However, in Spanish, the terms mean male pride, and boys are indoctrinated with the importance of being macho from a very early age.

One way the male child is socialized and reminded of his maleness [in the rural cultures of Puerto Rico and the Dominican Republic] is by his parents and other adults admiring and fondling the baby's penis. [Throughout the Latino world], little boys are valued for being male from the moment they are born into the family; even if there are older sisters, the male sibling is the dominant figure, both in the eyes of the parents and in sibling interactions. Mothers train their daughters early on to play "little women" to their fathers, brothers, and husbands; and train their sons to be dominant and independent in relationships with their wives as well as other women.

(Medina 1987:3)

The female equivalent of machismo is **etiqueta**, a complex value system that requires Latina women to be both feminine and pure and at the same time very sensual and seductive. Little girls are taught to hide their genitals and not to focus much attention on their vaginas. Yet girls are valued for and taught to enhance their sexual appeal. From birth, girls are adorned with earrings, bracelets, and special spiritual amulets. Their very feminine dress makes Latina girls extremely seductive and even provocative. A woman's virginity is highly valued, however, and families are careful to protect their daughters. Because girls are taught to be sensual and seductive, chaperons have the responsibility of making certain young women who are being courted do not stray.

Latina girls are constantly reminded of their inferiority and weakness, since a vital aspect of etiqueta is the concept of **marianismo**, the model of the obedient and docile female. A Latina woman is taught to center her life around her husband and children. She is not expected to enjoy sex herself—she is there to please her husband. In the marianismo value, sex is for procreation and not to be sought or enjoyed by the woman. A good woman is always ready for her man, but she should never be comfortable with sexual issues or with sexual intercourse. To do otherwise suggests a lack of feminine virtue.

For Latino men, their uncomfortableness with sex is expressed in ridicule and rejection of anything that hints of homosexuality. Even in the Brazilian culture, where everything sexual is explored, all men—even those who in the United States would be considered bisexual or homosexual—see themselves as *homens*, men in the sense of taking the active phallic sexual role (Medina 1987:3; Parker 1987:161).

Latino cultures also have a strong *pronatalist* value. In other words, large families with many children are preferred. The family is not structured like most American or European nuclear families. A girl who becomes pregnant out of wedlock is initially frowned on for violating *marianismo* and *etiqueta*, but she and her child are usually quickly accepted by her whole family. The pronatalist value is supported by the anticontraception and antiabortion position of the Catholic Church. Nevertheless, both contraception and abortion are commonly used (Kamenetzky 1990).

The Latino Experience Today

Like the other cultures we have looked at, today's Latino cultures, confronted with outside influences, are changing. Traditional female sexual mores, such as dependency, deference, passivity, and submissiveness, for instance, are being questioned or actively abandoned. In the private sexual domain, women are becoming more active partners rather than just the passive providers of pleasure. At the same time, Latino men are adjusting their traditional macho values to the changing expectations of Latina women and the value system of non-Latino Western societies.

Assimilation is a reality for Latinos as it is for all immigrant groups. For Latinos in the United States, the status of a minority creates a tension between the desire to maintain traditional values and the temptation to abandon these and adopt the prevailing value system of the majority. Changing values, accelerated by endemic poverty, limited opportunities, and marginalization in American society, has resulted in high rates of teen pregnancy, early sexual activity, and higher school dropout rates of Latino youths. At the same time, people of Latino descent are becoming more visible and influential in American culture, especially in the Southwest and Florida.

The Complexities of Sexual Customs

The varied ethnic traditions and values we have discussed remind us that no single set of sexual attitudes and behaviors are the norm for everyone. Each culture and society has evolved its own unique value system as a functional adaptation to the particular social, political, economic, and religious environment.

Despite the sometimes striking differences in sexual values and behaviors observed around the world, it is fascinating to note the similarities and draw some conclusions. For instance, every culture places a high premium on the family system and on structuring male/female relations. European-American families tend to be nuclear; the Latino and Eastern cultures value the extended family.

All cultures speak of human nature as having two aspects: a spiritual or mental side and a physical side. Eastern traditions take a rather holistic and positive view of the relationship between these two aspects. They tend to see these aspects more as complementary polarities than as opposing forces as Western traditions do. Eastern cultures have a more positive view of sexual pleasure and often stress the important role sexual relations and pleasure can play in achieving transcendence and cosmic awareness. Western traditions opt for a more dichotomous, compartmentalized view of human nature. European and American cultures use personal guilt and the concept of sin to control sexual behavior. Other cultures use shame and kin as control mechanisms.

At the same time, the striking transformation in human consciousness that gave birth to the religious visions of Hinduism, Confucianism, Islam, and Christianity are all characterized by masculine gods and patriarchal images. These male images appear to have replaced an earlier stage of human consciousness dominated by images of nature, the cosmic, and Mother Goddess. Primitive images of the female as sexual teacher and the celebration of sexuality can still be found in Hindu, Tantric, and Taoist beliefs. In Western Christianity female images and the early connection of sexual relations with cosmic experiences and transcendence have disappeared (Cousins 1987:45–46; Jaspers 1953:1–2). Yet most cultures, East and West, place a high premium on female virginity.

As communications and travel have turned our fragmented world into a global village, the assimilation of cultures has become a fascinating phenomenon. Geographic isolation allows cultures to develop distinct value systems, but these break down when social forces bring people from different cultures into contact. Hindus and Muslims who immigrate to the United States are forced to adapt to the prevailing Western values. Even the Chinese mainland has been jolted by Western influences. At the same time, American and Western cultures are altered and shaped by the experiences, cultures, and values of other ethnic groups. In recent years, dozens of books have popularized the Tantric and Taoist views of sexual pleasure and ecstasy by integrating these Eastern traditions with modern Western sexual therapy. Even as the cultures of Islam, India, and China adapt to Western influences, Americans have developed a fascination with non-Western views of sexuality. The exchange is two-way.

Key Concepts

1. The sexual behavior and relations endorsed by a particular culture are part of its whole social fabric and reflect the unique combination of religious, social, and economic conditions of that culture.

2. The Islamic tradition lacks a strong ascetic tradition, views women as very sexual and in need of control, and is more relaxed about sexual variation including homosexuality than the Judaeo-Christian tradition. Female seclusion, purdah, is practiced as a major control over the sexual power of women. Polygamy and temporary marriages are tolerated or accepted in many Islamic cultures.

3. The early Hindu view of sexuality as a very natural part of everyday life has been overshadowed by Muslim and British attitudes. Among the changes affecting traditional Hindu sexual values are a gradual shift away from arranged marriages to marriages based on love, the abolition of the dowry, and the growing economic independence of women.

4. Much of the change in sexual attitudes and behavior patterns in the People's Republic of China can be traced to two factors: (1) the political rejection by the Communist regime of the more positive attitudes and behavior toward sex that prevailed in imperial China, and (2) the economic necessity of population control and a resultant shift away from the large, extended family.

5. The sexual attitudes, gender roles, and male/female relations in the Latino cultures are deeply influenced by a common Catholic tradition, the values of *machismo, etiqueta, marianismo,* and *pronatalism,* and by the blend of indigenous pre-Columbian values with Spanish, Portuguese, African, and North American traditions.

Key Terms

arranged marriage (33)	marianismo (45)
dowry (38)	mut'a (34)
etiqueta (45)	patrilineage (33)
guilt culture (31)	purdah (32)
hijra (38)	shame culture (32)
machismo (45)	yin and yang (40)

Summary Questions

1. Using the description of sexual attitudes and customs in an Islamic nation, India, China, or the Latino world, explain one example of the interaction of religious traditions with politics and economics in creating a functional system of sexual values.

2. Compare the mechanisms for guiding sexual behavior in a shame culture and in a guilt culture as defined by Margaret Mead.

3. How do the views of women and their sexuality vary in the Islamic, Hindu, Tantric-Taoist, and Latino traditions?

4. Compare the attitudes toward homosexuality in Islamic, Hindu, Chinese, and Latino cultures.

Suggested Readings

Atiya, N. (1982). *Khul Khaal: Five Egyptian Women Tell Their Stories.* Syracuse, NY: Syracuse University Press.

Chia, M., & M. Chia. (1986). *Healing Love Through the Tao.* Huntington, NY: Healing Tao Books.

Chia, M., & M. Winn. (1984). *Taoist Secrets of Love*. Santa Fe, NM: Aurora Press. Chia's two books are the most readable introductions to ancient Taoist views of sex.

Deva, K. (1986). *Khajuraho*. New Delhi: Brijbasi Printers. A magnificent photographic tour of Hindu erotic sculptures and their significance.

El Saadawi, N. (1980). *The Hidden Face of Eve*. Boston: Beacon Press.

Gupta, B. (ed). (1987). *Sexual Archetypes, East and West*. New York: Paragon House. Examines male/female images in Eastern and Western religious traditions.

McGoldrick, M., J. Pearce, & J. Giordano (eds.). (1982). *Ethnicity and Family Therapy*. New York: Guilford Press. Insights into Iranian, Afro-American, Mexican, Puerto Rican, Cuban, and Asian families.

Mernissi, F. (1975). *Beyond the Veil: Women in the Arab World*. New York: Wiley.

*Values, Morals,
and Ethics*
Formal and Informal
Values
*Religion and Sexual
Values*
Guilt or Shame
Natural or Unnatural
Sex
Two Different
Worldviews
A Humanist View
*How We Develop
Our Values*
Social Development
and Values
Piaget's Model of Moral
Development
Kohlberg's
Developmental Model
Gilligan's View of Moral
Development
*Sexual Values
in the Future*

Chapter 3

Sexual Values and Moral Development

Special Consultants

Julian W. Slowinski, Psy.D., trained in Roman Catholic theology, Dr. Slowinski is a marital and sex therapist, Pennsylvania Hospital, and professor, Department of Psychiatry, University of Pennsylvania School of Medicine.

William R. Stayton, M. Div., Th.D., trained in Protestant theology, Dr. Stayton is assistant professor, Psychiatry and Human Behavior, Jefferson Medical College, and teacher, Human Sexuality Program, University of Pennsylvania and LaSalle University.

What motivated Americans in earlier times to condemn certain behaviors and lifestyles we now accept? Why do we make certain decisions about what is right and wrong in our sexual behavior? How do we learn to make decisions about when, where, with whom, and why to have sex, and what kind of sex to have? The values we develop deal with sex roles, sex stereotypes, the purposes of sexual intercourse, acceptable and unacceptable forms of sexual behavior, the role and position of the child in the family, the role of the family in society, and so on.

In this chapter we focus on the ways in which Judaeo-Christian religious traditions have molded the sexual values that are common in Europe and North America. To examine that impact we explore the difference between formal and informal values and guilt and shame. We will also look at the influence of fixed, process, and humanist worldviews and the different sexual values derived from these perspectives. Finally, we examine several important theories that seek to explain the stages we pass through in developing our sexual values.

Values, Morals, and Ethics

Values, morals, and ethics help us deal with the distinction between what is right and wrong. Although these terms are often used interchangeably, *values* represent the ideals, customs, and institutions that people find desirable and to which they have a strong emotional attachment. *Morals* focus on what is right and wrong in terms of fundamental religious or philosophical principles, rather than dealing with what is customary, legal, or socially accepted. The term *ethics* refers to a system of morals. Many examples of sexual values, morals, and ethics can be found in our survey of sexual customs in America and other cultures in Chapters 1 and 2.

Formal and Informal Values

Values, morals, and ethics may be expressed in public or personal terms. The American Constitution, our laws, and public statements of morality by religious groups often state specific values and summarize what a particular group considers to be acceptable behavior. These public statements represent **formal values**. But we also express our values in an individual, personal way. **Informal values** tell us what individuals in some society or group personally believe to be right, wrong, or important.

A formal public value may closely reflect the informal values of the majority of people, or it may conflict with informal personal values of people within a group. The Puritans, for instance, officially condemned premarital sex, even though, as we saw in Chapter 1, most of them accepted bundling, a custom that facilitated premarital sex. The formal religious endorsement of a strict code of sexually exclusive monogamy in the Latino cultures, which we discussed in Chapter 2, is not echoed by informal *macho* values that encourage a true man, *un hombre completo*, to have both a contractual wife and a consensual wife (see p. 487).

At times, when a large number of people adopt an informal value that openly contradicts and challenges some formal value, the formal value may change. For instance, prior to 1973, most of the 50 states had a variety of laws prohibiting or restricting women's access to abortion. Responding to growing pressure from women's groups and the changing understanding of what the Constitution means by privacy and freedom from government control, the U.S. Supreme Court declared restrictions of abortion unconstitutional and produced a new formal value that balances the rights of the pregnant woman and the fetus. In the aftermath of the Roe v. Wade decision, however, antiabortion groups have increasingly called for a restoration of the formal value that prevailed before 1973.

Formal values can have long-term consequences, long after they have been rejected and replaced with new values. For instance, in the Victorian era, masturbation was widely condemned as an unnatural and sinful indulgence in sexual pleasure. Although it is no longer a moral issue for the majority of Americans, the anxiety and guilt previously associated with masturbation still affects us. In one major survey of adolescent sexual behavior, men were quite willing to admit they had violated the formal value against premarital sex, but far fewer men were willing to admit they masturbated (Sorenson 1973). In another survey of college students, 82% of the males and 33% of the females admitted to masturbating, but two-thirds also felt guilty or anxious about this behavior (Gagnon 1977).

Religion and Sexual Values

Few would doubt that religion has been a major source of our morals and values (Figure 3.1). Even those who do not accept the Judaeo-Christian belief systems have been raised in a society which endorses values built on those beliefs. The influence of religion is often indirect, filtered through our parents, peers, the

Figure 3.1. *The beliefs that Moses received the ten commandments from God on Mount Sinai and that the sacred scriptures are inspired by God promotes a value system based on the unquestioned authority of male religious leaders.*

media, social trends, and our ethnic traditions. This filtering can mask the fact that the values and morals we learn from others are based on centuries of Judaeo-Christian traditions. In this tradition, several factors predominate: the use of guilt to control sex, the distinction between natural and unnatural sex, and fixed, process, and humanist influences which have given rise to different moral views of sexuality.

Guilt or Shame

In Chapter 2 we saw how Eastern religions—Islam, Hinduism, Confucianism, Taoism, and Tantrism—celebrate sexuality as a path to the divine and leave decisions about when and with whom to have sex to kin and a sense of shame. In our Western cultures, Judaeo-Christian religious beliefs have created an awareness of personal conscience, guilt, and the fear of divine punishment which help us decide what is right or wrong. In understanding Western sexual morality we need to be aware of this emphasis on a personal conscience and guilt.

Natural or Unnatural Sex

According to early Greek and Roman Stoic philosophers, sexual passion distorted a man's reason. The sole moral justification for sexual relations, in their view, was procreation. This view was developed and expanded by early Christian thinkers, particularly Augustine of Hippo around A.D. 300. Medieval Christian theologians adopted and extended this early Western view, classifying sexual acts as either natural or unnatural, depending on whether or not a particular behavior allowed the goal of procreation. In this perspective, fornication, rape, incest, and adultery were immoral and illicit indulgences in sexual pleasure because they occurred outside marriage and did not provide for the rearing of offspring. However, because they could result in procreation, they were **natural sins**. Masturbation, oral sex, and anal sex, on the other hand, were much more serious violations of the natural order because they were forbidden indulgences—occurring outside marriage—and contraceptive, hence deemed **unnatural sins**.

   This distinction between natural and unnatural sexual behavior is still very relevant today. It comes up most often in debates about the morality of homosexuality (Francoeur 1990b).

Two Different Worldviews

For centuries, two coexisting but quite different worldviews and beliefs about creation developed in Western thought. Since the early Greek and Roman philosophers, Western thinkers have chosen to picture our world in one of two ways. Some have interpreted the world in terms of a fixed worldview with unchangeable laws of nature. Others have pictured a world in the process of evolving with the nature of all things fluid and ever changing as creation continues. The *fixed* worldview, with its unchanging abstract archetypes, and the *process* worldview, with its emphasis on the reality of ever-changing environments and unique individual persons, represent two ends of a broad spectrum from which have been derived two different and often opposing sexual value systems (Francoeur 1965, 1970, 1988) (Highlight Box 3.1).

**HIGHLIGHT BOX 3.1.
A SPECTRUM OF
ETHICAL SYSTEMS**

The two worldviews outlined here, and the value systems they endorse, have evolved over centuries and can be found in varying degrees in all Western thought. They are in evidence in various official expressions of the Jewish and Christian belief systems and in the lifestyles of those who have incorporated these views, perhaps unknowingly, into their daily living.

It is interesting to note that there is often more agreement among different religious groups on the right or on the left side of this spectrum of fixed to process worldviews than between people within a religious tradition who are at opposite ends of the spectrum. Thus Catholics, Protestants, humanists, and Jews who accept a process worldview often agree on the morality of homosexuality, premarital sex, contraception, abortion, and so on, values that are rejected by members of their own traditions who adopt a fixed worldview.

Fixed or Absolutist Worldview	Process or Relativist Worldview
Expressed in orthodox Jewish, official Catholic, and fundamentalist Protestant belief systems	Expressed in humanist thought, and by liberal Protestant and Catholic theologians
1. The world and humans were created perfect and finished in the beginning	1. The world and humans have evolved and are still in the process of achieving their potential
2. Evil can be traced to the original sin commited by Adam and Eve in the Garden of Eden	2. Evil is a natural part of the life process and not due to some "original sin"
3. God punishes evil	3. Human laws and nature provide some punishment
4. The exercise of authority is in the hands of males who often take an absolutist view; hierarchical structure	4. Church authority is shared by male and female clergy and between clergy and lay members; egalitarian structure
5. Sacred texts and teachings are accepted in literal terms because the church possesses all the truth; there is only one true religion	5. Revelation is a gradual process achieved through sacred texts, communion with nature, other persons, and the ground of all being; many paths may lead to the truth
6. The purpose of life is to seek redemption and salvation from sin, to transcend the body and its emotions, to conquer death and reach the life "hereafter"	6. The purpose of life is to become, to reach your fuller potential; more emphasis on living an ethical, more creative life rather than on sin and a life hereafter
7. Static worldview	7. Dynamic, changing worldview

Fixed or Absolutist Worldview	Process or Relativist Worldview

The Sexual Values of These Two Systems

1. Sexuality is basically animal passion and lust, genital, and must be controlled	1. Sexuality is a natural and positive life force with both sensual and spiritual aspects
2. The main goal of sex is marriage and reproduction	2. Sex does not have to be confined to marriage; pleasure, love, and celebration are goals in themselves
3. Sex is only acceptable in heterosexual marriages	3. Tolerance or acceptance of same-gender relationships
4. Masturbation, oral sex, same-gender relationships, and contraception all thwart God's purposes for sex and are forbidden	4. God's purpose for sex is to celebrate life; masturbation, oral sex, and same-gender relationships can express the celebratory and communion nature of sex
5. Strict gender roles in relationships with male active and superior	5. Flexible, egalitarian gender roles
6. Emphasis on sex as genitality and on genital acts	6. Emphasis on people and their relationships rather than on what they do genitally

Source: Adapted from a summary by Linda L. Hendrixson, 1990.

The Fixed Worldview

Adherents of the **fixed worldview** claim that when the first humans were created, God established the nature of male and female, marriage, and heterosexual morality for all time. In the Jewish and Christian scriptures, the Genesis story explains that all humans have fallen from an original state of perfection and grace because of the rebellion of Adam and Eve. This corrupt nature can only be overcome by self-discipline, mortification of the flesh, and by avoiding indulgence in pleasure, especially sexual pleasure. With the archetypal story of Adam and Eve in the Garden of Eden, God established our heterosexual nature and the primacy of the male over the female. The command "Increase and multiply" identified the essential purpose of sexual relations (Figure 3.2).

Orthodox Jews and fundamentalist and evangelical Protestants commonly draw on this worldview in articulating their sexual values. In the Roman Catholic tradition, the Vatican adheres with unswerving vigilance to a natural law position as interpreted by the Magisterium or teaching authority of the church. These advocates of the fixed worldview commonly condemn contraception, masturbation, oral sex, premarital sex, divorce, consensual extramarital sex, and homosexuality, although individuals and some groups may be more tolerant in one or more of these areas.

In recent years, religious conservatives and fundamentalist Christians have become a revitalized force in American life. This group is diverse, including Mother Angelica's Eternal Word Television Network on cable television, Rev. Pat Robertson's "700 Club," the Moral Majority, the Council of National Righteousness, FLAG (Family, Life, America, and God), the Pro-Family Forum, and The Christian Voice. Cable television, communication satellites, over 30 gospel

Figure 3.2. *One traditional story of human origins depicts Adam and Eve being driven from the Garden of Eden as punishment for their disobedience. For centuries, this image of original sin led to a negative view of sex as sinful indulgence in pleasure that distracted men from more noble spiritual and intellectual endeavors. Women were viewed, like Eve, as dangerous seducers of men.*

television stations, and well over a thousand all-gospel radio stations reach out to millions of listeners who share many of the same values, especially in the areas of marriage and sexuality. This value system is also evident in the private schools and colleges which these groups support. For many Americans, such fixed values are unambiguous, authoritative, and provide reassurance and support in a very confusing world.

The Process Worldview

At the other end of the spectrum is the **process worldview** in which human nature is thought to be still evolving. The basic assumption in this worldview is that human nature has never been without flaws. Physical and moral evil are an unavoidable dark side of the struggle to fulfill our potential. Good and evil are linked together as people explore and discover deeper expressions of human potential and their sexual nature. Certain general principles of what is right and wrong in human behavior are acknowledged, but specific decisions about what is right and wrong depend on the ever-changing situation and context (Figure 3.3).

Figure 3.3. *When the early Protestants challenged the traditional Christian emphasis on celibacy and virginity with a positive view of marital sex, artists like the Dutch Hieronymus Bosch (1450?–1516) picked up this theme in paintings of the Garden of Eden and presented sex and sensuality in a positive way. This scene from Bosch's* Paradise *is part of his triptych of* The Garden of Earthly Delights.

A recent statement from the Episcopal Diocese of Northern New Jersey highlights the quite different role divine revelation, sacred texts, and traditional teachings play for those who adopt the process viewpoint.

> The Judaeo-Christian tradition is a tradition precisely because, in every historical and social circumstance, the thinking faithful have brought to bear the best interpretation of the current realities in correlation with their interpretation of tradition as they have inherited it. Thus, truth in the Judaeo-Christian tradition is a dynamic process to be discerned and formulated rather than a static structure to be received.
>
> The Bible is misunderstood and misused when approached as a book of moral prescriptions directly applicable to all moral dilemmas. Rather, the Bible is the record of the response to the word of God addressed to Israel and to the Church throughout centuries of changing social, historical, and cultural conditions. The Faithful responded within the realities of their particular situation, guided by the direction of previous revelation, but not captive to it.

(Thayer 1987:9–10)

Before we look at some specific examples of the conclusions people in the West have drawn from the fixed and process philosophies, it is important to point out that these two systems represent two ends of a spectrum. Few people, or for that matter religious groups, adhere completely to either of these two worldviews. Most of us fall somewhere along the spectrum between the two extremes. We may shift back and forth along the spectrum, holding to a fixed worldview on one issue and maintaining an opinion based on a process worldview on another. Despite this variation, overall most of us still tend to favor one or the other perspective and set our values accordingly (Francoeur 1965, 1970, 1987b, 1990a, 1990b) (Highlight Box 3.2).

HIGHLIGHT BOX 3.2.
A SAMPLING OF FIXED
AND PROCESS PERSPECTIVES

We can gain some idea of the relevance and wide influence these two opposing views have had on sexual morality and on current Western values by looking at some typical statements. The following statements are drawn from both religious and secular writings. Some of the statements represent formal, official values; others are statements of individuals expressing their views in terms of a fixed or process worldview.

Fixed Worldview

On male and female roles, from *Fascinating Womanhood* by Helen Andelin:

> The woman who becomes capable and independent suffers losses herself. As she takes on self-sufficient qualities, she tends to lose some of her feminine charm. A feminine woman is dependent and in need of protection from men. As she lessens her need for him, she lessens her femininity. As we view this generation of capable women, who are able to make it on their own in the world, it is not surprising to see the loss of respect men have for them, and that men no longer offer them the chivalry they did a generation ago.

On premarital sex, from *Your Half of the Apple: God and the Single Girl* by G. Andrews:

> Premarital sex amounts to spiritual destruction. It tears living fibers apart . . . when you get up and put your clothes on and go home (or he does), you are not the same as you were. There's been a real mingling of life itself, and because God intended this to be a permanent, one-for-life arrangement, you are damaged when you try to treat it as something casual.

(Andrews 1972:83–84).

On abortion, from *The Value of Life* by Senator Orrin B. Hatch:

> I have often had occasion to reflect on the calamity of abortion. While presiding as chairman of the Senate's Constitution Subcommittee during nine lengthy hearings exploring every philosophical, legal, moral, medical, and social aspect of this crisis, I thought about the plain commands of scripture on this subject. . . . All the insightful words from Senate debates on abortion, however, do not match the simple majesty of the Bible: "Thou shalt not kill."

On homosexuality, from the Congregation for the Doctrine of the Faith, Letter to the Bishops of the Catholic Church on the Pastoral Care of Homosexual Persons:

> The entire discussion of homosexuality is [based on] the theology of creation we find in Genesis. . . . Although the particular inclination of the homosexual person is not a sin, it is a more or less strong tendency ordered toward an intrinsic moral evil; and thus the inclination itself must be seen as an objective disorder.

Process Worldview

On masturbation, from the United Presbyterian Church Workstudy Document on Sexuality and the Human Community:

> The ethical significance of masturbation depends entirely on the context in which it takes place. Therefore, we can see no objection to it when it occurs as a normal developmental experience or as a deliberately chosen alternative to inappropriate heterosexual activity. We can see valid ethical questions raised about masturbatory practices which become or which inhibit normal heterosexual development. In most instances, however,

we believe that masturbation is morally neutral and psychologically benign.

On nonmarital cohabitation and sexually active single persons, from the *Report of the Task Force on Changing Patterns of Sexuality and Family Life,* Task Force of the Episcopal Diocese of Newark, New Jersey:

> Regarding the relationship itself, the following considerations are appropriate: a) the relationship should be life-enhancing for both partners and exploitative for neither. b) The relationship should be grounded in sexual fidelity and should not involve promiscuity. c) The relationship should be founded on love and valued for the strengthening, joy, support, and benefit of the couple and those to whom they are related.

On homosexual relations, from *Human Sexuality: New Directions in American Catholic Thought,* a study commissioned by The Catholic Theological Society of America:

> It bears repeating, without provision, that where there is sincere affection, responsibility, and the germ of authentic human relationships—in other words, where there is love—God is surely present.
>
> *(Kosnik 1977:218; see also Timmerman 1986:107).*

A Humanist View

In the Renaissance a third perspective on human nature and sexuality emerged. Some claim that this tradition, known as humanism, is rooted in Judaeo-Christian beliefs. However, the humanism of the Renaissance lost its religious basis as its advocates rejected divine revelations and the supernatural. Most humanists deny the authority of religious teachings and insist that values can be found only in the human experience. They generally agree that the basic goals of human life are happiness, self-actualization, self-awareness, and the avoidance of pain and suffering.

Joseph Fletcher, a leading humanist and author of *Situation Ethics* (1966), sums up the approach to sexual ethics most humanists accept.

> According to situation ethics, sexual behavior is morally acceptable in any form—heterosexual, homosexual, bisexual, autosexual (masturbation), or polysexual. What makes any sexual act right or wrong is what it is intended to accomplish and its foreseeable consequences. Sex is a means to an end beyond the sexual act itself. No sexual act is intrinsically

right or wrong. No sexual act, in and of itself, should be either blamed or praised, apart from whatever human values motivated and guided it.

(Personal communiqué)

In humanistic ethics, the morality of sexual acts depends on their context and outcome. It is not, however, a hedonistic, "anything goes," morality, because the morality of any act depends on the situation and context in which it occurs and on its consequences for all concerned.

We find similar values echoed in a secular humanist statement entitled "A New Bill of Sexual Rights and Responsibilities." This statement concludes, "We believe that freeing our sexual selves is vital if we are to reach the heights of our full humanity. But at the same time, we believe that we need to activate and nourish a sense of our responsibilities to others" (Kirkendall 1976).

How We Develop Our Values

Social Development and Values

We are not born with a sense of morality. Newborn infants do not know good or bad until they learn from parents, society, and others to recognize certain behaviors as being acceptable or unacceptable. We are not born with any innate knowledge about the morality of homosexuality, masturbation, premarital sex, oral sex, or any particular sexual expression or relationship. We acquire this awareness as we grow up.

Three developmental psychologists have described the stages of moral development that we negotiate as we emerge from an amoral infancy to adult responsibility and moral consciousness. Although these models developed by Jean Piaget, Lawrence Kohlberg, and Carol Gilligan share some similarities, they also highlight some important differences in how men and women approach decisions about morals and values.

Piaget's Model of Moral Development

Jean Piaget, a French developmental psychologist, theorized that infants begin life as completely *amoral* beings. In their first two years of life, they could hardly be less aware of the distinction between right and wrong. They are concerned only about having their basic needs met to be fed, dry, comfortable, and cuddled. At about age 2, children enter the *egocentric stage*. For the next five years or so, they have only a very general idea of what rules are. And children change the rules to satisfy their needs (Hersh et al. 1979).

The second major stage, the *heteronomous stage*, usually occurs between the ages of 7 and 12. Morality is now based on constraint (Figure 3.6). Guided by parents and other authority figures, children begin to assert some degree of logical and moral control over their behavior. This is Piaget's cognitive stage of formal operations, when children begin to think in terms of abstracts and distinguish between valid and invalid ideas. Authority is all-important—whether it be a parent, teacher, or older child. Children often accept an idea without question and see issues in terms of black and white. Children at this stage have little understanding of what is moral because they totally accept the morality imposed by others.

Between the heteronomous and the next stage, Piaget theorized a transitional phase in which children begin to comprehend values and apply them in original ways. This is mainly a rest station before they learn to accept full moral responsibility for their lives.

The *autonomous stage* begins somewhere after age 12 and continues throughout adulthood. People at this level of moral development think and act in terms of cooperation rather than constraint. Interactions, discussions, criticism, a sense of equality with peers, and a respect for others help us develop this sense of morality and values. We begin to see other perspectives on moral and ethical issues. We may question and struggle to verify rules and ideas. If we find a rule morally acceptable, we internalize it, making it an integral part of our values. We become autonomous, self-actualizing, and responsible adults.

Kohlberg's Developmental Model

Lawrence Kohlberg, a developmental psychologist at Harvard University, has expanded Piaget's model of moral development in some new directions. Instead of Piaget's egocentric, heteronomous, and autonomous stages, Kohlberg speaks of preconventional, conventional, and postconventional stages. He then divides each of these stages into two substages of moral development (Hersh et al. 1979; Kohlberg 1983).

On the level of *preconventional morality*, children respond to cultural rules and the labels of good and bad. This level is divided into two stages: (1) punishment and obedience orientation and (2) instrumental relativist orientation. In the first stage, we develop a total respect for the authority figure and have only a very primitive sense of morality based on rewards for obedience and punishment for disobedience. In the second stage of preconventional morality, we are concerned with satisfying our own needs rather than the needs of others or of society (Figure 3.4).

When we reach the level of *conventional morality*, our sense of values is characterized by a conformity to and maintenance of the moral conventions that are expected by our family, group, or nation—regardless of the consequences. When we first begin to think in terms of moral conventions, we are labeled "good" or "nice" if we conform our behavior to family and societal norms. As our understanding of conventional morality matures, we develop a sense of law and order, focusing on fixed rules and the social order. On this level, moral behavior consists of respecting authority and maintaining the social order so that society can function smoothly.

Finally, Kohlberg describes a *postconventional morality*, very similar to Piaget's autonomous level, where an individual tries to define his or her own morality apart from that of authoritative figures. Stage 5, the social contract stage, is reached when an individual puts an emphasis on what is legally binding, but realizes that laws may change to meet social demands. The last stage of moral development is the level of universal ethical principle orientation. Here a person's conscience serves as the arbiter of moral dilemmas. Abstract qualities such as justice, human rights, respect for the dignity of human life, and equality become important in making decisions. For some people, adherence to an inner conscience may require their breaking a law to achieve a higher purpose.

Although Kohlberg's theory is more detailed, it does compare in many ways with that of Piaget. In a revision of his work, Kohlberg implies that a higher

Piaget's Moral Development Model	Kohlberg's Moral Development Model			
	Level	Orientation Stage	Dominant Element	Personal Perspective
Amoral stage—ages 0 to 2				
Egocentric stage—a lack of morality, bends rules, and reacts instinctively to environment	Preconventional	1. Punishment and obedience orientation	Total respect for authority	"I must obey the authority figure, or else . . ."
		2. Instrumental relativist orientation	Satisfying one's own needs	"I might if I want to, but don't count on it."
Heteronomous stage—based on total acceptance of a morality imposed by others	Conventional	3. Good boy-nice girl orientation	Conformity to social conventions and expectations	"I probably should because everyone expects me to."
		4. Law and order orientation	Respect for authority and society's laws	"I ought to because of duty to obey the rules."
Autonomous stage—based on an internalized morality of cooperation	Postconventional or autonomous	5. Social contract orientation	Conformity to the ever-changing values and demands of society	"I may because of my role in society, but I often question the relative values of society."
		6. Universal ethical principle orientation	Personal conscience holds one responsible for doing what is right	"I will because I know it is the right thing to do."

Figure 3.4. Moral Development: Piaget and Kohlberg.

level, such as stage 5 or 6, is not necessarily better than a lower stage, and that most people do not operate on the postconventional level. In fact, in Kohlberg's research, most people seem to operate on stage 4, where law and order is the overriding orientation.

What connections, if any, can you see between these two models of moral development and the value systems based on either a fixed or process worldview?

Gilligan's View of Moral Development

Carol Gilligan, a Harvard psychologist, has criticized Kohlberg's theory and its conclusions, and by implication the model suggested by Piaget. She suggests that these theories do not apply to the ways in which women deal with moral issues. Studies have shown that when female solutions to hypothetical moral dilemmas are evaluated using Kohlberg's scheme, women appear to be "stuck" at level 2, that of conventional morality, where moral decisions are made in terms of pleasing and helping others (Kohlberg & Kramer 1969). Thus some have concluded that women fall short and do not attain the "higher" level of moral reasoning where values are derived from principles that transcend interpersonal concerns. This perception has led some to suggest that women commonly lack the quality of courage and a degree of conscience that some men demonstrate.

Gilligan contends that women are not deficient or immature in their moral development. Rather, she points out, the standard against which they are measured is biased. Kohlberg's model was derived from a 20-year study of moral development in 84 boys and did not include any girls, although the model has been generalized and applied to the moral sensitivity of *both* men and women (Colby 1983:14; Gilligan 1982, 1989; Lyons 1983).

As a result of her studies of moral reasoning in women, Gilligan suggests that there is another, equally valid, moral perspective besides Kohlberg's "justice and rights" framework. She calls it the *care perspective* because it emphasizes relationships and connections between people rather than an abstract hierarchy of rules and rights. This framework stresses nurturance and responsibility to others. For Gilligan, the justice and the care perspectives of morality are different, but equally valid. Neither is superior, or more or less mature, than the other. Both are needed for human survival (Gilligan 1982, 1989) (Highlight Box 3.3).

Gilligan points out that the two moral frameworks are gender-related, but not gender-specific. For the most part, women seem to be more comfortable within the care perspective, and men within the justice and rights perspective. However, in some instances, women reason from a justice/rights view and men from a care view.

Sexual Values in the Future

What does the future hold for sexual morality in the West? It is tempting to label the morality and views of those who adhere to fixed worldviews as the Old Morality, implying that this perspective is out of date and only for those who are willing to abdicate responsibility for their own lives and accept the dictates of others. Critics are quick to point out that legalistic rigidity commonly reduces human sexuality to our genitals and sexual morality to what we do with those genitals. Yet a morality based on universal, unambiguous rules is reassuring, especially when we are faced with sexual promiscuity, exploitation, sexual abuse, the breakdown of the family, divorce, reproductive technologies, and AIDS.

It is also equally tempting for critics of the process worldview to describe its advocates with their more flexible interpretations of traditional teachings as hedonists who reject the essence of traditional religious values. Humanists and

HIGHLIGHT BOX 3.3. GENDER AND MORALS

Carol Gilligan's research into moral development has highlighted two different perspectives in moral development: the justice perspective that stresses fairness and contractual obligations on which Piaget and Kohlberg focused, and a perspective that emphasizes caring and relationships. Review this outline and then answer the questions that follow.

	Justice	Care
Premise	Equality and fairness; objectivity, separation, and detachment	Avoidance of violence; subjectivity, connection, and attachment
Focus	Social contract or mutual agreements	People and their relationship to each other
Dominant element	Moral principles always prevail over individual situations	The circumstances of a situation may alter application of principles
Relationship to others	Stresses respect for individual rights, independence, and noninterference with others	Stresses relationships with others, involvement, and interdependence
	Others are seen in terms of one's self	Others are accepted in their own contexts
Obligation	To a hierarchy of prioritized principles and rules	To be unselfish and do no harm to others
Moral judgments	Judgments based on principles that downplay personal concerns	Reluctance to judge others, or to ignore personal considerations
Limits	"Just" resolutions, to which all can agree, are always possible	Not all conflicts can be resolved by mutual agreement and to the satisfaction of all parties

1. With which of these two perspectives are you more comfortable? Can you explain your preference?
2. How do these two perspectives fit in with the fixed and process worldviews of sexual morality?
3. What impact do you think these perspectives might have on judgments about sexual morality? Would they lead to different conclusions about the morality of sexual relationships outside marriage, in nonmarital, comarital, and extramarital relations?

Source: Outline adapted from a summary by Linda L. Hendrixson, 1990.

advocates of the process worldview call for each individual to take responsibility for his or her own moral decisions. This perspective requires that people operate most of the time on the autonomous or postconventional level of moral decision making, which is expecting a lot. Evaluating what is the most humane and responsible thing to do in every circumstance, when situations vary so much, takes time and a lot of thought. It also places a heavy, and possibly dangerous, reliance on the broad principles of love, respect, and interpersonal responsibility since human selfishness, self-deception, and outright dishonesty do exist. Obviously, there is no ideal, universally acceptable solution to the ongoing debate over the direction of sexual morality.

The tension between the fixed and process worldviews can be traced back to the earliest days of Western culture. It certainly is not going to disappear in the next 10 or 20 years, if ever. In view of the accelerating pace of change in our culture, we can safely predict that we will have to deal with a growing philosophical split within and between religious and humanist groups. This dissension will be increasingly evident in debates and conflicts on premarital sex, homosexuality, abortion, contraception, divorce, the ordination of homosexuals and women, and alternatives to the traditional sexually exclusive heterosexual marriage (Francoeur 1984:183–205).

Pessimistic as this prediction may appear at first sight, it is possible that the increasing tension will force our society into communicating more about sexual issues and toward a greater understanding among people. This ecumenism could very well focus

1. more on individuals and less on anatomy and gender in judging the morality of sexual acts;

2. on the responsibilities and rights of persons who are exploring new kinds of relationships; and

3. on respect for those who wish to follow traditional values and for those who wish to follow a more liberal value system.

How do you feel about these predictions? How do you think our sexual values will change in the 1990s?

Key Concepts

1. In the Western, Judaeo-Christian tradition, two basic philosophies or world visions, a *fixed philosophy of nature* and a *process view* of an ongoing creation, underlie all value systems. Within each religious tradition, Protestant, Jewish, Catholic, and others, sexual values often vary depending on the issue in question and on whether the individual or the group is working from a fixed or process worldview.

2. Statements of sexual morality based on the fixed philosophy of nature tend to adhere to unchanging religious truths and values in which the only acceptable sexual relations are heterosexual and limited to married couples.

3. Statements of sexual morality based on a process view of the world tend to be more open, flexible, and tolerant when judging masturbation, premarital sex, consensual extramarital sex, homosexuality, abortion, and contraception.

4. Humanists reject divine revelation and religious authority as the basis for sexual morality, but do not endorse a hedonistic "anything is acceptable" philosophy.

5. Piaget traces moral development from an amoral infant stage, ages 0 to 2, through an egocentric stage, ages 2 to 7, to the heteronomous stage, where morality is characterized by constraints which are imposed by others. In the final autonomous stage, we internalize rules after questioning them and become personally responsible for our actions.

6. After the amoral infant stage, Kohlberg speaks of three levels: a preconventional level emphasizing a total respect for authority and the satisfaction of our own needs, a conventional level emphasizing conformity to societal conventions and laws, and a postconventional level in which we internalize moral principles.

7. Gilligan suggests that whereas males tend to follow a moral reasoning based on justice and rights, women are more likely to base their moral decisions on a care perspective that stresses nurturance and interpersonal responsibilities.

Key Terms

fixed worldview (56)   natural sin (54)
formal value (52)   process worldview (57)
informal value (52)   unnatural sin (54)

Summary Questions

1. What is the difference between formal and informal values, and their relationship?

2. List five or more basic sexual values and attitudes associated with a fixed philosophy of nature. How are these values applied to specific sexual behaviors and relationships?

3. List five or more basic sexual values and attitudes associated with a process view of the world. How are these values applied to specific sexual behaviors and relationships?

4. List some core values humanists use as a basis for their sexual values.

5. Describe the similarities and differences in the models of moral development proposed by Piaget, Kohlberg, and Gilligan.

Suggested Readings

Bullough, V., and P. Gardella. (1987). A debate: Why is Christianity so hostile to sex? Christianity has given us a positive ethic of gender equality and sexual pleasure. In R. T. Francoeur (ed.), *Taking Sides: Clashing Views on Controversial Issues in Human Sexuality*. Guilford, CT: Dushkin.

Francoeur, R. T. (1990a). Current religious doctrines of sexual and erotic development in childhood. In M. Perry (ed.), *The Handbook of Sexology*. (Vol. 7). Amsterdam: Elsevier.

Francoeur, R. T. (1990b). New dimensions in human sexuality: The theological challenge. In R. H. Iles (ed.), *The Gospel Imperative in the Midst of AIDS: Towards a Prophetic Theology*. Wilton, CT: Morehouse.

Lawrence, R. J. (1989). *The Poisoning of Eros: Sexual Values in Conflict*. New York: Augustine Moore Press.

Nelson, J. B. (1978). *Embodiment: An Approach to Sexuality and Christian Theology*. Minneapolis: Augsburg.

Part Two

The Personal Context

4. Our Gender Development Before Birth
5. Sexuality in Childhood and Adolescence
6. Our Sexual Anatomy
7. Our Sexual Responses
8. Pregnancy and Birth
9. Contraception: Shared Responsibilities
10. Abortion: Our Shared Responsibilities
11. Your Sexual Health
12. Reducing Your Risk for Sexual Diseases
13. AIDS: Health and Social Issues

Gender and Sex
The Gates of
 Psychosexual
 Development
The First Two Months
 Nature's Basic Plan
 Gate 1: Chromosomal/
  Genetic Gender
 Gate 2: Gonadal Gender
 Gate 3: Prenatal
  Hormonal Gender
The Fetal Period
 of Psychosexual
 Development
 Gate 4: Our Internal
  Sexual Anatomy
 Gate 5: Our External
  Sexual Anatomy
 Gate 6: Neurological
  Tendencies
Psychosexual
 Development
 After Birth
 Gate 7: Gender
  Assignment
 Gate 8: Gender
  Scripting
 Gate 9: Gender Roles
 Gate 10: Gender Identity
 Gate 11: Gender
  Orientations
 Gate 12: Pubertal
  Gender Development
Variations
 Chromosomal Variations
 Genetic Variations
 A Postnatal Variation
An Integrating
 Framework

Chapter 4

Our Gender Development Before Birth

Special Consultants

John Money, Ph.D., director, Psychohormonal Research Unit, Johns Hopkins Medical School, and author of *Boy and Girl, Man and Woman, Lovemaps,* and *Gay, Straight, and In-Between.* Dr. Money is internationally renowned for his research on gender development.

Eli Coleman, Ph.D., associate professor of human sexuality, Department of Family Practice and Community Health, University of Minnesota Medical School, and editor, *Journal of Psychology and Human Sexuality* and *Psychotherapy with Homosexual Men and Women.*

Robert O. Hawkins, Jr., Ph.D., associate dean, School of Allied Health Professions, Health Sciences Center, State University of New York at Stony Brook, and coauthor of *Counseling Lesbian Women and Gay Men: A Life-Issues Approach.*

Timothy Perper, Ph.D., behavioral geneticist and author of *Sex Signals: The Biology of Love.*

James D. Weinrich, Ph.D., assistant research psychobiologist, Department of Psychiatry, University of California, San Diego, and author of *Sexual Landscapes: Why We Are What We Are, Why We Love Whom We Love.*

This chapter and the next chapter are a pair. This chapter describes the stages we pass through in developing our gender identity *before birth*. Chapter 5 deals with the stages of psychosexual development we pass through *after birth*. We use the model of a road map with 12 gates, 6 prenatal and 6 postnatal, to describe psychosexual development. Our main focus in this chapter is on the genetic, hormonal, and anatomical developments before we are born. Chapter 5 focuses on our responses to familial and social factors after we are born.

Several developmental variations provide helpful insights into the complexity of human gender. We emphasize the constant interactions and interdependence of nature (biological factors) and nurture (social conditioning and learning) that occur at critical turning points in our development. This chapter adds a biological dimension to the many examples of social conditioning we explored in Chapters 1–3.

Gender and Sex

What *sex* are you? What is your *gender*? We use these terms every day with different, often conflicting meanings. Sex may refer to the X or Y sex chromosomes in the cells of our bodies. It may refer to our genitals, or sexual anatomy, which we label male or female. Sex can also denote a behavior like sexual intercourse or oral sex, behaviors in which we use our genitals. Sex can also signify our status as a male or female when we see "Sex M F" on a job application. Here we use **sex** and **sexual** to mean our genital or reproductive anatomy, or to refer to activities involving that sexual anatomy.

Similarly, laypersons and professionals use the term *gender* with a wide variety of meanings which often overlap our use of the term sex. Some prefer to use gender to describe anatomy because they feel that using the term sex supports the biological, deterministic notion that "Anatomy is destiny." If someone has the sexual anatomy of a male, then that person is "designed to use" those organs in one way only, hetero*sexually* with a female.

We use **gender** or **psychosexual status** to refer to our biological, personal, social, and legal *status* as a male or female. The equally broad terms **gender identity** or **psychosexual identity** refer to our all-inclusive personal *conviction*, *awareness*, and *identification* of ourselves as female or male.

These two general concepts of *status* and *awareness* include the three following components or aspects:

1. our core gender identity;
2. our gender-role behaviors; and
3. our gender orientation (Figure 4.1).

By the time we were 3 years old, each of us had developed our basic sense or *awareness* of self as a boy or girl. This **core gender identity** developed after we were born, as we responded to the influence of gender hormones on the neural cells in our brains before and after birth, to our external anatomy, and to the conditioning we received from our parents and others. From birth onward, we also gradually developed our **gender-role** behaviors, all those things

**Gender
Orientation**

Figure 4.1. Components in Psychosexual Identity.

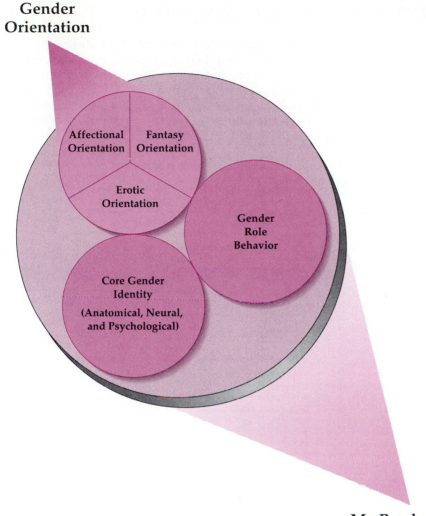

Affectional Orientation

Fantasy Orientation

Erotic Orientation

Gender Role Behavior

Core Gender Identity

(Anatomical, Neural, and Psychological)

**My Psychosexual
Identity and Status**

we say or do to indicate to others and to ourselves that we are either a female or male.

Gender identity and gender role are like two faces of one coin. Our core gender identity is the private, *personal experience* of our gender role. Our gender role is the *public expression* of our core gender identity and status as a female or male person. Some use the phrase **gender identity/role** or **G-I/R** to highlight the connection between these two aspects (Money 1980:15–42, 1988:52–78; Money in Reinisch 1987:15; Moses & Hawkins 1982; Shively & DeCecco 1978).

Here and in Chapter 5, we concentrate on the development of our core gender identity and gender-role behaviors. We leave to Chapter 16 the details of our gender and sexual orientations, the third major component in our psychosexual development and identity shown in Figure 4.1.

The Gates of Psychosexual Development

The process of gender or psychosexual differentiation has been described as a road map with a dozen gates arranged along two main paths, one producing a person of the female gender, the other producing a male-gendered person (Figure 4.2). The genetic and anatomical gates mark either/or forks in the road which lock tightly once we pass through them. Other gates, involving psychological and social factors, are more complex and flexible because they involve a variety of options spread out over time (Money in Reinisch 1987:15).

In species like [the fish] *Labroides dimidiatus*, all the gates [of psychosexual development] stay open so that it's possible for an individual to pass

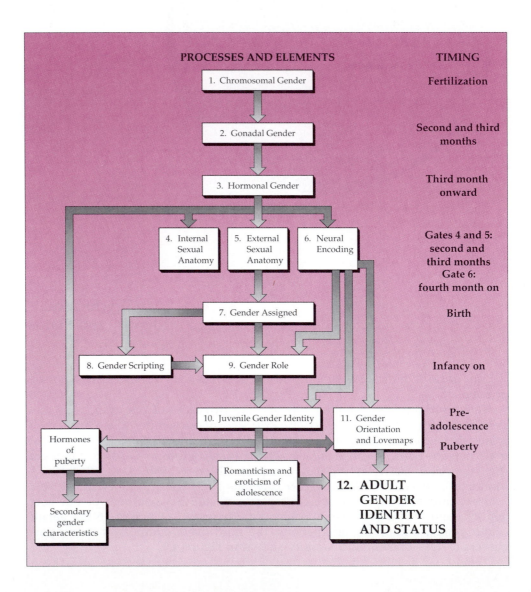

Figure 4.2. A Summary Roadmap of Our Psychosexual Development.

back and forth, able to function fully as either a male or a female throughout its adult life. [This gender change is not arbitrary; it only occurs under very specific conditions.]

In frogs and most fish, the gates may stay open for a considerable period but close tight at some point, locking the individual in as male or female both anatomically and behaviorally.

In the mammalian kingdom, some of the gates lock earlier, others stay open longer, and as you move up the scale to the primates, the sexual behavior gates gain some independence from the morphological anatomy of the genitals. In the primates, and especially in humans, some of the sexual behavior gates become barriers, solid lines, or broken lines on the development[al] road map, guides to the behavior on one side or the other of a lane, but no longer gates that lock.

As you approached each gated sex-differentiation point, you could have gone in either direction, but as you passed through, the gate locked, fixing the prior period of development as male or female. Your gonads, for example, could have become either testicles or ovaries, but once they became testicles, they lost the option of becoming ovaries, or if they became ovaries they could never again become testicles.

In behavior, however, at first you drove all over the highway, but as you proceeded you tended to stick more and more to the lanes marked out and socially prescribed for your sex. The lines and barriers dividing male from female for each kind of sex-linked [gender-role] behavior vary according to your culture and experience, and the kind of individual you have become makes a difference in the way you feel about crossing them, but you never lose these options entirely. A sufficiently strong stimulus [at a critical period of development]—physical, hormonal, neural, or social—can push you over practically any behavior line or barrier. Your own experience and alterations in the gender stereotypes of your culture can obscure established lines and lower barriers so that crossing becomes easier or harder.

(Money & Tucker 1975:73)

The First Two Months of Gender Development

Nature's Basic Plan

Before we discuss the details of our psychosexual development, we need to point out a general premise or principle. In the process of evolution, natural selection has made it much simpler for mammalian and human fetuses to differentiate as females than as males. Early in gestation, all mammalian and human fetuses have the potential to develop the reproductive, sexual system of either male or female. A fetus can develop the female anatomy and psyche without any hormones being needed to direct the development. If the ovaries, or the testes, of a fetus are removed before they begin producing gender-related hormones, that fetus will develop female sexual anatomy and neural templates, regardless of what sex chromosomes it has. This basic pattern of psychosexual development has been termed the **Eve Plan** (Money 1980).

On the other hand, for any fetus to develop the testes of a male, it must have a Y chromosome with gene(s) that direct the differentiation of the primitive gonads into testes. Subsequently, the testes must produce three hormones which override the Eve Plan and divert the undifferentiated internal and external anatomy and the brain into the male pathway.

In the **Adam Plan**, genes on the Y chromosome direct the primitive gonads, which would otherwise become ovaries, to develop into a pair of testes. The testes then produce testosterone and its DHT derivative which **masculinize** the fetus by triggering development of a penis and other structures found in the male. A third hormone, Mullerian Inhibiting Hormone or MIH, simultaneously blocks the natural female developmental pattern. MIH might be said to **defeminize** because it causes *degeneration* of those parts of the fetal anatomy which, in the *Eve Plan*, would naturally develop into a vagina, uterus, and fallopian tubes. Some believe that later in pregnancy, similar patterns of masculinization and defeminization occur as certain neural pathways in the hypothalamus and brain are "masculinized" or diverted into the male path; other neural pathways associated with the female gender, such as hormonal cyclicity and earlier puberty, are blocked or defeminized.

As we move through the gates of psychosexual development, keep in mind that *nature's contingency plan is to produce a female* (Figure 4.3). The Eve Plan has to be modified or overridden by the addition of male genetic and hormonal factors which actively direct the male system to develop while suppressing the female system. To emphasize the primacy of the Eve Plan, we have consciously reversed the customary phrases "male and female" and "masculine and feminine" to read "female and male" and "feminine and masculine" (Money 1980:5, 17).

Figure 4.3. Nature's Basic Tendency. *In the Middle East, 3,000 years ago, the male authors of the Bible pictured God creating Adam and then fashioning Eve from one of Adam's ribs (cartoon on left). In the cartoon on the right, the insights of modern embryology reverse this sequence. In the primal plan, Eve—woman—differentiates unaided. Angels appear with a syringe to give Eve an injection of testosterone, the masculinizing hormone and lo! Adam comes forth.*

In the first two months of human life, we grow from a single cell to an embryo measuring about 1¼ inches with millions of specialized cells. In eight weeks, the basis of all our organ systems is established. In these first eight weeks, we also pass through two gates in our psychosexual development and start moving through the third gate.

Gate 1: Chromosomal/Genetic Gender

The first gate in our psychosexual development occurs at fertilization when the chromosomes and genes of the *egg* (*ovum*) and *sperm* unite. Every body cell of our parents contains hereditary information arranged on 46 chromosomes set up in 23 pairs. Twenty-two of the 23 chromosome pairs, called *autosomes* or *body chromosomes*, are primarily responsible for the general development of the body and all its organs. The 23rd pair of chromosomes, the *gender chromosomes*, may be similar to or different from each other in both size and the type and amount of hereditary information they contain. The human female has two similar gender chromosomes, arbitrarily named X chromosomes. The human male has one X chromosome and a second, much shorter, Y chromosome.

In the ovaries, specialized cells known as primordial germ cells contain the same 46 chromosomes including two X chromosomes. The primordial germinal cells of the testes have 46 chromosomes with X and Y chromosomes. When these primordial germinal cells undergo a form of cell division known as meiosis, the sperm or ovum produced end up with one chromosome from each of the 23 pairs of chromosomes. All normal ova (eggs) contain 22 body chromosomes and an X chromosome. Normal sperm contain 22 body chromosomes plus either an X or a Y chromosome (Figure 4.4).

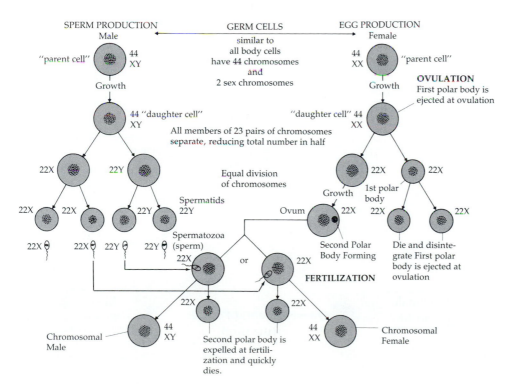

Figure 4.4. The Origins of Chromosomal Gender.

When fertilization brings the ovum and sperm together, the 23 chromosomes of the sperm join the 23 chromosomes of the ovum to give a normal chromosome complement of 46. If a sperm with an X chromosome unites with the X-bearing ovum, the outcome is XX plus 44 body chromosomes, a *chromosomal/genetic female*. If the sperm carrying a Y chromosome enters the ovum, the result is 44 body chromosomes plus XY, a *chromosomal/genetic male*.

In 1987, researchers discovered a gene on the Y chromosome they believed diverted the embryo away from the basic Eve Plan and into the male pathway. Because this gene was thought to make a protein that caused the sexually undifferentiated gonads to develop into testes at Gate 2, it was named the Testis Determining Factor (TDF). However, later research has failed to confirm this theory and we can now say only that a gene or several genes on the Y chromosome direct development along the male path (Page et al. 1987:1081–1082; Palmer et al. 1989).

The Eve Plan

If a zygote (egg/sperm) has no Y chromosome, it starts down the female gender path.

The Adam Plan

If a zygote (sperm/egg) has a Y chromosome, it starts down the male gender path.

This one-dimensional model suggests an either/or gate, with a *single axis* for Gate 1 (Figure 4.5). There are rare cases of individuals who fall in between the two extremes of genetic female and genetic male. These and other variations are discussed later, after we trace normal psychosexual development through all 12 gates.

The chromosomal/genetic gate in our psychosexual development is locked at fertilization and can never be changed.

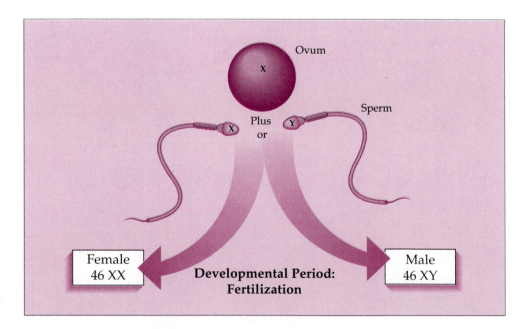

Figure 4.5. Gate 1: Chromosomal/Genetic Gender.

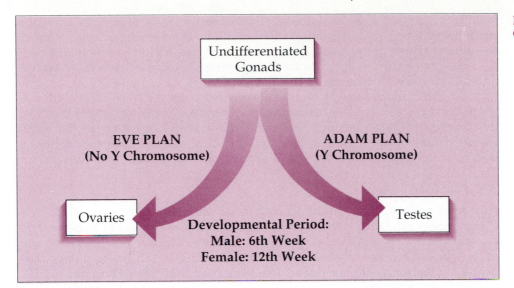

Figure 4.6. Gate 2: Gonadal Gender.

Gate 2: Gonadal Gender

During the second month of pregnancy, each embryo develops a pair of un-differentiated **gonads**, primitive reproductive glands which are neither male nor female. Although the embryo is already genetically a female or male, anatom-ically it has not yet differentiated along either path. As with Gate 1, Gate 2 represents a one-dimensional model with a single axis (Figure 4.6).

The Eve Plan

If the embryo has two XX chromosomes, and no Y chromosomes, the outer surface of the undifferentiated gonads develops into ovaries at about 12 weeks.

The Adam Plan

If the embryo has a Y chromosome, the inner core of the undifferen-tiated gonads develops into testes starting at 6 weeks.

Gate 2, gonadal gender, closes tightly and locks in the third month of preg-nancy. Even if the ovaries or testes are damaged or surgically removed after birth, it does not change the fact that from the third month to birth many organs in the body were feminized in the Eve Plan or masculinized and defeminized in the Adam Plan by hormones from the testes. Once a fetus starts down the path of female gender development, or prenatal hormones push a fetus into the male gender path, we have to negotiate four more gates in gender differ-entiation before we are born. As we pass through each of these four gates, they also close, locking us more firmly into the male or female pathway.

Gate 3: Prenatal Hormonal Gender

Further sexual differentiation now depends on the hormones produced by the testes. Hormones are powerful chemical agents, released directly into the blood-stream, which regulate development of many organs and their activities. We still do not know whether hormones from the mother's ovaries or from the placenta play any role in gender differentiation. Male fetal hormones control the differentiation of the sexual organs at Gates 4 and 5. They also help establish the male pattern of acyclic hormone and sperm production in the hypothalamus and possibly other pathways in the brain at Gate 6.

During the adolescence of females, hormones from the ovaries regulate sexual maturation, development of the breasts, menstruation, widening of the hips, development of subcutaneous fat, and sparseness of body hair. In the male, testicular hormones regulate male sexual maturation and the development of a deeper voice, muscular patterns, and the appearance of facial and body hair.

The Eve Plan

In a fetus with XX chromosomes and no Y, the ovaries produce (1) a predominance of *estrogens*, hormones which will feminize the girl at puberty, and (2) some *androgens* in amounts typical for females. The adrenal glands on top of the kidneys also contribute some androgens or masculinizing hormones. The ovaries and adrenals also produce a little **Mullerian Inhibiting Hormone (MIH)**, a defeminizing hormone. In females, the androgens and MIH levels remain below a critical threshold and have no known effect on fetal development. Because of this hormone balance, the fetus follows the female gender path and develops normal female anatomy and neural encoding in the brain for the menstrual cycle. This process happens whether or not estrogens are present in the embryo and fetus.

The Adam Plan

In a fetus with XY chromosomes, the testes and adrenal glands produce the same three types of hormones as the female fetus, but in a different balance. Genetic/gonadal male fetuses produce large amounts of: (1) *androgens* or masculinizing hormones, particularly testosterone, and (2) the defeminizing hormone Mullerian Inhibiting Hormone (MIH), along with (3) small amounts of feminizing *estrogens*. The balance and amount of these three hormones are critical in allowing the fetus to break away from the Eve Plan and follow the Adam Plan, developing as an anatomical male at Gates 4, 5, and 6.

To picture what happens at Gate 3, we need a diagram with two axes and two dimensions (see Figure 4.7). In the figure, the vertical axis indicates increasing amounts of MIH which suppress the female pattern or defeminize (move from the top to the bottom of the diagram). The horizontal axis shows increasing amounts of testosterone which promote male development or masculinize (move from left to right). In the upper left corner, low levels of both testosterone and MIH leave the Eve Plan intact and the path open for female gender development. An embryo with this prenatal hormone pattern will be feminized and not masculinized. In the lower right corner, high levels of testosterone and MIH combine in the Adam Plan, promoting male gender development. An embryo with this prenatal hormone pattern will be both masculinized and defeminized.

In the lower left corner is a fetus with little testosterone and a high level of MIH. The high MIH level overrides the Eve Plan and defeminizes some anatomical development, just as it does in most males. However, the low level of testosterone does not permit masculinization of other structures and neural pathways. This rare variation leads to a kind of asexual development as the

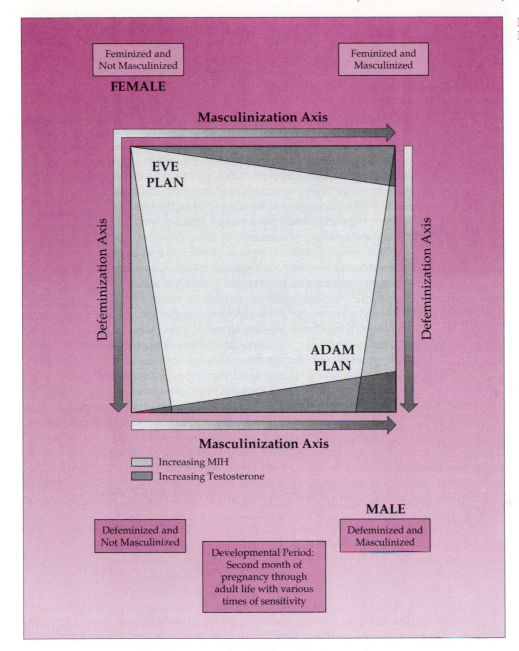

Figure 4.7. Gate 3: Hormonal Gender.

embryo passes through subsequent gates. For example, the androgen insensitivity syndrome involves an individual with XY chromosomes, testes, and a male balance of hormones whose body cells are incapable of reading the masculinizing message of the androgens and who thus ends up an anatomical, psychological female with little sex drive (see p. 97).

In the upper right corner are individuals with a high level of testosterone and a low level of MIH. The low MIH level keeps the Eve Plan in operation for certain characteristics which develop along the female path. Meanwhile, the testosterone masculinizes other structures. This phenomenon leaves the fetus with some female and some male development (see Retained Mullerian Syndrome, p. 85). You will understand these two rare variations better as we move through Gates 4 and 5 (Pillard & Weinrich 1987:432).

For both males and females, the window or gate for hormonal sexual development stays partly open until death. The balance of gender-related hormones can be altered by environmental influences. Programmed differences also occur. Until they are about six weeks old, infant boys produce a surge of masculinizing hormones; infant girls have no such hormonal surge. Yet, between the age of three months and puberty, boys and girls show little difference in the measurable levels of sex hormones.

The anatomical effects of hormones are much easier to detect and study than are their effects on neural and psychic functions. Medications and other environmental factors can alter the hormone balance even while the fetus is in the womb, and certainly after birth. But studying these effects is very difficult in humans.

Although many questions remain to be answered, exploratory studies suggest that severe maternal stress during the second trimester of pregnancy *may* masculinize a female fetus to some degree. Severe stress during pregnancy *may* also be accompanied by an increase in the incidence of male homosexual orientation. No parallel effect has been observed correlating maternal stress and lesbian orientation (Doerner et al. 1983; Ellis et al. 1988; Money 1988:25, 50, 112; Ward 1984). However, other researchers reject this conclusion (Coleman 1987; Gooren 1988).

Some research suggests that prenatal exposure to barbituates may inhibit or interfere with the Eve and Adam Plans for feminization and masculinization (Reinisch & Sanders 1982). After birth, medications and environmental factors can also modify our hormonal balance to some degree.

Keep in mind that the presence or absence of masculinizing and defeminizing hormones and their balance or ratio early in pregnancy influences all the subsequent development, both during pregnancy and after birth (Ehrhardt 1987; Ehrhardt & Meyer-Bahlburg 1981; Ehrhardt et al. 1984; Gooren 1988; Money & Ehrhardt 1972).

The Fetal Period of Psychosexual Development

The fetal period of human development extends from the beginning of the third month of gestation to birth. During these seven months, we encounter and pass through three more gates. At Gate 4, hormones determine our internal sexual anatomy. Soon thereafter, hormones direct our passage through Gate 5, when we develop our external sexual organs, a penis or clitoris. Some claim these hormones may also direct the encoding of male and female tendencies, patterns, and templates in our brain, at Gate 6, probably in three or four months before and after birth. However, clear evidence of neural encoding so far is limited to a few specific traits.

Hormonal masculinization and defeminization are the *two separate but interrelated processes* by which both the fetal sexual organs and the nervous systems are diverted from the basic female development path to the male path. To become a male anatomically and psychologically, some parts of the embryonic sexual system must be actively masculinized while other parts are actively defeminized. *Because this dual process starts during pregnancy and may continue after birth, a variety of combinations in the degree of masculinization and feminization can occur in the sexual anatomy and brain.* Although the anatomical effects of this process are fairly well documented, we can do little more than speculate about the neural and psychic effects of these hormones on such traits as aggression, spatial perceptions, and logical or intuitive thinking. However, it is important to remember that each step in the two processes of masculinization and defeminization is usually programmed to occur only at a specific critical period or "window" during embryonic development (MacLusky & Naftolin 1981; Pillard & Weinrich 1987:431; Taguchi et al. 1984).

Gate 4: Our Internal Sexual Anatomy

Each embryo has two sets of ducts or tubes developing in the abdominal cavity near the gonads. The paired Mullerian and paired Wolffian ducts develop originally in association with transitory fetal kidneys which soon degenerate as their excretory function is taken over by the definitive kidneys. The two Mullerian and the two Wolffian ducts then shift to provide connections between the ovaries or testes and the developing external sexual organs (Figure 4.8).

The Eve Plan	*The Adam Plan*
In the female (XX) fetus, the outer third of the *Mullerian ducts* fuse into a a single vagina. The middle portion also fuses to form the uterus. The inner third becomes the fallopian tubes for transport of the eggs.	In the male (XY) fetus, MIH causes the *Mullerian ducts* to degenerate.
Without a strong testosterone trigger, the *Wolffian ducts* degenerate.	In the male (XY) fetus, testosterone causes the *Wolffian ducts* to develop into the sperm ducts or vasa deferentia, prostate, seminal vesicles, and other male structures.
(Estrogen is not important in this development.)	

In describing Gate 4, we again need a two-dimensional diagram, Figure 4.9, similar to our hormone diagram for Gate 3 (Figure 4.7). The vertical axis indicates increasing amounts of MIH (move from the top to the bottom of the diagram). The horizontal axis shows increasing amounts of testosterone (move from left to right).

The upper left corner marks the Eve Plan, a female whose Mullerian ducts develop into a vagina, uterus, and fallopian tubes while simultaneously the absence of testosterone allows the Wolffian ducts to degenerate.

The lower right corner marks the Adam Plan, a male whose Wolffian ducts develop under the influence of testosterone into the vasa deferentia, seminal vesicles, epididymis, and prostate while a high level of MIH induces degeneration of the Mullerian ducts.

In the lower left corner, a genetic/gonadal male fetus can have a genetic mutation which makes it insensitive to high levels of masculinizing testosterone so that male anatomy does not develop. At the same time, MIH produced by the testes of this genetic/gonadal male causes defeminization as the Mullerian ducts degenerate (see p. 97).

Undifferentiated Condition at Six Weeks

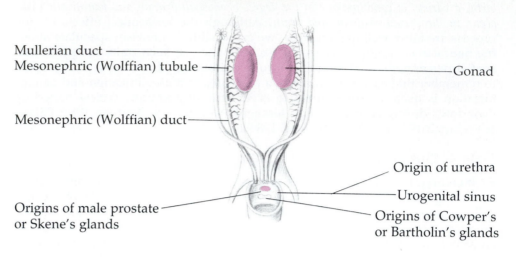

Mullerian duct
Mesonephric (Wolffian) tubule

Gonad

Mesonephric (Wolffian) duct

Origin of urethra

Urogenital sinus

Origins of male prostate
or Skene's glands

Origins of Cowper's
or Bartholin's glands

EVE PLAN
(Hormone-independent)

Female differentiation
after twelve weeks

ADAM PLAN
(Testosterone/MIS-induced)

Male differentiation
after six weeks

Fallopian tube   Uterus

Seminal vesicle

Vas

Ovary (1)

(2) Prostate

Ovarian ligament

Round ligament

(3) Cowper's gland

Vagina

Appendix testis

Skene's ducts
around urethra (2)

Urethra (4)

Epididymis

Bartholin's glands (3)

(4) Urethra   (1) Testis

Opening of vagina

Note: The numbers in parentheses indicate organs that are homologous in the male and female; organs with the same number in parentheses differentiate from the same embryonic origins.

Figure 4.8. Gate 4: Differentiation of Internal Sexual Anatomy.

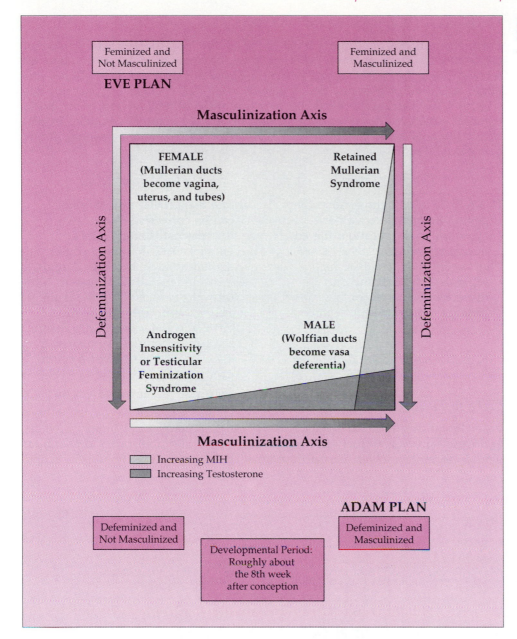

Figure 4.9. Gate 4: Internal Sexual Anatomy.

Because defeminization and masculinization are two different processes under the control of two different hormones, it is possible, though very rare, to have a male fetus in which the Mullerian ducts, instead of degenerating, develop into a uterus and fallopian tubes while the Wolffian ducts develop into the internal male anatomy. This possibility, a type of hermaphrodite with external male anatomy known as *Retained Mullerian Syndrome*, fits in the upper right corner of Figure 4.9. Since the vagina in this type of hermaphrodite may connect with the urethra, such an individual may menstruate through the penile urethra (Money 1980:16–17; Pillard & Weinrich 1987:432).

Gate 5: Our External Sexual Anatomy

If you examined a developing fetus at the end of two months, you could not tell from its external anatomy whether it was a female or male. At that age, all fetuses look alike, with a single protruding genital tubercle which will become either a clitoris or a penis, and a pair of swellings enclosing a pair of folds (Figure 4.10). During the third and fourth months of fetal development, these external structures develop as either female or male external genitalia. In picturing the fetal development at Gate 5, we again use a one-dimensional, single axis model (Figure 4.11).

The Eve Plan

In a female fetus, nature turns the genital tubercle into a clitoris, apparently without requiring any hormonal input.

The swellings and folds remain separated and become, respectively, the major and minor labia on either side of the vagina.

The Adam Plan

In the male fetus, testosterone can be converted into **dihydrotestosterone (DHT)**. If enough DHT is produced, the genital tubercle becomes a penis.

The swellings and folds fuse to form the underside of the penis and scrotum. (Shortly before birth, the testes move into the scrotum where, after puberty, a lower temperature allows sperm production.)

Gate 6: Neurological Tendencies

From tantalizing hints, it seems that the development of the brain in female and male fetuses is influenced and directed by the different ratios of the same gender hormones which, earlier in pregnancy, directed the defeminization and

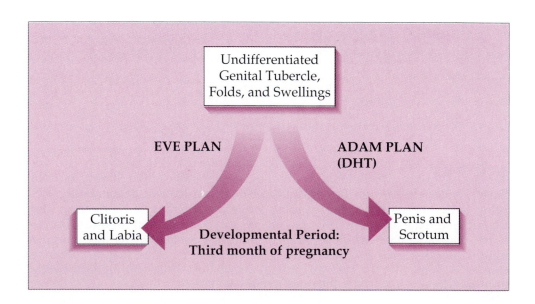

Figure 4.10. Gate 5: External Anatomy.

a. Undifferentiated Condition before Six Weeks

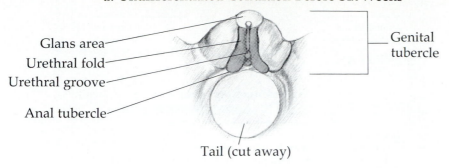

Glans area
Urethral fold
Urethral groove

Anal tubercle

Genital tubercle

Tail (cut away)

b. Six to Eight Weeks

EVE PLAN
(Hormone-independent)

ADAM PLAN
(DHT-induced)

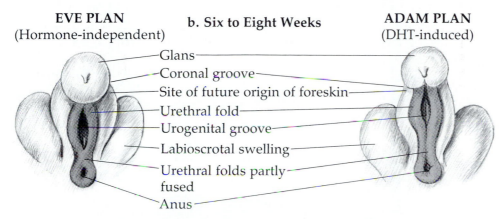

Glans
Coronal groove
Site of future origin of foreskin
Urethral fold
Urogenital groove
Labioscrotal swelling
Urethral folds partly fused
Anus

c. Full Development Twelve Weeks after Conception

Female   **Male**

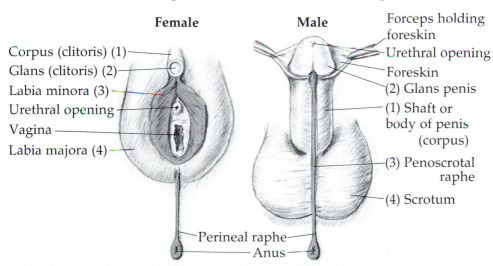

Corpus (clitoris) (1)
Glans (clitoris) (2)
Labia minora (3)
Urethral opening
Vagina
Labia majora (4)

Forceps holding foreskin
Urethral opening
Foreskin
(2) Glans penis
(1) Shaft or body of penis (corpus)
(3) Penoscrotal raphe
(4) Scrotum

Perineal raphe
Anus

Note: Homologous structures in the male and female are indicated by similar numbers in parentheses.

Figure 4.11. Gate 5: Differentiation of External Sexual Anatomy.

Figure 4.12. Gate 6: Encoding of Biobehavioral Neural Templates.

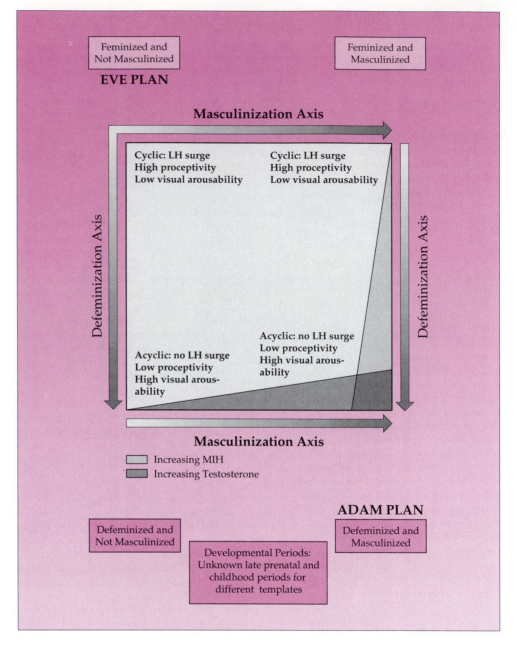

masculinization of the internal and external sexual anatomy (Figure 4.12). The hormones produced by the testes circulate in the bloodstream, not just to the internal and external sexual organs to program them into male structures, but also into the brain. These hormones only affect certain sensitive target cells. They are picked up by receptors in the target cells, enter the cytoplasm of the cell, are modified, and perhaps even enter the cell's nucleus. At each target organ, a gender-related hormone or its metabolite may have a specific and different masculinizing or defeminizing effect on the cell's functioning (Durden-Smith & Desimone 1983; Springer & Deutsch 1981).

The anatomical effects of gender hormones, in Gates 4 and 5, are well researched. Although a few effects of these hormones have been documented in the hypothalamus of the brain, the full extent of their effects on the brain and psyche remain a mystery and the subject of intriguing speculations and heated debate. Some believe that in fetal life, sexually dimorphic (female or male) binding sites in neural cells of the brain allow the hormones to encode permanent tendencies or templates in brain pathways. Later in life, when an activating stimulus is encountered, these different templates are thought to moderate communications and responses within the brain cells in ways which we describe as characteristic of females or of males (Pillard & Weinrich 1987:432). Other researchers, Gooren (1988) and Coleman (1987) among them, cite evidence which conflicts with this theory.

At first sight, the idea of neural templates appears to create a biological determinism in which even alleged differences between women and men can be attributed to an oversimplified biological reductionism. To avoid such a distortion, it is very important to recall our earlier remarks about *the impossibility of divorcing the social from the biological in our psychosexual development.* Before birth, the development of neural cells and the functioning in the brain is controlled by genes and probably modified by hormones. There are some important and specific differences in the genes males and females carry on their X and Y chromosomes which can affect the development of the brain cells and their programming. After birth, all our social experiences and learning flow through our senses to the brain where they pass through neural pathways and are processed by these same brain cells. With all the variables involved, there is no substance to claims of biological determinism. There is equally no substance to the belief that at birth the brain is a blank slate, a *tabla rasa*, which places no limits on the effects of social and environmental factors.

In one hypothesis of neural encoding, Perper defines a **brain (neural) template** as a "prenatal hormonally determined substrate *which is then overlaid by and elaborated on by postnatal determinants, social scripting, and one's personal experiences*" (1985:15–17). Neural encoding, some claim, is a type of developmental learning in which hormones or other prenatal influences set up biobehavioral tendencies in brain cells in such a way that a behavior only surfaces when the proper social/environmental stimulus activates those target cells and evokes the biobehavioral tendency. In this model, such neural tendencies and templates must be matched with an appropriate stimulus during a critical or sensitive developmental period after birth in order to become fully encoded. Once a biobehavioral pattern, such as gender identity, gender orientation, or an erotic preference, has been activated and expressed, some claim it becomes unusually resistant to change or extinction (Money & Ehrhardt 1972:286).

Since there are basic differences in the balances of the gender hormones in female and male fetuses, we can add the adjective **dimorphic** to the concept of neural encoding, neural tendencies, and templates. Since the dimorphic balance of prenatal hormones directs the anatomy of the fetus into either the feminized or masculinized path, it seems likely that similar dimorphic patterns might also occur during our neural development. Moreover, since masculinizing and de-feminizing processes do operate independently of each other at Gate 4, the sexual dimorphism of the brain may also allow the simultaneous development of both masculine and feminine templates, provided these involve different neurons the way different primordia are the source for the internal female and male sexual anatomy. This possibility gives some substance to discussion about an *androgynous* potential, the existence of both masculine and feminine traits in men and women (Durden-Smith & Desimone 1983; Money 1988:12–16; Singer 1976).

The Eve Plan—Feminization in the Brain

The best evidence of a dimorphic gender difference in neural encoding between males and females is the programming of hormones which control the menstrual cycle. The hypothalamus, in the floor of the brain, initiates and regulates the whole system of gender-related hormones. In mammalian development, the Eve Plan reflects a natural tendency which feminizes the fetal hypothalamus, encoding it with a cyclic template that produces a surge of luteinizing hormone (LH) once a month. After puberty, this LH surge is essential in the monthly production of eggs and in the regulation of the menstrual cycle.

Some believe that another Gate 6 element in the Eve Plan involves a higher level of proceptivity for females. **Proceptivity** is the behavioral scientist's term for a series of body language "statements," visual signs, and body movements which women and men use to flirt and indicate an interest in each other. Women usually make the first subtle moves in a "courtship dance" by letting a man know they are interested in him and therefore approachable (Moore 1985; Perper 1985, 1987, 1988; Perper & Fox 1981; Remoff 1984). But is this behavior primarily the result of hormonal effects in the brain before and after birth, the result solely of socialization, or the outcome of interactions between neuro-physiological and social factors?

The Adam Plan—Defeminization in the Brain

No one knows for sure what hormone is responsible for overriding or defeminizing the natural cyclic template in the hypothalamus. Nor do we know whether this process occurs before or after birth (Hutson & Donahoe 1983). Still, something overrides the Eve Plan so that males develop a neural program for acyclic or continuous production of gender-related hormones from the hypothalamus. Males do not have an LH surge. Males do not menstruate. Instead of a varying monthly cycle of hormones, male hormone production is relatively constant from puberty to death, although it may decline with age. Whereas women produce a single egg in a monthly cycle, men produce millions of sperm on a continuous basis (Pillard & Weinrich 1987:433; Weinrich 1987:150–160, 367–369).

Although the Eve Plan appears to give women the edge in proceptivity, men, too, can be proceptive. Men do flirt. But they are much more overt in their flirting, not nearly as subtle as women. When Perper and colleagues asked college men and women to describe how they flirt, they found that college women recognize and understand the early stages of flirtation very well. Men, for their part, often seem insensitive to or unaware of the early proceptive moves women make. Men almost invariably begin their description of courtship with their first overt physical contact (Perper 1985, 1987, 1988; Perper & Fox 1981). "It is as if men are blind—or have been blind*ed* by defeminization—to these initial proceptive steps" (Pillard & Weinrich 1987:434). For some, this behavior is the result of a biological difference. Others claim it is a cultural variable. What do you think? Are men *by nature* slower on the pickup? How might we prove this statement? (See Chapter 15 for more details on flirtation behavior.)

The Masculinization Axis in the Brain

Little is known at present about masculinization, the horizontal (left-to-right) axis of the two-dimensional model for Gate 6. Below the human level, masculinization appears to set up brain templates that favor males mounting and females engaging in lordosis (arching of the back) and presenting, a behavior which makes it easy for the male to mount the female. We have no idea what this phenomenon might mean, if anything, on the human level. There are questions about the apparent "insistent drive" of males to masturbate. Testosterone, which increases dramatically in males at puberty, has been clearly linked with libido or sex drive. Women certainly masturbate, but their drive to masturbate does not appear to be as insistent as it is in males. However, as with proceptivity, this difference might be because women are more socially conditioned against masturbating (Weinrich 1987, 1988).

There is some evidence that males may develop prenatal templates that make them more quickly and intensely aroused by visual stimuli while women develop templates that make them more responsive to touch. At the same time, critics challenge discussions of sex drive in terms of masturbation and response to visual stimuli.

Puberty and the Split Brain

In the 1960s, specialists working with epileptics found that violent seizures could be controlled by "splitting the brain in two," surgically separating the two cerebral hemispheres. In the process, researchers found that the *right hemisphere* specializes in processing spatial relationships, such as we encounter in mazes and solid geometry and the coordination needed in catching a football. The *left hemisphere* specializes in handling language and rote memory. In the hypothalamus of newborn rat pups, masculinized behavior is encoded on the right side and femininized behavior on the left side (Durden-Smith & Desimone 1983:58–61; Gazzaniga 1970; Gazzaniga & LeDoux 1978; Levy 1969, 1974; Levy & Trevarthen 1976, 1977; Levy, Trevarthen, & Sperry 1972; Nordeen & Yahr 1982; Rasmussen & Milner 1977; Springer & Deutsch 1981).

In the Eve Plan, females generally reach puberty two years before boys. As yet, we do not know the mechanism behind this difference. We don't know whether later puberty in males is part of the defeminizing, or a part of the masculinizing process. Some think the mechanism is set up before birth; others believe it develops in late childhood.

Some believe this female-male dimorphism in the onset of puberty gives the female brain less time than the male brain to specialize its two hemispheres. This idea might help explain so-called female intuition, since the intimate connection between the two hemispheres in women provides an advantage over males in quickly integrating the nuances and details of an intricate situation. With the path between the cerebral hemispheres less specialized and more open to communications, the brain can more quickly discern the overall picture in a complex situation. But males may have a different advantage because of their later puberty and more specialized hemispheres in being able to isolate the activities of the hemispheres and to zero in on a few details to the exclusion of everything else (Durden-Smith & Desimone 1983:72–74).

After birth, tendencies and templates encoded in the brain are constantly bombarded by our experiences and cultural conditioning. Anne Petersen has shown that boys who excel in athletics are also skilled in spatial reasoning, a function of the right cerebral hemisphere. Petersen asks whether a boy's involvement in sports where coordination and spatial perceptions are crucial might not stimulate and promote the functional separation of right and left hemispheres. If women become more involved in sports from early childhood, will this experience stimulate their brains to increase the specialization of the two hemispheres and thereby cut down on the communication between hemispheres through the corpus callosum bridge? (Naftolin et al. 1981; Weintraub 1981:17).

The underlying issue in all discussions about neural templates and what determines gender roles is not whether females and males develop different biobehavioral tendencies and subsequently different gender roles, but whether some of these differences are viewed as a superiority, particularly for the male. Are claims that anatomy is destiny used to support stereotyped gender roles, gender biases, and discrimination? Are documented or alleged differences used to restrict personal growth and freedom?

Psychosexual Development After Birth

We now need to complete our discussion by mentioning briefly the six postnatal gates in our gender development (Figure 4.2).

Gate 7: Gender Assignment

In the delivery room when you were born, the doctor or your parents looked at you and happily announced, "It's a girl!" or "It's a boy!" In three words, someone assigned you to the female or male gender. Like the genetic, gonadal, and external anatomy gates, this gate is one-dimensional and either/or. This **gender assignment** is a major turning point for every human because it immediately opens the door wide to a flood of social and cultural influences.

Gate 8: Gender Scripting

Parents and friends immediately respond to our gender of assignment by invoking all the expectations they have for the gender we were assigned as newborns. Every infant is slowly, but continually *scripted* (conditioned) to adopt certain behaviors considered suitable for its assigned gender. Parents and other caregivers treat infant girls and boys very differently (Pogrebin 1980) (Figure 4.13).

Baby boys are bounced around in a more physical way. In the United States, baby boys are usually not as pampered as baby girls because, we are told, pampering makes a boy a sissy and not strong like a man. Baby girls are handled gently, held and touched, cuddled and sung to more than baby boys are. There is also usually much more eye-to-eye contact between mothers and their daughters. Parents and relatives generally use more baby talk with infant girls than they do with baby boys. Later, if they continue using baby talk, little girls are thought to be "so cute" while little boys are encouraged to "talk straightforward, like a man" (Chodorow 1978; Rossi 1985; Schaffer & Crook 1985). All this complex conditioning may be summed up as **gender scripting**.

When the patterns of gender scripting for feminine or masculine behavior are deeply and clearly divided in a society, we find ourselves locked into *gender-*

Figure 4.13. *When a culture has clear and rigid stereotypes of what is appropriate for males and females, children are not free to explore aspects of their personalities as this boy is doing by playing with dolls or this girl is doing by pretending to shave.*

role stereotyping. We then have to follow certain roles and act in certain ways to convince others we are ''truly female'' or ''truly male.''

In recent years, many people have challenged the sexism of gender-role stereotyping (Figure 4.14). The strong male-biased gender-role stereotypes that have characterized Western culture for centuries press us to limit our personality and expression simply because we are told over and over again in so many ways that certain behaviors are appropriate for males or females. Until recently, elementary school textbooks showed Tom with toy guns, driving a truck, or leading a football rush through the line. Ann was shown cooking apple tarts in the kitchen, playing with a doll, or working as a secretary. Gender stereotyping is decreasing as we become more sensitive to its negative and limiting effect on the full expression of our personalities, but it is still very much alive in people's minds, in advertising, on television, and elsewhere (Pogrebin 1980).

Gate 9: Gender Roles

The infant usually responds to gender-differentiated scripting by adopting behaviors which it learns are considered appropriate for its gender as a male or female. By the end of their second year, children learn to prefer certain toys and clothes as appropriate for their gender. **Gender role**, whether it be in the choice of toys, clothes, or behavior, is what an infant does to tell others in nonverbal ways that it is a female or a male (Money in Reinisch 1987:16–17).

Whatever role prenatal influences may play in setting up tendencies for gender roles, these are primarily learned behaviors (Green 1979, 1987; Green & Money 1960, 1961; Green et al. 1982). After many years of studying gender roles in different cultures, anthropologist Margaret Mead remarked,

> Sometimes one quality has been [culturally] assigned to one sex, sometimes to the other. Now it is the boys who are thought of as infinitely vulnerable and in need of special cherishing care, now it is the girls. In some societies it is girls for whom the parents must collect a dowry or make husband-catching magic, in others the parental worry is over the

Figure 4.14.

"ACTUALLY IN OUR GROUP THE WHITE GUYS PLAY
LIKE BLACK GUYS, THE BLACK GUYS PLAY LIKE
WHITE GUYS, AND THE WOMAN PLAYS LIKE A MAN."

difficulty of marrying off the boys. Some peoples think of women as too weak to work out of doors, others regard women as the appropriate bearers of heavy burdens, "because their heads are stronger than men's." The periodicities of female reproductive functions have appealed to some people as making women the natural sources of magical or religious powers. . . . In some cultures women are regarded as sieves through whom the best-guarded secrets will sift, in others it is the men who are the gossips. Whether we deal with small matters or with large, with the frivolities of ornament and cosmetics or the sanctities of man's place in the universe, we find this great variety of ways, often flatly contradictory, in which the roles of the two sexes have been patterned. But we always find the patterning.

(cited by Money & Tucker 1975:39)

Gate 10: Gender Identity

By 24 months of age, the child has learned to distinguish between Mommy and Daddy, between girls and boys. Along the way, usually by three years of age, each of us develops a core gender identity, an internalized conviction that allows us to say with absolute certainty, "I'm a girl" or "I'm a boy." The roots of this core gender identity, the pathways and tendencies laid down in our brain before birth, have been molded, shaped, and reinforced by postnatal scripting. The infant identifies with the parent, siblings, and others who share its gender and counteridentifies with the family members who are of the other gender. At puberty, romanticism and erotic desires enrich this core gender identity to give the adolescent his or her juvenile gender identity.

Once our core gender identity is set, it appears to be completely irreversible. We know we are either a girl or a boy, a female or a male, and no one can convince us otherwise.

Gate 11: Gender Orientations

Gender orientation, the gender of the persons we fall in love with and whom we desire as sexual partners, is distinct and different from our *core gender identity*, our personal conviction that we are a female or a male. Persons with a clear gender identity may choose either males or females or both as sexual partners.

Despite this distinction, gender identity and gender orientation appear to share one similarity: They both appear to have their roots in tendencies which are set up in the brain before and/or shortly after birth. However, as we see in Chapter 16, these tendencies are molded and elaborated on by what happens to us after birth.

One factor in our emerging sexual interests is our experience with childhood sexual rehearsal play. Even in a culture such as ours which frowns on or punishes children for playing "doctor/nurse" or other games involving sexual curiosity, explorations, and adult role playing, children do manage to satisfy their need to find out about body differences and anticipate grown-up roles. The way parents react when they find their children playing such exploratory games helps mold our gender identity and self-image. Parental scripting, experiences with peers and adults, and our gender orientation all become part of our realization of who we are, of who we find sexually attractive, and of what we may prefer in the way of sexual activities (Money 1980:27–47, 51–60, 148–149; Perper 1985; Weinrich 1987).

In the juvenile years before the onset of puberty and adolescence, many children begin to focus on interpersonal relations, developing skills in pair-bonding and experiencing their first taste of erotic attraction. A rising surge of gender-related hormones moves us quickly into puberty, the twelfth and last gate in our psychosexual development.

Gate 12: Pubertal Gender Development

With puberty, the girl grows into a young woman, the boy into a young man. An increase in estrogens or androgens triggers development of the appropriate secondary gender characteristics. Voices change. Breasts develop. Beards grow. Hips broaden and curve. Erotic dreams and nocturnal emissions begin. Romance blossoms. Sexual desires become imperatives. The risks of pregnancy and sexually transmitted diseases become a concern. Passing through Gate 12 to our adolescent years, we face the wonders and risks of being a young but sexually mature man or woman.

Think about these 12 gates, these variables and their relationships with each other. The 6 gates before birth are predominantly genetic, hormonal, anatomical, and neural, without social input, but they are responsible for the foundations on which our social conditioning and learning must build.

Gate 1. Chromosomal/genetic gender

Gate 2. Gonadal gender

Gate 3. Prenatal hormonal gender

Gate 4. Internal anatomy

Gate 5. External anatomy

Gate 6. Neural encoding

After birth, through Gates 7 to 12, social and environmental factors become dominant, overlaying and building on our prenatal psychosexual development.

Gate 7. Gender assignment

Gate 8. Gender scripting

Gate 9. Gender roles

Gate 10. Gender identity

Gate 11. Gender orientations

Gate 12. Pubertal gender

Variations

In the linear flow suggested by the gate model, there is the possibility that an individual may shift to the other path in one or more aspects. Modern medicine and psychology have documented and studied a number of such variations in gender development. Because they have different outcomes, these variations can provide some important insights into the realities of gender. A brief description here of some key variations in chromosomal and genetic gender, in what appears to be neural encoding, and a case of postnatal variation add some important details to our gender landscape.

Chromosomal Variations at Gate 1

From puberty to death, males continuously produce billions of sperm. In each cell division, the 46 chromosomes and their over 100,000 genes are copied into two daughter cells. Mistakes are inevitable. About 20% of all sperm are abnormal. The same possibility exists, to a lesser extent perhaps, for ova. Sperm and ova may be missing a chromosome or have an extra chromosome. When the fertilized egg divides into millions of cells to become an embryo, individual cells can end up missing a chromosome or having an extra chromosome. If this chromosome happens to be the X or Y chromosome, gender development is affected.

Turner syndrome is the result of a missing chromosome. The affected individual is a female with 44 body chromosomes and a single X chromosome (45,X). Most 45,X fetuses miscarry or abort spontaneously early in pregnancy. Still, roughly 1 in 2,500 live female births is a girl with Turner syndrome. The absence of a Y chromosome and its genes allows female development, in keeping with the basic Eve Plan. The absence of a second X chromosome prevents development of ovaries. Without ovaries to produce estrogens at puberty, females with Turner syndrome do not develop secondary female characteristics or menstruate unless treated hormonally. They cannot produce eggs or conceive following intercourse. Despite their sterility and some minor physical differences, females with Turner syndrome do not have any confusion about their gender identity as females.

Klinefelter syndrome is a second, fairly common sex chromosome variation. This condition may develop when the zygote ends up with two X and one Y chromosomes, giving the individual 44 body chromosomes plus XXY, or 47,XXY instead of 46,XY. Screening of newborn infants shows that roughly 1 in every

500 live male births is 47,XXY. Until puberty, most Klinefelter boys appear normal. However, secondary male characteristics are not well developed. The testes cannot produce sperm, making them sterile. One-third of these boys develop enlarged breasts. With an even greater number lacking any interest in sex, few of them marry. Yet their gender identity as males is firmly established.

Other chromosomal variations are possible. Some individuals have the normal chromosome complement for a female, 46,XX, but end up functional males. These individuals may have inherited the TDF gene attached to a body chromosome or to the X chromosome received from the father. By contrast, an individual may have the male chromosome complement of 46,XY and develop as a female if the male-determining gene(s) was lost during sperm development (Page et al. 1987). Some individuals, known as chromosomal and sexual mosaics, end up with two different types of cells or cell lines, with some 46,XY male cells and some 46,XX female cells.

Genetic Variations at Gate 1

Androgen Insensitivity Syndrome

Sometimes gender development takes a detour because of a mutation in a single gene. The most common example is a recessive gene on the X chromosome which prevents production of a receptor protein needed to enable testosterone to enter the body cells with its masculinizing message. Since this recessive gene is found on the X chromosome, women can carry it on one of their two X chromosomes and not show its effects because they have an unaffected dominant gene on the other X.

When a male fetus receives this gene on the X chromosome from its mother, it starts off as a genetic male with testes and the hormones of a typical male. But since the mutated gene makes all the body cells insensitive to the masculinizing effect of testosterone, the Wolffian ducts fail to develop into the internal male system. At the same time, the Mullerian Inhibiting Hormone (MIH) gets its usual message through to the cells in the Mullerian ducts, so an internal female system also fails to develop. The external anatomy of a male cannot develop. Instead, a short vagina and the external sexual structures of a female take shape. Since the prenatal brain is also insensitive to the masculinizing messages of testosterone, its encoding is in keeping with the Eve Plan. The hypothalamus and other neural encoding follows the female path, even though there is no uterus and no possibility of menstruation (Figure 4.15).

At birth, the doctor usually identifies the infant as female (Gate 7). Passage through the remaining Gates 8 to 12 also follows the female gender path, hence the other name for this condition, *testicular feminization*. The twist to androgen-insensitive development is well stated by Money and Tucker who report, "There is enough estrogen in the testicular hormone mix to give any boy breasts like a pinup girl's and cause his body fat to deposit in a rounded pattern during adolescence if the estrogen is not dominated by the androgens that direct the emergence of masculine secondary characteristics" (1975:54–57). Plastic surgery may be needed to lengthen the short vagina. All in all, if raised as a female, the androgen-insensitive individual usually adjusts as a content, if sterile, female with little interest in sex. In Figure 4.12, the androgen-insensitive person would be in the lower left corner, defeminized and not masculinized (Pillard & Weinrich 1987:437–438; Weinrich 1987:153–154).

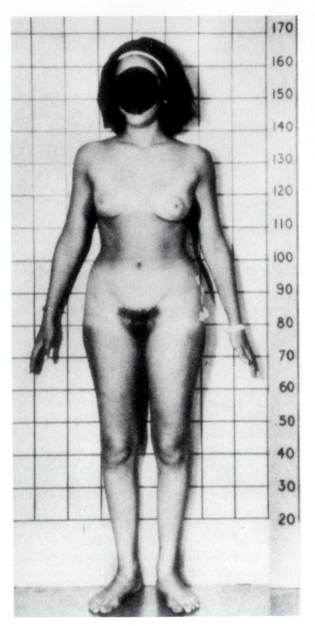

Figure 4.15. *This individual appears to be a female and was raised as a female. Although she has a male chromosome complement, 46,XY, and testes, her external anatomy, secondary sexual characteristics, and psyche are female. A genetic mutation made all the cells in her body incapable of being masculinized.*

DHT Deficiency

We first became aware of DHT deficiency, a controversial variation in gender development, in the 1960s when a type of male hermaphroditism was reported in two villages in the mountains of the Dominican Republic in the Caribbean (Imperato-McGinley 1976; Money 1976). Sporadic cases have since been reported elsewhere. In three generations of villagers, 38 children experienced a most unusual puberty. According to Imperato-McGinley et al. (1974, 1976, 1985:130), these infants had more or less ambiguous external sexual anatomy with a clitoral-like phallus and more or less fused labia. In the first generation, since these infants appeared female and no one suspected that they were genetic males with testes that had not fully descended, they were raised as girls. At puberty, they failed to develop secondary female characteristics and instead started developing some masculine characteristics. A liability to their parents, these individuals could not find husbands because of their masculine appearance. In the next generation, infants with this condition were referred to as *guevedoce*—"penis at 12," or as *machi-hembra*—"first woman, then man" (Imperato-McGinley et al. 1985:130).

The cause behind this type of male hermaphroditism is a mutant gene which prevents formation of the enzyme 5-delta reductase which converts testosterone into dihydrotestosterone or DHT. As we know from our discussion of external sexual anatomy at Gate 5, the hormone DHT directs development of male external anatomy. An infant with this mutant gene is a genetic male with undescended testes (Gates 1 and 2). With normal amounts of testosterone and MIH (Gate 3), the internal sexual anatomy differentiates in the male pattern (Gate 4). Only the external structures shift over partially into the female path (Gate 5).

At puberty, an increase in testosterone appears sufficient to trigger partial *virilization*. The clitoris-like structure enlarges into a small penis, and weak male secondary characteristics develop. By the end of puberty, the "girls" look like boys and have a sexual interest in girls (Imperato-McGinley et al. 1985; Peterson et al. 1977). Other researchers have challenged this report, questioning both the claim that the parents had raised these children with ambiguous genitals as normal girls and that the children raised as females were able to adapt successfully as males after puberty (Money 1976, 1988).

Some DHT-deficient children have been surgically feminized and socially raised as girls from birth onward. They become women with a heterosexual orientation, despite their male chromosomal and gonadal status.

Among the unanswered questions raised by these children is what role is played by the hormone-triggered neural encoding of gender identity tendency before birth (Money 1988:51). Does this condition and its management upset the theory that gender identity is irreversibly set between age 2 and 3, as is currently assumed? These children are reported to have had mixed feelings about their gender identity as girls and felt different from other girls. If their parents and everyone else were equally ambivalent in gender scripting these children as girls, could their gender identity have remained unsettled and only been irreversibly set much later than normal when they "converted" to boys at puberty? And how reliable are retrospective reports by the parents as to what they did and felt years earlier when they were raising these unusual children?

A Postnatal Variation

How are late infancy and prepubertal experiences instrumental in our developing gender identity? If an infant's gender is reassigned soon after birth, can it be successfully reared in the gender opposite to that of its development in the womb?

In 1965 identical twin boys were circumcised at the age of 7 months. One of the twins suffered a severe injury to his penis from the electric cauterizing needle. After a few days, the penis dried up and fell off, leaving only a stub. The parents were referred to Johns Hopkins Hospital where pioneering treatment of hermaphroditic babies had been going on for many years. At age 17 months, the accidentally castrated infant had surgery to create female external sexual structures. The testes were removed so they would not produce secondary male characteristics. Estrogen replacement and vaginal surgery in the adolescent years completed the work of gender reassignment (Money & Tucker 1975:91–99).

Early reports suggested a perfectly normal gender identity development for the reassigned girl. However, Williams and Smith reported that in her teen years the girl experienced considerable difficulty in adjusting to her female gender role. At age 15, "She does display certain features that would make me suspicious that she will ever make the adjustment as a woman." Diamond (1982) reported that her classmates taunted her as "cave woman" because of her unfeminine appearance and behavior. So the question remains: What is the relative importance of neural encoding for gender identity at Gate 6 and the finalizing of core gender identity in early childhood at Gate 10? In another society, where femininity in terms of physical attractiveness is described differently, would this girl experience a more "normal" psychosexual development?

An Integrating Framework

Many fascinating questions are being researched today about variations in psychosexual development. We have several theories, with very little or contradictory evidence. There are no clear answers. However, the dimorphic linear model used here represents one rather widely accepted way of structuring what we do know. At the same time, this model suggests some implications which reveal certain biases and assumptions.

A superficial reading of this linear model suggests that normal development requires everyone to pass through all the gates on one or the other side. Terms like *gender transposition* and *cross-coding* are frequently used to describe variations where development shifts from one path to the other. Such terminology can add to the implication that individuals who are not totally congruent in every aspect of this model of psychosexual development are somehow abnormal. But, as we saw in Chapters 1 and 2, words like normal and abnormal are very culturally biased. The Hindu culture accepts as a kind of third gender the *hijra*, men who adopt the female gender role on a full-time basis and relate with other men sexually. The male *berdache*, or shaman, who adopts a female gender role is likewise accepted and honored in American Indian cultures. Outside these cultures, the *hijra* and *berdache* would be considered to have an abnormal gender identity role.

This linear model with its two parallel paths may be interpreted as implying that persons with Turner, Klinefelter, androgen insensitivity, and DHT deficiency syndromes have a defective, incomplete, or abnormal gender identity. Similarly labeled are men and women who occasionally or continually experience a need to adopt the gender role of the other gender, transvestites and transgenderists who dress in the clothes of the other gender. Likewise labeled are transsexuals, persons with a male gender identity who are anatomically female, and those who have a female, gender identity with male anatomy. The linear model might be interpreted as implying that all the components of our gender identity/role *should be in agreement* and *should* follow consistently down one or the other path. But are we revealing some subconscious biases and assumptions in jumping to this conclusion? We study this question in Chapter 19, but it is worth mentioning here in the context of interpreting our model of psychosexual development.

A significant proportion, 5% to 10%, of all humans are drawn affectionally and erotically to persons of their own gender. These men and women are as convinced of their gender identity and status as are men and women who are attracted to persons of the other gender. Add to those with a homoerotic orientation the significant number of men and women who likewise have no trouble with their gender identity and are drawn erotically to persons of both genders, people we label bisexuals. How do we interpret different gender orientations in this model? The linear model need not be interpreted as implying that homoerotic and bisexual men and women are somehow abnormal because the majority of men and women have a heterosexual orientation. We continue our discussion of the issue of what is normal in gender orientations in Chapter 16.

Scientific models always have their limits. Beyond the cautions and questions just raised, the major limitation and danger of our linear model is that it can be interpreted to support sexist and heterosexist assumptions. It suggests that there are only two legitimate destinations in psychosexual development. At one destination, call it "New York," we find females who are assumed to be heterosexual and who adhere to all the gender roles assigned to the female path. At the other end of the continent, "Los Angeles," we find heterosexual males who follow all the male gender-role stereotypes prevalent in our culture.

Because real life offers more than these two destinations, we can expand the analogy between our gender development and the linear 12-gate model. Just as there are all kinds of legitimate destinations besides New York and Los Angeles, so nature presents us with a variety of persons besides the heterosexual male and female. Some men and women, heterosexually oriented transvestites, transsexuals, and transgenderists, may move from New York to Los Angeles, or the other way. Other transvestites, transsexuals, and transgenderists who are homoerotic or bisexual have different destinations. Some people never go to either of these destinations and still enjoy rich and full lives. Men and women who are drawn to persons of their own or to both genders have their own destinations and experiences as gendered persons. Persons whose genetic and gonadal gender conflict with their sexual anatomy or gender identity can also lead fulfilling lives on the broad landscape of our gendered experience.

Future research and theory will undoubtedly lead to a new model that will visualize new insights and evidence in a clearer and more valid way than the 12-gate model. Until that model is developed and tested for its perspective and value, we are left with a partial model which, despite its limitations and flaws, helps us understand a very complex developmental process involving the continual interaction of both nature and nurture at critical times in our gender development.

Becoming a sexual person is a lifelong challenge. The challenge begins when the egg and sperm first unite in fertilization. It continues before birth with the development of our gonads, sexual hormones, anatomy, and neural patterns. Along the way, environment, social interactions, and learning become increasingly important and influential, interacting always with our nature. These interactions continue until we die.

Key Concepts

1. Gender, not sex, is the umbrella term which includes a number of variables that make up our gender status and the awareness of our gender-identity/role.

2. Although some suggest a clear distinction between biological sex and psychosocial gender, a more integrative approach uses the concept of psychosexual or gender identity, which involves interaction of three factors: core gender identity, gender role, and gender orientation.

3. Fetal female gender development proceeds independently of hormone control; gender development of the male fetus, on the other hand, requires the addition of a Y chromosome, TDF gene, and above-threshold levels of testosterone, DHT, and MIH at critical times in fetal development.

4. Caution is important when we use the linear road map model and terms such as "natural," "normal," "transposition," and "cross-coding" in describing variations in gender development to avoid sexist and heterosexist assumptions.

5. Sex or gender roles vary greatly from one culture to another. What is thought to be feminine behavior in one society may be seen as masculine behavior in another culture.

6. The linear road map of human psychosexual development can be interpreted as implying the naturalness and legitimacy of only two destinations, heterosexual female and heterosexual male. However, a more careful reading of the evidence suggests that our psychosexual development involves a broader landscape with a variety of natural and legitimate destinations, or variations in psychosexual development.

Key Terms

Adam Plan (76)
brain (neural) template (89)
core gender identity (72)
defeminize (76)
dihydrotestosterone (DHT) (86)
dimorphic (89)
Eve Plan (75)
gender (72)
gender assignment (92)
gender identity (72)
gender-identity/role (G-I/R) (73)

gender role (72)
gender scripting (92)
gonads (79)
masculinize (76)
Mullerian Inhibiting Hormone (MIH) (80)
proceptivity (90)
psychosexual identity (72)
psychosexual status (72)
sex (72)
sexual (72)

Summary Questions

1. List the six *prenatal* gates of psychosexual development, giving a brief description of each stage and indicating when it occurs. Which of these gates are one-dimensional? Which are two-dimensional? Which of these gates lock irreversibly when the fetus crosses them?

2. List the six *postnatal* gates of psychosexual development, giving a brief description of each stage and indicating when it occurs. Which of these gates are one-dimensional? Which are two-dimensional? Which of these gates lock irreversibly?

3. What is sex role stereotyping? How does it affect our psychosexual development?

4. Discuss what we know and do not know about prenatal gender-dimorphic neural templates or encoding.

5. Describe the variations of Turner syndrome, Klinefelter syndrome, androgen insensitivity, and DHT deficiency syndrome. How do these variations fit into the linear model of psychosexual development?

6. How does the fact that boy babies and girl babies are treated differently affect the ways we experience our gender identity?

Suggested Readings

Durden-Smith, J., & D. Desimone. (1983). *Sex and the Brain*. New York: Arbor House.

Money, J., & P. Tucker. (1975). *Sexual Signatures: On Being a Man or Woman*. Boston: Little, Brown.

Rossi, A. (1985). The biosocial side of parenthood. In W. Williams (ed.), *Psychology of Women* (2nd ed). New York: Norton.

Springer, S. P., & G. Deutsch. (1981). *Left Brain, Right Brain*. San Francisco: Freeman.

Weinrich, J. D. (1987). *Sexual Landscapes: Why We Are What We Are, Why We Love Whom We Love*. New York: Scribners.

Weintraub, P. (1981). The brain: His and hers. *Discover*, 2(4):15–20.

Childhood Sexuality
    The Limits of What
        We Know
    Sexuality in Infants
        and Children
Puberty
    Puberty and Adolescence
        in the Western World
    The Hormones That
        Control Puberty
    Female Cycles
    Some Medical
        Complications
    Adjusting to the
        Changes of Puberty
Adolescent Sexuality
    Making Decisions
        About Sex
    Legal Rights of Children
        and Adolescents
    Sexuality Education
Theories of Child and
    Adolescent
    Development
    Sigmund Freud
    Erik Erikson
    Jean Piaget and
        Lawrence Kohlberg
    John Gagnon and
        William Simon
The Future of
    Childhood and
    Adolescent Sexuality

Chapter 5

Sexuality in Childhood and Adolescence

Special Consultants

Peggy Brick, M.Ed., director of education, Planned Parenthood of Greater Northern New Jersey, and author of *Positive Images: A New Approach to Contraceptive Education.*

Floyd M. Martinson, Ph.D., research professor of sociology, Gustavus Adolphus College, St. Peter, Minnesota. Dr. Martinson is an international expert on childhood and adolescent sexuality and the author of many papers on the subject.

Ronald Moglia, Ed.D., professor and director of the Human Sexuality Program, New York University, and a specialist in children and sexuality education.

Nelwyn B. Moore, Ph.D., professor of family and child development, Department of Home Economics, Southwest Texas State University, San Marcos, Texas.

Michael Perry, Ph.D., editor of Volume 7, *Childhood and Adolescent Sexology* in the *Handbook of Sexology.*

Ann Welbourne-Moglia, Ph.D., former executive director of the Sex Information and Education Council of the United States (SIECUS) and currently a sexuality education consultant.

Our sexual experiences as infants and children lay the foundation for that critical period in life we all experience at puberty and adolescence. This chapter explores the latest findings about our sexual development from birth through adolescence.

Childhood Sexuality

There are few human activities about which there is greater curiosity, greater social concern, and less knowledge than child sexuality.

Floyd M. Martinson (1980:30)

If eroticism is a legitimate experience for adults, it must be a legitimate aspect of growth.

A. Yates (1980:372)

The Limits of What We Know

Discussions of childhood and adolescent sexuality encounter several problems. First, we have limited empirical data on how children develop and experience their sexuality. Researchers who want to ask children questions about their sexual views and experiences are often seen as promoting early sexual experiences. This perception makes parents reluctant to give permission for their children to participate in such studies (Goldman & Goldman 1982a, 1982b). Government and other funding agencies are also reluctant to support such research.

Despite these problems, early research by Sanford Bell (1902), Albert Moll (1913), and Sigmund Freud; the work of Clellan Ford and Frank Beach, and Carlfred Broderick; Alfred Kinsey's surveys in the 1940s and 1950s; and others do give us some interesting insights into how children experience their sexuality (Jackson 1982:77; Martinson 1983; Money 1976a; Tabbutt 1987:15).

Sexuality in Infants and Children

Birth marks a turning point in our sexual development because social and psychological factors now come to the fore. In the first months after birth, parents incorporate their child into a family and a society. The infant learns nurturance, trust, and the simple pleasures its body and senses can provide as it interacts with others. Being nursed, cuddled, and played with affect a child's developing awareness and experience of its sexuality. The experience of toilet training can have long-term effects on our personality and sexuality. As the sphere of interaction with others expands, playmates and other children in nursery school, teachers, and religious influences complicate the socialization process. Messages about our bodies, about our being female or male, and about the kinds of behaviors others consider appropriate for our gender are absorbed and internalized. In countless nonverbal ways, parents and others communicate values about sexuality that influence us throughout life. Our sexuality cannot exist unless we are socialized and integrated into a community (Figure 5.1).

Even the best intentioned parents in the world tend to interfere with the natural evolution of their children's sexuality. One of our strongest cultural messages, at least until recently, has been the connection we maintain between

Figure 5.1. *Children pick up nonverbal positive messages about their bodies and sexuality when their parents are comfortable and positive about sexuality. Negative messages are also communicated nonverbally.*

sex, love, and reproduction in our value systems. With decreasing emphasis on reproduction and more flexibility in our lifestyles, parents and children are increasingly confronted with the challenge of dealing with sexual responses and pleasure apart from the few times in one's life when we use sex to reproduce (Calderone & Johnson 1981:18).

When Darling and Hicks asked college students to evaluate the messages about sexuality they received from their parents, the students agreed that the level of direct verbal communication on issues related to sexuality was "extremely low." More important, even when parents did talk about sex, they seemed more concerned about restraining their children's sexual interest and activity than with imparting information, especially when dealing with daughters. The major messages these college students received from their parents were (1) sex is bad; (2) sex should be delayed; (3) save sex for marriage; (4) love is a prerequisite for sex; and (5) there is a sexual double standard for boys and girls (Darling & Hicks 1983:240). Remember these students were recalling the messages they received from their parents roughly in the late 1960s and early 1970s. How does this report match the messages you recall receiving from your parents?

Socialization is a major factor in our developing sexuality, but parents and adults are not around all the time. Children interact among themselves. When left alone, they spontaneously explore their bodies, their genitals, and experience their developing sexual nature. Sex play and exploration are major factors in a child's development. Even when discouraged or prohibited by adults, as often happens in our culture, children manage to explore their bodies and their sexual organs. They explore the differences between boys and girls, whether or not parents and other adults provide an opportunity for this activity by

Figure 5.2. *Self-explora-tion is an expression of a young child's natural curiosity.*

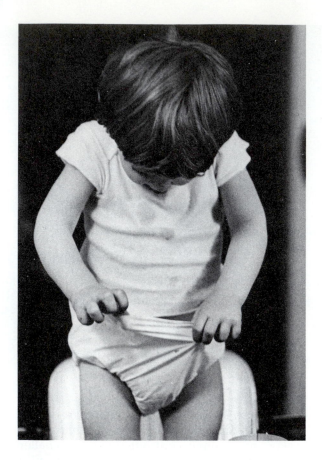

bathing with their children or bathing children together. Children masturbate, and they have love affairs, sometimes as early as age 3 (Bell 1902) (Figure 5.2).

Masturbation

The same reflex response that brings an erection to a boy or man has been seen functioning as early as 17 weeks in pregnancy when ultrasound pictures reveal erections of the tiny penis of male fetuses. Considering the analogies between the male and female genital systems, it is logical to assume that females also develop the capacity for cyclical vaginal lubrication while still in the womb (Calderone 1985:700; Colonna & Solnit 1981).

In one study of boys 3 to 20 weeks old, 7 of 9 infants had erections from 5 to 40 times a day (Conn & Kanner 1940). Girls as young as 7 months have been observed experiencing what to all appearances can only be judged to be a re-flexive orgasm induced by rubbing or putting pressure on their genitals (Bakwin 1974; Kinsey et al. 1953:104–105).

The natural reflexes that result in fetal and infant erections and vaginal lubrication are very much like the knee jerk and other reflexes, except they are accompanied by smiles and cooing that clearly suggests the infant is enjoying something quite pleasurable (Martinson 1980). Sooner or later, most children learn the pleasures of stimulating their genitals. Once that connection is made, the threat of punishment and sin may not be enough to keep a child from masturbating.

Most children seem to forget their early masturbation experiences. Two-thirds of the males in Kinsey's study reported hearing about masturbation from other boys in their prepubescent or early adolescent years before they tried it themselves. Fewer than 1 in 3 males reported they rediscovered masturbation entirely on their own. Two out of 3 females in Kinsey's sample learned about masturbation by accident, sometimes not until after they were married. Some women reported they had masturbated for some time before they realized what they were doing.

Sociosexual Play

The subject of sexual play among children and preadolescents is emotionally charged, mainly because adults tend to read into such play their own adult meanings. The sexual play of children is not sexual in the way it is for adults. It is more often oriented toward exploration, learning, and confirming their sexual identity than toward satisfying sexual urges (Borneman 1983; Kirkpatrick 1986; Martinson 1980). Researchers contend that very young children are capable of and seem to enjoy erotic and sexual activity, and that this early sensual stimulation contributes to both normal physical and psychological development. The evidence indicates that almost all childhood sexual experiences are positive, growth-promoting experiences. Unless they involve force or abuse, or trigger strongly negative reactions when discovered by adults, these experiences contribute to a smooth transition into adulthood and to satisfying adult intimacy (Figure 5.3).

Figure 5.3. *Self-exploration and curiosity often lead children to explore the differences in their bodies.*

(a)

Figure 5.4. The Evolution of Privacy. *In the 16th century, several families, single persons, married couples, and young and old all shared the same crowded space in the "big houses" of European urban life. Public baths, both indoors (a) and outdoors, provided another opportunity for children to learn about sexuality in a casual, relaxed way. This contrasts strongly with the evolution of domestic privacy that became dominant in the 19th-century Victorian home (b) with its public sitting room and private bedrooms.*

(b)

By age 2, children are naturally responding to each other, affectionately touching, hugging, and kissing each other. Whether this behavior is erotic or not, we have no way of knowing, even when it involves touching each other's genitals. By age 3, the child may take a casual interest in superficial examination of other children's genitals. Games of "playing house," "you show me yours and I'll show you mine," or "Mommy and Daddy" usually involve nothing more than undressing with some touching, or lying next to or on top of one another. When a few years of age separate the two children and the older child has lived in a small apartment where privacy is difficult, such games may mimic adult behavior and include mutual masturbation, oral-genital contact, and attempts at intercourse (Figure 5.4).

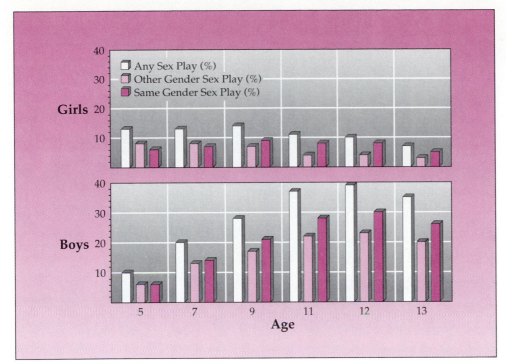

Figure 5.5. Sociosexual Play of Children. *These graphs show the percentages of boys and girls who engage in sociosexual play before the onset of puberty. The data is from the Kinsey surveys of 1948 and 1953.*

By age 5, about 10% of boys and 13% of girls have engaged in sociosexual play with other children (Figure 5.5). Before puberty, boys show the highest interest in sex play at age 12 when 39% engage in such activities. At age 9, 1 in 6 girls engages in sexual play. For those children who do engage in sex play with peers of their own sex or the other sex, such interactions are likely to be occasional. Research since Kinsey's studies suggests that children become increasingly interested in sexual topics and behaviors after age 5. However, they appear to be increasingly reluctant to engage in public displays of sex or their bodies as they approach puberty (Goldman & Goldman 1982b).

Sexual Play Between Siblings

When two or more children close in age grow up in the same family, there are many more opportunities for sociosexual exploration and interaction, especially if the children sleep in the same bed or room (Figure 5.6). Sexual exploration and play between a young brother and sister, two brothers, or two sisters might, strictly speaking, be labeled as incest or homosexual activity. However, most experts doubt that the terms "incest" and "homosexual" can be validly applied to the world of childhood sexuality.

In Finkelhor's 1980 study, 15% of the college women and 10% of the college men reported some childhood sex exploration with a sibling. Three out of four of these incidents were between brothers and sisters and the remaining quarter between same-gender siblings. About 25% of those who reported sexual experiences with a sibling were unhappy about the incidents because coercion was used. Women were more likely to have experienced coercive sex exploration as children.

Figure 5.6. *Children can satisfy their natural curiosity about their own bodies and those of others at their own pace when allowed some freedom to be themselves.*

The Importance of Touch

Psychologists today commonly recognize that hugs, loving touches, and lap sitting are a vital part of high quality child rearing. Yet, long before the recent hysteria over child sexual abuse, American parents typically backed off touching and hugging their children after age 4. John B. Watson's 1928 book, *Psychological Care of the Infant and Child*, was a major influence in promoting the "no touch approach" to child rearing, which came to dominate American family life.

When James Prescott examined child-rearing customs in 49 cultures around the world, including the United States, he found a very clear causal connection between nurturance, or the lack of it, in childhood and adolescence and the capacity of adults for intimacy. When children received a lot of nurturing body pleasure or when sexual relations were accepted for adolescents, they became socially well-adapted, peaceful adults. In cultures where children were deprived of nurturing touch and given negative messages about their bodies and sexual pleasure, the adults tended to be violent, to glorify war, and to use more drugs and alcohol. These findings confirmed what Harry and Margaret Harlow learned about the behavioral development of infant monkeys reared with wire mesh and fur dolls as surrogate mothers (see Chapter 15 for more details).

Unfortunately, our recent concern over the sexual abuse of children reenforces the antitouch philosophy of American child rearing. Anecdotal evidence suggests that many parents, and certainly many teachers and day-care professionals, are responding to the publicity about child sexual abuse by avoiding touching children and not giving them the physical nurturing they truly need. At the same time, parents and teachers have been warning children that there are "good touches" and "bad touches." Put these two reactions together and we could have a real problem in the future, according to Margaretta Dwyer, who coordinates the Sex Offender Treatment Program at the University of Minnesota Medical School.

Dwyer (1989) reminds us that sex therapists have found that negative messages about sex and lack of nurturing during childhood are common causes of sexual dysfunction today. Dwyer believes that "Twenty to 30 years from now, sex therapists may be seeing many female clients who internalized negative messages about their breasts and genitalia they received as young children in sex abuse prevention courses. A woman who has been deprived of touch in childhood and was told that letting someone touch her breasts or genitals is 'bad' may have difficulty switching off these negative messages when she marries."

To counter the current paranoia over sexual abuse of children and its negative consequences for the future, Dwyer suggests we talk about appropriate and inappropriate touches, instead of good or bad touches. She also stresses the need for teachers and day-care workers to deal with their own fears, and to discuss the importance of appropriate touching with parents.

Hyson and colleagues (1988) suggest that even a single warning may keep parents and other adults from providing the nurturing touch children need. Hyson showed videotapes of adults touching and hugging children to parents, day-care workers, and college students. Half of each group was told that

> Recent publicity about sexual abuse has made physical contacts between adults and children the focus of increased concerns. Every day, parents (or day-care providers) have many opportunities to touch, hold, caress, and engage in physical play with children. These interactions may have important consequences for later development.

Concerned parents and men were much more disapproving of affectionate adult-child touching after viewing the videotapes. Child-care professionals continued to approve such appropriate touching, despite the negative messages, even though they became more cautious because of the general societal messages.

The other half of each group was told that

> Recent research on young children's emotional needs has emphasized the importance of touch and warm physical affection between adults and children.

The adults who were given the positive message about touch were much more positive and accepting of the videotapes they saw of parents and day-care providers touching and hugging children. Even when day-care workers received positive messages about touch and had not changed their way of relating to children, many reported "feeling self-conscious or defensive about their affectionate behavior when parents are observing."

Hyson sees an important lesson in this research. "Many people seem ready to abandon all forms of physical contact with young children in the interests of safety, and to replace warmly affectionate care-giving behavior with a more formal teacher role. Fortunately, our study suggests that this negative behavior can be changed with positive public education."

In Sweden, research such as this is taken very seriously. Among Swedish sex educators and teachers, *Kramgohet* or "huggability" is a new watchword. The latest Swedish sex education program, which emphasizes *Kramgohet*, is designed to help children and adolescents realize the importance and the rewards of developing warm, tender, and intimate relationships as an end in themselves.

Puberty

Puberty and Adolescence in the Western World

Adolescence and puberty are the bridge between childhood and adulthood. Together, they mark a time of rapid physical and emotional changes. **Puberty** refers to the physical maturation of the sexual organs and the appearance of secondary sexual characteristics like breasts, beard, muscular development, and voice change. **Adolescence**, on the other hand, is a psychosocial process characterized by mental and social growth, the emergence of erotic and romantic feelings, and interpersonal sexual drives.

In the rural culture of medieval Europe, children were considered little adults by the age of 7 or 8 when they supposedly reached "the use of reason." Apprenticed out to learn a trade at an early age, they usually married in their midteens, often before reaching sexual maturity. Puberty appears to have occurred between ages 18 and 20. Thus, the idea of adolescence did not even exist (Aries 1962) (Figure 5.4).

During the Industrial Revolution of the 18th and 19th centuries, middle class children increasingly remained at home, attending the new public schools and remaining dependent on their parents. They began waiting until their late teens or even early twenties to marry. At the same time, the average age of puberty slowly dropped. Adolescence became a reality (Aries 1962).

In Europe and North America today, adolescence often extends from puberty in the early teens to somewhere between ages 24 and 28 (Goleman 1988b). With marriage often postponed to the mid or late twenties, or even early thirties, our society is finding it increasingly difficult to continue denying the sexuality of children and adolescents, as the Victorians did only 100 years ago.

The Hormones That Control Puberty

For girls, puberty usually begins between ages 8 and 12 when the breasts and pubic hair start developing. **Menarche**, the onset of menstruation, follows at an average age of 12.8 years. Menstruation will continue until **menopause** around age 50. A growth spurt starts between ages 9 and 14.

For boys, puberty generally begins about two years later than girls. Development of pubic hair and growth of the testes and scrotum occur first, followed by a growth spurt, facial hair, muscle development, a deepening voice, and growth of the penis.

The biological changes of puberty are triggered and controlled by hormones, particularly those from the hypothalamus and the pituitary in the brain. The **hypothalamus**, a specialized area in the floor of the brain, produces hormones known as **gonadotropin-releasing hormones** (**GnRH**). These hormones cause the pea-sized **pituitary gland**, located at the base of the brain just behind the

Table 5.1. *Endocrine Hormone Summary*

Hormone	Produced by	Functions
Gonadrotropin-releasing hormones	Hypothalamus	*M & F: Triggers anterior pituitary to produce FSH and LH*
Follicle-stimulating hormone	Anterior pituitary	F: Triggers ovary to produce eggs and estrogen M: Triggers seminiferous tubules to produce sperm
Luteinizing hormone or interstitial cell-stimulating hormone	Anterior pituitary	F: Causes release of mature egg, corpus luteum function, progesterone production M: Causes cells of Leydig to produce testosterone (male ICSH is same as female LH)
Growth hormone	Anterior pituitary	*M & F: Growth spurt in both male and female at puberty*
Prolactin	Anterior pituitary	F: Stimulates production of milk in the female breast
Oxytocin	Anterior pituitary	F: Causes ejection of milk from the breast to nipple when it is sucked
Estrogen	Ovarian follicles and adrenal	F: Female secondary sex characteristics, uterine lining growth, and menses
Progesterone	Ovarian corpus luteum	F: Preparation of uterine lining for implanting of fertilized egg and menses
	Placenta	F: Maintain pregnancy
Human chorionic gonadotropin	Placenta	F: Feedback to ovary, hypothalamus, and pituitary to suppress new egg development and maintain pregnancy
Testosterone	Testes and adrenal glands	*M & F: Sex drive in both male and female* M: Male secondary sex characteristics

eyes, to produce two gonadotropic hormones. (Gonadotropic means "gonad affecting.") These two hormones, **follicle-stimulating hormone (FSH)** and **luteinizing hormone (LH)**, then regulate production of hormones, and sperm or eggs by the testes or ovaries (Table 5.1).

In women, the production of the releasing hormones by the hypothalamus follows a monthly cycle (Figure 5.7). Cyclic production of FSH and LH by the pituitary then stimulates development of the egg inside the ovary. They also cause the ovaries to secrete two hormones, estrogen and progesterone. At pu-

Figure 5.7. The Female Hormone System. *A diagram of the hormonal control of estrogen secretion and egg production by the ovaries. The arrows on the right with the negative signs in circles coming from the ovary (progesterone) and from the placenta (HCG) indicate inhibition of GnRH production by the hypothalamus and FSH and LH suppression in the pituitary. Note the similarities with the male hormone system in Figure 5.8.*

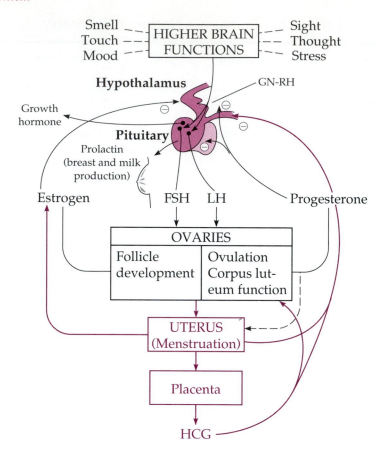

berty, **estrogen** triggers development of the secondary sexual characteristics, including breast development, the growth of pubic hair, and menstruation (Figure 5.7). Together, estrogen and **progesterone** regulate the menstrual cycle and pregnancy.

In men, FSH and LH are produced continuously with minor fluctuations. FSH controls sperm production in the seminiferous tubules of the testes. ICSH, interstitial cell-stimulating hormone, which is the same as LH in females, controls the production of testosterone from the interstitial cells of Leydig, which lie between the seminiferous tubules in the testes. **Testosterone** and its modified form DHT control anatomical and neural masculinization of the fetus, as we saw in Chapter 4. Testosterone also triggers development of male secondary sexual characteristics and sex drive or libido (Figure 5.8). In women, sex drive is activated by testosterone from the adrenal glands.

In addition to FSH and LH, the pituitary also produces a growth hormone, somatotropin, which triggers the growth spurt of puberty. The average age of growth onset for boys is between 13 and 14; the average age for girls is 11.

The dynamic, ever-changing balance of releasing hormones, FSH, LH, estrogen, progesterone, and testosterone, is controlled by a kind of biological "thermostat," a feedback communications network in which the level of each

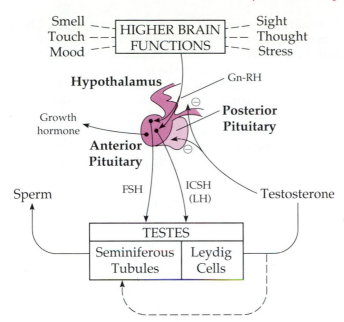

Figure 5.8. The Male Hormone System. *A diagram of the hormonal control of testosterone secretion and sperm production by the testes. The arrows on the right with the negative signs indicate inhibition of GnRH production in the hypothalamus and ICSH (LH) production in the pituitary.*

hormone in the blood is constantly monitored. If the level slips too high or too low, the hypothalamus, pituitary, and ovaries or testes are alerted to bring the system back into balance.

Female Cycles

The Menstrual Cycle

Human females have a menstrual cycle with a monthly **menses** or shedding of the uterine lining. Although females who menstruate may be interested in sex at any time in the monthly cycle, they ovulate and are fertile only one or two days in each cycle. Some women experience a peak of sexual interest just before the onset of the menstrual flow and/or at the time of ovulation.

Ovulation and menses are generally not affected by the environment although there are some suggestions that ovulation and menstruation may be synchronized with the moon's cycle for women with irregular cycles or cycles that average 29.5 days (Cutler 1980; Friedman 1981). Strenuous exercise and stress can also disturb the monthly cycle as we will see shortly in our discussion of menstrual cycle problems.

Ovarian and Uterine Cycles

The cyclic production of gonadotropin-releasing hormones (GnRH) by the hypothalamus controls the monthly cycle in a woman's ovaries and uterus. GnRH triggers the cyclic production of FSH and LH by the pituitary. The rising and falling production of FSH and LH from the pituitary is then mirrored in an *ovarian cycle* with its fluctuating production of estrogen and progesterone. Each ovarian cycle results in maturation of one or more eggs. The estrogen and progesterone from the ovaries regulate the *uterine cycle* and menstruation.

The **ovarian cycle** starts with the development of a new egg right after the release or ovulation of a mature egg in the previous cycle. About a month later, the new egg is ready to be released and a new ovarian cycle starts. Ovulation occurs 14 days before menstruation. In the **uterine cycle**, the lining of the uterus becomes spongy and vascular in preparation for a pregnancy. If pregnancy does not occur, it is shed in the menstrual flow, which actually marks the conclusion rather than the beginning of this cycle. However, our description of both the ovarian and uterine cycles will use the onset of menstruation as our starting point.

Menstruation (day 1 to day 4 in a model 30-day cycle counting from the start of menstruation)

Menstruation, the monthly shedding of the lining of the uterus, occurs when the egg released 14 days earlier is not fertilized and a pregnancy has not started. During menstruation, FSH and LH production in the pituitary increases. Estrogen from the ovaries rises and progesterone remains low. The menstrual flow, or menses, usually lasts from 3 to 7 days. It consists of cells, vaginal and cervical mucus, and the spongy, blood-filled lining of the uterus. The flow can be absorbed by external sanitary napkins or internal tampons (Figure 5.9).

The Follicular and Proliferative Phases (day 5 to day 16 in a model 30-day cycle counting from the start of menstruation)

Following average menstruation of 4 days, the ovaries enter into a *follicular phase* and the uterus starts its *proliferative phase*.

The Follicular Phase *in the OVARY*	*The* Proliferative Phase *in the UTERUS*
FSH production by the pituitary decreases noticeably while LH rises slightly. Both rise sharply before ovulation.	
Estrogen production peaks just prior to ovulation.	Under the influence of rising levels of estrogen, the lining of the
Progesterone remains low.	uterus becomes much thicker and
One, sometimes two or more, ovarian follicles develop, and migrate toward the center and then to the outer surface of the ovary.	rich with blood vessels that will make it possible for a fertilized egg to implant and begin a pregnancy. Progesterone also contributes.

(See Table 5.1 for the main sex hormones and their functions.)

Ovulation (day 16 in a model 30-day cycle counting from the start of menstruation)

The third stage in the model monthly cycle occurs 14 days before the end of the cycle. In the average 30-day cycle, that would be day 16 or day 17. During this phase, the levels of FSH, LH, and estrogen peak and then drop off sharply.

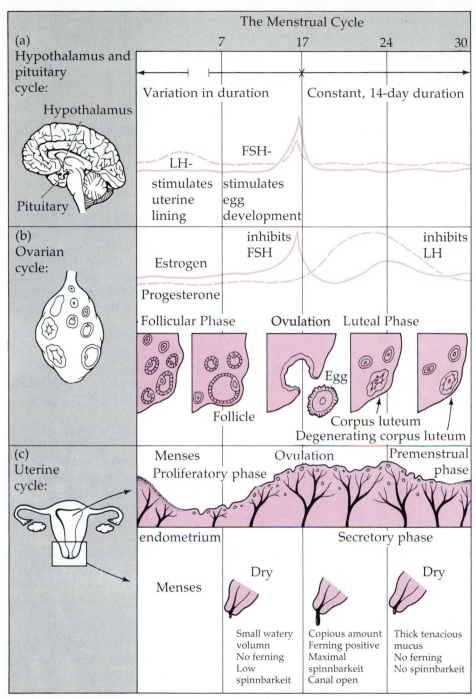

Figure 5.9. The Menstrual Cycle. *The three phases of the menstrual cycle: (a) the brain cycle involving the hypothalamus and pituitary, (b) the ovarian cycle of egg and hormone production, and (c) the uterine cycle involving the uterine lining and the cervical mucus. Changes in the cervical mucus involve "ferning," the development of a fernlike pattern in the cervical mucus when it is dried on a glass slide, and "spinnbarkheit," a stringy, stretchable cervical mucus. Both ferning and spinnbarkheit are signs of ovulation and the fertile period in the monthly cycle.*

At **ovulation**, the egg bursts from the mature ovarian follicle in which it has developed. Once freed from the ovary, it is pulled toward the opening of the fallopian tube.

The Luteal and Secretory Phases (day 17 to day 30 in a model 30-day cycle counting from the start of menstruation)

The Luteal Phase *in the* OVARY	*The* Secretory Phase *in the* UTERUS
The ruptured follicle and other cells produce a corpus luteum, a glandular body capable of producing progesterone. The rising level of progesterone inhibits pituitary LH and slows maturation of another egg.	The rising level of progesterone increases the development of blood vessels and nutrient glands in the uterine lining.
1. If the ovum does not implant in the wall of the uterus within 6 or 7 days, the corpus luteum degenerates and stops producing progesterone.	1. The decrease in progesterone triggers menstruation.
2. If the egg is fertilized and implants, the corpus luteum continues hormone production to maintain the pregnancy.	2. If pregnancy occurs, there is no menstruation and the uterine lining continues developing and becomes part of the placenta.

Some women have cycles that regularly match the model 30-day cycle just described. Most women, however, have longer or shorter cycles. Cycle lengths also vary with age. There is no absolute norm. Some women have cycles that last 24 days; others have cycles that run 35 or more days. Five out of 6 women have cycles that vary more than 7 days in length. Only 1 in 6 women has cycles that vary less than 6 days in their length. Whatever the length of the cycle, the luteal phase is relatively constant in length, with ovulation occurring 14 days before the start of the next menses. The follicular/secretory phases adjust by shortening or lengthening with the whole cycle (Chiazze et al. 1968; Moore 1988).

Some Medical Complications

Premenstrual Syndrome (PMS)

The many descriptions of **premenstrual syndrome (PMS)** are confusing both to experts trying to study this phenomenon and to the women who try to describe their experiences with it. The boundaries of discussion are blurred by a combination of viewpoints offered by biomedical researchers, doctors working with patients, social attitudes, legal applications, psychological concerns, and cultural attitudes toward menstruation (Boston Women's Health Collective 1984; Ginsberg & Carter 1987).

Many women experience breast tenderness and bloating for a few days before their menstrual periods due to fluid retention. Spasmodic cramps are most commonly experienced by women between ages 15 and 25 with PMS. Pregnancy and childbirth usually reduce this type of cramping. The acute pelvic pain and nausea sometimes associated with spasmodic cramping can be relieved by medication. A second type of PMS cramping, known as congestive cramping, begins several days before the menses and dissipates during the flow. Congestive cramping may bring a heavy, dull, aching sensation, water retention, backaches, constipation, irritability, breast sensitivity, lethargy, and sometimes depression.

Many women also have symptoms of PMS they describe as "tension," with headaches, irritability, nervousness, increased or decreased activity levels, fatigue, or exhaustion. Some women may experience crying spells, depression with no apparent cause, and an inability to concentrate.

Much has been written about these mood fluctuations. Some believe they are due to the shifting levels of estrogen, progesterone, and/or hormonelike prostaglandins. One theory blames depression on the lowered level of progesterone, which triggers cells to release potassium and retain sodium.

The 298 unmarried college women studied by Karen Paige (1973) disclosed some interesting correlations between menstrual mood fluctuations and religion. Catholic and orthodox Jewish women reported extreme fluctuations in anxiety levels during the cycle; Protestant women showed little or no change.

Cultural expectations may also promote mood changes prior to a woman's period. These are often reinforced by men who are brought up to expect and accept hostility and moodiness from women at "that time of the month." Some researchers think that women, raised in a society that "permits" premenstrual moodiness, may begin to act this way without realizing why they are moody.

Another cultural aspect of menstruation is the belief that sexual intercourse during menstruation may be unhealthy or even dangerous. In one survey cited by Paige (1973), over half of the couples reported they had never had intercourse during menstruation. Although there is no medical or biological reason for this avoidance, the naturalness of menstruation has been overshadowed by negative folklore and myths. Think about some of the slang expressions such as "that time of the month," "the curse," and "on the rag." You almost certainly know others. Although many of these expressions are not used as much today as they used to be, they still indicate something distasteful. Just think about how a young girl must feel when told about the "curse" that is soon to come upon her! (Delaney et al. 1976).

We need much more research before we understand PMS fully.

Dysmenorrhea and Amenorrhea

In the 35 or so years a woman has monthly menstrual cycles, most women occasionally experience painful menstruation or **dysmenorrhea**. The symptoms are similar to those of PMS, including headaches, backaches, nausea, pelvic pressure or bloating, and abdominal cramping. Even when a woman experiences dysmenorrhea regularly, her symptoms may vary greatly from one period to the next.

Maintaining general good health and nutrition can help reduce the symptoms of both dysmenorrhea and PMS. Restricting coffee and processed foods, particularly white sugar and flour, may help. Extra calcium, vitamin C, and vitamin B_6 daily, started a few days before the menstrual flow, may also be helpful. Ripe bananas and fresh orange juice relieve potassium depletion. Exercise has been found to reduce menstrual discomfort. A hot water bottle, lower back massage, and a sauna or steam bath may also be helpful (Harrison 1982). Masters et al. (1980:124) have reported that the buildup of sexual excitement and its release in orgasm from intercourse or masturbation can relieve the cramps and congestion sometimes associated with menstruation. Various over-the-counter pain relievers, some formulated specially for PMS, can also relieve the discomfort.

Sometimes a girl may go through puberty but not have a single menstrual period by the time she is 18. This complete lack of menstruation is technically known as primary amenorrhea. In secondary amenorrhea, a woman may stop menstruating after having one or more periods.

Amenorrhea, the lack of menstruation, can be caused by several factors including pregnancy, defects in the uterus, hormonal imbalance, stress, disease, cysts or tumors, and emotional factors. Women marathon runners, ballet dancers, gymnasts, skaters, and basketball players often stop menstruating. One theory suggests that strenuous physical activity causes a significant reduction in the level of body fat which, in turn, interferes with menstruation. Crash diets have also been associated with menstrual irregularities and amenorrhea. In such cases, normal menses usually return when the strenuous exercise is stopped (Sloane 1980:513).

Toxic Shock Syndrome (TSS)

Toxic shock syndrome (TSS) is a rare but serious condition that mainly strikes menstruating women under age 30 who are using high absorbency tampons. More rarely, it has been associated with use of a diaphragm or contraceptive sponge during menstruation or it strikes women shortly after they have given birth (Faich et al. 1986; Wallis 1985). TSS afflicts males as well as females, occurring in association with boils or abscesses.

TSS is probably caused by a new strain of the bacterium *Staphylococcus aureus*. This bacterium produces toxins or poisons that get into the bloodstream. Although the toxins rarely result in death, they can cause some serious symptoms. These are

- a high fever, usually over 102° F;
- vomiting, muscle ache, and diarrhea;
- a sudden drop in blood pressure, which may lead to shock;
- a sunburn-like rash which is more obvious on the upper body and neck; peeling of the rash usually occurs on the palms of the hands and soles of the feet one to two weeks after the onset of TSS.

If you get any of these symptoms during your period and you're using a tampon, remove it immediately and check with your doctor. TSS responds well to treatment when detected early.

Complications of Puberty for Males

Boys experience far fewer physical complications during puberty than girls. Maturation of the testes does bring the risk of testicular cancer (see Chapter 11 for a description of testicular self-examination). Boys are often anxious about physical differences and their own body image. "Am I keeping up with other boys? Is my penis at least as big as everyone else's?" Although acne tends to be short-termed in girls, it can continue through the teen years and into the early twenties for men.

Sexual maturation also brings boys the anxieties of peer pressure to become sexually active and prove one's manhood. The turmoil and stress some adolescents encounter in adjusting to a homosexual orientation may lead to suicide attempts.

Adjusting to the Changes of Puberty

During puberty, girls and boys are faced with body changes that they may find disturbing, particularly if these changes come at an earlier or later age than for their peers (Table 5.2). Although most girls anxiously look forward to their first bra, some may be totally unprepared for it at age 8 or 9. Some mothers today still do not tell their daughters about menstruation, assuming they will learn about it in school. When parents anticipate and prepare a daughter for her first menstrual cycle, the family can create a rite of passage to celebrate this event in a positive, reinforcing way. Parents can also prepare a son for his first wet dream or nocturnal emission as a way of celebrating his sexual maturation.

A boy or girl who begins maturing sexually well before his or her peers may be envied or made fun of. A delayed puberty can also cause problems for young people who are sensitive to their peers and the need to conform. A late-blooming boy often has difficulty coping with his smooth face, delayed growth spurt, and still childish voice. Obesity and acne in either sex are just two of the seemingly endless physical problems that may plague the maturing adolescent.

Parents also face problems adjusting as their children pass through puberty. The advent of puberty confronts parents with the fact that their children are maturing as sexual persons. The reluctance of parents to recognize this change may cause them to avoid any mention of sexuality in the home, or limit themselves to providing some information about menstruation for a daughter and warnings about the dangers of becoming pregnant or contracting a sexually transmitted disease for both sons and daughters.

Parents may also become concerned about showing affection for adolescents. Even if they were physically affectionate when their children were young, parents may be uncomfortable hugging or kissing a child after puberty. For some parents, this reaction stems from an unfounded fear of incest. For others, particularly men and their sons, there may be a fear of homosexual behavior. Fathers and sons may also feel a need to avoid behavior that may not be considered "manly." Sometimes the barrier to parent-child affection is raised by the adolescent. When a young person who has been sexually molested by an adult family member tells friends, "Don't let your father hug or kiss you," those friends may then avoid their father when he wants to hug or kiss them.

Young boys and girls need parental affection during the turmoil of puberty and adolescence. If physical affection is suddenly stopped, it may breed resentment and feelings of not being wanted or liked. Adolescents often feel uncomfortable with themselves. They may not have a strong, positive self-image. These feelings are compounded if their parents unconsciously reinforce these self-doubts. Creating barriers to *appropriate* expressions of affection and nurturance between parents and their children can result in barriers to intimacy and sexual problems later in life.

Table 5.2.
Development of Secondary Sex Characteristics During Puberty

Body Characteristic	Male Type	Age of Onset	Female Type	Age of Onset
Body size	On average, taller and heavier	10.5–16	On average, shorter and lighter	9.5–14.5
Head hair	Balding common		Seldom balding	
Facial hair	Beard begins with puberty		Noticeable in later years	
Neck, voice	Thicker, longer, with larynx one-third larger		Shorter, rounder, small larynx	
Body hair	More evident on chest and arms		Light	
Pubic hair	Triangular, pointing upward	10–15	Forms straight line across at top	8–14
Underarm hair	No difference	2 years after pubic hair	No difference	2 years after pubic hair
Breasts	Rudimentary		Well developed	8–13
Chest	Larger in every dimension		Smaller, narrower	
Shoulders	Broader, squarer		Rounder, sloping	
Muscles	More obvious		Largely hidden beneath fatty tissue	
Arms	Longer, thicker; straight "carrying angle"		Arm bent out somewhat at elbow	
Legs	Straight line from hip to foot		Slightly bent in at knees	
Gonads— uterus and penis	Growth of testes and scrotal sac; penis growth	10–13.5 11–14.5	Ovaries become functional; menstruation begins	10–16.5

Adolescent Sexuality

Making Decisions About Sex

Today's society gives young people conflicting messages about being sexually active. On one side, young people are told "Just say no!" At the same time, 1,043 teens cited television programming as the most common source of pressure pushing them to be sexually active. Over 90% of these teens could cite 1

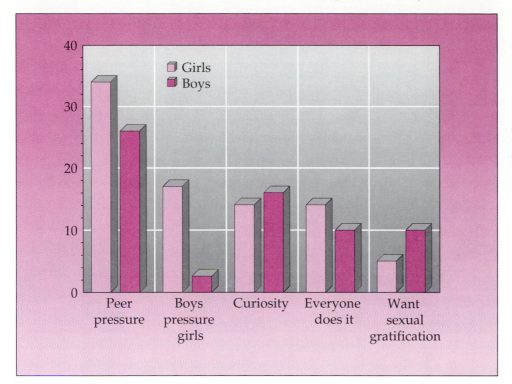

Figure 5.10. *This graph, based on a 1987 survey of 1,000 teenagers, indicates that pressure from peers is the main reason why both boys and girls engage in sexual relations before they want to. For girls, pressure from a boyfriend ranked second, followed by curiosity and the belief that everyone else is doing it. For boys, curiosity ranked second, followed by a desire for sexual pleasure and the belief that everyone else is doing it. For boys, pressure from a girlfriend was a minor reason.*

to 9 television programs that pressure teens to have sex. Four out of 5 teens in this study could cite at least one current popular song that promoted sexual activity. Pressure from peers was ranked third, followed by movies, TV commercials, and magazine ads (Howard 1985).

A different view is suggested by a 1986 poll conducted for the Planned Parenthood Federation (Peterson 1988). In this study, peer pressure was ranked first by boys and girls. Curiosity ranked second and "everyone does it" third. Boys pressuring girls was ranked fourth, and sexual gratification fifth (Figure 5.10).

At the same time, many educators wonder about the effectiveness of sexuality education programs that emphasize the risks and dangers of adolescent sexuality without ever mentioning or dealing with its pleasurable aspects. An interesting comparison has been drawn by some educators who suggest that European societies accept the fact that teenagers are sexually active and so they focus on reducing teenage pregnancies and venereal diseases. Americans are mainly concerned with keeping teenagers from being sexually active and enjoying it. How do you respond to discussions about premarital sex that ignore or do not deal openly with the delights and joys of sexual intimacy?

Legal Rights of Children and Adolescents

In 1984 several U.S. Supreme Court decisions established fairly clear guidelines that assured the access of adolescents to diagnostic services and contraceptives. However, the rights of minors to choose an abortion are more restricted. As of

Figure 5.11. *Today's youngsters get much of their information about sexuality from what they read, and what they see on television and in the movies.*

early 1990, 24 states had laws requiring parental notification or court consent. While all these laws allowed the minor to bypass parental notification or consent by obtaining court consent, only 9 states were enforcing the law. Meanwhile, the constitutionality of such laws was under appeal to the U.S. Supreme Court.

Sexuality Education

Home and Parents

The overwhelming majority of American parents favor sexuality education for the young. Some, like the conservative Eagle Forum headed by Phyllis Schlafly and the Moral Majority, oppose sex education in the schools and want it left solely in the hands of parents. Yet Gagnon (1965), Athanasiou et al. (1970), Hunt (1974), and other national surveys have found that roughly 60% of boys and 45% of girls obtain their sexual information from friends. About 20% learned about sex by reading. Television and movies play an increasing role in conveying sexual information. But only 3% of boys learned about sex from their mothers and 6% from their fathers. Sixteen percent of the girls were told about sex by their mothers and only 1% by their fathers. Unfortunately, most parents still avoid dealing with the sexual education of their children.

After interviewing 1,400 parents of 3 to 11 year olds in the mid-1970s, Roberts and Holt (1980) reported that most parents wanted their children to know about premarital sex, sexual intercourse, venereal disease, and contraception. Yet, only 14% of mothers and 8% of fathers talked with their children about premarital sex. They commonly avoided any mention of venereal diseases and contraception. Parents who did discuss some aspect of sexuality often assumed that bringing up the subject once is enough (Figure 5.11).

Typically, Gagnon (1985) found that a large majority of 1,482 parents of 3-to-11-year-old children accepted the fact that children masturbate. A smaller majority agreed that masturbation was all right for children. Yet less than half of these same parents wanted their children to have a positive view of masturbation.

Hepburn found a pattern when she analyzed the sex education of adolescent daughters in 48 two-parent upper and upper-middle class families. "The Big Talk" mothers have with their daughters somewhere between ages 8 and 12 establishes the tone and parameters of future communication about sex. It is followed by informal, occasional mother-daughter talks in which information is shared about birth control, abortion, teen pregnancy, responsibility, and values using other people's behavior as triggers. Later in adolescence, issues like abortion and homosexuality are discussed with the father and other family members present. Throughout this learning, the fathers are seldom directly involved. Instead, they communicate sexual attitudes and values through impersonal discussions of sociosexual issues and other people's behavior (Hepburn 1981, 1983).

Schools and Churches

In 1965 the Sex Education and Information Council of the United States (SIECUS) outlined the following nine goals for all sexuality education:

1. To provide for the individual an adequate knowledge of his or her own physical, mental, and emotional maturation processes as [they] relate to sex.

2. To eliminate fears and anxieties relative to individual sexual development and adjustments.

3. To develop objective and understanding attitudes toward sex in all of its various manifestations—in the individual and in others.

4. To give the individual insight concerning her or his relationships to members of both genders and to help him or her understand their obligations and responsibilities to others.

5. To provide an appreciation of the positive satisfaction that wholesome human relations can bring in both individual and family living.

6. To build an understanding of the need for moral values that are essential to provide rational bases for making decisions.

7. To provide enough knowledge about the misuses and aberrations of sex to enable individuals to protect themselves against exploitation and against injury to their physical or mental health.

8. To provide an incentive to work for a society in which such evils as prostitution and illegitimacy, archaic sex laws, irrational fears of sex, and sexual exploitation are nonexistent.

9. To provide the understanding and conditioning that will enable each individual to use his or her sexuality effectively and creatively in the several roles of spouse, parent, community member, and citizen. (Kirkendall 1965).

HIGHLIGHT BOX 5.1.
SEX EDUCATION IN NORWAY

In the following letter, a Norwegian mother of three teenagers comments on some striking differences between sex education in her country and in the United States based on her experience growing up in Norway.

Our school had required sex education for all children at the age of ten and again at twelve, but our teachers provided additional information, after-class counseling and discussion groups with films and other visual aids. The wife of the pastor also helped with these classes, as a volunteer. All the parents approved.

At the age of ten we learned all about our bodies and those of the opposite sex. We used many drawings and photographs, including some photographs of children and teenagers in the nude, to show development, as we grew older. This provided no special thrill or titillation for us, because almost everyone in town swam and sunbathed nude, and many families were nude at home. This included the pastor and his family, by the way, even though he was quite strict in religious matters.

During the class period we also learned all the technical words for organs and sex activities, and in the extra discussions we also learned the equivalents of these in our own languages—English, German, Swedish and Danish—the common four-letter words we might hear or use ourselves, so we would know what they meant.

We learned about boys' erections and saw pictures and photographs of them, and asked all the questions we wanted. Most of our sessions were with both boys and girls present, but there were a few in which the sexes would be segregated. We learned about menstruation. We learned about masturbation for both sexes, including how the other sex does it, and that it is pleasurable. We learned exactly how intercourse occurs, how the partners arouse each other by foreplay.

Of course we also learned how babies are conceived and born.

At twelve we had a longer project (about a month long, as I remember) reviewing all the previous information, but going on to include information about venereal disease and a lot of very detailed and explicit information about birth control—especially condoms and how to put them on, the purpose of the little reservoir at the end, about the care to be taken in removing them, and so on. The teachers showed us with real condoms on a large plastic natural-looking model of an erect penis. Again we were encouraged to ask questions, and both boys and girls practiced rolling a condom on the model in our own classes. Any child who had parental permission in writing was also told where to buy condoms easily through the health clinic.

We also were told at this age more about foreplay and afterplay and how to arouse a partner. We were told a lot about orgasms— one explanation being that they are rather like sneezes, because the tension builds up and you can't think of anything else and want it to happen and feel very good when it is over, but are so involved at the moment you are just about unconscious. I should have mentioned that we had both male and female teachers for these classes, and learned a great deal from the opposite sex in their discussions of orgasm, foreplay and other things based on their own experience.

At this age we also learned about several basic positions for intercourse, and even about oral sex as a kind of foreplay. The project always ended with a discussion of morality, and a reminder that the Church (Lutheran) holds that premarital sex is a sin and also forbids masturbation for pleasure, and other things we had been taught about. We were reminded even then, however, that masturbation is a way to avoid premarital sex by relieving tension, and that human beings had always been tempted to enjoy sex in their teen years, which was the reason for our classes. All of us knew that our parents and grandparents had typically married at fifteen or sixteen (sometimes younger, for the girls) after the girl was already pregnant, and the course made it clear to us that if we did engage in sex we could avoid pregnancy and the need for marriage in this time when it is no longer appropriate nor economically feasible for couples too young to support themselves. We learned that sex is fun and does no physical harm.

I think our classes were the right idea. They were matter-of-fact but not stodgy, and they told us things that were helpful. We all probably would have begun having sex anyway and not been so prepared—there were old proverbs, or jokes, about how hard it was to find a virgin in our part of Norway. None of our parents expected us not to have sex, not even the pastor and his wife for their four children. My own sex activity began at the

age of thirteen when I was completely mature physically and, because of my parents' support and the instruction at school, also mentally and emotionally. I really "bloomed out" from a full, happy sex life.

Needless to say, when my own children reached the age of ten, I began to wish there was the same opportunity for them as I had in Norway. I was disappointed that in this enlightened country, where sex is taken so much for granted, that the school sex education program is so limited. I think sex is too important in teenagers' lives not to be introduced to them as fully and supportively as possible. The schools should do this, and the churches, but if this does not happen, the homes must. My boy carries condoms and uses them willingly when they are needed, or if he isn't sure if his partner is on the Pill like most of his partners and both his sisters are.

Some may think sex is wrong, but surely ignorance of sex is *much* worse!

Source: Ms. K.H., Washington

Considerable progress has been made since the SIECUS goals were spelled out in 1965. Still, only 35% of the teenagers surveyed by Planned Parenthood in 1986 had had a sex education course that went beyond the simple facts of reproduction to deal with such issues as birth control, abortion, and the prevention of sexual abuse. Even today, only about 10% of American youths receive comprehensive, age-appropriate sex education.

Part of the reason for the inadequacies in American sex education, beyond the reluctance of Americans to recognize the sexuality of their children, is the vocal opposition of minority groups and the reluctance of elected school officials to open themselves up to controversy by introducing sex education programs. Parents who want sex education in our schools are reluctant to provide tax dollars to support teacher training in family life education. As a result, much of our efforts in sexuality education limp along.

The most comprehensive and revolutionary sex education programs for 11 to 13 year olds was introduced in 1971 by the Unitarian/Universalist Church. *About Your Sexuality*, now in its third edition, was, and still is, unique because it uses sexually explicit filmstrips and audiotapes of teens talking about their first sexual experience, masturbation, premarital sex, contraception, and homosexuality. Programs introduced by the Episcopal Church, the United Methodist Church, Catholic Church, the United Church of Canada, and others vary in their willingness to deal with controversial topics and to be open to masturbation, premarital sex, homosexuality, contraception, and abortion (*SIECUS Report* 1985).

Until recently, American sex education has been designed for middle class white students. Efforts to remedy this bias are producing new programs that are sensitive to and meet the needs of the 28 million blacks and 18 million Latino Americans in the United States (Darabi & Asencio 1987; Medina 1987). Likewise, a few efforts are being made to deal with the needs of the 5% to 10% of boys and perhaps 4% to 6% of the girls in junior and senior high school who are grappling with a homosexual or lesbian orientation they cannot share with their families or peers. In many colleges, gay and lesbian support groups work to change the content of psychology, history, and other courses to reflect the experiences of gay and lesbian persons. A few colleges are making tentative steps to develop lesbian/gay studies programs (Ellis 1985; Van Tassel 1989).

Theories of Child and Adolescent Development

In this century, several theories and some research have radically changed the way adults perceive childhood sexuality.

Sigmund Freud

Although many of Freud's theories are challenged or rejected today, his claim that children have sexual desires and experiences was truly revolutionary for the Victorian world. Freud claimed that our personality develops from the interplay of conscious and unconscious sensations, centering around our need to satisfy a basic pleasure principle. **Libido**, for Freud, is a major expression of that pleasure principle. Although he described it as a sexual drive, its focus is really sensual pleasure.

Freud pictured the developing psyche as having three dynamic elements, which he called the id, ego, and superego.

The *id* develops first in the personality. As the instinctual, pleasure-seeking part of our personality, it constantly seeks affection, nurturing, and sensual pleasure. Totally irrational, it resents any attempt to control its quest for pleasure.

The *ego* emerges as the infant begins to socialize and develop its personal identity. As the realistic, rational element of the mind, the ego mediates between the impulsive, pleasure-seeking id and the outside world represented in the mind by the superego.

The *superego* is the internal awareness of cultural norms, values, and sanctions that we gradually develop as our parents and society condition us. In our *conscience*, the negative side of the superego, guilt and punishment motivate us to do what is considered good and moral. Later, as we internalize this sense of morality and make it our own, we learn to do what is right out of pride that we are moral persons. Freud called this positive side of the superego the *ego ideal*.

According to Freud, the id, ego, and superego constantly interact as we move through five stages of psychosexual development: the oral, anal, phallic, latency, and genital stages.

During the *oral stage*, the infant gradually discovers its own body. Its pleasure drive is satisfied by sucking, being breast-fed, crying, and being held, cuddled, and nurtured.

In the *anal stage*, from age 1 to 2, the child shifts its focus of pleasure from the oral to the anal, gaining control over elimination as it responds to social conventions. Toilet training can become, in Freud's view, a battleground between the id and social values.

In the *phallic stage*, between ages 3 and 5 or 6, the child focuses on his or her genitals. Masturbation often becomes a conscious source of pleasure at this time.

For boys, this new sexual awareness triggers an erotic attachment to their mothers. Boys may then have an unconscious, even hostile, resentment of their fathers as sexual competitors. This reaction Freud called the *Oedipus complex*, drawing on the Greek myth and drama about Oedipus who kills his father and unknowingly marries his mother. Fearing castration as punishment for his incestuous desire, the boy is forced to break his ties with his mother and focuses on imitating the masculine role provided by his father.

Freud claimed that girls take a different track, experiencing penis envy and feeling cheated by not having a penis. Blaming her mother for "cutting off her penis," a girl rejects her mother and is drawn to her father, even having sexual fantasies about him. As the girl learns what society will and will not accept, her superego (conscience) helps her resolve these incestuous desires. As she matures and abandons masturbation, the girl replaces her incestuous fantasies with a desire for motherhood. This begins a transition from solo sex to a new and mature focus on vaginal intercourse.

Freud, however, viewed sexual intercourse as a painful, threatening event. This led him to propose the castration and Oedipus complexes for boys and the frightening primal scene for both sexes. Borneman (1983) has attacked this Victorian interpretation, pointing out that for thousands of years children have shared sleeping quarters with adults and observed adults engaging in sexual intercourse without suffering mass neuroses.

Between age 7 and puberty, Freud claimed both boys and girls experience a **latency period** when all interests in sexuality are dormant. Numerous studies refute the existence of a latency period (Borneman 1983; Goldman & Goldman 1982a, 1982b; Haaglund 1981).

Finally, in the *genital stage*, the mature adult focuses all his or her libido on penile/vaginal intercourse.

Freud expanded the concept of sexuality beyond the confines of copulation and allowed both physical and emotional sensations to be considered part of the sexual experience. However, his view of sexuality is penis-centered (Haaglund 1981). This led him to interpret early female sexual development from a masculine perspective, claiming that the clitoris is a small "masculine" organ and that women experience penis envy. Lerner (1977) has found that many parents pick up on this male bias and ignore their daughter's genitals mainly by not giving the child any words with which to identify her clitoris, labia, or vagina.

Despite many refutations of Freud's idea of a latency period, many adults insist that, because adolescents are essentially asexual, sex education in the schools is dangerous. Freud also believed that the psychosexual development

Table 5.3.
Childhood Psychosexual Development as Seen by Freud and Erikson

Age	Freud's Stages	Erikson's Crises or Choices	Psychosexual Abilities and Capacities
Birth–18 months	Oral stage	A basic sense of *trust or mistrust* of others	Sensuality and bonding by way of touching, being held and holding; genital exploration, erection and vaginal lubrication, and orgasmic capacity
18 months–3 years	Anal stage	Greater *autonomy or* a sense of *self-doubt and shame*	Bowel control and ability of males to stimulate an erection by genital touches; awareness of nongenital differences between boys and girls; gender identity as male or female established; use of sexually dimorphic language and terms for body parts
3–5 years	Phallic stage (Oedipal-Electra complex)	Continuing exploration and *initiative* when rewarded *or guilt* when initiative is discouraged	Deliberate pleasurable self-stimulation of the genitals; curiosity about sexual and reproductive processes; gender identity firmly established

of a child could be arrested at the oral or anal stage and not progress to the mature heterosexual genital stage of an adult. Hence, he saw male homosexuality as a psychosexual development that was "stuck" in the oral or anal stage. Masturbation, especially female masturbation, represented an immature fixation.

Despite these limitations and errors, Freud's theories helped open the way to a critical examination of all of human sexuality. Challenges to his theories have triggered new insights and exciting perspectives.

Erik Erikson

One of the first to criticize Freud's theories was his student Erik Erikson. Erikson explored the social environment in which our sexuality develops rather than focusing, as Freud did, only on the child's mind. Erikson divides our lifelong

Age	Freud's Stages	Erikson's Crises or Choices	Psychosexual Abilities and Capacities
5–11 years	Latency	*Industry* and self-accomplishment *or* sense of *inferiority*	Active sexual exploration with friends of same and/or other gender; active questioning about sexual information; onset of prepubertal growth spurt with initial growth of genitals
12–20 years	Genital stage	A firm *self-identity or role confusion*	Menstruation begins; ejaculation and nocturnal emissions begin; increasing romantic attachments; absorption in questions about self and self-identity
Young adulthood		Choices between *intimacy* with others *or isolation* and withdrawal	Long-term bonding and commitment; marriage and establishment of family; career decisions; separation from parental residence
Adulthood		*Creativity or stagnation*	
Mature years		*A sense of contentment and integrity, or despair*	

psychosocial development into eight stages. At each stage, he tries to see the interaction of the developing individual with parents, family, friends, lover, mate, and the universe. At each stage, we face a choice between two directions. Each choice builds on and draws its direction, more or less, from previous choices (Table 5.3).

Erikson's model suggests many applications and insights into our sexual development. A young child who is discovered exploring its genitals and masturbating, for instance, is expressing initiative. A positive parental response can head the child in the direction of autonomy, initiative, and industry, while suggesting that this behavior should be done in private. If the response from an adult is negative, it can lead to shame, doubt, guilt, and a sense of being inferior if the self-exploration is continued (Jackson in Perry 1990; Tabbutt 1987).

Erikson describes an adolescent crisis between identity and role confusion, followed by a choice between intimacy and isolation in the twenties. This sounds logical: You achieve self-identity and then learn to relate intimately with another person. According to Erikson, men define their self-identity and then look for an intimate relationship and start a family. However, Gilligan argues that women develop their self-identity through their relationships with others (Gilligan 1982:12).

Jean Piaget and Lawrence Kohlberg

After years of research, Jean Piaget, a French developmental psychologist, proposed a model that described how children develop the ability to think in the abstract, how we develop a sense of moral values, and how we make decisions that involve concepts of what is right and wrong. Lawrence Kohlberg, an American psychologist, used Piaget's theories and models of cognitive and moral development to outline the developmental stages we go through in trying to make sense of our social world. The insights of these psychologists were a major focus in Chapter 3 when we examined different systems of sexual values.

Anne Bernstein (1978) has found an interesting parallel to the Piaget and Kohlberg models in the way children learn about where babies come from. Instead of asking questions, she took the unusual approach of letting children tell *her* where babies come from. The simplest answers came from the "Geographers" who said babies came from a hospital or some specific place. A little later, children adopted a manufacturing explanation, explaining how babies were assembled from different parts. After acquiring a little more cognitive skill, children realized these early explanations didn't make sense, but they couldn't come up with a better answer. After they had received some information from others, children were able to repeat what others said about reproduction even though they did not understand it. Later, after reaching the level of abstract thought, the children began to offer theoretical explanations involving the role of sperm, egg, fertilization, and pregnancy. Finally, when the child's mental capacity had developed sufficiently in terms of abstract thought, the whole process comes together and the child can give a simple, complete, and accurate explanation of human reproduction.

John Gagnon and William Simon

In the early 1970s, Eric Berne, the originator of transactional analysis, suggested that much of our behavior, and our sexual behavior in particular, follows a script we learn from others just as an actor or actress follows a script in a theater play. Sociologists John Gagnon and William Simon developed this idea, suggesting that scripts are the mental plans we develop and use to organize our behavior along socially appropriate lines.

Scripting

From birth, parents influence the way children think and feel about sexuality. They provide parental models, or scripts, for the proper gender roles for boys and girls, men and women (Gagnon 1977:70). They handle baby boys more roughly than they do baby girls (Doyle 1985). They smile at and talk to girl babies more than they do boy infants (Thoman et al. 1972). Parents communicate, often in nonverbal ways, their attitudes about the child's body and how the child should view his or her genitals. The way parents express or don't express emotions and affection teaches their child to be expressive or controlled in close as well as casual relationships. Parents provide living examples of marriage, the family, and work roles. Parents also teach their children what is considered morally acceptable, both by example and by commenting on what others do. Simon and Gagnon describe all these messages as **scripting**. Once we internalize these messages, they become our sexual scripts, the blueprints that influence with whom we will be sexually intimate, what we will do sexually, when sexual behavior is appropriate for us, and where and why we relate sexually and have sexual intercourse (Gagnon & Roberts 1980:276; Gagnon & Simon 1973).

Scripting theory emphasizes learning and chance social influences and ignores biological factors. It argues that our sexual development is more episodic and not so much a continuous process. And finally, scripting theory rejects a sharp distinction between what is "sexual" and what is "nonsexual."

Erotophilia and Erotophobia

One type of sexual scripting involves the emotional responses we learn to associate with sexual cues and then gradually build into a value system that helps determine our adult sexual attitudes and behavior. By their very nature, sexual intimacy and erotic play are pleasurable, so one would expect every child to enjoy masturbating and other sexual explorations. However, this leaves parents and other adults out of the picture. Left alone, the child would naturally develop what Fisher and his colleagues calls **erotophilia**, a positive appreciation and enjoyment of a variety of erotic and sexual behaviors. However, parents and society can alter this natural erotophilia by providing the developing child with all kinds of negative messages. Messages that this or that sexual feeling or behavior is forbidden and sinful build a wall of guilt and shame around that feeling or behavior. The child learns to avoid it. When parents punish a child for some sexual feeling or behavior, they are scripting the child for **erotophobia**, a fear and anxiety about things sexual.

Adults who received messages of guilt and shame about sex as children may develop into erotophobic adults who respond negatively to sex. Erotophobic persons tend to be more limited in the kinds of sexual behavior they engage in. They find pornography and erotica distasteful, and avoid having sexual fantasies. They avoid opportunities of learning more about sex. They are also less likely to use contraception. These long-term consequences of early scripting showed up not just with American and Canadian college students and adults, but also with undergraduates in India, Hong Kong, and Israel (Fisher et al. 1988).

Scripting and Lovemaps

According to John Money (1988), each of us develops a special kind of sexual script as we grow up. He calls it a lovemap because this script represents or contains a kind of template of our idealized lover and the kind of erotic and sexual activities we would like to engage in with that ideal lover.

Our lovemaps are as personalized and unique as our faces and fingerprints. Each lovemap contains, as we will see in Chapter 15 on intimacy and love, some patterns of courtship that all humans share in common because of our shared ancestry. It also contains those prenatal tendencies we spoke about at Gate 6, in the previous chapter, when neural pathways in our brains formed the basis of our gender identity and our sexual orientation. Because each of us develops our own unique lovemap, each of us reacts differently to erotic stimuli. During childhood and adolescence, as we unconsciously elaborate our lovemap, we develop a script or template in which we are turned on by tall and thin, short and heavyset, long or short hair, large or small breasts, and so on. As we grow up, we also develop a script for the kind of sexual and erotic activities we want to engage in with that ideal lover, depending on the kinds of messages we pick up from parents, peers, and society about touching, intimacy, sexual intercourse, erotic play, and oral sex.

The lovemap encoded in our brain cells may fit what our society, culture, religion, and family consider a normal and acceptable sexual partner and range of sexual behaviors. But it can also be distorted as it is laid down. When a child's developing lovemap is traumatized or distorted, he or she may experience a long-term problem in relating intimately with another. The distorted template can also result in a paraphilia, an unconventional sexual expression, or in an illegal behavior such as pedophilia (see Chapter 20).

Gender Roles and Macho Scripting

Some parents and families maintain very clear gender role stereotypes that stress the differences between what is considered masculine and feminine. Mosher and Tompkins (1988) refer to this as the *macho script*. The macho script organizes childhood play and conditions the young boy to enjoy acting superior and masculine. Excitement, violence, aggression, danger, always winning, and being masterful and dominant are all part of the macho script, according to Mosher and Tompkins. Macho men are taught to avoid "feminine traits" like sensitivity and emotions. They approach women callously as servants of their pleasure.

Can you think of some adolescent rites of passage in the social networks of young males that might promote this kind of scripting? What factors in our culture promote macho scripting? Can you pick out any film or television trends that might promote overmasculinization? How might we counter the macho scripts?

Although the theories of psychosexual development proposed by Freud, Erikson, Piaget, Kohlberg, Simon, Gagnon, and others are intriguing, there is little research based on hypotheses derived from these theories. Their value, at least for the present, is thus limited in helping us understand childhood and adolescent sexual development.

The Future of Childhood and Adolescent Sexuality

Adolescence, Michael Carrera assures us, is much more than a "period of transition between childhood and adulthood characterized by the acting-out of emergent, difficult-to-control sexual urges." Adolescence is too new as a social phenomenon for adults to understand or appreciate fully what the roughly 39 million American teenagers experience in their years of rapid change. Although all adults remember their own adolescent experiences, most of what we know about adolescents today comes from problem-oriented clinical studies, Freud's commonly disputed theories of childhood sexuality, and the many studies of the experiences of adolescents with sexual intercourse, contraception, and abortion (Carrera 1984).

More important than their budding sexuality, most teenagers have compelling feelings and concerns about their self-esteem and self-worth. They have ambivalent ideas about the roles and experiences in the family and in friendships, their adjustment to divorcing, single, and remarrying parents, their school performance, employment, and their near- and long-term future (Constantine 1984).

Today's young people face the challenge of defining their own realities, apart from the genital-obsessed and problem-oriented view of adolescence that dominates adult thinking. Will today's children and adolescents develop a more integrated vision of young people in the 1990s? Will they be able to express their natural erotic interests and needs in a world filled with conflict, tension, mobility, leisure, and rapid change in a healthier way than their parents did? Will adolescents in the 1990s experience less stress and trauma, and more understanding and support than adolescents in the 1960s or 1970s?

The world of the adolescent in the 1990s may be more, or less, genitally focused than it is today. It may be more, or less, integrated with the world of adults. There may be a return to more restrictive values. Or we may see the emergence of more flexible and pluralistic options.

This chapter suggests some dimensions of the challenging future faced by today's youth. Some of them may be satisfied following patterns and lifestyles given them by their elders. Others may seek to create a new and more humane future for adolescents who are developing sexually but are not yet ready for long-term pair bonding or parenthood. How do you envision adolescence in the 1990s? What changes would you like to see occur? What can you do to promote these changes?

Key Concepts

1. Masturbation, play involving nudity and genital exploration, and sexual play between brothers and sisters are a common and natural occurrence in children before puberty.

2. Hugs, loving touches, and lap sitting are generally recognized as important parts of high quality child rearing. This nurturance, or its absence, appears to set the stage for adult intimacy and relationships.

3. The concepts of a sheltered childhood and a transitional period called adolescence are a recent development in Western societies.

4. Puberty or biological maturation occurs in the early teen years; adolescence or psychosexual maturation is a process that starts in the early teens and continues into the twenties.

5. Psychological factors can affect and alter the menstrual cycle.

6. Sexual decision making involves understanding the pleasures and allure of sexual expressions and relationships as well as the dangers.

7. Sexual scripts and scripting play a major role in ways we respond to our sexual nature, who we relate with sexually, what we do sexually, and in the macho gender role.

Key Terms

adolescence (114)
amenorrhea (122)
dysmenorrhea (121)
erotophilia (135)
erotophobia (135)
estrogen (116)
follicle-stimulating hormone (FSH) (115)
gonadotropin-releasing hormone (GnRH) (114)
hypothalamus (114)
latency period (131)
libido (130)
luteinizing hormone (LH) (115)

menarche (114)
menopause (114)
menses (117)
menstruation (118)
ovarian cycle (118)
ovulation (120)
pituitary gland (114)
premenstrual syndrome (PMS) (120)
progesterone (116)
puberty (114)
scripting (135)
testosterone (116)
toxic shock syndrome (TSS) (122)
uterine cycle (118)

Summary Questions

1. Describe the four stages of the menstrual cycle and one major development in the ovarian and uterine phases of each stage.

2. What conflicts or contradictions have been reported in the ways parents view sex education and the sexual maturation and behavior of their children?

3. Describe some basic goals of sexuality education and compare them with the realities of such education in the United States and Norway (see Highlight Box 5.1).

4. Which of Sigmund Freud's insights into childhood sexual development have stood the test of time, and which have been proven invalid?

5. Summarize and criticize the insights of Piaget, Kohlberg, and Erikson into childhood psychosexual development. Cite some practical applications.

6. Describe several ways scripting theory is used to explain our early psychosexual development.

Suggested Readings

Delaney, J., M. J. Lupton, & E. Toth. (1976). *The Curse: A Cultural History of Menstruation.* New York: New American Library. An absorbing history of attitudes about menstruation and menstruating women.

Constantine, L. L. (1984). Growing up slowly: Another century of childhood. In L. A. Kirkendall & A. E. Gravatt (eds.), *Marriage and the Family in the Year 2020*. Buffalo: Prometheus Books. An expert on childhood sexuality offers his views of what childhood will be like 30 years from now.

Constantine, L. L., & F. M. Martinson. (1981). *Children and Sex: New Findings, New Perspectives*. Boston: Little, Brown. An important report of recent research on how children develop sexually.

Goldman R., & J. Goldman. (1982). *Children's Sexual Thinking*. Boston: Routledge & Kegan Paul. How children learn about sex.

Harrison, M. (1982). *Self-Help for Premenstrual Syndrome*. Cambridge, MA: Matrix Press. A practical guide for PMS.

Person, E. S. (1988, March). Some differences between men and women. *Atlantic Monthly*, pp. 71–82. A review of the latest research on gender differences and their origins.

*T*he Evolution of
    Privacy
*F*emale Anatomy
    External Structures
    Internal Structures
    The Female Breast
A Sexual Fantasyland
*M*ale Anatomy
    Penis Myths
        and Realities
    Male Anatomy
*C*ircumcision
    Male Circumcision
    Female Circumcision

Chapter 6

*O*ur Sexual Anatomy

Special Consultants

Paul A. Fleming, M.D., D.H.S., director of the Fleming
Center, Raleigh, North Carolina.

Linda L. Hendrixson, M.A., Ph.D.(cand.), health educator
and adjunct professor of health and human sexuality,
Montclair State College, Upsala College, and Fairleigh
Dickinson University.

Norman A. Scherzer, Ph.D., professor, Department of
Biological Sciences and Allied Health Sciences, Essex
County College, and visiting professor, Rutgers, The State
University of New Jersey (Newark).

Beverly Whipple, Ph.D., R.N., associate professor, College of
Nursing, Rutgers, The State University of New Jersey
(Newark), and coauthor of *The G Spot and Other Recent
Discoveries in Human Sexuality* (1982) and *Safe Encounters*
(1989).

The reality of life, even in our "sexually liberated" times, is that most men and women don't fully understand their own bodies. At the same time, we probably know even less about the other sex. That's one reason why books about sexual health and human sexuality courses in high schools and colleges are so popular. Since the Boston Women's Health Collective published its pioneering book by and for women in 1976, *Our Bodies, Ourselves* has sold millions of copies in several editions; it also appears in a dozen foreign languages and in Braille for the blind. A similar and typical self-health book for men, *Man's Body: An Owner's Manual* (Diagram Group, 1976), sold out six printings in three years. Admitting we don't know everything we might about our bodies opens the door to learning some very helpful new insights into our sexuality and that of the person we love.

Modern books on heterosexual relationships invariably devote one or more chapters to understanding your own sexual anatomy and its functions, and include sections on the sexual anatomy of the other sex. Books for lesbians and gay men have similar sections devoted to practical knowledge and advice on the problems two persons of the same sex are likely to encounter. *The Male Couple's Guide to Living Together* (Marcus 1988), for instance, devotes a chapter to such topics as how to be affectionate and discrepancy in the needs for affection, as well as safe and risky behaviors. In *Lesbian Sex* (1984), JoAnn Loulan reminds her readers that they don't have to know Latin to know about their bodies when she discusses female physiology and what two women do in bed.

But understanding our sexual system and how its parts function is only a start. Understanding the variations in our anatomies can help us overcome the tyranny of stereotypes and expectations we encounter as males and females. Practically everyone has at least an occasional concern or doubt about his or her self-image. In a nation obsessed with weight control, breast enlargement, liposuction to reduce the buttocks and unwanted bulges, muscle building, and penis size, we are constantly reminded that we should look younger, thinner, and more sexy in very stereotyped ways.

The authors of *Our Bodies, Ourselves* make an important statement about these issues and why we should learn more about our bodies:

> Learning to understand, accept, and be responsible for our physical selves, we are freed and can start to use our untapped energies. If our image of ourselves is on a firmer base, we can be better friends and better lovers, better people, more self-confident, more autonomous, stronger and more whole.
>
> *(Boston Women's Health Collective 1976:13)*

In this chapter you may find some surprises. New research has uncovered major new insights into the sexual anatomy of both women and men. Two subsequent chapters will apply this anatomical information to sexual health and sexual responses. Taken together, these three chapters will help you use your resources effectively, be more confident about yourself, and take more control over your future. As a result, you can enjoy life more, make better friends, and be a better lover.

The Evolution of Privacy

A few years ago, an Ann Landers survey discovered that only about one-third of American mothers talk with their daughters about menstruation. If this is true of menstruation, it seems natural that fewer than a third of all mothers and fathers discuss sexual anatomy, sex, love play, and intercourse with their daughters and sons. As a result, many of us have to rely on friends, on magazines, or on a high school sexuality course. Along the way, we get some answers, but we also may pick up and accept as fact a number of sexual myths and a good bit of misinformation.

The sense of privacy about sexual anatomy and intercourse we are accustomed to is a recent development in Western society, as the sequence of household pictures in Figure 5.4 clearly shows. In colonial and pioneer America, sex was a commonly accepted everyday fact of life. Since most settlers had their own farm animals, children could hardly be sheltered from the facts of mating and birth. There was little privacy when parents, children, grandparents, and a hired hand or two shared a small log cabin or a sod house on the prairie.

Gradually, the growing affluence in the middle class and a Victorian sense of privacy set a pattern in which homes were divided into rooms open to friends and guests and a private domain of bedrooms and bathrooms. As sex was segregated from everyday life, it picked up negative messages. Sexual behavior became something people were not supposed to mention. Similar patterns of silence about sexual matters exist in some tribal cultures where middle class affluence and multiroom housing do not exist, so these changes do not fully explain the sense of privacy and the reticence of Victorian Americans in sexual matters. However it came about, men in the early 1900s were expected to know by "instinct" what to do when they married and the wife could find out from her husband on her wedding night.

The growing sense of privacy in the Victorian world probably contributed much to our prudery about the female body and its functions. This is clearly reflected in the approach the emerging profession of medicine adopted in the Victorian era toward female patients and their health concerns (Figure 6.1). The twentieth century has been marked by a radical change in this attitude as women have become more assertive in taking responsibility for their own bodies, health, and sexuality.

Although times have certainly changed, there are still many young people, as well as adults, who feel uncomfortable or insecure about their own bodies, about the bodies of others, and about sexuality in general. There are still cohabiting or married couples who have never had intercourse because they simply don't know what to do. Knowledge can help remedy this lack of comfort and ease with sexuality.

Female Anatomy

In Chapter 4, we examined the common embryonic origins that account for the many similarities in the development of female and male sexual anatomy. These similar origins are highlighted in Figure 6.2 with side-by-side frontal views of mature female and male sexual anatomy. Study these similarities for a few

Figure 6.1. *A hundred years ago, an accurate knowledge of human anatomy, especially female anatomy and physiology, rested on rather shaky grounds. This lithograph shows the proper procedure for an American physician to use in examining a pregnant woman. It was unthinkable and quite unprofessional for a physician of that era to see a woman undressed, even in his professional capacity as a doctor. Physicians were advised to inflict some pain on the female patient to assure that she would not be sexually aroused by this physical exam.*

minutes and then refer back to these drawings as you move through this chapter.

External Structures

Mons Veneris

The **mons veneris**, the Mount of Venus, is the soft, fatty pad covered by pubic hair at the front of the vulva. The mons lies over the point where the pubic bones come together. It protects the labia and clitoris behind it, and may also serve as a cushion between the pelvic bones during face-to-face sexual intercourse (Figure 6.3).

The pubic hair that covers the mons serves to spread pheromones, chemical sex attractants secreted by special apocrine glands in the vulval area. Apocrine glands in the armpits complement this function, producing both sweat and pheromones. Pubic hair usually begins to develop in both sexes around age 12. It varies in pattern, texture, color, and density. In many women, the pubic hairline forms a triangular patch with its apex pointing downward. The alternate pattern, with the apex pointing upward, is more usual in males.

Attitudes toward pubic hair vary greatly. In the early part of this century, pictures of the navel or belly button were considered obscene and any display of pubic hair was unthinkable. Until the early 1970s, pubic hair was carefully airbrushed from erotic photos of females or art such as the Vargas women in *Esquire* magazine. Less than 20 years ago, *Playboy* and *Penthouse* magazines broke this taboo with centerfolds and cartoons showing both female and male

Figure 6.2. Similarities in Female and Male Sexual Anatomy. *These drawings highlight the homologous organs in female and male sexual anatomy. Homologous structures develop from the same embryonic primordium but may specialize to serve different functions.*

1. Ovaries
2. Bartholin's glands
3. Clitoris
    glans
    corpora cavernosa (crurae or legs)
    clitoral shaft
4. Labia minora
5. Labia majora

1. Testes
2. Cowper's glands
3. Penis
    glans
    corpora cavernosa
    corpus spongiosum
4. Underside of the penis
5. Scrotum

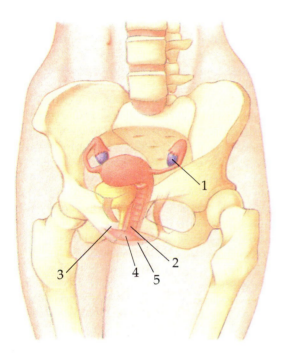
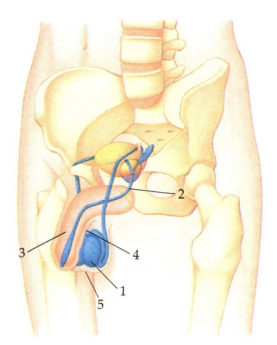

pubic hair. Although both classic and modern Japanese art is comfortable with showing sexual intercourse, the display of pubic hair is still considered taboo. Many women in Egypt and the Near East shave their pubic hair because it is considered more sensual and erotic.

There is a similar variation in attitudes toward female body hair in general. American men and women have a particularly difficult time accepting the naturalness of body hair. Women remove it from their underarms and legs, tweeze it from their eyebrows, pay for waxing of their arms and legs, and use

Figure 6.3. *The external female sexual anatomy— the vulva. Find each of the structures shown here in the photographs of vulvas in Figure 6.4.*

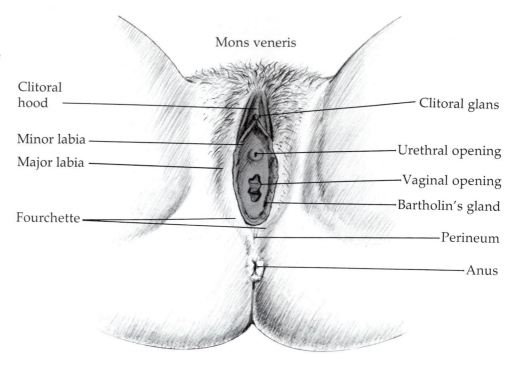

Mons veneris

Clitoral hood

Clitoral glans

Minor labia

Urethral opening

Major labia

Vaginal opening

Bartholin's gland

Fourchette

Perineum

Anus

depilatories. American men find this very sexy. Americans often find it strange that European women think it is sexier not to shave the underarms and legs.

The Vulva

The general term **vulva** is used for the external female sexual structure (Figures 6.3 and 6.4). This includes all external structures enclosed by the major labia, the clitoris, the clitoral hood, the minor labia, and the openings of the urethra, vestibular glands, and vaginal opening. Vulva, by the way, was the name of an ancient powerful Scandinavian goddess.

A variety of slang expressions are used for the vulva, such as box, beaver, bush, pussy, snatch, fur burger, twat, cunt, quim, and wazoo. Other slang expressions include verge, muff, gash, hole, hair pie, poozle, honeypot, twinkie, sweetmeat, pud or pudendum (literally, the shameful area), wound, flower, and snapper. What kinds of messages do these terms communicate? How do you feel when you hear or see them scrawled in graffiti? Do any of them have an obvious origin? What differences do you think there are, if any, in the way males and females react to these expressions? What is behind these reactions?

The Labia

A pair of major labia, or "lips," mark the outer edge of the vulva. Between the major labia is a more delicate pair of minor labia. The tip of the clitoris, the glans, is located in the midline, between and at the front of the paired major and minor labia, with the urethral and vaginal openings behind it (Figure 6.4).

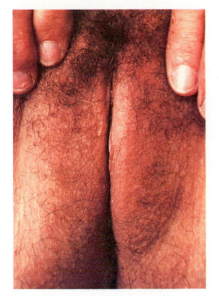

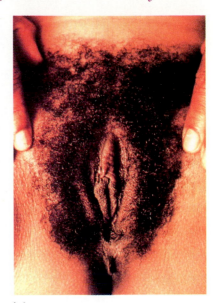

Figure 6.4. The Varieties of Female Sexual Anatomy. *This series of three photos of the vulva show some of the many healthy, normal variations in size, shape, texture, and color.*

Typical of the many slang expressions for the labia are bearded clam, muff, fur burger, snappers, jaws, and nut-breakers. What messages do these slang expressions convey?

The outer, **major labia** are paired fatty pads, covered with pubic hair, which reach from the mons in the front back to the region between the opening of the vagina and the rectum. They may swell and extend during sexual excitement. Like their homologue, the scrotum, the major labia contain sweat glands and are supplied with nerve endings that contribute to sexual arousal.

The inner, **minor labia** vary greatly in size, shape, and form. The inner labia are erectile, richly supplied with nerves, and very sensitive to erotic stimulation. The inner labia have natural glandular secretions that lubricate the vulval area. During sexual arousal, the inner labia are also lubricated by the paired **Bartholin's glands** (greater vestibular glands) and by a pair of lesser vestibular glands between the hymen and minor labia. Occasionally, these glands may become infected and their ducts blocked (Figure 6.5).

At the rear of the vulval area, the minor labia come together in front of the anus in the region known as the **perineum**, a sensitive and erotic area in both women and men.

The Clitoris

The **clitoris** is also referred to in slang as clit, little man in the boat, buzzer, and love button. Like the penis, this finger-shaped structure has a shaft with a **glans** or head and two cavernous bodies. The glans has a rich supply of nerves and is very sensitive. Stimulation of the clitoris can cause an orgasm in many women. In contrast with the reproductive, excretory, and pleasurable functions of its male homologue, the penis, the clitoris serves only a pleasurable function.

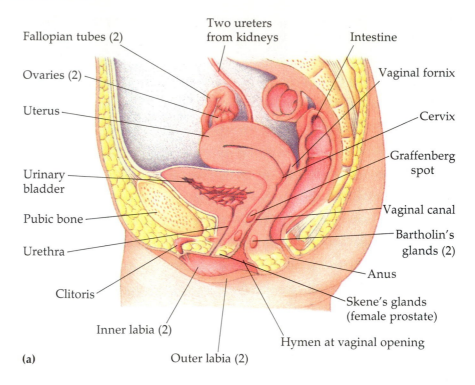

(a)

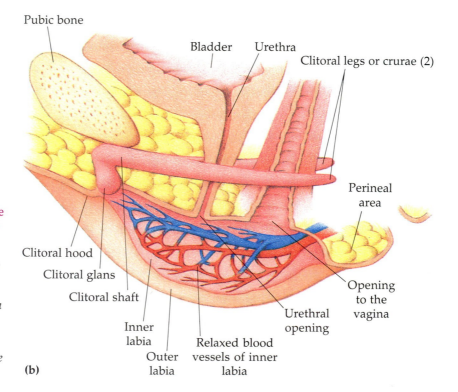

Figure 6.5. The Female Sexual and Reproductive Organs. *The first drawing (a) shows the position and relationship of the different organs, glands, and other structures in the pelvic region of a woman. The second drawing (b) shows the detail of a clitoris in its relaxed or non-erect state (Zaviacic 1990).*

(b)

A hood, foreskin, or **prepuce** formed by the juncture of the minor labia covers the glans. The area between the hood and clitoris should be kept clean of smegma because it can become irritated and infected. The size and shape of the clitoris vary and are unrelated to the ability to experience sexual pleasure (Figures 6.4 and 6.5).

Caressing and stimulating the breasts, neck, the mons, the labia, or the clitoris itself often result in blood congestion in the vulva and associated internal structures. This stimulation also causes the clitoral glans and the internal portions of the clitoris, the two cavernous bodies (crurae, or "legs"), and the bulb or vascular network surrounding the clitoris and vagina to become engorged with blood and "erect." Erection in the male is primarily external; erection in the female is mostly internal. During intercourse, if the thrusting of the penis does not provide sufficient stimulation of the clitoris, either partner can manually stimulate the clitoris.

The Hymen

Over the centuries, the **hymen** has played a major role in male/female relations despite the fact that it exists only as a vestigial remnant of vaginal development in the human female fetus. Known in slang as the cherry or maidenhead, this thin, tissuelike membrane may partially cover the opening of the vagina. It has one or more holes that allow the monthly menstrual flow to pass through from the uterus to the outside of the body (Figure 6.6). Some women are born without a hymen. In other women, the hymen spontaneously tears, breaks, or stretches open while participating in athletics, or as a result of masturbation or tampon use. If the hymen has not been previously ruptured, slight bleeding and discomfort may occur when a woman first has vaginal intercourse. If a woman is concerned about her hymen and the possibility of pain during her first intercourse, she can stretch and enlarge the opening by gradually inserting a clean, lubricated finger. If the hymen is so thick that it hinders intercourse, it can be stretched, dilated, or cut, if necessary, by a physician.

In many cultures, even today, an intact hymen is regarded as a sign of virginity. In some strongly patriarchal cultures, the bride's relatives, or the husband and his friends, still parade the bloodstained bedding from the wedding night through the village as proof to all that the bride was indeed a virgin. Naturally, women in such cultures have devised ways to compensate for a

Annular hymen

Septate hymen

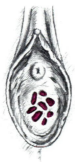

Cribriform hymen

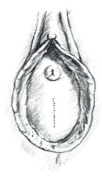

Imperforate hymen

Figure 6.6. *Only human females have a hymen—a structure with no known function. Some newborn females have very little or no hymen. The hymen also is frequently torn or ruptured in athletics or with tampons. A rare imperforate hymen can be opened with a simple incision.*

naturally ruptured hymen or for Mother Nature's failure to give them an adequate hymen. A bride may slip a small container with animal blood past her preoccupied husband and into the wedding bed so she can "bleed" at the appropriate time! In Japan, Morocco, and other countries, young women may have their virginity "restored" by plastic surgery to satisfy the concern of a new boyfriend or husband, although Italy has outlawed this practice. For many centuries in Europe, "deflowering" the virgin bride was a task too dangerous and demanding for the groom. By custom or some vague legal right, the local lord, prince, or priest might occasionally exercise his "right to the first night," thereby helping the groom out of his predicament (Murstein 1974:137). As with female circumcision, the customs that have evolved in different cultures for "deflowering" a virgin bride reflect patriarchal biases and concerns.

Internal Structures

The Vagina

The **vagina** is a collapsed muscular passageway that serves several purposes. The menstrual flow passes through it after leaving the uterus. The walls of the vagina are normally collapsed together, but they can easily expand to accept a tampon or a penis during sexual intercourse. The cervical canal is closed by a mucus plug except at the time of ovulation. As a birth canal, the vaginal walls stretch tremendously to allow passage of an infant that usually weighs 6 to 10 pounds (Figure 6.5).

The entrance to the vagina, or introitus, is rich with sensory neurons. The inner or cervical end of the vagina is not as sensitive. The inner surface of the vagina is covered with a mucosal membrane like that in the mouth. The mucosa is also surrounded by a muscular layer and by an outer membranous covering in the back. The front wall of the vagina is attached to the urethra and bladder.

Beneath the mucus membranes surrounding the vaginal entrance is the erectile tissue of the vestibular bulbs. During sexual arousal, the vestibular bulbs fill with blood, causing the vagina to "grip" the penis. This gripping action can be enhanced during intercourse if the woman contracts the diaphragm of voluntary muscles, the pubococcygeal muscles, which also surround the vaginal entrance (see Kegel exercises in Chapter 7).

The mucosal nature of the vaginal wall and the warm, moist environment of the vaginal canal make it a favorable pathway for pathogenic bacteria or viruses to enter the abdominal cavity (see Chapters 11 and 12).

Several myths have been associated with the vagina. One myth suggests that a petite woman may be injured if she has intercourse with a big man because his penis will be proportionately so big that her tiny vagina cannot accommodate it without pain or actual injury. When sexually aroused, the vagina lengthens to accommodate a longer penis that would otherwise not fit. Even in the few cases where a man's penis is actually too long for the vagina, a couple can experiment with different coital positions to give the woman full control over how deeply the man penetrates. The idea of a "trapped penis" is real for cats and some other animals. But in humans the fear that a woman's vaginal muscles might go into a spasm during intercourse and actually trap the penis has absolutely no basis in real life.

The Uterus

The **uterus**, or womb, resembles an upside-down, flattened pear about the size of two thumbs side by side (Figures 6.2 and 6.5). It is tilted forward over the bladder in a woman's pelvic cavity and held in place by ligaments. During pregnancy, the fetus develops in the uterus. At the base or "neck" of the uterus is the **cervix**. The cervical opening or *os* is very small and will not allow a penis, a tampon, or a finger to enter the uterus. However, it can stretch enough to allow insertion of a contraceptive intrauterine device (IUD) and instruments used in abortion. It opens slightly during ovulation, menstruation, and in labor to allow for passage of the infant from the uterus into the vagina during delivery. Except for a day or two when the ovary is releasing an egg and fertilization is possible, the cervix is blocked by a mucus plug. This provides a protective barrier against microorganisms that otherwise might easily pass through and infect the internal organs.

Like the vagina, the uterus has three layers. The inner lining, the endometrium, is rich in blood vessels and glands that play a major role in menstruation and implantation of the fertilized egg. Beneath the endometrium is a muscular middle layer, the myometrium, which can stretch to contain the fullterm fetus. It is also strong enough to contract and push the fetus through the cervix and into the vagina during delivery. The uterus is covered by an outer layer called the serosa or epimetrium.

Fallopian Tubes

The **fallopian tubes** are also called egg tubes, oviducts, or just "tubes." They are about 4 inches long, with a central canal about twice the diameter of a human hair. The end of the tube farthest from the uterus and closest to the ovary is shaped like a funnel. Fingerlike projections, called fimbriae, ring the funnel and beat rhythmically to pick up the egg when it is expelled from the ovarian follicle during ovulation. Rhythmic muscle contractions in the tube and cilia, microscopic hairs lining the inside of the tube, propel the egg along to the uterus. Fertilization usually takes place in the outer third of the fallopian tube, after which the fertilized egg travels to the uterus and becomes embedded in the uterine lining. Occasionally, a fertilized egg will implant in the fallopian tube, ovary, or abdominal cavity. Such ectopic pregnancies are discussed in Chapter 8.

The fallopian tubes are a common site of gonorrheal and other infections. Tubal infections are known as salpingitis. If the infection is not diagnosed and treated in time, one or both tubes may be blocked by scar tissue, resulting in sterility. Women with blocked fallopian tubes may still become mothers by having an egg fertilized in a small glass dish and reintroduced to the uterus through the vaginal canal. Surrogate mothers are another possibility (Chapter 8). Permanent sterility may be induced by tubal ligation: cutting, tying, or clamping the tubes (Chapter 9).

Ovaries

A pair of almond-sized **ovaries** are located at the ends of the fallopian tubes on either side of the uterus. Regulated by hormones from the pituitary gland, they operate on a monthly cycle to produce the female gonadal sex hormones, es-

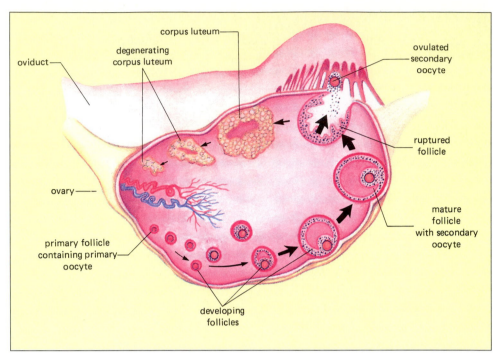

Figure 6.7. Egg and Hormone Production in the Ovary. *The development of follicles in an ovary, portrayed in a time sequence going counterclockwise from the lower left. A primary oocyte begins development within a follicle. The follicle grows, providing both hormones and nourishment for the enlarging oocyte. At ovulation, the secondary oocyte bursts through the ovary wall, surrounded by some follicle cells (now called the corona radiata). The remaining follicle cells develop into a secretory organ, the corpus luteum. If fertilization does not occur, the corpus luteum degenerates after a few days. The follicle cells surround the egg before ovulation and the cells of the corpus luteum produce two hormones, estrogen and progesterone, which are important in the woman's monthly cycle and in pregnancy.*

trogen and progesterone, which regulate the uterine menstrual cycle and secondary sex characteristics. Estrogen also helps prepare the breasts for nursing after the birth of an infant.

The ovaries also produce **eggs** (sing. **ovum**, pl. **ova**) on a monthly cycle (Figure 6.7). Half a million or more eggs start their development in the fetal ovaries, going through the first stage of meiosis before birth. Most of these are absorbed so that only 300,000 to 400,000 immature eggs remain at birth. These have stopped their development and remain dormant until after puberty. After reproductive maturity is reached in the early teens, each monthly cycle in the ovaries will usually result in the release of a single egg. In all, only about 400 eggs, one-tenth of 1% of the original total, will be released before menopause ends a woman's fertile years. The rest are reabsorbed by the ovary.

As the egg is released from the ovarian follicle, the fimbriae draw it into the tube and it moves toward the uterus. If the egg is fertilized in the tube, it will eventually implant in the uterus. If it is not fertilized, it will disintegrate and be reabsorbed or pass out in the menstrual flow. After the egg is released from the ovarian follicle, the nurse cells which are left behind in the ruptured follicle continue their hormone production as part of the corpus luteum or yellow body. The function of the corpus luteum in pregnancy is discussed in Chapter 8.

Skene's Glands and the G spot

Just inside the opening of the female urethra are the ducts that drain the Skene's or paraurethral glands. These glands come from the same embryonic origin as the male prostate and are thought to be associated with female ejaculation. The Grafenberg or G spot is located in the anterior wall of the vagina about halfway between the back of the pubic bone and the cervix, an inch or two inside the vaginal opening. The female ejaculation and the sensitivity of the G spot to sexual stimulation are discussed on pages 184–187.

The Female Breast

During puberty, the mammary glands of females develop into functional breasts capable of secreting milk when prompted by lactogenic hormone from the pituitary gland. Each breast consists of 15 to 20 clusters of grapelike mammary glands, surrounded by fatty and fibrous tissue (Figure 6.8). Ducts from these glands lead to the nipple. The areola, the area around the nipple, may be very dark in color. During nursing, sebaceous glands in the areola lubricate the nipple and keep it from cracking and drying. The small muscle around the nipple may contract when it is cold, when touched, or during sexual arousal. The nipples may be protruding, flat, or inverted. These variations are normal, although textbook diagrams invariably show only protruding nipples. Although

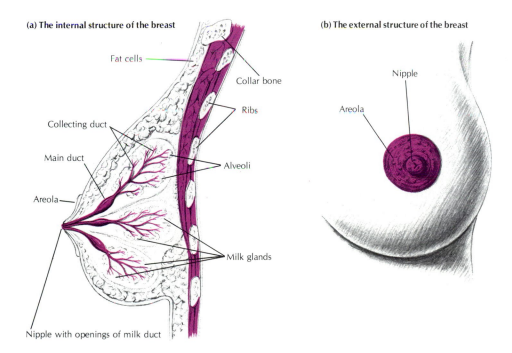

(a) The internal structure of the breast

Fat cells
Collar bone
Ribs
Collecting duct
Main duct
Alveoli
Areola
Milk glands
Nipple with openings of milk duct

(b) The external structure of the breast

Nipple
Areola

Figure 6.8. *The female breast. The breasts of most women are not perfectly symmetrical. They also follow different cycles of changes, depending on time of menstrual cycle and annual seasons, sometimes being larger or smaller in the summer or winter. Normal nipples may be inverted, flat, or protruding in the unstimulated state.*

most diagrams show nicely symmetrical and equal-sized breasts, few women have both breasts of the same size and shape (Figure 6.8).

Slang expressions for the female breasts include knockers, headlights, melons, tits, boobs, bubbies, and bazooms, a corruption of bosom.

In men, the mammary glands remain undeveloped, except for a temporary, slight enlargement at puberty. Breast development can be triggered in males by an abnormal hormone condition or by prolonged exposure to a chemical like THC in marijuana. As in females, male nipples respond to cold, touch, and sexual arousal.

There may be some normal discharge of a translucent white secretion from the nipple after a delivery, abortion, or miscarriage. Small discharges may also occur when a woman is taking birth control pills or when her breasts are being stimulated as part of love play. Although most discharges are normal, some may indicate a problem. If you notice a heavy nipple discharge or anything unusual about the discharge, have it checked by a doctor. The breast self-examination is described in Chapter 11.

American males are often accused of having a breast fetish, an attitude reinforced by the *Penthouse/Playboy* style centerfolds. Since myths about breasts abound, it is important to point out that the size or shape of a woman's breasts have nothing to do with her sexual desire or libido. Women with small breasts are just as erotically sensitive as women with larger breasts. And they are just as able to nurse an infant. In fact, the amount of glandular tissue is about the same in small and large breasts, with the difference being made up by fatty tissue.

A Sexual Fantasyland

Males and females have traditionally faced very different tasks as sexual persons. Until recently, being a female has meant accepting and fitting into a full set of gender roles, most of them passive, and most of them defined by men. This expectation started to change as women's liberation challenged women to define their own femininity and roles. The feminist and self-health movements have made women more conscious of their own bodies and more concerned about being responsible for their sexual health. At the same time, many women really know very little about the sexual anatomy of men and how it functions, even though they may have been sexually active for some time. Young women, curious about what males look like, have only a handful of magazines that exhibit the varieties of male anatomy, and most of them are designed for the male homosexual community.

On the other side of our patriarchal society, males have always had to prove themselves, not by passively accepting roles, but by being active and repeatedly proving their masculinity. Their male equipment, the penis, has been their starting point. But again, most men actually know very little about their own bodies. As Zilbergeld points out,

> The women in [this] fantasyland are all gorgeous and perfectly formed. A glance at the cartoons in any issue of *Playboy* or *Penthouse* makes the point succinctly: The women men desire are beautiful and flawlessly built; women who do not fit this mold are ridiculed.

Average-looking women, women who look older than twenty-two, those whose breasts sag or whose skin is not the model-conforming smooth, creamy, and silky—such women rarely appear in the world of sexual make-believe. It is a world where no one ages and no one wrinkles and no one loses her jutting breasts. . . .

Feminists and other women have long complained that men are too interested in [the female] physical appearance, paying more attention to "tits and ass" than to the personality and intelligence of women and being uninterested in women who do not fit the current standard of physical perfection.

(Zilbergeld 1978:26–27)

For males, there is an equally simplistic myth, summarized very nicely in a chapter title in Zilbergeld's book on *Male Sexuality*: "It's two feet long, hard as steel, and can go all night." This fantasy has no basis in reality. It has no connection with the way male sexual anatomy is constructed, or might be expected to perform. But it is a powerful fantasy, nevertheless.

We [men] all want to learn about sex since it seems like such an important part of being masculine and adult but, because of all the double messages we get from our parents and other sources, it is a subject loaded with anxiety. . . . And sex is one of the few areas of life where it is almost impossible to observe accurately how others are doing it. It is of course possible to obtain sexual information—we are deluged with it—but much of this information is absurdly exaggerated and inaccurate and the growing boy has no way of knowing this.

A crucial element that motivated our learning and fueled our anxiety was the necessity of proving we were men. In our society, manhood is a conditional attribute. The possession of a penis is necessary but not sufficient; you still had to prove, and keep on proving, that you were worthy . . . good enough, bold enough.

(Zilbergeld 1978:14-15)

Male Anatomy

Penis Myths and Realities

Because of the prevailing myth, men learn from their earlier years to measure their masculinity and sex appeal by the size of their penises. Bigger is inevitably better. Of course, this "pulsating, throbbing, ever-ready equipment" comes in only three sizes, "large, gigantic, and so big you can barely get them through the doorway" (Zilbergeld 1978:23). If this sounds silly and ridiculous, it is. But that does not deter men from believing it, just as women are seduced into their own sexual fantasyland (Highlight Box 6.1).

Part of the mythology of penis size has been the belief common among whites that black males are much more amply endowed than they are. This myth is evident in racist literature from the days of slavery on. It was also used to justify laws prohibiting interracial sexual relations and marriage. "Nature,"

HIGHLIGHT BOX 6.1.
THE SIZE OF A MAN

Dear Ann Landers: I would like to say something to "Rhode Island"—the young man who was afraid to pursue a romantic relationship with a woman because he was "underendowed." He said he couldn't take any more ridicule, he had had enough from the guys in the showers all through school.

I have been married four times. (Buried two and divorced one.) The best lover of the lot was the one who was the least generously endowed. Now what do you think of that, Ann Landers?—No Name, Just Pardeeville, Wis.

Dear Pardee: I think I have received about 10,000 letters on this subject, mostly from women saying the same thing. Please read on.

From Miami: "Rhode Island" has been victimized by locker-room baloney. The most exciting sex partner I ever had was a man with almost invisible parts.—Less Is More.

Los Angeles: I work as a hooker in Southern California and have been with thousands of men. Take it from someone who knows, the best performers are the ones with the least impressive equipment.—X-Peer-lence

From Philadelphia: Tell "Rhode Island" to concentrate on what he says and how he says it when he is making love. He will find it is much more important to a woman than what he is worrying about.—All Ears

Rapid City, S.D.: Bigger doesn't necessarily mean better.—Been Around

Long Island: I am a woman who sympathizes with "Rhode Island" because I had a similar problem, only it was my breasts. I was so flat-chested I was afraid to allow a man to get too friendly for fear it might lead to the bedroom and I would be humiliated. When I finally found the courage to let myself go, I discovered it didn't make one bit of difference.—Happy Lark

Cleveland: Better underendowed than over. I was married to both types and the one who was slightly "short-changed" was by far the more exciting lover.—Made Both Scenes

Melville, N.Y.: I went through the same humiliation in the showers when I was a GI. This caused me to shy away from women until I was 29. Tell R.I. not to fool around with trash because he thinks he's under par. When the right girl comes along, everything will fall into place.—Father Of Six

Spokane, Wash.: You gave "R.I." Wonderful advice. He needs counseling to get over his feelings of inadequacy. The problem is in his head, not lower down.—Mr. Also

Southern Illinois: Tell "Rhode Island" if he wants a wife or sweetheart, he had better get cracking. If she has never been to bed with anyone, she won't know the difference.

Bellingham, Wash.: The best measure of a man is how he treats a woman in the bedroom and out. It's the sharing and caring that matter. Nothing else.—Experienced

Troy, Ala.: Ann please tell "Rhode Island" that it's not the size of the ship that counts, it's the motion of the ocean.—Smiling Sally

Louisville, Ky.: If anyone complains that your column is too frank, ignore them. You are a master when it comes to handling hot topics with taste. You'll never know how many people you helped with that one.—Blessing You Regularly

Dear Blessing: Thanks, friend.

Ann Landers

Figure 6.9. Sexual Displays. *Men and women everywhere engage in sexual display. Skintight jeans accenting the buttocks or crotch, breast-revealing dress, and cosmetics all serve the same purpose. The Dani (New Guinea) man shown here (left) has chosen a penis sheath or extender to accent his manliness. The 16th-century Florentine nobleman shown on the right dons an elaborately embroidered codpiece to display his virility.*

it was argued, "never designed white women to have intercourse with blacks!" This alleged inferiority has not deterred white males from boasting of their manly endowments. Penis extenders and codpieces are only two of the fashions men have used to display and emphasize their virility to the ladies (Figure 6.9).

In the gay community there are two fantasyland images. The hairy macho type you expect to step out of an 18-wheeler represents one extreme. At the other end, and more popular, is the smooth-skinned, blond blue-eyed Aryan-type innocent youth. This second type is more likely to echo the heterosexual male fantasy, emphasizing the buttocks and "advertising the package up front" with tight jeans.

Adolescent males, who are uncertain and anxious about their budding sexuality and masculinity, suffer much from our myths and concerns about penis size. Even though our culture frowns on adolescent sexual activity, it is not uncommon for young boys to get together when adults aren't around to compare the size of their penises or hold a contest to see who can ejaculate or urinate the farthest. Such games and exploratory contests are a natural part of growing up as a male. They have nothing to do with a homosexual orientation, although some adults have unfounded fears that such games hint at a future homosexual orientation.

In general, the size of the penis is not related to greater sexual satisfaction for the female, although some women prefer a larger penis and deep thrusting. Although the whole length of the vagina is sensitive, the outer third is more sensitive, especially to tactile stimulation. On average, an erect penis of even 3 or 4 inches is sufficient to stimulate the outer vaginal nerves.

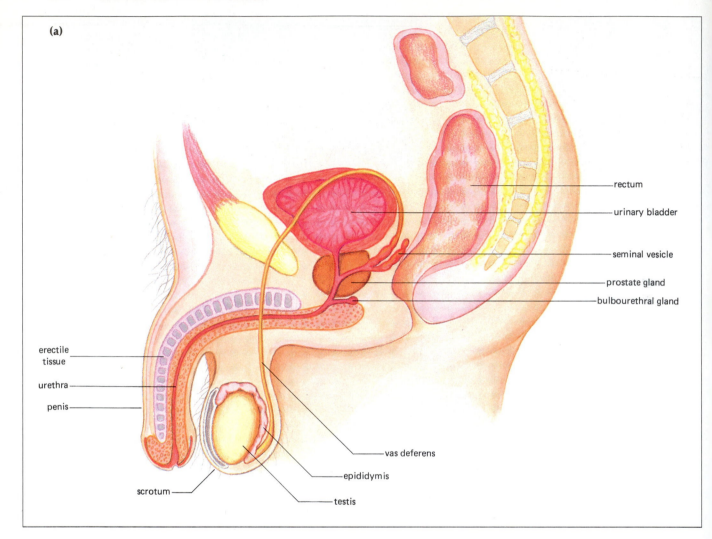

(a)

rectum

urinary bladder

seminal vesicle

prostate gland

bulbourethral gland

erectile tissue

urethra

penis

vas deferens

epididymis

scrotum

testis

Male Anatomy

The Penis

The **penis** is a cylindrical organ with three columns of spongelike tissue (Figure 6.10). Most of the shaft of the penis is taken up with the parallel columns of the **corpora cavernosa**. Beneath the corpora cavernosa is the urethra, the tube that carries the urine and semen, encircled by the **corpus spongiosum**. At the base of the penis, the corpus spongiosum enlarges in the penile bulb. Contractions of the penile bulb help in ejaculation of the semen. At the outer end, the spongy body enlarges into the glans of the penis.

As their names suggest, the tissue of the spongy and cavernous bodies is packed with thousands of tiny collapsed cavities capable of expanding tremendously when filled with blood under pressure. The penis enlarges and stiffens when the nervous system sends messages to the blood vessels controlling blood

(b)

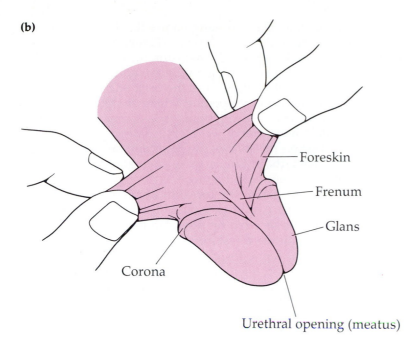

Foreskin

Frenum

Glans

Corona

Urethral opening (meatus)

Figure 6.10. The Male Sexual and Reproductive Glans. *The first drawing (a) shows the position and relationship of the different organs, glands, and other structures in the pelvic region of a man. Drawing (b) shows details of the penile glans and foreskin. Drawing (c) shows a cross section through the body of the penis with the erectile cavernous bodies and an erectile spongy body surrounding the urethra.*

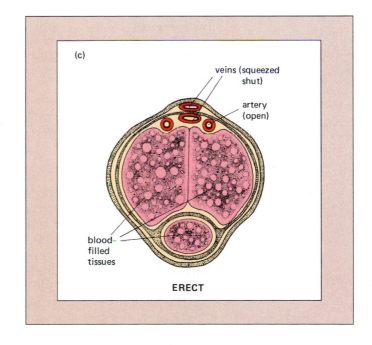

(c)

veins (squeezed shut)

artery (open)

blood-filled tissues

ERECT

flow into the cavernous and spongy bodies. When the arteries entering these bodies dilate, more blood flows into the collapsed tissue, causing it to swell. This partially constricts the veins in the penis, slowing the outflow of blood. The result is an erection—in slang terms, hard-on or boner. When the stimulus subsides, the veins relax, the blood drains out of the cavities, and the penis returns to its non-erect, flaccid state. Despite slang names like love muscle and boner, there is no muscle or bone in the human penis (Figure 6.11).

At the outer end of the penis, the corpus spongiosum forms the **glans**. The skin covering the glans is very sensitive, with many nerve endings. Especially sensitive are the corona, the crownlike ridge along the back edge of the glans, and the frenulum underneath the urinary opening where the glans joins the shaft of the penis. The shaft, or body, of the penis is less sensitive to touch than the glans, but does contain many nerve receptors for deep pressure. This is why most men squeeze and stroke the shaft of the penis and only occasionally involve the glans when they masturbate. Similarly, women stimulate the shaft of the clitoris and not the glans when masturbating.

The fold of skin that covers the glans, the **foreskin** or prepuce, can be retracted. This happens naturally when an uncircumcised man has an erection. **Smegma**, a cheeselike substance, is secreted by tiny glands behind the corona of the glans and on the underside of the foreskin. The smegma, a natural body product, also provides a congenial home for bacteria. If a man is not circumcised, he should pull back the foreskin regularly and clean the area under it.

Penises, like the female vulva, differ in size and shape. Some penises are small, others large. Some are long and thin. Others are short and stubby. Some penises have very prominent surface blood vessels; others are smooth. Some curve to the right, others to the left. Some are circumcised, with the foreskin removed; others are uncircumcised. When erect, some point almost straight up, others straight out, and the rest somewhere in between. Some erect penises are blunt, others bottle-shaped and still others turned up at the tip like the prow of a ship. All these variations are normal (Figure 6.11).

Among the more widely used slang expressions for the penis are prick, dick, wanger, cock, pecker, dong, meat, member, John Henry, hose, shlontz, peg, pink-eyed snake, horn, joystick, rocket, banana, turkey neck, poker, hot dog, dork, willie, wienie, and ya-ya. What messages do these expressions convey? How do these expressions compare with those we use for the female vulva or clitoris? What messages do they convey about male and female sex roles? Are men or women more likely to be offended by these terms?

The Scrotum, Testes, and Semen

The **scrotum** is a thin-walled pouch of dark-colored skin enclosing the **testes**. The testes or testicles—in slang terms, balls, nuts, family jewels, rocks, and shaboongies—are walnut-sized glands that produce testosterone and sperm. Their name comes from the ancient Biblical custom in which men swore an oath—testified—while holding their testes or the inside of the thigh (Genesis 24:1–5, 9). In most men, the left testicle hangs below the right testicle because of the length, angle, and source of the blood vessels supplying them.

The cremasteric muscle in the scrotum plays an important role in keeping the testes at the proper temperature for sperm production, about 5° below the normal 98.6° F. When the testes become too warm, the cremasteric muscle relaxes, and the scrotum and testes move away from the warm body wall to provide cooling. When the testes drop below the optimal temperature, when the skin of the scrotum or inner thigh is stimulated, and just before orgasm, the cremasteric reflex elevates and rotates the testes against the body wall. This same reflex occurs just before orgasm during sexual excitement.

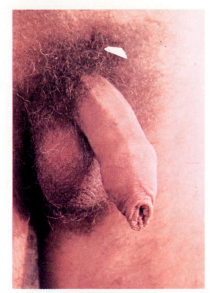

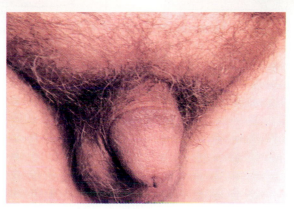

Figure 6.11. The Penis. *These three photos show the normal variety of size and shape of the penis. The penis on the upper left is uncircumcised.*

A cross section of a testicle shows triangular compartments packed with sperm-producing tightly coiled tubules (Figure 6.12). Packed in between the seminiferous tubules are blood vessels and the interstitial cells, or cells of Leydig.

After puberty, the **seminiferous tubules** produce millions of immature **sperm**, the male reproductive cell, every day. As the sperm cells develop over two months' time, they migrate from the outer edge of the seminiferous tubule toward the central cavity and out to the **epididymis**. The epididymis is a 20-foot-long tightly coiled tube located on top of each testicle. Sperm mature in the epididymis and can be stored there for up to six weeks. Sexual arousal will produce a rhythmic muscular movement that pushes the sperm into the **vas deferens**, the tubes leading from the epididymis upward, in front of and over the urinary bladder, and back down to the seminal vesicles and prostate gland.

With puberty, the interstitial cells of Leydig produce testosterone, other androgenic hormones, and a small amount of estrogen (Figure 6.12). These

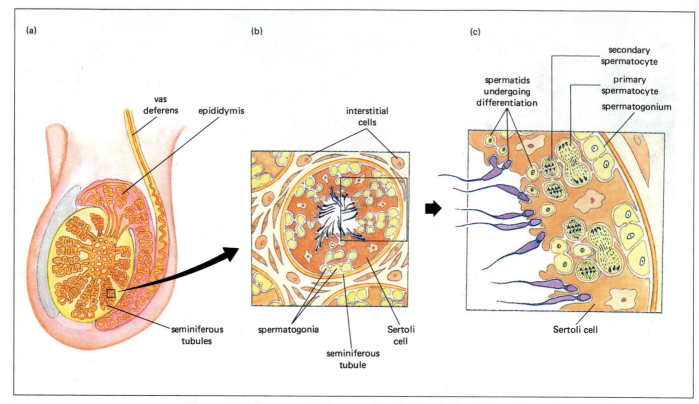

Figure 6.12. Sperm and Hormone Production in the Testes. *The male gonads, the testes, hang beneath the abdominal cavity in the scrotum. (a) A longitudinal section of the testicle, showing the location of the seminiferous tubules, epididymis, and vas deferens. (b) A cross section of the seminiferous tubules. The walls of the seminiferous tubules are lined with spermatogonia and Sertoli cells protruding into the lumen of the tubule. (c) As spermatogonia undergo meiosis, the daughter cells move inward, embedded in invaginations of the Sertoli cells. There they differentiate into sperm, drawing upon the Sertoli cells for nourishment. Mature sperm are finally freed into the lumen of the tubules for transport to the penis. Testosterone is produced by the interstitial cells found in the spaces between tubules.*

hormones control sex drive (libido) and the development of secondary male sex characteristics such as beard growth and a lower-pitched voice.

When a man is sexually aroused, blood accumulates in both the penis and testes. If sexual excitement continues for some time without the release of orgasm and ejaculation, the testes may become very sensitive, even painful. The slang expression for this condition is blue balls. Even without orgasm and ejaculation, this natural swelling will dissipate in a few hours.

Paired, saclike **seminal vesicles** behind the prostate gland open into the vas deferens just before they enter the prostate gland. The seminal vesicles produce 70% of the total seminal fluid or **semen**. This alkaline seminal fluid activates the sperm and contains sugars that supply the energy which allows the sperm to swim through the female reproductive tract to the egg. A powerful natural antibiotic, seminalplasmin, may protect women from vaginal infections and the male against infections of the urethra. This combined seminal fluid and sperm then enters the ejaculatory ducts, which are an extension of the vas deferens between the seminal vesicle openings and the urethra in the prostate.

The Prostate Gland

About the size of a large walnut, the **prostate gland** surrounds the urethra as it leaves the urinary bladder. Inside the prostate, two ejaculatory ducts carry the sperm and seminal fluid to the urethra, adding more seminal fluid from the prostate. The **Cowper's glands**, a pair of pea-sized glands at the base of the penis, secrete a small amount of clear, alkaline fluid into the urethra when there is mild sexual arousal. This neutralizes the acidic environment of the urethra, which can harm the sperm. Even without ejaculation or vaginal penetration, the secretions of Cowper's glands may leak from the partially erect penis with enough sperm to cause pregnancy if this fluid makes contact with the vagina or moist vulva.

At different times, the prostatic urethra receives urine and seminal fluid for transport to the penis. Two spinchter muscles regulate these processes. A bladder sphincter at the neck of the bladder, above the prostate, is normally closed to prevent leakage of the urine. A second, urethral sphincter, located in the urethra just below the prostate, normally remains open. Both sphincters are open during urination. During sexual arousal, both sphincters are at first closed. This allows the semen in the ejaculatory ducts and prostate to build up pressure during the emission phase of male ejaculation. The outer, urethral sphincter then opens to allow ejaculation or expulsion of the seminal fluid through the urethra, while the inner sphincter remains closed to prevent urine from passing out at this time. Ejaculation is aided by rhythmic contractions in the muscles surrounding the urethra. Ejaculation releases about 3 to 5 ml, about 1 teaspoon, of seminal fluid containing about 300 million sperm. Slang expressions for semen include cum, jism, and love juice. Details on male orgasm and ejaculation can be found in Chapter 7.

Circumcision

Male Circumcision

Prehistoric farmers ensured the fertility of their fields by offering their foreskins to the gods in the fields. The early Egyptians believed humans were created bisexual like some of their gods, with both a masculine and a feminine soul. The male's feminine soul was thought to be located in the foreskin and the woman's masculine soul in her clitoris. So, when an Egyptian boy or girl approached puberty, **circumcision** made the boy fully male by removing his foreskin and the girl fully female by removing her clitoris or at least the clitoral foreskin. African and Arabic cultures adopted circumcision from the Egyptians as a religious rite for both males and females. Male circumcision passed into the Jewish world through Abraham who had his sons circumcised. Joshua required it for all Jewish males as a sign of the covenant between the Jews and God, and to distinguish them from uncircumcised barbarians.

Until recently, about 80% of American males were circumcised. Yet in Canada less than 30% of males are circumcised, in Australia less than 25%, and in Great Britain less than 1%. It is rare in West Germany and Scandinavia.

Circumcision became popular in America in the 1800s when the Victorian culture became obsessed with sexual health and masturbation. According to medical and religious leaders of that era, circumcision would prevent or cure asthma, epilepsy, venereal disease, and cancer of the penis. Since a circumcised man did not have to retract the foreskin to clean under it when he bathed, circumcision, they thought, would reduce the temptation to masturbate (Money 1985a:99–102).

In the 1970s two studies reported the rate of cervical cancer was much lower in women married to circumcised men (Green 1977:403; Terris et al. 1974). But Rothkin (1973) asked whether the lack of circumcision, or other factors, promoted cervical cancer.

In 1975 the American Academy of Pediatrics said, "There is no absolute medical indication [to support] routine circumcision of the newborn" (Smolev 1984; Wallerstein 1980). This view fitted comfortably with the age-old myth that circumcision reduces a man's pleasure in intercourse. However, Masters, Johnson, and Kolodny found no difference in sexual sensitivity or pleasure reported by circumcised and uncircumcised men (1988:68–69).

The trend away from circumcision received a major boost when it was reported that 1 in 500 circumcisions is actually life threatening and half of all American circumcisions, 10,000 every year, have complications (Seligmann, 1979). By 1987 only 59% of newborn males were being circumcised.

In 1988 new research led the American Academy of Pediatrics to reconsider its earlier statement discouraging circumcision. Medical records from 427,698 infants born in U.S. Army hospitals indicate that boys who are not circumcised have 11 times as many urinary tract infections as males who are circumcised. Circumcision, it was reported, could prevent possibly 20,000 cases of urinary tract infection a year (Wiswell et al. 1987). Meanwhile, reports from Africa suggested that uncircumcised men may be 5 to 8 times more likely to get AIDS during heterosexual intercourse than men who have been circumcised (Marx 1989).

How do you feel about circumcision? How does your reaction relate to whether you are a male or female? Do you think female reactions are generally different from those of males? Would you have your son circumcised? Why? If you are circumcised, would you consider having your foreskin "restored" by plastic surgery? Some men have had such surgery, even though it takes a series of operations and leaves a "foreskin" that is noticeably different in color and texture from the skin on the penis (Greer et al. 1982).

Female Circumcision

In Victorian America, an "oversexed" female who expressed more interest in or enjoyment of sexual relations than her husband thought she should, was seen as a threat to male dominance and to motherly purity. Physicians had a simple remedy for "hyperesthesia": surgical removal of the clitoris (Sheehan 1981). In some ways, we still have remnants of this Victorian view of women. The term "nymphomania," for instance, is often erroneously used to describe a woman with a healthy sexual urge.

The term circumcision properly refers to removal of the foreskin or prepuce covering the glans of the penis or clitoris. When used in a nontechnical sense, **female circumcision** may refer also to clitorectomy, removal of the clitoris, and to Pharonic circumcision, the removal of the minor labia and sewing up of the vulva.

Today, clitorectomy is still common in many cultures. A 1980 survey by the Cairo Family Planning Association found that 90% of Egyptian women interviewed had had some part of their clitoris or labia removed. Usually an older female performs this surgery, without anesthesia, as part of a family rite of passage for a girl before she enters puberty. In rural areas and among the poor, the incision is often done under unsanitary conditions with a sharp stone, piece of glass, or knife. Millions of African, Indonesian, and Malaysian girls undergo some form of female circumcision every year. The mildest form involves removal of the clitoral hood or prepuce. In other cases, the whole clitoris and parts of the minor labia are removed. Obviously, this is not the equivalent of male circumcision because it removes the source of much of a woman's sexual pleasure. In some cultures, clitorectomy has a religious purpose, totally unrelated to male concerns about females enjoying sex. Some people believe that clitorectomy removes the remnant of the male in a woman and is necessary if she is to be fully female.

In Pharonic circumcision or infibulation, the minor labia are removed and the two sides of the vulva are pinned or sewn together, leaving only a small hole for urine and the menstrual flow. Infibulation ensures female virginity since the entrance to the vagina is not reopened until just before the wedding night by a midwife, a female relative, or on the wedding night by the husband himself (Atiya 1982; El Saadawi 1980; Mernissi 1975).

This centuries-old tradition is increasingly being challenged by emerging feminist movements in the Third World nations, and by the introduction of Western attitudes and medicine. When people whose families have traditionally practiced female circumcision immigrate to Europe and North America, Westerners find this custom shocking and barbaric. Doctors commonly refuse to perform the surgery, leaving the family to do it themselves. In some cases, immigrant parents have been charged with homicide because a child died of infection when doctors refused to circumcise their daughter and a member of the family performed this surgery as they would have in their native land (Morgan & Steinem 1980).

Key Concepts

1. Regardless of sexual orientation, men and women should be equally aware and understanding of their own sexual anatomy and that of their partners.

2. Slang terms for sexual anatomy reveal a definite bias against female sexuality as well as many negative images of human sexuality and functioning.

3. The size and shape of sex organs and breasts vary from person to person— there is no one "normal" or "ideal" model.

4. In women, the main erotic zones are the clitoris, the mons veneris, minor labia, entrance to the vaginal canal, the G spot, perineal region, breasts, neck, lips, and cheek areas. In men, the glans and frenulum of the penis

are the most erogenous zones, although the scrotum, perineum, anus, breasts, neck, lips, and cheek areas are also very sensitive.

5. Males often worry about myths that link penis size with virility, even though the ability of a male to stimulate and please a female partner during intercourse is not based on the size of his penis. Equally erroneous is the myth that absence of a hymen indicates a woman is not a virgin.

6. Male circumcision has no effect on sexual sensitivity, pleasure, or on the incidence of penile or cervical cancer, but urinary tract infections are 11 times more common in men who are not circumcised. Uncircumcised men, and women, should routinely wash under the foreskin to remove accumulation of smegma and other secretions.

7. Female circumcision can be traumatic, if not life threatening for many girls, yet it is widely practiced, mainly in Africa and the Middle East, to assure female virginity or for religious/philosophical reasons.

8. After puberty, the ovaries of women produce estrogen that controls the menstrual cycle, egg production, and secondary sex characteristics. The ovaries also produce some testosterone that controls sex drive.

9. After puberty in a male, the testes produce testosterone and other androgens that regulate sperm production, secondary sex characteristics, and sex drive.

Key Terms

Bartholin's glands (147)
cervix (151)
circumcision (163)
clitoris (147)
corpora cavernosa (158)
corpus spongiosum (158)
Cowper's glands (163)
egg (152)
epididymis (161)
fallopian tube (151)
female circumcision (165)
foreskin (160)
glans (147, 160)
hymen (149)
major labia (147)
minor labia (147)
mons veneris (144)

ovary (151)
ovum, ova (152)
penis (158)
perineum (147)
prepuce (149)
prostate gland (163)
scrotum (160)
semen (162)
seminal vesicles (162)
seminiferous tubules (161)
smegma (160)
sperm (160)
testes (testicle) (160)
uterus (151)
vagina (150)
vas deferens (161)
vulva (146)

Summary Questions

1. List some specific advantages of being aware of and understanding our sexual anatomy and how it functions.

2. How has the evolution of privacy in the home affected our sexual knowledge?

3. Discuss some myths associated with male and female sexual anatomy.

4. Describe the main components of female and male sexual anatomy. What specific parallels exist between male and female sexual anatomy?

5. Compare the structure of the clitoris and penis.

6. What are the origins of male and female circumcision?

7. What health risks are involved in male circumcision? How do health risks differ when a male is not circumcised?

8. Describe the varieties of female circumcision and why this practice is being increasingly denounced.

Suggested Readings

Boston Women's Health Collective. (1984). *The New Our Bodies, Ourselves*. (3rd ed.). New York: Simon & Schuster. A complete, intelligible book for women's sexual and health issues.

Brothers, J. (1981). *What Every Woman Should Know About Men*. New York: Simon & Schuster. A noted psychologist writes for women, and men too, about the differences between men and women.

Farrell, W. (1986). *Why Men Are the Way They Are*. New York: McGraw-Hill. A perfect companion for Dr. Joyce Brothers's book, for both men and women.

Federation of Feminist Women's Health Centers. (1981). *A New View of a Woman's Body*. New York: Simon & Schuster. Contains some revolutionary, if controversial, insights into female sexual anatomy and how it functions.

Kelley, G. (1979). *A Healthy Man's Guide to Sexual Fulfillment*. New York: Harcourt Brace Jovanovich. A basic book on male sexual health by a noted sexologist.

The Varieties of Human Sexual Responses
The Desire Phase (1)
The Excitement/Plateau Phase (2)
Two Arousal Processes
Excitement
Plateau
The Orgasm Phase (3)
Orgasmic Variations in Women
Orgasmic Variations in Men
Exercising the Pubococcygeal Muscles
The Resolution Phase (4)
An Integrated Psychophysiological Model
Cautions About Sexual Response Models
The Control of Sexual Responses
Two Types of Control
Reflexogenic Responses
Intermediate Controls
The Conscious Levels of Sexual Response

Chapter 7

Our Sexual Responses

Special Consultants

Norman A. Scherzer, Ph.D., professor, Department of Biological Sciences and Allied Health, Essex County College, and visiting professor, Department of Biology, Rutgers, The State University of New Jersey (Newark).

Beverly Whipple, Ph.D., R.N., associate professor, College of Nursing, Rutgers, The State University of New Jersey (Newark), and coauthor of *The G Spot and Other Recent Discoveries in Human Sexuality* (1982) and *Safe Encounters* (1989).

We are born into an environment filled with potential erotic stimuli. The people we see or meet, the situations we encounter, our different experiences, our varying moods and interests, chance events, the images we see on television or in advertisements, music, fragrances, and memories—each of these may trigger an erotic fantasy and sexual desire in our mind. Sometimes we are conscious of the erotic stimuli that come to us through our senses. At other times, we are distracted by more pressing activities, or deliberately shut off the erotic image before it has any real effect on us. We might also be asleep and unaware that some pressure on the sexual organs, or an erotic dream has started up a series of reflexive, automatic reactions in our bodies that will carry us through a cycle of sexual responses.

This chapter deals with the varieties of human sexual responses. There are many similarities in the sexual responses of men and women, in part because many sexual structures, like the penis and clitoris and the nerve pathways that regulate our sexual responses, have the same embryonic origins in males and females. But there are also some important differences. Although we still have much to discover, this chapter will raise some interesting new perspectives and questions.

The Varieties of Human Sexual Responses

Occasionally, in the everyday ebb and flow of erotic stimuli, an erotic trigger breaks through a certain threshold in our consciousness, or in the reflex arcs of our spinal cord. At that point, a natural cycle begins. The cycle may start when you consciously pick up on an erotic stimulus and turn it into a desire for the pleasures of sex (Figures 7.1 and 7.11). Sexual desire, the first phase in the **psychogenic** or conscious sexual response cycle, then leads us through the phases of excitement/plateau and orgasm followed by a resolution phase when we return to the gentle ebb and flow of everyday life. We can also go through the sexual response cycle, bypassing the conscious desire phase. The best example of the **reflexogenic** sexual response cycle is a male with an injury to the spinal cord above the erection center. The nerve damage prevents messages from the conscious brain from getting through to the sexual organs. It also blocks any sensations from the genitals from reaching the conscious regions of the brain. Despite this blockage and the fact that the brain cannot influence the sexual response cycle, pressure on genitals or manual stimulation can trigger reflex arcs in the lower spinal cord. When triggered, these arcs send messages back to the genitals, causing an erection. If the stimulation is sufficient, the genitals then move through the cycle of sexual excitement/plateau, ejaculation/orgasm, and resolution.

Wilhelm Reich (1897–1957), a controversial Austrian-American psychoanalyst, first proposed the division of the human sexual response cycle into four phases: (1) mechanical tension, (2) bioelectric charge, (3) bioelectric discharge, and (4) mechanical relaxation (1942). In the 1960s William Masters and Virginia Johnson gave these phases new names, which are now standard: the excitement, plateau, orgasm, and resolution stages (Figure 7.1).

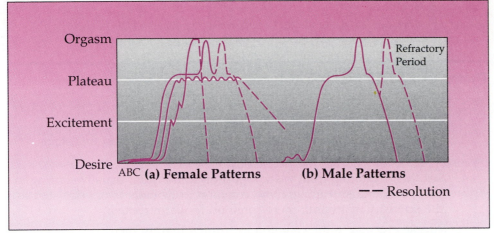

Figure 7.1. Variations in Female and Male Sexual Responses. *Masters and Johnson de-tected three common variations in the sexual response cycle of women (a). Pattern A involves two or more orgasms. Pattern B involves a prolonged plateau stage with minor orgasms. Pattern C involves a very rapid rise to orgasm followed by rapid resolution. See also the tenting, A-frame, and blended orgasm patterns described by Whipple, Perry, and Ladas in Figure 7.6. The typical male response is shown by the solid line in (b). Some males may experience a very short refractory period followed by arousal and a second orgasm.*

In 1979 Helen Singer Kaplan added a psychological stage, a desire phase, at the beginning of the Masters and Johnson model. Kaplan also saw no advantage in drawing a distinction between the excitement and plateau phases since the physiological processes that begin in the Masters and Johnson excitement phase continue and peak in the plateau phase. With the excitement/plateau phases combined, the result is a modified four-phase model of sexual arousal: (1) a desire phase, (2) an excitement/plateau phase, (3) an orgasm phase, and (4) a resolution phase (Figure 7.1).

The model of four phases in the sexual response cycle outlined here is an attempt to organize what we know about the changes we experience in our bodies when we become sexually aroused (in slang terms, turned-on or horny), when we allow that erotic tension to build, and when that tension triggers a natural climax and release we call orgasm or "coming." The process is the same whether we are sexually pleasuring ourselves in masturbation, or being sexually intimate with another person. Heterosexual couples, lesbian couples, and gay male couples experience the same stages of the sexual response cycle. It doesn't matter, either, whether our motive for being sexually active is true love or hot passionate lust. There is a danger in this model, however, which should be pointed out from the start. In dividing up the sexual response cycles of men and women and stressing similarities between the two sexes, one can wonder how much the desire to establish an equality between males and females influences our interpretation of what we know from clinical observations. Within this four-phase model, it is important to notice both similarities and differences in the male and female patterns (Table 7.1).

Table 7.1.
General Body Responses Shared by Men and Women
During the Sexual Response Cycle

During the EXCITEMENT STAGE, men and women share

1. An increase in muscle tension (myotonia), particularly in the voluntary muscles of the pelvis, arms, and legs;
2. Some tensing of smooth muscles of the abdomen late in this stage;
3. A moderate increase in heart rate and blood pressure;
4. Sex flush resulting from vasocongestion in the skin, usually starting in chest area and spreading; more common in women; may be related to the intensity of arousal; more common in warm rooms;
5. Nipple erection, more common in women than in men.

During the PLATEAU STAGE, men and women commonly experience

1. Muscle tension (myotonia), which becomes pronounced all over the body. Involuntary contractions of the hands and feet may occur, along with grimaces of the face, frowns, and scowls;
2. Vasocongestion, both superficial and deep, with an increase in sex flush;
3. Respiratory rate that may rise to over 40 breaths per minute; the mouth may open involuntarily in a gasping reaction to increase oxygen flow to the lungs;
4. A rise in heart rate to between 100 and 180 beats with continued elevation in blood pressure.

During the ORGASM STAGE, men and women commonly experience

1. Reduction in voluntary muscle control and an increase in involuntary muscle spasms throughout the body. Carpopedal spasm in foot with big toe held straight while other toes bend back and foot arches;
2. Heart rate may reach 160 to 180 beats per minute; breathing up to 40 per minute;
3. Sex flush may continue if already present;
4. External rectal sphincter contracts at 0.8-second intervals;
5. Involuntary rapid pelvic thrusting immediately prior to orgasm, especially in male.

During the RESOLUTION STAGE, in men and women:

1. All signs of muscle tension disappear within 5 minutes.
2. Sex flush disappears rapidly; loss of vasocongestion may trigger perspiration after orgasm.
3. Heart rate, breathing, and blood pressure return to normal.
4. Loss of nipple erection occurs.

There are also three problematic areas, or unresolved questions:

1. Do men and women have virtually identical four-phase cycles of sexual arousal and orgasm?
2. Is there more than one type of orgasm?
3. Do men and women have a similar capacity for multiple orgasms?

The Desire Phase (1)

Music, pictures, a fantasy, the sight of a sexy man or woman, or thoughts of a loved one that would start the average man or woman thinking about the delights and pleasures of sexual intimacy appear to have no effect on some people. Some persons never let themselves respond to erotic or sexual stimuli. They block or are inhibited long before their bodies start to respond to erotic stimuli and sexual excitement. They seem indifferent to sex, totally uninterested in it, or openly afraid of sexual emotions. Even the hint of a situation or relationship with the slight possibility of sexual intimacy developing may be enough to trigger anxiety and fear. Behind these negative reactions may be a traumatic early childhood incident, a bad experience in their early sexual explorations, or the internalizing of some very negative messages about sexual relations from their family, church, or peers. A strong fear of pregnancy or venereal disease, a sense of sin or guilt associated with sex, anxiety and fear of the unknown, and a variety of other emotions often result in a lack of sexual desire or even an aversion to sexual intimacy.

Although psychological causes are the more common cause of a lack of sexual desire or aversion to sexual intimacy, medications, drugs, and hormone imbalances can also turn off our sexual response system and suppress or block erotic desires and thoughts before they can trigger the normal reflexes of our sexual response cycle.

We will explore the organic and psychological causes of the lack of sexual desire or aversion to sex in some detail in Chapter 21. We also leave to a later chapter discussion of what different people find sexually attractive, sexual fantasies, and various outlets from masturbation to oral, anal, and vaginal intercourse in which we experience the sexual response cycle described in this chapter.

Here, we need only recall our earlier distinction between psychogenic and reflexogenic sexual arousal. The *psychogenic sexual response cycle* starts in the brain, with conscious sexual desires, with a **desire phase**. If, for whatever reason, people suppress or block out conscious sexual desires, they may not experience a psychogenic sexual response. Despite what you might expect, an occasional lack of sexual desire is perfectly normal. College students regularly block and suppress their sexual desires when they have other priorities, like the stress of studying for an exam. Some people may repress any sexual desire on a long-term basis and never experience conscious sexual arousal. Even though someone may block out all conscious sexual desires, if the body is healthy and the spinal cord functioning normally, this same individual will occasionally experience reflexogenic sexual arousal and orgasm. The *reflexogenic sexual response cycle* skips the conscious desire phase and involves automatic, unconscious reflexes in the spinal cord.

The Excitement/Plateau Phase (2)

Two Arousal Processes

From a clinical point of view, it is possible to divide the experience of sexual arousal into two stages, excitement and plateau, as Masters and Johnson first suggested. Because our concern here is with the way we experience sexual arousal rather than with clinical analysis, we prefer to treat excitement and plateau as a continuous process and concentrate on the development and consequences of two physiological changes that occur as we experience sexual arousal in the **excitement/plateau phase** (Katchadourian 1985:64). These two physical changes are known as vasocongestion and myotonia.

Vasocongestion

The most important change going on during the excitement/plateau phase involves **vasocongestion**, an increase in the flow of blood into the capillaries and sinuses within different body tissues, especially the genitals. The accumulation of blood in the cavernous tissues of the penis, clitoris, and vestibular bulb causes the tissue cavities to swell like balloons. The result is an **erection** or **tumescence.** Elsewhere in the genitals, vasocongestion forces fluid from the blood into the major and minor labia, the testes, the breasts, and the pelvic organs, causing swelling or **edema**. Tumescence and edema in the genitals and pelvic organs stimulate sensory receptors within these organs, which in turn transmit messages to the conscious brain where they are usually interpreted as pleasurable sensations. When sexual stimulation is continued, vasocongestion may increase until it is released by orgasm, or it may quietly fade away.

Myotonia

The second physiological change associated with the excitement/plateau stage is **myotonia**, an increase of tension in the muscles associated with the genitals and other body structures. Like vasocongestion, myotonia may increase to a peak before being released in orgasm, or it may simply fade away.

Excitement

Now and then, in the ebb and flow of daily erotic stimuli, either our conscious desires or a purely physical stimulation becomes intense enough to trigger a series of reflexive responses in the spinal cord's erection center. These nerve centers then send messages to sex organs, increasing the flow of blood into the sexual organs while reducing the outflow.

In females, erection of the clitoris increases its size two to three times that of the resting state (Figures 7.2a and 7.3a). Erection also occurs in the two elongated masses of erectile tissue, the vestibular bulbs, which lie underneath the bulbocavernosus muscles. The vestibular bulbs are connected at their anterior ends to the clitoris and extend back around the entrance of the vagina. Erection of the vestibular bulbs and the strength of the pubococcygeal muscles work together to determine the size, tightness, and feel of the vaginal canal for both partners during intercourse. The major labia flatten and separate while the minor labia increase two to three times in size and deepen in color.

(a) The Erect Clitoris

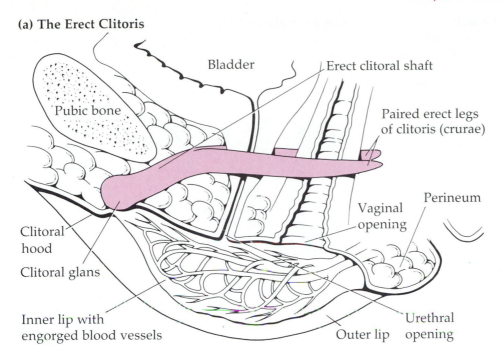

Bladder
Erect clitoral shaft
Pubic bone
Paired erect legs
of clitoris (crurae)
Perineum
Vaginal
opening
Clitoral
hood
Clitoral glans
Inner lip with
engorged blood vessels
Urethral
opening
Outer lip

(b) The Erect Penis

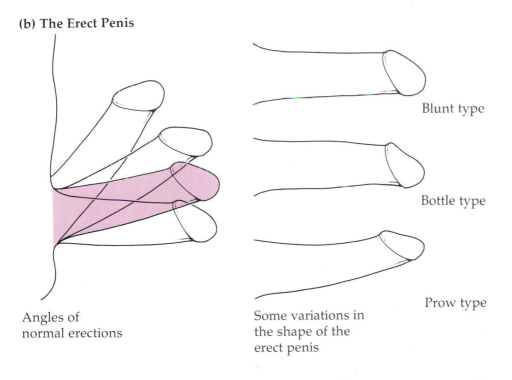

Blunt type

Bottle type

Prow type

Angles of
normal erections

Some variations in
the shape of the
erect penis

Figure 7.2. Erection in Males and Females. *(a) The erect clitoris, showing the clitoral glans, shaft, and crurae or paired legs. (See Figure 6.5b for a view of the non-erect clitoris.) (b) In normal, healthy men, both the angle and the appearance of the erect penis may vary greatly. All the variations shown here, and others in addition, are within the normal range (Zaviacic 1990).*

Figure 7.3a. Excitement Stage: Female.

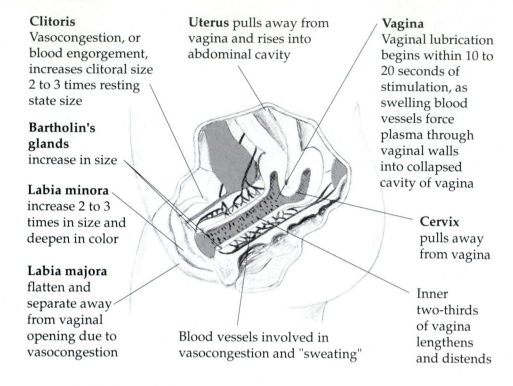

Clitoris
Vasocongestion, or blood engorgement, increases clitoral size 2 to 3 times resting state size

Bartholin's glands
increase in size

Labia minora
increase 2 to 3 times in size and deepen in color

Labia majora
flatten and separate away from vaginal opening due to vasocongestion

Uterus pulls away from vagina and rises into abdominal cavity

Vagina
Vaginal lubrication begins within 10 to 20 seconds of stimulation, as swelling blood vessels force plasma through vaginal walls into collapsed cavity of vagina

Cervix
pulls away from vagina

Inner two-thirds of vagina lengthens and distends

Blood vessels involved in vasocongestion and "sweating"

Detail of Vaginal Sweating

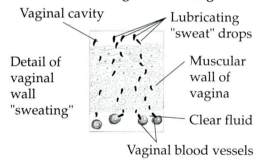

Vaginal cavity

Lubricating "sweat" drops

Detail of vaginal wall "sweating"

Muscular wall of vagina

Clear fluid

Vaginal blood vessels

MALE PARALLELS:
Vasocongestion causes erection of penis; scrotum elevates; testes may increase in size; Cowper's glands may produce some secretion.

In females, vasocongestion also causes **vaginal lubrication** as blood vessels in the vaginal walls and the major and minor labia expand with an increased blood flow. The surrounding tissue swells as fluid leaves the blood vessels and pushes between the tissue cells. In the vaginal walls, vasocongestion forces plasma out of the blood vessels and between the cells of the vaginal walls to the surface of the vagina. This type of "sweating" or vaginal lubrication prepares the vaginal canal for sexual intercourse. Even though moistening of the vaginal wall may begin 10 to 30 seconds after the start of sexual stimulation, most women do not become aware of this reaction, or of clitoral erection, until it is pronounced. The lubricating fluid is clear, slippery, and has a mild, natural scent. Its alkaline character helps neutralize the normal vaginal secretions whose acidic character reduce the risk of microbial infections reaching the internal organs through the vaginal canal. If penetration is attempted before the vagina is sufficiently lubricated, the woman may experience some pain. Lubrication

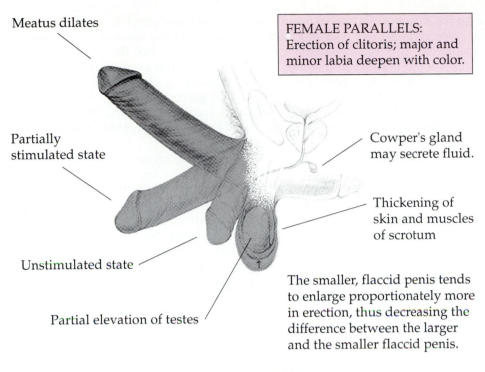

Meatus dilates

Partially
stimulated state

Unstimulated state

Partial elevation of testes

FEMALE PARALLELS:
Erection of clitoris; major and
minor labia deepen with color.

Figure 7.3b. Excitement Stage: Male.

Cowper's gland
may secrete fluid.

Thickening of
skin and muscles
of scrotum

The smaller, flaccid penis tends
to enlarge proportionately more
in erection, thus decreasing the
difference between the larger
and the smaller flaccid penis.

Cross section through
shaft of penis: Arteries
carrying blood into penis
dilate with sexual stimu-
lation, allowing blood to
fill spongy and cavernous
tissue and constricting three
veins carrying blood out of
penis. This vasocongestion
results in penile erection.

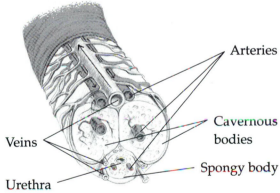

Arteries

Veins

Urethra

Cavernous
bodies

Spongy body

can be inhibited by a number of extraneous factors such as the woman's emotional state, fear, anxiety, health, and alcohol usage.

The female breasts also become engorged with blood, swelling and becoming more sensitive. This is more pronounced in women who have not nursed an infant. Wherever vasocongestion occurs, it stimulates sensory receptors within these organs, which in turn transmit messages to the conscious brain where they are interpreted as pleasurable sensations. Pleasurable sensations from swelling of the genitals, pelvic organs, and vaginal bulb increase as a woman approaches the tension release of orgasm.

Males quickly become aware of vasocongestion because the resulting erection of the penis is obvious (Figures 7.2b and 7.3b). **Erection** is not an all-or-nothing phenomenon. The cavities of the corpora cavernosa and corpus spongiosum do not fill instantly. Getting an erection is much like blowing up a balloon and letting a little air escape each time you take a breath to add more air to the balloon. The nerve impulses controlling the blood flow in and out of the three corpora may wax and wane depending on the intensity of the sexual stimulation. This causes fluctuations in the erection until the stimulation becomes intense enough to maintain a full erection. Men experience varying degrees of penile erection every day. It can be induced by physical exertions, while asleep, or at any time. For young men, a full erection may develop within 10 or 20 seconds. In older men erection usually comes slower and may not be as hard. Vasocongestion also causes the testes to swell and become tender to the touch.

Sexual stimulation also results in muscle tension, myotonia, in various parts of the body. In both women and men, this muscular tension increases in the voluntary muscles of the pelvic area, in the ischiocavernosa, transverse perineal, bulbocavernosa, and the levator ani, whose major portion is known as the pubococcygeal or PC muscles. Myotonia also affects the involuntary muscles associated with the uterus, seminal vesicles, and prostate. This muscle tension starts elevating the uterus into the abdominal cavity, and begins stretching the inner two-thirds of the vagina to form the seminal pool, which develops later in plateau stage. The release of myotonic tension in these muscles is an important aspect of orgasm (Figure 7.4). Myotonia also leads to an increase in the heart rate and blood pressure as the body compensates for the demands of increased blood flow and vasocongestion.

In men, the effects of myotonia during the excitement phase are most obvious in the scrotum where the dartos muscles tense, elevating the testes. The scrotal skin darkens in color. The Cowper's gland may exude a little alkaline secretion. Sexual excitement triggers nipple erection in about 60% of men. Nipple erection can occur in both men and women even when the breasts are not involved in love play and caressing. Figure 7.3 and Tables 7.1 and 7.2 summarize the results of vasocongestion and myotonia during the excitement stage for males and females.

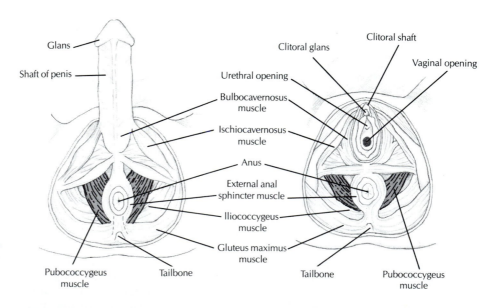

Figure 7-4. The Muscles of the Pelvic Floor. *Shown here are the pubococcygeal muscle and other muscles that surround the sexual organs and form the floor of the pelvic cavity.*

Glans

Shaft of penis

Pubococcygeus muscle

Tailbone

Pelvic Floor Muscles in Male

Clitoral glans

Clitoral shaft

Vaginal opening

Urethral opening

Bulbocavernosus muscle

Ischiocavernosus muscle

Anus

External anal sphincter muscle

Iliococcygeus muscle

Gluteus maximus muscle

Tailbone

Pubococcygeus muscle

Pelvic Floor Muscles in Female

Plateau

As vasocongestion and myotonia increase with continued sexual stimulation during the plateau phase in women, several changes occur in the internal organs (Figure 7.5). The increasing vasocongestion in the vestibular bulbs and increas-

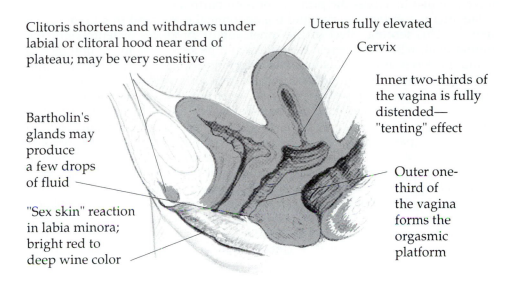

Clitoris shortens and withdraws under labial or clitoral hood near end of plateau; may be very sensitive

Bartholin's glands may produce a few drops of fluid

"Sex skin" reaction in labia minora; bright red to deep wine color

Uterus fully elevated

Cervix

Inner two-thirds of the vagina is fully distended— "tenting" effect

Outer one-third of the vagina forms the orgasmic platform

Figure 7.5a. Plateau Stage: Female.

MALE PARALLELS: Slight increase in coronal engorgement; deepening of reddish-purple color of glans; erection more stable; enlargement of testes by 50% with continued elevation and thickening of scrotum; Cowper's glands become active in many men.

FEMALE PARALLELS: Withdrawal of clitoris; sex skin coloring in minor labia; orgasmic platform; vaginal lubrication slows; uterus elevates; Bartholin's glands secrete.

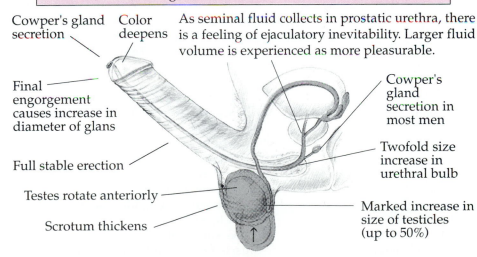

Cowper's gland secretion

Color deepens

As seminal fluid collects in prostatic urethra, there is a feeling of ejaculatory inevitability. Larger fluid volume is experienced as more pleasurable.

Final engorgement causes increase in diameter of glans

Full stable erection

Testes rotate anteriorly

Scrotum thickens

Cowper's gland secretion in most men

Twofold size increase in urethral bulb

Marked increase in size of testicles (up to 50%)

Testes fully elevated (orgasm never occurs without elevated testes)

Figure 7.5b. Plateau Stage: Male.

ing myotonia in the PC muscles around the vaginal entrance result in a swelling of the outer third of the vaginal barrel called the **orgasmic platform**. Because the orgasmic platform grips the penis during intercourse, it can provide stimulation to the man, facilitating orgasm and ejaculation. The strength of myotonia and voluntary contractions of the PC muscles create a tight fit for the penis in the vagina that increases the pleasure of both partners.

The uterus continues to rise into the abdominal cavity and the inner vagina expands. This **tenting** effect in the inner vagina produces a depression, the **seminal pool**, where the semen can collect and be kept close to the entrance to the uterine cervix after ejaculation. The clitoris and labia become fully erect and the labia separate. The minor labia become pink or bright red in women who have not given birth, and a more intense wine red color in women who have given birth. This change, known as **sex skin,** is a sign of impending orgasm. In women who have not given birth, the major labia flatten, thin out, and are more widely separated. In women who have given birth, the major labia become engorged, doubling or tripling in size. Vaginal lubrication decreases during the plateau phase. If sex play is too prolonged, it may even stop altogether, leaving the vagina without the desired lubrication for intercourse.

During the plateau phase, the entire clitoris retracts beneath the clitoral hood formed by the junction of the minor labia, losing about half the erection it had during the excitement phase and reemerging after orgasm. This withdrawal may protect the delicate and sensitive clitoris from overstimulation during penile thrusting and is not a sign the woman has lost her interest or desire for sexual intercourse.

Table 7.2.   Genital Changes in Men and Women During the Sexual Response Cycle

In addition to the general body changes men and women share during their sexual response cycles, they experience some parallel differences outlined here.

Excitement Phase	
Male	**Female**
VASOCONGESTION **Penis:** Flaccid to erect **Testes:** Swell **Nipples:** May erect	**Clitoris:** Flaccid to erect **Major Labia:** Flatten and move apart **Minor Labia:** Increase in size **Vagina:** Lubrication; inner two-thirds expands and lengthens **Uterus:** Elevates **Bartholin's Glands:** Secrete lubricant **G spot:** Enlarges
MYOTONIA General increase in pelvic muscle tension in both men and women.	

Table 7.2. continued

Plateau Phase	
Male	**Female**
VASOCONGESTION **Penis:** Glans size increases, full erection **Testes:** Swell, elevate, and rotate **Cowper's glands:** Secrete lubricant	**Clitoris:** May retract under clitoral hood **Minor Labia:** Increase 2–3 times in size with vivid color change **Vagina:**—Outer third swells and narrows, forming orgasmic platform —Inner two-thirds widens and deepens: tenting —Lubrication slows **Uterus:** Elevates **Areola:** Swells around erect nipple

MYOTONIA **General muscle tension**, particularly heart and respiratory rates and blood pressure, continue to increase in both men and women.

Orgasmic Phase	
Male	**Female**

VASOCONGESTION dissipates as muscle tension is released.

MYOTONIA	
Emission phase: **Vas deferens, seminal vesicles, ejaculatory ducts, and prostate:** Contractions build up pressure with feeling of ejaculatory inevitability *Propulsion phase:* **Outer urethral sphincter:** Opens **Prostate and muscles around the urethra:** Contract to propel the semen out.	**Vagina:** Muscle contraction in orgasmic platform **Uterus:** Rhythmic contractions **Pubococcygeal muscles:** Rhythmic contractions **Anal sphincter:** Rhythmic contractions **Ejaculation:** In about 10% of women

MYOTONIA **General muscle tension**, and specifically heart and respiratory rates and blood pressure, reach their peak in both men and women.

Resolution Phase	
Male	**Female**
Reversal of all vasocongestion and myotonic buildup, followed by a **refractory period** of variable duration.	Reversal of all vasocongestion and myotonic buildup, with the possibility of multiple orgasms and without a refractory period.

In males, during the plateau stage, the penis reaches a full, stable erection with the glans at its largest (Figure 7.5b). The testes swell, increasing about 50% in size. The congestion can become uncomfortable if sexual arousal is prolonged and its tension is not relieved by an orgasm. If orgasm does not follow, this congestion slowly subsides when sexual stimulation is stopped. During the plateau phase, the testes also elevate fully and rotate up against the body. This elevation, like sex skin in women, is a reliable sign of impending orgasm. Vasocongestion doubles the size of the urethral bulb, and muscle pressure on the Cowper's glands cause some of their secretions to seep through the urethra. Tension increases in both the voluntary and involuntary muscles of the body.

In both sexes, the plateau stage brings a slight rise in heart rate and blood pressure. Respiratory rate may start to rise. Some men and women experience a reddening of the skin, known as **sex flush**, as a result of vasocongestion, particularly in the skin of the neck and chest. Table 7.1 summarizes the results of vasocongestion and myotonia during the plateau stage.

The Orgasm Phase (3)

In terms of the physiological buildup and explosive discharge of tension, Kinsey, a meticulous biologist, could find only one parallel for a sexual orgasm, a hearty sneeze (1953:631). But there are two major differences between a sneeze and an orgasm. A sneeze is a localized event whereas a sexual orgasm involves the whole body. An orgasm may be as brief as a sneeze, but it is certainly much more pleasurable. In both men and women, an **orgasm** consists of a dozen or more rhythmic muscle contractions that affect all the sexual organs and the whole body (Figure 7.6). Muscles all over the body, but especially in the pelvic area, contract rhythmically at 0.8-second intervals, with three or four rapid and intense contractions followed by several slower and milder contractions. Women commonly report experiencing more intense orgasms with more frequent and stronger muscle contractions in the orgasmic platform. If a woman's sexual excitement is unusually intense, she may also experience several seconds of spastic or nonrhythmic contractions in the orgasmic platform before the rhythmic contractions take over.

The length of an orgasm has some variability. Male orgasms usually last about 10 to 30 seconds. Clinical monitoring of orgasm in women suggest the muscle contractions in female orgasms last between 13 and 51 seconds, although the same women reported their subjective perceptions of orgasms lasting between 7 and 107 seconds (Bohlen et al. 1982). Masters and Johnson have reported two to four orgasmic contractions in the anal sphincter of men; a more recent study found an average of 17 anal sphincter contractions occurring during the half minute of male orgasm (Bohlen et al. 1982). Another curious aspect of the orgasmic response is the carpopedal reflex. During orgasm, men and women sometimes experience a spastic contraction of the voluntary muscles of the hands and feet. The thumbs and big toes stiffen and straighten while the fingers and other toes bend upward.

In general, one might say that an orgasm is an orgasm, regardless of whether it is achieved by masturbation, oral sex, or intercourse, and whether it is a male or a female experiencing this intensely pleasurable release of erotic tension. But

(a) General Orgasmic Responses

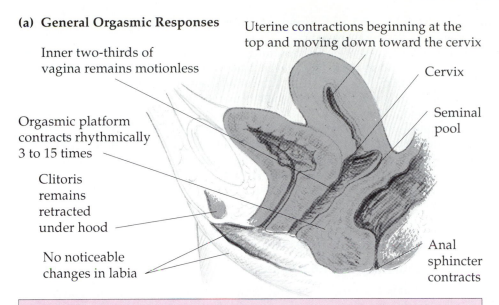

Inner two-thirds of vagina remains motionless

Uterine contractions beginning at the top and moving down toward the cervix

Cervix

Orgasmic platform contracts rhythmically 3 to 15 times

Seminal pool

Clitoris remains retracted under hood

No noticeable changes in labia

Anal sphincter contracts

MALE PARALLELS:
2 to 3 intense contractions to expel semen at 0.8-second intervals, followed by weaker and slower contractions; anal sphincter also contracts.

(b) Tenting and A-Frame Orgasms

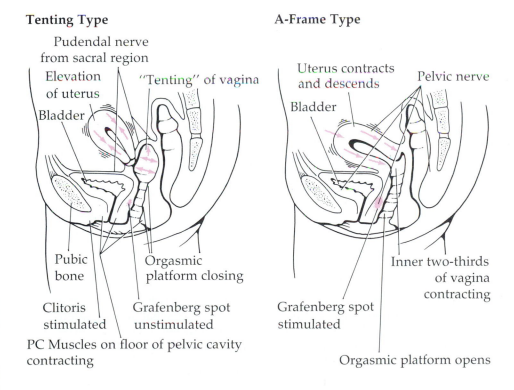

Tenting Type

Pudendal nerve from sacral region

Elevation of uterus

"Tenting" of vagina

Bladder

Pubic bone

Orgasmic platform closing

Clitoris stimulated

Grafenberg spot unstimulated

PC Muscles on floor of pelvic cavity contracting

A-Frame Type

Uterus contracts and descends

Pelvic nerve

Bladder

Inner two-thirds of vagina contracting

Grafenberg spot stimulated

Orgasmic platform opens

Figure 7.6 Orgasm Stage: Female. *(a) General orgasmic responses. (b) Tenting and A-Frame Orgasms. In the* tenting *type of orgasmic response,* stimulation of the clitoris passes by way of the pudendal nerve to the sacral region of the spinal cord. The buildup and discharge of myotonia occurs in the pubococcygeal muscles and the orgasmic platform closes.

In the A-Frame *or* uterine orgasm, *stimulation of the Grafenberg spot sends impulses along the pelvic nerve to the spinal reflex. The buildup and discharge of myotonia occurs in the deeper muscles of the vagina with the uterus contracting and pushing down and the orgasmic platform opening.*

A blended type of orgasm may combine these two types of stimuli and orgasm.

there are also intriguing and important differences, especially in the ways men and women experience orgasm.

Men usually have an **ejaculation** and expel semen as part of their orgasm. Before puberty and in their later years, however, males do experience orgasm without ejaculation. Men may also occasionally not ejaculate during intercourse because of fatigue or other extraneous reasons, even though they experience what they feel is an orgasm.

About one-third of American women report reaching orgasm as a result of vaginal intercourse without any other stimulation. For most women, direct clitoral stimulation during love play can trigger orgasm. For other women, direct clitoral orgasm may be painful. Some women experience orgasm as a result of stimulating a region in the vagina known as the Grafenberg spot. Some of these women may also expel fluid, although not with the regularity of men.

Orgasmic Variations in Women

Sequential and/or Multiple Orgasms

In the early 1900s Havelock Ellis and Sigmund Freud had trouble convincing their contemporaries that women experience much the same kind of sexual arousal and orgasm as men. Fifty years later, Kinsey found that 15% of the nearly 6,000 women he questioned claimed they occasionally experienced several orgasms during the same sexual encounter. Masters and Johnson confirmed this claim with laboratory studies showing that multiple female orgasm is a reality. After an initial orgasm, a woman may return to the plateau level and, with further stimulation, experience a second, third, or even more orgasms (Figure 7.6).

Some women can have *sequential orgasms*, a series of orgasms with short breaks in between. Rarer is the ability of a woman to have *multiple orgasms* with no break in between while the stimulation is continued. Some women are happy with a single orgasm during intercourse, but prefer having multiple orgasms when they masturbate, or vice versa. A woman may find that she is multi-orgasmic with one partner or in one situation, but has only one orgasm with a second partner or in a different situation. The sensitivity of the clitoris, which varies from woman to woman, is also a factor in what a woman prefers. For some women, being close, cuddling, and being emotionally satisfied is more important than having an orgasm. Much of the character of a woman's orgasmic response depends on her past experiences and her relationship with her partner. Women are more likely to experience multiple orgasms during masturbation than they are during intercourse, probably because masturbation makes it easier for them to continue sexual stimulation with fewer distractions, and they experience a greater comfort in using fantasies to enhance the experience than is possible when they are interacting with a partner.

Different Types of Female Orgasms

Freud used a value judgment in drawing a distinction between a "mature female orgasm" that resulted from vaginal intercourse and what he considered an "immature orgasm" achieved by clitoral stimulation. His Victorian contemporaries found this distinction quite acceptable because it emphasized the undesirable nature of masturbation and what they believed was the natural superiority of vaginal intercourse. In the 1960s Masters and Johnson challenged Freud's view, reporting no difference between the orgasms achieved through vaginal and clitoral stimulation. In fact, they argued from their clinical studies that vaginal stimulation in reality involved indirect stimulation of the clitoris and that all orgasms resulted from clitoral stimulation.

In resolving the controversies over different kinds of female orgasm popular since the time of Freud, Masters and Johnson (1966) helped end the tyranny of the "mature" vaginal orgasm. They legitimized women's personal experience with the clitoral orgasm and opened the way to a social acceptance of female masturbation. But there is a risk of authority, orthodoxy, and values in the Masters and Johnson model, just as there was with Freud or any other model that is used to "define" the "proper sexuality" for either females or males.

More recent studies suggest that women may indeed experience two main kinds of orgasm, one triggered as Freud suggested by clitoral and the other by vaginal stimulation. In 1972 Singer and Singer described three types of female orgasm. They called the orgasm Masters and Johnson described a *vulval orgasm* because it was characterized by involuntary rhythmic contractions of the vaginal entrance. A second kind of orgasm, the *uterine orgasm*, is distinguished by repeated displacement of the uterus during intercourse. Singer and Singer reported a third type, a *blended orgasm*, which combined the vulval and uterine orgasms.

Ladas, Whipple, and Perry (1982) suggest that we view female orgasm as a continuum. At one end of the spectrum would be the orgasm described by Masters and Johnson. In this **tenting orgasm**, the clitoris is the main focus of erotosexual stimulation leading to elevation or "tenting" of the uterus in the plateau phase (Figure 7.6b). Sensations from the stimulation of the clitoris travel by way of the pudendal nerve back to the spinal reflex center, which then discharges the myotonic tension that has built up in the pelvic muscles and in the orgasmic platform. At the other end of the spectrum would be the **A-frame orgasm**. This orgasm is triggered by stimulation of the Grafenberg spot, a sensitive region in the anterior wall of the vagina (see next paragraph). The erotosexual sensations from the Grafenberg spot travel along the pelvic nerve to the orgasm reflex center in the spinal cord. In the A-frame orgasm, the uterus contracts and descends, and the orgasmic platform remains relaxed. Subjective and clinical reports suggest tenting or clitoral orgasms are briefer but more intense than A-frame orgasms, which build up slower and have more subdued peaks. Tenting or clitoral orgasms subside quickly but can be part of a multiorgasmic experience; A-frame orgasms result in a deeper and fuller satisfaction and are unlikely to be multiple (Bentler & Peeler 1979; Fisher 1973; Ladas et al. 1982). A **blended orgasm** would combine the A-frame and tenting orgasms.

The **Grafenberg spot** is located in the front wall of the vagina, just under the bladder, an inch or two into the vaginal canal and about halfway between the back of the pubic bone and the front of the cervix. It varies in size from smaller than a dime to larger than a half dollar. Tiny and soft before stimulation, the spot swells and becomes more defined when stimulated. A woman's common first reaction to stimulation is a strong urge to urinate. This initial reaction is quickly replaced by a strong and distinctly sexual pleasure. At first, reports of the Grafenberg or G spot were greeted with outright incredulity and even ridicule. However, two studies have collaborated the existence of prostate-like glandular tissue in the autopsies of 60 females (Heath 1984; Mallon 1984).

Female Ejaculation

Over 200 years ago, the Dutch embryologist Reinier de Graaf described some small glands and ducts surrounding the urethra in women. These glands, de Graaf reported, produced a clear fluid "which makes women more libidinous with its pungency and saltiness." In the early 1900s, T. E. Van de Velde, reported that:

> . . . the majority of laymen believe that something is forcibly squirted or expelled from the woman's body in orgasm, and should so happen normally, as in the man's case. . . . I cannot venture to decide whether it should so happen, according to natural law. There is no doubt that it does happen to some women. But whether these are a majority or minority, I am unable to determine.
>
> *(cited by Sevely & Bennett 1978)*

Today, these tiny glands located just inside the urethral opening are known as the periurethral or Skene's glands. Embryologically, they develop from the same tissue as the male prostate. Ladas, Whipple, and Perry (1982) and other researchers suggest that the phenomenon of **female ejaculation** reported by Van de Velde is experienced by about 10% of women and is triggered by stimulation of the Grafenberg spot. In female ejaculation, the fluid may dribble out of the urethra at orgasm. It may also be ejaculated with some force, sometimes in a "gushing stream." According to Addiego and colleagues who observed a woman's husband massage her Grafenberg spot with his fingers,

> On none of these occasions did stimulation of the clitoris, direct or otherwise, appear to occur. Orgasmic expulsions occurred after less than a minute of stimulation; they were separated in a multiorgasmic series by similarly brief periods of time. The urethral area was clearly exposed in bright light, and there was absolutely no doubt that the liquid was expelled from the urethral opening. Sometimes it exuded from the urethra. At other times it was expelled from one to a few centimeters. On one observed occasion, expulsion was of sufficient force to create a series of wet spots covering a distance of more than a meter.
>
> *(Addiego et al. 1981:17)*

The nature of the fluid expelled from the urethra is, obviously, an important question. Addiego et al. (1981) and Belzer et al. (1984) have reported finding the enzyme prostatic acid phosphatase (AP) in samples of female ejaculation. However, the AP enzyme found in female ejaculate appears to be slightly different in structure from that produced by the male prostate. The ejaculate also contained very little urea, a characteristic component in urine. Goldberg et al. (1983), however, found no difference between their samples of female ejaculate and urine. Along with this unresolved issue, there are unanswered questions about where the ejaculate is stored before its release, how common the experience is among women, and what the connection is between the Grafenberg spot and female ejaculation.

Besides the Grafenberg spot, other factors related to female ejaculation include the strength of the woman's internal muscle contractions and the development and arrangement of the glands. Ladas, Whipple, and Perry (1982) report that voluntary contractions of the pubococcygeal or PC muscles are 49% stronger in women who ejaculate than in those who do not. Their uterine muscle contractions were 136% stronger. There is a growing opinion that strong pubococcygeal muscles and good control over them can facilitate and intensify the orgasmic experience, with or without sexual intercourse (Figure 7.4).

A woman can locate her Grafenberg spot using her own fingers if she has long fingers, a very flexible wrist, and short vagina (Figure 7.7). Otherwise, it is more practical to let a partner identify this region. This can be done by keeping the finger(s) on the upper or ventral surface of the vagina. Reach beyond the pubic bone, and press gently upward, sliding the finger(s) around until the most sensitive area is located. Then gently stroke the spot until it begins to swell. Usually the partner will need two fingers inserted deeply into the vagina (Heath 1984:205). As it swells, an initial response of wanting to urinate gives way quickly to intensely erotic and pleasurable sensations.

The initial response of wanting to urinate, or the fact that they once ejaculated and thought they had urinated, may be the reason some women hold back on their sexual responses. Without understanding this normal part of their

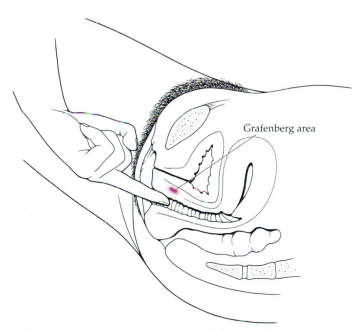

Grafenberg area

Figure 7.7. Finding the G Spot. *A woman may find the Grafenberg area or spot by inserting her middle finger into the vagina and pressing toward the pubic bone. When the area is stimulated with the finger, it may be easier to detect the G spot on the anterior vaginal wall.*

sexual response, women may find the initial feeling of wanting to urinate too embarrassing and resist any further stimulation. Understanding this stimulation and response is an important element in our growing understanding of female sexuality and our sexual pleasuring.

In some positions, particularly the male-above or so-called missionary position, the thrusting of the penis in the vagina does not stimulate the G spot. Rear entry may facilitate G spot stimulation during intercourse.

Orgasmic Variations in Men

A Two-Stage Orgasm

In men, the involuntary rhythmic contractions of orgasm begin when sexual arousal reaches a peak that triggers a reflexive, pleasurable release of the neuromuscular tension built up during the excitement/plateau phase. In men, orgasm appears to remain concentrated in the genital region. Ejaculation of seminal fluid may accompany male orgasm, but it is a distinct phenomenon. As orgasm approaches, rhythmic contractions start in the prostate gland, seminal vesicles, and the surrounding muscles. Before the start of orgasm, the two urethral sphincters, one above the prostate where the urethra leaves the urinary bladder and the other at the bottom of the prostate where the urethra enters the base of the penis, remain closed. This traps the seminal fluid so that when the prostate and surrounding muscles begin contracting, the pressure in the seminal fluid rises. This is the **emission phase** of male ejaculation (Figure 7.8).

As the pressure of the seminal fluid in the ejaculatory duct and urethral bulb of the prostate increases, the man gets a feeling that ejaulation is inevitable. During the **propulsion phase** of ejaculation, the outer urethral sphincter opens. Contractions in the penile shaft and throughout the pelvic area, at 0.8-second intervals, aid the ejaculation of seminal fluid. Throughout sexual arousal, erection, and orgasm, the inner urethral sphincter remains closed, preventing any leakage of urine or retrograde ejaculation.

Retrograde Ejaculation

Like prepubertal boys who experience a dry orgasm and older men with a decreased ejaculation, men in their sexual prime may also experience orgasm without a visible ejaculation. This does not mean they do not ejaculate. Men may be taking medication or have an organic condition that alters the nervous control over the two urethral valves so crucial in emission and ejaculation. In this case, the inner sphincter, leading from the prostatic urethra to the bladder, may open after the buildup of seminal fluid pressure during the emission phase, allowing for a retrograde ejaculation of the semen into the bladder. This seminal fluid is harmless and is released in the next urination.

Multiorgasmic Men

A number of the 5,300 men surveyed by Kinsey and his associates (1948) reported they were capable of several orgasms and ejaculations during a single sexual encounter. Kinsey also found the number of men reporting this experience declined from 15% to 20% of males in their teens and twenties to only 3% after age 60. As a neuromuscular discharge, orgasm can be physiologically and psychologically distinguished from ejaculation in both men and women. In ancient India and China, where sexual intercourse was viewed as a path to the

(a) **Emission phase** with a buildup of pressure caused by seminal fluid —
the result of early contractions of internal sexual organs. Semen
concentrates in urethral bulb of prostate.

Figure 7.8. Orgasm
Stage: Male. *The Emis-
sion and Propulsion
Stages of Ejaculation.*

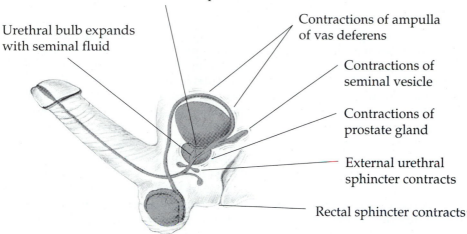

Internal urethral sphincter contracts

Contractions of ampulla
of vas deferens

Urethral bulb expands
with seminal fluid

Contractions of
seminal vesicle

Contractions of
prostate gland

External urethral
sphincter contracts

Rectal sphincter contracts

(b) **Propulsion phase** with expulsion of seminal fluid. External urethral
sphincter opens. Penile urethra and muscles around base of penis contract:
2 to 3 intense contractions at intervals of 0.8 seconds followed by weaker,
slower contractions.

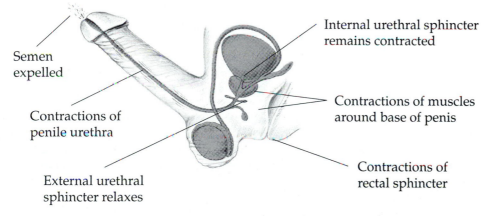

Internal urethral sphincter
remains contracted

Semen
expelled

Contractions of muscles
around base of penis

Contractions of
penile urethra

Contractions of
rectal sphincter

External urethral
sphincter relaxes

FEMALE PARALLELS:
Orgasmic platform; uterus and rectal sphincter contract at
0.8-second intervals, then weaker and slower contractions.

cosmic and divinity, yoga practices that prolonged intercourse without ejaculation were popular. Using breathing control, meditation, postures, and finger
pressure, men were able to prolong intercourse for hours and experience several
orgasms without ejaculation. The Oneida Community, mentioned in Chapter

HIGHLIGHT BOX 7.1.
ONE MALE'S EXPERIENCE
WITH BEING MULTIORGASMIC

Sam was a bright 10-year-old exploring his own body when he first learned the pleasure of orgasm. Of course, he didn't ejaculate. He was too young for that. But over and over again he reached a peak of enjoyment such as he had never felt in any other form of play. And it was so easy! All he had to do was continue stimulating his penis after the first intense reaction, and another followed soon after.

When he was eleven and a half he had his first orgasmic ejaculation. It, like the peaks of sexual excitement he had reached before, was very exciting. But it changed things as well. Somehow, he had difficulty going on to the second or third "peak" as he had done before. He continued stimulation, as he had in the past, and did, at last, reach an orgasm.

But it was not as satisfying as the second one had been in the past.

From then on, when he masturbated, he deliberately tried to avoid ejaculation the first time. It was not an easy task, but he persisted until, to his intense pleasure, he discovered that he could once more experience the high peaks to which he had become accustomed.

Sam has been multiorgasmic for twenty years. To him, it is natural. He was surprised when he heard us speak, that other men did not share his talent. He can have a single orgasm, if he chooses, when he hasn't enough time to enjoy more. He finds this ability useful for those times when he and his partner have to leave for work or an appointment but wish to share sex before they separate for the day.

Source: William Hartman and Marilyn Fithian, *Any Man Can*. New York: St. Martin's Press, 1984, pp. 16–17.

1, adopted this Tantric yoga practice of Karezza or Maithuna as part of its practice of group marriage.

Although Masters, Johnson, and Kolodny (1988:94) express some scepticism about multiple orgasm in men, even they admit ". . . it does appear that at least a few men have the capacity to have multiple orgasms before a true refractory period sets in, although it should be stressed that this does not happen once ejaculation has occurred." Their statement raises a question about the self-reported cases of multiple orgasm with ejaculation in the 1948 Kinsey report. Robbins and Jensen (1978), Katchadourian (1985:71), and Crooks and Bauer (1987:198) accept the possibility that men can learn to have multiple orgasms but without ejaculating with each orgasm.

The most extensive study of male multiorgasm is that of Hartman and Fithian whose 15 years research with thousands of subjects led to their book *Any Man Can* (1984). (See Highlight Box 7.1.) Although still controversial, the knowledge that men may experience multiple orgasm may legitimize an experience many men have but are unwilling at present to admit because they think it is abnormal. If this is the case—as seems to be happening with studies of orgasm variety and female ejaculation, future studies may reveal a greater similarity than we presently suspect between male and female ejaculation and between the percentages of men and women experiencing multiple orgasm.

Exercising the Pubococcygeal Muscles

Some sex researchers and therapists believe women and men can add to the pleasure of their orgasms by exercising their pubococcygeal or PC muscles.

For women three steps are recommended. To begin, you need to locate and identify your feeling of contracting the PC muscles. Insert two fingers into the vaginal opening and contract the muscles at the opening. You can feel these muscles squeeze your fingers if you are controlling the right muscles. Remove your fingers and contract the same muscles, for 3 seconds. Relax. Then repeat this contraction 10 times. Once you have identified the PC muscles and can contract them at will, you can exercise the PC muscles almost anywhere. Just quickly contract and release the muscles 10 to 25 times. Simply pretend you want to stop the flow of urine. The PC muscles are involved in stopping the flow of urine during urination.

Another exercise with the PC muscles can enhance your control. Imagine you are drawing something into your vagina using these muscles. Can you feel the muscles working? Repeating these exercises regularly will give you much better control over the muscles involved in orgasm and enhance your pleasure responses.

Men can easily exercise their PC muscles and achieve the same enhancement by alternately contracting and relaxing the muscles that control the flow of urine. As Figure 7.4 shows, the PC muscles in men and women are very similar in their location and function. Couples can exercise the PC muscles during love play and intercourse with a definite increase in their enjoyment and pleasure. The best position for this is with the woman sitting above the man who is lying on his back. In this position the man can contract his PC muscles and the woman can answer his contractions with her own (Perry and Whipple 1981a, 1981b).

As with any exercises, the PC muscles must be exercised for several weeks before a noticeable change occurs in their tone.

The Resolution Stage (4)

In the fourth stage, **resolution**, the clitoris and penis lose about half their fully erect size within 5 to 10 seconds after the end of orgasm (Figure 7.9). The labia lose their color, and vasocongestion in the orgasmic platform disappears in 10 to 15 seconds. Some sweating may occur as vasocongestion in the skin dissipates. Following these immediate responses to orgasm, all the organs and body parts affected by myotonia and vasocongestion slowly return to their resting state. The clitoris may take 5 to 30 minutes and the inner vagina and breasts 5 to 10 minutes to return fully to their resting condition. The cervix drops into the seminal pool as the uterus drops back into its normal position in the pelvis. The testes lose their vasocongestion and the dartos muscles of the scrotum relax.

You can use Table 7.2 to compare the changes in the genitals of females and males that come with vasocongestion and myotonia during the four stages of the sexual response cycle.

As noted earlier, the **refractory phase** most men experience immediately after orgasm may be more the product of ejaculation than orgasm. During the refractory phase no amount of sex play or stimulation can retrigger sexual arousal and erection. At times the refractory period may be very short, though it generally lengthens with aging.

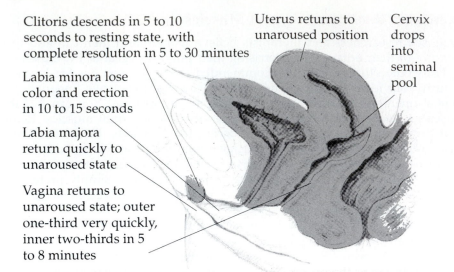

Clitoris descends in 5 to 10 seconds to resting state, with complete resolution in 5 to 30 minutes

Labia minora lose color and erection in 10 to 15 seconds

Labia majora return quickly to unaroused state

Vagina returns to unaroused state; outer one-third very quickly, inner two-thirds in 5 to 8 minutes

Uterus returns to unaroused position

Cervix drops into seminal pool

Figure 7.9a. Resolution Stage: Female.

MALE PARALLELS: Loss of penile erection in two stages, 50% decrease in vasocongestion within first minute followed by full return to resting state over several minutes; testes return to resting state; scrotum relaxes.

FEMALE PARALLELS: Two-stage return of clitoris to resting condition; labia return to resting state and lose their intense color.

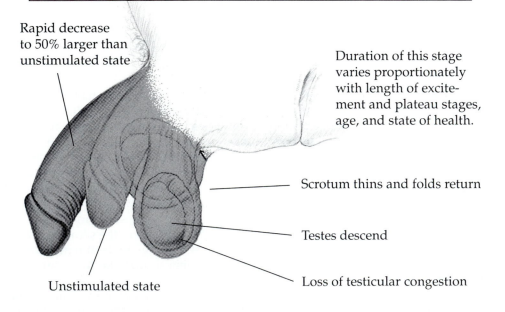

Rapid decrease to 50% larger than unstimulated state

Duration of this stage varies proportionately with length of excitement and plateau stages, age, and state of health.

Scrotum thins and folds return

Testes descend

Figure 7.9b. Resolution Stage: Male.

Unstimulated state

Loss of testicular congestion

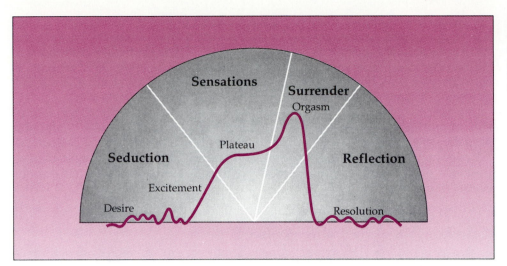

Figure 7.10. *The Erotic Stimulus Pathway Model of David M. Reed, integrating both psychological and physiological changes.*

An Integrated Psychophysiological Model

When Masters and Johnson described human sexual response in terms of excitement/plateau, orgasm, and resolution, they focused exclusively on the reactions of muscles, blood pressure, pulse, respiration, sweating, and other physiological measures. Zilbergeld and Ellison (1980) criticized the Masters and Johnson model for ignoring important subjective factors. They suggested a five-phase model: (1) interest or desire, (2) arousal, (3) physiological readiness (erection and lubrication), (4) orgasm, and (5) satisfaction. About the same time, Helen Singer Kaplan called attention to the role of sexual desire in human sexual responses.

This led David Reed, a psychologist at Jefferson Medical College in Philadelphia, to suggest a modification that stresses our psychosexual development and the connection between the physiological and psychological dimensions of our sexual responses. In Reed's **Erotic Stimulus Pathway (ESP) model**, the standard model of Masters and Johnson and Kaplan is enclosed in a psychological cycle of seduction, sensations, surrender, and reflection (Figure 7.10).

For Reed, the psychological component of the desire stage is *seduction*. We learn to seduce ourselves into being sexually interested in another person, at the same time trying to interest and attract the person who is turning us on. This seduction carries over into the excitement stage of the Masters and Johnson model. *Sensations* overlay the excitement and plateau stages. Our senses are nature's aphrodisiacs, triggering conscious messages of sexual arousal and pleasure in the brain. The sight and voice of a beloved, the erotic, pleasurable, healing touches, and the sights, tastes, smells, and sounds of sex play that are vital in the excitement/plateau stage are processed in the conscious centers of our brain. As the intensity of these psychological reactions builds to orgasm, we enter the third phase of *surrender*. For orgasm to be a pleasurable experience, one needs to let go and give control over to the shared experience. If one is overly concerned about remaining in control, or there is a power struggle in the relationship, then the psychophysiological response of orgasm will be inhibited or reduced (Stayton 1989).

During the resolution phase, *reflection* plays an important psychological role. How a person feels immediately after the sexual experience builds a background for future sexual experiences with that person. If the immediate reflection is positive, warm, loving, and pleasurable, then the desire will likely reoccur. If the love play was not what one expected or left a negative feeling about the partner or situation, then one will not be interested in repeating it.

By emphasizing the importance of stages and a cycle in the psychological side of our sexual responses, Reed's model provides an insight into a common sexual problem that will be obvious in our later discussion of sexual difficulties. "A common problem in long-term relationships is that couples forget the importance of the seduction phase and go right for the sensations or orgasm phase" (Stayton 1989).

Cautions About Sexual Response Models

Scientists find models help them communicate and share their experiences in therapy and research with others. The models create consistent categories, descriptions, and labels that make communication easier and more accurate. But they are limited because they represent our knowledge at a particular point in time and have to be constantly updated. With the current models primarily based on physiology and nervous controls, one should remember that many other factors affect our sexual responses, including age, state of health, psychological condition, level of general education, sexual experience, partner, quality of relationships, and possible effects of drugs or alcohol.

Unfortunately, these models may also suggest to some a new "goal" to be achieved or conquered. Discussions of multiple orgasms in men or the Grafenberg spot and female ejaculation can be interpreted as a new performance pressure. If a man or woman doesn't experience multiple orgasms, or she can't find her G spot or ejaculate, this doesn't mean they are in any way below average, abnormal, or suffering from some undiagnosed sexual problem.

The Control of Sexual Responses

Two Types of Control

There are both conscious and reflexive controls over our sexual responses. When input from our senses or from recollections and fantasies of some pleasant sexual encounter are processed in the brain, the result may be a conscious desire for sexual activity. But a simpler mechanism may also produce a sexual response. A pinprick sends impulses along sensory nerve fibers from nerve cells in the skin that sense pain to nerve cells in the central nervous system. The impulse may be transferred to a motor neuron that travels back to the muscles near where the pinprick occurred, and the finger is pulled away from the pin in a reflex reaction. A *reflex arc*, like that involved in a sneeze or knee jerk, operates below the level of the conscious brain although it may subsequently reach the conscious level of the brain.

Reflexogenic Responses

Erection Controls

In the erection reflex arc, receptors or *sensory cells* in the genitals are stimulated and send nerve impulses along *efferent neurons* to a *reflex center* in the spinal cord. In the spinal cord, at the erection centers, incoming sensory impulses stimulate the inhibiting *afferent neurons*, which innervate the smooth muscle within the walls of the genital blood vessels. These smooth muscles relax, the blood vessels dilate, and blood flow increases into the cavernous and spongy tissues of the genitals, producing vasocongestion and erection or vaginal lubrication. The primary erection center is located in spinal nerves (S_2 to S_4) in the sacral region of the spinal cord and is part of the parasympathetic nervous system (Figure 7.11).

A second *reflex center* regulating erection is located in the region of the T_{11} to L_2 region of the spinal cord. This reflex center is part of the sympathetic division of the autonomic nervous system, which operates as an antagonist to the parasympathetic division. The sympathetic and parasympathetic systems regulate the blood flow through the genital arteries into the cavernous tissues and the outflow through veins that is vital to erection, vaginal lubrication, and the return of the genitals to their resting condition after orgasm.

Ejaculation Controls

The pattern for the ejaculation reflex is similar. The main autonomic reflex is in the sympathetic division of the autonomic nerves of the spinal cord at the T_{11} to L_2 level. This reflex center involves the hypogastric nerve. This action triggers contractions in the vas deferens, seminal vesicles, and prostate gland, forcing their contents into the ejaculatory duct and prostatic urethra. This reflex controls the involuntary *emission phase* of ejaculation.

A second reflex controls the *propulsion phase* of ejaculation. This reflex involves the spinal nerves S_2 to S_4. This reflex sends impulses to the bulbocavernosa, ischiocavernosa, pubococcygeal, and other muscles of the urogenital diaphragm. Rhythmic contractions of these muscles help force expulsion of the semen.

The independence of the erection and ejaculation reflex centers does not mean they are totally independent of the conscious centers of the brain. The conscious activities of the brain can send impulses down the spinal cord to these reflex centers and stimulate, facilitate, or inhibit these reflexive centers. Usually, the conscious and reflexive aspects of our sexual responses complement and reinforce each other. We see something that triggers our erotic desires and the message goes down the spinal cord to trigger an erection. Someone walks in the bedroom and interrupts our fantasy, and an inhibiting message flashes from the brain down to the reflex center, shutting off our arousal. As we mentioned in the earlier brief discussion of the sexual desire phase, guilt, anxiety, fear, and other conscious emotions can inhibit the sexual reflexes.

Suppose neurons that carry sensory and motor information to and from the erection and ejaculation centers are injured or severed, as they sometimes are in sports and automobile accidents. This means a paralyzed male may still have erections and ejaculate. But he may have no conscious control over these re-

Figure 7.11. Nerve Pathways Involved in Sexual Arousal, Erections, and Vaginal Lubrications.

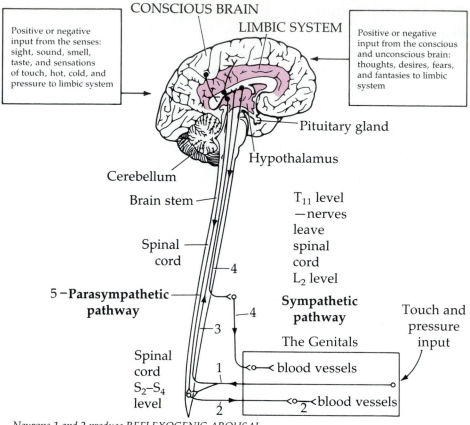

CONSCIOUS BRAIN

LIMBIC SYSTEM

Positive or negative input from the senses: sight, sound, smell, taste, and sensations of touch, hot, cold, and pressure to limbic system

Positive or negative input from the conscious and unconscious brain: thoughts, desires, fears, and fantasies to limbic system

Pituitary gland

Hypothalamus

Cerebellum

Brain stem

Spinal cord

T_{11} level
—nerves leave spinal cord
L_2 level

5 –**Parasympathetic pathway**

Sympathetic pathway

Touch and pressure input

The Genitals

Spinal cord S_2–S_4 level

blood vessels

blood vessels

Neurons 1 and 2 produce REFLEXOGENIC AROUSAL

a. A reflex arc occurs between the sensory neuron (1) and a motor neuron (2) of the parasympathetic pathway.

b. The parasympathetic impulses (2) cause blood vessels in the genitals to dilate— vasocongestion.

PSYCHOGENIC AROUSAL

Neuron 3. The sensory pathway transmits neural impulses to the limbic system and cerebral cortex. (If processed as pleasurable, this impulse will increase vasocongestion via the sympathetic and parasympathetic pathways.)

Neuron 4. The sympathetic pathway causes vasoconstriction and reduces vasocongestion. This pathway is probably always firing to some degree (tonic activity). When signals entering the limbic system are pleasurable, activity in this pathway decreases, lessening vasoconstriction and increasing vasocongestion. If input to the limbic system is unpleasurable, sympathetic activity increases, reducing vasocongestion.

Neuron 5. Parasympathetic impulses are activated by pleasurable input from the limbic system, increasing vasocongestion.

Summary:

Psychogenic erection and lubrication probably arise from inhibition of the sympathetic and facilitation of the parasympathetic pathway.

Reflexogenic erection and lubrication involve a reflex arc independent of the limbic system.

Under normal circumstances, all three pathways may be operating and the relative activity of each determines the final outcome, vasocongestion or no vasocongestion.

Source: Norman A. Scherzer, Ph.D., Essex County College, Department of Biology.

flexes. Since the nerve pathways in the spinal cord that normally carry sensory messages to the conscious centers of the brain are severed, such a male will have no sensations from his reflexive arousal or orgasm.

Because the physical consequences of these reflex centers are much more obvious in males, we can easily observe what happens when the nerves at different levels of the spinal cord are severed. Thus, we know a lot more about male sexual reflex mechanisms than we do about these reflexes in women. Neurologists assume that the spinal reflexes of women correspond to those for erection and ejaculation in men. But much more research and study is needed before we have an adequate description of the neurophysiology of our sexual response cycles.

Nocturnal Emissions and NPT

Reflexes may also be involved in **nocturnal penile tumescence** or **NPT** in men and a vaginal lubrication response in women that occurs during the normal cycle of sleep. The erection reflex center is activated during that portion of the sleep cycle known as REM or rapid eye movement sleep when we dream. REM sleep periods, lasting from a few minutes to a half an hour, alternate with periods of nonrapid eye movement or NREM sleep that accounts for about three-fourths of the sleep cycle. Thus, while we are asleep, men experience several reflexive erections of the penis and women several episodes of vaginal lubrication (Bixler & Vela-Bueno 1987).

These responses, probably initiated by the limbic system within the brain, can be detected with a penile plethysmograph, a thin mercury-filled plastic ring slipped around the base of the penis, or a vaginal photoplethysmograph, a tampon-shaped photocell inserted in the vagina. Both devices are attached to a polygraph to monitor the sexual arousal of a sleeping man or woman. If the monitor detects three or more episodes of sexual arousal, then the reflexive portion of the sexual response system is functioning. If the person is experiencing erectile problems or lack of vaginal lubrication, this evidence of normal reflexive function would suggest the cause is probably psychological rather than organic in origin.

An excellent example of reflexive ejaculation is the **nocturnal emission** or "wet dream." The stimulus of the penis pressed against a mattress during sleep can trigger the erection and ejaculation reflex arcs. This common, completely natural experience can cause anxiety and real worry in adolescent boys if the wet dream occurs without any warning and without any knowledge about how normal and expected this experience is. Kinsey et al. (1948) found that by age 45 nine out of ten males had had at least one nocturnal emission they could remember. But the college-educated males in Kinsey's study were seven times more likely to admit having nocturnal emissions. Several studies suggest that nine out of ten men and roughly half of all women can recall having at least one orgasm while sleeping (Hunt 1974; Peterson et al. 1983). These experiences may be more common when one is young.

Medieval writers reported that demons known as *incubus* and *succubus* caused nocturnal emissions. The incubi assumed the male-above position as they engaged sleeping women; the succubus assumed the female-below position in seducing men. It has been suggested that the buildup of sperm in the epididymis and semen in the seminal vesicles is the cause of nocturnal emissions. Some have suggested that a full bladder, heavy blankets, and certain sleeping positions might account for nocturnal emission, but again there is no evidence for or against this explanation. Nocturnal emission, like nocturnal penile tumescence, may be related to reflex responses associated with REM sleep, but if this is the main factor we need an explanation for the much higher incidence of nocturnal emissions in young men.

In 1953 Kinsey and his associates wrote that masturbation and nocturnal sex dreams to the point of orgasm are activities that provide the best measure of a female's "intrinsic sexuality" (1953:192). About 70% of the women in Kinsey's sample reported having had erotic dreams, although only half of these had had orgasms as a result of these dreams.

In her study of the nocturnal orgasm experiences of 245 college graduate and undergraduate women, Wells (1986) found that the women who reported having had nocturnal orgasms showed no anxiety or emotional disturbances. Thirty percent reported having had several nocturnal orgasms; another 30% had experienced at least one such orgasm in the previous year. Women who were sexually active, who had a positive attitude toward and knowledge of nocturnal orgasms, and who had liberal sexual views were the most likely to have nocturnal orgasms. Although we know little at present about female nocturnal orgasm, there appear to be some interesting parallels with male wet dreams.

Intermediate Controls

The human brain is the product of millions of years of evolution. Since that time, animals have evolved from very primitive nervous systems that reacted automatically and instinctively to stimuli to the highly complex functioning of the human brain with its capacity for emotions, feelings, abstract thought, and conscious reflection on the world we live in. In the higher vertebrates, the brain stem is overlaid with the limbic system and finally by the cerebral cortex. Some regions of the cerebral cortex handle motor and sensory functions. Other regions involve the emotions, thinking, problem solving, and memory (Figure 7.11).

The brain stem, or visceral brain, controls the most basic life-sustaining activities. Overlaying the upper portion of the brain stem and lying deep within the innermost edge of the cerebral hemispheres is the middle layer of the human brain, the **limbic system**. Interacting closely with the hypothalamus, the limbic system is involved in many activities associated with eroticism and mating behavior. The limbic system is involved in sociability, mating, procreation, preservation of the species, and "the selfish demands of feeding, fighting and self-protection" (Money & Ehrhardt 1972:238–239).

In this inner core is the all-important **hypothalamus**, the source of the gonadotropic-releasing hormones that regulate the production of hormones by the anterior pituitary. Pituitary hormones, in turn, regulate the ovaries, testes, and maturation of the ovum and sperm. The hypothalamus is also encoded with a neural template for either a cyclic or acyclic production of the gonadotropic-releasing hormone, and is thus responsible for the menstrual cycle in women and the continuous production of sperm after puberty in the male.

The limbic system also responds strongly to odors. In some lower vertebrates, **pheromones**, scents that activate sexual response, are vital in the mating process. In humans, smell appears to play a very minor role, but pheromones are found in human urine, smegma, apocrine sweat glands, and vaginal secretions.

Martha McClintock has suggested that human pheromones may have a prime role in synchronizing the menstrual cycles of women living in close association in college dormitories (1971). Women are far more sensitive to odor than men. They also have many more apocrine glands in their skin than men. These tiny glands are similar to exocrine sweat glands, but their secretions contain a higher proportion of solids and pheromones. Apocrine glands are concentrated in the armpits and around the sexual organs where hair tufts serve as traps for secretions. Like the moth that can smell a mate a mile or more downwind, humans may be able to detect subconsciously the presence of pheromones.

Is there a "chemistry" of love? Are you attracted to a man or woman because of his or her distinct odor? However further research answers this question, it is unquestionable that most Americans use so many deodorant products that their "true" smell is covered up!

Hormones also stimulate the libido or sex drive centers of the hypothalamus. Libido in both men and women is activated by testosterone. Men treated with estrogen to control prostate cancer often complain of reduced or lost sex drive. Although women treated with testosterone to control breast cancer often report increased sex drive such hormone treatments are no longer used because of other negative side effects.

The Conscious Levels of Sexual Response

The role of the conscious portions of the central nervous system, the cerebral cortex, will also come into focus in the chapter on sexual problems and difficulties. Here we need only recall the vital role the conscious part of the brain plays in sorting out and reacting to the countless sexual stimuli that bombard us through the sensory doors of our eyes, ears, nose, taste, and touch. Psychogenic sexual responses begin with those stimuli and their reception and sorting in the conscious centers of the cerebral cortex as well as in the subconscious centers of the limbic system.

In general, the conscious centers of the brain may override and inhibit sexual arousal that is reflexive or limbic in origin. The conscious brain can also facilitate or lower the level of sexual excitement. Understanding the roles and interactions of these conscious and subconscious centers is important in treating persons with sexual difficulties or problems.

In recent years, researchers have focused on the target cells and centers for sex hormones in the fetal and adult human brain. Neuroendocrinologists and neuropsychologists have sought to identify "sex centers" and learn how these might differ in male and female brains. Much progress has been made. However, it will be some time before we understand fully the dynamic interaction and integration of the three levels of the human brain and the spinal cord in regulating human sexual responses.

Key Concepts

1. Sexual arousal and orgasm can be reflexogenic and automatic, or psychogenic and conscious.
2. The human sexual response cycle is commonly described in four stages: desire, excitement/plateau, orgasm, and resolution. Men and women experience many similarities in their responses during each of these stages.

3. Vasocongestion causes erection of the penis and swelling of the testes in the male. In women, it causes erection of the clitoris, swelling and erection of the labia, vaginal lubrication, formation of the orgasmic platform, and swelling of the breasts. In both sexes, vasocongestion causes sex flush.

4. In both sexes, myotonia, the buildup of muscle tension, may increase to a reflexive release in orgasm, after which both muscle tension and vasocongestion fade in a pleasurable relaxation.

5. Males may experience a refractory period after orgasm during which they cannot be sexually aroused for some time.

6. Three types of female orgasm have been reported: the tenting orgasm described by Masters and Johnson, the A-frame or uterine orgasm described by Perry and Whipple, and a blended orgasm that combines both of these types.

7. Male ejaculation has two phases: the buildup of seminal fluid pressure in the prostate during the emission phase, and the release of seminal fluid during the propulsion phase. Two sphincters, above and below the prostate gland, regulate ejaculation.

8. Female ejaculation seems to involve fluid from the female prostate, the Skene's glands, around the urethra.

9. Nocturnal erection, nocturnal emissions, and erotic dreams with orgasm are common experiences for both men and women.

10. Several reflexive erection and orgasm centers in the spinal cord regulate sexual arousal and orgasm. These reflex responses may be moderated, enhanced, or inhibited by the hypothalamus and the conscious centers of the brain.

Key Terms

A-frame orgasm (185)
blended orgasm (185)
desire phase (173)
edema (174)
ejaculation (184)
emission phase (188)
erection (174)
Erotic Stimulus Pathway (ESP)
   model (193)
excitement/plateau phase (174)
female ejaculation (186)
Grafenberg spot (185)
hypothalamus (198)
limbic system (198)
myotonia (174)
nocturnal penile tumescence
   (NPT) (197)

nocturnal emission (197)
orgasm (182)
orgasmic platform (180)
pheromone (198)
propulsion phase (188)
psychogenic (170)
reflexogenic (170)
refractory period (191)
resolution (191)
seminal pool (180)
sex flush (182)
sex skin (180)
tenting (180)
tenting orgasm (185)
tumescence (174)
vaginal lubrication (176)
vasocongestion (174)

PART ONE:
CONCEPTION AND
PREGNANCY

Coitus and Conception
Fertilization
Ectopic Pregnancy
Twins
Pregnancy Signs
and Tests
The Embryonic Period
Embryonic Development
The Placental System
Fetal Development
The Second Trimester
The Third Trimester
Prenatal Care
Problems During
Pregnancy

PART TWO:
CHILDBIRTH AND
OPTIONS IN
DELIVERY

Vaginal Delivery
The Stages of Labor
Options in Vaginal
Delivery
Cesarean Section
Delivery
Breast Feeding
Custom-Made
Pregnancies
Infertility and Possible
Treatments
Artificial Insemination
and Frozen Sperm
Test Tube Fertilization
and Embryo Transfer
The Surrogate Mother
Controversy

Chapter 8

Pregnancy and Birth

Special Consultants

Paul A. Fleming, M.D., D.H.S., director, The Fleming Center, Raleigh, North Carolina.

Abraham Risk, M.D., director, Obstetrics and Gynecology, Morristown Memorial Hospital, Morristown, New Jersey.

The 12 gates of our psychosexual development outlined in Chapter 4 focused on the unfolding complexities of our psychosexual nature. Chapter 5 added rich details on the psychological and social dimensions of our sexual development during childhood, puberty, and adolescence. This chapter completes the picture of our early development by lifting the veil from the nine months of our physical development in and passage out of the womb.

**PART ONE:
CONCEPTION AND PREGNANCY**

Coitus and Conception

Fertilization

Whatever variations a woman has in her menstrual cycle, ovulation, the release of one or more eggs (ovum, ova), always comes with a surge of luteinizing hormone (LH) from the pituitary gland some 14 days before the beginning of the next menstrual flow. As ovulation approaches, the fingerlike tissue around the funnel-shaped opening of the fallopian tube becomes engorged with blood and gently strokes the egg follicle, sitting like a blister on the surface of the ovary. The egg is swept into the fallopian tube as soon as the ovarian follicle ruptures. Once inside, tiny hairlike cilia lining the inside of the tube push the egg along to the uterus (Figure 8.1).

Meanwhile, the 300 to 400 million sperm released in ejaculation face many obstacles in their effort to swim through the vagina, the cervix, and uterine cavity to reach their goal, the egg, in the outer end of the fallopian tube. Among those obstacles are staying in the vagina after ejaculation, finding a way through the cervical mucus, and surviving the acidic environment of the vagina and alkaline environment of the uterus. Sperm can get trapped in the pockets and folds of the vagina and uterine cavity. If ejaculation does not coincide with the time of ovulation, the sperm encounter a mucus plug, blocking their path at the cervix. Stymied in their effort to reach an egg, they languish and die. If, however, the sperm are released around the time of ovulation, they find the mucus plug has liquified and contains threads they can follow through the cervical canal into the cavity of the uterus. Half of the thousands of sperm that reach the fallopian tubes take the wrong turn and end up in the tube with no egg. **Fertilization**, the union of a sperm and egg, usually occurs in the outer third of the fallopian tube when one of a few hundred surviving sperm manages to penetrate the egg.

Normally, the sperm has to fertilize an egg within 24 hours of ejaculation and ovulation. After that first day, the sperm and egg start to deteriorate, even though they may be still able to join together for another day or two. Because the egg only completes its second meiotic division at fertilization when the sperm enters it, if the egg is two or three days old when fertilization occurs the separation of chromosomes in the second meiotic division may be abnormal. The result could then be an embryo with an extra chromosome, for example, causing Down or Klinefelter syndrome, or a missing chromosome, as in Turner syndrome (see p. 96). Several studies have linked a higher incidence of mental

(a) Location of internal female reproductive and sexual organs

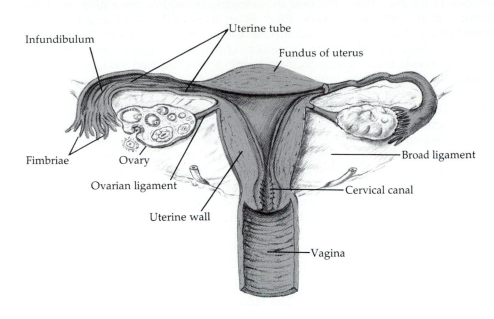

(b) Detail of egg production in one ovary, fertilization, and implantation

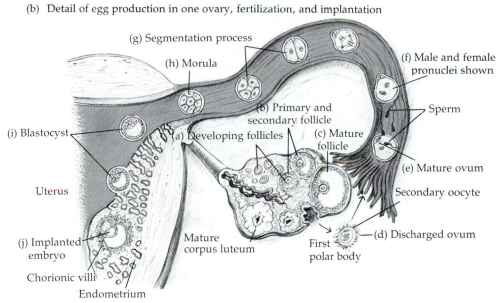

Primordial germ cells, egg nests on the surface of the ovary, begin developing, on average, two weeks before ovulation. A few follicles start but usually only one matures and ovulates. Check Chapter 4 and Figures 4.4 and 6.7 for genetic details of this development. If the egg is fertilized, it continues down the fallopian tube, hopefully to implanting 6 to 7 days later in the uterine lining.

Figure 8.1. Ovulation and the First Week After Fertilization.

retardation and physical defects in babies of couples who use natural or rhythm methods of contraception. Because these methods require abstaining from intercourse during the fertile days, there is an increased risk of a stale egg or sperm being involved in fertilization (Guest et al. 1979:109; Moore 1988:27–32).

Once the egg is fertilized, an immediate chemical reaction on the surface of the egg prevents other sperm from entering it. Fertilization also triggers cell division. At this point the new organism is called a **zygote**. Six or seven days later, when the zygote has gone through many cells divisions and is a hollow ball of cells, it is called a blastocyst. The blastocyst burrows into the spongy, highly vascular lining of the uterus. Pregnancy, which begins with implantation, has two unequal stages. The embryonic phase extends from the second through the eighth week (Figure 8.2). During this period, the **embryo** develops all its major organ systems, including the brain, heart, liver, lungs, limbs, and digestive tract. The fetal phase of pregnancy or gestation extends from the beginning of the third month to birth. During this period, the main organs and tissues of the **fetus** finish their development and the fetus is prepared for life outside the womb.

Ectopic Pregnancy

Occasionally, a fertilized egg will implant outside the main cavity of the uterus, resulting in an **ectopic** pregnancy. The fallopian tube is the most common site for ectopic pregnancies. The risk of tubal pregnancies is increased when previous infections have left "pockets" in the tubal wall and disrupted the ciliated cells of the tube that normally propel the zygote along to the uterus. In a tubal pregnancy, the implanted embryo continues to grow as it would in the uterus. As the embryo stretches the fallopian tube, the mother may experience a sharp pain, cramps, a dull, constant pain in the lower abdomen, or have no symptoms at all. When discovered before the tube ruptures, the developing fetus, and the tube if necessary, may have to be removed, although surgery that spares the tube is being perfected. In many cases, infertility results even though only one tube has been removed. If not discovered and remedied by surgery, the tube eventually ruptures, usually in the third month. The hemorrhaging that follows can result in serious complications, even death, for the woman.

Much rarer are ectopic pregnancies with implantation in the ovary, the cervix, the outer wall of the intestines, or the inner wall of the abdominal cavity. A small number of abdominal pregnancies have gone full term and babies have been delivered by laparotomy, an incision in the abdominal cavity. Since the placenta, the organ that permits transfer of nutrients and wastes between the fetus and mother, develops from the fetal tissue rather than from the mother's tissue, a normal placenta can form wherever the embryo implants as long as there is a good supply of maternal blood vessels. Embryologists have speculated about the possibility of transplanting a week-old embryo into the abdominal

Figure 8.2. The Human Egg and Young Embryo. *(a) A human secondary oocyte shortly after ovulation. Sperm must digest their way through the small follicular cells of the corona radiata and the clear zona pellucida to reach the oocyte itself. (b) At the end of the sixth week, the human embryo is about half head. The feet and hands have begun to develop fingers, and the tail is receding. (c) At the end of the eighth week, the embryo is clearly human in appearance and is now termed a fetus. Most of the major organs of the adult body have begun to develop.*

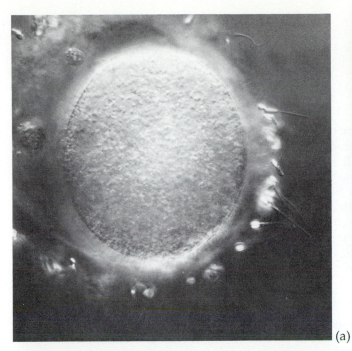
(a)

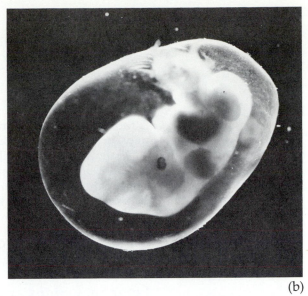
(b)

(c)

cavity of a male, and allowing a man to become a mother after a nine-month pregnancy and delivery by cesarean section! How would you feel about this possibility?

Twins

Although single pregnancies are the rule, multiple pregnancies can occur naturally, or as a consequence of infertility treatments.

Fraternal twins result from the fertilization of two different eggs by two different sperm. Fraternal twins are as different as any two children with the same parents. They can be two boys, two girls, or a boy and girl. Fraternal twins account for more than 70% of all twins. **Identical twins** are the result of a single egg fertilized by a single sperm. After about a week, the developing embryo divides into two separate embryonic masses. Identical twins have identical physical characteristics, blood type, and transplant tolerance. Some families have an inherited tendency for either identical or fraternal twins.

Pregnancy Signs and Tests

A pregnancy brings many physiological changes with wide-ranging consequences to the mother's hormonal system. Women who are sexually active and miss a menstrual period realize they may be pregnant. But this *presumptive sign* of pregnancy can also be due to a variety of other factors. Stress, emotional problems, illness, and strenuous daily exercise can disrupt the menstrual cycle and delay a period. *Probable signs* of pregnancy include swollen and sensitive breasts, tingling nipples, "morning sickness," increased urination and fatigue, enlarged uterus, and soft dark-colored cervix. In the third month of pregnancy, a sonogram showing the fetus in the womb and a detectable fetal heartbeat are *positive signs* of a pregnancy.

Pregnancy Tests

Of course, the traditional signs women looked for to alert them to a possibile pregnancy have lost most of their value because of the easy availability of new laboratory and home pregnancy tests. By the second week after fertilization, the embryonic mass embedded in the wall of the uterus has a primitive but functional placenta that is producing **human chorionic gonadotropin (HCG)**. The presence of the hormone HCG can be detected with immunologic tests of the blood or urine as early as the second or third week after fertilization. These new tests have replaced the crude and time-consuming pregnancy tests using rabbits, rats, and frogs common only 20 or 30 years ago. The most common clinical test detects HCG in the urine and is accurate in the fourth week after fertilization. A newer, more sensitive, and less common pregnancy test, known as the beta subunit HCG radioimmunoassay test, can detect the beta component of HCG in the blood 9 days after fertilization, or a few days after implantation. Even newer is the convenient, rapid, and sensitive ELISA test, a beta-specific monoclonal enzyme-linked immunosorbent assay test, which detects HCG as early as 7 to 10 days after fertilization.

Adding to the convenience of early clinical pregnancy tests are a variety of home pregnancy tests sold without prescription in pharmacies and elsewhere. Since a woman using a home pregnancy test kit does not have the expertise of a clinician, she should follow the instructions very carefully to make sure her results are valid. A positive home test should be confirmed by a clinical test as soon as possible.

In collecting a urine sample for a laboratory test, you should have no liquids after dinner the night before collection. A half cup of urine should be collected immediately on rising in the morning in a *very clean*, well-rinsed dry jar. The sample should be refrigerated until it can be taken to the lab or doctor's office that same day.

All pregnancy tests can give *false positive* or *false negative* readings if performed when the level of HCG is just starting to rise, if the urine or blood sample is contaminated, or if directions are not followed. If the test indicates an apparently false reading, a second test and examination by a physician can resolve the question.

The Importance of Early Pregnancy Tests

Pregnancy tests that measure the amount of HCG, rather than those that simply reveal a woman is pregnant, are important because they enable the woman to know approximately how long she has been pregnant. Since adequate prenatal care is crucial to both the mother and fetus, the sooner the woman sees a physician and begins a medical regimen, the more likely her pregnancy will be healthy. Prenatal care includes a complete physical examination, advice on diet, and instructions on medications to avoid during pregnancy. The physician, nurse clinician, or midwife can also offer support and discuss symptoms and side effects of the pregnancy which may be perfectly normal but not recognized as such by the pregnant woman. Prenatal care may also include genetic counseling and tests for German measles, diabetes, and for certain sexually transmitted diseases which the woman may be carrying even though she has shown no symptoms.

Early pregnancy detection is also necessary to allow adequate time for the woman to decide what to do in the event the pregnancy is unintended. Among the questions that may come up are the following:

- If the woman is single, should she discuss the pregnancy with the child's father, a close friend, and/or her parents?
- Should she carry to full term and keep the infant?
- Should she have an abortion?
- Should she deliver and give the child up for adoption?
- Is she making her own decision, or is it a response to pressures from others?
- Is the decision based on fact, or on fantasy and unfounded fears?
- What support systems and resources are available to help her with each of the options,

Every woman has her own unique combination of emotions and feelings when she finds out she is pregnant. If you have ever been pregnant, think back to the time when that first pregnancy was confirmed. What were your reactions? What was the mix of elation, depression, anxiety? Behind these emotions and reactions are a variety of factors: the woman's single or marital status, the emotional health of her relationship with her partner, her age and financial situation, and the impact the pregnancy is likely to have on her future life and on those around her.

Women who learn they are pregnant also confront some strong social stereotypes about how a woman ''should'' react to finding out she is expecting. If the woman is married or in a stable relationship, she is expected to exhibit a ''radiant glory'' of motherhood. With contraceptives readily available, most people assume that a married woman who is pregnant has planned her pregnancy and wants it, which may not be the case. Equally strong expectations come into play when a single woman becomes pregnant. The assumption often is she will have an abortion, even though many women today are choosing single parenthood.

Many Americans were surprised by an informal Ann Landers survey in 1979 when millions of readers said they *would not have had children if they had the chance to live that part of their life over again.* How do you think your parents would react to this question? What would you do if you were faced with being pregnant this year, two years from now, or five years from now? What factors would be most important in determining your reaction?

The Embryonic Period

Embryonic Development

The embryonic period includes the second through eighth weeks. Six or seven days after fertilization, the rapidly dividing embryonic mass burrows into the wall of the uterus. During the third week, about the time the woman realizes she is missing a menstrual period, the future spinal cord starts to form, along with the intestines and muscle tissue. By the end of the fourth week, the embryo is about 3/16 inch long and has developed a spinal cord, upper and lower limb buds, lungs, pancreas, digestive tract, and the beginnings of eyes. The fifth week of development is characterized by a two-chambered heart and brain development. By the end of the fifth week, the embryo is 1/3 inch in length. During the sixth week, the embryo grows to 1/2 inch, and the face begins to form (Figure 8.2). At this stage the embryo can be seen with ultrasound scanning.

By the end of the seventh week, a four-chambered heart, eyelids, liver, kidneys, and intestines are all formed and functioning. The embryo is now 3/4 inch long. In the eighth week, the embryo grows to over 1 inch and has well formed hands and feet with separated fingers and toes. The external sexual organs have started to form and the gonads have differentiated into testes if the embryo has a Y chromosome. The ovaries differentiate a little later than the testes. By the end of the embryonic stage, the infant is a complete miniature human that only needs to increase in organ maturity and general growth.

The Placental System

The support system for the developing embryo is the **placenta,** which develops from the embryonic cells that burrow into the uterine wall. The placenta specializes in moving nutrients and oxygen from the mother's circulatory system into the fetal circulation and waste products from the fetus into the mother's circulation. Three thin layers of fetal tissue separate the circulatory systems of mother and fetus so that the blood of the mother and the blood of the fetus do

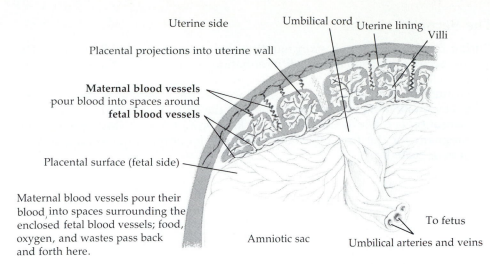

Figure 8.3 The Human Placenta.

Uterine side

Umbilical cord

Uterine lining

Villi

Placental projections into uterine wall

Maternal blood vessels pour blood into spaces around **fetal blood vessels**

Placental surface (fetal side)

Maternal blood vessels pour their blood into spaces surrounding the enclosed fetal blood vessels; food, oxygen, and wastes pass back and forth here.

Amniotic sac

To fetus

Umbilical arteries and veins

not mix. Oxygen, water, carbohydrates, fats, proteins, vitamins, hormones, antibiotics, drugs such as alcohol and tranquilizers, and viruses pass through this membrane between mother and embryo or fetus (Figure 8.3).

Besides being a nutrient-waste transfer structure, the placenta also produces hormones. It secretes increasing quantities of estrogen and progesterone that maintain pregnancy. The placenta secretes human chorionic gonadotropin (HCG), which regulates ovarian functions during pregnancy and provides the basis of pregnancy tests. The placenta also produces human chorionic somatomammotropin (HCS), which prepares the mother's body and breasts for nursing. HCS is sometimes known as human placental lactogen or HPL.

One end of the **umbilical cord** is attached to the navel in the center of the fetal abdomen. Two arteries and a vein carry fetal blood between the fetus and the placenta. The cord is about 20 inches long. Sometimes the cord becomes constricted or coiled around the fetus, causing it serious problems. When this occurs, the fetus may go into fetal distress, which can be fatal.

The fetus is surrounded by **amniotic fluid** that fills the amniotic sac, enclosing and guarding the fetus inside the expanding uterine cavity. This sac of fluid serves as an insulating buffer for the growing fetus, protecting it from bumps and shocks. The amniotic fluid can be used in detecting genetic diseases. (See the section on prenatal monitoring on page 218.)

Fetal Development

The fetal period extends from the third through the ninth month of pregnancy. The nine months are usually divided into trimesters of three or so months each. Thus the first month of fetal development falls in the first trimester. During the first month of the fetal stage, the face takes on human characteristics, and the male and female external genitals can be distinguished. In general appearance, the fetus is unmistakably human. It is about 4 inches in length and weighs approximately two-thirds of an ounce.

The Second Trimester

During the fourth through sixth months, the fetus grows rapidly in size. The organs become functional, and differentiation occurs within the basic organs (Figure 8.4).

Around the sixteenth or seventeenth weeks, the pregnant woman is often excited by **quickening**, the first movement of the fetus detectable by the mother. The sensation is often described as a "tickle" or a "tingle." Most women who are pregnant for the first time have difficulty identifying quickening until it happens repeatedly.

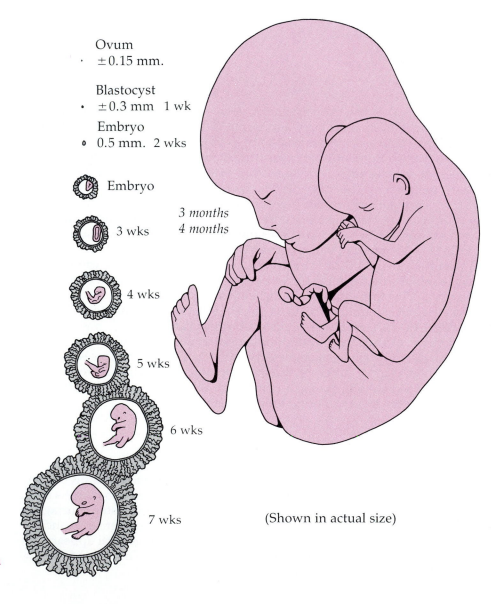

Ovum
± 0.15 mm.

Blastocyst
± 0.3 mm   1 wk

Embryo
0.5 mm.   2 wks

Embryo

3 wks

4 wks

5 wks

6 wks

7 wks

3 months
4 months

(Shown in actual size)

Figure 8.4. From Single Cell to Four-Month Fetus.

During the sixth month, the fetus becomes sensitive to both light and sound. It experiences cycles of sleep and wakefulness and definite periods of restless movement. Survival rate of premature births in the sixth month is about 1 in 10.

Generally, there are relatively few medical problems during the second trimester. Any spotting of uterine blood will usually have stopped, and often morning sickness, too, will have ceased. By this time the body has usually adjusted to the hormonal changes of the pregnancy. A few problems that may occur include constipation, edema or fluid retention (swelling), nosebleeds, and hemorrhoids. By the middle of the pregnancy, the breasts are prepared for nursing and are capable of producing *colostrum*, a thin, nutritious yellow fluid that is not milk.

If born prematurely, an 18-week fetus usually cannot survive. At 20 weeks, there is still a poor rate of survival, with roughly 1 in every 10,000 such births surviving long term.

As the fetus becomes larger, the woman has to adjust to the obvious signs of pregnancy. Although some women delight in showing their pregnancy, others find this stage to be both awkward and unattractive. Only 40 or 50 years ago, many middle class American women would not be seen in public after they began ''to show.''

The Third Trimester

During the last three months of pregnancy, the fetus gains weight rapidly. Although the average birth weight is about 7.5 pounds, there have been reports of babies born in excess of 20 pounds. After the seventh month, the fetus will usually slip into the birth position, with the head facing the cervix. The fetus has wrinkled skin and is covered by light, downy hair called *lanugo* and a protective waxy substance, *vernix caseosa*.

A premature infant faces some serious problems. With a weight under 5.5 pounds, a lack of insulating body fat, and immature lungs and nervous system, chances of survival are not good. Hyaline membrane disease of the lungs still takes the lives of many premature infants. Yet the statistics for survival of the premature infant are improving yearly. By the end of the seventh month, there is a 50% chance of survival. This jumps to 90% or 95% at the end of the eighth month. In the ninth month, the survival rate is around 99%. One of the major reasons for improvement in overall survival rates is the development of sophisticated intensive care units for premature infants (Kantrowitz 1988).

Research has found that most premature deliveries associated with teenage pregnancy are due not to the mother's young age but to her inadequate nutrition, heavy smoking, and general poor health. These factors can lead to long-term problems for the premature infant, even when it survives with intensive care.

During the last trimester, walking may be difficult for the near-term mother. She experiences shortness of breath and feels pressure on her heart, increasing pressure on the intestines, and constipation. Lower back pains may result from the stress of supporting the added weight of the fetus.

Psychological stresses also increase as the end of the pregnancy approaches. The woman may feel embarrassed because of the obvious pregnancy. She usually becomes more concerned about the health of the fetus. She may be anxious about the delivery and the pain that may attend it. She may also wonder about how she will be able to manage as a mother. She and her partner may worry how the new infant will affect their relationship and lifestyle. It is often difficult for a man to predict how he will react emotionally and sexually to the mother's changing body, the addition of a new member to the relationship, and the time and attention the mother gives their infant.

For the first 28 weeks of an uncomplicated pregnancy, a monthly checkup is customary. From the 28th to 36th weeks, biweekly exams are recommended with weekly or even semiweekly visits as term approaches. The position of the fetus, blood pressure, and preparation of the uterus for childbirth are checked by the obstetrician. Some women may have short, irregular, painless contractions during the final months. These contractions, known as Braxton-Hicks contractions, are sometimes confused with true labor pains, which are regular in their pattern with an increasing intensity.

Prenatal Care

Nutrition and Weight Gain

Proper nutrition is vital to the development of a healthy, normal fetus. One Canadian study indicated that poor diet during pregnancy resulted in a 300% increase in stillbirths and a 700% increase in miscarriages. This study also revealed that poor nutrition resulted in longer labor and four times as many health problems as the woman and fetus who had received adequate prenatal nutrition (Newton, cited in Boston Women's Health Collective 1976:253).

The effects of maternal malnutrition, impaired blood flow in the placenta, and multiple pregnancies on fetal growth are included in the **intrauterine growth retardation** (IUGR) syndrome. The rate of deaths among newborns is almost twice as high for women of color as it is for white women. In 1981 the infant mortality rate for black infants in Washington, D.C., was 25.5 per 1,000 infants compared with 14.1 for white infants. Among Native American women the effects of malnutrition are even more frightening. In 1979 38% of all pregnancies in one South Dakota Indian reservation resulted in excessive hemorrhaging or miscarriage before the fifth month. Sixty percent to 70% of the infants had respiratory problems (Boston Women's Health Collective 1984:331).

Dieting should be avoided during pregnancy because it can impair both the physical and mental development of the fetus. In addition, fat breakdown in the mother's body produces toxic substances known as ketones. About 80,000 additional calories are required during the pregnancy. This amounts to 300 additional calories per day, about the equivalent of one scoop of ice cream.

How much weight should a woman gain during pregnancy? Although it differs from woman to woman, the average desired weight gain is about 24 to 27 pounds. Thin women tend to gain less weight and have infants that may be dangerously small. On the other hand, obese women often gain too much weight and run the risks of high blood pressure and difficult pregnancies and deliveries (Brown 1983).

Even more important than the question of acceptable weight gain is what kinds of foods are eaten during the pregnancy. Certain foods should be eaten every day. A balanced diet with milk, dairy products, protein sources such as eggs, fish, chicken, or lean meat, peas or peanuts, dark green leafy vegetables, whole wheat bread, citrus fruits and/or juice, whole grain cereals, and yellow or orange vegetables is essential to the health of both mother and fetus.

What Causes Abnormal Development?

In the 10 weeks between the time the embryo begins to develop its nervous system and the end of the third month, all the embryo's major organs and organ systems are developing very rapidly. Exposure to a **teratogenic agent**, any drug or chemical that causes abnormal development, is especially dangerous at this time.

In the early 1960s hundreds of British and German infants were born without arms or legs because early in pregnancy their mothers had used thalidomide, a seemingly safe tranquilizer. Taken in the second month of pregnancy, thalidomide blocks the formation of the arms and legs. Fortunately, the medication was never approved by the FDA for sale in the United States.

In 1964 and 1965, more than 50,000 American infants died before birth or were born with serious defects because of an epidemic of **rubella** (German measles). Their mothers had not been vaccinated against rubella before becoming pregnant. Rubella is a minor inconvenience when an adult is exposed to it, but it is a serious problem for the fetus. Any woman of childbearing age should be vaccinated against rubella and then wait at least three months before becoming pregnant. Infants infected with herpes during delivery have a 40% to 50% mortality rate, and 30% will be retarded. Syphilis can also cause abnormal growth and mental retardation (Moore 1988:151–153).

Diethylstilbestrol (DES), a synthetic progesterone, was used between 1941 and 1971 to prevent miscarriage and in the treatment of diabetes. We now know that DES increases the risk of cervical cancer 15 to 28 years later in the daughters whose mother used this drug. Males may have an increased risk of testicular cancer and other problems. Infertility is a problem for offspring of both genders. Anyone who suspects their mother may have taken a medication for diabetes, or to prevent a threatened miscarriage, should check on what medication was used and what its possible side effects are.

The most common teratogenic agents today are alcohol and nicotine. The results of **fetal alcohol syndrome (FAS)** include low birth weight, defects in the face, heart, and limbs, and possible mental retardation. A glass or two of wine or beer, or an ounce or two of 80 proof alcohol per day at a crucial sensitive period early in pregnancy can result in some form of FAS. Smoking a pack of cigarettes a day is known to double the risk of premature delivery. Smoking is also known to interfere with normal sperm production.

Most prescription medications, including some antibiotics and drugs used for high blood pressure, diabetes, and allergies, can be dangerous to the fetus. Illegal street drugs, and even common over-the-counter medications like aspirin can also pose problems (Moore 1988:145–150). In brief, any and all drugs should be avoided during a pregnancy, unless carefully monitored by a physician.

Problems During Pregnancy

Several problems may be associated with pregnancy. Although many of these conditions are rare and caused by factors outside of the woman's control, some can be avoided if the causes are understood.

Miscarriage

A **miscarriage** is a spontaneous abortion of the embryo or fetus. Over 30% of all pregnancies may end in miscarriage. Three out of 4 known miscarriages occur in the first trimester, two-thirds of them before the woman or her doctor is aware she is pregnant. Sixty-five percent of all miscarriages are caused by gross chromosomal defects. The remaining 35% are usually caused by hormonal imbalance or by a weak cervix in the second trimester. When the cervix is unable to contain the developing fetus, the contents of the uterus tend to be expelled. Although minor physical discomfort may accompany spontaneous miscarriages, most are not dangerous to the mother. They do frequently trigger strong emotional reactions when the woman knows she has miscarried. A reassuring aspect of early miscarriages is that most of the women studied showed signs of high fertility just after the loss, with one-third of them becoming pregnant in the next menstrual cycle. Within two years, 95% of the women who had early miscarriages had a normal pregnancy carried to term (Beck 1988; Little 1988).

Fetal-Maternal Incompatibility

About 1 in 150 births can pose a serious problem for the infant because of incompatibility between a protein on the red blood cells of the fetus and the mother's immune system. Five out of 6 white Americans have a specific protein known as the **Rh factor** on the surface of their red blood cells (the protein was first discovered in rhesus monkeys). People with this protein are described as Rh positive. The other 1 in 6 does not have the protein and is Rh negative.

If an Rh-negative woman becomes pregnant and the father is also Rh negative, they will have no problem. However, if the father is Rh positive, there may be a problem (Figure 8.5). Anti-Rh antibodies leaking through the placental barrier into the blood system of the fetus destroy the fetal red blood cells,

Figure 8.5. The RH Factor Problem in Pregnancy. *Summary of events that occur during Rh incompatibility. (a) If a woman who is Rh⁻ carries an Rh⁺ child for the first time, placental rupture during childbirth may allow fetal red blood cells to leak into the mother's circulation. (b) The mother's immune system produces antibodies directed against the D antigens on the fetal red blood cells. (c) Upon a subsequent pregnancy with an Rh⁺ child, these antibodies enter the fetal circulation and destroy fetal red blood cells.*

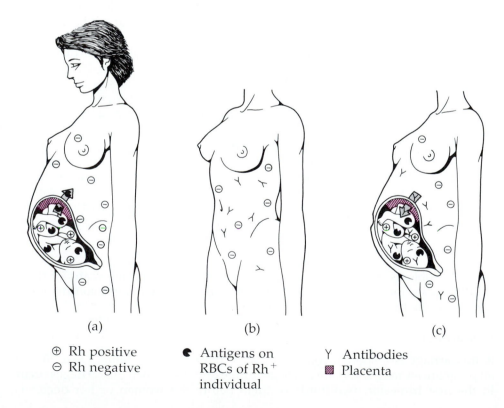

(a)   (b)   (c)

⊕ Rh positive   ● Antigens on   Y Antibodies
⊖ Rh negative   RBCs of Rh⁺   ▨ Placenta
                       individual

causing anemia, enlargement of the spleen and liver, mental retardation, cerebral palsy, and, in some cases, death.

Fortunately, the Rh factor problem can be prevented. Any Rh-negative woman who has an abortion, who suspects she has had a miscarriage, or who gives birth should get an injection of Rho-GAM (Rh factor antibodies) within 72 hours. The Rho-GAM antibodies combine with the fetal Rh-positive blood cells that may have leaked into the mother's circulation and remove them before they can trigger the mother's immune system. Rh-negative mothers with no anti-Rh antibodies are now given Rho-GAM during pregnancy with a booster shot for added protection after delivery. Unfortunately, once an Rh-negative woman's immune system has been triggered, nothing can be done to reverse the process of antibody production.

Toxemia

Toxemia is a metabolic complication of pregnancy, usually after the sixth month. Symptoms of *preeclampsia*, the first stage of toxemia, include elevated blood pressure, swelling of tissues (edema), and high protein levels in the urine. A severe case may be characterized by vision problems, mental slowness, headaches, and abdominal distress. In the final stage of the disease, *eclampsia* or convulsions may occur as well as coma and maternal death.

The causes of toxemia are unknown. Studies have indicated that poor women are more likely to die from toxemia than women with higher incomes. It is also more common among teenage mothers. Early warning signs of the disease include rapid weight gain and severe edema. Medical attention at an early stage can usually control it.

False Pregnancies in Men and Women

The interaction of the mind and body is one of the most intriguing mysteries of modern science. Nowhere is this interaction more perplexing than in the phenomenon of **couvade**. Couvade, a French term meaning "to brood or hatch," is commonly translated as "false pregnancy." In many nontechnological cultures, males go through a ritual pregnancy and delivery in order to draw the evil spirits away from the pregnant mother. These rituals may be so intense they trigger a psychosomatic condition in which the father actually experiences the symptoms of pregnancy and labor (Davenport 1965; Trethowan & Colton 1965).

In recent years, American fathers have adopted their own sort of ritualized participation in their wives' pregnancies by attending natural childbirth classes, learning to support their wives' exercises and preparations for labor, and participating as coaches in the actual delivery. For a significant number of these fathers-to-be, the emotional intensity of these prenatal experiences is enough to induce the psychosomatic symptoms of couvade. Various studies indicate that between 22% and 80% of American fathers experience some physical symptoms of pregnancy, with the most common being nausea, vomiting, heartburn, constipation, backache, abdominal swelling, unintentional weight gain and weight loss, an elevated heart rate, muscle tension, appetite changes, excessive fatigue, and general feelings of ill health. These same expectant fathers commonly reported headaches, depression, difficulty in concentrating, restlessness, irritability, generalized anxiety, and insomnia. Originally couvade was regarded as a neurotic phenomenon. Today, the more common interpretation is that the symptoms of false pregnancy are associated with a developmental crisis. But we could as well ask whether couvade may not be a quite natural psychosomatic outcome of an increasing emphasis on the emotional bonding and intensity of a shared pregnancy (Clinton 1987).

Pseudocyesis, or *false pregnancy,* occurs when a woman has such a strong desire to become pregnant, she experiences what psychologists call a psychic conversion and develops all the symptoms of a normal pregnancy. Menstruation may stop, and she may experience morning nausea, weight gain, abdominal expansion, and all the other signs of pregnancy. Psychotherapy may resolve this confusion, or the "pregnancy" may end on the expected "delivery day" with the expulsion of air and fluid from the uterus (McCary & McCary 1982:143; Taylor 1970:40,42).

Postpartum "blues" are also frequently shared by both the new mother and father. In one study, 89% of the new mothers and 62% of the new fathers reported postpartum depression. For the fathers the depression was usually related to a feeling of helplessness when confronted with caring for the infant, their inability to help their wives more with the nurturing, or with the reluctance of the mother to allow the father to share more in caring for their new child. Usually, such emotions pass quickly as the new parents adjust to their new roles. In a few cases, mothers have alleged that their postpartum depression was so severe it led them to injure or even kill their babies (Paige 1973).

Prenatal Monitoring

Today there are several relatively safe procedures for monitoring fetal development and diagnosing some genetic defects in the fetus (Francoeur 1985).

In **amniocentesis**, fluid is removed between weeks 16 and 18 of gestation from the amniotic sac that surrounds the fetus (Figure 8.6). The procedure involves inserting a needle through the abdomen and into the uterus, avoiding the placenta. The fetal cells are grown in a culture medium and then checked for normal chromosomes, genetic defects, and biochemical disorders. This testing usually takes between two and four weeks to complete. Blood tests for abnormal levels of alpha-fetoprotein, an indicator of neural tube defects, chorionic villi sampling, ultrasonography, and amniocentesis may reveal an abnormal fetus and prompt the woman or couple to decide on an abortion.

Amniocentesis is frequently used to determine if the fetus has Down syndrome, a condition in which an extra number 21 chromosome causes the child to be born mentally retarded and with major health problems, including congenital heart defects and an increased risk of leukemia. Down syndrome is more often associated with an older mother: The general risk is 1 in 700, whereas the risk for mothers over the age of 40 is 1 in every 30 to 50 births. New research has determined that in 20% to 25% of Down's children the father's chromosomes are the cause. At this point, the age of the father has not been proven as a contributory factor.

Amniocentesis should be considered,

- If you are over 35;.
- If you have had a previous abnormal pregnancy;
- If you have a family or personal history of genetic disorders;
- If you and your partner's ethnic background places the fetus at risk for a particular genetic disease.

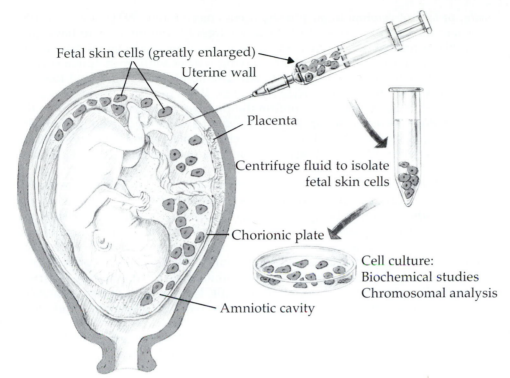

Fetal skin cells (greatly enlarged)
Uterine wall
Placenta
Centrifuge fluid to isolate fetal skin cells
Chorionic plate
Cell culture: Biochemical studies Chromosomal analysis
Amniotic cavity

Figure 8.6. Fetal Screening with Amniocentesis. *After 10 or 12 weeks of fetal development, an ultrasonic scan will reveal the location of the fetus and placenta in the uterus. The physician can then guide a hypodermic needle into the amniotic sac and withdraw a sample of amniotic fluid containing fetal cells. These cells are grown in tissue culture for chromosome and biochemical analysis. Several serious hereditary diseases can be detected in this way, allowing the woman to consider the options of continuing the pregnancy or having an abortion. Amniotic cells are much enlarged in this drawing.*

Amniocentesis has been adapted in a new technique known as *chordocentesis*. Instead of withdrawing a sample of amniotic fluid, a needle can be guided by ultrasound imaging into a blood vessel in the umbilical cord and a sample of the fetal blood withdrawn for direct analysis.

In **chorionic villi biopsy (CVB)**, developed in 1983, a catheter is passed through the vaginal and cervical canals to take a sample of the placental tissue. The biopsy can also be done through an incision in the abdominal wall, guided by ultrasound scanning. Since the cells of the placenta are fetal cells, they can reveal the existence of crucial fetal metabolic deficiencies or defects when grown in tissue culture. The chromosomes of these cells can also be checked to detect Down syndrome or other chromosomal variations. The increased risk of CVB when compared with amniocentesis may be offset by the advantage that it can be done in the eighth week or earlier, a factor which allows the woman or couple more time to make a decision about a possible abortion. First trimester abortions are much safer than those done in the second trimester.

In **ultrasonic scanning**, high frequency sound impulses are bounced off the fetus like radar and analyzed by a computer to reveal a picture of the fetus based on the different densities of its tissues (Figure 8.7). An amnioscope or fetoscope and thermography or heat-sensitive photography can provide a visual image of the fetus. None of these fetal monitoring methods are without some risk to the fetus, and possibly to the mother also.

Approximately 2 in every 1,000 American infants are born with serious neural tube defect (NTD). Usually, an NTD involves a spinal cord and neural tube that has not closed, called *spina bifida*. A more serious condition, *anence-*

Figure 8.7. *This ultrasonogram, taken with the mother lying on her side, shows the tiny erect penis of a 29-week-old fetus. The scrotum is visible in black beneath the erect penis. Ultrasonograms reveal male fetuses have the same rhythm of erections every 90 minutes as normal adult sleeping males.*

phaly, or lack of cerebral hemispheres, occurs more rarely. NTD always results in severe medical problems which require surgery if the infant is to have anything like a normal life. Even with surgery, paralysis and mental retardation are common consequences. Mothers carrying fetuses with open spinal cord or brain lesions have an elevated level of alpha-fetoprotein in their blood that can be detected with an *alpha-fetoprotein* (AFP) *test*. If the mother's blood tests positive for AFP, the physician will confirm the problem by checking for AFP in the amniotic fluid. To interpret an AFP test accurately, the doctor takes into consideration other factors like the mother's ethnic background, obesity, and the age of the fetus based on an ultrasound scan (Boston Women's Health Collective 1984:358).

Genetic counseling is a relatively new development that enables prospective parents who might be carriers of a genetic disease to find out more about the chances of their children being affected by the disease. Genetic counselors are trained in the principles of human heredity and in using new techniques to predict or detect genetic diseases in the fetus. One of these diseases, sickle cell anemia, primarily affects blacks, although some whites may also carry this trait. One out of every 10 black Americans has a mild form of this disease. Carriers of sickle cell anemia can be detected by a simple blood test. A genetic counselor can then discuss with prospective parents beforehand the risk for any child they might have.

The gene for Tay-Sachs disease occurs among Eastern European Jews. In order for a child to be affected, he or she must inherit a recessive Tay-Sachs gene from both parents. Tay-Sachs causes a degeneration of the nervous system, organs, and muscles, and death by age 3 or 4. Potential parents from this ethnic group should have a simple blood test that can detect whether or not they are carriers of the gene. Genetic screening has practically eliminated Tay-Sachs among Jewish-American infants.

In the 1990s the Human Genome Initiative Project will give us a detailed map of every gene carried on the 46 human chromosomes. This knowledge and our ability to detect genetics diseases during fetal development will raise many perplexing social and ethical questions.

Sexual Intercourse and Exercise During Pregnancy

In Victorian times, many physicians and most of the public believed that intercourse during pregnancy could harm the fetus, or at the least cause early labor. The present medical view is that most women can safely have intercourse until near the end of the pregnancy, when the cervix dilates during labor. Abstinence during the last three months, or even throughout the pregnancy, is encouraged for those women with a history of reproductive problems or premature thinning or opening of the uterus. If a woman has a high risk pregnancy and is prone to miscarriage, she should follow the advice of her physician (Naeye 1979).

Every expectant father and mother has his or her own unique psychological reactions to a pregnancy. Thus it is impossible to predict or anticipate how any one expectant mother or father might react to the changes pregnancy brings. A changed self-image for the mother, fear of hurting the woman or fetus during sexual activity, and an anticipated change in the man-woman relationship may need to be discussed. Different positions for intercourse may be tried, especially near term, along with alternatives to vaginal intercourse such as oral sex and mutual masturbation.

Figure 8.8. Pregnancy and Sexual Intimacy. *The physical changes that come with pregnancy may have a negative impact on the woman, distorting her image of herself as a sexually desirable partner. The man may also view the pregnancy as a sexual "turn-off." These negative reactions are rooted in the many sexual stereotypes common in our culture which focus on youth, slimness, and playboy/playgirl images. Pregnancy can add a new, rich dimension to the sexual lives of a couple.*

Moderate exercise during pregnancy is helpful. Although it is unwise for a woman to start a heavy program of exercise and training during pregnancy, there is usually no reason for her to discontinue a sport she has been practicing for some time. Ranking tennis players and Marines in the rigors of a 21-week officer training program have competed successfully while pregnant (Sloane 1980). A physician's advice obviously is very important in such decisions.

PART TWO: CHILDBIRTH AND OPTIONS IN DELIVERY

Vaginal Delivery

The Stages of Labor

The sign of impending birth is the onset of **labor**, the regular contractions of the uterus that expel the fetus into and through the vagina. Although the start of labor varies greatly, it is often accompanied by a bloody mucous discharge. This "show" is the plug that blocks the cervix during pregnancy and prevents bacteria from entering the uterus. In about 10% of women, the amniotic sac breaks ("breaking of the waters") before labor starts.

The First Stage of Labor

During the first stage, the cervix effaces or thins out and dilates to about 4 inches to allow passage of the fetus. The first stage of labor is divided into early, late, and transition phases. In the early phase, the uterine contractions occur every 15 to 20 minutes. Each contraction lasts less than a minute. In the late phase, the contractions increase in frequency and length. The transition phase, immediately prior to delivery, is the shortest and most difficult time in the first stage of labor.

Most women experience all three phases of this first stage of labor in the hospital labor room. Labor may last from 2 hours to 24 hours, or longer. In longer labors, the contractions may stop and start up again. First births average between 6 and 10 hours of labor. Subsequent labors are usually shorter, sometimes as brief as an hour or two.

The Second Stage of Labor

The second stage usually occurs in the delivery room and may take a few minutes, or an hour or more. If the baby is in the usual position, the head will come through the cervix first. In a breech delivery, the feet, knees, or buttocks come first. With coaching from the physician, midwife, or nurse and often the father or a friend, the woman can bear down, pushing the child out through the vagina (Figure 8.9).

To the rear of the vulva and in front of the anus is a muscular body of tissue called the perineum. As the fetus emerges from the vaginal canal, this tissue may be stretched to the tearing point. Tearing, especially if it extends into the rectal tissue, poses a risk of infection and slow recovery for the mother. Often the physician will prestretch the perineum in the early stages of labor to reduce the risk of tearing. Some physicians prefer to use a minor surgical incision in the perineum, an **episiotomy**, which can easily be repaired with a few surgical stitches after the delivery. Healing of an episiotomy usually takes about three weeks, although the area may remain sensitive to pressure for several weeks. A regular routine of the Kegel exercises will help the muscles regain their tone. In some European countries, episiotomies are rarely done. Many feminists and members of natural childbirth groups believe that episiotomy is unnecessary in most deliveries, even though it has been a routine American medical practice for years.

As the baby's head comes through the pelvic area, the body rotates so that the shoulders can exit. Once the baby's head has been delivered, mucus is removed from its mouth and nasal passages. After birth, a silver nitrate solution or an antibiotic ointment is routinely placed in the eyes to prevent damage from exposure to gonococcal-infected vaginal secretions. Breathing begins through the lungs. The umbilical cord is cut and clamped about 3 inches from the infant's body. The stub will dry up and fall off in a few days.

The Third Stage of Labor

During the third stage of labor, the **afterbirth**, the placenta and fetal membranes, are expelled by continued uterine contractions. This process may take a few minutes to an hour. The doctor examines the placenta and umbilical cord

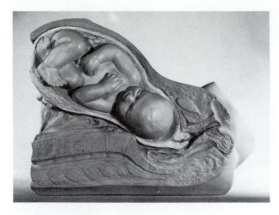

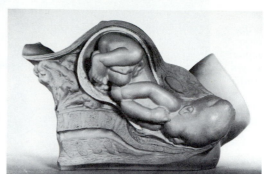

Figure 8.9. The Three Stages of Labor. *In the first stage, the fetus enters the cervical region of the uterus, usually head first. In the second stage, called crowning, the fetus begins to emerge from the birth canal. In the third stage, the placenta detaches from the uterine wall and is expelled as the afterbirth.*

to be sure that it has all been expelled. If any part of the afterbirth is retained in the uterus, it has to be removed by the physician. Otherwise, it will decay and cause an infection. After the afterbirth is fully expelled, the incision from an episiotomy, if done, is repaired.

Options in Vaginal Delivery

In the United States, hospital births are still the most common form of delivery. Obstetrical practices have changed considerably, however, in recent years. Instead of a woman giving birth flat on her back with her feet in stirrups and her arms tied down, special birthing beds or chairs are used (Figure 8.10). The use of anesthesia and episiotomy is declining, and involvement of both parents in labor and delivery is being encouraged.

Natural or Prepared Childbirth

Natural childbirth is quite common in Europe and is increasingly popular in the United States. The term was coined by Dr. Grantley Dick-Reed, an English obstetrician, in his 1932 book *Childbirth Without Fear.*

In **prepared childbirth**, the expectant mother is taught to relax, using exercises for breathing and muscle control so she can assist during delivery. The breathing reduces the tension and pain caused by the fear a woman commonly experiences when she is unprepared for what happens during labor and deliv-

Figure 8.10. The Return of the Birthing Chair or Bed. *After nearly 200 years during which American women have given birth lying on their backs, some doctors are reviving an ancient method of delivery in which the woman sits upright in a "birthing chair." The birthing chair shown here is designed with molded knee braces, adjustable footrests, and completely motorized controls. Use of the birthing chair often cuts in half the time spent in second-stage labor.*

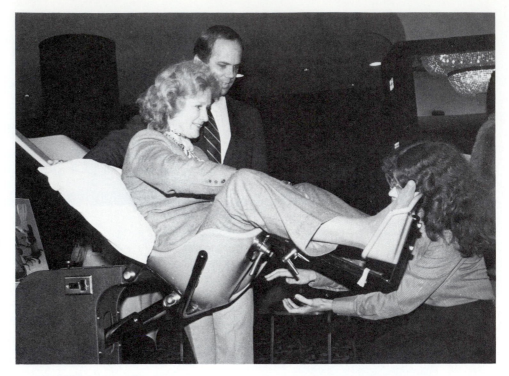

ery. Preparation for natural childbirth includes learning about possible complications and options including cesarean section, anesthetics, forceps delivery, and episiotomy. Anesthetics are discouraged because of the possible danger to the child and because they can lessen the awareness and cooperation of the mother. The father, a relative or friend takes classes with the mother, learns how to assist in delivery, and coaches and comforts her during labor and delivery. In uncomplicated pregnancies, midwives may replace obstetricians in assisting at the delivery.

Sometimes the couple's other children are allowed to be present at a natural delivery. There is some controversy about this practice and its long-term effects on a young child. With new fast-speed films and video camcorders, many couples today record the birth of their babies for posterity.

The Lamaze Delivery

The **Lamaze method of childbirth** was introduced to the United States in the early 1950s by the French obstetrician Fernand Lamaze. Popular in many hospitals and clinics today, the Lamaze method emphasizes relaxation and controlled breathing. The woman is prepared to take control of the delivery, with the physician assisting her. During the pregnancy, the expectant mother and father learn about all aspects of the birth process. The father is trained to help as a guide or mentor during the birth. In the Lamaze method, a regional anesthesia may be used to eliminate pain and leave the mother fully aware and able to participate in the delivery.

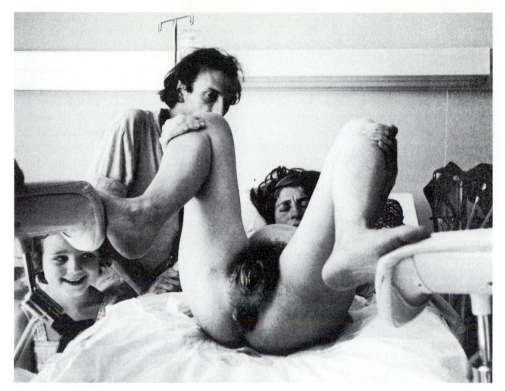

Figure 8.11. A Gentle Birthing. *A woman giving birth at the Maternité des Lilas in Paris using the techniques of "gentle birthing" developed by the French physician Frederick Leboyer. In this technique the birth is a family affair, with the young children of the family participating and watching. Do you think this procedure would have any effect on sibling jealousy?*

Leboyer's "Gentle Birthing"

Frederick Leboyer, a French physician, introduced his method of delivery to the United States with his books *Birth Without Violence* and *The Traditional Indian Art of Baby Massage*. **Leboyer Gentle Birthing** focuses on the comfort of the infant and the development of a strong bonding between the infant and parents by making massage a part of the birth.

The room is dim and warm, with soft music playing. As the infant emerges from the birth canal, father and mother both assist, drawing the baby up and over the mother's abdomen without losing any physical skin-to-skin contact with it. The child is massaged by both parents, gently sponged with warm water, and then put to nurse. Later the umbilical cord is clamped and cut, and the baby is given a gentle warm bath (Figure 8.11). Throughout the birth, the importance of physical intimacy shared by the parents and the infant is stressed, a point we return to in Chapter 15 when we discuss the important role our early experiences with nurturance and touch play in our quest for intimacy and in our relationships later in life.

Birthing Clinics

Birthing clinics are special facilities designed to allow childbirth to occur in a natural, homelike atmosphere. They permit family and friends to be with the mother and attend to her both before and after the birth. Some clinics are located near hospitals; others are part of a hospital but separate. In birthing clinics, the baby is not separated from the mother, and the mother makes a natural transition to begin caring for her child. Unnecessary drugs and medical procedures are also avoided.

Birth in the Home

Until this century, babies were regularly delivered at home. In the 1960s and 1970s, especially in California, there was a move to return birthing to the comfort of the home where the whole family and even friends can share in the delivery aided by a midwife. However, should a problem arise, few communities have adequate emergency services to allow safe transport of a woman in the midst of birthing to a hospital. Although the American College of Obstetricians and Gynecologists opposed home delivery in 1982, a matched, controlled study of 2,092 home and hospital births found no significant differences in maternal or infant mortality or morbidity (Mehl 1978).

Midwives

Whether a baby is delivered in a hospital, a birthing center, or at home, the midwife is playing an increasingly visible and important role. Many hospitals and communities today have *certified nurse midwives* (CNMs) available. These midwives have taken a graduate program in assisting in a normal pregnancy and birth and in caring for the mother. Some states have examinations and license CNMs to practice with a physician. Most *lay midwives* were eliminated during the 1960s by pressure from the medical profession. However, they still serve an important need in rural areas and among poor and minority women who have limited access to health care.

Forceps-Assisted Deliveries

In the early 1900s different kinds of forceps, scissorlike paddles, were widely used to ease delivery. Forceps were sometimes used even before the head of the fetus emerged from the cervix. Today, only 10% to 15% of all deliveries are forceps-assisted, and the forceps are only used after the cervix is fully dilated and the head of the infant can be seen.

Cesarean Section Delivery

Although the varieties of vaginal delivery we have described are options for the mother to choose, there are deliveries in which a **cesarean section** (C-section) may be required because of the condition of the mother or the fetus. Cesarean section is usually performed when

- The fetus is too large or the woman's pelvis is too small;
- The cervix is not dilating;
- Labor is too long and strenuous and is exhausting the woman;
- The umbilical cord is tangled or coming out first;
- There is fetal distress;
- Fetal position poses a risk to mother or fetus.

Table 8.1.
How Common Is
Cesarean Section Delivery?

	1984	1990	2000*
All ages	21.1%	28.8%	40.3%
Under 20	16.5%	22.2%	31.4%
20–24	19.6%	26.9%	38.3%
25–29	20.8%	29.1%	40.8%
30–34	24.6%	32.3%	45.1%
35 and older	28.7%	35.4%	48.6%

*Projected.
Sources: U.S. Census Bureau and the National Center for Health Statistics.

A cesarean section is performed by making incisions in the abdominal and uterine walls through which the baby is removed. The incisions are then stitched, with recovery taking between 7 and 10 days.

Around 1970 less than 5% of American births were by cesarean section. In 1976 the percentage was close to 12%, in 1984, 21%, and in 1990, 29%. By the year 2000, over 40% of all American babies are expected to be delivered by cesarean section (Table 8.1). These statistics include first time and repeat cesarean sections. Some defenders of this trend say it is because we provide the very best in prenatal electronic monitoring and surgery. Opponents argue that the United States ranks 17th among the industrialized nations in infant mortality, and that Holland, which has a much lower infant mortality rate, has only 2% to 4% cesarean sections and seldom uses anesthesia or prenatal electronic monitoring (Table 8.2). The maternal mortality rate in the United States is also much higher than in many other nations (Table 8.3).

The main reason for the frequent use of cesarean sections is that a very real fear of malpractice suits encourages physicians to use the latest equipment even when it is not needed, or to intervene rather than risk losing the baby. In 1987 Dr. Warren H. Pearce, executive director of the American College of Obstetricians and Gynecologists, agreed with a report from the Public Citizen Research Group that only 12 to 16 births out of 100 births to women who have not previously had a cesarean section medically require the procedure. Whatever the reasons for the rising use of cesarean section, the controversy is likely to continue.

Hospitals and physicians have become so comfortable with cesarean section delivery that they will sometimes allow the father in the operating room during the birth. With the latest techniques, women may choose a natural delivery for a subsequent birth if another cesarean section is not mandated.

The Forced Cesarean Controversy

In the late 1980s antiabortion forces began urging the lower courts and state legislatures to refocus the debate on the fetus and its rights. The argument is that when the U.S. Supreme Court recognized women's constitutional right to the privacy of their bodies in 1973, it also recognized the interest of the states

Table 8.2.
How Does the United States Compare on Infant Mortality Rates?

In 1986 the United States had a higher infant mortality rate than 16 other nations. The figures given are the number of deaths for infants under one year of age per 1,000 lives births in 1986.

Finland, Japan, Iceland	6.2
Sweden	6.3
Denmark, Switzerland	7.7
Norway	7.9
The Netherlands	8.3
Canada, France	8.5
Hong Kong	9.2
Singapore	9.4
Australia (including 30 deaths per 1,000 births estimated for the aborigines)	9.6
Ireland	9.8
England & Wales	10.1
East Germany, West Germany	10.3
United States	10.6 *

*In 1981 infant mortality rates in 10 urban and poor areas ranged between 16.7 and 32.5 deaths per 1,000 live births.
Sources: Demographic Office of UNICEF, The Economic and Social Council of the United Nations, and "Sisterhood Is Global."

Table 8.3.
How Does the United States Compare on Maternal Mortality Rates?

Number of Maternal Deaths per 100,000 Live Births in 1982	
Canada	1.9
Israel	3.1
Hong Kong	3.5
Sweden	4.3
Finland	4.5
Ireland	5.6
The Netherlands	6.4
England & Wales	6.7
Kuwait	7.4
Belgium	7.5
United States	7.9

Source: 1985 United Nations Demographic Yearbook.

in the potential human life in the three months before birth. In 1987 the *New England Journal of Medicine* reported on 21 cases in 11 states where women had been forced to undergo cesarean section to protect the life of a potential human being. Most of the court orders forcing these operations on pregnant women were granted within six hours. All of the women were poor; black and Hispanic women accounted for 47% of the forced operations (Bonavoglia 1987; Gallagher 1987; Johnsen 1986; Kolder et al. 1987).

Breast Feeding

After decades in which bottle feeding was popular, many American mothers are choosing to breast-feed their infants. This shift is part of a growing awareness of the importance of nutrition and of the nurturing bonding between infant and mother. Today, about one-third of American infants are breast-fed. Most, however, are breast-fed only through the second month with a sharp decline after the third month. Breast feeding is fulfilling for both mother and child. It also provides an opportunity for holding and cuddling, a vital factor in promoting the emotional development of the infant. However, bottle-fed babies also are held and cuddled and, despite statements to the contrary, there is no proof of long-term differences between bottle-fed and breast-fed infants (Figure 8.12).

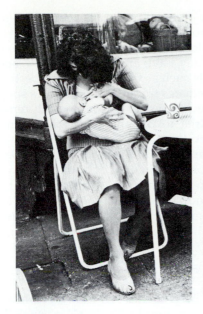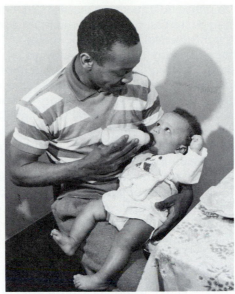

Figure 8.12. *More positive social attitudes toward breast feeding and a new emphasis on a father's involvement in child care add new dimensions to parenting.*

The production of breast milk is stimulated by the hormone *prolactin*. Another hormone, *oxytocin*, stimulates the expulsion of milk from the breasts. Oxytocin is produced by the pituitary in response to sucking on the breast. The first fluid produced by the breast is colostrum. This protein-rich nutrient contains maternal antibodies that protect the baby against certain infections. This acquired immunity lasts about as long as breast feeding continues. Although breast feeding usually delays the return of ovulation, it should not be relied on as a form of contraception. Groups like the La Leche League provide information on techniques and aids to breast feeding.

Custom-Made Pregnancies

Infertility and Possible Treatments

Infertility is the inability of a male to produce sperm capable of fertilization or of a woman to conceive and bear a child. Contrary to popular opinion, infertility is common in the United States and is increasing. Between 15% and 20% of all couples trying to have children, 2 million to 3 million Americans, are infertile. Studies show that sterility has tripled in the past 20 years and that 10 million American men suffer from low sperm counts or total lack of sperm. In the 20- to 24-year-old age group, female sterility is up by 177% since 1965. The Office of Technology Assessment reported Americans spent a billion dollars on infertility treatments in 1988.

In a male, the inability to produce normal viable sperm in sufficient amounts to assure fertilization may be due to many causes, including an infection with a high fever during puberty, X-ray exposure in large doses, undescended testes, varicocele, low motility or movement of sperm, blockage of the vas deferens, emotional stress, poor nutrition, or obesity. The most common causes of female infertility include anovulation (lack of ovulation) and blocked fallopian tubes due to pelvic inflammatory disease (PID) or endometriosis. Poor nutrition, uterine polyps, stress, and obesity may also cause infertility in women.

A controversial study of 132 males at Florida State University suggests that perhaps as many as 1 in 4 young males may have an abnormally low sperm count due to accumulation of toxic chemicals such as PCBs, DDT, and pesticides in the testes (Dougherty 1979). Informal estimates from infertility clinics suggest a similar high rate of female sterility in young women. Much research remains to be done on environmental and industrial toxins and their effects on the fertility of both men and women exposed to them.

Couples facing an infertility problem can often find help at a clinic specializing in treating sterility. A thorough clinical examination of both the man and the woman may reveal a problem that can be remedied with hormonal treatment, medication, or counseling. Or the couple can sometimes find a solution in one of the new reproductive technologies. Artificial insemination, frozen sperm and eggs, embryo transplants, and surrogate mothers are among the several remedies available.

Artificial Insemination and Frozen Sperm

The reproductive technology most widely used today, **artificial insemination**, was first used 200 years ago. The technique is simple: The male partner, husband, or a male donor masturbates, and his semen is inserted into the vagina of the woman with a plastic syringe. The only problem is to coordinate the artificial insemination with the time the woman is ovulating and fertile. Artificial insemination was seldom successful until the 1930s when scientists first realized that ovulation does not occur just before menstruation as they previously believed but 14 days before. Even after this discovery, using fresh semen had its limits.

In 1942 human semen was frozen without damage, although the first "frozen sperm baby" was not born until 1954. Frozen semen made artificial insemination much more practical and flexible. If the man has a low sperm count, several ejaculates can be concentrated and stored for a single insemination. Using frozen donor semen also is easier than relying on fresh semen from a donor.

By the mid-1980s, commercial frozen sperm banks were operating in most large cities. Sperm banks provide a backup for men who have had a vasectomy, but then divorce, remarry, and decide to have a child with their new wives. Men in contact sports and chemical industries where sterility is a risk use sperm banks as a backup. Couples who know they are carriers for Tay-Sachs, sickle cell anemia, cystic fibrosis, and similar diseases may use frozen donor semen to avoid the risk of passing these defective genes on to their child. There is even a eugenics-oriented sperm bank designed to improve the quality of the human gene pool by using frozen semen of high IQ men to inseminate equally intelligent women. In the 1980s the growing reality of increasing sterility among men and women in their twenties has added to the popularity of artificial insemination.

Artificial insemination is now used by single women and lesbian couples who wish to have a child of their own without resorting to heterosexual intercourse. In one classic case, a lesbian in California was artificially inseminated by her lover using semen from the lover's brother and a turkey baster. The lover was listed on the birth certificate as the "father" because she inseminated or impregnated the mother. Later, when the couple split up, the court awarded the lover "paternal visiting rights."

Figure 8.13.

LOOK, LADY — YOU'RE THE ONE WHO ASKED FOR A FAMOUS MOVIE STAR WITH DARK HAIR, STRONG NOSE AND DEEP SET EYES...

We still do not have reliable ways of sorting out the male-determining sperm from the female-determining sperm, but progress is being made. When an effective method is found—and it will be—couples who want a child of their own but also want to avoid the risk of an X-linked trait in their genetic background like hemophilia, Duchenne muscular dystrophy, or Lesch-Nyhan disease will be happy to use it. Couples who want only one or two children may use it to determine the sex of their first child, which could create an imbalance in the sex ratio. If it is used to any extent to produce firstborn sons and then daughters, a different kind of imbalance may result. There is some evidence that firstborns have significant biological and intellectual advantages over second-born children, probably because firstborn children are given more attention than subsequent children.

Although artificial insemination has many valuable uses, it may have some unexpected consequences. Between 1975 and 1983, the number of unmarried Canadian women ages 25 to 39 who became single mothers rose by 600%! Commenting on this significant increase, one knowledgeable physician suggested, "The growing use of artificial insemination reflects the growing trend in women to bear children of their own," without being married (Francoeur 1985:4).

Test Tube Fertilization and Embryo Transfer

Microsurgery techniques to open minor blocks in the fallopian tubes are successful in 3 out of 4 cases, although the success rate with major blocks is between 0% and 20%. Another common cause of female infertility, the failure to produce fertile eggs regularly, can sometimes be solved by stimulating the ovaries with hormones. When drugs are used, the ovaries produce an average of 5 eggs, with 17 being the maximum reported. To fertilize these eggs, a woman may have intercourse with her partner, or be artificially inseminated with a donor's semen.

If a woman can ovulate but cannot carry a child to full term, her eggs may be removed surgically. They can also be flushed from the fallopian tube or uterus. The eggs can be matured in a nutrient solution for 4 to 8 hours before being mixed with the male partner's or donor semen. If a man's sperm cannot

Figure 8.14.

get inside his partner's egg, the sperm can be injected into the egg to facilitate fertilization. Within a day of exposure to sperm, 80% of the eggs show signs of fertilization. The tiny embryo can then be transferred through the cervical canal into the cavity of the uterus. Within two weeks, the success or failure of this venture is known. In nature, up to 75% of fertilized eggs fail to implant in the uterine wall. In **IVF** (**in vitro fertilization**) (or test tube fertilization) followed by embryo transfer of 3 or more embryonic masses, about a third of the women with normal hormone cycles become pregnant. The miscarriage rate, however, is relatively high, about 25%.

In 1978, Lesley Brown, aided by Drs. Edwards and Steptoe, gave us the world's first IVF or "test tube" baby (Edwards & Steptoe 1981) (Figure 8.15). By 1990, there were an estimated 15,000 IVF babies born around the world, including many sets of twins and triplets, as well as several sets of quadruplets. In 1990 there were over 150 IVF clinics in the United States. The most successful American clinic, the Jones Institute for Reproductive Medicine at the Eastern Virginia Medical School in Norfolk, reported over 200 IVF babies in 1989. Although nearly half of all U.S. IVF clinics had not produced their first IVF baby, the chances of success with IVF continue to improve.

Advances in IVF, accompanied by new legal and social complications, have come with a speed no one expected. Australian researchers pioneered the use of donor eggs for women who could not be induced to ovulate. At first, the donor eggs were fertilized *in vitro* with her partner's semen before transferring them into the woman's womb. Then California researchers found they could artificially inseminate the donor as she ovulated, flush the embryos from her womb five days after fertilization, and transfer them into the womb of the childless woman. This technique combines natural or hormone-induced ovulation and artificial insemination of a **surrogate mother**, embryo lavage, and embryo transplantation to the childless woman. If the woman is ovulating normally but cannot carry a normal pregnancy, she can be naturally or artificially

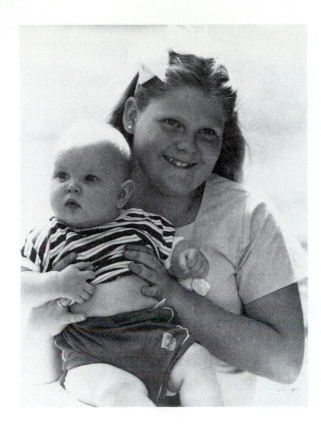

Figure 8.15. *Eleven-year-old Louise Brown, the world's first test-tube baby, holds six-month-old Andrew Patrick Macheta. Both were attending a 1989 New Year's Day party for the 600 children born at the test-tube baby clinic near Cambridge, England. Andrew was named after Patrick Steptoe, the doctor who pioneered this reproductive technique in 1978.*

inseminated with her partner's or a donor's semen. The embryo can be flushed from her womb and transferred to a surrogate mother for a nine-month pregnancy. This combination is known as *artificial embryonation*. In 1984 researchers found a way to avoid wasting the extra eggs produced by hormone-induced ovulation. Surplus eggs can now be fertilized in the test tube and frozen in liquid nitrogen at −196°F until needed.

The more common form of surrogate motherhood is *embryo adoption*. In this procedure, a surrogate mother is artificially inseminated with the semen of a childless male partner. She then serves as a "prenatal wet nurse" and carries the child to term before giving it up for adoption by the childless couple. This is the technique that exploded into nationwide headlines in 1986 and 1987, when Mary Beth Whitehead, a surrogate mother, refused to give up "Baby M" to the natural father and adoptive mother, Elizabeth and William Stern.

The Surrogate Mother Controversy

On November 24, 1979, an anonymous couple ran a classified ad in *The Louisville Courier-Journal*, seeking a "surrogate mother." An Illinois mother of three in her mid-thirties responded to the ad and became America's first (as far as we know) paid legal surrogate mother. Elizabeth Kane, her public pseudonym, was artificially inseminated with the childless husband's semen, after she persuaded her husband to let her help out this couple who so desperately wanted a child.

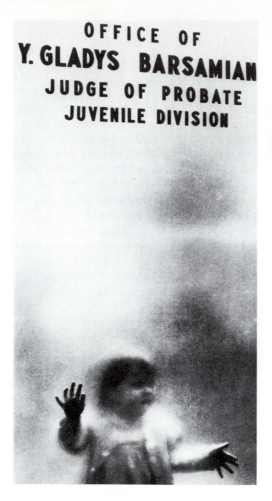

Figure 8.16. The Mysterious World of Reproductive Technologies. *Fourteen-month-old Elizabeth Ann tries to peer through the frosted door of Wayne County Juvenile court. Inside, her parents, a Detroit area couple who were unable to produce their own offspring, are completing the first legal proceedings in the nations's history to adopt a child carried for them by a surrogate mother. Elizabeth Ann's parents, identified only as Deborah and George, established a legal precedent for surrogate motherhood in March 1979.*

After giving her 8-pound, 4-ounce infant boy up for adoption, Ms. Kane explained her decision on an NBC television show (Kane 1988).

Ten years later over 1,000 women had followed Elizabeth Kane's lead. The vast majority of these cases went smoothly, with all parties happy with the outcome. This majority included several unusual cases: women who served as surrogate mothers for a childless sister, and a South African woman who was artificially inseminated with her son-in-law's semen and gave birth to her own semigrandchild whom her daughter raised as her own child. Television and newsmagazines carried frequent stories about the newest twist to surrogate motherhood. Lori Andrews, a research attorney at the American Bar Foundation and professor of medical law, wrote a "Consumer's Guide to the Newest Infertility Treatments" (Andrews 1985). America seemed to have negotiated a startling new medical advance with minor hitches.

Then came the Baby M case. In October 1986 Elizabeth Kane read about Mary Beth Whitehead's "nightmare" as a surrogate mother and her legal battle in the New Jersey Supreme Court to retain custody of the child she had contracted to bear for Elizabeth and William Stern. The case dragged on for months with Baby M and the contending parents becoming international news celebrities (Chesler 1988). When Elizabeth and Mary Beth met, Kane summed up the views of many feminists and others who have come to oppose the payment of fees to surrogate mothers:

> We have to come face-to-face with the fact that wealthy men are taking advantage of women from lower-middle-income families. The baby brokers and judges are well aware of the financial status of women being hired as breeders, smug in the fact that few will have the financial means to engage in long legal battles to regain custody of their own children. This is reproductive prostitution.
>
> *(Kane 1988)*

By the early 1980s a Feminist International Network on the New Reproductive Technologies and other groups had organized to urge legislatures to outlaw surrogate motherhood (Arditti et al. 1984; Corea 1985; Holmes et al. 1981). By mid-1988 four states had outlawed surrogate mother contracts and forbade payment for their services. More than 20 other states were considering such legislation to outlaw any payment for surrogate mothers beyond reimbursement for medical expenses (Andrews 1984; Keane & Breo 1981; Singer & Wells 1985; Zukerman Overvold 1988).

Surrogate motherhood has raised cultural, political, legal, and ideological questions for which no one appears to have answers. Women have a constitutional right to privacy that gives them sole power to decide to terminate a pregnancy at any time. Yet once artificially inseminated, does a surrogate mother retain this right? On the other hand, doesn't a woman have the legal right to rent her uterus and be paid as a prenatal wet nurse? If we were to outlaw surrogate motherhood, or at least outlaw payment for surrogate moth-

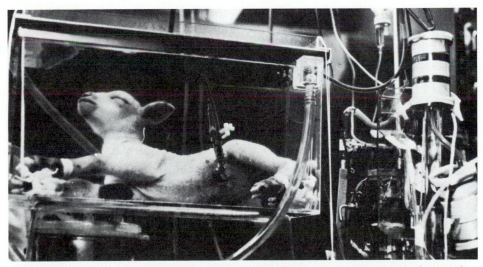

Figure 8.17. Is the Artificial Womb Our Next Step? *Twenty years ago, researchers at the National Heart and Lung Institute's Laboratory of Technical Development were wrestling with ways to improve the chances of a premature infant's survival. One approach was a complete "artificial womb," such as the one shown here. In the not-too-distant future, this experimental technique for saving premature infants may be used to sustain human life throughout the nine months of fetal life.*

ers, how could we possibly enforce such a law? (Andrews 1984, 1985; Singer & Wells 1985). We will all be affected by the answers our society arrives at for these questions. And arriving at answers, or compromises, will be far from easy (Francoeur 1985).

Technologies like the computer, television, and nuclear power have altered our environment, forcing us to adapt and change our lifestyles and the ways we relate to each other in order to survive. The reproductive technologies surveyed here have a much more immediate effect on our lives. Unlike the mechanical technologies, the reproductive technologies radically impinge on our personhood and on the way we experience and view our life as sexual, parental persons.

Critics of these reproductive technologies like to create scenarios of a depersonalized, loveless Brave New World in which humans have been driven by Faustian madness to demonic attempts to "play God." They picture the government issuing licenses for "making babies" and putting restrictions on the poor and minorities. They fear a complete separation of sex and reproduction, the creation of a new social class of professional surrogate parents, of enforced genetic screening, and sterilization with infanticide of defective newborns. Others anticipate a brighter world in which individuals have expanded choices, a greater personal involvement in creating a more healthy future for the next generation, and a more responsible approach to both sexual intercourse and human reproduction.

Key Concepts

1. A woman should have a reliable pregnancy test done as soon as she suspects she may be pregnant so she can make whatever decisions or preparations that are best for herself, her partner, and the fetus.

2. Prenatal care and proper nutrition are essential for a healthy mother and child.

3. Smoking, alcohol, simple medications, and other drugs can seriously harm the fetus, especially in the first two months of pregnancy.

4. Being certain that the fetus, where possible, has the best genetic health is becoming an increasing concern of prospective parents; genetic tests may help in achieving this goal.

5. Conception and pregnancy mark turning points which can have a major impact on the sexual relationship of a woman and her partner.

6. Infertility appears to be a growing problem for both young men and women. Environmental toxins, increased sexual activity with a variety of partners, and unsuspected subclinical pelvic infections are likely factors.

Key Terms

afterbirth (222)
amniocentesis (218)
amniotic fluid (211)
artificial insemination (230)
cesarean section (226)

chorionic villi biopsy (219)
couvade (217)
ectopic (206)
embryo (206)
episiotomy (222)

fertilization (204)
fetal alcohol syndrome (FAS) (215)
fetus (206)
fraternal twins (208)
human chorionic gonadotropin
   (HCG) (208)
identical twins (208)
infertility (229)
intrauterine growth retardation
   (IUGR) (214)
IVF (in vitro fertilization) (232)
labor (221)
Lamaze method of childbirth (224)

Leboyer Gentle Birthing (225)
miscarriage (215)
placenta (210)
prepared childbirth (223)
quickening (212)
Rh factor (216)
rubella (215)
surrogate mother (232)
teratogenic agent (215)
toxemia (217)
ultrasonic scanning (219)
umbilical cord (211)
zygote (206)

Summary Questions

1. What hormone is used in all pregnancy tests? What kinds of pregnancy tests are available and what are the advantages of early pregnancy testing?

2. Describe the various methods of childbirth available today, and the advantages and disadvantages of each of these options.

3. List the arguments pro and con in the current controversy over delivery by cesarean section.

4. What are some benefits and risks posed by our growing ability to detect genetic diseases in the developing fetus?

5. List the various reproductive technologies available today, and describe situations or problems in which couples and single women might choose to use them.

Suggested Readings

Andrews, L. B. (1989). *Between Strangers: Surrogate Mothers, Expectant Fathers, and Brave New Babies.* New York: Harper & Row. A consumer's guide to the complexities of today's reproductive technologies by a knowledgeable lawyer.

Arditti, R., R. D. Klein, & S. Minden. (1984). *Test-Tube Women: What Future for Motherhood?* Boston: Pandora Press. Feminist views of reproductive technologies.

Chesler, P. (1988). *Sacred Bond: The Legacy of Baby M.* New York: Times Book. Behind the national scandal and headlines of Baby M, her surrogate mother, and adoptive parents.

Grad, R., et al. (1981). *The Father Book—Pregnancy and Beyond.* Washington, DC: Acropolis Books. A guidebook filled with information, advice, and support for men.

Neilson, L. (1965). *A Child Is Born.* Boston: Seymour Lawrence. Stunning color photographs of embryonic and fetal development.

Wertz, R., & D. Wertz. (1977). *Lying-In: A History of Childbirth in America.* New York: The Free Press. How a male-dominated medical profession took over obstetrical practice.

They did it 20,000 times on television last year.

How come nobody got pregnant?

Teenage pregnancy in the U.S. has reached epidemic proportions, shattering hundreds of thousands of lives and costing taxpayers $16 billion per year. Instead of helping to solve this problem, the TV networks have virtually banned any mention of birth control in programs and advertising. We need to turn this policy around. You can help.

I. On television, sex is good, contraception is taboo.

There's a lot of sex on television. We all know that. What most people don't realize is that while the networks have been hyping sex, they've banned all mention of birth control in advertising, and censor information about it in programming. (It is permitted in the news.) Millions of dollars in sexually alluring ads are okay. Ads for vaginal sprays and hemorrhoidal products are okay. So are the ads which use nudity here and there to sell products. And characters like J.R. Ewing have been seducing women a few times an hour for eight years.

In 1978, researchers counted 20,000 sexual scenes on prime-time network television (which does not even include soap operas), with nary a mention of consequences or protection. It's even higher today. The only sexual mystery left seems to be how all these people keep doing it without contraception while nobody gets pregnant.

With all that worry-free hot action on television, it's no wonder American youngsters are having sex earlier and more often. *And* getting pregnant. Kids watch an average of four hours every day. That's more time than they spend in school or doing anything else in life, except sleeping. That's four hours per day inside a world where no one ever says "no," where sex is loose and often violent, and where sexual responsibility is as out-of-date as hula-hoops. Today's TV message is this: "GO FOR IT *NOW.* GO FOR IT AGAIN. AND DON'T WORRY ABOUT ANYTHING."

But there is plenty to worry about. The teen pregnancy rate in this country is now the highest of any country in the industrialized world. In the U.S. more than a million teens get pregnant every year. The consequences are tragic: high rates of school drop-outs, broken families, welfare and abortion. Who pays the tab? You do. About $16 billion yearly.

Of course television is *not* the only cause. When it comes to sex, there's a terrible breakdown of communications between parents and kids. There's also an appalling lack of timely, comprehensive sex education in schools. So kids are learning about sex the hard way—by experience. But television is making matters worse. Both because of what's on TV, and because of what is not.

II. Censorship by the Networks

The television industry is very sensitive about people telling them what they cannot broadcast. But the TV industry itself feels free to censor content.

Last year, the American College of Obstetricians and Gynecologists (ACOG)—a most prestigious physicians organization—prepared an ad campaign to educate kids about how to prevent pregnancy. They wanted to use print media, radio, and television. The brochure for the campaign said this: (1) Kids *can* resist peer pressure. They can take the option of postponing sex until they're ready. (2) The pill *is* a safe contraceptive for young women. And (3) sexually active young *men* should also be responsible—use condoms. These were useful statements.

The TV commercials ACOG prepared were even milder. All they suggested was that *unintended pregnancy* can interfere with career goals for women, and they offered to send the brochure. But, amazingly, the network execs said the ads were too "controversial," because they made mention of the word "contraceptives." These are the same networks which routinely show thousands of murders, rapes and acts of kinky sex. And 94% of the sexual encounters in soap operas are among people not married to each other. Are *those* presentations non-controversial? Do *those* represent some kind of higher moral value?

Finally, after long negotiations, the three networks agreed to let the spots run. But only after the dreaded "C-word" – "contraception" – was censored. Instead, the networks substituted this dynamic phrase: "There are many ways to prevent unintended pregnancy."

As for network policies censoring "birth control" within programs? No change. As for the rejection of commercials for contraceptive products like condoms, foams, the pill? No change. As for the reduction of irresponsible sexual imagery? No change. As for a sense of balance between sexual hype and realistic useful information? No change.

III. Blaming the public tastes

Network executives argue that they've a responsibility to uphold high standards of public taste. The mention of birth control (except in the news) would somehow violate that. Is that true? Does the public really want uneducated pregnant teenagers? And a tax bill for $16 billion?

A recent Louis Harris Poll showed exactly what the public wants. Most Americans believe that television portrays an unrealistic and irresponsible view of sex. And 78% would like to see messages about contraception on TV. A similar percentage wants more sex education in schools. So it's not the public which resists more responsible sexual imagery. It's the television executives who resist it. Why? Maybe it's just a creative problem for them. We think they can solve it. Right now they don't even mention birth control when it's exactly appropriate. Why can't J.R. ask his latest conquest if she is prepared? Why can't she ask him? The screenwriters can work it out.

The television industry once said the public couldn't handle images of people wearing seatbelts, and they figured that one out. The case of birth control should be simpler than seatbelts, since 90% of adults already accept its use. It's mainly teenagers who don't.

IV. What you can do

Television executives keep trying to avoid their own responsibility, telling us that TV imagery has nothing to do with shaping teens' attitudes, that television doesn't influence them. But this is ridiculous. Television is the most powerful medium ever invented to influence mass behavior. It's on that basis that the networks sell their advertising.

Television influences all of us every day. And it is a major influence on teenagers about sexuality and responsibility. It may now be a more important influence than school, parents, or even peers. The problem is that television is putting out an unbalanced view which is causing *more* problems for teenagers and society. The situation has got to change.

It's time we turn to the small number of men who control this medium and tell them they have a responsibility to the public beyond entertainment, titillation, pushing products and making money.

They need to know you are out there, and that you are concerned. It will make a tremendous difference. Use the coupons. Write letters and make phone calls. And join Planned Parenthood's efforts in your area.

Thank you.

Planned Parenthood®
Federation of America, Inc.

*T*he Struggle to Control
   Human Reproduction
*D*eciding to Use a
   Contraceptive
Erotophiles and
   Erotophobes
Why Contraceptives
   Aren't Used
Sharing the
   Responsibility
Contraceptive
   Effectiveness
*C*ontraceptive Choices
   1. *Outercourse*
   2. *Barrier and*
      Spermicidal
      Contraceptives
   3. *Hormonal*
      Contraceptives
   4. *Natural*
      Contraception
   5. *Surgical Methods*
*C*hoosing a
   Contraceptive You
   Will Use
*U*nreliable
   Contraceptive
   Methods
*T*eenage Pregnancy
   and Contraceptives
*T*he Ambivalence
   of Americans
School-Based Health
   Clinics
A Fuller Picture
The Costs of Accidental
   Pregnancy
*C*ontraception in the
   1990s
*C*oping with the New
   Reality

Chapter 9

*C*ontraception: Shared Responsibilities

Special Consultants

Peggy Brick, M.Ed., director of education, Planned Parenthood of Greater Northern New Jersey, and author of *Positive Images: A New Approach to Contraceptive Education* (1987).

Sylvia D. Diehl, M.D., medical director, Planned Parenthood of Greater Northern New Jersey, and staff physician, Student Health Services, Fairleigh Dickinson University.

Linda L. Hendrixson, M.A., health educator and adjunct professor of health and human sexuality, Montclair State College, Upsala College, and Fairleigh Dickinson University.

Berta Numata, R.N.C., Ob/Gyn Nurse Practitioner, Planned Parenthood of Greater Northern New Jersey.

Mary Jane St. Peter, R.N., director, Student Health Services, Fairleigh Dickinson University.

In the past century, we have come close to solving a problem our ancestors have struggled with since the beginning of recorded history, and likely since the start of the human race. We can now control human reproduction and still enjoy sexual intercourse as a uniquely intimate way for a man and woman to relate because we have invented a wide range of relatively effective and safe **contraceptives**. Condoms, diaphragms, and surgical vasectomy were developed in the 1800s. In the 20th century, we have devised natural birth control methods based on a scientific understanding of the reproductive cycle. Chemicals that kill sperm were created. In the past 30 years, hormonal contraceptive pills, long-term implants, and improved intrauterine devices have been developed. Surgical sterilization for men and women has become available. In many countries abortion became a legal option for women faced with an unwanted pregnancy.

This wide range of relatively effective and safe contraceptives marks a major social revolution in human history. Women and men can now have the number of children they really want when they want them. For the first time in human history, women and men can enjoy sexual intercourse without the risk of an unwanted pregnancy. Our ability to separate heterosexual intercourse and reproduction now forces us to face three new challenges and one old controversy.

1. We face the challenge of developing new social attitudes and personal values to guide heterosexual men and women in their enjoyment of nonreproductive sexual relations.

2. We face the challenge of developing new social attitudes and moral values to guide our control of human reproduction in a world where overpopulation threatens everyone.

3. We face the challenge of using old and new contraceptives in new ways, in both heterosexual and homosexual love play, to prevent the spread of sexually transmitted diseases.

4. Finally, the ability of heterosexual couples to separate sexual intercourse and the enjoyment of erotic pleasure from reproduction forces our society to reexamine its traditional, now controversial justification of sexual pleasure only in terms of reproduction and its condemnation of homosexual and lesbian sexuality as unnatural because they are not procreative.

For heterosexual men and women, this chapter provides a variety of practical information about ways to experience and enjoy your sexuality while avoiding an unwanted pregnancy. We discuss outercourse and intercourse, and the communication and mutual responsibilities a heterosexual couple can share in choosing and using an effective contraceptive. The information in this chapter can help you broaden your options and choices as a sexual person.

The Struggle to Control Human Reproduction

Nearly 4,000 years ago, upper-class Egyptian women inserted small balls of crocodile dung into their vaginas to prevent conception. A few centuries later, tampons made from linen moistened with fermented acidic plant juices became popular. An early Greek physician recommended a woman hold her breath when the man ejaculated and then immediately get into a squatting position and sneeze to expel the semen. Aristotle recommended covering the cervix and inside of the vagina with oil before intercourse. Little progress was made in the next 1,500 years, until the Renaissance when new scientific and medical advances began in earnest (see Highlight Box 9.1).

Even though we do not yet have 100% safe and effective contraceptives, we are close to that goal. Think about what it would have been like living 100, 500, or 2,000 years ago and wanting to limit the size of your family.

For centuries, Christian leaders struggled with the question of sexual pleasure. Augustine, probably the most influential early Christian writer, denounced it and only reluctantly tolerated sexual intercourse for reproduction within marriage. The only acceptable and natural expression of human sexuality was heterosexual vaginal intercourse that was open to procreation.

Civil authorities were equally opposed to contraception. Large families and many offspring were essential to survival of those in power. In feudal times, local princes and lords exercised control over the marriage of their serfs and encouraged early marriage to provide many offspring to work the lord's land and serve in his armies (Gordon 1976; Himes 1963; Murstein 1974:136; Reed 1978).

As the feudal system declined, concepts of personal freedom and rights slowly emerged. Improved medical care allowed more children to survive, reducing the need for a woman to bear a dozen children so she and her partner might be able to rely on the few who survived for care in their old age. Previously, children were apprenticed at age 7 and married by 14. Today, children are dependent on their parents and often postpone living independently until they are in their twenties. From preindustrial times through the Victorian age, children were an economic benefit. Today, the financial cost of raising a large family of children can be prohibitive. The industrial age is yielding to the age of computers. Brains replace brawn. Agricultural economies dependent on brute manpower have given way to massive mechanized farms.

The result of these radical social and economic changes is a new type of person, the sexually mature but single man or woman. Today, it is not just married couples who want to limit the number of children and plan, if they want any children at all, when they will have one, two, or more children. Contraception is an important concern for heterosexual single persons of all ages who want to engage in sexual intercourse, but who are not ready for or do not want the responsibility of having and raising a child.

Young people, who are only beginning to explore and express their sexual natures, are pulled in many directions by the radical changes in our society. In many ways they are expected to behave as independent adults. At the same time they often remain financially dependent on their parents. Society and parents are often uncomfortable or unwilling to recognize the growing sexual maturity of teenagers and young adults. The official view of society is still that sexual intercourse should occur only in marriage. This attitude places a tremendous responsibility on young people as they step out on their own. Deciding how you are going to express your sexual nature and needs inevitably raises the question of decisions and choices about contraceptive options.

HIGHLIGHT BOX 9.1.
FOUR HUNDRED YEARS
OF CONTRACEPTIVE PROGRESS

1564: Fallopius, an Italian doctor, describes a condom made of linen as a preventative for venereal disease, although condoms made from animal tissue were used in ancient Rome and elsewhere.

1700s: Casanova, an Italian diplomat and associate of Boswell, Benjamin Franklin, and Voltaire, popularizes the use of condoms in his 12-volume memoirs of countless love affairs with women.

1798: Malthus warns of the impending threat of starvation in an overpopulated world, urging sexual abstinence.

1838: The diaphragm is invented.

1843: Goodyear vulcanizes rubber, opening the way for rubber condoms to replace condoms made from animal intestines.

1873: The "Comstock Laws" make it a crime to mail, display, sell, or use contraceptives, and to provide information about contraception and family planning in the United States.

1880s: The diaphragm becomes popular among middle and upper class women who can afford a private doctor. A London chemist produces a popular vaginal contraceptive suppository made of cacao butter and quinine.

1882: The first birth control clinic opens in Holland.

1893: The first surgical male sterilization (vasectomy) is performed.

1909: First modern versions of intrauterine device (IUD) appear.

1912: Margaret Sanger campaigns to make contraceptives available to all women, including the working class.

1914: Margaret Sanger coins the term *birth control*.

1916: Margaret Sanger opens first birth control clinic in Brooklyn.

1930s: A new understanding of the menstrual cycle leads to the rhythm method of family planning based on "safe" periods for intercourse. Effective chemical spermicides developed.

1937: The American Medical Association ends its 25-year opposition to contraception and begins teaching birth control in medical schools.

1951: India becomes the first nation to have a government-supported birth control program.

1950s: Hormonal birth control pill is developed.

1962: Food and Drug Administration approves birth control pill.

1966: U.S. Supreme Court declares unconstitutional a law prohibiting sale of contraceptives to married women. Pro-choice advocate Bill Baird is jailed in New Jersey for displaying a condom in public. United Nations urges governments to become actively involved in population control.

1970s: The Minipill provides protection with lower hormone doses.

1972: U.S. Supreme Court strikes down laws prohibiting sale of contraceptives to single persons.

1984: Contraceptive sponge becomes available commercially.

1985: Contraceptive progestin implants approved by WHO.

1986: Ads for contraceptives and condoms appear on television and in popular magazines.

1989: Progestin implants are approved by the FDA.

Deciding to Use a Contraceptive

It might be wonderful if sex could be completely spontaneous and without consequences. Television and the other media bombard us with pictures of sex as impulsive and exciting, but the consequences of unplanned, unprotected sex are seldom shown. How often have you seen a television show or movie where a man asked the woman he was in bed with whether she was using a contraceptive or whether she would mind his using a condom? How many shows have you seen where the woman asked the man to use a condom, or help her insert a contraceptive foam before they went on with their passionate love play? (Figure 9.1).

When couples think about the possible consequences of having sexual intercourse, then they are planning to do something society, and their families, may not find acceptable. In a society still uncomfortable with sexuality, it is difficult not to have some residue guilt about sexual relations outside marriage. This feeling of guilt may not prevent you from becoming sexually involved and having intercourse, but it often does lead to a neglect of contraception. If "it just happens," if you "just get swept away," then you don't have to worry about "being bad or immoral." To talk about using contraceptives or being

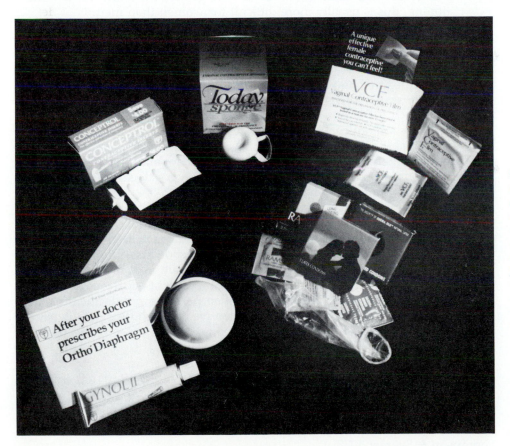

Figure 9.1. *Sexually active persons who want to avoid an unwanted pregnancy can choose from a wide variety of barrier, chemical, and hormonal contraceptives. As the frequency of intercourse increases or decreases, and one's partner(s) change, the choice of contraceptive should be reevaluated. Whatever contraceptive is used, it should be one that both partners are comfortable with. It should also be used according to instructions every time the couple has intercourse.*

prepared may be construed as deliberately planning to violate the norms of your family and society (Brick & Cooperman 1987:31; Cvetkovich et al. 1975) (Figure 9.1).

Erotophiles and Erotophobes

People generally handle their sexual behavior either by openly acknowledging it, or by denying and hiding it. Donn Byrne, a social psychologist, calls these two types of people erotophiles and erotophobes. **Erotophiles** are comfortable with their sexuality. They can discuss sexual issues with comfort, have little sexual guilt, and enjoy sex and being erotic. **Erotophobes**, on the other hand, do not discuss sex. They are strongly influenced by guilt and fear of social or parental disapproval (Byrne 1977; Byrne & Fisher 1983).

It is easier for erotophiles to make effective decisions about their sexual behavior and the possible need for contraceptive protection. Byrne suggests that the effective use of contraceptive options can be broken into five stages:

1. Acquiring and remembering basic accurate information about contraceptive options.
2. Acknowledging that there is a possibility you might engage in sexual intercourse sometime soon. Given our gender roles and social conditioning, this is usually more difficult for women than men.
3. Deciding which contraceptive you are going to use and obtaining it.
4. Communicating with your partner about the possibility you may engage in sexual intercourse and the need for an effective contraceptive.
5. Being prepared and actually using the contraceptive every time you engage in sexual intercourse.

Erotophobes are not comfortable seeking out information on contraception. They would find it difficult to admit the possibility of being "swept away" and pressured into intercourse, although it commonly happens. They are ill at ease buying condoms or foam at the drugstore, or going to a doctor for the Pill or a diaphragm. They find it very hard, if not impossible, to talk with their partners about the possibility of having sex and needing a contraceptive. And finally, erotophobes are less likely to use any contraceptive consistently and properly.

Erotophiles, on the other hand, are more comfortable in negotiating each of the five steps and more successful in accepting responsibility for their sexual behavior and its possible consequences. They find out what contraceptive options are available. They can more easily admit they might decide to have sexual intercourse sometime soon. They talk with their partners and decide on a suitable contraceptive. And they use the contraceptive they choose more effectively (Byrne 1977; Byrne & Fisher 1983).

Why Contraceptives Aren't Used

Being comfortable with your own sexuality and being able to communicate with your partner are critical factors in sexual responsibility. It means overcoming the fear that "talking about sex and contraception will give him or her the impression one is ready to jump into bed" (Delamater & Maccorquodale 1978; Thompson & Spanier 1978).

In 1976 the "major reasons for not using contraception were that teenagers [mistakenly] thought that they could not become pregnant because of the time of month, age, or infrequency of intercourse or because contraceptives were not available when they needed them." For 30%, obtaining contraceptives was a major problem. Other reasons given included the interference with pleasure and moral or medical objections. Nine percent of the girls "didn't mind getting pregnant," and 6.5% wanted to get pregnant. Some emotionally deprived girls dreamed of having someone to love and take care of, so they deliberately tried to become pregnant. Some young men looked on making a woman pregnant as proof of their manhood (Guttmacher Report 1976). Which of these reasons do you think may be still valid today?

Although you might suspect that religious beliefs are an important reason some people do not use a contraceptive, it does not seem to be the case. Although the Vatican has repeatedly and forcefully condemned the use of artificial contraceptives, numerous surveys indicate that about the same percentages of Catholic, Protestant, and liberal Jewish women use artificial contraceptives (Ostling 1984). However, a sense of guilt may affect the use of contraceptives. Having intercourse may violate a person's moral training, but it may not appear as bad as having sex and using a contraceptive. Mosher and Vinderheide (1985) found that college women who felt particularly guilty about masturbation were more likely to have difficulty accepting a diaphragm, cervical cap, or condom because these devices require touching the genitals.

Traditional sex roles have an interesting effect on contraceptive use. In a 1977 study of Midwest college students, men with strong traditional gender attitudes showed the strongest sense of contraceptive responsibility. In contrast, college women who accepted the personal responsibility for contraception had nontraditional gender attitudes and a strong commitment to accept responsibility for what happens to them in any area of their lives (Fox 1977).

For some women, the decision to engage in unprotected intercourse is a conscious one, based on weighing what they see as the relative risks, costs, and benefits of becoming pregnant and using a contraceptive. When contraceptive risk takers become pregnant and have an abortion, they may think they have been successful and leave the abortion clinic with no plans to use a contraceptive. This decision can be costly in the long run because repeat abortions have been clearly linked with infertility (Luker 1975).

A 1980 alumni magazine survey of college students at Rutgers University, The State University of New Jersey, revealed that the "majority [of students] have traditional attitudes toward marriage, are sexually inactive, and trust [their] luck or unreliable contraceptive methods when having coitus." College women who were having vaginal intercourse often did not use an effective contraceptive. Unless the male partner used a condom, the female partner was unprotected most of the time. One of the reasons given for not using an effective contraceptive when having sexual intercourse is that the women still tend to have intercourse on impulse and do not take the necessary precautions. Do you think this situation has changed since 1980? What can you do in your relationships to improve communications about sexual matters and contraception?

Some people do not use contraceptives because they mistakenly believe they are dangerous, messy, or not worth the trouble. But what are the real hazards of using contraceptives? How does the very small risk of the new contraceptive pills stack up against other risks in everyday life? Your chances of dying in an automobile accident are 1 in 6,000 compared with a 1 in 63,000 chance of dying as a result of using an oral contraceptive if you are a nonsmoker! There is no risk of death associated with the use of a condom, diaphragm, cervical cap, or the natural methods of contraception. There are greater risks of death in smoking, motorcycling, power boating, and playing football. The risk of dying as a result of an unwanted pregnancy are small but real. One in 10,000 women dies as a result of a full-term pregnancy and delivery. Legal abortions have smaller risk, ranging from 1 in 400,000 for abortions before 9 weeks to 1 in 10,000 for an abortion performed after 16 weeks. The risk of death from any contraceptive method is far below the risk of an unwanted pregnancy (Table 9.1).

Table 9.1.
Putting the Voluntary Risks of Contraception into Perspective

Risk	Chance of Death in a Year (U.S.)
Smoking	1 in 200
Motorcycling	1 in 1,000
Automobile driving	1 in 6,000
Power boating	1 in 6,000
Rock climbing	1 in 7,500
Playing football	1 in 25,000
Canoeing	1 in 100,000
Using tampons (toxic shock)	1 in 350,000
Having sexual intercourse (PID)	1 in 50,000
Preventing pregnancy:	
Oral contraception (nonsmoker)	1 in 63,000
Oral contraception (smoker)	1 in 16,000
Using IUDs	1 in 100,000
Using barrier methods	None
Using natural methods	None
Undergoing sterilization:	
Laparoscopic tubal ligation	1 in 20,000
Hysterectomy	1 in 1,600
Vasectomy	None
Deciding About Pregnancy:	
Continuing pregnancy	1 in 10,000
Terminating pregnancy:	
Nonlegal abortion	1 in 3,000
Legal abortion:	
Before 9 weeks	1 in 400,000
Between 9–12 weeks	1 in 100,000
Between 13–16 weeks	1 in 25,000
After 16 weeks	1 in 10,000

Sharing the Responsibility

Despite the shift toward equality and away from the double moral standard, many men still expect the woman to protect herself against an unwanted pregnancy. Many women resent this attitude as chauvinistic, yet they feel safer when they are in control of the contraception. Communication can turn a couple's contraceptive decision into a mutual, shared experience. Talking about the possible need for a contraceptive with each other often makes it easier for the couple to seek out the information they need to make a decision (Figure 9.2).

Quite often the choice of a contraceptive involves a primary and a backup method. If the man agrees to use a condom and the woman uses a foam or diaphragm as a backup, both are involved. A woman may decide to use the Minipill and let her partner use a condom as a backup. If a couple discusses their options and decides to use a diaphragm or cervical cap with a contraceptive foam, they can eroticize these and incorporate their use into their love play. Putting on and taking off a condom can be erotic play. There are many possibilities a couple may explore. Talking about the need for contraceptive protection beforehand allows a couple to express their respect and sense of responsibility for each other.

Contraceptive Effectiveness

Although abstinence from vaginal intercourse is a 100% effective method of avoiding an accidental pregnancy, many couples feel that it is not an acceptable method despite its guaranteed effectiveness. Other contraceptive options must

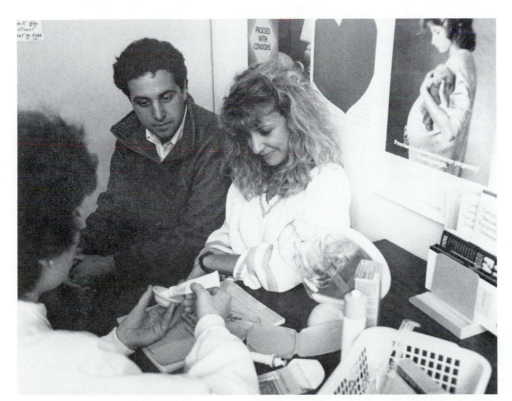

Figure 9.2. Contraceptive Counseling. *Hospital clinics, college health services, Planned Parenthood clinics, and other public health organizations offer free or inexpensive counseling for individuals or couples who want to avoid pregnancy.*

then be considered. But how effective are other methods? How often do they fail? Answering that question is not easy.

Obviously, the effectiveness statistics for any contraceptive method are meaningless unless the couple or person uses the method every time sexual intercourse occurs and uses the method as instructed. Using a backup method,

Table 9.2.
What Real Protection Do Different Contraceptives Offer?

Method	Percentage of Typical Users Who Avoid an Accidental Pregnancy Using Method for One Year	Percentage of Typical Users Who Experience Accidental Pregnancy Using Method for One Year	Highest Reported Percentage of Protection Against Pregnancy
No intercourse	100%	0%	100%
Hormone implants			
Rods	99.8	0.2	100
Capsules	99.7	0.3	
Injectable progestin			
DMPA	99.7	0.3	100
NET	99.6	0.4	100
Female tubal ligation	99.6	0.4	100
Male vasectomy	99.6	0.4	100
Combination pill	96.0 (93.8)*	4.0 (6.2)	100
Progestin only (Minipill)	97.5 (83.8)	4.6 (6.2)	99.0
Condom with spermicide	95.0 or higher	4	99.0
IUD	95.0	5	97 to 99.5
Condom alone	90.3 (87.4)	9.7 (12.6)	96.0
Natural family planning	87.4 (83.4)	12.6 (16.2)	
Ovulation method			92.0
Sympto-thermal			89.0
Calendar			89.0
Diaphragm with spermicide	82.0	18	98.0
Withdrawal	82.0	18	93.0
Cervical cap	82.0	18	92.0
Foams and suppositories	82.0 (73.7)	18 (26.3)	100
Sponge with spermicide	72 to 82	18 to 28	72 to 86
Douching postintercourse	60.0	40	
Unprotected Intercourse	**11**	**89**	

Sources: Adapted from Hatcher et al. 1986:102 and 1988:151 and from a 1989 (October) Alan Guttmacher Institute Report.
*User failure rates in parentheses are based on a 1989 Alan Guttmacher Institute reevaluation of previous data. Those failure rates given for oral contraceptives, condoms, diaphragms, rhythm, spermicides, and withdrawal are 30% higher than rates previously cited.

such as a contraceptive foam with an IUD or condom, or a condom with the Minipill, increases the chance of avoiding an accidental pregnancy. But, in reality, motivation, responsibility, and proper consistent use are the key to effective use of contraceptives.

After examining the data on contraceptive effectiveness, Trussell and Kost (1987) concluded that the data are misleading and only marginally useful in helping people decide which method to use. On balance, they suggest that most contraceptive methods are extremely effective and differ mostly in whether they are used properly and consistently. A couple is more likely to have a strong motivation and use their chosen method consistently and correctly when they have openly discussed and explored their options.

The actual success rate that the average man or woman can expect in using a particular contraceptive should be compared with the risk of using no protection. *Ninety percent of the women who are having sexual intercourse and use no contraceptive protection can expect to become pregnant by the end of one year.* Using any contraceptive method is better than not using any protection (Table 9.2).

Contraceptive Choices

This section discusses contraceptives arranged in the following five categories:

1. Abstinence or outercourse;
2. Barrier and spermicidal contraceptives;
3. Hormonal contraceptives;
4. Natural contraception;
5. Surgical methods.

The basic information provided here gives you an overview of all the options and choices available to someone who is in, or might soon be in, a sexual relationship and who wants to avoid becoming pregnant if and when he or she decides to have sexual intercourse (Table 9.3).

Table 9.3. Who Uses What Kind of Contraceptive?

Country/Region	Tubal Ligation	Vasectomy	Pill	IUDs	Condoms	Other Methods
United States	23.2%	11.4%	30.0%	7.9%	12.9%	14.8%
China	37.5	12.9	4.8	41.1	2.0	1.6
India	40.0	40.0	2.9	8.6	5.7	2.9
Caribbean & Latin America	36.8	2.6	36.8	5.3	7.9	10.5
Middle East & Africa	14.3	0	57.1	14.3	7.1	7.1
All developed countries	13.0	7.4	26.9	11.1	24.1	17.6

Source: Population Crisis Committee data, 1985.

1. Outercourse

Abstinence or Outercourse

The only 100% guaranteed way of not becoming pregnant is to avoid vaginal intercourse and keep semen away from the vaginal opening. Abstaining from vaginal intercourse does not mean you can't enjoy being sexual. Instead of seeing sexual intimacy only, or mainly, in terms of vaginal intercourse, a couple can explore the many rewards of **outercourse**. Outercourse may include enjoying erotic caresses, kissing, cuddling, full body massages, shared sexual fantasies, mutual masturbation, and oral sex. The possibilities of outercourse are limited only by the sensual imagination of a couple and their willingness to explore their sensual and erotic potential.

There is no risk of an unwanted pregnancy when you engage in outercourse, provided all semen is kept away from the vaginal opening. Outercourse also greatly reduces the risk of transmitting a sexual disease. However, for outercourse or abstinence to be 100% effective, both partners must be determined that they will use this method of avoiding pregnancy without any exceptions, such as getting carried away by passion or urgency of the moment to have vaginal intercourse (Hatcher et al. 1988:371–374).

Before the advent of the contraceptive pill and the sexual revolution of the 1960s, necking and petting offered couples a way to express their affection and enjoy being sexually intimate without risking an unwanted pregnancy. At a time when virginity was considered important for a woman before marriage, outercourse allowed a woman to enjoy being sexual and at the same time remain a "technical virgin." When the birth control pill suddenly reduced the risk of unwanted pregnancy, many Americans plunged into a sexual revolution. Vaginal intercourse was often expected by the third date, or earlier. Outercourse was quickly replaced by intercourse. Necking and petting became passé. "Why waste time on first, second, or third base, when you can score?" In the 1980s many men and women began to wonder whether we had become obsessed with jumping into bed and having vaginal intercourse without taking time to enjoy the pleasures of love play. A return to romance, a growing disillusionment with sexual liberation, and the risk of AIDS and other STDs are other factors cited by men and women who are rediscovering the pleasures and eroticism of outercourse (Bailey 1988; Richardson 1971:83–92).

2. Barrier and Spermicidal Contraceptives

Condoms for Men

In 1987 an estimated 46 million couples worldwide were using condoms. Of all the people in the world who use contraceptives, 1 in 3 uses condoms. One out of every 2 Italians, and 4 out of 5 Japanese men who use contraceptives use condoms. Women buy 40% of the condoms sold in the United States, up from 10% in 1980. In parts of California, women buy almost 60% of all condoms sold. The condom is second only to the birth control pill in popularity for single Americans (Gallen et al. 1987; Leinster 1986; Stokes 1980).

Condoms, made from latex rubber or from the processed intestines of young lambs, measure about 7.5 inches long and 1 inch wide. They easily stretch to accommodate any size erect penis. Some slang terms for condoms are prophylactic, sheath, skin, pro, safe, safety, and a rubber (Hatcher et al. 1988:332–353).

Cost   Condoms are inexpensive, 25 to 50 cents, and as little as 5 or 10 cents at some family planning clinics. Some people spend a little more for lubricated or spermicide-coated latex condoms, or for "designer" or "atmosphere" condoms in exotic colors or fancy textured surfaces.

How the Condom Works   Since the condom covers the penis during ejaculation, it traps the semen in the space at the end of the sheath. *Used consistently and correctly,* condoms can be 97% or 98% effective, especially when used with a spermicidal foam, a diaphragm, sponge, or with the Minipill. Latex condoms are also good protection against some sexually transmitted diseases and the AIDS virus.

How to Suggest Using a Condom   A light touch of humor may help when a relationship is getting intimate and you want to raise the issue of using a condom for pregnancy and STD protection. Greeting cards with a condom inside are becoming popular: "Sweetheart, why don't you slip into something more comfortable?"—for both of us!" (Figure 9.3). Some men and women may simply agree to use a condom and not have to worry (Grieco 1987). What kind of approaches can you think of to open up discussion of using a condom?

Figure 9.3. *Efforts to promote the use of condoms for safer sex have turned from scare tactics to humor. Each of the cards shown in this display contains a condom.*

Figure 9.4. Using a Condom. *Most condoms, lubricated and plain, come packaged in foil and rolled, ready for easy use. The condom is placed over the head of the penis, with a space left at the tip to hold the semen when ejaculated. Either partner can unroll the condom down over the glans and shaft of the penis to the base of the scrotum. The condom should be in place before any vaginal contact and should be removed immediately after ejaculation and withdrawal.*

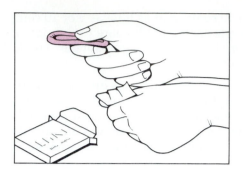
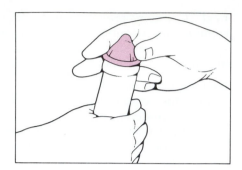
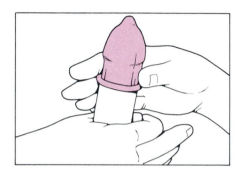
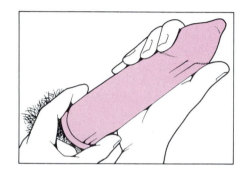

How to Use a Condom   Hold the tip of the condom with two fingers and your thumb to squeeze out the air in the last half inch—which will fill with the ejaculate—and unroll the condom over the erect penis (Figure 9.4). Practice taking a few condoms out of their packages and unrolling them over two fingers or a small banana so you know which way they unroll and how to make the space for the ejaculate. A creative couple can turn unwrapping and putting on a condom into an erotic game and a fun part of their love play.

Avoid any contact between the penis and vulva before the condom is on the penis. Don't start intercourse until the vagina is well lubricated. If you plan on using a lubricant, then use only a water-soluble one such as K-Y Jelly or Astroglide, or a contraceptive foam. Using Crisco or petroleum jelly can cause problems in the vagina.

Immediately after ejaculation, hold the condom securely at the base of penis and withdraw the penis from the vagina completely. This is an important precaution since most men lose about 50% of their erection immediately after ejaculation. After removing the condom from the penis, tie a knot in it near the open end so the semen doesn't leak out. Also wash the penis to remove any semen before continuing love play. Discard all used condoms.

Precautions   Buy fresh merchandise and avoid vending machines unless you know they have a high turnover. Condom vending machines in college dormitories usually have fresh stock. Inspect the package for broken seals. Women can carry condoms in their purses, but men should not carry them in a wallet for a long period of time because body heat will deteriorate the latex. *Use a fresh condom each time. Don't try to wash a condom out and reuse it!*

Possible Side Effects   Some men complain that condoms reduce their pleasure during intercourse. Extra thin latex condoms may help. If an allergic reaction to the latex or other chemicals in the condom occurs, try a different brand. Condoms with "wet" lubricants tend to dry out when exposed to air.

Noncontraceptive Benefits   Condoms provide good protection against four major sexually transmitted diseases: AIDS, herpes, gonorrhea, and chlamydia. Because many people have sexually transmitted diseases but show no symptoms, they can unknowingly infect their partners. Using a condom with a foam or cream containing the chemical nonoxynol-9 increases protection against both pregnancy and sexually transmitted diseases. In addition, condoms probably reduce the risk of cervical cancer and a rare female allergic reaction to male semen (Hatcher et al. 1982a:52–53).

Condoms can be purchased in pharmacies, food stores, newsstands, vending machines, and even by mail order. Using a condom can enhance a male's self-esteem by involving him in the shared responsibility for contraception and STD prevention. Sex therapists sometimes recommend condoms for men who ejaculate too quickly because a condom can reduce stimulation to the penile glans and prolong intercourse pleasure for both partners (Hatcher et al. 1988:343–344).

Possible Complications—What to Do If the Condom Breaks   If the vagina is well lubricated before intercourse begins, there is very little chance of the condom breaking (Hatcher et al. 1988:341). If a condom does break, don't panic! If your main concern is pregnancy, an extra application of a contraceptive foam will reduce the risk of an accidental pregnancy. Do not douche because it might force sperm through the cervix. However, if the condom breaks and the male partner has tested positive for the AIDS virus or is at high risk, immediate douching will reduce the infection risk.

A Condom for Women

Reality (TM), a new female condom, is now available in some parts of the United States. This condom is a soft, loose-fitting polyurethane sheath with a flexible ring at both ends (Figure 9.5). Reality (TM) is inserted into the vagina so that the smaller ring at the closed end covers the cervix and inner vagina while the larger outer ring stays outside the vagina, covering the labia and the base of

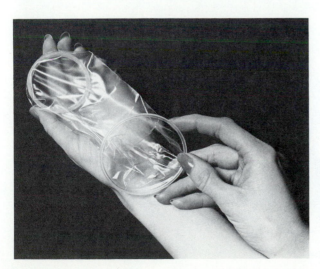

Figure 9.5. A Condom for Women. *The female condom shown here is easy to use, convenient, and inexpensive. Inserted in the vagina before sexual intercourse, it provides reliable protection against both conception and sexually transmitted diseases.*

the penis during intercourse. The device is inserted in the vagina before intercourse and removed after ejaculation. Like male condoms, Reality (TM) is sold over the counter. It has several advantages over the male condoms, including its broad cover, ease of use, and the extra strength of the polyurethane (Family Planning Perspectives 1988:20(3)).

Spermicidal Foams

The most obvious advantages of spermicidal foams, used alone or with a diaphragm or condom, are that they are safe and simple to use. You can buy them at pharmacies and food stores without a prescription or visit to a physician.

Cost   Spermicidal foams sell for a few dollars, whether in the larger economy size for use at home or in the convenient small six-application containers that fit easily in a purse or pocket.

How Foams Work   The active ingredient in **vaginal foams** is a **spermicide**, a chemical that kills sperm. The foam also acts as a physical barrier to keep the sperm away from the cervix. The effectiveness of contraceptive foams is ''extremely high,'' perhaps as good as the Pill, especially when used with a condom or diaphragm. But to be effective, the foam must be deposited at the cervix and used every time you have intercourse (Hatcher et al. 1988:323).

How to Use Foam   Directions for using a contraceptive foam come in the package, often with clear diagrams. First shake the aerosol can at least 20 times to mix the spermicide with the propellant. Then fill the applicator and insert it as deep as it will go in the vagina. Withdraw the applicator half an inch so that when the plunger is depressed the foam is deposited right at the cervix. The foam should be applied 15 minutes or less before intercourse. Don't use a tampon or douche for at least six hours after intercourse. A minipad will catch any slight discharge. Another application of foam should be used if intercourse is repeated (Figure 9.6).

Figure 9.6. Using a Contraceptive Foam. *Contraceptive foams come in tubes with an applicator that screws on for filling; under aerosol pressure, the applicator automatically fills after shaking. The applicator should be inserted fully into the vaginal canal and withdrawn half an inch before foam is ejected. Apply no more than 15 minutes before intercourse.*

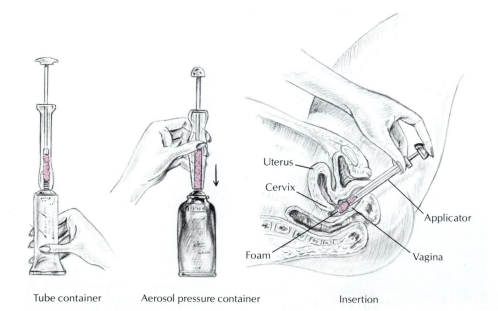

Tube container   Aerosol pressure container   Insertion

Possible Complications If a foam causes an allergic reaction, try a different brand, one without a scent. Using a flavored foam may avoid an unpleasant taste when engaging in oral sex before or after intercourse. To avoid interrupting the romantic or erotic mood, make application of the foam a part of love play.

Noncontraceptive Benefits Spermicidal foams with nonoxynol-9 provide "dramatic" protection against gonorrhea, some protection against other sexually transmitted diseases including the AIDS virus, and a reduction in the normal risk of pelvic inflammatory disease (Hatcher et al. 1988:326). Older women may find the foam's lubricating quality helpful, since their decrease in estrogen production may decrease their natural vaginal lubrication.

Precautions Do not confuse contraceptive foams with feminine hygiene products, douches, and vaginal deodorants. These other products *do not provide pregnancy prevention.*

Vaginal Suppositories

Suppositories are sold over the counter in pharmacies, supermarkets, and many convenience stores (Figure 9.7).

Cost Encare Oval, Semicid, and Intercept suppositories usually cost under $5 for a package of 12, less than 50 cents per use.

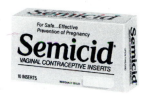

Figure 9.7. *Vaginal contraceptive inserts provide a convenient alternative to contraceptive foams.*

How a Contraceptive Suppository Works When the suppository dissolves, it releases its sperm-killing active ingredient and provides a thick physical barrier around the cervix. Vaginal suppositories may be used with a condom, diaphragm, or an IUD as a backup method and to increase protection.

How to Use a Supporitory Insert the suppository deep into vagina and wait at least 10 minutes before having intercourse. The directions on some brands suggest waiting up to 30 minutes, so read the directions carefully. These contraceptives provide protection against conception for about two hours after insertion. If you want to have intercourse a second time in that two-hour period, insert a second suppository and wait the required time for it to dissolve. You should not douche for 6 to 8 hours after intercourse. If the suppository is soft, hold the sealed package under cold water until it hardens enough for insertion.

Possible Complications The suppository may generate a small amount of heat as it dissolves, which some women find a pleasant sensation. For others, it is brief mild discomfort. If the suppository does not dissolve completely before intercourse, it may cause a gritty effect with some irritation or increased friction during intercourse that would also reduce the contraceptive effectiveness. Any slight vaginal leakage after intercourse can be contained by a minipad.

Noncontraceptive Benefits Incorporating insertion of the suppository as part of the couple's love play involves the male partner in this important aspect of their relationship. Some prefer this method because of its convenient size, its premeasured dose, pleasant scent, and because it is available without a prescription.

Precautions If either partner feels something solid that indicates the suppository has not yet fully dissolved, the man should refrain from ejaculation and withdraw his penis from the vagina until it is dissolved. Do not have pointed or sharp fingernails which might injure the vagina when the suppository is inserted. Do not use these suppositories for anal intercourse.

Vaginal Contraceptive Film

VCF or **C-film** is a new product on the American scene. It has been used in Europe and England since the mid-1970s and was approved for over-the-counter sale in the United States in 1988 (Hatcher et al. 1988:329).

Cost   A packet of 12 films runs about $7, a little over 50 cents per use.

How a VCF Film Works   The VCF, a thin 2-inch-square sheet of translucent material, contains the spermicide nonoxynol-9 and two inactive ingredients. When the film dissolves in the normal vaginal fluids, it becomes a tenacious gel that clings to the cervix. It also disperses into the folds of the vagina around the cervix and into the cervical canal. Sperm coming in contact with the gel are killed and blocked from getting into the uterus. There are no American studies of the effectiveness of the VCF as yet, but European and English experiences suggest that it is as effective as other vaginal spermicides. VCF films can be used with a condom for added protection.

See for yourself how the film works by putting a film in a saucer and adding half a teaspoon of warm water. Shake the saucer gently and watch what happens.

How to Use a VCF Film   Wash your hands with soap and water and make sure they are completely dry. Fold a single film over your middle finger, holding it in place with the tip of your thumb. Quickly insert the middle finger with the film over its tip into the vagina and push it in deep until you feel the cervix. You can also insert the film using your index and middle fingers. Withdraw your finger(s), leaving the film to dissolve over the cervix. You may want to practice finding the cervix several times before trying to insert a film. You can insert the film while lying down, while crouching, or standing with one leg bent and your foot on a stool or chair (Figure 9.8).

(a)   (b)   (c)

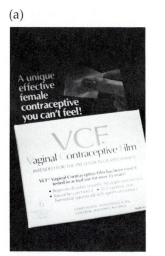
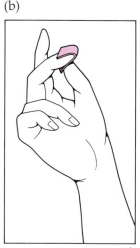
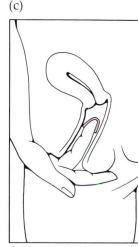

Figure 9.8. Using a Vaginal Contraceptive Film. *(a) Vaginal contraceptive films provide a new alternative for pregnancy protection. (b) Although there are several ways to hold the VCF for insertion, the best way is shown here, folded over one or two fingers. (c) The VCF may be inserted with middle or middle and index fingers. The fingers should be dry before touching the VCF. Insertion should be swift to avoid having the VCF stick to the finger(s). Some practice without the VCF may be necessary to gain confidence in finding the cervix and placing the VCF deep in the vagina.*

The film takes 5 minutes to dissolve into a gel, and provides contraceptive protection for 2 hours after insertion. Wait 15 minutes after insertion before having vaginal penetration. Use one VCF for each act of intercourse. If douching is desired, wait 6 hours after intercourse.

Possible Complications   Like other vaginal spermicides, VCF may occasionally cause a slight vaginal or penile irritation. Some couples may have difficulty finding the cervix or inserting the film. A little practice usually solves this problem.

Noncontraceptive Advantages   The small size of the film, its ease of use, and lack of messiness are major advantages. Either partner can insert the film as part of love play. Because the film produces a gel that clings to the cervix and surrounding tissue, it does not leak out as other vaginal spermicides tend to do.

Precautions   Inserting the film with the penis doesn't assure proper placement of the film at the cervix or allow sufficient time for the film to dissolve.

Diaphragm with Spermicidal Cream or Jelly

The **diaphragm** is a dome-shaped latex cup with flexible metal spring rim. Even though diaphragms must be fitted by a physician or at a clinic or family planning center, they are popular with both single and married couples. A diaphragm is much cheaper than the Pill.

Cost   A diaphragm, which costs about $15 to $20, can last a year or two if you take proper care of it. It is custom-fitted to your cervix and vaginal canal during an initial checkup by a physician or health care professional. Cost of diaphragm fitting may be kept down by including it in an annual checkup with a Pap smear and pelvic exam.

How a Diaphragm Works   The diaphragm provides a physical barrier between penis and cervix while the spermicidal cream or gel kills sperm.

How to Use a Diaphragm   Always wash your hands with soap and water first. Cover the outside of the diaphragm with spermicidal cream or jelly. Put a blob of spermicide inside the dome. Insert the diaphragm in the vagina up to two hours before intercourse. The diaphragm should cover the cervix and fit behind the pelvic bone at the front of vagina. When you are fitted for the diaphragm, ask the health practitioner to check your technique as you practice inserting it (Figure 9.9).

Leave the diaphragm in place 6 hours after intercourse. Do not leave your diaphragm in place more than 24 hours. Do not douche or use petroleum jelly or foam with a diaphragm. Six hours after intercourse, remove the diaphragm, wash it with a mild soap, pat dry, and powder with cornstarch. Do not use talcum or a perfumed powder. Store your diaphragm in a cool place until you need it again.

Noncontraceptive Benefits   A diaphragm may be used for intercourse during menstruation or to retain menstrual flow for up to 12 hours. Use of a diaphragm helps familiarize a woman with her genitals. If the male inserts it as part of love play, he can also learn more about female anatomy. The diaphragm may offer some protection against sexually transmitted diseases, but not against syphilis, herpes, or AIDS.

Figure 9.9. Using a Contraceptive Diaphragm. *Vaginal diaphragms come in many sizes and must be fitted by a physician. Contraceptive cream or jelly is placed in the bowl and around the rim. The diaphragm can then be inserted by the woman while standing, squatting, or lying on her back, or by her partner as part of love play. Insert not more than two hours before intercourse and leave in place six to eight hours afterward.*

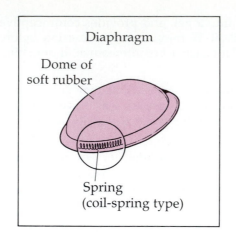

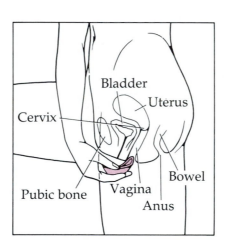

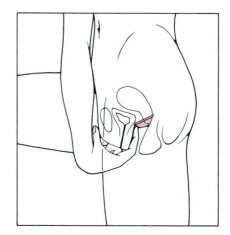

Precautions   Inspect your diaphragm regularly for pinholes or tears by holding it up to the light before insertion. Replace it every two years. Some women experience pain when using a diaphragm after pregnancy, abortion, or pelvic surgery. If you get a vaginal infection, buy a new diaphragm and throw the old one away to avoid reinfection after treatment. If you gain or lose more than 15 pounds, see your physician to have the diaphragm size checked.

Contraceptive Sponge

Although women have used sponges with various sperm-killing agents for centuries, they did not become available in the United States until 1983 (Figure 9.10).

Cost   Sponges cost between $1 and $1.50 each.

How the Sponge Works   Modern **contraceptive sponges** contain sperm-killing nonoxynol-9, which is released by vaginal secretions during sexual activity. The sponge also physically blocks the sperm's passage to the uterus and traps sperm (Hatcher et al. 1986:222).

Figure 9.10. *Contraceptive sponges are easy to use and provide protection for a day or more.*

How to Use a Sponge   Whether the woman or her partner inserts the sponge, clean hands and smooth, round fingernails are a must. Moisten the sponge with tap water and insert it into the vagina so that it covers the cervix at the upper end of the vagina. A sponge can be inserted up to 24 hours before intercourse. It should be left undisturbed in the vagina for at least 6 hours after intercourse. If multiple intercourse occurs, the sponge should be left for at least 6 hours after the last intercourse.

Possible Complications   Outside of a rare allergic reaction to either the polyurethane foam or the spermicide, clinical reports indicate no negative side effects of the contraceptive sponges.

Noncontraceptive Benefits   Incorporating insertion of the sponge in love play allows a male partner to be involved in the responsibility for contraception. The sponge is easier to use than the diaphragm with cream or jelly, and less messy than the contraceptive foams. It should be inserted hours before intercourse so that the time for love play and intercourse is less restricted.

Precautions   The sponge should not be used as a contraceptive during the menstrual flow or if you have any unusual vaginal discharge. Use another method during your menstrual period to be safe. For reasons unknown, the sponge appears to be more effective with women who have not had a child than for women who have given birth. Do not reuse a contraceptive sponge.

You may hear someone mention that women who use the contraceptive sponge or diaphragm have eight times the risk of toxic shock syndrome as women in the general population. But what does that mean? Clinical reports suggest 10 out of 100,000 women using the sponge for a year develop TSS. The death rate from TSS is only 3%. That means 1 out of 300,000 women using the sponge may die of TSS. But 25 women out of 300,000 who use no contraceptive die of pregnancy complications! More important, this very low risk is further reduced if a woman does not leave the sponge in place for more than 24 hours (Hatcher et al. 1988:300–312).

If the sponge is accidentally left in for more than a day, it may break up, so examine the sponge to make sure you have not left a piece behind.

Cervical Cap

A rubber or soft plastic cup-shaped device, the **cervical cap** is a miniature diaphragm with a high dome that fits over the cervix. Its firm rim and suction hold it in place. Custom-fitted caps with a one-way valve to allow escape of the cervical mucus and menstrual flow allow continuous wear. The FDA approved the cervical cap for marketing in the United States in 1988 (Figure 9.11)

Cost   Since the cervical cap must be fitted by a health care professional, cost must include the office fee for initial fitting and instructions on how to insert and remove the cap plus $15 to $20 for the cap itself.

How the Cap Works   Since it covers the cervix, the cap prevents semen from reaching the cervical passage and uterine cavity. Spermicide on the inner side of the cap kills any sperm that get around the cap. So far, very little data is available to indicate the true effectiveness of the cap, although it appears to be about the same as the diaphragm, with a proper fit and insertion being major factors.

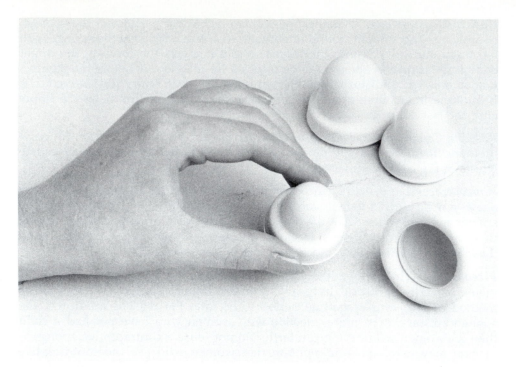

Figure 9.11. *Several types of cervical caps, a variation on the diaphragm, provide effective contraceptive protection.*

How to Use a Cervical Cap   A health professional who is experienced in fitting cervical caps can recommend the best type for you. When you are fitted for a cap, you should practice inserting and removing it with a health professional watching to make sure it is properly situated on the cervix. Inserted sometime before intercourse, the cap should be left in place 6 hours after ejaculation. Because of the very slight possibility of toxic shock syndrome or changes in the cervix, some doctors do not recommend leaving the cap in more than 24 hours at a time or using the cap during menstruation.

Possible Complications   Allergic reactions to the plastic or rubber in the cap are rare. Urinary tract infections (UTI) are twice as common in women using the cap as they are in women on the birth control pill, but this may be because the woman did not wash her hands with soap and water before inserting or removing the cap. Cervical inflammation or erosion and a foul-smelling discharge can occur if the cap is left in for a long period of time. (*Contraceptive Technology Update* 1985:76).

Noncontraceptive Benefits   Since the cap can be inserted hours before lovemaking, its use cannot interrupt or interfere with the romantic/erotic mood. Some women report a stronger orgasm when using the cap.

Precautions   Douching with the cap in place is not recommended.

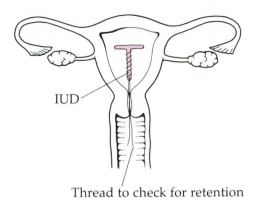

Thread to check for retention

Figure 9.12. *The only IUD currently available in the United States is a copper-impregnated, plastic, T-shaped IUD shown here in the uterine cavity. A plastic thread extends into the vagina so the woman can check to make sure the IUD is in place.*

Intrauterine Devices

In the 1960s and 1970s, **intrauterine devices (IUDs)** were a popular contraceptive for women who had had at least one pregnancy. In 1982 2.2 million American women were using IUDs. These plastic shields, coils, and T-shaped devices were inserted through a relaxed cervix into the uterine cavity. The contraceptive effects of the IUD may result from speeding up movement of the egg through the fallopian tube, reducing the chance of fertilization, immobilizing the sperm, preventing implantation of a fertilized egg, and dislodging it if it should implant. Some IUDs are wrapped with fine copper wire or contain hormones that prevent fertilization and/or implantation. A fine plastic string, extending through the cervix, allows a woman to check whether the IUD is still in place or has been expelled (Figure 9.12).

In the early 1970s the Dalkon Shield IUD was implicated in a high number of cases of pelvic inflammatory disease (PID) and spontaneous miscarriages, as well as some deaths. Although the Dalkon Shield was withdrawn in 1974, thousands of women still use it. Because of the debate over risks associated with IUDs, only two IUDs were available in the United States in the late 1980s: Progestasert, which slowly releases progestin, and the Copper-T380A. Although IUDs provide no protection against sexually transmitted diseases, they remain "a medically sound and excellent contraceptive method for many women" (Hatcher et al. 1988:267–294). A woman interested in using an IUD should familiarize herself with the latest information available on the pros and cons.

3. Hormonal Contraceptives

According to the latest available figures (1984), oral contraceptive pills were being used by over 56 million women worldwide. Currently about 10 million American women are using the Pill.

Since 1960 when the Food and Drug Administration approved the first hormonal contraceptive pills, there has been a clear trend toward reducing the doses of both estrogen and progestin. Early fears about the Pill were based on the possible effects of high levels of both hormones, especially estrogen. In 1985 a Gallup poll sponsored by the American College of Obstetrics and Gynecology reported that 76% of American women they sampled mistakenly believed there was a substantial risk in using the Pill. Thirty-one percent mistakenly thought the Pill caused cancer. Because there are many different contraceptive pills on the market, each with its own combination and hormone doses, we cannot generalize here about the possible risks.

Two general types of oral contraceptives are currently prescribed in the United States. **Combination pills** supply both estrogen and progestin over 21 days. They inhibit ovulation, interfere with transport of both the egg and sperm, thicken the cervical mucus to prevent sperm entry, and prevent implantation of a fertilized egg. **Progestin-only pills** do not inhibit ovulation. Instead, they prevent pregnancy by changing the cervical mucus and inhibiting the development of the uterine lining.

Combination Pills

The combination pills provide a daily dose of estrogen and a synthetic progesterone, progestin, every day for 21 days with 7 days of placebos or no pills to allow for the menstrual period.

Cost   Cost of the Pill varies widely depending on where it is purchased. At a pharmacy, a month's supply may run up to $20. Planned Parenthood and other clinics usually have sliding fees, and services be free for women who cannot pay.

How a Combination Pill Works   Five days after her menstrual period begins or on the Sunday after her period starts, a woman takes the first pill. The estrogen stops the pituitary from producing FSH and prevents ovulation in that cycle. The small amount of progestin in each pill keeps the mucus in the cervix thick and dry so sperm have a hard time getting through. It also keeps the lining of the uterus from developing so that if an egg does mature and is fertilized it cannot implant. When the last hormone-containing pill is taken on day 26, a sudden drop in estrogen and progestin produces a lighter than normal menses. The next series of 21 hormone pills is started on day 5 of the next cycle.

Possible Complications   The major factor for contraceptive failure is not the Pill itself, but the fact that many women using the Pill start and stop and do not protect themselves with another method. Twenty-five to 50% of the women who start with the Pill stop taking it in their first year. Most women who stop using the Pill do so for *nonmedical* reasons. Because of this high dropout rate, many doctors and clinics urge their patients going on the Pill to use a second contraceptive method simultaneously as a backup (Hatcher et al. 1988:195).

Because hormones are potent biological agents and circulate in the bloodstream, they can have varied side effects. Although side effects were more common with the earlier high dose Pill, they still may occur with the newer Pills. A physician should explain the more common side effects when prescribing a particular Pill. Although serious side effects are rare, there are five danger signs that should be checked out with a physician if a woman experiences any of the following symptoms while on the Pill:

- **A** Abdominal pain (severe);
- **C** Chest pain (severe), cough, shortness of breath;
- **H** Headaches (severe), dizziness, weakness, numbness;
- **E** Eye problems blurred or loss of vision, speech problems;
- **S** Severe pain in the calf or thigh (Hatcher 1988:216).

Noncontraceptive Benefits   The contraceptive protection provided by the Pill has had a profound effect on the lives of millions of women by freeing them from unwanted pregnancies. Many women find that the Pill evens out their mood swings and enhances their libido. Women taking the Pill tend to have more regular and shorter menstrual periods with less bleeding and cramping, and a decrease in iron-deficiency anemia. Premenstrual tension (PMS) tends to decrease. Benign breast growths are less frequent. The Pill may also protect against pelvic inflammatory disease (PID), and may give some protection against ovarian and endometrial cancer, functional ovarian cysts, and rheumatoid arthritis (Boston Women's Health Collective 1984:241–246; Hatcher et al. 1988:239–241).

Precautions   If you forget a Pill, check with your physician. Be sure your doctor is aware if you are using a tranquilizer, ampicillin, Dilantin, Rifampicin, or phenobarbital. The results of some laboratory tests are altered by the Pill, so if you have any tests run, make sure the clinician knows you are on the Pill.

A semiannual checkup is highly recommended, even if everything seems fine. If you want to get pregnant, use another contraceptive method for at least three months after you stop the Pill until your natural hormones return to their normal cycle.

Progestin-Only Pills

Progestin-only or Minipills are not widely used in the United States because of breakthrough bleeding and failure to prevent pregnancy. They are popular in Third World countries because they can be taken for protection while a woman is nursing.

4. Natural Contraception

Couples who are highly motivated and in long-term relationships can use several methods of avoiding conception that do not involve hormones, spermicides, or barrier devices (Boston Women's Health Collective 1984:235–237; Hatcher et al. 1988:354–367).

The Rhythm Method

The **rhythm method** relies on estimating the time of ovulation based on mathematical calculations of the length of the menstrual cycle for the previous eight months. Used alone, this method is not reliable.

Basal Body Temperature Method (BBT)

In the **BBT method**, the time of ovulation is estimated by the woman who checks her temperature each morning before getting out of bed. When the basal body temperature (BBT) shows a slight dip followed by a 0.5° to 1.0° F rise, ovulation has occurred. After three days at the higher temperature, the unsafe or fertile period is over and sexual relations can be resumed.

The Cervical Mucus (Billings') Method

The **cervical mucus method** works like this: As ovulation approaches, the vulva becomes moist and even wet, and normally cloudy mucus becomes clear and slippery. This mucus increases in volume and a sample can be stretched 2 to 3 inches between the fingers. At the same time, cervical mucus, if smeared on a glass slide, dries in a fernlike pattern. The fertile period is over when the ferning stops, the cervix closes and becomes firm, and when the mucus again becomes mostly cloudy (Figure 9.13).

The Sympto-Thermal Method

The BBT method can be combined with the cervical mucus or Billings' method and is called the **sympto-thermal method**. This combination method is much more effective than any single natural method.

Effectiveness These natural methods indicate when ovulation is likely to occur, but to be used effectively, a woman must be consistent in checking her symp-

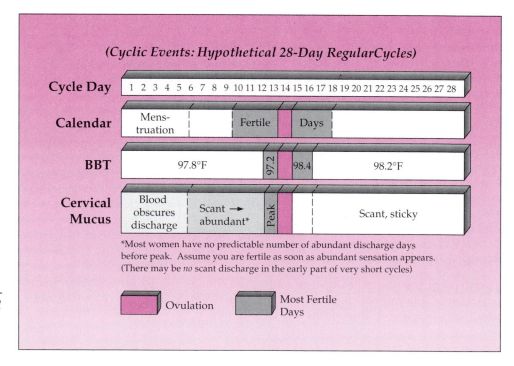

Figure 9.13. Using Natural Family Planning Methods. *The calendar, basal body temperature (BBT), and cervical mucus methods can be combined to plan a pregnancy or avoid one.*

toms. The couple must also refrain from intercourse during the fertile period. Studies of a select sample of highly motivated married women suggest that the effectiveness of the sympto-thermal method can approach 92%, with single methods providing 80% to 85% protection.

Noncontraceptive Benefits   Using natural contraceptive methods involves co-operation and a daily sharing of responsibility. These methods also encourage a couple to explore outercourse and alternative ways of giving and receiving sexual pleasure. With the Billings' method, women become more aware of their body changes. Also, when the couple decide to have a child, they can use these methods to increase the chances of conception by having intercourse during the fertile period.

Precautions   Most couples need training sessions with someone who is skilled in the finer points of these methods. However, many who provide training in these methods disapprove of premarital sexual activity and may be reluctant to provide proper instruction for single women.

   The cyclic mucus changes should not be confused with midcycle secretions, or with semen, lubricants, or infectious discharges. Douching will wash out the natural cervical mucus and change the results observed. The accuracy of temperature readings can be compromised by infections, electric blankets, and other factors.

5. Surgical Methods

Tubal Ligation

Tubal ligation is a routine and safe operation even though it involves abdominal surgery. The object is to cut and tie, clamp, or otherwise block the fallopian tubes in order to prevent the sperm from reaching the egg. The tubes can be reached by several routes, through an incision in the cervical end of the vagina or through a small incision in the abdominal wall (Boston Women's Health Collective 1984:257–259; Hatcher et al. 1988:409–420).

Laparoscopy   Laparoscopy, the so-called Band-Aid operation, is now the most common surgical sterilization for American women. It takes about 30 minutes with a spinal or general anesthesia. The woman's abdomen is inflated with carbon dioxide or nitrous oxide through a small incision in or below the navel (belly button). A laparoscope (lighted viewing tube) allows the doctor to cut and cauterize the fallopian tubes, or clamp them with plastic clips. The small incision is then closed. Although the sperm can no longer reach the egg, ovulation, hormone production, menstruation, and orgasmic response are unaffected (Figure 9.14).

Minilaparotomy   Instead of the two incisions as in laparoscopy, a minilaparotomy is done with a single small incision just above the pubic hairline. A local anesthesia is used. The tubes are pulled one at a time through the incision and clamped or cut.

Cost   Because it involves abdominal surgery, anesthesia, a battery of tests, and one-day hospitalization, a tubal ligation may cost $1,000 to $1,500. Medical and surgery insurance may cover most of the cost, depending on the deductible. Hospitals and doctors often have a sliding scale for those who find the cost prohibitive.

(a) Side view   **(b) Front view**

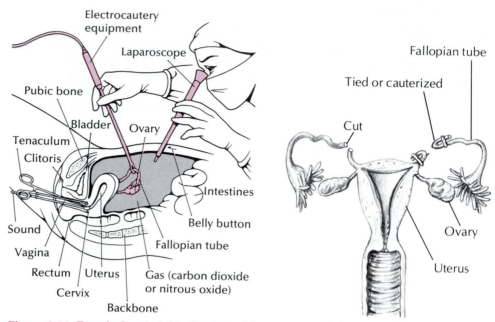

Figure 9.14. Female Surgical Sterilization. *A laparoscope with fiber optics is used to locate the fallopian tubes. The tubes are then cut and tied, cauterized, or closed with plastic clips. The incision in the abdominal wall may be only ½ inch long.*

Possible Complications   Normal postoperative pain and discomfort usually disappear within a day or two as with any surgical procedure. Most clinicians consider tubal ligation permanent. However, new microsurgery can rejoin severed tubes and possibly restore fertility.

Noncontraceptive Benefits   Tubal ligation provides freedom from pregnancy with no long-term side effects.

Precautions   In 1988 12% of the single women using a contraceptive chose tubal ligation. This growing popularity of tubal sterilization among single women opens the possibility for later regrets if it is chosen too hastily (Darroch Forrest & Fordyce 1988; Medical Journal Australia 1986).

Vasectomy

Blocking or cutting and tying the vas deferens to prevent passage of the sperm is **vasectomy**, the simple procedure of male sterilization (Hatcher et al. 1988:400–408).

Cost   A vasectomy can cost between $300 and $400, but usually less in family planning clinics.

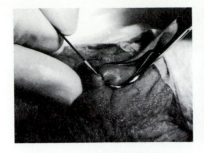

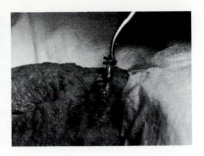

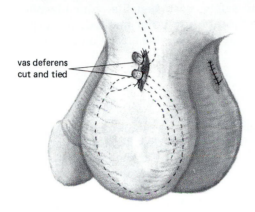

vas deferens
cut and tied

Figure 9.15. Male Surgical Sterilization. *The procedure for a vasectomy involves minor surgery with a local anesthetic. From left to right: an incision is made in the scrotum, the vas deferens is located and exposed, the vas is severed and tied before it is returned to the scrotal sac, and the incision is sewn shut.*

How a Vasectomy Is Done   Vasectomies are usually performed in a doctor's office with a local anesthesia. An incision is made in both sides of the scrotum to gain access to the two vasa deferentia. After the tubes are cut and tied, or clamped off, the scrotal incisions are sewn up. Sperm are prevented from leaving the testicles and are reabsorbed. Seminal fluid is still produced by the prostate and seminal vesicles, so ejaculation still occurs. Hormone production, erection, and orgasm remain unaffected (Figure 9.15).

Possible Complications   Recovery may take a day or two, but most men can drive a car and return to work the day after surgery. Infection, blood clots, and testicular inflammation are rare complications. Although 50% to 66% of men develop antibodies to their own sperm after a vasectomy, there is no evidence that it causes any problem.

Despite presurgery counseling, some men may feel emasculated. Remarriage after a divorce, the death of a child, and a new desire for more children are the main reasons why some men seek out ways of having their fertility restored after a vasectomy. Although men considering a vasectomy should look on it as permanent and irreversible, new microsurgery techniques may restore fertility in some cases.

Noncontraceptive Benefits   Vasectomy provides freedom from the fear of pregnancy with no side effects.

Precautions   At least 15 ejaculations are necessary after surgery before the tubes are free of sperm. A backup contraceptive should be used until two negative sperm counts by a laboratory confirm sterility.

Choosing a Contraceptive You Will Use

The best contraceptive method is the one you and your partner are most comfortable with and most likely to use consistently.

For those of you who have decided to have intercourse and who want to be protected from an accidental pregnancy, the choice of a contraceptive is an important, personal decision that requires some real discussion between you and your partner. Your age, the amount of expected sexual activity, state of health, moral or religious and family considerations are all part of the decision.

Once you choose a method, talk it over with your partner. Have you given sufficient consideration in your choice to safety, cost, benefits, your lifestyle, previous experience with the chosen method or any other method, the experience of friends, possible effects on menstruation, possible effects on emotional or mental outlook, and convenience?

Unreliable Contraceptive Methods

No contraceptive method, except total abstinence from vaginal intercourse, is guaranteed protection against an unwanted pregnancy. Some methods are significantly less effective than others, but the major factor in the effectiveness of any contraceptive is the consistency with which the couple uses it properly whenever they have intercourse.

Withdrawal or interrupted intercourse in which the male withdraws the penis from the vagina before ejaculation can be 75% to 80% effective if used without fail. But consistent use requires the male partner to be highly motivated, very aware of his sexual responses, and have the self-control and responsibility to always withdraw before ejaculation. The female partner needs a lot of confidence in her partner to rely solely on this method to avoid an unwanted pregnancy. Even when used consistently and carefully, withdrawal runs the risk of a pregnancy because the pre-ejaculatory secretions produced during sexual arousal do contain some sperm. Also, even though a male may think he has not ejaculated, some semen may escape before he withdraws. The effectiveness of withdrawal when used by a sexually inexperienced and nervous couple may be far below the 70% to 80% claimed for this method.

Other very risky methods of preventing an unwanted pregnancy include vaginal douching after intercourse. Douching is only about 60% effective because some sperm can get through the cervix before the woman douches. Although daily breast feeding stimulates a woman's endocrine system to suppress ovulation, pregnancy occurs in about 40% of women who are breast feeding and do not use a contraceptive.

Some people mistakenly believe they can avoid an unwanted pregnancy by having sexual intercourse with the woman standing up or sitting astride the prone male partner. Although some seminal fluid may run out of the vagina in these positions, most of it quickly thickens and stays near the cervix. Another contraceptive myth claims that a woman will not become pregnant if she does not have an orgasm. Whether or not a woman reaches orgasm, the seminal fluid will enter the uterus and fallopian tubes where fertilization can occur if an egg is present.

Although 9 out of 10 women having intercourse without protection will become pregnant within a year, many men and women continue to take chances. Their reasons include many vague, unfounded hopes that "It can't, or won't happen to me"; "I'm too young to become pregnant"; or "It can't happen if you only have sex occasionally."

Teenage Pregnancies and Contraception

Roughly half of the 11 million American teenagers are having sexual intercourse. Each year over a million teenagers become pregnant. One in 5 American mothers is a teenager (Guttmacher Report 1976, 1981). The media has seized on these statistics and deplored "the epidemic of teenage pregnancy." At the same time, commentators have failed to make some important distinctions in analyzing the data (Table 9.4; Figure 9.16).

Three-quarters of the teenage mothers are 18 or 19 years old. Most of these women are married, or marry the fathers of their child. Even though the average age for first marriage is now in the early twenties, many American women still marry right after high school graduation, at age 17 or 18.

A little less than a quarter of "the million teenage mothers" are between ages 15 and 17. For many of these teenagers, pregnancy and motherhood may not be a problem (Figure 9.17). In some subculture and ethnic groups, bearing a child outside wedlock is not viewed negatively because of an extended family support system involving older women who share in the parenting. For others, teenage motherhood creates major personal, social, and economic dilemmas. At the same time, some critics point out that our social welfare system may contribute to the incidence of teenage mothers by inadvertently supplying financial incentives in child support without providing alternatives in educational and job training.

For the 13,000 new mothers under age 15, pregnancy and motherhood poses serious medical and social problems. Reducing the number of unwanted preg-

Table 9.4.
Where Does the United States Stand on Teenage Pregnancies?

15- to 17-Year-Old Females	Pregnancies Per 1,000	Births Per 1,000	Abortions Per 1,000
United States Total	62	32	30
Whites	51	25	26
Blacks	128	71	57
Canada	28	14	14
England & Wales	27	13	14
Sweden	20	5	15
France	19	8	11
The Netherlands	7	3	4

Sources: Data adapted from Dryfoos 1985:3; Jones et al. 1985, 1986.

Figure 9.16. Contraception Among Teenage Girls. *(Adapted from a* Chicago Tribune *graphic based on data from the National Research Council.)*

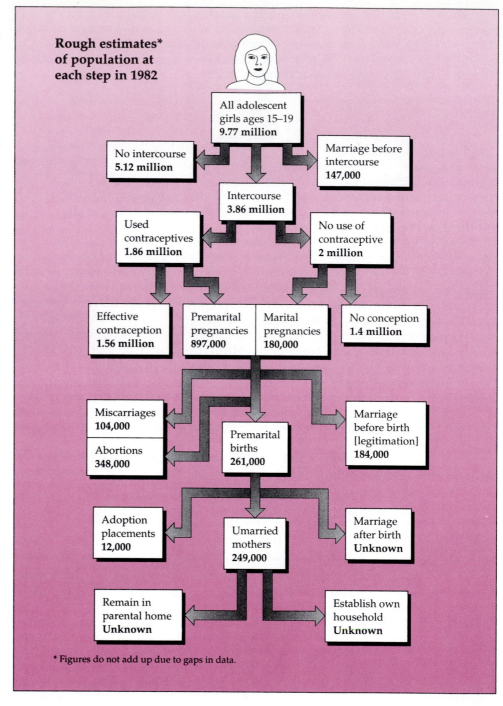

Rough estimates* of population at each step in 1982

All adolescent girls ages 15–19
9.77 million

No intercourse
5.12 million

Marriage before intercourse
147,000

Intercourse
3.86 million

Used contraceptives
1.86 million

No use of contraceptive
2 million

Effective contraception
1.56 million

Premarital pregnancies
897,000

Marital pregnancies
180,000

No conception
1.4 million

Miscarriages
104,000

Abortions
348,000

Premarital births
261,000

Marriage before birth [legitimation]
184,000

Adoption placements
12,000

Umarried mothers
249,000

Marriage after birth
Unknown

Remain in parental home
Unknown

Establish own household
Unknown

* Figures do not add up due to gaps in data.

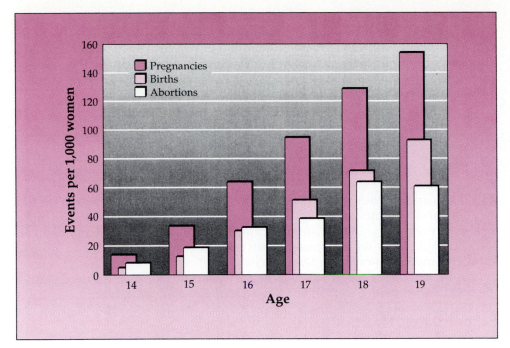

Figure 9.17. Teenage Pregnancies, Births and Abortions. *This graph shows the incidence of pregnancies, births, and abortions per 1,000 women for American women ages 14 through 19, in the year 1981, the most recent statistics available. The number of pregnancies shown here is simply the sum of the known births and abortions. In reality, there are more teenage pregnancies than estimated here.*

nancies is a primary goal of contraceptive education, family life programs, and holistic programs designed specifically for inner city teenagers. The predicament also exists in rural areas where support and prevention programs are far fewer (Guttmacher Report 1976, 1981).

Important progress in dealing with teenage pregnancy is being made by new public policies. In the Harlem section of New York City, one such program addresses the issues of adolescent sexuality, pregnancy, and childbearing before children reach puberty. It provides family life and sex education for parents and teens, medical and health services, and help in dealing with interpersonal, family, and personal problems. Self-esteem is built by participation in the performing arts and lifetime individual sports programs. Teenagers are given help with their school work, career planning, and college applications. Early results suggest that restructuring our approach to teenage sexuality in terms of the whole social environment in which teens live and are sexually active can reduce the number of unwanted pregnancies and single mothers (Carrera & Dempsey 1988; Sandoval 1988).

In the past decade, the number of teenagers using effective contraceptives has increased significantly. However, teenagers who did use contraceptives waited, on average, about nine months after they first started having sexual intercourse before using a contraceptive. More than half the pregnancies reported to teenagers in the late 1970s occurred within six months of the first sexual intercourse. Nearly one-third of all teenage females had at least one premarital pregnancy (Dawson 1986).

The statistics clearly suggest that many young couples recognize the risk of unprotected sexual intercourse only after they have experienced an unwanted pregnancy or thought the woman was pregnant, and decided then to use an effective contraceptive. Reducing the number of teenage pregnancies and abortions means convincing men and women *to think about contraception before they decide to have sexual intercourse and to use an effective contraceptive the first time and every time they have intercourse* until they decide they are ready and want to have a child and devote 20 years of their lives to raising that child.

The Ambivalence of Americans

The average American television viewer sees more than 9,000 scenes of suggested sexual intercourse, sexual comment, or innuendo each year. Yet rarely do these same television programs refer to the need for contraception or the consequences of unprotected sexual activity. Movies, music, radio, and television tell everyone sex is romantic, exciting, and titillating. How many popular songs do you know whose lyrics openly refer to sex? While the media propagates the myth of pervasive sexual activity and almost encourages it, many people in our society prefer a "Just say no!" policy rather than acknowledging the need for providing early education in sexuality and contraception.

School-Based Health Clinics

In 1982 when 28% of all births in Baltimore were to teenagers, Johns Hopkins University Hospital received a pioneer grant to provide free contraceptives to two Baltimore junior and senior high schools. By 1988 well over 100 such inner city school clinics nationwide were providing comprehensive health care, contraceptive services, and a sense of community for students who might otherwise never see a counselor or doctor.

The focus of the expanded school-based clinic is on prevention. The range of services includes general physical examinations, hearing and eye examinations, immunizations, first aid, nutrition advice, sex counseling, reproductive health information, drug and alcohol abuse programs, and other services tailored to low income students. In most clinics, only a third or a quarter of the services provided relate to sexuality and pregnancy. Yet, because some school-based health clinics dispense contraceptives and provide abortion counseling and referrals, they have triggered major opposition from conservatives (see Highlight Box 9.2).

A Fuller Picture

Sexual values and behavior are an integral part of the whole social fabric. Dryfoos (1985) suggests that Americans need to acknowledge and accept the fact that teenagers and single persons commonly engage in sexual intercourse. If our society recognized this reality, it might accept a moral obligation to provide education and access to contraceptives so teenagers can act responsibly. Yet even this initiative would not eliminate unplanned pregnancies which are the result of complicated social conditions.

The compounding effects of poverty and minority status are grinding under a whole generation of young people whose options are severely limited by segregation, school failure, and lack of employment oppor-

HIGHLIGHT BOX 9.2.
CLASHING VIEWS ON SCHOOL-
BASED HEALTH CLINICS

Phyllis Schlafly, founder of The Eagle Forum, vehemently denounces in-school health clinics that provide contraceptive information and services. Rather than encouraging teenage chastity, Schlafly claims, sex education has legitimized teenage promiscuity and caused the horrifying rise in teenage pregnancies since the 1950s (Schlafly 1987).

Schlafly's strong objections were shared by the Reagan administration, the National Right to Life Committee, several Roman Catholic bishops, a variety of black and Hispanic community leaders, the executive director of the national board of the YWCA, and William J. Bennett, U.S. Secretary of Education in 1986.

Richard Kenney, a physician working with adolescents in North Carolina, argues from his observations of these school-based health clinics that they address important health needs of teenagers otherwise ignored in our society. These clinics save $25 for every dollar invested (Kenney 1987).

Over 120 national organizations, including the National Parent-Teacher Association, American Baptist Churches, Child Welfare League for America, Campfire Girls, Girl Scouts, National Education Association, and the Association of School Nurses have endorsed school-based health clinics. In defending the school-based clinics in New York City, former Mayor Koch pointed out that the premise is to encourage abstinence but "You would have to be an ostrich if you believe that if you simply advocated abstinence that every teenager is going to do that."

tunities. For many of them, parenthood is about the only alternative they perceive, so that when a pregnancy occurs, even unintentionally, parenthood is accepted as the hand of fate. So in addition to changing the sexual climate, we have to do something to alleviate the social and economic problems of the children in the inner cities and the Appalachias of America.

(Dryfoos 1985:7)

When people, especially young people, feel they have no control over their environment or future, when they have to live from day to day and accept what fate brings, they are not likely to plan ahead and take precautions when it comes to having sex. At the same time, we need to remember that teenage pregnancies and motherhood, in some subcultures, are a positive and integral part of the value system (Levinson 1986).

The Costs of Accidental Pregnancies

Lack of access to proper prenatal care and balanced nutrition, and not age, is the prime reason babies born to teenagers have an increased risk of dying in their first year. Infants born to teenaged mothers are more likely to have a low birth weight, be premature, have birth defects, and experience respiratory problems. Infants born to young mothers are also at greater risk of being neglected and even physically abused when the young mother confronts new stresses in her life.

Mothers under age 15 are 60% more likely to die as result of the pregnancy than mothers in their early twenties. Mothers between 15 and 19 have a 13% higher risk of maternal death. Many pregnant teenagers drop out of school, become alienated from their friends, and have difficulty gaining employment.

The teenage marriage has its own high risks. Brides age 17 or younger are three times more likely to divorce than women who marry in their early twenties. For men age 17 or younger, the divorce rate is twice as high as for men who marry in their early twenties. In one study, 3 out of 5 women age 17 or younger who were pregnant when they married were separated or divorced within six years of marriage. One-fifth of these marriages broke up within the first year (Guttmacher Report 1976).

The young male involved in a teenage pregnancy is rarely considered, which in itself is a major problem. Although he is equally responsible for the pregnancy, he often has little or nothing to say in deciding whether the fetus is aborted or the pregnancy ends in birth. If the couple marries, he may have to drop out of school to support his new family. This responsibility often leads to resentment and a rather bleak outlook for the family's financial security (Guttmacher Report 1976, 1981; Hendrixson 1979).

Contraception in the 1990s

The future of new contraceptive methods depends to a great extent on what happens with the threat of medical liability suits. The IUD has been practically eliminated from the American scene by lawsuits. Some of the most effective and simplest contraceptives may go undeveloped because there is not a sufficient financial incentive for the pharmaceutical companies to invest in their developing, testing, and marketing.

Several implants and injections containing only progestin are awaiting approval from the FDA for marketing in the United States. Norplant, consisting of six hollow strawlike silastic capsules, 1.3 inches long, can be implanted under the skin of the arm to give contraceptive protection for five years. Because these implants are not biodegradable, they must be removed by surgery and replaced by fresh straws. Several biodegradable implants currently being tested will, if approved, eliminate the problem of surgical removal and provide daily protection for one, three, or six months. Five million women are using two injectable progestins that provide two- to three-month protection.

Silastic vaginal rings can release a combination of estrogen and progestin to provide protection for up to three months. The ring, inserted in the vagina like a diaphragm, is removed during intercourse.

RU 486, a contraceptive sponsored by the World Health Organization (WHO), mimics the structure of the female hormone progesterone. This characteristic allows RU 486 to block the normal action of progesterone, which is to prevent menstruation during a pregnancy. When combined with prostaglandins, RU 486 can be used to induce menstruation or sloughing of the uterine lining in a woman who suspects she may be pregnant. Some object that this drug opens the possibility of "do-it-at-home abortions." Still, RU 486 appears to be "one of the most exciting advances in the family planning field in a number of years," according to Dr. Wayne Bardin, director of the Center for Biomedical Research of the Population Council.

Efforts are also being made in India to immunize women against human chorionic gonadotropin (HCG) hormone. HCG is produced by the placenta and signals the ovary to stop the next menses because a pregnancy is under way. If the HCG signal is not received, menstruation will sweep out the implanted zygote. Vaccines are also being developed against other hormones involved in pregnancy.

Another new contraceptive now being tested is a miniaturized battery-powered "satellite" that stuns and kills sperm as they swim into the cervix on their way to the egg. Microchip technology has led to several devices that may make using the Billings', BBT, and sympto-thermal methods much easier. A hand-held minicomputer can be used to calculate fertility based on the viscosity of the cervical mucus and temperature. Another hand-held minicomputer has oral and vaginal sensors to determine fertility based on ionic concentration in cells. A wristwatch with sensor displays the time of day and the word "fertile" or "infertile" at the press of a button. A chemically treated dipstick measures the luteinizing hormone in vaginal secretions, turning blue to indicate the fertile period. Other, more convenient aids to natural contraception will inevitably be marketed in the 1990s (*Contraceptive Technology Update* 1986).

Also possible are liquid silicone plugs that are injected into the uterine openings of the fallopian tubes and harden to completely block the tubes. These plugs have embedded miniature loops so they can be removed when the woman wants to become pregnant. Clam extracts that paralyze sperm are another possibility, but many doubt that a male contraceptive pill will be popular with either women or men.

Coping with a New Reality

In the past century, tremendous economic and social changes have created a population of millions of sexually mature young people who, although they may be unprepared and economically unable to marry or become parents, nevertheless are expressing and exploring their sexuality. These same social and economic changes have also contributed to the emergence of a large population of single men and women in their middle and later years. Although modern medical technology has provided us with a wide range of relatively safe and effective contraceptives, many Americans have not adjusted their thinking and their values to accommodate the realities of today's world. We hope this chapter has provided some practical insights into this ongoing tension and development.

Key Concepts

1. A century of rapid medical advances has provided us with a variety of relatively safe and effective contraceptives, including barrier, hormonal, natural, and surgical methods.

2. Social and economic changes have produced a new phenomenon, the sexually mature single person. As a society and as individuals we have yet to work out our attitudes and values about nonmarital and nonreproductive sex.

3. Erotophobes, men and women who have negative attitudes about sex, are less likely to use contraceptives than erotophiles, who have a positive view of their sexuality.

4. For a variety of reasons, many young people tend to delay their use of contraceptives until after they have engaged in unprotected intercourse for some months.

5. The effectiveness of any contraceptive method depends primarily on the motivation of the user and the consistent and proper use of the method.

Key Terms

BBT method (264)
cervical cap (259)
cervical mucus method (264)
C-film (256)
combination pill (262)
condom (250)
contraceptives (240)
contraceptive sponge (258)
diaphragm (257)
erotophile (244)
erotophobe (244)

intrauterine device (IUD) (261)
outercourse (250)
progestin-only pill (262)
rhythm method (263)
spermicide (254)
sympto-thermal method (264)
tubal ligation (265)
vaginal foam (254)
vasectomy (266)
VCF film (256)

Summary Questions

1. In general terms, which contraceptive methods are most effective and which are least effective? Which would be more practical for a woman or man who has vaginal intercourse only occasionally? Which would be more practical for a young couple or older couple who are having intercourse regularly?

2. What is outercourse and how is its practice related to the use of contraceptives by persons who are sexually intimate?

3. What social and cultural variables affect the incidence of teenage pregnancies and any proposed attempt to reduce this incidence?

4. From what you may know about sexual attitudes and sex education in various countries, can you suggest any reasons for the wide differences in the incidence of teenage pregnancy shown in Table 9.4?

5. What misinformation about "risks" of certain contraceptives and the "safety" of intercourse without contraceptive protection are commonly accepted, even though they are not supported by medical facts?

Suggested Readings

Balis, A. (1981). *What Are You Using? A Birth Control Guide for Teenagers.* New York: Dial Press. How to make decisions about contraceptives.

Everett, J., & W. D. Glanze. (1987). *The Condom Book: The Essential Guide for Men and Women.* New York: New American Library Signet. Everything you need to know about condoms.

Gordon, L. (1976). *Women's Body, Women's Right: A Social History of Birth Control in America.* New York: Grossman.

Hendricks, P. (1987, September). Condoms: A straight girl's best friend. *Ms.* magazine, pp. 98–102. Brief and practical advice.

Reed, J. (1978). *The Birth Control Movement in America: From Private Vice to Public Virtue.* New York: Basic Books. The politics of birth control.

A History of Abortion
  Religious Views
  Who Has Abortions?
  Legal Aspects
*A*bortion Controversies
  The Antiabortion and
    Prochoice Movements
  A Human Life
    Amendment or
    Statute
  When Does Human
    Life Begin?
  The Rights of Minors
    and Their Parents
  The Rights of the Poor
  The Rights of People in
    the Third World
  Abortion and Sex
    Selection
*M*aking Decisions
  About Pregnancy
  The Single Parent
    Option and Adoption
  The Abortion Choice
*A*bortion Options
  Postcoital Hormonal
    Contraception
  Medical Procedures
  Medical and Emotional
    Aftercare
A National Dilemma

Chapter 10

*A*bortion: Our Shared Responsibilities

Special Consultants

Sylvia D. Diehl, M.D., medical director, Planned Parenthood of Greater Northern New Jersey, and staff physician, Student Health Services, Fairleigh Dickinson University.

Paul A. Fleming, M.D., D.H.S., director, The Fleming Center, Raleigh, North Carolina.

Berta Numata, R.N.C., Ob/Gyn nurse practitioner, Planned Parenthood of Greater Northern New Jersey.

Mary Jane St. Peter, R.N., director, Student Health Services, Fairleigh Dickinson University. She has also served as assistant supervisor, Department of Gynecology, St. Francis Hospital, Hartford, Connecticut, and coordinator of maternal/child health, Morristown Memorial Hospital, Morristown, New Jersey.

No doubt, even the advocates of a woman's right to choose an abortion and the women who have abortions would prefer not to be faced with this choice. Yet, until we have a perfectly safe, 100% reliable, convenient, and fully reversible contraceptive available to all women who would like to avoid all unintended pregnancies, there will be a need for **abortion**, medical and surgical procedures that terminate a pregnancy before birth. Even if we had the perfect contraceptive, some women who knowingly become pregnant would later decide to have an abortion for various reasons, including detection of a genetic disease in the fetus.

With well over half of the 40 million men and women between the ages of 15 and 24 sexually active, and with 1.3 million abortions in the United States each year, chances are the information in this chapter may, sooner or later, be very practical for you or someone close to you.

A History of Abortion

History provides an important context for understanding the current debates about abortion in today's society.

In ancient Greece, Aristotle found abortion completely acceptable, but only when used as a backup in cases of contraceptive failure. Hippocrates disagreed with the common viewpoint of the time and rejected abortion as a means of population control. In fact, the original Hippocratic oath taken by physicians until the 1970s prohibited giving a patient any substance that would induce an abortion. The oath has since been revised to eliminate the prohibition against the physician's involvement in an abortion.

In ancient Rome, population control was also a matter of public policy. Abortion up to the fifth month was not only acceptable but encouraged by the state. However, it was practiced almost exclusively by the ruling class, which caused great concern that the lower classes might someday outnumber those in power.

Religious Views

In ancient Judaism, there were no Talmudic laws against abortion. In fact, Jewish law considered the fetus as not being a viable human being until sometime after birth. Today, orthodox Judaism only permits therapeutic abortion in order to save the mother's life, in cases of rape, and when mental anguish may occur if the pregnancy is not terminated. Conservative and reform Jews are more liberal in accepting abortion for other reasons (Callahan 1970; Simmons 1986, 1987).

Until the fifth century, Christian theologians were unanimous in condemning abortion under all circumstances. However, after 500, the philosophy and scientific views of the Greek philosopher Aristotle began to attract Christian theologians. As an embryologist, Aristotle had argued, probably from his anatomical studies of miscarried fetuses, that the male fetus developed its sexual and human structure about 40 days after conception and the female fetus its form about 80 days after conception. Philosophically, Aristotle said it was not logical for a human animating principle or soul to be present until the human form was present. When Thomas Aquinas, the greatest of medieval theologians, accepted Aristotle's view that the human fetus first has a vegetative soul, then an animal life principle, and finally after quickening, a human soul, many theologians decided to accept abortion in the first trimester, with a small religious penalty, and to punish abortion after that point with excommunication.

In the 1700s some embryologists claimed they could see a preformed human figure curled up in the human egg or sperm with their new microscopes (Figure 10.1). Since this "evidence" refuted the position of Aristotle and Aquinas, Pope Sixtus V outlawed all abortions regardless of their timing. If the human form was present in the egg or sperm, then the human soul must also be there from fertilization on. Three years later, however, Pope Gregory XIV reaffirmed the Aristotelian position and again allowed first trimester abortions. But the new embryologists again convinced the theologians that Aristotle was wrong. A hundred years later, with better microscopes and less imagination, the embryologists returned to Aristotle's view of a gradual development of the human form. For their part, Catholic theologians continued to condemn all abortion, believing the human soul was present from fertilization on (Doncell 1970; Francoeur 1970:68–80).

The Eastern Orthodox Church takes a position on abortion similar to that of recent Roman Catholicism. Both churches strongly oppose abortion under any circumstances. There is, however, a marked discrepancy between dogma and practice because American Catholics have abortions at the same rate as Protestants and others.

Although some Protestant sects also strictly prohibit abortion, the mainstream of the Protestant Church accepts abortion as a matter of individual conscience. Most denominations oppose any state or national laws that would interfere with or restrict abortion, which they see as a threat to freedom of religion and to the separation of church and state.

Who Has Abortions?

Since 1980, 3 out of every 10 pregnancies in the United States have ended in an abortion, which means about 1.3 million abortions each year. Six out of 10 abortions are had by young women, including 26% by teenagers. White women account for 70% of all abortions. Unmarried women have 81% of the abortions. Half of all abortions were performed in the first 6 weeks of gestation and 91% by the 10th week. The more disturbing statistic is that close to 4 out of 10 abortions in the United States represent repeat abortion. Women who have had two, three, or more abortions do face a clear risk of infertility (Henshaw 1986, 1987).

Women 18 and 19 years old continue to have the highest abortion rate of any age group. Although most abortions are had by white women, the nonwhite abortion rate is twice that of whites. However, nonwhite and white teenagers have about the same abortion ratios (Henshaw 1986, 1987; Isaacson 1981).

Around the world, an estimated 30 to 40 million abortions are performed each year. Adding an estimate of the illegal abortions increases the total number of abortions worldwide to between 40 and 60 million abortions a year. Three out of 4 women in the world live in countries that allow abortion at least for health reasons. Four out of 10 women live in nations that allow abortion on request at least in the first trimester. A third of all women in the world have no access to legal abortion. Most of these women live in Central and South Africa, Latin America, and fundamentalist Islamic nations. Illegal abortions result in 200,000 deaths each year (Henshaw 1986, 1987).

Figure 10.1. The "Little Person" in the Sperm. *From the late 1600s to the late 1700s, biologists debated whether the human sperm, or egg, contained a fully formed human body. If the human form was present, it was argued, then the human soul was also present. This "scientific" conclusion led theologians to condemn abortion, which had been previously tolerated prior to quickening. Improvements in microscopes subsequently showed that the homunculus or "little person" was actually a figment of the early scientists' imaginations.*

Obviously, abortion is a reality that cannot be ignored in this country or around the world.

Legal Aspects

Before Roe v. Wade

Under English common law and colonial American law, abortion prior to the fifth month was not considered a crime. However, in the 1800s, a humanitarian movement began, seeking to protect women from the dangerous and crude methods then used in performing abortions.

Before the advent of the Industrial Revolution, the number of children a couple had was of little interest to the state. Families were generally quite large, although the infant, child, and maternal mortality rates were very high—1 in 5 women died in pregnancy and 1 in 5 infants did not survive its first year. Still, children were an economic advantage for the family working a farm. With the onset of the Industrial Revolution in the 1800s, government and the business world encouraged large families. With child labor an important economic consideration in the mines and mills, anticontraception and antiabortion movements began to grow. Using both religious and economic arguments, these groups succeeded in getting the English government to declare abortion a crime in 1803, except when the woman's life or health was in danger. The first American antiabortion law was passed in 1821. By the late 1800s, abortion was a crime throughout the United States except when deemed necessary to protect a woman's health.

The movement to liberalize American abortion laws began in the 1960s as a result of several factors. A new way of doing abortions became available: the vacuum curettage method developed in Hungary. Because this technique was safer than delivery, it negated the argument that abortions had to be illegal to protect women. Another factor was the thalidomide tragedy. An excellent sedative and tranquilizer, thalidomide unexpectedly turned out to have a devastating side effect. Early in pregnancy, thalidomide prevents development of the arms and legs. American women, who brought the tranquilizer home from abroad and found themselves faced with the possibility of carrying a severely crippled fetus, created a lot of pressure in the mass media for reform of the abortion laws (Figure 10.2). A 1964 epidemic of German measles caused many pregnant women to seek and obtain legal abortions. The American Law Institute took a formal position advocating the legalization of abortion. The newly vocal feminist movement endorsed a woman's right to control her own body, pointing out the social and personal advantages of safe legal abortions over dangerous illegal ones. In 1970 Alaska, Hawaii, New York, and Washington legalized abortion on request.

Roe v. Wade

On January 22, 1973, the U.S. Supreme Court voted 7 to 2 in the case of **Roe v. Wade** to legalize abortion throughout the nation. Basing their position on the right to privacy, the justices ruled that a woman and her physician have the sole decision on abortion in the first trimester. In the second trimester, a state may intervene only to protect the woman's health. In the third trimester, a state may regulate abortion to protect fetal life. In a second decision on the same day, Roe v. Bolton, the court also struck down in a 7 to 2 decision all

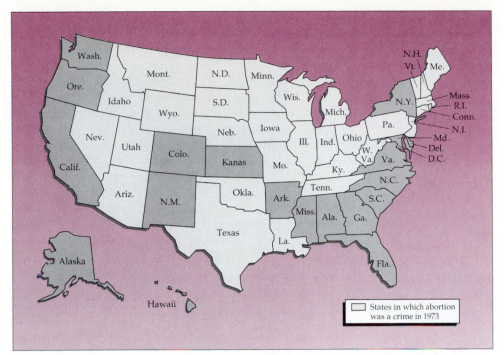

Figure 10.2. Abortion before 1973 and after 1989. *Before the Supreme Court legalized abortion in 1973, 18 states, with 41% of the population, allowed abortion. Thirty-one states still considered it a crime, but 3 out of every 4 Americans could get a legal abortion within 100 miles of where they lived. If Roe v. Wade was reversed, what might be the consequences? This question became paramount in 1989 when the U.S. Supreme Court began dismantling Roe v. Wade in the Webster decision. Janet Benshoff, an attorney for the American Civil Liberties Union, believes Utah, Louisiana, Illinois, and Missouri would very likely outlaw abortions. New Hampshire, Connecticut, Kentucky, Idaho, and South Dakota might also activate antiabortion laws, making it necessary for women in those states to travel to another state if they wanted a legal abortion. States shown in gray allowed abortion prior to Roe v. Wade. In the states shown in white, abortion was a crime before 1973.*

restrictions on the facilities that can be used for abortion. Several controversial issues immediately emerged in public debate.

Abortion Controversies

The Antiabortion and Prochoice Movements

Since the Supreme Court legalized abortion in 1973, the prochoice and antiabortion controversy has not slackened. A variety of antiabortion groups have politically identified themselves as "prolife," supporting "the right to life." This coalition includes such constituents as Eastern Orthodox, Roman Catholic, fundamentalist, and some Protestant groups, like the Moral Majority, as well as orthodox Jews (Figure 10.3).

Prochoice advocates believe that the final word in deciding whether or not to continue a pregnancy to term must rest with the individual woman. They

Figure 10.3. Antiabortion and Prochoice Demonstrations. *Since the U.S. Supreme Court decision legalizing abortion in 1973, the controversy has intensified. Although the prochoice advocates do not like abortion, they see it as the lesser of two evils—the more serious consequence of unwanted pregnancies being battered and abused children. Because we have ineffective education on contraceptives, these advocates claim we need the free choice of abortion as a backup. On the other side, the antiabortion advocates see themselves as defenders of the right to life of the embryo and fetus. They see abortion as homicide, and never morally acceptable.*

believe that the rights of a woman take precedence over the assumed rights of the fertilized human egg, the embryo, or even the fetus whose human status and rights are not as clearly established or recognized. Prochoice groups generally agree that abortion needs to be an option in a society where sex education is not as effective as it should be and where fully acceptable and effective contraceptives still remain to be developed. Prochoice advocates include Protestant and Jewish organizations, Catholics for Free Choice, Planned Parenthood, National Organization for Women (NOW), National Abortion Rights Action League (NARAL), and the American Civil Liberties Union (ACLU).

An analysis of correlations in the voting records of legislators supporting the antiabortion movement reveals some interesting patterns of thought. Canadian and U.S. senators who have voted in favor of the restriction or abolition of abortion have consistently voted for bills supporting capital punishment and the war in Vietnam and against bills that would regulate handguns and the exercise of "no knock" police searches. In an analysis of voting on 15 bills in the U.S. Senate, which the Farmers Union viewed as supporting family life, senators voting against abortion choice had the lowest scores of votes for family support, on bills for school lunch and milk programs, and for aid to the elderly. These patterns, coupled with an analysis of voting on abortion, homosexuality, and prostitution legislation, led Prescott to suggest that the basic motivation of the antiabortion movement is not the protection of human life, but rather an unacknowledged antisexual bias (Prescott 1975b, 1978, 1986; Prescott & Wallace 1978).

Despite heated debate and controversy, there has been no significant change in the attitudes of Americans on the abortion issue. In the midst of the 1980 presidential campaign, George Gallup found that nationwide attitudes on abortion had not changed significantly in five years. The findings also found almost no differences in the attitudes of men and women on abortion, between Protestants and Catholics, or between Republican and Democrat voters (Gallup 1980).

A Human Life Amendment or Statute

Within months of the Roe v. Wade decision, 200 versions of a Human Life Amendment were introduced into Congress in an attempt to prohibit all abortions. In the next two years, hearings were held, but none of the proposed amendments was voted out of committee. In 1981 antiabortion groups decided to push for a Human Life Statute that would declare human life begins at the moment of fertilization or conception instead of attempting to amend the Constitution. This statute was defeated in a full Senate vote in 1982. The next year, the Senate defeated a Human Life Statute that would have protected the fetus from conception on.

When Does Human Life Begin?

When a human egg and sperm unite at fertilization there is no doubt that a human organism begins its growth, controlled by distinctly human chromosomes. But is this cell mass a "human"? Is the zygote, or even the embryo, a person with inalienable rights? In removing the veil from the embryo and fetus in the womb, modern fetology has revived the age-old argument about when human life really begins. The debates of Aristotle, Aquinas, and the embryologists of the 1500s and 1600s return to haunt us with their perplexity (Francoeur 1989).

The modern twist to the question of when human life begins is the issue of **personhood**. Persons have rights, but human cells do not. If human cells had the same rights as persons, we could not morally accept tissue and organ transplants.

Some argue, on the basis of religious belief, that a human person is present from the first moment of conception and must have our unequivocal protection. Abortion, therefore, is homicide. Abortion is the same as infanticide, killing the newborn.

Others argue that although the embryo and fetus certainly deserve respect, a pregnancy may be terminated to avoid a greater evil in the birth of an unwanted child that cannot or would not be provided with a decent standard of living. A zygote or embryo may, or may not, develop into a person. If a pregnancy is terminated before the fetus becomes a person, it is argued, the abortion is not the same as homicide (Simmons 1986, 1987).

Personhood, then, becomes the issue if the brain is the real seat of personhood. We cannot have a person without a brain. Had they known what we know today about the development of the fetus in the womb, Aristotle and Aquinas would likely have argued that until the fetus has a functioning brain, there is not person, mind, or soul present. The central nervous system first

HIGHLIGHT BOX 10.1.
THE TURNING POINT
OF VIABILITY

When the Supreme Court ruled on the Roe v. Wade case, the question of when the fetus could survive outside the womb, its **viability**, was a serious concern. In 1973 few premature newborns weighing less than 2 pounds (1,000 grams) could survive even with the medical care then available in perinatal intensive care units. Today, with sophisticated intensive care, nearly all 28-week-old, 1000-gram newborns can survive. A few newborns weighing only 1 pound (500 grams) may survive (Harris & Snowden 1985).

A fetus usually weighs about 600 to 800 grams by the end of six months gestation (24 weeks). Somewhere between 20 and 22 weeks, a fetus normally reaches the 500 gram mark, about 1 pound. About 20% of the newborns weighing less than 1000 grams, under 2 pounds, survive. Since the Roe v. Wade decision defined viability as existing at six months, do the recent advances in medical science and a new viability standard mean the courts should change the time period for legal abortion? Sandra Day O'Connor, associate justice of the U.S. Supreme Court, has suggested that

the definition of fetal viability in the 1973 Roe v. Wade decision is on "a collision course" with modern medical advances in perinatal intensive care. Fetal viability depends on the lungs and kidneys being mature enough to function and support life outside the womb. The air sacs in the lungs are not able to function independently until somewhere between 26 and 28 weeks. The kidneys mature enough to support life outside the uterus between weeks 22 and 26. Even the most sophisticated perinatal intensive care cannot compensate for the immature, poorly functioning kidneys and lungs of a very premature infant (Bennett 1989:83–86; Flower 1989:71–82).

Although a premature infant between 500 and 1,000 grams may indeed be kept alive for some time after delivery, these newborns are usually severely handicapped and seldom survive to leave the hospital and live a normal life. Some physicians question the morality of making an all-out effort to extend the lives of these tiniest of newborns (Harris & Snowden 1985; Schechner 1980; Strong 1983).

appears in the third week of pregnancy as a structure, but it does not begin functioning until months later. The neocortex, where our conscious thinking processes are based, does not begin to function in a rudimentary way until around the end of the fifth or beginning of the sixth month of gestation (Bennett 1989; Flower 1989). Identifiable, functional connections between nerve cells do not develop in the brain until sometime between 18 and 21 weeks. But does that make the fetus a "person" in the full sense, or is personhood a quality society defines?

Another aspect of the debate about personhood is the fact that in some cultures the biological birth of a fetus does not make it a person. To be a person, the newborn must undergo a **social birth**, a public ritual in which it is formally presented to and accepted by the elder(s) of a family or community. In some cultures like China, a newborn who dies or is killed before it goes through a social birth is not mourned. In the orthodox Jewish tradition, a male infant who dies before its circumcision eight days after its biological birth is not given a name or a formal burial because circumcision is a necessary sign of the covenant between Yahweh and his chosen people and of incorporation into the people of God (Minturn 1989:87–88; Morgan 1989:97–114).

The Rights of Minors and Their Parents

One ongoing debate is over the conflict between the rights of the more than 1 million American teenagers who become pregnant each year and the rights and responsibilities of their parents. About 400,000 of these teenage women exercise their constitutional right to privacy and choose to have an abortion. State legislatures have repeatedly considered laws requiring pregnant teenagers to obtain parental permission for an abortion and requiring doctors to inform the parents 24 hours before performing an abortion on a minor. The problem is how to respect a minor's legal right to privacy and the parents' moral, legal, and financial responsibility for their child's health.

In 1976 the U.S. Supreme Court, in Planned Parenthood of Central Missouri v. Danforth, ruled that a woman does not need the consent of her parents or husband before having an abortion. In 1979 the U.S. Supreme Court, in Belloti v. Baird, overturned a Massachusetts law requiring parental consent. In 1981 another ruling from the Supreme Court, in H.L. v. Matheson, upheld a Utah law popularly known as the squeal rule. This law permitted states to require doctors to notify the parents of "immature minors" seeking an abortion, but stipulated that the states provide prompt and confidential judicial hearings for teenagers who do not want to seek their parents' permission. When Minneapolis passed a parental notification law in 1981, the birthrate for 15 to 17 year olds in that city went up 38%. In the same period, the birthrate for 17 to 19 year olds, who were not covered by the law, went up only 0.3%.

The debate over parental notification has continued in the courts and state legislatures for over 15 years and promises to remain a point of heated contention through the 1990s.

The Rights of the Poor

Does the taxpayer and the government have an obligation to provide health care for the poor who cannot afford it? Does this obligation extend to elective abortions?

On the federal level, generally speaking, the Senate has favored no prohibitions on the use of federal or state funds to pay for abortions for poor women. However, in the House of Representatives, antichoice legislators regularly attach to annual budget bills amendments prohibiting federal funds from being used in any program supporting abortion as an option, including Medicaid. In the subsequent Congressional compromises, the antiabortion restrictions usually remain in effect. As a result, poor women are often forced to continue an unwanted pregnancy and give birth to a child they cannot support because Medicaid funds are not available to pay for an abortion.

In 1977 the U.S. Supreme Court, in Beal v. Doe and Maher v. Roe, ruled that the federal government and the states cannot be compelled to pay for elective abortions for poor women. The U.S. Congress also passed the Hyde amendment banning use of Medicaid funds to pay for abortions for poor women. By 1979 40 states had passed laws restricting Medicaid funds for abortion. In 1982 the New Jersey Supreme Court ruled that the state must pay for "medically necessary" abortions for poor women. The U.S. Supreme Court refused to hear an appeal of the law, saying that a State Constitution can guarantee more rights than the U.S. Constitution.

In 1983 the U.S. Supreme Court provided some protection for poor women seeking abortions by overturning a law requiring that all abortions beyond the third month be done in hospitals. But then Congress eliminated funds for abortion services in the health benefit plans of federal employees. By 1985 only 14 states and Washington, D.C., continued to fund abortions for Medicaid-eligible women, and 36 states prohibited tax monies from being used to fund abortion services.

In 1989 the U.S. Supreme Court upheld a Missouri law which prohibited abortions in any hospital or facility receiving public funds, unless the abortion was necessary to save the woman's life. This decision made abortion all but impossible to obtain in Missouri. Ninety-seven percent of all abortions in Missouri were performed at Truman Medical Center in Kansas City. Because this private hospital was built on land leased from the state, it is considered a "public facility" and subject to the law prohibiting abortion.

The Rights of People in the Third World

At a 1984 international family planning meeting in Mexico City, the United States announced that no American funds would be given to any international family planning group that includes abortion among approved methods of population control, or which is even associated with groups that do. There had been a law against giving funds directly for abortion since 1973, but the policy from 1983 on said funds could not be given to an organization even if their overseas abortions programs were entirely funded by other, private means. This policy immediately cut off $15 million annually from the funding of International Planned Parenthood for its programs in Third World countries where population problems are overwhelming. U.S. funds that in the past had supported a wide variety of population programs were suddenly shut off.

With India facing the prospect of surpassing China as the world's most populated country, Bangladesh's population approaching a breaking point, and China rumored to be using enforced abortion to help control its birthrate, the "Mexico City Policy" seriously limited the prospects of the more populous, and usually poverty-ridden, nations gaining control over their growth.

Abortion and Sex Selection

Amniocentesis, discussed in Chapter 8, can be used to learn the sex of a fetus at 16 to 18 weeks of gestation. If tests reveal that the fetus has Down syndrome, other chromosomal disorders, or a neural tube defect, the parents may decide to have an abortion rather than bring a seriously handicapped infant into the world. But what if a couple wants a boy for their first child, or the couple has had two or three girls, and the test now reveals the woman is carrying a healthy, normal girl? Should a physician, and society, allow abortion of a healthy fetus simply because it is of the "wrong" sex?

In mid-1988 the relatively affluent state of Maharashra, India, where the city of Bombay is located, outlawed fetal tests for sex selection. Experts believed that tens of thousands of such abortions had been performed in recent years throughout India for affluent and poor women alike. Old and new cultural values clashed when advertisements warned prospective parents that it is better to spend 500 rupees for amniocentesis and an abortion now rather than pay 50,000 rupees in an illegal dowry to get a daughter married. The law could serve as a model for the rest of India and for other Asian countries where the practice is widespread. Yet the problem remains how to enforce such a law. Even though the American medical community is opposed to abortion for sex selection, it does occur (Hoskins & Holmes 1984; Roggencamp 1984; Weisman 1988).

Making Decisions About Pregnancy

Before any decisions are made regarding a suspected pregnancy that may be unplanned or unwanted, the pregnancy should be confirmed by a pregnancy test and an examination that will establish the length of the pregnancy. Once the pregnancy is confirmed, a variety of options need to be considered.

The Single Parent Option and Adoption

As recently as the 1940s, a single women who became a mother was a social outcast. Today, with divorce and a growing economic independence at least for middle class women, single parenthood has become a common reality of American society. In many cases, the single mother does not set out to become a single parent, but rather is caught up in a net of circumstances, especially in the inner city ghetto, that are part of and contribute to a cycle of poverty. One positive sign of coping is that inner city public schools are beginning to develop programs allowing single mothers to complete their secondary schooling and graduate with some skills. The decision to become a single mother and raise the child, especially if the mother is still in her teen years, means making a commitment to a whole set of limitations and responsibilities that can be frightening and overwhelming if the woman does not have some kind of support system and family to call on for help (Figure 10.4).

"THEY SAY I NEED PARENTAL CONSENT BEFORE THEY CAN GIVE ME AN ASPIRIN. I'LL JUST GET AN ABORTION, INSTEAD."

Figure 10.4. Whose Choice? *This cartoon illustrates the conflicting dimension posed by the debate over women's rights to control their own reproductive functions. In most states, minors have confidential access to contraceptive counseling. In 1990, the U.S. Supreme Court ruled that state laws requiring girls under 17 to have the consent of at least one parent or a court before having an abortion were constitutional.*

Within the antiabortion movement, there is a growing realization that some viable options must be offered to reduce the number of abortions. Generally, this recognition has not led to support for sex education in the schools or for endorsement of condom use. It has, however, led to a growing number of programs that provide prenatal care, housing, and financial support for single mothers who are willing to carry their pregnancy to term and give the child up for adoption.

The Abortion Choice

Once the pregnancy has been confirmed, it is important to consider carefully all of the options available. Such important decisions are often made easier if the pregnant woman can talk with a supportive family member or friend. A counselor, doctor, clinician, or member of the clergy can also be helpful in getting an objective overview of the options. If the decision is to have an abortion, then the various choices can be explored. Decisions should be based on solid information and an exploration of feelings rather than on fear or guilt.

Abortions today are safer than ever before. In fact, early abortion, in the first three months, is considerably safer than carrying a child to term. The word *early* is stressed here because first trimester abortions are safer and simpler than those performed in the fourth to sixth month. Decisions regarding abortion, therefore, are best made as soon as possible after the pregnancy is established.

If you decide to have an abortion, don't forget to discuss with your partner what you are going to do to avoid facing a repeat decision in the future. Despite your anxieties and overriding concerns about the abortion, you should also get information on contraceptives and *decide which contraceptive method you are going to start using immediately after the abortion.* If you were using a contraceptive method and it failed, discuss with the doctor why it may have failed and whether another method might be more effective for you in the future. **Remember:** *Four out of 10 abortions in the United States are repeat abortions. Repeat abortions do increase the risk of fragments of uterine/fetal tissues lodging in the openings of the fallopian tubes and blocking them.*

Psychological Considerations

Deciding whether or not to have an abortion often brings with it a combination of conflicting emotions. What kinds of feelings might you be experiencing if you were faced with an unplanned or unwanted pregnancy? Elation with your body? A desire to be a parent? A feeling of completeness or fulfillment? Fears of disapproval by family or friends? Fear of being rejected by your partner? Concern over having another child because of the economic situation, or an already strained marriage? Fear of becoming a parent? Fear of having an abortion? Usually a woman experiences a mix of such emotions and questions. Young women may be angry with their partner or themselves for not using effective contraception, or at their parents for not providing adequate birth control information. Frustration and indecision are also common, particularly if neither partner feels ready or mature enough to raise a child. Feelings of loneliness, isolation, and guilt are also common in an early, unwanted pregnancy. Because the partners are often under great stress, nonjudgmental counseling and support can be very helpful. Although an early decision is important, it is better to take time to weigh the options and reach a decision that is best for the specific case.

The Male Role in Abortion

Although women are the primary focus of an abortion decision, the unplanned or unwanted pregnancy is usually the result of a relationship. The partner may be just as involved as the woman. He may share many of the same frustrations and mixed emotions as his partner.

Only recently, however, have counselors become sensitive to the specific pressures that may affect the male partner. The male may feel isolated from the situation because he is not the one who will, in most cases, make the decision. He may be unfamiliar with abortion and be concerned about its safety. He may also have strong feelings of wanting the child and may not be able to do anything about it. Or he may feel that it is his male role to act nonchalant and unconcerned, even though he cares very much and cannot express his feelings. In addition, some men may be concerned about influencing the partner's decision. They may hold back and fail to communicate their feelings adequately.

What can the male do in this situation? The best solution is to be open and willing to communicate. Listening to one's friend or lover is always important. Being able to listen, and trying to remain open to each other's views and feelings will help in making a decision both can live with. If the decision is to have an abortion, then the woman may need support and assistance in making arrangements, as well as in the days and weeks that follow the abortion. The decision and the abortion must be integrated into the relationship, if it is to continue. Of course, both partners should make plans to prevent a second unwanted pregnancy so that abortion is not relied on as a means of contraception in the future (Wade 1979).

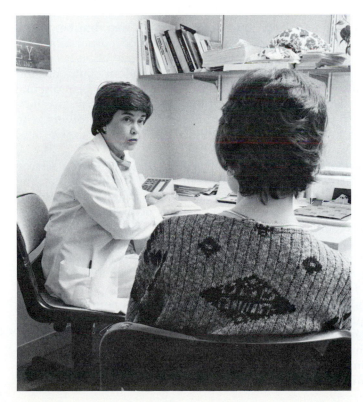

Figure 10.5. Abortion Counseling. *Women or couples faced with an unwanted pregnancy can benefit greatly from discussing their options with a professional, nonjudgmental counselor. Counseling after an abortion can also help a woman or couple work through their emotional reactions and go on with their lives.*

Choosing Where to Have an Abortion

A woman who decides to have an abortion does have options in selecting where to have it done. There are freestanding abortion clinics that specialize in performing first trimester abortions. These clinics are not connected with hospitals. They charge lower fees and still have very experienced personnel. However, you must be careful to select a clinic that has a good reputation. Some abortion clinics may be too large, or more interested in making a profit than in providing sensitive care with a good follow-up. Try to talk with someone at the clinic to find out as much as you can before deciding to have an abortion there. Also, check with a local hospital or medical society to make sure the clinic is legitimate and legal.

In some states, gynecologists perform first trimester abortions in their offices. These physicians are often known in the community, and you can check their credentials through a county medical society. Again, interview the doctor before deciding. If you're not comfortable with a particular doctor, try to find another one who relates better to your concerns and questions if possible. Also check to make certain the anesthesiologist (if one is needed) is board certified.

Abortion services are either outpatient or inpatient. Outpatient clinics perform abortions up to 14 to 16 weeks without requiring an overnight stay. Some outpatient clinics may also perform second trimester abortions, up to 20 to 24 weeks. Inpatient services are usually reserved for second trimester saline injection or prostaglandin abortions, or when there are no clinics or private physician facilities available and usually require an overnight stay. Costs for a hospital abortion may range from $1,200 to $1,500.

There are many questions you should ask when you decide to have an abortion. First, find out as much as possible about abortion facilities in your community. There may be a local abortion hot line in your area, but be careful that it is not a captive referral service for a profit-oriented corporation that receives kickbacks for its referrals. The National Abortion Federation has a toll-free hot line and provides free referrals to reliable independent clinics around the country. (The number can be dialed from anywhere in the continental United States, 800–223–0618.) Planned Parenthood and your community hospital may also be able to provide information. If possible, talk to others who have had abortions and find out about the facilities used, the personnel, and the general attitudes toward abortion at the facility.

In checking out an abortion clinic, find out if it is affiliated with a nearby hospital or has arrangements with it in case of an emergency. Is there counseling before and after the abortion? Is a laboratory test to confirm pregnancy required? Some clinics do misrepresent and have been known to perform an "abortion" even if the woman turned out not to be pregnant. In addition, a VDRL test for syphilis and an HIV-I test are also standard today before any abortion. A blood typing should be done in the event that a transfusion is needed and to determine whether you have Rh-negative blood (see Chapter 8). You can also ask to see the recovery room and discuss the length of stay, possible complications, and provisions for such complications. A facility with ultrasound equipment available is usually well equipped to handle most problems. The choice of a facility is important to future health and should not be taken lightly.

You should also find out about the follow-up procedures. Is a pathology report filed to determine that the abortion was complete? Is there a provision for a follow-up examination? Is birth control information available? Choosing an effective, acceptable contraceptive that can be started right after the abortion is essential to avoiding a repeat abortion in the future.

In metropolitan areas in 1990, an average fee for a first trimester abortion was between $200 and $350, more if general anesthesia or RhoGAM was needed. Staff at the facility can help determine what part of the fee will be covered by insurance. If necessary, friends and family may be able to help with the cost. Since abortion centers expect to be paid before they do the procedure, it is important to find out what is required and to make financial arrangements as soon as possible after you make the decision. Some centers accept only cash or a certified check. Some will not accept cash. Some accept payment with a major credit card. Some accept Medicaid, but most do not.

Abortion Options

The choices available to a woman who decides not to carry a pregnancy to term depend very much on how far the pregnancy has advanced by the time she makes her decision (Figure 10.6).

Postcoital Hormonal Contraception

Two emergency procedures may be used to prevent implantation of the zygote in the case of rape, incest, or unprotected intercourse. The more commonly used "morning-after pill" or injection containing a combination of estrogen and progestin is effective if taken within 72 hours after unprotected intercourse. Many health professionals do not recommend a pill or injection with diethyl-stilbestrol (DES) (see p. 317). The DES pill is taken for three to seven days, starting the day after unprotected intercourse. These hormones may prevent ovulation or implantation. Because these pills can cause medical complications, they should not be relied on for regular contraception. A third method is to have an IUD inserted within 24 hours, again to prevent implantation.

We discussed **RU 486** in Chapter 9 as one of the more promising future contraceptives. As a chemical alternative to surgical abortion, it is effective and has very few side effects. Administered in the early weeks of pregnancy, it is 90% to 95% effective, and 80% effective in the seventh week. When prosta-glandins, which induce uterine contractions, are used with RU 486, the rate of successful nonsurgical abortions is 95% in the first 12 weeks. Because it mimics the structure of the female hormone progesterone, RU 486 blocks the proges-terone receptor sites in the uterus, which in turn prevents implantation of the embryonic mass in the uterine lining. If the blastocyst has already implanted when RU 486 is administered, the drug prevents normal maintenance of the uterine lining by allowing menstruation. Because RU 486 prevents pregnancy or gestation, it is more accurately described as a **contragestive** or an abortifacient rather than a contraceptive.

If approved by the FDA and marketed in the United States, RU 486 could replace 80% to 90% of the 1.5 million first trimester surgical abortions performed every year. RU 486 looks promising as a treatment for endometriosis, and may be used to prevent almost a third of cesarean sections. Despite strong advocacy by feminist groups, as of mid-1990, no American pharmaceutical company had expressed an interest in investing $125 million to get the drug approved by the FDA. The basic cost is not what worries possible investors. Because RU 486 is

Figure 10.6. Pregnancy and Abortion: Time-tables in Law and Medicine.

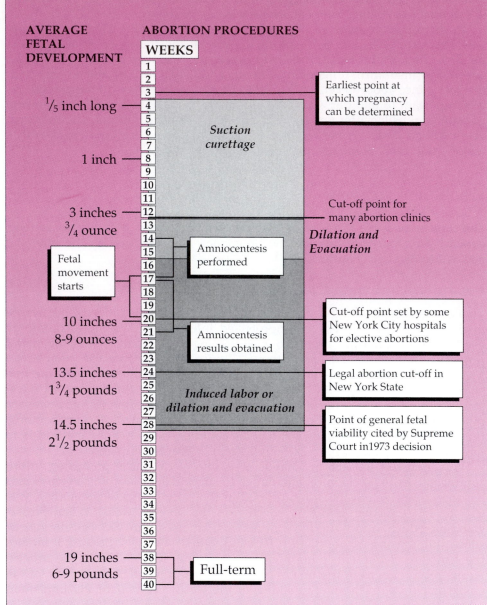

AVERAGE FETAL DEVELOPMENT

ABORTION PROCEDURES

WEEKS

Earliest point at which pregnancy can be determined

1/5 inch long — 4

Suction curettage

1 inch — 8

3 inches — 12
3/4 ounce

Cut-off point for many abortion clinics

Dilation and Evacuation

Amniocentesis performed

Fetal movement starts

10 inches — 20
8-9 ounces

Cut-off point set by some New York City hospitals for elective abortions

Amniocentesis results obtained

13.5 inches — 24
1 3/4 pounds

Legal abortion cut-off in New York State

Induced labor or dilation and evacuation

14.5 inches — 28
2 1/2 pounds

Point of general fetal viability cited by Supreme Court in 1973 decision

19 inches — 38
6-9 pounds

Full-term

Abortion procedures and times at which they are usually performed are from the Centers for Disease Control's "Abortion Surveillance" issued in May 1983. The type of abortion varies and is a decision made by the physician and the patient.

viewed as a "do-it-at-home abortion drug," any company that applies for a license to market RU 486 would face an immediate nationwide boycott of all its products. Twelve years after the National Right to Life Committee began a nationwide boycott of its products in 1973, Upjohn Pharmaceuticals was finally forced to give up marketing one of its three prostaglandin abortifacients (Kolata 1988; Lang 1988).

Medical Procedures

Three basic medical procedures are used for abortion today: vacuum curettage, dilation and evacuation, and intra-amniotic infusion.

Vacuum Curettage

Vacuum curettage, also known as suction or vacuum aspiration (Figure 10.7), is performed after a positive pregnancy test and during the first trimester, between 6 and 12 weeks after the last menstrual period. A local is definitely to be preferred over a general anesthesia because the latter does have a certain, if very low, mortality risk. Some physicians insert laminaria, a seaweed plug, into the cervix for 6 to 12 hours prior to the abortion. The plug absorbs moisture from the surrounding tissue, swells up, and painlessly dilates (stretches) the cervix so the plastic vacuum curette can be inserted into the uterus. The embryo/fetus and placenta is then removed by suction, and the lining of the uterus lightly scraped, in a procedure known as **dilation and curettage** or **D&C**. This scraping is done to be certain that all fetal and placental material from the

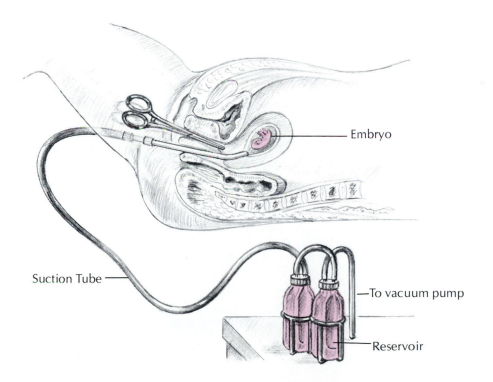

Embryo

Suction Tube

To vacuum pump

Reservoir

Figure 10.7. Vacuum Curettage Abortion. *In a first trimester abortion, an instrument holds the cervix in position while it is dilated and a vacuum curette inserted. The curette is used to dislodge the embryo and its amniotic sac, which are then removed by suction. A variation of this technique, known as dilation and evacuation, is also used in second trimester abortions.*

pregnancy has been removed. The procedure takes about 5 to 10 minutes and can be done in a doctor's office or clinic.

Complications using the method are rare, but may include hemorrhage, perforation of the uterine wall, infection accompanied by fever and chills, an incomplete abortion (part of the fetal material remains in the uterus), and very rarely an incomplete abortion after which the fetus continues to grow and pregnancy signs remain. Following the doctor's instructions and precautions after the abortion is important to reduce the chance of infection and other complications. It is also essential to be aware of warning signs, such as severe abdominal pain, fever, and bleeding, and to call the doctor if these occur.

Dilation and Evacuation (D&E)

From the 13th to the 24th week after the last menstrual period, dilation and evacuation is used for abortion. The cervix is dilated and several hours later the contents of the uterus are removed by instruments and suction, usually under general anesthesia, but local anesthesia is effective and safer. Vacuum-assisted D&E procedures can now be safely performed in clinics as well as in hospitals.

Intra-amniotic Infusion

Intra-amniotic infusion is used for pregnancies between 16 and 24 weeks. A saline (salt) solution or prostaglandins are injected directly into the amniotic sac through the abdominal wall (Figure 10.8), causing uterine contractions. After several hours the fetus and placenta are expelled. This method is only used for second trimester abortions and is performed in hospitals. There are greater risks and complications in these induced abortions. Women with high blood pressure, heart disease, kidney or liver problems, and sickle cell anemia should not have saline abortions. Many physicians do not like the method because of the complications and contraindications for many women. There is also the psy-

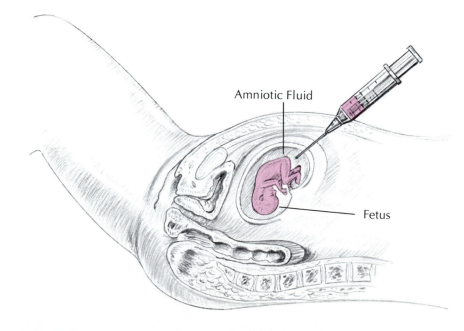

Figure 10.8. Saline Injection Abortion. *In an intra-amniotic infusion abortion (second trimester), a saline solution or prostaglandins are injected into the amniotic sac to cause uterine contractions that expel the fetus and placenta within a few hours.*

Amniotic Fluid

Fetus

chological stress involved in passing the lifeless fetus in surroundings that are often not supportive—the fetus may often be delivered in a hospital ward where the staff may be opposed to abortion.

Amniocentesis and other monitoring techniques are commonly used today when the mother's and father's medical histories indicate a risk of genetic or developmental (see Chapter 8). An abortion in the fifth or sixth month, especially when the child was wanted and planned for, can be very traumatic and stressful for both partners. Considering the complications of a saline infusion and the fact that a skilled physician can usually perform a D&E in pregnancies up to 24 weeks, a woman should explore the possibility of a D&E in preference to a saline abortion.

Medical and Emotional Aftercare

Aftercare following an abortion is as important as the procedure itself. Since infection is a possibility, antibiotics may be prescribed. Follow the directions for taking them carefully. It is important not to stop taking the medication early even if you feel well. You may be given another drug, Ergotrate or Methergine, to contract the uterus. In most cases, you can resume normal activities the same day. Iron supplements are often prescribed after an abortion.

It is also important to monitor your temperature for a week following the abortion. Be sure to take your temperature before taking such fever-reducing drugs as acetaminophen (e.g., Tylenol) or aspirin. If your temperature reaches 101° F or higher, call the doctor or clinic. Other reasons to notify the doctor or clinic include:

- Severe lower abdominal cramps or pain.
- Heavy bleeding (heavier than during your normal menstrual period).
- Your menstrual period does not begin within eight weeks after the abortion.

Light bleeding or spotting may continue for two weeks after the abortion and is not a cause for concern. Slight cramping may occur, but should be similar to menstrual cramps. In order to prevent infection, be sure to avoid douching, tub baths, and sexual intercourse for two weeks. You should get adequate nutrition and sleep. A follow-up examination should be done about three weeks after the procedure. Be sure to ask any questions and tell the doctor about any unusual symptoms.

Emotional aftercare will vary depending on the feelings you experience. Some women feel guilty about having had an abortion, others feel great relief. Many women have mixed feelings—being happy not to be pregnant but sad about aborting the fetus. Some of the highs and lows may be related to hormonal adjustments. These mood swings will disappear as the endocrine system returns to its normal cycle.

After the abortion is an important time to talk about your feelings to a good listener. The intensity of the feelings will diminish as time passes, but frustration and anger can last a long time if not dealt with adequately. Some women may have temporary negative feelings about resuming a sexual relationship, which their partner needs to understand and accept. A man whose partner or close friend has an abortion is also deeply involved and needs to express and deal with his feelings and reactions both before and after an abortion.

A National Dilemma

U.S. Supreme Court Justice Potter reportedly joined six other justices in voting to legalize abortion in the 1973 Roe v. Wade case because he saw "abortion was becoming one reasonable solution to population control." His comment typifies an American posture on family, contraception, and abortion that sets the United States apart from its European counterparts. In no European country do women have the sovereign right in abortion decisions that American women are guaranteed by Roe v. Wade. But in no European country does the government fail to provide pregnant and child-rearing women with the wherewithal to lead decent lives and care for their children as American society has failed to do (Glendon 1988; Luker 1975, 1984).

Recall the voting pattern of many legislators, mentioned earlier, who consistently vote against abortion and against school-based health clinics that provide contraceptive services, family planning programs, school lunches, and family support (Prescott 1986). Because Americans resist the intrusion of society into the domain of family planning, and because we also refuse to deal with the result of not providing family planning services, prenatal care, and family support for those who cannot afford a decent living, abortion has unfortunately, according to many critics, become the quintessentially American solution to the problem of family planning, putting us on a par with the Soviet Union where contraceptives are almost impossible to obtain and most women have five or six abortions in a lifetime.

In all the controversy over abortion, it is well to remember that many women will seek abortion no matter what the risk when they are confronted with an unwanted pregnancy. Governments cannot stop abortions. They can only make abortion more or less dangerous and costly.

Key Concepts

1. The United States ranks fourth among the nations of the world in the frequency of abortions. Between 1973 and 1979 the number of U.S. abortions doubled, with three-quarters of the abortions experienced by single women. Since then the numbers have remained fairly stable.

2. The 1973 U.S. Supreme Court Decision in Roe v. Wade legalized abortion. Later decisions and legislation have restricted the use of federal funds to pay for abortions for poor women and to support programs that provide abortion counseling.

3. Legislators who oppose abortion commonly vote in favor of capital punishment, a strong military, the abolition of gun control laws, "no knock" police searches, and limited funding of family support systems.

4. It is important in any decision about an unwanted pregnancy that both parties be involved. If all options are weighed in making the decision, there is less risk of postabortion depression.

5. The earlier an abortion is performed the safer it is. Delaying a pregnancy test and decision on abortion only increases the risk unnecessarily.

6. Women will seek abortion no matter what the risk if they are confronted with an unwanted pregnancy. Governments cannot stop abortions. They can only make abortion more or less dangerous and costly.

Key Terms

abortion (280)
contragestive (293)
dilation and curettage (D&C) (295)
personhood (285)
Roe v. Wade (282)

RU 486 (293)
social birth (286)
vacuum curettage (295)
viability (286)

Summary Questions

1. How did religious views on abortion change from the time of ancient Greece and Rome, to early Christianity, the Middle Ages, and the advent of embryological science in the 16th century?

2. What is the present medical position on fetal viability in terms of neural and respiratory development?

3. Why is the issue of fetal personhood a central controversy in the abortion debate?

4. What is the connection between repeat abortions and infertility?

5. Describe the basic procedure for dilation and curettage abortions and saline injection abortions. When is each used?

Suggested Readings

Doerr, E., & J. W. Prescott. (1989). *Abortion Rights and Fetal "Personhood."* Long Beach, CA: Centerline Press. A comprehensive review by experts in different fields.

Luker, K. (1984). *Abortion and the Politics of Motherhood.* Berkeley: University of California Press. An excellent review of the politics of abortion.

Luker, K. (1975). *Taking Chances: Abortion and the Decision Not to Contracept.* Berkeley: University of California Press. Looks at why women don't use contraceptives.

Nathanson, B. (1979). *Aborting America.* Garden City, NY: Doubleday. An anti-abortion leader argues against legal abortion.

Prescott, J. W. (1986). The abortion of *The Silent Scream. The Humanist, 46*(5):10–28. A critical review of a popular anti-abortion film.

Self-Image and Sexual
    Health for Women
Vulval and Vaginal
    Self-Examinations
The Bimanual Pelvic
    Examination
Sexually Related
    Disorders of the
    Female Pelvis
Breast Self-Examination
Sexually Related
    Disorders of
    the Breast
Some Health Problems
    Men and Women
    Share
Self-Image and Sexual
    Health for Men
Self-Health
    Examinations
Prostate and Rectal
    Examinations
Sexually Related
    Diseases
Choosing the Right
    Doctor

Chapter 11

Your Sexual Health

Special Consultants

Linda L. Hendrixson, M.A., Ph.D.(cand.), health educator and adjunct professor of health and human sexuality at Montclair State College, Upsala College, and Fairleigh Dickinson University.

Berta Numata, R.N.C., ob/gyn nurse practitioner, Planned Parenthood of Greater Northern New Jersey.

Norman A. Scherzer, Ph.D., professor, Department of Biological Sciences and Allied Health, Essex County College, and visiting professor, Department of Biology, Rutgers, The State University of New Jersey, (Newark).

Beverly Whipple, Ph.D., R.N., associate professor, College of Nursing, Rutgers, The State University of New Jersey (Newark), and coauthor of *The G Spot and Other Recent Discoveries in Human Sexuality* (1982) and *Safe Encounters* (1989).

This chapter builds on your new knowledge about male and female sexual anatomy, raising practical issues about your sexual health. We stress the importance of regular self-examinations for both men and women. Simple directions are provided. The symptoms and treatment of several important sexually related diseases (SRDs), which you can have even though you're not sexually active, are described. Finally, we offer guidelines on finding the right doctor for your sexual health needs.

Self-Image and Sexual Health for Women

In the male culture, men, young men in particular, tend to have a macho view of themselves as perfectly healthy and invulnerable to any disease. "I'm young, healthy, into sports and exercise, so I don't need to worry. Why waste my time?" Yet, the statistics on sexually related diseases among young men show they should be concerned. Behind the bravado and indifference, there may be a subconscious fear that if they ask questions, or do a monthly testicular-penile and breast self-examination, they might someday find something wrong.

Women, on the other hand, still frequently refer to their sexual organs as "down there," implying something ugly, dirty, shameful, or just not nice. Many women have no idea what is really "down there," or what their external genitals look or feel like. Although women may have annual pelvic examinations, these are often done with a drape that makes it hard to see what the doctor is doing. And, "Nice girls and ladies don't ask questions about their private parts!"

The idea of women and men examining their own sexual organs is a relatively new concept. Self-examination is not meant to replace a physician's examination, but it can help us have a more positive attitude toward our bodies. Regular self-exams also help us find out what is normal for our own bodies. When you know what your sexual organs normally look like and what your personal variations are, you can more easily recognize a potential problem. Regular self-exams put you in a better position to give a detailed, accurate picture to the physician and to ask better questions. As a result, you are more likely to receive a more accurate diagnosis, and to understand your condition and treatment better.

Vulval and Vaginal Self-Examinations

When someone first said to me two years ago, "You can feel the end of your cervix with your finger," I was interested but flustered. I had hardly ever put my finger in my vagina at all, and felt squeamish about touching myself there, in that place "reserved" for lovers and doctors. It took two months to get up my nerve to try it, and then one afternoon, pretty nervously, I squatted down in the bathroom and put my finger in deep, back into my vagina. There it was (!), feeling slippery and rounded, with an indentation at the center, through which, I realized, my menstrual flow comes. It was both very exciting and beautifully ordinary at the same time.

(Boston Women's Health Collective 1979:26)

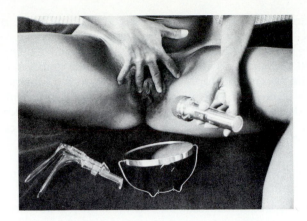

Figure 11.1. Female Self-Examination. *One position a woman can use during a self-examination of her sexual organs.*

Although it is easy and painless to examine your vulva and vagina, you may share the feelings of the woman just quoted. The first time you do almost anything, you're likely to be uncomfortable. Despite all the negative conditioning women are given about their sexual organs, you can consciously disagree with those messages and decide to take your own health "in hand," starting with regular self-examinations.

If you're a man and your partner asks you to join her in her self-examination so you can understand her sexuality better, it is likely that you may have similar negative feelings. If you decide to try a self-examination, it may be helpful to talk with your partner, or with someone who has already done it to get their reactions and thoughts. Some women find it more supportive to do the self-examination with a small group of friends. Others prefer doing it alone, or with their sexual partner.

For a vulval self-examination, you need only a bright flashlight, a fairly large hand mirror, and some pillows (Figure 11.1). You should take notes and keep a record of your observations, so have a pad and pencil handy. Before you examine the vulva, wash your hands thoroughly, make sure your nails are short, and empty your bladder. You can squat over the mirror which can rest on the floor. Or you can put the pillows against the back of the bed and lean against them with your legs flexed and the mirror propped at an angle as in Figure 11.1. Examine and spread the outer and inner labia. Find your clitoris, its hood, and the opening of the vagina. The urethral opening may be hard to find—it looks like a dimple between the clitoris and vagina. Note the color, size, and shape of these structures. Is your hymen visible at the opening of the vagina? In women who use tampons or who are athletic, the hymen may not be evident. Also note if there are any secretions from the vagina. Vaginal secretions are normally scant, sticky, and clear or white. For several days around the time of ovulation the discharge increases and is clear and slippery. The normal discharge has a mild odor and dries to a yellowish color on underclothes. Note also the size and shape of the inner and outer labia or lips. Is one inner lip larger than the other? This is common and perfectly normal.

To continue the self-examination internally, you will need a speculum and water-soluble lubricant. With a metal or plastic speculum you can open the vaginal walls and examine them and the cervix. You can buy a disposable plastic speculum in medical supply stores, women's health clinics, and in many pharmacies. They are inexpensive, sterile-packaged, and come in different sizes. Astroglide or K-Y Jelly is available in all pharmacies.

If you decide to proceed with this internal exam, practice using the speculum first so you will be familiar with its operation. Once you're comfortable with manipulating the speculum, apply a little water-soluble lubricant to the tip of the speculum blades so it will glide into the vaginal canal smoothly. These blades are not sharp! Lie back on a firm support, bend your knees, and keep your feet flat on the bed or floor. Keep the mirror handy. Get comfortable and relax. Then,

1. Insert the speculum into the vagina with the blades in the closed position and the handle to the side.

2. Rotate the speculum so that the handle is in the downward position.

3. Squeeze the handle to open the blades and push into a locked position. You will hear a click when this occurs.

4. Hold the mirror in one hand, the flashlight in the other. The speculum will stay in its locked position without holding it.

5. Examine the interior walls of the vagina, the cervix, and the opening to the cervix. It may be necessary to turn the speculum slightly in order to see the cervix. Keep it in the locked position. The cervix changes during the monthly cycle and will not always look the same.

6. After examining yourself, move the speculum out slightly before closing the blades.

7. Check the speculum for any discharge before disposing of it. Use a new plastic speculum each time. If you use a metal speculum, wipe it thoroughly with alcohol before and after each self-examination.

The Bimanual Pelvic Examination

A more thorough internal pelvic examination is usually done by an internist or a gynecologist, a physician specializing in female health issues (Figure 11.2). Many women fear the pelvic examination and tend to put it off for "later." This can be a dangerous habit because early detection of medical problems is the best way of avoiding serious complications. In addition, the physician will perform a Pap smear during the vaginal examination. It is important to have a regular Pap smear to detect any infection or unusual condition of the cervix and allow early treatment. In the past 40 years, deaths from cancer of the uterus and cervix have fallen by 70 percent to less than 10,000 a year, mainly because most women get regular Pap tests (Boston Women's Health Collective 1984:477–481; Budoff 1983:116–120).

In taking a **Pap smear**, the physician inserts a small plastic or wooden spatula into the vagina while the walls are separated by a speculum, and scrapes several samples of cells from the lining of the cervical canal, the cervix itself, and the outer wall of the vagina. This is a completely painless procedure. There may be some very light bleeding after the scrapings have been taken but this quickly stops. The cells are then spread on microscope slides and examined. It may take a few days to a week to get the results back. A Pap smear may show all normal cells, signs of an inflammation, which could be due to a variety of causes, suspicious cells suggesting a risk of cervical cancer, or an actual case of

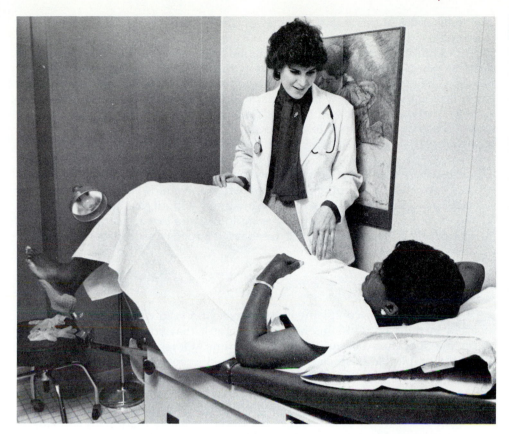

Figure 11.2. The Pelvic Examination. *Several techniques are part of a regular pelvic examination for women, but most important is comfortable communication between the physician and patient and a sensitivity on the part of the physician.*
(a) The speculum is used for vaginal and cervical examinations; here a spatula is shown taking a sample of cervical cells for a Pap smear. (b) The bimanual technique.

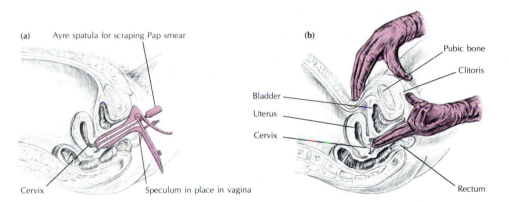

(a) Ayre spatula for scraping Pap smear

Cervix

Speculum in place in vagina

(b) Pubic bone

Clitoris

Bladder

Uterus

Cervix

Rectum

cervical carcinoma. Obviously, since a cancerous condition does not appear overnight, a Pap smear once a year can detect an abnormal condition at an early stage. Early detection allows for early treatment and a much more optimistic prognosis. Women who started having sex at an early age, who have had multiple partners, or who have had several children have a higher risk of cervical and uterine cancer, making annual Pap smears for them especially important. However, Pap smears tell us nothing about the possibilities of infections or problems in the uterus, tubes, or ovaries. That's why a full annual pelvic exam is useful.

Although the routine pelvic examination may take only five minutes and is painless when properly done, too many women avoid it. They expect it will be painful. They find it embarrassing. They once had a physician who was insensitive or rough in giving a pelvic exam. Some fears and embarrassment are normal, particularly if it is a teenage girl's first examination. However, most women become accustomed to the procedure, as a 33-year-old woman suggests in this quote:

> I must have had about 30 pelvics by now, and I'm beginning to feel as blasé about them as my doctor does. After one child, two diaphragms, and a yeast infection I think I'll go to my grave with, it just doesn't bother me anymore. Last time, right in the middle of the exam, I caught myself wondering if Dr. Jackson dyed his hair! It proves you can get used to anything, I suppose.
>
> *(Stewart et al. 1979:323)*

A not uncommon complaint is the shock of a cold metal speculum being inserted in the vagina. If this happens, suggest that your physician or nurse warm the speculum before insertion next time. Other women are concerned about the drape that is spread over their flexed knees. This effectively isolates the woman from her examination and may create a psychological barrier to her asking questions she may have. Some physicians may be uncomfortable doing the examination with the woman watching, which may be one reason the practice continues. Other women believe the drape provides them with a desirable sense of privacy. Many women do not like the nurse to be in the room during the examination. They feel the nurse inhibits them from talking openly to the doctor. However, most doctors require the presence of a third person to protect them in case of an accusation concerning their conduct during the exam. A third person is also handy in case the doctor needs some assistance during the procedure (Stubin-Stein & Debrovner 1975).

How do you feel about the speculum, the draping, and a third person in the examining room? Have you found that pelvic exams become easier, or more difficult, as you get older? How comfortable are you about asking questions?

A few simple preparations are worth keeping in mind when you schedule a pelvic examination with your physician. Many physicians recommend that a woman not have intercourse for 48 hours prior to the examination and that tampons and douching be avoided for at least 24 hours. This leaves the vaginal environment undisturbed, and gives the physician a more accurate picture.

When should you have a pelvic exam? Most physicians like to see a patient annually, but others may want to do so more or less frequently, depending on a woman's age and physical condition. There is a consensus among health specialists that the first pelvic exam should take place in the early teen years. Some parents are reluctant to have a daughter undergo a pelvic exam for fear that it might compromise her virginity, even though the lack of an intact hymen is not a sign the girl has had sexual intercourse. This concern may be a problem in some ethnic groups. However, pelvic examinations for teenage girls accustom them to the exam and its importance. It is also crucial for young women who are sexually active, so that they can discuss and obtain appropriate birth control methods and check on suspicious symptoms.

Sexually Related Disorders of the Female Pelvis

Whether or not they are sexually active, women can experience one or more sexually related diseases (SRDs).

Pelvic Inflammatory Disease

Each year over 2.5 million American women visit a physician seeking relief from **pelvic inflammatory disease** or **PID**. Each year, PID also causes 250,000 women to be hospitalized and results in 150,000 operations. Yet these statistics are only part of the PID story because the symptoms of this infection are so varied. The primary symptom is pain, but that can be so mild it's hardly noticed, or so severe that a woman heads straight for a hospital emergency room. Unfortunately, women often ignore an initial mild pain in the middle of the abdomen. PID is usually not diagnosed until the infection has spread into the fallopian tubes and a strong pain is felt on one or both sides of the lower abdomen (Boston Women's Health Collective 1984:251–252, 420–421; Budoff 1983).

Because several different microorganisms can cause PID and because the inflammation can involve the cervix, uterus, fallopian tubes, ovaries, and/or the abdomen (Figure 11.3), women with PID may experience a variety of other symptoms besides primary abdominal pain. Among other possible symptoms are

- a sudden high or low-grade fever that occurs periodically;
- chills;
- pain in the lower back or legs;
- increased urination, with burning sensation;
- an abnormal discharge from the vagina or urethra;
- pain or bleeding during or after intercourse;
- increased menstrual cramps, or irregular bleeding or spotting;
- pain during ovulation;
- swollen abdomen or lymph nodes;
- loss of appetite, nausea, or vomiting; and
- feelings of weakness, tiredness, and depression.

With this variety of possible symptoms it is understandable why the statistics cited are much lower than the actual incidence of PID.

The primary cause of PID is usually one of several sexually transmitted diseases (STDs).

My husband had no symptoms at all although I had been suffering from chronic PID for years. Neither of us could figure out how I got sick. It took us a long time to find a doctor who cultured both of us for orga-

Figure 11.3. Pelvic Inflammatory Disease. *PID may cause a sharp pain at the most infected site, and/or cause pain in a broader area throughout the abdomen.*

(a) Full view

(b) Detail

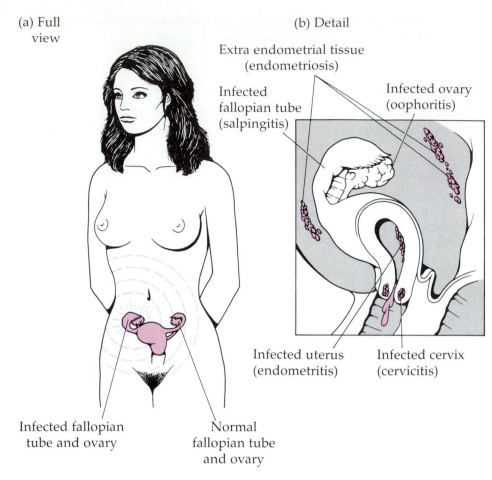

Extra endometrial tissue (endometriosis)

Infected fallopian tube (salpingitis)

Infected ovary (oophoritis)

Infected uterus (endometritis)

Infected cervix (cervicitis)

Infected fallopian tube and ovary

Normal fallopian tube and ovary

nisms. I finally got over it when we both started getting tested and treated according to what organisms were found: chlamydia, mycoplasma, staph, strep.

(Boston Women's Health Collective 1984:503)

The microorganisms that cause PID can come from sexual intercourse with an infected partner, even if that partner has no symptoms. They can also be a side effect of an IUD, an abortion, miscarriage, childbirth, surgery, artificial insemination, or a variety of medical and diagnostic procedures that involve the abdominal organs. If untreated, PID can have serious consequences, including abscesses in the ovaries and tubes, ectopic pregnancy, infertility, and life-threatening peritonitis.

Finding out what causes a particular case of PID and getting an effective treatment is usually very difficult, for several reasons. First, a wide variety of microorganisms can cause PID. Second, these microorganisms can infect several different organs inside a woman's body where they are difficult to identify and diagnose. Third, we do not have reliable, inexpensive, and easily available tests for many of these microorganisms. Finally, not all doctors are well informed about PID. Here, more than in any other issue of female health, women must learn as much as they can about PID so they can ask questions and keep looking until they find the best and most knowledgeable physician available. Equally important, if you suspect PID, is the need to involve any male partner(s) in both the diagnosis and treatment. Often, in cases of PID, the male partner is a silent reservoir for reinfection. Men can harbor pathogenic microorganisms even though they have no symptoms at all. They can pass these infections to their partners every time they have sex, so unless the man is also treated his female partner will be continually reinfected.

Vaginitis

Because the vagina provides a moist and convenient passage from a woman's abdominal organs to the outside world, it also makes women vulnerable to a variety of vaginal irritations and infections. The general term **vaginitis** covers them all, whether or not the irritation or infection has anything to do with being sexually active. Sometimes a distinction is made between nonspecific vaginitis and cases of vaginitis that are due to known specific infections like chlamdydia, trichomonas, gardnerella (hemophilus), yeast (monilia), and venereal warts (discussed in Chapter 12). Frequent douching or douching with an overly strong acidic solution is a common cause of vaginitis because the acid may irritate the vaginal wall and leave it open to infection. Small objects inserted into the vagina as part of masturbation experiments, especially by children, may lead to infection when the object cannot be removed and is then forgotten. Vaginitis can also result from, or be aggravated by penile penetration without sufficient lubrication.

Should men be concerned about a partner who has vaginitis? Yes, because the same organisms that infect the vagina can invade the male urethra during intercourse and spread to the prostate and other internal sexual organs. If a woman has vaginitis, her sexual partner(s) should also be tested.

Simple common sense and a little preventive medicine provide easy ways to reduce the risk of pelvic inflammatory disease and vaginitis. Keep yourself in general good health. Get adequate sleep and exercise. Eat a well-balanced diet, and reduce your consumption of carbohydrates and refined (white) sugar. Find channels for expressing your emotional stresses instead of suppressing them. The following suggestions are also helpful:

1. Shower or bathe regularly with mild soap. Avoid bubble baths.
2. Avoid feminine hygiene deodorant sprays, colored toilet paper, and shared washcloths and towels.
3. Wear cotton panties and avoid pantyhose. Synthetic fabrics do not "breathe" and retain both heat and moisture on which bacteria thrive. Avoid tight-fitting jeans and clothes that may irritate the vulva and prevent normal air circulation. Use loose nightwear and don't wear underpants while you sleep. This allows the vulva to air and dry.
4. Wash the vulva carefully and dry it thoroughly.
5. Wipe the anus from the front of the vulva backward to avoid spreading rectal bacteria into the vaginal and urethral openings.

6. Allow sufficient time for love play and arousal to produce adequate natural vaginal lubrication or use a water-soluble lubricant such as K-Y Jelly or Astroglide. Do not use Vaseline or other petroleum-based lubricants since these do not mix with vaginal secretions and may harbor bacteria. Sufficient water-soluble lubrication also reduces the risk of the condom tearing.

7. Use a condom and spermicidal foam containing nonoxynol-9 during vaginal intercourse to reduce the risks of both pregnancy and SRD/STD transmission. Condoms coated with nonoxynol-9 do not contain enough of this agent to protect against STDs without the added protection of a spermicidal foam or jelly.

8. Wash the penis after anal intercourse and before vaginal contact, or better, use a double condom and spermicidal jelly or cream for anal intercourse.

9. Make sure your hands and sexual organs and those of your partner are clean. Wash the genitals before and after sex.

10. Do not douche unless your doctor recommends it. Douching washes away the normal, protective organisms in the vagina. However, if you are prone to yeast infections (candida), douching once a month after the menstrual flow stops will help restore the normal acidic condition of the vagina and inhibit yeast growth. You can use 1 or 2 tablespoons of white vinegar in a quart of warm water.

11. If you or someone in your immediate family has diabetes, be sure your physician knows about it. It increases your risk of candida infections.

Endometriosis

Endometriosis is a very painful and serious condition for over 10 million American women, most of them in their twenties and thirties. The problem may begin when tiny pieces of the endometrial lining of the uterus accidentally move into the fallopian tubes or abdominal cavity instead of leaving through the cervix and vagina during menstruation. If these tissue bits find a new home and nourishment in the abdominal cavity, they grow, spreading to other sites and organs. Bits of uterine tissue can also implant in the vulval area and Bartholin's glands. Whether they are in the uterus, in the abdominal cavity, or in the vulvar area, endometrial cells respond to the monthly hormone cycle. In the first part of the cycle, they multiply. When menses begins, these cells are shed. If they are inside a gland or the abdominal cavity, they cannot get out. Inflammation results until the body can reabsorb the dead and degenerating debris. Backaches, abdominal pains, painful intercourse, enlarged cysts, and regular and severe menstrual pain are common symptoms of endometriosis.

Synthetic androgens are sometimes prescribed for endometriosis. In the past, treatment for endometriosis required a large abdominal incision and surgical removal of the wandering tissue. If the pain was severe, the surgeon might also have severed some of the nerves in the lower back. A new technique, known as videolaseroscopy, requires only three tiny incisions (Figure 11.4). If left untreated, the condition may disappear after menopause, but this depends on the amount of endometrial tissue that is growing outside the uterus. Although the tissue does not return in the areas where it was burned out, it can

(a) Laparoscope with laser and camera probes pelvic organs and relays picture to TV screen.

(b) Red dot on TV monitor screen shows laser's aim. When dot is on endometrial tissue, surgeon fires the laser. Seared tissue is irrigated with liquid and residue is suctioned away.

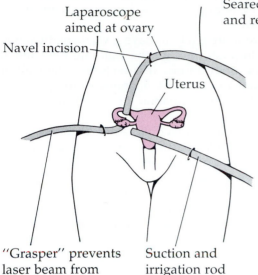

Laparoscope aimed at ovary

Navel incision

Uterus

"Grasper" prevents laser beam from penetrating other organs

Suction and irrigation rod

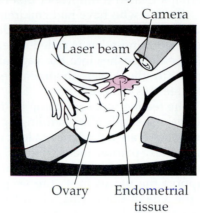

Camera

Laser beam

Ovary   Endometrial tissue

Figure 11.4. Curing Endometriosis with Videolaseroscopy. *Unlike treatments necessitating major surgery, videolaseroscopy requires only a small incision in the navel so a laparoscope can be inserted and focused on the endometrial tissue. Two other small incisions allow insertion of a grasper and irrigation/suction tube. A single stitch closes each incision. Often less than an hour is needed to remove the endometrial deposits compared to several hours for the older procedures.*

return in unaffected areas, even after a hysterectomy. In 1980 a National Endometriosis Support Group was started with local chapters around the country (Boston Women's Health Collective 1984:500–502).

Cystitis

Cystitis is a common infection of the bladder with a variety of causes. Although the symptoms can be frightening, cystitis is usually not a serious problem. The urge to urinate every few minutes and a burning sensation when you try to urinate even though only a little urine is passed are signs of cystitis. Blood and pus in the urine also indicate a bladder infection. "Honeymoon cystitis" may occur when a woman begins to engage in frequent sexual intercourse. Pressure from the penis during intercourse may displace and irritate the bladder and urethra, which lie directly above the vagina.

When caused by sexual intercourse, symptoms of cystitis may occur within 24 to 48 hours. In mild cases, the symptoms disappear in a day or two. Emptying the bladder before and after intercourse and use of a lubricating jelly for intercourse may also be helpful. Drinking a lot of fluids, especially cranberry juice, will help flush the urinary tract of bacteria. A heating pad applied just above the pubic bone can relieve urethral spasms. If the symptoms last more than 48 hours, or recur frequently, an ordinary urinalysis should be done to find out if bacteria are causing the irritation. Most urinary tract infections respond quickly to antibiotics in a single large dose or in smaller doses spread over 10 to 14 days. If antibiotics are prescribed, a secondary yeast infection may occur in the vagina. (See advice under Candida in Chapter 12.)

Ovarian Cysts, Hernias, and Prolapsed Uterus

An ovarian cyst is an ovarian follicle that has failed to rupture and release its egg. Cysts may be filled with water, or solid benign tumors. Usually they disappear in a cycle or two. Recurrent cysts may indicate a hormone imbalance, perhaps related to improper diet or stress.

Women who have had children are more likely to have a weakened vaginal wall that allows the urinary bladder to push through the wall into the vaginal canal, forming what is called a hernia, or cystocele. In a rectocele, the wall of the rectum pushes into the vaginal wall and canal. A dragging or tugging sensation in the lower abdomen and frequent urination or incontinence may indicate this kind of hernia.

The feeling that something is "falling out" and a dull heavy sensation in the vagina, especially after standing up for a while, may indicate a prolapsed uterus. Other signs are a tendency to leak urine when coughing, sneezing, or laughing, backaches, painful menstruation, pelvic congestion, and uncomfortable intercourse. The problem comes from weakened uterine ligaments that no longer support the uterus in its proper place. Normally, the uterus is at right angles to the axis of the vagina, almost horizontal above the bladder. When not supported by its ligaments, the uterus pushes down into the vagina, pulling the bladder with it. Maintaining good tone in your pelvic muscles by practicing the Kegel exercises (p. 191) is good insurance against hernias and uterine prolapse. A diaphragm-like rubber device, known as a pessary, may be used to help support the uterus. Surgery may be a last resort in rare severe cases.

Fibroids

Fibroids are benign, not cancerous, growths composed of muscle cells, not fibrous tissues. One in five women is likely to develop these growths in the uterus before age 35. Black women are more at risk than white women. Almost one-third of all women approaching menopause have uterine fibroids. Although no exact cause is known, the fact that fibroids grow faster if a woman is pregnant, taking a hormonal contraceptive, or using estrogen replacement during menopause, suggests a link with estrogen levels.

Small fibroids usually cause no symptoms. However, if a woman has several fibroids, or they are very large, she may have abdominal or lower back pains, urinary problems, and bleeding between periods or excessive menstrual bleeding. Because fibroids vary in number, size, and growth rate, regular six-month or annual consultation with a gynecologist is recommended to learn how best they can be managed.

Hysterectomy is often suggested as a remedy for uterine fibroids. But unless the fibroids are causing a serious problem, it may be better to leave the fibroids alone, knowing that the reduction in estrogen during menopause will cause them to shrink. In this conservative approach, avoiding caffeine and keeping one's weight under control will help reduce fibroid growth (Boston Women's Health Collective 1984:509–512; Budoff 1983:110–112, 126–129).

Breast Self-Examination

Regular breast self-examination can mean the difference between life and death. A regular breast self-exam is simple, painless, and takes only a few minutes of your time each month. If caught early, breast cancer can be controlled and is seldom fatal. Early detection usually means the growth has not spread. This may allow a simpler, less disfiguring lumpectomy instead of a modified or radical mastectomy. Despite this optimistic outcome for early detection, one-third of the 110,000 American women diagnosed every year with breast cancer will die because the growth was not discovered early enough to control it. Regular breast self-examination could significantly reduce this death rate, which is disproportionately high among black women. In women over the age of 30, an annual mammogram can also help detect a lump even before it can be palpated.

Equally important is the fact that regular breast self-exams can check for benign cysts or a fibrocystic condition, which are common among young and middle-aged women.

By examining your breasts regularly, you will learn how your breasts feel and will be able to notice any changes. Breast tissue varies depending on the time of the menstrual cycle, so the best time to examine yourself is five days after your menstrual period has ended when any fullness or tenderness has subsided (Figure 11.5).

You can start your self-exam during a shower or bath. Glide your flat hand over the whole surface of each breast, using the right hand to check the left breast and left hand for the right breast. Notice any lumps, hard knots, or thickening.

Next, stand in front of a mirror, with your arms held at your sides. Visually check the size and contour of each breast for any swelling, dimpling, or change in the nipple. Repeat this visual inspection with your arms raised above your head. Then, rest your palms on your hips and press down firmly to flex your chest muscles. Remember few women have matching breasts. Squeeze the nipple to check for any discharge. Any irregularities should be checked medically.

The third phase of the examination involves palpation, feeling the breasts for unusual lumps or thickness. A lump may be a normal gland, a benign cyst, a normal fibroadenoma, or indication of an early and treatable malignancy. As you palpate the breasts, follow the directions here and in the diagrams in Figure 11.5. In order to palpate your breasts, you will need a bed or flat surface and a pillow or folded towel. If you have small breasts, place your left hand under the back of your head. If your breasts are larger, place a small pillow or folded towel under your left shoulder and your left hand under the back of your head. You can then use your right hand to examine your left breast. With the three middle fingers of your right hand, press gently using small circular motions to examine the breast. Begin at the breastbone and work around the outside of the breast until a complete circle has been formed. Continue to examine in a circular motion until the entire breast has been covered. Do not use the fingertips. Notice any lump, thickening, hardening, soreness, or tenderness of the breast tissue. If you feel something unusual, check to see if it has a boundary or whether it gradually blends into surrounding tissue. If it "melts" into a surrounding tissue, then it is probably just a gland. Lumps in the breast, especially very small ones, are most likely to be discovered when the exam is done while the breasts are wet from bathing or moistened with a lotion.

Reverse your position and repeat the procedure to examine your right breast.

It will take a few months before you know what is natural for your breasts. Once you are familiar with your breasts, you will be able to detect a suspicious condition. Remember, most breast lumps are benign, and not malignant.

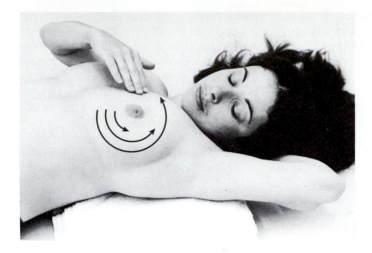

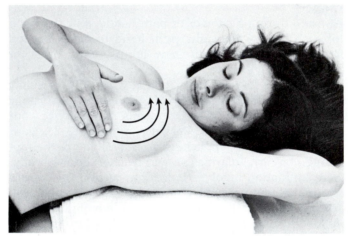

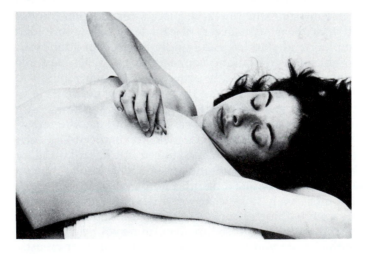

Figure 11.5. Breast Self-Examination. *Monthly self-examination of the breasts is an important aspect of a woman's responsibility for her own health. These photographs illustrate the directions given in the adjoining text.*

Sexually Related Disorders of the Breast

Fibrocystic Disorder

When a woman finds a suspicious lump in her breast, the immediate and frightening thought is of cancer. But at least half of all women experience some swelling, discomfort, or lumpiness in the breasts during their monthly cycle. Just before menstruation begins and during ovulation, hormone changes may cause some breast cells to retain fluid. The result is small swollen sacs or cysts, especially on the sides nearest the arms. These cysts quickly disappear as the cycle continues. Some doctors have given this natural condition the rather ominous name of fibrocystic disease. Others call it **fibrocystic disorder.**

Some women experience this cystic condition beginning in puberty. For others, it develops in their twenties or thirties. The condition may stabilize, with some months better or worse than others, until menopause ends the condition. For a few women, the cysts may increase with age. A fibrocystic condition can usually be managed by keeping your weight under control because being overweight seems to aggravate cyst development. Caffeine, coffee, tea, chocolate, and alcohol also seem to promote cyst development. Watching one's diet and using specific vitamin and mineral supplements often reduce any problems associated with a fibrocystic condition. It is important for women with cysts, and their male partners, to be aware that a fibrocystic condition is not a prelude to cancer. Most women with cysts do not develop cancer of the breast.

Fibroadenomas

If you are in your teens or twenties, finding a lump that remains constant may be as frightening as finding a cyst which comes and goes. Such stationary lumps are called fibroadenomas and can develop in one or both breasts. Their origin is not known, although they seem to be related to fat in the diet. Although fibroadenomas may feel like a cancerous lump, they are not cancerous. Thus, any persistent lump should be checked by a doctor to make sure it is only a cyst or fibroadenoma. The odds are it will be a normal lump, but only a medical exam can answer your question.

Breast Cancer

If a clinical breast exam, **mammogram**, and biopsy reveal that a suspicious lump is not a cyst or fibroadenoma, and is in fact malignant, surgery may be recommended. A second opinion is always in order when there is a question of surgery. For breast cancer, a second opinion is essential because treatment of breast cancer continues to change. Catalyzed by pressure from feminist health groups, a conservative trend has led to extensive clinical comparisons of simple lumpectomy coupled with chemotherapy or radiotherapy with the more extensive surgery of modified and radical mastectomies (Figure 11.6). When a malignancy is diagnosed, early radical surgery and lumpectomy give similar survival rates. The advantage of a lumpectomy is that it is far less disfiguring and creates less problems because the underlying muscles and lymph nodes are left intact (Budoff 1983:68–109).

Figure 11.6. Mastectomy and Reconstruction. *(a) In a* radical *mastectomy, the whole breast and the lymph nodes of the chest and underarm are removed. (b) The same woman after breast reconstruction. In many cases, regular monthly breast self-exams can prevent the need for radical surgery.*

(a)

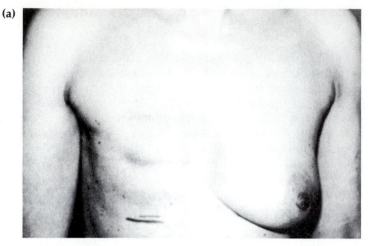

(b)

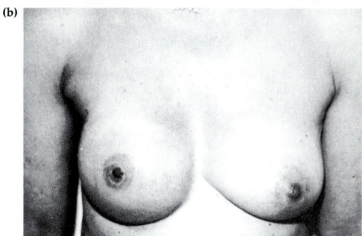

Women who have the greatest risk of developing breast cancer are those who

- have cysts in the breasts;
- started menstruating early in life;
- have a history of breast cancer among relatives;
- are considerably overweight;
- have had no children, or their first child after age 30;
- have not breast-fed their children; and
- experience a late menopause.

These are only risk factors. If you have any of them, that is an added reason to examine your breasts monthly and have an annual medical breast examination.

Breast self-examinations can also be an enjoyable part of a sexual relationship, if a couple is comfortable with this. Your sexual partner can learn to examine your breasts. This will enable your partner to better know your body and to share actively in maintaining your good health. How would you feel about involving a lover in your breast self-examination? If you are a male, how would you feel about being asked to participate?

Some Health Problems Men and Women Share

Infectious Mononucleosis

The "kissing disease," **mononucleosis**, is an acute infection of the lymph glands caused by a virus in the same family as herpes. Spread by saliva, there is no known prevention, although a vaccine is being developed. The onset is sudden, with fever, fatigue, chills, sweating, headache, sore throat, and loss of appetite. The fever usually lasts about five days with the other symptoms disappearing in two or three weeks, although full recovery may take months. Although "mono" is a common disease among men and women ages 15 to 24, it can be serious, even fatal. Following the physician's advice is, therefore, very important.

Genital Tuberculosis

Although tuberculosis usually starts in the lungs, the tubercular bacillus can spread to other tissues including the genitals. When it invades the prostate, it causes a painless, crumbly fibrous growth and calcification. The bacteria can also spread into the epididymis and testes. In women, 2% of all diseases of the upper genital tract involve tuberculosis, usually in the uterus and fallopian tubes.

DES Mothers, Daughters, and Sons

Between 1941 and 1975, 3 to 6 million American women were given a synthetic form of estrogen for diabetes or to prevent miscarriage. **Diethylstilbestrol (DES)** is now known to increase the risk of vaginal and cervical cancer in the daughters born to mothers who used DES during their pregnancies. The risk is small and decreasing because the children of women who were given DES before 1971 are getting older. However, for women in their late twenties and older, the risk is still significant. A significant percentage of women whose mothers used DES will experience side effects. These effects may include problem pregnancies, structural changes in the cervix and uterus, and various abnormal cell conditions. For the sons of DES mothers, the consequences include underdeveloped and undescended testes, benign cysts on the epididymis, abnormal semen, and low sperm counts. Some studies suggest that the women who used DES have an increased incidence of breast, uterine, and ovarian growths and cancers.

If you were born between 1940 and the mid-1970s, ask your mother if she had diabetes or a problem pregnancy. If so, can she remember what medications she was given? Prescriptions for DES were written under about 200 different trade names, so you may need help from experts to find out whether your mother was exposed to DES and what your risk might be. For information about DES, send a business size self-addressed stamped envelope to DES Action, Long Island Jewish Hospital, New Hyde Park, NY 11040 (Boston Women's Health Collective 1984:487–500; Stewart et al. 1979:488–499).

Self-Image and Sexual Health for Men

Self-Health Examinations

Testicular and Penile Self-Examinations

There are three good reasons why every man should take a few minutes to examine his testes and penis regularly. Spotting infections, especially sexually transmitted diseases, is the most obvious reason. When infections are caught early, they can often be easily treated.

The second reason may surprise you: Young men have a real risk of testicular cancer. Cancer of the testes is the most common solid tumor found in men between the ages of 20 and 34. It is more common in this age group than Hodgkin's disease and leukemia. One in every 6 men who dies of cancer in his twenties and early thirties dies of testicular cancer. Each year 25,000 males are known to develop testicular cancer, but the number is probably much higher because most cases are not diagnosed until after the malignancy has spread to other organs, in which case the death is attributed to cancer in the secondary organ even though it started in the testes. Testicular lumps are almost always malignant. If detected early, however, this is one of the most curable of cancers. If not caught early by a regular self-examination, it is one of the most deadly.

Although quite rare, the risk of penile cancer is a third reason for men giving themselves a regular self-exam. This cancer is usually associated with a genital herpes infection or poor personal hygiene. Early signs of an unusual localized lump in the shaft or glans of the penis or a small bleeding ulcer may be easily detected in a monthly self-examination. If detected early, the malignancy may be controlled without resorting to partial or total amputation of the penis.

Every male, young or old, should examine his testes at least once a month, looking for any difference in size or texture (Figure 11.7). To examine your testes, take a warm shower to relax the scrotal muscles. Then lie down in a warm comfortable setting. Using the fingertips, gently touch the entire surface of the testicle. It should feel like a shelled hard-boiled egg, smooth but firm. Along the back of the testes is the epididymis and vas deferens. Check this area, too, and note any pain or sensitivity. The epididymis will feel irregular, so do not be alarmed. Note any firm lumps, however. Sometimes the scrotal sac may become infected and swollen. This condition may require treatment.

Examine the penis also. Check for any infections or other irregularities. Because of the dark, moist environment of these organs, they are subject to skin infections and lesions. Too vigorous handling during masturbation can also cause minor skin irritation and reddening. If something seems unusual or suspicious, have it checked by your physician as soon as possible. It may be nothing that requires treatment, or only a minor, easily treated problem. Letting it slide by could lead to a serious problem later.

Breast Self-Exam for Men

Whereas breast cancer accounts for 26% of all cancers in women, slightly less than 1 in 100 cases of breast cancer occurs in a male. That may sound like nothing for you to be concerned about, especially when you are young and healthy. But if you happen to be the occasional male who develops breast cancer, you could be very happy you did a monthly breast exam along with your penis/testes/scrotum self-examination. All you need to do is follow the

Figure 11.7. Self-Examination for Men. *(a) A man has located the spermatic cord containing the vas deferens and is checking it and the epididymis for any tenderness. (b) Shows details of the testes and epididymis. (c) A good self-examination includes both a visual inspection for rashes or open sores on the penis and scrotum and a palpating of the testes, scrotum, and associated structures for unusual soreness, sensitivity, or tenderness. Any unusual or suspicious development can be checked by a physician.*

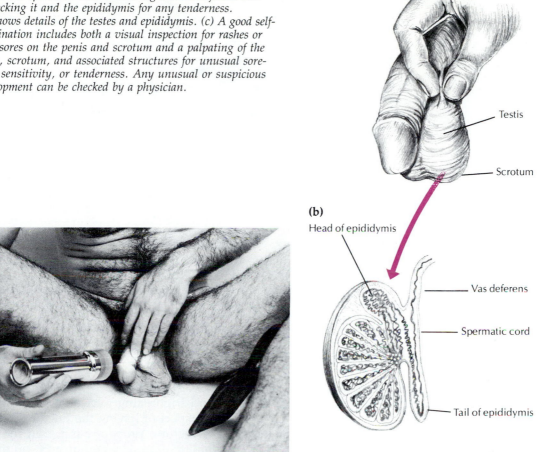

(a)

Testis

Scrotum

(c)

(b)

Head of epididymis

Vas deferens

Spermatic cord

Tail of epididymis

directions given earlier for the three-step breast self-examination for women. Don't confuse your ribs for a breast lump, however.

Prostate and Rectal Examinations

Some male sexual problems can be serious, even life threatening. But if women are reluctant to have an annual pelvic exam because it is embarrassing and makes them feel vulnerable, the prospect of a rectal-prostate exam is equally distasteful for men. Benign growths, infections, and cancers of the prostate, colon, and rectum are major killers of men. Three-fourths of the 53,000 American men who die every year from these cancers could be saved by early diagnosis.

The problem is that the most effective early detection test is a digital rectal-prostate exam every year after age 30, with a fecal blood test every year and a proctoscope examination every three to five years after age 50. It sounds simple, but for a male, the thought of bending over a table with his buttocks fully

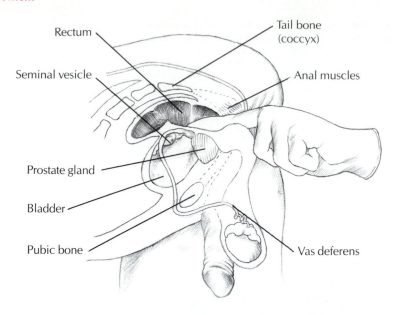

Figure 11.8. Rectal/Prostate Exam. *In a rectal examination the health care professional lubricates the anal sphincter and inserts a gloved finger into the rectal canal to check the condition and possible enlargement of the prostate and the presence of any unusual masses in the rectum. Both conditions are common in middle-aged and older men.*

exposed carries all kinds of powerful and frightening overtones of homosexuality in our culture (Figure 11.8). The prospect of having the doctor insert his or her gloved, lubricated finger into the rectum, probe around, and massage the prostate gland for a three- or four-minute exam is a real turnoff, no matter how convinced a man is that this procedure is necessary for his continued good health. It may also be that the man is afraid the doctor may detect that the exam turns him on. If a man experiences an erection during a rectal-prostate exam, he should simply try to ignore it, because that is what the examining doctor will do. It is a simple reflex, and not the result of a latent homosexual tendency.

Each year, 138,000 new cases of colon, rectal, and prostate cancer are diagnosed, the vast majority too late to save a life. Only the younger generation of men can change this devastating picture. But that means young men will have to change their attitudes and accept the brief embarrassment of having the annual medical exam they need for continued good health.

Sexually Related Diseases

I had this dull pain in my balls and just all over down there. It even hurt to walk. I finally went to the campus doctor. It was a small religious college, and he only came once a week. He examined me, did all kinds of blood tests, and put his finger up my rectum to check my prostate. "Everything's normal," he said, "Nothing wrong at all." But the pain continued. I went back a second and third time, and got the same line.

Then I read about the buildup of semen causing swollen testes—"blue balls"—and prostatitis. I began wondering about all the messages I had heard about the evils of wet dreams and masturbation. I wondered about the doctor too, and his religious views. After I masturbated a couple of times, my pain disappeared. Happily, I cured myself!

(Author's files)

Prostatitis

An estimated 30% to 40% of American men ages 20 to 40 suffer from chronic **prostatitis**. A bacterial infection or congestion in the prostate from infrequent ejaculation can lead to an enlargement of the prostate. It can also come from a prolonged infection in other parts of the body. A dull, persistent pain in the lower back, testes, scrotum, and glans, and a thin mucous discharge, usually present early in the morning, are symptoms of this common condition. Antibiotics and prolonged warm baths will help relieve both the infection and the congestion (Brosman 1976; Finkle 1967; Mobley 1975; Stiller 1963).

Most people associate prostatitis with their fathers and grandfathers. In this condition, known as benign prostatic hyperplasia, fibrous nodules push from the prostate gland into the urethral canal and block the passage of urine. Characteristic symptoms are increased frequency of urination especially at night, a reduced urinary stream, a burning sensation during urination, chills, and fever. The common treatment for this noncancerous condition today is transurethral resection, a kind of minor "Roto-Rooter" clearing of the blocked urethra. Although this treatment sounds cruel and painful, it is a simple surgical procedure with relatively few risks and far fewer side effects than the earlier surgeries where entry was made through either the abdomen or rectum.

Epididymitis

Each year over 600,000 American men have an inflammation of the epididymises, known as **epididymitis**. Half of these cases are due to chlamydia, a sexually transmitted bacterial disease. Gonorrhea, tuberculosis, abnormalities in the urinary tract, and generalized infections may result in varying degrees of epididymitis. A slight swelling and tenderness in the epididymis may indicate a mild infection, but an escalating infection can involve the whole testis and result in sterility. If you are sexually active and not using a condom, your chances of picking up a mild chlamydial infection and epididymitis are definitely increased. The high incidences of chlamydia and epididymitis are a major reason why men should examine their testes every month (Berger 1980).

Cryptorchidism

Although males are concerned about their penis and testes, the privacy we associate with our sexual anatomy makes it possible for 1 in 50 boys to go into puberty with one or both of their testes still in the abdominal cavity or inguinal canal. One in 500 adult men has an undescended testis or cryptorchidism. A variety of prenatal and postnatal factors can lead to undescended testes. But whatever the cause, it is important that the condition be remedied as soon as possible. After puberty, undescended testes degenerate, and secondary sex characteristics of the male will remain undeveloped. Hormones or surgery can be used to bring the testes into their normal position in the scrotum (Ellis 1960; Engel 1981; Sperling 1980).

Balanitis, Varicocele, Dermatoses, and Priapism

A regular examination of your sexual organs may turn up other problems which, if detected early and treated, can be easily cured. Infections, irritations, drugs, sexually transmitted diseases, and other factors can lead to an inflammation of the glans and foreskin known as balanitis. A black, brown, rust, or reddish coloring in the urine or semen may indicate a problem in the kidneys, bladder, urinary tract, prostate, or associated sexual glands.

An estimated 1 in 10 males will experience an enlargement or **varicocele** in the spermatic vein that supplies the testis. The left spermatic duct, which supplies the left testis, contains more blood than the right vein because of its angle with the left renal vein into which it empties. This normally causes the left testis to hang below the right and increases the risk of varicocele, 99% of which occur in the left epididymis. Again, regular self-examination can detect any early indication of this common male problem (Clark 1962).

As athletes quickly learn, skin infections, dermatoses, in the genital region are fairly common. Tinea cruris or jock (strap) itch is a fungal infection with reddish, scaly patches that become inflamed, very itchy, and painful. Tight clothing, sweating, and not drying the genitals thoroughly after showering may trigger this common infection that can be easily cured with over-the-counter medications.

Black males are more susceptible than white males to priapism because of their risk for sickle cell anemia and its effect on blood supply to the penis. In priapism, a problem in the blood supply to the corpora cavernosa causes these tissues suddenly to fill with blood and remain erect. The glans and corpus spongiosum are not affected. The onset of priapism is sudden, painful, and not related to any sexual desire. Because continued partial erection can permanently damage the erectile tissues of the penis, any indication of priapism should be immediately checked by a physician.

Choosing the Best Doctor for Your Sexual Health

You need a doctor with whom you can feel comfortable. You need a doctor you can ask questions, and a doctor who is willing to take time to answer your questions. That doctor may be a man or a woman. Some women much prefer going to a female physician, but other women would not even consider it. Males sometimes are uncomfortable with a female doctor, especially if they have sexual questions or problems.

It may be more difficult than you think to find a doctor who not only has knowledge of the sexual organs but also understands the emotional factors involved with sexuality. Until recently, most medical schools did not have courses on human sexuality. Thus, a physician's knowledge may be limited to the mechanics of the sexual organs, with little understanding of sexual attitudes and behaviors. In addition, physicians tend to be conservative and may have a difficult time accepting anything they consider "unusual" in sexual behavior.

Not all doctors are comfortable counseling a single young woman who is sexually active. Some doctors are uncomfortable treating a homosexual patient. Since sexual relations and behaviors are an important part of general health, your doctor may need to inquire or advise you. That discussion may be difficult for your doctor if he or she is not comfortable with your orientation or lifestyle.

Most internists can examine and treat conditions of the sexual/urinary organs. However, you may need a specialist. Urologists specialize in male urogenital problems; gynecologists specialize in female health care.

You can take some steps to find out how knowledgeable a doctor is before you pick him or her as your physician. Asking for references from your college health clinic, a local Planned Parenthood office, or the adolescent health clinic at a local hospital is a good place to start. Friends can often direct you to a physician they have found particularly good. If you are gay, lesbian, or bisexual, local gay helplines and gay/lesbian activist groups can provide reliable leads. To narrow your choices, you may want to talk with two or three of the recommended doctors. A 10- or 15-minute consultation should give you a good idea whether or not you will be comfortable with a particular physician and he or she with you. Ask what he or she does to keep up with new developments in sexual medicine. Does he or she have additional training as a sex educator or counselor? Does she or he read *Medical Aspects of Human Sexuality*, a monthly journal for health care professionals? Does he or she seem to be a good listener? Is she or he concerned about individuals? If you ask about having tests for some sexually transmitted disease and the doctor suggests that's not necessary because you're not from the "big city" or aren't "that kind of woman," find yourself another doctor.

Choosing a doctor, a health clinic, or a self-help group is your responsibility. It may take some time to find a good doctor, but that time will be well worth it.

Key Concepts

1. Both men and women can gain a more positive image of themselves as sexual persons, learn what is normal in their sexual anatomy, identify health problems early, and improve their health care if they take a few minutes each month to do a genital and breast self-examination.

2. An annual or semiannual Pap smear can identify a variety of possible problems, both noncancerous and malignant, in the cervix.

3. The risk of vaginitis and cystitis, common health problems for women, can be greatly reduced by following a few simple guidelines, particularly not douching.

4. Ovarian cysts, vaginal hernias of the bladder and rectum, prolapsed uterus, and uterine fibroids are among the other important sexually related disorders occurring in women.

5. Fibroadenomas and fibrocystic breast disorders can often be controlled by diet without resorting to surgery.

6. A woman can greatly reduce risks to her health by doing a monthly breast self-exam and having an annual mammogram after age 30.

7. Early detection of STDs, penile cancer, and testicular cancer, the most common solid tumor found in men between the ages of 20 and 34, are three good reasons for men to do a monthly genital self-exam.

8. The risk of infections and cancers of the epididymis, prostate, colon, and rectum can be reduced by a regular genital self-exam and by having an annual rectocolon-prostate exam.

Key Terms

cystitis (311)
diethylstilbestrol (DES) (317)
endometriosis (310)
epididymitis (321)
fibrocystic disorder (315)
mammogram (315)
mononucleosis (317)

Pap smear (304)
pelvic inflammatory disease
    (PID) (307)
prostatitis (321)
vaginitis (309)
varicocele (322)

Summary Questions

1. What factors create a greater risk of breast cancer in a woman?
2. Describe the steps in genital and breast self-exams for a woman, for a man.
3. Describe the symptoms and causes of PID, endometriosis, and cystitis.
4. How many American men die needlessly each year of infections and cancers of the prostate, colon, and rectum?
5. What characteristics should one look for in a physician? Where can one usually find out about such a physician?

Suggested Readings

American Cancer Society. Pamphlets on cancer facts for men, testicular cancer, and male self-examinations, as well as similar pamphlets for women, are available from a local ACS office.

Boston Women's Health Collective. (1984). *The New Our Bodies, Ourselves*. New York: Simon & Schuster. The essential book for women concerned about their health.

Budoff, P. W. (1980). *No More Menstrual Cramps and Other Good News*. New York: Penguin. A down-to-earth woman physician offers advice on PMS and other problems.

Budoff, P. W. (1983). *No More Hot Flashes and Other Good News*. New York: Putnam. New insights into conservative health care for women by a woman physician; a sequel to *No More Menstrual Cramps*.

Federation of Feminist Women's Health Centers. (1981). *How to Stay Out of the Gynecologist's Office*. Culver City, CA: Peace Press. A useful complement to *The New Our Bodies, Ourselves*.

Kelley, G. (1979). *A Healthy Man's Guide to Sexual Fulfillment*. New York: Harcourt Brace Jovanovich. An excellent guide for men's sexual health.

Zilbergeld, B. (1978). *Male Sexuality: A Guide to Sexual Fulfillment*. Boston: Little, Brown. A worthwhile complement to Kelley's book.

*T*he STD Scene
  Who Gets Them?
  Why We Haven't
    Controlled Them
  Where Did They
    Come From?
  Reducing Your Risk
  STDs as a Weapon
A Summary of Sexually
  Transmitted Diseases
  Sexual Diseases Caused
    by Bacteria
  Sexual Diseases Caused
    by Fungi or Yeasts
  Sexual Diseases Caused
    by Parasites
  Sexual Diseases Caused
    by Viruses
*G*etting Help
  Where to Go
  What to Expect
A Look to the Future

Chapter 12

*R*educing Your Risk for Sexual Diseases

Special Consultants

Roger Cooper, M.D., medical training officer, Centers for Disease Control and director, STD/AIDS Clinic, St. Michael's Hospital, Newark, New Jersey.

Berta Numata, R.N.C., Ob/Gyn nurse practitioner, Planned Parenthood of Greater Northern New Jersey.

Newton Richards, health education specialist, New Jersey Department of Health, and coauthor of *Foundations for Decision Making: A VD Teaching Guide*, published by the American Council for Healthful Living.

Anne Tripp, M.S., former executive director of the American Council for Healthful Living.

In Chapter 11 we discussed SRDs, sexually related diseases which can affect various sexual and reproductive organs at any time whether or not you are genitally intimate. In this chapter we discuss the diseases known as **sexually transmitted diseases (STDs)** because in the vast majority of cases they are spread through sexual intimacy and intercourse. You may also know these diseases as venereal diseases, or VD.

When we are caught up in romantic fantasies, in the throes of falling in love, having a lighthearted summer fling, or otherwise being carried aloft from the real world by lust, erotic attraction, or just a desire for a new experience, STDs are not a popular topic. Whether you are gay, straight, or bisexual, this chapter can show you how you can reduce the risk of getting STDs when you are sexually active and how to avoid complications by getting prompt treatment. Each year millions of average young Americans pick up an STD.

Even if you are not having sexual intercourse or being genitally active with someone now, knowing about STDs still makes good sense for your health. Take the case of yeast infections, or candidiasis, a common STD. Yeast lives quite peacefully in every human digestive tract and in every female vagina. Normally, it causes no problem. If it gets out of control, the result is a painful, itching infection. Women can get a candidal infection from vaginal intercourse or oral sex with an infected partner. But a woman can also get candidiasis if she has a penicillin shot for a cold and the antibiotic upsets the balance of microorganisms in her vagina. The birth control pill, diabetes, and obesity can also upset the population balance of *Candida* and other flora in the vagina for some women and allow the yeast cells to take over. Some STDs, like candidiasis, can also be described as sexually related diseases (SRDs).

In this chapter we discuss bacteria, fungi, yeasts, parasites, and viruses which cause a variety of STDs/SRDs you may never have heard of but may encounter. We outline how to reduce the risk of contracting these infections, how they can be cured or treated, and what happens when you do not get prompt treatment.

The STD Scene

Who Gets Them?

Men and women of every type, tall and short, overweight and underweight, people of every racial and ethnic background, every economic level from the richest to the poorest, religious people and atheists, gays, straights, and bisexuals—in brief, if you're a man or woman you may, sooner or later, get an STD or SRD. STDs are transmitted by vaginal, oral, and anal sex, but persons who are not genitally active do get some of these same diseases in other ways. The stress of final exams or your menstrual period may trigger a candidal infection, or reactivate a genital herpes. Cases of young children getting STDs as a result of sexual abuse are also increasing.

Table 12.1 gives an insight into the **Silent Epidemic**. Many men and women are unaware they have a bacterial, viral, or parasitic infection because they have an **asymptomatic** infection (no significant symptoms). Whether or not the infection is having any immediate effect in their bodies, these **carriers** can infect their partners. Unfortunately, we usually only worry about the risk of getting

Table 12.1.   The Silent Epidemic

Disease	Percentage of Infected Males with No Symptoms	Percentage of Infected Females with No Symptoms
Candidiasis	Seldom any symptoms	Symptoms usually obvious
Chlamydia	10%	60% to 80%
Gonorrhea	5%–20%	Up to 80%
Hemophilus	May be asymptomatic	Frequently no symptoms
NGU	Sometimes so mild, males ignore them	Often no symptoms
Syphilis	Obvious symptoms	Cervical/vaginal chancres often unnoticed
Trichomonas	Rarely show symptoms	Half of all women may have this parasite, usually with no symptoms
Warts	Not noticed if warts are internal	Internal warts on cervix and in vagina not noticed

an STD from a partner with symptoms. Too often, we forget about the real risk of asymptomatic carriers, the main part of the STD iceberg that lies hidden from view.

Figure 12.1 suggests the dimensions of the Silent Epidemic. When you are genitally intimate with someone, there are usually several, maybe even many, hidden partners, unless you are both virgins. You or your partner may have had a previous sexual partner who was asymptomatic and a carrier. He or she may also have had symptoms of an STD and ignored them because they seemed unimportant. Or that earlier sexual partner may have noticed symptoms, been treated, but was then too embarrassed to tell you or your partner of the risk. So you get an STD and wonder what happened. If your sexual partner has had sexual relations with other persons before you, then those persons are silent partners who might put you at risk for an STD.

Multiply Figure 12.1 by the 7 million teenage men, the 5 million teenage women, and the millions of men and women over age 20 who are genitally intimate in the United States, and you have some idea why STDs are a serious problem today. In 1984, 850,000 new cases of gonorrhea were reported, although various researchers estimate the actual number of new cases to be between 2 and 3 million each year. In recent years, the Centers for Disease Control in Atlanta, Georgia, have reported about 30,000 new cases of syphilis each year, but again, researchers estimate another 60,000 cases went unreported. Since most reported cases occur among young Americans ages 15 to 29, your chances of contracting syphilis or gonorrhea before you are 25 may be about 1 in 6 for these two diseases. This estimate says nothing about the nonreportable diseases such as genital herpes, genital warts, or *Chlamydia,* the most common cause of nongonococcal urethritis (NGU) in men. An estimated one-third of all cases of female infertility are due to STDs.

Figure 12.1. The Hidden Network Behind the Spread of STDs. *Although you may have been very selective and limited in your sexual relationships, a dozen or more persons may have been, directly or indirectly through your sexual partners, potential channels for sexually transmitted diseases. Your sexual partners may not have been as careful in their sexual contacts as you have been. Some of the people in this network may have been infected and did not show any symptoms, even though they could transmit the disease to others through sexual contact.*

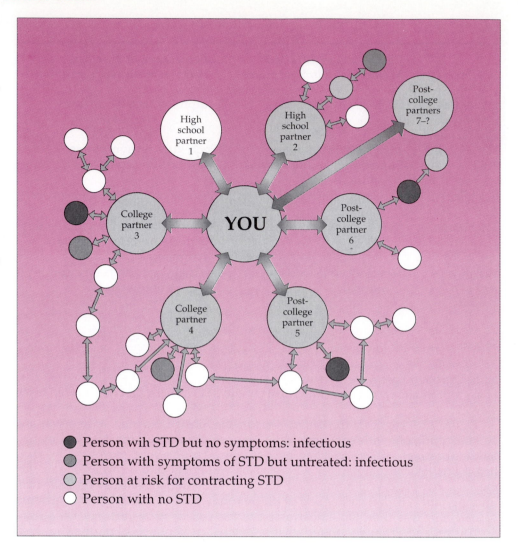

- ● Person wih STD but no symptoms: infectious
- ● Person with symptoms of STD but untreated: infectious
- ● Person at risk for contracting STD
- ○ Person with no STD

Why We Haven't Controlled Them

There are many reasons why, despite all our medical technology, we haven't done a better job in controlling some of the simple bacterial and parasitic diseases associated with sex. Among the factors listed here, which do you think are the most important? Is there one factor that you would rank as the major problem preventing us from facing up to the silent STD epidemic? Do your friends, classmates, or parents agree with your choices?

1. Young people having sexual intercourse at an earlier age than ever before and more people having several sexual partners before they get married, and sometimes after marriage.

2. An increase in sexual freedom and mobility, which means we often get involved with people about whose background and previous sexual relations we know very little.

3. A macho attitude among many men who refuse to use condoms and spermicidal foam even though they have heard their use can reduce the spread of STDs.

4. Denial of sexual desires and an unwillingness to prepare for sexual relations by many young women who do not use spermicidal foam with condoms even though their use can reduce their risk for STDs.

5. Teenagers who believe "It'll never happen to me," the parents of teenagers who prefer to ignore STDs because "It'll never happen to my son or my daughter," and school boards and teachers who avoid discussing STDs and contraception because "That would only promote promiscuity" or trigger protests from parents. The belief that "Only poor, unclean, or promiscuous people get STDs."

6. The hypocrisy of our society which is willing to show sexual scenes and situations in movies and on television, but avoids any mention of pregnancy and STDs and ways to prevent them (Figure 12.2).

7. A common moralistic view that says "You play, you pay!" which leads to financial support to find cures for cancer and funding for research on artificial hearts, but not to support research on STDs.

8. A common lack of knowledge about the symptoms of STDs and a reluctance to see a doctor or be tested.

9. The very nature of most STDs, the fact that many times the symptoms do not appear until weeks or months after the infection was contracted and that many infected persons have only mild symptoms, or no symptoms at all.

Where Did They Come From?

Diseases with symptoms characteristic of both gonorrhea and syphilis are described in the Old Testament of the Bible. The ancient Romans gave the name of their goddess of love, Venus, to these classic "venereal" diseases.

The common theory today is that syphilis started as a tropical disease somewhere in Europe or Asia. Because it is always easy to blame someone else, syphilis has been called the "French disease," the "Spanish disease," the "Polish pox," the "German pox," the "Christian disease," or the "Muslim/Persian fire." For centuries, before we knew what bacteria were and how many different kinds there were, syphilis and gonorrhea were thought to be the same disease, known as lues or the plague. Most STDs probably originated when bacteria or viruses that normally occurred in the human body mutated into disease-causing forms. Since the tissues of the vulva, penis, urethra, and mouth are not nearly as resistant as the rest of our skin to infections, and since bacteria and viruses enjoy such moist tissues, it is natural that they are now commonly transmitted from one person to another during sexual intimacy.

The incidence of STDs often fluctuates widely. Wars and massive migrations often bring epidemics. Gonorrhea, for instance, was a worldwide epidemic after World War I. Its incidence leveled off during the 1930s, and then rose sharply during World War II and later during the Vietnam War.

Penicillin and other antibiotics have helped control the bacteria that cause some STDs, which has lulled us into a false sense of security. As a result people forget about commonsense prevention and diagnosis. "It would never happen to me, or my loved one." So the incidence of STDs starts to increase. When an

Figure 12.2. An Age-Old Problem. *These examples from the May 28, 1892,* National Police Gazette *offer a plethora of medical aids "guaranteed" to remedy the "errors of youth" and "weaknesses of men." The aids promised to cure self-abuse, small penises, syphilis, gonorrhea, glect, Whites, Spermatorrhea, small or weak potency, and opium addiction.*

epidemic is declared, everyone suddenly wakes up and the incidence starts to drop again. The cycle may take 15 to 20 years, unless, as with AIDS, we get bombarded with dire warnings from every side, including the evening TV news.

Reducing Your Risk

The following suggestions involve common sense and basic health principles. These suggestions can save you, and those you love, much pain and suffering if you follow them. Moreover, the suggestions work equally well for men and women, for lesbians, gay men, and heterosexuals. Because of the nature of their sexual relations, lesbians are much less at risk for the transmission of STDs.

Being genitally intimate in a responsible way means taking into consideration ways to reduce the risk both of an unwanted pregnancy and of contracting a sexually transmitted disease.

1. Complete abstinence is a certain way to avoid both an unwanted pregnancy and STDs, but with well over 50% of the population having sex by age 19, that approach alone is not very realistic.

2. Some persons limit their sexual intimacy to a single partner, remaining sexually exclusive throughout a courtship and lifelong marriage, but it is not the most common pattern for premarital and marital relations. A significant percentage of young Americans have more than one sexual partner between their early teens and the time they marry.

3. Being selective about your sexual partner(s). One night stands, casual pickups, and sexual intimacy with persons you hardly know pose a much greater risk than long-term monogamous relations with someone you know well (Figure 12.3).

4. The more sexual partners you have the greater the risk of contracting an STD.

5. Unless you and your partner are and have been strictly monogamous, use a condom and spermicidal foam for STD protection until you know each other and are sure of each other. Use FDA-tested American brand condoms, not foreign brands.

6. If you're using the Pill, use a condom and spermicidal foam to counter the increased risk of vaginal infections and STDs caused by the hormonal pill altering the vaginal environment (Cates 1984a, 1984b). (See p. 261 in Chapter 9.)

7. If you're using an IUD for contraception, use a condom and spermicidal foam to counter the increased risk of STD transmission associated with the IUD (Cates 1984a). (See p. 261 in Chapter 9.)

8. Watch for sores, rashes, or discharge around the vulva or penis, or elsewhere on your body, especially the mouth. When cold sores are present, avoid kissing or oral sex.

9. Wash your genitals and hands with soap and warm water immediately before and after sexual contact.

10. Both men and women should urinate soon after intercourse to clean any infectious organisms out of the urethra.

11. Some STDs can be transmitted by fellatio (oral stimulation of the penis) with an infected partner. Use a condom if you have any doubts about the possibility of either partner having an STD. Some condoms are

Figure 12.3. The Image of the "Promiscuous Male." *Traditionally, so-called promiscuous men were blamed for the spread of sexually transmitted diseases; women were assumed to be sexually naive and innocent. Hence, the focus of this 1936 advertisement from the American Society for Social Hygiene.*

flavored, which may make them more acceptable for fellatio. Rinse your mouth and gargle with salt water or a mouthwash. Do not brush your teeth before or after fellatio, since it may cause tiny tears in the gums through which microorganisms may enter.

12.   Penile-anal contact or intercourse should never be engaged in without a double condom and ample lubrication with K-Y Jelly or Astroglide.

13.   Oral-anal contact is high risk behavior for STD transmission. Use a dental dam or condom to reduce the risk.

14.   If you're sexually active with more than one partner in a year's time, have regular STD checkups. Most doctors and health clinics will not perform STD tests unless you request them. Many doctors assume that their patients don't get STDs because they are married or come from "nice" families.

15.   If you have any reason to suspect an infection, find a good health clinic and have the appropriate tests as soon as possible. Remember, each STD has its own dormancy or incubation period after the initial infection when the test cannot yet detect the bacteria or virus even if it is present. If the test(s) are performed at the correct time and are negative, you can stop worrying. If they are positive, get the proper treatment. Don't delay because of embarrassment or fear. Don't mistake the spontaneous disappearance of symptoms as a sign that you are cured. If you have a negative test, at least you know that you mistook the supposed symptoms. This knowledge is worth the small investment in a test.

16.   If the test(s) prove positive, notify your sexual partner(s) so they can be treated immediately. Your doctor or a Health Department counselor may help with this difficult task. Avoid sexual intercourse, oral sex, and other forms of intimate contact until both of you are treated and a physician says both of you are no longer infectious. In most cases, both partners should be treated at the same time. If you or your partner just can't wait, and you're willing to take some risk of reinfection, at least use a condom and nonoxynol-9 foam for vaginal intercourse or two condoms and a good lubricant for anal intercourse.

17.   You can usually get free or very reasonable cost treatment for STDs at state-run clinics in all states. Call your local health department or hospital for information.

STDs as a Weapon

The legal concepts of assault and battery have been part of English common law for many years. Assault is a threat to do bodily harm to a person with the present and immediate ability to do the harm threatened. Battery, on the other hand, is any unconsented, unjustified touching of another person. Can STDs be used as a weapon in sexual assault and battery? This is a new possibility, although the law is not clear. Clearer, but still open to debate, is negligence, a failure to protect others against "unreasonable great risk of harm . . . in determining whether an individual has acted negligently towards another, it must be decided whether the individual owed the other a 'legal duty.' This is the threshold issue in any negligence action. The focus of concern is on whether the plaintiff's interests are entitled to legal protection from the defendant's conduct" (Alexander 1984; Dalton 1985:793; Gold-Bikin 1985; Reidinger 1987; Taylor 1987).

What is now obvious from legal precedents is that if someone knows he or she has an STD infection, that person may well have a legal responsibility to inform any sexual partner of that risk. If the partner is not informed and contracts an STD as a result of intimate contact, he or she can sue and may win damages.

A Summary of Sexually Transmitted Diseases

Over 20 STDs are known today. We supply specific, practical information here on the more common diseases, divided into four categories depending on the nature of the organism causing the disease. Since the exact status of some microorganisms, like *Chlamydia* and *Candida*, is not clear, you may find them listed under different categories in other sources. We discuss AIDS in Chapter 13.

1. STD/SRDs caused by bacteria: *Chlamydia*, NGU, *Hemophilis vaginalis*, gonorrhea, syphilis.
2. A STD/SRD caused by a fungus-like yeast: *Candida albicans*.
3. STD/SRDs caused by parasites: *Trichomonas*, pubic lice, scabies or mites, and lymphogranuloma venereum.
4. STD/SRDs caused by viruses: venereal warts or condyloma, genital herpes, and hepatitis B.

Sexual Diseases Caused by Bacteria

Chlamydia, a bacteria-like intracellular parasite, is the main cause of STD-associated cervicitis, an infection that starts in the cervix and spreads, and of nongonococcal urethritis (NGU), an infection of the urethra of both men and women. With more than 3 million Americans newly infected each year with *Chlamydia trachomatis*, this dangerous organism is the most prevalent STD today, and the one you are most likely to encounter if you are young and genitally intimate.

Cervicitis

An estimated 1 out of every 5 or 6 American women has a chlamydial cervicitis infection. It is also one of the most serious STDs because 60% to 80% of the infected women show no symptoms until the infection has spread beyond the cervix, where it usually starts. Chlamydial infections are also a major cause of pelvic inflammatory disease (PID), an inflammation of the pelvic organs which hospitalizes more than 200,000 American women each year. Over a million more women are treated for PID as outpatients each year. Women with PID may experience a pain deep inside the abdomen during penile penetration, nausea and vomiting, a foul-smelling vaginal discharge, abnormal menstruation, or

Table 12.2.
Summary of Bacterial or Bacterial-Like STDs

Disease	How Transmitted	Symptoms	Detection
Chlamydia and cervicitis	Vaginal intercourse	60%–80% of infected women have no symptoms; cervical infection and symptoms of PID	Monoclonal antibody test
Gonorrhea	Vaginal or anal intercourse; oral-genital contact	80% of women and 5%–20% of men have no symptoms; greenish vaginal discharge, vulvar irritation; penile discharge and painful urination; sore throat and swollen glands	Quick Gram stain of a smear or culture taken from suspected area
Nongonococcal urethritis	Intimate contact; possible spontaneous infection	Slight white, yellow, or clear discharge from penis or vagina; females usually have no symptoms; mild pain when male urinates	Lab test for *Chlamydia, Trichomonas,* and *Candida*
Syphilis	Vaginal or anal intercourse; oral-genital contact	Primary stage: chancres Secondary: rash, flulike symptoms, mouth sores	Examination of chancre fluid; blood test after 4–6 weeks
Hemophilus	Direct sexual contact; females often asymptomatic; males serve as carriers	Profuse creamy white or gray vaginal discharge; foul odor	Microscopic examination of vaginal, anal, or penile smear

pain when urinating. Besides the risk of PID from chlamydial infections, an estimated 11,000 young women with untreated chlamydial infection develop blocked fallopian tubes and become sterile each year. Estimates suggest that 1 in 10 pregnant women has a chlamydial infection and that 3,600 women suffer annually from ectopic or tubal pregnancies because of it. Every year, an estimated 155,000 infants contract this infection during pregnancy or delivery. It causes eye infection, infant pneumonia, premature delivery, and low birth weight. When women do have symptoms, they include vaginal discharge, pelvic pain, abnormal bleeding, and painful urination.

Until 1987, chlamydial infections were commonly confused with gonorrhea and often mistreated. The only test for *Chlamydia* was expensive, difficult, and largely unavailable. Fortunately, we now have a new monoclonal antibody test that is accurate, fast, and relatively inexpensive. When detected, *Chlamydia* can be successfully treated with an appropriate antibiotic.

You should be concerned about chlamydial infection especially if you

- are under 24 years of age and have a new sexual partner;
- are not using condoms and a spermicidal foam with nonoxynol-9 which appears to kill *Chlamydia* and other organisms that cause a variety of STDs;
- have more than one sexual/genital partner, or your partner has had other partners;
- have a cervical discharge or bleed during a vaginal exam; or
- have been exposed to another STD.

If you fit any of these situations, you should consider being tested for *Chlamydia* at least once or twice a year. Remember, if caught early, chlamydial infection is easily cured. If not, it will lead to major problems for your health and future fertility.

Nongonococcal Urethritis (NGU)

Nongonococcal urethritis (NGU) or nonspecific urethritis (NSU), an infection of the urethra, becomes a new health problem for 2 million American men each year. *Chlamydia* is the leading cause of NGU in men, although it can be caused by other microorganisms like *Ureaplasma urealyticum*, *Trichomonas vaginalis*, and *Candida albicans*. In addition to being transmitted by sexual contact with an infected partner, the infection can be spread by infected fingers to the eyes. A rectal infection can result from anal intercourse.

Symptoms appear within one to three weeks: usually a slight white, yellow, or clear discharge from vagina or penis, and, for males, mild to moderate pain when urinating. Although 9 out of 10 men infected with *Chlamydia* have noticeable symptoms, many men ignore the mild discomfort of painful urination and a watery discharge. Unfortunately, females often experience no symptoms even though they are infected and can transmit the infection to a partner.

Like chlamydial cervicitis, chlamydial NGU is frequently misdiagnosed as gonorrhea. A chlamydial or other NGU infection can exist at the same time with a gonorrheal infection. Thus, it is very important to ask questions and return to your doctor for further testing if your symptoms do not respond to treatment. Since the infection can recur within two to six weeks after treatment, possibly due to reinfection or to the life cycle phase of the bacteria at time of treatment, retesting may be advisable. Infants born to infected women should be routinely treated for disease.

If undiagnosed and untreated, NGU can lead to severe pelvic infection for women (PID), infertility, and a tendency to miscarry. Each year, NGU results in epididymitis, an inflammation of the epididymides of the testes, for half a million American men. Epididymitis may affect fertility. For the fetus of an infected woman, the risks include pneumonia, conjunctivitis of the eye, miscarriage, low birth weight, infant death, and infections of the middle ear, rectum, intestines, and sexual organs.

Hemophilus vaginalis

Hemophilus (*Gardnerella*), a bacterial STD, is becoming more common, mainly because women who are infected frequently show no symptoms. Men can also be asymptomatic carriers. A profuse creamy white or gray vaginal discharge with a foul odor is a clear warning of this bacterial infection.

Hemophilus can easily be found by microscopic examination of smears taken from an infected vagina, anus, or penis. Treatment is equally simple and effective with antibiotics and other drugs. As with any STD, sexual abstinence or use of condom is important until all symptoms are gone and both partners are cured. There are no known complications or danger for a fetus born to an infected woman.

Gonorrhea

In slang terms, the clap, drip, or dose, **gonorrhea** is one of our most common STDs. You can contract it by vaginal, oral-genital, or anal intercourse with an infected person who may or may not have any symptoms. You can also get a gonorrheal infection in your eye if you touch it with a moist hand after touching an infected area. However, gonococcal bacteria die quickly when exposed to air, so it is not spread by contaminated moist towels, toilet seats, and other mythic sources (Figure 12.4). Symptoms usually appear between three to five days after contact. However, up to 80% of infected women and 5% to 20% of men may show no symptoms! In women the main symptoms are a greenish or yellow-green vaginal discharge and irritation of the vulva. Men can experience painful urination and a urethral discharge (see the color insert, Figure A). Oral sex with an infected partner can result in a throat gonorrheal infection with sore throat and swollen glands, although asymptomatic infections of the throat are also common. The bacteria can also cause anal irritation, discharge, and painful defecation.

If you either have symptoms, or have no symptoms but have had sex with someone who has or might have gonorrhea, a bacterial culture test is easy to get and 70% to 90% reliable, depending on the culturing site. Cultures should be taken from the cervix, urethra, anus, and/or throat if these are possible sites of infection. Cultures done in a hospital usually take 48 hours for results. If done by a private physician who uses an outside laboratory, results may take three days.

Penicillin, the standard treatment for gonorrhea, is usually effective. Unfortunately, a strain of the gonococcal bacterium has "learned" that penicillin can be lethal and has managed to mutate so it produces penicillinase, an enzyme that inactivates penicillin. As a result, other antibiotics may be needed to treat this STD. Nationwide, in 1986, only 1.8% of all gonorrheal cases were due to

The contagious disease gonorrhea is caused by this bacterium, *Neisseria gonorrhoeae.*

Figure 12.4. The Gonorrhea Bacterium.

PPNG, penicillinase-producing *Neisseria gonorrhoeae*, the mutant strain. However, in New York City, Los Angeles, and some counties in Florida, as many as 1 in 5 cases is due to the PPNG strain. In 1987 a new strain of gonococcal bacterium was reported in 8% of the U.S. servicemen who contracted gonorrhea in Korea. This new strain, which is resistant to penicillin and other antibiotics, will soon be spreading in the United States. In Holland today, over 25% of all cases of gonorrhea are penicillin-resistant (Boslego 1987).

The risks of not being tested for a suspected gonorrheal infection can be serious. Forty percent of the women with untreated gonorrhea develop PID with the possibility of sterility (Hatcher et al. 1986:51). Severe inflammation of sexual organs, sterility, arthritis, and blindness are other possible consequences for men and women if the infection is not treated. Since an infant's eyes can become infected in passage through the vaginal canal, silver nitrate eyedrops or an antibiotic salve is applied to the eyes of all newborn infants.

Syphilis

Known in street terms as the pox, siff, syph, lues, bad blood, and old Joe, **syphilis**, like other bacterial STDs, is transmitted by vaginal, oral-genital, or anal contact with an infected person. The corkscrew-shaped spirochete or bacterium dies if exposed to air so you only get it by direct contact with an open syphilitic sore (Figure 12.5). After declining for five years, cases of syphilis increased by 23% in the first quarter of 1987. California and New York City reported increases of more than 40%, mainly among heterosexuals. In the same areas, syphilis cases among homosexual and bisexual males decreased by almost 50%. Florida also showed a dramatic increase in syphilis among white heterosexual males.

Syphilis goes through three stages, each with characteristic symptoms and consequences. *Primary Stage*: Within 9 days to 4 weeks after exposure to an infected person, a **chancre** or painless round sore with a craterlike, depressed center will appear where the bacteria entered (see the color insert, Figures B and C). That could be on the fingertips, breast, mouth, or wherever you made direct contact with a chancre or other lesion on the body of an infected partner. This chancre disappears naturally without treatment in one to five weeks, but the microorganism continues to spread in the bloodstream throughout the body. *Secondary Stage*: About three weeks later, new symptoms appear: a rash, flulike symptoms, mouth sores, and maybe patchy loss of hair. Again, these symptoms will also disappear naturally even without treatment. About two-thirds of the untreated cases have no further problems. *Tertiary Stage*: Several years later, 1 in 3 untreated persons will experience new and more serious symptoms, with

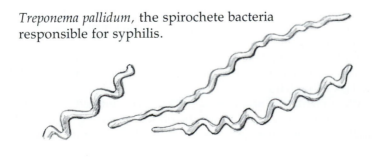

Treponema pallidum, the spirochete bacteria responsible for syphilis.

Figure 12.5. The Syphilis Bacterium.

Table 12.3.   Summary of Fungal or Yeast STDs

Disease	How Transmitted	Symptoms	Detection
Candidiasis or vaginitis	Vaginal or anal intercourse; oral-genital contact; spontaneous infection from rectum or after antibiotic treatment	Vulvar irritation; thick, white vaginal discharge with yeasty odor; males seldom have symptoms	Microscopic examination of vaginal, anal, or throat smear

loss of muscle coordination, heart disease, blindness, deafness, paralysis, insanity, and eventual death.

Depending on the stage of the disease, the presence of the *Treponema* organism which causes syphilis can be detected by microscopic examination of the chancre fluid, by blood tests, or, in the tertiary stage, by a spinal tap. The common screening test for syphilis is the VDRL (Venereal Disease Research Laboratory) test. If a blood sample contains syphilis bacteria, they will clump together when exposed to VDRL antibodies. Since both false positives and false negatives may result with the VDRL test, a positive finding should be confirmed by a more definitive test.

Carefully prescribed penicillin is the standard treatment for syphilis. If you are allergic to penicillin, another antibiotic can be used. Follow-up blood tests should be done at regular intervals to make sure the syphilis bacteria are eliminated.

Infants born to an infected woman can be born deformed, stillborn, or die shortly after birth. If the mother is treated before the 16th week of pregnancy, her fetus is not likely to be affected because the infective organism is not usually transmitted to the fetus before that time.

Sexual Diseases Caused by Fungi or Yeasts

Candida albicans Vaginitis

Also known as **candidiasis**, monilial vaginitis, moniliasis, vaginal or oral thrush, or simply as yeast, *Candida albicans* vaginitis normally lives quietly in the mouth, vagina, and rectum where it causes no problem as long as its population growth is controlled by other naturally competitive microorganisms (Figure 12.6). It can also live in the smegma under the foreskin of an uncircumcised male. It can travel from the rectum to the vagina by way of menstrual pads or from wiping from the anus toward the vulva after a bowel movement. Active infections may follow antibiotic therapy, oral sex, or vaginal or anal intercourse. Taking oral contraceptives, pregnancy, stress, and being diabetic or overweight also increases the risk of infection.

In women, an irritation and itching in the vulva with a thick, white discharge resembling cottage cheese and a yeasty odor are telling signs of candidiasis. Infected males seldom have any symptoms. A yeast infection can easily be

Figure 12.6. The Candida Microorganism.

Candida albicans, a yeastlike organism, slightly larger than bacteria, is a common cause of vaginitis.

confirmed by microscopic examination of vaginal, anal, or throat smears or in a sample of smegma.

Candidiasis can be cured with antibiotic-antifungal vaginal or oral tablets. In stubborn cases, treatment may last up to two months. Cool tub baths, petroleum jelly, and cool, wet compresses can be used to soothe the irritated tissues. Feminist health advocates suggest eating yogurt and vaginal insertion of plain, unflavored yogurt with active bacterial cultures to reestablish proper bacterial balance. Douching with 2 tablespoons of white vinegar in 1 quart of warm water can be helpful during an infection. Chances of recurrence can also be lessened by reducing your sugar and carbohydrate intake, and by wiping the anus backward, away from the vagina, after a bowel movement. Secondary bacterial infections can occur if candidiasis is not treated. Newborn infants can pick up a candidal infection of the mouth and throat (often called "thrush") as they pass through an infected vaginal canal.

Sexual Diseases Caused by Parasites

Pubic Lice

Very efficient in finding new hosts, **pubic lice**, or "crabs" can crawl from one person to another during love play or sexual intercourse, causing intense itching in the pubic area. They also hide in mattresses, bed linens, towels, furniture, clothing, and around toilet seats waiting for an unsuspecting victim to come along. College dormitories are likely sites for infestation (Figure 12.7).

The lice lay their eggs on pubic hairs where you can find evidence of an infection (see the color insert, Figure D). Once you know they are there, an application of an over-the-counter cream or lotion, or shampooing with Kwell,

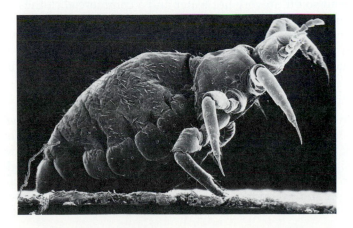

Figure 12.7. *This electron microphotograph shows a pubic louse.*

Table 12.4.   Summary of Parasitic STDs

Disease	How Transmitted	Symptoms	Detection
Pubic lice	Contact with infected clothes, bed linens, towels, furniture, or person	Intense itching in pubic area	Visual examination of pubic hairs and area
Scabies	Intimate contact; infected clothes, towels, etc.	Itchy rash and pimples in genital region, but also arms, feet, chest, and buttocks; pinhead blood spots on underwear	Visual examination of affected areas
Trichomonas	Intimate contact; infected moist towels, bathing suits, underwear	Usually no symptoms until person is stressed; foul-smelling, thin, yellow-green or gray vaginal discharge, burning vulva, abdominal pain	Microscopic examination of discharge or smear from infected area
Lympho-granuloma	Sexual intercourse with infected person	Transient small ulcers or lesions on genitals, groin lymph node swelling; headache, fever, nausea, and malaise	Antibody test

a prescription medication, will rid you of these pests. However, to keep them at bay, you will have to take other precautions. Adult lice die within 24 hours and their eggs take about 6 days to hatch, so you will have to wash all clothing, bed linens, and so on, in very hot water and a commercial clothes dryer, which is hotter than the usual home dryer. Then leave the clothes in sealed plastic bags for 7 days before using them again. Any article that is dry cleaned or boiled can be used immediately. Use an iron to give your mattress and upholstered furniture a good hot treatment, especially around any seams and buttons.

Scabies

When the insidious and very contagious female mite, *Sarcoptes scabiei*, burrow under the skin to lay eggs, the result is a very itchy rash and pimples. Tiny blue or dark red spots under the skin, pinhead blood spots on underwear, and rashes are signs of **scabies**. Scabies usually occur in the genital region, but can also develop on the hands, arms, feet, chest, and buttocks. The itching is often worse at night and secondary infections commonly follow intense scratching. To treat a mite infestation, a prescription ointment is applied to the entire body as directed by a dermatologist or other physician. Clothing and linen must be disinfected by washing, dry cleaning, or by removing them from human exposure for one to two weeks.

Trichomonas vaginalis

Known in slang as trich (pronounced ''trick'') or TV, **Trichomonas** *vaginalis* is a very nasty, irritating one-celled parasite that lives naturally in the urethra and prostate of some men and half of all women. Usually no symptoms occur, until a pregnancy, stress, the Pill, or hormonal change just before or during menstruation triggers a population explosion. Then, a foul smelling, yellow-green or gray, thin, foamy vaginal discharge brings a burning sensation in the vulva and lower abdominal pain that often seems unbearable. If you pick up a second STD at the same time, the discharge may be thicker or whiter.

The *Trichomonas* parasite is hardier than gonorrhea bacteria and can survive for a few hours—and be transmitted—by moist towels, bathing suits, underwear, and washcloths. It also gets passed back and forth sexually between men and women who are infected but show no symptoms. Lesbians, gay men, and heterosexuals can transmit it in their love play.

The fast-swimming parasites can easily be spotted with a microscopic examination of the discharge itself or in a smear from the vagina, cervix, urethra, smegma, or glans/foreskin (Figure 12.8).

Flagyl, in pill form, is the most commonly prescribed treatment. Ask your doctor about possible side effects. Feminist health groups suggest using a vaginal douche of 2 tablespoons of white vinegar in 1 quart of warm water twice daily to help inhibit the parasite, but this remedy should be checked with a physician. You can lessen the risk of recurrence by taking tub baths during menstruation and rinsing the vulva with clear warm water when changing hygiene pads, applying petroleum jelly to the irritated vulvar tissues, wearing loose clothing and clean cotton underwear, and avoiding tampons and vaginal hygiene sprays.

Trichomonas vaginalis, a single-celled organism that causes vaginal inflammations.

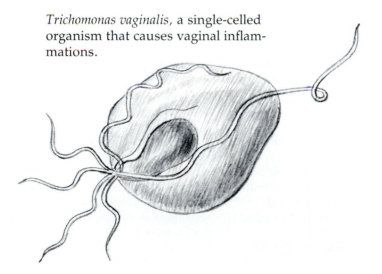

Figure 12.8. The Trichomonas Parasite.

Lymphogranuloma Venereum (LGV)

The initial symptoms of an infection of *Chlamydia trachomatis*, an intracellular parasitic microorganism, are transient small ulcers or lesions on the genitals, followed by a marked swelling of the lymph nodes of the groin, headache, fever, nausea, and malaise. Until recently, LGV was limited to the tropics and the southern United States. However, its incidence in temperate zones has been increasing. Transmitted by sexual contact, a blood test can easily identify the specific antibodies to the LGV organism, which can then be treated with antibiotics.

Sexual Diseases Caused by Viruses

Venereal Warts

Venereal warts (*Condyloma acuminatum*) are the unheralded STD champion of the late 1980s. People don't talk about genital warts, but they are very common and extremely contagious. More important, the human papillomavirus (HPV) which causes venereal warts is probably one of the leading causes of cancers in the lower abdominal organs (Barrasso et al. 1987; Richart 1987).

Table 12.5. Summary of Viral STDs

Disease	How Transmitted	Symptoms	Detection
Venereal warts	Oral, vaginal, and anal intercourse	Small, hard, yellow-gray warts on penis or around anus changing to soft, pink or red cauliflowerlike clustered or single warts; in women, usually in vaginal wall or cervix	Pap smear in women; visual examination in men
Hepatitis B	Blood transfusions; sexual contact; sharing contaminated needles in IV drug use	Flulike symptoms with jaundice, dark urine, abdominal and gastric discomfort, pain	Laboratory analyses
Genital herpes	Sexual or other contact with open blisters; kissing; shared towels and drinking cups; oral sex	Tender, painful blisters, slight fever, enlarged lymphs glands in groin; reoccurrence signaled by tingling sensation in region of first infection	Visual examination of blisters confirmed by examination of smear
AIDS	See Chapter 13		

The virus is easily spread by an infected person to the partner during oral, vaginal, or anal intercourse. The first warts appear between three weeks and three months after exposure, but the infection can be transmitted even before they appear. In males, the small, hard, and yellow-gray warts are easy to see on the tip and shaft of the penis and around the anus (see the color insert, Figure E). In males, the lesions may also go unnoticed if they are internal. Venereal warts are more common in uncircumcised than in circumcised men. As the warts grow, they may appear soft, pink or red, cauliflower-like, in single or multiple clusters. In women, the first warts are small, painless, nearly invisible hard spots on the cervix or vaginal wall (see the color insert, Figure F). If warts are suspected, a Pap smear is usually needed to detect their presence in women.

Several treatments are available; the most common is a chemical that burns off the growths. If the growths are large or extensive, surgery, freezing, or laser beams may be used to destroy them. Abstinence or use of a condom is essential until all the warts are removed. Because the virus is so highly contagious, the warts will continue to spread, if not removed, eventually blocking the vaginal, urethral, and/or rectal openings. Vaginal or cervical warts can infect a newborn during delivery. Because of the link with cervical and other cancers, women who are treated for venereal warts should have a Pap smear every six months. Equally important, the male partner(s) should be checked by a urologist or dermatologist who understands the need for internal examination with a colposcope and a close follow-up (Richart 1987).

Hepatitis B

When the flulike symptoms and jaundice of a friend are diagnosed as a liver infection caused by the hepatitis B virus, we don't usually think of a sexually transmitted disease. The hepatitis virus is more commonly transmitted in a blood transfusion. But like the AIDS virus, it is also transmitted by sexual contact, or by intravenous (IV) drug users sharing contaminated needles. A 1986 report from the Centers for Disease Control pointed out that **hepatitis B** (serum hepatitis) afflicts about 150,000 Americans each year. The study also showed that white heterosexuals with three or more different partners in four months were up to 11 times more likely to have hepatitis B than the general population. The rapid onset of acute symptoms may be severe, resulting in prolonged illness, destruction of liver cells, and degeneration of the liver. It can be fatal. A high protein diet, rest, and injections of hepatitis B antibodies (immune globulin) are the standard treatment.

Genital Herpes

Only a few years ago, **genital herpes** was the most talked about and feared STD. When herpes first made the national headlines, the stories were scary and often exaggerated. People with herpes reported feeling like social outcasts. They found it hard to date or to be sexually intimate. Now we know that one-fourth or more of all adult Americans have the herpesvirus. In the spring of 1986, an estimated 98 million Americans were infected with oral herpes and 9 million with genital herpes. Between 300,000 and 600,000 new cases of genital herpes appear annually in the United States (Becker et al. 1985). However, some researchers estimate that a quarter to a half of all sexually active Americans carry

Figure 12.9. The Herpes Virus.

A *Herpes simplex* virus, only a few billionths of a meter in diameter.

one of the herpesviruses, and are unaware they have it because they have suffered no noticeable effects.

Genital herpes may be a lifelong incurable infection, but it can be little more than a minor irritation if you understand its pattern. Generally, it is said that genital herpes is caused by the *herpes simplex* II virus (HSV-2); cold sores are caused by the closely related *herpes simplex* I virus (HSV-1) (Figure 12.9). But in reality, both viruses can infect the genitals. Oral herpes (HSV-1) can be transmitted by kissing, shared towels or drinking cups, and oral sex. Both kinds of HSV are known to survive for up to 3 days on dry gauze, for 24 hours in distilled water, and for 2 to 4 hours in tap water, on toilet seats, and moist plastic. So, although direct physical contact with a person with open blisters is the usual path of transmission, a herpes infection need not be sexually transmitted. It could be transmitted by direct skin contact with the moist plastic-coated seats at a health spa, pool, or gym. The growing popularity of oral-genital sex has brought the two strains together, so that there is now about a 20% crossover (Neinstein et al. 1984; Nerurkar et al. 1983).

Once the genital herpesvirus enters your body, it follows a cyclic pattern, spending most of its time resting in the nerves at the base of the spine where it cannot infect anyone or cause you any problems. The dormant periods alternate with an occasional active period marked by infectious blisters (see the color insert, Figures G and H). Herpes can be reactivated by physical or emotional stress, hormone changes, sunbathing, food allergies, a cold, fatigue, and menstruation.

A tingling sensation at the site of the original infection usually signals a new outbreak and the renewed risk of infection. If the herpes blisters occur in the genital area, you should abstain from contact with that area, or use a condom at the first sign of an outbreak. Kissing, hugging, and outercourse are safe, as long as you avoid contact with the herpes blisters. Within a day, tender, painful blisters appear on sexual organs, buttocks, thighs, or within the urethra. Blisters in the vagina or on the cervix may go unnoticed. A primary outbreak may also bring a slight fever and tender, enlarged lymph glands in the groin region. Fortunately, recurrent symptoms are usually milder than the original ones. Some people have no recurrences, but the average is four to five outbreaks a year, each lasting a few days. Contact with the infected area(s) should be avoided during these times.

A genital herpes infection can be identified by a viral culture and examination of a smear taken from active sores. Pregnant women should be checked before delivery, and if active lesions are present, a cesarean section may be recommended to reduce the risk of transmitting the virus to the baby.

If you test positive for herpes, there is no cure. Most antibiotics have no effect on viruses. However, antibacterial ointments can be used to prevent secondary infections, and pain-relieving pills and ointments can be prescribed. An antiviral drug, acyclovir, sold under the brand name of Zovirax, speeds healing and possibly shortens the infective period by entering infected cells and halting their ability to reproduce the virus. But it must be applied at the first sign of an outbreak. Maintaining good health, practicing good nutrition, and learning stress management is important. Warm water sitz baths help. Cool, wet dressings, and wearing loose clothing can provide relief during an outbreak. Women should not wear pantyhose. Cotton underwear is recommended instead of synthetics which retain moisture. Petroleum jelly can keep acidic urine from irritating the open sores. For males, boxer shorts are better than skintight briefs.

Women should have a Pap smear every 6 to 12 months because herpes may be associated with an increased risk of cervical cancer. If you become pregnant, be sure to let your obstetrician know you have herpes. If you get an outbreak close to delivery time, you may need a cesarean section to avoid infecting your child. Males with herpes may be at greater risk for prostatic, penile, and testicular cancer.

Getting Help

Where to Go

If you are concerned about sexually transmitted diseases and want more information or advice, a variety of resources, hot lines, and support groups are listed in the appendix, pages 651–653. In seeking help, you will find that many medical practitioners are understanding and will respect your need for confidentiality. Just to be on the safe side, however, be sure to ask the physician his or her position on confidentiality before you discuss your particular problem. This precaution is especially important if you are a minor because, although most states permit you to consent to medical treatment without parental permission, some states do have age or other limitations. Also, some physicians have problems in dealing with sexually active minors, and may take a parental attitude toward a young person, and regardless of the law, may feel they have an obligation to inform the parents.

You should check on your rights to medical treatment and confidentiality in the state in which you live. Health clinics or Planned Parenthood may be preferable to a private physician for a young person. If your physician is judgmental or threatening, or does not answer your questions, find another doctor you can trust and respect. It is important to remember your rights as a patient. Ask direct questions about the purposes of tests, procedures, and follow-up. If you are nervous, write down your questions beforehand and write down the answers as you get them. You may find it helpful to take a friend along.

Although most STDs can be cured, you can easily be reinfected because the body does not develop an immunity to these infectious organisms. Be sure to ask for full information on ways to protect yourself against subsequent reinfection.

What to Expect

The diagnosis and treatment of sexually related and transmitted diseases is a specialized area of medicine. STD or VD clinics are a good place to go when you need help. If you prefer going to a private physician, look for a dermatologist, urologist, or ob/gyn physician who frequently treats STDs. In both situations, you can expect confidential handling of all information about your condition. A physician, nurse, or other intake person will start by asking you for pertinent personal information, a brief medical history, and whatever information you can give on symptoms and development of the infection.

Most clinics provide same-day service, so you usually don't have to wait too long for the outcome of the test(s). If the test results are positive, you will be given a full explanation of the infection and told how it can be treated. The medication will be explained, including how and when to take it and possible side effects. You may be advised to avoid alcohol while under treatment because it can interfere with specific medications. You should also get information and arrange for follow-up visits and retests to make sure the treatment is successful. Advice about precautions to take with a sexual partner while you are under treatment is also important.

If you get a positive result back on your STD test, the next step is sharing this important information with your partner(s). STDs don't cure themselves. If you need treatment, your partner also needs it. Sexuality carries with it a responsibility of caring for your own health and for the health of your sexual partner(s). If you find out that you have an STD, be honest with your partner(s). It can be very embarrassing and awkward to say to one you like or love deeply, "I've got gonorrhea, herpes, venereal warts, or whatever. I know because I got tested. Now you have to be tested and we both may need treatment." Be sure to tell your partner(s) to pass this information along to any other partners he or she has had recently, so they can get tested. Try to avoid the trap of finding a scapegoat and blaming someone, either yourself or your partner. Remember, some sexual diseases can result from a spontaneous infection, and may not be due to "cheating" or "playing around." Your partner, or you, may have picked up an infection months or years ago and only find it out because symptoms suddenly show up. If you are in a new relationship, your partner may not even suspect he or she picked up an asymptomatic infection in a past relationship. Give yourself and your partner the benefit of the doubt and do not become accusatory.

There is an alternative to telling your partner directly, which is worth considering. A physician who is experienced with STDs and the staff at a STD clinic can be very helpful. After talking it over, you may decide to have a disease intervention specialist at the clinic or the Department of Health help you. A disease intervention specialist can inform your contact(s) if providing this information directly by you could create serious emotional, legal, or relationship problems. Because of his or her training and experience in counseling, the specialist may be able to locate or convince a partner to seek medical treatment which you might not be able to do. Also, the specialist will be certain to give all the important information accurately and make sure your partner(s) really understand the situation, are tested, and follow through on treatment if needed.

The long-term risks of an untreated STD far outweigh any possible embarrassment you might have in telling your partner(s) about their risk and need for testing. Even if it was a casual sexual encounter, your partner deserves to be told right away about a possible infection he or she may have. Having an STD, like experiencing an unplanned pregnancy, is a couple problem. It should not be handled as if it only affects you. Remember the implications of Figure 12.1. Accepting responsibility for your sexual partner's health and being honest even when it is difficult and embarrassing will help reduce the incidence of sexually related diseases.

A Look to the Future

Although no one has a clear picture of the future, we can suggest some interesting insights about the future of STDs by asking a few key questions.

Why do you think we might be more or less effective in dealing with the STD epidemic in the years ahead? What impact will AIDS have on our willingness to talk about and deal with other STDs? To what extent do you think our elementary and high schools might start dealing with STD education? What effect do you think the fear of STDs and AIDS will put on our dating, premarital, and extramarital relations? What message about social attitudes versus medical facts are conveyed by the cartoon of the singles bar on page 363? Why might this message change in the near future? To what extent might parents, religious groups, and others who have traditionally opposed sex education in the schools because they disapprove of premarital sex, begin to admit and recognize an increase of sexual activity of teenagers and the need for more education? Will the conservative message of sexual abstinence be accepted by more people because of the fear of AIDS and other STDs?

In the next 10 years, medical research may give us simple, accurate, inexpensive monoclonal antibody tests and DNA probes to replace many of our current STD tests. Research may also give us vaccines for herpes and other STDs, although experts say a vaccine for gonorrhea is unlikely because of the nature of the organism. Could new vaccines allow sexually active persons to reduce their STD risk to near zero? With the age of first sexual intercourse coming earlier and earlier, we may see the day, in the not too distant future, when children in elementary school will be required to have STD vaccinations along with the standard measles, smallpox, and polio vaccinations we now require. But all these changes would require a major adjustment in our social consciousness, attitudes, and values. You might want to consider what this shift would mean for yourself and society in general. Would you agree to having your child vaccinated against certain sexual diseases as a condition for attending kindergarten?

Key Concepts

1. Infections produced by bacteria, viruses, parasites, and yeasts can be transmitted by sexual intimacy or triggered by stress, hypertension, antibiotics, diabetes, the contraceptive pill, and other medications. The same infection may be classified as a sexually transmitted disease (STD) or as a sexually related disease (SRD), depending on its origins.
2. The risk of contracting an STD from an infected person varies and depends on many factors, including the recipient's state of health, his or her possible

resistance or immunity to the bacteria or virus, and the type of sexual activity involved.

3. STDs are a problem for sexually active men and women, regardless of their social class or sexual orientation, although lesbian couples run less risk of infection than persons in heterosexual or gay male relationships.

4. Any suspicion or symptoms of an STD should be confirmed as soon as possible by the appropriate test performed by a physician or at a VD/STD clinic.

5. STD and SRD infections can occur in any of the genital organs, in the rectum or anus, mouth or throat. When an infection is suspected and the person has engaged in oral or anal sex, these sites should also be checked for possible infections.

6. When a person suspects an STD or tests positive, he or she should have no further sexual contact involving the infected area(s) until the infection is definitely cured or under control.

7. However embarrassing it may be to have an STD, it is very important that the infected person immediately inform his or her sexual partner(s) of their risk and urge them to have tests performed as soon as possible in case they are infected. A disease intervention specialist may help with advice or do the actual informing.

Key Terms

asymptomatic (328)
candidiasis (340)
carrier (328)
chancre (339)
Chlamydia (335)
genital herpes (345)
gonorrhea (338)
Hemophilus (338)
hepatitis B (345)

nongonococcal urethritis (NGU) (337)
PPNG (339)
pubic lice (341)
scabies (342)
sexually transmitted disease (STD) (328)
Silent Epidemic (328)
syphilis (339)
Trichomonas (343)
venereal warts (344)

Summary Questions

1. What is meant by the Silent Epidemic?

2. List and discuss some of the reasons for the increasing incidence of STDs.

3. How may use of the Pill or antibiotic treatment be related to the incidence of a sexual disease?

4. What are some common warning symptoms for STDs?

5. List and discuss briefly some safer sex practices which reduce the risk of contracting an STD.

Common Symptoms of Sexually Transmitted Diseases

There are some common warning signs that indicate the possibility of a sexually transmitted infection. Any tenderness or irritation in the genitals, genital sores or blisters, or an unusual discharge from the urethra or vagina should be checked by a physician who is familiar with diagnosing and treating STDs. A variety of these common symptoms of STDs are shown here. Remember, STDs are common, easily treated, and often easily cured.

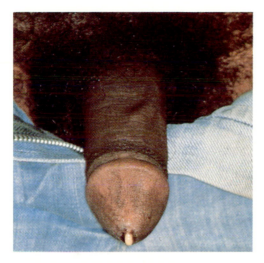

(A) A thick, creamy discharge from this penile urethra indicates a gonorrhea infection.

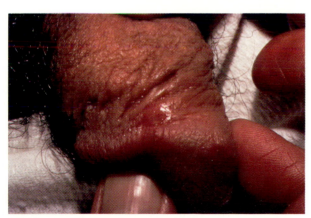

(B) The open sore or chancre on this foreskin indicates the primary stage of syphilis.

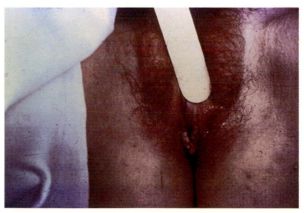

(C) A primary chancre on the right labia indicates a syphilis infection. A cluster of venereal warts appear below the chancre.

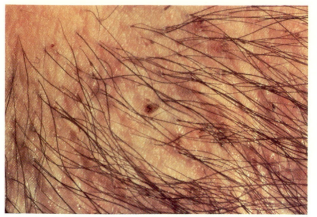

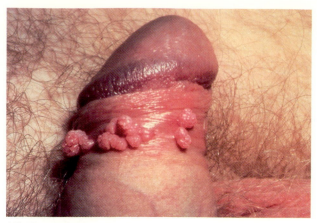

(D) *Intense itching can result from the pinhead bites of pubic lice that enjoy the shelter of pubic hairs where they lay eggs. Secondary infections and small open sores are common consequences of scratching.*

(E) *Venereal warts on a penis.*

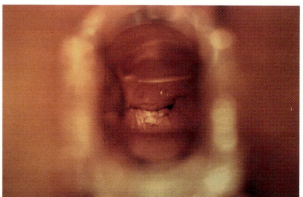

(F) *Women often have internal venereal warts—as this woman does on her vaginal wall near the cervix—without realizing they have this virus.*

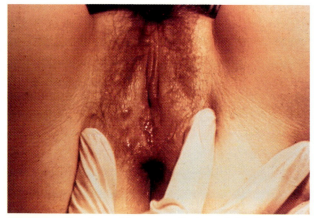

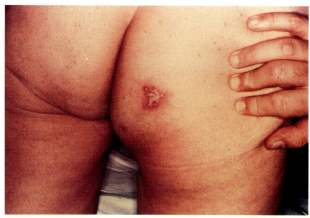

(G) *Crater-like ulcers of herpes on the inner labia during the infectious stage.*

(H) *A cluster of herpes blisters on the buttock.*

Suggested Readings

Hamilton, R. (1988). *The Herpes Book.* Boston: Houghton Mifflin.

Kilby, D. (1986). *Manual of Safe Sex.* Philadelphia: B. C. Decker. Distributed by C. V. Mosby. The many color photographs make this small book especially valuable.

Lumiere, R., & S. Cook. (1983). *Healthy Sex and Keeping It That Way: A Complete Guide to Sexual Infections.* New York: Simon & Schuster.

Rosebury, T. (1973). *Microbes and Morals: The Strange Story of Venereal Disease.* New York: Ballantine Books. A classic, readable history of sexual diseases before the advent of AIDS.

Warren, T. G., & R. Warren. (1985). *The Updated Herpes Handbook.* Portland, OR: Portland Press.

YOU CAN'T LIVE ON HOPE.

You hope this guy is finally the right guy.

You hope this time she just might be the one.

And you both hope the other one is not infected with the AIDS virus. So, what should you do?

Of course you could ask. But your partner might not know. That's because it's possible to carry the AIDS virus for many years without showing any symptoms.

The only way to prevent getting infected is to protect yourself. Start using condoms. Every time.

AIDS Ask him to use them. If he says no, so can you.

If you think you can't get it, you're dead wrong.

NEW YORK CITY DEPARTMENT OF HEALTH. FOR MORE INFORMATION CALL: **1 (718) 485-8111**

Plagues, Past
  and Present
HIV and What It Does
  The Viruses That
    Cause AIDS
  How HIV Is Spread
  HIV and the Immune
    System
  The Consequences
Testing for HIV
  Two Tests
  When Should You
    Be Tested?
High Risk Behaviors
  and Risk Reduction
  Risky Behaviors
  HIV Prevention and
    Risk Reduction
Personal and Social
  Issues
  Educating the Young
  Public Health Issues
  Who Pays?
  The Global Consequences
What You Can Do
  to Help

Chapter 13

AIDS: Health and Social Issues

Special Consultants

Roger Cooper, M.D., medical training officer, Centers for Disease Control, and director, STD/AIDS Clinic, St. Michael's Hospital, Newark, New Jersey.

Norman A. Scherzer, Ph.D., professor, Department of Biological Sciences and Allied Health, Essex County College, and visiting professor, Department of Biology, Rutgers, The State University of New Jersey (Newark).

William Yarber, H.S.D., professor, Department of Applied Health Science, Indiana University, Bloomington, Indiana, and author of *AIDS: What Young Adults Should Know* (1987).

In 1980 no one had even heard of a disease called **acquired immune deficiency syndrome**, or **AIDS**. Within a few years, AIDS became a major public health issue around the world. Today, AIDS threatens everyone, including newborn infants, with its devastation and death.

Comparisons are made between AIDS and plagues like the Black Death that several times swept across Europe, at times killing two-thirds to three-quarters of the people. But there are some important differences between the plagues and epidemics of the past and the current AIDS epidemic. The human race will always have diseases and occasional epidemics. However, today, we know how the human immunodeficiency virus (HIV) spreads. We know what behaviors carry a high risk of contracting the HIV virus. We can diagnose the infection early on and reduce the risk of opportunistic infections with antibiotics and other medicines.

AIDS will continue to be a problem for the foreseeable future because of the hundreds of thousands of people already infected around the world. But it is a disease that can be prevented by changing our behaviors. This is an option people in past epidemics did not have.

This chapter puts the AIDS epidemic in perspective. It reviews what we know about the disease and the behavior changes essential to avoid it. Problems of increasing violence against gays, mandatory testing, and the needs and rights of persons with HIV are also examined.

Plagues, Past and Present

Although we know modern medicine is capable of "miracles," disease and epidemics are an unavoidable part of the human experience. The Middle Ages began and ended with massive plagues. People were completely helpless during the reign of Justinian the Great (527–565) when bubonic plague, the Black Death, spread from Asia across Europe, killing one-half the people in those areas. In panic, people sealed up houses where inhabitants were dying. Because no one knew about bacteria or that bacteria could be spread by rats and fleas, the panic of people only helped spread the disease. When a person was discovered dying with the plague, neighbors often fled, taking with them infected fleas in their clothes and possessions. Houses where persons had died of the plague were often burned, causing the resident rats to escape to new areas where their fleas spread the disease.

In the 1300s the Black Death again spread across the Western world, killing over 25 million people in less than five years. Terrified citizens blamed Jews and other minorities for the disease and massacred them. In the next 200 years, occasional outbreaks of the bubonic plague wiped out whole villages and cities in a matter of weeks. In the 1600s the Great Plague of London decimated that city, again in a few weeks.

In 1793 a yellow fever epidemic turned Philadelphia into a ghost town. Cholera devastated London in 1849 and again in 1853. Cholera was a problem for the armies of both the North and the South during the American Civil War. Typhus and dysentery helped defeat Napoleon's army in Russia, and again devastated Russia after the 1917 revolution.

In 1918 a new strain of the influenza virus swept around the world. One billion people were infected, over 25 million died, half a million in the United States. In two or three days, a person could die of the flu. The dead could not

Figure 13.1. *Thousands of men and women who have died of AIDS are remembered in the ever-growing AIDS Memorial Quilt displayed here in front of the White House in October 1988.*

be buried fast enough. People had to seal the bodies of their dead relatives in coffins before the undertaker would take them to the cemetery.

Epidemics and plagues make headlines, but other less sensational diseases regularly kill millions. Every year, over 200 million people are infected, and a million die of malaria. In the history of the human race, more people have died of malaria than from any other cause. Millions die of dysentery every year.

Every epidemic has triggered rational and irrational fears and attempts to find scapegoats who can be blamed for the new threat. In the case of AIDS, people's fears have led to violence against homosexuals and to threats of quarantining any person infected with HIV. In facing the lethal threat of AIDS, it is important to keep this devastating disease and our fears in perspective.

In past epidemics, infected persons showed warning symptoms very quickly. Persons with HIV may show no symptoms for years, even though they can pass on the infection. Past epidemics killed very quickly. HIV may take years to kill. Modern medicine has been able to develop vaccines for the bacteria and viruses behind past epidemics. There is only a very slim chance of developing a vaccine for HIV. Yet we can reasonably hope for some medical breakthroughs to prevent the opportunistic infections that kill persons with AIDS and we can reduce the spread of HIV by altering our behavior (Figure 13.1).

HIV and What It Does

The Viruses That Cause AIDS

Viruses cause many common diseases. Some viruses, like those for the common cold, mumps, and sore throats, are merely a passing nuisance. Those that cause polio, influenza (the flu), and AIDS can be lethal. Two viruses have been linked with a variety of symptoms we now describe as AIDS. Because they interfere directly with the body's immune system and its ability to fight off infections, these viruses have been named **human immunodeficiency viruses,** or HIV I and HIV II for short, or simply **HIV** (Monmaney 1988). Much of the discussion you hear about AIDS and the virus that causes it is not precise. We use the terms AIDS and acquired immune deficiency syndrome only to refer to the set of symptoms defined by the Centers for Disease Control (CDC) which mark the terminal stage of this infection. HIV, HIV I, HIV II, or simply, the virus, will be used to refer to the infective virus. This distinction may seem minor, but it is important. In testing for AIDS we are actually testing for the presence of antibodies to the HIV virus. When we talk about getting AIDS from anal sex or some other behavior with an infected person, we are actually talking about the risk of becoming infected with the HIV virus.

The viruses that cause AIDS probably evolved first in Central Africa 100 or more years ago. HIV may have mutated from a much older virus, SIV, which causes similar symptoms in monkeys in the same region. The disease spread along trade routes, often wiping out entire villages. Some time in the 1970s, the virus reached Haiti in the Caribbean. From there, it spread into the United States around 1977 or 1978. The first American cases were diagnosed in 1981. In 1982 officials at the Centers for Disease Control identified a handsome blond steward for Air Canada who could be linked with 9 of the first 19 cases of AIDS in Los Angeles, 22 cases in New York City, and 9 more cases in 8 other cities. Gaetan Dugas traveled widely and had an estimated 250 sexual partners a year. He continued the same behavior until he died in March 1984, even after developing Kaposi's sarcoma in June 1980 and being warned he was endangering his sexual partners. If this man had not been Patient Zero, the disease would still have spread around the world, perhaps slower than it did, but with the ease of air travel just as inevitably (Shilts 1987).

Like all viruses, HIV I and HIV II are very primitive life-forms and can only exist as parasites inside a living host cell (Figure 13.2).

1. In its *particle stage*, HIV has a core of nucleic acids, RNA. This short chain of hereditary information is surrounded by four protein coats. The protein coats protect the very delicate hereditary information when the virus particle passes from one person to another. They also help the virus particle get into a host cell.

2. Once inside a host cell, the virus enters its *reproductive stage*. Its protein coats dissolve. An enzyme known as reverse transcriptase uses the RNA as a template to make viral DNA inside the host cell.

3. In the *provirus stage*, the viral DNA is spliced into the DNA of the host cell. When the segment of the host cell chromosome containing the viral DNA is activated, new viral RNA and viral proteins are produced. The new viral RNA is wrapped in protective protein coats and released to infect other cells. But unused fragments of the protein coats not used in making whole new viruses also play a role in the disease.

How the Virus Is Spread

HIV is not easy to catch. It is not spread like the cold and flu viruses, by sneezing, coughing, sharing dishes or eating utensils, or by being around a person with AIDS even if that contact is daily family living. People can work with, use public toilet seats and swimming pools, eat at restaurants, and attend public affairs with persons who have the HIV virus, or have ARC or AIDS with no risk of getting the virus. You cannot get HIV from hugging a loved one with AIDS or shaking the hand of a person with AIDS. HIV is not spread by mosquitoes or flies. Although the HIV virus has been found in human tears and saliva, it has not been found in high enough concentrations to be transmitted through these fluids.

Health workers, morticians, emergency squad workers, police, and fire fighters are more at risk for hepatitis and spinal meningitis than they are for con-

(a)

(b)
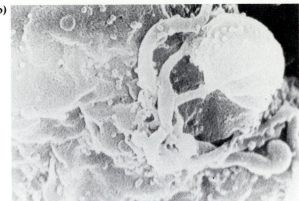

(c)
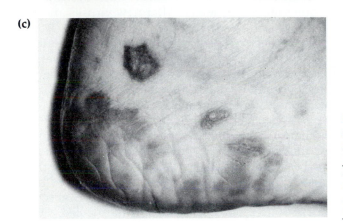

Figure 13.2. The HIV Virus and Its Consequences. *Scanning electron micrographs show (a) a population of white blood cells infected with HIV and (b) an HIV virus budding from the surface membrane of a T-4 lymphocyte (white blood cell). The skin ulcers of Karposi's sarcoma on the heel and foot are shown in (c).*

tracting HIV in their routine work. There are standard precautions we should all follow when assisting or working with possibly infectious persons in situations where we might be exposed to blood and body fluids. Remember, HIV is hard to transmit.

- *Sexual contact*: HIV is transmitted by anal and vaginal intercourse and by oral sex with an infected partner. The virus is passed by infected semen, vaginal secretions, and blood. As of mid-1988, less than half of the physicians doing artificial insemination tested donor semen for HIV. Because only a quarter of the doctors reported testing donated semen for gonorrhea, hepatitis, and chlamydial infection in mid-1988, some states now mandate such testing.

- *Exchange of blood*: Blood-to-blood contact between an infected person and someone else is the second most common way HIV is transmitted. Sharing contaminated IV needles and syringes used with illegal drugs is an obvious risk.

  Early in the AIDS epidemic, some hemophiliacs and patients needing blood transfusions were inadvertently given HIV-contaminated blood. Since March 1985, all blood supplies are carefully screened for the virus. Organs donated for organ transplant are also tested. Today, chances of contracting HIV from a blood transfusion are about 1 in 25,000. The blood-clotting factor given hemophiliacs is now given a special treatment that kills the virus. You cannot get the virus from donating blood because only sterile needles and equipment are used to draw the blood.

- *From mother to newborn infant*: Only about 1.5% of the AIDS cases in the United States are infants, but the actual number of children born with HIV may be three to five times higher. An HIV-infected mother has a 40% to 50% chance of passing the virus to her fetus in the womb, during birth, or during breast feeding. Infants born with HIV are most common in low-income inner city areas (Levine 1988).

HIV and the Immune System

The main target of HIV is a type of white blood cell known as the T_4 lymphocyte. Normally, T_4 cells multiply quickly and in large numbers when the body is challenged by an infection. They then help launch an attack which destroys the invading bacteria, viruses, or other microorganisms. After new viruses are produced in the T_4 host cell, they break out, destroying the T_4 lymphocyte. At the same time, fragments of the viral protein coat are also released. These proteins stick to specific membrane receptors on the surface of other T_4 cells, setting them up for destruction by antibodies. This direct and indirect destruction of T_4 lymphocytes weakens the body's immune defense system, leaving the person with little defense against infections and certain cancers (Figure 13.3).

Our immune system has two divisions, a cell-mediated response and a humoral response. In the cell-mediated response, T_4 helper cells regulate all other T lymphocytes which produce chemicals that help in the destruction of infected cells whose membranes have been altered by the entry of the virus. In the humoral response, T_4 helper cells promote antibody production by B lymphocytes. Antibodies circulate in the blood and other body fluids but cannot get into the infected cells. They destroy free viral particles outside the cell. Often when antibodies destroy microorganisms, they also inadvertently damage the host cell as well. To minimize this effect, another type of T cell, the T_8 or suppressor lymphocyte, dampens the immune response. A healthy person has twice as many T_4 cells as T_8 cells. Since HIV attacks only the T_4 cells, it reverses the normal 2-to-1 ratio, reducing the immunity given by the T_4 cells and at the same time increasing the suppression of immunity by the T_8 lymphocytes.

Normally, invading viruses and bacteria, and some cancers, are controlled by this two-part immune system. An immune system that has been weakened by HIV opens up the opportunity for microorganisms to gain a foothold in the body. Hence the term **opportunistic infections**. In AIDS, the main opportunistic infection is a lung infection known as **pneumocystic pneumonia**, technically *Pneumocystis carinii pneumonia* or PCP. Since the immune system also normally controls the growth of certain cancers, a weakened immune system also allows some cancers to develop, particularly a rare cancer of the blood vessels known as **Kaposi's sarcoma** or KS. Evidence indicates that the products of the AIDS virus may directly cause Kaposi's sarcoma by stimulating abnormal blood vessel growth.

Normally, the body's immune system recognizes the foreign protein coat of an invading virus like HIV and quickly builds antibodies to attack it. But the protein coat around HIV is not immediately recognized as a foreign protein, so it may take months to trigger the body's immune system. Even when some antibodies are made, they are not very effective in neutralizing HIV again because the protein coat on HIV does not bind strongly with the antibody. One

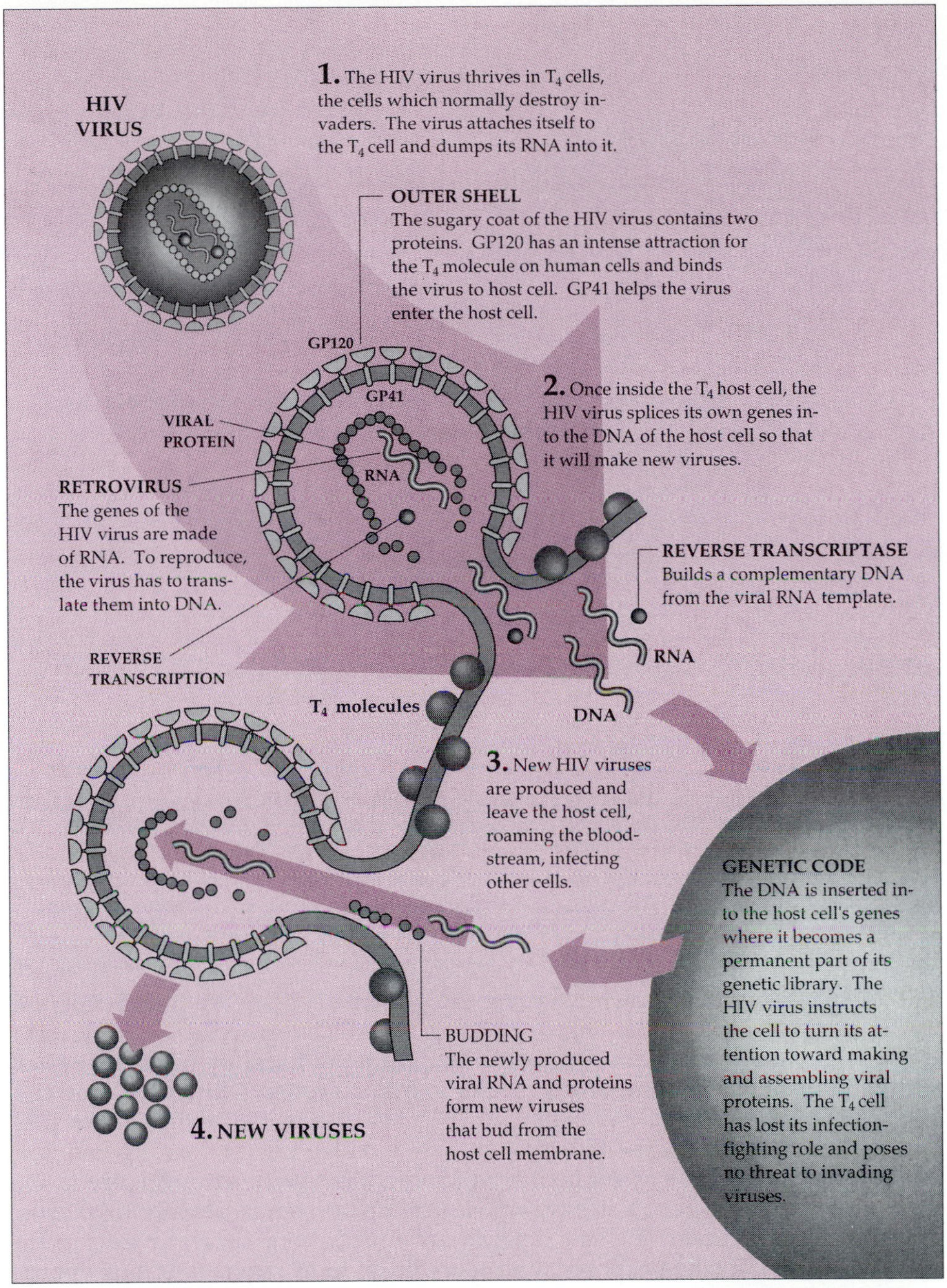

Figure 13.3. How the HIV Virus Operates.

HIV VIRUS

1. The HIV virus thrives in T_4 cells, the cells which normally destroy invaders. The virus attaches itself to the T_4 cell and dumps its RNA into it.

OUTER SHELL
The sugary coat of the HIV virus contains two proteins. GP120 has an intense attraction for the T_4 molecule on human cells and binds the virus to host cell. GP41 helps the virus enter the host cell.

GP120

GP41

VIRAL PROTEIN

2. Once inside the T_4 host cell, the HIV virus splices its own genes into the DNA of the host cell so that it will make new viruses.

RETROVIRUS
The genes of the HIV virus are made of RNA. To reproduce, the virus has to translate them into DNA.

RNA

REVERSE TRANSCRIPTASE
Builds a complementary DNA from the viral RNA template.

REVERSE TRANSCRIPTION

RNA

T_4 molecules

DNA

3. New HIV viruses are produced and leave the host cell, roaming the bloodstream, infecting other cells.

GENETIC CODE
The DNA is inserted into the host cell's genes where it becomes a permanent part of its genetic library. The HIV virus instructs the cell to turn its attention toward making and assembling viral proteins. The T_4 cell has lost its infection-fighting role and poses no threat to invading viruses.

BUDDING
The newly produced viral RNA and proteins form new viruses that bud from the host cell membrane.

4. NEW VIRUSES

reason for this weak reaction is that the genes producing the protein coat mutate very often. By the time antibodies are made, HIV has mutated to a new and slightly different virus with a different protein coat the antibody does not recognize. Recent research indicates that after the initial response to HIV, the immune system does not produce new types of antibodies for the new mutant strains in the same person.

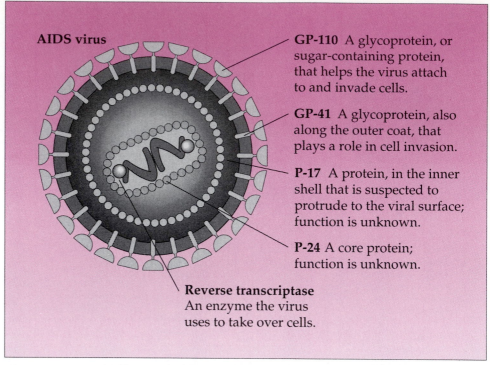

AIDS virus

GP-110 A glycoprotein, or sugar-containing protein, that helps the virus attach to and invade cells.

GP-41 A glycoprotein, also along the outer coat, that plays a role in cell invasion.

P-17 A protein, in the inner shell that is suspected to protrude to the viral surface; function is unknown.

P-24 A core protein; function is unknown.

Reverse transcriptase
An enzyme the virus uses to take over cells.

Figure 13.4. Developing an AIDS Vaccine. *The human immune system normally identifies invading foreign organisms by distinguishing proteins on the surface of the invading bacteria or virus. The immune system then builds antibodies that will recognize and attack the foreign cells before they do much damage. However, the surface proteins in the HIV virus are very similar to normal human proteins. The immune system responds very slowly to the invading HIV cells and does not produce effective antibodies. Scientists hope to build an effective antibody and vaccine by locating parts of the HIV virus that, when injected into the body, will stimulate production of protective antibodies. Scientists are working with various combinations of the four protein subunits shown here to make a vaccine they can test in animals and then humans.*

The frequency with which the protein coat genes mutate is a major problem facing scientists who are trying to develop an effective vaccine. Vaccines are made from whole dead viruses, weakened whole viruses, or from natural or synthetic parts of viruses that trigger the immune system without causing the disease. The difficulty in developing an HIV vaccine is identifying genes that make up a stable part of the HIV protein coat and also trigger a strong immune reaction and production of antibodies which can destroy the virus (Figure 13.4).

As you might suspect, a person whose immune system is already weakened by other factors related to their lifestyle are much more susceptible to being infected with HIV when exposed, and more likely to experience serious opportunistic infections. Poor nutrition and the prevalence of untreated sexually transmitted diseases probably play a major role in the spread of HIV in Africa. Other infections that attack the immune system may make an individual more susceptible to HIV and AIDS. These infections include both types of herpes, hepatitis, the Epstein-Barr virus, and cytomegalovirus.

Drug and alcohol abuse, stress, and poor nutrition definitely make a person more susceptible to HIV and its consequences if they are exposed to it. Alcohol appears to stimulate multiplication of HIV after infection. Use of alcohol, amphetamines (speed), marijuana, and nitrites (poppers) may also weaken the immune system and increase vulnerability to HIV (Yarber 1987:12–13). Although the popular belief is that anyone who gets AIDS will soon die of opportunistic infections, Dr. Larry Siegel, chairman of the AIDS Taskforce of the American Medical Society on Alcoholism and Other Drug Dependencies, and other AIDS experts now suggest that patients with AIDS who do not use alcohol and illegal drugs may have a much better chance of long-term survival (Scott 1988a, 1988b).

The Consequences

Sero-Positive Persons

The fragile, delicate HIV particle cannot live long outside a host body. Proper moisture and temperature are critical to its survival. When a person is exposed to the virus, it often gets into the tissues of the body through a break or open sore in the skin. However, recent research shows that the virus may be able to enter the body even in the absence of a lesion in the skin. Once inside the body's cells, it usually takes three to four months before the level of HIV antibodies can be detected by either the ELISA or Western Blot tests. New, experimental tests may soon give earlier results.

A person who tests **sero-positive** has HIV antibodies, indicating that he or she has been infected and may infect other persons. Such persons have no symptoms other than the antibodies in the blood. Experts suggest that some sero-positive persons may go 15 years or more before showing any signs of the infection.

Persons with AIDS-Related Complex

In addition to having the HIV antibodies, a person with **AIDS-related complex (ARC)**, experiences damage to the immune system which may lead to swollen lymph nodes, night sweats, prolonged diarrhea, unexplained weight loss, weakness, persistent sore throat, and/or mental confusion. There are roughly 5 persons with ARC for every 1 person with the full AIDS condition. Although the CDC is gradually dropping the distinction of ARC, the concept is useful. Some people die while in the ARC category without developing the full-blown symptoms of AIDS. Others, for unknown reasons, have not yet gone on to develop the full symptoms of AIDS despite having had the virus for many years.

Persons with AIDS

Persons who die of AIDS do not die as a direct result of the virus, but as the result of cancers and/or opportunistic infections that appear when the immune system is severely damaged. The four symptoms of this terminal stage are

- Opportunistic infections, including PCP, tuberculosis, candidiasis, toxoplasmosis, herpes zoster, and many other infectious diseases.
- Certain cancers, as listed by the Centers for Disease Control, especially Kaposi's sarcoma.
- Emaciation, or wasting away of the body and its muscles.
- Dementia, a progressive mental deterioration.

HIGHLIGHT BOX 13.1.
WHEN FEAR TAKES CHARGE

He got sick in Dallas, and sought refuge in his native West Virginia. But a small town, he soon learned, is no haven for an AIDS victim.

Steve Forrest can [still] see the faces of the people at the pool that day, their mouths drawn taut and eyes granite-hard and flecked with fear. A cop was there, too, his hands planted on his hips, and a woman screamed, "Why don't they lock him up?" as Forrest [not his real name] walked past the glaring crowd from the locker room to his car, pretending nothing was wrong but inwardly wishing he could hide. By the next day, the newspaper had bannered the story across the front page: "Williamson pool closed after swim by AIDS victim."

By then, he wasn't just Steve any more, the kid who'd gone to West Williamson Elementary School and bagged groceries at Kroger's and played trumpet in the Belfry High School band. He was "the AIDS Victim," and lifelong friends no longer said hello, vandals shot out his car windows and others (he never knew just who, they never gave names) called the newspaper editor and the mayor with rumors that he was licking the fruit at Food City and spitting in the salad bar at Wendy's—so many rumors that even the police chief speculated that Steve was trying to infect people in the town. "I don't know this person," the chief told a newspaper reporter, "but he might be the type who, if he knows he's going, he might want to take some of us with him."

That was Steve Forrest's public humiliation. The familial indignities—a hurtful and confusing blur of averted eyes and unreturned phone calls—were less overt. No one except his father's cats would touch him. And then rumors spread that the cats had AIDS, and no one would touch them either.

Two months [later] Forrest, 26, the first known AIDS case in Williamson, West Virginia, fled to live in a new city.

Source: Reprinted from AIDS: When fear takes charge. *U.S. News & World Report.* 1987 (October 12) p. 63.

A person is classified as having AIDS when he or she is HIV positive and exhibits any of the four symptoms listed. The fatality rate for persons with AIDS is extremely high, with 80% dying within three or four years of an AIDS diagnosis.

Roughly 5% of the persons who test sero-positive will develop the full symptoms of AIDS within 3 years of infection (Highlight Box 13.1). By 5 years, 25% to 30% will have developed AIDS. Estimates are that 65% to 100% of all sero-positive persons will die of AIDS within 25 years after infection. Infants with AIDS live about 9 months to 3 years.

Testing for HIV

Two Tests

The **ELISA test**, used in the initial screening for infection with HIV, detects an antibody to HIV I in the blood. **False negative** results occur when the test is performed before the body's immune system has had time to respond to the virus by producing antibodies in amounts the ELISA test can detect. This window is usually three to four months, but can last up to a year before the antibodies reach a detectable level. A false negative result indicates no HIV infection

Figure 13.5.

when the virus is actually present. A false positive test result indicates there is an infection when in fact HIV is not present. **False positive** results may occur because other infections can produce antibodies that are very similar to the one HIV antibody the ELISA test detects. False positives also result from faulty preparation of the test antigen. Any positive result with the ELISA test should be confirmed with a Western Blot Test (Figure 13.5).

The **Western Blot test** detects several specific antibodies for proteins in the HIV-I structure and is used to confirm positive findings from the mass screening results of the ELISA test which detects only one HIV-I antibody. Second-generation experimental tests are now being developed that will detect the presence of HIV directly by detecting specific stable genes or segments of HIV-I genetic code.

When Should You Be Tested?

Unless you have serious reason to believe you have been exposed to HIV by having vaginal, anal, or oral sex with a person who may be infected, or by sharing needles or syringes, chances are you shouldn't bother getting tested. But if you are involved in such high risk behaviors, a call to the Public Health Service's hot line, 1-800-342-AIDS, will provide a tape recorded message with basic information and a number to call for direct advice. Two nationwide hot lines provide details on testing. The Public Health Service operates a national resource and information service, 1-800-342-7514, 7 days a week, 24 hours a day. A second national AIDS hot line is based at St. Clare's Hospital in New York City. Its number, 1-800-433-2437, is open between 9 A.M. and 8 P.M. (EST) on weekdays and until 4 P.M. on Saturdays. Trained counselors answer all calls to this number. (See the appendix for more resources.)

The counselor will not ask you to give your name or otherwise identify yourself. If the information provided suggests a test may be warranted, the test will be explained. You will be given a code number to protect your anonymity, and an appointment will be made for you to be tested at a health department facility in your area. Procedures differ from state to state. Regulations on confidentiality may also vary.

Private physicians and hospitals also may offer confidential testing, with fees usually running between $35 and $100. In some areas, not all physicians can provide HIV testing because local regulations require physicians and labs to be certified for HIV testing. When a test comes back sero-positive, the physician or clinic should provide counseling. Putting the sero-positive person in touch with a support group helps in coping with the emotional shock.

Early detection of an HIV infection allows early treatment with the drug AZT, which has been clearly shown to prolong the life of HIV-positive persons (Figure 13.6).

High Risk Behaviors and Risk Reduction

The risk of contracting HIV depends on several factors, some of which we have already mentioned. The two most important considerations are the partner or partners you have sex with and the kinds of sexual behavior you engage in. If you are not involved in vaginal, anal, or oral sex with a person at risk and not sharing needles or syringes, there is no risk of contracting HIV. Working or living with a person with HIV or AIDS does not pose a risk, unless you engage in high risk behaviors with that person.

Risky Behaviors

In 1988 63% of all AIDS cases were homosexual and bisexual men who contracted the HIV virus by engaging in high risk behaviors with an infected partner. Heterosexual intravenous drug users accounted for 19% of HIV-positive persons. Seven percent were male homosexual and bisexual IV drug users. Four percent of AIDS patients contracted the virus by engaging in high risk behaviors in a heterosexual relationship. Twenty-nine percent of the women with AIDS contracted HIV through heterosexual intercourse. Close to 60% of the women who contracted HIV through heterosexual intercourse are black or Hispanic (Hatcher et al. 1988:2).

The odds are not equal for all persons who engage in risky behaviors. Some studies suggest that uncircumcised males are four times more likely than circumcised males to become infected with HIV after exposure. Women are more likely to become infected from vaginal intercourse with an infected male than a male is to be infected by intercourse with an infected female partner. Having intercourse many times with an infected partner logically increases the risk of being infected. But in one study, a women was infected after having unprotected sex with her sero-positive husband only once; other women did not pick up the virus despite having unprotected sexual intercourse with an infected partner over 100 times.

Women and men with genital lesions caused by herpes and syphilis are more at risk of contracting the HIV virus than others if they engage in high risk behaviors. Other sexually transmitted diseases may affect the immune system

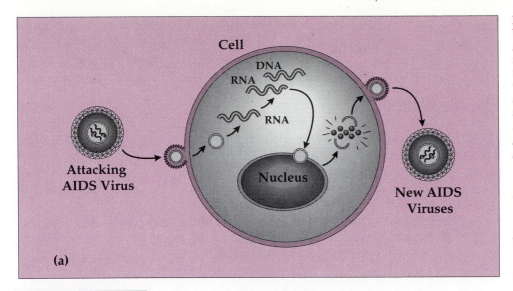

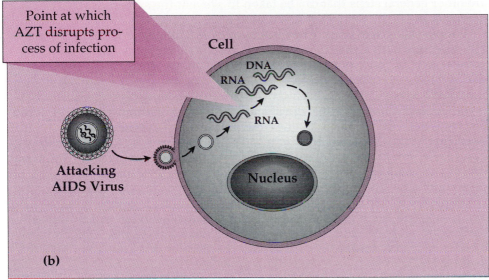

Figure 13.6. How AZT Works to Stop the AIDS Virus. *(a) Normally, when an HIV virus attacks a cell, the virus uses an enzyme known as reverse transcriptase to translate its RNA code into a DNA genetic code. This DNA genetic material then enters the nucleus of the cell and diverts the cell's genetic machinery to produce new viral particles. The new viruses bud from the surface of the infected cell and move to other cells where they repeat and expand the cycle of infections. The infected cells are usually killed as the new viral buds break out. (b) AZT prevents the enzyme reverse transcriptase from translating the HIV viral RNA code into a DNA genetic code.*

and thereby reduce the resistance to an HIV infection. Another important fact to remember is that the use of alcohol and illegal drugs both interfere with the immune system. A weakened immune system appears to increase the chances a person will become infected with HIV if exposed to it, and the chances of the sero-positive person getting opportunistic diseases that cause an early death (Scott 1988a, 1988b).

HIV Prevention and Risk Reduction

Even though the fragile nature of HIV makes it difficult to transmit, some sexual behaviors are totally safe whereas others present some risk, or a very high risk. There are two factors to consider in talking about HIV prevention and risk reduction: sexual behaviors and partners who present an infection risk. A popular term for this prevention and risk reduction is **safer sex**. *HIV prevention* means

- Abstaining from any sexual activity that could result in exposure to blood or body fluids that might contain HIV.

Risk reduction means

- Practicing complete and mutual monogamy, limiting one's vaginal, oral, and anal sexual relations to one uninfected partner.
- Using latex condoms for all vaginal, oral, and anal intercourse unless both partners are monogamous, non-IV drug users, and known to be free of the virus.
- Using latex condoms coated with nonoxynol-9 spermicide, or a nonoxynol-9 vaginal foam for all vaginal and anal intercourse unless both partners are monogamous and known to be free of the virus (Figure 13.7).

Not sharing unsterile needles and syringes and testing women before pregnancy are other general steps that can be taken to prevent the spread of HIV (Hatcher et al. 1988:4–5).

Simple changes in your sexual behavior can significantly reduce your risk of HIV infection with a partner you are not absolutely certain is not at risk. When you are not celibate or in a completely monogamous relationship, the primary risk reduction practice is the use of a latex condom and a spermicidal foam containing nonoxynol-9. Using a condom is recommended in any sexual activity involving exposure to seminal or vaginal fluids with a partner whose past sexual history is not totally known. In one study, none of the spouses of AIDS patients practicing sexual abstinence became sero-positive. In couples that used condoms, 17% sero-converted. These couples reported condom breakage, improper use of the condom, and fellatio without a condom. In couples who used no protection, 82% later tested sero-positive for the virus (Fischl et al. 1987).

Some sexual behaviors like hugging, masturbation, full body massage, and dry kissing are completely safe even with a partner who has AIDS. Other behaviors are probably safe, although they may have a small risk. Certain behaviors are high risk unless you are certain the partner does not have HIV (McIlvenna 1987).

Completely Safe Sexual Practices

Sexual fantasies

Flirting

Erotic bathing together

Watching sex movies and videos

Masturbation without contacting the semen or vaginal secretions of the partner

Sharing erotic books and magazines

Sex talk in person or on the telephone

Reading aloud or listening to erotic books or magazines with a partner

Acting out sexual fantasies like voyeurism, exhibitionism, and bondage and dominance

Figure 13.7.

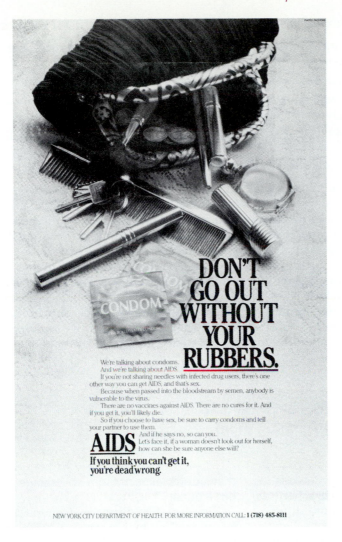

Hugging

Social kissing (dry)

Body massage

Low Risk If Partner Has HIV

French (deep) kissing

Fellatio without ejaculation—safer with a condom

Oral-vaginal sex—safer with a latex barrier or female condom

Vaginal intercourse with a condom—safer with condom and nonoxynol-9 spermicide

Contact with urine on unbroken skin

Anal intercourse with a condom and adequate lubrication—a double condom and withdrawal before ejaculation greatly reduces the risk

Risky Sexual Behaviors Clearly Linked with HIV Transmission

Vaginal intercourse without a condom; unprotected intercourse during menstruation is even riskier

Anal intercourse without a condom and adequate lubrication

Taking semen in the mouth, or swallowing it (not yet documented, but strongly suspected)

Unprotected oral-anal contact (analingus) (See Highlight Box 13.2)

What To Do If the Condom Breaks

Condoms and spermicidal foams can be used both for contraceptive purposes and to reduce the risk of becoming infected with HIV. If the condom breaks during vaginal intercourse, you have to make a quick judgment whether, in that situation and relationship, you are more concerned about the risk of an unwanted pregnancy or about the risk of possible exposure to an HIV infection. If you decide an unwanted pregnancy is the greater risk, then a second application of contraceptive foam should be used. If you decide the risk of exposure to HIV might be greater than an unwanted pregnancy—which, if it occurs, could be resolved by an early abortion—then immediately douching with a mild vinegar solution (2 tablespoons of white vinegar in 1 quart of warm water) will help flush most of the possibly infected semen from the vagina and reduce the

---

HIGHLIGHT BOX 13.2.
CONFLICTING PUBLIC POLICIES

The ambivalence of public policy in dealing with AIDS was highlighted in 1988 when two major federal officials adopted quite different approaches to AIDS prevention.

Secretary of Education William J. Bennett argued for a policy of sexual restraint. Children, he believes, should not be told about AIDS and its risks until at least the eighth grade or later. His booklet, *AIDS and the Education of Our Children: A Guide for Parents and Teachers*, talks a lot about sexual abstinence. One page, out of 28 pages, deals with safer sex practices, mentioning only condoms and not spermicides. His message about condoms emphasizes that "many people" object to condoms for moral or religious reasons. Two studies are referred to, out of context, to emphasize that condoms have an "extraordinarily high" failure rate. The concluding paragraph stresses that advising teenagers to use condoms "can suggest to teenagers

that adults expect them to engage in sexual intercourse."

In early 1988 Surgeon General C. Everett Koop mailed his report on AIDS to every household in the United States. Koop argued that AIDS education should begin "at the lowest grade possible," probably in the third grade. The surgeon general's report emphasizes sexually exclusive monogamy and abstinence. For those who do not find these practical, the surgeon general is quite explicit about safer sex practices and use of condoms. Koop's report contains a number of pictures and drawings that make very clear what he is talking about. His recommendations for safer oral, vaginal, and anal sex are brief and to the point. Masturbation and other noncoital erotic pleasures are mentioned as alternatives.

Which approach do you believe is more effective?

risk of infection through the vaginal mucosa. Since douching after intercourse may help some semen through the cervix, it is not recommended when the prime concern is avoiding conception. An application of a spermicide containing nonoxynol-9 is recommended after douching.

Knowing Your Partner

Much of the educational material on HIV stresses knowing your partner. Articles in popular magazines give detailed advice on how to raise the issue of HIV with a new sexual partner, and how to probe his or her past sexual and drug history (Nelson 1987). Although establishing communication and getting to know your partner is essential in any relationship, communication *alone* cannot be depended on for protection from contracting HIV.

The desire to make a good impression on a potential sexual partner leads many to lie about their sexual past and/or drug use. Effectively asking direct questions may not produce honest answers. Yet the majority of sexually active women admit they rely heavily on this approach to assess their risk. If there is any doubt whatsoever about the partner's possible exposure to the disease, a condom and spermicide should be used every time.

In one study, 35% of the men admitted they had lied to a woman in order to have sex with her. One in 5 men would lie if asked about having had a HIV test, telling the woman they had tested negative when they had never been tested. Two out of 3 men at higher risk for HIV said condoms were unnecessary because they relied on the woman to use a contraceptive. The risk women run in relying on what men say is probably much higher than the admissions of men suggest because 60% of the women said they believed a man had lied to them (Mays & Cochran cited by Goleman 1988a). Officials at the Centers for Disease Control agree that relying on what a potential sexual partner says about his or her sexual and drug past is impractical and dangerous.

In talking about avoiding risky sexual behaviors, the emphasis must be on a *comprehensive plan of risk reducing behaviors,* and not on avoiding just one high risk behavior. Take the case of 19 middle-class educated women who knew the risk of multiple partners and so limited themselves to one sexual partner at a time and averaged 2.5 partners over a three-year period. These 19 women avoided sexual relations with IV drug users and bisexuals. Yet 11 of the 19 women tested positive for HIV. The 19 women had all had sex with the same man, a civil engineer who probably contracted the HIV virus while working in Africa. "Emphasizing only sexual relations with multiple partners as a risk factor for women may be irrelevant and even counterproductive since it implies that the absence of multiple partners makes women safe" (Clumeck et al. 1989). To reduce your risk for HIV infection, you must know your partner(s) and avoid risky behaviors all the time in all relationships.

The Knowledge-Behavior Gap

Despite the many efforts to inform the public about the risk of HIV and ways of reducing those risks, many people continue to flirt with HIV infection. Typical of the gap between what people know about the risk of HIV and what they actually do or do not do to reduce their risks is shown in a 1988 survey of 500 heterosexual women, ages 20 through 45. About half of the women were married or living with someone and half were single. They were not typical of American women in general, but their views highlight a problem (Avery 1988).

Single Women

- The 50 single women who were dating more than one man were the least concerned and least likely to follow preventive or risk reducing practices. As a whole these women had an average of 1.7 sexual partners in the past year. One-quarter of these women did not postpone having sexual intercourse, and only half waited until they knew the man well. "It appears that many of these women have unrealistic notions about their invulnerability. They are rationalizing risky behavior."

- 85% of all the single women admitted being worried about HIV or AIDS, but only 38% said they usually bring up the subject with a date.

- 88% of all the single women thought condoms were effective against HIV. Only 37% of the women bought and carried condoms. Knowing how reluctant many men are to use condoms, 53% of the single women still relied on their dates to be prepared with condoms.

- Four of 10 single women said they would have sexual intercourse even if they or their partner did not have a condom. Women who carried a condom would still have intercourse without it, if the man resisted.

- Almost one-fifth of the women reported having had anal sex, but 45% said they now avoid it because of fear of HIV and AIDS. That means 1 in 10 single women was still having unprotected anal sex.

Married Women

- The women who had been married more than 10 years were not worried about HIV or AIDS. This lack of concern is realistic only if the wife and her husband have not had extramarital sex. Yet 13% of the wives said they knew their husbands had been unfaithful. And that is far below the standard estimates of 50% to 70% infidelity for married men. Not to mention that 20% of the wives or living-together women in this survey admitted they had had outside sex. Another 20% probably had had extramarital sex and didn't admit it.

- In the Kinsey survey in 1948, 46% of the men surveyed had had sexual relations with both women and men. Husbands who are closet bisexuals are not uncommon in today's society. Gay men frequently report that many of the men who show up in gay bars are married men whose wives have no idea their spouses are bisexual.

- Seven out of 10 married women said they would insist their partner be tested if they knew he had had an affair. Half would insist he use a condom. But only 4 of 10 women would tell their partner if they had an affair, leaving him unaware of any risk for him.

Yet two-thirds of the women in this survey believed there will be a major AIDS epidemic among heterosexuals, and 1 in 5 already knew someone with AIDS or ARC. How do we explain this gap between what men and women know, and their reluctance, or failure to protect themselves? *The real risk of HIV lies in denying any risk exists.* This denial has much more to do with people's attitudes than with their knowledge. A person may be knowledgeable about the risk of HIV infections and the need for safer sex practices, but then continue to engage in risky behaviors because of erotophobic attitudes and an uncomfortableness in dealing with the realities of homosexuality, bisexuality, and IV drug use in their own social group.

Cultural attitudes also play a major role in the ways women react to the threat of HIV. Among Latin Americans, the strong negative image of homosexuality causes most bisexual husbands to hide this fact from their wives. Also, the gender roles endorsed by the Latin cultures see the male as innately superior to the female.

> This encourages female dependence and women deferring to men in decisions related to sexual practices. Furthermore, communications between men and women, or parents and children regarding sex is not the norm. Latina women traditionally define themselves primarily through their role as mothers. Attractiveness is seen as being synonymous with sexual inexperience or "purity." The males are seen as the "seducers" of the inexperienced (sexually uneducated) women. A woman "prepared" for sex (e.g., carrying condoms) is perceived to be experienced, "loose" and therefore unattractive . . . Puerto Rican women interviewed in drug treatment programs professed the wish to have their partners use condoms, but felt unable to ask them to do so for fear of being rejected or superseding their defined role. Conversely, men may not want to be seen as proposing protected sex, which carries the connotation for women of not being "serious," in other words, desiring sex which does not lead to pregnancy and marriage, the desired goal of [many] Puerto Rican women.
>
> *(Worth & Rodríquez 1987:6)*

Personal and Social Issues

Educating the Young

We can educate children about AIDS, even though it means dealing with social attitudes that are uncomfortable about homosexuality. Talking about condoms and oral and anal sex may raise some objections from religious minorities, but it can still be done when school administrators and teachers work with parents. Teens also have a sense of invulnerability that may make discussions of HIV and AIDS seem unimportant.

Sexuality educators have been coping for years with the erotophobic attitudes in our society, the uneasiness of parents in recognizing the sexuality of their children, and the opposition to sexuality education. Skilled sexuality educators have effective methods for decreasing the discomfort in discussing sexual behaviors candidly and explicitly, for demonstrating the effectiveness of condom use, and for dealing with homophobia. Research and experience indicates that sexuality education can be effective in helping young people assess their risks and vulnerabilities for HIV infection and then make responsible decisions based on this awareness (Gross et al. 1987b) (Figure 13.8).

Public Health Issues

When the issue of testing for HIV is raised, conflicts between the rights of society, the rights of innocent parties, and the rights of individuals who might be infected are inevitable. In 1988 some hospitals reported testing all their patients for HIV without informing the patients or getting their consent. Doctors,

Figure 13.8. Effective Teaching About How AIDS Isn't Spread. *Helen Kelly, a teacher at Woodrow Wilson High School in San Francisco, hugs Christian Haren as she introduces him and Edgardo Rodríguez (right) to her family life class. Both men have AIDS, and Ms. Kelly is demonstrating that the disease cannot be spread by casual contact.*

psychologists, and other professionals debate their responsibility to inform the spouse or sexual partner of a client who has tested sero-positive. When a patient or client refuses to tell a sexual partner he or she is engaging in high risk behavior, what is the responsibility of the doctor, psychologist, or social worker? In California, the physician is now required by law to notify partners at risk.

Should HIV testing be required for all prostitutes, customers of prostitutes, rapists, and those convicted of incest? Should prostitutes with HIV be locked up because they pose an imminent danger to public health? Can insurance companies require HIV testing before issuing medical or life insurance policies? Are there any limits or qualifications on the right to patient confidentiality when it comes to results of a HIV test? Should public health services provide sterile needles and syringes free to IV drug users?

Who Pays?

The costs of caring for persons with AIDS has dropped dramatically since 1986, mainly because of the shift from hospital care to home care. The average cost of hospital care for the first 10,000 cases of AIDS in the United States was $147,000 per person. In 1987 several studies indicated hospital costs had dropped to about $45,000 per case. In many cities, a case manager can now adapt the health care system to the particular needs of individual patients instead of just putting them in a hospital. Even so, the issue of who will pay, the federal government, Medicare, states, or individuals, is rapidly becoming a major social and political issue.

In 1988 expiration of a $30 million federal grant to provide AZT, a costly drug that may prolong the lives of persons with AIDS, threatened the lives of 6,000 patients around the country. A one-year supply of AZT for one person costs between $8,000 and $10,000. Many AIDS patients may be reduced to poverty if they have to bear the full cost of their care (Dentzer 1988; Smilgis, Wallis, & Serrill 1987:54). In 1989 the pharmaceutical company that manufactures AZT was pressured to lower its prices while another company which manufactures a drug used to treat pneumonia in HIV-positive persons announced it would give the drug free to uninsured persons but not reduce its cost for the insured.

But the social costs of AIDS is not limited to the direct costs of medical care and drugs. There is also the loss in productivity and creativity from the death of people in the prime of their lives.

The Global Consequences

Worldwide, an estimated 5 to 10 million people carry HIV. As of January 1989, the World Health Organization estimated there were about 400,000 adults with AIDS, half of these in sub-Saharan Africa. In Africa, an estimated 2 to 5 million people are already infected. By the year 2000, some African nations could lose 25% or more of their population, often the young, the educated, and future leaders. Heavy losses in the educated and professional classes could destroy the efforts of some developing nations, matching the economic and social ruin the Black Death wrought in medieval Europe (Fumento 1990). In the United States, by the end of 1990, an estimated 150,000 Americans had AIDS and between 700,000 and 1.5 million were infected with the virus.

What You Can Do to Help

Beyond reducing your own risks, there are several things you can do to help others cope with the threat of HIV. You can speak up when you hear someone repeat a myth about AIDS and make sure they have the facts straight. You might create an AIDS information and prevention program or public lecture for your school, fraternity, sorority, or local community. Hospices, hospitals, and AIDS support groups always need volunteers and financial support. As our care of persons with AIDS shifts away from hospitals to home care and hospices, volunteers who can help provide emotional support and help in daily household chores are becoming more essential.

Prepare yourself for the day when you may learn that a relative or friend has tested sero-positive, or has ARC or AIDS. That loved one or friend will definitely need your understanding and support as they struggle to express their fears and concerns. They will need someone to listen, someone to advise and support them if they are rejected at work, at school, or by other loved ones (Yarber 1987:13–14).

Key Concepts

1. The current HIV epidemic has some similarities with past epidemics, but also some important differences, because we know what causes AIDS and what behaviors put a person at risk for contracting the virus.

2. HIV attacks the body's immune system by destroying T lymphocytes. Since its protein coat has only a weak effect in triggering the immune system to produce neutralizing antibodies, the body is vulnerable to a variety of opportunistic infections and cancers, especially pneumocystic pneumonia and Kaposi's sarcoma, which are the primary cause of death in most persons with AIDS.

3. HIV infection follows three stages: an infective sero-positive stage with no symptoms, an ARC stage with a damaged immune system but mild symptoms, and the terminal AIDS stage.
4. The spread of the HIV virus can be controlled and limited by following safer sex practices and knowing your sexual partner.

Key Terms

acquired immune deficiency
   syndrome (AIDS) (354)
AIDS-related complex (ARC) (361)
ELISA test (362)
false negative (362)
false positive (362)
human immunodeficiency virus
   (HIV) (355)

Kaposi's sarcoma (358)
opportunistic infections (358)
pneumocystic pneumonia (358)
safer sex (365)
sero-positive (361)
Western Blot test (363)

Summary Questions

1. List the behaviors which put a person at moderate or high risk of becoming infected with the HIV virus.
2. Describe safer sex practices. What role does knowledge of your sexual partners and their past sexual history play in preventing the spread of the HIV virus?
3. What are the two tests for HIV infection? What are their advantages and limitations? What is one major advantage of early testing and diagnosis of an HIV infection?
4. What are the differences in how you handle a situation in which the condom breaks?
5. What are some major questions the AIDS epidemic raises about educating the young, public health issues, who pays, and the global consequences of this epidemic?

Suggested Readings

Alyson, S. (1989). *You CAN Do Something About AIDS*. Boston: Alyson Publications. (The Stop AIDS Project, 40 Plympton St., Boston, MA 02118.)

Gadsby, P. (1988, April). Mapping the epidemic: Geography is destiny. *Discover*, pp. 28–31.

McIlvenna, T., ed. (1987). *The Complete Guide to Safe Sex*. San Francisco, CA: Specific Press, The Institute for the Advanced Study of Human Sexuality.

Scientific American. (1988). What science knows about AIDS. A single topic issue, *259*(4). Articles on AIDS in 1988, the biology and origins of HIV, epidemiology in the United States and worldwide, the clinical and cellular pictures, AIDS therapies and vaccines, and the social dimensions.

Shilts, R. (1987). *And the Band Played On: Politics, People, and the AIDS Epidemic*. New York: St. Martin's Press.

Part Three

The Interpersonal Context

14.   Sexual Desire and Love Play
15.   Intimacy and Love
16.   Gender and Erotic Orientations
17.   Lifestyles of Singles and Couples
18.   Sexuality, Aging, and Health
19.   Gender Conflicts
20.   Unconventional Sexual Expressions
21.   Sexual Problems and Therapies

*S*exual Desire
  The Nature of Desire
  The Enemies of Desire
  Aphrodisiacs
*S*olo Sexual Pleasures
  The Erotic Mind
  Sex for One
*S*haring Sexual
  Pleasures
  Erotic Touches
  Intercourse Positions
  Oral Sex
  Love Play and Gender

Chapter 14

*S*exual Desire and Love Play

Special Consultants

Joan E. Blank, M.A., M.P.H., editor-in-chief, Down There Press, and author of *The Playbook for Women about Sex* and *Good Vibrations: A Complete Guide to Vibrators.*

Martha Cornog, M.A., M.S., former secretary for the Society for the Scientific Study of Sex, former editorial assistant, *Journal of Sex Research,* and editor, *Libraries Erotica and Pornography.*

Deborah Eve Grayson, M.S., R.P.T., mental health counselor and sex therapist, and author of *Parents and Other Strangers: A Creative Guide to Better Relationships* and *Breath Marks in the Wind,* a book of erotic poetry created to promote healthy sexual attitudes.

Timothy Perper, Ph.D. behavioral biologist specializing in the ethological and ethnographic study of courtship and the North American singles scene, and author of *Sex Signals: The Biology of Love.*

This chapter deals with the nature, origins, and enemies of sexual desire. We also examine solo sexual pleasures—erotic dreams, sexual fantasies, and masturbation—and the sharing of sexual pleasures.

Sexual Desire

The Nature of Sexual Desire

For centuries, philosophers and poets have debated the nature of sexual desire and love. Ancient Greek philosophers like Plato and Aristotle spoke of four kinds of love: (1) *philia* or the nonsexual love between friends, (2) *storge* or the love of a parent and child, (3) *eros* or the physical passion of lusty, lecherous sexual desire, and (4) *agape* or the intellectual, spiritual experience of love. Plato believed that the first humans had both male and female sexual organs and psyches. When these first humans threatened the gods, the gods solved the threat by splitting humans into two sexes who would then spend their lives searching for their partners and leave the gods alone. Because some of these first humans were male/male and female/female, their division explained homosexuals and lesbians.

In the early part of this century, Freud speculated about a fundamental libido, or pleasure drive, that motivates all human behavior. For Freud, this pleasure principle was rooted in the sexual and erotic, although it could be sublimated into all forms of creativity and higher expressions of love.

In more recent times, psychologists and social scientists have examined the various expressions of love and analyzed the phenomenon of limerence or falling in love. Historians have sought to trace the origins of romantic love in the Arabic poets and the troubadors of southern France in the early Middle Ages.

Biologists and evolutionary theorists have sought explanations for the mating urge in animals. Why do young animals engage in sex rehearsal play long before they reach sexual maturity? Why do animals, and humans, engage in sexual stimulation and various forms of intercourse, including same-gender stimulation and intercourse, when reproduction is not possible? Experimental psychologists and hormone specialists have tried to find causal connections between testosterone and hormone cycles and the libido or sex drive.

In our Western cultures, in Europe and the Americas, all our questions and speculations about the nature and origins of sexual desire and love have been deeply and permanently influenced by a philosophical perspective that came into our thinking from the philosophy of the ancient Greeks. This perspective pictures human nature in terms of a dualism, a dichotomy of body and soul. There is a spiritual love that originates in the mind and heart, and a lusty, lecherous carnal love that springs from the groin (Lawrence 1989; Money 1985a; Singer 1984a, 1984b, 1987).

Love above the belt deals with the spiritual, with falling in love or limerence, with a togetherness of the mind, and with the intimacy of two companions, two friends, or two lovers. Love above the belt is lyrical and romantic. It is expressed in whispers, caresses, hugs, and gentle kisses. This love is celebrated in public. Love above the belt springs from our need for companionship, nurturance, and intimacy. We are by nature social creatures. We need close companions to survive and develop (Money 1985a:125–128) (Figure 14.1).

Love below the belt deals with biological urges or drives we describe as passionate, erotic, lusty, and carnal. Lust below the belt is epic, noisy, sweaty,

Figure 14.1. *Sexual attraction and desire are a part of life, regardless of one's age.*

fleshy, bawdy, and playful. Lust is hidden in private. The wellsprings of love below the belt remain unknown and hotly debated, although they appear deeply rooted in our biological nature and evolutionary origins. Animals experience a mating drive that impels them to overcome all obstacles and reproduce even if they die in the process. Do humans share a similar kind of biological drive to reproduce? What is the balance and interplay of hormonal and social factors in the erotic life? How many men and women pair-bond or marry because society says they should?

This crucial distinction between romantic limerent love above the waist and lust below the belt permeates all Western thinking. It has some serious consequences for our attitudes and behavior. In much of Western religious beliefs, love above the belt springs from a divine creator, a God, who is pure spirit. True love, then, is asexual. It is above and beyond the physical and the sexual. It is not distracted or contaminated by erotic passions. Lust below the belt, on the other hand, is associated with the flesh, passion, lechery, and with sin.

Historians commonly acknowledge that the roots of the love/lust split in our Western culture continues in the dilemmas of the madonna/whore and the saint/playboy. Eve, the first woman of the Genesis story, was both the virginally innocent helpmate of Adam and the naive servant of the serpent who seduced man. Women, then, are either nurturing, asexual, virginal madonnas, or they are passionate, seductive whores. Adam, or man, likewise had two faces. He is either the patriarch and provider, made in God's image, or the sinful playboy, powerless to resist the voluptuous Eve who causes his downfall.

The chasm between love and lust is deep and treacherous. It is a split between the spirit and the body that Western cultures have yet to resolve. As a result, most boys and girls are openly prepared by their parents and society to deal with saintly pure love. At the same time, they get covert messages about sinful lust. The integration of these two forms of love is tricky, and not always successful. This dilemma is obvious in the often repeated sarcasm that although lusty love is of the flush and sinful, we should reserve it exclusively for our true love and for marriage.

One interpretation of this conflict between romantic saintly love and lusty erotic love and the many different ways people handle it has been offered by John Money, a prominent analyst of psychosexual development (Money 1985a, 1986:31–39, 1988:133–185). The ideal outcome, Money suggests, is to overcome the conflicting messages of our culture and integrate these two forms of sexual desire by focusing them harmoniously on one person.

When we cannot integrate saintly and lusty love, the cleavage and continued tension between the two are incorporated into our adult experiences of intimacy, love, bonding, and passion. Compromises are made in which either love or lust are displaced, temporarily or on a permanent basis. When love wins out, guilt suppresses lust. As a result, the organs of lust, the sexual organs, may not function normally, or they may be used rarely. When lust displaces love, the sexual organs may be used repeatedly with a variety of partners and with compulsive frequency.

A third compromise may leave the image of the loved one pure and intact while the lover displaces the focus of his or her lust away from the partner to some nonsexual part of the loved one or includes a nonsexual object as the focus of lusty love. Money suggests this kind of compromise leads to what he calls vandalized lovemaps, or paraphilias (see Chapter 20). A man who is sexually turned-on by a woman's foot focuses his lusty love in a way that leaves his loved one pure and untouched by his sinful love. Others learn to express their lusty love by focusing it on some nonsexual object. A shoe, a piece of rubber, or an enema becomes the stimulus for the expression of lusty love.

Men and women, Money suggests, can engage in any of these compromises between love and lust on a temporary or permanent basis, in their fantasies, or by acting out the compromise. A man who has not resolved the conflict, for instance, may fantasize that his loved one is a prostitute. A woman who has not accepted the possibility that lusty love is not sinful, but good, may fantasize that her loved one is a stranger who forces her to enjoy forbidden sexual pleasures. The possibilities of compromise are limited only by the human imagination (Money 1986:31–39).

The Enemies of Desire

Sexual Guilt and Erotophobia

Men and women who base their views of sexual morality on some outside authority tend to have more guilt than those who, after observing the behavioral codes of society, family, and their religion, develop their own personal, internalized value system (see Chapter 3, pp. 61–64). The more sexual guilt we have, the less frequently we are inclined to engage in sexual behavior and the more that behavior is likely to be restricted to a few acceptable forms (Gerrard & Gibbons 1982; Propper & Brown 1986). Recall our discussion in Chapter 5 about erotophobia, a fear and anxiety about things sexual. Negative messages about sex and feelings of guilt, fear, and shame can put a damper on sexual interest and behaviors.

Lack of Self-Confidence

To be sexually intimate with another person we have to open ourselves up to another person. We must become vulnerable and accept the possibility that the relationship may not work out. Having a positive, confident image of ourselves is a key factor in being sexually intimate (Figure 14.2 and Highlight Box 14.1).

Although self-confidence has traditionally been a hallmark of masculinity and something women expect in a man, the self-confidence of some male bravado strikes today's women as insensitive and lacking in finesse. At the same time, the growing economic and sexual liberation of women has made self-confidence and self-sufficiency important for women. Even though some men continue to look for dependent, submissive women, most men today prefer a woman who is confident about herself and self-assured. Today's woman has a distinct advantage both in her career and in her social and romantic life when she feels confident about her abilities and can interact well with others.

The central challenge in building a strong self-image and self-confidence is learning to like and love ourselves. To be self-confident, we also need to be our own strongest supporter. A person with self-confidence and a good self-image will answer the question "Who loves you?" with "I do," and then add "—and Mom and Dad do, or my partner does . . ."

Unwarranted fears of unattractiveness are a common cause of the lack of self-confidence. Some men feel that no woman would even find them attractive because they are too short, too tall, bald, or have too small a chin. Fear that his penis is too small is a common reason for a man's lack of self-confidence when it comes to sexual intimacy. Women also experience a lack of self-confidence because their breasts are too small, their hips too flat or too large, and so on. These fears may be totally irrational, but their effect is real. To remedy such fears, we need to recall that we humans exhibit an incredible, unlimited variety in our lovemaps. For every self-perceived physical peculiarity, there are several potential partners for whom that physical characteristic is genuinely appealing.

Figure 14.2. *Cathy, © 1983 Universal Press Syndicate. Reprinted with permission. All rights reserved.*

BILL HASN'T CALLED TO ASK ME OUT AGAIN. HE HATES ME.

I DROVE HIM BACK TO HIS GIRLFRIEND, SHIRLEY... HE MET SOMEONE HE LIKES BETTER... I DID SOMETHING ON OUR LAST DATE THAT DISGUSTED HIM...

HE HATES ME! HE'S SORRY HE EVER MET ME!!

CATHY, WHY DON'T YOU JUST CALL AND ASK HIM OUT?

I'M AFRAID I'LL FEEL REJECTED.

HIGHLIGHT BOX 14.1.
A SEX APPEAL SURVEY

The following results are from a survey sent to psychiatrists by the editors of *Medical Aspects of Human Sexuality*. Although no breakdown was given on the sex of the 400 respondents, it can be assumed, based on the predominance of male psychiatrists, that the results represent a predominantly male view. How would you answer these questions? Do you agree or disagree with these findings?

Is sex appeal primarily innate or acquired?

Chiefly innate	9%
Some innate components, but largely acquired	46%
Mostly innate, but can be improved	46%
Chiefly acquired	11%

What is the most influential component in a woman's sex appeal?

Sensuality	59%	Physical beauty	33%
Self-esteem	15%	Empathy	8%
Grace	7%	Intelligence	1%

What is the most influential component in a man's sex appeal?

Sensuality	33%	Physical attractiveness	31%
Self-esteem	18%	Achievement	17%
Empathy	15%	Intelligence	6%

Are individualists or conformers more likely to be perceived as having sex appeal?

Individualists	73%	Conformers	6%
No appreciable difference	26%		

Does shyness contribute to or detract from sex appeal?

No consistent effect	46%
Detracts in both men and women	41%
Contributes in both sexes	6%
Contributes in women, detracts in men	2%
Contributes in men, detracts in women	1%

Are people with a high interest in and responsiveness to sexual activity generally perceived as having above-average sex appeal?

Not particularly	56%	Yes	44%

When a spouse's sex appeal diminishes in marriage, what is the usual cause?

Familiarity	38%	Lack of effort	28%
Failure to escape routines	23%	Quarreling	14%
Neglect of grooming	9%	Aging	5%
Other	11%		

Do men maintain their sex appeal with age better than women?

Much more so	8%	Considerably more so	37%
Slightly more so	29%	No	23%

Source: A. Pietropinto. (1983). Sex appeal. *Medical Aspects of Human Sexuality, 17*(4):195–210. Reprinted with permission from *Medical Aspects of Human Sexuality* © Cahners Publishing Company. Published March 1983. All rights reserved.

Figure 14.3. *In recent years, many college officials have recognized that students are coming to campus confused about values and relationships. Increasingly, colleges are setting up programs designed to help freshmen form bonds with each other. Students are provided with small group settings, such as this one, where they can discuss values, stress, and human relations with the help of older students and staff.*

Ineffective Communication

Few people are naturally good communicators. Most of us have to learn the art of communicating. Couples seeking help with their relationships or sex therapy often have communications problems (Zimmer 1983). A major part of relationship, marital, and sex therapy is helping couples improve their communication and empathy. Learning to communicate more effectively means learning to be sensitive to and understand our own thoughts, needs, and feelings. It means being able to communicate these to our partners. It also means being able to listen and appreciate a partner's thoughts, needs, and feelings, without judging them as good or bad. Establishing good communication early in a relationship can help prevent relationship problems later on. Good communication also establishes a strong foundation for intimacy and makes for a richer, more enjoyable life (Figure 14.3).

Those who have studied communications skills commonly suggest some basic, practical guidelines. Which of the following guidelines have you used?

1. Think before bringing up an issue that the listener may respond to emotionally and defensively.
2. Make sure that what you want to say is actually conveyed by the words you choose and clearly understood by your partner.
3. State your thoughts and feelings in simple, clear, honest words.
4. Zero in on the important issue. Forget the irrelevant.
5. Edit out statements that would deliberately and needlessly hurt your partner. Avoid sarcasm and insults.
6. Find a way to avoid accusing or blaming your partner.

7. Start your sentences with "I," not "You." Starting a sentence with "You" makes it easy to slip into blaming or accusing, or being interpreted as blaming even if you don't mean to.

8. Don't try to read your partner's mind. When you're tempted to make an assumption, clear the air and ask, "Are you trying to say . . ." Check with your partner to make sure he or she understood what you tried to say. Ask him or her what they heard you say.

9. Listen to your partner. If he or she is silent, searching for the right word or struggling with an idea, don't jump in. Wait. Give your partner time to find the best way to say what he or she wants to say.

10. Even when your partner says something that sets off an emotional reaction, don't walk away and get angry. Paraphrase what you heard and ask whether you heard and interpreted it accurately.

11. Avoid playing amateur psychologist, psychoanalyst, or therapist.

These guidelines may be difficult to put into practice in intimate relationships, but being aware of them can help improve communication.

Sexual Inexperience

Everyone learns about sexuality from experience. Some have more sexual experience than others, but may have learned less about the meanings of sexual intimacy and how it is achieved. Although being sexually inexperienced may appear to be a handicap, there are ways you can compensate for a lack of sexual experience. There are a variety of inexpensive self-help manuals on sexual relations which can provide information, insights, and encouragement. College courses, many of which use sexually explicit films, can provide answers to questions and help build self-confidence.

Open communication and a sensitive partner can help overcome the lack of sexual experience. A person who has self-confidence but lacks experience might complement a more experienced partner by saying, "I've never tried . . . , but you know—I'd sort of like to try it with you." Letting the more experienced partner take the lead and sharing your responses also helps, provided you feel free to express your reactions to new experiences.

There is no one in this world who cannot learn something new about sexual intimacy if they are sensitive and open to exploring new dimensions. If a couple is venturesome, they may discover that their mutual chemistry can lead to something totally new and unique, something neither has ever experienced with anyone else.

Intrapsychic Factors

Our Puritan tradition says "Cleanliness is next to godliness," but Americans often turn cleanliness into an obsession with deodorants and feminine hygiene sprays that mask the natural odors of a clean body. The natural secretions of the genitals and armpits contain pheromones, natural sex attractants, which can be a real, if subconscious, turn-on. Still, many men and women approach sexual intimacy with some fear, distaste, or even disgust. When someone finds the wet, sweaty, and messy aspects of sexual intimacy and intercourse distasteful, sexual desire can often be blocked or suppressed.

In the 1960s and 1970s, a common message was that sex could be liberated and enjoyed without fear, guilt, responsibility, or commitment. However enjoyable and liberated sexual intimacy may be, like any human activity or relationship it carries with it certain responsibilities and risks. Today, the real fear of AIDS, especially among the naive and sexually inexperienced, is a major hindrance to sexual desire. In some cases, it may even paralyze sexual desire. Learning about the realities of AIDS, herpes, and other STDs and how to reduce risks in a new relationship are important considerations for any sexually active person today.

Aphrodisiacs

The folklore of **aphrodisiacs** appears unlimited, although men have traditionally been more interested than women in finding that magic sex or love potion. Since prehistoric times, men have searched for some food, drug, or scent guaranteed to improve their sex drive or sexual capacity, or make them irresistible to a woman. Eating oysters, clams, and orchids was claimed to improve one's sex drive and performance because they resemble the female vulva. Oysters, clams, peanuts, olives, and bananas have likewise been recommended as aphrodisiacs because they resemble the testicles or penis. Ground rhinoceros horn, a famous Chinese aphrodisiac, may have given us our slang expression horny, although it does nothing to improve anyone's libido. Ginseng and mandrake roots, licorice, fennel seed, and a variety of other substances have been praised for their alleged effect on libido. None of these claims hold up in scientific experiments (Covington & McClendon 1987; Pechter 1988).

Some claim that alcohol is a good aphrodisiac. One or two drinks may, in fact, lower inhibitions and allow sexual desire to surface because alcohol depresses the central nervous system, the brain, and one's conscience. Sometimes, however, more than a drink or two of alcohol interferes with sexual response. Chronic alcoholism can result in erection problems in men and reduced sexual desire and lack of orgasm in women (Buffum 1990; Klassen & Wilsnack 1986; Lang 1985; Wiseman 1985).

Marijuana use can prolong and intensify sensations. Sensations of touch and taste are particularly enhanced. A normal libido and sperm count both depend on a normal level of testosterone. Smoking marijuana at least 4 days a week for 6 months or more without using any other drug significantly lowers testosterone levels. Heavy smokers, 10 or more joints a week, have both lower testosterone levels and lower sperm counts than light smokers. Fortunately, both libido and sperm count appear to return to normal when smoking stops (Buffum 1990).

Users of amyl nitrate, or "poppers," report that the drug produces more intense sensations during orgasm, probably by increasing the blood flow in the genitals. Poppers, however, can cause dizziness, headaches, and fainting. They also increase the risk of stroke, and occasionally have led to death. Butyl nitrate, sometimes used by disco dancers, has similar effects (Buffum 1990; Covington & McClendon 1987).

Cocaine in its many street forms is popular and addictive because these drugs are very effective in stimulating the pleasure systems of the brain and causing powerful psychological highs. These drugs also enhance the natural highs, such as orgasm, which may occur when a person is using cocaine or one of its derivatives. However, when the effects of cocaine wear off, during the so-called crash between drug-induced highs, normal impulses of pleasure are either reduced, or suppressed altogether in the case of a heavy user.

In experiments, yohimbine, an extract of the bark of an African tree, doubled the copulation rate of sexually experienced rats. It made virgin rats more sexually active and previously asexual rats suddenly eager to mate. In humans, less than half of the men suffering psychogenic erectile problems improved when they took yohimbine for 10 weeks (Buffum 1985, 1990).

Lack of sexual desire or a low sexual drive affects millions of Americans, but sexual desire depends on having enough testosterone in the right form. It also requires a variety of known and as-yet-unidentified neurotransmitters, chemicals that allow the brain to turn sexual images and sensations into sexual arousal (Goleman 1988c). Desire also depends on the images we have in our brain of who and what we interpret as sexy.

Solo Sexual Pleasures

Mention sex, and many people think immediately of sexual intercourse—of two persons caught up in the hot passion of sexual play or the more relaxed sensuality of love play. However, as we saw in our examination of childhood and adolescent sex, much of our sexual activity does not fit this description. The average man and woman has many private sexual thoughts and fantasies every day. Infants, children, adolescents, and adults of all ages enjoy solo masturbation for its release of tension or its erotic pleasure. Over a lifetime, sexual fantasies and solo sex are likely the most common sexual outlets for men and women, single and married persons, and homosexual, heterosexual, and bisexual persons.

The Erotic Mind

Erotic Dreams

Almost all males and 2 out of 3 females have had erotic dreams (Kinsey, Pomeroy, & Martin 1948, Kinsey et al. 1953). Nocturnal emissions, known familiarly as wet dreams, are a common experience, especially for young men. Many women, especially women who masturbate or have had sexual intercourse, have similar experiences with erotic dreams and nocturnal orgasms (Fisher et al. 1983; Wells 1983).

Erotic dreams can be surrealistic, nonsensical, even deliriously erotic. They can also be realistic scenarios involving people the dreamer knows. The creativity of the sleeping mind is limitless. The mind can weave together fragments from the subconscious psyche with yesterday's experiences and shadowy memories of experiences and persons known, perhaps long ago (Figure 14.4).

Vivid images of illicit and forbidden, even frightening behaviors, sometimes rise from the subconscious to float through our erotic dreams. Coming as they do from our subconscious, these taboo elements certainly are not grounds for feelings of shame, embarrassment, or guilt. Occasional dreams of forbidden or undesirable sexual behaviors are a natural part of our lives. If they become recurring images that trigger anxiety or guilt, discussing them with a psychologist or trusted counselor may help you learn to interpret and deal with such dreams. Psychoanalysts and psychologists often find fertile insights in the subconscious world of such dreams. Many maintain that besides the obvious content of a dream there are latent or hidden symbols, which, when interpreted, can provide insights into the motivations behind many of our behaviors.

Figure 14.4. *In Tantric yoga, sexual energies are coiled and resting at the base of the spine. When aroused they need to be channeled upward through animal centers and into the human sphere of the heart and mind. This drawing from an 18th-century Japanese print shows a sexual dream arising from the throat, halfway between the heart and the mind, a region in Tantric physiology where sexual energy is transformed into life-force energy. Unlike Western sexual thought, Eastern traditions view the lusty images of sexual dreams and sexual fantasies as an integration of lust and love.*

Erotic Fantasies

In gathering women's sexual fantasies for the book *My Secret Garden*, Nancy Friday wrote that fantasies

> exist only for their elasticity, their ability to instantly incorporate any new character, image or idea—or, as in dreams, to which they bear so close a relationship—to contain conflicting ideas simultaneously. They expand, heighten, distort or exaggerate reality, taking one further, faster in the direction in which the unashamed unconscious already knows it wants to go. They present the astonished self with the incredible, the opportunity to entertain the impossible.
>
> *(1973:3–4)*

A sexual fantasy can be relaxing or exciting. Ranging from the unreal and forbidden to realistic, lusty, and romantic scenarios, they may involve a stranger, someone you know, or someone you would like to know in a sexual way. Unlike the dreams of sleep, our sexual daydreams and fantasies are constructed for maximum sexual arousal. They can even add sparkle to a sexual encounter with a partner. Table 14.1 summarizes some intriguing similarities and differences in the content of the masturbation fantasies of men and women.

Men and women create erotic fantasies for a variety of reasons. In one study, 60% of both male and female college students reported they used sexual fan-

Table 14.1.
Male and Female Masturbation Fantasies

	Men		Women	
	(Sue)	(Hunt)	(Sue)	(Hunt)
Sex with a loved one		75		70
former lover	43		41	
imaginary lover	44		24	
stranger		47		21
Oral-genital sex	61		51	
Sex with two or more persons of the opposite sex		33		18
Group sex	19		14	
Sexual activities one would not do in real life		19		28
Being observed having intercourse	15		20	
Observing others engaging in sex	18		13	
Being irresistible to another	55		53	
Having another give in to you after initial resistance	37		24	
Forcing someone to have sex	24	13	16	3
Being forced to have sex	21	10	36	19
Being rejected or sexually abused	11		13	
Homosexual activity	3	7	9	11
Sex with animals	1		4	

Sources: Sue (1979) and Hunt (1974).

tasies as part of their love play with a partner. Sue (1979) also reported 38% of the men and 46% of the women said they used sexual fantasies during intercourse to increase their sexual arousal. Eighteen percent of the men and 13% of the women used fantasies to experience activities in their imagination that they did not engage in with their partner. A third of the men and 22% of the women used fantasies to heighten their partner's attractiveness; 3% to 5% used them to relieve boredom.

In our culture where sex often has the aura of the forbidden and sinful, sexual fantasies can also trigger guilt, shame, or anxiety. In Sue's study, 20% of the college men and women felt uneasy or ashamed about having sexual fantasies during intercourse. As for fantasies about taboo behaviors, thinking is not the same as doing. The person who has control over his or her actions doesn't have to worry about a fantasy involving force or violence because he or she is not likely to act out that fantasy. However, a rapist or pedophile who fantasizes about raping someone or molesting a child in order to become sexually aroused may indeed act out his fantasies and, in the process, seriously harm another person.

Men and women who place a strong emphasis on being emotionally and sexually faithful to their spouse may find a fantasy of another partner particularly disturbing and unacceptable. For those who think it is a crime, unfaithful, or sinful to retreat consciously into the secret garden of the mind while in the arms of a loved one, Ray Birdwhistle suggests that an overly closed idea of a relationship can be dangerous.

> If the couple wants intimacy, both partners need to refresh themselves with privacy. That implies also being allowed to withdraw without guilt. It is only in the private kingdom of the mind that one can enjoy fantasies.
>
> *(In Friday 1973:9)*

Sexual fantasies can be used to overcome anxieties about sex and smooth the way to exploring new sexual outlets. Fantasizing about meeting, flirting, and making the first overtures to someone can help us overcome hesitation and be more confident. Sexual fantasies can bolster our self-image. In fantasies, we can be as sexual, attractive, powerful, loved, or desired as we want to be. Sexual fantasies can break us out of our culturally imposed feminine/masculine roles. The dark side of sexual fantasies is that they can lead to unrealistic expectations or become a troublesome turn-on (Follingstas & Kimbrell 1986). Couples who are comfortable with their sexual fantasies sometimes find sharing some of these fantasies with each other adds new life and vigor to a long-term sexual relationship.

The frequency with which people have sexual fantasies appears, in general, to be related to their ability for genital arousal. Women who reported having frequent sexual fantasies while masturbating also demonstrated greater intensity in their sexual arousal than women who used masturbation fantasies less frequently. Clinical studies suggest that persons who enjoy creating sexual fantasies usually have a higher sexual interest and are more easily aroused than people who don't have many sexual fantasies. The problem with this conclusion is that we don't know whether this latter group who do not fantasize very much necessarily have a lower sexual drive, or enjoy sex less than those who fantasize a lot (Brown & Hart 1977; Davidson & Hoffman 1986; Knafo & Jaffe 1984; Nutter & Condron 1983; Stock & Geer 1982).

Men appear to spend more time on sexual fantasies and have more sexually explicit fantasies than women. However, we can ask whether the so-called romantic fantasies of women would be described as sexually explicit fantasies if they were reported by males. Sexually experienced women are more likely than virgins to have explicit sexual fantasies. For both men and women, the frequency of sexual fantasies appears to decrease with age (Halderman & Zelhart 1985).

Male fantasies often deal with male sexual power, aggressiveness, and submission (Crepault & Couture 1980). The sexual fantasies of men often reveal core emotions and a conflict between love and rage far deeper and vastly more complex than the cliché of women as madonnas or whores (Friday 1980). The sexual fantasies of women are quite varied. They may, for example, involve a faceless stranger, being watched while having sex, or being forced to have sex. Women also fantasize about being dominant or submissive, being out of control or doing the forbidden, or being an irresistible earth mother; their fantasies may involve incest, interracial sex, fetishes, and other expressions of lust and love (Barbach 1984; Friday 1973, 1975).

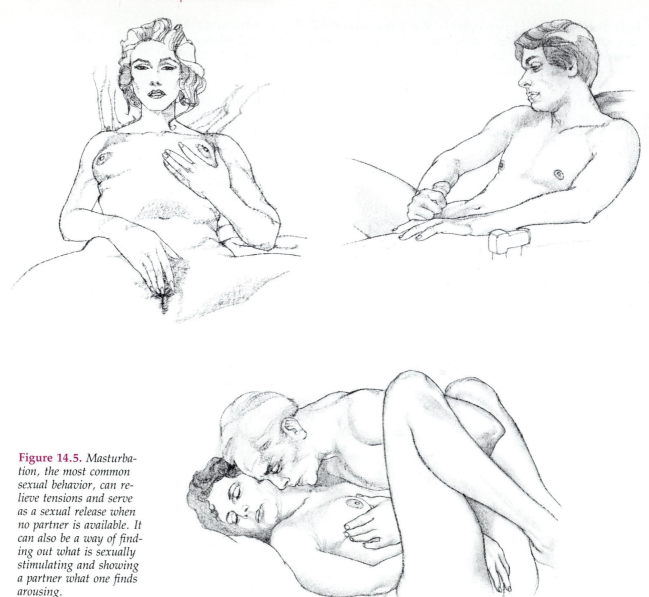

Figure 14.5. *Masturbation, the most common sexual behavior, can relieve tensions and serve as a sexual release when no partner is available. It can also be a way of finding out what is sexually stimulating and showing a partner what one finds arousing.*

Sex for One

Masturbation is "the on-going love affair that each of us has with ourselves throughout our lifetime." It is "a way for all of us to learn about sexual response . . . the way we discover our erotic feelings . . . the way we learn to like our genitals and build our sexual self-esteem. . . . For women especially, it's a way to build confidence so we can communicate clearly with our lovers" (Dodson 1987:3–5). A technical definition of **masturbation** is self-stimulation and self-pleasuring of one's genitals to produce sexual arousal and/or orgasm (Figure 14.5).

Masturbation is not mentioned in the Bible, but Christian philosophers have traditionally condemned it as a sinful enjoyment of sexual pleasure (see Chapter 3, p. 54). Traditionally in the West, sexual pleasure was tolerated by moralists as an inducement for couples to have and raise children. It was not embraced as a good in and of itself. Masturbation was then often viewed as sinful and unnatural because it was not aimed at reproduction within marriage (Lawrence 1989; Phipps 1977).

In recent years, the official Catholic position on masturbation has continued to condemn this "narcissistic self-indulgence" while mainstream Protestant churches have adopted a more positive approach. Recent Protestant statements reflect a 1984 position statement from the Sex Information and Education Council of the United States which summed up the current medical view of masturbation as follows:

> It is the generally accepted view of the medical and mental health professions that masturbation is a natural and nonharmful behavior for individuals of all ages and both sexes. Masturbation can be a way of becoming more comfortable with and enjoying one's sexuality by getting to know and like one's body. It can be a form of sexual pleasure and/or release for people who are not involved in a relationship and, in either the presence or absence of their partner, for those who are involved in a relationship.

Even though the incidence of masturbation tends to decline with age, about half the unmarried men and women in their seventies and eighties surveyed by Brecher (1984) and the editors of Consumer Reports Books reported they still enjoyed masturbating.

Despite the fact that self-loving is our most common mode of sexual outlet (Markus & Francis 1975),

> most persons who masturbate remain more or less guilt-ridden about it, and nearly all of them are extremely secretive about their masturbating and would be horribly embarrassed to have anyone know the truth. . . . It is far easier to admit that one does not believe in God, or was once a Communist, than [to admit] that one sometimes fondles a part of his [or her] body to the point of orgastic release.
>
> *(Hunt 1974:66–67)*

Kinsey's data from 1948 and 1953 indicate that persons in the lower socio-economic class and with less education tended to have more negative attitudes toward masturbation. Attitudes were also more negative in certain ethnic and religious groups. Today, many Americans still consider masturbation sinful, immature, narcissistic, unnatural, unmanly, unladylike, hedonistic, and/or self-indulgent. For many people, especially the young, masturbation still brings an undefined sense of guilt and shame (Table 14.2).

Self-Loving and Women

If masturbation has been a taboo subject for men, it has been even more so for women, at least until the 1960s when the feminist movement and sex therapists began endorsing masturbation for women. Films showing masturbation are

Table 14.2. Masturbation and Today's Teenagers

This data, drawn from Aaron Haas's 1979 survey of 600 15- to 18-year-old males and females, mainly in California, compares their approval of masturbation—a formal value—with the informal value—what they actually do. Data is also given on the age at which these teenagers began to masturbate.

	Approve of Masturbation		Have Masturbated		Age When Teenagers First Masturbated			
	Boys	Girls	Boys	Girls	Boys by Age 13	Boys by Age 15	Girls by Age 13	Girls by Age 15
Age 15–16	76%	70%	75%	52%	52%	75%	37%	44%
Age 17–18	85%	72%	80%	59%	41%	70%	28%	47%

commonly used in college sexuality courses. When one group of college women were shown a female masturbation film, they later reported no effect on their attitudes on behavior. Nevertheless, they did report masturbating significantly more often after viewing the film. Whether these women actually masturbated more often, or were just more willing to admit it after seeing the film, remains a question (Heiby & Becker 1980).

In masturbating, some women prefer to stimulate the clitoris, its glans, or shaft directly with the hand, a vibrator, or other object. Some women avoid direct clitoral stimulation, preferring to massage, squeeze, or rub rhythmically the minor labia and mons area to stimulate the clitoris indirectly and achieve orgasm. Women who masturbate by directly stimulating the clitoris carry this preference over into sex with a partner and prefer clitoral rather than vaginal stimulation in reaching orgasm (Leff & Israel 1983). Women seldom insert their fingers, a dildo, or dildo-shaped vibrator in the vagina when masturbating (Hite 1976). Some women can masturbate to orgasm by massaging and stimulating their breasts and nipples without touching their genitals.

The average woman masturbating has an orgasm in less than 4 minutes, some in less than 30 seconds. Men are similar and usually masturbate to orgasm in 2 or 3 minutes (Kinsey, Pomeroy & Martin 1948, Kinsey et al. 1953).

There appears to be no relationship between either the capacity to masturbate or masturbatory styles and a woman's orgasms during intercourse. However, middle-class women who masturbate are more likely to have orgasm during intercourse than those who do not masturbate (Leff & Israel 1983).

Self-Loving and Men

Men are generally less varied than women in their self-loving. A slow up-and-down movement of the hand encircling the penis, gradually increasing the pace, tightness, and contact with the glans as arousal heightens, is by far the most popular method. Some men also masturbate by pressing or rubbing against a pillow or the mattress, or with a vibrator or hand-held shower head.

Sharing Self-Love

Masturbation can release sexual tension. It can provide sexual pleasuring and intimacy without jumping to sexual intercourse before both partners are ready. As a form of outercourse, masturbation shared with a partner is a safe alternative to unprotected intercourse. It provides a safe outlet when there is a risk of HIV infection.

Masturbation can be shared as part of a sensuous, full-body massage that gradually builds in pleasure and excitement to sharing and watching each other masturbate. It can be a way of exploring each other's sexual responses and learning how to pleasure each other. It can precede or follow intercourse. It can mimic intercourse, as when the partner uses his or her fingers to stimulate the G spot and clitoris. Self-loving or digital stimulation can also help a woman reach orgasm during intercourse. Whether prompted by a near-term pregnancy, a health problem, or just the mood of the moment, sharing self-love can be another way of expressing intimacy and closeness.

Sex Toys

When Alex Comfort's *Joy of Sex* was published in 1972, electric vibrators were sold by medical supply stores for scalp massage and arthritis. Within a few years, sophisticated department stores were advertising vibrators without hinting at their possible use for sexual pleasuring. Today, the focus of sex toys has broadened from "magic orgasm producers" to enhancing sensual and sexual pleasure. Vibrators of every conceivable kind, sexual lubricants, massage manuals, dildos (artificial penises), erotic music cassettes, incense, sex toys, and sexual aids are sold in "adult stores," sex boutiques, and mail-order catalogs (Figure 14.6). Soft- and hard-core videos can be rented or purchased locally or by mail order.

Some view vibrators and other sex toys as vaguely unnatural. Some heterosexual men may be uneasy when they learn their lover uses a vibrator or dildo. But the sales figures on sex toys suggest that many persons, of all ages, enjoy using adult toys for masturbation, or to enhance and vary their sexual pleasure with a partner. Preorgasmic women may be introduced to a vibrator as part of their therapy. Older couples and men with erectile problems often find a vibrator enhances their ability to pleasure one another. Battery and electric-powered vibrators of all kinds and prices are available today (Blank 1989).

For those who are hesitant about experimenting with a vibrator or other sex toy, Lonnie Barbach, a noted sex therapist working with women who have trouble reaching orgasm, suggests that "You don't know what you like until you're willing to try something that may not work."

Sharing Sexual Pleasures

Erotic Touches

Kissing

Kisses can be casual and friendly, familial or parental, respectful and religious, but they can also be a major source of sensual and sexual pleasure, hot and passionate or gentle and sensual, dry or wet, brief or prolonged, nibbling or

Figure 14.6. *Pleasure boutiques in larger cities sell a wide variety of sex toys, dildos, vibrators, and body lotions to enhance erotic play and fantasy.*

sucking, shallow or deep. Kissing lips can linger, wandering over the body from forehead, cheeks, and earlobes, to neck, nipples, and breasts. They can visit fingers and toes, vulvas and penises. Lovers welcome kisses anywhere. The only limit is the lover's imagination and the appropriate degree of privacy (Halpern & Sherman 1979).

Touches and Massages

From the moment we leave the womb until we die, physical contact—touch—is the most powerful way we communicate intimacy, togetherness, empathy, support, tenderness, concern, and love. Without touch, sexual pleasure cannot exist. Mind and body come together in touch. We don't need words when we touch.

HIGHLIGHT BOX 14.2. KISSING

Safe

Safe from the sear of savage nails
Your back settles into the pillow
like a cat's purr.

Eyes blurred from swapping sweat
We blink ourselves back
to the comfort of kisses,
snug as the suction of lust

Knowing the "o"
of our lips.

Source: Reprinted from *Breath Marks in the Wind, a Book of Erotic Poetry and Illustrations.* Deborah Eve Grayson. Fort Lauderdale, FL: Breath Marks/IDF, Inc. 1988.

Figure 14.7. *In much of the Orient, massage is a part of everyday life. Massage is used to cure headaches and nervous exhaustion. In today's world, a face, hand, or foot massage can relax a loved one in a few minutes, but the pleasures of a full body massage are worth the time.*

Some areas of our bodies are more erotically sensitive than others, but every inch of our skin responds to the emotion-conveying range of touch. There is nothing more appreciated after a hard day's work that a leisurely back massage. Caressing hands are much better at refreshing tired feet than a buzzing, plastic foot bath. The bones, sinews, muscles, and skin of our overworked hand tingle to a sensuous massage. A head massage is much better than aspirin for relieving a headache and nervous exhaustion.

Massages can focus on one part of the body for a few minutes, or envelope the whole body in relaxing caresses. You can be dressed or undressed. A quiet time with the phone silenced and door locked, the right music, and a light vegetable oil scented and warmed to body temperature are all one needs. A massage manual helps, but tenderness, sensitivity, and a willingness to explore are basic.

Massages can be relaxing or erotic. A whole body massage will take an hour or two of leisure. A hand, foot, or facial massage brings its own delights and rewards in a few minutes. When loving caresses and kisses move to nongenital erogenous zones, the cheeks, neck, lobes of the ears, nipples, and buttocks, new pleasures are experienced. When the massage involves the breasts, vulva, and penis, sensual, nurturing touches can be either relaxing or sexually arousing. Lovers who set aside time for love play and forget about "scoring" can explore the landscape of each other's body. Exploration leads to discoveries, to unexpected treasures of sensual and erotic pleasure.

All touches, but especially genital touches, benefit from verbal and nonverbal guides, at least when lovers are getting to know each other's bodies. If one observes a partner masturbating, it will be obvious which genital touches he or she finds most pleasurable. A hand or finger can direct a lover's explorations and let him or her know whether you prefer feather-light, firm, or vigorous touches. Moods and tempos change, so good communication is important.

Intercourse Positions

A common opinion mistakenly attributes the so-called *missionary position* for sexual intercourse to Christian missionaries in Africa or the South Pacific. In creating Adam before Eve and giving man dominion over woman, God allegedly required the male-above-female prone position. In reality, 1,500 years before Christian missionaries went to the South Pacific, the Greek Stoic philosopher Artemidorus advocated the face-to-face, man-on-top position as the only proper one for Greeks because it affirmed the domination of men over women.

Unlike Western traditions, the classic love manuals of the Orient, India, and Middle East pictured literally hundreds of different positions for mutual pleasuring, oral sex, and both vaginal and anal intercourse. Centuries of human experience with these different positions are summed up in manuals like the 4th-century Hindu *Kama Sutra* translated into English in 1883 by Sir Richard Burton, the 15-century *Theater of God* or *Ananga Ranga* from India, and the 16th-century Arabic classic *The Perfumed Garden*. The creative genius of the human mind and our continual desire for intimacy and sensual pleasure make human sexual relations a continual venture. Figure 14.8 illustrates the variety of intercourse positions possible. The key is for lovers to explore, experiment, be playful, and discover those positions they enjoy most.

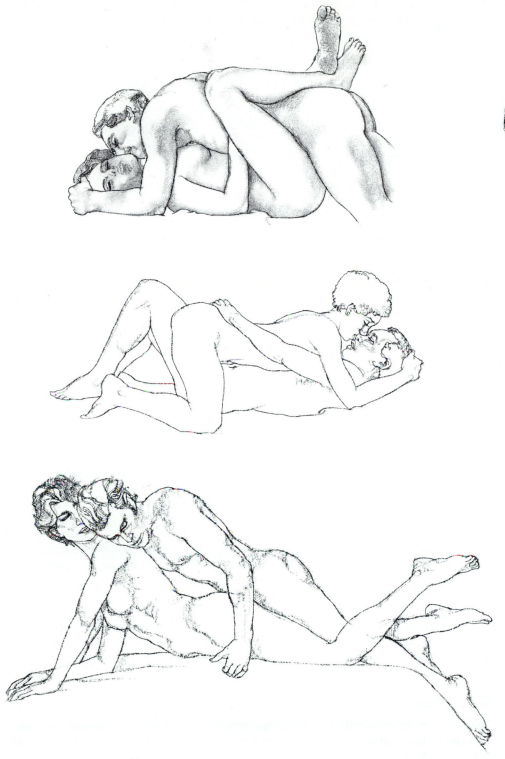

Figure 14.8. *When a couple relaxes and approaches their loveplay without an agenda or goal other than expressing their intimacy and love, they can explore an infinite variety of possibilities and positions. A couple can discover many different ways of expressing their sensuality and meeting their erotic needs that also add newness and variety to their erotic relationship.*

HIGHLIGHT BOX 14.3.
TWO POEMS

i like my body when it is with your
body. It is so quite new a thing.
Muscles better and nerves more.
i like your body. i like what it does,
i like its hows. i like to feel the spine
of your body and its bones, and the trembling
-firm-smooth ness and which i will
again and again and again
kiss, i like kissing this and that of you,
i like, slowly stroking the shocking fuzz
of your electric fur, and what-is-it comes
over parted flesh. . . .   And eyes big love-
    crumbs,

and possibly i like the thrill

of under me you so quite new

Reprinted from e.e. cummings. Copyright 1925. *Complete Poems 1913–1962.* Harcourt Brace Jovanovich.

My Want You Eyes

My want you eyes
thinly disguised
grow wide
with wishes
that take
you in and
devour you whole.
No signs of life
or lust are left,
just
love puddles

everywhere.

Reprinted from *Breath Marks in the Wind, a Book of Erotic Poetry and Illustrations.* Deborah Eve Grayson. Fort Lauderdale, FL: Breath Marks/IDF, Inc. 1988.

Oral Sex

One of the more obvious changes in sexual behavior that came with the sexual revolution of the 1960s and 1970s is the growing acceptance and popularity of mouth-genital or **oral sex**. The 2,436 college students who participated in a study of *The Sex Lives of College Students* (Segal 1984) expressed few inhibitions about oral sex. Generally, however, these students reserved oral sex for a sexual partner who would "return the favor." A greater proportion, especially of the women, enjoyed receiving more than giving. Only a small percentage of the women said they thoroughly enjoyed giving. The women typically said, using the common slang expressions for oral sex, that they felt obliged to "give some head" to their partner after he "went down on them." The women's main motive for giving oral sex was to please their partner; men used it to support their own belief in their sexual prowess and competency as a lover. Most college students rated their first experience with oral sex rather poorly, but experience with the scent and taste of female and male secretions often became a turn-on after some practice. Preconceptions and myths are a major deterrent for those who have not tried oral sex (Segal 1984) (Figure 14.9).

Cunnilingus

Male-to-female, or female-to-female oral-genital sex is known technically as **cunnilingus**; slang expressions include going down, giving head, muff diving, and eating at the Y.

Figure 14.9. *Americans have become more accepting of oral sex in recent years, although we are still not as comfortable with this form of sexual pleasure as other cultures. In Chinese erotic literature, fellatio, or "playing the flute" is often recommended as a way of evoking the sexual control necessary to achieve the heights of ecstasy. Taoism teaches that mutual oral-genital sex creates a special energy circuit that can help harmonize body elements.*

A woman who has been given negative messages about her sexual organs and not taught to take pride in or view her vulva as beautiful may wonder why a man would want to pleasure her this way. Men may be hesitant because of negative messages and concern about what it will taste like. However, after some initial explorations and experimenting, many men and women learn to enjoy the variations and possibilities for pleasuring and orgasm that cunnilingus offers (Kitzinger 1985; Legman 1969).

A woman receiving oral sex is in a unique position of being able to direct her partner and not worry about him losing his erection or having an orgasm too soon. A woman can easily direct and encourage her partner with verbal and nonverbal signals, so that he can provide the greatest pleasure with kisses and oral caresses to her inner thighs, mons, clitoris, labia, and vaginal entrance. In cunnilingus, a man can concentrate all his energies and focus on pleasuring his partner. Encouraged by the sexual liberation of recent years, many women have become enthusiastic about cunnilingus. Some women report that, for them, oral sex is the best, and sometimes the only way they can have an orgasm (Hite 1976).

As for health concerns, the vagina has fewer bacteria and is cleaner than the mouth. Presence of a venereal infection, a herpes outbreak, or a woman who has tested sero-positive for the AIDS virus do raise important health questions (see safer sex practices in Chapter 13, pp. 365–371).

Fellatio

Female-to-male, or male-to-male oral-genital sex is technically known as **fellatio**. Slang expressions include blow job, sucking cock, and giving head.

The glans of the penis, its shaft, the testicles, the inner thighs, and the region just behind the scrotum are all erogenous areas. The pleasurable variations of sucking, licking, nibbling, and caressing are limitless. The receiving partner can guide his partner with verbal and nonverbal feedback. Whether or not the giver continues stimulation to orgasm and takes the ejaculate into the mouth or outside is a matter of personal preference and experimentation. Since many women are concerned about the taste of semen, gagging, ejaculation in the mouth, and swallowing semen, it is best if the couple discuss and explore their feelings about this variation before trying it. The ejaculate has the consistency of egg white. It may have a distinctive, slightly salty aftertaste (Kitzinger 1985).

As with cunnilingus, presence of a venereal infection, a herpes outbreak, or a man who has tested sero-positive for the AIDS virus do raise important health questions (refer again to Chapter 13).

Sixty-Nine

The joys of simultaneous fellatio and cunnilingus, known as 69 in slang, are often extolled in erotic literature and are a common element in many sexual fantasies. Some couples find 69 a delightful variation, whether they do it side by side or with one partner above the other. Some find having the woman above gives her more control. More couples say that 69 is just not worth the trouble—"Too many distractions," "Too much going on," or "Too much to choreograph."

Anal Sex

Many heterosexual couples occasionally engage in **anal intercourse** as a variation. Over a third of the men and women in the 1983 *Playboy* reader survey had tried anal stimulation and intercourse. Many more couples try it as an experiment. Unlike the vagina, the anus is surrounded by strong muscles, and the rectum contains no natural lubrication. Thus inserting a finger or penis in the rectum requires relaxation and lots of water-soluble lubricant.

Health precautions are more important with anal sex than with other sexual activities. *E. coli* bacteria are a normal inhabitant of the rectum, but can cause infections elsewhere. The rectum can also harbor the hepatitis virus. The greater risk of small tears in the rectal lining increases the risk of AIDS if either partner is HIV sero-positive (see Chapter 13). Never insert the penis in the vagina or mouth without washing it after it has been in the rectum. **Analingus**, known in slang as rimming, involves stimulating the perineal and anal region with the tongue. Stimulating the anus and rectum with the finger is another variation some couples engage in (McIlvenna 1987; Morin 1987).

Love Play and Gender

The ways in which two persons can sexually pleasure each other are very much the same whether the two people are a man and woman, two women, or two men. Kissing, hugging, being close, cuddling, sensuous massage, touching one's own and the partner's genitals and erogenous parts, petting, and solo and shared masturbation are much the same regardless of the partner's genders. Oral sex and mutual oral sex are the same, even though the two partners have the same sexual organs. Gay men, as well as straight couples, may engage in *interfemoral intercourse*, climaxing with the penis between the partner's closed thighs. Less frequent is anal sex (Silverstein & White 1977; Walker 1977). Lesbians engage in mutual masturbation, oral sex, and *tribadism* with one partner lying on top of or next to the other and rubbing the mons and clitoral areas together or against another part of the partner's body, for example, the hip or leg (Loulan 1987).

Lesbians and gay men are apparently more relaxed in their love play and less goal-oriented than heterosexual couples. Lesbian couples spend much more time caressing the breasts than do heterosexual couples. As mentioned earlier, some women can be sexually satisfied to orgasm when their breasts and nipples are stimulated. Gay men also spend much more time stimulating each other's nipples. Lesbian and gay couples communicate more about sexual matters than heterosexual couples (Masters & Johnson 1979).

Key Concepts

1. Between birth and death, erotic dreams, sexual fantasies, and masturbation are undoubtedly the most common sexual outlets for men and women. Because these experiences are often frowned upon, if not condemned, they may be associated with uneasiness or guilt.
2. There are no known effective and safe aphrodisiacs. A little alcohol may dampen sexual inhibitions, but more than two or three drinks can interfere

with erection. Chronic abuse of alcohol and heavy use of marijuana can reduce the level of testosterone or affect libido or sperm count. Use of cocaine breaks down the brain's ability to enjoy ordinary pleasurable experiences when the drug is not being used.

3. In Western cultures an unresolved split between spiritual love and lust creates tensions for many people. This conflict leads some to find compromises that result in nonfunctional, reduced, or compulsive/repetitive sexual activity. Compromises may also involve refocusing one's lust and finding a sexual stimulus in some nonsexual part of the loved one or in a nonsexual object.

4. The creative genius of the human mind and our continual desire for intimacy and sensual pleasure make human sexual relations an ongoing venture limited only by the partners' imagination and willingness to explore.

Key Terms

analingus (401)   fellatio (400)
anal intercourse (401)   masturbation (390)
aphrodisiacs (385)   oral sex (398)
cunnilingus (398)

Summary Questions

1. Describe the major tension in our views of limerent and lusty love. What is the likely origin of this tension? What are some typical outcomes of this conflict and tension?
2. Describe four common enemies of sexual desire.
3. Describe some conflicting views of masturbation.
4. Describe some ways in which we use sexual fantasies.
5. How do the sexual fantasies of college students reported by Sue (1979) fit in with Money's interpretation of compromises we make between love and lust?

Suggested Readings

Barbach, L. (1984). *For Each Other: Sharing Sexual Intimacy.* New York: New American Library.

Barbach, L. (1984). *Pleasures: Women Write Erotica.* New York: Harper & Row.

Blank, J. (1989). *Good Vibrations: The Complete Guide to Vibrators* (3rd rev. ed.). Burlingame, CA: Down There Press.

Dodson, B. (1987). *Sex for One: The Joy of Self-Loving.* New York: Harmony Books.

Friday, N. (1980). *Men in Love* (men's sexual fantasies). New York: Delacorte.

Gottman, J., et al. (1976). *A Couple's Guide to Communication.* Champaign, IL: Research Press.

Halpern, J., & M. A. Sherman. (1979). *Afterplay: A Key to Intimacy.* New York: Stein & Day.

Kennedy, A. P., & S. Dean. (1988). *Touching for Pleasure.* Chatsworth, CA: Chatsworth Press.

Kitzinger, S. (1985). *A New Approach to Woman's Experience of Sex.* New York: Putnam.

Legman, G. (1969). *Oragenitalism: Oral Techniques in Genital Excitation.* New York: Julian Press.

Segal, J. (1984). *The Sex Lives of College Students.* Wayne, PA: Miles Standish Press.

The Evolution of Love
Making Contact
  A Different Past
  The Dating Scene Today
Developing Intimacy
  Skills
  Intimacy, Nurturance,
    and Violence
Partner Choice
  Two Models of Mate
    Selection
  Lovemaps
  The Dance of Intimacy
Intimacy and Love
  Four Types of Intimacy
  Conflicting Gender
    Experiences of
    Intimacy
  Jealousy
The Paradoxes of True
  Intimacy

Chapter 15

Intimacy and Love

Special Consultants

Anne Bolin, Ph.D., a symbolic cultural anthropologist and author of *In Search of Eve,* Dr. Bolin is an assistant professor in the Department of Sociology at Elon College, North Carolina.

Martha Cornog, M.A., M.S., former secretary for the Society for the Scientific Study of Sex, former editorial assistant for the *Journal of Sex Research,* and editor of *Libraries, Erotica, and Pornography.*

Timothy Perper, Ph.D., behavioral biologist specializing in the ethological and ethnographic study of courtship and the North American singles scene, and author of *Sex Signals: The Biology of Love.*

James W. Prescott, Ph.D., developmental neuropsychologist internationally known for his neurological and cross-cultural studies of the effects of nurturance and somatosensory affectional deprivation on adult social skills and intimacy.

David L. Weis, Ph.D., associate professor, Human Development and Family Studies, Department of Applied Human Ecology, Bowling Green State University, and author of a number of research articles in the areas of extramarital sexuality and intimate lifestyles.

Intimacy and love are among our most ambiguous and misinterpreted words. *Intimacy* may mean privacy, familiarity, closeness, sharing, or sexual relations, although we can be intimate with someone on a purely intellectual, emotional, or spiritual level without being sexually involved.

The *Oxford English Dictionary* defines *love* rather abstractly as:

> that disposition or state of feeling with regard to a person which (arising from recognition of attractive qualities, from instincts of natural relationship, or from sympathy) manifests itself in solicitude for the welfare of the object and usually also in delight in his presence and desire for his approval; warm affection, attachment.

A Woman's New World Dictionary offers a more down-to-earth three-fold definition of *love* from a feminist viewpoint:

> 1. [Trad.] The profoundly tender and passionate feelings one person may have for another person. 2. A deep personal experience no longer considered the viable foundation for a woman's existence. 3. To be cared for, thought of and valued, not abstractly, as men often value women, but in the accumulation of daily minutiae that make life dense and intricate and worthy.

> *(Kramarae & Treichler 1985)*

How does one distinguish between love and affection, liking, fondness, caring, concern, infatuation, attraction, passion, or desire? Love may refer to an emotion, an attitude, a sentiment, a neurotic manifestation, a way of looking at the world, a means of emotional manipulation, a sublime passion, a peak experience, a religious dedication, a mental state, a desire, a mystical experience, a weakness of the will, an obsession, an aesthetic reaction, a universal thirst, and a glimpse of heaven (Tennov 1980:5–15).

This chapter discusses our quest for intimacy, including a brief history of love and courtship and the relationship of intimacy to nurturance and violent behavior. We examine the dance of flirtation and how we select a partner. We also look at various types of intimacy and at jealousy.

The Evolution of Love

Part of learning about the factors which influence our intimate behavior involves understanding the cultural evolution behind our present concepts of sex, love, and intimacy. The idea of marriage based on romantic love is relatively new. For centuries, marriage was an economic arrangement between families. In ancient Greece, true passionate sexual love could exist only between two men. But the Greeks also gave priority to selfless love of the mind. In the Stoic tradition, physical love distracted men from their higher intellectual endeavors. In the Greek world, women were believed to be incapable of any truly intense love (Lawrence 1989:9–16).

Christianity rejected the homosexual love of the Greeks, but continued the Stoic suppression of physical love. Christianity glorified spiritual celibate love and at the same time reduced sexual love to a second-rate lifestyle, tolerated

Figure 15.1. The Pain of "True Love." *The classic parting of Humphrey Bogart and Ingrid Bergman in the movie* Casablanca *is typical of the romantic view of true love as doomed from the outset. The premature death of the heroine in the novel/movie* Love Story, *the tragedy of Romeo and Juliet, and the disastrous fate that befell Lancelot when he finally declared his love for the Lady Guinevere in the Arthurian legend, musical, and film* Camelot, *all echo the principles of of medieval courtly love.*

only because it could produce more souls for the kingdom of heaven (Hunt 1967; Lawrence 1989; Singer 1984a, 1984b, 1987).

In the early Middle Ages, a new type of love appeared with the troubadours in southern France. **Courtly love** had four roots: the lusty male-dominated Teutonic values of the Franks who viewed women as playthings for men's enjoyment, a certain hedonism introduced by Eleanor of Aquitaine, a new interest in and misinterpretation of Ovid's classic Roman poem *The Art of Love*, and the growing veneration of the Virgin Mary. Medieval knights vied for the honor of their ladies in jousting tournaments and sang of their love. But these ladies were unattainable, the wives of a noble or king. Sex, the expression of physical love, however, was still the mortal enemy of true, noble love. True love still had nothing to do with marriage, which was arranged by the family and based on property and power motives, or simple practicalities (Figure 15.1).

During the Renaissance, romantic courtly love began to mingle more and more with human sexuality. By the 14th century, the extramarital affair was recognizable as we know it today, as an illicit sexual and emotional relationship outside marriage. Prior to this period, adultery was male lust without any emotional involvement or interest. Protestantism was responsible for adding a new dimension by fusing romantic love with marriage. The early Protestants rejected the medieval ascetic view of marriage as an inferior way of life and restored the Jewish view of the family as the center of religious life and nurturance. Many of the virtues of courtly love now became part of marriage (Branden 1980; Lawrence 1989; Singer 1984, 1987).

The new concept of romantic love was particularly popular in the new middle-class families of Europe. This bourgeois-puritan tradition flourished in 19th-century American society. Family historians believe that a major step in the evolution of love occurred during the Victorian period in America around 1880. They have no explanation for the sudden burst of popular literature, novels, poetry, and advice manuals which glorified romantic and marital love. The shift away from communal living in "big houses" to the privacy of a single couple, a husband and wife with their children, was ideologically completed with the adoption of two new values. First was the expectation that a man or a woman should be responsible for satisfying all of the partner's needs—the "knight in shining armor" and his "princess." The second idea was the belief that the two parents can and must meet all the needs of their children. These new values were very much in tune with the emergence of industrialized, growth-oriented capitalism and the nuclear family.

Something unique happened to love and lust in the American experience, which is quite unequaled anywhere else in the world. In the United States especially, an attempt was made to combine sexual passion, commitment, intimacy, love and marriage into one unique experience between one man and one woman (McCary 1975). If we visualize love as a triangle with the three components of commitment, intimacy, and passion, as Robert Sternberg suggests, we can see some of the dynamics and varieties of what we call love (Figure 15.2). The levels of intimacy, passion, and commitment change over time. Commitment, the cognitive aspect of love, tends to increase gradually at first and then more rapidly as a relationship develops. It eventually levels off in a long-term relationship, or falls back to zero if the relationship fails. Intimacy, the emotional component of love, grows steadily and then levels off. It may not be expressed much, but if it disappears, the relationship is likely to fail. Passion, the motivation of love, builds quickly as a positive force in a relationship, peaks, and then drops to a fluctuating lower level (Walster & Walster 1978:37–78). There is also a negative passion that takes hold more slowly and lasts longer. This negative force accounts for the heartache that remains after love is gone (Sternberg 1985; Trotter 1986; Walster & Walster 1978:79–206).

Recent years have brought two more changes to our conception of love and sex. Feminists have

> challenged the old definition of sex as a physical act. Sex, or "normal sex," as defined by the medical experts and accepted by mainstream middle class culture, was a two-act drama of foreplay and intercourse which culminated in male orgasm and at least a display of female appreciation. We rejected this version of sex as narrow, male-centered, unsatisfying. In its single-mindedness and phallocentrism, this [view of sex] . . . reminds us simply of work: "Sex" as narrowly and traditionally defined, is obsessive, repetitive, and symbolically (if not actually) tied to the work of reproduction.
>
> We insisted on a broader, more playful notion of sex, more compatible with women's broader erotic possibilities, more respectful of women's needs.
>
> *(Ehrenreich, Hess & Jacobs 1987:153)*

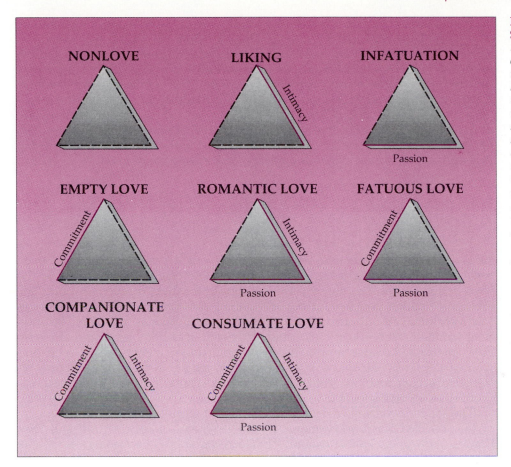

Figure 15.2. The Shapes of Love. *Robert Sternberg, IBM Professor of Psychology and Education at Yale University, has visualized love as a triangle with commitment, intimacy, and passion forming the three sides. A larger triangle could be used to show more commitment, intimacy, and passion in a relationship. Eight combinations are possible, ranging from a non-existent relationship, nonlove, through the one-dimensional liking, infatuation, and empty love, to two-dimensional romantic, fatuous, and companionate love, to balanced, full-dimensional consumate love. Solid lines indicate presence of a particular element; a dotted line indicates its absence.*

Even when the three components are all present in a relationship, they can be unbalanced. To show such imbalances, one can use a triangle with unequal sides, and partially dotted lines to show deficient aspects of the relationship.

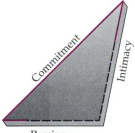  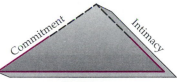

Thus some couples have a very strong commitment, even though their intimacy and closeness have faded and the passion has died down.

Other couples have a very strong emotional intimacy and can bare their souls to each other all the time, even though they have little in the way of commitment or passion. This is little more than a high-grade friendship.

A third unbalanced possibility occurs when passion rules a relationship. This might be an affair, a one-night stand, or a fling in which there is little intimacy and even less commitment.

At the same time, we have also become aware of the role of brain chemistry in our emotions of passion and love. During emotional states, our brain produces chemicals remarkably similar to opiates and amphetamines. The sudden release of one of these chemicals, a morphinelike endorphin, contributes to the pleasurable sensations and euphoria of orgasm. These chemicals can also play a part in the unbridled elation of the "head-over-heels," "blinded-by-love," "swept-away" infatuation Carol Cassell (1984) writes about. The brain chemistry of devastating depression that comes with the end of a love affair, that "broken heart" effect, may be a kind of amphetaminelike withdrawal (Liebowitz 1983). Perhaps there is something to the phrase "the chemistry of love."

Making Contact

A Different Past

As recently as 200 years ago, most marriages were arranged by parents. Even today, many young persons whose parents have recently immigrated to the United States from Asia marry someone chosen for them by their parents. The concept of young people courting and dating someone of their own choice is relatively new. At the turn of the century, young people often met through their families, the schools, formal introductions, or church and community socials. In rural America and tight-knit ethnic urban communities, men and women met in similar ways. But as American society became more industrialized and urban, mobility, college life, or work increasingly provided new opportunities for young people to meet without parental supervision (Bailey 1988).

The modern concept of dating only emerged with the urban-based flappers of the so-called Roaring Twenties. In the 1950s era of rock 'n' roll and Dick Clark's "All-American Bandstand," adolescents shifted to "going steady," a pattern that meshed well with their emergence as consumers in our urban, industrialized economy.

The 1970s carried this evolution of intimate relations and sexual behavior even further. The number of single, never married, separated, or divorced people rose dramatically. The number of women attending college increased significantly. Gradually, more and more young people with financial independence began to think of marrying only after they started a career. However, the workplace seldom offers the same variety and numbers of suitable partners to select from that exists on a college campus.

The Dating Scene Today

In a random sample of East Carolina University students, one-third of the college students met their partners through a friend. "Establishing relationships with same-sex peers may be the best way to meet someone of the opposite sex" (Knox & Wilson 1981). In this same study, 22% of the women and 13% of the men found their dating partners at parties, 12% and 5% met at work, and 6% and 9% met in class.

The commonly accepted images of the college pub, singles bar, and disco are that they are places young people, particularly men, go looking for sex without involvement or emotional meaning. This stereotype may be true for some, but the majority of people going to such places use them to find partners for long-term, stable, emotional, and sexually rewarding relationships. Health

Figure 15.3. *Cathy,* © 1983 Universal Press Syndicate. Reprinted with permission. All rights reserved.

and fitness clubs and the laundry room of a singles condo or apartment are choice meeting places today. So are singles groups like Club Med and Parents Without Partners. Travel agencies and resorts sponsor singles weekends and cruises for singles (Figure 15.3).

"It pays to advertise" is the slogan of many newspapers and magazines, including the classy *New York Review of Books* and *Harper's Magazine.* Many people today, especially those in their middle years, find that a brief ad under the "Personals" heading in the classified section of a local paper can link up like-minded persons. Meeting someone through a personal ad may be almost as haphazard as meeting someone on the street, but it works often enough to be popular. Increasing numbers of gay men and lesbians are turning to personal ads because a post office box number lets them remain anonymous until they find a congenial person.

Dating services claim to match your personality profile and your image of an ideal partner with the profiles of other singles (Figure 15.4). Computer matching, videotaped profiles, and personal introduction services are part of our modern dating scene. The tradition of the marriage broker, common in the

Figure 15.4. *Cathy,* © 1983 Universal Press Syndicate. Reprinted with permission. All rights reserved.

18th- and 19th-century European upper and upper middle class, continues today among Orthodox and Hassidic Jews. Marriage brokers may also specialize in finding brides in the Philippines and Orient for American and European men who want a wife whose values are more traditional than their Western counterparts (Belkin 1986; Breen, Breen, & Ehrlich 1986; Joseph 1984).

If meeting a suitable partner is less structured and more difficult today, so too is communicating with that partner about what we expect. Negotiating the ground rules for sexual intimacy often creates tensions. Knox and Wilson (1981) found that less than 15% of both sexes shared an understanding with their dates of how long they would wait before engaging in kissing, petting, and intercourse. For many of these students, the nature of the relationship and not the number of dates determined when sexual intimacy began and its extent.

Developing Intimacy Skills

Intimacy, Nurturance, and Violence

How do we develop the ability to be open with another person, to have an intimate relationship? Is it a purely natural process, or do we have to go through certain developmental stages, with all the risks of not reaching our goal? In Chapters 4 and 14 we touched on some of the developmental stages we go through in building a strong self-identity and our gender-identity role during childhood and adolescence. Particularly important here is the connection between nurturance and intimacy in the early years and our intimacy skills as adults (Figure 15.5; Table 15.1).

An essential factor influencing our ability to develop intimate, loving, and committed relationships with other adults is the nurturance we receive, or do not receive, as infants, children, and adolescents. The physical and emotional

Figure 15.5. *Most adults are unaware that they are providing an important preparation for the intimacies of adult relationships when they are physically close to their children, cuddling and holding them, as this father is doing while shopping.*

nurturance, the touching and cuddling we experience early in life flows through our senses to our brains where behavioral tendencies or pathways are traced which prepare us for later adult intimacy. Children deprived of nurturance early in life often develop neural roadblocks that make it difficult for them to trust and become intimate with others later in life (Gambrill 1989; Prescott 1975a, 1989).

Insights about early nurturance began 40 years ago with Harry and Margaret Harlow's experiments with monkeys (Harlow 1964, 1971). The Harlows took some newborn monkeys from their mothers and raised them with only a cold metal mesh and nursing bottle as a surrogate mother. Other newborns were raised with a furry surrogate mother and nursing bottle. Control animals were raised by their natural mothers. The infants deprived of normal touching and cuddling grew up with a fear of being touched. They became depressed and antisocial, withdrawn, even "autistic-like." Other researchers have compared newborn monkeys raised with a furry, free-swinging surrogate mother suspended from the top of the cage and with a stationary surrogate. Again, the deprivation of somatosensory input, this time motion, produces a withdrawn, antisocial animal, incapable of interacting or being intimate with others (Gambrill 1989; Mason & Berkson 1975; Prescott 1975a, 1989).

Researchers have identified two neural systems in the limbic region of the brain which are primary centers for processing sensations of pleasure and pain. These areas operate as if they were at the ends of a seesaw—when the neural pleasure system is stimulated, the neural system that mediates pain and violence is inhibited. The reverse is also true. When a young animal receives a lot of pleasurable stimulation from being cuddled, stroked, and rocked, its neural pleasure system develops and regulates the neural pain/violence system. The result is a friendly, social animal. When an animal is deprived of pleasurable input, its neural pain/violence system is unregulated since the neural pleasure system remains relatively undeveloped. If the infant is physically abused, the effect is even more direct. Lack of nurturing sensory input and physical abuse imprint the brain, producing a violent, antisocial monkey. Prescott calls this phenomenon the **Somatosensory Affectional Deprivation (SAD) syndrome**.

Evidence of the SAD syndrome in humans helps us better understand the issue of intimacy. Prescott and his associates have found evidence of neurobiological damage in the neural systems of the brains of isolation-reared monkeys. Other investigators have found similar damage in violent criminals. Neuronal spiking, large voltage discharges found in deep brain structures of isolation-reared, violent monkeys, has yet to be confirmed in humans with violent personality disorders and a history of SAD syndrome (Kruesi et al. 1986; Prescott 1971; Saltzberg 1985; Saltzberg et al. 1969).

There is also cross-cultural evidence for the SAD syndrome. In 80%, 39 out of 49, of the societies for which Prescott found data, the absence of physical affectional nurturance is associated with violence in particular cultures. Societies that provide child nurturance tend to be peaceful societies.

But what about the remaining 20%, those 10 societies which do not appear to support this conclusion? In 4 out of these 10 societies, adults provide a lot of infant nurturance, but the children grow up to be quite violent. All 4 societies have strong taboos against premarital sexual relations and place a high value on premarital virginity. "It appears," Prescott concludes, "that *the beneficial effects of infant physical affection can be negated by repression of physical pleasure [premarital sex] later in [adolescent] life.*" In the remaining 6 cultures, there is little physical affection shown for the young, and yet these cultures exhibited low levels of adult physical violence. These 6 societies accept or tolerate premarital sex. "Thus, *the detrimental effects of infant physical affectional deprivation seem to be compensated for later in life by sexual body pleasure experiences during adolescence*" (Prescott 1975a, 1989).

The evidence suggests that when societies and individual families promote nurturance and intimacy during childhood and adolescence, they prepare their young for intimacy and love as adults. When societies and families deprive their young of body pleasure and nurturance, they set the stage for adult problems in intimacy (Prescott 1989) (Table 15.2).

Table 15.1.
One View of Intimacy

The editors of Medical Aspects of Human Sexuality *surveyed 400 physicians for their thoughts about intimacy. Following are some of their answers. Taking into consideration the quite different social worlds of physicians and today's college students, do you think you would get significantly different answers if these questions were answered by a group of 400 college students?*

What is the best indicator of emotional intimacy?

Good understanding of one another's feelings			54%
Trust	28%	Deep affection	14%
Complete honesty	6%	Leisure spent together	5%

What is the chief barrier to emotional intimacy?

Fear of rejection	40%	Hostility toward spouse	40%
Lack of common interest	12%	Traditional sex roles	8%
Need for privacy	2%		

What is the best way to improve intimacy?

Frank discussions	51%	More nonsexual affection	35%
Sharing leisure time	12%	More frequent sex	3%

Is frequent intercourse a good indicator of strong emotional intimacy?

No	68%	Yes	29%

Should spouses be totally honest with each other about their feelings?

No, discretion is needed in expressing sentiments that would hurt or anger partner	57%
Yes, with rare exceptions 45%	

For true intimacy, should a spouse be one's best friend as well as partner?

Preferable, but not essential	48%	Yes, essential	43%
Not relevant to intimacy	8%	Not preferable	3%

Do men or women have a stronger need for emotional intimacy?

About equal	53%	Women	44%	Men	3%

Do men or women have more difficulty in being frank and open with their partner?

Men	49%	About equal	39%	Women	12%

Does having a close friend and confidant tend to impair marital intimacy?

No, may even promote emotional harmony			51%
No bearing usually	31%	Yes	17%

Source: Reprinted with permission from *Medical Aspects of Human Sexuality.* © Cahners Publishing Company. Published March 1983. All rights reserved.

Table 15.2.
Attitudes, Moral Values, and Behaviors of Violence-Oriented Persons

In 1974, 96 college students filled out a questionnaire and personality profile which allowed James Prescott to relate certain attitudes toward sex and pleasure with the attitudes, values, and behaviors of violence-oriented persons.

In this table, attitudes and behaviors which showed a factor loading greater than 0.50 are very significant. All the items shown in this table are statistically significant and typical of violence-oriented persons. Violence-oriented persons typically reject physical pleasure and seek emotional relief through drugs and alcohol.

Violence Approved

0.85   Hard physical punishment is good for children who disobey a lot.
0.81   Physical punishment and pain help build a strong moral character.
0.80   Abortion should be punished by society.
0.76   Capital punishment should be permitted by society.
0.75   Violence is necessary to really solve our problems.
0.74   Physical punishment should be allowed in the schools.
0.69   I enjoy sadistic pornography.
0.54   I often feel like hitting someone.
0.43   I can tolerate pain very well.

Physical Pleasure Condemned

0.84   Prostitution should be punished by society.
0.80   Responsible premarital sex is not agreeable to me.
0.78   Nudity within the family has a harmful influence upon children.
0.73   Sexual pleasures help build a weak moral character.
0.72   Society should interfere with private sexual behavior between adults.
0.69   Responsible extramarital sex is not agreeable to me.
0.61   Natural fresh body odors are often offensive.
0.47   I do not enjoy affectional pornography.

Alcohol and Drugs Rated Higher Than Sex

0.70   Alcohol is more satisfying than sex.
0.65   Drugs are more satisfying than sex.
0.60   I get hostile and aggressive when I drink alcohol.
0.49   I would rather drink alcohol than smoke marijuana.
0.45   I drink alcohol more often than I experience orgasm.

Political Conservatism

0.82   I tend to be conservative in my political points of view.
0.77   Age (Older).
0.51   I often dream of either floating, flying, falling, or climbing.
0.45   My mother is often indifferent toward me.
0.42   I often get "uptight" about being touched.
0.40   I remember when my father physically punished me a lot.

This pattern carries over into our modern Western societies. Those Western societies which discourage nurturance consistently share negative attitudes toward gun control, abortion, nudity, sexual pleasure, masturbation, premarital and extramarital sex, breast-feeding, and women. These same societies also tend to glorify war and have a high level of drug and alcohol abuse.

On the other side, societies which encourage nurturance and have a positive view of body pleasure also advocate prolonged breast-feeding, have a strong sense of humor, and accept abortion, premarital, and extramarital sex. These same societies show a low anxiety about sex, little sexual dysfunction, and treat women and men as equals. They also have small families, do not glorify war or violence, favor gun control laws, and deemphasize private property.

Partner Choice

Two Models of Mate Selection

There are several theories seeking to explain how we choose a partner. One folklore theory suggests that "opposites attract." In fact, just the opposite seems to be true! We tend to be attracted to people who are similar to us in economic and social position, intelligence, attractiveness, background, values, expectations, and attitudes (Byrne 1971; Lauman 1969; Reiss 1960; Vandenberg 1972).

One model of partner selection, the **stimulus/value/role (SVR) theory**, stresses the similarity of values and roles and their negotiation as an intimate relationship develops. Selecting a mate, according to Murstein, requires that we move through three stages: a *stimulus* stage, a *value* exploration stage, and a *role* negotiation stage. Hence the acronym SVR. In the first stage, we respond to initial physical, social, intellectual, or other attraction or stimuli. Next is the value stage where we explore the compatibility of each other's values in religion, lifestyle, politics, sex, hobby interests, and other value areas. After successfully negotiating these two steps, we can work out the roles with which we are both comfortable (Murstein 1970, 1974:389–398). Selecting a partner with similar background and values appears to increase the chances of a quality relationship, regardless of whether the couple is heterosexual and married or cohabiting, gay, or lesbian (Kurdeck & Schmitt 1987) (Figure 15.6).

In recent years, the **social exchange theory** has gained popularity as a way of explaining the formation and development of intimate relationships (Nye 1979, 1980). In the view of exchange theorists, all relationships involve an exchange of rewards and costs. Each partner experiences some events in the relationship as rewarding or enjoyable: Your partner smiles at you, or says "I love you." Your partner tells you a funny joke or does something special for you. You think your partner is beautiful or rich. Other events are experienced as negative: Your partner makes odd noises while eating, or grinds his or her teeth during a horror movie. Your partner fails to notice when you go out of your way to be nice. Your partner embarrasses you in front of your friends.

No relationship is perfect in the sense that it generates only rewards. All relationships include some costs for each partner. When the rewards exceed the costs, the relationship generates "profit." Such relationships tend to be satisfying and to grow more intimate. We like to be with persons we experience as highly rewarding. When the costs are greater than the rewards, the relationship operates at a loss. It tends to be dissatisfying. We pull back and become less intimate.

"REMEMBER WHEN YOU WENT BACK TO WORK, AND I DECIDED TO STAY HOME AND TAKE CARE OF THE HOUSE, HOW WE THOUGHT IT WOULDN'T WORK OUT?"

Exchange principles operate at various stages of a relationship. They influence who we find attractive, who we are willing to date a second time, who we are willing to "go with," and whether we believe a relationship is ready for marriage. Moreover, the exchange of rewards and costs can shift over time. A relationship that was once highly rewarding can grow to become costly—even to the point of a breakup.

Lovemaps

The particular person we select out of the crowd, that one person we choose to date and pair up with for life is probably not a purely random choice. We may select that one person because he or she matches a very personal, unique lovemap we have developed over the years in our mind and brain. This image, which depicts our idealized lover and our idealized program for relating sexually with that idealized lover, is as personalized as our faces and fingerprints. This brain template or image, this **lovemap**, started developing before we were born (see Gate 6 in Chapter 4).

After birth, this tendency was overlaid and detailed by our own unique combination of sexual and erotic scripting. Part of our lovemap appears to involve the gender of the persons to whom we are emotionally and sexually attracted. As part of our lovemap, this orientation tendency also appears to be laid down before birth and elaborated by a variety of social factors after birth (Money 1986:127–130) (Figure 15.7).

A lovemap, which falls within the range of what our community or authorities say is statistically normal, can be called a *normophilic lovemap*. The range of

Figure 15.7. *Much of the detail in our lovemap, the image we develop in our brain of the ideal love partner, develops from associations and relationships we have as children and young adolescents.*

normophilic lovemaps is quite wide. The ideal lover might be thin or weigh 250 pounds, have short or long hair, be clean-shaven or bearded (Goode & Preissler 1982; Silverstein et al. 1986). Lovemaps that have a homosexual or lesbian orientation are considered normal by many today.

Since lovemaps are the product of a long process of development, it is natural that some lovemaps are distorted or vandalized. Voyeurism and exhibitionism, for example, are often normal, healthy behaviors in courtship and loveplay. When elements like voyeurism, exhibitionism, and other sexual stimuli become dominant and replace the partner as the focus of sexual arousal and satisfaction, the result is a paraphilic or distorted lovemap for the unconventional or "kinky sex" discussed in Chapter 20.

Limerence is a term coined by Dorothy Tennov (1979) to describe the intense emotional state of falling in love and being love-smitten. Limerence is beyond conscious control. A romantic love, it is preoccupied with the loved one to the point of being oblivious and blind, at least temporarily, to reality (Walster & Walster 1978).

Weinrich (1988) has made an interesting distinction between romantic limerence and the lust of physical passion. Limerent sexual attraction, he suggests, eroticizes the personality and physical traits of the particular person with whom we fall in love. A lusty sexual attraction, on the other hand, produces erotic arousal when a new object of lust appears. Weinrich claims that men and women experience both kinds of sexual attraction. But he suggests that, in our culture, most women experience limerence as a general desire and physical passion or lust mostly as a reaction to a particular person. Most men in our culture, on the other hand, experience a general lusty desire and limit their limerence to a particular person. The gender of the person with whom we fall in love may not be important, but lusty attraction is rarely indifferent to the gender of its object.

The Dance of Intimacy

Flirtation Patterns

How do people make contact in a singles bar, a club, an old age home, retirement community, or college pub? After observing over 500 couples, Perper and Fox found there is a common pattern in the way we flirt and make contact which cuts across class distinctions, age levels, and sexual orientations.

Flirtation may seem to be a complex, unstructured, and unpredictable phenomenon if we walk into a crowded and noisy disco. However, a skilled observer of behavior and body language can peel away the extraneous details and get to the core of how we all flirt (Eibl-Eibesfeldt cited in Money 1988:129). Successful **flirtation** behavior depends on negotiating five escalation points. These are objectively observable events, points at which the flirtation either escalates upward toward increasing intimacy or deescalates toward decreased intimacy and the end of the relationship. Flirtation continues and intimacy develops only if the couple mutually negotiates each of five escalation points in the dance of intimacy (Perper 1985; Perper & Fox 1981; Perper & Weis 1987).

We know practically nothing about the behavior patterns two women engage in when flirting because their courtship usually occurs in the privacy of women's spaces. What little is known about lesbian flirtation comes from lesbian writers and not from scientific observations. Gay male courtship, on the other hand, is often quite public, involving cruising with elaborate posturing and eye contact. At the same time, gay men do not have a set of cultural scripts for flirtation. Unlike dancing, there's no problem if two men simultaneously take the lead when it comes to sexual encounters. But how do two men communicate the early stirrings of interest? Which male expresses an interest first? In heterosexual courtship, the female is proceptive and makes the first subtle overtures by letting her interest be known. The courtship of gay men is more complicated than heterosexual flirtations (Weinrich 1987:270–277).

Heterosexual Flirtation

Step One: The Approach   The first step in flirtation requires that one person approach the other. One person enters and quickly scans everyone present to select a potential partner. Long-distance eye contact may be part of this selection process, or the potential partner may be selected without being aware of it. Closing the physical gap may involve a meandering path, but the approach is nevertheless very obvious in its ultimate goal. Often, it is the woman who moves into proximity with a man she finds attractive. The person approached must acknowledge the other person, by moving toward her or him, looking briefly, tilting the head slightly, or in some other way recognizing the new presence.

Step Two: Talk   An inconsequential conversation typically follows, for example, "The band is loud tonight, isn't it?" or some other opening line that requires a response. If the other person does not reply, he or she has rejected the attempt to escalate the relationship. The interaction is over.

Step Three: Swivel or Turn   If the second step leads to some casual conversation, one or the other person will try to escalate the flirting a bit further. As they talk, body language comes into play. If they are mutually attracted, they gradually shift from standing side-by-side to face each other. The turning process contains its own minor escalation points. Every time one person turns more toward the other, thus closing the angle between their bodies, the movement must be reciprocated if the intimacy is to grow. A man who turns away from a woman who has just shifted her weight toward him is rejecting her escalation, even though he may not be aware of his message.

Step Four: Touch   Because it is our most basic form of communication and intimacy, the first touch between two persons marks a major escalation point. Typically, the woman touches first. It may be as innocuous as picking an imaginary piece of lint or hair from his suit, or "accidentally" brushing his thigh with her hand. This initial touch must be accepted by returning it, by smiling, or by turning more face to face. Otherwise, the interaction slows down and stops. Occasionally, a man freezes or appears startled when a woman touches him. Both are subtle rejections. Even if he simply does not respond or acknowledge the touch, the relationship will wind down. Escalations must be accepted and actively returned; otherwise, the interaction has no future.

Step Five: Synchronization   Following the swivel and touch, or sometimes simultaneous with one or the other, the two people begin to synchronize their body movements, mirroring each other's actions. They lift their drinks or fold their hands almost simultaneously. Later on, they sway back and forth in synchrony with each other. Often the two adopt identical postures, crossing their legs or shifting their weight together. The degree and type of body synchronization provide the observer with a remarkably accurate index of the developing intimacy. This final, and most important step, cannot be faked.

If all goes well, in an hour or two the interaction pattern is stabilized. The two people are facing each other, moving in synchronization, looking into each other's eyes and at each other's bodies, and regularly touching each other.

Flexible as this five-step dance may seem, it cannot be rushed or forced. Intimacy, whether lifelong or lasting only a few evenings, develops mutually.

> Each person must enjoy the dance of intimacy with the other, for its own sake and for the pleasure of being with the other person. Which makes sense, if you think about it. When we dance, we want to enjoy dancing for itself, and not race through the steps just so we can get back to the table as fast as we can. So it is with courtship. The dance of intimacy should be enjoyed for how it brings us close together, talking, touching, synchronizing with another person, just as we can enjoy sexual intimacy for its shared touching and feeling, as an end in itself.
>
> *(Perper 1987:24)*

Women typically are much more aware than men of what is happening in flirtation. Even successful men frequently have no idea how they attract women, or of what happens as they flirt. Women characteristically say they know a man is interested by how he moves, dances, looks at her, or generally handles himself. Men focus on the fact that a woman will do something publicly with them to demonstrate their interest. A man does not want to risk saying the woman is interested until she makes some kind of public commitment, like dancing or having a drink with him.

Although a man may be tempted to interpret a woman's flirting as a sign of promiscuity, a woman who flirts has already chosen her target. Even if she temporarily stalls escalation of the flirtation dance, it is only to test the man's sensitivity and his potential as a long-term partner. Men who fail such a test by pressing a woman for sex will be unequivocally, and often contemptuously, rejected (Perper & Weis 1987:477).

Once the initial contact has been made and the relationship has developed to the point of becoming sexually intimate, the importance of body language and nonverbal communication continues. The process of communicating sexual interest is more complex than making initial contact, but it is still predominantly nonverbal and conveyed by touch. When Jesser asked sexually experienced college students how they communicated their sexual interest to another person, 98% said they relied on touching, snuggling, and kissing. Nine out of 10 said allowing their hand to wander was the next best way of communicating an interest in sex. Three out of 4 women felt comfortable simply stating their interest in sex. About half used familiar code words for sex to set a mood atmosphere. Forty percent to 50% resorted to eye contact, compliments, removing some clothing, teasing, and suggestive postures, especially lying down (Jesser 1978).

Females, The Initiators

Traditionally, men have believed that they, and not women, are the sexual initiators. The myth is that women are reluctant, hesitant, or coy. Whether it is the woman who more often selects and touches first, as Perper and Weis observed, or whether it is the woman who is more direct than the male in communicating sexual interest by touching and directly asking for sex, as Jesser found, it seems that women are the prime initiators. Remoff (1984) suggests that "female choice" is an evolutionary mandate given to women so that she may select the best mate and thus assure the survival of the species. Women, Remoff contends, are the "active initiators of the majority of encounters that lead to sexual contact."

Monica Moore's observations of more than 200 randomly selected women provide an insight into the wide range of nonverbal solicitation signals women use regularly to get the attention of a man they find interesting. The fact is that men think they are taking the initiative when, in reality, they are actually responding to women's nonverbal overtures (Moore 1985) (see Table 15.3). In the dance of flirtation and intimacy, it is important to remember that two people interact, communicate, and respond to each other. Regardless of which partner initiates the escalation, either party can call off the process.

Table 15.3.
How Women Invite Intimacy

When Monica Moore observed the nonverbal flirtation behaviors of more than 200 randomly selected women between the ages of 18 and 35, she found that the women who sent out more visual and tactile displays were most often approached by a man. Also, the more courtship signals the woman used, the more likely the man was to continue the contact. Following is a catalog of the behaviors she observed. The number after each behavior is the number of times each signal was used by the 200 women Moore observed. How do these observations fit in with the five stages in the dance of flirtation described by Timothy Perper?

Facial and Head Patterns		Gestures		Body Posture Patterns	
A smile	511	Hand gestures	62	Dancing alone	253
A room-encompassing glance	253	Caressing an object	56	Leaning toward man	121
A laugh	249	Primping	46	"Accidental" brushing or touching	96
A short, darting glance	222	Caressing the man's leg	32	Pointing to a chair, inviting him to sit	62
A hair flip	139	Caressing his arm	23	Accepting a dance request	59
A fixed gaze	117	Holding his hand	20	Parading with exaggerated hip movement, etc.	41
A head toss	102	Caressing his back	17	Soliciting his aid	34
A nod of the head	66	Patting his buttock	8	Playful behavior	31
Whispering to man	60	Tapping to get his attention	8	Hugging his shoulder	25
Tilting the head, touching exposed neck	58			Placing man's hand on her lap, etc.	19
Licking lip(s)	48			Approaching with two feet	18

Source: Moore, M. M. (1985). Nonverbal courtship patterns in women: Context and consequences. *Ethology & Sociobiology.* 6:237–247.

Intimacy and Love

Four Types of Intimacy

How do we go about choosing a partner for a long-term intimate relationship? Much of our choice depends on how we define and describe what we mean by intimacy. Intimacy may be intellectual, physical, and emotional. All three of these dimensions may exist in any long-term relationship, but they probably exist in different degrees. Some couples have little intellectual intimacy but a great deal of physical intimacy. Physical intimacy can also exist without much emotional involvement. Erik Erikson says that **intimacy** is the task of every maturing young adult to evoke caring from a committed peer partner (Renshaw 1984).

A fourth type of intimacy is spiritual intimacy (Assagioli 1971). Many people find a type of transcendent, religious, or spiritual intimacy or nurturance in the vitality of their church or synagogue community. These intimacies may also be found in the privacy of a direct relationship and experience with the transcendent or divine. At times, as we see in discussing the varieties of sexual and erotic outlets in later chapters, these spiritual experiences may have a very sensual and even erotic character with no genital expression whatsoever.

Intimacy can be varied by controlling the scope of activities shared with the other person or by limiting the amount of self that we choose to disclose and share. Think about how much of your core self you share with a person with whom you are intimate. Many of us choose to keep much of our personal selves from the other person. There is no right or wrong response here, since private space is as essential to many people as openness is to others.

Conflicting Gender Experiences of Intimacy

Man is a social animal, and the ordinarily healthy human finds prolonged isolation a severe punishment. Short of physical torture or death, solitary confinement is the worst agony that can be inflicted on a prisoner. Such is the need for basic intimacy. For intimacy breeds understanding, and most of us want to be understood, at least by a few people.

(Morris 1971)

Unfortunately, in our Western culture, expressing affection and intimacy that is not sexual is something few of us have learned. And when we have learned it, we find that others more often misinterpret our intent. For many men, there is often an all-or-nothing equation: "touch = sex = intercourse." As a result, we usually limit nonsexual affection and intimacy to children, deathbeds, funerals, and family reunions (Renshaw 1984).

When it comes to intimacy, Renshaw (1984:74) notes, "It has often been said that girls use sex to get love, and boys use love to get sex. With these cross-purposes they mate and alienate, and wonder what went wrong." Carol Gilligan (1982) has observed that young girls learn to experience themselves as part of a network of relationships and are threatened by anything that might rupture these connections. Men are trained to find their security in themselves. They are taught to be self-sufficient and dominant. They are allowed all sorts of options. Yet most men are willing to trade this freedom for mortgages, child care, ulcers, and monogamy because they need a woman as their emotional outlet and main source of love. Nancy Friday believes this conditioning is why men's love for women is so often filled with unexpressed rage, even though love wins out over rage (Friday 1980:5).

Men are constantly threatened by their fears of female rejection. Women may flirt and tease, but men complain when they are unresponsive or refuse to be sexually intimate. Women are viewed as moody and bitchy, self-absorbed, always fussing about their appearance, and spending too much money on their clothes. Women, on the other hand, are put off by the sexual pressure and demands from men which leave them with a feeling of having been used. Women complain that men are condescending and treat them as inferior or stupid. Women are upset that men too often hide their emotions and act tough. Men, women complain, are thoughtless, messy, unreliable, belchy, and insensitive (Buss 1989; Farrell 1988; McGill 1985).

Women tend to look for intimacy and mutual emotional support in their friendships and marriages. Men tend to look to friendships, not for emotional

If you want to avoid intimacy with another person, Bryan Strong, a psychology professor, suggests ten rules that are quite effective. Of course, *if you want to be intimate with another person, you should not follow these rules!*

RULE 1: Don't talk!   This is the basic rule for avoiding intimacy. If you follow this one rule, you will never have to worry about being intimate again.

RULE 2: Never show your feelings!   Showing your feelings is almost as bad as talking because sharing your feelings is a way of communicating. If you cry, show emotion, express sadness or joy, you are giving yourself away. You might as well talk, and if you talk, you could become intimate. So hide your emotions.

RULE 3: Always be pleasant!   Always smile, always be friendly, especially if something is bothering you. You'll be surprised at how this will prevent you from being intimate and will fool your partner into thinking that everything's perfect in your relationship. If everything is okay, you and your partner won't have to change.

RULE 4: Always win!   Never compromise. Never admit that your partner's view may be as good as yours. If you start compromising, that's an admission that you care about your partner's feelings, which is a dangerous step toward intimacy.

RULE 5: Always keep busy!   If you keep busy at school or work, your work will keep you from being intimate with your partner. Because our society values hard work and success, your partner won't be able to complain that you're putting all your time and energy into your work and ignoring him or her.

RULE 6: Always be right!   There is nothing worse than being wrong. That would indicate that you're human. If you admit you're wrong, you'll have to admit your partner is right, and that will make him or her as good as you. Then you will have to take your partner into consideration, and before you know it, you're intimate.

RULE 7: Never argue or disagree!   If you argue or disagree, you'll discover you and your partner are different. If you're different, you may have to talk about your differences and make adjustments for them. That means revealing your feelings and needs, which requires talking and leads to intimacy.

RULE 8: Make your partner guess what you want!   Never tell your partner what you want. That way, when your partner tries to guess and is wrong, you can tell him or her that he or she really doesn't understand or love you. If your partner did love you, he or she would know what you want without asking. Not only will this prevent intimacy, it will drive your partner crazy as well.

RULE 9: Always look out for number one!   Remember, you are number one. All relationships exist in order to fulfill *your* needs, no one else's. Whatever you feel like doing is okay. If your partner can't satisfy your needs, he or she is selfish. After all, you're the one who's making all the sacrifices in this relationship.

RULE 10: Keep the television on!   Keep the television on at all times, while you're reading, when you're in bed, while you're talking—especially if your partner's talking about something important. This may sound petty, but it's important to keep you from noticing that you and your partner are not talking with each other.

We want to caution the reader that this list is not complete. You undoubtedly know other ways of avoiding intimacy. These may be your own unique invention, or rules you've learned from others. To complete this list, add your own rules for avoiding intimacy, and don't share them or these ten rules with your "Significant Other."

Source: Adapted from the *FLEducator*. (1985, Winter). 4:2.

intimacy, but for shared activities and for help in doing what they want to do (Blyth & Foster-Clark 1987). In a long term relationship, women equate intimacy with sensitivity, shared emotions, and talking about the relationship itself. Men equate intimacy with fulfilling their responsibilities and doing things for their wives. Marriage allows a man to break ties with his family and bind to his woman. Marriage allows a woman to resolve tensions with her parents, especially her mother, even as her husband moves to the center of her network (Goleman 1986; Lerner 1989).

Jealousy

Eight hundred years ago, when romantic love appeared in Western Europe, the noble ladies of Languedoc used to say, "Real jealousy always increases the worth of love." Many would agree that jealousy is a normal, natural part of true love. It is seen as an emotion that strengthens marriage and monogamy. In the 1960s and 1970s, this traditional view was challenged by people exploring alternative, nonmonogamous lifestyles, such as swinging, sexually open marriages, and group marriages.

Psychologists Gordon Clanton and Lynn Smith (1977a, 1977b) have suggested that much of what we call jealousy is actually a mask for other negative emotions. They believe we use jealousy to express ulterior motives we do not want to admit to ourselves. Behind the mask of jealousy we often find a gnawing sense of inadequacy, insecurity, and threatened self-identity. The mask may mean that a person cannot tolerate hearing about the partner's earlier relationships and loves, envies the time a loved one spends at work or with other persons, or feels insecure and threatened by the potential competition of others. We may feel resentful when a loved one becomes engrossed with another person and leaves us out. This feeling is not jealousy, but a mask for our resentment at being excluded and for our unwillingness to encourage our loved one to enjoy an experience we might not be able to provide.

The traditional sense of jealousy is based on the idea that we must provide for all the needs of our loved one, no matter how impossible that goal might be. The traditional sense of jealousy ignores the possibility that another person might be able to share or bring out some aspect of our beloved's personality that we cannot touch. Traditional jealousy creates guilt when we do not meet this impossible responsibility of being everything to our partner.

A more serious form of jealousy stems from a personal sense of insecurity and the fear of being abandoned. Jealous feelings and reactions may be a mask for deeper feelings of our own insecurity. A feeling that "She (he) may leave me, so I have to hang on" may actually mean "I am unwilling to deal with my own lack of self-identity and self-confidence." It may also mean that "I really don't trust the strength of our love."

There are some societies where jealousy is an unknown emotion. The amorous Lepcha of Sikkim and some of the Polynesian cultures in the South Pacific find our concepts of romantic love, the broken heart, and jealousy incomprehensible, so we know that jealousy is an emotion we learn by social scripting. In cultures where infants and children are nurtured openly by many adults in the village, children are not threatened by loss when their parents are not around or are playing with their brothers and sisters and ignoring them.

In the privacy of the American family, sibling rivalries and jealousies are common emotional responses. The way parents handle these emotional reactions can set the stage for the way their children cope with jealousy as teenagers and adults. If your parents punished your jealousy of their attention to a brother or sister, you may tend to repress your jealous feelings as an adult. If they ignored you or deprived you of affection in response to your jealousy, you may have an even deeper feeling of insecurity and jealousy in later life. If, on the other hand, they recognized and respected your reactions, reassured you of their love, and tried to help you put it in perspective, you were being conditioned to cope with your jealous emotions in a broader perspective.

Coping with jealousy in a culture that provides mixed messages about the emotion is not easy. To say that jealousy is a childish, immature, or a negative emotion does not solve the problem. Clanton and Smith (1977a, 1977b) suggest two ways we can deal with this real emotion.

As an example of the *insecure, defensive reaction*, consider the following thoughts that might run through your mind when you see your loved one engaged in an enthusiastic, bubbling conversation with a person of the other sex:

> His interest in her confirms my suspicion that he is on the make. I never did trust him. Her interest in him shows she is dissatisfied with me. He's quite attractive. I guess she's grown tired of me. And he's so attentive to her, so appreciative. I guess I've come to take her for granted. No wonder she's so turned on by his courtesies. They want to go to the opera together, and I feel left out. I wonder what other excuses they'll find to spend time together. Maybe she'll take time away from me to be with him. Maybe I'll have to cook dinner and take care of the kids while she's off at the "opera." If I can't count on my own wife, what the hell can I count on?
>
> *(Clanton & Smith 1977a:44)*

On the other hand, you might react in a *constructive* way, trusting in your own self-image and in your partner's love:

> His interest in her confirms her attractiveness. I'm proud of her. Her interest in him shows she is alert and alive. I'm glad for that. An inert partner, no matter how secure the relationship, is a bad deal. He's like me in some ways, so I am affirmed by her choice of him. He's different from me in some ways, which suggests she has some needs that I don't meet. I must consider these needs carefully and try to find out if I could do a better job of meeting them. But I realize I cannot meet all of her needs without violating my own autonomy, so I must work to become glad she has other friends who can fulfill her in ways I do not and would rather not. Thank God, she's found someone who wants to go to the opera with her. I want to be reassured that our relationship means as much to her as it does to me, but I won't demand that she renounce all others in order to demonstrate that to me.
>
> *(Clanton & Smith, 1977a:44)*

How do you handle jealousy? Do you give your partner the silent treatment, not wanting to demean yourself by admitting that your feelings have been hurt? Or do you take the opposite tack, cut in on the conversation, grab your partner by the arm and snap, "Okay, Don Juan, let's go!"?

Some people use jealousy to get attention, as a reminder to their loved one that someone else thinks they are just the most fascinating person around. However, insecurity and jealousy can turn us into supersleuths, always looking for signs of betrayal. Sometimes our jealousy hides a masochistic need to play the "poor me" martyr role. Martyrdom is an excellent cover for insecurity.

In recent years, the traditional defenses men and women used in dealing with jealousy have crumbled as the liberation of women gained strength and patriarchy waned. Men and women have been left staring into the red-hot heart of rage, envy, and jealousy. The goal, Nancy Friday contends, is not to try to eliminate jealousy but to understand its destructiveness in our search for intimacy and love (Friday 1985).

The Paradoxes of True Intimacy

In analyzing *Love and Intimacy*, R. L. Coutts comments on the paradoxes inherent in our quest for intimacy.

> I've come to realize that the most compelling aspect of my life has been my search for intimacy. I've come to realize that the possession of intimacy has been the source of both my moments of greatest happiness and well-being, and of greatest pain and misgivings.
>
> *(Coutts 1973)*

Happiness, Coutts suggests, comes from the unending marvel of understanding and being understood by another person. The misgivings he sees are in the fear of being made foolish, the fear of having done something wrong, of being different, and most of all, the fear of being rejected.

Key Concepts

1. In the past most intimate relationships began in the safe confines of the family, church socials, and community gatherings. Today, many relationships begin by chance, in the workplace, on college campuses, at singles clubs, or through personal ads. Many people also turn to dating services and matchmakers as a way of making contact.

2. Neurophysiological and cross-cultural evidence supports the theory that sensory input and nurturance in childhood or adolescence can strongly inhibit the brain's pain/violence centers and lead to socially adapted, nonviolent adult behavior.

3. The negative effects of somatosensory deprivation in childhood may be reversed by physical-affectional nurturance and sexual/sensory pleasuring during the crucial adolescent years, just as the beneficial effects of infancy nurturance may be reversed by strong sexual taboos and a negative attitude toward women in the teen years.

4. Negative attitudes toward sex, body pleasure, premarital and extramarital intercourse, equality of the sexes, nudity, abortion, masturbation, breastfeeding, gun control, and women are all correlated. These attitudes are also

  linked with a glorification of violence and war and the frequent use of drugs and alcohol as a substitute for nurturance and body pleasure.

5. Factors associated with high physical-affectional infant or adolescent nurturance include a lack of strong social stratification, prolonged breast-feeding, a good sense of humor, an acceptance of abortion and of premarital and extramarital sex, low anxiety about sex, little sexual dysfunction, a lack of emphasis on private property, little war, and a peer relationship between men and women.

6. According to Perper, successful flirtation requires that we negotiate several escalation points, including the approach, body swivel, body movement synchronization, and touching. Women are more likely than men to lead in flirtation and to be aware of the escalation points and body language.

7. Intimacy has been defined as the ability to relate to another person as an equal on an emotional, physical, spiritual, and/or intellectual level. The extent and depth of sharing may vary with time.

8. The emotion of jealousy is a culturally conditioned, scripted reaction, often associated with a culture's emphasis on private property and women as men's possessions. Scripting for jealousy can often be traced back to the parents' handling of childhood jealousy and sibling rivalry. Jealousy often masks other emotions, such as envy, insecurity, and fear of loss.

Key Terms

courtly love (407)
flirtation (419)
intimacy (422)
limerence (418)
lovemap (417)

social exchange theory (416)
Somatosensory Affectional Deprivation
 (SAD) syndrome (413)
stimulus/value/role (SVR) theory (416)

Summary Questions

1. Sketch a brief history of the evolving concept and experience of love. What were two or three major turning points?

2. How has courtship changed as a result of the changing concept of love? What were some important factors in this changing experience?

3. Compare the stimulus/value/role (SVR) model with the social exchange theory of partner selection.

4. Describe some of the combinations of commitment, passion, and intimacy described by psychologist Robert Sternberg.

Suggested Readings

Buscaglia, L. (1972). *Love*. New York: Fawcett Crest.

Cassell, C. (1984). *Swept Away: Why Women Fear Their Own Sexuality*. New York: Simon & Schuster.

Friday, N. (1985). *Jealousy.* New York: Morrow.

Lerner, H. G. (1989). *The Dance of Intimacy: A Woman's Guide to Courageous Acts of Change in Key Relationships.* New York: Harper & Row.

Liebowitz, M. R. (1983). *The Chemistry of Love.* Boston: Little, Brown.

McGill, M. E. (1985). *The McGill Report on Male Intimacy.* New York: Harper & Row.

Tennov, D. (1979). *Love and Limerence: The Experience of Being in Love.* Briarcliff Manor, NY: Stein & Day.

Trotter, R. J. (1986, September). The three faces of love. *Psychology Today,* pp. 46–54.

Gender and Erotic
   Orientations
   A Question of Labels
   A Historical Perspective
   Research Perspectives
What Is Normal Sexual
   Behavior?
   The Personal View
   Other Perspectives
      and Views
Gender Orientation
   Research
   Biological Theories
   Psychoanalytic Theories
   Social Learning Theories
   Biobehavioral
      Interactions
Variations on a Theme
   Lesbians and Gay Men
   Gay Teens
   Gay Politicians
      and Clergy
   Bisexualities
Adjusting to a
   "Different"
   Orientation
   Social Issues
   Family Issues
   Legal Issues
   Coming Out
Are We Born with a
   Panerotic Potential?

Chapter 16

Gender and Erotic Orientations

Special Consultants

Nancy J. Barbara, M.A., sexologist, psychotherapist, lesbian counselor, and professor, College of Social and Behavioral Sciences, University of Southern Florida (Tampa).

Richard A. Friend, Ph.D., assistant professor, Human Sexuality Education Program, Graduate School of Education, University of Pennsylvania, and author of articles in the *Journal of Homosexuality, Holistic Nursing Practice,* and other journals.

Robert O. Hawkins, Jr., Ph.D., associate dean, School of Allied Health Professions, Health Sciences Center, State University of New York at Stony Brook, and coauthor of *Counseling Lesbian Women and Gay Men: A Life-Issues Approach.*

Fritz Klein, M.D., director, Institute for Sexual Behavior, San Diego; author of *The Bisexual Option*; and coauthor of *Bisexualities: Theory and Research.*

James D. Weinrich, Ph.D., assistant research psychobiologist, Department of Psychiatry, University of California, San Diego, and author of *Sexual Landscapes: Why We Are What We Are, Why We Love Whom We Love.*

This chapter explores what we know and do not know about the particular mind-sets that incline and draw us affectionally, emotionally, erotically, and sexually to other persons, whether the persons we are attracted to are members of our own or the other gender. In common parlance, this chapter deals with sexual orientation, with homosexuality, heterosexuality, and bisexuality, with persons society labels as gay, straight, lesbian, or bi. The lifestyles, joys, and concerns of persons who are attracted to members of their own gender or to both genders are the main focus because many people in the "straight" majority are not aware of the many joys and biases gay, lesbian and bi persons encounter.

Gender and Erotic Orientations

A Question of Labels

Labels can be useful, misleading, or even dangerous. On the negative side, we sometimes use labels to squeeze things into convenient, neat boxes so that we can be comfortable with them, even though our labels may distort reality by focusing on a single aspect rather than the whole.

Thus we talk about sexual orientation and then label people as homosexual, bisexual, or heterosexual. However, these four terms focus on *sexual activity*, and not on whole people and their lifestyles. They define individuals in terms of their genitals and what they do with them, much as the proverbial blind sages of China tried to describe the elephant in terms of the trunk, leg, or tail they could feel.

Homosexual, heterosexual, and bisexual are misleading terms when applied to a person who is not sexually active with another person. In the context of sexual or genital relations, many so-called heterosexual, homosexual, and bisexual persons would be more accurately described as asexual. Some gay men, particularly younger ones, are sexually attracted to men and emotionally attracted to women. Other gay men and lesbians are emotionally and sexually attracted to persons of their own gender. The variations are endless, as they are with men and women who are attracted to members of the other gender, the so-called heterosexuals or straight men and women.

We use the term **gender orientation** to avoid focusing on the sexual or genitals and to allow us to distinguish between

1. **affectional orientation**—the gender of the persons we bond with emotionally;
2. **sexual fantasy orientation**—the gender of the persons we fantasize having sex with; and
3. **erotic orientation** —the gender of the persons we prefer to have sex with.

Even though these three aspects are interrelated, they are distinct aspects of our gender orientation (Moses & Hawkins 1982:42–44). (See Figure 16.1.)

Gender orientation is, in turn, one of three parts in our psychosexual or gender identity:

**Gender
Orientation**

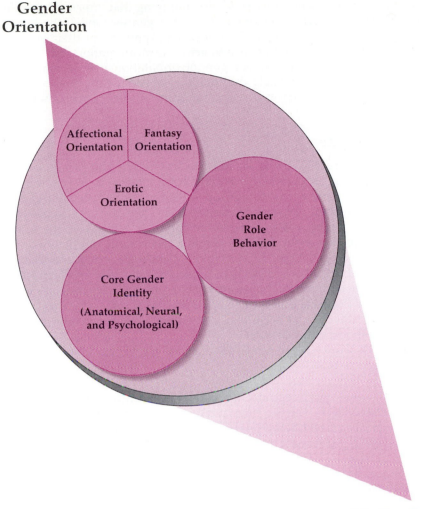

**My Psychosexual
Identity and Status**

1. our **gender orientation**;
2. our **core gender identity**, the conviction we have of being either female or male; and
3. our **gender-role behavior** by which we tell the world in a culturally appropriate way which gender we are (Moses & Hawkins 1982:43).

Development of our core gender identity and our gender orientation begins months before we are born. These two aspects, along with our sexual identity, continue developing after birth as we pass through the remaining six gates of our psychosexual development as outlined in Chapter 4 (Figure 16.1).

A second problem associated with using the terms sexual orientation, homosexual, heterosexual, and bisexual is more an issue of implication. Many people use the term *orientation* to mean *sexual preference,* implying that "normal" people *choose* to be sexually attracted to persons of the other gender while others, the homosexuals and bisexuals, *choose* to fall in love with persons of their own or both genders. We may or may not choose to act on our orientation, but we do not *choose* our gender orientation. If our gender orientation were a matter of personal choice, it hardly seems likely that millions of Americans would chose a lifestyle that leaves them open to discrimination, prejudice, and sometimes violence.

A Historical Perspective

The concept that some people can or should be classified by the gender of the person they love or have sex with is a recent development in Western psychology. From ancient Greece and Rome, up until the 1860s, people did not refer to each other as homosexual or heterosexual. They did use terms like *sodomite* or *buggery* to describe sexual behavior between persons of the same gender, without suggesting a psychological condition or erotic orientation.

In the 1860s a German gay writer K. M. Benkert coined the term *homosexuality* to emphasize a natural sexual orientation, in hopes that the new Prussian leaders would continue to allow sexual behavior between persons of the same gender which had been acceptable under the Napoleonic legal code. The maneuver failed and the term homosexual became a derogatory label for certain people who were deemed abnormal or deviant.

The origins of the word *gay* are not clear, but Yale University historian John Boswell (1980) suggests that

> The Provincal word "gai" was used in the thirteenth and fourteenth centuries in reference to courtly love and its literature and persists in Catalan-Provencal's closest living relative [language] as a designation for the "art of poesy"("gai saber"), for a "lover" ("gaiol"), and for an openly homosexual person. . . . The cult of courtly love was most popular in the south of France, an area noted for gay sexuality, and some troubadour poetry was explicitly homosexual. Moreover, both troubadour poetry and courtly love were closely associated with southern French heretical movements, especially the Albigensians, who were internationally suspected of favoring homosexuality. In the early twentieth century "gay" was common in the English homosexual subculture as a sort of password or code. Its first public use in the United States outside of pornographic fiction appears to have been in the 1939 movie *Bringing Up Baby,* when Cary Grant, wearing a dress, exclaimed that he had "gone gay." . . . Presumably "straight" is derived from "straight arrow," a slang term suggesting adherence to conventional values.

> (Boswell 1980:43–45)

In 1948 Kinsey urged that we use the words homosexual and homosexuality to refer only to behavior, and not as a label for a person, condition, or role.

> It would encourage clearer thinking on these matters if persons were not characterized as heterosexual or homosexual, but as individuals who have had certain amounts of heterosexual experience and certain amounts of homosexual experience. Instead of using these terms as sub-

stantives which stand for persons, or even as adjectives to describe persons, they may be better used to describe the nature of overt sexual relations, or of the stimuli to which an individual erotically responds.

(Kinsey, Pomeroy, & Martin 1948:617)

Unfortunately, we are seldom this clear in our everyday language. And so the terms homosexual, bisexual, and heterosexual continue to be used, sometimes to refer specifically to a particular sexual behavior, but most of the time as a general reference to gender orientation and persons (Bell & Weinberg 1978).

Research Perspectives

Kinsey's Findings

Although there has been a great deal of research regarding gender orientation, most people still believe that the human race is split into two or three distinct groups: a heterosexual majority and a homosexual minority, with some who fall in between these two boxes in the shadowy world of bisexuals. Forty years ago Kinsey's research proved this stereotype had no basis in reality. He found that

- It is very common for children to have sexual contact with peers of their own gender. In fact, prior to puberty, it is not at all unusual for individuals to have more sexual contact with members of their own gender than with the other gender.

- Sexual experiences with a same-gender person are not at all uncommon, especially in the adolescent years, and do not indicate a same-gender (homosexual) orientation.

- Occasional fantasies or daydreams of same-gender contact may, or may not, be a sign of a same-gender orientation.

- As young people with a true homosexual orientation recognize the standards of society, they are often pressured into adopting heterosexual contacts and relationships.

After interviewing 5,300 men and 5,940 women, Kinsey and his associates decided their data could be best displayed as a continuous scale, a range based on the ratio of sexual contacts with one's own gender and the other gender. This spectrum, now known as the **Kinsey Six Scale** (Figures 16.2 and 16.3), classifies individuals on the ratio of their same- and other-gender sexual experiences and fantasies. A "Kinsey 0" indicates a person whose behavior and fantasies have always involved persons of the other gender. "Kinsey 6" indicates a person whose sexual experiences and fantasies have always involved persons of their own gender.

According to Kinsey's data, half of all American males were exclusively heterosexual in their experience and fantasies. Four percent of the males and 2% of the females were exclusively oriented to persons of their own gender. The remaining 46% of American males had varying proportions of sexual activities with both males and females. The three diagrams in Figure 16.3 show more details on men and women between ages 20 and 35.

Kinsey's work suggests a question that highlights some important distinctions we have already made. If a person has had a few sexual experiences with

Components of Gender Orientation and the Kinsey Six Scale

The concept of Gender Orientation includes
1. Sexual fantasy orientation, past and present;
2. Affectional orientation, past and present; and
3. Erotic (sexual) orientation, past and present.

KINSEY ZERO	KINSEY ONE	KINSEY TWO	KINSEY THREE	KINSEY FOUR	KINSEY FIVE	KINSEY SIX
Exclusively Heteroerotic	Predominantly Heteroerotic	Ambisexual Heteroerotic	Ambisexual Bisexual	Ambisexual Homoerotic	Predominantly Homoerotic	Exclusively Homoerotic
Preference for other-gender partners only	Primary preference for other-gender partners, occasional preference for same-gender partners	Usual preference not based on gender, occasional preference for same-gender partner	Preference not based on gender	Usual preference not based on gender, occasional preference for other-gender partners	Primary preference for same-gender partners, occasional preference for other-gender partners	Preference for same-gender partners only

Figure 16.2. The Kinsey Six Scale of Gender Orientation.

persons of his or her own gender, or a few fantasies about a homosexual experience, does that mean he or she is meant to fall in love, or enjoy sex only with members of his or her own gender? If this conclusion were true, then 50% of American men and 20% of the women Kinsey interviewed would be considered "homosexual." Remember, we have been making a distinction between sexual fantasies, sexual experiences, and emotional or affectional orientation, as three elements in our gender orientation. Unfortunately, Kinsey didn't ask his subjects about their emotional orientations. Even so, his findings show how inappropriate it is to label people as homosexual, bisexual, or heterosexual.

Some men and women may *appear* to shift back and forth across the Kinsey scale at different times in their lives. A woman or man may have a consistent pattern of same-gender sexual fantasies and same-gender emotional attachments, but be sexually active with her or his spouse. Later in life, that same person may become more comfortable being sexually involved with a person of his or her own gender. Has that person then jumped from a heterosexual or bisexual box to the homosexual box? The way we answer this question has interesting implications when we realize that recent statistics indicate that more than 30 million Americans have had both heterosexual and homosexual experiences (Bell & Weinberg 1978; Klein 1978). Although some people will never have a homosexual experience, they may have a strong emotional and/or sexual attraction to someone of their own gender. Psychologists have sometimes called such persons *latent* homosexuals. Does this label mean a person who fantasizes about a homosexual experience is a latent homosexual? Would we call someone a latent heterosexual when he or she has a heterosexual fantasy but has not yet had a sexual experience with a person of the other gender?

FEMALE HETEROSEXUAL-HOMOSEXUAL RATING (AGES 20–35)

0	1	2	3	4	5	6
Single 61–72%						1–3%
					2–6%	
Married 89–90%				3–8%		
			4–11%			
Previously married 75–80%		6–14%				
	11–20%					

HETEROSEXUAL AND HOMOSEXUAL BEHAVIOR AND FANTASIES

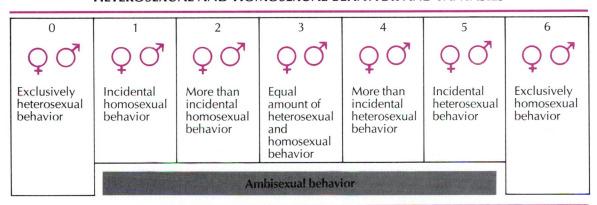

0	1	2	3	4	5	6
Exclusively heterosexual behavior	Incidental homosexual behavior	More than incidental homosexual behavior	Equal amount of heterosexual and homosexual behavior	More than incidental heterosexual behavior	Incidental heterosexual behavior	Exclusively homosexual behavior
	Ambisexual behavior					

MALE HETEROSEXUAL-HOMOSEXUAL RATING (AGES 20–35)

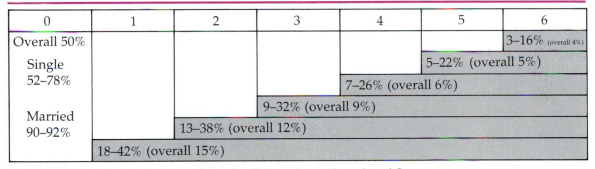

0	1	2	3	4	5	6
Overall 50%						3–16% (overall 4%)
Single 52–78%					5–22% (overall 5%)	
				7–26% (overall 6%)		
			9–32% (overall 9%)			
Married 90–92%		13–38% (overall 12%)				
	18–42% (overall 15%)					

Figure 16.3. The Kinsey Surveys of Gender Orientations. *The scale and figures are adapted from Kinsey's data on males and females published in 1948 and 1953. The ranges of percentages result from different ratios in various subgroups within the seven categories. These categories themselves are somewhat arbitrary, and the whole scale should therefore be viewed as a spectrum.*

Situational "Homosexuality"

Some men and women engage in sexual activities with persons of their own gender because no partners of the other gender are available. Men who engage in sex with other men in prisons usually do so because they are isolated from women and because sex can be very effectively used as a demonstration of power and control (Long & Sultan 1987). For women in prison, sexual activity is more often part of an ongoing relationship than an expression of control and power (Giallombardo 1974). Heterosexual men and women in the military may also engage in this kind of **situational homoerotic behavior**. In most cases, these men and women quickly revert to other-gender relations when the opportunity arises.

Experimental Same-Sex Behavior

Since as many as 1 in 5 of Kinsey's subjects reported they had had one or more sexual experiences with a person of the same gender during their teen years, we need to include in our perspective of gender and erotic orientation a kind of **same-gender sexual experimentation**. A few sexual explorations with a peer of the same gender are normal for teenagers who are trying to figure out and cope with their emerging sexual needs. If such experiences were evidence of a same-gender orientation, then the majority of Americans would have to be so classified. In reality, our gender and erotic orientations are not a matter of choice.

Klein's Sexual Orientation Grid

Although the Kinsey Six Point Scale gives us a basic insight, it still tends to categorize individuals by specific types of behavior and sexual responses. It ignores the ever-changing expression of gender orientation over time. Fred Klein, a physician and expert on gender orientations, has tried to allow for this time dimension and at the same time include other aspects of gender orientation besides fantasy and erotic orientation in a quasi three-dimensional **Sexual Orientation Grid** (1978; Klein, Sepekoff, & Wolf 1985:35). Klein includes seven factors in his grid.

1. Sexual attraction (erotic attraction): Who turns you on? Who do you find attractive as a real or potential sexual partner?
2. Sexual behavior—kissing, petting, intercourse: Who are your sexual contacts (partners)?
3. Sexual fantasies: Who do you enjoy fantasizing about in erotic daydreams or while masturbating?
4. Emotional or affectional preference: With whom do you prefer to establish strong emotional bonds?
5. Social preference: With which gender do you prefer to socialize?
6. Lifestyle: Do you spend most of your time with persons who see themselves as heterosexually, homosexually, or bisexually oriented?
7. Self-identification: How do you identify yourself in terms of sexual orientation on the Kinsey scale?

These seven aspects, or facets, of gender orientation have a dynamic character as well—a past, a present, and a future (Moses & Hawkins 1982:37). These aspects are shown in the grid in Highlight Box 16.1, which you can copy and fill out to gain an insight into the complexities of your own gender orientation.

The Sexual Orientation Grid, proposed by Fred Klein, M.D., highlights the complex aspects of our gender orientations. You can copy out the grid and fill it in for yourself, using the 0 to 6 number scale in the Kinsey 6 rating scale as follows:

- Putting a 0 in any of the 21 boxes indicates that your sexual behavior, attraction, fantasies, emotional or social preference, lifestyle, or self-identification has been, is, or ideally would be exclusively with members of the other gender.

- Putting a 1 in any box indicates that your sexual behavior, attraction, fantasies, emotional or social preference, lifestyle, or self-identification has been, is, or ideally would be primarily with members of the other gender, but with incidental involvement with persons of your own gender.

- A 2 in any box indicates that your sexual behavior, attraction, fantasies, emotional or social preference, lifestyle, or self-identification has been, is, or ideally would involve mostly members of the other gender, but with significant involvement with members of your own gender.

- A 3 in any box indicates an about equal involvement with members of both genders.

- A 4 in a box indicates involvement mostly with members of the same gender, but with significant involvement with members of the other gender.

- A 5 is the reverse of a 1, predominantly same-gender involvement with incidental sexual involvement with or orientation toward the other gender.

- A 6 in any box indicates an exclusive involvement with or orientation toward members of the same gender.

- Because the Kinsey scale doesn't allow for asexual behavior (no behavior, experience, or fantasy), indicate it by placing a dash (—) in the appropriate box.

	Past (five years ago)	Present (in the past year)	Ideal Future Goal
Sexual attraction			
Sexual behavior			
Sexual fantasies			
Emotional preference			
Social preference			
Lifestyle			
Self-identification			

Overall Kinsey Average = Total divided by 21 or _____

To find where you fit on the Kinsey Six Scale, add up your score and divide by the number of boxes you rate 0 to 6. As you complete this grid remember that these categories are not discrete or distinct. They are arbitrary points in or on an ever-changing continuum.

What Is Normal Sexual Behavior?

For a variety of reasons, when it comes to sexual behaviors most people are very concerned about what is "normal" or "abnormal." In terms of sexual normality, there is probably no sexual activity, including heterosexual marriage, which has not been at some time condemned as deviant. In reality, it is impossible to define the terms normal and deviant unless we clearly explain the basis for the judgment. In the process, we may find that what we consider unnatural and abnormal, another person or society accepts as perfectly natural and normal.

Normal, according to one dictionary, means "conforming with or constituting an accepted standard, model, or pattern; especially, corresponding to the median or average of a large group in type, appearance, achievement, behavior, function. . . ." How, then, do we decide what is normal sexual behavior? Do we use a statistical base? Do we label a particular sexual behavior normal or abnormal based on our medical knowledge, on the law, or do we ask what society approves? How important are our religious beliefs in deciding what is normal, moral, and acceptable? What about our personal views, and the rights of individuals?

The Personal View

We often tend to view what we and our friends do as normal. People who behave differently are abnormal. This classic insider/outsider judgment is often dictated by fear of the unknown, by ignorance of others as persons, or by the tendency to see the world as a mirror of ourselves.

How do you react to a sexual behavior or to a person with a lifestyle you haven't encountered before and therefore know little about? Many people feel so uncomfortable, so uneasy, they ridicule the behavior, or make fun of the person. Fear, hostility, and violence are defense mechanisms against the unknown, or what is perceived of as threatening. Labeling persons who are attracted to individuals of their own gender as abnormal, sick, or mentally unbalanced is a defense strategy designed to "isolate the enemy." Terms like queer, fag, dyke, or lezzie become weapons. In our society, until recently at least, normal was a term used to describe someone sexually attracted only to persons of the other gender. All other orientations, therefore, automatically became abnormal or deviant.

Other Perspectives and Views

A Developmental Perspective

The model of gender-identity/role development outlined in Chapter 4 suggests that there are two natural outcomes of our development, male or female. But what does this statement mean?

The fact that the majority of humans pass through the 12 gates on one or the other side says nothing about the significant number of persons who move to the other path in one or the other aspect of their personality. Current estimates suggest that between 5% to 10% of males and 4% of women find themselves attracted sexually only to persons of their own gender. Many gay men and lesbian women may fall in love and bond with someone of their own gender, much as straight men and women fall in love and bond with someone of the other gender. There are also gay men and lesbian women who are sexually drawn to men but do not fall in love or bond with them. Similarly, some straight men are sexually drawn only to women, but find their strongest bonds, friendship, and love with a "best buddy." Some gay men are sexually attracted to men, but emotionally bond with women. Sometimes a man loves his wife but is sexually attracted to men. When we distinguish between affection or emotional orientation and sexual orientation, a rich variety of gender expressions becomes evident. Edward Brecher once observed that ours is "a homosocial, heterosexual society."

Although it appears that the majority of males and females grow up to be sexually attracted to persons of the other gender, making a distinction between emotional, affection, and sexual attraction breaks us out of the either/or picture. Most experts believe that something happens to the neural pathways of the fetal brain before birth and that prenatal neural tendencies are elaborated on and become fixed in early childhood and the preadolescent years. But, as we saw earlier, this biobehavioral encoding involves our core gender identity, as well as tendencies and scripting for gender-role behaviors and emotional and sexual attraction. At present, we have a fair understanding of what gender orientation is, and when it develops. However, we have no idea how or why it develops the way it does in different men and women. We do know, however, that persons with different gender orientations are found in almost every culture studied (Blackwood 1985; Ford & Beach 1951).

A Statistical View

Would you say that a behavior is statistically normal when most people do it? Would you consider something only a few people do to be statistically abnormal? If so, consider that in 49 of the 76 societies, other than our own, for which information is available, homosexual behavior is considered normal and socially acceptable for certain members of the community (Ford & Beach 1951:130). If 49 of 76 societies accept homosexual behavior, then is our society statistically abnormal because it does not accept this behavior and lifestyle? Does the acceptance of **homoerotic** behavior—sexual activity between persons of the same gender—in 64% of these societies make this behavior statistically normal (Blackwood 1985)?

Statistics on anal intercourse offer another example. If Mexican homoerotic men prefer anal intercourse and English homoerotic men do not, what does the concept of statistically normal mean when applied only to these two male populations? Even if anal sex is statistically normal for some gay male cultures, what do we make of the statistics on anal sex among heteroerotic men and women? Two-thirds of American married couples at least occasionally engage in anal intercourse. In Brazil, where there is a very small identifiable gay male population, men who identify themselves as "heterosexual males" commonly engage in anal intercourse with their wives, with female prostitutes, and with other men (Parker 1987:160–166). If the majority of these **heteroerotic** men and women engage, at least occasionally, in anal sex, then are those who do not engage in anal sex statistically abnormal? As you can see, using statistics as a criterion for what is normal has its risks.

A Clinical View

Faced with growing clinical evidence that the majority of gay men and lesbians are just as comfortable with their orientation as straight men and women are with theirs, the American Psychiatric Association (APA) removed homosexuality from its list of mental disorders in 1973. If someone accepts his or her sexual orientation, doesn't want to change it, and functions quite well in society, then it is hardly accurate to label their orientation abnormal and a mental disorder. The APA manual also contains no clinical description that fits "homosexuals," so it is impossible to use the term in a clinical diagnosis (Moses & Hawkins 1982:57).

The Legal Perspective

Since the civil rights movement of the 1960s, many states have revised their laws defining and regulating criminal behavior. Many states have adopted so-called consenting adult laws, which consider perfectly legal any sexual activity engaged in by two or more consenting adults in private. In 1989 the New York State Appelate Court recognized the right of a gay male couple to be considered a family in terms of rental leases. On the other hand, in a 5 to 4 decision in Bowers v. Hardwick, the U.S. Supreme Court ruled that the state of Georgia could constitutionally prohibit anal intercourse, "regardless of whether the parties who engage in it are married or unmarried, or of the same or different sexes" (Francoeur 1987a:202–213).

A Sociological View

Homoerotic behavior and relationships were quite acceptable in ancient Greece and Rome. They appear to have been tolerated in the early years of Christianity and openly accepted in the Christian Middle Ages (Boswell 1980). From the late Middle Ages on, homosexuality was more or less repressed in European countries. Today, in the aftermath of our new awareness of civil rights and the sexual revolution of the 1960s and 1970s, "For the first time in American society, most adults feel no discomfort at having a friend who is homosexual" (Yankelovich 1981:59). Although some might question Yankelovich's conclusion about "most adults" and "no discomfort," there is probably more acceptance of homosexuals and lesbians today than ever before in Western civilization.

A Religious Perspective

In recent years, a major religious controversy has emerged over homosexuality. In the early 1900s there was unanimous agreement among Christians that sexual behavior between two males was a sin against nature and God. About 30 years ago, Protestant and Catholic scholars began reexamining the biblical texts in terms of their social context and very precise linguistic analyses. In the 1970s gay and lesbian people began pressing the churches to deal with them in less dogmatic and condemning terms. As a result, the British Council of Churches, the United Presbyterian Church of the United States, the United Methodist Church, the Episcopal Church, the United Church of Christ (Congregationalists), and others have moved from condemnation to tolerance to acceptance of gay and lesbian Christians (Figure 16.4).

Gay men and lesbian women who are open about their orientation have been ordained in some churches and synagogues. The Episcopal Diocese of

(a)

(b)

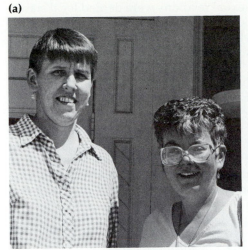 

Figure 16.4. Lesbian and Gay Clergy. *Religious communities are debating the issue of whether practicing lesbians or gay persons should be ordained as members of the clergy. Shown here in (a) is the Reverend Rose Mary Denman (right) and Winnie Weir of the United Methodist Church in Dover, New Hampshire, and in (b), the Reverends Kerr (left) and Greisel at Trinity Episcopal Church in San Francisco. Both couples share their ministries and are domestic partners.*

Newark, New Jersey, has asked the church to recognize and bless gay unions. In 1989 this same Episcopal Diocese established a parish in Newark to provide a congenial and comfortable faith community for lesbian and gay people (Batchelor 1980; Edwards 1984; Gramick and Furey 1988; Kosnick et al. 1977; McNeill 1976; Nugent 1984; Thayer et al. 1987).

This trend has been vehemently opposed by traditionalist-minded persons. In 1988 national conventions of the Episcopal Church and the Methodists avoided a split by hedging on the issue. Many conservatives maintain that homosexual relations are specifically condemned by the biblical tradition. For them, the ordination of openly avowed gay men and lesbian women to the ministry is totally unacceptable, along with any recognition of gay and lesbian unions.

The history of Christian thinking on homosexual behavior is not as clear as we might think. Yale University historian John Boswell (1980), for instance, contends that Christian dogma did not always condemn homosexual behavior. People in different eras, Boswell claims, used and misinterpreted Christian writings to justify the oppression of homosexuals and others considered to be social deviants for practical, economic, or political reasons which had nothing to do with religion.

Biblical texts, Boswell contends, were never used directly to support an antihomosexual philosophy. Only one statement, in the book of Leviticus, specifically condemns homosexual behavior, and that text may have been rewritten or misinterpreted by later scholars. In the 4th century A.D., some Christian advocates of homoerotic love stated that it was far superior to the love of a man for a woman. Men, it was argued, should only engage in sexual relations with women to produce children necessary for survival of the human race.

In this same era, social restrictions on people who engaged in homosexual behavior began to appear, although it was several centuries before persons who endorsed and engaged in same-gender sexual relations were denied legal status. In the Middle Ages, some strange biological theories were used to condemn oral and anal sex. The "unclean weasel" allegedly practiced oral sex and the promiscuous rabbit grew a new anal canal each year so it could practice anal intercourse (Boswell 1980:137–138).

Yet, other Christians argued that homosexual behavior was "unnatural" because animals did not engage in it. Even as homosexual behavior was condemned as violating the natural law, incest, which occurs in many animal species, was also thought to be unnatural. The penalties attached to various activities are also enlightening. During the 8th century, for instance, Pope Saint Gregory III ordered 160 days of penance for lesbian behavior, one year penance for male homosexual behavior, and three years penance for any priest who went hunting! This discrepancy says something about the moral norms of that era.

In the early Middle Ages, homosexual behavior flourished and was openly tolerated by the Christian church. Gay priests were numerous. As the Middle Ages continued, a very literate homoerotic subculture developed. Knights and clerics publicly debated the relative merits of gay and nongay love and argued which group was more skilled in lovemaking. The ranks of prominent Christians in gay subcultures between 1050 and 1150 included monks, archbishops, and saints.

In the 1200s, as Europe's social order and political stability began to crumble, intolerance of homosexual behavior grew. The Crusades, the decay of the cities, the shift back to rural life, and a revival of the vehemently antihomosexual opinions of some earlier church leaders increasingly forced homosexually oriented persons and their culture underground. Other minorities, Jews, Muslims, witches, and dissidents of all kinds suffered a similar fate.

Throughout Boswell's interpretation of history runs the thesis that intolerance of people who differ from the norm increases as political, social, and economic stability decline.

Gender Orientation Research

In many cases, our judgment about what is or is not normal in sexual orientation and behavior hinges on what we believe about how we develop psychosexually. We have many theories about what may cause gender orientations, but we really don't know definitively. We have good animal research, but these findings cannot be incorporated into a theory of human sexual orientation without extreme caution. Some may talk about prenatal masculinizing and defeminizing of the brain, but we know little about that hypothesized process. We know even less about the effects of postnatal behavior in elaborating on neural templates that may exist in the brain. And we know that behavior can modify neural tissue. Remember, the concept of nature/critical period/nurture is not a one-way model.

Social and behavioral scientists trying to find out what determines our sexual orientations naturally focus on behavioral and social factors. Other researchers have a biological bias and focus on genes and hormones. Is nurture more important than nature? Or does nature have the upper hand? When we explored this question in Chapter 4, our conclusion was that it is more accurate to represent our psychosexual development as the continual interaction of nature and nurture at critical periods in our development: nature/critical period/nurture instead of nature versus nurture. The influences occur in both directions, with nature influencing nurture and nurture affecting the biological at critical periods, so that our psyche and behavior are the result of both aspects interacting (Money 1988:86–87).

Despite an ongoing heated debate between advocates of biological and social determinism (De Cecco 1987a, 1987b; Gagnon 1987; Meyer-Bahlburg 1987; Perper 1987), there is no convincing evidence to support any explanation that does not include both biological and social factors working together. Our gender orientations develop in stages, and have more than one cause. At the same time that people are very concerned about what causes a child to "become" a homosexual, few of us ask the other, parallel question: What causes some people to have a heterosexual orientation? (Money 1988:123).

Biological Theories

It would be simple if we could trace gender orientation to genes, but the evidence from twin studies in no way supports this explanation (Heston & Shields 1968; Kallman 1952). A genetic disposition may exist in some families, but the outcome of this tendency is dependent on learning experiences. When Pillard and Weinrich (1987) interviewed the brothers and sisters of predominantly heterosexual and predominantly homosexual men, they found only 4% of the brothers of heterosexually oriented persons were predominantly homoerotic or gay. Almost a quarter of the brothers of the gay men, 22%, were predominantly homosexual in their orientation. But this study doesn't tell us to what extent this difference is due to heredity, family conditions, or a combination of both.

Although a few tantalizing details about the role of prenatal hormones in encoding prenatal neural tendencies have been uncovered, this process is hotly debated. Some claim that the male sex hormone somehow masculinizes before birth, but does not defeminize the brain. A decrease in the normal levels of masculinizing hormone at critical periods in fetal life might then leave certain pathways in the brain unmasculinized, but not defeminized (Money 1988:50, 123–124). Severe stress on the mother during pregnancy, for instance, has been linked with a postnatal tendency to homosexuality in males, but not in females (Doerner et al. 1980, 1983; Ellis et al. 1988; Money 1988:110–112; Van Wyk 1984). After birth, the hormone balances in persons with heterosexual and homosexual orientations show no significant or consistent differences.

Psychoanalytic Theories

In one of the earliest attempts to explain homosexuality, Sigmund Freud did not see homosexuality as a mental illness. He saw little prospect of converting homosexuals into heterosexuals. For Freud, as for earlier thinkers, the *quality* of sexual expression, not its *object* is what counts. He even supported civil rights for homosexuals in Austria and Germany (Lewes 1988).

On the other side, drawing on his patients and the self-reports of unhappy homosexuals, Freud suggested that same-gender-oriented men tend to have weak, ineffectual, or absent fathers and seductive, domineering mothers. This theory has been completely refuted by several recent studies. Freud also claimed gay men sought out effeminate men as partners to avoid the "castrating vagina" whereas lesbians, in general, preferred the stereotype "butch" or masculine-appearing lesbian. Again, the evidence contradicts Freud's assumptions (Bell & Weinberg 1978; Freedman 1971; Mendola 1980; Tollison & Adams 1979).

Lewes (1988) and Stoller (1979) have criticized some contemporary psychoanalysts like Socarides (1978) and Bergler (1959), for assuming that the only normal outcome of resolving the Oedipal complex and progress through the oral, anal, and genital phases is heterosexuality. In denying that homosexuality is any more or less an illness than the wide range of heterosexualities, Stoller cites Freud's statement that "In the psychoanalytic sense the exclusive interest of the man for the woman is also a problem requiring an explanation."

Social Learning Theories

McGuire (1965) believes that the path to homosexuality starts with an unpleasant early other-gender experience or feelings of inadequacy coupled with the fear of not being able to relate sexually with persons of the other gender. The child then has a positive same-gender sexual experience that provides meaning to homoerotic fantasies previously linked to masturbation. Finally, scripting links the successful homoerotic experience and masturbation with homoerotic fantasies as a sexual outlet.

This is an interesting theory, but it does not explain why many men and women, with little or no actual early same-gender experience, who appear to have had a successful marriage, later in life find more fulfillment with persons of their own gender. The assumption in this theory is that men only turn to other men when they can't find a suitable female partner. The straight person may ask, "Why settle for second best?" But the homoerotic person sees partners of the same gender as the best and most natural for him or her.

In another unsupported social learning theory, Bandura (1969) suggests that a homoerotic orientation may result from the lack of a strong male role image and a domineering, seductive mother who encourages and reinforces her son's effeminate behavior. Here we can ask why many heteroerotic men who had this type of family environment did not end up gay.

In 1976 Bieber originated the concept of the "homoseductive mother," suggesting that a male teenager turns to same-gender relations out of fear of his mother's seductiveness and her jealous possessiveness. More recently, Bieber has suggested that the son with a detached or openly hostile father may come to hate and fear his father while yearning for his father's love and acceptance, which, he claims, may trigger a gay orientation. Again, we encounter a theory unsupported by any evidence.

Tripp (1975) and Storms (1980) have suggested that boys who begin to mature sexually before their peers, when the preadolescent males play together and avoid girls, are more likely to associate sexual arousal with males, and thus become homosexual. But again, there is no evidence to support this theory.

There are hardly any theories which attempt to explain the origin of lesbian orientations. Charlotte Wolff (1971) suggests that when a girl receives inadequate love from her mother, she may continue throughout her life to seek out the missing love in a relationship with a woman. Wolff also feels a distant or absent father may make it difficult for the teenage girl to learn how to relate to men in a loving way. This theory does not explain why many women with such a background are heteroerotic (Chapman & Brannock 1987).

At the same time, there are no theories which attempt to explain heterosexual orientation, a result of the belief that there is no need to explain what is defined as normal.

Biobehavioral Interactions

Gender Nonconformity

In 1981 Bell, Weinberg, and Hammersmith admitted that their interviews of 1,500 men and women did not solve the mystery of the origins of gender orientation, although they did turn up one important clue. They found no evidence that unresolved Oedipal feelings, a lack of sufficient heterosexual opportunities, rape (for lesbianism), seductive other-gender parents, seduction by an older same-gender person, or a domineering mother and weak father cause homosexuality. Parents also appeared to have little influence on their children's developing gender orientation. A cold, detached father may predispose a boy to homosexuality, but only if this situation is followed by a long chain of other events.

When their interviews revealed no social factor(s) as a cause of an exclusive homosexual orientation, Bell, Weinberg, and Hammersmith suggested the prime factor might be a biological tendency or predisposition. "If there is a biological basis for sexual orientation—and this study points in that direction—it probably is stronger for exclusive homosexuals than for bisexuals. This biological predisposition also probably accounts for sissy behavior in boys and tomboyishness in girls—gender nonconformity— as well as sexual orientation." (Note the tentative wording: *if, points in that direction, probably.*)

In pursuing the idea that gender nonconformity is a key factor in the development of an exclusive homosexual orientation, these researchers pointed out that so-called sissy boys and tomboy girls who adopt the gender-role behavior of the other gender would also tend to be less involved with and accepted by their peers because of their gender nonconformity. Bell thinks this nonacceptance may also contribute to a homoerotic orientation. The object of our romantic interest, he contends, must be essentially different from oneself in terms of gender-related attributes. If a child is not accepted by his or her same-gender peers in preadolescence, he or she will not come to view the other gender as really different. Males who spend their early childhood involved with a male peer group would find it virtually impossible to be fascinated by other males as the object of their romantic and erotic interest. Bell believes that this theory applies equally to males and females, and to both heteroerotic and homoerotic orientations.

Gender nonconformity has also been implicated as a factor in homosexual orientation by another major clinical study. In 1987 Richard Green reported the results of a 15-year study of gender nonconformity in so-called sissy boys. Green compared the development of a very select sample of 44 "sissy boys" with a parallel group of "conventionally masculine" boys over the course of 15 years, from between ages 4 and 11 to adulthood. The sissy boys liked to dress in girls' or women's clothes. They played with girls. They preferred Barbie dolls to trucks. In Mommy-Daddy games, they played Mommy. They avoided sports and rough-and-tumble play. These boys even told their parents they would prefer being girls. They were, in the eyes of their peers, sissies. In psychological or behavioral terms, they were expressing **gender nonconformity**. The boys in the control group were the exact opposite. For whatever reasons, their gender role behavior conformed to the conventionally masculine role model *for our culture*, just as the behavior of the sissy boys did not conform. Among Green's conclusions were the following:

1. Three-quarters, possibly more, of the 44 very effeminate boys studied grew up to be homosexual.

2. Parental discouragement of cross-gender (girlish) behavior in boys and therapies designed to discourage extremely feminine behavior and enhance male self-concept appeared to result in an increase in heterosexual behavior for some very effeminate boys. This finding suggests that homosexual behavior tendencies might be lessened, but not necessarily reversed.

3. Counseling may not divert homosexual tendency, but it can result in more conventional masculine behavior for extremely effeminate boys. It certainly can enhance an individual's social and psychological comfort with being a male.

4. Sissy boys have an inborn "receptivity" to environmental factors that encourage homosexual orientation.

To give this study its proper weight, we must keep in mind that the 44 boys were very carefully selected for their "very effeminate traits." Given their strong gender role discomfort, it is not surprising most of them had a same-gender orientation. But the characteristics of these sissy boys *is not typical of the vast majority of homoerotic men*. In summing up his research, Green has highlighted the ongoing mystery of gender and erotic orientations.

> I doubt that a biological factor can completely explain the development of these boys' different patterns of sexual identity. Nor do I believe that a biologic factor can completely explain the emergence into homosexuality of some of the previously "feminine" boys. . . . Reciprocally, I doubt that socialization influences fully explain the development of "femininity" and/or homosexuality. There are too many exceptions for every rule.
>
> *(Green 1987:384)*

Variations on a Theme

Lesbians and Gay Men

Traditionally, all homosexuals have been grouped under one cultural umbrella, although in real life lesbians and gay males have quite different lifestyles. Although the distinction may appear subtle, the dividing line in terms of economics, politics, and sexual values and practices is as wide as it is powerful and boldly visible among lesbians and gay men.

Historically, the romantic and sexual lifestyles of gay men have differed markedly from those of lesbians. American men have been socialized to play dominant, orgasm-oriented roles; women have been socialized to be the passive, intimacy-oriented partner. These patterns occur among straight men and women, lesbians and gay men. Gay male relationships typically have emphasized sexual compatibility, initially and throughout the life of the relationship. Lesbian couples traditionally have emphasized sensuality as opposed to sexuality. In lesbian relationships, even though the sexual aspects may slacken, the emotional and sensual bond tends to keep the relationship together.

In the wake of the AIDS crisis, gay men have changed their sexual values significantly, bringing the two subcultures of lesbian and gay men closer together. In the past, lesbians were noted for their emphasis on long-term intimate relationships and gay men for just the opposite. That has changed significantly in recent years (McWhirter & Mattison 1984; Peplau 1981; Peplau & Amaro 1982; Peplau et al. 1982).

One of the most common misconceptions about gay male and lesbian relationships is that they mirror their straight counterparts via active/passive male or butch/femme lesbian roles. In real life, the most common pattern in both lesbian and gay male relations is a shifting of gender roles and behavior, depending on the situation, need, and availability.

Peplau and others report most lesbians and gay men actively reject the traditional male/female gender roles of husband and wife as a model for homosexual love relationships. Interestingly, there are no real role models for lesbians and gay males to follow or pattern their relationships after. Homosexual unions seem simply to flow with no real set of external norms.

Community is important in both the lesbian and gay male culture. The cultural bonding of community means unity, mutual support, progress, cohesion, and family. Oppression, homophobia, and heterosexism have been major factors in creating the sense of community among lesbians and gay men. However, the lesbian experience of community is quite different from the gay male community, serving a different function both in the gay culture and in society in general.

Gay Teens

Because heterosexism dictates that homosexuality is not an acceptable orientation, it is often very difficult for gay and lesbian people to develop a positive self-image. Lesbian and gay youths, particularly those from small communities, seldom receive support from their peers or from the sex education and family life courses in their schools. Counselors and teachers assume that all of their students are heterosexually oriented, even though anywhere between 1 in 10 and 1 in 20 in any school have a same-gender orientation. Along with the normal tensions and uncertainties of adolescence, gay and lesbian teenagers have to confront the question of whom they are sexually attracted to. Do they give into peer pressure and date members of the other gender? Do they tell a best friend they are gay, and risk losing that friend or, worse, get ostracized or beaten up? Should they get sexually involved to prove they are straight? If they find themselves attracted to someone of the same gender, what do they do?

> I'm a 20-year-old male and am growing more worried by the week. My best friend Ben is heterosexual. I am bisexual. He is very attractive with blond hair topping a well-built body. Every time I see him I'm overcome with a strong desire to make love to him. I don't know how to let him know about my feelings. I don't want to lose him as a friend. I don't want to put anything on the line. Please help. I need advice!—
>
> *(Forum 1988:17(8):67)*

Fortunately, the number of resources gay teens can turn to are increasing, both on the national and local levels. Knowledgeable and sensitive members of the gay community have published practical guides and insights into what gay persons should know about dating and living together, and coping in a straight world (Loulan 1984; Marcus 1988; McWhirter & Mattison 1984).

About 10% of heterosexual boys and girls attempt suicide. Three to four times that many gay teenagers and twice as many lesbian teenagers attempt suicide (Youth Suicide National Center Report 1989). The lack of acceptance and support for gay and lesbian teenagers is undoubtedly a factor. When people know others hate them, they can easily come to hate themselves and think life is not worth living.

Many colleges today provide student activities funds and recognition for a Gay and Lesbian Alliance (GALA) or a Lesbian and Gay Organization (LAGO). Several chapters of gay fraternities and lesbian sororities have been organized. However, even where such organizations exist, many lesbian and gay collegians avoid them or keep their membership quiet. Unfortunately, on many smaller college campuses, even in large metropolitan areas, gay and lesbian students may still have to hide their orientation (Lubenow 1982; Middleton & Roark 1981).

Gay Politicians and Clergy

The growing visibility of homosexuals in American society and the scrutiny of the press probing the private lives of public figures has led some politicians to acknowledge publicly their gay orientation. In 1980 Robert E. Bauman, a leading conservative Republican Congressman from Maryland, lost his bid for reelection after revealing his homosexual orientation (Bauman 1986). About the same time, Congressman Gerry E. Studds from Massachusetts revealed his homosexuality and continued to serve in the House of Representatives (Figure 16.5). When Massachusetts Representative Barney Frank freely disclosed his homosexual

Figure 16.5. Gay Politicians. *Gerry Studds, Democratic Congressman from Massachusetts, has been re-elected several times and is openly homosexual. He was one of the first elected officials to openly acknowledge his sexual orientation.*

orientation in 1987, his colleagues echoed the comment of Representative Studds that Frank's orientation was "essentially non-news."

Homosexuality in the clergy has been equally controversial, with emotional debates on ordaining homosexuals to the ministry and accepting homosexual behavior and gay relationships as moral. In the late 1980s several studies suggested that the incidence of homosexuality was much higher among the clergy than in the general population. Estimates of the percentage of gay clergy ranged from 20% to 40% of Catholic priests and upward of 50% among Episcopal clergy in large urban areas (Woodward 1987). Such estimates naturally caused considerable controversy and even outrage, especially when they appeared as cover stories in national newsmagazines or were widely reviewed, for example, the autobiographical stories of lesbian nuns (Curb & Manahan 1986; Gramick 1990).

Bisexualities

Much less is known about the lifestyles of men and women who are sexually and emotionally attracted to persons of both genders (Fast & Wells 1975; Klein 1978, Klein, Sepekoff, & Wolf 1985).

> Fundamental to [the concept of] **bisexuality** [our emphasis] is the belief that in each of us there is a masculine-feminine polarity, a masculine side and a feminine side, whatever our gender. Most people, both heterosexuals and homosexuals, go through life attempting to deny this masculine-feminine polarity. They try to complete themselves by finding someone of the opposite (or same) sex who is playing the same game. Such relationships are extremely limited in potential, at best, and are usually unfulfilling. Many argue that the differences between men and women are mostly illusionary, burdensome, restrictive roles that close doors to new ways of relating, and stand in the way of living a more fulfilling life.
>
> Most persons interested in bisexuality support development of relationships with both females and males. These may include spiritual, social, emotional, sensual, sexual and intellectual ties. Although the open expression of affection and touch among people can occur in these relationships, it does not necessarily have sexual implications.
>
> *(Barr 1985:231–232)*

A major issue for many bisexual men and women is the lack of acceptance they have on one side from gay men and lesbians who argue they "just haven't had the courage to come out" and, on the other side, from heterosexuals who despise the bisexual for the homoerotic part of their own personality. We discuss the issue of bisexual husbands and wives in Chapter 17.

Adjusting to a "Different" Orientation

Social Issues

Individuals with unconventional gender orientations face problems similar to those of any minority group whose existence is not fully recognized, only slightly tolerated, and often discriminated against by social traditions and the law.

Heterosexism and Homophobia

Heterosexism, the assumption that everyone is or should be heterosexual, is a prevalent bias in our culture. This viewpoint sets the stage for individual, institutional, and cultural oppression of nonheterosexual persons. **Homophobia** is an intense dislike and fear of homosexual men and lesbian women and of sexual intimacy engaged in by persons of the same gender. Homophobia also refers to the fear of being perceived as homosexual. We usually think of a phobia as an *irrational* fear, a fear that interferes with everyday living. The fear of homoerotic men and women and of homosexual behavior is quite real for many people. It is carefully taught and reinforced by elements in our culture. It reflects often a person's fear of their own homoerotic feelings. "If one of them comes on to me, does that mean that I'm gay/lesbian?" Considering the cultural forces that support homophobia, it is certainly not an unexpected fear and dislike.

Stereotypes of homosexual persons reinforce and are reinforced by cultural homophobia and heterosexism. One typical stereotype is the belief that gay men are effeminate or "swishy." Yet 40% of the male college athletes in one survey admitted they had engaged in homosexual activities to orgasm twice or more in the previous two years (Garner & Smith 1977). Another stereotype is the gay male as a child molester. Although most adolescents who have same-gender relations do so with other teenagers, the myth persists that a gay or lesbian teacher is likely to seduce students and convert them into homosexuals (Highlight Box 16.2). In fact, 80% of teachers and child-care personnel charged with child molestation are heterosexual. Moreover, 90% of pedophiles are heterosexual in their orientation (McCaghy 1971).

Homophobia can lead to "gay bashing." In 1988 a man in Chicago was hospitalized after being attacked in a park by a man wielding a broken bottle and screaming epithets about AIDS. In New York, a gang attacked a man in Central Park, shouting antigay slurs as they stabbed him to death. The National Gay and Lesbian Task Force reported 7,008 antigay incidents in 1987, 42% more than in 1986. Of the 64 local groups who contributed data to the study, 23 said antigay violence was increasing, 30 said they weren't sure whether it was in-

---

HIGHLIGHT BOX 16.2.
GAY AND LESBIAN TEACHERS

In a 1970 nationwide survey, over three-quarters of adult Americans believed that sexual relations between two adults of the same gender were wrong, and a slight majority felt homosexuals should not be allowed to be teachers, judges, ministers, or physicians (Levitt & Klassen 1974). Between 1970 and 1984, there was little change in the disapproval of homosexual acts although Americans did become a little more tolerant of homosexuals and lesbians teaching in colleges and universities. How do you think this tolerance translates when the issue is whether lesbians and gay men should be teachers in high schools? In elementary schools? Are these responses and concerns about youth based on what we actually know about the factors involved in gender orientation and where these factors come into play?

Question and Responses	Percentage of Sample	
	1973	1984
1. Are sexual relations between two adults of the same sex		
Always wrong	74	73
Almost always wrong	7	5
Wrong only sometimes	8	7
Not wrong at all	11	14
2. Should an admitted homosexual man be allowed to teach in a college or university?		
Yes	49	59
No	51	41

Source: J. A. Davis and T. Smith. (1984). *General Social Surveys,* 1972–1984: *Cumulative data.* New Haven: Yale University, Roper Center for Public Opinion Research.

One of the fears most frequently encountered in discussions of gay rights is the fear that gay teachers will entice impressionable young children into a homosexual life. While incidents of gay teachers or camp counselors being sexually involved with students occasionally appear in the news, there are far more incidents of heterosexually oriented teachers sexually harassing or becoming sexually involved with students. The job insecurity most gay teachers experience because of their orientation is usually more than enough cause for them to avoid any sexual involvement with students. Moreover, since sexual orientation is believed to be set by age 5 or 6, there is little chance of a heterosexually oriented student being converted to a gay lifestyle. (Cartoon by Mike Peters, reprinted by permission of United Feature Syndicate.)

creasing or decreasing, and 11 said they thought this type of violence was decreasing. In Baltimore, 1 in 6 of the gay and lesbian people surveyed reported being harassed or assaulted by someone who mentioned AIDS.

In the late 1980s a flurry of government studies confirmed what many homosexuals said they already knew: Harassment, violence, and crimes against homosexuals have been increasing in recent years. A New York State Task Force reported, "One of the most alarming findings in the youth survey is the openness with which the respondents expressed their aversion and hostility toward gays and lesbians." More than 30% of the New York high school students said they had witnessed harassment of students and teachers thought to be homosexuals. It is hard to say from present surveys whether this is just a surge in reporting, or whether it represents a real increase in gay bashing. The Philadelphia Lesbian and Gay Task Force has reported that gay/lesbian Philadelphians are 10 times more likely to be victims of violence than other citizens. In 1989 the U.S. Justice Department identified gay and lesbian people as the number-one victims of hate crimes.

Many claim the growing hostility to homosexuals is linked with fear and anxiety about AIDS. But, according to David Wertheimer, the executive director of the New York City Gay and Lesbian Anti-Violence Project, "AIDS is [just] a convenient new excuse to attack the gay community." At the same time, there is evidence of increased acceptance of homosexuality, at least among well-educated professionals. Does this finding remind you of Boswell's conclusion about people using religion to attack homosexual persons when they are really motivated by other subconscious reasons?

Family Issues

For some families, homosexuality is considered the worst possible thing that can happen to their child. Parents sometimes disown a homosexual child. Orthodox Jews have been known to "bury" the child with a funeral service and a "death" announcement in the obituary column. Some family members may adjust rather easily, others very painfully, when a son or sibling falls in love and wants the gay or lesbian partner to be included in their family life.

Many gay men and women find it easier to give into parental and family pressure to get married and produce grandchildren. Some homosexuals marry in an attempt to deny or "cure" their homoerotic orientations. Sex researchers estimate that about 20% of gay men, about 4 million men, may marry at least once (Dullea 1987). Many homosexual men and women may lead a closet bisexual life, having an extramarital homosexual or lesbian relationship at the same time their spouse is convinced they are in a typical heterosexual marriage (Hill 1989). Sometimes, to avoid problems like these, a gay man and lesbian agree to a marriage of convenience. They present themselves as a traditional married couple, but live as roommates and have separate sexual lives.

After some years of marriage and a double life, a gay or bisexual spouse may decide to "come out." If the marriage ends in divorce, the children and grandparents, as well as the husband and wife, are forced to confront and accept or walk away from the new reality. It may be even more difficult when a grandparent decides to acknowledge his or her homosexual orientation (Bozett 1987; Friend 1987; Jones 1978; Mendola 1980).

Legal Issues

Lesbian and gay people face specific legal problems, since there are no sexual orientation/preference clauses in most U.S. civil rights laws. This lack of legal protection allows for discrimination in areas such as employment and housing. Sodomy laws are used to harass gay men, although they are rarely used against heterosexual men and women. Divorcing lesbian and gay parents often encounter legal challenges when they seek to retain or share custody of a child. However, some states now allow gay and lesbian couples to retain custody of their children after a divorce, or to adopt heterosexual or gay adolescents. Older lesbian and gay persons have to deal with hospitals or health facilities which do not recognize the right of a partner to determine the course of treatment or to visit in an intensive care unit unless they have obtained power of attorney rights in advance. The wills of gay and lesbian couples are frequently contested by surviving blood relatives (Curry & Clifford 1986; Friend 1987).

Figure 16.6. *Kim Klausner (left) and Debra Chasnoff, shown here with their son Noah, are lesbian parents who arranged for artificial insemination with a gay friend's sperm. Today, many gay and lesbian couples are opting to be parents. Some couples retain custody of a child from a previous marriage or adopt.*

Coming Out

The process of acknowledging and accepting one's gender orientation and publicly "coming out (of the closet)" involves several steps. A gay or lesbian person may pass through, or pause, at any one or more of these stages. The first step is self-recognition, acknowledging that one is, in fact, exclusively or predominantly oriented toward persons of one's own sex. This stage may be followed by a full acceptance and a desire to share this new awareness with close friends and family. Simple honesty and a need to shed the burden of secrecy may come into play at this point. In our homophobic culture, parents are often the *last* to know that a son or daughter is gay or lesbian, or at least are often the last in whom the young person confides that information. Usually, in such situations, the parents have given some message that leads the child to believe that the disclosure will hurt his or her parents severely (Borhek 1983; Chapman & Brannock 1987; Friend 1987; Moses & Hawkins 1982:80–98).

Somewhere in the coming out process, the gay or lesbian person has to face the question of how open or public he or she wants to be about their orientation. Should fellow students, co-workers, employees, or employers be told? Coming out requires considering the many personal and professional consequences. Having negotiated these hurdles, gay and lesbian persons can integrate their sexuality into their total lifestyle, much as their nongay counterparts do with their gender orientation. In this stage, the gay man or lesbian is open to all who care to know, but view their gender orientation as about as significant as their political, religious, ethnic, or racial identification. In a realistic way, they give each of these aspects, including their gender/erotic orientation, as much attention as the times and other external factors dictate. Once comfortable with their orientation and sensitive to the political realities of today's society, some gay and lesbian persons then become active in political or social organizations where they can work with others to oppose oppression and discrimination based on gender orientation and help build peer support.

In a social context, coming out today is much easier than it was 30 or 40 years ago because of the gay activism of recent years. It is still a difficult personal step for many, however.

Although gays and lesbians are often discriminated against, most are happy and content with their lifestyles and do not want to change their orientation, even if they could. They have negotiated the crisis of coming out. They have found access to an empowering gay/lesbian community and culture. And they have reconstructed their identity in their own terms.

Yet, for some homosexuals, a homophobic and heterosexist society makes their gender orientation extremely painful. They would like to change, but can't. The pain was obvious when former Congressman Robert E. Bauman wrote, "I did not choose to be homosexual. I would change my sexual orientation if that were within my power" (1986) (Figure 16.5). Masters and Johnson (1979) claimed they were able to help some male homosexuals become heterosexuals. But these few cases involved people who did not enjoy their homosexual activity and were very afraid of and ignorant about heterosexual activity. They also had some degree of bisexuality and a very strong desire to change (Money 1988:87).

Counseling, support groups, and psychotherapy can help a gay or lesbian person adapt to and accept his or her orientation, cope with society's heterosexist prejudices, and overcome feelings of guilt and gain self-respect.

Given the history of the civil rights movement and our knowledge of gender orientations, the real social problem is not the acceptance of people of different racial or gender orientation but the racism, heterosexism and homophobia that continues to divide our society into ''we'' and ''them.''

Are We Born with a Panerotic Potential?

In talking about our gender orientation, we invariably focus on what leads us to seek sensual and erotic pleasure and nurturance in close, intimate, and loving relations with other persons. However, there are other dimensions or sources of nurturance and sensuality which are important in giving meaning to our everyday lives. We distort our sexuality when we limit it to the genitals and what we do with them.

According to William Stayton (1980), we are in fact born ''totally sexual,'' with a pansensual or **panerotic potential.** ''Nature's intent seems to be to produce persons who are sexual [and sensual] in the fullest sense of the word.'' With the entire universe as a potential erotic turn-on and a source of sensual nurturance of all kinds, Stayton sees any sensual/erotic activity that ''keeps a creative balance between serving one's own needs and being able to delay or substitute gratification'' as basically a healthy response (Figure 16.7).

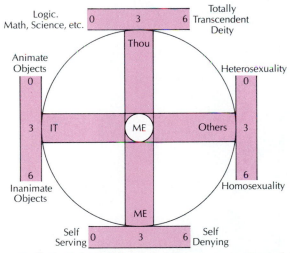

RELATIONSHIPS AND POTENTIAL EROTIC RESPONSES

Figure 16.7. A Panerotic Potential Model. *Men and women can express their erotic/affectional drives in a wide variety of ways, in sensual/erotic experiences with oneself, with persons of the same or other gender, with animate and inanimate objects, and in such intellectual and creative experiences as science, the arts, and spiritual, transcendent, and mystical experiences. William Stayton's model shows that almost anything in the universe has the potential to satisfy our sensual and erotic drives, depending on one's individual needs.*

Before we can be intimate with another person, we first have to develop a healthy relationship with ourselves: This is the personal dimension of intimacy and nurturance in Stayton's model. He suggests that each of us needs to achieve a balanced approach to the sensual and erotic potential of our own body. We need a balance between total self-serving narcissism (0) and total self-sacrifice (6).

Our quest for intimacy can also be met by turning to the world outside. Stayton talks of a range between the sensuality expressed in the love of nature and the cosmos and the sensual potential we have in relating to the animal world.

Other persons provide us with a third outlet, one we are much more familiar with and often equate with "orientation." Here, Stayton suggests that our human potential is, by nature, basically bisexual, somewhere in the Kinsey 1 or 2 categories for the majority of persons. The bell-shaped distribution curve for what we have called gender orientation would then taper off in either direction, toward the exclusive heteroerotic 0 and the exclusive homoerotic 6, with very small percentages of the population in either category.

The fourth, and most controversial, dimension of this panerotic potential model, the transcendental, is not very evident in Western civilization. A few artists and poets, like the Pre-Raphaelite Dante Gabriel Rossetti (1828–1882) and the romantic William Blake (1757–1827), England's greatest visionary poet, have captured the transcendental dimension of human sensuality and eroticism. The mystical writings of two medieval Spanish saints, Teresa of Avila and John of the Cross, contain examples of transcendental erotic expressions in poetry and meditations (Figure 16.8). In more recent times, the work of anthropologist poet

Figure 16.8. The Erotic Potential of the Mystical Experience. *Both the setting and the expression of Giovanni Bernini's 17th century sculpture of* The Ecstasy of St. Teresa of Avila *show the close connection between eroticism or sensuality and the mystical experience. The spiritual ecstasy of Teresa, experienced in her meditations and her relationship with God, is clearly given erotic and orgasmic expression in her writings, which recall the highly sensual, openly erotic and passionate* Song of Songs *by King Solomon in the Old Testament of the early Jewish tradition.*

Loren Eiseley and the astronomer/poet Carl Sagan have touched on the domain of transcendental and cosmic sensuality, as does some New Age thinking. The New Age music of Kitaro and Andreas Vollenweider are good examples of this dimension. The Taoist and Tantric Buddhist tradition of sexuality with its symbolic lingam/yoni or yin and yang—the complementary male and female principles—and the Hindu temple sculptures of northern India express this transcendental/erotic dimension in the Eastern cultures.

Viewing the human quest for intimacy as a panerotic potential helps us escape the reduction of our sexual nature to the genitals and what we do with them.

Key Concepts

1. People do not fit into neat groups such as heterosexual/normal and homosexual-or-bisexual/abnormal, mainly because there is as much variety among gay, lesbian, and bi persons as there is among the so-called straight majority.

2. Kinsey viewed the possibilities of sexual orientation as a spectrum ranging from exclusively heterosexual experiences and fantasies, Kinsey 0, to the exclusively homosexual experiences and fantasies, Kinsey 6. Half of American men fell in the Kinsey 0 category, 4% were in the Kinsey 6 category, and the remaining 46% were bisexual, Kinsey 1 through 5.

3. Kinsey advised that we not characterize persons as either heterosexual or homosexual, but rather as individuals who have had certain amounts of heterosexual and homosexual experiences. The terms heterosexual and homosexual should be used only to describe behaviors or the stimuli that trigger erotic responses.

4. The Sexual Orientation Grid, developed by Fred Klein, involves a Kinsey 0 to 6 rating for seven aspects of sexual orientation: past, present, and ideal. The seven aspects are sexual attraction, sexual behavior, sexual fantasies, emotional preference, social preference, lifestyle, and self-identification.

5. Stayton's theory of panerotic potential is similar to Freud's polymorphic perversity theory, with four dimensions: the self, other persons, nature and things, and the transcendental.

6. John Boswell's study of homosexuality and social tolerance suggests that economic factors and the shifts between predominantly urban and rural social structures are key factors in the tolerance or condemnation of homosexual lifestyles. Tolerance and acceptance characterized the early Christian era to A.D. 600. A major flowering of gay culture occurred in the Middle Ages, during the 11th and 12th centuries, after which the gay community was very much suppressed in European culture.

7. The term *normal* requires careful use and definition. There are statistical, clinical, religious, legal, social, cross-cultural, and personal definitions of normality. The term *unconventional* is used in a nonjudgmental way for sexual behaviors and relationships that in some way deviate from social conventions and the formally accepted standards of society.

Key Terms

affectional orientation (432)
bisexuality (451)
core gender identity (433)
erotic orientation (432)
gender nonconformity (447)
gender orientation (432)
gender-role behavior (433)
heteroerotic (432)
heterosexism (452)
homoerotic (438)

homophobia (452)
homosexuality (434)
Kinsey Six Scale (435)
normal (440)
panerotic potential (457)
same-gender sexual
    experimentation (438)
Sexual Orientation Grid (438)
situational homoerotic behavior (438)

Summary Questions

1. Describe briefly the three components of our psychosexual identity or gender, and the three aspects of gender orientation.

2. Describe different aspects of heterosexism and homophobia. How do they promote a hostile environment and encourage violence against persons with socially unacceptable gender orientations?

3. Describe what we know and don't know about the prenatal/postnatal and biological/social factors which affect our psychosexual development and gender orientation.

4. Why are psychological and behavioral therapies generally ineffective in changing gender orientation? What practical use might counseling have for a gay or lesbian person?

5. Describe the process and stages of coming out.

6. What kinds of family, social, and legal problems do same-gender-oriented persons encounter in a heterosexist society?

Suggested Readings

Borhek, M. V. (1983). *Coming Out to Parents: A Two-Way Survival Guide for Lesbians and Gay Men and Their Parents.* New York: Pilgrim Press. The mother of a gay son offers down-to-earth advice and support for coming out.

Bozett, F. W., ed. (1987). *Gay and Lesbian Parents.* New York: Praeger. A variety of perspectives on homosexuals as effective parents.

Clark, D. (1973). *Loving Someone Gay.* New York: New American Library. A compassionate, supportive guide when you discover a friend or family member is gay or lesbian.

Curry, H., & D. Clifford. (1986). *A Legal Guide for Lesbians and Gay Couples* (4th ed.). Berkeley, CA: Nolo Press.

Edwards, G. R. (1984). *Gay/Lesbian Liberation: A Biblical Perspective.* New York: Pilgrim Press. A theologian examines biblical statements on homosexuality in contemporary terms.

Jones, C. (1978). *Understanding Gay Relatives and Friends*. New York: Seabury. A compassionate introduction of family members who happen to be homosexual in their orientation.

Loulan, J. (1987). *Lesbian Passion*. San Francisco: Spinsters/Aunt Lute. A book about lesbian sex written by a lesbian counselor.

McNaught, B. (1988). *On Being Gay: Thoughts on Family, Faith and Love*. New York: St. Martin's Press. A wise, pithy primer on what it means to be gay.

Two Novels of Special Interest

Brown, R. M. (1977). *Rubyfruit Jungle*. New York: Bantam Books. The story of one young lesbian.

Warren, P. (1974). *The Frontrunner*. New York: Bantam Books. A novel about a gay male track star, his coach, and the Olympics.

*T*oday's Relationships
  A Changing Society
  A New Ecosystem
*S*ingles
  The Singles Population
  Deciding Whether To Be
    Sexually Active
  Creative Singlehood
*C*ouples
  Monogamy and Its
    Evolution
  Variations on a Theme
*S*ingle Again
  The Divorced and
    Widowed
*H*ow to Define a Family
*S*hifting Sex Ratios
  and Values

Chapter 17

*L*ifestyles of Singles and Couples

Special Consultants

Wayne Carpenter, Ph.D., counselor at Western New England College in Springfield, Massachusetts, author of a 12-year retrospective study of cohabiting and noncohabiting college students.

Arno Karlen, author of *Sexuality and Homosexuality* and *Threesomes: Studies in Sex, Power, and Intimacy*; coauthor of *Sexual Decisions*, a college text; and editor, *Sex Education in Medicine* with Harold Leif, M.D.

Teresa Donati Marciano, Ph.D., professor of sociology, Fairleigh Dickinson University. Author of numerous papers and chapters on alternate lifestyles.

Robert L. McGinley, Ph.D., founder and director, The Lifestyles Organization and the North American Swing Club Association.

Joseph W. Scott, Ph.D., professor, American Ethnic Studies, University of Washington (Seattle), and author of several studies of sexual customs and lifestyles among black Americans.

David L. Weis, Ph.D., associate professor, human development and family studies, Department of Applied Human Ecology, Bowling Green State University. Author of several research articles on extramarital sexuality and intimate lifestyles.

In the 1990s our lifelong search for intimacy, belonging, and nurturance invariably leads us into a variety of interpersonal relationships. Some are superficial and short-lived. Others are long-term committed relationships. Whatever form they take, these relationships all express and try to satisfy basic personal needs. This chapter examines our changing social environment and the pressure it places on both traditional marriage and the nontraditional lifestyles many men and women are exploring in an attempt to meet their intimacy needs in a rapidly changing world.

Today's Relationships

A Changing Society

In 1941, when the Great Depression was over and World War II began, the ideal and certainly most common American lifestyle was to marry and have a large family. As young people matured sexually, they were encouraged to double date and then go out with a single person (Bailey 1988). Dating was expected to be emotionally monogamous. All other friendships were casual. As a couple approached marriage, their expectations as an engaged couple were clear. They might express their growing love in petting, so-called making out, but premarital sex was still somewhat taboo. Marriage followed, with a more intense emotional and sexual exclusivity which emphasized the couple and downplayed their individual needs. The husband was the breadwinner and the wife stayed home, finding her identity as wife and mother. In old age, there would be a period of celibate widowhood. Divorce was a possibility, as was remarriage, but those options were hardly discussed and statistically rare.

In the 1990s we can look back over 50 years and honestly say no other period in human history has witnessed more upheavals and radical changes in the social ecosystem than today's college students, their parents, and their grandparents have experienced.

A New Ecosystem

Life Expectancy

Two thousand years ago, the average life span was about 18 years. By the Middle Ages, the average life expectancy of Europeans at birth was about 33 years. Only a few people lived to a ripe old age, the proverbial three score and ten. Childbirth, war, plagues, natural calamities, and inadequate diet and shelter made life hard and short. By 1900 the average American could expect to live about 47 years. Today, the average life expectancy at birth has pushed into the seventies and early eighties.

Already, 1 in 5 Americans is over the age of 60. Women in the 65-and-older age group are the fastest-growing segment of our population. In retirement communities, the average woman-man ratio is 7 to 1.

Mobility

In 1990 over half of all Americans enjoyed the mobility, affluence, and leisure only 1% or 2% of Americans enjoyed in 1900. Many young people leave home and move into college dormitories or off-campus apartments. The farther young people geographically distance themselves from their parents, the more likely they are to cohabit. Even young adults who continue living with their parents have more freedom than ever before. Mobility has weakened once strong family control over the lifestyles of young adults. With family members often scattered across the country, we live in a very different world from that which provided support and social control only two or three generations ago when all our relatives lived in the same neighborhood, or at least in the same city. Many people find themselves creating their own intentional family, an intimate network of friends.

Leisure and Retirement

A hundred years ago, the average American male worked 70 or 80 hours a week and 6 days every week. Work on the farm, in the factory, or mine meant work from sunup to sundown. With no social security, pensions, or retirement benefits, most people worked until they died, or could no longer keep going (Piotrkowski, Rapoport, & Rapoport 1987:251–268).

By 1890 many American businesses had adopted a 10-hour workday, although a 12-hour day was not uncommon even as recently as 1923. During World War II, the present 5-day, 40-hour week became popular. Today the average work week is 37.5 hours.

Recent decades have witnessed a marked increase in the number of retirees. Twenty years ago, General Motors had 10 active workers for each retiree. Ten years ago, the ratio was 4 workers to 1 retiree. In the 1990s the ratio may well approach 1 to 1. More people are living longer and retiring earlier, or picking up a second career. Many unions and the military service allow retirement after 20 or 30 years. The number of young people entering the work force is declining. Retraining for a second career in midlife is not an uncommon experience today.

Women's Growing Financial Independence

At the turn of the century, very few middle- and upper-class women worked outside the home. In 1940 only 17% of married women had outside jobs. World War II provided a catalyst for change, opening new economic options for women. Today, most women expect to work and have a career, even though they plan to take a few years off for a "nesting period" when they have one or two young children. Or they may choose not to have any children (Houseknecht 1987:369–392). For a variety of reasons, most women expect to work outside of the home. The growing emphasis on self-actualization represents a major ideological change in our understanding of human relationships.

Economic opportunities provide some women with financial independence. Despite these gains, women are represented in disproportionate numbers among the poor. Single-parent families, most of which are headed by women, are very often at or barely above the poverty level. In addition, a high percentage of older people are classified as poor, and a major part of the older poor are women.

Professional opportunities for women are at an all-time high. Never before have we had as many women doctors and lawyers. Women now work in construction and mines. They are police officers, fire fighters, and truck drivers—blue-collar jobs previously closed to them. Yet they still represent only about 3% of those employed in the better paying "male" jobs. It is important to remember that women still have not achieved pay equity with men; half of all working women are employed in low-paying service jobs such as waitresses and clerical workers. Because of social changes and their growing financial potential, women are not forced into marriage. They can remain single, marry and stay at home, marry and work outside the home, live with someone and remain single, and so forth.

A Contraceptive Culture

Any American under age 40 has grown up taking for granted our contraceptive technology. Ours is the first generation in human history capable of separating sexual intercourse from the risk of pregnancy. It is also the first generation to face the psychological separation of sex and reproduction via frozen embryos, embryo transplants, and debates over surrogate motherhood. This revolution, symbolized by the Pill and surrogate mothers, has had a tremendous effect on the way men and women relate sexually as well as socially.

Adapting to Our New Environment

To survive, any animal must adapt to its environment. And since environments are constantly changing, each animal species is forced to change. In the past century, we have taken an active role in creating and modifying our social environment. With startling speed, we discovered antiseptics and antibiotics to extend our life expectancy and improve our quality of life. Industrial technology, and the more recent shift to an information and service-oriented workplace, have increased leisure and mobility. At the same time we separated sex and reproduction, we extended adolescence to the mid-twenties. The sexual revolution of the 1960s and 1970s was followed by STDs like herpes and AIDS. In the midst of this new environment, our expectations and lifestyles, our attitudes and values, inevitably change (Figure 17.1).

Until the 1960s, young people were expected to follow a sort of primrose path of courtship, marriage, and family. Figure 17.1 gives an insight into how radical that one path has splintered. Today, we have to make repeated decisions, choosing the lifestyle which best suits us at this particular time, knowing full well our situation and choice of lifestyle may be different a few years from now. Today, there is no regular progression from one type of relationship to another. If a person begins with a traditional exclusive courtship, he or she probably will move into a traditional marriage. But there are many other options. Cohabitation and/or one or more premarital relationships might precede a traditional or nontraditional marriage. We might also choose to remain single, perhaps becoming a single parent by choice.

After marriage, traditional expectations may change. Twenty years ago, in his 1970 book *Future Shock*, Alvin Toffler forecast that "Instead of wedding 'until death do us part,' couples will enter matrimony knowing from the start that the relationship is short-lived. And when the opportunity presents itself, they will marry again . . . and again . . . and again." In the 1990s this forecast has become reality. Clifford Sager, a noted family psychiatrist, reports we are seeing much more short-term bonding, with an increasing number of men and women going through serial marriages. A divorce may lead to remarriage, or a revitalized single life. A sexually exclusive living-together or marital relation may be opened up to become part of a close personal network with intimate satellite relations. Today, many people move back and forth and around the circle of intimacy, commitment, and dependency shown in Figure 17.1.

Our Changing Social Environment

Increasing life expectancy

Women's liberation—women in the work force, economic
 independence of women, single mothers by choice

Contraceptive technologies: separation of sex from reproduction

Increasing mobility

Increasing leisure—shorter work week, retirement

Television and global communications

Legalized abortion

No-fault divorce

Smaller families—shift from rural to urban life

Lower infant mortality rates

Lower maternal mortality rates

Prolonged adolescence

Earlier age of puberty

Later age of marriage

Emergence of singles as economic independent consumers

Our Adaptive Behaviors in Relationships

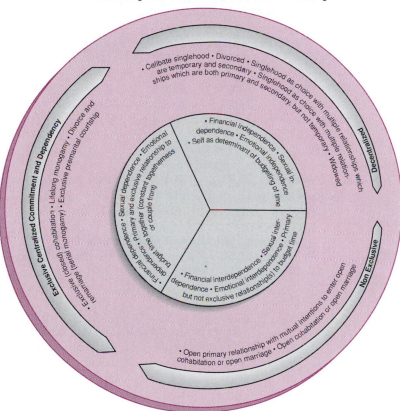

Figure 17.1. Adapting to Our Changing Social Environment. *Radical changes in our so-cial environment over the past 100 years or more have led to the emergence of a variety of lifestyles and relationships more functional in today's world than the rigid sex roles and monog-amous Victorian marriage of the past. The circle of intimacy and commitment has no particular path, no normal sequence. Individuals follow their own unique path, moving from one lifestyle to another. Thus a traditional exclusive courtship may move into cohabitation or into a sexually exclusive marriage. This relationship may produce a lifelong commitment, or end in divorce or widowhood, followed in turn by remarriage, creative singlehood, or a celibate life. Any combina-tion or sequence is possible. Try tracing the path some of your relatives or friends have followed.*

Singles

The Singles Population

Well over 50 million, over 20% of adult Americans, are single. Between 1960 and 1986, the number of adult Americans living alone tripled to 21 million. Although marriage still remains a goal for the majority, marriage now comes later than ever before in American history (Shostak 1987:355–366). (See Table 17.1.)

Table 17.1.
The Way We Live

In a study that examines trends in American households and families, the Census Bureau reported that American men and women are marrying later than ever before and that more than 1 American adult in 10 lives alone—three times as many as in 1960.

Men	**Percentage of Men and Women Never Married**					
	1950	1960	1970	1980	1985	1986
20 to 24 years	59.0%	53.1%	54.7%	68.8%	75.6%	75.5%
25 to 29 years	23.8	20.8	19.1	33.1	38.7	41.4
30 to 34 years	13.2	11.9	9.4	15.9	20.8	22.2
Women						
20 to 24 years	32.3	28.4	35.8	50.2	58.5	57.9
25 to 29 years	13.3	10.5	10.5	20.9	26.4	28.1
30 to 34 years	9.3	6.9	6.2	9.5	13.5	14.2

One-Person Households **(as a Percentage of All Households)**				
1960	1970	1980	1985	1986
13%	17%	23%	24%	24%

Unmarried Couples Living Together **(as a Percentage of All Households)**				
1960	1970	1980	1985	1986
0.8%	0.8%	2.0%	2.3%	2.5%

	Median Age at First Marriage						
	1960	1965	1970	1975	1980	1985	1986
Men	22.8	22.8	23.2	23.5	24.7	25.5	25.7
Women	20.3	20.6	20.8	21.1	22.0	23.3	23.1

Source: Bureau of the Census

A growing number of singles plan never to marry. The number of single cohabiting couples has tripled since 1960. Some single persons have been married, but are now separated, widowed, or divorced. Single persons are found in every age group, among middle-aged and older persons as well as among college students and graduates just entering the business world (Green 1987).

Americans today spend much of their lives as single persons. Our longer life span and the increasing frequency of divorce are only part of the reason. In the days of Romeo and Juliet, 500 years ago, the average age of first marriage was 13 for girls and 15 for boys. In 1986 the median age for first marriage was 25.7 for men and 23.1 for women. Added to these factors is our more permissive attitude toward premarital sex. In 1937 only 1 in 5 Americans accepted premarital sex in any circumstance. Forty years later, 3 out of 4 young people found it acceptable (Hass 1979; Hunt 1974).

Deciding Whether to Be Sexually Active

Singlehood can be very exciting, fresh, and challenging. It is also, like any other lifestyle, sometimes lonely, frustrating, and difficult. One of the ongoing stresses of a single life is exclusion from the community of married couples. The fact that single persons are often viewed as being sexually threatening to married couples is a major reason for the isolation of many singles in certain communities, but many singles also prefer not to socialize with married couples (Shostak 1987:355–366).

There are great pressures on singles today to become involved in sexual relationships, and saying "no" is not easy. In the 1979 Hass survey, young women gave many different reasons for acting contrary to their feelings or convictions when it came to having sex. Not wanting to hurt a man's feelings, feeling pressured or intimidated, afraid of losing him, a sense of obligation, being high on alcohol, not wanting to appear a tease, and compromising are common reasons. A man's reasons for not saying "no" are somewhat different: not wanting to hurt a woman's feelings, being afraid she would think he didn't like her, proving his manhood, peer influence, "nothing else to do," and a socialization that places few restraints on male libido (Hass 1979:64–82). (See Highlight Box 17.1.)

It is interesting to compare these reasons for having sex when they really didn't want to with the reasons another group of young people gave Sorensen in his 1973 survey. Some of their motives had nothing to do with sex. Instead, they used sexual relations for nonsexual goals, such as rewarding or punishing a partner, rebelling against parents, and challenging social or family values. Other reasons included seeking a new experience, the desire to escape tensions, communication, physical pleasure, exploring one's sexual potential, and proving one's heterosexuality in an age when homosexuality is more open.

The majority of sexual interactions of young people occur in a positive emotional climate where personal feelings and the meaning of intercourse are discussed beforehand (Christopher & Cate 1984, 1985). However, singles also encounter dating situations where they experience forced, sometimes violent sexual encounters (Korman & Leslie 1982; Koss & Oros 1982). Over half of the undergraduate single women in Christopher's 1988 study reported being pressured into kissing, breast and genital manipulation, and oral sex at least once. (See Chapter 22 for a discussion of sexual coercion and assault in dating relationships.)

Celibacy

Popularization of the sexual revolution has led to the common misconception that everyone is sexually involved and that virginity and sexual abstinence or **celibacy** are out of date, and even harmful to one's mental and physical health (Lee 1980). This shift in social expectations from sexual abstinence and monogamous lifelong marriage to sexual involvement in a series of multiple relationships, some claim, has brought a natural swing of the pendulum back to more conservative values. *The Joy of Sex, More Joy, Sex and the Single Woman (Man), Swinging Singles,* and *Open Marriage* were followed by *The Sexual Revolution Is Over* (Leo 1984), *Sex Is Dead* (Leonard 1982), *The New Celibacy* (Brown 1980), and "The National Chastity Association."

Some observers have argued that the new emphasis on sexual abstinence represents a kind of "sexual burnout," "a backlash to the performance and genitally focused imperatives inherent in American sexual beliefs" (Hite 1976; Lee 1980; Whelehan & Moynihan 1982; Zilbergeld 1978). To avoid reducing this "new celibacy" to a simple sexual cop-out or a negative withdrawal from sexual pressures, Whelehan and Moynihan (1982) redefine celibacy as "a modified sensate focus approach to pleasuring one's self or one's partner in a manner that is neither directed toward sexual arousal nor orgasm." (See p. 565 or the Glossary for a definition of sensate focus.) Despite the media hype, none of the recent surveys indicate a sizable increase in sexual abstinence in the 1980s. On the other hand, celibacy and sexual abstinence can be for some a very positive, thoughtfully chosen lifestyle.

Celibacy may be temporary or long term. A man or woman may be sexually intimate but choose not to engage in sexual intercourse (Darling & Davidson 1987). Men and women in many religious traditions have endorsed celibacy or sexual abstinence as a way of concentrating their energies on spiritual concerns and service to others. Yet church dictums which required celibacy are being changed by clergy who want their celibacy to be a free choice. Other men and women freely adopt a lifestyle of secular celibacy in order to devote all their time and energies to a career or artistic work, without having to be concerned about responsibilities to a spouse or children.

Most persons, both single and married, go through periods of temporary celibacy (Pietropinto 1987). A newly divorced person or a single person who has just broken off a relationship may be angry and distrustful, or simply need time to heal before becoming sexually involved again. In the years of a long-term relationship, it is natural for occasional periods of little or no sexual intercourse to occur for a variety of reasons. Abstinence from sexual intimacy may occur when individuals are depressed or under great stress. Sometimes one partner needs a break from sexual intimacy. It is important that this need be discussed openly so that the other partner can better understand the reasons for the change and not take it as a personal rejection.

First Sexual Experience

The age of first intercourse has continued to drop to younger ages. In the early 1950s Kinsey reported that 3% of women and 40% of men had intercourse by the age of 16. Contrast this finding with Sorensen's 1973 statistics indicating that 30% of women and 44% of men had intercourse by age 16. In three national surveys, a majority of teenagers were found to be sexually active between ages 16 and 19 (Hofferth, Kahn, & Baldwin 1987; Kahn, Kalsbeek, & Hoffert 1988).

HIGHLIGHT BOX 17.1.
AMERICAN SINGLES SPEAK OUT

For their 1982 study of *Singles: The New Americans*, Jacqueline Simenauer and David Carroll interviewed a representative nationwide sample of singles from ages 20 to 55. The following are some of their main findings.

- Integrity, sensitivity, and a sense of humor are more important than physical attractiveness, money, status, or position in terms of initial attraction.

- Most singles dislike singles bars, although almost 40% of single men and women make their initial contacts at bars and singles functions.

- Over 90% of singles believe nonsexual friendships can and should exist between men and women.

- More than 75% of single men feel women should pay or help pay for a date *occasionally*. Four out of 5 women under 25 do not want a man to pay. Older women did not feel as strongly.

- Three out of 4 singles reported that being independent helped their careers. Divorced and single mothers cited prejudice on the job and having children as real problems.

- Most single parents report that their dates don't mind their having children.

- Almost 70% of single men said they were indifferent or actively opposed to sleeping with a woman on the first date, although over two-thirds *do* sleep with a woman on their first to third date.

Another nationwide survey, conducted by the National Institute of Child Health and Human Development in 1986, gives additional insights into the lifestyles of single women.

- One in 3 single women in their twenties has been pregnant at least once.

- The average unmarried 20-year-old has had sexual relations with four or five men, half of them serious long-term relations and the other half more casual acquaintances.

- Half of the white women and 1 in 10 black women aborted their first pregnancy.

- One-third of single women have lived with a man.

- One out of 6 single women habitually risks pregnancy by having sexual intercourse without using contraceptives.

- One-fifth of the single women do not start using contraceptives until they have been pregnant.

Contrary to what many people think, first intercourse is given a highly favorable rating. Ninety percent of the teenage males and 70% of the females in the 1979 Hass survey said their first experience was "very enjoyable." Nine percent of the males and 18% of the females said it was moderately enjoyable. About 1 in 10 girls reported their first experience was not enjoyable and even painful.

The tendency for women to find their first sexual intercourse somewhat less enjoyable than men is probably the result of anxiety, physical discomfort, and pain. A lack of experience and lovemaking skills on the part of both individuals may lead to rushed intercourse without enough time for the woman to achieve sufficient vaginal lubrication or to reach orgasm. In Sorensen's survey, teenage girls reported attaching less significance to their first sexual intercourse than boys did. On the other hand, twice as many males had positive reactions to their first experience when compared with teenage girls. For boys the immediate reaction was anticipation and excitement; for the girls, the reaction was one of some fear and anxiety. The girls frequently felt guilty, sad, and disappointed. David Weis termed this reaction the "Peggy Lee syndrome," referring to Lee's song "Is That All There Is?" (Weis 1983b).

More often than not, the boys were completely oblivious to the girl's negative feelings and hesitations. Boys, however, also experience some tensions and pressures, particularly when they grapple with their "need to prove themselves" and to perform like experienced men. In some cases, this need to meet a stereotype of masculinity can render a man impotent. It may also lead to a premature ejaculation, either before or within a few seconds of vaginal penetration. Both the male and female may feel "let down" and disappointed with their experiences.

Despite the growing acceptance of premarital intercourse, it is important to remember that premarital virginity is still highly valued, particularly in orthodox Judaism, Roman Catholicism, fundamentalist Protestantism, and among Mormons and Muslims.

Single Parents

Statistics about single parents regularly make news. In 1988 the U.S. Census Bureau reported that 26% of all American children, 8.8 million, live in a single-parent family. One in 5 infants born to white women and 3 out of 4 black infants were born to single mothers. On the surface these numbers could be interpreted as a disaster, implying that both mother and child are locked into a never-ending cycle of welfare. However, behind these raw statistics are some interesting insights into the changing American family. The most obvious fact is that since 1970, the rate of white single mothers has risen by 67% while the rate for black single mothers has declined by 15%. Almost half of all black and white single mothers marry within 5 years, and nearly 70% are married within 15 years. In addition, almost one-fourth of out-of-wedlock births occur among unmarried couples who are living together (Gongla & Thompson 1987:397–415; U.S. Census Bureau 1989; Wattenberg 1989). (See Figure 17.2.)

Contrary to the common image of single mothers, Glick found a sharp decline starting 20 years ago in the proportion of poorly educated single mothers and a doubling in single-parent families whose mother was a college graduate. When Furstenberg tracked a sample of black single mothers in the mid-1960s, he found that by 1987, 71% had graduated from high school, 68% were employed, 71% were not on welfare, and their family size was relatively small. Most of the children of these single mothers, Furstenberg found, had graduated from high school and had not become single mothers (Wattenberg 1989). Still, families headed by single women are most likely to be below poverty level (Figure 17.3).

Adding to the variety of single mothers are single mothers by choice. Increasing numbers of never-married and divorced women are deciding in their thirties to become single parents. Some single women choose to adopt; others have their own baby via intercourse with a friend or artificial insemination using donor semen. In some states, lesbians and gay men can adopt babies or older children. Lesbians also use artificial insemination to have a child. In response to this new trend, support groups like Single Mothers by Choice and Single Adoptive Parents are appearing in many larger cities.

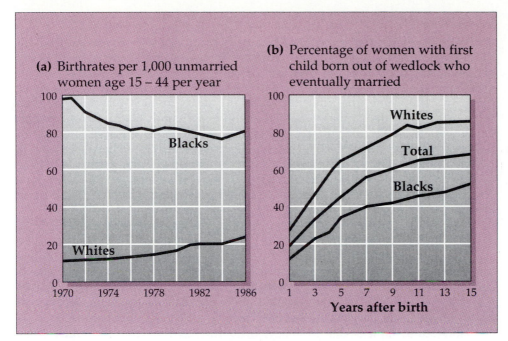

(a) Birthrates per 1,000 unmarried women age 15 – 44 per year

(b) Percentage of women with first child born out of wedlock who eventually married

Figure 17.2. Single Mothers. *Graph (a) shows the annual birthrates per 1,000 unmarried women between ages 15 and 44. Graph (b) shows the percentage of women with a first child born out of wedlock who eventually married. These figures are cumulative and based on a study since 1970 of 13,017 adults in the United States of which 1,625 were unwed mothers not previously married.*

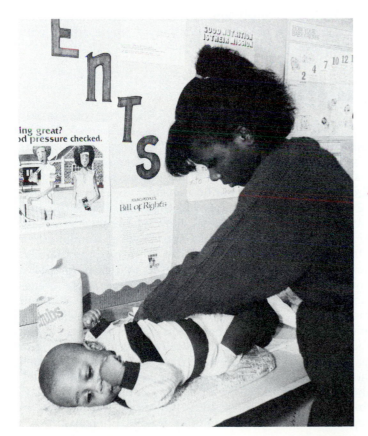

Figure 17.3. *Special programs in many schools now allow teenage mothers to continue their education while taking care of their babies as this young mother is doing in the Parenting Room at a New York high school.*

Creative Singlehood

With the flexibility and mobility of today's world, many men and women are in intimate, sexual relationships, dating, or living with someone without being married. This trend is simply an extension of the monogamous, sexually exclusive marriage. Some single persons are involved with or date two or more persons at the same time, meeting different needs in each relationship. One relationship may be primarily sexual, another primarily social, professional, emotional, or intellectual. Roger Libby calls this lifestyle **creative singlehood** (Libby & Whitehurst 1977:37). A person is creatively single when he or she is not emotionally, financially, or sexually dependent on any one person. Creative singlehood, in this context, describes the lifestyle of a single person who does not have a commitment to any particular monogamous relationship, but is open to multiple relationships of varying degrees of intimacy.

The hallmark of creative singlehood is being nonexclusive and available both sexually and emotionally for relations of varying intimacy and intensity. The creatively single person believes that his or her sexual relations are not determined by and limited to the particular couple relations in which he or she is currently involved. Thus any relationship this person develops may, or may not, become sexually intimate. People choose creative singlehood because it allows them to be open to all the possibilities life brings and because it does not isolate and limit sexual intimacy, even though they may be much more cautious now because of AIDS.

The old image of single adults as lonely and isolated no longer holds, if for no other reason than the existence of a large number of single adults with financial independence, mobility, and leisure.

Couples

Monogamy and Its Evolution

The concept of **monogamy**, the marriage of one man and one woman, has evolved over thousands of years, during which time the experience and expectations of monogamous couples have changed radically, as we saw in Chapters 1 and 14. One hundred years ago, a romantic, sexually exclusive, lifelong monogamous marriage with four to six children was the ideal. It was the only socially acceptable lifestyle for middle-class adults. Men who enjoyed wandering and the single life headed for the western frontier. Young women either married and had children or became the maiden aunt in an extended family. This "normal, average" American family was expressed in classic television series like "Father Knows Best" and "Leave It to Beaver." There was a bread-winner husband, a wife as domestic support system, and two or three children, living in a private home or apartment with separate bedrooms for the children.

Despite the prevailing belief, a careful examination of U.S. Census Bureau statistics indicate this ideal was always more mythical than real. According to the latest Census Bureau figures, less than 15% of American households match this mythic model. Allowing for a conservative estimate of 50% marital infidelity, this model accounts for less than 7% of all American households today. Families without children outnumbered those with children for the first time in 1985. In 1988 the average size of the American family was 2.62 persons.

Closed Marriage and "Traditional" Values

The American experience of Victorian values added romantic expectations and images of the one and only "knight in shining armor" and his "fair princess" who would totally meet each other's every need. Anthropologists Nena and George O'Neill (1972) called this model a **closed marriage,** describing it as a romantic, emotionally, and sexually possessive relationship, with very clear and rigid roles for the husband and wife. It is male-dominated and quite concerned with the couple's identity. The couple exists as a unit shaped in status and emotional temperature by the man, and not as two distinct persons who relate as equals. Fidelity and trust are static and "nervous" concerns abound, with both parties concerned about the possibility of "losing" one's love in competition with others. The assumption is that two persons will be able to grow on parallel tracks in an exclusive relationship for 30, 40, or more years.

Dual-career or "two-paycheck" marriages, where both partners work full time, whether or not they have children, have had a major impact on the traditional conception of marriage and its expectations. As recently as the 1950s, nearly two-thirds of all American households consisted of a breadwinner husband and a homemaking wife. Today, over half of all wives are employed outside the home. Dual-career couples tend to maintain more individual lives, because of their work and because they often come to marriage after they have established their identities. Dual-career couples may negotiate some time they can spend alone, aside from the time they devote to their work, marriage, and family. Some therapists see this inclination as a healthy remedy against the oppressive togetherness of the traditional marriage (Macklin 1987:330–332; Myers & Leggitt 1975; Piotrkowski et al. 1987:251–268).

Providing for child care while both parents work is a major social dilemma. Few couples can arrange flexible work schedules that allow both partners to design their work hours to meet their family needs and the spouses' work schedules (Piotrkowski et al. 1987:251–268).

Extramarital Sex

Hovering on the edge of the ideal world of the traditional romantic and sexually exclusive relationship or marriage are the specters of infidelity, adultery, or extramarital affairs. Once two people have developed a relationship to the point of making a commitment to each other, whether in a dating relationship, living with someone, or being married, that commitment can be violated. In the romantic, monogamous model, both parties are expected to be emotionally and sexually exclusive. The traditional concept of romance and marriage cannot tolerate the possibility of either partner being emotionally or sexually involved with another person. "Cheating" on that commitment requires extramarital affairs that are secretive and hidden from the spouse and society in general (Atwater 1982; Lampe 1987; Richardson 1985; Taylor 1982; Weis 1983b).

Traditionally, men have been more active extramaritally than women, but recent surveys indicate some changes. In the 1940s Kinsey projected that at least half of all married men would have some experience with extramarital sex sooner or later. One in 4 married women under 40 reported extramarital experience. In 1970 a survey of *Psychology Today* readers showed 40% of husbands and 36% of wives had had affairs (Athanasiou et al. 1970). Married men and

Figure 17.4. *The custom of arranged marriages has deep roots in many cultures. Shown in (a) is the Holy Wedding of 2075 couples in New York's Madison Square Garden in July, 1982. This was one of many mass weddings held by the Unification Church for its members, whose marriages are arranged by the Reverend Moon and other church leaders. There are also some groups within the Jewish community that still arrange marriages for young couples. In (b), the matchmaker from the movie* Crossing Delancey *shows an eligible pickle merchant photos of possible mates in the hope of making a match.*

(a)

(b)

currently divorced males under age 45 in Hunt's 1974 nationwide survey reported a 47% rate of infidelity. A year later married women, 40 and older, in a Tavris and Sadd survey for *Redbook*, reported a 39% frequency. In Linda Wolfe's "Sexual Profile of That Cosmopolitan Girl," 69.2% of the married women over age 35 reported an extramarital experience. Both the 1975 *Redbook* and the 1980 *Cosmopolitan* surveys were special groups and hardly representative of American women in general. It may be that the increasing sexual experience of women in college and before marriage predisposes them to view multiple and nonexclusive relationships in a more positive framework than in the past when extramarital sex was considered a male prerogative tolerated by women. Also, many single women prefer having affairs with married men because they do not want a man around all the time (Lampe 1987:165–198, Richardson 1985; Thompson 1983).

Most of the surveys of marital fidelity were done before heterosexuals became concerned about AIDS, so little can be said for certain about extramarital affairs in recent years. The few surveys we do have, many of them done by popular magazines, may give us some indication of the incidence of extramarital sex, but they tell us very little about how extensive this experience is, whether it is a chance one-night stand, several different relations, or long-term relationships. Of the persons reporting extramarital sex in these surveys, 40% to 50% had only 1 outside partner, 40% to 45% had 2 to 5 partners, 5% to 11% had between 6 and 10 partners, and 3% to 5% had more than 10 extramarital partners. In the *Redbook* survey, 1 in 5 women reported a one-night stand, 1 in 5 reported seeing each partner more than 10 times, and the rest reported between 2 and 9 meetings with each partner. In some respects, women now seem to be reversing the picture of extramarital sex, equaling or surpassing the males. In one study of 200 couples in marital therapy, Humphrey found that the affairs of husbands lasted an average of 29 months as against 21 months for the affairs of wives, hardly fitting the image of one-night stands (Hall 1987).

Traditionally, men found it much more difficult than women to accept a partner's affair. Despite traditional sex roles and socialization, the affairs of men and women are becoming more and more similar in their motivation and character. No longer are men motivated by sex while women seek to meet their emotional or communication needs in an affair (Atwater 1982; Glass & Wright 1985).

In her survey, Atwater (1982) tried to uncover the process by which women move into an extramarital relationship. She found that, first, the woman became aware of the possibility, usually when a man directly or indirectly let her know of his interest or when a female friend confided her own extramarital experience and discussed it with her. Three-quarters of the women gave this possibility much thought, considering how interested they were, and weighing both the negative and positive consequences if they did take the step. This thinking phase might last a couple of months or years before the woman made her decision. A casual attraction, or liking the person, was often sufficient reason for making the move when the situation and opportunity arose.

Although many studies indicate that an overwhelming majority of Americans consider adultery to be wrong, some psychotherapists see women's greater access to sexual choices as potentially positive because it equalizes power within the marriage (Hall 1987).

Consent and Tolerance

Despite our cultural values and the obvious trauma caused by many affairs, 116 marital therapists ranked having an affair only ninth in terms of harmfulness. More important were such issues as poor communications, unrealistic expectations, and power struggles. Surveys and media discussions of the prevalence of extramarital sex and realization of the costs of divorce and remarriage may be slowly altering our consciousness and expectations of marriage couples (Myers & Leggitt 1975).

Atwater (1982) found that about 25% of the women in her sample had discussed the possibility of having an extramarital affair with their husbands before going ahead. Still, most men and women prefer to ignore the issue and not be told anything about it. As long as the primary relationship is successful and for the most part satisfying, many partners tend to ignore the fact that their partner is emotionally and/or sexually involved with another person (Thompson 1983:17–19).

Cohabitation

Between 1970 and 1987, the number of unmarried Americans who were living with someone of the other sex, **cohabitation,** increased fivefold, from 500,000 to 2.5 million. The number of people who cohabit before marriage continues to rise, especially for those who marry more than once. Of those who remarried between 1980 and 1987, 60% had lived with someone, usually the new spouse, before remarrying. One-quarter of those who lived together married within the first year; half married within three years.

In the early 1980s high school dropouts led the cohabitation trend. Among those who reached age 25 between 1980 and 1984, nearly half of the high school dropouts, a third of high school graduates, and nearly a quarter of college graduates had cohabited. About 40% of the unmarried cohabitors married or split up within a year. Only a third continued through a second year without marrying or splitting up. Only 1 in 10 cohabiting couples stayed together for five years without marrying or splitting up (Bumpass & McLanahan 1989).

In 1968 Linda LeClair, a sophomore at Barnard College in New York City, became a national celebrity when she was expelled for living off campus with a former Columbia University student. Today, anywhere from less than 10% to more than a third of college students are cohabiting at any one time. College students in the East and West are more likely to cohabit than those in the Midwest and South. Cohabitation is also more common at larger schools and public colleges than it is in smaller and religious-affiliated colleges. Housing arrangements, the presence and enforcement of dorm visitation regulations, and the ratio of males and females on campus also affect cohabitation (Macklin 1974).

Comparing the findings of three independent studies of cohabiting couples and noncohabitors, Newcomb (1986) found that cohabitors are sexually active earlier and have more sexual experience than noncohabitors. They also tend to be more socially competent and have parents with more positive sexual attitudes than noncohabitors. Religious affiliation is a factor. Almost half of the college cohabitors studied by Macklin expressed no religious preference, 35% were Jewish, 12% Catholic, and 10% Protestant.

Most cohabiting couples see living together as a natural outgrowth of a loving, affectionate friendship and not as a "trial marriage." Although some cohabitors may not rule out marriage with their present partner as a future possibility, most do not equate living together with eventual marriage. Many analysts see the increase in cohabitation, along with divorce and the tendency to delay marriage, as symptoms of our growing uneasiness with marriage.

In the 1960s and 1970s social analysts expected the increase in cohabitation to lead to happier marriages and fewer divorces. But Bumpass and McLanahan (1989) found that within 10 years of the wedding, 38% of those who lived together before marrying had divorced whereas only 27% of those who simply married had divorced. Does this finding mean that cohabiting with someone increases your odds of getting divorced? Not so, say the experts. Spanier and Furstenberg (1987) point out, "People who cohabit and then marry may have higher expectations of what marriage ought to offer in the way of personal intimacy, shared experience, friendship, sex, and the like." The marriages of cohabiting couples may not be less happy than those of noncohabiting couples. They may simply be more willing than noncohabitors to end an unsatisfying marriage. This interpretation gains some weight from the fact that cohabitors are less likely to be religious or have strong family pressure keeping them in an unhappy marriage (Barringer 1989; Clayton & Voss 1977; Demaris 1984; Newcomb 1983; Watson 1983; Watson & DeMeo 1987).

Twelve years after Macklin completed her pioneering studies of cohabiting students at Syracuse University, Wayne Carpenter (1989) interviewed some of these same alumni. The 38 cohabitors and 70 noncohabitors in his sample showed no real differences in gender, race, religion of rearing, home background, or parents' education. Their overall involvement in college activities and academic performances had been quite similar. College cohabitors, however, had been more involved in dating and in dating relationships with intercourse which lasted three or more months.

In the 12 years following their graduation, 43% of the Syracuse cohabitors had lived with another partner, usually someone of the other sex who had not been previously married. Those who had not cohabited in college were less likely to do so after graduation. Unlike Bumpass and McLanahan (1989) who found less marital satisfaction among previous cohabitors, the Syracuse cohabitors and noncohabitors revealed few differences 12 years later. In marriages of 7 to 12 years duration, prior cohabitation had little or no effect on subsequent marital satisfaction. Those who had cohabited in college, however, reported greater satisfaction, fewer sexual problems, and fewer problems in developing and maintaining their intimacy and reaching their intimacy goals. Both groups reported similar overall satisfaction with their lives, similar postcollege problems, overall attainment of life goals, drug use, marital status, number of children, employment status, family income, and strength of religious affiliation.

Cohabitation in college, then, appears to have little real effect on one's life and relationships, although clear answers can only come when experts have had time to study and repeat the preliminary longitudinal reports of Carpenter, Bumpass and Sweet, and others.

Premarital Contracts and Palimony

In 1977 Michelle Triola Marvin, a former singer, sued actor Lee Marvin in a highly publicized court case that drew on little-known but long-standing legal precedents in common law marriages. Ms. Marvin—she had legally changed her last name—had openly lived with Marvin for six years and gave up her singing career to devote herself to being his mate. An initial court judgment awarded her $100,000 in support while she developed a new career and retrained for a single life. This award of **palimony** was based on the existence of an implied contract, expressed verbally and publicly during their six years together. Prior to this court decision, alimony had been limited to legally recognized marriages. According to the *SexuaLaw Reporter* (1977), "The Marvin decision effectively encourages contractual marriages and heralds the acceptance of alternative lifestyles."

In the years since the Marvin v. Marvin decision, unmarried straight, gay, and lesbian couples have found their way into court to resolve issues of support and equitable distribution of property and income gained during the duration of a cohabitation. Cohabitation support suits have revived an age-old custom of engagement/marital contracts, common in Europe until the 19th century. In the Jewish community, there is a long tradition of the wedding contract, the *ketubah*. For centuries, the Jewish families stipulated the conditions of the marriage, even down to details of its possible dissolution. Monetary arrangements were primary because other elements of the marriage were too well established and uniform in the community to need repetition.

Today, couples entering a second or third marriage are increasingly working out prenuptial contracts to define provisions and responsibilities for previous partners and children and protect their individual preunion finances. Obviously, negotiations of this kind just prior to a marriage can result in considerable stress because they run counter to the norms of "romantic love" (Dullea 1988).

Variations on a Theme

Open Relations and New Values

The values and expectations our society has until recently associated with love and marriage have been clearly spelled out. The values and expectations we are evolving in response to radical changes in our social environment are still emerging in our consciousness and experience. As we become increasingly aware of ourselves as individuals with a real existence outside the socially imposed stereotypes of dominant male, passive female, and male-dominated marriage, we struggle to define our own sexual identity, role, values, relationships, and behavior patterns. No longer is sex defined in the simplistic terms of anatomy and vaginal intercourse. Sex becomes sexuality, a diffused *sensuality* that permeates our whole personality and everything we do. Sex transcends genital performance. It is integrated into a holistic lifestyle, spreading its warmth of intimacy in a wide range of sensual communication. Contemporary values are rooted in the equality of men and women and in a single—as opposed to double—moral standard. There is a growing awareness that our relationships are dynamic and require constant communication and renegotiation. Marriage becomes one of several options, and marriage itself can assume a variety of quite different patterns (Francoeur 1984, 1987b; Francoeur & Francoeur 1974, 1976; Macklin 1987:317–343).

Swinging

One form of consensual extramarital sex, which is based on the togetherness value of traditional romantic monogamy, is **swinging,** recreational social-sexual sharing among consenting adults. In swinging, two or more couples mutually agree to engage in sex with each other's partners. The extent of swinging is not well documented, but surveys indicate that somewhere between 2% and 5% of American adults have participated at one time or another in this lifestyle (Athanasiou et al. 1970; Hunt 1974; Jenks 1985; Macklin 1987:334–335; Macklin & Rubin 1983; Smith & Smith 1970, 1974; Spanier & Cole 1974; Tavris & Sadd 1977).

Although single men and some single women are involved in swinging, it is predominantly a recreation and lifestyle for couples. For many couples, swinging is a catalyst for positive growth, a sharing activity that promotes understanding, communication, and intimacy in their relationships. They report that it helps free their relationship of routine, sex-role playing, and socially imposed inhibitions. Yet these same swingers are quick to point out that this lifestyle is not for all couples (McGinley 1979). Other writers, principally those involved in marriage counseling, report that swinging was a negative factor in the lives of those they investigated.

The North American Swing Club Association lists over 100 active, organized American swing clubs in its directory, as well as dozens of publications catering to the swing community. Annual Lifestyles Conventions in the South, Midwest, and West draw several thousand swingers each year.

Swing clubs report that close to one-third of all calls for information come from women. The majority of calls are from married couples. Although some reports claim that swinging is generally initiated by the male with the woman reluctantly going along, swing club owners report that most couples have discussed swinging, sometimes for months, before mutually agreeing to contact a club.

It also has been suggested that, because of biological differences, men may feel pressure to perform whereas women, sensing permission from their mate and having less limited biological capacity for sex, become enthusiastic participants. Observation at swing parties and discussion with participants suggests an entirely different picture. Men and women enjoy swinging equally, with no discernible difference in sexual capacity. This is because sex in swinging is varied and not limited to vaginal intercourse and orgasm. The emphasis is on mutual pleasure.

Some couples have self-imposed rules for their swinging. They may, for example, elect to swing only as a couple with another couple in the same room. This arrangement is the most common. Some prefer a threesome, generally with a second woman. Others may prefer group sex with several couples sharing. For the most part, swingers are flexible and do what seems appropriate at the time.

Swinging is not all sex. It is a social activity. Whether attending a party or meeting with another couple privately, swingers enjoy talking, dining, drinking, laughing, and sharing stories of their lives, work, and experiences. Swinging may or may not follow such socializing. Swingers tend to make friends and socialize with other swingers and their social involvement may extend into the business world. This finding is contrary to Bartell's 1971 observation that "Almost without exception, the swingers we met were constantly looking for new partners because the typical couples swings with another couple just once."

The educational level of swingers is relatively high compared with the national average. Smith and Smith (1970) found 52% of the swingers they studied in the San Francisco/Oakland Bay Area were college graduates and 30% had postgraduate training. Only 4% had not finished high school. McGinley's 1979 analysis of 1,470 new members of the Wide World Club members indicates a similar profile. Seventy percent of the new members of Wide World were ages 26 through 45, with the median being 36; 93% fell in the age bracket between 21 and 50.

A different view is offered by outside observers of the swinging scene (Bartell 1971; Gilmartin 1977; Jenks 1985; Karlen 1988:71–94). These reseachers report that organized swingers are generally *not* liberal, highly educated, or sophisticated. They are predominantly conservative or moderate in their politics, and far from permissive on a wide range of social and political issues. Most of the women are typical housewives, with few outside interests. Swingers also tend to be churchgoers. Typical of all lifestyles we have described, swingers cannot be lumped together. In reality, there are several distinct and very different subcultures among swingers (Jenks 1985; Karlen 1988:73–77).

Interest in swinging is increasing, according to McGinley and other observers, despite the threat of AIDS, possibly because most swingers are rather traditional in their concept of family, and participating in swinging leaves intact the values of the nuclear family. The only adjustment is the agreement to share sexually (Jenks 1985). Because swinging typically increases trust, openness, and the equalitarian perception of sex and male/female roles, advocates of swinging see this lifestyle preserving the basic structure of the family while providing a catalyst for greater understanding and acceptance between mates.

Sexually Open Marriages

The **open marriage** described by anthropologists Nena and George O'Neill (1972) is based on "an equal partnership between two friends" who respect each other as persons. It is flexible and allows each partner to grow and develop, even in unexpected directions. It stresses communication, an open trust, spontaneity, and the right to privacy for personal growth. Only later, when the media popularized the idea, did the concept of open marriage become associated with sexual openness.

One hundred years ago, the harsh demands for survival made a sexually open marriage impossible, even inconceivable, for all but a few in the aristocratic, upper social class. Today, this lifestyle is becoming more popular among the middle-class men and women who value equality of the sexes and often have dual-career relationships (Macklin 1987:335–336).

Blumstein and Schwartz (1983) reported that when spouses filled out separate questionnaires, 15% stated that they have a **sexually open marriage** or relationship (SOM). Nearly 30% of the cohabiting couples in this same study reported they are sexually open. Although the United States appears to be in a conservative period with a swing back to so-called traditional values, what little evidence we have suggests that "there are as many sexually open relationships today as in the recent past, and perhaps even more, although they are much less visible" (Libby 1987).

An SOM modifies the romantic courtly love tradition discussed in Chapter 14. The couple accepts the probability that they cannot satisfy all their partner's needs completely and totally throughout the many years of their relationship. They recognize that their partner may have certain interests or needs that do not match theirs. Instead of struggling to grow on perfectly parallel tracks, they accept a variety of intimate relationships on all levels, for both the husband and wife. Whether these secondary relations are called satellite, comarital, or compartment 4, they are intended to reinforce and complement the primary couple relationship (Francoeur & Francoeur 1974; Myers & Leggitt 1975; Roy & Roy 1967). In the traditional closed marriage, these outside relationships would be seen as competitive and described negatively as affairs, whether or not they involved sexual intimacy.

Because of the more diffused concept of sexuality and sensuality in an SOM, persons with satellite relationships are not driven by the compulsion to affirm their sexual identity in genital intercourse. As a result, genital intimacy is probably much less frequent within an intimate network of single and married people than it is among traditional married couples and single persons for whom extramarital "cheating" has the strong lure of "forbidden fruit."

In a five-year study of 82 couples in SOM, Rubin and Adams (1986) compared sexually monogamous and SOM couples in terms of marital happiness, extramarital sex, jealousy, changeableness, job changes, and education. The only real difference between the two groups was that SOM couples had changed jobs more, sought additional education, and had either additional or fewer people in their households. In both groups, marital stability was associated with women who had a higher education and worked outside the home.

After studying persons in successful SOM, persons divorced or separated after being in an open relationship, and the third party in open relationships, Watson (1981:18) suggested that "Open marriage may best be conceived as a stage, perhaps recurring, in the developmental process of a couple's relationship, rather than as an ongoing lifestyle." In reality, this statement describes most relationship patterns discussed in this chapter. The dynamics of our social environment and the constant changes most people experience in our mobile society force most couples and singles to adapt and change repeatedly in their relationships. (See Figure 17.1).

Intimate Networks

An **intimate network**, as defined by James Ramey (1975, 1976), is a cluster of intimate friends, some single, some married, bound together by a definite commitment and involvement with each other. In some respects it is a kind of intentional family, but without the incest or adultery taboos associated with a blood kinship family. The married couples see their marital fidelity in broader terms than sexual exclusivity and often accept sexual intimacy as an appropriate expression in deep committed friendships. Diagrams of typical intimate networks are shown in Figure 17.5.

People become involved with intimate networks because they see emotional and sexual exclusivity as too limiting and restricting of personal growth. They also do not think that sexual relationships should be exclusive. This type of relationship provides a variety of support for individuals, with each member contributing some degree of emotional, social, financial, and/or sexual involvement. The network provides outlets for more of one's needs through contact with several persons rather than by relying on only one individual.

Some studies indicate that intimate networks could be the wave of the future because they enable both singles and married couples to have open relationships with each other, even with the reality of AIDS. No longer would the single person, for example, be isolated among married couples or exclusive cohabitors (Macklin 1987:340–341).

Figure 17.5. How Intimate Networks Develop. *Diagram (a) shows a simple woman-sharing intimate network involving a woman and two men studied by Ramey (1975). Diagram (b) illustrates a more complex intimate network.*

Code: Married couple with date of marriage

Married and divorced with dates

Heterosexual cohabitation

Gay union: date of friendship with date of sexual intimacy in ( )

Nonsexual friendship with date of start and end

Sexually intimate friendship with date of initial friendship and date for start of sexual intimacy in ( ) if different

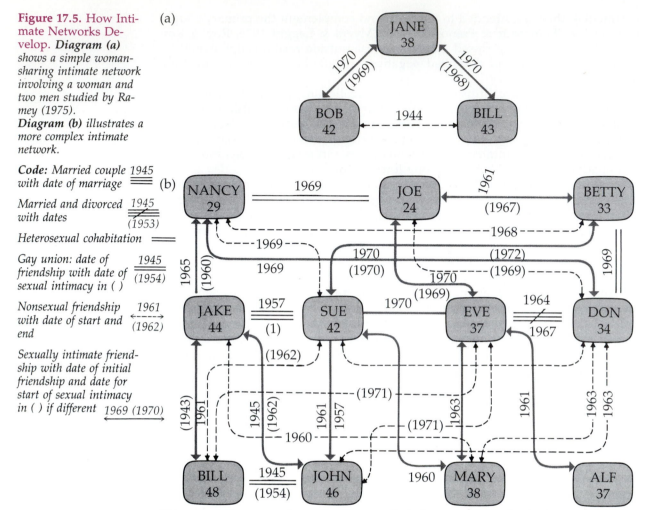

This type of diagram can be used to illustrate the intimacy networks of swingers, couples in sexually open relationships, man-sharing, and so on. You can gain some valuable insights into the complexity of our lives today by drawing a similar diagram of your own intimate network in high school, college, and postcollege years.

Threesomes, Group Marriages, and Other Variations

Many men and women fantasize about a *ménage à trois*, a threesome or sexual relation involving two women and a man, or two men and a woman. This fantasy, according to Karlen (1988), becomes a reality for 1 in 20 or 25, or roughly 10 million Americans. Karlen estimates that perhaps as many as 4% to 5% of all Americans will experience a threesome at least once.

In his 20-year study of threesomes, Karlen uncovered two main patterns that appear in striking frequency in the sexual histories of people who experience

Figure 17.6. An Open Bisexual Marriage. *When Barry Kohn and Alice Matusow married, they had all the traditional images and expectations of any newlywed American couple. Barry graduated from Temple University and Dickinson School of Law and served as Deputy Attorney General in Pennsylvania. Alice also graduated from Temple and received her master's degree in social work and research from Bryn Mawr College. As their marriage evolved, both agonized as they uncovered their own and each other's bisexual orientation.*

threesomes. Erotic adventurers are sexually active from an early age, and eventually have many partners and a wide variety of sexual experiences. The number of erotic adventurers is likely to remain about the same in the future, despite AIDS, herpes, and a more conservative atmosphere. They may, according to Karlen, even increase in number. The other pattern, those Karlen calls "the timid late starters at sex" did a lot of determined catching-up in their thirties, forties, and even fifties. In a society that seems somewhat more permissive than in the 1950s and 1960s, there may be fewer late-starter threesomes in the future.

In a threesome, each person has to relate with the other two persons separately and together, which means balancing nine relationships with the timing and tact of a high wire artist. Consequently, most threesomes are short-lived experiments. However, Karlen did find some long-term threesome marriages in his 20-year study.

A bisexual husband or wife may not share that interest with his or her partner, but still engage in homosexual or lesbian relations on the side. Other couples in bisexual marriages may chose to swing, to have a sexually open marriage, or become part of an intimate network in which they can express their sexual interests (Figure 17.6) (D.Dixon 1985; J.Dixon 1985; Kohn & Matusow 1980).

Group marriages and communal living have had a perennial appeal for some, as evidenced by the Oneida Community and other utopian experiments in 19th-century America and the rebirth of communes in the 1960s and 1970s (Bartell 1971; Constantine & Constantine 1973; Macklin 1987:338–340).

Figure 17.7. A Modern Polygamous Family. *Although the Church of the Latter-day Saints (Mormons) gave up the practice of polygamy 100 years ago, many Mormon groups outside the mainstream church still practice polygamy. Alex Joseph, 52, shown here with 9 wives and 5 of his children, served two terms as mayor of Big Water, Utah. Down from 13 wives in 1975, Joseph admits that ''Marriage doesn't always work out.'' Several of his wives are college graduates. He currently lets his wives take the initiative when it comes to sexual relations. This poses no problem, according to Elizabeth, 35, a lawyer and one of his wives who also ran for public office: ''We simply make an appointment.''*

Polygamy, or more specifically polygyny, the marriage of one man and several wives, was quite common in early Jewish times and continued well into modern times. The Anabaptists, precursors of the Baptists, established polygamous communes in Germany in the 1500s; the Mormons or Church of the Latter-Day Saints endorsed this lifestyle in the late 1800s (Lawrence 1989) (Figure 17.7). Even today, some splinter groups of Mormons continue to practice polygamy (Belkin 1989), and polygyny is widespread in Africa and Asia.

Man-Sharing

Another lifestyle, called **man-sharing,** is motivated by quite different factors, and has been documented in the American black community by Joseph W. Scott, professor of American ethnic and African-American studies at the University of Washington. On the surface, the marital and family lifestyles among black Americans may seem to fit patterns and labels commonly used in white middle-class structures, but there are some important differences based on demographics, economics, and ethnic values (Rao & Rao 1980). There are about 1.8 million more black females than males in the United States. Blacks have 2.5 to 5.3 times more widows than whites in the age groups from 25 to 44. There are roughly 85 black males for every 100 black women in their twenties and thirties in the lower middle-class black community. In the lower class, the shortage of marriageable black males is even greater (Noble 1983). Forty-five percent of black families are single-parent families, usually headed by single, never-married women who became pregnant in high school (Scott 1980, 1986).

> The single [black] mother often leaves home before age 20. On her own, she finds it difficult to support herself. A good paying job is not likely because of her interrupted education, and the cost of child care further cuts into her income when she is able to work.

Under ideal conditions, her choices include getting married to a responsible male with a job who is willing to take on a ready-made family. But these are not ideal times; such men are scarce. Since young black men in America are perhaps the most unemployed group in the American labor force, they are generally not marriage material—if a woman is looking for a steady provider for her child and herself. . . . Thus, she is trapped. One recourse is for her to find a "sponsor." (A sponsor is a man who has the economic means to help support her and her child.) Keeping in mind that the "sponsor" does not have to be the sole support, she often seeks a married man willing to "help" in exchange for sexual companionship. Sexual companionship is not just a "commodity" since she often seeks out such sexual satisfaction herself—without any exchange of money ever taking place. She too needs sexual companionship; she also needs male companionship as protection against those predatory males who seek out and exploit single never-married women whether on welfare, or with jobs of their own. In addition, she needs a good role model for her child, one who is comfortable at home rather than in the streets. Married men are said to have these qualifications and appear to be highly desirable—to the never-married single mother.

The single mothers I have interviewed seem to argue that married men are more desirable than single men because they are more generous, more stable, more family-oriented and more willing to have part-time relationships. The net result is that married men seeking to have extramarital affairs will find it relatively easy to start up relationships with single never-married mothers with children, especially those with their own independent households.

As it often happens, a young woman eventually becomes pregnant by and has a baby for her married companion. The child goes a long way toward elaborating their relationships further by adding paternal obligations to all the other commitments. As the commitments of parenting and child support become more and more operative, what was once an extramarital affair becomes an extramarital family. This changes the social obligations in such a way that a polygamous family is now existent.

(Scott 1980)

Scott distinguishes this lifestyle from consensual polygamy in which a man and two or more women mutually agree to create a single multiparent family. Man-sharing or extramarital polygamy is not an arrangement that most black women willingly accept. It is tolerated by women because of economic circumstances and pressures that make this lifestyle more functional than a total dichotomy between single-parent families struggling to survive and more affluent two-parent families.

Man-sharing among blacks has many social similarities with man-sharing, by choice or force of circumstances, among white middle- and upper-class women. Although economic factors are not a major element in man-sharing among whites as they are among blacks, a shortage of available males is an important consideration for both groups (Chapman 1986; Richardson 1985).

Man-sharing has parallels with quasi-polygamous patterns common in Mediterranean and Latin American societies. Although these patriarchal cultures often openly accept the tradition of *"un hombre completo"* having a "consensual wife" as well as a "contractual wife," the parallel phenomenon among women is much more hidden. Nevertheless, woman-sharing, in which a husband and one or more other men share sexual access to the same married woman, exists as a complement to man-sharing.

Covenants and Polyfidelity

As personal agreements in an ongoing relationship, **covenants** enable two individuals to agree on those elements which are essential to their living arrangement. A covenant allows individuals the freedom and flexibility to renegotiate their commitment in order to meet changing needs. In general, covenants are based on personal commitment, open to renegotiation, and concerned with mutual decisions within a religious framework and rite (Brill, Halpin, & Genne 1979; Thayer 1987).

There is a growing interest in the Protestant, Catholic, and Jewish communities today in adapting the idea of covenants to the new unconventional lifestyles of the 1990s. The United Methodist Church adopted an unofficial divorce ritual, reminiscent of the Jewish divorce covenant or *get*. This covenant ritual includes a promise to free the former spouse from "claims and responsibilities" and especially from the "burdens of guilt and sterile remorse." With both ex-spouses vowing their "I do's," wedding bands are switched from the left to the right hand. In 1988 the United Church of Canada recognized gay, lesbian, and other intimate relationships outside marriage so long as they are based on a "commitment." Also in 1988 the Lambeth Conference of the Episcopalian Church reversed its 100-year-old ban on baptizing polygamists and their families (Francoeur 1990; Francoeur & Shapiro 1979).

Even as men and women grapple with a great variety of lifestyles, and both civil and religious authorities debate whether or not to recognize or embrace them, the basic premise of human relationships, commitment, and fidelity is being rethought and reworked (Francoeur & Francoeur 1974/1976:118–145). As an alternative to sexual exclusivity and jealousy, some have argued for a redefinition of fidelity. One such attempt, developed in the context of a group marriage, involves the concept of **polyfidelity.** A polyfidelitous family is a "group of best friends, highly compatible, who live together as a family unit, with sexual intimacy occurring equally between all members of the opposite sex, no sexual involvement outside the group, an intention of lifetime involvement, and the intention to raise children together with multiple parenting" (Pines & Aronson 1981).

This strict definition of polyfidelity has been adapted, sometimes consciously and more often emerging in a sort of parallel evolution, by men and women in a wide variety of lifestyles, in sexually open marriages, intimate friendships, swinging networks, threesomes, and man-sharing relationships. The original definition of polyfidelity assumes that a person can have several primary relationships simultaneously. The adaptive definitions of polyfidelity often make a distinction between a primary relationship and satellite or comarital relationships. Because of the variety of lifestyles possible today, couples are often compelled to discuss and define their commitment to each other and agree on what fidelity means in the context of their lifestyle.

Fidelity, in this context, means a commitment to the agreed upon covenant or contract. Adultery, which etymologically means "polluting the relationship," may be viewed as any action or behavior that violates the couple's commitment to each other. Where couples have agreed to have a sexually open marriage, the terms extramarital and adultery are not applicable to a satellite or comarital relationship, since these are incorporated within the dynamics of the primary relationship.

Single Again

The Divorced and Widowed

Divorce Trends

Alvin Toffler's comment, cited earlier, about Americans "marrying again . . . and again . . . and again" highlights a major myth that Americans are a monogamous people. If anything, the past 100 years have brought us close to serial monogamy or serial polygamy, where a series of two, three, or four monogamous marriages is common for many men and women (Weis 1983b). This observation reminds us that most men and women today find that, as the years pass, they move here and there, back and forth, around the circle of intimacy and commitment shown in Figure 17.1.

One hundred years ago, when 1 in 5 women died in childbirth and most families had six or more children, divorce was rare. Women had few alternatives to staying married. Their lives were spent in childbearing and child rearing. In 1920 there was 1 divorce for every 7 marriages. By 1940, 1 in 6 marriages ended in divorce. In 1960 it was 1 in 4. In the early 1980s there was 1 divorce for every 2 marriages. Each year since 1974, over a million American marriages have ended in divorce (Raschke 1987:597–620) (Figure 17.8).

Figure 17.8. *Divorced single parents often use special interest groups like this Parents Without Partners meeting to make contact with potential new mates.*

In 1970 20% of teenage marriages ended in divorce. By 1985 1 in 3 teenage marriages resulted in divorce. In 1987 demographers at the U.S. Census Bureau projected that as many as 60% of women in their thirties in 1985, 36% of those in their forties, and 24% of those in their fifties will divorce. At the same time, wives were twice as likely as husbands to take the initiative in seeking divorce, filing almost two-thirds of all divorce applications. First marriages lasted an average of 10.7 years before divorce and second marriages, 6.7 years. Third marriages did a bit better, lasting on average 7.2 years (National Center for Health Statistics 1989).

Many reasons might be cited for this change: the Vietnam War, the civil rights movement, the women's movement, and a general trend toward independent living. Population experts think that the divorce rate has reached its peak and will continue to level off and perhaps decline slightly in the 1990s. One reason is that teen marriages, the most vulnerable to divorce, are declining. The increasing numbers of couples living together and the rise in dual-career marriages may also contribute to more durable marriages (Prince 1987; Raschke 1987:597–620; Spanier & Furstenberg 1987:419–432).

Surveys indicate that the majority of divorced women, 90% by some statistics, have sexual relations after divorcing, most within the first year and usually with more than one partner, four a year on average according to Hunt (1974). Divorced women also report a higher frequency of orgasm than in marriage. The feelings of inadequacy, communication problems, and financial stress some experience in a disintegrating marriage may resolve after divorce to allow a fuller sexual life (Witkin & Lehrenbaum 1985). But the reverse might also result, with the trauma of the divorce leading to feelings of sexual inadequacy, doubt, and dysfunction (Simernauer & Carroll 1982:371–399).

Statistics indicate that close to 100% of divorced men under 55 have sexual relationships after they divorce. Divorced men report an average of eight partners per year. Although divorced women have been falsely depicted as lonely and sex-starved, divorced men have been wrongly accused of having wild sex lives with dozens of partners. Many divorced men and women may engage in a short period of sexual abandon but, in most cases, they soon settle down, often remarrying. However, about 40% of the women who separate in their thirties will never remarry, nor will about 70% who separated after age 40. In the long term, 72% of divorced women will eventually remarry. A major social factor in these projections is the tendency for men to marry younger women (Bumpass and McLanahan 1989; Simernauer & Carroll 1982:371–399; Spanier & Furstenberg 1987:419–432).

Widowhood

Losing a mate after a satisfying long-term relationship is a trauma many gay, lesbian, and straight people face. AIDS has made this experience particularly painful for gay couples (Friend 1987). Older persons who lose a partner may be reluctant to begin a new relationship out of loyalty to the deceased mate. For heterosexual widows and widowers, negative family pressures are often a major deterrent to a new relationship. Sons and daughters sometimes feel they need to protect a widowed parent, when in reality they are protecting themselves from the new relationship. Many adult children also have difficulty in viewing a widowed parent as a sexual person with real needs for intimacy (Witkin 1985).

How to Define a Family

In the last decade of the 20th century, the growing pluralism of socially acceptable lifestyles is pushing us to redefine the meaning of family. In 1985 the Minneapolis section of a White House Conference on Families defined the family in traditional terms as "two or more persons related by blood, heterosexual marriage, or adoption." The American Home Economics Association responded by defining the family as "two or more persons who share resources, share responsibility for decisions, share values and goals, and have a commitment to one another over time. The family is that climate that one 'comes home to' and it is this network of sharing and commitments that most accurately describes the family unit, regardless of blood, legal ties, adoption, or marriage." One could hardly find two more opposing definitions.

In May of 1989 San Francisco became the first major American city to provide public registration of the "domestic partnerships" of gay man, lesbian, and unmarried heterosexual couples. The law defines **domestic partners** as any "two people who have chosen to share one another's lives in an intimate and committed relationship." The immediate impact of this act is to bar discrimination in favor of married couples and to extend to all domestic partnerships the same hospital visitation rights and bereavement benefits accorded married couples. The New York Court of Appeals adopted a similar definition of family in recognizing the right of a surviving partner in a long-term gay relationship to keep a rent-controlled apartment lease. Lawmakers in other cities quickly announced their intent to introduce similar legislation in their cities.

Commenting on these initiatives, John D'Emilio, professor of history at the University of North Carolina and coauthor of a history of American sexual customs, suggests that in the 1990s "There will be much opposition . . . but these are the first institutional signs of change [in the way we view family]" (Marciano 1988).

**HIGHLIGHT BOX 17.2.
FACE-OFF: RECOGNIZING
"DOMESTIC PARTNERS"**

Bring Families Out of Shadows

By Thomas B. Stoddard
Guest columnist

NEW YORK—Millions of Americans live their lives in shadow. The relationships they most cherish are accorded no recognition at all by the law and, therefore, very little by the society generally.

Consider this recent call: A woman in her 30s, suddenly gravely ill, had entered a hospital in suburban New York. She was unmarried and had no children. But she did have a companion of nine years—another woman who was in spirit, if not law, her "next of kin."

Since they were related by neither blood nor marriage, the companion felt compelled to lie to the hospital about her identity: She said she was the woman's sister. She believed that otherwise she would have been excluded from her partner's bedside.

The fact the women are lesbians is of less

significance than the emotional and social bond they share. They live together, love one another and regard their mutual relationship as paramount. They ought to be able to secure and protect that relationship. But at present, virtually all relationship rights flow only from the concepts of marriage or blood relationship. A "household" under tax law covers only married couples. Employers limit health benefits to spouses and children. Apartment leases typically permit additional occupants only if formally related to the named tenant.

Perhaps there was a time when everyone's central relationships were by blood or marriage, but that time, if it ever existed, has ended. For many, many adults, marriage is un-available, inadvisable or simply undesired. Parenthood is similarly limited.

Los Angeles and San Francisco have enabled unmarried couples to register as "domestic partners." The New York Legislature has passed a law nullifying leases that limit occupancy by blood or marriage. And now New York's highest court has interpreted "family" in a rent-control law to cover "two adult lifetime partners whose relationship is long term and characterized by an emotional and financial commitment and interdependence."

Such steps are not only practical and humane. They are socially wise—for they affirm the basic human values of love and commitment.

Don't Put Real Families in Shadows

By Bruce Fein
Guest columnist

GREAT FALLS. Va.—"The law is the witness and external deposit of our moral life. Its history is the history of the moral development of the race." Those insights of Oliver Wendell Holmes make recent assaults on the traditional definition of family alarming.

New York's highest court has ruled that a married couple and long-term homosexual partners are legal equivalents under rent-control laws. New York Mayor Edward Koch plans to issue an executive order granting bereavement-leave rights to both homosexual and heterosexual city workers whose "domestic partners" die. A San Francisco ordinance officially recognizes homosexual couples. The next step may be an Internal Revenue Service authorization to unmarried partners to file joint income tax returns at reduced rates.

These seemingly magnanimous gestures are woefully misguided. The law should encourage traditional family arrangements because of the precepts they teach: that joint endeavors should not be casually jettisoned at the drop of disagreement or fleeting unhappiness; that fulfillment generally demands long-term commitment, through thick or thin, to persist and adapt to unforeseen or uncontemplated events; that compromise and tolerance of foibles are indispensable to the success of any collaborative undertaking; and that intimate relationships should be entered only with great care—the consequences of misjudgments can be irreparable.

Giving legal dignity to homosexual or heterosexual partnerships is philosophically at war with the virtues husbanded by traditional family life. It grants rights without obligations, fostering intimacies based on impulse or impetuosity, a formula for turmoil and emotional scars. The lack of legal obligations also reinforces the too-prevalent penchant instantly to give up on any undertaking when difficulties arise.

Patience, persistence and reflection over adjustments to make a mission constructive are often unnurtured virtues in uncemented relationships. They accentuate the malaise of drifting from one intimacy or task to another for light and transient causes, resulting in a lifetime of immaturity, intolerance and unfulfillment.

(Source: USA Today, July 12, 1989)

Shifting Sex Ratios and Sexual Values

In the 1980s demographers and sociologists reported and hotly debated "the Great American Man Shortage," "too many women," and a shortage of men in the available marriage pool (Guttentag & Secord 1983; Johnson 1986; Noble 1983; Novak 1984; Salholz 1986; Westoff & Goldman 1984). As we might expect, a surplus of men, or of women, in an culture inevitably leads to changes in the attitudes with which men and women view their respective roles and their expectations in marriage.

Sociologists Marcia Guttentag and Paul Secord (1983) report that in societies with a **high sex ratio,** those with a male surplus, the male-dominated political structure supports social norms and attitudes that favor marital stability. Monogamy, female virginity, and sexual fidelity for women are highly prized. Strong barriers prevent women from exploring alternative lifestyles other than marriage, from divorcing once they are married, and from challenging male dominance in any way.

In societies with a **low sex ratio,** like the United States in recent years when we had a surplus of women looking for partners, sexual permissiveness is more acceptable for both men and women. Both sexes are free to have multiple or successive relationships with different partners. Sexual intimacy is not limited to the marital bed. Women may be less valued and protected, but they are also freer to explore independent lives and to seek intimacy in a variety of lifestyles.

As we enter the 1990s there are five young women for every six young men. The U.S. Census Bureau estimates there are about 2.3 million more unmarried men in their twenties than women in the same age group (Bradsher 1990). Given these social tendencies and the possibly "irreversible" social changes outlined in the beginning of this chapter, what do you foresee in the 1990s, when demographers predict the sex ratio will shift to a surplus of men and a shortage of women? To what extent might we return to the patriarchal value system of exclusive monogamy and competition in our relationships? Will women be willing to give up the freedom and independence they have experienced in recent decades? Fowles (1988) predicts "a resurgence of the conventional family by the year 2000" with the father working and the mother staying at home with the children.

Key Concepts

1. What is changing in American society is not so much the variety of intimate and marital patterns, which has always existed, but the widespread character, visibility, and open tolerance of this pluralism.

2. The alternatives to monogamous marriage run the gamut from a freely chosen single life with or without sexual intimacy, cohabitation, voluntary childlessness, homosexual and lesbian relations, a variety of open marital patterns, networks, and multilateral relationships.

3. The number of single adults has increased dramatically in the 1970s and 1980s, opening up new lifestyles including single parenthood and creative singlehood.

4. The traditional lifelong, sexually exclusive marriage is being altered by voluntary childlessness, dual-career marriages, the incidence of extramarital relations, divorce and reconstituted families, cohabitation, and premarital contracts.

5. The number of Americans exploring alternatives in the traditional pattern of marriage appears to be increasing.

6. Although the divorce rate seems to be leveling off, divorce and remarriage patterns indicate a continuing evolution of marriage.

Key Terms

celibacy (470)
closed marriage (476)
cohabitation (478)
covenants (488)
creative singlehood (474)
domestic partners (491)
high sex ratio (493)
intimate network (483)

low sex ratio (493)
man-sharing (486)
monogamy (474)
open marriage (482)
palimony (480)
polyfidelity (488)
sexually open marriage (482)
swinging (480)

Summary Questions

1. Describe some of the changing social factors which you believe have been most influential in forcing adaptations in the ways we relate and structure our families today.

2. What are some of the legal complications of today's alternate or nontraditional lifestyles and family patterns?

3. What similarities and differences occur in man-sharing, intimate networks, sexually open marriages, swinging, and similar traditions of extramarital or quasi-polygamy?

4. What social factors have contributed to the rapid increase in the number and proportion of single adults and single parent families?

5. What role does celibacy play in the life of the average American?

Suggested Readings

Blumstein, P., & P. Schwartz. (1984). *American Couples: Money, Work, Sex*. New York: Pocket Books. A 10-year study of how we pair off and the new ambiguities of love and sexual expectations and behavior among married, unmarried, straight, gay, and lesbian couples.

Green, T. (1987, November 15). Why wed? The ambivalent American bachelor. *New York Times Magazine*, pp. 24ff. Insights into modern single males and their hesitations over intimacy, commitment, and marriage.

Johnson, C. (1986, September). Exploding the male-shortage myth. *New Woman*, pp. 46–50. A critical look at the Westoff and Goldman report.

Lampe, P. E., ed. (1987). *Adultery in the United States.* Buffalo: Prometheus Press. The past, present, and future of extramarital relations in the United States.

Richardson, L. (1985). *The New Other Woman: Contemporary Single Women in Affairs with Married Men.* New York: Free Press (Macmillan). An intelligent, thoughtful analysis of the lives and agendas of many contemporary women.

Simenauer, J., & D. Carroll. (1982). *Singles: The New Americans.* New York: Simon & Schuster. A major study of single Americans.

Westoff, C. F., & N. Goldman. (1984). Figuring the odds in the marriage market. *MONEY* magazine, *13*(12):34–35.

Sexuality in the Middle
   and Later Years
   Love, Sex and Aging
   Social Dimensions
   Health Issues
Sexuality and Persons
   with Disabilities
   The Double Social Taboo
      of Sex and Disability
   The Impact of
      Disabilities
   Chronic Illness
      and Sexuality
A More Humane
   Perspective

Chapter 18

Sexuality, Aging, and Health

Special Consultants

Pamela S. Boyle, M.S., ACSC, president, Coalition for Sexuality and Disabilities, Inc., New York City.

Sandra S. Cole, Ph.D., coauthor of *Sexual Options for Paraplegics and Quadriplegics,* and professor, Sexuality Training Center, Department of Physical Medicine and Rehabilitation, and director, Human Sexuality Curriculum, University of Michigan Medical School.

Paul A. Fleming, M.D., D.H.S., director, The Fleming Center, Raleigh, North Carolina, and editor, *Sex over Forty Newsletter.*

The relevance of this chapter for young people is nicely summed up by the president of the Coalition for Sexuality and Disabilities who reminds us, "We all need to remember that we will all grow old, and that most of us will become disabled in some way, to some degree, before we die" (Boyle 1986:3).

Sexuality in the Middle and Later Years

In 1860 over half of the American population was under age 20 and only 13% over age 45. In 1990 less than one-third of all Americans were under age 20 and 21% were over age 45. In the 1950s our birthrate was over 25 babies per 1,000 population. These baby boomers are now in their middle years, and our birthrate has dropped to less than 15 babies per 1,000, well below the replacement level. America is a graying society (Thomas 1986).

Love, Sex, and Aging

Although persons over age 50 are the fastest growing segment of our population, research on their lifestyles and patterns of intimacy has been almost exclusively limited to studies of the chronically ill, the socially isolated, and the poor. Edward Brecher made one of the first attempts to study and describe active, healthy Americans in their middle and later years. Brecher's sample of 4,000 persons between the ages of 40 and 92 was largely white and affluent, although he did include a low-income group. His overall conclusion was that the sexual interest and activity of older persons is the best kept secret in America. Although there is a taboo about researching the sexual lives of grandparents who supposedly no longer are interested in "that sort of thing," older persons were just as much affected by the sexual revolution and changing attitudes of the 1960s and 1970s as young people.

As Brecher (1984) discovered, healthy older people today are "enormously different from the older person of 40 or 50 years ago." They are very much interested in intimacy and sexual relations. They live all the lifestyles found in the young and middle-aged populations. Not one of Brecher's 4,000 respondents was sexually inactive, although masturbation was the most common sexual outlet. Satisfaction with sex among those over age 50 was rated very high. Of the 4,000 respondents, 1,850 rated their satisfaction most enjoyable. Only 37 rated their sexual activity not enjoyable. Good health was a major determinant in whether or not older persons enjoy an active sexual life (Figure 18.1).

In another study of healthy upper-middle-class men and women ages 80 to 102 living in residential retirement communities, 14% of the men and 29% of the women were still married. Sexual touching and caressing, followed by masturbation and then intercourse were the most common sexual activities. Of these outlets, only touching and caressing declined with age, and it was more evident for men than for women. Men and women who had been sexually active earlier in life tended to remain so in their eighties and nineties, although the frequency of sexual intercourse was sometimes limited by their current physical health and by social circumstances including the lack of an available partner (Bretschneider & McCoy 1988).

The *Starr-Weiner Report on Sex and Sexuality in the Mature Years* (1981) examined the sexual lives and attitudes of 800 persons ages 60 to 91 from four regions of the United States. When the sexual activities of these 60 to 90 year olds are

Figure 18.1. *The image of older persons has changed dramatically in recent years as they participate in marathons, mountain climbing, and special Olympics. Most older persons lead active, fulfilling lives.*

compared with the 40 year olds Kinsey studied 35 years earlier, there is no significant decline as long as the opportunities exist. "Sex remains pretty much the same unless some outside event intrudes, such as a health problem, the loss of a spouse, impotence, or boredom." A reliable predictor of the sexually active life of older persons is their acceptance or rejection of the social stereotype of dependent, sickly older person. Older persons who maintain an active participation in life in general tend to be more sexually active in their later years (Highlight Box 18.1).

Starr and Weiner brought into focus two major problems for which there appears to be no easy remedy. The first problem is the tendency for older men to become asexual when they encounter an occasional erection or orgasmic problem. Instead of exploring noncoital pleasuring with their partners, too many older men simply give up all interest in sex. The second problem is the ever-growing number of older women who are without sexual partners and thus deprived, against their will, of sexual intimacy and pleasure. Dimensions of this second problem are explored shortly.

Very little is known about sexuality and aging among the estimated 3.5 million American men and women over age 60 who are homosexual. For gay men and lesbians, aging can create unique conflicts and problems, depending

HIGHLIGHT BOX 18.1.
SEX AND THE OLDER PERSON

The editors of *Medical Aspects of Human Sexuality* asked physicians to answer the following questions. The responses shown are those of the first 400 doctors to return the questionnaire. Which of the responses surprises or disturbs you? Why were you surprised or disturbed?

Are men over 65 more interested in sex than women of the same age?

About the same	52%	Slightly more	22%
Significantly more	18%	Much more	8%

Are men over 65 more likely to engage in sexual activities than women of the same age with a similar level of interest?

Yes	61%	No	39%

Are people over 65 more sexually active than elderly people were a generation ago?

Slightly more	34%	About the same	29%
Significantly more	29%	Much more	11%

What is the biggest deterrent to sexual activity in the elderly?

For Men:

Potency problems	33%	Medical illness/disability	27%
Lack of available partners	20%	Self-imposed taboos	9%
Lack of interest	6%	Disapproval of family/society	5%

For Women:

Lack of available partners	38%	Lack of interest	18%
Gynecological discomfort	13%	Medical illness/disability	11%
Self-imposed taboos	11%	Disapproval of family/society	9%

Do widows or widowers usually have more difficulty engaging in sexual relations with a new partner?

No significant difference	50%	Widows	32%	Widowers	18%

What generally happens to a woman's interest in sex after menopause?

No consistent pattern	59%	Decreases	21%	Increases	20%

Are elderly people engaging in sexual activity without marriage more often than a generation ago?

Significantly more	40%	Slightly more	36%
Much more	13%	No appreciable change	11%

Do elderly men and women without sexual outlets suffer from more psychophysiological symptoms than their sexually active counterparts?

Both sexes	45%	No appreciable change	40%
Chiefly men	11%	Chiefly women	4%

Should nursing homes and homes for the aged provide facilities that enable the elderly to engage in sexual activities?

Yes, for all who wish it	52%	Only in specific selected cases	20%
Only for married couples	19%	No	9%

Source: A. Pietropinto. (1987, June). Sex and the elderly. *Medical Aspects of Human Sexuality*, pp. 110–117. Reprinted with permission from *Medical Aspects of Human Sexuality* © Cahners Publishing Company. Published March 1983. All rights reserved.

on their individual lifestyles. The death of a partner in a long-term relationship may bring out homophobic reactions among family members that lead these relatives to ignore the bereaved partner or contest a will. Gay men and lesbians who decide to acknowledge their orientation after years of passing as heterosexual face the possibility of quite different reactions when loved ones, children, and grandchildren learn of their relative's sexual orientation. Gay men, who are fearful that their orientation will be discovered as it becomes evident they are not going to marry, may adopt a loner life with relatively little sexual and social intimacy. Lesbian couples have to cope with two female incomes, which is typically less money than most dual-career gay male or heterosexual couples earn (Friend 1987).

By necessity, gay men and lesbians develop skills in coping and crisis management which give them an advantage in the aging process. More flexible gender roles, which are common among homosexuals, may allow older homosexuals to take aging more in stride and develop ways of taking care of themselves that feel comfortable and appropriate. "These skills may not be developed to the same degree among heterosexual men or women, who may be used to having or expecting a wife or husband to look after them" (Friend 1987:311). Gay people tend to plan ahead for their own independence and security, whereas heterosexuals are more likely to assume that their children will take care of them in their old age. Homosexual men and women have significantly more close friends than do heterosexuals, friends who serve as a surrogate family. In larger urban areas, organizations like the New York-based Senior Action in a Gay Environment (SAGE) provide a variety of social and support services for older homosexuals (Friend 1987).

Although American society as a whole places an inordinate value on youth, some observers contend that segments of the gay male community place still greater emphasis on this fleeting characteristic. "Accelerated aging," some claim, brings this value into painful focus for many homosexuals, as gay men are more likely to feel they are "over the hill" at a younger age than heterosexual men (Gagnon & Simon 1973:149). The pain of losing a loved one to AIDS is a possibility many older gay men have to face.

At the same time, some lesbian women are not as concerned about physical appearance as homosexual men or heterosexual women. The confidence and sense of achievement many lesbians gain from their careers make aging and the question of security less problematic for them than it might for most heterosexual women (Friend 1987).

Social Dimensions

Desexing Older Persons

A comparison of sexuality in older persons from other cultures offers an interesting contrast with our culture. In 70% of 106 traditional societies, older men were expected to continue being sexually active until very late in life. In 84% of the societies for which data was available, older women shared this expectation of remaining sexually active (Winn & Newton 1982).

Why, then, does our society assume older persons to be invisible, inactive, and, above all, asexual? First, in a youth-obsessed culture, younger people are afraid that their sexual abilities will fade as they age. One way of dealing with this fear is to deny that sex is important in the later years. Second, our youth-obsessed culture results in a self-fulfilling prophecy. With everyone saying that sexual interest and performance disappear with aging, many people accept this cliché as reality as they grow older. Finally, whether or not we accept the Oedipus complex theory, children in our Western culture often find it difficult to imagine their parents, let alone grandparents, enjoying masturbation, oral sex, and intercourse on a regular basis (Charatan 1982). In addition, although only a small percentage of older persons are dependent on others for care, there is a strong tendency for younger people to extend their stereotype of older people as dependent, asexual children to all older persons. This false image is under attack from many sources, including the media and the pioneering prime-time television show "The Golden Girls."

In one sense, denial of the sexual rights and needs of older persons makes management of retirement and nursing homes easier. By withholding from residents the right to express their sexual needs and develop intimate relationships, even prescribing constant tranquilizing medications, administrators and staff avoid having to deal with sensitive situations like masturbation, dating, and sexual intimacy. Older persons without partners who have control over their environment do masturbate more than those in nursing homes where privacy is at a premium (Catania & White 1982).

Denying or ignoring the sexuality and sexual needs of older persons allows administrators to avoid the cost of restructuring antiquated facilities to provide "privacy rooms." Desexing older residents also avoids confrontations with the relatives of residents who may be uncomfortable and condemning of a parent or grandparent in his or her seventies, eighties or nineties being "interested in that sort of thing!" Note, in Highlight Box 18.1, the response of 400 doctors to the question "Should nursing homes and homes for the aged provide facilities that enable the elderly to engage in sexual activities?" A little over half said, "Yes, for all who wish it," but 20% said, "Only in specific selected cases," 19% said, "Only for married couples," and almost 1 in 10 doctors opposed the idea.

And yet, providing opportunities for dating greatly enhances the quality of life for older persons. Dating in later life offers companionship, opportunities for self-disclosure, and emotional and sexual outlets otherwise denied older persons. Dating is a major hedge against loneliness in later life, which can contribute to depression and poor health (Bulcroft & O'Connor 1986).

The Shortage of Older Men

American women traditionally married men who were on average four years older than themselves. These women now outlive their husbands by about eight years. Many women, about 50% by age 65, are thus widowed at a relatively young and healthy age. The thinning ranks of older men, coupled with the tendency of older men to seek much younger wives if they divorce or are widowed and for younger women to find older men attractive, leaves older women with dimming prospects (Butler 1983). Masturbation, seeking out a younger partner, sharing a man with another woman, or lesbian relations are about all we can suggest as solutions for this increasing problem.

The Feminization of Poverty

As Americans live longer and women experience a longer life expectancy than men, more and more older women are left on their own. This situation is compounded by the fact that "no-fault divorce," which was supposed to give women an equal share in a divorce, has actually pushed more and more women into poverty or near poverty. The **feminization of poverty** means that divorced and older women are increasingly put at an economic disadvantage and that among the poor the proportion of divorced and older women is constantly increasing. In the United States, 2 out of 3 poor adults are women and 1 out of 5 children is poor. Single women head half of all poor families, and over half the children in female-headed households are poor.

Abuse of the Elderly

Elderly parents living with their children oftentimes reverse the traditional roles, with the parent becoming a dependent child and the middle-aged child forced into being a parent to the parent. The tensions and strains this reversal produces may lead to psychological, and even physical, abuse of the older parent. Despite almost no statistics on this little reported crime, activist groups such as the Gray Panthers and the American Association for Retired Persons have brought this issue to public attention and discussion.

Health Issues

The Consequences of Aging

Between ages 45 and 60, *midlife crisis* may hit some men and women with a decline in sexual interest, disappointments in not having achieved earlier dreams, and wrinkles and changes in physical appearance leading to restlessness and depression. Myths and misinformation about what to expect sexually as we grow older and lack of communication between a couple who have been together for years may compound the problem (Rienzo 1985). At the same time, the pressure of traditional sex roles may wane. Older couples often feel freer to express aspects of their personality associated with the other gender which they suppressed in younger years (Hubbard & Young 1987).

The sexual frustrations of older women stem mostly from social and cultural factors, rather than from physical difficulties. Older women experience relatively little change in their sexual capacities. What does change most frequently, as we mentioned earlier, is the decreasing availability of sexual partners (Figure 18.2).

Figure 18.2. *The older couple in the sexually explicit film "A Ripple in Time" is known to hundreds of thousands of college students and professionals since the film was produced 20 years ago. The film's message that older persons can be just as interested in sexual intimacy and just as sexually involved as younger persons is still surprising, even shocking, to some people.*

Women usually experience **menopause**, the cessation of the menstrual cycle, in their early fifties. The sexual hormone system gradually slows and stops, sometimes smoothly, sometimes in jumps and starts. Accustomed to the monthly cycle of hormones, the brain and other organs recognize the drop in hormones and suffer a set of withdrawal symptoms. Hot flashes occur in 85% of menopausal women. Depression and mood swings are common. Some women, especially those who accept the traditional female role, may see the end of their childbearing years as a sign of a loss of sexual attractiveness. For other women, the end of childbearing potential is welcomed as a new experience, devoid of concern about contraception.

Vaginal lubrication and elasticity may decrease, although "a substantial number" of the women in Brecher's study did not experience this effect. Reduced acidic secretions and **vaginal atrophy**, a drying up of the tissues and glands in the vaginal wall, may result in infections and painful intercourse. A water-soluble lubricant, an estrogen ointment, or estrogen replacement therapy can remedy this problem.

Osteoporosis, a progressive deterioration of the strength of the bones as they lose calcium, is another consequence of menopause. Broken hips and fragile bones are a serious health problem for older women. In cultures where the diet is low in fats and high in fruits, vegetables, and grains, osteoporosis is almost nonexistent. Thus a carefully designed diet combined with regular exercise may control this possible outcome of aging. **Estrogen replacement therapy** (ERT) can relieve hot flashes, vaginal atrophy, and osteoporosis. Progesterone may also be used to complement the benefits of estrogen and counter its slight risks (Lalich & Scommegna 1988). When questioned about their priorities and the slight risks of ERT, most of the women in Brecher's study said they preferred using estrogen therapy and being sexually active to being celibate.

A positive view of sex, an optimistic outlook on life, good nutrition, and proper exercise are important factors in older women remaining sexually active.

Men reach their peak sexually around age 20, women in their thirties. Older men normally find it takes longer to get an erection, and they are not as firm as when they were young. They need more physical stimulation to get an erection. Surgery to improve blood circulation in the penis is now an option for men with organic impotence. Ejaculation may come slower, and many older men, especially those over age 70, have intercourse with orgasm but do not ejaculate. Sexual desire does not diminish. The testes may shrink, although sperm production continues into the nineties. Remaining sexually active in the later years means adapting to these changes. Being creative, exploring, and having a sense of humor obviously helps.

One of the problems older men face is benign or malignant enlargement of the prostate. A variety of new surgical methods and drugs for these conditions has improved the outcome of prostatic treatments. No longer is impotence or the loss of erections a necessary or even common outcome of prostate surgery.

Boredom and routine may affect a long-term marriage. Yet despite all the problems of growing old in a youth-oriented society, many older men and women continue to lead very active, fulfilling lives. They may expand their experiences and explore new forms of intimacy they would have rejected in their younger years. The beliefs of many children and grandchildren that "It's all over after 50, and your grandparents never think of sex" do not hold true for many older persons.

Erection Aids

In the later years, a variety of organic conditions can affect the ability of the penis to respond to normal stimulation. Diabetes, decreasing blood circulation in the penis, reactions to some medications, multiple sclerosis, and spinal cord injuries from sporting and automobile accidents are common causes for erection problems in younger men. For older men, surgery on the prostate or in the pelvic region, kidney dialysis, and radiation therapy for cancer may affect the normal functioning of the penis.

Until recently, the inability to have an erection was handled with sexual and hormonal therapy. In the past few years, several aids have been developed and tested. One type of erection assistance device is simple, inexpensive, and non-invasive. If the blood supply to the penis is normal, such nonsurgical aids can be effective. The nonsurgical erection aid is a soft, condom-like sheath of semirigid silicone that slips over the penis. A collar at the open end forms a seal at the base. When a vacuum is created by a small pump, the penis is pulled into the device to give "the natural stretched feeling of an erection." The penis remains erect without restricting its circulation as long as the vacuum is maintained, even after ejaculation.

Today, we have several types of surgically implanted erection aids. The simplest involves two silicone rods with flexible stainless steel cores implanted in the cavernous bodies of the penis. This gives a permanent erection, but the penis can be bent so it hangs down naturally most of the time, and then bent up at the right angle for intercourse when needed.

A more sophisticated implanted aid has two acrylic cylinders, one in each of the cavernous bodies of the penis. They run from the glans back into the base of the penis just in front of the rectum. Each cylinder has an inflation pump at its tip under the glans. A couple of squeezes of the glans and the penis has an erection. Squeeze the deflation valves in the cylinders just behind the glans, and the penis goes flaccid.

The closest we come at present to mimicking the normal process of erection is a device with two inflatable cylinders in the cavernous bodies, a fluid reservoir implanted under the skin of the abdomen, and a pump and release valve hanging next to the testes in the scrotum. Squeezing the pump in the scrotum a number of times produces an erection. The release valve on the side of the pump lets the penis go flaccid.

In 1987 close to 1 in 5 surgically implanted erection aids was in a male under age 40. In the near future, erection aids will likely include electrobionic inflatable devices powered by 10-year batteries implanted under the skin or with rechargeable batteries that can be left in permanently. The pumps and release valves may be replaced by an inflatable device turned on and off by remote control with transponders, much like the kind we now use to turn our televisions on and off and change channels by remote control.

Sexuality and Persons with Disabilities

- ''With all the emphasis on youth and beauty, will anyone be attracted to me? Will anyone be able to fall in love with me?''
- ''Where do you meet a partner when you're in a wheelchair?''
- ''How do you flirt when you can't see?''
- ''How do you figure out how to 'do it' when you're paralyzed, blind, crippled with arthritis, or otherwise physically limited?''
- ''What is it like to have sex and not feel anything below your waist?''
- ''Do you know what it's like having to depend on your partner to undress you, or empty your fecal or urinary bag before you make love?''
- ''What is it like making love without ever being able to have vaginal intercourse?''
- ''What happens when two persons are too handicapped to have sex by themselves and require the assistance of a third person?'' (Sutherland 1987).

The Double Social Taboo of Sex and Disability

Our society denies the sexuality of older persons, and it even more consistently refuses to recognize the sexuality and the sexual needs of persons with any kind of disability. We associate physical and mental disabilities with dependence and sickness, with being childlike and helpless. None of these characteristics are particularly sexy. Telethons and poster children exploit these attitudes to raise money, without ever hinting that persons of any age with a disability are sexual persons with sexual needs. Women with disabilities are even more victimized than disabled men, because of our traditional denial of female sexuality and linking feminine sex appeal with beauty and perfect bodies.

In the 1980s we began to see a few role models in films, television, or novels which provide insights and encouragement for persons with a disability. Biographic films of a paralyzed Vietnam veteran and Olympic skier Jill Kinmont opened the door. *Love Letter*, a stage play by Bobbi Linn, describes the first love experiences of an adolescent girl with cerebral palsy. In 1989 Christopher Burke, a teenager with Down syndrome, played a lead role in the television series "Life Goes On" about an average family struggling to give their three children a normal life.

Along with changes in the media have come other important advances. In the mid-1980s dating services for persons with disabilities began appearing in larger cities. Likewise, designer clothes became available, with wedding gowns for brides using wheelchairs, modified designer dresses for women in wheelchairs, and trousers with decorative expandable slats for persons with leg braces. Even more important for the social and sexual lives of people with disabilities were changes in federal laws requiring transportation systems and public facilities to accommodate their needs. The opportunity to socialize publicly and to travel independently can increase and strengthen self-esteem.

The Impact of Disabilities

When a child is born with a disability or the condition develops in early childhood, sexual maturation and sexual education may be affected. Parents and other adults may believe that a disabled child or adolescent is better off not being interested in relationships, intimacy, and sex. "Why encourage disabled children's sexual interests and let them risk even more rejection?" This belief can restrict children's opportunity to develop the psychosexual social skills they will need as adults. Children with congenital disabilities are often left out of the kinds of activities which are most important to young people and their sociosexual development, such as dances, sports, cheerleading, hanging out at the mall, and getting a driver's license (Cole & Cole 1982).

Parents may further try to protect the child by not providing sex education which they believe the child would never be able to use. Parents often avoid taking pictures of their child in a wheelchair. They avoid buying attractive clothes and do not encourage pride in the child's body as it is, disability and all, because then they would be forced to deal openly with the sexual needs of the child. Being born disabled means being exposed to many negative attitudes and diminished expectations about social and sexual potential from parents, professionals, and society as a whole (Bullard & Knight 1981; Rousso 1986).

At the same time, being disabled from birth or early childhood means growing up with a disability and having many years to integrate that disability into one's identity, sense of self, and life.

On the other hand, a young man or woman who has enjoyed a full and unlimited life and then is suddenly paralyzed in an automobile, skiing, or diving accident or other trauma has already established his or her gender role and sexual maturity. The task then is to adapt to the impact of the injury on physical capabilities, social status, and sexual self-image. Masculine or feminine self-images and gender-role behavior may be challenged or reversed. The style of daily living and preferred sexual behaviors can be altered, convoluted, or terminated (Leyson 1990). A sudden onset of multiple sclerosis or crippling arthritis can force major changes in attitudes and coping mechanisms. Cancer of the colon may require surgery and a colostomy with an external bag to collect urine or feces, again forcing dramatic changes in sexual lifestyle.

The impact of a physical disability, injury, illness, or disease also depends on whether the condition is stable or progressive. If, as in a spinal cord injury, the disability is stable, then it is quite possible to plan life around the altered body condition. When the disability is progressive, as is the case with multiple sclerosis, it is more difficult to plan daily living, including sexual intimacy and behaviors. It is not always possible to be in control of the changing, unpredictable state of our physical health. The fluctuating pain of arthritis and bursitis can limit energy level, mobility, and desire to be socially active.

Chronic Illness and Sexuality

Medical Conditions

The most common disability to strike young adults is trauma from an automobile or sporting accident resulting in spinal cord or brain injury. There are well over 120,000 paralyzed Americans, more young men than women. Yet as more women participate in sports, we see an increase in injured women too. It is difficult to give a person with a congenital disability like cerebral palsy or an acquired progressive disability such as multiple sclerosis or a paralyzing stroke a clear picture of the future. In the case of spinal cord injuries, however, the outcome of therapy and the posttrauma adjustment are quite predictable and stable. All these conditions can alter sexual images and personal lives. The attitudes and values of one's partner and family, the age of onset, and the personality character of the person before onset also affect how someone adjusts to a perhaps radically altered self-image (Leyson 1990; Mooney et al. 1975; Shover & Jensen 1988; Woodhead & Murph 1985).

Thousands of young Americans, not just the elderly, deal every day with the chronic limitations of pain and movement associated with arthritis and bursitis. Medical experts point out that the morphinelike endorphins produced by orgasm can provide pain relief for six to eight hours. Communicating with one's partner to relieve a natural concern about causing pain during love play and intercourse is important. Choosing the best time of day for love play and timing the use of pain-killing medication can help. Loosening up with stretching exercises and exploring different positions to find the more comfortable ones for intercourse are other useful recommendations.

Chronic diabetes affects 11 million Americans, with half a million new cases each year. Those over age 40 are more at risk, but Afro-Americans have a 33% higher risk and Hispanic Americans a 300% greater risk than whites for non-insulin-dependent diabetes. More women than men are affected. Diabetic women may experience decreased vaginal lubrication, difficulty or loss of orgasm ability, and more frequent vaginal infections (Strodtman & Knopf 1983). For men, diabetes can mean erectile problems, especially when they complicate their condition with poor nutrition and being overweight.

Emphysema, asthma, and chronic lung diseases also affect the sexual lives of young and old (Francoeur 1988; Hossler & Cole 1983). A quarter of all men who have heart attacks give up sex, even though 80% could safely resume their customary sexual activity and the remaining 20% only need to adjust their lovemaking style to fit their exercise tolerance as indicated by their physicians (Rosenthal 1988).

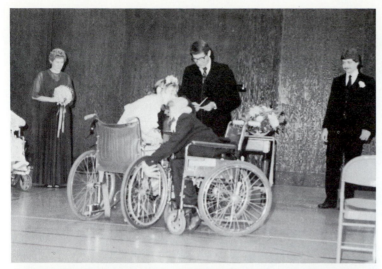

Figure 18.3. *"Why would you want our wedding picture for your textbook? We're no different from any other couple!" Bill asked me. Bill Heyer and Margo Bouldin are just like any other couple, except, as Margo said, "We have a little more difficulty getting around." Until recently, disabled persons' need for intimacy and the sexual rights of handicapped persons were not recognized by the nondisabled. Institutions frequently tried, and still try, to reduce the disabled to the state of asexual dependent children. Margo was told as a child she would never be anything more than "a vegetable." Today, cerebral palsy keeps both of them in wheelchairs. Yet on Halloween 1982—"a good night for mischief" Margo told me—she and Bill became the first married couple at the Cheshire Home, a New Jersey residence that tries to provide a normal environment for handicapped persons.*

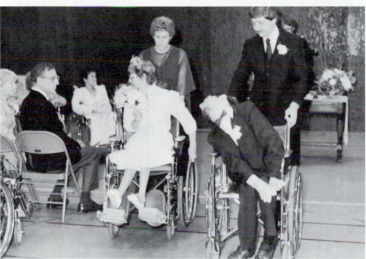

The Visually Impaired and Deaf

Young people who are blind do not have the early sexual experiences which normally contribute to sexual identification, knowledge, and development. They are not exposed to the variety of visual information and nonverbal communications others benefit from daily, the images of sexuality on television, and in movies, magazines, and pornographic literature. They also do not have the benefit of everyday observation of body image and nudity in the locker room and showers (Figure 18.4). Blind youths often have limited knowledge of their own bodies and much less knowledge of the other sex because of the social taboos that prevent them gaining such knowledge by touch in the family or outside (Doughten, Minken, & Rosen 1978; Knuth & Smith 1984).

Figure 18.4. *Blind teenagers face a unique challenge in learning about their sexuality because they are not exposed to the many visual messages about how males and females differ and interact. Teachers and parents can now use realistic models to help blind teenagers gain insight into sexual anatomy.*

Attempts in the 1940s to promote sex education for deaf and hearing impaired children were not very successful. By 1966 only half of the larger American residential schools for the deaf had any family education, and this figure is likely exaggerated. Isolation is the single most important factor impacting on the emotional adjustment of the deaf child. Children who are hearing impaired have difficulty establishing meaningful relationships with their peers and tend to be less mature and socially competent than hearing children. More important, it appears that hearing impaired children do not internalize normal sexual taboos, because they do not receive the extra verbal innuendos that characterize everyday conversations. Having a hearing impairment may also interfere with a child's gender-role development because of restricted identification with the same-gender parent and peers. Although some progress has been made in recent years, Max and Della Fitzgerald (1980) not too long ago described the state of our professional knowledge and understanding of deafness from a psychosexual viewpoint as "in its infancy."

Sexual Enrichment Aids for the Disabled

Some persons with physical disabilities and chronic illnesses find that *sexual enrichment aids* can be helpful. Some adult magazines and mail-order catalogs feature special adaptive devices for use by persons with disabilities who may have difficulty with hand movements. Vagina-shaped vibrators, dildos, and training aids to increase vaginal grip or erection are available from catalogs and some medical supply companies. Given time and a participating partner, most people with physical disabilities create the opportunities to explore their own potential in sexual activities and learn how to give and receive pleasure and enjoy intimacy (Goodman 1980).

Developmental Disabilities and Mental Retardation

There are many differences between a physical disability and a developmental disability or mental retardation (DD/MR). Each year, an estimated 100,000 developmentally disabled persons are sexually abused in America. By age 18, 99% of all youths with mental retardation have been sexually exploited and misused at least once, almost always by someone they knew. Physically disabled persons experience a similar very high rate of sexual abuse (Cole 1984–1986).

Two factors make this problem unusual. First, persons who are developmentally disabled learn early in life that passivity and cooperation make survival and independence easier. Second, the more severely retarded are institutionalized because they need constant supervision, attention, and protection. Both factors make these people vulnerable to sexual abuse (Cole 1984–1986).

People with DD/MR are considered either asexual or hypersexual. They are seldom seen as having feelings very similar to the norm in the general society. Although sometimes overly protected by well-meaning parents or institutional staffs, these individuals need specific and consistent education, counseling, and guidance to make up for their lack of natural and spontaneous everyday opportunities to learn about relationships, feelings, sex, and sexuality. Many individuals with mild to moderate DD/MR can enjoy loving, tender, and joyous relationships with the guidance and help of caring professionals and families (Bernstein 1985; Moglia 1986).

A More Humane Perspective

Drawing on many years of work in the field of rehabilitation medicine and sexuality, Sandra and Theodore Cole (1982:904) suggest eight positive statements about the sexuality of older persons and persons with disabilities:

1. Genital function alone does not make a functional relationship.
2. Urinary incontinence does not mean genital incontinence.
3. Absence of sensation does not mean absence of feelings.
4. Inability to move does not mean inability to please or be pleased.
5. The presence of deformities does not mean the absence of desire.
6. Inability to perform does not mean inability to enjoy.
7. Loss of one's genitals or the ability to have penile/vaginal intercourse does not mean loss of sexuality.
8. Sexual dysfunction is not synonymous with personal inadequacy.

Alex Comfort, the author of *The Joy of Sex*, offered a similar view in his preface to *Sexual Options for Paraplegics and Quadriplegics* (Mooney et al. 1975:viii).

Virtually nobody is too disabled to derive some satisfaction and personal reinforcement from sex—with a partner if possible, alone if necessary. When a disabled person is unable to enjoy sex, the greatest obstacle to enjoyment usually isn't the difficulty or impossibility of making particular movements, but the social convention that sex consists of putting the penis in the vagina and that all the rest of the rich range of human and mammalian sexual responses—oral, manual, and skin stimulation—are abnormal. Human sex is widely versatile and not limited to the genitalia.

Key Concepts

1. Older persons are increasingly demanding recognition of their sexual needs and rights as their numbers increase.

2. Denying the sexual rights and needs of older persons and persons with disabilities is costly for society and the individuals themselves because being able to meet one's needs for nurturance and intimacy is a major factor in an active life and rehabilitation.

3. Maintaining a positive self-image and an active outlook on life help us maintain an active social and sexual life in the later years and when we are faced with a disability.

4. The sexual adjustments persons with disabilities need to make depends on whether they are born disabled, or are disabled in childhood, before adulthood, or later. The severity of the disability and its visibility are two other factors that determine what kinds of adjustments are needed.

Key Terms

estrogen replacement therapy (ERT) (504)

feminization of poverty (503)

menopause (504)

vaginal atrophy (504)

Summary Questions

1. What five factors increase the chances that a person will be sexually active in their later years?

2. What kinds of barriers do older persons commonly encounter in their effort to lead sexually fulfilling lives?

3. What kinds of barriers do persons with disabilities commonly encounter in their effort to lead sexually fulfilling lives? How does the person's age affect this effort?

4. Reword and summarize the positive conclusions about the sexuality of older persons and persons with disabilities offered by Alex Comfort and Sandra Cole.

Suggested Readings

Brecher, E. M., & the Editors of Consumer Reports Books. (1984). *Love, Sex, and Aging: A Consumers Union Report.* Boston: Little Brown. A major study of sexuality in the later years.

Kilmartin, M. (1984, May). Disabled doesn't mean no sex. *Ms.*, pp. 114–118, 158. The personal story of a college coed who finds herself in a dorm for disabled students because it was the only way she could get a single room.

Rosenthal, S. H. (1988). *Sex over Forty.* Los Angeles: J. P. Tarcher.

Gender Discomfort
Gender Identity/Role
  Transpositions
  Transvestism
  Transgenderism and
    Transsexualism
  Therapies and Support
    Groups
The Gender Rainbow

Chapter 19

Gender Conflicts

Special Consultants

Paul Hanson, founding member and current board member of The Renaissance Education Association, Inc., a support and information service for tranvestites and transsexuals.

Roger E. Peo, Ph.D., a New York therapist working with transgendered clients and their partners.

JoAnn Roberts, Ph.D., founder and a director of The Rennaisance Education Association, Inc.

Leah Cahan Schaefer, Ed.D., charter member of the Harry Benjamin International Gender Dysphoria Association, past president of the Society for the Scientific Study of Sex, and author of *Women and Sex*.

Connie Christine Wheeler, M.S., Ph.D.(cand.), charter member of the Harry Benjamin International Gender Dysphoria Association and co-editor of *Progress in Sexology*.

This brief chapter deals with persons who experience a dissatisfaction or conflict in their gender identity or in their gender role. In simple terms, this chapter discusses transvestites, men and women who feel compelled to crossdress as the other gender, and transgenderists and transsexuals who experience a tension or conflict in their gender identity.

Gender Discomfort

Gender dysphoria is a collective term used to describe a form of gender discomfort, or dissatisfaction with one's gender. Gender is fundamental to most everything in human life. The very first question we ask about any newborn is ''What is it?—a boy or girl?'' The issue of gender dysphoria is one of the most interesting and controversial areas of study in the human personality because here the focus is on gender at its extremes. In studying these extremes, we can learn a great deal about the middle, the average, or so-called normal.

Before we examine the extreme examples of gender development, we need to remind ourselves of the three elements of what we call **gender**. Our **core gender identity** is our personal, basic, immutable conviction or awareness of being either female or male. Some refer to core gender identity simply as gender identity. **Gender role behavior**, or simply gender role, allows us to tell the world in a culturally appropriate way who we are. Gender role is the public expression of our personal awareness of being masculine or feminine. The third element, **gender orientation**, includes our sexual fantasy and affectional orientations as well as the gender orientation of our sexual activity.

It may be difficult to keep these three elements distinct in our minds, but, if we want to understand our gender and its many variations, we must always remember that the gender orientations of our sexual fantasies, our falling in love, and our choice of sexual partner are all part of our gender, but they are not all of our gender. Although core gender identity, gender role, and gender orientation combine to make up our gender, they are distinct aspects.

Most researchers today believe that our gender identity/role is the result of the ongoing interaction of nature and nurture at critical periods in our development before and after birth. Thus, persons with gender dysphoria are born with their condition, even though their social experiences after birth impact on their gender discomfort or conflict. At present, we have a fair understanding of what gender dysphoria is, and when it develops. However, we have no idea how or why it occurs. Nor do we have any idea which mothers might be at risk for having a child with gender dysphoria. Gender dysphoria is not inherited or acquired. It is, in the words of Harry Benjamin, a pioneer in gender dysphoria and transsexualism, best described as a ''phenomenon.''

Gender Role Transpositions

The conditions most commonly associated with gender dysphoria are transvestism, transgenderism, and transsexualism. These conditions are generally thought to be related. They do fall along the same developmental scale. However, their symptoms differ and emerge at different ages. A transsexual or transgenderist experiences a *constant and continuous discomfort* with his or her gender, which leads him or her to adopt the full-time role of the other gender. The conviction that one's sexual anatomy doesn't match one's gender identity as male or female can lead to sex-change surgery. A transvestite man or woman has *recurring episodes* of gender discomfort, which are expressed in crossdressing, with or without overtones of sexual arousal (Money 1988:79–125).

A gender dysphoria begins somewhere during the third or fourth month of pregnancy, when the fetal brain is masculinized or feminized. A gender element is transposed to the other gender path, so that this one element is in conflict with the genetic, gonadal, and anatomical gender path taken by the fetus. A transsexual is aware as far back as he or she can remember that he or she is not like other members of their gender. Before birth, a transsexual's *core gender identity is transposed to the other path*, leaving a "male imprisoned in a female body" or a "female imprisoned in a male body." In a transvestite, *the neural template for gender role behavior is partially transposed to the other path*, leaving a male or female who occasionally feels compelled to crossdress. A transvestite does not recognize his or her gender role cross-coding until the onset of adolescence when other secondary sexual characteristics appear in all humans. Both conditions are prenatally programmed, so that transvestites do not develop into transsexuals, and vice versa.

Transvestism

Many people still confuse transvestism with homosexuality and transsexualism. Remember, gender orientation is different from both gender role behavior and gender identity. Many people also mistakenly think that all transvestites are sexually aroused by wearing clothes of the other gender. Remember, a person's gender role behavior is related to but definitely distinct from his or her sexual turn-ons. Transvestites usually have a relatively solid gender identity that matches their anatomical gender, with perhaps occasional shift to the other gender identity (Highlight Box 19.1).

An Episodic Lifestyle

A **transvestite**, known in the subculture as a TV, is a person who occasionally experiences an irresistible need to dress as a member of the other gender.

Most people think transvestites are males who dress as women. But Schaefer and Wheeler note that there are more female-to-male crossdressers than most people suspect, although little is known about the female TV. It is much easier for a genetic female to dress in male clothing and be accepted in society "as a woman who likes to wear male-type attire." Some professional and even famous women have passed for years as men. Mary Walker, for instance, had a successful career as surgeon general in the U.S. Army and was awarded the Medal of Honor without anyone suspecting she was not a man (Sullivan 1985). When Billy Tipton, a jazz musician, died in 1989, the doctor informed his wife and three adopted sons that their husband and father was in reality a woman. From age 16 until his death, for 48 years, Billy had successfully passed as a man (Highlight Box 19.2).

Most transvestites are men who seek women as sexual partners. Some are women who seek male sexual partners. Bisexual men and women can be transvestites. Some gay men, known as "drag queens," and lesbians are also transvestites. Most observers of the TV scene believe that the number of gay

HIGHLIGHT BOX 19.1.
SIX MYTHS OF TRANSVESTISM

MYTH 1: Transvestites are gay.

REALITY: Although there is no definitive research surveying the entire TV population, observers believe that the proportion of gay and straight men and women in the transvestite subculture parallels the proportion of gay and straight men and women in the general population.

MYTH 2: Male transvestites want to be women.

REALITY: Male transvestites, as opposed to M-F transsexuals, enjoy being men. They would not accept a sex-change operation. Transgenderists, on the other hand, have a female gender identity and role, but do not have sex-change surgery because for them gender, not sex, is a prime concern.

MYTH 3: Male transvestites crossdress because they were dressed like girls in childhood.

REALITY: Although many crossdressers recall crossdressing when they were children, not all boys who dress up in their mother's or sister's clothes become transvestites. The parents of Ernest Hemingway, the notoriously macho writer, dressed him as a girl when he was young.

MYTH 4: Male transvestites act like women even when wearing men's clothes.

REALITY: In fact, transvestites are no more effeminate, or more masculine, than any other men. Because many TVs fear being found out, they consciously try to act as traditionally "masculine" as possible, some even acting "supermacho."

MYTH 5: Transvestites suffer from sexual dysfunction.

REALITY: For many TVs, crossdressing and eroticism are strongly linked. However, they are not directly related, and often exist independently. Although transvestism usually has an erotic root, this link may fade in the older TV who uses crossdressing for nonerotic, gender-related purposes.

MYTH 6: Transvestism is a mental illness.

REALITY: Some TVs do suffer mental anxiety, but it is the result of inappropriate guilt they feel because of society's disapproval of their behavior. These symptoms frequently disappear, or may never arise, when a TV is in an accepting or tolerant environment.

Source: JoAnn Roberts and Paul Hanson, The Renaissance Education Association, 1989.

transvestites is about the same as the number of gay persons in the general population, about 5% to 10%. Many transvestites are happily married and successful parents. Others are single. Some are sexually active with a partner. Others are not.

For some transvestites, crossdressing is a fetish. These transvestites need to crossdress in order to be sexually aroused and satisfied. These men may wear one or more articles of feminine apparel for sexual arousal, but they do not usually try to emulate a woman. For other transvestites, crossdressing is a gender role behavior with no sexual or erotic motive. These men may adopt a full feminine attire with lingerie. They may remove their body hair and have electrolysis for beard removal. To the best of their ability and within the constraints of their male physique, they try to emulate a woman. Older men may crossdress as an escape from the pressures and expectations of being a male in our society. Some transvestites crossdress to express hidden personality char-

Figure 19.1. *In the film "La Cage aux Folles," Monsieur Charrier (seated), Chairman of the Morals Squad, is given a new identity by a friendly Zaza Albin.*

acteristics, out of envy for women's role as "sex kitten" or "bitch goddess," to fool the world, or to express their creativity in fashion. Whether they are gay or straight, and whether their motive is a fetishistic arousal or not, transvestites do not want a sex-change operation.

Another gender expression, often confused with transvestism, is the female impersonator, or FI as they are called in the subculture. Often a **female impersonator** is a talented heterosexual male who makes a living as a performer mimicking females. Flip Wilson's "Geraldine" and Benny Hill's many female incarnations are classic expressions of this type of female impersonation (Figure 19.1). Some FIs adopt a female persona only on stage. Dressing in female clothing, they "lip-sync" to recordings of female stars. Some FIs live full time as women, on and off stage, but would never think of having genital reassignment surgery. Some FIs are true transvestites. Still others are transsexuals and use female impersonation to make money to pay for sex-change surgery.

Relationships

The homosexual crossdresser shares many lifestyle traits with other gay men who do not crossdress. A gay TV sometimes considers having a sex reassignment operation to give him female sexual anatomy in the hope that the procedure will make him more attractive to his same-gender partner. Such surgery, however, leads to tragedy when the TV discovers that his partner is really looking for a *man* who dresses as a woman, and not for a woman.

A heterosexual TV may marry in the hope that a heterosexual relationship with a woman will cure his desire to crossdress. Often he does not tell his wife before marriage. Once married, he finds that being exposed to femininity on a constant basis only arouses his need to crossdress more. Then the dilemma— to tell his wife or not. Either approach has its risks. If he tells her, she may feel betrayed and lose her trust. Her femininity may be threatened and she may wonder if perhaps she is a lesbian. She worries that discovery of his secret may jeopardize his job or lead to social ostracism. She may feel trapped in the relationship, both financially and emotionally, with no way out. Yet, faced with this "terrible secret," she may have no one she can turn to for advice and support. If the marriage is to survive, and some do, both husband and wife will require much counseling. Most marriages, however, do not survive this damaging revelation.

A TV husband may also keep his secret, living a masquerade that is constantly threatened by the danger of exposure. And yet the compulsion to crossdress must be satisfied, at least occasionally, no matter the risks.

If a woman finds out beforehand, she may go ahead with the marriage, feeling she can cure him, or, if not, that it won't be so bad. Neither turns out to be true. The more she supports his crossdressing, the more it expands, until it takes over the whole relationship. Even if this does not happen, the crossdressing invades all aspects of a relationship in ways that no other behavior does. We are first and foremost sexual beings and programmed early on to expect certain behaviors from others depending on their gender. Crossdressing violates these expectations and causes problems in a relationship as intimate as marriage.

A transvestite parent faces a similar decision about whether or not to let his children in on Dad's secret.

Transsexuals who marry before they are fully aware of their true situation face similar problems, including the risk of total rejection by their partner, children, parents, and siblings.

Cultural Aspects of Crossdressing

Transvestites are found in every culture and in every period of history. Unlike Western cultures that have great difficulty dealing with transvestites, other cultures almost welcome the transvestite. Some American Indian tribes honor the crossdressing berdache or shaman because he is blessed by the gods. In 1624 a Japanese decree installed men as Kabuki actresses. Similarly, in the time of Shakespeare only men were allowed to play the role of girls and women on the Elizabethan stage.

Transgenderism and Transsexualism

Transgenderism is a term coined by Virginia Prince (1979), grande dame of the TV/TS scene. Used as a synonym for transsexualism, the term transgenderism recognizes that not all persons with gender identity conflicts are interested in sexual intimacy. Since all persons with a gender dysphoria are fundamentally and totally concerned with gender, Schaefer and Wheeler suggest that trans-

HIGHLIGHT BOX 19.2.
BILLY TIPTON

To his many fans, Billy Tipton was an extraordinary jazz pianist and saxophonist. To his wife Kitty, he was the perfect husband. Their three adopted sons thought of him as the perfect father. When he died in February 1989, his wife, sons, and fellow musicians were all shocked to learn that Billy was a woman. Born in Oklahoma City, Billy found her female gender was a barrier to her budding career in jazz music. At age 16, she persuaded her family to move to St. Louis and let her pass as a male.

For over 50 years, no one suspected Billy was really a woman. He told his wife he had been in an accident that made sexual intercourse impossible. Kitty had had pelvic surgery as a teenager and could not have sex, so it was, as she said, "A marriage made in heaven." No one really knows why Billy decided to pass as a man. He may have been a true transsexual who did not seek sex-change surgery. He may have been a life-long male impersonator, a transgenderist, or a transvestite. Whatever the case, his life highlights the complexities of gender dysphoria discussed in this chapter.

Photograph of Billy Tipton (jazz musician extraordinaire, died February 1989).

genderism may be a more appropriate general term for this condition of gender identity/role transposition. The term **transgenderism** does not exclude those who *are* interested in sex and sexual relationships, the **transsexuals**, but it also includes those who are not so inclined and do not want sex-change surgery.

As mentioned earlier, transgenderism and transsexualism are birth phenomena, resulting from gender transposition or neural **cross-coding** early in pregnancy. We don't know what causes this cross-coding, or why it happens. We only know that one is born with a gender dysphoria. Thus, a person does not become a transsexual by adopting the other gender role behavior, dressing as the other gender, or having a sex-change operation. These steps merely help the transgenderist and transsexual live more comfortably in society.

A **transgenderist**, or TG, is often described as a "female imprisoned in a male body," or the reverse. As with crossdressers, transgenderists may be oriented to fall in love and relate sexually with persons who have the same sexual anatomy as they do, with persons who have the other sexual anatomy, or with both genders. Often, this gender orientation remains unchanged following

Figure 19.2. *Twenty-seven years after her transsexual surgery in Denmark in December 1952, Christine Jorgenson shows the front page of a New York newspaper announcing her sex-change surgery. At a 1979 press conference in San Diego, California, Christine said she would have killed herself if she had not been able to have the surgery, which at that time was only available in Europe. Today sex-change counseling and surgery are available at several medical centers in the United States.*

transsexual surgery. For example, a genetic/anatomical male whose gender identity is female and who is living with a woman could be described as having an other-gender or heterosexual orientation. If this person continues living with the woman after transsexual surgery, her gender orientation would be described as same-gender or lesbian. Yet, the surgery only changed the sexual anatomy, not the person's gender orientation. The same would be true if a genetic/anatomical male was living with a male before surgery and continued living with him after surgery. This also holds for female-to-male transsexuals.

The earliest recorded sex-change surgery was done in the 1930s. In 1952 the operation gained worldwide attention in the case of George Jorgenson who became Christine Jorgenson in Copenhagen. More than 4,500 Americans have had transsexual surgery (Figure 19.2).

Support Groups and Therapies

Regardless of how gender transpositions arise, they generally are not "curable." Once the gender identity is established in early childhood, it is fixed and cannot be changed. Similarly, once the desire/drive to crossdress is established, it cannot be eliminated.

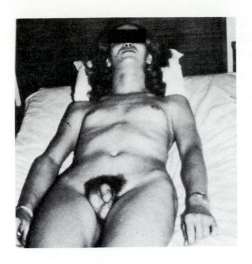

Figure 19.3. *A male-to-female transsexual. Left, a 24-year-old male after 15 weeks of estrogen treatment to obtain female breast development, but before surgery. Right, the same person after Dr. Roberto C. Granato performed sexual surgery. Since this individual did not respond well to the hormone treatment, implants were used to provide the desired breast enlargement.*

Therapy for crossdressers, then, is aimed at management of the drive so that it does not disrupt other aspects of life. Heterosexual crossdressers have a nationwide "sorority without sisters," The Society for the Second Self, and other self-help support groups. With local chapters across the country, TRI-ESS and similar organizations sponsor social events and support groups where wives and significant others of TVs, TGs, and TSs can meet and find help in coping with their feelings and experiences in loving someone with a gender dysphoria. Several national and international support groups provide information and referrals for transvestites, transsexuals, and their families and partners.

Since gender identity appears to be irreversibly set in the first couple of years after birth, the remedy for a transsexual's conflict may involve plastic surgery to give the individual a sexual anatomy corresponding to his or her gender identity.

For a male-to-female (M–F) transsexual, this procedure entails a careful physical and psychological evaluation, hormone treatment to produce female secondary sex traits, living a year or more as a woman, followed by surgical removal of testes and penis and plastic surgery to construct labia, a clitoris, and a vaginal canal (Figure 19.3). The only problem is one of voice timbre. The hormones of puberty alter the vocal cords long before most male-to-female transsexuals have their surgery. With appropriate voice training, this effect can be minimized.

In some respects, the female-to-male (F–M) transformation fares better. Hormones can produce masculine muscle growth, deepening of the voice, and growth of body hair. The breasts, ovaries, and uterus are surgically removed. Labial and clitoral tissues, augmented by skin grafts from elsewhere on the body, are used to create a penis and scrotum. A fully functioning, erectile penis, capable of intercourse, is beyond the current state of the art. However, surgically implanted, flexible silicone rods or a prosthetic penile pump may make intercourse possible. Such erection aids are widely used with diabetic and spinal-cord-injured men (see Chapter 18). Both M–F and F–M transsexuals report being able to have orgasms after surgery, although neither can function reproductively in their new gender role.

The Gender Rainbow

It is useful to remember that within every so-called normal person—persons with no definitive gender conflicts—there resides, either consciously or not, a portion of the other gender. Social scientists often allude to this phenomenon as the "androgynous" soul. Schaefer and Wheeler suggest that our androgynous nature may also give us an insight into persons with gender conflicts:

> With imagination, one could consider that people endowed with a gender conflict may be uniquely privileged. In a unique way, they experience the two *persona*, male and female, which each of us has. Those with a gender dysphoria have the rare opportunity to know at the deepest level the thoughts and feelings of both genders and all the configurations in between. Yet, when we extend this concept to include a deeper recognition of the male in us if we are female—or the converse, the female in us if we are male, we often tend to at best devalue it, or at worst fear and attempt to expunge it. Yet, to be aware of the place each of us occupies on the gender continuum, to know our unique color on the gender rainbow, and to better integrate these special attitudes, talents and ideas into our lives, is to know a more enhanced and enriched sense of being.
>
> *(Personal communication, 1989)*

Key Concepts

1. In passing through the fixed and flexible gates of psychosexual development before and after birth, some people develop an unconventional gender identity/role, in which they express one or more aspects of gender identity/role usually associated with the other gender.

2. Transvestites generally become aware in their adolescent years of their need to crossdress. Transvestites, like non-crossdressers, include heterosexual, homosexual, and bisexual men or women, single and married, celibate and sexually active persons.

3. A transsexual person experiences a core gender identity that is in conflict with his or her chromosomal and anatomical sex. This conflict may be resolved by sex-change surgery.

4. A variety of local and national support groups and services are available for persons who experience a total or partial transposition in some aspect of their gender identity/role.

5. Since gender cross-coding also affects the significant others in the lives of a transvestite, transgenderist, or transsexual, counseling and support groups are also important for involved family members.

Key Terms

core gender identity (516)
cross-coding (521)
female impersonator (519)
gender (516)
gender dysphoria (516)
gender orientation (516)

gender role behavior (516)
transgenderism (521)
transgenderist (521)
transsexual (521)
transvestite (517)

Summary Questions

1. Describe and give an example of gender dysphoria. What three factors may be involved in this phenomenon?

2. How is the concept of gender transposition related to gender dysphoria?

3. List some key differences and similarities between transvestites and transsexuals.

4. What kinds of problems do transvestites and transsexuals encounter? What resources are available for them?

Suggested Readings*

Bolin, A. (1988). *In Search of Eve: Transsexual Rites of Passage*. S. Hadley, MA: Bergin & Garvey. An award-winning study of how male-to-female transsexuals learn to express their gender identity as females, by a cultural anthropologist.

Morris, J. (1974). *Conundrum*. New York: Harcourt Brace Jovanovich. The autobiography of a famous British journalist who underwent a sex-change operation to become a woman.

Newton, E. (1979). *Mother Camp: Female Impersonation in America*. Chicago: University of Chicago Press. A solid, readable exploration of the varieties of crossdressing and tranvestism.

Stuart, K. E. (1983). *The Uninvited Dilemma*. Lake Oswego, OR: Metamorphous Press. Explores a wide range of personal problems encountered by male-to-female transsexuals in their careers, family life, and relationships.

Sullivan, L. (1985). *Information for the Female to Male Crossdresser and Transsexual*. San Francisco: L. Sullivan. A down-to-earth exploration of the female-to-male transsexual by someone who has been through this experience.

*For resources on gender issues, see the Appendix, page 652.

*N*ormal and
Unconventional
Sexual Behaviors
Four Patterns of
Response
How Normal Lovemaps
Are Vandalized
Pedophilia
Other Paraphilias
*T*he Controversy over
Sexual Addiction
*W*hen the
Unconventional
Is a Problem

Chapter 20

*U*nconventional Sexual Expressions

Special Consultants

Margaretta Dwyer, R.S.M., M.A., licensed psychologist and instructor, Program in Human Sexuality, Department of Family Practice and Community Health, University of Minnesota Medical School (Minneapolis).

Sharon E. King, M.S.Ed, R.C.H., C.A.S., abuse and incest counselor, The Starting Point, Collingswood, New Jersey.

Roger E. Peo, Ph.D., New York therapist working with persons with gender dysphorias and unconventional sexual preferences.

Norman A. Scherzer, Ph.D., professor, Department of Biological Sciences and Allied Health, Essex County College, and visiting professor, Department of Biology, Rutgers, The State University of New Jersey (Newark).

William R. Stayton, M. Div., Th.D., assistant professor, Psychiatry and Human Behavior, Jefferson Medical College, and adjunct professor, Human Sexuality Program, University of Pennsylvania Graduate School of Education, and LaSalle University.

Flashers, obscene phone callers, child molesters, sadists, masochists, transvestites or crossdressers, and people with sexual fetishes are sexually aroused in ways that society considers unconventional, or not within its norms of acceptable sexual response. This chapter deals with unconventional sexual responses, their origins, and their treatment.

Normal and Unconventional Sexual Behaviors

Four Patterns of Response

In Victorian society, the range of sexual behaviors that was accepted as "normal" was rather narrow. Today, what is generally considered normal by custom, and by both civil or religious authorities, encompasses a much broader range of sexual behaviors. John Money calls this culturally variable range of normal sexual behavior normophilic or **normophilia**.

In any society, some men and women have sexual interests and engage in sexual behaviors which fall outside the range of responses considered normal in a particular society. People who experience an overly active sexual response, significantly higher than a society's standard, are said to have a hyperphilia. The term **hyperphilia** combines *philia*, the Greek word for attraction or love, with the prefix *hyper*, meaning excessive or above the normal range. Clinically, psychologists talk about two types of hyperphilia: *nymphomania*, a woman with an unusually high sexual drive, and *satyriasis* or Don Juanism, a male with a similarly high libido. These hyperphilias are characterized by a recurring need for multiple sexual partners and the inability to develop a durable pair-bond with any one partner. Lust displaces love and pair-bonding (Money 1986:31). Some, but not all swingers, and some people who enjoy group sex, may fit into this clinical category of hyperphilia.

Hyperphilias can become a problem when a man or woman finds he or she is thinking about sex and trying to find sexual outlets much of the time, to the detriment of other aspects of his or her life. A hyperphilia may also be a problem if the long-term partner cannot keep up with the high level of sexual activity desired by the hyperphilic partner.

The opposite of a hyperphilia is a **hypophilia**. An early sexual trauma or very negative messages about sex may cause a person to shut off much or all of his or her sexual response. When this negative response is significantly below the normal range of sexual responses for a society it is viewed as hypophilic. A person with a hypophilia may express no interest at all in sex. He or she may even be physically and emotionally disturbed by the possibility of being sexually involved with someone. Even if such a person expresses some sexual desire, a normal response may be blocked during the excitement or orgasm stages of the sexual response cycle. Hypophilic women may have a normal desire for sexual intimacy, but then experience vaginal dryness, vaginal spasms that prevent intercourse, dyspareunia (pain during intercourse), lack of orgasm, or lack of any sensation in their genitalia. Hypophilic men may experience normal sexual desire but have trouble achieving an erection. Such men may also experience premature ejaculation, an inability to achieve vaginal penetration, pain during intercourse, or a lack of orgasm.

There is a third type of unconventional sexual response in which a person's level of sexual interest and activity lies within the normal range, but exhibits a

(a)   **(b)**

Figure 20.1. *In the 18th century, Lord Cornbury (a), Royal Colonial Governor of New York and New Jersey, was well known for his cross-dressing as in this official portrait. In (b), a modern cross-dressing male in New York's Greenwich Village.*

dependence on some unusual and personally or socially unacceptable sexual stimulus (Figure 20.1). Some might describe a man who is sexually turned on only by a woman's foot or shoe or by wearing women's clothing as "kinky" or "perverted," but the technical term used by psychologists is paraphilia. A **paraphilia** is a chronic dependency on an unconventional object or sexual stimulus for sexual arousal and/or gratification. A person with a paraphilia can only be sexually aroused by a particular nonsexual object, by a particular nonsexual part of the partner's body, by repetitive sexual activity involving real or simulated suffering or humiliation, or by repetitive sexual activity with nonconsenting partners (*Diagnostic & Statistical Manual*, 1980:266; Money & Lamacz 1990).

A person with a paraphilia is usually dependent on a particular stimulus for his or her sexual arousal and satisfaction. Some paraphiliacs require the immediate experience of a particular stimulus in order to be aroused. Usually, however, paraphiliacs can be aroused by a fantasy of an earlier experience with this stimulus. A husband with a rubber fetish who can only get sexually turned on by the smell, texture, and ritual of wearing rubber clothing may resort to a fantasy recalling doing this some time in the past in order to have intercourse with his wife who objects to his fetish (Money & Lamacz 1990).

Stayton's panerotic potential model (Figure 16.7, p. 457) suggests that anything within the universe can become an erotic turn-on. That model sheds some light on our discussion here of paraphilias. If we are born with a panerotic potential, then it is easy to see how paraphilias can fit into the total picture of human sexual responses. **Fetishes** develop when a person's sexual orientations and turn-ons are out of balance and become focused on some animate or inanimate object. Other paraphilic obsessions can develop in a distorted or unbalanced relationship with oneself, with other persons, or even perhaps with the spiritual or religious.

How Normal Lovemaps Are Vandalized

Before exploring various kinds of paraphilias, we need to say something about how a person develops a paraphilia. The origin of hypophilias is fairly easy to understand. A wide variety of negative messages, antisexual attitudes, and early, unresolved sexual traumas, as well as different physical factors, can leave an adolescent with a sexual desire significantly below the normal range. Although we know much less about the origins of hyperphilias, similar factors may be involved in this type of sexual response (Money 1985a:184–188).

Although every person with a paraphilia has his or her own unique turn-on, the variety of paraphilias are limited. Clinical and police reports suggest some general categories of paraphilias occur much more often in men, although some cases have been reported in women. In reality, paraphilias may be just as common in women as in men, but the paraphilias of women may be less violent and better hidden, often being expressed under the guise of a hypophilia.

This difference between the sexes raises a question about how paraphilias develop. At present, the evidence suggests that the male brain is developmentally programmed, beginning with the hormones of prenatal life, to develop a greater dependence on and a lower threshold for visual imagery as a sexual turn-on than is the female brain. Females appear to be more dependent on touch. But this difference is not an absolute. Not all men are more turned on by sight and not all women are more responsive than men to touch. What we mean is rather a relative, generally accurate difference (Money 1986:29–30).

How do men develop their sexually arousing images? The content of such images is to some extent unique and different for every man. Although the capacity for visual turn-ons, like the capacity to learn a language, may be laid down in the brain before birth, there is no evidence to support the theory that we are born with these sexually arousing images preprogrammed in our brain any more than we are born with a native language programmed in our brains. After birth, we learn a native language. After birth, we develop the actual content of sexually arousing stimuli. During the preadolescent and early adolescent years, individual experiences are associated with sexual arousal and particular images or stimuli that trigger sexual arousal become programmed in neural pathways within the brain.

A paraphilic response may result when a normal lovemap is distorted or "vandalized" during its development. We described a lovemap in Chapter 5 as a neural template in the brain and mind that depicts the idealized lover and the idealized program for love play and sexual arousal with that partner. Normal or normophilic lovemaps can be defaced, distorted, traumatized, or vandalized before they are firmly established in the neural pathways of the brain. Psychoanalysts believe paraphilias grow out of unresolved and misdirected hostility. Behaviorists believe they are learned behaviors. Both explanations, however, agree on the importance of traumatic events that sidetrack or distort the development of eroticism and result in unconventional sexual turn-ons.

Developing lovemaps appear to be most vulnerable to distortion when a child is between ages 5 and 8. Many, perhaps most, children who experience a traumatic episode like incest, physical abuse or neglect, emotional abuse or indifference, or seduction by a much older person during this vulnerable period emerge relatively unscathed. Others are permanently traumatized (Money 1986:16–23; Money & Lamacz 1990).

A lovemap can be distorted by **displacement** when a normal element in courtship and sexual foreplay is displaced in the brain's programming from its normal role and given an abnormal importance. Genital display provides a good example of this type of paraphilic distortion. Among primates, genital display is an ordinary part of seduction, an invitation and prelude to sexual play and mating. For the exhibitionist or "flasher," genital display is no longer a normal part of intimate love play with a partner. The exhibitionist has become obsessed with genital display and can only be sexually aroused and satisfied by shocking women in this way. For the voyeur, the normal sexual turn-on of watching one's partner be sexy while undressing becomes the whole focus of sexual arousal and satisfaction (Money 1986:34–39).

A lovemap may also be distorted by **inclusion** when an extraneous, non-sexual element is incorporated in our psychosexual behavioral development during childhood. When a nonsexual element becomes so important that a person cannot be sexually aroused and satisfied without it being part of the sex play, at least in fantasy, we are again dealing with a distorted, paraphilic lovemap.

If a child experiences sexual arousal while being given an enema during the period when his lovemap is forming in his brain, he may as an adult be dependent on repeated enemas as a way of becoming sexually aroused. This paraphilic lovemap is called klismaphilia. When spanking or being punished becomes associated with sexual arousal during the critical, vulnerable period before puberty, a boy may find that later in life his sexual arousal depends on being spanked. This paraphilic lovemap is known as masochism. A person with a zoophilic lovemap is dependent on having sex with an animal. In another form of *inclusion paraphilia*, persons with fetishes have incorporated a shoe, a foot, a piece of clothing, or some other nonsexual element into their pattern of sexual arousal to the point where they can only become aroused and satisfied when this element is included into their sex play actually or in fantasy (Table 20.1).

Once established in the brain, a paraphilic lovemap is remarkably persistent and very difficult, if not impossible, to change. Even the threat of years in prison cannot induce an exhibitionist or a pedophile to give up his paraphilic compulsion (Money 1985:189;1986:34–39).

Pedophilia

Pedophilia is the compulsive and repetitive sexual attraction of an adult for a child. The sexual contact that results from this paraphilia may involve exposing the victim's or the abuser's genitals, fondling the genitals of either, and seduc-

Table 20.1.   Some Paraphilias

The development of lovemaps that fall within the range of society's norms is sometimes distorted as the child matures. In some way, the child is prevented from integrating the lusty aspects of sex with the spiritual aspects of love. The result is a vandalized lovemap that allows participation in lusty sex, but only if the partner is somehow protected from the lust or made the unwilling victim of it. In some paraphilias, sexual arousal is projected on a nonsexual object, on the partner having a certain characteristic, or on a particular behavior. Listed here are a variety of paraphilias.

Acrotomophilia: Aroused by an amputee partner.

Adolescentilism: Aroused by imitating an adolescent.

Asphixophilia: Aroused by self-strangulation.

Automasochism: Aroused by self-inflicted pain.

Autopedophilia: Aroused by impersonating a child during sex play.

Chrematisophilia: Aroused by being charged or forced to pay for sexual services.

Coprolagnia, coprophilia: Aroused by thinking about, seeing, smelling, handling, or eating feces or by seeing someone defecate.

Erotic pyromania: Aroused by setting fires.

Hybristophilia: Aroused by having a sexual partner who is a criminal.

Infantilism: Aroused by being treated as an infant or a baby.

Juvenilism: Aroused by impersonating a juvenile and being treated as such by a sexual partner.

Klismaphilia: Aroused by being given an enema.

Mysophilia: Aroused by soiled, filthy, sweaty underwear or used menstrual pads.

Necrophilia: Aroused by sexual activity with a corpse.

Nepiophilia: Aroused by playing the role of a parent with an infant.

Retifism: Aroused by women's shoes.

Troilism: Aroused by watching one's loved one have sex with a third party.

Undinism, urophilia: Aroused by urine and urination.

tive or forced sexual intercourse. Usually the pedophile trys to seduce the child and win his or her acceptance and friendship. The extreme outcome of pedophilia shows up in child lust murder.

Children between ages 8 and 12 who feel they have no friends are especially vulnerable. Pedophiles readily admit they can walk into a school playground and within minutes pick out an ideal victim for seduction simply by looking for the poorly dressed or dirty child who is not being taken care of by his or her parents. Pedophiles may prey on strangers, but many children are sexually molested by adult friends or family members. Some 90% of all reported sexual molestations are committed by adult males on female minors. Most of the sexual abuse of male children is committed by men who are not closely related to their victims. There are also cases of adult women seducing or abusing young boys or girls. Despite popular myths about homosexuals molesting young boys, pedophilia and child sexual abuse is predominantly a heterosexual problem (Bell & Hall 1971; Rossman 1976).

Recent media coverage of scandals in day-care centers, boys' clubs, and schools raises a question whether sexual abuse of children is actually increasing, or whether we are just seeing more cases reported because people are more sensitive to the warning signs. Kinsey and his colleagues (1953) found about a quarter of the women in their samples reported having been sexually approached in childhood by an adult. Other more recent studies suggest that between 12% and 55% of females and 3% to 6% of males have been victims of childhood sexual abuse (Finkelhor 1984; Hrabowy & Allgeier 1987). The wide variation in these statistics is due in part to sampling different populations and to the use of different definitions of abuse with different cut-off ages, that is, before age 14, 16, or 18. So we are left with our question about the incidence of sexual abuse of children unanswered, but it does suggest that our heightened sensitivity to the issue and publicity about cases may increase reporting of incidents by giving victims permission to speak out.

Working with college students, Finkelhor (1984) identified eight factors that increase the risk of children being sexually abused. When none of these factors were present, very few students reported being victimized. Two-thirds of the students who had at least five of the eight factors reported being victimized. Each risk factor increased a child's vulnerability by 10% to 20%.

Factors That Increase the Risk of Child Sexual Abuse

1. Having a stepfather during childhood.
2. Having a sex-punitive or sex-denying mother.
3. Not being close to the mother.
4. Having a mother who did not finish high school.
5. Living without one's mother for some time.
6. No physical affection from the father.
7. A family income under $15,000.
8. Two or fewer friends in childhood.

In Finkelhor's study, half of the girls with stepfathers reported being victimized, *although not necessarily by their stepfathers*. In Russell's 1984 study, 1 out of 6 women with a childhood stepfather was sexually abused whereas only 1 out of 40 women was abused by her biological father.

Girls whose mothers warned or scolded their daughters for masturbating or for asking questions about sex or looking at sexual pictures were 75% more likely to be victimized than the typical girl in Finkelhor's sample. This finding is very important when we listen to objections against sex education in the schools. "If mothers have repressed all the healthier ways of satisfying sexual curiosity, these daughters may be more vulnerable to an adult or authority figure who appears to give them permission and opportunity to explore sex, albeit in the process of being exploited. . . . Whatever the precise mechanism, it is clear from this finding that it is not the sexually lax, but the sexually severe, families that foster a high risk for sexual exploitation" (Finkelhor 1984:27).

There is considerable dispute over the long-term consequences of childhood sexual abuse (Finkelhor 1979b). Biased samples and speculation by researchers with pet theories or advocates of a child's right to be sexually active with an adult often distort what little is published on the subject. According to Finkelhor (1979a), the degree of sexual contact, exhibitionism, fondling the genitals, or sexual intercourse may not be as important in producing a traumatic or negative outcome as are the use of force and a wide difference in the ages of the adult and child. However, another study of college women found that although being physically forced into sexual activity as a child was traumatic, the absence of force sometimes intensified the trauma (Fritz, Stoll, & Wagner 1981). When force is used, the child can at least retain some self-respect. When no force is used, the child's sense of guilt and loss of self-respect may be much more devastating. This is especially true when the child "enjoys" the sexual experiences; the enjoyment compounds the sense of guilt and trauma.

In trying to understand the sexual misuse of children, it is helpful also to look at factors that contribute to the making of a pedophile. Many pedophiles have a weak sense of their own masculinity and low self-esteem. They distrust other adults and lead lonely lives. They find it difficult, if not impossible, to relate intimately with adults. Sexual inadequacy is a common characteristic whether it is due to marital or occupational stress or to inhibited social development when young. Pedophiles are found in all age groups, with every educational and professional background. Most are heterosexual, although some are homosexual. Many incidents of pedophilia are impulsive, often occurring when a person has had too much to drink or is using drugs.

Although legislators, the media, and others focus the public's attention on the dangers of kiddie pornography, those who work with sex offenders report that most pedophiles can easily find sexually stimulating material in the rash of advertisements that portray young girls, and sometimes boys, as sex objects (Figure 20.2).

Researchers at the Johns Hopkins University Hospital clinic for sexual disorders have found some pedophiliacs have hormonal, brain, or chromosomal disorders. Initial studies suggested that intensive therapy coupled with use of Depo-Provera, a libido-suppressing drug, may be the most effective way of dealing with this sexual compulsion (Berlin & Meinecke 1981; Money 1986:135–146). Today other drugs have replaced Depo-Provera and are commonly used in treating pedophiliacs.

Other Paraphilias

Exhibitionists and Voyeurs

Most of us have at least a touch of exhibitionism in our personalities. In its mildest forms, sexual exhibition is part of the ritual of sexual display and courtship. We indulge in various forms of socially acceptable exhibitionism in our clothes, at the beach, in gyms and health spas, and dancing. Codpieces, penis extenders, and bikinis may be socially acceptable forms of genital exhibitionism, depending on the culture. At the edge of the socially acceptable, exhibitionism may be part of the motivation of go-go dancers and both male and female strippers. It may also play a role in the sexual responses of swingers who enjoy having sex in the presence of others and of people who are into the role playing of bondage and dominance or sadomasochism.

For some persons, however, genital exhibitionism has become a compulsive behavior they must repeat in order to achieve sexual arousal and orgasm. For these individuals, display of the genitals has been displaced from its normal role in courtship and lovemaking rituals and become the focus of intense sexual arousal and satisfaction. As a paraphilia, **exhibitionism** refers to a man who can only become sexually aroused and reach orgasm by exposing his genitals

Figure 20.2. *After a nationwide operation drastically reduced the production and distribution of kiddie porn, pedophiles found a new source of arousal in advertisements (for jeans, perfumes, and even prestigious chocolates) that pose young girls in provocative ways.*

and shocking women (Highlight Box 20.1). The exhibitionist, the "weany-wagger," or "flag-poler," is always a male, since exhibitionism is legally defined as a male activity (Money 1986:77–85).

The compulsive, repetitive behavior of an exhibitionist may be motivated by anger and hatred, in which case he wants to shock his unwilling victim. This type of exhibitionist may also fantasize about sexually assaulting his victim. A second type of exhibitionist, motivated by the need for acceptance, may actually hope to attract a woman or seduce her by exposing his sexual organs. Or he may do it strictly to gain attention with little or no sexual content in mind. Many exhibitionists have difficulty with social and sexual relations, having failed to develop normal social skills. Exhibitionism allows them to prove their masculinity in a nonverbal statement (Gebhard et al. 1965).

Although exhibitionists account for roughly a third of all arrests for sexual offenses in the United States, they are often taken lightly by society. Cartoons and television often poke fun at this behavior (Figure 20.3). Since most exhibitionists are timid, shy, nonaggressive individuals, the best way to cope with this type of person is not to get emotionally upset. Ignore it if you prefer, or at least treat it casually (Brecher 1978). However, the rare exhibitionist who is motivated by hatred and anger may fantasize about sexually assaulting his victim. This type of exhibitionist may be provoked by ridicule.

HIGHLIGHT BOX 20.1.
THE IRRESISTIBLE URGE
OF AN EXHIBITIONIST

By definition, a paraphilia is a compulsive behavior in which sexual arousal and satisfaction depends on the ritual repetition of a particular behavior. This compulsion is evident in the following statement of an exhibitionist who despite being repeatedly arrested for exposing his genitals in public places, nevertheless continued to experience and give in to this irresistible urge.

When the urge does come, it comes so strong that you really want to do it. It just blocks off everything that makes sense. . . . everything else that could maybe stop you. . . . You want to do it so bad. . . . I was driving, and the urge just came out of nowhere to do it. . . . I must have passed up about 10 or 15 places where I could have done it, trying not to do it. . . . But it just kept tingling with me. Stop here! Stop there! Stop here! Go ahead! You can do it! And the feeling that I had inside was one like, if I didn't do it, I'd be missing out on something very, very great. It just kept on going. I ended up driving halfway to Annapolis, trying not to do it, just passing up places. And it got so strong I just had to do it. I just had to get out and do it. (Money 1986:35)

Voyeurism is the flip side of exhibitionism. Its milder forms range from woman-watching on the street or at the pool or beach, to the devotees of X-rated videos, adult magazine centerfolds, and topless-bottomless bars. Like exhibitionism, voyeurism is legally an exclusively male behavior. If a man stands naked in a window and a woman watches from the street, he can be arrested as an exhibitionist. If the situation is reversed, and a man in the street watches a woman undressing, he can be arrested for voyeurism.

The voyeur is sometimes referred to as a "Peeping Tom" in recognition of the one male citizen who watched as Lady Godiva rode naked through town to protest her husband's unjust taxing of the people of Coventry, England in 1057. The paraphilic **voyeur** gets sexual gratification from watching others naked or having sex. In watching a woman undress or a couple making love, the voyeur will frequently fantasize that he is making love to the woman and that she will embrace him because he is such a fantastic lover. Voyeurs commonly masturbate to fantasies of having sex with the person they are watching.

The voyeur is turned on by the anonymity of the woman, the risk of being caught, and the fact that the woman does not know she is being watched. Most sexologists today accept voyeurism as a normal behavior when the fantasies are within the range of socially acceptable behavior and when it is not compulsive, an avoidance mechanism, or a substitute for other sexual outlets.

Those voyeurs who are arrested tend to be young, shy, and sexually inadequate. They generally have difficulty relating to women. They also tend to have few friends and are likely to be the youngest member of their family.

In one study, 18% of college men and 13% of college women reported having fantasies of observing others engaging in sex (Sue 1979). Many couples today fulfill this fantasy by renting X-rated videotapes to watch at home as a sexual turn-on.

Figure 20.3.

"FORGET IT, NED. YOU'LL NEVER BE A FLASHER. YOU'RE TOO SLOW."

Fantasies of or actually watching a couple engage in sexual intercourse, being watched by a third party while having intercourse, or watching one's partner have sex with a third party were clearly regarded as disturbed and perverted behavior only 30 years ago. This judgment began to change in the 1960s and 1970s when group sex, threesomes, swinging, and mate swapping were common topics for discussion on television and in sex magazines. Elements of voyeurism and exhibitionism combine in *troilism* where a person is aroused by watching his or her partner have sexual intercourse with a third party. For some today troilism is no longer a paraphilic behavior.

Obscene phone callers are sexually aroused by shocking a stranger with a combination of sexually explicit talk and verbal abuse. Some obscene phone callers direct their attention to children; others try to find vulnerable women. Probably the most frightening aspect of such calls is their anonymity and the fact that the receiver of the call cannot fight back or respond.

The simplest way to handle such calls is to hang up immediately. Never give any information about yourself, especially not your name or address, until the caller has properly identified him- or herself. If such calls persist, inform the telephone company or local police. An unlisted number may solve the problem, although it has some inconveniences. Telephone companies now market a new device that attaches to your phone and instantly displays the caller's telephone number. This system allows you to screen all calls and not answer calls from numbers you don't recognize if you suspect they are obscene callers. If you do answer and the caller is abusive, you know the telephone number and can report it. Some telephone companies offer a "Call Block" service that allows you to program your phone not to receive calls from one or more specific phone numbers.

The **frotteur** is usually a male who achieves sexual gratification by rubbing against the clothing or body of a woman from behind. Frotteurs operate in the safety of a crowded bus, train, elevator, or other places where people gather in the anonymity of a crowd. This situation often makes it impossible to tell whether one is being sexually used by a frotteur, or is just the victim of a very crowded bus or subway car. It is difficult for the victim to do or say anything, even if she is certain what is happening.

Variations in Sadomasochism and Bondage and Dominance

Sadomasochism, or S&M, is a catchall phrase that covers a wide range of sexual behaviors and needs ranging from voyeuristic and exhibitionistic aesthetics and games of bondage and submission to a compulsive paraphilic dependence, and the rare psychopathic lust murder. A **sadist** derives sexual pleasure and stimulation from humiliating psychologically and/or physically abusing his or her partner, or even inflicting severe pain. A **masochist** is sexually aroused by receiving humiliation, abuse, and even pain (Weinberg & Levi Kamel 1983).

In classic S&M, the sadist inflicts heavy whipping and pain on his or her victim and never gives up control. The other person is a victim, not a partner. In the more common form of S&M today, the submissive partner controls the whole ritual, which in the subculture is called a "scene."

Psychoanalytically, masochism is thought to be a "twisted" sadistic impulse. For example, if a child witnesses adult lovemaking and interprets it as aggression and punishment, he may twist this experience around so that he becomes the victim of aggression in his sexual relations. Others have suggested that the sadist is actually performing "symbolic castration" on his partner. Orgasm then comes from inflicting pain and rage on the partner (Green & Green 1974).

A neurophysiological theory suggests that the pain and pleasure centers in the hypothalamus are so close that an overflow of nerve impulses to the pain center may affect the sexual pleasure center (Prescott 1975a). If this overflow occurs, the person might come to associate pain with sexual pleasure. There are other theories, but whether one or a combination of factors actually results in a proclivity for S&M remains to be determined (Highlight Box 20.2, Table 20.2).

In the milder forms of **bondage and dominance**, bondage and discipline, and dominance and submission (D&S), aesthetics and role playing are given a priority and actual pain is avoided. The sexual turn-on of role playing in B&D and D&S is enhanced by very elaborate costumes and psychosexual drama. Masks, jackets, leather jockstraps and G-strings, belts, laces, wrist straps, and other paraphernalia are an important part of the role playing. Couples may spend thousands of dollars a year on their costumes (Mains 1988).

In recent years, because of the AIDS threat, many swingers have shifted to the aesthetics and games of dominance and submission, with exchangeable roles. Bondage and dominance (B&D) plays on erotic elements of being tied up and "forced" to participate in sexual acts. Although often a part of S&M, B&D can also be a separate behavior. B&D may involve the mild use of restraints, spankings, and humiliation without physical pain. Another recent development in this subculture are women who provide telephone sex services and often advertise their willingness to fulfill S&M fantasies for their callers. In many cities, branches of the Eulenspiegel Society and other clubs have a loyal clientele who enjoy the role playing, voyeurism, and exhibitionism of B&D and D&S.

HIGHLIGHT BOX 20.2.
AN S&M COUPLE

The childhoods of Carl and Toby provide an insight into how a man and woman could have their lovemaps scripted in a complementary way that makes them quite sexually compatible. This New York couple belongs to the Eulenspiegel Society, a group of people devoted to S&M. They are a typical suburban couple with children and indistinguishable from their neighbors except for their private sexual preferences. As a child, Carl was small and frequently picked on by neighborhood girls. He became sexually aroused by thoughts of being beaten by women and often masturbated while thinking of this fantasy. He enjoyed the submissive role of sexual slave. When his first wife did not share his role playing and the marriage ended, Carl met Toby who complemented his expectations by enjoying the dominant role (Goleman & Bush 1977).

Toby grew up in an area of New York City where at an early age she had to learn to defend herself. As a teenager she fantasized about dominating men and forcing them to engage in oral sex with her. Her first marriage also ended in divorce because of her sadist interests. She and Carl married and together made a perfect sexual match.

Toby and Carl are an excellent example of the scripting and conditioning that can play an important role in sexual orientation, particularly in adolescence when sexual images and behavior are taking shape.

Table 20.2.
Two Common Sadomasochistic Responses

The Kinsey surveys of 1948 and 1953 revealed that an erotic response to being bitten was a mild masochistic reponse for about half of the men and women interviewed. Only 1 in 10 females and 1 in 5 males reported being sexually aroused by reading sadomasochistic stories.

Erotic Responses to Being Bitten	By Females (%)	By Males (%)
Definite and/or frequent	26	26
Some response	29	24
Never	45	50
Number of people interviewed	2,200	567

Erotic Arousal from Sadomasochistic Stories	By Females (%)	By Males (%)
Definite and/or frequent	3	10
Some response	9	12
Never	88	78
Number of people interviewed	2,800	1,016

Source: Adapted from Kinsey, A. C., Pomeroy, W., Martin, C., Gebhard, P. *Sexual Behavior in the Human Female*, pp. 677–678. Philadelphia: Saunders, 1953. By permission of the Kinsey Institute for Research in Sex, Gender, and Reproduction, Inc.

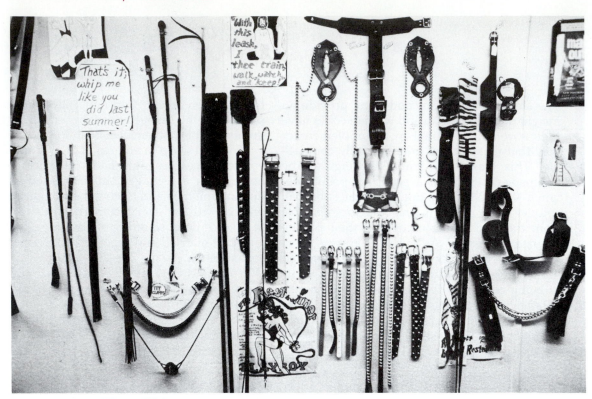

Figure 20.4. *Mail-order catalogs, specialty shops like the one shown here, and clubs like the Eulenspiegel Society cater to the needs of persons who enjoy the role playing of bondage and dominance or sadomasochism in their sex play.*

Forced crossdressing may be another part of the D&S scene when the woman or dominatrix forces the man to crossdress as a woman (Breslow, Evans, & Langley 1985; Spengler 1977).

Some women with strict religious upbringing may only be able to reach orgasm when "forced" to have sex in their fantasies or symbolically when their partner ties them up (Green & Green 1974). It has been shown that both S&M and B&D seem to be more common among people in positions of power and authority in business and politics, most of whom want to play the subservient role. For some, this role reversal seems to provide an outlet to work out the guilt they suffer because of their power. Dominants, or "tops," in the S&M, B&D, and D&S subcultures have no trouble finding submissive or "bottom" partners. Although some women are willing to play the top, there are far fewer true dominants than submissive females.

Kinsey's research in the 1940s revealed that 20% of men and 12% of women were aroused by sadomasochistic fantasies (Table 20.3). Twenty years later, Hunt (1974) found that 22% of men and 18% of women were aroused by S&M fantasies, although these fantasies were rarely expressed in real life. These statistics suggest that many people are willing to fantasize about an unconventional behavior like an S&M relationship, without wanting to actually have the ex-

Table 20.3.
Sadomasochistic Sexual Interests of Men and Women

Men and women contacted through sadomasochistic clubs and magazines by N. Breslow, L. Evans, and J. Langley reported they enjoyed a wide range of activities.

Interest	Male (%)	Female (%)
Spanking	79	80
Master-slave relationships	79	76
Oral sex	77	90
Masturbation	70	73
Bondage	67	88
Humiliation	65	61
Erotic lingerie	63	88
Restraint	60	83
Anal sex	58	51
Pain	51	34
Whipping	47	39
Rubber/leather	42	42
Boots/shoes	40	49
Verbal abuse	40	51
Stringent bondage	39	54
Enemas	33	22
Torture	32	32
Golden showers	30	37
Transvestism	28	20
Petticoat punishment	25	20
Toilet activities	19	12

Source: Archives of Sexual Behavior, 14:315. Copyright 1985 by Plenum Publishing Company. Reprinted by permission.

perience. No matter how unconventional, fantasies of S&M or B&S are not harmful, nor do they indicate mental instability.

Fetishes and Transvestism

A fetish develops when a person learns to attach erotic significance to an object that is not of itself sexual in nature. Rubber and leather fetishes are good examples of pure fetishes. Crossdressing may be a fetish and used as a sexual turn-on, but it may also be enjoyed as a political statement. High heels, garters, leather or vinyl boots, women's shoes, tight jeans, and seductive lingerie may also become fetishes. They are often used to heighten eroticism in pornographic movies and photographs, as well as in advertisements (Gosselin & Wilson 1980).

Some men do not focus on the whole person they are sexually involved with, but rather on a particular part of their partner's body which then becomes a fetish object. Foot fetishists are not uncommon. Much rarer are individuals who are erotically aroused by amputees, or being an amputee. There has yet to be a well-documented clinical report of a woman with a fetish (Wise 1985).

The psychological origin for some fetishes may be the inability of a person to cope with a sexual relationship. This inability may result from a fear of rejection. The body part or object is seen as a safe focus for erotic behavior because it is not threatening—a shoe cannot reject sexual advances!

Most so-called normal people have some mild fetishes—often unrecognized and unconscious. The advent of telephone sex services has brought a new dimension to the ways a man can satisfy his fetish. Most fetishists are harmless, socially functional people. A fetish only becomes a problem if it results in guilt or anxieties, or if it becomes an obsession and obstacle in other areas of a person's life (Rosen 1964; Tollison & Adams 1979).

Crossdressing or, transvestism, only qualifies as a true fetish when a male wears one or more items of women's clothing to achieve sexual arousal. In such cases, wearing a brassiere or panties is sufficient to gain sexual arousal and satisfaction. A man who dresses completely as a woman usually is doing so to gain relief from the pressures of the male gender role. In such cases, sexual arousal appears to be at a minimum.

Gerontophilia and Ephebophilia

Our culture dictates that two sexual partners should be roughly about the same age, usually with the man a few years older than the woman. In *gerontophilia*, a young adult is drawn to find a partner old enough to be his or her parent or even grandparent. In the reverse paraphilia, *ephebophilia*, an older person feels compelled to find an adolescent sexual partner.

However, the increase in divorce and the more permissive attitudes of recent years have made it more acceptable for two persons of quite disparate ages to engage in sex or marry. Today, it is common for men confronted with midlife crisis to end their marriage and marry a much younger woman—the "Jennifer syndrome" (Gordon 1988). Younger women, regardless of their physical attributes, are commonly viewed as more sexually attractive than older women (Palmer 1988:524). Faced with the shortage of available men in their forties, fifties, and sixties, increasing numbers of middle-aged women are finding younger sexual partners and marrying much younger men (Houston 1987). Given today's social context, these behaviors are no longer necessarily viewed as paraphilic or deviant.

Some Rare Paraphilias

Rarely an individual may be sexually turned on by feces, urine, enemas, even vomit. Sexual contact, masturbation, oral sex, and intercourse between a human and an animal (zoophilia) is quite rare and decreasing in frequency. It was much more common when most Americans lived on farms. In a rural society, young males not only observe animals mating but can also use farm animals for sexual release when sex with a woman is not possible. Necrophilia, sexual attraction to and contact with dead bodies, is also very rare.

The Partners of Paraphiliacs

Because the lovemap of a paraphiliac is so uniquely individual, it is often difficult, if not impossible, for paraphiliacs to find partners whose lovemaps complement their sexual turn-on and imagery. Although an exhibitionist enjoys exposing himself and some females may enjoy voyeurism, the exhibitionist wants to expose himself to an unwilling victim or to a stranger, not to a partner he knows. Some women will tolerate a partner who is into fetishistic cross-dressing, but few wives of transvestites are enthusiastic about such behavior in a spouse. Men with a fetish for a part of the female body are often able to find a suitable partner. Long-term pair-bonding between a sadist and a masochist or a submissive and a dominant partner is not uncommon.

The Controversy over Sexual Addiction

Some sexual counselors and therapists today talk about a pathological dependence on repetitive compulsive sex with a variety of partners as a sexual addiction similar to that of alcoholism or substance (drug) abuse. Sexual addicts have such a preoccupation with sex that it interferes with thinking about other things. They have lost control. Even when they set rules for themselves, trying to limit their sexual encounters, they succeed only by counting the seconds between encounters and constantly struggling to resist their urges, according to Mic Hunter, the coordinator of a Compulsivity Clinic in Minneapolis.

Patrick Carnes (1983, 1986) suggests that **sexual addicts** progress through an ever-accelerating cycle that involves

1. A trancelike preoccupation with sex that creates a compulsive search for sexual stimulation;

"WHAT DO YOU RECOMMEND TO SLOW DOWN A NYMPHOMANIAC?"

Figure 20.5.

2. The creation of special rituals that precede sexual behavior and intensify the arousal and excitement;

3. A compulsion to have sex no matter the risk or cost; and

4. A feeling of utter hopelessness and inability to control the compulsive behavior.

Specialists in sexual addiction find that a large percentage of sex addicts were sexually abused as children. In trying to cope with loneliness, low self-esteem, and anxiety, some individuals, they argue, seek a "high" or "fix" in sex the way others compensate with highs from alcohol or drugs. Sexual addicts may also be trying to recapture the intoxication of a young love by creating a trancelike fantasy with each ritual encounter (Carnes 1983; Edwards 1986; Goleman 1984; Schwartz & Brasted 1985).

As with other paraphilic conditions, the sexual addict may attract a partner who comes from a similar background. The wife of a sexual addict may be aware of her husband's many affairs, but assume that all men act similarly. Or the spouse may blame him- or herself, thinking if he or she changed or behaved differently, the partner's addiction pattern would change.

In one Midwest group, 84.5% of the sexual addicts in treatment were males ages 19 to 66 with a mean age of 36.7. Almost 9 out of 10 had some college education, half were employed as "professionals," and a quarter in business, with a median income of $27,000. Carnes advocates a treatment that involves both partners, family therapy, and an adaptation of the Twelve Steps in the Alcoholics Anonymous program.

But can an individual really be addicted to sex, as some are addicted to drugs or alcohol? Sex is an experience, not a substance. In treating substance abuse, the addict is expected to give up all use of alcohol or drugs. Thus abstinence is part of the treatment of sexual addict. Sex certainly can produce a "high," but its absence brings no withdrawal symptoms like those experienced with the withdrawal of an addictive drug. Finally, critics of this concept of sexual addiction suggest that what some therapists and psychologists judge to be abnormal, compulsive behavior may fall outside the norms of acceptable behavior because it involves multiple sexual partners and sex without affection or love. However, these criteria have no absolute value. What some term "sexual addiction" in American culture would be considered the social norm among the Mangians and other Polynesians in the South Pacific (Coleman 1986; Levine & Troiden 1988).

When the Unconventional Is a Problem

The wide range of unconventional sexual behaviors we have discussed can run the gamut from borderline acceptable, to a mild paraphilia that is considered harmless if "kinky," to a compulsive obsessive extreme prohibited by law. At any point along this spectrum, an unconventional sexual behavior may become a problem to the individual, to his or her partner, or to society. A mild type of behavior, such as occasional crossdressing, may not be a problem to society, but can be extremely disturbing to a partner. A more extreme behavior, such as child molestation, is a problem to society and the victim, and the individual must be treated and, if possible, rehabilitated.

Many persons with unconventional sexual orientations are comfortable with their lifestyle and have negotiated accommodations with their partners. Other partners find they cannot adjust or accept an unconventional behavior. In such cases, if therapy does not resolve the problem, separation or divorce may be inevitable.

Some individuals with unconventional sexual orientations desire to change their behavior, even though they are not in trouble with the law and have no immediate problems with society. They may want to change because they or their partner is unhappy. They may feel a need to adopt the sexual standards of the majority. Guilt may be a major problem and working through the guilt associated with a paraphilia can be an important step in the paraphiliac gaining control over his or her compulsive behavior. For those who have legal problems because of their sexual orientation, treatment or therapy is often mandated as part of a rehabilitation program.

Traditional psychoanalytic therapies, analysis, group therapy, and hypnosis may help a person give up a paraphilic behavior much as they may be useful for persons with alcohol or drug addictions (Kilmann et al. 1982). Behavioral therapies assume that unconventional sexual behavior, whether functional or dysfunctional, is learned and not innate. This type of therapy is often short term and operates on the principles of behavior modification: Any behavior that can be learned can also be unlearned. It has been most successful with persons who are strongly self-motivated.

In aversion therapy, the client is conditioned to associate a pleasant or compulsive sexual behavior with an unpleasant outcome. At the same time, the therapist tries to help the paraphiliac develop and enjoy a more conventional lovemap. A person with a sexual fetish, for example, may be shown erotic pictures that would ordinarily be stimulating. Along with the pictures, a mild electrical shock is applied. The individual begins to associate the shock with the fetish until an aversion to the fetish object develops. Negative learning has taken place, and the person eventually becomes "turned off" by the fetish (Kushner 1977). Maletzky (1980; 1984) has reported an 87% success in treating exhibitionists with noxious odors and unpleasant images while the patient fantasizes about exposing himself. Other clinicians are less optimistic about the success of aversion therapies in "curing" compulsive paraphilias.

Some people are disturbed by unconventional fantasies and fear they may begin to act on these impulses. Such fantasies include adultery, homosexual acts, incest, or masochistic thoughts or dreams. Counterconditioning substitutes the conventional sexual behavior for the unconventional. A married woman who is disturbed or feels guilty because she fantasizes about making love to another man while making love to her husband may be counseled to substitute the husband's image in her fantasy (Davison 1977).

In recent years, progestins (synthetic forms of progesterone) have been used in helping paraphilics seeking to alter their lovemaps to more socially acceptable patterns. These drugs, which substitute for testosterone in the target cells that control libido, seem to reduce the urgency of the paraphilia and allow more normal sexual fantasies and activities to occur and be enjoyed. This allows the therapist to work with the paraphiliac to construct a new normophilic lovemap in the brain. Although still quite experimental, this combination treatment has proven useful with some paraphiliacs, especially male pedophiles. Unfortunately, not much research has been done on the treatment of female pedophiles (Money 1986:135–145).

Key Concepts

1. A lovemap, our pattern of sexual response, may be distorted or vandalized during childhood, leaving the adult with a compulsive dependence on an unconventional sexual stimulus.
2. Exhibitionism and voyeurism can range from socially acceptable expressions to illegal outlets.
3. Sadomasochism is a general term for sexual behaviors ranging from voyeuristic/exhibitionist role playing of bondage and submission to a compulsive paraphilic dependence on giving or receiving pain in order to become sexually aroused and satisfied.
4. In a fetish, a nonsexual object or a particular nonsexual part of the partner's body becomes the focus of sexual arousal.
5. Except in the area of sadomasochism, a person with an unconventional sexual interest may have trouble finding a partner whose lovemap complements theirs.
6. True paraphilic lovemaps are extremely resistant to attempts to alter them.

Key Terms

bondage and dominance (538)	masochist (538)
displacement (531)	normophilia (528)
exhibitionism (534)	paraphilia (529)
fetish (541)	pedophilia (531)
frotteur (538)	sadist (538)
hyperphilia (528)	sadomasochism (538)
hypophilia (528)	sexual addicts (543)
inclusion (531)	voyeur (536)

Summary Questions

1. How do the three general types of vandalized lovemaps differ from each other and from a normophilic lovemap?
2. Describe some theories and interpretations of sadomaschism.
3. Describe the formation of a paraphilia by inclusion and by displacement.
4. What factors increase the risk of child sexual abuse?

Suggested Readings

Carnes, P. J. (1986, July). Progress in sexual addiction: An addiction perspective. And Coleman, E. Sexual compulsion vs. sexual addiction: The debate continues. *SIECUS Report, 14*(6):4–10. Two sides of an ongoing controversy.

Mains, G. (1988). *Urban Aboriginals: A Celebration of Leather-Sexuality.* East Haven, CT: Gay Sunskine/Inland Book Co. Insights into leather fetishes.

Money, J. (1985). *The Destroying Angel.* Buffalo: Prometheus Press. A nontechnical survey of fetishes and their causes.

*S*exual Health
  Sexual Unfolding
  Sexual Skills
*S*exual Adequacy
  Definition
  Work or Play?
  Sexual Communications
*W*hen the Sexual
  Becomes Problematic
  Sexual Difficulties
    and Problems
*W*hat Causes a
  Sexual Problem
  or Difficulty?
  Some Biological Factors
  Some Psychological
    Causes
  Some Social or
    Interpersonal Causes
*S*ex Therapies
  The PLISSIT Model
  Combined Therapies
  Sex Therapy for Gay
    Persons
  What To Look for
    in a Therapist
*T*ypes of Sexual
  Difficulties
  Desire Phase Difficulties
  Sexual Arousal
    Difficulties
  Orgasm Difficulties
  Other Sexual Difficulties
*D*ealing with the
  Unavoidable

Chapter 21

*S*exual Problems and Therapies

Special Consultants

Sandra R. Leiblum, Ph.D., professor, Clinical Psychiatry; Co-director, Sexual Counseling Service, University of Medicine and Dentistry of New Jersey, Robert Wood Johnson Medical School; and co-editor of *Sexual Desire Disorders* and *Principles and Practice of Sex Therapy*.

Julian W. Slowinski, Psy.D., marital and sex therapist, Pennsylvania Hospital, and faculty member, University of Pennsylvania School of Medicine, Department of Psychiatry.

How common are sexual problems and difficulties? Many clinicians would say, "More common than the common cold." Sooner or later, almost every man and woman is bound to experience some kind of sexual problem or dysfunction. Men may have difficulty getting an erection or not have an erection when they want one. Men may also experience early ejaculation or not be able to reach orgasm. Women may have difficulty becoming aroused. Vaginal lubrication may not be sufficient for comfortable intercourse. Women may have difficulty or not be able to reach orgasm. Women and men may experience painful intercourse. Both men and women may experience a lack of sexual desire, differences in the level of sexual desire with a partner, and sexual aversion.

This chapter discusses sexual problems and difficulties. As a framework we explore some factors in sexual health and what it means to be sexually adequate. Next we discuss the general causes of sexual problems and difficulties and therapies used to treat them. Finally, common sexual problems and difficulties are described with some specific therapies.

Sexual Health

Sexual Unfolding

After working with college students for many years, Lorna and Philip Sarrel identified six aspects of personal development, what they call *sexual unfolding*, which they believe are important in developing a healthy sexuality. Although these aspects of sexual development overlap and affect each other, separating them in a brief list may help us see how each applies in our own lives. The six aspects of sexual unfolding are as follows:

1. Growing intellectually and developing an understanding of our sexual nature;
2. Developing a set of moral principles and personal values;
3. Learning to make decisions about our lifestyle, career, and the kinds of relationships we want;
4. Developing a growing sense of our personal sexual identity;
5. Separating ourselves gradually from our family and from the role of a child to become more independent; and
6. Becoming aware of the role sexuality plays in the framework of our life, including its spiritual aspects.

In our early years, we develop these six aspects of our sexuality at our own pace. We manage some of these tasks quite well, with a minimum of problems. In others we may lag behind and falter momentarily. But, to appreciate and enjoy our sexual potential in healthy, rewarding relationships, we need to develop and balance our progress in all six areas (Sarrel & Sarrel 1979).

Sexual Skills

When the Sarrels asked college students about the challenges these basic aspects posed, the students came up with a list of specific skills. Although all of us grapple with these tasks more or less throughout our lives, some of them are more important for young adults. Which of the following challenges are most

Figure 21.1. In our childhood and adolescent years, we gradually develop the skills we need to relate intimately with others. The give-and-take of early casual friendships builds our self-confidence and prepares us for closer and more intimate friendships in adult life.

difficult at this point in your life? Which tasks were more difficult for you five or ten years ago? Where have you made the most progress? Have you been avoiding the challenge of any one area?

1. To what extent have you developed a secure awareness of yourself as a male or female? Are you as comfortable and as positive as you would like to be with your body?

2. To what extent have you learned to deal with, overcome, or moderate the guilt, shame, and childhood inhibitions associated with sexual thoughts and behavior?

3. How have you adjusted to the gradually loosening of your ties to parents and family, and with taking responsibility for your own life?

4. How comfortable and clear are you about your gender orientation? How comfortable are you with persons who do not share your gender orientation?

5. To what extent have you learned what you enjoy and find pleasurable, or do not enjoy, in a sexual relationship? Are you comfortable with your present level of sexual expression?

6. How have you learned to avoid or deal with sexual problems? To what extent have you become comfortable with the eroticism of your own body, with self-pleasuring? Are you comfortable with expanding this eroticism in relations with others?

7. Are you comfortable with your changing awareness of your sexuality and sexual behavior? To what extent have you seriously considered your options as a sexual adult? How much have you thought about the advantages and disadvantages of remaining single, living with someone, being married, having an open or a closed marriage, or remaining celibate?

8. How responsible are you for yourself? How aware are you of your potential or actual role in the sexual unfolding of a partner? If you are having genital intercourse, how have you taken responsibility for contraception and sexually transmitted diseases?

9. Finally, to what extent have you learned to experience eroticism as one aspect of an intimate relationship? We do not mean that all satisfying eroticism must occur in an intimate relationship. However, given our culture and conditioning, increasing our ability to find love and eroticism in the same relationship is one way of achieving a mature sexual personality (Sarrel & Sarrel 1979).

Despite the common impression that sexual desire and expression are natural and almost instinctive, it is obvious from these six tasks and nine challenges that reaching our full potential as sexual persons is not all that simple. Sexual problems and difficulties can often be traced back to our failure to accomplish one or more of these tasks and challenges as well as to other factors, both organic and psychological.

Sexual Adequacy

Definition

Sexual adequacy can be defined as the ability of two people to relate with each other in a sexual way that is satisfying and rewarding to both. But for many people, this simple definition is complicated by the unrealistic expectations that are often associated with sexual performance. For many men, adequacy is defined as how quickly they can have an erection or bring their partner to orgasm. For women, adequacy may mean how quickly they can achieve orgasm. For many, a rewarding and satisfying sexual encounter is defined by vaginal intercourse, even though orgasm can also be achieved in other ways. Some couples who achieve orgasm before or after intercourse by manual or oral stimulation or with a vibrator think there may be something wrong with them because the woman doesn't have orgasm during vaginal intercourse. Other couples feel inadequate if they enjoy all kinds of sexual pleasuring but one or the other partner doesn't always reach orgasm. There is also the myth that a person should be able to "perform" 100% every time he or she has the opportunity for or wants sex. In trying to decide whether we are sexually adequate, we are often misled by unrealistic expectations of what others, especially the media, tell us lovemaking *should be*.

Work or Play?

Good sex is often equated with "scoring," "conquering," "going all the way," or "getting home." In this context, orgasm during intercourse is the supreme *goal*, an obsessive need (Highlight Box 21.1).

Figure 21.2.

"You're impotent? Darling, we're made for each other. I'm frigid."

When the work ethic elevates some aspect of sexual intimacy to an obsessive goal, we quickly forget that intimacy is a process of play, communication, and love. Caressing, sharing, and pleasuring of all kinds are as much a part of sex as intercourse and orgasm. All sexual activities do not necessarily have to culminate in intercourse. Masturbation is a classic form of solo or shared sexual play. A sensual massage or noncoital love play may provide more intimacy and enjoyment than the rush to score (Figure 21.3).

In *Total Sex*, Herbert and Roberta Otto reject the sexual work ethic. They describe sexual intimacy as a "spontaneous, free-flowing, creative, joyous, or pleasure activity. Relatively devoid of structure and without the element of competition, sexual play is essentially a leisure activity with directions emerging from within the persons" (Otto & Otto 1972:299). Feminists and others have also insisted on a broader, more playful notion of sex, more compatible with women's greater erotic possibilities, and more respectful of women's needs. In today's culture, normal sex is no longer restricted to a two-act drama of foreplay and intercourse that culminates in male orgasm and at least a display of female appreciation (Ehrenrich, Hess, & Jacobs 1987:183).

Sexual Communications

Men and women are remarkably alike when it comes to sexual arousal and response. The labia, clitoris, and vulva and the penis and scrotum all respond to erotic stimulation. Vasocongestion of erectile tissues occurs in both men and women, producing pleasurable reactions. Men cannot fake an erection, but neither can a woman fake vaginal lubrication. Men and women may pretend

HIGHLIGHT BOX 21.1.
WHAT IS THE GOAL OF SEX?

Traditionally intercourse and orgasm have been the dominant goal of sexual intimacy. (a) Progress toward this goal was typically described as getting from first to second to third base and home, scoring with intercourse and an orgasm, at least for the male. Scoring then becomes a performance pressure, especially for men, and the measure of one's manhood, or femininity.

(b) When sexual intimacy is approached as a non-goal-oriented game, with an ethic of playfulness, whatever happens is accepted for what it brings in the way of sexual pleasure, communication, intimacy, and oneness. There is no set game plan, no set objective, except to enjoy the moment and what it brings.

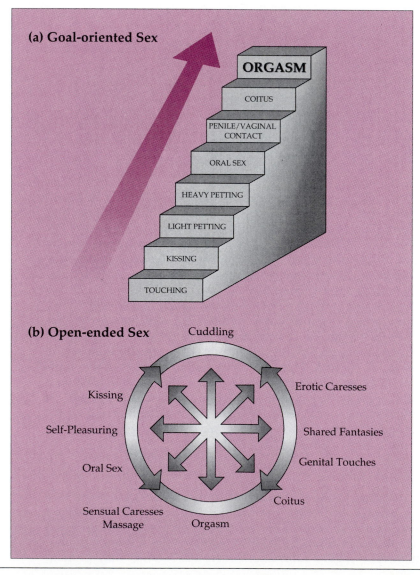

(a) Goal-oriented Sex

ORGASM
COITUS
PENILE/VAGINAL CONTACT
ORAL SEX
HEAVY PETTING
LIGHT PETTING
KISSING
TOUCHING

(b) Open-ended Sex

Cuddling
Erotic Caresses
Kissing
Self-Pleasuring
Shared Fantasies
Oral Sex
Genital Touches
Sensual Caresses Massage
Coitus
Orgasm

Figure 21.3. *Noncoital erotic play, or outercourse, can add variety to a couple's intimacy.*

to have an orgasm and to enjoy lovemaking because of performance pressures, or because they don't want to hurt or disappoint their partner. Continually pretending to have orgasms can and often does lead to resentment and even anger. Yet, whether a relationship is just starting or has been going on for many years, men and women may be hesitant to tell their partner some position or some touch is a sexual turn-off or unpleasant when the partner assumes that what he or she is doing is the ultimate turn-on. Open communications and trust are vital in a healthy sexual interaction. A message that might be taken as a reflection on the partner's lovemaking skills can be turned into a positive message when you use "I language," such as "I feel . . . ," "I would like to . . . ."

When the Sexual Becomes Problematic

Sexual Difficulties and Problems

A sexual disorder or dysfunction is a recurring inhibition or lack of a natural healthy response at either the desire, the excitement, or the orgasm stage in the sexual response cycle (Chapter 7; DSM-III-R:290). Although some still use the technical terms disorder and dysfunction, many therapists today prefer the less negative term **sexual difficulty**. We will use this less technical term, speaking of sexual difficulties instead of sexual disorders or dysfunctions.

In the desire stage, a sexual difficulty may involve a chronic lack of interest in sex, an interest in but avoidance of sexual intimacy, an aversion to sex, or a conflict about the amount or type of sexual intimacy a couple desires. A person may also experience a sexual difficulty with heightened or "excessive" sexual desire.

A man or woman experiencing a sexual difficulty in the excitement stage wants to engage in sexual relations but can't become sexually aroused enough to have an erection or vaginal lubrication that allows him or her to have an orgasm. An excitement stage problem may also involve the subjective sense of a lack of arousal. Spastic contractions of the vaginal muscles which prevent penile penetration are another form of inhibited sexual arousal in women.

A man who has an erection but ejaculates early or cannot reach orgasm during intercourse, or during masturbation, has an orgasmic difficulty. A woman with an orgasmic difficulty has a natural sexual desire and becomes sexually aroused during love play but then cannot reach orgasm during intercourse or during masturbation.

Sexual problems are less specific than sexual difficulties or dysfunctions because their effects are not evident in the lack of an erection, vaginal lubrication, or an orgasm. A couple with a sexual problem function perfectly well, experiencing no difficulty with the level of their sexual desire, with any lack of erection or vaginal lubrication, or with achieving orgasm. But they feel "something is wrong." Even as they function naturally, one or the other, or both feel(s) anxious, guilty, or just uncomfortable about their sexual behavior. Following are some examples:

- A young unmarried couple or a gay or lesbian couple very much enjoys their sexual intimacy, but both partners feel somehow uneasy about their intimacy because of unresolved conflicts with their own and their families' religious values.

- A wife thoroughly enjoys sex with her husband but feels that her intense pleasure and multiple orgasms are somehow not befitting her role as a "good wife and mother."

- One partner wants to try a new sexual technique. The other partner goes along but feels very uncomfortable, somewhat guilty, or "dirty" about it.

The definition of a sexual difficulty or dysfunction mentioned earlier included a component which requires some qualification. The concept of a *natural healthy response* includes different degrees of response, of desire, arousal, and orgasm intensity, within a natural range. The existence of a natural range means that we don't have to always function sexually at 100% all the time. Athletes use their natural strengths to function regularly. They exert themselves in peak performances occasionally. We allow and expect competitive athletes to have some slack days. Yet, when it comes to sex, there is a common expectation, based on what we call a natural response, that suggests we should always be ready, willing, and capable of responding fully to any sexual stimulus or opportunity at any time. In real life, everyone encounters occasions when we don't function sexually the way we would like. That is a natural occurrence, and does not mean we have a sexual problem or dysfunction.

The term *natural* also alerts us to different cultural expectations which change over time. In our contemporary culture, a woman who has difficulty reaching orgasm may be said to experience inhibited female orgasm which *The Diagnostic and Statistics Manual* lists under "Orgasm Disorders or Dysfunctions." In Victorian times, however, such a woman would not have been considered sexually dysfunctional. Instead of being treated, a Victorian woman with inhibited orgasm would have been held in esteem by her husband and others as a "good woman and mother." Our focus on sexual desire problems today is a cultural artifact, as is the recent concern with what some term an excess of sexual desire or sexual addiction.

Figure 21.4.

Sexual problems and difficulties have a history. When a person has always experienced a particular dysfunction, it is called a **primary sexual dysfunction**. A man who has never been able to achieve an erection sufficient for intercourse, for instance, is said to have a primary **erectile difficulty** (dysfunction). A primary arousal problem would mean that a woman has never had vaginal lubrication sufficient to facilitate intercourse. A **secondary** or acquired **sexual difficulty**, on the other hand, means that the man or woman has been able to achieve and enjoy sexual intercourse in the past or with another partner, but now has a difficulty regularly or with a particular partner. Sexual problems can also be primary or secondary.

In the next two sections, we examine what causes sexual problems and difficulties and then describe specific types.

What Causes a Sexual Problem or Difficulty?

Sexual problems, as you might suspect, may have a very simple cause, being triggered by some misinformation, an unfounded fear, anxiety, or by some stressful situation. But because sexual problems involve vague feelings, their actual nature and cause may be difficult to track down, identify, and resolve. Sexual problems always have a psychological rather than organic or physical cause. They are rooted in feelings, emotions, beliefs, and the like.

HIGHLIGHT BOX 21.2.
THE CAROUSEL DYNAMICS

When two persons are interacting in an intimate relationship they can easily get caught up in what sex therapist Don Sloan calls the carousel dynamics. A fear of inadequate sexual performance and communication problems are two factors that often work together in a merry-go-round effect that keeps building to a breaking point in the relationship. Either partner can climb on the carousel as a result of a single frustrating experience. When lack of communication leads to hurt, anger, and getting even, with both partners not discussing the problem but reacting emotionally, the couple may experience a major sexual difficulty.

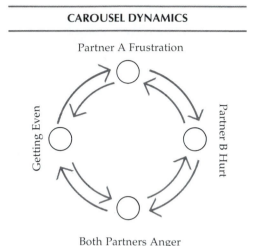

CAROUSEL DYNAMICS

Partner A Frustration

Getting Even

Partner B Hurt

Both Partners Anger

Sexual difficulties, on the other hand, usually result from the interaction of several factors. Different biological, psychological, and interpersonal factors can combine to produce any one of several different difficulties in the desire, arousal, or orgasmic stages of the sexual response cycle. The same factor may produce quite different results in two different persons. For example, one victim of rape who has not worked through this experience may not feel any sexual desire and may avoid sex altogether. Another rape victim may still desire sex but experiences a mental/physical block at arousal and does not respond naturally to love play or has vaginal spasms that prevent penile penetration. A third rape victim may have natural responses of desire and arousal but experience inhibited orgasm.

Usually it takes a combination of biological, psychological, and social factors interacting over an extended period of time to produce a sexual difficulty. It is simplistic and misleading to try to trace any sexual difficulty, except perhaps a mild simple one, to a single cause. For this reason, many sex therapists today speak of the *biopsychosocial* origins of sexual difficulties. Biological factors usually interact with personal and interpersonal factors to produce sexual difficulties.

Some people experience good sex in a bad relationship, and others have bad sex in a good relationship. When someone seeks help with a sexual problem or difficulty, the therapist tries to piece together the combination of circumstances that led to its development or emergence (Engel 1980; Leiblum & Pervin 1980, 1989; Messer 1986).

Some Biological Factors

A variety of biological factors can be a major or contributing factor in a sexual difficulty. Most therapists today believe that biological factors are often as important as psychological factors in causing sexual problems. They may be the primary factor in a quarter of all sexual difficulties.

Diabetes, kidney dialysis, stress, poor nutrition, hormone imbalances, cancer therapies, pelvic, vaginal, and abdominal infections, spinal cord injuries, obesity, and abdominal surgery are other biological factors often associated with a variety of sexual difficulties (Bullard in Leiblum & Rosen 1988).

The other major category of biological or organic factors involve medications which may interfere with or block natural sexual responses. Tranquilizers, sedatives, and hypnotics prescribed for anxiety, muscle spasms, and insomnia may reduce sexual desire. These same drugs may also inhibit sexual arousal, ejaculation, or orgasm. Antidepressants may cause erectile problems, delayed ejaculation, and lack of ejaculation in men and inhibited arousal or delayed orgasm in women. Medications for high blood pressure, migraine headaches, and angina may decrease sexual desire in both men and women, create erectile and ejaculation difficulties, and produce bizarre erotic dreams. Diuretics used for high blood pressure and fluid retention commonly cause erectile difficulties.

Amphetamines used as a diet aid and antispasmodics used in treating ulcers can decrease sexual desire and bring about erectile difficulty in men. Sex hormones, both those in the contraceptive pill and those used in the treatment of cancer, bone, and menstrual problems, may increase or decrease libido.

Because many doctors today are aware of these possible side effects, they are able to change the prescription and reduce or eliminate these problems before the patient decides to give up taking the medication because of the side effect on his or her sexual responses (Leyson & Francoeur 1990; Seagrave 1988).

On-the-street illegal drugs have their own sexual side effects. Although marijuana may increase sexual desire in the first half hour, its more lasting effect is to depress libido. Cocaine and LSD have a similar effect, with erectile difficulties as an added consequence. Alcohol and barbituates may reduce inhibitions in small doses, but they also depress the central nervous system and commonly interfere with sexual responses. Chronic use of alcohol and barbituates can result in loss of sexual desire and arousal problems.

Some Psychological Causes

In most cases, the psychological causes of sexual problems are not deeply rooted in mental disorders. In many cases, they have obvious causes that are easily treated (Highlight Box 21.2).

Negative Sexual Experiences

Many of us have had negative sexual experiences, particularly in adolescence or young adulthood. Anxiety, nervousness, and a lack of experience may be compounded by too much alcohol, leaving a young male incapable of having an erection when he desperately wants one. Is he impotent? Not likely. However, this negative experience may lead to feelings of inadequacy and a fear of trying again under better circumstances. If this fear continues, the young man may end up with a persistent erectile problem.

A child who is sexually molested may be puzzled or even disregard the experience, but if parents and other adults react very emotionally when they find out about the incident, what might be a neutral experience can be turned into a very traumatizing event which then builds into a long-term sexual difficulty. Many people suppress or forget traumatic experiences until a problem emerges that brings the negative experience to the surface where it can no longer be ignored.

Negative Learning

Despite our more open attitudes toward sexuality today, some children still receive negative messages about their bodies and sex. Parents who never say anything about sex may still convey a subtle but convincing message that sex is dirty, animalistic, something unmentionable, or at best unimportant. At other times, the negative message is more direct, as when a mother warns her daughter to never let a man touch her "down there" because sex only causes trouble and pregnancy.

What effect do you think a parent has on a child's view of sex when the child's father or mother yells and slams the door on a child who accidentally walks into the bathroom and catches a parent naked? How would you avoid giving a negative message about sexuality if you were a parent and your child wandered into your bedroom in the middle of the night when you were making love?

Body Images

When people have a poor body image and do not feel comfortable or happy with their looks, it often translates into a general insecurity that makes them reluctant to get sexually involved. Avoidance then becomes an effective defense mechanism.

Not infrequently, healthy and sexually active persons find themselves faced with a new body image and the problem of adjusting to a new situation. An automobile or skiing accident can suddenly put us in a wheelchair. A natural event like pregnancy or aging can alter our body image. Breast surgery, cancer, crippling arthritis, or multiple sclerosis can change our image of being sexually desirable. Coping with an altered body image means developing an awareness that, whatever the handicap, we can still be attractive to others and can still enjoy relating sexually.

Stress and Fatigue

Occasional periods of stress or fatigue are inevitable. Stress can so preoccupy someone that any interest in sex disappears. Mental and physical fatigue are a common cause for decreased sexual desire and sexual problems. Family or financial worries and the depression that may follow failing an exam, losing a job, or having a fight with a close friend or partner can easily interfere with our sexual responses.

Exercise, yoga, meditation, and a change of environment are good ways of coping with stress and fatigue. Counseling and training in stress management can be helpful. Couples trying to balance careers and limited time together may find it helpful to adjust their schedules so that their sexual activity is not relegated to a time when a couple is most tired and tense.

Performance Fears

Men, more than women, are likely to suffer from performance fears. This fear includes the pressure on the male to orchestrate, initiate, and be ever-ready to perform sexually. Another problem for men is that they are less likely than women to admit their fears of perhaps not being sexually functional (Barbach 1982; Zilbergeld 1978).

Performance pressures may lead to **spectatoring**. Like a spectator at a sports events, we sometimes become sexual spectators. We carefully watch, monitor, grade, and compare both our own sexual performance and that of our partner. It is almost as if we were withdrawing from our bodies and hovering over the sexual experience as an observer. Spectatoring can be a destructive behavior because it takes away from the spontaneity of the experience and sets up standards of performance we expect to meet or exceed each time we have sex. Spectatoring can also produce anxiety and tension that inhibit our sexual responses (Highlight Box 21.3).

HIGHLIGHT BOX 21.3.
SEX AS A STATUS SYMBOL

Are you having mutual orgasm, mutual simultaneous orgasm, multiple orgasms, or just plain orgasm? Are you ready to go all the way every time the slightest opportunity arises? Have you found the G spot? Have you experienced female ejaculation? Are you sexually inadequate because sometimes you would rather cuddle than have hot, passionate sex? Do you sometimes feel that you are not as sexy or attractive as a friend or acquaintance?

Somehow these kinds of questions and comparisons always leave us coming out on the short end, not quite measuring up to some assumed performance standard. These questions and comparisons may seem important and real but in everyday life they only create problems. We are tempted to feel that others are enjoying more and better sex than we are. We begin to feel sexually unfulfilled. Sex then becomes something we have to work at. We feel we always have to improve our track record. We have to keep up with our peers and friends because they somehow set the standard for our sexual lifestyles and enjoyment. In the process,

"I CAN'T REMEMBER THE FIRST TIME I HAD AN ORGASM. I CAN'T REMEMBER THE LAST TIME, EITHER."

we forget that people characteristically improve on reality when they tell others about their sexual lives.

Some Social or Interpersonal Causes

Social and Peer Pressures

Social pressures on women begin at birth. Many girls are still taught to be sweet, delicate, and ladylike, meaning sexually passive, nonassertive, and accepting of certain feminine roles. Women raised with this stereotype may find it difficult to shift gears suddenly and become an active, interesting sexual partner on a par with their partners.

Men, on the other hand, often learn to measure their masculinity against certain standards of sexual performance. A young man who does not measure up to the expected standard of sexual activity and variety may feel inadequate and insecure.

Ignoring Issues of Personal Risk

The growing numbers of single and divorced persons and the increasing acceptance of nonmarital sex naturally increases the number of men and women who have several sexual partners over a period of months or years. Before the emergence of herpes and AIDS, men and women could move into a new relationship with little worry. Men assumed that women were using the Pill, an IUD, or a diaphragm. Today, regardless of what contraceptive a woman or couple uses, condom protection for both partners is a realistic issue that needs to be discussed in a new relationship. Gay men seeking a partner are confronted with this problem often.

Ignoring or repressing a realistic fear about AIDS and other STDs may create hidden worry or anxiety that may interfere with natural sexual functioning. Although it may be awkward or uncomfortable to raise the issue of reducing our risk for AIDS and other sexually transmitted diseases, dealing with this reality up front can enhance the sexual interaction and make for a more responsible and healthy relationship. Coleman and Reese (1988) note that the fear of AIDS has had a major effect on the sexual lives of gay men. Fear of contracting the AIDS virus can be a major barrier to sexual desire. Obviously, living with a partner who has either tested sero-positive or who has ARCS or AIDS can be a strong deterrent to the experience and expression of sexual interest.

Conflicts and Tensions in a Relationship

A sexual difficulty may develop as a symptom of a basically unhealthy relationship. Unresolved tensions and conflicts in nonsexual areas of a relationship are often reflected in a couple's sex life. Repressed hostility to a parent or other authority figure may be unconsciously transposed into a hostility toward one's sexual partner. For instance, a man who resents working for a female supervisor may find this attitude surfaces in his sexual relationship with his female partner (Kaplan 1974, 1979, 1983).

For many couples, erotic desire depends on the unexpected. Even the most loving couples can suffer from a relationship that has become routine and monotonous. Researchers have found that the intensity and emotions of romantic love usually last only from six months to two years before fading. The relationship, and its sexual expression, then either ends, matures into a deep, intimate friendship, or turns into a routine relationship (Ramey 1976; Rubin 1973, 1977; Tennov 1979).

The routine relationship may be alleviated by developing and sharing a richer fantasy life or by exploring new ways of making love and enjoying non-coital outercourse. Some people find the familiar to be monotonous and unexciting when compared to the lure of a new relationship. However, the new relationship may soon become familiar, and the pattern often repeats itself. Increased life expectancy, pressures of a dual-career relationship, and heightened expectations of intimacy and sexual fulfillment have redefined the meaning of commitment, love, and fidelity for many couples. For some, this redefinition has meant opening up the relationship to allow sexual relationships with other persons besides the primary partner. There is no way that a couple can predict the outcome of nonexclusive sexual intimacy. For some couples, the experience is positive and strengthens the primary relationship. For others, it is disastrous and leads to a breakup of the primary relationship. Thus a couple should carefully weigh all aspects before entering into secondary relationships (Knapp & Whitehurst 1978; Murstein 1978; Ramey 1976).

It is important to stress that many couples who have lived together for many years do not become bored with their sexual lives. If intimacy has become routine, it may still be pleasurable and fulfilling.

Situations That May Trigger a Sexual Difficulty

The lack of privacy in a college dormitory, a roommate who wants to study, or parking in a lovers' lane can result in an uneasiness that may inhibit one's sexual responses. Couples forced by finances to live with parents may find the spontaneity of their love play inhibited by parental proximity. Couples who do not have their own place to go may find their only option is a budget motel or their parents' living room sofa before the parents come home from work. Although such situations can be negative and stressful, they can be a source of sexual arousal for some people who associate sex with risk.

Sex Therapies

The PLISSIT Model

Twenty years ago when sex therapies were just being developed, we had little understanding of the varieties of sexual difficulties and the range of causes from very simple to serious personality disorders that could cause them. However, therapists soon realized that many people did not require intensive therapy. Sometimes even the simplest intervention could prove quite effective.

This realization was incorporated into the PLISSIT model of sex therapy (Annon 1974, 1976). Very often, simple sexual problems and difficulties can be resolved without resorting to intensive sex therapy. Using the PLISSIT filter model, a psychologist, counselor, or sex therapist can sort out the large number of people with simple sexual problems who can profit from simple therapies.

The acronym **PLISSIT** refers to four stages in sexual therapy:

- Permission giving (P);
- Limited Information (LI)—this second step is often used at the same time with permission giving;

Figure 21.5. The PLISSIT Model of Sexual Therapies. *The PLISSIT filter model of sexual therapies illustrates how persons with mild sexual problems and difficulties can be handled with brief interventions and simple therapies. If a brief therapy involving permission giving and limited information does not work, the person or couple can seek further help designed to address their particular problem. In most cases brief interventions and specific suggestions will resolve the difficulty. If not, professional help and intensive therapy are available.*

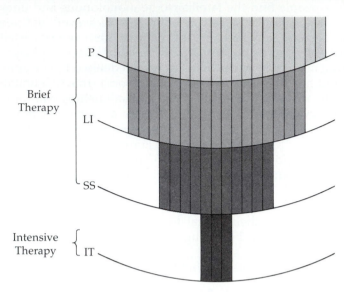

PLISSIT FILTER MODEL OF SEXUAL THERAPIES

Brief Therapy

P

LI

SS

Intensive Therapy — IT

Permission giving and receiving from an authority or someone we respect.

Limited information picked up from a friend, sexuality course, or reading.

Specific suggestion (behavior exercise or suggestion on reducing stress or situation).

Intensive therapy with a trained certified sex therapist or counselor.

- Specific Suggestions (SS); and
- Intensive Therapy, (IT), required by relatively few persons with sexual problems (Figure 21.5).

Permission Giving and Limited Information

In our sex-negative society, many of us occasionally get the feeling that what we are doing or would like to do sexually is somehow perverted, or deviant. All we may need is reassurance from a friend or an authority figure that what we are feeling or doing is perfectly natural. Many people in our sex-negative culture need an authority figure to say, "Yes, it is natural. If you enjoy it and are comfortable with it, then why not continue doing it?" To reinforce this permission giving, the authority figure may add some factual information about the feeling or concern. Both permission giving and limited information focus on a specific sexual concern. Reassurance, support, and information are provided so that the person can comfortably continue the behavior, or change it if so desired.

Permission giving and limited information are often helpful in dealing with sexual problems that result from anxieties and misinformation about sexual thoughts, fantasies, feelings, and behaviors. Television talk shows dealing with sexual issues like spouse abuse, sexual dysfunctions, and relationship problems can prevent or resolve many sexual difficulties by providing limited information and permission for listeners to discuss their concerns and seek help. Human sexuality courses in colleges are another source for these two levels of sexual therapy. These courses give permission for students and their friends to express, discuss, and ask questions about their sexual concerns. Textbooks for such courses contain considerable information that can prevent or resolve concerns that might otherwise turn into sexual difficulties. This same permission giving and limited information is a major source of sexual enrichment as well as therapy and preventive medicine.

There is one situation in which permission giving is not appropriate, however. In a situation that involves criminal activity or some behavior that could harm someone, permission giving would be inappropriate. Outside this exception, a friend, family member, or even an acquaintance can give us a helping hand toward a more rewarding and satisfying sexual life by sharing a piece of information about sex that answers a question or removes some guilt or anxiety we might feel.

Specific Suggestions

When permission giving and limited information do not resolve a sexual problem, *specific suggestions* which address the problem may resolve it. Before offering a specific suggestion, a friend, therapist, or counselor needs to know exactly what the problem is. A counselor or therapist usually uncovers this essential issue by taking a brief history of the problem. A sex problem history contains the following five questions:

1. Describe the problem you experience.
2. When did it start and how has it developed?
3. What do you think caused it?
4. What kind of medical, professional, or self-treatment have you used?
5. How would you like this problem resolved?

Once the problem and its history has been identified, a solution may be obvious to a counselor who has some knowledge of human sexual behavior. For instance, a couple in a college dormitory may experience a lack of sexual desire, inhibited arousal, or a problem with orgasm. When they examine the history of their problem it may become apparent that they are uncomfortable and inhibited by the dorm setting and its lack of privacy. A useful specific suggestion might focus on helping the couple find a more relaxing and comfortable place for their love play. A married or gay couple with a similar problem might be advised to take a weekend vacation, even if it's just at the motel around the corner. Specific suggestions like those just described may seem too simplistic to be helpful, but remember, many sexual problems have relatively simple, often superficial causes that can easily be eliminated once they are identified.

One specific suggestion commonly recommended by sexual counselors involves the sensate focus exercises. These exercises may be helpful when a couple has a conflict in the levels of their sexual desire, or experiences a lack of desire for sexual relations. They are particularly helpful in dealing with performance pressures and inhibited sexual arousal. Therapists also use the sensate focus exercises to help couples overcome problems caused by poor body image, negative learning, inexperience, poor communications, boredom, and fatigue. In addition, some couples with no sexual difficulty occasionally use the sensate focus exercises to enrich their sexual communications and pleasuring skills.

In the sensate focus exercises a couple is asked to approach sexual intimacy as mutual pleasuring instead of focusing on the goals of sexual arousal, intercourse, and orgasm. The **sensate focus exercises** concentrate on sensual play

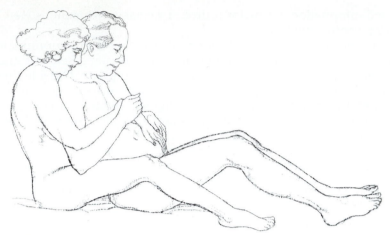

Figure 21.6. *The sensate focus exercises are a behavioral therapy that can help a couple with a variety of sexual problems and difficulties, including an uneasiness with nudity, genital touches, sexual inexperience, poor body image, an earlier sexual trauma, negative messages about sexual intimacy, and so on. In the position shown here the male is directing his partner in genital exploration and touching.*

(Figure 21.6). Neither partner is expected to become sexually aroused or have genital intercourse. The emphasis is on relaxation and playfully learning what gives your partner pleasure without expecting anything in return. This focus makes the exercises equally useful for gay, lesbian, and straight couples with a sexual problem or difficulty.

Each partner takes the opportunity to show the other what kinds of touches he or she enjoys most, where his or her most sensitive and erotic places are, and how he or she likes to be touched. Each partner knows best what is most enjoyable and stimulating, and each needs to communicate this information verbally or by directing the partner's hand.

The exercises are done in the nude and with the lights on. The couple moves from simple body exploration, to nongenital pleasuring, to genital/sexual pleasuring without any need to be aroused, to more intense sexual pleasuring. The sensate focus exercises are not an exercise in penile-vaginal intercourse but rather guided lessons in becoming more comfortable with erotic play and sexual pleasuring. The performance pressures to become aroused and to have an erection or orgasm are removed because the couples are forbidden to expect or demand these outcomes.

Some other specific ideas recommended by sex therapists are different coital positions, the PC muscle exercises (see Chapter 7), the partner sexual exam, and the stop-go technique used in treating difficulties with early ejaculation (Figure 21.7).

Intensive Therapy

Relatively few people who encounter occasional mild sexual problems and difficulties need intensive therapy, the fourth level in the PLISSIT model. Today, sex therapists use a variety of techniques including behavioral therapy, psychotherapy, hypnosis, and biofeedback, and focus on broader issues of relationship and systems counseling.

Figure 21.7. *Varying the position for sexual pleasuring, oral, anal, and vaginal sex allows the partners to alternate in the active or receiving role, to be more or less active or in control, and to engage in erotic touches of all types. The position shown here allows the woman to control penetration and thrusting while allowing her partner to pleasure her clitoris, vulva, and breasts with his fingers or a vibrator.*

Combined Therapies

Sex therapy, as originally proposed by William Masters and Virginia Johnson in 1966, was a brief, intensive reeducation process that focused on behaviors and behavior-oriented exercises like sensate focus. It appeared to be highly successful because Masters and Johnson worked with a select population of healthy people in basically solid relationships. After their success with these relatively simple cases, they and other therapists began to encounter more difficult cases which could not be solved with the original behavioral approach. A broader therapy, using different techniques including psychological counseling, was needed.

In the early 1970s, Joseph LoPiccolo advocated the use of additional approaches designed to reduce anxiety within the behavioral therapy suggested by Masters and Johnson. William Simon and John Gagnon stressed the importance of dealing with social scripting in sex therapy. Harold Lief pointed out the importance of nonsexual interpersonal issues and communications problems as factors in sexual difficulties. Lief also advocated incorporating the principles of marital therapy into sex therapy. As therapists began to integrate other modes of psychotherapy, such as cognitive, gestalt, and imagery therapies, it soon became apparent that there was no single official form of sex therapy. In the early 1980s, some sex therapists were sensitized to the possible impact and influence ethnic values can exert on a sexual problem by the pioneering work of family therapists like M. McGoldrick, J. K. Pearce, and J. Giordano (1982).

Helen Singer Kaplan made what may be the most profound contribution to sex therapy since Masters and Johnson's original work when she blended traditional concepts from psychotherapy and psychoanalysis with cognitive psychology and behavioral therapy. Kaplan's "New Sex Therapy" (1979) dealt with such important therapeutic issues as resistance, repression, and unconscious motivations. This new approach focused not only on altering behavior with techniques like the sensate focus exercises but also with exploring and modifying covert or unconscious thought patterns and motivations which underlie a sexual difficulty (Engel 1980; Messer 1986).

Modern sex therapy has also incorporated important advances in medicine and pharmacology. More precise knowledge and techniques now allow a therapist to develop a hormone profile for a patient, monitor nocturnal penile tumescence, and check penile and vaginal blood flow. As patients reported the negative side effects of medications on their sexual responses, doctors developed strategies for altering the course of medication. New surgical methods could improve penile blood supply; prosthetics and other aids like injections and electrical devices to stimulate erection were developed. Antidepressants, antianxiety, and antipanic medications are being explored for use in conjunction with psychotherapy in treating desire phase problems.

Today, few therapists who deal with sexual difficulties see themselves as pure sex therapists. More and more, the term *sex therapy* refers to a focus of intervention rather than to a distinctive and exclusive technique. Individual psychologists, psychotherapists, marriage counselors, and family therapists may be more or less skilled in dealing with sexual problems, but each tends to apply those interventions and techniques they are more comfortable with.

Informal support groups also provide opportunities for dealing with sexual problems and difficulties. Many hospitals and service organizations provide workshops and support groups for patients recovering from heart attacks and for persons with diabetes, emphysema, multiple sclerosis, cystic fibrosis, arthritis, and other chronic diseases. These support groups usually include both patients and their partners.

Sex Therapy for Gay Persons

Gay and bisexual men and lesbian women experience many of the same sexual difficulties as heterosexually oriented men and women. We all share the same culture, with the same sex-negative conditioning, the same possibility of positive or traumatic early sexual experiences, and the same combination of good and bad fortune in our sexual unfolding. The same biopsychosocial factors that lead to loss of sexual desire, arousal problems, and orgasmic difficulties for straight couples produce similar results for gay and lesbian couples. The sexual therapies and behavioral exercises used with straight couples are equally helpful in treating the sexual problems of lesbian, gay, and bisexually oriented persons, but there are some important differences (Figure 21.8).

Margaret Nichols notes that lesbian women report the lowest level of sexual exchange of pair-bonded couples. She wonders whether lesbian women are much less inclined to engage in sex because their relationship lacks male sexual initiative and orchestration. In the case of lesbian couples, the very intimacy that seemingly provides justification for sexual desire may discourage it because of the intimate nature of the lesbian relationship. Nichols suggests that the tendency of lesbian couples to fuse with each other leads them to ignore, discourage, or deny differences between themselves.

Tripp (1975) suggested that sexual desire is dependent on "barriers" and "differences" that two people overcome in sexual relations. This idea led Nichols to note that "One can only desire to have sex with another person when that person in fact *exists* as a distinct, separate reality." Therapy, in this case, means helping the partners in a lesbian relationship to become emotionally autonomous and comfortable with tolerating distance from each other and personal differences (Nichols 1988:387–412).

Gay men face some unique challenges. In addition to the fear of AIDS mentioned earlier, gay men may experience more difficulty than straight men with

Figure 21.8. *Men and women in same-gender relationships encounter similar sexual problems and difficulties as heterosexual couples. Sensate focus exercises can help a gay or lesbian couple overcome performance pressures and arousal and orgasm difficulties, as well as enrich their love play.*

achieving a positive sexual identity, or with fears and conflicts about intimacy; they may experience internalized homophobia, overly rigid male sex-role stereotyping, a failure to resolve early traumas involving sexual or physical abuse, unresolved hostility and fear of men, unresolved grief, and inadequate coping with aging. These factors may lead to desire and arousal problems, but they can also trigger sexual compulsion with very high levels of sexual activity. These factors, along with the lack of social acceptance for homosexuals, puts gay men at special risk for developing chemical dependency patterns, which can cause desire and arousal phase difficulties (Coleman & Reese 1988).

It is much easier today for people with a gay, bi, or lesbian orientation to find a sex therapist who is sensitive to their needs. Informal referral networks and gay activist groups can usually provide names of trained professionals who are sensitive to the needs of the gay, lesbian, and bisexual person.

What to Look for in a Therapist

When you need help with a sexual problem, it is important that you have confidence in the counselor or therapist you choose. Certification as a psychologist, psychotherapist, psychiatrist, family, or marital counselor is essential. In addition, inquire about the counselor's special training in sex therapy. Some counselors and psychologists list AASECT Certified Sex Counselor or Therapist in their credentials. They are certified by the American Association of Sex Educators, Counselors, and Therapists.

Community health departments, health centers in colleges and universities, and hospital community services or health education departments can often provide useful leads to find trained sexual counselors or therapists. Professors of health and sexuality courses and psychology faculty can sometimes recommend a reputable professional.

Types of Sexual Difficulties

As mentioned earlier, sexual problems and difficulties are very common (Highlight Box 21.4). And although the factors behind them share a certain similarity, the same negative learning or experience, fear, bit of misinformation, or situation may produce quite different dysfunctional effects in different persons. Natural functioning may be disrupted, inhibited, or blocked in the desire phase, in the arousal stage, or in the orgasm stage. We look briefly at the different possible problems and some therapies that have proven effective in their treatment.

Desire Phase Difficulties

According to Harold Lief, a pioneer in identifying and treating problems of desire, "Sexual desire is an extraordinarily complicated part of life and there is an enormous range of differences."

Sexual desire depends on adequate hormone levels and the proper functioning of specific circuits and centers in the brain. Even when these factors are functioning properly, psychological factors can inhibit or shut down sexual desire. Some men and women have few sexual fantasies and little or no desire to engage in sexual intimacy because of negative messages they received about sex as children. Emotional tensions and conflicts in a couple relationship may destroy sexual desire in people who, in another situation or relationship, may have a strong sexual desire. In any intimate relationship, differences in the level of sexual desire may create tension and frustration that negatively affect the relationship unless the problem is dealt with (Kaplan 1979, 1983:242).

Sexual Aversion

Some people are completely turned off to any kind of sexual intimacy. For these men and women, any situation or relationship that suggests the possibility of sexual involvement can trigger strong emotions of disgust and fear. **Sexual aversion** may be so strong the person sweats and trembles if he or she cannot escape the threatening situation.

The causes of sexual aversion are always psychological. A traumatic sexual experience, such as rape or sexual abuse, may have left the person with deeply rooted fears about any kind of sexual involvement. The fear of pregnancy or an STD may drown out any sexual desire. Strong sex-negative messages from parents, family, friends, or religion—guilt and shame—may also kill sexual desire. Even though treating sexual aversion means counseling to eliminate the phobia for sex, anxiety-reducing medication may be helpful (Kaplan 1979, 1983; Leiblum & Rosen 1988:7–8).

HIGHLIGHT BOX 21.4.
HOW COMMON ARE SEXUAL PROBLEMS AND DIFFICULTIES?

Four out of 5 of the 100 predominantly well-educated, white, middle-class couples interviewed by Frank, Anderson, and Rubinstein (1978) described themselves as happily married. Yet over half the women and over a third of the men admitted they had some sexual problem or difficulty. The results of these interviews, shown here, are similar to the results of 20 other general sex surveys, although these surveys did reveal considerable variability in the frequency of problems and difficulties reported (Nathan 1986).

	WOMEN (%)	MEN (%)
Difficulty		
Difficulty getting excited/getting erection	48	7
Difficulty maintaining excitement/erection	33	9
Reaching orgasm/ejaculation too soon	11	36
Difficulty reaching orgasm/ejaculation	46	4
Inability to have orgasm/ejaculation	15	0
Other Problem		
Partner chooses inconvenient time	31	16
Inability to relax	47	12
Attraction to person(s) other than mate	14	21
Disinterest	35	16
Attraction to person(s) of same sex	1	0
Different sex practices or habits	10	12
"Turned off"	28	10
Too little foreplay	38	21
Too little tenderness after intercourse	25	17
Sexual Satisfaction		
"How satisfying are your sexual relations?"		
Very satisfying	40	42
Moderately satisfying	46	43
Not very satisfying	12	13
Not satisfying at all	2	2
"How satisfactory have your sexual relations with your spouse been in comparison to other aspects of your marital life?"		
Better than the rest	19	24
About the same	63	60
Worse than the rest	18	16
"Do you have [sexual dissatisfaction] in your marriage?"		
Yes	21	33
No	79	67

Based on Frank, E., Anderson, C., and Rubinstein, D. (1978). Frequency of sexual dysfunction in normal couples. *New England Journal of Medicine*, 299:111–115.

Inhibited Sexual Desire (ISD)

Everyone occasionally experiences a period when they have little or no interest in sexual activity. The ebb and flow of sexual desire is natural. Some women experience increased desire at the time of menstruation and ovulation, perhaps with comparatively little desire in between. Other women have different cycles. Men also may experience cycles in their level of sexual desire. Some people deliberately shut off their sexual desire because it distracts them from other more important aspects of their lives. Such fluctuations are usually temporary and are not viewed as a problem if they are put in perspective.

However, an estimated 20% of men and women have **inhibited sexual desire (ISD)**, with little or no sexual fantasies or desire (DSM-III-R 1987:291). In one study of couples seeking sex therapy, too little or too much sexual desire was the second most common complaint, reported by 28% of the patients (Goleman 1988c).

What causes sexual desire to operate at a level below natural, or not at all, is one of the major questions still waiting to be answered. Low levels of testosterone, the hormone that controls sex drive, may occur with ISD. However, simple testosterone injections seldom solve inhibited sexual desire problems, although in some cases they may help.

For women, the hormonal factors behind sexual desire are more complicated and poorly understood. We do know that sexual desire in women is more susceptible than it is in men to psychological variables, such as relationship problems, anger, hostility, fear, and guilt. This tendency is probably a reflection of social factors. In most cases ISD is probably the result of combined biological and psychological factors (Leiblum & Rosen 1988:3–5).

Sexual Desire Conflicts

A recent survey of 289 sex therapists found that 31% of couples seeking sex therapy complained of a discrepancy or conflict in their desire for sex, making it the most common sexual complaint today (Goleman 1988). **Sexual desire conflicts** in long-term relationships are common because seldom can two persons have matching, parallel tracks of sexual desire over years.

Lack of communication, different perceptions of individual sexual desire, and the inability to compromise can result in conflicting levels of sexual desire in a dysfunctional situation. Woody Allen's movie *Annie Hall* offers a classic example of different perceptions. When their therapist asks Annie how often they have sex, she answers, "All the time—three times a week." When the therapists asks Alfie the same question, he says, "Hardly ever—three times a week!"

Differences in sexual desire are natural and to be expected in any intimate relationship. It is only when communications and the ability to negotiate and adjust to these differences break down that these differences become conflicts which may require professional counseling or sex therapy (Kaplan 1983).

Sexual Arousal Difficulties

Unlike sexual desire which is primarily a psychological reaction and much more affected by interpersonal conflicts and negative emotions, especially anger, sexual arousal and orgasm are primarily biological reflexes and therefore more susceptible to biological factors than sexual desire. However, sexual desire is the starting point for arousal and orgasm. Thus what may appear to be a problem with sexual arousal or orgasm may in fact be a lack of sexual desire stemming from an unresolved conflict, anger, a power struggle, boredom, or monotony.

Inhibited Sexual Arousal

Both men and women may experience **inhibited sexual arousal**, an inhibition in their responses during the arousal stage of the sexual response cycle. For a woman, it may mean she regularly experiences no sense of being sexually excited and enjoying love play and intercourse. Or it may be that her sexual excitement is not sufficient to produce or maintain vaginal lubrication until the completion of sexual activity. For a man, it may mean he regularly has difficulty attaining an erection sufficient for intercourse, or cannot maintain it long enough to allow him to complete intercourse. (The old terms frigidity and impotence are no longer used for this condition because of their negative connotations.)

Most healthy men and women experience an occasional problem becoming sexually aroused. It is only when this difficulty is persistent or recurs more than occasionally that we talk about it being a sexual problem. Like other sexual difficulties, inhibited sexual arousal may be described as either primary or secondary.

Orgasm Difficulties

Early Ejaculation

The critical feature of **early (premature) ejaculation** is a lack of voluntary control over when an ejaculation will occur. Only a few years ago, a man who reached orgasm before his female partner did was often labeled a premature ejaculator. Today, early ejaculation is not described in terms of how many thrusts a man can have before orgasm, or whether he reaches orgasm before his partner. Early ejaculation is currently defined as the inability of a man to maintain control over his responses to the stimulation that triggers ejaculation (Perelman in Leiblum & Pervin 1980:199–233). An estimated 30% of the male population experience some form of early ejaculation (DSM-III-R 1987:292) (Highlight Box 21.5).

Inhibited Male Orgasm (IMO)

Because two distinct reflex arcs control ejaculation and orgasm, a male may experience ejaculation without orgasm, or orgasm without ejaculation. Before puberty, boys commonly experience dry orgasms with no ejaculation. However, therapists today use the terms *retarded ejaculation* and **inhibited male orgasm** (**IMO**) interchangeably for a male who has difficulty reaching orgasm and ejaculating during sexual intercourse.

Most therapists and patients regard erection as a definite sign of sexual arousal. When a man engages in vaginal intercourse it is assumed that he is aroused and wants to have intercourse in order to enjoy an orgasm. Hence a man who cannot reach orgasm during intercourse is often treated by having his partner apply intense stimulation to his penis to overcome the inhibition of ejaculation.

HIGHLIGHT BOX 21.5.
THE STOP-GO EXERCISE

The Stop-Go exercise is used to help a man learn to pace his genital stimulation so he does not ejaculate before he and his partner are ready. Using the position shown here the male or female partner can stimulate the man's penis manually or orally. He signals the partner to stop just before he feels ejaculation is inevitable. After his sensitivity slackens, the partner resumes stimulation. This alternating of stimulation and rest may be repeated several times in one session before ejaculation is finally triggered. Repeating this exercise over several weeks or months helps teach the man to control his stimulation and time his ejaculation more comfortably.

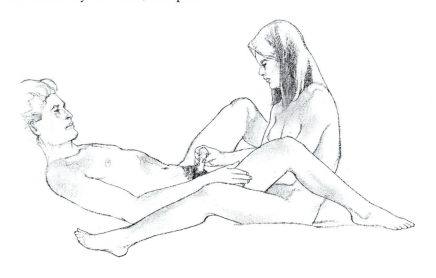

Men with IMO who can easily reach orgasm while masturbating may, according to Bernard Apfelbaum, find vaginal intercourse disgusting, or, at best, a chore they must put up with because society and the partner expects it. An erection in this case is not a sign of sexual arousal or of a desire for sexual intercourse. Instead it is the result of a pressure to perform. A man with IMO, Apfelbaum believes, is actually turned off by the touch of a woman and his orgasm inhibited instead of stimulated by vaginal intercourse. In this interpretation, treating inhibited male orgasm means dealing with performance anxieties. The man may be afraid of losing control if he has an orgasm. He may not actually want to have intercourse with this particular woman. He may be angry with her, or he may be turned off by vaginal penetration. There is also the possibility of nerve damage and other organic factors causing IMO. All factors considered, inhibited male orgasm is much more difficult to treat than early ejaculation (Apfelbaum in Leiblum & Pervin 1980:264–296; 1989).

Inhibited Female Orgasm (IFO)

Today many women may experience the performance pressure men have known for years. The recent celebration of female sexuality and orgasm has unfortunately been undermined by a host of subtle factors. Mixed messages and cultural contradictions have made orgasmic concerns real and urgent for many women, especially for those who repeatedly achieve high levels of stimulation but find themselves unable to reach orgasm during penile-vaginal intercourse. One estimate suggests that about 30% of all women experience orgasmic problems (DSM-III-R 1987:292).

Few parents and religious traditions promote and encourage girls to celebrate their sexuality. Men who masturbate are viewed as practicing for intercourse. Women who masturbate are too often viewed as indulging in illicit pleasure they should only enjoy during intercourse with a man. A lack of trust and a fear of being vulnerable or hurt in a relationship is a common barrier for female orgasm.

Another social factor complicating our perspective on female orgasm is the assumption that any woman should be able to reach orgasm every time she has vaginal intercourse. We have no evidence that penile thrusting is the most effective or most natural way for a woman to reach orgasm. Penile-vaginal thrusting may be a power trigger for male orgasm, but women's sexual responses rely on a variety of erotic stimuli that allow her a much greater choice of paths to orgasm. These different paths, including manual and oral stimulation of the clitoris, vulva, and breasts, are just as legitimate as penile thrusting during intercourse.

There is little agreement and much controversy about whether the inability to experience orgasm during vaginal intercourse constitutes a sexual problem. Is a woman sexually dysfunctional because she does not reaches orgasm with penile thrusting but very much enjoys orgasm when she or her partner stimulates her manually or orally before or after vaginal intercourse? There is even an ongoing debate about what constitutes an orgasm for women, and how to identify reliably whether or not a woman is experiencing orgasm (Barbach in Leiblum & Pervin 1980:107–146; 1989).

Although the debate over female orgasm and its relationship with penile-vaginal intercourse continues, inhibited orgasm, whether primary or secondary, is a major concern for many women who seek a solution in sex therapy. Short-term therapies are quite effective in helping women with inhibited orgasm problems. Support groups may help a woman explore and appreciate her own sexual responses. Counseling to build trust with the partner and masturbation workshops are also helpful (Barbach in Leiblum & Pervin 1980:107–146; 1989).

Other Sexual Difficulties

Dyspareunia

Painful intercourse, technically known as **dyspareunia**, refers to recurrent or persistent genital pain experienced before, during, or after sexual intercourse. Although this condition does occur in men, it is much more common in women (Lazarus in Leiblum & Pervin 1988:147–166).

In men, dyspareunia may be due to a tight foreskin that does not retract during erection and causes pain in the glans of the penis. It can also result from vascular problems in the penis.

Since many women are willing to accept some pain or discomfort in the mistaken belief that it is an unavoidable part of what they consider to be their marital duty, we do not have good statistics on the actual incidence of painful intercourse among women. When a woman does report this problem to her gynecologist, it is often due to physical factors which, once diagnosed, can be easily remedied. A vaginal or pelvic infection or irritations from contraceptive foams may be factors. Painful intercourse may also be due to a lack of vaginal lubrication resulting from a hormonal imbalance or declining hormones during menopause. When a thorough medical examination reveals no physical factor, the cause may be psychological. A variety of past experiences, an unresolved traumatic sexual experience, one's upbringing, and relational tensions or conflicts may combine to cause painful intercourse.

Vaginal Spasms (Vaginismus)

Recurrent or persistent spastic contractions in the muscles surrounding the entrance of the vagina, **vaginal spasms**, can prevent or interfere with vaginal intercourse. A woman may be so anxious and tense about having sexual intercourse that her brain sends neural impulses to her vaginal muscles causing involuntary spasms which prevent penetration by a penis. Although the causes of this disorder are almost always psychological, therapists commonly agree on a treatment that includes insertion of fingers or vaginal dilators of increasing size in a step-by-step conditioning to overcome the woman's fears (Leiblum et al. in Leiblum & Pervin 1989:167–193).

Dealing with the Unavoidable

Every man and woman who becomes sexually intimate with another person sooner or later experiences some kind of sexual problem or difficulty. The sexual problems or difficulties we usually encounter are not serious or deep rooted in the psyche. Thus they can often be resolved if we share the problem and find the information that will allow us to put the problem in perspective and resolve it. Sometimes a specific suggestion may solve the difficulty and allow us to function naturally again. More serious sexual problems and difficulties may require professional help to identify the complex interaction of biopsychosocial factors causing the problem and to work out a solution.

Key Concepts

1. Although learning to become a sexual person is a lifelong task, the sexual unfolding that occurs during adolescence is crucial, involving critical progress in both intellectual and moral growth, a choice of life work (with its impact on our sexual choices), a growing sense of one's sexual identity as a dynamic reality, an increasing distance from one's family which allows the development of new intimate relations, and a spiritual growth which internalizes and personalizes moral principles.

2. Sexual problems or difficulties occur in one of the three phases of the sexual response cycle: the desire, arousal (excitement), or orgasmic phase. Sexual

problems and difficulties can be primary and complete or secondary and situational.

3. Sexual aversion is an emotional anxiety reaction to the threat of sexual involvement with strong physiological reactions. Lack of sexual desire and conflicts in the levels of sexual desire can have both psychological and organic causes.

4. Three common sexual problems of men are erectile difficulties, early ejaculation, and inhibited male orgasm. For women the three main problems are painful intercourse (dyspareunia), inhibited orgasm, and vaginal spasms (vaginismus).

5. The psychological causes of desire, arousal, and orgasm difficulties are similar and the outcome depends on the individual person. The causes include negative sexual experiences, negative learning, misinformation, specific situations, social and peer pressures on men and women, performance pressures and fears, and interpersonal conflicts and tensions.

6. Organic or physical causes of sexual difficulties include the side effects of certain medications, poor nutrition, hormone imbalances, the use of alcohol and drugs, obesity, spinal cord injuries, genital infections, arthritis, kidney dialysis, and the consequences of abdominal surgery.

7. A therapeutic filter model (PLISSIT) emphasizes brief therapies and non-professional management of simple sexual problems. Steps include permission giving, limited information, specific suggestions, and intensive therapy.

8. Behavioral exercises for both sex therapy and sexual enrichment include the sensate focus exercises, the stop-go technique for early ejaculation, mutual masturbation, partner sexual examination, and massage exercises.

Key Terms

dyspareunia (575)
early (premature) ejaculation (573)
erectile difficulty (557)
inhibited female orgasm (IFO) (575)
inhibited male orgasm (IMO) (573)
inhibited sexual arousal (573)
inhibited sexual desire (ISD) (572)
painful intercourse (575)
PLISSIT (563)

primary sexual dysfunction (557)
secondary sexual difficulty (557)
sensate focus exercises (565)
sexual aversion (570)
sexual desire conflict (572)
sexual difficulty (555)
sexual problem (556)
spectatoring (561)
vaginal spasms (576)

Summary Questions

1. Compare the psychology and value system that supports the intercourse/orgasm goal-oriented view of sexual intimacy and the non-goal-oriented ethic of sexual playfulness.

2. List a dozen possible psychological causes for sexual problems and difficulties. Rank them according to what you think is their importance.

3. Explain the use and meaning of the term biopsychosocial in connection with the origins of sexual problems and difficulties.

4. List the sexual difficulties of men and women, and compare them in terms of which stages in the sexual response cycle are affected.

5. Which sexual difficulties are always the result of psychological or social factors?

Suggested Readings

Barbach, L. (1982). *For Each Other: Sharing Sexual Intimacy.* Garden City, NY: Anchor/Doubleday.

Cassel, C. (1984). *Swept Away: Why Women Fear Their Own Sexuality.* New York: Simon & Schuster.

Castleman, M. (1980). *Sexual Solutions.* New York: Simon & Schuster.

Comfort, A. (1972). *The Joy of Sex.* New York: Crown.

Comfort, A. (1974). *More Joy.* New York: Crown.

Raley, P. (1976). *Making Love: How To Be Your Own Sex Therapist.* New York: Dial Press.

Silverstein, C., & E. White. (1978). *The Joy of Gay Sex.* New York: Simon & Schuster.

Sisley, E., & B. Harris. (1978). *The Joy of Lesbian Sex.* New York: Simon & Schuster.

Zilbergeld, B. (1978). *Male Sexuality: A Guide to Sexual Fulfillment.* New York: Bantam.

Part Four

The Social Context

22. Sex and the Law
23. Sexual Coercion
24. Prostitution and Pornography

American Sex Laws
How Our Laws
Regulate Sex
Why Do We Have Laws
Regulating Sexual
Behavior?
Protecting Marriage
Protecting Public
Morality and Health
Protecting Against
Sexual Assaults
Protecting Minors
The Reform of
Sex Laws
Rape Penalties
Privacy and Minorities
Victimless Crimes
The Trend Toward
Consenting Adult
Laws

Chapter 22

Sex and the Law

Special Consultants

Lori B. Andrews, J.D., research fellow in medical law, American Bar Foundation; senior scholar, University of Chicago Center for Clinical Medical Ethics; and author of *New Conceptions: A Consumer's Guide to the Newest Infertility Treatments* (1985) and *Between Strangers: Surrogate Mothers, Expectant Fathers, and Brave New Babies* (1989).

Margaretta Dwyer, R.S.M., M.A., licensed psychologist and instructor in the Program in Human Sexuality, Department of Family Practice and Community Health at the University of Minnesota Medical School; works with sex offenders and their victims.

Many of our laws dealing with sexual behavior were written 50, 100, or more years ago when society's values and attitudes toward sex and marriage were quite different from what we find acceptable today. Yet many of these laws remain on the books and are sometimes applied by special interest groups, politicians, and law enforcement officials in discriminatory ways. The American Bar Association and the American Correctional Association have both called for updating and reform of our laws, especially those dealing with sexual behavior. In the last 20 years, we have made considerable progress, even though many conflicts and tensions remain. This chapter examines the principles behind our sexual laws and outlines the types of sexual behavior, human relations, and responsibilities currently affected by our legal system.

American Sex Laws

How Our Laws Regulate Sex

It has taken over 200 years for the American people to clarify the meaning of the "self-evident" statement in the Declaration of Independence that "all Men are created equal." Early interpretations allowed for slavery and denied slaves the right to marry and have families. It also denied women the right to sue for divorce, even on the grounds of adultery, although men could seek a divorce if their wives were unfaithful.

According to the First and Fourth Amendments to the Constitution, citizens have a right to peaceful assembly, and "to be secure in their persons, houses, papers, and effects, against unreasonable search and seizure." But the 1873 Comstock Law prohibited anyone from buying, selling, or distributing information about contraception, family planning, and abortion. The last vestiges of the Comstock Law were only declared to be unconstitutional infringements of the right to privacy of American citizens in the early 1980s. Although the Fourteenth Amendment of 1868 mandated equal protection of all citizens, this protection was not fully applied to women until the 1970s when 14 states amended their constitutions to include statutes prohibiting discrimination based on sex. Changing attitudes and values have led to many changes in the laws regulating sexual behavior.

But the changes have come about on several levels. In our democratic structure, laws are enacted by four different government branches or **legal jurisdictions**. Federal laws are passed by Congress, approved by the president, and enforced by federal law agencies. State laws are passed by the legislatures of individual states and enforced by state law agencies. There are also local laws passed and enforced by local communities or municipalities. Finally, all military personnel are regulated by military law while they are in active service. As you might suspect, communcations and coordination between legislators in these four different jurisdictions is not always the best. State laws on the same issue often show wide discrepancies.

Adding to the confusion of laws regulating sex are the different **legal codes** found within these jurisdictions. In our federal, state, and local laws, you can find relevant laws written in three distinct codes of criminal, civil, and family laws. Like the jurisdictions, these operate rather independently of each other. A criminal code contains laws designed to protect innocent people from injury or harm. Violation of a criminal law can bring the convicted offender a fine or imprisonment. Laws in a civil code are designed to regulate and resolve disputes over property rights, slander, libel, and other personal suits. In the family codes, laws regulate marriage, divorce, child custody, and adoption. Family laws also regulate responsibilities for financial support within the family, and protect spouses and minors in the family against neglect and abuse.

A further complication comes from what we call **case law**. Once enacted by a particular jurisdiction, a law is subject to modification as it is applied by the courts. Case law may also develop as disputes are resolved in areas where there are no statutes covering the situation, as, for instance, with the new reproductive technologies. Court decisions and appeals to a higher court all the way up to the U.S. Supreme Court can clarify and modify the law considerably. No law is absolute, and every law is continually subject to challenge, appeal, and reinterpretation. Case law leads to legal precedents, which then guide judges in future rulings.

Why Do We Have Laws Regulating Sexual Behavior?

Every society finds it necessary to regulate sexual behavior and the way in which families, the basic unit of a society, are structured and function. Formal laws are one way of providing order, but equally effective are informal social and religious taboos.

Even sexual intercourse, the central expression of human sexuality, has been subject to restrictions in various cultures. Religious prohibitions and civil laws may attempt to restrict this central expression to married couples, condemning both premarital and extramarital sex. Equally common, however, are societies that have more open regulations that allow both premarital and extramarital sex. Some societies, like China and the Oneida Community, have at times tried to regulate the reproductive outcome of marital intercourse. The Oneida Community had informal guidelines that allowed their concept of group marriage and amative intercourse to function smoothly. Beliefs about menstruation and ritual cleanliness are the basis of Orthodox Jewish taboos restricting marital intercourse to certain times of a woman's monthly cycle.

Social **taboos** are often more effective than civil laws in regulating sexual behaviors. Taboos rely on triggering a strong sense of shame and guilt in a person who violates a taboo and a parallel community response which may involve ostracizing the guilty party. In a tight-knit community, social or religious taboos can be more effective than laws, whereas in a large, more anonymous society people may be tempted to "get away" with whatever they can if it is to their advantage.

Unlike informal taboos and religious beliefs, laws are discussed, debated, voted on, written down, and published. Most of our sexual laws were designed to protect the moral values of our society, or that of our ancestors. Laws punishing adultery, fornication, rape, sodomy, and incest reflect a society's particular vision of sex, marriage, and the family. Understandably, in a pluralistic society such as ours, there is no shortage of opinions on what constitutes acceptable or unacceptable sexual behavior or what justifies a law regulating or prohibiting a particular behavior or activity. (See Figure 22.1.)

Some reasons commonly cited to justify laws regulating sexual relations and their outcome are

- to protect citizens against forced sexual behavior;
- to protect children and minors from sexual exploitation;

Figure 22.1.

"MASTURBATION IS LEGAL? THEN THEY'VE BEEN LYING TO ME."

- to prevent conduct that is socially offensive or harmful;
- to protect public morality and the family unit; and
- to protect public health.

Although most people would agree that there is a need to protect individuals from certain types of sexual behavior and their consequences, many of our sex laws are not based on any of these five reasons. Think about which of these five reasons apply when we talk about laws that make it a crime

for a husband and wife to engage in oral sex in their bedroom;

for a heterosexual or homosexual couple to engage in anal sex;

for a married woman to buy a contraceptive;

for an unmarried man or woman to purchase a contraceptive;

for a pharmacy or supermarket to display condoms;

for a newsstand to sell *Penthouse, Playgirl, Playboy,* or other sexually explicit magazines;

for a couple to kiss or hold hands in public;

for a doctor to prescribe a contraceptive;

for a woman to have an abortion;

for anyone to publish a manual for married couples that describes sexual intercourse and family planning.

The Roots of American Sex Laws

Many of our laws regulating sex are based on English common law and can be traced back to colonial or revolutionary times. Remember that in England, the church and state were for centuries considered a single entity. The king or queen was also the head of the Church of England. A sinful act from a moral and religious point of view was therefore also a criminal act against the state.

Although the United States supports the complete separation of church and state, there was and still is sufficient church influence to continue pressure for laws that regulate private sexual behavior between consenting adults. Groups affiliated with the Moral Majority, antiabortion groups, groups working for the censorship of books in public libraries and schools, and groups opposing legislation that would eliminate discrimination against persons because of their sexual orientation make a strong point that this is a "Christian nation" and they are only trying to preserve the "tradition of our Founding Fathers." As a result,

> there is a sharp clash between what modern society considers permissible sexual behavior and what the law says is forbidden. Judged by any civilized standards, many of our sex laws are primitive, outdated, and unworkable. Many, in fact, are carryovers from days when superstition and myth played a role more important than they play now. Moreover, there is a sharp conflict between our sexual preachings and our sexual practices which tends to make many of us moral as well as legal hypocrites.
>
> *(Kling 1969:v)*

In 1962 the first of many calls for a complete revision of our penal codes was issued by the American Law Institute. In the 1970s a few states accepted the challenge and revised their penal codes. That trend continues today, and the task is far from finished.

Protecting Marriage

Age of Majority

Since colonial days, we have had laws stating the minimum age at which a man and woman could enter into a legal marriage. Until 1987, a 14-year-old girl in New Mexico could get married. The age of consent was 12 in many southern states until recently. For males, legal status as a consenting adult is usually a little later than it is for females.

Adultery

The most common sex laws have been those designed to protect the integrity of marriage and family by limiting sexual relations to persons married to each other and prohibiting any "unnatural," nonreproductive sexual behavior. **Adultery**, sexual intercourse between a married person and someone other than his or her legal spouse, has always been considered an immoral act in the Judaeo-Christian tradition. Traditionally, husbands could charge a wife with "criminal communications" or adultery and her accomplice with "alienation of affections." Wives did not gain this right until passage of the Fourteenth Amendment in 1868. Even then, this right and other rights of women were honored more in theory than in practice (Hall & Hall 1987:78). In 1969 it was also a criminal offense in 45 of our 50 states. Adultery was grounds for divorce in all 50 states, and often the only grounds. Today, cruelty and desertion are the most common grounds for divorce in those states that still require grounds. In many states, no-fault divorce laws allow a couple to divorce by mutual consent and without any need to document a cause such as adultery.

In the late 1880s opposition to the patriarchal biases of American society led to enactment of Emancipation Acts and Married Women's Acts which restored to married women the rights they had enjoyed as single women, including the right to own and control property and to sue and be sued without male consent or participation. But the controversy over the Equal Rights Amendment in recent years suggests that the fight for legal and social equality of the sexes is not over.

Fornication

In 1969 **fornication**, sexual relations between unmarried persons, was illegal in 38 states. Today, many state criminal codes ignore adultery and fornication. Laws making certain sexual relations between adults a crime have been replaced by **consenting adult laws**. Such laws remove all criminal sanctions attached to any sexual behavior engaged in by two or more consenting adults in private.

Cohabitation

A similar fate has fallen on laws regulating cohabitation and common law marriages. The prevalence of cohabitation on college campuses and among single persons, both young and old, has made these laws largely unenforceable. In their stead, cohabiting couples are finding themselves guided by, and in some cases protected by, the emerging case law of cohabitation contracts. The legal value of these implied, verbal, or, in some cases, written contracts was first established in 1977 when Michelle Triola Marvin filed a "palimony" suit against actor Lee Marvin. Since then, the legal status and responsibilities of couples living together without being legally married has become clearer in case law, if not in actual legislation. In 1989 several large cities passed legislation or had court rulings which recognized various legal rights of "domestic partners."

Interracial Sex

Thirty years ago many states still prohibited sexual relations and marriage between couples of different racial origin. In 1967 the U.S. Supreme Court declared such laws an unconstitutional invasion of the right to privacy.

Artificial Insemination and Surrogate Motherhood

In 1986, before the Baby M case (see p. 233), the Family Law Section of the American Bar Association began work on a Model Surrogacy Act. Discussion of the proposal was tabled at the mid-1988 meeting of the American Bar even though about 40 state legislatures were considering legislation that would regulate surrogate motherhood. The key issue in surrogacy is whether payment to the surrogate for her nine months service constitutes "buying a baby" or whether a woman has a right to accept payment for her services and the "rental of her womb." We could argue that since men have traditionally been paid for donating their sperm for artificial insemination, women should be allowed to gain financially from allowing use of their reproductive capabilities. Any laws enacted in the future will have to deal with this issue. Such laws will also have to spell out minimum and maximum payments, requirements for screening women before they are allowed to sign a surrogacy contract, the rights and responsibilities of all parties, what happens if the child is born with a defect, and adoption procedures.

As of late 1988, five states—Indiana, Kentucky, Louisiana, Michigan and Nebraska—had laws that make paid surrogate contracts unenforceable. In Florida, unpaid surrogates were allowed if screening and adoption laws are complied with. In Nevada, a surrogate may be legally paid. In Arkansas, a couple contract with an unmarried surrogate, and the genetic father of the child and his wife are the legal parents, not the surrogate mother. In 30 states, a child conceived by artificial insemination with donor semen is the legal child of the sperm recipient and her consenting husband.

Prenuptial Contracts

With over half of all American marriages ending in divorce, moving in and out of marriage has raised the issue of **prenuptial contracts**. The bride-to-be may be in her thirties, the groom somewhat older, divorced, and with a child or two from the previous marriage. If he has been successful and brings to the second marriage a substantial estate as well as obligations for child support and alimony, he may want to protect himself against possible future liabilities. It is not romantic, but more and more couples getting married for the second time are writing prenuptial contracts. One out of 5 prenuptial contracts is initiated by the woman to protect her estate and rights.

Prenuptial contracts may include an assurance that the new wife will, or will not bear children. Their main focus, however, is the division of joint and individual estates, and the right to spousal support and its amount in case of a divorce. Contracts in which one spouse waives the right to support in case of a divorce are legal in many states including New York, Connecticut, and New Jersey, but not in California and 10 other states (Allen 1988; Dullea 1988).

Oral and Anal Sex

In the past, when sexual intercourse was socially justified only in terms of reproduction in marriage, laws prohibiting oral and anal intercourse even for married couples were commonly included in our statutes. In 1986 the U.S. Supreme Court upheld a Georgia antisodomy law in the case of Bowers v. Hardwick, citing condemnations of oral and anal sex dating back in English common law to the days of King Henry IV (1399). In Georgia, oral and anal sex is a criminal offense "regardless of whether the parties who engage in it are married or unmarried, or of the same or different sexes." Yet in 26 states, oral and anal sex is no longer a crime when engaged in by consenting adults (Francoeur 1987a:202–213).

Protecting Public Morality and Health

Contraceptives and Family Planning Information

The 1873 Comstock Law was so broadly worded in its concept of "obscene matter" that mailing or distributing books, advertisements, and contraceptive information was a federal crime. As late as the mid-1960s, 22 states had laws forbidding or restricting the sale of contraceptives to anyone. In 1965 the U.S. Supreme Court ruled that it was an unconstitutional invasion of the right to privacy for a state to prohibit the sale of contraceptives to married women. The constitutional right of single women to purchase contraceptives was not recognized until 1972! Today, contraceptives are openly sold in pharmacies and supermarkets, even though many television stations and magazines refuse to carry advertisements for condoms.

Lewd Behavior

At times lawmakers have been so embarrassed by the sexual activities they were trying to outlaw, they could not even state clearly what the law prohibited. Laws may talk about "lewd and lascivious acts," "criminal conversation" or acts that are "unmentionable among Christians." The vague terms "sodomy and buggery" are used in older law to refer to oral sexual relations between two men, two women, or between a man and a woman. Anal intercourse may also be included under either sodomy or buggery laws, without distinction as to whether the two persons are heterosexual or gay, married or unmarried. Even when a state has adopted consenting adult laws, legislators often receive considerable pressure to introduce new laws that will severely penalize sodomy.

Some states do not have specific laws against nonreproductive sex but use laws against disorderly conduct, carnal abuse, lewdness, lascivious behavior, public indecency, loitering, and indecent exposure to prosecute crimes of oral and anal sex. There is a great deal of "prosecutor's discretion" in sodomy cases, particularly when it involves homosexual males.

Pregnancy and Work

With our growing knowledge about the environmental hazards of the workplace, there is a question of how to protect women and men of childbearing age, pregnant women, and fetuses from possibly dangerous exposure in the workplace. Existing labor laws, sex discrimination statutes, and health regulations do not directly address this new issue. Is it legal or discriminatory to bar women from certain jobs that may pose a health threat to a fetus or to a woman's reproductive future? It may be cheaper to take this approach than to clean up the dangers. What are the rights of women who become pregnant and demand to be transferred out of a job they believe to be hazardous? What are the legal liabilities of the employer to provide a safe workplace? Often ignored in these discussions is the fact that man's sperm production and reproductive capacity can also be endangered by exposure to toxins in the workplace (Andrews 1987; Lewin 1988).

Sterilization Laws

In the past, some states allowed or required mentally handicapped persons, epileptics, and the insane to be sterilized (vasectomy for men; tubal ligation for women). The goal was to prevent the spread of these conditions, which were wrongly thought to be inherited. Other laws tried to protect institutionalized women from unwanted pregnancy by sterilizing them while ignoring the sexual abuse they sometimes experienced from staff and other patients. There have been many controversies about the constitutionality of such laws. Some mentally handicapped individuals want to marry and feel they can raise a child in a loving family.

In 1980 a major scandal resulted when it became public knowledge that sterilization was a common practice in many state facilities. In Virginia, from 1920 to 1972, 8,300 women were sterilized ostensibly to "raise the intelligence level of the state's citizens." In one hospital and training school, more than 4,000 men, women, and children were sterilized over a 50-year period. These individuals were told only that the operations were being done to correct medical problems.

Sexually Transmitted Diseases

Individual states and the federal government have laws requiring the reporting of statistics on certain STDs. Some states also require a couple who are applying for a marriage licence to be tested for certain STDs, including in some cases AIDS. Additionally, some states have considered laws requiring persons in particular occupations to be tested for the AIDS virus. The AIDS epidemic has led to major debates about whether the federal or state governments can or should require AIDS testing for teachers, restaurant workers, health workers, and military personnel. As mentioned in our earlier discussions of herpes and AIDS, new case law is being generated by suits brought by men and women charging their sexual partners knew they were infected but were criminally negligent in not informing them of their risk. In most cases, the charge is criminal negligence, but it may also be a charge of sexual assault and battery.

Protecting Against Sexual Assaults

Rape

As noted earlier, the traditional concept of rape was limited to a male forcing sexual intercourse on a female who is not his wife and against her will. The assault was often legally defined as forced penis-in-vagina intercourse without any mention or consideration given to the psychological force or other kinds of sexual acts that could be forced on a woman. Traditional rape laws also did not recognize the possibility of a male raping another male, or of a female raping a male or female. Many of these laws have been changed. In 1986 30,780 males and 348 females were arrested for forcible rape (*Information Please Almanac* 1988:799). In the 1980s new applications of laws against sexual assault were made in cases of dating or acquaintance rape and marital rape. However, many states still do not recognize marital rape.

Some states still allow the lifestyle and past sexual experience of the victim to be used in evidence by the defense in sexual assault trials. However, Congress passed the Rape Victim's Privacy Act in 1979 that limited the extent to which evidence of a victim's previous sexual experiences with persons other than the defendant could be introduced. Fortunately, as more states revise their penal codes to bring them in line with our new views of sexual assault, this discriminatory practice is becoming less common.

Sexual Harassment

Title VII of the 1964 Civil Rights Act and many State Fair Employment Practice Laws protect workers from sexual harassment, but many companies are now spelling out policies on this issue. Although the Supreme Court widened the definition of sexual harrassment in 1986 and many companies now have policy statements and procedures designed to protect employees, only 5% of workers who say they have been sexually harrassed file a complaint (Saltzman 1988).

Indecent Exposure and Voyeurism

Laws prohibiting **indecent exposure** are designed to protect citizens from other, less violent kinds of sexual assault. Women are seldom arrested, however, no matter how tiny the bikini, because exhibitionism and voyeurism are both considered a male prerogative. Recent debates about nude bathing at public beaches have added another dimension to our laws against indecent exposure. It is often difficult to define what constitutes indecent exposure; laws that prohibit loitering and disorderly conduct are even more vague. This lack of definition makes it possible to apply them to prostitutes working the streets, "Peeping Toms," customers of adult bookstores, and a whole range of what some consider unacceptable behaviors.

Protecting Minors

Statutory Rape

Protecting minors from sexual abuse and exploitation requires defining who is a minor. The age at which a minor reaches legal majority and is legally capable of giving consent to sexual relations varies widely in the 50 states, in some cases with laws dating back to the social environment of the 1800s. In Holland, changing social conditions recently prompted a lowering of the age of consent to age 12. **Statutory rape** laws make "carnal knowledge" of a female who is a legal minor a crime regardless of whether or not the female consents to or even invites the relations. Legally, a minor cannot give consent to sexual relations. Minor males are protected by laws which prohibit pedophilia, incest, and adults of either gender from "corrupting the morals of youth."

Sexual Abuse

The 1980s witnessed an explosion in the awareness of child sexual abuse by family members, day-care and school personnel, family members, and strangers. Commenting on the kidnapping of children for sexual exploitation by male and female adults, Nicholas Groth, director of the sex offender program at the Connecticut Correctional Institute, warned that despite stringent laws, "There is an epidemic of sexual abuse of children in the country."

Sexual abuse often begins when a pedophile seeks out a vulnerable victim. Often a particular child is chosen because he or she gives signs of being neglected and looking for attention and love. A child who is shabbily dressed or sitting alone on a school playground while peers play games is a good target for a child molester. Sexual abuse usually begins with seduction, the offer of attention or some candy. When the adult manages to get the child alone, the pedophile usually begins by exposing his or her genitals to the child, or asking the child to expose him or herself. In later encounters, the adult may mastur-

Figure 22.2. *Getting court testimony from children who are victims of incest and other sexual abuse presents problems of constitutional rights and sensitivity to the victim. Here a counselor uses an anatomically correct doll to elicit testimony in a court trial.*

bate, or fondle the child's genitals. Oral sex and vaginal or anal penetration may follow. Throughout the abuse, the adult commonly stresses the need for secrecy, perhaps threatening to injure or kill the child's parents or family if he or she tells anyone.

The sexual abuse is likely to continue unless the victim becomes tired of the relationship, is injured, becomes pregnant, or otherwise decides to disclose the abuse. Often the disclosure is indirect or accidental, being picked up from clues by a perceptive teacher, counselor, health care worker, or other adult. State laws commonly require adults who have reasonable cause to suspect a child is being sexually abused to report it to a state youth and family agency, which will then investigate.

In recent years, local law enforcement agencies, adolescent clinics in hospitals, and state youth and family agencies have developed sensitive procedures for handling cases of child sexual abuse. Gaining the child's confidence after he or she has been violated by a pedophile requires sensitivity and skill so that the trauma is not compounded as evidence is gathered for use in court (Figure 22.2). Although our courts traditionally require the victim to testify in the presence of the accused, courts are increasingly allowing the child victim of sexual molestation or incest to testify on videotape and thus avoid a face-to-face confrontation with the perpetrator in the courtroom. (See pp. 615–616 for discussion of reporting and treatment of child molestation.)

Contraceptive and Abortion Rights

Federal courts have consistently supported the rights of sexually active minors to confidential contraceptive information. Efforts to enact "squeal laws" that require doctors providing contraceptives for minors to report to the parents have not met with success. However, the courts have also supported laws that require teenagers seeking an abortion to notify one or both parents or to get judicial permission before going ahead (Associated Press 1988; Taylor 1988).

Incest

Sexual intercourse between persons related by blood or marriage, or incest, is a crime in all states. "Related by blood or marriage" usually means parent and child, brother and sister, grandparent and grandchild, aunt and nephew, and uncle and niece. In some states, the prohibition also extends to first cousins and to stepparents and their stepchildren. (See pp. 615–616 for discussion of reporting and treatment of incest.)

"Kiddie Porn"

In 1984 Congress passed the Child Protection Act that established penalties of up to 10 years in prison and fines up to $250,000 for those convicted of producing, distributing, or possessing pornography involving children. In 1985, according to one estimate, at least 300,000 children under age 16 were involved in the nationwide child pornography racket. U.S. Customs officials estimate that up to 20,000 pieces of "kiddie porn" enter the country every week, with sales amounting to "at least several million dollars a year." In 1987 a nationwide sting operation, organized by the Child Pornography Protection unit of the Customs Service and the U.S. Attorney General, produced 100 indictments (U.S. Surgeon General's Report 1986:52–55). This enforcement has made it very difficult and dangerous for pedophiles to obtain their usual stimulus material. In its place sex offenders are using the readily available advertisements that depict children posed in underwear or in what the pedophile considers seductive poses (see Figure 20.2, page 535).

The Reform of Sex Laws

In most states, the existing civil and penal codes are not designed to deal with today's sexual lifestyles. Still, there has been some progress and reform. Case law is having a major effect in many areas we have outlined. Legal definitions of sexual assault, rape, harassment, and the rights of victims are being clarified, although many inequities remain. There has also been some reform in laws regarding the sentencing and rehabilitation of sex offenders.

Rape Penalties

One major issue is the serious discrepancies in the penalties attached to violations of different criminal laws. In many states, rapists and murderers serve shorter prison terms than robbers or car thieves in other states. In West Virginia, the average car thief served 41 months, nearly three times the prison time served by a rapist in the same state. The average car thief in West Virginia also served more time in prison than the average rapist in Alaska, Arizona, Colorado, Delaware, Kansas, Kentucky, Maine, Massachusetts, Minnesota, Nebraska, Nevada, New York, North Dakota, Pennsylvania, Puerto Rico, and Wisconsin. The most time rapists spent in prison on average was 119 months in Arkansas and 109 months in North Carolina. In Puerto Rico, the average time spent in prison for rape was 18 months; in West Virginia, 16 months; and in Nevada and Alaska, only 14 months (Winer 1981).

This same study by the National Law Journal also revealed that rapists convicted in the strictest states served eight times longer sentences in prison than rapists in the most lenient states. Blacks served more time on average for the same crime than whites or Hispanics. And women served less time for the same offenses than men when convicted.

Privacy and Minorities

A major factor in the reform of our sex laws is the growing sense of the individual's right to privacy. To be constitutional and legal, any restriction of our personal freedom by the government must be justified by some clear, compelling social need. Today, many people do not see any social benefit or need for laws that prohibit oral and anal sex. Sexual minorities and civil rights groups have become increasingly active in lobbying against the discretionary actions of law enforcement agencies and the courts, and the use of sex laws to discriminate against individuals and minority groups. Despite the setback of the Bowers v. Hardwick Supreme Court decision, gay rights groups are trying to eliminate sodomy laws which are seldom applied to married couples, but may be used to harass homosexuals. Efforts to get local legislatures to pass ordinances pro-

---

HIGHLIGHT BOX 22.1.
SHOULD CONGRESS CENSOR ART?

In the autumn of 1989 the U.S. Congress was embroiled in a major controversy: Can the U.S. government censor works of art if the artist is the recipient of federal funds? The immediate issue was an amendment Senator Jesse Helms (R-NC) attached to an appropriations bill. The amendment would bar federal money for "obscene or indecent art." Helms was reacting to two exhibitions financed by the National Endowment for the Arts. The first, at Washington's Corcoran Gallery of Art, known for its interest in contemporary artists, was a retrospective of Robert Mapplethorpe's photography including some homoerotic photographs. The second exhibition included Andres Serrano's photograph of a crucifix submerged in urine.

After the Mapplethorpe retrospective was canceled, Congress passed legislation forbidding federal grants to art considered obscene. This action sent a chill down the spine of the arts community. In the aftermath, major artists across the nation called for resignation of the director of the Corcoran Galley of Art. Seven key staff members resigned in protest of the legislation, and several major exhibits were canceled as artists protested by withdrawing their works. Self-censorship quickly became an undercurrent for directors of museums, artists, and their sponsors.

Although the art of Mapplethorpe, Serrano, and other contemporary artists may shock some people today, the history of art is filled with works that were originally denounced as outrageous and later adored by the public. Critics of the all-encompassing Helms amendment argue that it would put many of our classics in jeopardy. Federal funds to support productions of Shakespeare's "Merchant of Venice" could be banned because of the portrayal of Jews, Wagner's Ring Cycle could be banned for its depictions of incest, and countless nudes by Rubens, Rembrandt, and others could also be banned.

The issue of the law and censorship is a recurring controversy in our society that will continue to emerge when artists and social critics break with tradition. Where do you stand on this issue?

hibiting discrimination in housing and employment based solely on sexual orientation have met with mixed results, although the fight for equality continues.

Victimless Crimes

Another trend is to abolish laws that deal with **victimless crimes**. By definition, a criminal law is designed to protect an innocent person from harm. But many of the behaviors prohibited by our sex laws do not inflict any harm on the consenting participants. A man who visits a prostitute and pays for her services, a person who wants to buy a pornographic magazine, any adult couple who enjoys a particular way of relating sexually—all may be engaging in sexual behaviors that others may not agree with or want to engage in, but, if no one is harmed and there is no victim, then we can ask what "compelling need" exists to justify the state restricting a citizen's personal freedom of association and their right to be secure in their own houses.

The Trend Toward Consenting Adult Laws

The civil rights movement of the 1960s and 1970s has been a major factor in the growing trend toward consenting adult laws in sexual matters. In 1962 the American Law Institute recommended a Model Penal Code which would abolish all criminal sanctions for any sexual behavior engaged in by consenting adults in private. Sexual crimes would still include sexual intercourse when forced or imposed, sexual assault of all types, the seduction, corruption, and abuse of minors, and prostitution.

The first consenting adult penal code was adopted in 1962 by Illinois. It removed all adult consensual sexual behavior from the criminal code. By 1981 more than 20 states had adopted similar codes or were considering them.

It has often been said that the best government is the one with the fewest laws. A study of history suggests that the more repression there is of personal and sexual rights in a society, the more laws there are to enforce these restrictions. The ongoing challenge for any society is to constantly reevaluate its laws and find the most effective balance between individual rights, freedom, and privacy and the common good. Considering that our sexual drive or libido is so central to the human experience, and so powerful, it is worth asking what are the social and personal costs of laws that unnecessarily restrict and repress this energy, and whether we as a society are willing to pay those costs.

Key Concepts

1. Ideally, the social taboos and laws a society develops will provide guidelines for the integration of sexual behaviors and relationships in the broader context of everyday life, allowing the maximum freedom to the individual while protecting the rights of others and the public good. However, negative religious and moral views of sex often lead to laws which repress and restrict sexual behavior even in private.

2. The justification for laws regulating private sexual behavior is contained in the phrases "compelling interest" and "protection of public welfare."

3. The rights of the state to enact laws regulating or prohibiting sexual behavior is most evident in laws that (1) protect the public interest in the stability of

marital and family life, (2) protect minors and other citizens against sexual assaults and exploitation, and (3) protect public health.

4. There is a growing trend toward the enactment of consenting adult laws for sexual behavior.

Key Terms

adultery (585)

case law (583)

consenting adult laws (594)

fornication (586)

indecent exposure (590)

legal codes (582)

legal jurisdictions (582)

prenuptial contracts (587)

statutory rape (590)

taboos (583)

victimless crimes (594)

Summary Questions

1. Describe the four jurisdictions and three separate codes which characterize the American legal system. How is the American model similar to or different from legal systems in Canada or European countries? Why are conflicting or different laws regulating sexual behavior and relationships enacted in different jurisdictions and codes?

2. Describe some laws that (1) protect the public interest in the stability of marital and family life, (2) protect minors and other citizens against sexual assaults and exploitation, and (3) protect public health.

3. How are recent changes in our sexual attitudes raising new questions about the ''compelling interest'' and ''protection of public welfare'' used to justify laws which regulate or prohibit private sexual behavior between consenting adults?

Suggested Readings

Allen, C. L. (1988, August 15). Planning for failure with prenuptial pacts. *Insight,* pp. 54–55.

Andrews, L. B. (1989). *Between Strangers: Surrogate Mothers, Expectant Fathers, and Brave New Babies.* New York: Harper & Row.

Dullea, G. (1988, July 6). Prenuptial stress over the contract. *New York Times,* pp. C1, C8.

Lewin, T. (1988, August 2). Protecting the baby: Work in pregnancy poses legal frontier. *New York Times,* pp. A1, A15.

Saltzman, A. (1988, August 1). Hands off at the office. *U.S. News & World Report,* pp. 56–58.

TODAY'S GREEKS CALL IT DATE RAPE.

Just a reminder from Pi Kappa Phi. Against her will is against the law

Rape
  Rape in History
  What Constitutes Rape?
  What Motivates
    Rapists?
  Types of Rape
  Reducing the Risk
    of Sexual Assault
  A Developmental-
    Descriptive Profile
    of the Rapist
  Resisting a Rape
    Attempt
Incest
  Sexual Abuse Within
    the Family
Coping During and
  After a Sexual
  Assault
  During an Assault
    Attempt
  Reporting Rape or Incest
  The Trauma of Rape
    and Abuse
Sexual Harassment
  Sexual Harassment from
    1964 to the Present
  Two Definitions
  What Constitutes Sexual
    Harassment?
  Dealing with Sexual
    Harassment

Chapter 23

Sexual Coercion

Special Consultants

Peter Anderson, Ph.D., assistant professor, Department of Human Performance and Health Promotion, University of New Orleans.

Margaretta Dwyer, licensed psychologist and instructor, Program in Human Sexuality, Department of Family Practice and Community Health at the University of Minnesota Medical School; works with sex offenders and their victims.

Sharon E. King, M.S.Ed., R.C.H., C.A.S., abuse and incest counselor, The Starting Point, Collingswood, New Jersey.

Andrea Parrot, Ph.D., assistant professor, Human Services Studies, Cornell University, and author of *Acquaintance Rape and Sexual Assault Prevention Training Manual.*

Sexual relations are more often than not an expression of love, affection, friendship, curiosity, mutual exploration, and pleasuring, and a variety of other creative, positive motives. But some people use their sexuality in a destructive way, as a weapon, to degrade and control another person, to express anger and rage, or to compensate for feelings of inadequacy and an unresolved childhood sexual trauma.

Sexual assaults are not pleasant to think about, but they do represent some important realities of life and sexual relations. Understanding how some people use sex to assault, control, and abuse other people can help you recognize warning signs and avoid such situations and relationships. Our topics include rape by a stranger and by an acquaintance, friend, date, or partner. We also deal with sexual harassment and incest. We provide practical advice on how to deal with these quite different kinds of sexual assault and how to find help if you or a friend is a victim. Unfortunately, sexual assaults are far more common than most people think, so it is important for every adult to know how to avoid, prevent, and cope with sexual assaults.

Rape

Rape in History

In the 1700s and 1800s black women slaves were fair game for rape by their white masters. They were the master's property and used as "breeding machines" to produce more slaves, particularly after the importation of slaves was halted in the early 1800s (D'Emilio & Freedman 1988:85–104; Gates 1987).

Rape has been commonly used to humiliate and control a defeated enemy. In the 1971 war between Bangladesh and Pakistan, for example, Pakistani soldiers were shown pornographic movies before going into battle to incite them to rape the Bangladesh women. Because ancient Bangladesh custom dictates that any woman who is raped is a source of shame to her family and/or husband, these women were generally abandoned and ostracized. After the war, a government proclamation that all rape victims of the war were national heroines did little to reestablish their honor, social position, or mental health (Brownmiller 1975). On the American frontier, most sexual contact between white males and Indian and Mexican women took the form of rape. After winning a battle in 1869, Lieutenant Colonel Custer allegedly invited his officers to "avail themselves of the services of a captured squaw" while he indulged himself with a Cheyenne woman (D'Emilio & Freedman 1988:91–92). In wars, the ultimate humiliation is for the victorious soldiers to rape the enemy's women and sodomize the defeated males. Control and power also appear as a major motive for homosexual rape in prisons.

Male competition and affirming macho self-identity are often motives in gang, fraternity, party, and group rapes (Erhart & Sandler 1985). This same psychology may take a less violent form when females, seeking membership in a gang, are subjected to a gang rape that establishes male dominance as well as the macho self-identity of the male gang members (Figure 23.1).

Figure 23.1. *In the past 10 years, women's groups, feminist groups, and conservative antiabortion groups have protested the availability of pornography which degrades and exploits women. They claim that pornography provides a cultural milieu that promotes sexual assault and rape.*

What Constitutes Rape?

Definitions

The term *rape* suggests a menacing "creep in the bushes" who leaps out to tear the clothes off an unsuspecting, attractive young woman and force her to have sex with him. The Federal Bureau of Investigation (FBI) uses the phrase "forcible rape," which it defines as

> the carnal knowledge of a female forcibly and against her will. Assaults or attempts to commit rape by force or threat of force are also included; however statutory rape (without force) and other sex offenses are excluded.

This definition implies that there may be such a thing as "consensual rape." It also implies that only women can be raped. The meaning of "forcibly" and "force" are left unexplained. Because of this confusion, some suggest using the general term *sexual coercion* or *sexual assault* instead of rape (Allgeier 1987:12).

Since there is much confusion and little agreement, we accept the common usage of the term rape and define it to include stranger rape, marital rape, date rape, and acquaintance rape regardless of the participants' genders. **Rape**, for our purposes, means any form of sexual contact or intimacy forced on one person by another person using actual physical force, a weapon, or the threat of physical force. In marital, date, and acquaintance rapes, coercion is more common than physical force.

Definitions of rape differ considerably. There are casual, colloquial, and feminist uses of the term. Legal definitions vary from state to state. They may limit rape to vaginal intercourse, or use the term to include other sexual activities. The relationship between the two parties involved may also be a factor, as it is with statutory rape, incest, acquaintance, date, and marital rape.

Recently, there has been a trend to view rape, not as an either/or phenomenon, but on a continuum with normal male behavior within a culture. Rape, or sexual aggression, then represents a range of behaviors from sexual intimacy achieved through persuasion and verbal coercion to sexual intimacy and intercourse achieved through the use of force (Koss & Oros 1982). This trend has led to revision of criminal codes which avoid the term rape and speak instead of a general category of sexual assault with varying degrees of sexual contact and force. The New Jersey criminal code, for instance, has four categories: (1) sexual assault, (2) aggravated sexual assault, (3) criminal sexual contact, and (4) aggravated criminal sexual contact. In each of these categories, the age of the actor and the victim, their relationship, and the position of authority held by the perpetrator or assailant affect the seriousness of the crime.

Although some laws limit the term rape to a male sexually assaulting a female, other laws are gender neutral and allow for rape to include homosexual, lesbian, and female heterosexual assaults on males.

Use of the term *victim* in rape situations has also been challenged. Talking about a a rape victim implies a sense of powerlessness, of permanent damage, and little or no hope of recovery. It is considered more constructive and supportive to avoid the term victim and refer instead to the *survivor* of a sexual assault.

Force, Coercion, and Consent

The most difficult aspect of defining rape is the issue of force and lack of consent. To what extent can rape be alleged if the adult victim is impaired by the use of alcohol or drugs? Alcohol and drug use are major factors in date and party rapes. To what extent can the term rape be applied to an adult victim who is developmentally disabled? Some would regard rape of a mentally retarded adult as a type of statutory rape and date rape with a victim under the influence of alcohol as a type of sexual assault lacking the full forcible aspect of rape. In some states sexual intercourse with a woman who is under the influence of alcohol is defined as rape. In feminist literature, there is considerable debate over extensions of the term rape to include sexual harassment and unwanted flirtation (Dworkin 1987).

Equally difficult to define is the concept of "psychological coercion." **Coercion** may include using a position of power or authority, getting someone intoxicated, using verbal pressure, or lying to gain sexual intimacy from someone. In a dating situation, when does seduction become persuasion become coercion? When does acceptance become hesitation become reluctance become rejection?

Or, when does a "maybe" mean "yes" or "no?" These gray areas remain deeply perturbing to anyone dealing with sexual assault and rape.

Psychologically, some forms of rape involve addictive and compulsive repetitive behavior (see p. 530 for a discussion of paraphilic behavior). This kind of rapist uses physical violence along with psychological terror and threats to achieve control over the victim and usually needs to repeat his violence, at least in fantasy, to achieve sexual arousal and possibly orgasm, even when masturbating or having intercourse in a nonrape situation.

What Motivates Rapists?

The common belief today is that rape is always and foremost an aggressive act, motivated by the rapist's anger and need to control (Groth 1979).

Prior to the early 1970s most researchers of rape assumed that the primary motive behind rape was sexual pleasure. Feminism challenged this view by arguing that rape is a political act that indicates nothing about male sexual desire. Rape was seen as a political act of violence and domination, characteristic of American patriarchal and sexist traditions (Figure 23.1). This view was pioneered by Kate Millet, Suzanne Griffin, and Germaine Greer and soon became a focal point of feminist theory. Susan Brownmiller's book *Against Our Will* (1975) popularized the "not sex" explanation of rape.

The "not sex" explanation of rape then became the central theme in work on rape and child abuse. The argument was that rapists use sex to express their anger and rage at women. They use sex to regain control and power over women. And, in the extreme case of sadistic rape, men use pain, degradation, and even murder to achieve sexual pleasure.

In 1979 Nicholas Groth, Director of the Sex Offender Program at the Connecticut Correctional Institution, provided evidence for the "not for sex" explanation with clinical data on convicted rapists. By 1980 the not for sex theory of rape was "generally accepted by criminologists, psychologists, and other professionals working with rapists and rape victims that rape is not primarily a sexual crime, it is a crime of violence" (Warner 1980).

This belief that some sexual assaults are motivated by the male drive for power and control over women fits comfortably with the strong evidence of socialization of males for violence and patriarchy. Ours is a society that tolerates or accepts considerable violence on television and in films, the widespread sale of handguns and rapid-firing attack guns, and plea bargaining in the prosecution of rapists and murderers.

Recently researchers questioned the evidence offered to support the claim that rape is always and foremost an aggressive act in which sexual desire and pleasure are, when present, a very negligible factor (Hagen 1979). In a detailed critique of the not for sex theory, Palmer (1988) concludes that the arguments are flawed because they are either illogical, based on inaccurate definitions, untestable, or inconsistent with the actual behavior of rapists. Although the not for sex motivation may be valid for many *repetitive and compulsive sex offenders* who have been studied in our prison system, its validity for the majority of rapists who are never arrested is questionable. The not for sex motivation is even more questionable in acquaintance, date, and marital rapes. Forced sexual intercourse is for some rapists a way of sexual fulfillment rather than simply an expression of rage and anger.

The question of what motivates different types of rape is crucial if we are to develop effective programs to reduce the incidence of all kinds of rape and to rehabilitate rapists. Some rapists, particularly those who qualify psychologically as sociopaths, can never be rehabilitated.

Types of Rape

Stranger Rape

The stranger stalking an unsuspecting young woman and forcing her to have sex with him is the most common image of rape. Stranger rape is *not* the most common form of rape. It is, however, the kind of rape most frequently prosecuted and punished by prison sentences.

Rapists of this type tend to be compulsive repetitive sex offenders. Psychologists believe they have a paraphilic addiction called rapism. Behind their compulsive, repetitive use of sex is a need to regain control in their lives, to express anger, to degrade, or to win acceptance. Some rapists compensate for their inadequate self-image by trying to gain control, using their penis as a weapon. Others want to degrade the victim and will quickly switch to forced oral sex if they think the woman they are assaulting dislikes oral sex more. The attempt to degrade the woman may also involve forcing the woman to engage in anal sex. Urination or defecation on the victim may also occur. In a large percentage of these rape situations, vaginal intercourse never occurs. Males are also victims of degradation and anal rape, with similar psychological consequences.

Some Facts About Stranger Rape   Block and Skogan (1982) report that

- The typical survivor of stranger rape is a white female, aged 18 to 26.
- Half of all stranger rapes attempted are completed.
- Thirty-five percent of all rape targets are between ages 12 and 19, although this age group constitutes much less than a third of the general population.
- Over half of all rapists are white.
- Black women are less likely to resist rape and robbery attempts; they are also more likely to be the object of assaults involving weapons.
- Almost a quarter of rapists are under age 21.
- Weapons are used in over a quarter of stranger rapes.

Myths about sexual assault abound. A common myth is that most rapists do not know their victims. The problem is that the survivors of sexual assaults tend to report assaults by strangers much more often than they report rapes by acquaintances, dates, and spouses. The racist myth that suggests the most common rape by a stranger involves a black assailant and white female survivor is refuted by data showing that attempted or completed stranger rapes are more often committed by persons of the same race as the victim (Block & Skogan 1982; MacKellar 1975).

Date and Acquaintance Rape or Coercion

Definition   As a working definition, we can say that **date rape** involves the use of psychological and/or physical coercion to pressure an unwilling partner into engaging in sexual intimacies and/or intercourse in a relationship where the couple are dating. The definition of date rape is narrower than the definition of stranger rape because it is situation-specific. The definition of date rape is also broader because the force used is more often emotional, persuasive, seductive, and manipulative than physical. Lines like "You would if you loved me" and "If I don't, he (or she) may drop me" are common in date rapes. **Acquaintance rape** refers to sexual activity forced on a person by someone who is known to the victim, for example, by a classmate, teacher, neighbor, or friend.

How Common Is Date Rape?   Kanin (1969) found that 25% of the male university students he interviewed admitted they had tried to force intercourse on a date, girlfriend, or fiancée. In 1985 Kanin found college male date rapists avoided using weapons and their fists, but described their quest for intercourse as a "no-holds barred contest." Rappaport and Burkhart (1984) found that 43% of the 201 men they questioned said they had used a "sexually coercive method" at least once or twice. Fifteen percent said they had physically forced intercourse. At other colleges, 20% to 30% of those surveyed had experienced courtship violence (Figure 23.2).

At one large university in the Southwest, Laner found 60% of the students surveyed had experienced some form of sexual violence while dating. A quarter of the students, male and female, said they expected slapping, hitting, and scratching to be part of a serious relationship. "We're taught to accept violence from people who say they love us" (cited by Joseph 1981).

In a study of close to 4,000 university students, 71% of the women and 53% of the men reported their messages about not wanting sexual intercourse had been misinterpreted. A third of the women and 23% of the men admitted to being in a situation where they felt the man was so sexually aroused it was useless to try to stop him or to try to stop, even though the woman did not

Figure 23.2. *College students and administrators are becoming more aware of the realities of acquaintance or date rape and party or frat rape, and of the need for rape prevention workshops.*

want to have intercourse. About a quarter of the women reported having un-wanted sex because of continual pressure or actual use of physical force (Koss & Oros 1982; Koss, Gidycz, & Wisniewski 1987).

Date Rape and Coercion of Men   There are two parties in a dating or courtship relationship, usually a male and a female. Given our cultural biases, we assume that when date rape occurs, it is with a male assailant and a female victim. Recent evidence suggests our changing sex roles and values have altered the realities of date rape (Anderson 1989). When Muehlenhard and Cook surveyed 507 men and 486 women, 93.5% of the men reported they had experienced unwanted sexual activity, including unwanted kissing and petting. Two-thirds of the men reported they had experienced unwanted sexual intercourse; inter-estingly, only half of the women reported unwanted intercourse.

Why Rape Occurs in Dating Situations   When Los Angeles teenagers were asked ''Under what circumstances is it OK for a guy to hold a girl down and force her to have sexual intercourse,'' 82% of the boys and girls said this kind of force was never justified. However, when details were added to the scenario, the students were much more accepting of rape. There was a startling willing-ness to justify male violence when the boy and girl had been dating some time, when he had paid for an expensive evening, or when she appeared to be teasing him (Figure 23.3). A significant number of both boys and girls felt that the girl was in part to blame even when the boy beat her (Kikuchi 1988; Malamuth 1981; Zellman et al. 1979). What might these results tell us about the social condi-tioning of both males and females in our culture?

Our stereotyped standards dictate that a real man should always make a sexual advance whenever he can. Otherwise, the woman might think he is homosexual or think she lacks sex appeal. The men in Muehlenhard and Cook's 1988 survey cited some familiar factors for their unwanted sexual activity. These included enticement, peer pressure, a negative value on male virginity, the

Figure 23.3. Who's Responsible for Date Rape? *How do you feel about the approval of violence in the following situations? Why do you think more than twice as many girls as boys accepted date violence?*

Situation	Percentage Finding Force Justified	
	Girls	Boys
She leads him on	54	27
She gets him sexually excited	51	42
She is stoned or drunk	39	18
She's had sex with other boys	39	18
He's spent a lot of money on her	39	12

pressure to gain sexual experience, physical coercion, fear that refusal might have a negative effect on the relationship, being drunk and unaware or unable to resist, a desire to be accepted, and not wanting to appear gay, unmanly, or shy and afraid (Anderson 1989).The individual motivations that come into play in date rape and the interpretations of these motives are extremely complex. Both the perpetrator and the victim have conscious and unconscious desires at the time of the incident. The motivations of the person forcing sexual intimacy may range from a need to control, dominate, and degrade the partner to sexual desire and arousal. The victim may be dealing with ambivalent feelings about sex, or with a need to conciliate and please the partner.

After the assault, faulty memories, rationalizations, and, at times, sincere but distorting reconstructions and reinterpretations may affect the understanding of what happened and why it happened. After the assault, the victim of a date rape may also be influenced by the definitions, ideologies, and interpretations of her or his family, peers, the media, a counselor, or therapist.

Anger, seeking power, and a sense of male privilege may provide subconscious or unconscious motives for date rape. The assailant may say, "I was aroused and couldn't stop!" when actually he means, "I paid plenty for this evening and had a right to expect sex" (Korman & Leslie 1982).

The victim's interpretation at the time of the incident and afterward also varies widely (Adams & Fay 1984; Pritchard 1988). The victim may cooperate because he or she perceives the risk of physical harm, because of an internalized desire for dominance by the partner, or an inability to admit a partially formed desire for intercourse. The victim may also cooperate because the incident is not perceived as an assault at the time, or out of a need to be accepted or liked. The victim's postrape reinterpretation of her or his motivations and of the perpetrator's motives may also lead to accepting full responsibility for the assault (Korman & Leslie 1982).

The assailant's interpretations and reinterpretations are also complex. He or she may totally deny using any force or coercion and blame the incident on the victim. He or she may not interpret what was done as force. Or guilt feelings caused by accepting full blame for the incident may lead to a sexual dysfunction or a complete aversion to any sexual intimacy. The basic point here is that the reactions, interpretations and reinterpretations of both the perpetrator and the victim are seldom simple.

Factors in Date Rape A crucial finding of several researchers is that alcohol and/or drug use by both the assailant and the victim are a common factor in rapes (Allgeier 1987:25 & 49; Russell 1984). The majority of incarcerated rapists studied by Wolfe and Baker (1980) were drinking or drunk when they raped.

Stress and jealousy are factors in date rape. More important is our expectation and acceptance of violence in courtship. At a large university in the Northwest, 1 in 3 students had at some time considered physical abuse a sign of love, perfectly normal, and even a healthy part of a love affair. Surprisingly, over a third reported that violence had improved their relationship (Barrett 1982; Carmody 1989; Joseph 1981; Story 1986).

The inability or failure to communicate one's actual desires and current limits on intimacy in the dating situation is another major factor in date rape. Muehlenhard and Hollabaugh (1988) found that, given our double moral standard, women often say "no" when they really mean "yes." Among the reasons women gave for saying "no" when they meant "yes" were not wanting to appear too aggressive or eager, being afraid of being hurt or used, not wanting to appear loose or easy, being unsure about how much the man liked them, and not being ready emotionally. Women also said "no" meaning "yes" when they wanted the man to be more aggressive or talk them into it, when they wanted him to beg, or wanted to make him more aroused by waiting. Women also said "no" meaning "yes" when they were angry with the man, wanted to get back at him, or wanted to be in control. Since men are aware of this ambivalence, it makes it easy for them to rationalize forcing or coercing a date into sexual intercourse.

Allgeier (1987) believes that young people should use role playing to learn (1) how to communicate clearly what their sexual expectations and needs are up front in a dating situation and (2) how to negotiate a mutually acceptable arrangement that is open to renegotiation as the relationship develops.

How do you think persons who are dating can use an awareness of these two skills to reduce their risk of date rape?

Male Rape

Early surveys of sexual experience seldom asked if men had ever been rape victims. Recently, cases have been reported of men who were forcibly raped by women, men who had been intimidated into having sex, abused by a babysitter, or seduced into incest by a female relative. Despite their strong emotional reactions of anger, embarrassment, or terror, many of these men were able to continue functioning sexually because, unlike female rape victims, they were not troubled by the thought that they may have invited their victimization. Other men had the same rape trauma syndrome experienced by female victims (Cochran & Druker 1984; Muehlenhard & Cook 1988; Musialowski & Kelley 1987; Sarrel & Masters 1982).

The vast majority of male rape victims are the subject of rape by other males. They are often abused more violently and sustain more serious injuries than female victims. The victims of same-sex rapes tend to be the young and the elderly rather than middle-aged males. Every day, at least 1,200 men are raped in the jails, prisons, and juvenile detention centers in the United States. The average age of these victims is 17. These victims are likely to come back onto the streets full of rage and desire for revenge (Donaldson 1985).

These rape victims experience the same reactions as females (see discussion of rape trauma syndrome, p. 615). However, men don't grow up with a fear of rape, so it comes as a greater shock. Male homosexual rape is also a shattering assault on a male's concept of himself as masculine. Postrape depression and suicide attempts are not uncommon.

Group or Party Rape

The common image of gang rape is that it only occurs in wild motorcycle clubs, in the ghetto, or among drug users. In fact, when Erhart and Sandler investigated the phenomenon of gang rape on college campuses for the Association of American Colleges, they made the following statement:

> [We] began to realize that these events were not single aberrations but events that happen all too commonly on too many campuses. The Project identified more than 50 incidents occurring at a wide range of institutions:

public, private, religious affiliated, Ivy League, large and small. On some campuses, Project staff were told "it happens almost every week." Apparently, no institution is immune from the potential of "fraternity gang rape" or "party gang rape."

(Erhart & Sandler 1985)

Although most gang rapes were found to be associated with fraternities, they were also reported in dormitories and at off-campus parties. Voyeurism and peer pressure are factors. Those who are not directly involved may watch and urge on younger students and group members. Fraternity gang rapes are often planned in advance so that the only question is finding a suitable victim. That victim is often a female whose use of alcohol or drugs makes her vulnerable. Unfortunately, a woman who is drunk or high is often seen as easy prey and fair game for a party rape; a male under the influence also may be a victim of a party rape (Pritchard 1988:24–27).

Marital Rape and Abuse

Traditionally, the marriage contract assumed that the husband had a right to sexual relations with his wife any time he wanted. Since the wife's legal status was often defined as "chattel"—property of her husband—she had a conjugal duty and could not refuse. Thus the very thought of what we now call marital rape was inconceivable. The reverse situation, a wife forcing sexual relations on her husband, was simply never thought of.

In 1980 the California Marital Rape bill altered its rape statutes to include **marital rape**, sexual intercourse with one's spouse if accomplished under force, violence, or threat of great and immediate bodily harm. Over 25 states have passed laws making it a felony for a husband to force his wife to engage in sexual relations against her will. Some of these statutes are gender-neutral and leave open the possibility that either the husband or wife may be the assailant.

Each year close to 2 million women are beaten by their husbands, approximately 1 every 18 seconds. Half of all American wives will be beaten at least once in their married lives. Each year a quarter of a million men are beaten by their wives (Hunter 1979).

Unfortunately, a complementary psychology of subconscious attraction often creates the opportunity for marital abuse and rape. A spouse or partner who is inclined to use abuse, beatings, and rape to compensate for his or her needs and inability to cope with stress commonly seeks out a partner who will accept this kind of behavior and interpret it as a sign of love and devotion. The victim of spouse abuse and marital rape may be "addicted" to this kind of relationship and will often seek out another abusive partner, if divorced (Anderson 1983; Fields & Lehman 1982; Fleming 1979).

Statutory Rape

Traditionally, **statutory rape** has referred to sexual intercourse between an adult and a legal minor. In law, a minor cannot consent to sexual intercourse so whether the minor consented or not is irrelevant to the crime. In some legal jurisdictions, such as the New Jersey Penal Code, sexual intercourse between a consenting minor female and an older male is classified as "sexual assault." If force is used, the crime is "aggravated sexual assault." The degree of the crime increases if the older person holds a position of authority, such as a minister, teacher, or Boy Scout leader. It also depends on the relationship between the two and on the difference in their ages.

Rape Fantasies

Sexual fantasies involving forced sexual activities appear to be common for both men and women. In a sexually repressive, moralistic culture, some people may enjoy fantasies of being forced to engage in and enjoy sexual practices that would otherwise be forbidden. Needless to say, the vast majority of persons who occasionally indulge in a rape fantasy as a sexual turn-on do not want to be raped or rape. Both men and women may occasionally choose to enjoy a rape or masochistic fantasy without actually being a rapist or masochist (Greendlinger & Byrne 1987; Marshall 1988).

Although rape fantasies are common for both men and women in our culture, they are also evidence of a belief that men are expected to be dominant, aggressive, unemotional, and controlling while women are expected to be submissive and nonassertive. Teaching women to express their sexual needs and desires, to be assertive about their sexuality, and to take control of their own bodies is an important factor in reducing the sexual violence of our culture. Equally important is the task of raising the consciousness of men about our prevailing values of macho masculinity, our tendency to view women as sex objects, and the need for men to express their emotions and to improve their communications skills (Highlight Box 23.1).

Reducing the Risk of Sexual Assault

Avoiding High Risk Situations

The most effective way of reducing your chances of sexual assault is to avoid putting yourself in known high risk situations. If you are at a party, make sure you watch your alcohol use and do not lose your self-control. If you are alone on a deserted street or subway platform especially late at night, walking across a dark parking lot, or strolling through an unlighted part of the campus, you may be putting yourself at risk of being mugged or sexually assaulted. Hitch-hiking carries a high risk. Leaving your doors and windows open or unlocked may facilitate an assault (McCombie 1980).

Avoiding Silent Signals

The image you present, especially the way you walk, can send out a clear message advertising your vulnerability to a potential assailant. Betty Grayson (1981) videotaped 60 persons walking in a high-crime area of New York City and asked prisoners convicted of repeated assaults and rapes to rate each person for vulnerability to assault. The scale ran from "a very easy rip-off" to "avoid, too risky, not vulnerable enough."

A second set of prisoners then rated each of the 60 videotapes using Grayson's scale. The body movements were also analyzed against standards of nonverbal communications. The persons the prisoners picked as highly vulnerable and safe candidates for mugging or rape all showed similar patterns in the way they walked and carried themselves. These people were sending out silent body language messages telling a would-be assailant they were vulnerable. The five most obvious traits were

HIGHLIGHT BOX 23.1.
WHAT MEN CAN DO
TO HELP STOP RAPE

Men Stopping Rape, Inc. started in Madison, Wisconsin, when a group of college men decided to take action on issues of sexuality, masculinity, friendships between men and women and between men, sexual assault, violence awareness, and homophobia. They talk with men in high schools and colleges about these issues, organize conferences and rallies, and network with other antirape and antiviolence groups.

Members also distribute pamphlets and posters with information about factors that pro-mote sexual violence and practical ways men can fight rape and sexual violence. Their one-page summary of what every man can do to help create a rape-free culture is reproduced here. How do you feel about the factors listed in the Rape Spectrum? What can you do, as a man or as a woman, to shift our culture and individuals from the Rape Spectrum to the Support Spectrum?

Information on Men Stopping Rape, Inc. can be obtained by writing Box 316, 306 N. Brooks St., Madison, WI 53715.

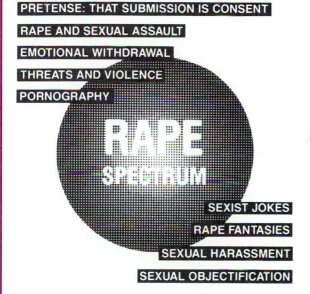

PRETENSE: THAT SUBMISSION IS CONSENT
RAPE AND SEXUAL ASSAULT
EMOTIONAL WITHDRAWAL
THREATS AND VIOLENCE
PORNOGRAPHY

RAPE SPECTRUM

SEXIST JOKES
RAPE FANTASIES
SEXUAL HARASSMENT
SEXUAL OBJECTIFICATION

DEVELOP FULL RELATIONSHIPS WITH MEN AND WOMEN
RECOGNIZE AND INTERRUPT SEXUAL ASSAULT
CONFRONT WOMAN-HATING ATTITUDES
DISCUSS YOUR EXPECTATIONS
RESPECT OTHERS' FEELINGS
TALK ABOUT SEX

SUPPORT SPECTRUM

JOIN MSR
GIVE WOMEN SPACE
TAKE "NO" FOR AN ANSWER
SUPPORT ANTI-RAPE ORGANIZATIONS
ASK WOMEN WHAT MAKES THEM FEEL UNSAFE
ENCOURAGE WOMEN'S EFFORTS TO EMPOWER THEMSELVES

1988 © Men Stopping Rape, Inc.
Designed by Gardner Grady

- A stride that is either too long or too short for one's overall build and leg length.
- Swinging the right arm and leg forward, and then the left arm and leg, instead of swinging the right arm forward as the left leg takes a step forward, and vice versa.

- Walking by lifting the whole foot and setting it down rather than using the more graceful heel-to-toe step.
- Moving individual parts of the body in a disjointed way, instead of moving the whole body smoothly in an integrated way.
- Moving the upper and lower halves of the body as if they were separated; for instance, letting the lower part of the body move freely while holding the body above the waist rigid.

Have a friend study your way of walking to see if you exhibit any of these silent invitations. Study the way other people walk and see if you can recognize these signals.

Practical Suggestions

Every rape prevention pamphlet or booklet offers detailed advice on "how to play it smart and safe" and reduce your risk of stranger rape. These same rules apply to men who want to reduce their risk of being robbed or mugged. Sources for these more detailed safety guides are listed at the end of this chapter.

When walking or jogging: Avoid dark, unlighted areas. Have a companion at night if possible. Walk or jog in the open, not near bushes where someone can hide. Never hitchhike or accept a ride from a stranger. If attacked, defend yourself, scream, run, strike—aim for the face, groin, or foot with your keys, a book, a pen, your knees, hands, or feet.

When driving: Park in lighted areas. Have your keys in hand as you approach your car. Check the backseat before getting in. Keep your doors locked and windows up when driving. Check the area before getting out of your car and then lock it. If you see a disabled motorist, don't stop; inform the police and give them a location. If you have car trouble on a major highway, raise the hood, return to your car, roll up the windows, lock the doors and wait for the police or a tow truck.

At home: Keep your doors and windows locked. Use your initials on your mailbox and in your telephone listing. Never open your door to a stranger. Have a peephole installed in your door. Keep a telephone by your bedside with the number for the police handy or on automatic dial.

An Important Caution

Sexual assaults somehow trigger a need to blame someone, as if that would somehow make some sense out of it. This reality makes discussions about safety guidelines, about factors that put one at risk for sexual assaults and incest, and about behavior and attitudes that may signal a victim's vulnerability quite risky. Such discussions are subjective, emotional, moralistic, and often political. They are loaded with serious risk of what is now called **victim precipitation**, blaming the victim of a rape and absolving the assailant. No matter what people do, it does not justify being forced into unwanted sexual activity. Leaving a patio door unlocked may be foolhardy, but it does not excuse the robber or rapist.

A Developmental-Descriptive Profile of the Rapist

Developmental-descriptive profiles of sex offenders who have served time in prison indicate that adult patterns of repetitive violent behavior and sexual assaults are quite often associated with two developmental factors. Many rapists have a persistent, unresolved perception of themselves as socially inadequate, what psychologists term an *inadequate personality*. They also have an *early sexual trauma* that has not been faced and worked through (Groth 1979; McCombie 1980; Prendergast 1979). This developmental profile does not apply to psychopath and sociopath rapists who follow a different developmental path.

Some people with an inadequate personality and/or early sexual trauma get help to work through these problems and adapt socially. They may also compensate in socially acceptable ways by *denial*, becoming overachievers, or by accepting their inadequacies and remaining underachievers.

When *deniers* turn to antisocial behavior, they use force and terror to control and degrade their victims. *Acceptors* use seduction to control their victims by winning their acceptance.

Deniers who are only trying to cope with an unresolved inadequate personality may turn to spouse and child abuse, robbery, murder, or terrorism. Acceptors coping with an unresolved inadequate personality may become victims of abuse, con artists, forgers, or embezzlers.

Deniers with unresolved feelings of inadequacy plus an early sexual trauma may turn to sexual assault, anger-motivated exhibitionism, obscene phone calls with violent fantasies and language, or rape. Acceptors may turn to seductive exhibitions and phones calls, voyeurism, and seductive pedophilia.

Resisting a Rape Attempt

In a rape situation, the most important thing to do is remain calm and not panic. If you think you can escape, do so. But this decision must be made quickly (Bart & O'Brien 1985). Be sure the assailant doesn't have a weapon. Several studies indicate that the more women resist an assault as soon as it begins, the more likely they are to escape the attacker. Among 915 assault cases, Selkin (1975, 1978) found that one-third successfully escaped by immediately running away, screaming for help, and fighting and resisting physically. In three studies by Ageton (1983), men reported the primary reason for not completing an assault was the victim's resistance. According to Mary Lystad, chief of the National Center for the Prevention and Control of Rape at the National Institute of Mental Health, "The thing not to do is to act utterly passive. A woman who behaves as if she is weak and defenseless appears to increase her risk of rape."

If you think that it is too dangerous to try to escape, then accept the assailant as a person and try to talk him out of it. It is important to give the assailant the illusion of being in control. Do not directly challenge his need for control or insult him.

Many feminists strongly advocate self-defense training for women (Offir 1975). Despite the prevalence of this training, many women are still reluctant to use their new skills in self-defense because of their early social conditioning. Sexual assailants are aware of this reluctance and are not as intimidated or put off by the new emphasis on self-defense for women as you might expect. Whether or not a woman is willing and ready to use these forms of defense, common sense suggests that she will have more self-confidence and present a less vulnerable image to the would-be assailant if she knows self-defense.

In a major study of attempted rape and robbery by strangers, women who did not resist an attempted rape were raped 58% of the time compared with only one-third of the women who physically resisted. When the rapist was not armed, only 19% of the women who offered verbal resistance, screamed, or ran away were raped. Physical resistance, especially when the assailant was armed, not only increased the risk of injury but also the success of the rape attempts (Block & Skogan 1982).

Whatever your views on the conflicting suggestions of how to cope with an assault situation may be, it is important to examine all the suggestions and options. The consequences of making the wrong choice can be a matter of life and death. Keeping in mind the varieties of motives and personalities involved in sexual assault, the risk of physical resistance should be carefully weighed (Bart & O'Brien 1985).

Incest

Sexual Abuse Within the Family

Every year in the United States 2 million children are physically abused and 2,000 die of abuse (Figure 23.4). Pedophilic sexual abuse of children by nonfamily members is a major social concern, as we saw in Chapter 20. **Incest** involves any form of socially prohibited sexual activity between family members, including stepparents and significant other adults. Incest involves not only prohibited behavior, but also a willful perpetrator who uses his or her power and authority to abuse a relatively powerless victim.

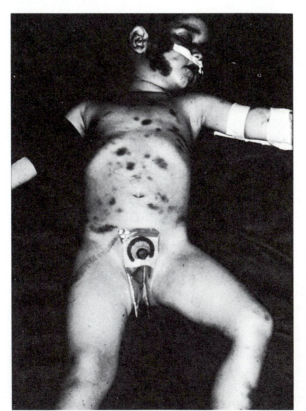

Figure 23.4. *This child has been battered and burned with lighted cigarettes and scalded milk. Studies have shown that parents who physically abuse their children were themselves often physically abused when they were young. Such violence-prone men and women also are likely to be afraid to touch and receive physical pleasure. Often they are intolerant of premarital and extramarital sex and have extremely poor sex lives.*

Eighty-five percent of incest victims are female, with the most common form occurring between a father or stepfather and daughter (Stark 1984). Incest is seldom a onetime event. It is usually repeated over the years (Daugherty 1984; Vander Mey & Neff 1986; Ward 1985).

But what constitutes sexual activity, and who are considered family members? In other cultures, adults may masturbate a restless infant or child instead of giving it a pacifier. In our culture, that would be considered incestuous abuse. Our culture also prohibits forcing a child to masturbate an adult, exposing a child to pornography or pornographically exploiting a child, "talking dirty" to a child, and adult-child vaginal, oral, or anal intercourse. Overt incest involves a parent or adult who is sexually stimulated by invading a child's privacy, observing a child fully or partially undressed, or by nudity deliberately engaged in for sexual stimulation. Covert incest may be verbal, involving inappropriate sexual talk with or in the presence of a child, or a boundary violation, in which the privacy of a child is violated. Emotional incest occurs when a parent uses a child to meet the emotional needs a spouse normally meets (Bradshaw 1988; Kempe & Kempe 1984; Vander Mey & Neff 1986).

We have no reliable statistics on the incidence of incest, but it does occur at all socioeconomic levels and in all kinds of families. A 1965 national survey suggested a low incidence of 4%. In Morton Hunt's 1974 national survey, 20% reported noncoital incest and another 7% reported having engaged in incestuous vaginal intercourse. In Finkelhor's 1979–80 study of students at six New England colleges, 32% reported incest. Morgan (1982) estimates that between 30% and 70% of children with alcoholic parents encounter some form of sexual abuse. The figures are also high for prison populations.

Gaining an insight into the realities of incest is not easy. When Freud encountered incestuous experiences in two of his female patients, he chose not to attribute their hysteria to the trauma of incest but to declare the women were suffering from childhood fantasies. Although approximately 24% of Kinsey's subjects reported frightening childhood sexual experiences, Kinsey concluded that ". . . children should not be upset by these experiences. If they were, this was not the fault of the aggressor, but of prudish parents and teachers who caused the child to become 'hysterical' " (Herman 1981:16). For many years, viewpoints like the ones we cite here offered by respected pioneers in the field of sexuality curtailed deeper studies of incest.

The incestuous father/stepfather is usually a dominating patriarchal figure, isolated from his family, an introvert with few friends, a hardworking, good provider. He is an insecure man who has trouble relating to people his own age. He often considers females as inferior and sees his children as objects. He also is opposed to seeking sex outside the home from prostitutes or in an affair (Blake-White & Kline 1985; Daugherty 1984; Vander Mey & Neff 1986). Fathers commonly rationalize their incestuous behavior, saying they couldn't help themselves: "She was too attractive, too sexy" or "There was this romantic compulsion." Some justify their incest by claiming it is better to "keep-it-in-the-family" and preferable to adultery, or a way of protecting the daughter from the dangers of sex with a male her own age. When caught, incest offenders commonly deny their involvement, leaving the daughter with the guilt and shame (Meiselman 1979:39).

The role of the mother in father-daughter incest has received little attention. Some clinicians and researchers see the mother as overtly facilitating or at least silently accepting the incest out of fear or because she lacks the courage to confront it. In some families, the daughter may be groomed to become the primary female or to take the mother's place sexually. There are cases where mothers have put their daughters in jeopardy because this is the sort of relationship they had as a child. However, Chandler (1982) and Ward (1985:164) deny that the mother has any significant involvement at all with incestuous affairs.

Incestuous relations develop gradually, beginning on average between ages 9 and 11, before puberty and often before the child has completed the developmental stages of trust, autonomy, initiative, and industry described by Erikson. Despite the media images of the seductive daughter in novels and films like *Lolita* and *Pretty Baby*, the 12-year-old prostitute in *Taxi Driver*, and the use of female children as seductive high fashion models, only rarely does a daughter actually "seduce" the father (Chandler 1982:64; Meiselman 1979; Rush 1980).

Why don't daughters tell? Threats, promises, and/or rewards from their father are part of the reason. Many children simply don't understand what is being done to them, or that it is wrong. Many believe they are protecting younger sisters.

The immediate impact of incest leaves the child feeling confused, angry, afraid, ashamed, and guilty. Kempe and Kempe suggest that:

> Sexually abused children . . . are all stunted in their emotional growth, their personal timetable of normal learning, and in the caring, affection, safety, and support that a family and friends can give. They all, in their own way, are hindered or are unsupported and [left] alone to face developmental tasks and so lose essential parts of their childhood. They also lose the joy of discovery, of tenderness, of compassion which form such a vital part of personality development. (1984:204)

Father/daughter incestuous affairs may end when the daughter refuses to continue it, when she tells her mother who puts an end to it, when she becomes pregnant, when the affair is reported to legal authorities, or when she simply leaves home.

Other forms of incest involve brothers and sisters, cousins, and very rarely mothers and their sons.

Coping During and After a Sexual Assault

During an Assault Attempt

Unfortunately the best prevention strategies sometime fail. If you can't escape a rape situation, observe and try to remember the attacker's face, build, age, clothing, and other features. A few strands of hair or a little skin under your fingernails can provide forensics experts with fragments of chromosomes that are as unique and irrefutable as fingerprints. Make it clear to the assailant that you are not condoning the act, and that it is not pleasurable (Grossman & Sutherland 1982; McCombie 1980).

Reporting Rape or Incest

Many communities today have hot lines and shelters for victims of rape, spouse abuse, child abuse, and incest. These aids are listed in telephone books under Emergency Services, Victim Assistance Programs, or Social Services.

In the case of rape, contact a friend who can provide emotional support as soon as you can. Then contact the police and a rape crisis center or a woman's health center. Although rape victims often want to shower, douche, and dispose of their clothes to remove reminders of the rape, it is vital not to destroy important clues that can bring a conviction in a trial.

Quick medical care is also important. Hospital emergency room personnel, who are often trained to deal with sexual assaults, may be more helpful than your own personal physician. All injuries and bruises should be documented. Vaginal and anal smears should be taken if penetration occurred. Clothes which might have semen on them should be examined. To eliminate the risk of pregnancy, a drug can be taken that will prevent pregnancy. Tests for STDs should be done as part of the follow-up treatment.

Although many victims are reluctant to report sexual assault, particularly if it is an acquaintance, a prompt report makes it possible to press legal charges later if you decide to do so. Reporting an assault as soon as possible also makes the report more believable because the details are fresh in your mind and a sensitive, skilled investigator can obtain more details and support for the charge. Police departments often have trained officers who are sensitive to the survivor's situation. Remember you do not have to answer any questions that are not directly related to the incident. You will be asked to make a complete statement concerning the assault. If the assailant is apprehended, you will be asked to identify him or her in a lineup from behind a one-way mirror. In federal courts and many states, the victim's past conduct and lifestyle cannot be brought up in a rape trial.

Cases of child abuse and incest may be reported anonymously to health departments, social services, or the police. Teachers, doctors, nurses, and other health workers must by law report any cases of child abuse that come to their attention.

The Trauma of Rape and Abuse

Rape may or may not result in physical injury, but the psychological effects are inescapable and devastating for female rape victims who range in age from infants to women in their nineties. Boys and men who are raped by other males, and to a lesser extent males raped by women, also experience **rape trauma syndrome**. These reactions include strong emotions and feelings of shame, humiliation, rage, personal violation, fear, confusion, the sense of having lost power or control over one's life, sexual phobias, a compulsion to wash the body in an attempt to wash off the degradation and shame, sexual dysfunction, and fear of sexual intimacy. A rape victim may fear being alone and worry about being followed. Nightmares, phobias, trouble eating, and disrupted sleep patterns are common reactions. A rape victim may not want to discuss the attack with others, and may even deny anything ever happened (Burgess & Holstrom 1975).

Possibly the most common and difficult aspect of rape trauma syndrome to work through is the feeling of the victim that she or he somehow caused or

Figure 23.5. *Many social service groups and police departments are now trained to handle the trauma of sexual assault and provide needed counseling and support for the survivors of rape, incest and sexual abuse.*

unknowingly invited the attack. "If I had only not gone to that bar, not opened the door, not walked into that elevator . . ." This feeling is particularly true for heterosexual adolescent males who are raped by another male. "Why did he choose me? Did he, perhaps, see something in my behavior that suggested I might be gay? Why did I have an orgasm, when I know I am straight and have never wanted a homosexual experience?" The victim's family, husband, wife, girlfriend, or boyfriend may blame the victim for what happened, implying that the assault was somehow invited. Some men react in a matter-of-fact way because they cannot understand the humiliation and violence a friend or loved one experiences after being raped (Figure 23.5).

The trauma of incest is perhaps even more devastating than rape because of the victim's immaturity and the disruption of normal family functions. In incest, the fundamental trust a child has in a parent is demolished. This violation makes it extremely difficult for the incest victim to trust someone close ever again. Blume (1986) calls the victims of incest the "walking wounded." The long-term effects of incest "are similar to those described in the rape-trauma syndrome, but may be longer lasting and more severe" (Goodwin 1985:165).

Working through the trauma of any sexual assault usually requires the help of a professional counselor who is trained to recognize the many different symptoms that can follow a rape, sexual abuse, or incest, and who can then help the victim work these through either in a one-on-one counseling situation or in a support group.

Sexual Harassment

Sexual Harassment from 1964 to the Present

A 1976 *Redbook* survey reported that 88% of the women stated that they had experienced overt sexual harassment and regarded it as a serious work-related problem. A 1988 *Men's Health* survey reported 57% of its male readers stated they had been sexually propositioned at work, and 58% admitted they had at least occasional sexual fantasies about co-workers.

Sexual discrimination was prohibited by Title VII of the Civil Rights Act of 1964. But it took over 15 years for the government to figure out how to enforce the sexual harassment implications of the act, and even longer for business corporations to understand the law. In a 1981 *Redbook-Harvard Business Review* survey, 63% of the top level managers and 52% of middle managers believed that "the amount of sexual harassment at work is greatly exaggerated." Although the amount of sexual harassment in the workplace has probably decreased because of the growing awareness of its risks, *Working Woman* reported some business managers stating that "More than 95 percent of our complaints have merit" (Sandroff 1988).

Two Definitions

The interim guidelines issued by the Equal Employment Opportunity Commission in 1980 defined **sexual harassment** as "unwelcome sexual advances, requests for sexual favors, and other verbal or physical conduct of a sexual nature" when

1. submission to such conduct is made either explicitly or implicitly a term or condition of an individual's employment;

"NOTICE? THEY'RE A LOT MORE
SENSITIVE THAN THEY USED TO BE?"

Figure 23.6.

2. submission to or rejection of such conduct by an individual is used as the basis for employment decisions affecting such individual; or when

3. such conduct has the purpose or effect of substantially interfering with an individual's work performance or creating an intimidating, hostile, or offensive working environment (Deane & Tillar 1981).

Notice that this definition, and those for date rape, are gender-free. They can apply to a man sexually harassing or raping a woman or another man, or to a woman sexually harassing or raping a man or another woman.

What Constitutes Sexual Harassment?

Sexual harassment exists throughout the business and the academic world. Although both men and women can be victims, women are more often the target because men are usually in positions of greater power and women are in the vulnerable position of being subordinates. The woman most likely to be victimized can be of any age, but she tends to be vulnerable, young, belonging to a minority group, and unable to afford to resist because she needs the job. In this rapidly changing scene, sexual harassment by subordinates of the supervisors or managers is becoming more common.

Sexual harassment includes a number of activities that tend to control, influence, and frustrate one's career, job, or grades (Highlight Box 23.2). These activities may include

- verbal abuse and sexist remarks;
- leering or ogling a co-worker, subordinate, or supervisor;
- fondling or touching a co-worker, subordinate, or supervisor;
- pressure to have sexual intimacy or intercourse in return for promotions or better grades; and
- threatening demotion or firing for not cooperating sexually.

Dealing with Sexual Harassment

Fortunately, many companies and colleges have developed statements defining and prohibiting sexual harassment, often in response to protests and court action by employees. These policy statements usually explain specific procedures and remedies employees and students can pursue in case they become victims of this type of sexual assault. Many state Fair Employment Practices protect workers from sex discrimination. Careful documentation, a diary noting the details of each episode, and witnesses are important elements to have in hand when you decide to file a complaint of sexual harassment with academic officials, an employer, or the courts.

Another way of solving the problem of sexual harassment suggested by Mary Rowe, a labor economist at the Massachusetts Institute of Technology, is to write the harasser a letter. In the first part of the letter, the victim gives a straightforward record of what has happened. The term sexual harassment is never used, but the detailed record, with dates, circumstances, and a simple statement of what happened each time, gives a clear message.

HIGHLIGHT BOX 23.2.
MYTHS AND FACTS
ABOUT SEXUAL HARASSMENT

MYTH 1: Women should ignore sexual harassment when it occurs.

REALITY: In one survey, 33% tried to ignore the unwanted attentions. In 75% of these cases, the harassment continued or became worse. One-quarter of the women who ignored the sexual propositions received unwarranted reprimands from their bosses or had their workloads increased.

MYTH 2: Men don't have to worry about sexual harassment at work.

REALITY: Fifty-seven percent of the male readers of *Men's Health* magazine reported they had been sexually propositioned at work.

MYTH 3: If a woman really wants to discourage unwanted sexual attention, she can do so. If she's sexually harassed, she must have asked for it.

REALITY: Many men believe a woman's "no" is really "yes" and therefore do not accept her refusal. Moreover, when a man is in a position of power, such as an employer or teacher, the victim may feel forced to submit.

MYTH 4: Most charges of sexual harassment are false. Women use these charges as a way of "getting back" at a man with whom they are angry.

REALITY: Women who openly charge harassment are often not believed, may be ridiculed, may lose their job, be given a bad grade, or be mistreated in some other way. Women have little to gain from false charges.

MYTH 5: Sexual harassment is really not harassment at all. It is a fact of life, a purely personal matter between men and women.

REALITY: When a woman is harassed or coerced by a professor or her employer, she is not always in a position to reject such overtures. And, if she does, she may face severe consequences. Several courts have ruled that sexual harassment constitutes sex discrimination under Title VII of the Civil Rights Act, and in some instances have awarded damages to the victim. Whether sexual harassment against students constitutes sex discrimination under Title IX of the education amendments is now under litigation.

The second part of the letter calmly states the writer's candid reactions to these facts, without emphasizing the negative effects of the harassment. Stressing the negative effects may aggravate the situation if the person doing the harassing is motivated by aggression and now has evidence that the harassment is working. The letter can end with a brief statement of what the writer wants to happen. "I want our relationship to be purely professional from now on," "Please review my papers and grade in a more objective way," or "Please withdraw my last evaluation until we can work out a fair one." A copy of the letter should be kept as documentation.

Rowe reports that the typical reaction to such a letter is no reaction. The harassment just stops. Writing the letter often gives the victim a renewed sense of control and takes the person out of the passive role. If the letter is ignored, it can become the first step in a formal complaint process.

Several organizations offer counseling and referral services in cases of sexual harassment. Some groups deal specifically with harassment on the college campus. See list in the Appendix, page 651.

Key Concepts

1. The black and white legal use of the term rape is being replaced by "sexual assault," which is not restricted to forced vaginal intercourse but includes a continuum of behaviors ranging from exploitive behavior, persuasion and threats used with a reluctant partner, sexual coercion, sexual harassment, and acquaintance rape, to actual physical force and stranger rape.

2. Both men and women can be the perpetrators in sexual assaults and coercive sex.

3. Sexual assault may be motivated by quite different motives. Rage and the desire to control and degrade the victim are dominant among convicted rapists. Various factors are cited in the case of date rape, including the use of alcohol and/or drugs, a distorted macho self-image, peer pressure, the need of the male to control, the feeling that a man's sexual drive cannot be controlled once a certain point is reached, and other beliefs.

4. Incest is not an uncommon experience for many Americans, with estimates ranging from 4% to 7% for coital incest and a higher frequency for other sexual contact. The most common type of incest occurs between siblings or cousins of the same age; next in frequency is father-daughter incest; and much less frequent is mother-son contact.

5. Date rape and courtship coercion are the most common form of forcible sexual activity. Misinterpretation of messages by both men and women, changing roles and expectations, and old values carried over into new, often less structured male-female relationships where the ground rules have yet to be worked out are important factors in these assaults.

6. Sexual harassment has been defined as any unwelcome or unsolicited sexual advance, request for sexual favors, or other verbal or physical conduct of a sexual nature whose acceptance or rejection is explicitly or implicitly used as a condition for employment, recognition, promotion, or grades.

7. A developmental/descriptive personality profile of *convicted rapists and other sexual assailants* very often includes strong feelings of personal inadequacy and unresolved early sexual traumas for which the individual has not learned to compensate in a socially acceptable way. In such cases, the rapist selects a vulnerable, controllable victim on which to vent his suppressed rage over these traumas as a way of gaining control.

8. Five out of 6 women and many men experience sexual harassment in the business and academic environment. Most victims, especially women, are selected because of their vulnerability to psychological coercion and because of their subordinate position. But the reverse can also occur with the subordinate sexually harassing a person in a supervisory position.

Key Terms

acquaintance rape (603)
coercion (600)
date rape (602)
incest (612)
marital rape (607)

rape (600)
rape trauma syndrome (615)
sexual harassment (616)
statutory rape (590)
victim precipitation (610)

Summary Questions

1. What are some common myths about rape? What are the facts?

2. To what extent, and in what types of sexual assault, are control, violence, and degradation the goal of the perpetrator? To what extent, and in what types of sexual assault, is sexual gratification and pleasure the goal?

3. What steps can a woman or man take to reduce the risk of being sexually assaulted or coerced into sexual intimacy she or he does not want?

4. What factors are known to be commonly associated with most party or fraternity rapes?

5. What strategies are recommended for a person who is confronted with a situation in which she or he is being coerced into unwanted sexual intimacies? When and how should a woman physically resist a rape attempt?

6. What procedure is recommended for handling incidents of sexual harassment?

Suggested Readings

Adams, C., & J. Fay. (1984). *Nobody Told Me It Was Rape.* Santa Cruz, CA: Network Publications.

Bart, P. B., & P. H. O'Brien. (1985). *Stopping Rape: Successful Survival Strategies.* Elmsford, NY: Pergamon Press.

Bass, E., & L. Davis. (1988). *The Courage to Heal: A Guide for Women Survivors of Child Sexual Abuse.* New York: Harper & Row.

Bradshaw, J. (1988). *Bradshaw On: Healing the Shame That Binds You.* Deerfield Beach, FL: Health Communications, Inc.

Crewdson, J. (1988). *By Silence Betrayed: Sexual Abuse of Children in America.* New York: Harper & Row.

Daughterty, L. B. (1984). *Why Me? Help for Victims of Child Sexual Abuse (Even If They Are Adults Now).* Racine, WI: Mother Courage Press.

Dzeich, B. W., & L. Weiner. (1984). *The Lecherous Professor, Sexual Harassment on Campus.* Boston: Beacon Press.

Pritchard, C. (1988). *Avoiding Rape On and Off Campus.* (2nd ed.). Wenonah, NJ: State College Publishing Company.

PART ONE: PROSTITUTION

Prostitution in America
The Varieties of
  Prostitution
The Customers Who
  Buy Sex
The Economics of
  Prostitution
Three Ways of
  Handling Prostitution
A Declining Future?

PART TWO: PORNOGRAPHY, EROTICA, AND OBSCENITY

Defining Obscenity
  in Legal Terms
Pornography's Impact
  on Individuals and
  Society
Pornography, Sexism,
  and Violence

Chapter 24

Prostitution and Pornography

Special Consultants

Bonnie Bullough, Ph.D., R.N., dean of Nursing, State University of New York at Buffalo, and coauthor of *Sin, Sickness, and Sanity: A History of Sexual Attitudes* and *Women and Prostitution: A Social History*.

Vern L. Bullough, Ph.D., R.N., dean of Natural and Social Sciences and New York Distinguished Professor at the State University of New York (Buffalo) and coauthor of *Sin, Sickness, and Sanity: A History of Sexual Attitudes* and *Women and Prostitution: A Social History*.

Depaul Genska, O.F.M., board member, Genesis House, an outreach facility for prostitutes in Chicago.

Douglas E. Mould, Ph.D., psychologist in Wichita, Kansas, and author of *A Critical Analysis of Recent Research on Violent Erotica*.

Carol A. Pollis, Ph.D., sociologist and dean of Humanities, Social Sciences, and General Education, University of Wisconsin (Green Bay), and author of several studies of feminism and pornography.

The issues of prostitution and pornography raise perplexing and controversial questions about the freedom and rights of individual citizens and the social values a society promotes in its laws. Streetwalkers, call girls, teen prostitutes, male prostitutes, homosexual prostitutes, pimps, massage parlors, and the customers who patronize these forms of prostitution have all been the subject of legal regulation. The social and financial cost of this legal regulation are examined in this chapter. Comparisons of the ways European countries and the United States have tried to control prostitution suggest the American policy is not the most effective, but also not the worst.

Recurring debates about what pornography and obscenity are and to what extent they should be regulated by law provide a second focus for this chapter. The conclusions of two White House Commissions and the U.S. Surgeon General's report on pornography shed some light on the varieties and meanings of pornography and obscenity. This chapter also examines what we know and don't know about the sexist character of most pornography and about the causal connection between the use of pornography and sexual violence. Some comparisons are also made between the European and American experience with pornography.

PART ONE
PROSTITUTION

Prostitution is the exchange of sexual favors for money. Although most prostitution involves females providing sexual services for males, there are male prostitutes, mostly in their teens and twenties, who exchange sex for money with older male homosexuals. Some male prostitutes also provide sexual services for women.

Prostitution in America

Commercialized prostitution thrives when there is a concentration of population and when women have limited viable alternatives to support themselves.

Prostitution did not prosper in the sparse, spread out rural population of America before 1800. In the cities, despite a shortage of women, there were always women on the financial fringe of urban life—unattached, single women with few skills, for whom prostitution provided a way of survival and at times a way to find a husband. In the colonies, servants, apprentices, and slaves were not allowed to marry, a custom that encouraged prostitution. Indentured male servants, apprentices, and even slaves could use the tips they earned—they received no salary—to buy a little pleasure at the local tavern (Bullough & Bullough 1987:211–221).

When industrialization began in the 19th century in New England and the mid-Atlantic states, women, mostly young and unmarried, provided the main work force for the textile mills. Though wages were lower, women preferred the freedom mill work gave them to the tightly regulated life of a domestic servant. There was little if any social life available after work hours for these single persons living apart from their families. Since they often shared a boardinghouse room with six to eight women, sometimes sleeping three to a bed, they often found their only relief at the local tavern. With men leaving for the frontier and a surplus of women, young women sometimes turned to prostitution for escape or affection.

In the mid-1800s, waves of immigration created a surplus of males trying to save enough money to bring their wives and families over from the old country. At the same time, in each new wave of immigration, many of the first women to arrive were already involved in "the trade." Other unattached immigrant women turned to prostitution in an effort to survive (Bullough & Bullough 1987:216–217).

In the frontier towns and mining camps of the West, men far outnumbered women. Thousands of women were imported from Mexico, Chile, Peru, the South Pacific, and China to work in the flourishing brothels. After the Civil War, American cities tried to follow the example of their European counterparts by segregating prostitutes to certain areas, requiring them to register or be licensed. In an attempt to control venereal diseases, they were also required to have regular physical examinations. For a while, licensing seemed to work. Between 1880 and 1920, prostitution was commonplace and legal. Since few prostitutes bothered to register, licensing was not effective in controlling disease. Police supervision only spawned bribes and payoffs. Gradually, most European nations and the United States took steps to make the importation of women for the purposes of prostitution, called white slavery, a crime. In many nations including the United States, regulation or licensing gave way to criminalization of prostitution (Bullough & Bullough 1987:220–231;259–280; Smith 1978:102–112).

The Varieties of Prostitution

Prostitution is a commercial venture. The sellers have to know their market and what their customers want. Since the product is illegal in all states but Nevada, there is a distribution problem. To make a living, prostitutes have to find ways of getting their product to their customers. This situation has made it profitable for some people in legal businesses to make extra income by providing support services for prostitutes and their managers. With prostitution a crime, the women and men who engage in it often are forced to turn to those in the criminal system for protection and support.

The central issue in prostitution, however, is the product: sexual services in exchange for money. The women and men involved in the business of prostitution cater to a wide variety of customers and customer interests. Some prostitutes are in the business full time. They have no other job skills and are locked into this way of earning a living. Others, both female and male, have additional jobs and engage in prostitution to supplement their incomes. Some prostitutes enjoy their work; others despise it and would get out if they could find a viable alternative. Some entered prostitution by choice, some by accident, and some as the almost inevitable outcome of circumstances.

Prostitutes may be classified according to how visible they are to the public, who their clients are, the kinds of service they offer, and their age (Alexander 1983:2–4).

Figure 24.1. *Annie and her friends on Pike Street in Seattle, Washington, are typical of thousands of teenagers who have either been kicked out of their homes or have chosen to escape physical and sexual abuse at home. They often band together and become a sort of family, using drugs and sex to survive on the street.*

Female Prostitution

Streetwalkers

Prostitutes who solicit on the street, in bars, and in hotel lobbies have limited overhead with matching low fees. *Streetwalkers* usually come from the lower socioeconomic classes or are runaway teenagers (Figure 24.1). Drug addiction is a major problem among streetwalkers and with drug addiction comes the increased risk of HIV infection and AIDS. Prostitutes in Newark, New Jersey, have one of the highest HIV infection rates in the nation because of the widespread IV drug usage.

Because their work is illegal, they often become involved with a *pimp*, a manager who provides the necessities of everyday life, housing, food, and clothing, plus the all-important protection of bail and a lawyer in the case of an arrest, in return for a large cut of the prostitute's fees. Because of their visibility, streetwalkers are the most vulnerable to harassment and arrest, but rarely spend much time in jail. They are usually released through the so-called revolving doors of the courts as soon as their bail is paid by the pimp. The usual picture of a pimp with a "stable" is that of a male who physically and emotionally abuses his "girls." This stereotype is often true of streetwalkers, where the relationship is one of accepted dependence and exploitation. Many streetwalkers do not have pimps but live with men who provide similar services in return for the women's plying their trade to support their drug habits. Streetwalkers who use prostitution to support drug habits often trade sex for drugs. Since they have no health insurance and may not be able to pay for medical care, they rely on being arrested occasionally and sent to a hospital for a check-up and STD treatment before trial or release.

Some prostitutes specialize in catering to certain types of client interests. "Amazons," for instance, provide S&M domination. Such specialists may operate out in the open, in a particular area known for this service, or they may work out of a house or hotel.

Brothels and Bordellos

Houses of prostitution are less common today than they were in the past. The famous houses of the Storyville area of New Orleans or the Barbary Coast of San Francisco were often very luxurious, and women both lived and worked in the same brothel for many years. Because of legal problems, most whorehouses today are seedy and in disrepair. If they are tolerated by the local police, they may be better maintained. The hostess and business manager, usually called the madam, is often a former prostitute. Brothels sometimes advertise their services in "underground" newspapers or in the "free press." The only legal bordellos or houses of pleasure in the United States today are in Nevada where a 1971 court decision allowed counties the discretion of legalizing and licensing prostitution (Bullough & Bullough 1987:284–285; Lerner 1988).

In most cities today, bars and massage parlors may double as "fast-service" brothels. Bars usually offer the whole range of sexual services, from masturbation, "handworks," and fellatio to intercourse. Clients are asked to be fully undressed before the service and before a fee is agreed upon, which helps to eliminate arrests by undercover police.

Escorts and Call Girls

Escorts and *call girls* are considered the "class" of the profession. Their "dates" are arranged by an intermediary or by personal referral. Call girls do not solicit on the street. They may come from middle-class suburban families and may be housewives moonlighting to earn extra money. Call girls may also provide escort services for men who require a woman companion for a social or business event. They usually have regular clients who contribute to their maintenance by providing clothes and other gifts, in addition to high hourly charges—often in excess of $100 an hour for sexual services. In 1984 this form of prostitution made headlines across the nation with the arrest of "The Mayflower Madam," Sydney Biddle Barrows. Barrows had run an elegant escort service, providing flawlessly dressed and polished "girls" as companions for leaders in business and politics (Barrows 1986) (Figure 24.2).

Lifestyles of Female Prostitutes

Although prostitutes often say they are in the profession only for economic reasons, outside observers have found that the economic motive is usually accompanied by other factors in the prostitute's background which also contribute to her moving into prostitution (Laner 1974). Depaul Genska, a Franciscan priest who works with prostitutes in Chicago, has found that most of the women prostitutes he meets come from sexually repressed families. Women who work on the street or in bars and massage parlors often were sexually abused as children (James 1976; Satterfield & Listiak 1982). The work gives them feelings of personal worth as desirable women. The money they earn is visible proof of

Figure 24.2. *Front-page headlines reported the arrest and trial of the "Mayflower Madam," Sidney Biddle Barrows, for "promoting prostitution." Barrows is a wealthy New York socialite whose ancestors came here on the Mayflower. The "girls" in her escort service were flawlessly dressed and trained to please their rich, prominent, and powerful clients. Many of Barrows's employees attended diplomatic and society functions on the arms of the world's business and political leaders.*

that worth as well as a way of making a living. Other motives may also come into play, such as a supposedly glamorous life, good income from nonroutine work, support for a drug or alcohol habit, and the urging of a boyfriend or husband who sees the financial advantages (Alexander 1983:8).

In some societies, all women who are not part of the traditional marriage system are candidates for prostitution. With no viable ways of supporting themselves, widows who cannot rely on children or relatives, women without dowries, orphans, and poor women are forced to turn to prostitution. Immigrant and minority women are also sources of recruits. "Prostitution tends to be symptomatic of economic inequality rather than uniform poverty in a society" (Bullough & Bullough 1987:296).

Although we hear a lot about young girls being forced into a life of prostitution, studies reveal that few women are actually coerced into this way of life. Only about 4% of the prostitutes in Gebhard's sample (1969) were forced into prostitution. Most women appear to become prostitutes by "enlistment rather than recruitment" (Gagnon & Simon 1968). Suffering in an unstable lower-class or lower-middle-class family, they often hear about prostitution from a friend or acquaintance, or actively seek out a prostitute to gain entry into the profession. Although they may have been more promiscuous in their teen years than their age peers in college, their attitudes toward premarital sexual intercourse and sexual intimacy are often more conservative than found in the college environment (Coleman 1972; Tollison & Adams 1979). Many of the prostitutes in Gebhard's study (1969) had no regrets over their decision to become a prostitute, even after being exposed to physical and mental abuse, drugs, blackmail, and jail.

According to Savitz and Rosen (1988), prostitutes consistently describe their sexual relations with customers and lovers as usually or extremely enjoyable and highly orgasmic, certainly higher than reported by the general population. Most women reported enjoying oral and anal sex with current lovers all or most of the time. A considerable percentage reported enjoying sadomasochism but usually not with their lovers. In Gebhard's study (1969), married prostitutes reported being more orgasmic with clients than with their husbands, but 20 percent also reported being nonorgasmic. On the other hand, the sociologist Nancy Lee reports that the hundreds of streetwalkers she has interviewed in a large New Jersey city reported little if any enjoyment of their sexual relations, whether with customers or their lovers. Their sole interest in life was to get money to pay for their next drug high, and providing sex for men just happened to be the easiest means to this goal.

As a career, prostitution is not a profession in which seniority counts. Age, disease, and drug addiction take their toll. "Squaring up" and returning to a more legitimate lifestyle is not easy. Some may escape by marrying a client. But few full-time prostitutes have a skill they can put to use. Married women and part-time prostitutes have it much easier, since they are not fully committed to prostitution and have continued to keep contact with "straight" society (Benjamin & Masters 1964; Winick & Kinsie 1971; Young 1970).

Teenage Prostitution

Almost half of all runaway children are believed to spend at least some time as prostitutes. According to a 1982 U. S. General Accounting Office Report, there are 2.4 million American teenagers involved in prostitution. These teenagers share some common characteristics. They have poor self-images. Lured by the glamor of the big city and a call to adventure, they usually are running away from homes where they were left unsupervised and on their own. Rejected by their peers and with few friends, teenage prostitutes need adult attention and affection, and try to find these in prostitution (Alexander 1983:8–10; Satchell 1986).

Juveniles who move into prostitution or participate in making pornography frequently experience a kind of psychological paralysis. They may, or may not, hate what they are doing. Being coerced into prostitution or pornography, coupled with a poor self-image, rejection by peers, and the lack of friends often results in teenage prostitutes having no sense of being able to control their lives. Many teenage prostitutes simply accept being trapped and victimized, and cannot conceive of any alternative (Silbert 1986:29–30).

Male Prostitution

Most heterosexual male prostitutes are not street hustlers. They usually have steady customers, or relationships that are ongoing and similar to those of a high-priced call girl. A male prostitute or "gigolo" often provides an escort service or acts as a social companion for single, wealthy women. Frequently, a younger man is "kept" by a wealthy, older woman. The relationship is openly convenient, and there is usually no pretense of love or commitment. In 1972, when a special "Yellow House" opened in Hamburg, West Germany, 1,600 males volunteered to provide sexual services for women who entered the brothel through a beauty parlor (Bullough & Bullough 1987:303).

In large cities, gay male prostitutes may be as visible in sections where homosexuals gather as female streetwalkers are in other areas. These men make their contacts "cruising" in gay bars, gay baths, and public toilets, in bus and train stations, and on the streets. Often the hustler is heterosexually oriented, but seeks the homosexual trade to earn some fast money. These prostitutes are usually very flexible in their sexual activities, work without a pimp, and keep all their earnings (Harris 1973; Humphreys 1970; Reiss 1961). Today, along with heterosexual female prostitutes who are IV drug users, gay male prostitutes pose a serious risk of AIDS.

Commerical Exhibitionism/Voyeurism

In the Bible, Samson enjoyed the seductive dances of Delilah, King David watched Bathsheba undress, and King Herod was seduced by the dancing Salome. Men have long been willing to pay to see beautiful young women remove their clothes in tantalizing, seductive dances. Although they do not engage in direct sexual contact with their customers, strippers, both female and male, offer a blend of commercial sex that combines elements of both prostitution and pornography. By the mid-1980s, male strip joints had become an acceptable, almost routine part of the female consumer culture. In some respects, male strippers shatter macho male stereotypes (Figure 24.3).

The impact of the scene is distinctly feminist: Men are not such a big deal after all. In fact, reduced to bikini shorts while dancing around to a disco beat,

Figure 24.3. *In the late 1970s, a new entertainment form appeared. Housewives and businesswomen began to attend clubs where they viewed male strippers.*

they're fun to watch and a little silly, too. And what is most important is that it's up to the *women* to tip the stripper. In a parody of male behavior, women clutch at the performer's bikini and pull it to tuck a folded bill inside. ''Thus is the phallus—the awesome centerpiece of fifties sexuality—demystified in the sexual marketplace'' (Ehrenreich, Hess, & Jacobs 1987:111–113).

''Though male stripping may be seen by some as a case of role reversal and the dancers might be viewed as sex objects, it bears noting that male strippers still make better money and work under better conditions than female strippers'' (Clark 1985:54). Others dispute this statement, claiming that most female strippers and certainly female porno stars are paid more than males.

The Customers Who Buy Sex

The customer, known in slang terms as the john, trick, or date, is the most ignored person in prostitution. Society tends to keep the client out of sight without questioning why he or she seeks a prostitute for sexual services.

Men go to prostitutes for any number of reasons. They may want quick, anonymous, uninvolved sex with a guaranteed sexual release. Many men will pay for the complete attention of a woman who has no claim on them other than financial payment for specific services (Stein 1974). Some men go to prostitutes for sexual activities that their wives or partners reject. This motive is especially true of men with fetishes. Others seek prostitutes for novelty, excitement, or to learn about sex. Some men, who view their wives, female friends, and mothers as Madonnas and above the profanities of sex, can only have sex with women they consider to be tramps and whores (Bullough & Bullough 1987:299–300).

It is not uncommon for men who have had an active sexual life and then suddenly been paralyzed by an accident to decide the simplest way to find out just what they can now do sexually is to seek out a prostitute who will help them explore new sexual outlets. For some severely disabled men, prostitutes may be the only available sexual outlet (Smith & Bullough 1975).

The men who buy sex are seldom arrested. Some cities have attempted to implicate the clients by publishing their names in newspapers with the idea of embarrassing them and their families. This policy, however, raises questions of discrimination, since the names of other unconvicted felons are not published.

The Economics of Prostitution

The Criminal Element

Several factors work against any major involvement of organized crime in prostitution. As long as it is not licensed and segregated in distinct districts as it once was, prostitution is too spread out to be easily controlled. Secondly, in our much more permissive society, men do not have to pay for sex the way they had to in Victorian times. Finally, criminal groups do not take a great interest in prostitution because it doesn't pay enough, there are too many amateurs in it, and there are more lucrative fields in which to operate. However, by making prostitution a crime, American laws have forced prostitutes to associate with other criminals. In those cities where organized prostitution exists on a large scale, organized crime will be involved at some level. When prostitution functions on a large scale despite existing laws, it is only with the tolerance of police and politicians. That means bribery and intimidation. Although organized crime may not be involved, the petty criminal certainly finds prostitution a major source of income (Alexander 1983:11–12; Bullough & Bullough 1987:304).

The Costs and Politics of Enforcement

There are an estimated 450,000 female prostitutes working in the United States. They do not pay taxes. Nor are taxes paid on any of the monies that pass back and forth in the underground economy associated with prostitution, the monies that pass between prostitutes or their pimps and the hotel and motel owners and clerks, the massage parlors, the recruiters, cab drivers, doormen, and rental agents who make prostitution possible (Alexander 1983:5–7,11–12).

To get a clearer idea of the costs of making prostitution a crime, consider the costs of enforcing prostitution laws in our 16 largest cities in 1985.

Police Enforcement Costs	$53,155,688
Court Costs:	$35,627,496
Correction Costs:	$31,770,211
TOTAL 1985 COSTS	**$120,553,395**

In 1985 Dallas, Texas, police made only 2,665 arrests for the 15,000 violent crimes reported. But they made 7,280 prostitution arrests at a cost of over $10 million and almost 800,000 hours of police work. In 1986 Boston, Cleveland, and Houston police arrested twice as many people for prostitution as they did for all homicides, rapes, robberies, and assaults combined. Meanwhile, 90% of perpetrators of violent crimes evaded arrest. Between 1976 and 1985, violent crimes in the 16 largest cities rose by 32% while arrests for violent crimes rose only 3.7% and arrests for robbery and homicide actually dropped by 15%. Equally important, our 16 largest cities frequently spend more on enforcing prostitution laws than they do on either education or public welfare (Pearl 1987).

It costs about $300 to prosecute a woman each time she is arrested for prostitution. *But an arrest seldom has any effect.* In frustration, San Francisco police gave one prostitute 54 citations over a three-month period for "obstructing the sidewalk," before she finally received a 60-day jail sentence. Nine out of 10 convicted prostitutes pay a fine of $100 to $1,000. Only 11% of all convicted prostitutes get short jail terms. Prostitutes make up 30% to 50% of the population in most women's jails. Each prostitute in prison costs taxpayers $15,000 a year. Investing this money in education could provide viable alternatives for prostitutes who want to leave the profession (Pearl 1987).

Working in pairs, police spend an average of 21 hours to obtain a solicitation, make an arrest, transport the prostitute to the detention center, process her papers, write up a report, and testify in court. Undercover police cruising the street looking for a solicitation need frequent changes of disguises and rented cars. Making an arrest of a call girl is even more difficult, requiring greater expense for false identification and credit cards, hotel room, luggage, and other paraphernalia to convince the call girl that the agent is a legitimate customer and not a police officer. The hotel room is usually wiretapped and the solicitation videotaped. Arrests of prostitutes working in massage parlors present their own difficulties. It usually takes half an hour for an undercover officer to undress, shower, and get into the massage before an illegal service is offered. For a while, Houston police ran their own parlor. When that was declared entrapment by the courts, teams of 10 undercover officers began working existing modeling studios as customers. "Ten officers at a time, at $60 each, with no guarantee that we'd get solicited. . . . we could spend $3,000 or $4,000 and not make a case" (Pearl 1987:779).

Every tax dollar and every hour of police work devoted to enforcing prostitution laws means less money available for other law enforcement. In 1985 83% of all reported violent and property crimes failed to result in an arrest. In Cleveland, 18 officer hours were spent on prostitution duty for every violent crime that went without an arrest (Pearl 1987).

Typical of the politics of prostitution are periodic preelection antiprostitution campaigns. In 1978–79, New York politicians announced a Times Square Action Plan to clean the prostitutes out of the theater district. Arrests for prostitution doubled. But, in the same area, the number of rapes increased by 30% without a parallel increase in arrests for rape. Burglaries went up 22% but burglary arrests dropped by 40% (Pearl 1987:784).

Three Ways of Handling Prostitution

The history of prostitution around the world reveals three ways of coping with the inevitability of the world's oldest profession: licensing or regulating it, making it a crime, and decriminalizing it (Alexander 1983:10–15; Bullough & Bullough 1987:259–290, 302–305, 317–321).

Licensing

After many years of regulating and licensing prostitution, the United States, Italy, and France abandoned this approach because of organized pressure from women and because there are other, more effective ways to control venereal diseases. Most other European countries have also moved away from licensing to decriminalize prostitution. Only West Germany and the Netherlands still license prostitutes and restrict them to special areas. Although it allows the government to tax all aspects of the prostitution trade, mandatory registration stigmatizes prostitutes and limits their leaving the profession and their social mobility. Some suggest that licensing may reduce the transmission of diseases including AIDS, but there are other more effective ways of accomplishing this goal. As of mid-1988, 9,000 tests of Nevada's licensed prostitutes had not turned up one case of AIDS (Lerner 1988) (Figure 24.4).

The legalization of prostitution would transfer the present controls from the pimps and criminal element to the government. Physical exams for STDs, licensing, regulation of areas for prostitution, and numerous other bureaucratic matters would have to be worked out, opening the door to bribery and corruption.

Criminalization

Making prostitution a crime, **criminalization,** has done nothing to reduce its incidence in the United States or elsewhere. When prostitution is a crime, those who engage in it are forced to deal with other criminals. Bribery of law enforce-

Figure 24.4. *Two prostitutes share drinks with customers at the Salt Wells Villa, a legal house of prostitution in Nevada. Some argue that legalizing prostitution could reduce the incidence of AIDS and other sexually transmitted diseases as it has in Nevada, where legal prostitutes are required to have regular checkups.*

ment officials to look the other way is encouraged. Criminalization also discourages prostitutes from having regular health checkups. Some argue that criminalization increases the risk of prostitutes getting involved with illegal intravenous drugs, thus adding to the spread of AIDS.

Decriminalization

Great Britain appears to have adopted the most rational and effective approach by **decriminalizing** prostitution and removing all criminal penalties for prostitution as of 1959. Uniformed police can still make arrests for soliciting on the street, which greatly reduces the more blatant forms of prostitution from view. Statutory rape and age of consent laws still protect minors just as laws protect adults from being forced into prostitution or any other activity. Decriminalization would do nothing directly to reduce the spread of diseases, but with the stigma of crime out of the way, educational programs and other efforts could be focused on this problem. It is well to remember that national health officials attribute only 3% to 5% of venereal diseases to prostitutes.

If prostitution were decriminalized, law enforcement personnel could concentrate on protecting citizens against violent crimes. Some of the $120 million saved from ineffective pursuit of prostitutes could be channeled into helping women move out of prostitution by providing job training so they could earn a decent living. Even with this effort, it is unlikely that highly paid call girls would be enticed to leave their profession to take up lower paying and more demanding work.

Many groups support decriminalization, including feminists and unions of prostitutes like COYOTE (Call Off Your Old Tired Ethics) in California and

PONY (Prostitutes of New York) (Alexander 1983). Decriminalization, they claim, would protect the civil rights of prostitutes and their adult clients. It would also free our court system from the revolving-door practice of arrests, bail, and "back on the streets." It would liberate the prostitute from harassment, discrimination, abuse by pimps, and the stigma of society.

After studying the costs of criminalized prostitution in the United States, Pearl concluded that "Many Americans may never wish to condone prostitution, but the time has come to ask whether we can afford to keep it illegal. In the face of rising complaints of violent crime in virtually all major cities, the thousands of highly skilled vice officer hours devoted weekly to prostitution represent tremendous opportunity costs" (Pearl 1987:789).

A Declining Future?

In spite of continued economic inequities in the United States and other countries, some observers believe prostitution will decline because of the availability of effective contraceptives, a continued liberalization of sexual attitudes, and the decline in the double standard. However, the sexual liberation of women and their interest in enjoying satisfying sexual relations may make prostitutes an attractive outlet for men who do not want to bother relating with a woman as an equal, or who are not interested in the love play women expect. As women become more cautious about casual sex because of the threat of AIDS, men may not find sex as readily available as it was in the 1960s and 1970s (Bullough & Bullough 1987:288–289).

PART TWO
PORNOGRAPHY, EROTICA, AND OBSCENITY

Few issues generate more controversy and emotion today than debates about what is obscene, what is pornographic, what the effects of exposure to pornography are, and how our society should regulate this material. Fifteen years ago, the word *pornography* was a generic term for anything with a sexually explicit content. Today, **pornography** is increasingly used to refer to sexual material that contains a sexist message and/or violent, coercive content.

Obscenity, in the general sense, refers to anything that is offensive to public taste and morality. But obscenity also has a precise legal definition. Pornography usually refers to written or pictorial material designed to elicit sexual arousal. Material that is sexually explicit is protected by the First Amendment. Obscenity is not protected by the constitutional right of freedom of speech.

Defining Obscenity in Legal Terms

The current legal definition of obscenity was established by the Supreme Court in the 1957 **Roth v. the United States** decision. For a book, movie, magazine, or picture to be legally **obscene**,

- Its dominant theme of the work, as a whole, must appeal to prurient interest in sex—key words for this definition: dominant theme, whole, and prurient interest.

- The work must be patently offensive to contemporary community standards—key phrase: community standards.

- The work must be devoid of serious literary, artistic, political, or scientific value—key word: devoid.

However, this so-called definition left a critical issue unresolved. The meaning of the phrase "community standards" is still unclear. What may be considered offensive by some people in the community might be quite acceptable to others. A community, for example, might include a college where sexually explicit films are shown in a sex education course. Meanwhile, on Main Street, sexually explicit films may be prohibited because they are offensive to the "community."

In the 1973 **Miller v. the United States** decision, the Supreme Court attempted to tighten the restrictions on obscene material by requiring that defenders of an alleged obscene work prove that it has "serious literary, artistic, or scientific merit." Despite this clarification, the courts still faced the near-impossible task of determining what has "literary, artistic, or scientific merit," who represents the "average community member," and what the "community" is. In 1987 the Supreme Court attempted to refine the Roth and Miller decisions by saying "a reasonable person," not "an ordinary member of the community," could decide whether some allegedly obscene material has any serious literary, artistic, political, or scientific value (Taylor 1987).

In 1969 the Supreme Court ruled that private possession of obscene material was not a crime and is not subject to legal regulation. In 1990 the Supreme Court ruled that possession of child (kiddie) pornography in one's home is not protected by the right to privacy and the First Amendment. Federal laws continue to prohibit obscene material from being broadcast on radio and television, mailed, imported, or carried across state lines. Local communities also control obscenity through zoning regulations that limit the location of adult bookstores and pornographic theaters to one area of a city (Figure 24.5).

Pornography's Impact on Individuals and Society

What are the effects of viewing sexually explicit materials, pornography, and sexual violence? Do we react differently to soft-core and hard-core pornography, the sexually explicit films used in many college courses, kiddie porn, and visual materials that link sex and violence? Does violent pornography cause an increase in rape and other sexual abuse? In trying to interpret what researchers have found on these questions, it is important to examine the premises on which a particular research report is based.

Some Models of Pornography

One psychological theory, the **catharsis research model,** assumes that pornography and other sexually explicit materials provide a safety valve in a sexually repressive society. This safety valve enables people to reduce the tension of sexual repression in ways that do not harm others. This model views pornog-

Figure 24.5. *In the 1990s, the sale and rental of "adult" videos trail only children's tapes and new releases in popularity. In some areas, particularly the Northeast and the West Coast, adult videos often account for 20 percent of a store's rentals.*

raphy and other sexually explicit materials as "not so good, perhaps disgusting, but still useful" in diverting tensions that otherwise might trigger aggressive antisocial behavior.

A different hypothesis of the psychological effects of pornography suggests an **imitation research model.** Proponents of this model believe that sexually explicit books, pictures, and movies provide powerful role models that can, by conditioning and scripting us, promote antisocial, sexually aggressive behavior (Bart & Jozsa 1980; Griffin 1980; McCormack 1978; Russell, 1980a, 1980b, 1983).

Another model of pornography addresses its personal and societal uses in different cultures, as a product designed as an alternative source of sexual arousal gratification, and as a way of enhancing masturbation (Reiss 1986:186–190). There are also models of pornography based on communication, Marxist, psychoanalytic, feminist, and religious theories (Kappeler 1986; Malamuth & Billings 1984, 1986; Soble 1986; Valverde 1986).

Since researchers and those who comment on the effects of pornography can be using any one of these models as the basis for their remarks and conclusions, we need to know what model and what suppositions are being used, either consciously or implicitly, in order to understand and appreciate what is being said about pornography and its effects.

Three Federal Studies

The 1970 White House Commission

Appointed in 1968, the White House Commission spent two years with a $2 million budget that supported independent research into the effects of pornography. After finding that neither hard-core nor soft-core pornography leads to antisocial behavior, the commission recommended that all obscenity laws except those protecting minors be abolished. The majority of the commission concluded that pornography provides a useful safety valve in an otherwise sexually repressive culture.

This conclusion was rejected by three commissioners in a minority report. President Richard Nixon also rejected the majority report as "morally corrupt." The Senate, in a 60 to 5 vote, also rejected it.

The 1986 Meese Commission

In 1984, when he signed the Child Protection Act of 1984, President Ronald Reagan announced a new White House Commission that would reexamine the connection between pornography and child abuse, incest, and rape. The 11 commissioners chosen by U.S. Attorney General Edwin Meese were given one year and a half-million-dollar budget for its study, which forced the commission to rely on research already done by social scientists instead of allowing the commission to do its own research as the 1970 commission had done. Based on testimony, the commission concluded that there is a causal connection between viewing sexually explicit materials, especially violent pornography, and the act of rape and other sexual assaults. The commission recommended stricter penalties to regulate the pornography traffic, enactment of laws to keep hard-core pornography off home cable television and home telephone service, more vigorous prosecution of obscenity cases, and encouraged private citizens to use protests and boycotts to discourage marketing of pornography.

The Meese Commission was widely criticized because it was set up to determine the extent of the harm caused by pornography, rather than to find out whether or not pornography caused any harm. The commission was also criticized for relying on the concept of "the totality of evidence" which gave equal weight to the testimony of fundamentalist ministers, police officers, antipornography activists, and putative victims of pornography. This research method allowed the commission to conclude there is a "proven" causal connection between violent pornography and sexual assaults. Based on an examination of the April 1986 issues of top-selling men's sex magazines, the commission ignored the testimony of social scientists and concluded that sexual violence in these magazines has been increasing since the 1970s. The American Civil Liberties Union provided evidence that only 0.6% of the imagery involved "force, violence, or weapons." Two women commissioners refused to sign the final report and issued their own dissenting statement (Lynn 1986:41–42; Nobile & Nadler 1986).

Among the many criticisms of the Meese Commission, Robert Staples, a black sociologist, pointed out that in the black community, pornography is a trivial issue. It is "a peculiar kind of white man's problem" because blacks see the depiction of heterosexual intercourse and nudity, not as a sexist debasement of women, but as a celebration of the equal rights of women and men to enjoy sexual stimuli and pleasure (in Francoeur 1987a:258).

The 1986 Report of the U.S. Surgeon General

Surgeon General C. Everett Koop's 1986 report candidly admits that "we still know little about the patterns of use or the power of attitudes in precipitating sexually aggressive behavior. Much research is still needed in order to demonstrate that the present knowledge [of laboratory studies] has significant real world implications for predicting behavior." The report does not call for censorship, boycotts, and other tactics advocated by the Meese Commission. Rather it recommends development of "street-based, innovative approaches" to educate the public about the different types of sexually explicit material and their possible effects.

Erotica Versus Pornography

Some feminists have drawn an important distinction between pornographic material and erotica. Pornography, as defined by some feminists, *endorses* sexism and degrades women. It treats them as sex objects, and advocates violence as a good way to control women and maintain the power of a patriarchal society. **Erotica**, in this usage, refers to sexually explicit material that celebrates free choice and mutual participation in the quest for sensual and sexual pleasure.

In a political statement, Gloria Steinem (1980) offers one feminist's interpretation of why many people confuse and condemn both erotica and pornography:

> Both [erotica and pornography] assume that sexuality can be separated from conception, and therefore can be used to carry a personal message. That's a major reason why, even in our current culture, both may be called equally "shocking" or legally "obscene," a word whose Latin derivative means "dirty, containing filth." This gross condemnation of all sexuality that isn't harnessed to childbirth and marriage has been increased by the current backlash against women's progress. Out of fear that the whole patriarchal structure might be upset if women really had the autonomous power to decide our reproductive futures (that is, if we controlled the most basic means of production—the production of human beings), right-wing groups are not only denouncing prochoice abortion literature as "pornographic," but are trying to stop the sending of all contraceptive information through the mails by invoking obscenity laws.
>
> Sex as communication can send messages as different as life and death; even the origins of "erotica" and "pornography" reflect that act. After all, "erotica" is rooted in "eros" or passionate love, and thus in the idea of positive choice, free will, the yearning for a particular person. (Interestingly, the definition of erotica leaves open the question of gender.) "Pornography" begins with a root "porno," meaning "prostitution" or "female captives," thus letting us know that the subject is not mutual love, or love at all, but domination and violence against women. Erotica celebrates the equality of persons sharing the positive aura of sexuality and physical pleasure. Erotica ignores as irrelevant the traditional need to justify sexual relations on the basis of reproduction and stresses freedom of choice. The message of pornography, in contrast, is one of violence, male dominance, and conquest, of sex being used as a weapon or tool to maintain or create an inequality between men and women. By reinforcing the message of violence, pornography tells us that to experience our sexual/sensual nature and enjoy sexual pleasure, we must

adopt either a sadistic or masochistic role, getting our sensual pleasure by giving or receiving pain.

This feminist distinction between mutual pleasure-oriented erotica and sexist, violent pornography has had a profound impact on our research and conclusions. One interesting aspect of the distinction is the feminist equation of prostitution with "female captives." The differentiation has allowed some researchers to exempt certain kinds of sexually explicit material from their research (Soble 1986).

Some critics view traditional male-oriented sexually explicit material as treating women as spectators of male erections and as objects useful only for male pleasure. Devoid of personality, the women are either distasteful or excruciatingly dull. Their only function is to please men and serve as "physical receptacles for showers of sperm." But others argue that the emphasis in traditional pornography has been to focus on women's pleasure. The fantasy of the male in such films is ultimately to send his sexual partner into erotic ecstasy. Such film classics as *Deep Throat* and *The Devil in Miss Jones* tell of a sexually frustrated or inexperienced woman who is helped to find the erotic paradise she has been missing. Such diverse interpretations of the basic image of women in traditional pornography suggest that subjective biases are often very influential in the way we interpret pornography.

Some Types of Pornography

Deciding whether a particular book, film, or video is sexist pornography or an erotic celebration of mutual sexual pleasure is a subjective and personal judgment. For this reason, we use pornography as a generic term in our descriptions here of various types of sexually explicit materials.

Feminist Pornography

The new feminist soft-core pornography portrays women as persons who enjoy sexual pleasure as much as men. It appears in the pages of such mainstream women's magazines as *Cosmopolitan* and more overtly in *Playgirl*. It is promoted by sex boutiques with names like Eve's Garden, Adam and Eve, and Good Vibrations which cater to women. Across the country, a variation on the Tupperware and Mary Kay Cosmetics home parties now brings women the opportunity to examine and purchase a whole line of sex toys, love lotions, and lingerie in the privacy of their homes. Exotic lingerie is also available in specialty stores and by mail order from such stores as Victoria's Secret and Frederick's of Hollywood (Ehrenreich et al. 1987:113–117).

Candida Royalle, the key figure in Femme Productions, openly strives to produce true erotica. She makes a point of using actresses with "strong personalities and intensity" and designs her films to appeal to women. The emphasis of these videos is on mutual pleasuring and often on the male pleasuring the woman, without the usual obsession with male erections and ejaculations so common in traditional pornography.

Romance Novels

Erotic romantic novels have become an acceptable form of soft-core pornography for women. Far outselling gothic novels, science fiction, self-help, and other books aimed at women, erotic romantic novels often center around a traditional rape myth, a story in which the woman is at first unwilling but finally yields in a sensual rapture to a man. In nonsexual characteristics, women who read erotic romantic novels are very much like women who do not. However, they appear to enjoy sex more and have a richer sexual fantasy life (Coles & Shamp 1984; Lawrence & Herold 1988).

But is this the only function of these novels? To what extent do these endlessly repetitious fairy tales of desire help the housewives who read them resolve fundamental sexual and cultural ambiguities in their own lives? To what extent are romantic novels and feminist erotica allowing some women to create a new culture? These two questions are too complex to examine here but they have been studied by Janice Radway (1984) and others.

Gay and Lesbian Porn

Researchers and theorists, feminists and nonfeminists have almost completely ignored the existence of gay pornography.

Lesbian pornography tends toward two extremes, about evenly divided in popularity, with little middle ground. Small independent presses publish a lot of soft-core pornography or erotica. Erotica on audiocassettes are very popular among lesbians. On the other side is a hard-core lesbian literature with a strong S&M character that makes some feminists uncomfortable. *Off Our Backs*, a tabloid magazine, is the largest publication of this type. *Eidos*, another tabloid, carries numerous ads for lesbians who desire B&D or S&M relations.

There is much more pornography designed for homosexual men. Most of this genre is hard-core pornography with a lot of emphasis on leather, S&M, and younger males. At the same time, gay videos pioneered in eroticizing the condom, nonoxynol-9, and safer sex practices. Telephone sex is another form of gay pornography growing in popularity.

Kiddie Porn

In 1982 the U.S. Supreme Court upheld laws barring the use of children in an sexually explicit film, photograph, or performance, whether or not these materials meet the legal standard of being obscene. Child pornography, the court ruled, is not protected by the First Amendment. Its exploitation of minors eliminates any possibility that it might be tolerated under the three criteria in the Roth and Miller Supreme Court decisions. A 1990 Supreme Court decision made possession of sexually explicit material showing minors a criminal offense even in one's home.

Dial-a-Porn

Dial-a-porn, telephone sex, is a multimillion dollar a year business producing massive profits for telephone companies and the companies providing phone-in services (Figure 24.6). In one year, dial-in-services including dial-a-porn earned Pacific Bell $24.5 million and the phone-in companies $47.2 million. Because of constitutional concerns, the Public Utilities Commission and Federal Communications Commission (FCC) do not allow telephone companies to censor telephone messages or to discriminate among dial-for-a-message 1–900 services on the basis of content. Telephone companies cannot legally deny telephone lines to adults willing to pay the bill, although at least one court has ruled that it is not unlawful discrimination for a telephone company to refuse to provide services for dial-a-porn services. The FCC does require dial-a-porn

Figure 24.6. *Telephone sex is now a multi-million-dollar business, with services catering to a wide variety of male needs, as these two advertisements clearly indicate. Credit cards or automatic payment on 1-900 numbers have made dial-a-porn very accessible.*

services to screen out calls by minors by supplying their customers with special access numbers or having them pay by credit card. One suggested solution is to have concerned parents pay a onetime $5 fee to block all phones in a residence from dial-a-porn.

Popular discussions of dial-a-porn often focus on the assumed legal responsibilities of the dial-a-porn companies and the telephone companies to protect minors against this kind of sexually explicit material. Such discussions assume that there is clear evidence that exposure to the sexually explicit verbal messages of dial-a-porn is harmful to minors, just as we often assume that exposure of minors to sexually explicit magazines is harmful. When a 12-year-old California boy sexually assaulted a 4-year-old girl two weeks after spending two and a half hours listening to dial-a-porn messages, the parents of both children filed a $10 million lawsuit against the telephone company and two dial-a-porn services. But such a case raises a question about the family environment and about parents who would allow a child to be on the telephone for two and a half hours.

Pornography, Sexism, and Violence

The Censorship Question

Censorship has always been a touchy issue in the American democratic tradition. Freedom of speech and the right to privacy are protected by the Constitution. Debates over the real impact and consequences of pornography and obscenity present a particular challenge for this tradition (Highlight Box 24.1).

Censorship tends to create a "vacuum cleaner" effect. Once a particular type of material is censored, then the same law is often used to prohibit any and all

HIGHLIGHT BOX 24.1.
PUBLIC ATTITUDES ON PORNOGRAPHY AND CENSORSHIP

In 1987 Media General-Associated Press conducted a nationwide poll on pornography asking for opinions about the effects of pornography, attitudes toward the sexual content of advertising, novels, shows, and movies, and support for banning such material. How would you answer each of the following 14 questions? Why do you agree, or disagree, with the majority in each question?

Here are the questions used in the Media General-Associated Press poll on pornography:

1. First, do you think reading or looking at pornography is generally harmful to adults, or not?

Yes: 29 percent. No: 64 percent. Don't know, no answer: 7 percent.

2. (If yes) In what way? (Multiple answers OK)

Leads to sexual crimes: 27 percent. Causes psychological problems: 27 percent. Is against religious or moral beliefs: 23 percent. Other: 35 percent.

3. What do you think of stores that remove magazines like *Playboy* and *Penthouse* from newsstands? Do you think such action is appropriate or inappropriate?

Appropriate: 48 percent. Inappropriate: 41 percent. Don't know, no answer: 11 percent.

4. (If appropriate) Why do you feel that way? (Multiple answers OK)

Should not be accessible to young people: 45 percent. Don't like magazines: 23 percent. Seller should be allowed to decide: 16 percent. Other reasons: 31 percent.

5. Are you offended by sexual content in advertising, or not?

Yes: 35 percent. No: 58 percent. Don't read or watch: 1 percent. Don't know, no answer: 6 percent.

6. Contemporary novels?

Yes: 16 percent. No: 70 percent. Don't read: 10 percent. Don't know, no answer: 4 percent.

7. Television shows?

Yes: 39 percent. No: 52 percent. Don't watch: 4 percent. Don't know, no answer: 5 percent.

8. Hollywood movies?

Yes: 33 percent. No: 56 percent. Don't watch: 7 percent. Don't know, no answer: 4 percent.

9. Do you think magazines that show nudity should be banned in your community, allowed as long as they are carried out of sight or under the counter, or allowed with no restrictions?

Banned: 22 percent. Allowed out of sight: 55 percent. Allowed with no restrictions: 18 percent. Don't know, no answer: 5 percent.

10. How about magazines that show adults having sexual relations? Should they be banned from your community, allowed as long as they are under cover, or allowed with no restrictions?

Banned: 41 percent. Allowed under cover: 47 percent. Allowed with no restrictions: 8 percent. Don't know, no answer: 4 percent.

11. Should theaters that show X-rated movies be banned or allowed in your community?

Banned: 49 percent. Allowed: 44 percent. Don't know, no answer: 7 percent.

12. How about the sale or rental of X-rated home videocassettes? Should they be banned or allowed in your community?

Banned: 33 percent. Allowed: 60 percent. Don't know, no answer: 7 percent.

13. Have you ever read or looked through a magazine that features nudity?

Yes: 81 percent. No: 17 percent. Don't know, no answer: 2 percent.

14. Have you ever seen an X-rated movie or videocassette?

Yes: 61 percent. No: 37 percent. Don't know, no answer: 2 percent.

Source: Associated Press.

similar types of material. It took 100 years for the court system to reclaim the many rights and freedoms censored by the Comstock Law. Many people feel that our rights under the First Amendment to the Constitution are so precious, and in many ways so fragile, that they must be protected even at the cost of permitting blatantly offensive material to be published and sold without restriction to consenting adults. Limiting the access of minors to such material can be handled without getting into censorship legislation.

Despite its view of pornography as a safety valve and the lack of a strong violence component in pornography at the time, the 1970 White House Commission described the distinguishing characteristic of pornography as "the degrading and demeaning portrayal of the role and status of the human female . . . as a mere sexual object to be exploited and manipulated sexually." Sexist images that degrade and demean women and portray both women and men as sex objects are obvious in some pornography, but the question of what is degrading is a subjective one. Some blacks feel that "The Bill Cosby Show" and the preponderance of black football players degrades blacks. There is also a misleading assumption about sexual violence in pornography. Discussions of sexually violent pornography usually assume that the violence is by men toward women, but an examination of the many sexual cartoons in men's magazines reveals a good amount of violence by women against men.

How much sexual violence is actually portrayed in pornography, and what are its effects on the viewer? The circulation rates of *Playboy*, *Penthouse*, and *Hustler* closely correlate with the incidence of rape around the country. In cities and states where these magazines are highly popular, the incidence of rape is correspondingly high (Bart & Jozsa 1980; Johnson & Shirer 1987:236–240; Scott & Schwalm 1988). But does this connection mean that reading these magazines causes rape? A statistical correlation between two events does not necessarily mean the two are related in a cause-and-effect way. Consider a hypothetical study of the growth of membership in a local social club, or political party, and the increase in rape in the same locality. A researcher says there is a statistical correlation of 0.96 between the two statistics, meaning the increasing membership in the club matches almost perfectly the increase in the number of rapes. Does this correlation mean that the increase in rape is causing an increase in club membership? Does increased club membership cause more rape? Or are the two observations independent and the correlation meaningless? According to the imitation theory, mass exposure to sexually violent material should condition men to associate violence with sexual pleasure by modeling sexual violence and reducing inhibitions for it. But a correlation between increasing rape and increasing use of pornography might be unrelated in the sense that pornography causes rape.

Of the 10 largest sex magazines, *Playboy* has the highest correlation of circulation rates with rape rates (Scott & Schwalm 1988). Sexual violence did increase in *Playboy* magazine between 1973 and 1977. But since 1977, the amount of sexual violence has been declining (Scott & Cuvelier 1987). More important, an analysis of sexual violence in 30 years of *Playboy* magazines found only one page of sexually violent pictorials or cartoons per 3,000 pages. Fewer than 4 sexually violent pictorials out of every 1,000 seems hardly sufficient influence to cause an increase in rape. We might also conclude that there are underlying social and demographic factors which cause high rates for both rape and sex magazine readership (Baron & Straus 1986:352). Unfortunately, no similar study has been done of the sexual violence in regular and pornographic films and videos. More important, although most of the increase in sexual violence studied was found in cartoons, much of the cartoon violence shows women exploiting and degrading men rather than the reverse, which is implicitly assumed in most discussions of violent pornography (Mould 1988).

Are rapists sexually aroused by violent pornography? Men who have been diagnosed as compulsive and repetitive rapists, or pedophiles, are only sexually turned on by sexually explicit material that matches their distorted, paraphilic lovemap. Erotic materials that stress an interpersonal relationship produce strong feelings of guilt and anxiety in compulsive, repetitive sex offenders. Compulsive, repetitive rapists are turned on by violent pornography, but not by sexually explicit films that portray a mutual relationship unless they can turn this positive image into a rape fantasy. In addition, convicted sex offenders appear to have had little exposure as youngsters to sexually explicit material. "Of course, there are aggressive and violent people who use sex as a means of expressing aggression, but images of sex do not cause such violence" (Baron & Straus in Francoeur 1987a:262). These factors need to be considered in dealing with the question of the connection between sexually violent material and rape.

Japanese films and novels offer an interesting insight. Bondage and rape, usually of a teenage girl, is a recurring theme in Japanese pornography. Yet Japan has one of the lowest rates of rape of any industrialized country in the world. With strong socialization for respect, responsibility, and commitment, the "Japanese view erotic rape and bondage films as a cathartic escape valve that provides vicarious satisfaction for unacceptable behavior" (Abramson & Hayashi 1984; Reiss 1986:188).

What effect might we expect if we legalized all pornography except kiddie porn? (Figure 24.7). In the late 1960s, Denmark decriminalized and then legalized pornography. After an initial rise, sales of pornographic materials dropped

Figure 24.7. Pornography's Audience. *The typical customer of massage parlors, peep shows, and porno theaters is the middle-class, conservative, middle-aged businessman.*

significantly. There was also a reduction in reported sex crimes, particularly child molestation which dropped more than 80%. Critics suggest that these statistics are misleading and that many minor sex crimes went unreported because of the more liberal and changing sexual environment of the times (Bart & Jozsa 1980; Kutchinsky 1983).

Over a dozen researchers have found that under experimental laboratory conditions, exposure to sexually explicit violent material can later promote sexually aggressive attitudes and behavior of men toward women. Most of these researchers have emphasized the relationship between exposure to sexually violent material and the increased likelihood of certain men either condoning aggressive acts against females or acting aggressively toward them. But this research is in an experimental laboratory setting. There are as many or more studies showing that exposure to nonviolent sexual material may actually reduce aggressive tendencies in men. Equally important, most researchers have found that the key factor is the violent nature of the material and not whether it depicts sexual or nonsexual violence (Scott & Schwalm 1988:242). When the research literature, the types of films used, and the experimental setting are critically evaluated, Mould (1988) concludes, "There is precious little evidence showing that violent pornography causes an increase in aggression."

In a more general perspective, aside from the 1980 pornographic violence of *Caligula*, "Pornographic features thus far have rarely reached the levels of violence equivalent to those in *Indiana Jones and the Temple of Doom*, a film rated PG. A pornographic feature will almost certainly borrow the plot of the latter, however, just as *Blonde Goddess* (1982) ripped off *Raiders of the Lost Ark*" (Slade 1984).

In 1985 Andrea Dworkin, Catherine MacKinnon, and Women Against Pornography joined forces with local citizens' groups in Minneapolis and Long Island, New York, to promote a new kind of pornography legislation. Using a civil rights argument, the legislation stated that

> Pornography is sex discrimination. [Where it exists, it poses] a substantial threat to the health, safety, peace, welfare, and equality of citizens in the community. . . . Pornography is a systematic practice of exploitation and subordination based on sex that differentially harms women. The harm of pornography includes dehumanization, sexual exploitation, forced sex, forced prostitution, physical injury, and social and sexual terrorism and inferiority presented as entertainment.

The proposed legislation would have made producing, selling, or exhibiting pornography an act of sex discrimination. Women forced to participate in pornographic films, exposed by force of circumstances to view pornography "in any place of employment, education, home, or public place, or assaulted by a male inspired by pornography" could sue in civil court for damages based on sex discrimination. The American Civil Liberties Union (ACLU), Feminist Anti-Censorship Taskforce (FACT), and others challenged this kind of legislation. After considerable nationwide debate about civil rights, sex discrimination, and the constitutional right to free speech, these legislative efforts were abandoned (Blakely 1985).

In a postscript to this legislative attempt, Andrea Dworkin (1987) argued that sexual "intercourse is the pure, sterile formal expression of men's contempt for women." Men use intercourse, according to Dworkin, to "occupy," "violate," "invade," and "colonize" women's bodies. Because this is a world ruled by men who hate women, women cannot freely consent to any act of sexual intercourse. Dworkin's position has disturbed many other feminists who readily recognize the reality of misogyny and rape, but are unpersuaded by her view of sexual intercourse and her conclusion that impotent men are the only good men (Sternhell 1987).

A more positive alternative to censorship of violence and sexual violence in television programming was an important part of considerations at the Surgeon General's 1986 Workshop on Pornography and Public Health. Documentaries on incest, rape, and rape myths can be used to educate the public about the subtle conditioning of depictions of violence in the media. Educational programs can be designed to sensitize children to the distortions of TV and film violence. Using shows like "Miami Vice," "Starsky and Hutch," and "The A-Team," children can be taught that the violent behavior of the characters in such shows does not represent the behavior of most people. They are shown that the violence captured by the camera is an illusion that would have devastating consequences for persons if it were real, and that people can solve problems much easier without violence (Donnerstein & Linz 1986, 1988).

How would you resolve the tension between freedom of speech, pornography, and censorship?

Key Concepts

1. The range of commercialized prostitution includes female streetwalkers and male hustlers, prostitutes who work in bars and massage parlors, runaway teenagers, and high-class escort and call girls.

2. Although female prostitutes report experiencing pleasure in their business and private sexual relations, they are also troubled by the risks of being a prostitute, abuse by their customers and pimps, harassment by police, and by health risks, especially from AIDS and drug usage.

3. Men engage in sexual relations with prostitutes for a variety of reasons, but most enjoy having guaranteed, quick, uninvolved sex that satisfies their fantasies in exchange for money.

4. The economics of prostitution includes referral agents, recruiters, pimps, hotel clerks, cab drivers, doormen, rental agents, and the owners and staff of hotels, massage parlors, and other facilities where prostitution occurs. The economics of prostitution also involves major investment of taxpayer dollars in the enforcement of laws prohibiting prostitution.

5. Most of the research on the effects of pornography and erotica has been carried out using the catharsis, or "safety valve" model. New research done with the imitation model suggests that the degradation and objectification of women and the endorsement of such degradation and objectification in sexual violence may provide powerful role models. These role models may be factors in scripting antisocial, sexually aggressive behavior.

6. Violence in films and on television, sexually oriented advertisements, sexist and violent pornography, child pornography, and dial-a-porn raise as-yet-unanswered questions about their effects and about how society, minors, and the constitutional right to privacy can be protected.

Key Terms

catharsis research model (636)
criminalization (633)
decriminalization (634)
erotica (639)
imitation research model (637)

Miller v. the United States (636)
obscene (635)
pornography (635)
prostitution (624)
Roth v. the United States (635)

Summary Questions

1. What are the direct financial costs of enforcing the laws against prostitution in the United States? How effective are the laws against prostitution in promoting the welfare of society?

2. How do the expenditures of large cities on controlling prostitution compare with their expenditures on education and public welfare?

3. What are the differences between decriminalizing and legalizing prostitution? What advantages and disadvantages might be associated with decriminalization of prostitution? with its legalization?

4. What are the three criteria in the legal definition of obscenity established by the 1957 U.S. Supreme Court decision in Roth v. the United States? How has this been modified by the 1973 Miller v. the United States decision?

5. How do the premises of the catharsis and imitation models affect the outcome of research on the social effects of pornography? Why are these premises important in understanding the meaning of various research?

6. Compare the conclusions of the 1970 White House Commission on pornography, the 1986 Meese Commission, and the 1986 Report of the U.S. Surgeon General.

7. What connections have been demonstrated between sexually violent pornography, the circulation of adult sex magazines, and the incidence of rape in the United States? What insights does Japanese pornography offer?

Suggested Readings

Prostitution

Barrows, S. B. (1986). *Mayflower Madam: The Secret Life of Sydney Biddle Barrows*. New York: Arbor House.

Bullough, V., & B. Bullough. (1987). *Women and Prostitution: A Social History*. Buffalo, NY: Prometheus Press.

Clark, R. (1985, summer). Male strippers: Ladies' night at the meat market. *Journal of Popular Culture, 19*:51–55.

Hall, S., & R. Adelman. (1972). *Gentlemen of Leisure: A Year in the Life of a Pimp*. New York: Quadrangle/The New York Times Book Co.

Pornography

Blakely, M. K. (1985, April). Is one woman's sexuality another woman's pornography? *Ms. Magazine*, pp. 37ff.

Burstyn, V. (ed.). (1985). *Women Against Censorship*. Toronto: Douglas & McIntyre.

Feshback, S., & N. Malamuth. (1978, November). Sex and aggression: Proving the link. *Psychology Today*, pp. 111–117, 122.

Mosher, D. L. (1986, May). Misinformation on pornography: A lobby disguised as an educational organization. *SIECUS Report*, *14*(5):7–10.

Weatherford, J. (1986). *Porn Row*. New York: Arbor House.

Appendix:
Resources and Hot Lines

1. Abortion

- Birthright. 761 Coxwell Avenue, Toronto, Ontario M4C 3C5, Canada.
- National Abortion Federation. 110 East 59th Street, Suite 1011, New York, NY 10022. Toll-free hot line: 1-800-223-0618.
- National Abortion Rights Action League. 825 15th Street, N.W., Washington, DC 20005.
- Planned Parenthood Federation of America. 810 7th Avenue, New York, NY 10022.
- Religious Coalition for Abortion Rights. 100 Maryland Avenue, N.E., Washington, DC 20002.
- Right-to-Life National Headquarters. 529 14th Street, N.W., Suite 341. Washington, DC 20045.

2. Acquired Immune Deficiency Syndrome (AIDS)

- In the United States: Centers for Disease Control, a toll-free national hot line: 1-800-342-AIDS.
- Public Health Service: a hot line for questions about AIDS: 1-800-447-AIDS.
- AIDS Action Council. Federation of AIDS-Related Organizations. 1115½ Independence Avenue, S.E., Washington, DC 20003. Phone: 1-202-547-3101.
- Gay Men's Health Crisis. P.O. Box 274, 132 West 24th Street, New York, NY 10011. Phone: 1-212-807-6655.
- National Lesbian and Gay Health Foundation. P.O. Box 65472, Washington, DC 20035. Phone: 1-202-797-3708.

Many states and Canadian provinces have their own local AIDS councils or programs which can be reached by calling the local state or provincial Department of Health.

3. Disabilities and Sexuality

• Handicap Introductions. P.O. Box 232, 22 N. Main Street, Coopersburg, PA 18036. A nationwide network of handicapped and nonhandicapped people for whom physical disability is no barrier to romance and an active social life.

• Networking Project for Disabled Women and Girls. YWCA of the City of New York. 610 Lexington Avenue, New York, NY 10022.

• The Coalition for Sexuality and Disabilities. 122 East 23rd Street, New York, NY 10010.

4. Gender Conflict Issues

• The Educational TV Channel. P.O. Box 6486, San Francisco, CA 94101. Publishes the *International Gender Support Directory* for persons with gender dysphoria questions.

• The Renaissance Education Association. P.O. Box 1263, King of Prussia, PA 19406. An information and outreach support group.

• TRI-ESS. Box 194, Tulare, CA 93275. A nationwide sorority for heterosexual crossdressers and publisher of *Femme Mirror*, a quarterly.

• Outreach Institute. Box 368, Kenmore Station, Boston, MA 02215.

• The International Foundation for Gender Education. P.O. Box 367, Wayland, MA 01778. Provides referrals and publishes *TV-TS Tapestry Journal*.

5. Gender Orientation

• Gay Parents Legal and Research Group. Box 1723, Lynnwood, WA 98036.

• Gay Teachers Association. 204 Lincoln Place, Brooklyn, NY 11217.

• Lambda Legal Defense and Education Fund, Inc. 132 West 43rd St, New York, NY 10036.

• National Gay and Lesbian Task Force. 1517 U Street, Washington, DC 20009.

• Parents of Gays. Metropolitan Duane Methodist Church. 201 West 13th St, New York, NY 10011.

Local social, political, and education groups such as the Gay Activist Alliance (not a national organization) can often be found in the telephone directory and in the Yellow Pages under Social Services along with other gay and lesbian organizations. There are also numerous gay and lesbian religious organizations comprised of members of almost every sect and denomination. They include the Metropolitan Community Church (Christian), Dignity (Roman Catholic), Integrity (Episcopal), Presbyterians for Gay Concerns, Lutherans Concerned, Friends for Lesbian and Gay Concerns (Quaker), Church of the Beloved Disciple (Eucharistic Catholic, New York), and Gay Synagogue (New York and other major cities).

6. Sexual Abuse and Incest

• Incest Survivors Anonymous (ISA). P.O. Box 1653. Long Beach, CA 90805.

• SARAH, Inc. (Sexual Assault Recovery through Awareness and Hope). P.O. Box 20353. Bradenton, FL 34203. 1-813-746-9114.

• Survivors of Incest Anonymous. P.O. Box 21817. Baltimore, MD 21222. 1-301-282-3400.

• VOICES in Action, Inc. P.O. Box 148309. Chicago, IL 60614. Provides free referrals nationwide, a newsletter, and information on local self-help groups.

7. Sexually Transmitted Diseases

• **A nationwide STD hot line:** 1-800-227-8922, except in California 1-800-982-5883.

• The U.S. Public Health Service also has a toll-free hot line for general information about STDs: 1-800-342-2437.

• American Foundation for the Prevention of Venereal Disease, Inc. 799 Broadway, New York, NY 10013. Free pamphlet: *The New Venereal Disease Prevention for Everyone*.

• American Social Health Association (American Venereal Disease Association). 260 Sheridan Avenue, Palo Alto, CA 94306. Quarterly publication: *Sexually Transmitted Diseases*. Free pamphlets: *Some Questions and Answers About VD, Women and VD, The Sexually Active and VD*, and *How to Cope with Herpes*.

• Canadian Public Health Association. 1335 Carling Avenue, Suite 210, Ottawa, Ontario K1A OL2, Canada. 1-613-725-3769.

• Centers for Disease Control, Bureau of State Services, The Venereal Disease Control Division, Atlanta, GA 30333. The Technical Information Services of the CDC publishes abstracts and a bibliography.

• National Lesbian and Gay Health Foundation. P.O. Box 65472, Washington, DC 20035. 1-202-797-3708.

• National Coalition of Gay STD Services. P.O. Box 239, Milwaukee, WI 53201.

• The Public Health Department, Venereal Disease Division: listed in your telephone book under state government offices.

• Helpline for Herpes, 1-415-328-7710, between 8 A.M. and 4:30 P.M., Pacific time or between 11 A.M. and 7:30 P.M. Eastern time. The Herpes Resource Center publishes *The Helper*, a quarterly newsletter free to members and $1.50 per copy for nonmembers (P.O. Box 100, Palo Alto, CA 94302). HRC offers support groups and counseling through more than 45 local chapters in many large cities. Your local health department or mental health center may have information about a support group in your area.

Glossary

The definitions in this glossary are based on *A Descriptive Dictionary and Atlas of Sexology* by Robert T. Francoeur, author of this textbook, Timothy Perper, and Norman A. Scherzer (Westport, CT: Greenwood Press, 1990).

abortion (280):   Medical or surgical termination of a pregnancy before the fetus is sufficiently developed to survive outside the uterus.

acquaintance rape (603):   Sexual intimacy forced on an individual by an acquaintance; see *date rape*.

Acquired immune deficiency syndrome (AIDS) (354):   Lethal infection of the human immunodeficiency virus (HIV) which damages the body's immune system, leaving it incapable of fighting off opportunistic infections and certain cancers; transmitted by infected semen, body fluids, and blood.

Adam Plan (76):   Theory of embryonic/fetal development which holds that the natural tendency is for a fetus to differentiate as a female and that the addition of testosterone and its derivatives is needed for development of a male; see *Eve Plan*.

adolescence (114):   That period of psychosexual development between the onset of sexual maturation (puberty) and early adulthood during which young people refine their self-identity, sexual identity, sex roles, and erotosexual relationships with other persons.

adultery (585):   Sexual intercourse engaged in by a married person with a partner other than his or her spouse.

affectional orientation (432):   Emotional attraction an individual experiences toward persons of their own, the other, or both genders; that aspect of gender orientation referring to the gender of the person with whom one falls in love.

A-frame orgasm (185):   Uterine-centered orgasm believed to result from stimulation of the Grafenberg spot.

afterbirth (222):   Placenta, fetal membranes, blood, fluid, and the umbilical cord expelled from the uterus after an infant is born.

AIDS: See *Acquired immune deficiency syndrome*.

AIDS-related complex (ARC) (361):   Intermediate stage in an HIV infection in which the immune system is damaged, but there is not yet dementia, emaciation, opportunistic infections, or cancers, which characterize the full syndrome of AIDS.

ambisexual (451): Condition of being sexually, erotically, and/or affectionally oriented to both men and women; also known as bisexuality.

amenorrhea (122): Complete lack of the monthly menstrual cycle; also irregular menstrual cycles; see *dysmenorrhea*.

amniocentesis (218): Test in which fetal cells, obtained by a syringe from fluid in the amniotic sac, are grown in tissue culture and checked for defects in the chromosome number and gene-controlled enzyme activity; usually performed between the 16th and 20th weeks of pregnancy.

amnion (211): Thin membrane sac that develops around the fetus in the uterus; filled with fluid that protects the fetus; combines with the chorion to form the placenta.

amniotic fluid (211): Insulating, protective fluid contained in the amniotic sac surrounding the fetus.

analingus (401): Oral stimulation of the anal region.

anal intercourse (401): General term for penile penetration of the rectum and/or oral or digital stimulation of the anal region.

aphrodisiac (385): Any chemical, drug, or scent alleged to increase sexual interest, desire, or response.

ARC: See *AIDS-related complex*.

arranged marriage (33): Negotiation of a marital contract by the parents or relatives of a man and woman.

artificial insemination (230): Introduction of fresh or frozen semen into the vaginal canal by any means other than sexual intercourse in order to produce a pregnancy.

asymptomatic (328): Lacking in observable or clinically significant symptoms.

B&D: See *bondage and dominance*.

Bartholin's glands (147): Two small glands on either side of the vaginal opening that secrete lubricating fluid.

BBT method (264): Natural contraceptive method that ascertains by daily checks of the basal body temperature the times when sexual intercourse is not likely to result in pregnancy.

bio-psycho-socio-cultural phenomenon (4): Development of psychosexual identity and status as the outcome of biological, psychological, sociological, and cultural factors interacting at critical periods before and after birth.

birth control: See *contraceptive*.

bisexuality (451): Condition of being erotically, and/or affectionally oriented to both men and women; also known as ambisexuality.

blended orgasm (185): Combination of the tenting orgasm triggered by clitoral stimulation and the A-frame orgasm triggered by stimulation of the Grafenberg spot.

bondage and dominance (B & D, B/D) (538): Sexual relationship in which sexual arousal and orgasm are facilitated by or dependent on role playing, with one person in a passive, submissive role and the other in a dominant, controlling role.

brain (neural) template (89): Pattern or behavioral tendency developed before birth in the brain cells of the fetus by hormones that affect behavior after birth when activated by various social and learning stimuli.

bundling (10): Colonial American courtship custom that allowed a young man and woman to sleep together provided they were fully clothed, but which also facilitated premarital intercourse.

candidiasis (340): Infection of the sexual organs, rectum, or mouth caused by an excess growth of a naturally occurring yeastlike fungus, *Candida*; infected males usually have no symptoms; infected females have a vaginal discharge with a yeastlike odor.

carrier (328):   Person who has a recessive genetic defect but does not show it, or who has a disease-producing organism, shows no symptoms of infection, but can infect others.

case law (583):   The meaning and application of laws as they have been interpreted in specific court decisions.

catharsis research model (636):   Hypothesis which suggests that pornography provides a healthy and necessary release of sexual tension in a sexually repressive society.

celibacy (7, 470):   Complete abstinence from sexual activity, especially sexual intercourse.

cervical cap (259):   Small plastic or rubber thimble-like device worn on the cervix as a barrier form of contraception.

cervical mucus method (264):   Natural contraceptive method in which the safe time for sexual intercourse is ascertained by daily checks of changes in the slipperiness, stretchability, and opaqueness of the cervical mucus.

cervix (151):   Narrow neck of the uterus which contains a passage leading from the upper (inner) end of the vagina into the uterine cavity to allow passage of sperm, the menstrual flow, or a baby during delivery.

Cesarean section (226):   Surgical procedure in which a fetus is removed from the uterus through an incision in the abdominal wall because vaginal delivery is not medically advisable or possible.

C-film: See *vaginal contraceptive film.*

chancre (339):   Small, painless, crater-like, open sore with a hard rim which appears in the primary stage of a syphilitic or chancroid infection.

Chlamydia (335):   A microscopic parasite; the cause of the most common sexually transmitted disease in America; infected females usually show no symptoms although the infection is a major cause of pelvic inflammatory disease; infected males usually experience painful urination with nongonococcal urethritis.

chorionic villi biopsy (CVB) (219):   Technique for monitoring the development of a fetus by analyzing chromosomes and gene activity in fetal cells obtained from the placenta through the cervical canal; most useful when performed in the 6th to 10th week of pregnancy.

circumcision (163):   Surgical removal of the foreskin or flap of skin covering the glans of the penis or clitoris; see *female circumcision.*

clitoris (147):   In a female, the small erectile, hooded organ at the front of the vulva whose sole function is sexual pleasure; homologous to the male penis.

closed marriage (476):   Marriage which emphasizes traditional male/female sex roles and emotional and sexual exclusivity.

coercion (600):   Use of a position of power or authority, of psychological persuasion, verbal pressure, intimidation, or alcohol and/or drugs to induce an unwilling person to engage in some activity, such as sexually intimate behavior or intercourse.

cohabitation (478):   Act of living with another person as a sexually intimate couple in a primary relationship without benefit of civil or religious recognition.

combination pill (262):   Hormonal contraceptive pill containing both estrogen and progestin in daily doses that prevents ovulation.

Comstock Prohibition (15):   Antiobscenity law passed by the U.S. Congress in 1873 which made it a criminal offense to distribute, sell, or promote use of any product or information "designed, adapted, or intended for preventing conception or producing abortion, or for any indecent or immoral use." Last vestige of this law was declared unconstitutional in 1977.

condom (250): Latex or natural membrane sheath used to cover the penis during vaginal intercourse to prevent conception and to cover the penis during anal or oral sex to prevent exposure to the AIDS virus.

consenting adult laws (21, 594): Code of laws which contains no criminal penalties for sexual acts engaged in by consenting adults.

contraceptive (240): Any natural, barrier, hormonal, or surgical method used to prevent conception and pregnancy.

contraceptive sponge (258): Synthetic sponge containing a spermicide inserted into the vagina before sexual intercourse to cover the cervix and prevent conception.

contragestive (293): Hormonal agent, such as RU 486 or an intrauterine device, which prevents inplantation and gestation of an embryo; an abortifacient.

core gender identity (72, 433): Innermost experience of oneself as a male or female, established in the first two or three years after birth; see *gender identity*.

corpora cavernosa (**sing. *corpus cavernosum***) (158): Paired cylindrical bodies composed of spongy, erectile tissue which run the length of the penis and clitoris; responsible for the mechanical function of penile or clitoral erection.

corpus spongiosum (158): Cylindrical body of spongy erectile tissue surrounding the urethra in the penis and expanding to form the glans of the penis. Lies under the paired corpora cavernosa in the penis; when filled with blood during sexual arousal, it contributes to penile erection.

courtly love (407): Revolutionary medieval view of love which placed woman in a status far superior to the man, almost unattainable and beyond the reach of passion; precursor of the concept of romantic love which emerged after the 17th century in European and American cultures.

couvade (217): Psychologically induced symptoms of pregnancy experienced by a male.

Cowper's glands (163): Two pea-sized glands at the inner base of the penis, just beneath the prostate, which secrete a clear alkaline fluid that neutralizes the acidic urethra in preparation for ejaculation.

creative singlehood (474): A lifestyle that includes two or more close relationships without an exclusive emotional, sexual, and/or financial dependence on any one person.

criminalization (633): Law which makes a particular behavior a crime punishable by imprisonment and/or a fine.

cross-coding (521): Developmental pattern in which a person's psychosexual and gender-identity role development shifts from the predominant gender path to the other gender pattern for one or more of the 12 gates of psychosexual development, so that his or her genetic, gonadal, hormonal, anatomical, and neural encoding for gender identity, gender role, and affectional, gender, or sexual orientations are not consistent and harmonious; see *gender dysphoria*.

cunnilingus (398): Oral stimulation of a female's genitalia by a partner.

cystitis (311): Infection of the urinary bladder.

date rape (602): Use of psychological and/or physical coercion to pressure or force an unwilling partner into sexual intimacy and/or intercourse in a dating or courtship relationship.

decriminalization (634):   Abolition or revoking of criminal penalties for an activity previously defined as illegal and a crime, as in the decriminalization of prostitution.

defeminize (76):   Prenatal developmental process in which nature's natural tendency to follow the female path of psychosexual development, the Eve Plan, is inhibited or suppressed; in the male fetus, anatomical defeminization occurs when Mullerian Inhibiting Hormone causes degeneration of the Mullerian ducts.

DES: See *diethylstilbestrol.*

desire phase (173):   First of the three general divisions of the sexual response cycle, in which the desire for sexual pleasure and activity increases and leads to the physiological changes of sexual arousal and orgasm; may also be included in Masters and Johnson cycle of excitement, plateau, orgasm, and resolution.

diaphragm (257):   Dome-shaped latex cup with a flexible spring steel rim inserted into the vaginal canal to cover the cervix and serve as a contraceptive barrier against sperm.

diethylstilbestrol (DES) (317):   Synthetic female hormone used in the 1950s and 1960s to prevent miscarriage and currently as a so-called morning-after contraceptive pill, despite its rare but significant side effects.

dihydrotestosterone (86):   Powerful androgenic hormone, derived from testosterone, responsible for masculinization of the external genitalia in a male fetus.

dilation & curettage (D&C) (295):   Medical procedure in which the cervix is dilated and the inner surface of the uterus scraped in performing an abortion or to treat a menstrual or uterine problem.

dimorphic (89):   Having two distinct forms, as in the sexual dimorphism of the male and female sexes or masculine and feminine genders.

displacement (531):   Distortion of a lovemap when a normal element in courtship and sexual foreplay, such as genital display, is given an abnormal importance and becomes the focus of sexual arousal and satisfaction.

domestic partners (491):   New legal term applied to gay and lesbian couples or to cohabiting heterosexual couples.

dowry (38):   Money or property given to the groom by a bride's family at the time of engagement or marriage.

dysmenorrhea (121):   Painful menstruation; see *pelvic inflammatory disease.*

dyspareunia (575):   Difficult or painful sexual intercourse.

early ejaculation: See *premature ejaculation.*

ectopic (206):   Something that is not in its usual, or normal, position, as an ectopic pregnancy in which the fetus develops in the fallopian tube, ovary, or abdominal cavity instead of in the upper uterine cavity.

edema (174):   Swelling or bloating of tissue due to water retention.

egg: See *ovum.*

ejaculation (184):   In the male, the expulsion or release of seminal fluid following the emission phase when myotonic contractions in the prostate and seminal vesicles build up pressure on the seminal fluid; see *emission phase, propulsion phase.*

ELISA test (362):   General screening test for an infection with HIV, the AIDS virus; positive test result should be confirmed with the Western Blot test.

embryo (206):   Early stage of development of an organism during which all major organ systems are established; in humans, the first two months after conception is the embryonic period; see *fetus, zygote*.

emission phase (188): Buildup of seminal fluid pressure in the prostate and seminal vesicles prior to release of the semen into the penile urethra and its subsequent ejaculation; see *ejaculation, propulsion phase*.

endometriosis (310): Painful condition in which tissue from the inner surface of the uterus is displaced through the fallopian tube into the abdominal cavity where it is subject to the menstrual cycle and results in inflammation, secondary infections, and sterility.

epididymis (161): Tightly coiled tubes on the back side of the testes where sperm are normally stored.

epididymitis (321): Infection of the epididymis.

episiotomy (222): Surgical incision made in the posterior outer edge of the vagina and perineum to prevent tearing during childbirth.

erectile difficulty (557): Inability to have and maintain an erection sufficient to allow vaginal intercourse.

erection (174): Stiffening and projection of the penis or clitoris as a result of sexual stimulation and vasocongestion.

erotica (639): Sexually explicit material celebrating mutuality, consent, and sexual pleasure, as distinct from pornography defined as sexist, depersonalizing, and degrading sexually explicit material.

erotic orientation (432): Gender of the persons with whom we prefer to have sex; also known as sexual orientation; see *affectional orientation, bisexuality, gender orientation, heterosexual, homosexual*.

Erotic Stimulus Pathway (ESP) model (193): Model of the human sexual response cycle which parallels psychological responses with the phys-iological changes: *seduction* during the desire and excitement phases, pleasurable *sensations* during the excitement and plateau stages, *surrender* during orgasm, and *reflection* during the resolution stage.

erotophile (erotophilia) (135, 244): Person who feels comfortable with and positive about his or her sexual nature and responses; the opposite of an erotophobe.

erotophobe (erotophobia) (135, 244): Person who feels guilt and fear about his or her sexual nature and responses; the opposite of an erotophile.

ESP model: See *Erotic Stimulus Pathway model*.

estrogen (116): Generic term for a group of feminizing hormones responsible for the secondary sexual characteristics of the female; one of two major hormones found in females, the other being progesterone; males also produce small amounts of estrogens.

estrogen replacement therapy (504): Use of estrogens to alleviate vaginal atrophy and other symptoms of menopause.

etiqueta (45): In Latino cultures, the social and gender scripting of a girl for a docile and yet sexually seductive role as a woman.

Eve Plan (75): Hypothesis that there is a natural tendency for mammalian fetuses to differentiate sexually as a female spontaneously rather than in response to sex hormones; see *Adam Plan*.

excitement/plateau phase (174): Combined first and second stages of the sexual response cycle described by Masters and Johnson. In the female, vasocongestion leads to erection of the clitoris, flattening and separating of the labia minora, deepened color and increase in the size of the labia majora, lengthening and distention of the inner two-thirds of the vagina, formation of the orgasmic platform, elevation of the uterus, nipple erection, breast enlargment, vaginal sweating, sex skin, and withdrawal of the clitoris under its hood. In the male, the flaccid penis becomes erect, the skin and muscles of the scrotum thicken as the testes elevate, the Cowper's glands secrete an alkaline fluid, seminal fluid is released by the seminal vesicles into the ejaculatory ducts, and at the end, there is a feeling of ejaculatory inevitability.

exhibitionist (534):   Person who is psychologically dependent on publicly exposing his or her genitals in order to achieve sexual arousal and satisfaction.

fallopian tubes (151):   Pair of 3- to 4-inch-long tubes which run from the upper corners of the uterus toward the ovaries; these tubes carry the ovum from the ovary to the uterine cavity where, if it is fertilized in the outer portion of the tube, it can implant in the uterine wall.

false negative (362):   Test result which does not detect a condition and wrongly indicates it is not present when in fact it is.

false positive (362):   Test result which wrongly indicates a condition that is not actually present.

FAS: See *fetal alcohol syndrome*.

fellatio (400):   Oral stimulation of a man's penis by his partner.

female circumcision (165):   Ritual in many cultures, especially African and Moslem, in which the clitoris, and sometimes the minor labia, of a young girl are removed; in some cases the vulva is sewn up to ensure female virginity.

female ejaculation (186):   Controversial phenomenon of fluid expulsion from the female urethra reported by some women following stimulation of the Grafenberg spot.

female impersonator (519):   Male who dresses in feminine clothing and adopts a feminine role as part of an entertainment or comedy act, for sexual arousal in transvestism, or as a homosexual "drag queen"; see *cross-coding*.

feminization of poverty (503):   Recent social and economic phenomenon in which divorce, single parenthood, and the increasing number of women surviving into their later years increases the proportion of women among the poor.

fertilization (204):   Union of a sperm and ovum, combining their haploid chromosome complements to produce a zygote which develops into an offspring; see *embryo, fetus*.

fetal alcohol syndrome (FAS) (215):   Combination of facial, neural, and cardiac abnormalities in a newborn resulting from the consumption of alcohol by the mother at critical periods during pregnancy.

fetish (541):   Attribution of erotic or sexual significance to some nonsexual inanimate object or to a nongenital body part, or the reliance on such a nonsexual object for sexual arousal and satisfaction.

fetus (206):   Unborn offspring from the 9th week of pregnancy to birth; see *embryo, zygote*.

fibrocystic disorder (315):   Single or multiple benign cysts, or growths, in a woman's breast.

fixed worldview (56):   Philosophical view of the world, humans, and sexuality which stresses the immutability of human nature, sex roles, and sexual morality, and emphasizes the unnaturalness of homosexual, bisexual, nonmonogamous, nonmarital, and nonprocreative sex.

flirtation (419):   Ritualized pattern of behavior whereby two people make initial contact in a courtship. Human flirtation involves five stages: physical approach, making verbal contact, swiveling of both persons from shoulder-to-shoulder to face-to-face position, touch, and finally synchronization of bodily movements.

follicle-stimulating hormone (FSH) (115): Steroid hormone produced by the pituitary in both males and females that stimulates development of the ova and sperm.

foreskin (160): Thin membrane-like flap covering the glans of the penis or clitoris.

formal value (52): Value or principle that is officially expressed by some authority in a public statement; see *informal value*.

fornication (586): Sexual intercourse engaged in by two unmarried persons.

fraternal twins (208): Two infants delivered in the same birth but resulting from the fertilization of two separate eggs; see *identical twins*.

"free love" movement (8): Philosophical, often anarchistic movement in the late 19th century which advocated abolishing marriage and endorsed equality of men and women, a distinction between reproductive and relational sex, and both self-health and sexual freedom for women.

frottage (frotteur) (538): Person who depends on rubbing up against another person's body, especially a stranger, in a crowded or public place in order to achieve sexual arousal and satisfaction.

FSH: See *follicle-stimulating hormone*.

gender (72, 432, 516): One's personal, social, and/or legal status as a male or a female, or as a person of mixed gender. In its simplest usage, *gender* is one's social role as a sexual person as opposed to the genital or sexual anatomy with which one is born.

gender assignment (92): Public assignment of male or female sex and gender status to a newborn, usually based on external genital anatomy.

gender dysphoria (516): Subjectively experienced state of conflict between one's genital anatomy and one's gender-identity/role; see *cross-coding*, *transgenderism*, *transsexualism*, *transvestitism*.

gender identity (72, 516): Internalized conviction that one is a male, a female, or has an ambiguous sexual status; the private experience of one's gender role.

gender-identity/role (73): Term which emphasizes the inseparable nature of one's gender identity—the private experience of one's maleness or femaleness—and one's gender role or public manifestation of gender identity as a male, female, or ambivalent individual.

gender nonconformity (447): Behavioral pattern in which an individual adopts the gender role of persons of the other *sex*, either chronically as in a transgenderist, or episodically as in a transvestite; see *cross-coding*.

gender orientation (432, 516): Concept which includes (1) erotic (sexual) orientation—the gender of the persons we prefer to have sex with; (2) sexual fantasy orientation—the gender of the persons we fantasize having sex with; and (3) affectional orientation—the gender of the persons we bond emotionally with.

gender role (72, 93, 433, 516): Combination of everything one does and says to indicate to others and to oneself the extent to which one's gender identity is male, female, or ambivalent; the public expression of one's gender identity.

gender-role behavior (72, 433, 516): Behavior associated with one's gender role as a male or female.

gender scripting (92): Social conditioning for behavior deemed suitable to and acceptable for a male or a female.

genital herpes (345):   Sexually transmitted, incurable viral infection characterized by intermittent, mildly painful outbreaks of open sores or blisters at the site of infection in the sexual organs, during which the individual is infectious; caused by *Herpes simplex* II virus.

glans (147, 160):   Smooth, dark-colored, erectile enlargement at the tip of the clitoris or penis; in the male, the glans is an enlargement of the corpus spongiosum.

gonadotropin-releasing hormone (GnRH) (114):   General term for hormones produced by the hypothalamus which control the production and release by the pituitary of follicle-stimulating, and luteinizing or interstitial cell stimulating hormones.

gonads (79):   The ovaries which produce eggs and a female balance of sex hormones and the testes which produce sperm and a male balance of sex hormones.

gonorrhea (338):   Common sexually transmitted bacterial infection of the vagina, penis, rectum, throat, and/or eyes caused by the bacterium *Neisseria gonorrhoeae*; many infected females and 5% to 20% of infected males show no early symptoms; male symptoms include painful urination, penile discharge, swollen glands, and/or sore throat.

Grafenberg spot (185):   Very sensitive tissue located in the anterior wall of the vagina, just under the urinary bladder, an inch or two beyond the vaginal orifice, and usually halfway between the back of the pubic bone and the front of the cervix.

group marriage (8):   Lifestyle in which two or more couples live together as spouses.

guilt culture (31):   Culture in which the average person's integrity and sense of responsibility and guilt are deemed sufficient to keep him or her from violating the sexual mores of the culture; see *shame culture*.

HCG: See *human chorionic gonadotropin*.

Hemophilus vaginalis (338):   Sexually transmitted bacterium which causes a profuse, foul-smelling vaginal discharge, although it frequently occurs with no symptoms in women and is asymptomatic in males.

hepatitis B (345):   Viral-caused, possibly lethal liver infection transmitted by sexual contact, contaminated blood transfusion, and the use of contaminated needles or instruments.

herpes: See *genital herpes*.

heteroerotic (432):   Sexually but not affectionally attracted to persons of the other gender as sexual partners.

heterosexism (452):   The personal or cultural bias and assumption that everyone is or should be heterosexual.

heterosexual(ity) (435):   Condition of being sexually attracted to persons of the other gender as sexual partners.

high sex ratio (493):   Society in which males outnumber females, particularly in the 20- to 30-year-old age group; such societies tend to be patriarchal and to emphasize strict gender roles, monogamy, sexual exclusivity, and virginity for women.

hijra (38):   Indian term for a full-time female impersonator; member of a traditional Hindu social class; type of third gender alongside males and females.

HIV (355):   Human immunodeficiency virus, the causative agent for acquired immune deficiency syndrome; see *sero-positive*.

homoerotic (438):   Sexually attracted to persons of one's own gender as sexual partners.

homophobia (452):   Intense dislike and fear of homosexually oriented persons, often expressed as an obsessive hostility for those whose love, lust, and sexual bonding are directed to persons of their own gender.

homosexual(ity) (434): Condition of being sexually attracted to persons of one's own gender as sexual partners.

human chorionic gonadotropin (HCG) (208): Sex hormone, produced in large amount by the placenta, which maintains hormone production by the ovaries that supports pregnancy; used as the basis of all pregnancy tests.

human immunodeficiency virus (HIV) (355): Causative agent for acquired immune deficiency syndrome (AIDS).

hymen (149): Functionless fold of skin that partially covers the entrance to the human vagina.

hyperphilia (528): Syndrome with varied causes and diagnoses in which sexual activity is significantly above a social or cultural standard, or beyond the level preferred by the individual.

hypophilia (528): Syndrome with varied causes and diagnoses in which sexual activity is significantly below a social or cultural standard, or below the level preferred by the individual.

hypothalamus (114, 198): Region in the floor of the brain which activates, controls, and integrates the peripheral autonomic nervous system, hormone processes, and many somatic functions such as body temperature, sleep, appetite, and sexual and mating behaviors.

identical twins (208): Two offspring developing from the same zygote, a single ovum fertilized by a single sperm, which subsequently separates into two embryos to produce two infants with identical hereditary traits.

imitation research model (637): Research hypothesis theorizing that people learn patterns of exploitation and violence from the role models provided by pornography; see *catharsis research model*.

incest (612): Sexual contact between two persons of close kinship for whom such intimacy is forbidden by custom, law, and/or religious tradition.

inclusion (531): Distortion of a love-map when an extraneous, nonsexual element is incorporated into one's psychosexual development during childhood so that the person becomes dependent on this element for sexual arousal and satisfaction.

indecent exposure (590): Legal term for the public display of a part of the body which is prohibited by law, usually the genitalia, buttocks, or breasts in a woman, and the male genitalia.

infertility (229): Inability to conceive and carry a fetus to term and delivery.

informal value (52): Moral judgment or value expressed by what a person actually does; may conflict with the formal value endorsed by the family or ethnic group, society, or church to which that individual belongs; see *formal value*.

inhibited female orgasm (575): Inability of a female to reach orgasm during or in association with vaginal intercourse, due to psychogenic or organic factors or a combination of the two.

inhibited male orgasm (ejaculation) (573): Inability of a male to reach orgasm and ejaculate during vaginal intercourse, due to psychogenic or organic factors or a combination of the two.

inhibited sexual arousal (573): In the male, the inability to obtain or maintain an erection capable of allowing penile/vaginal intercourse and ejaculation; in females, the inability to achieve vaginal lubrication sufficient to allow sexual intercourse without pain or physical discomfort. Both conditions may have an organic, psychological, or a combined etiology.

inhibited sexual desire (572):   Persistent or temporary lack of sexual desire or libido caused by organic, psychological, or a combined etiology.

intimacy (422):   Close, personal relationship between two persons who relate as equals; intimacy may involve intellectual, physical (sexual), emotional, and spiritual aspects of the personality, and vary from superficial to very personal and fulfilling.

intimate network (483):   Group of single and married friends who accept sexual intimacy as part of their ongoing relationships.

intrauterine contraceptive device (IUD) (261):   Device made of plastic inserted into the uterine cavity and left there; it appears to speed up transport of the ovum through the fallopian tube and prevent implantation of a fertilized ovum.

intrauterine growth retardation (IURG) (214):   Inhibition of the normal growth rate of the fetus due to maternal malnutrition, impaired blood flow in the placenta, and multiple pregnancies; once physical retardation has occurred at critical developmental periods, it cannot be remedied.

in vitro fertilization (IVF) (232):   Procedure in which an ovum is removed surgically from the ovary or by lavage from the fallopian tube, fertilized in a culture medium with sperm, artificially cultured for two days, and then transferred to the uterus of the original woman to bypass her blocked fallopian tubes. It may also be transferred to a surrogate mother if the ovum donor does not wish to or cannot carry a gestation full term.

IUD: See *intrauterine contraceptive device.*

IURG: See *intrauterine growth retardation.*

IVF: See *in vitro fertilization.*

Kaposi's sarcoma (358):   Rare malignancy of the skin and connective tissue; an opportunistic cancer commonly associated with acquired immune deficiency syndrome (AIDS).

kiddie pornography (592):   Sexually explicit films and pictures showing pubescent and prepubescent children in sexual situations.

Kinsey Six Scale (435):   Discontinuous scale of 0 to 6 rating the proportion of heterosexual and homosexual experiences and fantasy, with 0 the rating for an exclusively heterosexual person, 3 the rating for a true bisexual (equally attracted to both men and women), and 6 indicating an exclusively homosexually oriented person.

Klein Sexual Orientation Grid (438):   Two-dimensional grid designed to describe gender orientation in terms of seven factors (sexual attraction, sexual behavior, fantasies, emotional preference, social preference, lifestyle, and self-identification) arranged on the vertical axis and three time frames (five years ago, the current year, and ideal or future goal) arranged on the horizontal axis. Individual is rated in each of the 21 boxes, using the 0 to 6 rating criteria of the Kinsey Six Scale. Total sum of the 21 ratings is then divided by the number of ratings to give an overall sexual orientation rating from 0 to 6.

labia: See *major labia, minor labia.*

labor (221):   Period and the processes during parturition from the beginning of cervical dilation through childbirth to the delivery of the placenta or afterbirth.

Lamaze method of childbirth (224): Most popular form of natural childbirth, involving instruction on all aspects of childbirth, practice of relaxation, breathing, and muscle control exercises, and coaching during labor and delivery.

latency period (131): In Freud's psychoanalytic theory of psychosexual development, a stage alleged to last from about age 6 until puberty during which there is supposedly little interest in sexual activity.

Leboyer Gentle Birthing (225): Approach to childbirth which stresses (1) a gentle, controlled delivery in a quiet, dimly lit warm room; (2) avoidance of pulling the newborn's head; (3) avoidance of overstimulating the newborn's sensory intake; and (4) encouragement of maternal/paternal/infant bonding.

legal codes (582): Division of legal responsibilities to cover specific areas of human behavior; criminal, civil, and family codes are central to the system of jurisdiction in the United States and most Western countries.

legal jurisdictions (582): Division of legal responsibilities to specific authorities; in the United States, federal, military, state, and local jurisdictions.

LH: See *luteinizing hormone*.

libido (130): Subjectively experienced and self-reported sexual drive or urge; the primary, possibly instinctual, seeking of sexual gratification activated by testosterone. Although libido is innate, the behaviors which allow its gratification are learned.

limbic system (198): That portion of the primitive mammalian brain which governs emotions such as fear, rage, pleasure, anger, and sexual arousal; see *hypothalamus*.

limerence (418): An intense love beyond the person's rational control, the state of falling in love and being love-smitten; a romantic love that is preoccupied with the loved one to the point of being oblivious, at least temporarily, of all other reality.

lovemap (417): Personalized, developmental template or representation in the mind and brain depicting an idealized lover and the idealized program of sexual activity.

low sex ratio (493): Society in which females outnumber males, particularly in the 20- to 30-year-old age group. Such societies tend to grant more equality of the genders, allow for more sexual freedom, and accept lifestyle options for women that are not limited to marriage and child rearing.

luteinizing hormone (LH) (115): Gonadotropic hormone secreted by the pituitary. In females, it works with follicle-stimulating hormone to activate production of ovarian estrogens. After ovulation, it stimulates conversion of the follicle to a corpus luteum. In males, LH is known as interstitial cell stimulating hormone (ICSH) because it stimulates testosterone production in the interstitial cells of the testes.

machismo (45): Mystique and cultural imperatives associated with masculinity in Latin American cultures. Stresses male physical aggressiveness, high risk taking, breaking the rules, and casual and uninvolved sexual relations with women.

major labia (147): Two long, liplike pads of skin, one on either side of the vaginal opening outside the minor labia and extending from the front to the back of the vulva. These labia contain areolar tissue, fat, a thin layer of nonstriated muscle, and may be covered with pubic hair; see *minor labia*.

mammogram (315): Diagnostic X ray of the soft tissues of the breast.

man-sharing (486): Form of informal polygyny originally observed among American blacks, in which a married man with a wife and family develops a second household/family, typically with a single mother; usually a response to economic pressures and a shortage of marriageable males.

marianismo (45):   Latin American ideal of feminine spiritual superiority which teaches that women are semi-divine and morally superior to men; the complement of machismo; see *etiqueta*.

marital rape (607):   Act of forcing the spouse, usually the wife, to engage in sexual relations against her will.

masculinize (76):   Developmental differentiation of masculine features and characteristics, involving a constant interaction of both biological and sociological factors at critical periods. Before birth, affects the sexual anatomy and neural pathways in the brain. After birth, involves a continual interaction of hormonal, neural, and social factors.

masochism (masochist) (538):   Paraphilic response to or dependence on receiving punishment, bondage, discipline, humiliation, and/or servitude in order to become sexually aroused and reach orgasm.

masturbation (390):   Self-stimulation of the genitals by touch or pressure, usually with the hands or vibrator, and with orgasm as a common but not inevitable or necessary outcome.

menarche (114):   Onset of the monthly menstrual cycle and menses in a female during puberty.

menopause (114, 504):   Natural and gradual cessation of menstruation in a human female, usually between ages 45 and 60.

menses (117):   In women between menarche and menopause, the monthly discharge consisting of cells from the uterine lining, blood, and vaginal and cervical mucus. The menstrual flow begins 14 days after ovulation when fertilization and pregnancy does not follow ovulation. It usually lasts 3 to 7 days.

menstruation (118):   Physiological process whereby the disintegrating inner lining of the uterus is shed and expelled from the uterus; also known as *menses, period*.

Miller v. the United States (636):   1973 decision of the U.S. Supreme Court which attempted to tighten the restrictions on obscene material by requiring that defenders of an alleged obscene work prove that it has "serious literary, artistic, or scientific merit." This decision did little to change the criteria of the 1957 Roth v. the United States decision.

minor labia (147):   Two delicate folds of skin between the major, or outer, labia, which extend from the clitoris posterior on both sides of the urethral and vaginal orifices; very sensitive, erectile, and varied in shape and color; see *major labia*.

MIS: See *Mullerian inhibiting hormone (substance)*.

miscarriage (215):   Spontaneous, natural abortion, usually before the 28th week of gestation.

monogamy (8, 474):   Sexually exclusive marriage of a man and woman.

mononucleosis (317):   Acute herpes-type viral infection; symptoms include fever, malaise, sore throat, swollen lymph glands, enlargement of the spleen and liver, and abnormal liver function.

mons veneris (144):   In human females, a soft, fatty, triangular-shaped mass of tissue covering the pubic bone, above and anterior to the vulva; covered with pubic hair after puberty.

Mullerian inhibiting hormone (substance) (MIH or MIS) (80):   Hormone produced by the testes of male fetuses which prevents the differentiation of the primordial paired Mullerian ducts into the upper vagina, uterus, and fallopian tubes.

mut'a (34):   Moslem tradition which allows a man to contract with a woman for a "temporary marriage," a marriage of pleasure, in return for a certain payment; may last a single night, several weeks, or longer.

myotonia (174):   Buildup of muscle tone or tension during sexual arousal; see *vasocongestion*.

natural sin (54):   Sexual act which, although considered sinful and immoral, nevertheless does not violate the procreative goal of sexual relations (e.g., rape, incest, adultery, and fornication); oral and anal sex, masturbation, and contraceptive coitus are considered unnatural.

NGU: See *nongonococcal urethritis*.

nocturnal emission (197):   A wet dream; subconscious and involuntary sexual arousal and ejaculation during sleep occurring in roughly 80% of adolescent males.

nocturnal penile tumescence (NPT) (197):   Spontaneous and natural erection of the penis associated with the rapid eye movement (REM) phase of sleep. Healthy men typically experience such erections every 90 minutes for a total duration of two to three hours.

nongonococcal urethritis (337):   Common sexually transmitted infection of the male or female urethra that is not caused by the *Neisseria gonorrhoeae* bacterium, but by other microorganisms such as *Chlamydia*, *Herpes*, or *Candida*.

normal (440):   Conforming with or constituting an accepted standard, model, or pattern for a particular group, population, or species; the criterion for what is considered normal may be personal, religious, statistical, legal, or social.

normophilia (normophilic) (528):   Condition of conforming erotosexually with the norms dictated by custom or religious or civil authorities; the opposite of paraphilia or deviant.

obscene, obscenity (15, 635):   A social or moral concept referring to anything that is offensive to modesty or decency. For the current legal definition, see *Roth v. the United States*.

open marriage (482):   An equal, flexible partnership between two friends that stresses communication, open trust, spontaneity, and the right to privacy for personal growth; may include sexual openness.

opportunistic infections (358):   General term for various infections associated with depression of the body's immune system and AIDS; see *Kaposi's sarcoma*, *pneumocystic pneumonia*.

oral sex (398):   Any love play involving the mouth and genitals; see *cunnilingus, fellatio*.

orgasm (182):   Intense, reflexive, physiological, and pleasurable release of sexual tension, following sexual stimulation and the buildup of sexual arousal in intercourse, oral sex, or masturbation; the third and shortest of the four phases of the sexual response cycle as described by Masters and Johnson.

orgasmic platform (180):   Thickening of the walls and tightening and elevation of the outer third of the vagina due to vasocongestion during sexual arousal; the orgasmic platform facilitates gripping of the penis during intercourse, increasing the pleasure for both partners.

outercourse (250):   Any form of sexual pleasuring or expression of sexual intimacy other than penile/vaginal intercourse.

ovarian cycle (118):   That portion of the female monthly cycle centered in the ovaries, involving their production of a Graafian follicle with a mature ovum during the follicular phase, ovulation, and formation of a hormone-producing corpus luteum during the luteal phase.

ovary (151):   The paired female reproductive glands which produce ova, estrogens, and progesterone, located in the lower abdominal cavity on either side of the uterus.

ovulation (120, 204): Release of one or more ova from the ovary; followed 14 days later by the onset of the next menstrual flow if the ovum is not fertilized.

ovum (pl. *ova*) (152, 204): The female reproductive cell, containing 22 body chromosomes and one X chromosome; fertilized by a sperm to produce a zygote.

painful intercourse (575): Sexual intercourse which is accompanied by physical pain resulting from a lack of vaginal lubrication, a vaginal infection, or allergic reaction in women, from a sexual deformity in men, or from a psychogenic cause in both men and women.

palimony (480): Colloquial term for financial compensation and support awarded by a court or mutual agreement to a woman or a man after breakup of a nonmarital heterosexual cohabitation, or a gay or lesbian union.

panerotic potential (457): Theory that the newborn infant has a potential to react erotically to and receive nurturance from one's self, other persons, inanimate and animate objects, and the transcendent; social pressures and scripting narrow down this potential to a socially acceptable range.

Pap smear (304): Routine cytological smear used most often to test for a cancerous or precancerous condition of the cervix.

paraphilia (529): Psychological condition in which a person responds to and is dependent on an unusual or socially unacceptable stimulus, either actual or reenacted in fantasy, for sexual arousal and satisfaction.

patrilineage (33): Pattern of kinship in which descent is traced through the father and his male ancestry.

pedophilia (pedophilic, pedophile) (531): Paraphilic condition in which an adult is dependent for sexual arousal and satisfaction on sexual activity with a prepubertal or early pubertal boy or girl, or fantasy of such.

pelvic inflammatory disease (307, 335): Any inflammatory condition of the female pelvic organs, usually due to a bacterial infection.

penis (158): Male urinary and copulatory organ composed of an internal root and an external shaft; the shaft contains two parallel, cylindrical, and erectile bodies, the corpora cavernosa, and beneath them, surrounding the urethra, the erectile corpus spongiosum with a glans penis and the foreskin at the distal end.

perineum (147): Region bordered on the sides by the thighs, between the scrotal base or vulva and the anus; an erogenous zone.

period: See *menses.*

personhood (285): Those biological, legal, social, and/or religious characteristics used to designate a human infant as an acceptable member of its social group, included under the protection of its laws, and worthy of the effort and expense necessary to support and educate it until it becomes an adult; a critical concept in the abortion debate.

pheromone (198): Odorous secretion that acts as a chemical and sexual messenger and attractant between individuals.

PID: See *pelvic inflammatory disease.*

pituitary gland (114): Endocrine gland located under the brain, known as the "master gland" because its hormone products, including a growth hormone and follicle-stimulating and luteinizing hormones, regulate many vital functions of the body including growth, sexual activity, and reproduction.

placenta (210): Highly vascular fetal/maternal organ formed early in pregnancy on the inner wall of the uterus through which the fetus receives oxygen and nutrients and gets rid of waste products; see *afterbirth*.

plateau phase: See *excitement/plateau phase*.

PLISSIT (563): Filter model for sex therapy. Acronym stands for four levels of therapy, starting with Permission giving often accompanied by Limited Information, moving to Specific Suggestions, and, when necessary, Intense Therapy.

pneumocystic pneumonia (358): Opportunistic form of pneumonia occurring when the immune system is suppressed; characterized by fever, cough, rapid breathing, and, frequently, cyanosis; a major symptom of acquired immune deficiency syndrome (AIDS).

polyfidelity (488): Mutually agreed upon commitment and fidelity shared by more than two persons in a closed group marriage or in an ongoing intimate network incuding both primary and secondary, comarital, and satellite relationships.

polygyny (7): Marriage of one man with two or more women; commonly referred to as polygamy.

pornography (635): Generally speaking, writings, pictures, images, or films that depict erotic behavior with the intent of sexually arousing the reader or viewer; see *obscene*.

PPNG (339): Acronym for a strain of gonorrhea-causing bacterium which is resistant to penicillin.

premature ejaculation (573): Sexual difficulty in which a male regularly reaches orgasm sooner than he or his partner would prefer.

premenstrual syndrome (120): Combination of mild-to-severe physical and psychological symptoms including fatigue, bloated feeling, depression, irritability, and lowered self-esteem experienced by some women a few days before menstruation and/or during the first day or two of menstruation.

prenuptial contract (587): Verbal or written agreement, usually detailing financial matters, entered into by a man and woman prior to their marriage; see *palimony*.

prepared childbirth (223): Any method of childbirth stressing involvement of the mother and avoiding use of anesthesia, episiotomy, and forceps; variously known as natural childbirth and the Bradley, Lamaze, or Read methods.

prepuce (149): Hairless foreskin or loose, retractable skin covering the penile glands in the male, often surgically removed in circumcision; the skin of the minor labia covering the top of the clitoris in the female.

primary sexual difficulty (problem) (557): Any sexual problem that a person has always experienced, as opposed to a secondary sexual problem which is episodic, situational, or short term.

proceptivity (90): Solicitation of a male by the female; in a more general sense, the initial phase in which the two persons engage in a ritual of soliticitation and courtship, mutually attracting and responding to overtures using bodily positions and movements and both visual and verbal signs.

process worldview (57): Worldview and philosophy of life which accepts change and does not see sexual roles, behavior, and values in terms of a rigid morality established in the beginning of time by God or nature; see *fixed worldview*.

progesterone (116): One of the two major female sex hormones; produced by the ovarian corpus luteum following ovulation and by the placenta during pregnancy, and also by the adrenal gland. Responsible for preparing the uterus for implantation of the fertilized ovum and for maintaining a pregnancy; see *estrogen.*

progestin-only pill (262): Any of a growing number of oral hormonal contraceptives containing only progestin; progestin-only pills and implantables are not yet readily available in the United States.

propulsion phase (188): Expulsion or ejaculation of the seminal fluid from the penile urethra when the external or outer prostatic sphincter opens following the buildup of pressure in the prostate during the emission phase.

prostate (163): Golfball-sized gland in males which elaborates a secretion that liquefies the compacted sperm and semen received from the testes and seminal vesicles. The prostate surrounds the neck of the bladder and urethra and is associated with two sphincters which control the flow of semen and urine.

prostatitis (321): Acute or chronic infection or inflammation of the prostate, treatable with antibiotics, sitz baths, bed rest, and fluids.

prostitution (624): Commercial exchange of sexual favors in return for money.

psychogenic (170): Originating in the mind; sexual excitement, arousal, and erection resulting from consciously perceived psychological stimuli—visual, aural, olfactory, and tactile.

psychosexual identity (72): Alternate term for gender identity.

psychosexual status (72): One's social expression and acceptance by others as a male, female, or indeterminate gender.

puberty (114): Transitional biological stage marking the end of childhood and the start of adolescence, when a surge in sex hormones triggers development of secondary sexual characteristics and the achievement of reproductive capacity.

pubic lice (341): Blood-sucking louse *Pediculus pubis* that infects the pubic areas and possibly the eyelids and eyelashes, scalp, and skin.

purdah (32): Islamic custom and institution of "female exclusion" which requires that Moslem women be fully veiled when in public and remain unseen by any male except close relatives.

Puritan (5): Value system named for an English and colonial American Protestant separatist group of the 16th and 17th centuries which emphasized the family and severely punished any sexual activity outside of marriage.

quickening (212): First fetal movements perceived by a pregnant woman, usually occurring in the 16th to 20th week of pregnancy.

rape (600): In English common law, forced sexual intercourse with a nonconsenting female other than one's own wife. The modern definition is more inclusive: vaginal, oral, or anal sexual intercourse, or other sexual intimacies or contact forced on one person by another using either physical force, the threat of physical force, coercion, and/or a weapon.

rape trauma syndrome (615): Reaction pattern following a sexual assault involving strong emotions and feelings of shame, humiliation, rage, personal violation, fear, confusion, the sense of having lost power or control over one's life, and possibly the feeling that one somehow caused or unknowingly invited the rape.

reflexogenic (170): Originating in a nerve reflex; sexual arousal resulting from tactile stimulation activating a reflex arc leading to relaxation of blood vessels of the cavernous tissues of the genitalia, thereby producing erection of the penis, clitoris, and/or minor labia.

refractory phase (191):   Temporary period, immediately following ejaculation, during which a male cannot be sexually aroused; duration may be very brief in the teen years and longer in the later years.

resolution (191):   Last of four phases in the Masters and Johnson model of the sexual response cycle during which the sexual system returns to its unaroused state.

Rh factor (216):   Protein on the surface of red blood cells which, when it occurs in a fetus, can trigger an Rh negative mother's immune system to produce antibodies that destroy the fetal blood and can result in fetal problems and death.

rhythm (263):   Natural method of preventing conception which relies on abstinence from sexual intercourse during fertile times estimated from records of the shortest and longest cycle in six or more previous monthly cycles.

Roe v. Wade (282):   1973 decision of the U.S. Supreme Court which legalized abortion.

Roth v. the United States (635):   1957 decision of the U.S. Supreme Court which established three criteria for legal obscenity: (1) the dominant theme of a work must appeal to prurient interests; (2) it must be offensive to the average community member; and (3) it must lack any social value; see *Miller v. the United States*.

RU 486 (293):   Drug used to induce a very early abortion when pregnancy is suspected; not currently available in the United States.

rubella (215):   German measles, a viral infection of little consequence to children and adults but a serious danger to a fetus exposed during the first three months of pregnancy.

sadism (sadist) (538):   Paraphilic need for inflicting humiliation, punishment, torture, restraint, and pain on one's partner in order to achieve sexual arousal and facilitate orgasm; see *sadomasochism*.

sadomasochism (sadomasochistic) (538):   Consensual, sometimes paraphilic, sexual activity involving polarized role playing, intense sensations and feelings, actions and fantasies that focus on the forbidden, and playing out or fantasizing dominant and submissive roles as part of a sexual scenario.

safer sex (365):   Sexual behaviors recommended to reduce the risk of contracting the AIDS virus in sexual relationships: use of condoms with spermicidal nonoxynol-9, avoidance of anal and oral sex with high risk partners, and avoidance of needle sharing.

same-gender sexual experimentation (438):   Sexual intimacies occurring during adolescence and motivated by curiosity rather than a true homosexual orientation.

scabies (342):   Contagious skin condition caused by a parasitic mite and characterized by intense itching.

scripting (92, 135):   Psychological linking of an early sexual experience with a particular circumstance, stimulus, or person; in a more general sense, the social conditioning a person is subjected to by parents, family, peers, society, culture, and religion.

scrotum (160):   Loose-skinned pouch containing the testes, epididymis, and part of the spermatic cords.

secondary sexual difficulty or *problem* (557):   Sexual problem or dysfunction which has not always existed, but occurs sporadically or in certain situations or relationships.

semen (162):   The male ejaculate: thick, whitish nutrient secretions of the prostate, seminal vesicles, epididymis, and Cowper's gland mixed with sperm produced by the testes.

seminal pool (180): Cavity which forms at the cervical end of the vagina during the plateau and orgasmic stages, serving as a receptacle for the ejaculated semen and facilitating its access to the cervical canal; see *tenting*.

seminal vesicles (162): Two saclike structures behind the prostate gland which secrete nutrient seminal fluid (semen) into the ejaculatory ducts for transport to the prostatic urethra.

seminiferous tubules (161): Long, thin, coiled tubules within the testes which produce sperm.

sensate focus exercises (565): Noncoital, nondemand, graduated pleasuring exercises used in behavioral therapy for various sexual dysfunctions. Exercises stress playful, non-goal-oriented touching and caressing, exploration of the partner's body, and sensual responses with continual verbal feedback. The object is for the couple to become comfortable with each other, without the male needing to have an erection or the female needing to become aroused.

sero-positive (361): Test result which indicates the presence of HIV antibodies and an infectious AIDS condition.

sex (72): One's biological status as a male or female based on one's external sexual anatomy; sexual intercourse; see *gender*.

sex flush (182): Temporary reddish, measles-like rash that sometimes develops as a result of vasocongestion during the plateau stage; usually begins on the abdomen and breasts before spreading to other regions including the neck, face, hands, and soles of the feet as arousal increases.

sex role (72): Patterns of behavior and expectations which are culturally stereotyped as typical of or especially suited to one or the other gender; also known as gender role.

sex skin (180): Darkening color of the minor labia occurring during sexual arousal.

sexual addiction (543): Concept of compulsive dependence on frequent repetition of highly ritualized sexual activity. Analogy of sexual addiction with alcohol and drug addictions is challenged by many experts.

sexual aversion (570): Severe phobic reaction in which a sexual situation or even the possibility of sexual involvement triggers an anxious avoidance in an individual, often with strong reactions of disgust, anger, sweating, and fear.

sexual desire conflict (572): Conflict in the amount or type of sexual activity desired by two persons in a relationship.

sexual difficulty (dysfunction) (555): Condition in which a person does not function as the average healthy person would be expected to in terms of sexual desire, sexual arousal, or orgasm; desire phase difficulties include lack of desire, desire conflicts, and sexual aversion; arousal difficulties include inhibited sexual arousal, erectile difficulty, and lack of vaginal lubrication; orgasm phase difficulties include inhibited orgasm and early (premature) ejaculation; vaginal spasms and dyspareunia (painful intercourse) are also included under this term; see *sexual problem*.

sexual problem (556): Condition in which a person is not sexually dysfunctional, but feels uneasy, uncomfortable, or guilty about his or her sexual behavior, or has a communication problem with his or her mate; see *sexual difficulty*.

sexual harassment (616): Any unwelcome or unsolicited sexual advance, request for sexual favors, or other verbal or physical conduct of a sexual nature whose acceptance or rejection is explicitly or implicitly used as a condition for employment, recognition, promotion, or grades.

sexuality (4): The experiential combination of one's biological sex and psychosocial gender, coextensive with one's gendered personality as a male, female, or indeterminate gender.

sexually open marriage (SOM) (482): Marriage that allows for comarital relationships, friendships which may be emotionally and/or sexually intimate.

sexually transmitted disease (328): Any one of a variety of diseases which is transmitted primarily by sexual contact, including gonorrhea, syphilis, chlamydia, venereal warts, nongonococcal urethritis, trichomoniasis, herpes, candidiasis, hemophilus, pubic lice, and AIDS.

Sexual Orientation Grid (438): Sexual orientation ascertained by rating a person's sexual attraction, sexual behavior, sexual fantasies, emotional preference, social preference, lifestyle, and self-identification, using the Kinsey Sex Scale for the present, five years prior, and one's ideal.

shame culture (32): Term created by social anthropologist Margaret Mead for a culture in which strict, external restraints are deemed necessary to prevent people from violating sexual mores; see *guilt culture*.

Silent Epidemic (328): Concept that there is a major risk of contracting common sexually transmitted diseases because persons with chlamydial infection, genital herpes, venereal warts, gonorrhea, and candidiasis often show no symptoms and do not know that they are infectious and can pass these diseases on to their sexual partners.

situational homoerotic behavior (563): Sexual activity engaged in by persons of the same gender because the environment in which they find themselves, for example, a boarding school, summer camp, aboard ship, or in prison, does not allow for sexual contact with persons of the other gender.

situational problem (438): Sexual problem or dysfunction caused by a particular situation, such as the lack of privacy.

smegma (160): Cheesy, foul-smelling secretion of sebaceous glands found under the foreskin around the raised edge of the penile and clitoral glans; contains pheromones or sex attractants.

social birth (286): Public ritual in which a newborn or child is accepted into the family or community and granted full status as a person with certain rights and responsibilities.

social exchange theory (416): Theory that seeks to explain the formation and development of all relationships in terms of the balance and dynamics of their rewards and costs. If the rewards of a relationship outweigh the costs, the relationship is likely to continue and become more intimate. If the relationship becomes too problematic, it is likely to wane and break up.

SOM: See *sexually open marriage*.

somatosensory affectional deprivation (SAD) syndrome (413): Developmental changes in the brain resulting from the lack of body pleasure experienced when a child is not touched, caressed, and gently rocked or moved; has been correlated with an increased tendency to violent adult behavior and a difficulty or inability to relate with others in ways that involve body pleasuring.

spectatoring (561): Psychological process whereby a person acts as an observer, monitor, or judge of one's own sexual performance and/or that of one's partner; a common outcome and cause of sexual dysfunction.

sperm, spermatozoon (115, 160):   The male reproductive cell, containing 22 body chromosomes and either an X or a Y chromosome in the head with a contractile tail providing motility through the female reproductive tract; joins with the ovum in fertilization to produce a zygote.

spermicide (254):   Chemical such as nonoxynol-9 which kills sperm; widely used in contraceptive foams, gels, vaginal suppositories, contraceptive films and sponges, and in coating some condoms.

statutory rape (590):   Legal concept of sexual intercourse between an adult and a legal minor; a legal minor cannot consent to sexual intercourse, hence the criminal concept of rape.

stimulus/values/role (SVR) model (416): Theory explaining partner choice in terms of initial physical, mental, or emotional stimulus/attraction, followed by selection based on compatible values and negotiation of compatible roles.

surrogate mother (232):   Woman who volunteers and may be paid to carry a child for a woman who cannot bear her own child.

swinging (480):   Exchange of partners for social/sexual recreation; mate or wife swapping.

SVR model: See *stimulus/values/role model*.

sympto-thermal method (264):   Natural method of family planning using the cervical mucus changes and basal body temperature to ascertain the time when a woman should abstain from sexual intercourse because of the risk of ovulation and conception.

syphilis (339):   Sexually transmitted infection that may affect all systems of the body including the brain if left untreated; initial bacterial infection is characterized by painless chancres.

taboo (583):   Any act, relationship, or person that is forbidden or with whom contact is prohibited; violation of a taboo involves strong social guilt and risk of serious punishment.

tenting (180):   Elevation of the uterus from the pelvic cavity into the abdominal cavity during sexual arousal, resulting in expansion of the inner vaginal cavity and formation of a seminal pool where semen gathers after coital ejaculation.

tenting orgasm (185):   Orgasm triggered by stimulation of the clitoris, formation of the orgasmic platform, and a myotonic discharge in the various pelvic muscles including the pubococcygeal muscles; see *A-frame orgasm, blended orgasm*.

teratogenic agent (215):   Any chemical, drug, or other agent that causes abnormal development of the fetus.

testes (sing. *testis*) (160):   Paired walnut-sized male reproductive glands responsible for production of sperm and androgenic hormones; also known as testicle(s); see *ovary*.

testosterone (80, 116):   The most potent masculinizing hormone, produced in the male by the testicular cells of Leydig and in the female by the adrenal glands. Stimulates masculine differentiation of internal fetal sexual anatomy, male secondary sexual characteristics following puberty, and, in both sexes, libido. Also diverts the fetal brain from the Eve Plan into the Adam Plan.

Tijuana bible (16):   Wallet-sized, 8-page, cartoon-style sexually explicit booklets popular among boys in the 1930s and 1940s, illustrating every form of sexual activity.

toxemia (217):   Infrequent complication of pregnancy that can endanger the mother's life.

toxic shock syndrome (TSS) (122): Serious medical condition in which vaginal inserts, particularly superabsorbent tampons, allow the growth of life-threatening bacteria; symptoms include fever, sore throat, nausea, vomiting, diarrhea, red skin flush, dizziness, and high blood pressure.

transgenderism (transgenderist) (521): Psychological/behavioral condition in which a person, usually a male, enacts the social role of the other gender; a transsexual who does not have sex change surgery.

transgenderist (521): See *transgenderism*.

transsexualism (521): Psychological condition in which the sexual anatomy is in conflict with a person's gender or psyche; "a male psyche imprisoned in a female body," or a "female psyche imprisoned in a male body"; may be resolved by sex change surgery.

transvestitism (517): Dependence on dressing in the clothes of the other gender, either as an expression of gender discomfort or in order to achieve sexual arousal and satisfaction.

Trichomoniasis (343): Sexually transmitted infection caused by a flagellate parasite, resulting in a burning, itching, a frothy, thin, foul-smelling vaginal discharge, and sometimes in urethritis for an infected male.

tubal ligation (265): Surgical sterilization of a woman; fallopian tubes are cut and tied or otherwise blocked to prevent passage of the ovum and union of ovum and sperm.

tumescence (174): Erection and enlargement of the sexual organs, particularly the clitoris, orgasmic platform, and the penis, resulting from the vasocongestion during sexual stimulation.

ultrasonic scanning (219): Use of high frequency sound to create a moving image of the fetus in the uterus and monitor its development.

umbilical cord (211): Flexible tubular structure which carries blood between the fetus and the placenta, allowing wastes to pass from fetus through the placenta to the mother's kidneys and nutrients to pass from mother to fetus.

unnatural sin (54): In religions which emphasize the natural law theory that sexual activity is only moral when it is heterosexual and open to procreation, the belief that masturbation and oral and anal sex are unnatural whereas rape and incest are less immoral because they involve heterosexual vaginal intercourse and may be procreative.

uterine cycle (118): Monthly or near-monthly cycle of proliferation and shedding of the uterine endometrium, regulated by ovarian estrogens and progesterone; see *menses, menstruation*.

uterus (151): Hollow pear-shaped muscular organ in the female pelvis in which the fertilized ovum or zygote normally implants and where the resulting embryo develops during pregnancy.

vacuum curettage (295): First trimester surgical abortion, performed by scraping the uterine lining and suctioning out the fetal and other material.

vagina (150): Collapsed, highly expandable, tubular structure leading from the uterus to the vulva; provides passage for the menstrual flow and the infant during birth as well as receiving the penis during sexual intercourse.

vaginal atrophy (504): Degeneration and inflammation of the vaginal lining in women resulting from a reduction in estrogen secretion during menopause.

vaginal contraceptive film (VCF) (256): 2-inch-square gel film containing a spermicide which provides protection against conception when placed over the cervix during sexual intercourse.

vaginal foam (254):   Aerosol contraceptive with a spermicide which is inserted near the cervix in the vagina less than two hours before intercourse and left undisturbed for six hours after intercourse.

vaginal lubrication (176):   "Sweating" of slippery fluid from blood vessels through the walls of the vagina into the vaginal canal during sexual arousal, thus facilitating sexual intercourse.

vaginal spasms (576):   Recurrent and spastic contractions of the muscles surrounding the vaginal entrance which prevent vaginal penetration and intercourse; a sexual dysfunction due to psychological inhibitions and fear of sexual intercourse.

vaginitis (309):   Infection of the vagina.

variocele (322):   Enlarged, twisted condition in the blood vessel supplying the testes and epididymis; most common in men ages 15 to 25 as a cause of infertility.

vas deferens (pl. vasa deferentia) (161):   Paired tubes that carry the mature spermatozoa from the epididymis above the testes out of the scrotum to the seminal vesicles and prostate in the early part of the ejaculation process.

vasectomy (266):   Male sterilization operation in which the vasa deferentia in the scrotum are cut and tied or otherwise blocked.

vasocongestion (174):   Increase in the amount of blood concentrated in certain body tissues, especially in the female breasts and minor labia and in the cavernous and spongy bodies of the penis and clitoris during the excitement and plateau phase of the sexual response cycle.

VCF: See *vaginal contraceptive film.*

venereal warts (344):   Highly contagious, viral-caused soft growths on the surface of the genitals which can be transmitted through sexual contact; a common and serious, but easily controlled sexually transmitted disease.

viability (286):   Medical term for the ability of a fetus to survive and live outside the uterus; a key concept in determining the legal status of an abortion; see *personhood.*

victimless crime (594):   Illegal activity, such as prostitution, sodomy, oral or anal sex, engaged in by two consenting adults with no harm incurred by third parties.

victim precipitation (610):   Belief that a rape or incest victim is at least partially responsible for the attack, either inviting or precipitating it; although the victim of a sexual assault may do something foolhardy that puts her or him at risk, it does not excuse the behavior of the rapist or incest perpetrator.

Victorian (6):   Undefined but clear set of conservative, even antisexual, social values prevailing in northern Europe and the United States in the last half of the 19th century; named for Queen Victoria who reigned in England from 1837 to 1901.

voyeurism (voyeur) (536):   Paraphilic dependence on secretly watching another person undress or engage in sexual behavior in order to achieve sexual arousal and satisfaction.

vulva (146):   General term for the external female sexual structures, including the mons veneris, major and minor labia, clitoris, and vaginal opening.

Western Blot test (363):   Highly accurate test for presence of the HIV virus which causes acquired immune deficiency syndrome (AIDS); used to confirm a positive result of the less accurate ELISA test; see *sero-positive*.

yang (40): In oriental philosophy, one of two complementary vital energies, found in all nature; the force of heaven, the positive, male principle, light, and heat.

yin (40): In oriental philosophy, one of two complementary vital energies, found in all nature; the force of earth, the negative, female principle, dark, and cold.

zygote (206): Developing, fertilized egg prior to its embedding in the uterine wall.

Bibliography

Abramson, P. R., & H. Hayashi. (1984). Pornography in Japan: Crosscultural and theoretical considerations. In N. M. Malamuth & E. Donnerstein (eds.), *Pornography and Sexual Aggression*. Orlando, FL: Academic Press.

Adams, C., & J. Fay. (1984). *Nobody Told Me It Was Rape.* Santa Cruz, CA: Network Publications.

Addiego, F., et al. (1981). Female ejaculation: A case study. *J. Sex Res.*, 17(1):13–21.

Ageton, S. S. (1983). *Sexual Assault among Adolescents.* Lexington, MA: Heath.

Alexander, L. A. (1984). Liability in tort for the sexual transmission of disease: Genital herpes and the law. *Cornell Law Rev.*, 70(1):101–140.

Alexander, P. (1983). *Working on Prostitution.* California NOW Inc. National Organization for Women.

Allen, C. L. (1988, August 15). Planning for failure with prenuptial pacts. *Insight*, pp. 54–55.

Allgeier, E. R. (1987). Coercive versus consensual sexual interactions. In V. P. Makosky (ed.), *The G. Stanley Hall Lecture Series. Vol. 7.* Washington, DC: American Psychological Association.

American Psychiatric Association. (1978). *Diagnostic and Statistical Manual of Mental Disorders* (3rd ed.). Washington, DC: American Psychiatric Association.

Anderson, K., et al. (1983, September 5). Private violence: Child abuse, wife beating, rape. *Time*, 122(10): 18–29.

Anderson, P. (1989). Adversarial Sexual Beliefs and the Past Experience of Sexual Abuse of College Females as Predictors of Their Sexual Aggression Toward Adolescent and Adult Males. Ph.D. dissertation, New York University.

Andrews, L. B. (1984, August). The stork market: The law of the new reproductive technologies. *Amer. Bar Assoc. J.*, 70:50–56.

Andrews, L. B. (1985). *New Conceptions: A Consumer's Guide to the Newest Infertility Treatments* (rev. ed.). New York: Ballantine.

Andrews, L. B. (1987, October/November). The aftermath of Baby M: Proposed state laws on surrogate motherhood. *Hastings Center Report*, pp. 31–40.

Andrews, L. B. (1988). Surrogate motherhood: Should the adoption model apply? *Children's Legal Rights J.*, 7(4):13–20.

Annon, J. S. (1974, 1976). *The Behavioral Treatment of Sexual Problems. Volume 1. Brief Therapy.* Honolulu, HI: Enabling Systems; New York: Harper & Row.

Ardehali, P. E. (1990). Personal communication with R. T. Francoeur on sexual customs in Iran.

Arditti, R., R. D. Klein, & S. Minden. (1984). *Test-Tube Women: What Future for Motherhood?* Boston: Pandora Press.

Aries, P. (1962). *Centuries of Childhood: A Social History of Family Life.* New York: Random House.

Assagioli, R. (1971). *Psychosynthesis*. New York: Viking.

Associated Press. (1988, August 9). Parental notification for abortion upheld by federal appellate court.

Athanasiou, R., et al. (1970, February). Sex. *Psychology Today*, 4(2):39–52.

Atiya, N. (1982). *Khul Khaal: Five Egyptian Women Tell Their Stories*. Syracuse, NY: Syracuse University Press.

Atwater, L. (1982). *The Extramarital Connection: Sex, Intimacy, and Identity*. New York: Irvington.

Avery, C. S. (1988, July). Flirting with AIDS. *Self*, pp. 80–84.

Bailey, B. L. (1988). *From Front Porch to Back Seat: Courtship in Twentieth-Century America*. Baltimore: Johns Hopkins University Press.

Bakwin, H. (1974). Erotic feelings in infants and young children. *Med. Aspects Human Sex.*, 8(10):200–215.

Bandura, A. (1969). *Principles of Behavior Modification*. New York: Holt.

Barbach, L. (1982). *For Each Other: Sharing Sexual Intimacy*. Garden City, NY: Doubleday/Anchor.

Barbach, L. (1984). *Pleasures: Women Write Erotica*. New York: Harper & Row.

Baron L., & M. A. Straus. (1986). Two false principles. In P. Noble & E. Nadler (eds.), *United States of America vs. Sex*. New York: Minotaur Press.

Barr, G. (1985). Chicago Bi-Ways: An informal history. *J. Homosexuality*, 11(1–2):231–234.

Barrasso, R., et al. (1987). High prevalence of papillomavirus-associated penile intraepithelial neoplasia in sexual partners of women with cervical intraepithelial neoplasia. *New Eng. J. Med.*, 317(15):916–922.

Barrett, K. (1982, September). Date rape—Campus epidemic? *Ms.* magazine, pp. 48 ff.

Barringer, F. (1989, June 9). Divorce data stir doubt on trial marriage. *New York Times*, pp. A1, A28.

Barrows, S. B. (1986). *Mayflower Madam: The Secret Life of Sydney Biddle Barrows*. New York: Arbor House.

Bart, P., & M. Jozsa. (1980). Dirty books, dirty films, and dirty data. In L. Lederer (ed.), *Take Back the Night: Women on Pornography*. New York: Morrow.

Bart, P. B., & P. H. O'Brien. (1985). *Stopping Rape: Successful Survival Strategies*. Elmsford, NY: Pergamon Press.

Bartell, G. (1971). *Group Sex*. New York: Wyden.

Bass, E., & L. Davis. (1988). *The Courage To Heal: A Guide for Women Survivors of Child Sexual Abuse*. New York: Harper & Row.

Batchelor, E. (ed.). (1980). *Homosexuality and Ethics*. New York: Pilgrim Press.

Bauman, R. E. (1986). *The Gentleman from Maryland: The Conscience of a Gay Conservative*. New York: Arbor House.

Beck, M. (1988, August 15). Miscarriages: A medical mystery. *Newsweek*, pp. 46–52.

Becker, T., et al. (1985). Genital herpes infections in private practice in the United States, 1966 to 1981. *J. Amer. Med. Assoc.*, 253:1601–1603.

Belkin, L. (1986, May 11). The mail-order marriage business. *New York Times Magazine*, pp. 28 ff.

Belkin, L. (1989, June 12). Custody battle in Utah's top court shines rare spotlight on polygamy. *New York Times*.

Bell, A., & C. Hall. (1971). *Personality of the Child Molester*. Chicago: Aldine Atherton.

Bell, A., & M. Weinberg. (1978). *Homosexualities: A Study of the Diversity among Men and Women*. New York: Simon & Schuster.

Bell, A., M. Weinberg, & S. Hammersmith. (1981). *Sexual Preference: Its Development in Men and Women*. Bloomington: Indiana University Press.

Bell, S. (1902). A preliminary study of the emotion of love between the sexes. *Amer. J. Psychology*, 13:325–354.

Belzer, E. G., B. Whipple, & W. Moger. (1984). On female ejaculation. *J. Sex Res.*, 20(4):403–406.

Benjamin, H., & R. Masters. (1964). *Prostitution and Morality*. New York: Julian Press.

Bennett, M. V. L. (1989). Personhood from a neuroscientific perspective. In E. Doerr & J. W. Prescott (eds.), *Abortion Rights and Fetal "Personhood."* Long Beach, CA: Centerline Press.

Bentler, P. M., & W. H. Peeler. (1979). Models of female orgasms. *Archives Sexual Behavior*, 8:405–423.

Berger, R. E. (1980, February). Diagnosis and treatment of epididymitis. *Med. Aspects Human Sex.*, pp. 131–132.

Bergler, E. (1959). *Homosexuals*. Patterson, NJ: Pageant.

Berlin, F., & C. F. Meinecke. (1981). Treatment of sex offenders with antiandrogenic medication: Conceptualization, review of treatment modalities, and preliminary findings. *Amer. J. Psychiatry*, 138:601–607.

Bernstein, A. C. (1978). *The Flight of the Stork*. New York: Delacorte.

Bernstein, N. R. (1985, November). Sexuality in mentally retarded adolescents. *Med. Aspects Human Sex.*, pp. 50–61.

Bieber, I. (1976). A discussion of "Homosexuality: The ethical challenge." *J. Consulting & Clinical Psychology*, 44:163–166.

Bixler, E. O., & A. Vela-Bueno. (1987). Normal sleep: Physiological, behavioral, and clinical correlates. *Psychiatric Annals*, 17(7):437–445.

Blackwood, E. (ed.). (1985). *Anthropology and Homosexual Behavior*. New York: Haworth Press.

Blakely, M. K. (1985, April). Is one woman's sexuality

another woman's pornography? *Ms.* magazine, pp. 37–47 ff.

Blake-White, J., & C. M. Kline. (1985). Treating the dissociative process in adult victims of childhood incest. *Social Casework*, 66(7):394–402.

Blank, J. (1989). *Good Vibrations: The Complete Guide to Vibrators*. Burlingame, CA: Down There Press.

Block, R., & W. Skogan. (1982). *Resistance and Outcome in Robbery and Rape*. Evanston, IL: Northwestern University, Center for Urban Affairs & Policy Research.

Blume, E. S. (1986). The walking wounded: Post-incest syndrome. *SIECUS Report*, 15(1):5–7.

Blumstein, P., & P. Schwartz. (1983). *American Couples: Money, Work, Sex*. New York: Pocket Books.

Blyth, D. A., & F. S. Foster-Clark. (1987). Gender differences in perceived intimacy with different members of adolescents' social networks. *Sex Roles*, 17(11–12):689–717.

Bohlen, J. G., et al. (1982). Development of a woman's multiorgasmic pattern: A research case report. *J. Sex Res.*, 18(2):130–145.

Bolin, A. (1988). *In Search of Eve: Transsexual Rites of Passage*. S. Hadley, MA: Bergin & Garvey.

Bonavoglia, A. (1987). Reproductive rights: The ordeal of Pamela Rae Stewart. *Ms.* magazine, pp. 92 ff.

Borhek, M. V. (1983). *Coming Out to Parents: A Two-Way Survival Guide for Lesbians and Gay Men and Their Parents*. New York: Pilgrim Press.

Borneman, E. (1983). Progress in empirical research on children's sexuality. *SIECUS Report*, 12(2):1–5.

Boslego, J. W. (1987). Effect of spectinomycin use on the prevalence of spectinomycin resistant and penicillinase-producing Nisseria gonorrhoeae. *New Eng. J. Med.*, 317(5):272–277.

Boston Women's Health Book Collective. (1973, 1976, 1979). *Our Bodies, Ourselves*. New York: Simon & Schuster.

Boston Women's Health Book Collective. (1984). *The New Our Bodies, Ourselves* (3rd ed.). New York: Simon & Schuster.

Boswell, J. (1980). *Christianity, Social Tolerance and Homosexuality*. Chicago: University of Chicago Press.

Bouhdiba, A. (1985). *Sexuality in Islam*. London: Routledge & Kegan Paul.

Boyle, P. S. (1986, March). Sexuality and disability: Looking backward and forward. *SIECUS Report*, 14(4):1–3.

Bozett, F. W. (1987). *Gay and Lesbian Parents*. New York: Praeger.

Bradshaw, J. (1988). *Bradshaw On: Healing the Shame That Binds You*. Deerfield Beach, FL: Health Communications.

Bradsher, K. (1990, January 17). For every five young women, six young men. *New York Times*, pp. C1, C10.

Branden, N. (1980). *The Psychology of Romantic Love*. New York: J.P. Tarcher.

Brecher, E. M. (1969). *The Sex Researchers*. Boston: Little, Brown.

Brecher, E. M. (1978). *Treatment Programs for Sex Offenders*. Washington, DC: National Institute of Law Enforcement and Criminal Justice, U.S. Department of Justice, pp. 89–90.

Brecher, E. M., & the Editors of Consumer Reports Books. (1984). *Love, Sex, and Aging: A Consumers Union Report*. Boston: Little, Brown.

Breslow, N., L. Evans, & J. Langley (1985). On the prevalence and roles of females in the sadomasochistic subculture: Report on an empirical study. *Archives Sexual Behavior*, 14:303–317.

Bretschneider, J. G., & N. L. McCoy. (1988). Sexual interest and behavior in healthy 80- to 101-year-olds. *Archives Sexual Behavior*, 17(2):109–129.

Brick, P., & C. Cooperman. (1987). *Positive Images: A New Approach to Contraceptive Education* (2nd ed.). Hackensack, NJ: Planned Parenthood of Bergen County.

Brosman, S. A. (1976, March). How frequency of coitus affects the prostate. *Med. Aspects Human Sex.*, p. 143.

Brothers, J. (1981). *What Every Woman Should Know about Men*. New York: Simon & Schuster.

Brown, G. (1980). *The New Celibacy*. New York: McGraw-Hill.

Brown, J. (1983). *Nutrition for Your Pregnancy*. Minneapolis: University of Minnesota Press.

Brown, J., & D. Hart. (1977). Correlates of females' sexual fantasies. *Perceptual Motor Skills*, 45:819–825.

Brown, R. (1977). *Rubyfruit Jungle*. New York: Bantam.

Brownmiller, S. (1975). *Against Our Wills: Men, Women and Rape*. New York: Simon & Schuster.

Budoff, P. W. (1983). *No More Hot Flashes and Other Good News*. New York: Putnam.

Buffum, J. (1985). Yohimbine and sexual function. *J. Psychoactive Drugs*, 17(2):131–132.

Buffum, J. (1986). Pharmacosexology update: Prescription drugs and sexual function. *J. Psychoactive Drugs*, 18(2):97–106.

Bulcroft, K., & M. O'Connor. (1986). The importance of dating relationships on quality of life for older persons. *Family Relations*, 35:397–401.

Bullard, D. (1988). Treatment of desire disorders in the medically ill and physically disabled. In S. R. Leiblum & R. C. Rosen, eds. *Sexual Desire Disorders*. New York: Guilford Press, pp. 348–385.

Bullard, D. G., & S. E. Knight (eds.). (1981). *Sexuality and Physical Disability: Personal Perspectives*. St. Louis: C.V. Mosby.

Bullough, V. (1980). Woman's changing role: Technology's child. *Sexology Today*, 47(1):50–55.

Bullough, V. (1987a). Technology for the prevention of "les maladies produites par la masturbation." *Technology and Culture*, 28(4):828–832.

Bullough, V. (1987b). Why is Christianity so hostile to sex? In R.T. Francoeur (ed.), *Taking Sides: Clashing Views on Controversial Issues in Human Sexuality*. Guilford, CT: Dushkin.

Bullough, V., & B. Bullough. (1977). *Sin, Sickness, and Sanity: A History of Sexual Attitudes*. New York: New American Library.

Bullough, V., & B. Bullough. (1987). *Women and Prostitution: A Social History*. Buffalo, NY: Prometheus Press.

Bullough, V., & F. F. Ruan. (1988, June 8). China's children. *Nation*, pp. 48–49.

Bumpass, L. L., & S. McLanahan. (1989). Unmarried motherhood. *Demography*, 26:279–286.

Burgess, A. W., & L. L. Holmstrom. (1975). Sexual trauma of children and adolescents. *Nursing Clinics North Am.*, 10:551-663.

Buscaglia, L. (1972). *Love*. New York: Fawcett Crest.

Buss, D. M. (1989). Evolution of human intrasexual competition: Tactics of mate attraction. *J. Personality & Social Psychology*, 54:616–628.

Butler, R.N. (1983). Sexual frustrations of older women. *Med. Aspects Human Sex.*, 17(4):65–71.

Butterfield, F. (1980, January 13). Love and Sex in China. *New York Times Magazine*, pp. 15 ff.

Byrne, D. (1971). *The Attraction Paradigm*. New York: Academic Press.

Byrne, D. (1977). Social psychology and the study of sexual behavior. *Personality & Social Psychology Bulletin*, 3:3–30.

Byrne, D., & W. Fisher. (1983). *Adolescents, Sex and Contraception*. Hillsdale, NJ: Erlbaum.

Calderone, M. (1985). Adolescent sexuality: Elements and genesis. *Pediatrics Supplement*, pp. 699–703.

Calderone, M. S., & E. W. Johnson. (1981). *The Family Book about Sexuality*. New York: Harper & Row.

Calhoun, A. W. (1945). *A Social History of the American Family*. New York: Barnes & Noble.

Callahan, D. (1970). *Abortion: Law, Choice and Morality*. New York: Macmillan.

Carmody, D. (1989, January 1). Increasing rapes on campus spur colleges to fight back. *New York Times*, pp. 1, 12.

Carnes, P. (1983). *Out of the Shadows: Understanding Sexual Addiction*. Minneapolis: CompCare Publications.

Carnes, P. J. (1986, July). Progress in sexual addiction: An addiction perspective. *SIECUS Report*, 14(6):4–6.

Carpenter, W. D. (1989). College cohabitors and non-cohabitors twelve years later: A comparative analysis of life course variables. *Dissertation Abstracts*, 50(2), Book A.

Carrera, M. A. (1983). Some reflections of adolescent sexuality. *SIECUS Report*, 11(4):1–2.

Carrera, M. A. (1984). Reconceptualizing adolescence. *SIECUS Report*, 12(4):10.

Carrera, M. A., & P. Dempsey. (1988). Restructuring public policy on teen pregnancy. *SIECUS Report*, 16(3): 6–9.

Cassell, C. (1984). *Swept Away: Why Women Fear Their Own Sexuality*. New York: Simon & Schuster.

Castleman, M. (1980). *Sexual Solutions*. New York: Simon & Schuster.

Catania, J. A., & C. B. White. (1982). Sexuality in an aged sample: Cognitive determinants of masturbation. *Archives Sexual Behavior*, 11(3):237–245.

Cates, W. (1984a). Family planning and STD programs: Can their efforts be merged? *Contraceptive Technology Update*, 5:4–71.

Cates, W. (1984b). Sexually transmitted diseases: The national view. *Cutis.*, 33:69–80.

Chandler, S. M. (1982). Knowns and unknowns in sexual abuse of children. *J. Social Work & Human Sex.*, 1(1–2):51–68.

Chapman, A. B. (1986). *Man-Sharing: Dilemma or Choice*. New York: Morrow.

Chapman, B. E., & J. C. Brannock. (1987). Proposed model of lesbian identity development: An empirical examination. *J. Homosexuality*, 14(3/4):69–80.

Charatan, F. B. (1982). Geriatric sexuality. *Med. Aspects Human Sex.*, 16(7):68W-68DD.

Chesler, P. (1988). *Sacred Bond: The Legacy of Baby M.* New York: Times Books.

Chia, M., & M. Chia. (1986). *Cultivating Female Sexual Energy: Healing Love Through Tao*. Huntington, NY: Healing Tao Books.

Chia, M., & M. Winn. (1984). *Cultivating Male Sexual Energy: Taoist Secrets of Love*. Sante Fe, NM: Aurora Books.

Chiazze, L., et al. (1968). The length and variability of the human menstrual cycle. *J. Amer. Med. Assoc.*, 203:377–380.

Chodorow, N. (1978). *Reproduction of Mothering: Psychoanalysis and the Sociology of Gender*. Berkeley: University of California Press.

Christopher, F. S., & R. M. Cate. (1984). Factors involved in sexual decision-making. *J. Sex Res.*, 20: 363–376.

Christopher, F. S., & R. M. Cate. (1985). Premarital sexual pathways and relationship development. *J. Social & Personal Relationships*, 2:271–288.

Clanton, C., & L. Smith. (1977a, October). The self-inflicted pain of jealousy. *Psychology Today*, 10(10):44 ff.

Clanton, G., & L. Smith. (1977b). *Jealousy*. Englewood Cliffs, NJ: Prentice Hall.

Clark, H. R. (1982, February 15). Untying the knot in China. *Time*, p. 52.

Clark, R. (1985, Summer). Male strippers: Ladies' night at the meat market. *J. Popular Culture*, 19(1):51–56.

Clayton, R., & H. Voss. (1977). Shacking up: Cohabitation in the 1970s. *J. Marriage & Family*, 39:273–283.

Clinton, J. (1987). Couvade. *Med. Aspects Human Sex.* 21(11):115,132.

Clumeck, N., et al. (1989). A cluster of HIV infection among heterosexual people without apparent risk factors. *New Eng. J. Med.*, 321(21):1460–1462.

Cochran, D., & L. A. Druker. (1984). *Women Who Rape*. Boston, MA: Massachusetts Trial Court, Office of Commissioner of Probation.

Colby, A. (1983). A longitudinal study of moral judgment. *Monographs of the Society for Research in Child Development*, 4(1–2), Serial No. 200.

Cole, S. S. (1984–1986). Facing the challenges of sexual abuse in persons with disabilities. *Sexuality and Disability*, 7(3–4):71–87.

Cole, T. M., & S. S. Cole. (1982). Rehabilitation of problems of sexuality in physical disability. In F. S. Kottke et al. (eds.), *Krusen's Handbook of Physical Medicine and Rehabilitation*. Philadelphia: Saunders.

Coleman, E. (1986, July). Sexual compulsion vs. sexual addiction: The debate continues. *SIECUS Report*, 14(6): 7–10.

Coleman, E. (1987). Identity formation: Assessment of sexual orientation. *J. Homosexuality*, 14(1/2):9–24.

Coleman, E., & R. Reese. (1988). Treating low sexual desire among gay men. In S. R. Leiblum & R. C. Rosen (eds.), *Sexual Desire Disorders*. New York: Guilford Press, pp. 413–445.

Coleman, J. (1972). *Abnormal Psychology and Modern Life*. New York: Scott, Foresman.

Coles, C. D., & M. J. Shamp. (1984). Some sexual, personality, and demographic characteristics of women readers of erotic romances. *Archives Sexual Behavior*, 13:187–209.

Colonna, A. B., & A. J. Solnit. (1981). Infant sexuality. *SIECUS Report*, 9(4):1–2.

Comfort, A. (1972). *The Joy of Sex*. New York: Crown.

Comfort, A. (1974). *More Joy*. New York: Crown.

Conn, J., & L. Kanner. (1940). Spontaneous erections in childhood. *J. Pediatrics*, 16:337–340.

Constantine, L., & J. Constantine. (1973). *Group Marriage*. New York: Macmillan.

Constantine, L. L. (1984). Growing up slowly: Another century of childhood. In L. A. Kirkendall & A. E. Gravatt (eds.), *Marriage and the Family in the Year 2020*. Buffalo: Prometheus Books.

Constantine, L. L., & F. M. Martinson. (1981). *Children and Sex: New Findings, New Perspectives*. Boston: Little, Brown.

Contraceptive Technology Update. (1985, May). Cervical caps. 6(5):76.

Contraceptive Technology Update. (1986, June). Natural family planning programs can capitalize on high-tech aids, pp. 71–73.

Corea, G. (1985). *The Mother Machine*. San Francisco: Harper & Row.

Cousins, E. H. (1987). Male-female aspects of the trinity in Christian mysticism. In B. Gupta (ed.), *Sexual Archetypes, East and West*. New York: Paragon.

Coutts, R. (1973). *Love and Intimacy*. San Ramon, CA: Consensus Publishers.

Covington, T. R., & J. F. McClendon. (1987). *Sex Care*. New York: Pocket Books.

Crepault, C., & M. Couture. (1980). Men's erotic fantasies. *Archives Sexual Behavior*, 9(6):565 ff.

Crewdson, J. (1988). *By Silence Betrayed: Sexual Abuse of Children in America*. New York: Harper & Row.

Crooks, R., & K. Baur. (1987). *Our Sexuality* (3rd ed.). Menlo Park, CA: Benjamin/Cummings.

Curb, R., & N. Manahan. (eds.). (1986). *Lesbian Nuns: Breaking the Silence*. New York: Warner Books.

Curry, H., & D. Clifford. (1986). *A Legal Guide for Lesbians and Gay Couples* (4th ed.). Berkeley, CA: Nolo Press.

Cutler, W. (1980). Lunar and menstrual phase locking. *Amer. J. Obstetrics & Gynecology*, 137:834–839.

Cvetkovich, G., et al. (1975). On the psychology of adolescents' use of contraceptives. *J. Sex Res.*, 11:256–270.

Dalton, J. (1985). The consequences of an uninformed ménage à trois extraordinaire: Liability to third parties for the nondisclosure of genital herpes between sexual partners. *St. Louis University Law J.* 29:787–815.

Darabi, K. F., & M. Asencio. (1987). Sexual activity and childbearing among young Hispanics in the U.S. *SIECUS Report*, 15(4):6–8.

Darling, C. A., & J. K. Davidson. (1987). The relationship of sexual satisfaction to coital involvement: The concept of technical virginity revisited. *Deviant Behavior*, 8:27–46.

Darling, C. A., & M. W. Hicks. (1983). Recycling parental sexual messages. *J. Sex & Marital Therapy*, 9(3): 233–243.

Darroch Forrest, J. R., & R. R. Fordyce. (1988). U.S. Women contraceptive attitudes and practices: How have they changed? *Family Planning Perspectives*, 20(3):112–118.

Daugherty, L. B. (1984). *Why Me? Help for Victims of Child Sexual Abuse (Even If They Are Adults Now)*. Racine, WI: Mother Courage Press.

Davenport, W. (1977). Sexual patterns and their regulations in a society of the Southwest Pacific. In F. Beach, (ed.), *Sex and Behavior*. New York: Wiley.

Davidson, J. K., & L. E. Hoffman. (1986). Sexual fantasies and sexual satisfaction. *J. Sex Res.*, 22:184–205.

Davison, G. (1977). Elimination of a sadistic fantasy by a client-controlled counter-conditioning technique. In J. Fischer & H. Gochros (eds.), *Handbook of Behavior Therapy with Sexual Problems*. New York: Pergamon Press.

Dawson, D. (1986). The effects of sex education on adolescent behavior. *Family Planning Perspectives*, 18(4): 162–170.

Deane, N. H., & D. L. Tillar. (1981). *Sexual Harassment: An Employment Issue*. Washington, DC: College & University Personnel Association.

DeCecco, J. P. (1987a). Homosexuality's brief recovery. *J. Sex Res.*, 23(1):106–114.

DeCecco, J. P. (1987b). The two views of Meyer-Bahlburg: A rejoinder. *J. Sex Res.*, 23(1):123–127.

Degler, C. L. (1980). *At Odds: Women and Family in America from the Revolution to the Present*. Oxford: Oxford University Press.

Delamater, J., & P. Maccorquodale. (1978). Premarital contraceptive use: A test of two models. *J. Marriage & Family*, 40(2):235–247.

Delaney, J., M. J. Lupton, & E. Toth. (1976). *The Curse: A Cultural History of Menstruation*. New York: New American Library/Mentor.

Demaris, A. (1984). A comparison of remarriages with first marriages on satisfaction in marriage and its relationship to prior cohabitation. *Family Relations*, 33: 443–449.

D'Emilio, J., & E. B. Freedman. (1988). *Intimate Matters: A History of Sexuality in America*. New York: Harper & Row.

Dentzer, S. (1988, January 18). Why AIDS won't bankrupt us. *U.S. News & World Report*, pp. 20–21.

Diagnostic and Statistical Manual (DSM III). (1980). Washington, DC: American Psychiatric Association.

Diagnostic and Statistical Manual (DSM III-R). (1987). Washington, DC: American Psychiatric Association.

Diamond, M. (1982). Sexual identity: Monozygotic twins reared in discordant sex roles and a BBC follow-up. *Archives Sexual Behavior*, 11(2):181–186.

Dixon, D. (1985). Perceived sexual satisfaction and marital happiness of bisexual and heterosexual swinging husbands. *J. Homosexuality*, 11(1/2):209–223.

Dixon, J. K. (1985). Sexuality and relationship changes in married females following the commencement of bisexual activity. *J. Homosexuality*, 11(1/2):115–133.

Docter, R. F. (1988). *Transvestites and Transsexuals: Toward a Theory of Cross-Gender Behavior*. New York: Plenum.

Dodson, B. (1987). *Sex for One: The Joy of Self-Loving*. New York: Harmony Books.

Doerner, G., et al. (1980). Prenatal stress and possible aetiogenetic factor homosexuality in human males. *Endokrinologie*, 75:365–368.

Doerner, G., et al. (1983). Stressful events in prenatal life and bi- and homosexual men. *Exper. Clinical Endocrinology*, 81:83-87.

Donaldson, S. (1985). Male victims of rape. An unpublished report to the Sex Information and Education Council of the U.S.

Donceel, J. F. (1970). Animation and hominization. *Theological Studies*, 31(1):76–105.

Donnerstein, E., & D. Linz. (1986). Techniques designed to mitigate the impact of mass media sexual violence on adolescents and adults. A paper prepared for the Surgeon General's Workshop on Pornography and Public Health.

Donnerstein, E. & D. Linz. (1988). A critical analysis of "A critical analysis of recent research on violent erotica." *J. Sex Res.*, 24:348–352.

Dougherty, R. C. (1979). Sperm counts decreasing in American men. *Sexual Med. Today*, 3(11):14–15.

Douglas, N., & P. Slinger. (1979). *Sexual Secrets: The Alchemy of Ecstasy*. New York: Destiny Books.

Doyle, J. (1985). *Sex and Gender*. Dubuque, IA: W. C. Brown.

Dryfoos, J. (1985). What the United States can learn about prevention of teenage pregnancy from other developed countries. *SIECUS Report*, 14(2):1–7.

Dullea, G. (1988, July 6). Prenuptial stress over the contract. *New York Times*, pp. C1, C8.

Dullea, G. (1987, April 27). Wives confront spouses' homosexuality. *New York Times*, p. B11.

Durden-Smith, J., & D. Desimone. (1983). *Sex and the Brain*. New York: Arbor House.

Dworkin, A. (1981). *Pornography: Men Possessing Women*. New York: Perigee/Putnam.

Dworkin, A. (1987). *Intercourse*. New York: Free Press.

Dwyer, M. (1989). Guilty as charged: or are they? Unpublished paper, Program in Human Sexuality, Department of Family Practice and Community Health, University of Minnesota Medical School.

Edwards, G. R. (1984). *Gay/Lesbian Liberation: A Biblical Perspective*. New York: Pilgrim Press.

Edwards, S. R. (1986, July). A sex addict speaks. *SIECUS Report*, 14(6):1–3.

Ehrenreich, B., E. Hess, & G. Jacobs. (1987). *Re-Making Love: The Feminization of Sex*. New York: Doubleday/Anchor.

Ehrhardt, A. A. (1987). A transactional perspective on the development of gender differences. In J. M. Reinisch, et al. (eds.), *Masculinity/Femininity: Basic Perspectives*. New York: Oxford University Press.

Ehrhardt, A. A., & H. F. L. Meyer-Bahlburg. (1981). Effects of prenatal sex hormones on gender-related behavior. *Science*, 222:1029–1031.

Ehrhardt, A. A., et al. (1984). Sex-dimorphic behavior in childhood subsequent to prenatal exposure to exogenous progestogens and estrogens. *Archives Sexual Behavior*, 13:457–477.

Elkholy, H. (1990). Personal communication with R. T. Francoeur on sexual customs in the Islamic traditions.

Elliott, D., & P. Gries. (1988, August 8). Frank talk about S-x. *Newsweek*, p. 40.

Ellis, A. (1960). *The Art and Science of Love*. New York: Lyle Stuart.

Ellis, L., et al. (1988). Sexual orientation of human offspring may be altered by severe maternal stress during pregnancy. *J. Sex Res.*, 25(1):152–157.

Ellis, M. J. (1985, Spring/Summer). Eliminating our heterosexist approach to sex education: A hope for the future. *J. Sex Ed. & Therapy.* 11(1):61–63.

El Saadawi, N. (1980). *The Hidden Face of Eve*. Boston: Beacon Press.

Engel, G. L. (1980). The clinical application of the biopsychosocial model. *Amer. J. Psychiatry*, 137:535–544.

Engel, R. M. E. (1981, April). Treatment of cryptorchidism. *Med. Aspects Human Sex.*, pp. 51–52.

Erenberg, L. A. (1984). *Steppin' Out: New York Nightlife and the Transformation of American Culture*. Chicago: University of Chicago Press.

Erhart, J. K., & B. R. Sandler. (1985). *Campus Gang Rape: Party Games?* Project on the Status and Education of Women, Association of American Colleges, 1818 R. St., NW, Washington, DC. 20009.

Faich, G., et al. (1986, January 10). Toxic shock syndrome and the vaginal contraceptive sponge. *J. Amer. Med. Assoc.*, 255(2):216–218.

Family Planning Perspectives. (1988). The female condom. 20(3).

Farrell, W. (1984). The evolution of sex roles: The transformation of masculine and feminine values. In L. A. Kirkendall & A. E. Gravatt (eds.), *Marriage and the Family in the Year 2020*. Buffalo: Prometheus Books.

Farrell, W. (1988). *Why Men Are the Way They Are*. New York: Berkley Books.

Fast, J., & H. Wells. (1975). *Bisexual Living*. New York: M. Evans & Co.

Federation of Feminist Women's Health Centers. (1981). *A New View of a Woman's Body*. New York: Simon & Schuster.

Fellows, W. J. (1979). *Religions East and West*. New York: Holt.

Ferm, D. W. (1971). *Responsible Sexuality Now*. New York: Seabury.

Fields, M., & E. Lehman. (1982). *Handbook for Beaten Women*. Spanish and English editions. Brooklyn, NY: Brooklyn Legal Services Corp.

Finkelhor, D. (1979a). *Sexually Victimized Children*. New York: Free Press.

Finkelhor, D. (1979b). What is wrong with sex between adults and children? *J. Orthopsychiatry*, 49:692–697.

Finkelhor, D. (1984). *Child Sexual Abuse: New Theory & Research*. New York: Free Press.

Finkle, A. L. (1967, October). The relationship of sexual habits to benign prostatic hypertrophy. *Med. Aspects Human Sex.*, pp. 24–25.

Fischl, M. A., et al. (1987). Heterosexual transmission of human immunodeficiency virus (HIV), relationship of sexual practices to seroconversion. The Third International Conference on AIDS, Washington, DC, June 1-5.

Fisher, C., et al. (1983). Patterns of female sexual arousal during sleep and waking: Vaginal thermo-conductance studies. *Archives Sexual Behavior*, 12(2):97 ff.

Fisher, S. (1973). *The Female Orgasm*. New York: Basic Books.

Fisher, W. A., et al. (1988). Erotophobia-erotophilia as a dimension of personality. *J. Sex Res.*, 25(1):123–151.

Fitzgerald, M., & D. Fitzgerald. (1980, September & October). Sexuality and Deafness—An American overview, Parts I & II. *British J. Sexual Med.*, 7:30–34, 24–30.

Fleming, J. (1979). *Stopping Wife Abuse*. Garden City, NY: Anchor/Doubleday.

Fletcher, J. (1966). *Situation Ethics: The New Morality*. Philadelphia: Westminster.

Flower, M. J. (1989). Neuromaturation and the moral status of human fetal life. In E. Doerr & J. W. Prescott (eds.), *Abortion Rights and Fetal "Personhood."* Long Beach, CA: Centerline Press.

Follingstas, D. R., & C. D. Kimbrell. (1986). Sex fantasies revisited: An expansion and further clarification of variables affecting sex fantasy production. *Archives Sexual Behavior*, 15(6):475–486.

Ford, C. S., & F. A. Beach. (1951). *Patterns of Sexual Behavior*. New York: Harper & Row.

Forum (Penthouse). (1988, April). A man in love. 17(8):67.

Fowles, J. (1988, June 5). Coming soon: More men than women. *New York Times*, p. C 3.

Fox, G. L. (1977). Sex-role attitudes as predictors of contraceptive use among unmarried university students. *Sex Roles*, 3(3):265–280.

Francoeur, A. K., & R. T. Francoeur. (1974, 1976). *Hot and Cool Sex: Cultures in Conflict*. New York: Harcourt Brace Jovanovich; Cranbury, NJ: A. S. Barnes.

Francoeur, R. T. (1965). *Perspectives in Evolution*. Baltimore: Helicon Press.

Francoeur, R. T. (1970). *Evolving World Converging Man*. New York: Holt.

Francoeur, R. T. (1972). *Eve's New Rib: 20 Faces of Sex, Marriage and Family*. New York: Harcourt Brace Jovanovich.

Francoeur, R. T. (1984). Moral concepts in the year 2020. In L. A. Kirkendall & A. E. Gravatt (eds.), *Marriage and the Family in the Year 2020*. Buffalo, NY: Prometheus Press.

Francoeur, R. T. (1985). Reproductive technologies: New alternatives and new ethics. *SIECUS Report*, 14(1):1–5.

Francoeur, R. T. (ed.). (1987a). *Taking Sides: Clashing Views on Controversial Issues in Human Sexuality*. Guilford, CT: Dushkin.

Francoeur, R. T. (1987b). Human sexuality. In M. B. Sussman & S. K. Steinmetz (eds.), *Handbook of Marriage and the Family*. New York: Plenum.

Francoeur, R. T. (1988a, March/April). Sexual components in respiratory care. *Respiratory Management*, 18(2):35–39.

Francoeur, R. T. (1988b). Two different worlds, Two different moralities. In J. Gramick & P. Furey (eds.), *The Vatican and Homosexuality*. New York: Crossroad.

Francoeur, R. T. (1989). Summing up the linchpin question: When does a human become a person, and why? In E. Doerr & J. W. Prescott (eds.), *Abortion Rights and Fetal "Personhood."* Long Beach, CA: Centerline Press.

Francoeur, R. T. (1990a). Current religious doctrines of sexual and erotic development in childhood. In M. Perry (ed.), *The Handbook of Sexology. Volume 7*. Amsterdam: Elsevier.

Francoeur, R. T. (1990b). New dimensions in human sexuality: The theological challenge. In R. H. Iles (ed.), *The Gospel Imperative in the Midst of AIDS: Towards a Prophetic Theology*. Wilton, CT: Morehouse-Barlow.

Francoeur, R. T., & R. Shapiro. (1979). Recognition of alternatives to traditional monogamy in new religious and civil rites. *J. Sex Ed. & Therapy*, 1(5):17–20.

Frank, E., C. Anderson, & D. Rubinstein. (1978). Frequency of sexual dysfunction in normal couples. *New Eng. J. Med.*, 299:111–115.

Frayser, S. G. (1985). *Varieties of Sexual Experience: An Anthropological Perspective on Human Sexuality*. New Haven, CT: HRAF Press.

Freedman, M. (1971). *Homosexuality and Psychological Functioning*. Belmont, CA: Wadsworth.

Friday, N. (1973). *My Secret Garden: Women's Sexual Fantasies*. New York: Pocket Books.

Friday, N. (1975). *Forbidden Flowers. More Women's Sexual Fantasies*. New York: Delacorte.

Friday, N. (1980). *Men in Love: Men's Sexual Fantasies: The Triumph of Love over Rage*. New York: Delacorte.

Friday, N. (1985). *Jealousy*. New York: Morrow.

Friedman, E. (1981). Menstrual and lunar cycles. *Amer. J. Obstetrics & Gynecology*, 140:350.

Friend, R. A. (1987). The individual and social psychology of aging: Clinical implications for lesbians and gay men. *J. Homosexuality*, 14(1–2):307–331.

Fritz, G. S., K. Stoll, & N. A. Wagner. (1981). A comparison of males and females who were sexually molested as children. *J. Sex & Marital Therapy*, 7:54–59.

Fumento, M.A. (1987, November). AIDS: Are heterosexuals at risk? *Commentary*, 84(5):21–27.

Gagnon, J. H. (1965). Sexuality and sexual learning in the child. *Psychiatry*, 28:212–228.

Gagnon, J. H. (1977). *Human Sexualities*. Glenville, IL: Scott, Foresman.

Gagnon, J. H. (1985). Attitudes and responses of parents to pre-adolescent masturbation. *Archives Sexual Behavior*, 14(5):451–466.

Gagnon, J. H. (1987). Science and the politics of pathology. *J. Sex Res.*, 23(1):120–123.

Gagnon, J. H., & E. J. Roberts. (1980). Parents' messages to pre-adolescent children about sexuality. In J. M. Samson (ed.), *Childhood and Sexuality: Proceedings of the International Symposium*. Montreal: Editions Etudes Vivantes.

Gagnon, J. H., & W. Simon. (1968). Sexual deviance in contemporary America. *Annals Amer. Academy Political & Social Sciences*, 376:106–122.

Gagnon, J. H., & W. Simon. (1973). *Sexual Conduct: The Social Sources of Human Sexuality*. Chicago: Aldine.

Gallagher, J. (1987). Prenatal invasions and interventions. *Harvard Women's Law J.*, 10:9–58.

Gallen, M. E., L. Liskin & N. Kak. (1987, January). Men—new focus in family planning. *Population Report*, p. 33.

Gallup, G. (1980, July 11). Unchanging views on abortion. A national news release.

Gamarekian, B. (1987, September 7). Getting together: Dating for the disabled. *New York Times*, Style Section.

Gambrill, L. (1989). Can more touching lead to less violence in our society? *The Truth Seeker*, 1(1):23–25, 36.

Gardella, P. (1985). *Innocent Ecstasy: How Christianity Gave America an Ethic of Sexual Pleasure*. New York: Oxford University Press.

Garner, B., & R. W. Smith. (1977). Are there really any gay male athletes? *J. Sex Res.*, 13(1):22–34.

Gates, H. (ed.). (1987). *Classic Slave Narratives*. New York: New American Library/Mentor.

Gazzaniga, M. S. (1970). *The Bisected Brain*. New York: Appleton-Century-Crofts.

Gazzaniga, M. S., & J. E. LeDoux. (1978). *The Integrated Mind*. New York: Plenum Press.

Gebhard, P. (1969, March). Misconceptions about female prostitutes. *Med. Aspects Human Sexuality*, 3:24–30.

Gebhard, P., et al. (1965). *Sex Offenders: An Analysis of Types*. New York: Harper & Row.

Gerrard, M., & F. X. Gibbons. (1982). Sexual experience, sex guilt, and sexual moral reasoning. *J. Personality*, 50:345–359.

Giallombardo, R. (1974). *Social World of Imprisoned Girls*. New York: Wiley.

Gilligan, C. (1982). *In a Different Voice: Psychological Theory and Women's Development*. Cambridge, MA: Harvard University Press.

Gilligan, C. (1989). *Mapping the Moral Domain: A Contribution of Women's Thinking to Psychological Theory and Education*. Cambridge, MA: Harvard University Press.

Gilmartin, B. (1977). Swinging: Who gets involved? and how? In R. Libby & R. Whitehurst (eds.), *Marriage and Alternatives: Exploring Intimate Relationships*. Glenview, IL: Scott, Foresman.

Ginsberg, B. E., & B. F. Carter (eds.). (1987). *Premenstrual Syndrome*. New York: Plenum.

Glass, S. P., & T. L. Wright. (1985). Sex differences in type of extramarital involvement and marital dissatisfaction. *Sex Roles*, 12(9/10):1101–1119.

Glendon, M.A. (1988). *Abortion and Divorce in Western Law*. Cambridge, MA: Harvard University Press.

Goldberg, D. C., et al. (1983). The Grafenberg spot and female ejaculation: A review of initial hypotheses. *J. Sex & Marital Therapy*, 9:27–37.

Gold-Bikin, L. Z. (1985). Herpes new legal epidemic: Fraud and negligence suits. *Family Advocate*, 26(4): 26–27.

Goldman, R., & J. Goldman. (1982a). Children's sexual thinking: Report of a cross-national study. *SIECUS Report*, 10(3):1–2.

Goldman, R., & J. Goldman. (1982b). *Children's Sexual Thinking*. Boston: Routledge & Kegan Paul.

Goleman, D. (1984, October 16). Some sexual behavior viewed as an addiction. *New York Times*, pp. C1, C9.

Goleman, D. (1986, April 1). Two views of marriage explored: His and hers. *New York Times*, pp. C1, C11.

Goleman, D. (1988a, August 14). Lies men tell put women in danger of AIDS. *New York Times*, p. 29.

Goleman, D. (1988b, November 8). Therapists find last outpost of adolescence in adulthood. *New York Times*, pp. C1, C13.

Goleman, D. (1988c, October 18). Chemistry of sexual desire yields its elusive secrets. *New York Times*, pp. C1, C15.

Goleman, D., and Bush, S. 1977. Liberation of sexual fantasy. *Psychology Today*, 11(5):48 ff.

Gongla, P. A., & E. H. Thompson, Jr. (1987). Single-parent families. In M. B. Sussman & S. K. Steinmetz (eds.), *Handbook of Marriage and the Family*. New York: Plenum.

Goode, E., & J. Preissler. (1982). Admirers of fat women. *Med. Aspects Human Sex.*, 16(3):140–145.

Goodman, R. E. (1980). Sex aids and the disabled. *Sexuality & Disability*, 3(3):232–235.

Goodwin, J. (1985). Post-traumatic symptoms in incest victims. In Grayson, B., & M. Stein. (1981, Winter). Attracting assault: Victims' nonverbal clues. *J. Communications*, pp. 68–75.

Gooren, L. J. G. (1988). An appraisal of endocrine theories of homosexuality and gender dysphoria. In J. M. A. Sitsen (ed.), *Handbook of Sexology. Vol, 6. The Pharmacology and Endocrinology of Sexual Function*. Amsterdam: Elsevier.

Gordon, B. (1988). *Jennifer Fever: Older Men, Younger Women*. New York: Harper & Row.

Gordon, L. (1976). *Woman's Body, Woman's Right: A Social History of Birth Control in America*. New York: Penguin Books.

Gordon, L., & A. Gordon. (1987). *American Chronicle: Six Decades in American Life 1920–1980*. New York: Atheneum.

Gosselin C., & G. Wilson. (1980). *Sexual Variations: Fetishism, Sadomasochism, Transvestism*. New York: Simon & Schuster.

Gramick, J. (1990). *Homosexuality in the Priesthood and the Religious Life*. New York: Crossroad.

Gramick, J., & P. Furey. (eds.). (1988). *The Vatican and Homosexuality*. New York: Crossroad.

Grayson, B., & M. I. Stein. (1981, winter). Attracting assault: Victims' nonverbal cues. *J. Communications*. pp. 68–75.

Great Britain Committee on Homosexual Offenses and

Prostitution. (1963). *The Wolfenden Report*. New York: Stein & Day.

Green, G., & C. Green. (1974). *The Last Taboo*. New York: Grove Press.

Green, R. (1979). Childhood cross-gender behavior and subsequent sexual preference. *Amer. J. Psychiatry*, 136:106–108.

Green, R. (1987). *The "Sissy Boy Syndrome" and the Development of Homosexuality*. New Haven: Yale University Press.

Green, R., & J. Money. (1960). Incongruous gender role: Nongenital manifestations in prepubertal boys. *J. Nervous & Mental Diseases*, 130:160–167.

Green, R., & J. Money. (1961). Effeminacy in prepubertal boys: Summary of eleven cases and recommendations for case management. *Pediatrics*, 27:286–291.

Green, R., et al. (1982). Ninety-nine "tomboys" and "nontomboys": Behavioral contrasts and demographic similarities. *Archives Sexual Behavior*, 11:247–266.

Green, T. (1987, November 15). Why wed? The ambivalent American bachelor. *New York Times Magazine*, pp. 24 ff.

Green, T. H., Jr. (1977). *Gynecology: Essentials of Clinical Practice*. Boston: Little, Brown.

Greendlinger, V., & D. Byrne. (1987). Coercive sexual fantasies of college men as predictors of self-reported likelihood to rape and overt sexual aggression. *J. Sex Res.*, 23(1):1–11.

Greer, D. M., et al. (1982). A technique for foreskin reconstruction and some preliminary results. *J. Sex Res.*, 18:324–330.

Grieco, A. (1987, March). Cutting the risks for STDs. *Med. Aspects Human Sex.*, pp. 70 ff.

Griffin, S. (1980). Sadism and catharsis: The treatment is the disease. In L. Lederer (ed.), *Take Back the Night: Women on Pornography*. New York: Morrow.

Gross, J. (1987a, October 21). AIDS threat brings new turmoil for gay teen-agers. *New York Times*, pp. B1 & B5.

Gross, J., et al. (1987b). "AIDS: The next phase." A 4-part series. *New York Times*. March 16, pp. A1, A16-A17; March 17, pp. A1; March 18, pp. A1, B5; March 19, pp. A1, B10.

Grossman, R., & J. Sutherland (eds.). (1982). *Surviving Sexual Assault*. New York: Congdon & Weed.

Groth, A. N. (1979). *Men Who Rape: The Psychology of the Offender*. New York: Plenum.

Guest, F., et al. (1979). *My Body My Health*. New York: Wiley.

Gutman, H. (1976). *The Black Family in Slavery and Freedom*. New York: Random House.

Guttentag, M., & P. Secord. (1983). *Too Many Women? The Sex Ratio Question*. Beverly Hills, CA: Sage.

Guttmacher Report. (1976). *11 Million Teenagers: What Can Be Done About the Epidemic of Adolescent Pregnancies in the United States?* New York: Alan Guttmacher Institute.

Guttmacher Report. (1979). *Abortions and the Poor: Private Morality, Public Responsibility*. New York: Alan Guttmacher Institute.

Guttmacher Report. (1981). *Teenage Pregnancy: The Problem That Hasn't Gone Away*. New York: Alan Guttmacher Institute.

Guttmacher Report. (1989). *Facts in Brief: Abortion in the United States*. New York: Alan Guttmacher Institute.

Haaglund, V. (1981). Feminine sexuality and its development. *Scandinavian Psychoanalytical Rev.*, 4:127–150.

Haeberle, E. (1978). *The Sex Atlas*. New York: Seabury Press.

Hagen, R. (1979). *The Biosocial Factor*. New York: Doubleday.

Halderman, B. L., & P. F. Zelhart. (1985). A study of fantasy: Determinants of fantasy function and content. *J. Clinical Psychology*, 41(3):325–330.

Hall, S., & R. Adelman. (1972). *Gentlemen of Leisure: A Year in the Life of a Pimp*. New York: Quadrangle—New York Times Book Co.

Hall, S. M., & P. A. Hall. (1987). Law and adultery. In P. E. Lampe (ed.), *Adultery in the United States: Close Encounters of the Sixth (or Seventh) Kind*. Buffalo, NY: Prometheus Press.

Hall, T. (1987, June 1). Shifting patterns of infidelity. *New York Times*, p. B 8.

Halpern, J., & M. A. Sherman. (1979). *Afterplay: A Key to Intimacy*. New York: Stein & Day.

Harlow, H. F. (1964). Early social deprivation and later behavior in the monkey. In A. L. Adams, et al., (eds.), *Unfinished Tasks in the Behavioral Sciences*. Baltimore: Williams & Wilkins.

Harlow, H. F. (1971). *Learning to Love*. San Francisco: Albion.

Harris, C. C., & F. Snowden, eds. (1985). *Bioethical Frontiers in Perinatal Intensive Care*. Shreveport: Northwestern Louisiana State University Press.

Harris, M. (1973). *The Dilly Boys: Male Prostitution in Piccadilly*. London: Croom Helm.

Harrison, M. (1982). *Self-Help for Premenstrual Syndrome*. Cambridge, MA: Matrix Press.

Hartman, W., & M. Fithian. (1984). *Any Man Can*. New York: St. Martin's Press.

Hass, A. (1979). *Teenage Sexuality: A Survey of Teenage Sexual Behavior*. New York: Macmillan.

Hatcher, R. A., et al. (1982a). *Contraceptive Technology 1982–1983* (11th ed. with special section on infertility). New York: Irvington.

Hatcher, R. A., et al. (1982b). *It's Your Choice: A Personal Guide to Birth Control Methods for Women . . . and Men Too!* New York: Irvington.

Hatcher, R. A., et al. (1986). *Contraceptive Technology 1986–1987* (13th ed. with special section on sexually transmitted diseases). New York: Irvington.

Hatcher, R. A., et al. (1988). *Contraceptive Technology 1988–1989* (14th ed. with special section on AIDS and family planning). New York: Irvington.

Heath, D. (1984). An investigation into the origins of a copious vaginal discharge during intercourse—"enough to wet the bed"—that "is not urine." *J. Sex Res.*, 20:194–215.

Heiby, E., & J. D. Becker. (1980). Effect of filmed modeling on the self-reported frequency of masturbation. *Archives Sexual Behavior*, 9(2):115–120.

Heiman, J. (1975, April). The physiology of erotica. *Psychology Today*, pp. 91–94.

Hendricks, P. (1987, September). Condoms: A straight girl's best friend. *Ms.* magazine, pp. 98–102.

Hendrixson, L. L. (1979, May). Pregnant children: A socio-economic challenge. *Phi Delta Kappan*, pp. 663–666.

Hendrixson, L. L. (1989). Care versus justice: Two moral perspectives in the Baby "M" surrogacy case. *J. Sex Ed. & Therapy*, 15(4):247–256.

Henshaw, S. K. (1986). Induced abortion: A worldwide perspective. *Family Planning Perspectives*, 18(6):250–253.

Henshaw, S. K. (1987). Characteristics of U.S. women having abortions, 1982–1983. *Family Planning Perspectives*, 19(1):5–11.

Henshaw, S. K., J. D. Forest, & J. Van Vort. (1987). Abortion services in the United States, 1984–1985. *Family Planning Perspectives*, 19(2):63–70.

Hepburn, E. H. (1981). The father's role in sexual socialization of adolescent females in an upper and upper-middle class population. *J. Early Adolescence*, 1(1):53–59.

Hepburn, E. H. (1983). A tree-level model of parent-daughter communication about sexual topics. *Adolescence*, 18:523–534.

Herman, J. L. (1981). *Father-Daughter Incest*. Cambridge, MA: Harvard University Press.

Hersh, R., D. Paolitto, & J. Reimer. (1979). *Promoting Moral Growth: From Piaget to Kohlberg*. New York: Longman.

Heston, L., & J. Shields. (1968). Homosexuality in twins: A family study and registry study. *Archives Gen. Psychiatry*, 18:149–160.

Hill, I. (ed.). (1989). *The Bisexual Spouse: Different Dimensions in Human Sexuality*. McLean, VA: Barlina.

Himes, N. E. (1963). *Medical History of Contraception*. New York: Schochen/Gamut Press.

Hite, S. (1976). *The Hite Report on Female Sexuality*. New York: Macmillan.

Hofferth, S. L., J. R. Kahn, & W. Baldwin. (1987). Premarital sexual activity among U.S. teenager women over the past three decades. *Family Planning Perspectives*, 19(2):46–53.

Holmes, H. B., B. B. Hoskins, & M. Gross. (1981). *The Custom-Made Child? Women-Centered Perspectives*. Clifton, NJ: Humana Press.

Hoskins, B. B., & H. B. Holmes. (1984). Technology and prenatal femicide. In R. Arditti, R. Klein, & S. Minden (eds.), *Test-Tube Women: What Future for Motherhood?* Boston: Pandora Press.

Hossler, C. J., & S. S. Cole. (1983). *Intimacy and Chronic Lung Disease*. Ann Arbor, MI: University of Michigan Hospitals, Department of Physical Medicine and Rehabilitation, Patient Education Advisory Committee.

Houseknecht, S. K. (1987). Voluntary childlessness. In M. B. Sussman & S. K. Steinmetz (eds.), *Handbook of Marriage and the Family*. New York: Plenum.

Houston, V. (1987). *Loving a Younger Man*. Chicago/New York: Contemporary Books.

Howard, M. (1985). Postponing sexual involvement among adolescents. *J. Adolescent Health Care*, 6:271–277.

Hrabowy, I., & E. R. Allgeier. (1987, May). Relationship of level of sexual invasiveness of child abuse to psychological functioning among adult women. A paper delivered at the Midwestern Psychological Association Meeting, Chicago.

Hubbard, B., & M. Young. (1987). Androgyny in later life. *FLEducator* 5(3):17–19.

Humphreys, L. (1970). *Tearoom Trade: Impersonal Sex in Public Places*. Chicago: Aldine.

Hunt, M. (1967). *The Natural History of Love*. New York: Minerva Press.

Hunt, M. (1974). *Sexual Behavior in the 1970s*. Chicago: Playboy Press.

Hunter, M. (1979, December 13). House passes bill to aid victims of family violence. *New York Times*, p. A26.

Hutson, J. M., & P. K. Donahoe. (1983). Is Mullerian-inhibiting substance a circulating hormone in the chick-quail [*Coturnix coturnix japonica*] chimera? *Endocrinology*, 113:1470–1475.

Hyson, M. C., L. C. Whitehead, & C. M. Prudhoe.

(1988). Influences on attitudes toward physical affection between adults and children. *Early Childhood Res. Quarterly*, 3:55–77.

Imperato-McGinley, J. (1976). Gender identity and hermaphroditism: An exchange with J. Money. *Science*. 191:872.

Imperato-McGinley, J., et al. (1974). Steroid 5 alpha-reductase deficiency in man: An inherited form of male pseudohermaphroditism. *Science*, 186:1213.

Imperato-McGinley, J., et al. (1985). The impact of androgens on the evolution of male gender identity. In Z. DeFries et al. (eds.), *Sexuality: New Perspectives*. Westport, CT: Greenwood Press.

Imperato-McGinley, J., R. E. Peterson, & T. Gauthier. (1976). Gender identity and hermaphroditism. *Science*, 191:872.

Information Please Almanac. (1988). Boston: Houghton Mifflin.

Isaacson, W. (1981, April 6). The battle over abortion. *Time*, pp. 22–28.

Jackson, S. (1982). *Childhood and Sexuality*. Oxford: Blackwell.

James, J. (1976). Prostitution: Arguments for change. In S. Gordon & R. Libby (eds.), *Sexuality Today and Tomorrow*. N. Scituate, MA: Duxbury.

Jaspers, K. (1953). *The Origin and Goal of History*. New Haven, CT: Yale University Press.

Jenks, R. J. (1985). A comparative study of swingers and nonswingers: Attitudes and beliefs. *Lifestyles: J. Changing Patterns*, pp. 5–20.

Jesser, C. (1978). Male responses to direct verbal sexual initiatives of females. *J. Sex Res.*, 14:118–128.

Johnsen, D. E. (1986). The creation of fetal rights: Conflicts with women's constitutional rights to liberty, privacy and equal protection. *Yale Law J.*, 95(3): 599–625.

Johnson, R. L., & D. Shrier. (1987). Past sexual victimization by females of male patients in an adolescent medicine clinic population. *Amer. J. Psychiatry*, 144(5): 650–652.

Jones, C. (1978). *Understanding Gay Relatives and Friends*. New York: Seabury.

Jones, E. F., et al. (1985). Teenage pregnancy in developed countries: Determinants and policy implications. *Family Planning Perspectives*, 17(2):53–63.

Jones, E. F., et al. (1986). *Teenage Pregnancy in Industrialized Countries*. New Haven, CT: Yale University Press.

Joseph, N. (1981, June 23). Campus couples and violence. *New York Times*, p. 20.

Joseph, R. A. (1984, January 25). American men find Asian brides fill the unliberated bill. *Wall Street J.*, pp 1, 22.

Kahn, J. R., W. D. Kalsbeek, & S. L. Hofferth. (1988). National estimates of teenage sexual activity: Evaluating the comparability of three national surveys. *Demography*, 25(2):189–204.

Kallman, F. (1952). Comparative twin study on the genetic aspects of male homosexuality. *J. Nervous Mental Disease*, 115:283–298.

Kamenetzky, S. (1990). Personal communication to R. T. Francoeur regarding pronatalist and population policies and practices in Latin America.

Kane, E. (1988). *Birth Mother: The Story of America's First Legal Surrogate Mother*. San Diego: Harcourt Brace Jovanovich.

Kanin, E. J. (1969). Selected dyadic aspects of male sex aggression. *J. Sex Res.*, 5:12–28.

Kanin, E. J. (1985). Date rapists: Differential sexual socialization and relative deprivation. *Archives Sexual Behavior*, 14:219–231.

Kantrowitz, B. (1988, May 16). Premies. *Newsweek*, pp. 62–70.

Kantrowitz, B., et al. (1987, February 16). Kids and contraceptives. *Newsweek*, pp. 54–68.

Kaplan, H. S. (1974). *The New Sex Therapy*. New York: Brunner/Mazel.

Kaplan, H. S. (1979). *Disorders of Sexual Desire and Other Concepts and Techniques in Sex Therapy*. New York: Brunner/Mazel.

Kaplan, H. S. (1983). *The Evaluation of Sexual Disorders*. New York: Brunner/Mazel.

Kappeler, S. (1986). *The Pornography of Representation*. Minneapolis: University of Minnesota Press.

Karlen, A. (1988). *Threesomes: Studies in Sex, Power, and Intimacy*. New York: Beech Tree/Morrow.

Katchadourian, H. (1985). *Fundamentals of Human Sexuality* (4th ed.). Fort Worth, TX: Holt.

Katz, J. (1976). *Gay American History*. New York: Thomas Crowell.

Keane, N., & D. Breo. (1981). *The Surrogate Mother*. New York: Everest House.

Kempe, R. S., & C. H. Kempe. (1984). *The Common Secret: Sexual Abuse of Children and Adolescents*. New York: Freeman.

Kikuchi, J. J. (1988, April). What do adolescents know and think about sexual abuse? Paper presented at the National Symposium on Child Victimization, Anaheim, CA.

Kilmann, P. R., et al. (1982). The treatment of sexual paraphilias: A review of the outcome research. *J. Sex Res.*, 18:193–252.

Kinsey, A. C., et al. (1953). *Sexual Behavior in the Human Female*. Philadelphia: Saunders.

Kinsey, A. C., W. B. Pomeroy, & C. E. Martin. (1948). *Sexual Behavior in the Human Male*. Philadelphia: Saunders.

Kirkendall, L.A. (1965). *Sex Education*. SIECUS Study Guide No. 1. New York: Sex Information and Education Council of the United States.

Kirkendall, L. A. (1976, January/February). A new bill of sexual rights and responsibilities. *The Humanist*, 26(1):4–6.

Kirkpatrick, A. C. (1986). Some correlates of women's childhood sexual experiences: A retrospective study. *J. Sex Res.*, 22(2):221–242.

Kitzinger, S. (1985). *A New Approach to Woman's Experience of Sex*. New York: Putnam.

Klassen, A. D., & S. C. Wilsnack. (1986). Sexual experience and drinking among women in a U.S. national survey. *Archives Sexual Behavior*, 15(5):363–384.

Klein, F. (1978). *The Bisexual Option*. New York: Arbor House.

Klein, F., B. Sepekoff, & T. J. Wolf. (1985). Sexual orientations: A multi-variable dynamic process. In F. Klein & T. J. Wolf (eds.), *Bisexualities: Theory and Research*. New York: Haworth Press.

Kling, S. G. (1969). *Sexual Behavior and the Law*. New York: Pocket Books.

Knafo, D., & Y. Jaffe. (1984). Sexual fantasizing in males and females. *J. Res. Personality*, 19:451–462.

Knapp, J., & R. Whitehurst. (1978). Sexually open marriage and relationships: Issues and prospects. In B. Murstein (ed.), *Exploring Intimate Relationships*. New York: Springer.

Knox, D., & K. Wilson. (1981). Dating behavior of university students. *Family Relations*, 30:255–258.

Knuth, J. L., & S. E. Smith. (1984). Sexuality from the perspective of the visually impaired. *SIECUS Report*, 12(5):5–7.

Kohlberg, L. (1983). *The Psychology of Moral Development: Essays on Moral Development*. San Francisco: Harper & Row.

Kohlberg, L., & R. Kramer. (1969). Continuities and discontinuities in childhood and adult moral development. *Human Development*. 12:93–120.

Kohn, B., & A. Matusow. (1980). *Barry and Alice: Portrait of a Bisexual Marriage*. Englewood Cliffs, NJ: Prentice-Hall.

Kolata, G. (1988, February 16). Drug combination gains support as alternative to surgical abortion. *New York Times*, p. C3.

Kolder, V., et al. (1987). Court-ordered obstetrical interventions. *New Eng. J. Med.*, 316(19):1192–1196.

Korman, S. K., & G. R. Leslie. (1982). The relationship of feminist ideology and date expense sharing to perceptions of sexual aggression in dating. *J. Sex Res.*, 18(2):114–129.

Kosnick, A., et al. (1977). *Human Sexuality: New Directions in American Catholic Thought*. New York: Paulist Press.

Koss, M. P., & C. J. Oros. (1982). Sexual experiences survey: A research instrument investigating sexual aggression and victimization. *J. Consulting & Clinical Psychology*, 50:455–457.

Koss, M. P., C. A. Gidycz, & N. Wisniewski. (1987). The scope of rape: Incidence and prevalence of sexual aggression and victimization in a national sample of higher education students. *J. Consulting & Clinical Psychology*, 55:162–170.

Kruesi, M. J. P., et al. (1985). Carbohydrate craving, conduct disorder and low 5HIAA: A case report. *Psychiatry Res.*, 16:83–86.

Kurdeck, L. A., & J. P. Schmitt. (1987). Partner homogamy in married, heterosexual cohabiting, gay and lesbian couples. *J. Sex Res.*, 23(2):212–232.

Kushner, M. (1977). The reduction of a long-standing fetish by means of aversion conditioning. In J. Fischer & H. Gochros (eds.), *Handbook of Behavior Therapy with Sexual Problems*. New York: Pergamon Press.

Kutchinsky, B. (1983). The effect of easy availability of pornography on the incidence of sex crimes: The Danish experience. In D. Copp & S. Wendell (eds.), *Pornography and Censorship*. Buffalo: Prometheus Books. Also in *J. Social Issues*, 29(3):163–181.

Ladas, A., B. Whipple, & J. Perry. (1982). *The G Spot and Other Recent Discoveries about Human Sexuality*. New York: Holt.

Lalich, R. A., & A. Scommegna. (1988, July). Progestin after menopause—Yes or No? *Med. Aspects Human Sex.*, 115–122.

Lampe, P. E. (ed.). (1987). *Adultery in the United States: Close Encounters of the Sixth (or Seventh) Kind*. Buffalo, NY: Prometheus Press.

Laner, M. (1974). Prostitution as an illegal vocation: A sociological overview. In C. Bryant (ed.), *Deviant Behavior: Occupational and Organizational Basis*. New York: Clover.

Lang, A. R. (1985). The social psychology of drinking and human sexuality. *J. Drug Issues*, 15(2):273–289.

Lang, S. S. (1988, August). The abortion pill: French women will have it—why can't we? *Vogue*, pp. 231–232.

Lauman, E. (1969). Friends of urban men. *Sociometry*, 32:54–69.

Lawrence, K., & E. S. Herold. (1988). Women's attitudes

toward and experience with sexually explicit materials. *J. Sex Res.*, 24:161–169.

Lawrence, R. J. (1989). *The Poisoning of Eros: Sexual Values in Conflict*. New York: Augustine Moore Press.

Lee, E. (1982). A social systems approach to assessment and treatment for Chinese American families. In M. McGoldrick, et al. (eds.), *Ethnicity & Family Therapy*. New York: Guilford Press.

Lee, R. V. (1980). The case for chastity. *Med. Aspects Human Sex.*, 14(12):57–58.

Leff, J. J., & M. Israel. (1983). The relationship between mode of female masturbation and achievement of orgasm in coitus. *Archives Sexual Behavior*, 12(3):227 ff.

Legman, G. (1969). *Oragenitalism: Oral Techniques in Genital Excitation*. New York: Julian Press.

Leiblum, S., & L. Pervin. (1980; 2nd ed. 1989). *Principles and Practice of Sex Therapy*. New York: Guilford Press.

Leiblum, S. R., & R. C. Rosen (eds.). (1988). *Sexual Desire Disorders*. New York: Guilford Press.

Leinster, C. (1986, November). The rubber barons. *Fortune*, pp. 105–118.

Leo, J. (1984, April 9). The sexual revolution is over. *Time*, 123:74–78.

Leonard, G. (1982, December). Sex is dead. *Esquire*, pp. 70–80.

Lerner, H. E. (1977). Parental mislabeling of female genitals as a determinant of penis envy and learning inhibitions in women. In H. P. Blum (ed.), *Female Psychology: Contemporary Psychoanalytic Views*. New York: International Universities Press.

Lerner, H. G. (1989). *The Dance of Intimacy: A Woman's Guide to Courageous Acts of Change in Key Relationships*. New York: Harper & Row.

Lerner, M. A. (1988, June 13). A move to ban bordellos. *Newsweek*, p. 34.

Levine, A. (1988, February 1). AIDS and the innocents. *U.S. News & World Report*, pp. 49–51.

Levine, M. P., & R. R. Troiden. (1988). The myth of sexual compulsivity. *J. Sex Res.*, 25(3):347–363.

Levinson, R. A. (1986). Contraceptive self-efficacy: A perspective on teenage girls' contraceptive behavior. *J. Sex Res.*, 22:347–369.

Levitt, E., & A. Klassen. (1974). Public attitudes toward homosexuality: Part of the 1970 national survey by the Institute for Sex Research. *J. Homosexuality*, 1:29–43.

Levy, J. (1969). Possible basis for the evolution of lateral specialization of the human brain. *Nature*, 224:614–615.

Levy, J. (1974). Psychobiological implications of bilateral asymmetry. In S. Dimond & G. Beaumont (eds.), *Hemispheric Function in the Human Brain*. New York: Halsted Press.

Levy, J., & C. Trevarthen. (1976). Metacontrol of hemispheric function in human split brain patients. *J. Experimental Psychology: Human Perception and Performance*, 2:299–312.

Levy, J., & C. Trevarthen. (1977). Perceptual, semantic language processes in split-brain patients. *Brain*, 100:105–118.

Levy, J., C. Trevarthen, & R. W. Sperry. (1972). Perception of bilateral chimeric figures following hemispheric disconnection. *Brain*, 95:61–78.

Lewes, K. (1988). *The Psychoanalytic Theory of Male Homosexuality*. New York: Simon & Schuster.

Lewin, T. (1988, August 2). Protecting the baby: Work in pregnancy poses legal frontier. *New York Times*, pp. A1, A15.

Leyson, J. F. J. (ed.). (1990). *Sexual Rehabilitation of the Spinal Cord Injury Patient*. Clifton, NJ: Humana Press.

Leyson, J. F. J., & R. T. Francoeur. (1990). Pharmacosexology: Sexual side effects of medications and other drugs. In J. F. J. Leyson (ed.), *Sexual Rehabilitation of the Spinal Cord Injury Patient*. Clifton, NJ: Humana Press.

Li, Jing-wei, et al. (1987). *China Medical Encyclopedia: Medical History*. Shanghai: Shanghai Scientific & Technological Publishing House.

Libby, R. W. (1987, September). Open marriage. *Med. Aspects Human Sex.*, p. 74.

Libby, R. W., & R. Whitehurst (eds.). (1977). *Marriage and Alternatives: Exploring Intimate Relationships*. Glenview, IL: Scott, Foresman.

Liebowitz, M. R. (1983). *The Chemistry of Love*. Boston: Little, Brown.

Little, A. B. (1988). There's many a slip 'twixt implantation and the crib. *New Eng. J. Med*, 319(4):241–242.

Liu, D-l. (1987). Science of sex and liberation of women. *Frontier of Social Sciences*, 1:125.

Long, G. T., & F. E. Sultan. (1987). Contributions from social psychology. In L. Diamont (ed.), *Male and Female Homosexuality: Psychological Approaches*. Washington, DC: Hemisphere.

Loulan, J. (1984). *Lesbian Sex*. San Francisco: Spinsters/Aunt Lute.

Loulan, J. (1987). *Lesbian Passion*. San Francisco: Spinsters/Aunt Lute.

Lowry, T. P., & T. S. Lowry (eds.). (1976). *The Clitoris*. St. Louis: Warren H. Green.

Lubenow, C. (1982, April 5). Gays and lesbians on campus. *Newsweek*, pp 75–77.

Ludwig, T.M. (1989). *The Sacred Paths: Understanding the Religions of the World*. New York: Macmillan.

Luker, K. (1975). *Taking Chances: Abortion and the Decision*

Not to Contracept. Berkeley: University of California Press.

Luker, K. (1984). *Abortion and the Politics of Motherhood*. Berkeley: University of California Press.

Lynn, B. (1986). *Polluting the Censorship Debate: A Summary and Critique of the Final Report of the Attorney General's Commission on Pornography*. Washington, DC: American Civil Liberties Union.

Lyons, N. P. (1983). Two perspectives: On self-relationships and morality. *Harvard Educational Rev.*, 53(2): 125–145.

Mace, D., & V. Mace. (1960). *Marriage East and West*. New York: Doubleday.

MacKellar, J. (1975). *Rape: The Bait and the Trap*. New York: Crown.

Macklin, E. (1974, November). Cohabitation in college: Going very steady. *Psychology Today*, pp. 53–59.

Macklin, E. (1980). Nontraditional family forms: A decade of research. *J. Marriage & Family*, 42:905–922.

Macklin, E. D. (1987). Nontraditional family forms. In M. B. Sussman & S. K. Steinmetz (eds.), *Handbook of Marriage and the Family*. New York: Plenum.

Macklin, E., & R. Rubin (eds.). (1983). *Contemporary Families and Alternative Lifestyles: A Handbook on Research and Theory*. Beverly Hills, CA: Sage.

MacLusky, N. J., & F. Naftolin. (1981). Sexual differentiation of the central nervous system. *Science*, 21 (4488):1294–1303.

Mains, G. (1988). *Urban Aboriginals: A Celebration of Leather-sexuality*. East Haven, CT: Gay Sunshine/Inland Book Co.

Malamuth, N. M. (1981). Rape proclivity among males. *J. Social Issues*, 37:138–157.

Malamuth, N. M., & V. Billings. (1984). Why pornography? Models of functions and effects. *J. Communication*, 34(3):117–129.

Malamuth, N. M., & V. Billings. (1986). The functions and effects of pornography: Sexual communications versus the feminist models in light of research findings. In J. Bryant & D. Zillman (eds.), *Perspectives on Media Effects*. Hillsdale, NJ: Erlbaum.

Maletzky, B. M. (1980). Assisted covert sensitization. In D. J. Cox & R. J. Daitzman (eds.), *Exhibitionism: Description, Assessment and Treatment*. New York: Garland.

Maletzky, B. M., & R. Price. (1984). Public masturbation in men: Precursor to exhibitionism? *J. Sex Education*, 10:31–36.

Mallon, R. (1984, October). Demonstration of vestigial prostatic tissue in the human female. A paper presented at a meeting of the American Association of Sex Educators, Counselors & Therapists, Las Vegas, NV.

Marciano, T. D. (1988). Families wider than kin or marriage. *Family Science Review*, 1(2):115–124.

Marcus, E. (1988). *The Male's Guide to Living Together: What Gay Men Should Know about Living Together and Coping in a Straight World*. New York: Harper & Row.

Markus, E., & J. Francis. (1975). *Masturbation from Infancy to Senescence*. New York: International Universities Press.

Marshall, W. L. (1988). The use of sexually explicit stimuli by rapists, child molesters, and nonoffenders. *J. Sex Res.*, 25(2):267–288.

Martinson, F. M. (1980). Childhood sexuality. In B. B. Wolman (ed.), *Handbook of Human Sexuality*. Englewood Cliffs, NJ: Prentice-Hall.

Martinson, F. M. (1983). Sensory/erotic development: Embryo, fetus, infant, child. Theories of sexual motivation and conduct in infants and young children. Papers delivered at the 6th World Congress of Sexology, Washington, DC, May 24.

Marx, J. L. (1989). Circumcision may protect against the AIDS virus. *Science*, 245:470–471.

Mason, W. A., & G. Berkson. (1975). Effects of maternal mobility on the development of rocking and other behaviors in rhesus monkeys: A study with artificial mothers. *Dev. Psychobiology*, 8:197–211.

Masters, W. H. (1986). Sexual dysfunction as an aftermath of sexual assault of men by women. *J. Sex & Marital Therapy*, 12(1):35–45.

Masters, W. H., & V. Johnson. (1966). *Human Sexual Response*. Boston: Little, Brown.

Masters, W. H., & V. Johnson. (1979). *Homosexuality in Perspective*. Boston: Little, Brown.

Masters, W. H., V. Johnson, & R. C. Kolodny. (1980). Unpublished observations.

Masters, W. H., V. Johnson, & R. C. Kolodny. (1988). *Human Sexuality* (3rd ed.). Glenview, IL: Scott, Foresman.

McCaghy, C. (1971, August). Child molesting. *Sexual Behavior*, 16–24.

McCary, J. (1975). *Freedom and Growth in Marriage*. New York: Hamilton Press/Wiley.

McCary, J. L., & S. P. McCary. (1982). *McCary's Human Sexuality*. Belmont, CA: Wadsworth.

McClintock, M. (1971, January 22). Menstrual synchrony and suppression. *Nature*, 229:244–246.

McCombie, S. (ed.). (1980). *The Rape Crisis Intervention Handbook, A Guide for Victim Care*. New York: Plenum.

McCormack, T. (1978). Machismo in media research: A critical review of research on violence and pornography. *Social Problems*, 25(5):552–554.

McGill, M. E. (1985). *The McGill Report on Male Intimacy*. New York: Harper & Row.

McGinley, R. L. (1979). Swinging in the United States with reference and challenge to published reports. An unpublished doctoral dissertation, Newport International University.

McGoldrick, M., J. Pearce, & J. Giordano (eds.). (1982). *Ethnicity and Family Therapy*. New York: Guilford Press.

McGuire, R., J. M. Carlisle, & B. G. Young. (1965). Sexual deviations as conditioned behavior: A hypothesis. *Behavior Res. & Therapy*, 2:185–190.

McIlvenna, T. (ed.). (1987). *The Complete Guide to Safe Sex*. San Francisco: Specific Press, The Institute for the Advanced Study of Human Sexuality.

McNeill, J. (1976). *The Church and the Homosexual*. Kansas City: Sheed Andrews & McMeel.

McWhirter, D. P., & A. M. Mattison. (1984). *The Male Couple: How Relationships Develop*. Englewood Cliffs, NJ: Prentice-Hall.

Medical J. Australia. (1986). Tubal sterilization often chosen too hastily. 145(1):4–7.

Medina, C. (1987). Latino culture and sex education. *SIECUS Report*, 15(3):1–4.

Mehl, L. E. (1978). The outcome of home delivery: Research in the United States. In S. Kitzinger & J. A. Davis (eds.), *The Place of Birth*. New York: Oxford University Press.

Meiselman, K. (1979). *Incest: A Psychological Study of Causes and Effects with Treatment Recommendations*. San Francisco: Jossey-Bass.

Mendola, M. (1980). *The Mendola Report: A New Look at Gay Couples*. New York: Crown.

Mernissi, F. (1975). *Beyond the Veil: Women in the Arab World*. New York: Wiley.

Messer, S. B. (1986). Behavioral and psychoanalytic perspectives at therapeutic choice points. *American Psychologist*, 41(11):1261–1272.

Meyer-Bahlburg, H.F.L. (1987). Psychoendrocrine research and the societal status of homosexuals: A reply to DeCecco. *J. Sex Res.*, 23(1):114–120.

Middleton, L., & A. Roark. (1981, July 13). Campus homosexuals out of the closet but not out of trouble. *Chronicle Higher Ed.*, pp. 3–4.

Minturn, L. (1989). The birth ceremony as a rite of passage into infant personhood. In E. Doerr & J. W. Prescott (eds.), *Abortion Rights and Fetal "Personhood."* Long Beach, CA: Centerline Press.

Mobley, D. F. (1975, November). Relation of sexual habits to prostatitis. *Med. Aspects Human Sex.*, p. 75.

Moglia, R. (1986, March). Sexual abuse and disability. *SIECUS Report*, 14(4):9–10.

Moitoza, E. (1982). Portuguese families. In M. McGoldrick et al. (eds.), *Ethnicity and Family Therapy*, pp. 412–437.

Moll, A. (1913). *The Sexual Life of the Child*. New York: Macmillan.

Money, J. (1976a). Childhood: The last frontier in sex research. *The Sciences*, 16(6):12–15, 27.

Money, J. (1976b). Gender identity and hermaphroditism. *Science*, 191:872.

Money, J. (1980). *Love and Love Sickness: The Science of Sex, Gender Differences, and Pair Bonding*. Baltimore: Johns Hopkins University Press.

Money, J. (1983). Pairbonding and limerence. In B. B. Wolman (ed.), *International Encyclopedia of Psychiatry, Psychology, Psychoanalysis and Neurology. Progress Volume I*. New York: Aesculapius.

Money, J. (1985a). *The Destroying Angel: Sex, Fitness & Food in the Legacy of Degeneracy Theory, Graham Crackers, Kellogg's Corn Flakes & American Health History*. Buffalo, NY: Prometheus Press.

Money, J. (1985b). Gender: History, theory and usage of the term in sexology and its relationship to nature/nurture. *J. Sex & Marital Therapy*, 11(2):71–79.

Money, J. (1986). *Lovemaps: Clinical Concepts of Sexual/Erotic Health and Pathology, Paraphilia, and Gender Transposition in Childhood, Adolescence, and Maturity*. New York: Irvington.

Money, J. (1988). *Gay, Straight, and In-Between: The Sexology of Erotic Orientation*. New York: Oxford University Press.

Money, J., & A. A. Ehrhardt. (1972). *Man & Woman Boy & Girl*. Baltimore: Johns Hopkins University Press.

Money, J., & M. Lamacz. (1990). *Vandalized Lovemaps*. Buffalo: Prometheus Press.

Money, J., & P. Tucker. (1975). *Sexual Signatures: On Being a Man or Woman*. Boston: Little, Brown.

Monmaney, T. (1988, January 4). Another AIDS virus appears. *Newsweek*, pp. 60–62.

Montagu, A. (1969). *Sex, Man and Society*. New York: Putnam.

Mooney, T. O., et al. (1975). *Sexual Options for Paraplegics and Quadriplegics*. Boston: Little, Brown.

Moore, K. L. (1988). *The Developing Human: Clinically Oriented Embryology*, (4th ed.). Philadelphia: Saunders.

Moore, M. M. (1985). Nonverbal courtship patterns in women: Context and consequences. *Ethology & Sociobiology*, 6:237–247.

Morgan, L. M. (1989). A cross-cultural perspective on the personhood of fetuses and young children. In E. Doerr & J. W. Prescott (eds.), *Abortion Rights and Fetal "Personhood."* Long Beach, CA: Centerline Press.

Morgan, P. (1982). Alcohol and family violence: A review of the literature. *Alcohol and Health Monograph No. 1*, pp. 223–259.

Morgan, R., & G. Steinem. (1980, March). The international crime of genital mutilation. *Ms.* magazine, pp. 65–67.

Morin, J. (1987). *Anal Pleasure and Health* (2nd ed.). San Francisco: Down There Press.

Morris, D. (1971). *Intimate Behavior*. New York: Random House.

Morris, J. (1974). *Conundrum*. New York: Harcourt Brace Jovanovich.

Morrison, J., & R. K. Morrison. (1987). *From Camelot to Kent State: The Sixties Experience in the Words of Those Who Lived It*. New York: Times Books.

Moses, A. E., & R. O. Hawkins, Jr. (1982). *Counseling Lesbian Women and Gay Men: A Life-Issues Approach*. Columbus, OH: Chas. Merrill.

Mosher, D. L., & S. S. Tompkins. (1988). Scripting the macho man: Hypermasculine socialization and enculturation. *J. Sex Res.*, 25(1):60–84.

Mosher, D. L., & S. G. Vonderheide. (1985). Contributions of sex guilt and masturbation guilt to women's contraceptive attitude and use. *J. Sex Res.*, 21(1): 24–39.

Mould, D. E. (1988). A critical analysis of recent research on violent erotica. *J. Sex Res.*, 24:326–340, 353–358.

Muehlenhard, C. L., & S. W. Cook. (1988). Men's self-reports of unwanted sexual activity. *J. Sex Res.*, 24: 58–72.

Muehlenhard, C. L., & L. C. Hollabaugh. (1988). Do women sometimes say no when they mean yes? *J. Personality & Social Psychology*, 54:872–879.

Murstein, B. (1970). Stimulus-value-role: A theory of marital choice. *J. Marriage & Family*, 32:465–481.

Murstein, B. (1974). *Love, Sex and Marriage Through the Ages*. New York: Springer.

Murstein, B. (ed.). (1978). *Exploring Intimate Lifestyles*. New York: Springer.

Musialowski, D. M., & K. Kelley. (1987). Male rape: Perception of the act and the victim. A paper presented at the Eastern Regional meeting of the Society for the Scientific Study of Sex, Philadelphia.

Myers, L., & H. Leggitt. (1975). *Adultery and Other Private Matters: Your Right to Personal Freedom in Marriage*. Chicago: Nelson Hall.

Naeye, R. (1979). Coitus and associated amniotic fluid infections. *New Eng. J. Med.*, 301:1198–1200.

Naftolin, F., et al. (1981). Understanding the bases of sex differences. *Science*, 211(4488):1263–1317.

Namazi, J. (1990). Personal communication with R. T. Francoeur on sexual customs in contemporary Iran.

Nanda, S. (1984) The hijras of India: A preliminary report. *Med. & Law*, 3:59–79.

Nathan, S. (1986). The epidemiology of DSM-III psychosexual dysfunctions. *J. Sex & Marital Therapy*, 12(4): 267–281.

Nathanson, B. (1979). *Aborting America*. Garden City, New York: Doubleday.

Neilson, L. (1965). *A Child Is Born*. Boston: Seymour Lawrence.

Neinstein, L., et al. (1984). Nonsexual transmission of sexually transmitted diseases: An infrequent occurrence. *Pediatrics*, 74:67–76.

Nelson, J. B. (1978). *Embodiment: An Approach to Sexuality and Christian Theology*. Minneapolis: Augsburg.

Nelson, S. (1987, September). Sex, AIDS and pillow talk. *Glamour*, pp. 350–351, 416–417.

Nerurkar, L. et al. (1983). Survival of herpes simplex virus in water specimens collected from hot tubs in spa facilities and on plastic surfaces. *J. Amer. Med. Assoc.*, 250:3081–3083.

Newcomb, M. D. (1983). Relationship qualities of those who live together. *Alternative Lifestyles*, 6(2):78–101.

Newcomb, M. D. (1986). Sexual behavior of cohabitors: A comparison of three independent samples. *J. Sex Res.*, 22(4):492–513.

Newton, E. (1979). *Mother Camp: Female Impersonation in America*. Chicago: University of Chicago Press.

Nichols, M. (1988). Low sexual desire in lesbian couples. In S. R. Leiblum & R. C. Rosen (eds.), *Sexual Desire Disorders*. New York: Guilford Press.

Nobile, P., & E. Nadler. (1986). *United States of America vs. Sex: How the Meese Commission Lied About Pornography*. New York: Minotaur Press.

Noble, K. B. (1983, September 9). One approach to the shortage of men is sharing. *New York Times*, p. B4.

Nordeen, E. J., & P. Yahr. (1982). Hemispheric asymmetries in the behavioral and hormonal effects of sexually differentiating mammalian brain. *Science*, 218: 391.

Nugent, R., ed. (1984). *A Challenge to Love: Gay and Lesbian Catholics in the Church*. New York: Crossroad.

Nutter, D., & M. Condron. (1983). Sexual fantasy and activity patterns of females with inhibited sexual desire versus normal controls. *J. Sex Marital Therapy*, 9: 276–282.

Nye, F. I. (1979). Choice, exchange, and the family. In W. R. Burr et al. (eds.), *Contemporary Theories about the Family. Volume II. General Theories/Theoretical Orientations*. New York: Free Press.

Nye, F. I. (1980). Family minitheories as special instances of choice and exchange theory. *J. Marriage & Family*, 42:479–489.

Offir, C. W. (1975, August). Don't take it lying down. *Psychology Today*, 8(8):73 ff.

O'Neill, N., & G. O'Neill. (1972). *Open Marriage: A New Lifestyle for Couples*. New York: Evans.

Ostling, R. N. (1984, December 3). A bold stand on birth control. *Time*, p. 66.

Otto, H. A., & Otto, R. (1972). *Total Sex*. New York: Peter H. Wyden.

Page, D. C., et al. (1987). The sex-determining region of the human Y chromosome encodes a finger protein. *Cell*, 51:1091–1104.

Paige, K. (1973, April). Women learn to sing the menstrual blues. *Psychology Today*, 7(4):41–42.

Palmer, C. T. (1988). Twelve reasons why rape is not sexually motivated: A sceptical examination. *J. Sex Res.* 25(4):512–530.

Palmer, M. S., et al. (1989, December 21/28). Genetic evidence that ZFY is not the testis-determining factor. *Nature,* 342:937–939.

Parker, R. (1984). The body and the self: Aspects of male sexual ideology in Brazil. A paper presented at the 83rd Annual Meeting of the American Anthropological Association, Denver.

Parker, R. (1987, June). Acquired immunodeficiency syndrome in urban Brazil. *Med. Anthro. Q.*, n.s. 1(2): 155–175.

Parker, R. A. (1935). *A Yankee Saint*. New York: Putnam.

Parrinder, G. (1980). *Sex in the World's Religions*. Don Mills, Ontario, Canada: General Publishing Co.

Parrot, A. (1989). Acquaintance rape among adolescents: Identify risk groups and intervention strategies. In P. Allen-Meares & C. Hoenk Shapiro (eds.), *Adolescent Sexuality: New Challenges for Social Work*. New York: Haworth Press.

Pearl, J. (1987). The highest paying customers: America's cities and the costs of prostitution control. *Hastings Law J.*, 38:769–800.

Pechter, K. (1988, Spring). The new aphrodisiacs. *Men's Health*, pp. 43–44.

Peplau, L. A. (1981, March). What homosexuals want in relationships. *Psychology Today*, pp. 28–38.

Peplau, L. A., & H. Amaro. (1982). Understanding lesbian relationships. In W. Paul et al. (eds.). *Homosexuality: Social, Psychological and Biological Issues*. Beverly Hills, CA: Sage.

Peplau, L. A., et al. (1982). Satisfaction in lesbian relationships. *J. Homosexuality*, 8:23–35.

Perper, T. (1985). *Sex Signals: The Biology of Love*. Philadelphia: iSi Press.

Perper, T. (1987, April). The dance of intimacy. *Penthouse Forum*, pp. 18–24.

Perper, T. (1988). Assumptions and implications of the linear and landscape psychosexual development models. Personal letter to the author.

Perper, T. (1989). Theories and observations on sexual selection and female choice in human beings. *Med. Anthro.*, 11:409–454.

Perper, T., & S. V. Fox. (1981). *Flirtation Behavior in Public Settings: Final Report*. New York: The Harry Guggenheim Foundation.

Perper, T., & D. L. Weis. (1987). Proceptive and rejective strategies of U.S. and Canadian college women. *J. Sex Res.*, 23(4):455–480.

Perry, J. D., & B. Whipple. (1981a, May). The varieties of female orgasm and female ejaculation. *SIECUS Report*, 9:15–16.

Perry, J. D., & B. Whipple. (1981b). Pelvic muscle strength of female ejaculators: Evidence in support of a new theory of orgasm. *J. Sex Res.*, 17(1):22–39.

Perry, M. E. (ed.). (1989). *Childhood and Adolescent Sexuality. Handbook of Sexology. Vol. 7*. Amsterdam: Elsevier. See particularly J. Money: Current scholarly concepts of sexual and erotic development in childhood; S. Jackson: Historical doctrines and concepts of children's sexual and erotic development; R. T. Francoeur: Current religious doctrines of sexual and erotic development in childhood; E. Galenson: Early infantile observations of sexual and erotic development; T. Langfeldt: Early juvenile sexual rehearsal play; L. Kirkendall & L. McBride: Erotosexual imagery and adolescent experience.

Peterman, D., et al. (1974). A comparison of cohabiting and noncohabiting college students. *J. Marriage & Family*, 36:344–354.

Peterson, J. R., et al. (1983). Playboy readers sex survey. *Playboy*, 30(1 & 3).

Peterson, L. (1988). The issue—and controversy—surrounding adolescent sexuality and abstinence. *SIECUS Report*, 17(1):1–8.

Peterson, R. E., et al. (1977). Male pseudohermaphroditism due to steroid 5delta-reductase deficiency. *Amer. J. Med.*, 62:170.

Phipps, W. E. (1977). Masturbation: Vice or virtue? *J. Religion & Health*, 16(3):183–195.

Pietropinto, A. (1987, July). Sexual abstinence. *Med. Aspects Human Sex.* pp. 115–118.

Pillard, R. C., & J. D. Weinrich. (1987). The periodic table model of the gender transpositions: Part I. A theory based on masculinization and defeminization of the brain. *J. Sex Res.*, 23(4):425–454.

Pines, A., & E. Aronson. (1981). Polyfidelity: An alternative lifestyle without jealousy? *Alternate Lifestyles*, 4(3):373–392.

Piotrkowski, C. S., R. N. Rapoport, & R. Rapoport. (1987). Families and work. In M. B. Sussman & S. K. Steinmetz (eds.), *Handbook of Marriage and the Family*. New York: Plenum.

Pogrebin, L. (1980). *Growing Up Free, Raising Your Child in the 80's*. New York: McGraw- Hill.

Pomeroy, W. B. (1972). *Dr. Kinsey and the Institute for Sex Research*. New York: Harper & Row.

Prendergast, W. (1979). The sex offender: How to spot him before it's too late. *Sexology*, 46(2):46–51.

Prescott, J. W. (1971). Early somatosensory deprivation as an ontogenetic process in the abnormal development of the brain and behavior. In I. E. Goldsmith & J. Moor-Jankowski (eds.), *Medical Primatology*. Basel/New York: S. Karger.

Prescott, J. W. (1975a). Body pleasure and the origins of violence. *The Futurist*, 9(2):64–74.

Prescott, J. W. (1975b, March/April). Abortion of the unwanted child: A choice for a humanistic society. *The Humanist*, pp. 11–15.

Prescott, J. W. (1978, July/August, & November/December). Abortion and the right to life. *The Humanist*, pp. 11–15, 8–12.

Prescott, J. W. (1986, September/October). The abortion of *The Silent Scream*. *The Humanist*, pp. 10–28.

Prescott, J. W. (1989). Affectional bonding for the prevention of violent behaviors: Neurological, psychological and religious/spiritual determinants. In L. J. Hertzberg et al. (eds.), *Violent Behavior. Volume 1: Assessment and Intervention*. New York: PMA Publishing Corp.

Prescott, J. W., & D. Wallace. (1978, July/August). Abortion and the "right-to-life." *The Humanist*, pp. 18–24.

Prince, D. (1987, June 1). Marriage in the '80s: What love's got to do with it. *New York*, pp. 31–38.

Prince, V. (1979). Charles to Virginia: Sex research as a personal experience. In V. Bullough (ed.), *Frontiers of Sex Research*. Buffalo, NY: Prometheus Books.

Pritchard, C. (1988). *Avoiding Rape On and Off Campus* (2nd ed). Wenonah, NJ: State College Publishing Co.

Propper, S., & R. A. Brown. (1986). Moral reasoning, parental sex attitudes, and sex guilt in female college students. *Archives Sexual Behavior*, 15(4):331–340.

Quadagno, D. M. (1988, August). Update on the G-spot. *Med. Aspects Human Sex.*, 22(8):93–94.

Radway, J. A. (1984). *Reading the Romance: Women, Patriarchy and Popular Literature*. Chapel Hill: University of North Carolina Press.

Raley, P. (1976). *Making Love: How To Be Your Own Sex Therapist*. New York: Dial Press.

Ramey, J. (1975). Intimate networks. *The Futurist*, 9(4): 174–182.

Ramey, J. (1976). *Intimate Relationships*. Englewood Cliffs, NJ: Prentice-Hall.

Rao, V. V. P., & V. N. Rao. (1980). Alternatives in intimacy, marriage and family lifestyles: Preferences of black college students. *Alternative Lifestyles*, 3(4):485–498.

Rappaport, K., & B. R. Burkhart. (1984). Personality and attitudinal correlates of sexually coercive college males. *J. Abnormal Personality*, 93:216–221.

Raschke, H. J. (1987). Divorce. In M. B. Sussman & S. K. Steinmetz (eds.), *Handbook of Marriage and the Family*. New York: Plenum.

Rasmussen, T., & B. Milner. (1977). The role of early left-brain injury in determining lateralization of cerebral speech functions. In S. Dimond & D. Blizzard (eds.), *Evolution and Lateralization of the Brain*. New York: New York Academy of Sciences.

Reed, J. (1978). *The Birth Control Movement in America: From Private Vice to Public Virtue*. Princeton, NJ: Princeton University Press.

Reidinger, P. (1987, April 1). Negligent sex: Herpes victims sue their partners. *American Bar Assoc. J.*, 75(1): 73.

Reinisch, J. M., & S. A. Sanders. (1982). Early barbiturate exposure: The brain, sexually dimorphic behavior, and learning. *Neuroscience & Biobehavioral Reviews*, 6: 311–319.

Reinisch, J. M., & S. A. Sanders. (1984). Hormonal influences on sexual development and behavior. In B. Schwartz & A. F. Moraczewski (eds.), *Sex and Gender: A Theological and Scientific Inquiry*. St. Louis: Pope John Center.

Reinisch, J. M., et al. (eds.). (1987). *Masculinity/Femininity: Basic Perspectives*. New York: Oxford University Press.

Reiss, A. (1961). The social integration of queers and peers. *Social Problems*, 9:102–120.

Reiss, I. L. (1960). Toward a sociology of the heterosexual love relationship. *Marriage & Family Living*, 22: 139–145.

Reiss, I. L. (1986). *Journey into Sexuality: An Exploratory Voyage*. Englewood Cliffs, NJ: Prentice-Hall.

Remoff, H. T. (1984). *Sexual Choice: A Woman's Decision*. New York: Dutton/Lewis.

Renshaw, D. C. (1984). Intimacy and intercourse. *Med. Aspects Human Sex.*, 18(2):70–76.

Richardson, H. W. (1971). *Nun, Witch, Playmate: The Americanization of Sex*. New York: Harper & Row.

Richardson, L. (1985). *The New Other Woman: Contemporary Single Women in Affairs with Married Men*. New York: Free Press.

Richart, R. M. (1987, October 15 supplement). Causes and management of cervical intraepithelial neoplasia. *Cancer*, 60(8):1951–1958.

Rienzo, B. A. (1985). The impact of aging on human sexuality. *J. School Health*, 55(2):66–68.

Robbins, M. B., & G. D. Jensen. (1978). Multiple orgasm in males. *J. Sex Res.*, 14(1):21–26.

Roberts, E. J., & S. A. Holt. (1980). Parent-child communication about sexuality. *SIECUS Report*, 8(4):1–2, 10.

Robertson, C. N. (1970). *Oneida Community: An Autobiography, 1851–1876*. Syracuse, NY: Syracuse University Press.

Rodman, H., S. H. Lewis, & S. B. Griffith. (1984). *The Sexual Rights of Adolescents: Competence, Vulnerability, and Parental Control*. New York: Columbia University Press.

Roggencamp, V. (1984). Abortion of a special kind: Male sex selection in India. In R. Arditti, R. Klein, & S. Minden (eds.), *Test-Tube Women: What Future for Motherhood?* Boston: Pandora Press.

Rosellini, L., & E. E. Goode. (1987, October 12). AIDS: When fear takes charge. *U.S. News & World Report*, pp. 62–70.

Rosen, I. (1964). *Pathology and Treatment of Sexual Deviates*. Fairlawn, NJ: Oxford University Press.

Rosen, R. C., & J. G. Beck. (1988). *Patterns of Sexual Arousal: Psychophysiological Processes and Clinical Applications*. New York: Guilford Press.

Rosenthal, S. H. (1988). *Sex Over Forty*. New York: J. P. Tarcher.

Rossi, A. (1985). The biosocial side of parenthood. In W. Williams (ed.), *Psychology of Women* (2nd ed.). New York: Norton.

Rossman, P. (1976). *Sexual Experiences Between Men and Boys*. Chicago: Association Press.

Rothkin, I. D. (1973). A comparison of key epidemiological studies in cervical cancer related to current searches for transmissible agents. *Cancer Res.*, 33: 1353–1367.

Rousso, H. (1986, March). Confronting the myth of asexuality: The networking project for disabled women and girls. *SIECUS Report*, 14(4):4–6.

Roy, R., & D. Roy. (1967). *Honest Sex*. New York: New American Library.

Ruan, F. F. (1990). Personal communication with the author.

Ruan, F. F., & K. R. Chong. (1987, April 14). Gay life in China. *The Advocate*, pp. 28–31.

Ruan, F. F., & Y. M. Tsai. (1988). Male homosexuality in contemporary mainland China. *Archives Sexual Behavior*, 17(2):189–199.

Ruan, F. F., & Y. M. Tsai. (1987). Male homosexuality in traditional Chinese literature. *J. Homosexuality*, 14 (3/4):21–33.

Rubin, A. M., & J. R. Adams. (1986). Outcomes of sexually open marriages. *J. Sex Res.*, 22(3):311–319.

Rubin, Z. (1973). *Liking and Loving: An Invitation to Social Psychology*. New York: Holt.

Rubin, Z. (1977, February). The love research. *Human Behavior*, pp. 27–30.

Rush, F. (1980). *The Best Kept Secret: Sexual Abuse of Children*. New York: McGraw-Hill.

Russell, D. (1980a). Pornography and violence: What does the research say? In L. Lederer (ed.), *Take Back the Night: Women on Pornography*. New York: Morrow.

Russell, D. (1980b). Testimony against pornography: Witness from Denmark. In L. Lederer (ed.), *Take Back the Night: Women on Pornography*. New York: Morrow.

Russell, D. (1983). Research on how women experience the impact of pornography. In D. Copp & S. Wendell, (eds.), *Pornography and Censorship*. Buffalo, NY: Prometheus Books.

Russell, D. (1984). *Sexual Exploitation: Rape, Child Sexual Abuse, and Workplace Harassment*. Beverly Hills, CA: Sage.

Saltzberg, B. (1985). Special electrophysiological tests: Brain spiking, EEG spectral coherence. In R.C. Hall et al. (eds.), *Handbook of Psychiatric Diagnostic Proc. Vol. 2*. pp. 137-150.

Saltzberg, B., et al. (1969). Detection of focal depth spiking in the scalp EEG of monkeys. *Electroencephalography & Clinical Neurophys.*, 31:327–333.

Saltzman, A. (1988, August 1). Hands off at the office. *U.S. News & World Report*, pp. 56–58.

Sandoval, J. A. (1988). Impact 88: Dallas' countywide plan for reducing teen pregnancy. *SIECUS Report*. 16(3):1–5.

Sandroff, R. (1988, December). Sexual harassment in the Fortune 500. *Working Woman*, pp. 69–73.

Sarrel, L., & P. Sarrel. (1979). *Sexual Unfolding: Sexual Development and Sex Therapies in Late Adolescence*. Boston: Little, Brown.

Sarrel, P. M., & W. H. Masters. (1982). Sexual molestation of men by women. *Archives Sexual Behavior*, 11(2):117–177.

Satchell, M. (1986, July 20). Kids for sale. *Parade Magazine*, pp. 4–6. Reprinted in O. Pocs (ed.) (1987). *Human Sexuality 87/88*. Guilford, CT: Dushkin, pp. 223–225.

Satterfield, S., & A. Listiak. (1982). Juvenile prostitution: A sequel to incest. Paper presented at the 135th meeting of the American Psychiatric Association, Toronto, May 15–21.

Savitz, L., & L. Rosen. (1988). The sexuality of prostitutes: Sexual enjoyment reported by "streetwalkers." *J. Sex Res.*, 24:200–208.

Schaefer, L. C., & C. C. Wheeler. (1983). The non-surgical true transsexual: A theoretical rationale. Paper presented at the Eighth International Symposium of the Harry Benjamin International Gender Dysphoria Association, Bordeaux, France.

Schaefer, L. C., & C. C. Wheeler. (1988). Harry Benjamin's first ten cases, 1938–1953—Historical influence. In W. Eicher & G. Kockott (eds.), *Sexology*. Berlin/Heidelberg: Springer-Verlag.

Schaffer, H. R., & C. K. Crook. (1985). The role of the mother in early social development. In W. Williams (ed.), *Psychology of Women* (2nd ed.). New York: Norton.

Schechner, S. (1980). For the 1980s: How small is too small? *Clinics in Perinatology*, 7:143.

Schover, L. R., & S. B. Jensen. (1988). *Sexuality and Chronic Illness: A Comprehensive Approach*. New York: Guilford Press.

Schwartz, M. F., & W. S. Brasted. (1985). Sexual addiction. *Med. Aspects Human Sex.*, 19:103–107.

Scientific American. (1988, October). What science knows about AIDS. A single topic issue.

Scott, J. E., & S. J. Cuvelier. (1987). Sexual violence in Playboy Magazine: A longitudinal content analysis. *J. Sex Res.*, 23(4):534–539.

Scott, J. E., & L. A. Schwalm. (1988). Rape rates and the circulation rates of adult magazines. *J. Sex Res.*, 24:241–250.

Scott, J. W. (1980). Black polygamous family formation. *J. Alternative Lifestyles*, 3(1):31 ff.

Scott, J. W. (1986). From teenage parenthood to polygamy: Case studies in black polygamous family formation. *Western J. Black Studies*, 10(4):172–179.

Scott, N. (1988a, May–June). Is AIDS always fatal? Siegel says "No!" *Alcoholism & Addiction*, pp. 14–16.

Scott, N. (1988b, May–June). AIDS and Addiction: Policies, politics, and prevention. *Alcoholism & Addiction*, pp. 18–20.

Seagrave, R. T. (1988). Drugs and desire. In S. R. Leiblum & R. C. Rosen (eds.), *Sexual Desire Disorders*. New York: Guilford Press.

Segal, J. (1984). *The Sex Lives of College Students*. Wayne, PA: Milet Standish Press.

Selkin, J. (1975, August). Rape: When to fight back. *Psychology Today*, 8(8):70–76.

Selkin, J. (1978). Protecting personal space: Victim and resister reactions to assaultive rape. *J. Community Psychology*, 6:263–268.

Sevely, J., & J. Bennett. (1978). Concerning female ejaculation and the female prostate. *J. Sex Res.*, 14(1):1–20.

SexuaLaw Reporter. (1977, March/April). Lee Marvin vs. Michelle Marvin. pp. 1–2.

Sheehan, E. (1981). Victorian clitorectomy: Isaac Baker Brown and his harmless operative procedure. *Med. Anthro. Newsletter*, 12(4):9–15.

Sherman, A. (1975). *The Rape of the A.P.E.* Chicago: Playboy Press.

Shilts, R. (1987). *And the Band Played On: Politics, People, and the AIDS Epidemic*. New York: St. Martin's Press.

Shively, M. & J. DeCecco. (1978). Components of sexual identity. *J. Homosexuality*, 3(1):41–48.

Shon, S. P., & D. Y. Ja. (1982). Asian families. In M. McGoldrick et al. (eds.), *Ethnicity and Family Therapy*. New York: Guilford Press.

Shostak, A. B. (1987). Singlehood. In M. B. Sussman & S. K. Steinmetz (eds.), *Handbook of Marriage and the Family*. New York: Plenum.

Silbert, M. H. (1986). The effects on juveniles of being used for prostitution and pornography. Paper prepared for the Surgeon General's Workshop on Pornography & Public Health.

Silverstein, B. et al. (1986). The role of the mass media in promoting a thin standard of bodily attractiveness for women. *Sex Roles*, 14(9–10):519–532.

Silverstein C., & E. White. (1977). *The Joy of Gay Sex*. New York: Simon & Schuster Pocket Books.

Simenauer, J., & D. Carroll. (1982). *Singles: The New Americans*. New York: Simon & Schuster.

Simmons, P. D. (1986). *A Theological Response to Fundamentalism on the Abortion Issue*. Washington, DC: Religious Coalition for Abortion Rights Educational Fund.

Simmons, P. D. (1987). *Personhood, the Bible and the Abortion Debate*. Washington, DC: Religious Coalition for Abortion Rights Educational Fund.

Singer, I. (1984a, 1984b, 1987). *The Nature of Love. Volumes 1–3*. Chicago: University of Chicago Press.

Singer, J. (1976). *Androgyny: Toward a New Theory of Sexuality*. Garden City, NY: Anchor Press/Doubleday.

Singer, P. & Wells, D. (1985). *Making Babies: The New Science and Ethics of Conception*. New York: Scribners.

Sisley, E., & B. Harris. (1978). *The Joy of Lesbian Sex*. New York: Simon & Schuster.

Slade, J. W. (1984). Violence in the hard-core pornographic film: A historical survey. *J. Communication*, 34(3):148–163.

Sloane, E. (1980). *The Biology of Women*. New York: Wiley.

Smilgis, M., C. Wallis, & M. Serrill. (1987, February 16).

"The Big Chill: Fear of AIDS: How heterosexuals are coping with a disease that can make sex deadly." *Time*, pp. 50–60.

Smith, B. (1978). *The American Way of Sex. An Informal History*. New York: Two Continents/Gemini.

Smith, J., & B. Bullough. (1975). Sexuality and the severely disabled person. *Amer. J. Nursing*, pp. 2194–2197.

Smith, J. R., & L. S. Smith. (1970). Co-marital sex and the sexual freedom movement. *J. Sex Res.*, 6:131–142.

Smith, J. R., & L. S. Smith (eds.). (1974). *Beyond Monogamy: Recent Studies of Sexual Alternatives in Marriage*. Baltimore: Johns Hopkins University Press.

Smolev, J. (1984). Male reproductive anatomy and physiology. In J. M. Swanson, & K. Forrest (eds.), *Men's Reproductive Health*. New York: Springer.

Soble, A. (1986). *Pornography: Marxism, Feminism, and the Future of Sexuality*. New Haven: Yale University Press.

Socarides, C. (1978). *Homosexuality*. New York: Jason Aronson.

Sorenseon, R. C. (1973). *Adolescent Sexuality in Contemporary America*. New York: World.

Spanier, G., & C. Cole. (1974). Comarital mate-sharing and family stability. *J. Sex Res.*, 10:21–31.

Spanier, G. B., & F. F. Furstenberg, Jr. (1987). Remarriage and reconstituted families. In M. B. Sussman & S. K. Steinmetz (eds.), *Handbook of Marriage and the Family*. New York: Plenum.

Spengler, A. (1977). Manifest sadomasochism of males: Results of an empirical study. *Archives Sexual Behavior*, 6:441–456.

Sperling, E. (1980, June). Psychosexual development and cryptorchidism. *Med. Aspects Human Sex.*, pp. 93–94.

Springer, S. P., & G. Deutsch. (1981). *Left Brain, Right Brain*. San Francisco: Freeman.

Stark, E. (1984, May). The unspeakable family secret. *Psychology Today*, 17:(5)38–46.

Starr, B. D., & M. Bakur Weiner. (1981). *The Starr-Weiner Report on Sex and Sexuality in the Mature Years*. Briarcliff Manor, NY: Stein & Day.

Stayton, W. R. (1980). A theory of sexual orientation: The universe as a turn-on. *Topics Clinical Nursing*, 1(4):1–7.

Stayton, W. R. (1985). Religion and adolescent sexuality. *Seminars Adoles. Med.*, 1(2):131–137.

Stayton, W. R. (1989). A theology for sexual pleasure. *Amer. Baptist Q.*, 8(2):94–108.

Stein, M. L. (1974). *Lovers, Friends, Slaves: Nine Male Sexual Types: Their Psycho-Sexual Transactions with Call Girls*. New York: Berkley/Putnam.

Steinem, G. (1980). Erotica and pornography: A clear and present difference. In L. Lederer (ed.), *Take Back the Night: Women on Pornography*. New York: Morrow.

Sternberg, R. J. (1988). *The Triangle of Love: Intimacy, Passion, Commitment*. New York: Basic Books.

Sternhell, C. (1987, May 3). Ice and fire, intercourse. *New York Times Book Review*, pp. 3, 50.

Stewart, F., et al. (1979). *My Body My Health: The Concerned Woman's Guide to Gynecology*. New York: Wiley.

Stiller, R. (1963, July). Common prostate problems. *Sexology*, pp. 817–819.

Stock, W. E., & J. H. Geer. (1982). A study of fantasy-based sexual arousal in women. *Archives Sexual Behavior*, 11(1):33–45.

Stokes, B. (1980, December). Men and family planning. *Worldwatch Paper 41*.

Stoller, R. J. (1979). *Sexual Excitement: The Dynamics of Erotic Life*. New York: Pantheon.

Storms, M. (1980). Theories of sexual orientation. *J. Personality Social Psych.* 38:783–792.

Story, M. D. (1986). Factors affecting the incidence of partner sexual abuse among university students. An unpublished paper.

Strodtman, L., & R. Knopf. (1983). *Sexual Health and Diabetes*. Ann Arbor: University of Michigan, Michigan Diabetes Research and Training Center.

Strong, C. (1983). The tiniest newborns. *Hastings Center Report*, 13(1):14–19.

Stubin-Stein, R., & C. Debrovner. (1975, March). Psychological aspects of vaginal examination. *Med. Aspects Human Sex.*, 9(3):163 ff.

Sue, D. (1979). Erotic fantasies of college students during coitus. *J. Sex Res.*, 15:299–305.

Sullivan, L. (1985). *Information for the Female to Male Crossdresser and Transsexual*. San Francisco: L. Sullivan.

Sutherland, P. (1987, April 7). "I want sex—just like you." [*Village*] *Voice*, pp. 25–27.

Tabbutt, J. E. (1987). Childhood sexual learning. Unpublished independent study paper, the Human Sexuality Program, New York University.

Taguchi, O., et al. (1984). Timing and irreversibility of Mullerian duct inhibition in the embryonic reproductive tract of the human male. *Develop. Biology*, 106:394–398.

Tannahill, R. (1980). *Sex in History*. New York: Stein & Day.

Tavris, C., & S. Sadd. (1977). *The Redbook Report on Female Sexuality*. New York: Dell.

Taylor, G. (1987, October 5). Herpes victim seeks $1.3 million from his ex-wife's lover. (Smith v. Jones) (Texas). *National Law J.*, p. 8.

Taylor, G. R. (1970). *Sex in History*. New York: Harper & Row.

Taylor, R. (1982). *Having Love Affairs*. Buffalo, NY: Prometheus Books.

Taylor, S. (1987, May 5). Justices refine standard in determining obscenity. *New York Times*, p. B5.

Taylor, S. (1988, August 9). Curbs for minors seeking abortion upheld on appeal. *New York Times*, pp. A1, A13.

Tennov, D. (1979). *Love and Limerence: The Experience of Being in Love*. Briarcliff Manor, NY: Stein & Day.

Terris, M., et al. (1974). Relation of circumcision to cancer of the cervix. *Amer. J. Obstetrics Gynecology* 117: 1056–1066.

Thayer, N. S. T., et al. (1987, March). Report of the Task Force on Changing Patterns of Sexuality and Family Life. *The Voice* (Newark, NJ: Episcopal Church).

Thoman, E,. et al. (1972). Neonate-mother interaction during breast feeding. *Developmental Psychology*, 6: 110–118.

Thomas, E. (1986, May 19). Growing pains at 40. *Time*, pp. 22-43.

Thompson, A. P. (1983). Extramarital sex: A review of the research literature. *J. Sex Res.*, 19(1):1–22.

Thompson, E. H., & P. A. Gongla. (1983). Single-parent families: In the mainstream of American society. In E. D. Macklin & R. H. Rubin (eds.), *Contemporary Families and Alternative Lifestyles: Handbook on Research and Theory*. Beverly Hills, CA: Sage.

Thompson, L., & G. Spanier. (1978). Influence of parents, peers, and partners on the contraceptive use of college men and women. *J. Marriage & Family*, 40(3): 481–491.

Tietze, C. (1981). *Induced Abortion: A World View*. New York: The Population Council.

Timmerman, J. (1986). *The Mardi Gras Syndrome: Rethinking Christian Sexuality*. New York: Crossroad.

Tollison, C. D., & H. E. Adams. (1979). *Sexual Disorders: Treatment, Theory, Research*. New York: Gardner Press.

Trethowan, W. H., & M. F. Colton. (1965). The couvade syndrome. *British J. Psychiatry*, 111:57–66.

Tripp, C. (1975). *The Homosexual Matrix*. New York: McGraw-Hill.

Trotter, R. J. (1986, September). The three faces of love. *Psychology Today*, pp. 46–54.

Trussell, J., & K. Kost. (1987, December). Contraceptive failure in the United States: A critical review of the literature. *Studies Family Planning*, 12(5):246–249.

Turner, E. S. (1955). *A History of Courting*. New York: Dutton.

United Presbyterian Church in the U.S.A. (1970). *Sex-uality and the Human Community*. Philadelphia: United Presbyterian Church.

U.S. Surgeon General's Report. (1986). *Pornography and Public Health*. Prepared by E. P. Mulvey & J. L. Haugaard. Washington, DC: U.S. Dept. of Health & Human Services.

Valverde, M. (1986). *Sex, Power and Pleasure*. New York: The Women's Press.

Vandenberg, S. (1972). Assortative mating, or who marries whom? *Behavior Genetics*, 2:127–158.

Vander Mey, B. J., & R. L. Neff. (1986). *Incest as Child Abuse: Research and Applications*. New York: Praeger.

Van Tassel, P. (1989, March 5). Rutgers panel seeks ways to assure gay rights. *New York Times*, pp. 1, 6.

Van Wyk, P. (1984). Psychosocial development of heterosexual, bisexual, and homosexual behavior. *Archives Sexual Behavior*, 13:505–544.

Vicinus, M. (ed.). (1972). *Suffer and Be Still: Women in the Victorian Age*. Bloomington: Indiana University Press.

Wade, R. (1979). *For Men about Abortion*. Boulder, Colorado: R. Wade (P.O. Box 4748, Boulder, CO 80306).

Walker, M. (1977). *Men Loving Men*. San Francisco: Gay Sunshine.

Wallerstein, E. (1980). *Circumcision: An American Health Fallacy*. New York: Springer.

Wallis, C. (1985, June 17). The magnesium connection. *Time*, p. 77.

Walster, E., & G. Walster. (1978). *A New Look at Love*. Reading, MA: Addison-Wesley.

Ward, E. (1985). *Father-Daughter Rape*. New York: Grove Press.

Ward, I. L. (1984). The prenatal stress syndrome: Current status. *Psychoneuroendocrinology*, 9:3–11.

Warner, C. (ed.). (1980). *Rape and Sexual Assault: Management and Intervention*. Germantown, MD: Aspen Systems Corporation.

Warren, P. (1974). *The Frontrunner*. New York: Bantam.

Watson, M. A. (1981). Sexually open marriages: Three perspectives. *Alternative Lifestyles*, 4(1):3–21.

Watson, R. E. L. (1983). Premarital cohabitation vs. traditional courtship: Their effects on subsequent marital adjustment. *Family Relations*, 32:139–147.

Watson, R. E L, & P. W. DeMeo. (1987). Premarital cohabitation vs. traditional courtship and subsequent marital adjustment: A replication and follow-up. *Family Relations*, 36:193-197.

Wattenberg, B. J. (1989, July 3). The changing face of out-of-wedlock births. *U.S. News & World Report*, p. 29.

Weinberg, T. S. (1987). Sadomasochism in the United States: A review of recent sociological literature. *J. Sex Res.*, 23(1):50–69.

Weinberg, T. S., & G. W. Levi Kamel. (1983). *S and M: Studies in Sadomasochism*. Buffalo, NY: Prometheus Press.

Weinrich, J. D. (1987). *Sexual Landscapes: Why We Are What We Are, Why We Love Whom We Love*. New York: Scribners.

Weinrich, J. D. (1988). The periodic table model of the gender transpositions: Part II. Limerent and lusty sexual attractions and the nature of bisexuality. *J. Sex Res.*, 24:113–129.

Weintraub, P. (1981). The brain: His and hers. *Discover*, 2(4):15–20.

Weis, D. L. (1983a). Affective reactions of women to their initial experience of coitus. *J. Sex Res.*, 19(3): 209–237.

Weis, D. L. (1983b). ''Open'' marriage and multilateral relationships: The emergence of nonexclusive models of the marital relationship. In E. D. Macklin & R. H. Rubin (eds.), *Contemporary Families and Alternative Lifestyles: Handbook on Research and Theory*. Beverly Hills CA: Sage.

Weis, D. L. (1985). The experience of pain during women's first sexual intercourse: Cultural mythology about female sexual initiation. *Archives Sexual Behavior*, 14(5):421–437.

Weisman, S. R. (1988, July 20). No more guarantees of a son's birth. *New York Times*, pp. A1 & A9.

Wells, B. (1983). Nocturnal orgasms: Females' perceptions of a ''normal'' sexual experience. *J. Sex Ed. & Therapy*, 9:32–38.

Wells, B. L. (1986). Predictors of female nocturnal orgasms. *J. Sex Res.*, 22(4):421–437.

Whelehan, P. E., & F. J. Moynihan. (1982). Secular celibacy as a reaction to sexual burnout. *J. Sex Ed. & Therapy*, 8(2):13–16.

White, W., & P. J. Spencer-Phillips. (1979, March 19). Recurrent vaginitis and oral sex. *Lancet*, 1(8116):621.

Williams, P., & M. Smith. (1979). Interview in ''The First Question.'' London: British Broadcasting System Science and Features Department film.

Wilson, J. D. (1979). Sex hormones and sexual behavior. *New Eng. J. Med.*, 300(22).

Winer, J. (1981, February 23). Huge disparities in jail time. *National Law J.*, 3(24):1,28–30.

Winick, C., & P. Kinsie. (1971). *The Lively Commerce*. Chicago: Quadrangle.

Winn, R. L., & N. Newton. (1982). Sexuality in aging: A study of 106 cultures. *Archives Sexual Behavior*, 11(4):283–298.

Wise, T. N. (1985). Fetishism—Etiology and treatment: A review from multiple perspectives. *Comprehensive Psychiatry*, 26:249–257.

Wiseman, J. P. (1985, Spring). Alcohol, eroticism and sexual performance: A social interactionist perspective. *J. Drug Issues*, 15(2):291–308.

Wiswell, T. E., et al. (1987). Declining frequency of circumcision: Implications for changes in the absolute incidence and male to female sex ratio of urinary tract infections in early infancy. *Pediatrics*, 79(3):338.

Wolfe, J., & V. Baker. (1980). Characteristics of imprisoned rapists and circumstances of the rape. In C. G. Warner (ed.), *Rape and Sexual Assault*. Germantown, MD: Aspen Systems Corporation.

Wolff, C. (1971). *Love Between Women*. New York: Harper & Row.

Women Speak Out about Abortion. (1983). Miller Place, NY: Rose Soma/Americans United To Save Abortion (P.O. Box A-W).

Woodhead, J. C., & J. R. Murph. (1985). Influence of chronic illness and disability on adolescent sexual development. *Seminars Adoles. Med.*, 1(3):171–176.

Woodward, K. L. (1987, February 23). Gays in the clergy. *Newsweek*, pp. 58–60.

Worth, D., & R. Rodríguez. (1987, January–February). Latina women and AIDS. *SIECUS Report*, 15(3):5–7.

Yankelovich, D. (1981). New rules in American life: Searching for self-fulfillment in a world turned upside down. *Psychology Today*, 15(4):35–91.

Yarber, W. (1987). *AIDS: What Young Adults Should Know. A Student Guide, and An Instructor's Guide*. Reston, VA: American Alliance for Health, Physical Education, Recreation & Dance, 1987.

Yates, A. (1980). The effect of commonly accepted parenting practices on erotic development. In J.-M. Samson (ed.), *Childhood and Sexuality: Proceedings of the International Symposium*. Montreal: Editions Etudes Vivantes.

Yi, J-c. (1980). Annotated notes on *Tian-xia-zhi-tao-tan: Qi-sun Ba-yi. J. Hunan Traditional Chinese Medical College*. Special series on the studies of Ma-wang-tui Medical Books. 1:27–32.

Young, W. (1970). Prostitution. In J. Douglas (ed.), *Observations of Deviance*. New York: Random House.

Youth Suicide National Report. (1989). Gay teenagers and suicide, pp. 16–32.

Zaviačič, M. (1990). Personal communication with R. T. Francoeur about clitoral anatomy and homologies.

Zaviačič, M., et al. (1988a). Female expulsions evoked

by local digital stimulation of the G-Spot: Differences in the response patterns. *J. Sex Res.,* 24:311–318.

Zaviačič, M., et al. (1988b). Concentrations of fructose in female ejaculate and urine: A comparative biochemical study. *J. Sex Res.,* 24:319–325.

Zellman, G., et al. (1979). Adolescent expectations for dating relationships: Consensus and conflict between the sexes. Paper presented at the American Psychological Association Meeting, New York City.

Zilbergeld, B. (1978). *Male Sexuality: A Guide to Sexual Fulfillment.* Boston: Little, Brown.

Zilbergeld, B., & C. R. Ellison. (1980). Desire discrepancies and arousal problems in sex therapy. In S. R. Leiblum & L. A. Pervin (eds.), *Principles and Practice of Sex Therapy.* New York: Guilford Press.

Zimmer, D. (1983). Interaction patterns and communication skills in sexually distressed and normal couples. *J. Sex Marital Therapy,* 9:251–265.

Zuckerman Overvold, A. (1988). *Surrogate Parenting.* New York: Pharos Books.

Credits

Source Notes

Ann Landers. Creators Syndicate. The size of a man.

Associated Press. Media General-Associated Press poll on pornography. Copyright © 1987 by Associated Press. Reprinted by permission of Associated Press.

Breslow, N., L. Evans, & J. Langley. Men and women contacted through sadomasochistic clubs and magazines. *Archives of Sexual Behavior*. Copyright © 1985 by *Archives of Sexual Behavior*, vol. no. 14, pg. 315. Reprinted by permission of Plenum Publishing Corporation.

Davis, J. A., & T. Smith. *General Social Surveys, 1972–1984: Cumulative Data*. Copyright © 1984 by Yale University, Roper Center for Public Opinion Research.

Family Life Educator, Volume 4, Number 2 (Winter 1985), coordinated by ETR Associates, Santa Cruz, CA. Adapted with permission. For information on other publications, call toll-free 1–800–321–4407.

Fein, Bruce. Don't put real families in shadows. *USA Today*. Copyright © 1989 by Bruce Fein. Reprinted by permission of Bruce Fein.

Grayson, Deborah Eve. "My Want You Eyes." *Breath Marks in the Wind, a book of erotic poetry and illustrations*. Copyright © 1988 by Breath Marks/IDF, Inc.

Grayson, Deborah Eve. "Safe." *Breath Marks in the Wind, a book of erotic poetry and illustrations*. Copyright © 1988 by Breath Marks/IDF, Inc.

Hatcher, Robert. Putting the voluntary risks of contraception into perspective. *Contraceptive Technology*. © Irvington Press.

Reprinted by permission of Robert Hatcher.

"i like my body when it is with your" is reprinted from TULIPS & CHIMNEYS by E. E. Cummings, edited by George James Firmage, by permission of Liveright Publishing Corporation. Copyright 1923, 1925 and renewed 1951, 1953 by E. E. Cummings. Copyright © 1973, 1976 by the Trustees for the E. E. Cummings Trust. Copyright © 1973, 1976 by George James Firmage. Reprinted by permission of Liveright Publishing Corporation.

Medical Aspects of Human Sexuality. Current thinking on intimacy. Reprinted with permission of *Medical Aspects of Human Sexuality*. © Cahners Publishing Company. Published March 1983.

Moore, M. M. How women invite intimacy. *Ethology and Sociobiology*, vol. no. 6, pp. 237–247. Copyright © 1985 by Elsevier Science Publishing Company. Reprinted by permission of Elsevier Science Publishing Company, Inc.

National Institute of Child Health and Human Development. Survey on Lifestyles of Single Women. Copyright © 1986 by National Institute of Child Health and Human Development. Reprinted by permission.

Oxford English Dictionary. Definition of "love". Copyright © 1990 by Oxford University Press. Reprinted by permission of Oxford University Press.

Penthouse Forum. Sex education in Norway. Reprinted by permission of *Penthouse Forum*. Copyright © 1990.

Pietropinto, A. Sex and the elderly. *Medical Aspects of Human*

Sexuality. Reprinted with permission from *Medical Aspects of Human Sexuality*. © Cahners Publishing Company. Published June 1987.

Pietropinto, A. Survey; Sex Appeal. *Medical Aspects of Human Sexuality*. Reprinted with permission from *Medical Aspects of Human Sexuality*. © Cahners Publishing Company. Published March 1983.

Simonauer, Jacqueline & David Carroll. *Singles: The New Americans*. Copyright © 1982 by Jacqueline Simonauer and David Carroll. Reprinted by permission of Simon & Schuster, Inc.

Stoddard, Thomas B. Bring families out of shadows. *USA Today*. Copyright © 1989 by *USA Today*. Reprinted by permission of Thomas B. Stoddard.

US News and World Report, October 12, 1987, pg. 63. AIDS: When fear takes charge. Copyright © 1987 by *US News and World Report*. Reprinted by permission of *US News and World Report*.

A Woman's New World Dictionary. Definition of *love*. Copyright © 1973 by 51% Publications.

Photographs and Figures

Chapter 1 American Sexual Customs

page 2: © Elliott Erwitt/Magnum Photos. *page 5*: Library of Congress. *page 7*: U.S. Patent Office. *page 9*: Bettmann Archives. *page 12*: National Police Gazette. *page 13*: The State Historical Society of Wisconsin. *page 16*: Reprinted from *The Kinsey Institute for Research in Sex, Gender, and Reproduction Guidebook*. 1984. Indiana University. *page 19*: Brown Brothers. Stock Photos. *page 20*: © Charles Trainer/Globe Photos, Inc. *page 22*: © Burt Uzzle/Picture Group. *page 23*: Equinox (Oxford) Ltd. and first published in *Manwatching* by Desmond Morris, Jonathan Cape, Ltd., London and Harry N. Abrams, Inc. NY.

Chapter 2 Sexual Customs in Other Cultures

page 28: © Seth Hammer. *page 31*: Art Resource/Giraudon. *page 33*: © Bernard Pierre Wolf/Photo Researchers, Inc. *page 36*: © Seth Hammer. *page 39*: Wide World Photos. *page 40*: Healing Tao Center. *page 43*: (both) © Terry Lennon. *page 44*: © K. Thomas.

Chapter 3 Sexual Values and Moral Development

page 50: © de Ardrade/Magnum Photos, Inc. *page 53*: Art Resource. *page 57*: Art Resource. *page 58*: El Prado, Madrid, Spain.

Chapter 4 Our Gender Development Before Birth

page 70: Mary Cassatt. "The Caress," 1902, oil on canvas, 83. 4 × 69. 4 cm. National Museum of American Art, gift of William T. Evans. *page 76*: Adapted from J. Money, *Gay, Straight, and in-Between: The Sexology of Erotic Orientation*. New York: Oxford University Press, 1988. *page 93-L*: © Chuck Ashley/Photo Researchers, Inc. *page 93-R*: © Myron Papiz/Photo Researchers, Inc. *page 94*: Sidney Harris. *page 98*: Dawn DeLozier.

Chapter 5 Sexuality in Childhood and Adolescence

page 104: Edgar Degas (1834–1917). "The Young Spartans," National Gallery, London. Photo courtesy of The Bridgeman Art Library. *page 107*: © Ursula Markus/Photo Researchers, Inc. *page 108*: © Warren D. Jorgensen/Photo Researchers, Inc. *page 109*: © Hella Hammid/Photo Researchers, Inc. *page 110-B*: New York Public Library. *page 112*: © Ursula Markus/Photo Researchers, Inc. *page 126*: © Joel Gordon, 1978.

Chapter 6 Our Sexual Anatomy

page 140: Culver Pictures. *page 144*: The Bettmann Archive. *page 147-L*: Multi-focus. *page 147-C*: Multi-focus. *page 147-R*: Multi-focus. *page 152*: Macmillan Publishing Company. *page 157-L*: © Henry H. Bagish/Anthro-Photo. *page 157-R*: Art Resource. *page 161-TL*: © Justin Hill. *page 161-TR*: © Justin Hill. *page 161-B*: © Justin Hill. *page 162*: Macmillan Publishing Company.

Chapter 7 Our Sexual Responses

page 168: Utamaro. "Poem of the Pillow," Victoria and Albert Museum, London. Photo courtesy of The Bridgeman Art Library.

Chapter 8 Pregnancy and Birth

page 202: Georges de la Tour. "The New Born," Musée des Beaux-Arts, Rennes. Photo courtesy of The Bridgeman Art Library. *page 207*: all © Lennart Nilsson. *page 219*: Deborah Alley, RDMS (Registered Diagnostic Medical Sonographer), Department of Maternal-Fetal Medicine, Children's Hospital of the King's Daughters, Norfolk, VA. Reprinted by permission of Dr. Mary Steichen Calderone. *page 221*: © Robin Schwartz. *page 223*: The Cleveland Health Museum. *page 224*: United Press International, Inc. *page 225*: © Irene Barki, 1981/Woodfin Camp & Associates. *page 229-L*: © Tequila Minsky. *page 229-R*: United States Department of Labor. *page 231*: United Media. *page 232*: Marlette. *page 233*: © Topham/The Image Works. *page 234*: The Bettmann Archives. *page 235*: Warren Zapol, M.D. Massachusetts General Hospital. Department of Anesthesia. Boston, MA.

Chapter 9 Contraception: Shared Responsibilities

page 238: Planned Parenthood. *page 243*: © John Schultz/PAR/NYC, Inc. *page 247*: © Rhoda Sidney/Monkmeyer Press. *page 251*: © Flanzy Chodkowski/Kitchen Cards. *page 253*: Courtesy Wisconsin Pharmaceutical Company. *page 255*: Courtesy Ortho Pharmaceutical Corporation. *page 256*: Courtesy Apothecus, Inc. *page 258*: Courtesy Whitehall Laboratories. *page 260*: Prentif Cervical Cap. *page 267-T*: William M. Foss, M.D., FACS, Assistant Clinical Professor of Surgery, University of California Medical School, Irvine, CA. *page 267-B*: Macmillan Publishing Company. *page 271*: Adapted from E. F. Jones et al (1986), "Teenage Pregnancy in Industrialized Countries." New Haven, CT: Yale University Press.

Chapter 10 Abortion: Our Shared Responsibilities

page 278: Henri Matisse. "Venus," 1952, paper on canvas, National Gallery of Art, Washington, DC. Alisa Mellon Bruce Fund. *page 284*: © Fitzpatrick/Reuters/Bettman Newsphotos. *page 289*: Copyright Steve Bensen. *page 291*: © Robert Hauser/Comstock.

Chapter 11 Your Sexual Health

page 300: "Krishna with the Cow Girl's Clothes," by an anonymous Garhwal artist, c. 1790 watercolor. Victoria and Albert Museum, London. Photo courtesy of The Bridgeman Art Library. *page 303*: © Kathy Bendo. *page 305*: © Blair Seitz/Photo Researchers, Inc. *page 316*: Randolph H. Gunthrie, MD. *page 319*: © Ken Karp/Ken Karp Photography.

Chapter 12 Reducing Your Risk for Sexual Diseases

page 326: © Erich Hartmann/Magnum Photos, Inc. *page 332*: Public Domain. *page 333*: American Social Health Association.

*I*ndex

A

Abortion
  aftercare
    emotional care, 297
    medical care, 297
  antiabortion movement, 24, 25
  beginning of human life issue,
    285–286
  death from illegal abortion, 281
  decision-making about, 290–293
    choosing facility for, 292–293
    male role in, 291
    psychological aspects, 290
  definition of, 280
  dilation and evacuation, 296
  historical view
    ancient era, 280
    religious views, 280–281
  intra-amniotic infusion, 296–297
  legal aspects
    pre-1970s, 282
    Roe v. Wade, 282–283
  minor rights, 287
  as national dilemma, 298
  options to, 289–290
  poor, rights of, 287–288

  postcoital hormonal contraception,
    293–295
    DES pill, 293
    RU 486, 293, 295
  prochoice movement, 283–285
  Roe v. Wade, 22
  sex selection and, 288–289
  statistical information, 281
  third world and, 288
  vacuum curettage, 295–296
Abortion pill. *See* RU 486
About Your Sexuality program, 129
Absolutist worldview. *See* Fixed
    worldview
Abstinence, 250
Acquired immune deficiency syndrome.
    See AIDS
Acrotomophilia, 532
Acyclovir, 347
Adam and Eve, 56
Adam Plan
  feminization in brain, 90
  prenatal gender differentiation, 76,
    78, 79, 80
Adjustment, to puberty, 123
Adolescence, definition of, 114
Adolescentilism, 532

Adolescents
  gay teens, 449–450
  See also Puberty.
Adolescent sexuality
  decision-making about sex, 124–125
  legal rights of adolescents, 125–126
Adoption, as option to abortion, 290
Adultery, legal aspects, 585–586
Affectional orientation, 432
A-frame orgasms, women, 185
Afterbirth, 222–223
Agape, 378
Aging
  health aspects
    menopause, 504–505
    prostate enlargement, 505
  midlife crisis, 503
  social aspects
    desexing of elderly, 502
    elderly abuse, 503
    feminization of poverty, 503
    males, shortage of, 503
Aging and sexuality
  erection aids, 505–506
  erection problems, 505
  homosexuals, 499, 501–502
  limited research on, 498

Aging and sexuality (*Continued*)
  problems of, 499, 502
  sexual satisfaction, 498
  survey on, 500–501
  vaginal lubrication and, 504
AIDS
  AIDS-related complex, 361–362
  costs of, 372–373
  education and, 371
  fear of, 562
  global implications, 373
  hot line, 363
  human immunodeficiency virus
      (HIV), 355–361
    geographic origin of, 356
    immune system and, 358–361
    particle stage, 356
    provirus stage, 356
    reproductive stage, 356
    sero positive persons, 361
    spread of, 356–358
    susceptibility to, 360–361
  issues related to, 25
  knowing partner, importance of, 369
  knowledge-behavior gap and,
      369–371
  opportunistic infections, 358, 361
    Kaposi's sarcoma, 358
    pneumocystic pneumonia, 358
  public health issues, 371–372
  public policies and, 368
  risk reduction, 365–368
  risky behaviors related to, 364–365,
      368
  statistical information, 373
  terminal stage, signs of, 361
  tests for
    ELISA test, 362
    false negative results, 362–363
    false positive results, 363
    information about testing, 363
    Western Blot test, 363
  women's attitudes/behavior and,
      370–371
Alcohol use
  as aphrodisiac, 385
  HIV and, 360–361, 365
  prenatal effects, 215
Alpha-fetoprotein tests, 220
Amenorrhea, 122
American Psychiatric Association
    (APA), on homosexuality, 442
Amniocentesis, 218–219
  indications for, 218
Amniotic fluid, 211
  labor and, 222
Amoral beings, 61

Amyl nitrate, as aphrodisiac, 385
Anabaptists, 486
Anal sex, 401
  analingus, 401
  health precautions, 401
  homoerotic vs. heteroerotic, 441
  legal aspects, 442, 587
Anal stage, 131, 132
Ananga Ranga, 396
Ancients
  circumcision, 163
  homoerotic behavior, 442
  view of abortion, 280
  view of love, 406
  view of sex, 54
  view of sexual desire, 378
Andelin, Helen, 24
Androgen insensitivity syndrome, 97
Androgens, synthetic, 310
Androgyny, 524
Anencephaly, 219–220
Anovulation, 229
Antibiotics, discovery of, 10, 11
Antibodies, 358, 360
Any Man Can (Harman and Fithian), 190
Aphrodisiacs, 385–386
  alcohol, 385
  amyl nitrate, 385
  cocaine, 385
  foods/herbs, 385
  marijuana, 385
  yohimbe, 386
Apocrine gland, 144
Apocrine glands, 144, 198, 199
Areola, breast, 153
Aristotle, view of abortion, 280
Arousal phase difficulties, inhibited
    sexual arousal, 573
Arranged marriage
  definition of, 33
  in Hinduism, 37–38
  Islamic, 33–34
Artificial insemination, 230–231
Arts, sexual customs and, 18
Asphixophilia, 532
Asymptomatic infection, 328–329
Augustine of Hippo, 54
Autonomous stage, in moral
    development, 62
Autopedophilia, 532
Aversion therapy, paraphilias, 545
AZT, 372–373

B

Baby boom, sex ratio imbalances, 13
Baby M case, 234–235, 586–587

Balanitis, 322
Bartholin's glands, 147
Basal body temperature method, 264
Bauman, Robert E., 450, 456
Beal v. Doe, 287
Belloti v. Baird, 287
Benkert, K.M., 434
Berdache, 100
Berne, Eric, 134
Billings' method, 264
Biological theories, of gender
    orientation, 445
Bio-psycho-cultural phenomenon,
    human sexuality as, 4
Birth control, historical view, 10, 11
Birth control pill, 261–263
  combination pill, 262–263
    complications, 262–263
    cost, 262
    noncontraceptive benefits, 263
    precautions, 263
    proper use of, 262
  development of, 11
  progestine-only pills, 262, 263
Birthing clinics, 225–226
Birth Without Violence (Leboyer), 225
Bisexuality, 451
  bisexual marriages, 485
  issue of, 451
Blake, William, 458
Blended orgasms, women, 185
Blood transfusion, AIDS, 357–358
Bloody show, 221–222
Body chromosomes, 77
Body image, poor, sexual difficulty and,
    560
Bondage and dominance, 538–541
Bordellos, 627
Boswell, John, 434, 443, 444
Bowers v. Hardwick, 442, 587, 593
Brain
  gender differentiation, 86, 88–92
    defeminization in brain, 90
    feminization in brain, 90
    masculinization axis, 91
    neural template hypothesis, 89
  lack of nurturance and, 413
  limbic system, 198
  pleasure/pain processing, 413
  puberty, 114
  split brain and puberty, 91–92
Breast cancer
  diagnosis of, 315
  risk factors, 316
  treatment options, 315
Breast disorders
  breast cancer, 315–316

fibroadenomas, 315
fibrocystic disorder, 315
mammogram, 315
Breast feeding, 228–229
production of breast milk, 229
Breasts
anatomical aspects, 153–154
masturbation and, 392
in pregnancy, 213
self-examination of
female, 312–314
male, 318–319
vasocongestion, excitement phase,
177
Brothels, 627
Brown, Lesley, 232
Buddhism, 39
Bundling, practice of, 10
Burton, Sir Richard, 396

C

Call girls, 627
Cancer
breast cancer, 315–316
penile cancer, 318
testicular cancer, 318
Candidiasis, 340–341
symptoms of, 340–341
treatment of, 341
Cardopedal reflex, orgasm phase and,
182
Care perspective, moral development
and women, 64, 65
Carriers, of disease, 328
Case law, 583
Catharsis research model, pornography,
636–637
Celibacy, 470
definition of, 7, 470
as religious practice, 7
time span in, 470
Cell-mediated immunity, 358
Censorship
art, 593
Comstock Prohibition, 15
obscenity, legal criteria, 15
pornography, 642–647
Certified nurse midwives, 226
Cervical cap, 259–260
complications, 260
cost, 259
effectiveness, 259
noncontraceptive benefits, 260
precautions, 260
proper use, 260
Cervical mucus method, 264

Cervicitis, 335–337
Cervix, 151
Cesarean section, 226–228
forced Cesarean controversy, 227–228
incidence of, 227
indications for, 226
rise in use, 227
C film. *See* Vaginal contraceptive film
Chador, 32–33, 35
Chancre, in syphilis, 339
Childbirth
afterbirth, 222–223
birthing clinics, 225–226
Cesarean section, 226–228
forceps-assisted delivery, 226
home birth, 226
midwives, 226
postpartum depression, 218
prepared childbirth, 223–224
Lamaze delivery, 224
Leboyer delivery, 225
stages of labor, 221–223
Childbirth Without Fear (Dick-Reed), 223
Childhood sexuality
infants, 106
masturbation, 108–109
messages from parents about sex,
107
research limitations, 106
sexual dysfunction in adulthood and,
113
sibling sexual play, 111
socialization factors, 107–108
sociosexual play, 109–111
touch, importance of, 112–113, 114
Child Protection Act, 592, 638
China
homosexuality, 40, 42
marriage, 41–42
view of sex, 39–41
western influences, 42
Chlamydia, 321, 335–336
risk factors, 337
sterility and, 336
symptoms of, 335–336
Chordocentesis, 219
Chorionic villi biopsy, 219
Chrematisophilia, 532
Christianity
homosexuality as issue, 443–444
view of abortion, 280–281
view of love, 406–407
Chromosomal abnormalities
androgen insensitivity syndrome, 97
Klinefelter syndrome, 96–97
Turner syndrome, 96
variations in, 97

Chromosomes
body chromosomes, 77
gender chromosomes, 77
of ovum and sperm, 77–78
prenatal gender differentiation, 75–79
Churches, sex education programs, 129,
130
Cigarette smoking, prenatal effects, 215
Circumcision
female circumcision, 164–165
historical view, 163
male circumcision, 163–164
trends related to, 164
Cleanliness, obsession about, 384
Clergy, gay clergy, 451
Clitorectomy, 7, 164, 165
Clitoris
anatomical aspects, 147, 149
erection, excitement phase, 176
during plateau phase, 180
Closed marriage, 475
Cocaine, as aphrodisiac, 385
Cohabitation, 478–480
college cohabitors, 479
domestic partners, legal definition,
491
later divorced and, 479
legal aspects, 586
palimony, 479–480
statistical information, 478–479
Colonial era, attitude about sex, 9
Colostrum, 213, 229
Combination pill, 262–263
complications, 262–263
cost, 262
noncontraceptive benefits, 263
precautions, 263
proper use of, 262
Comfort, Alex, 24, 393
Coming out process, gay person, 456
Communal living, group marriage, 485
Communication, guidelines for good
communication, 383–384
Comstock, Anthony, 15
Comstock Law, 582, 588, 644
Comstock Prohibition, 15
Conception
ectopic pregnancy, 206
fertilization, 204, 206
Concubinage, 40
Condoms, 250–253
AIDS prevention, 366–368
breaking during intercourse, 253
breaking of, 368
cost, 251
effectiveness, 251
female condom, 253–254

Condoms (*Continued*)
　historical view, 10
　noncontraceptive benefits, 253
　precautions, 252
　proper use of, 252
　raising issue for use, 251
　side effects, 252–253
　slang expressions, 250
Confucianism, view of sex, 40–41
Confucius, 39
Consensual wife, 487
Consenting adult laws, 21, 586, 594
Conservation, Reagan era, 25
Constitution, women's rights and, 14
Contraceptives
　abstinence, 250
　basal body temperature method, 264
　birth control pills, 261–263
　cervical cap, 259–260
　cervical mucus method, 264
　condoms, 250–253
　contraceptive sponge, 258–259
　decision-making about, 243–244, 268
　definition of, 240
　diaphragm, 257–258
　effectiveness of, 247–249
　erotophiles vs. erotophobes and, 244
　future view, new methods, 274–275
　historical view, 240–242
　intrauterine device (IUD), 261
　legal aspects, 591
　Reality (TM), female condom,
　　253–254
　reasons for lack of use, 244–246
　rhythm method, 263
　shared responsibility in, 247
　spermicidal foams, 254–255
　sympto-thermal method, 264–265
　teenage pregnancy, 269–274
　tubal ligation, 265–266
　unreliable methods, 268
　vaginal contraceptive film, 256–257
　vaginal suppositories, 255
　vasectomy, 266–267
Contraceptive sponge, 258–259
　complications, 259
　cost, 258
　effectiveness, 258
　noncontraceptive benefits, 259
　precautions, 259
　proper use, 259
Contractual wife, 487
Contragestive, 293
Conventional morality, in moral
　　development, 62
Copper T380A IUD, 21
Coprophilia, 532

Core gender identity, 433
Corpora cavernosa, 158
Corpus spongiosum, 158
Couples, 474–480
　cohabitation, 478–480
　　palimony, 479–480
　　statistical information, 478–479
　marriage
　　closed marriage, 475
　　extamarital sex, 475, 477–478
　　monogamy, 474–475
Courtly love, 407
Courtship, historical patterns, 8–10
Coutts, R.L., 427
Couvade, 217
Covenants, 488
Cowper's gland, 163, 178, 182
Creative singlehood, 474
Cremasteric muscle, 160
Criminalization, prostitution, 633–634
Cross-cultural views
　Chinese, 39–42
　female circumcision
　　clitorectomy, 165
　　infibulation, 165
　Hindu world, 35–39
　Islamic world, 30–35
　jealousy, 425–426
　Latin cultures, 43–47
　teenage pregnancy, 269
　transvestism, 520
　See also individual cultures.
Crossdressing, 518–519
　as fetish, 541, 542
　forced in S & M scene, 540
Cryptorchidism, 321–322
　causes of, 321
　treatment of, 322
Culture
　guilt cultures, 31–32
　shame cultures, 32
Cunnilingus, 398, 400
Cystitis, 311–312
　honeymoon cystitis, 311
　symptoms of, 311
　treatment of, 311
Cysts, 312

D

Dalkon Shield IUD, 261
Date rape, 602–606
　common factors in, 605–606
　definition of, 602–603
　frequency of, 603–604
　male coercion, 604
　reasons for, 604–605

Dating, 410–412
　past practices, 410
　present methods of, meeting people,
　　410–412
Dating services, 411
Decriminalization, prostitution, 634–635
Depo-Provera, 534
Dermatoses, 322
DES. *See* Diethylstilbestrol
Desire phase, 171, 173
Desire phase difficulties
　inhibited sexual desire, 572
　sexual aversion, 570
　sexual desire conflicts, 572
DES pill, 293
Developmental disability, 511
DHT deficiency, 98–99
Diabetes, 508
Diaphragm, 257–258
　cost, 257
　effectiveness, 257
　noncontraceptive benefits, 257
　precautions, 258
　proper use, 257
Dickinson, Robert L., 17
Dick-Reed, Dr. Grantley, 223
Diethylstilbestrol (DES)
　information source in, 317
　prenatal effects, 215
　sons/daughters of mothers taking, 317
Dihydrotestosterone (DHT), 86
　DHT deficiency, 98–99
Dilation and curettage (D & C)
　abortion, 295–296
　complications of, 296
Dilation and evacuation, procedure in,
　296
Dimorphism, 89, 91
Disabled
　developmental disability, 511
　hearing impairments, 510
　impact of disability, 507—508
　media attention and, 507
　medical conditions of, 508
　mental retardation, 511
　sexual enrichment aids for, 510–511
　visual impairments, 509
Divorce, 489–490
　sexual relationships, post-divorce, 490
　trends related to, 489–490
Doctors, choosing right doctor, 322–323
Domestic partners, legal definition, 491
Douching, 268
Down syndrome, amniocentesis,
　218–219
Dowry
　antidowery laws, 38

definition of, 38
in Hinduism, 38
Drag queens, 517
Dreams, erotic dreams, 386
Drug use
prenatal effects, 215
sexual difficulty and, 559
Dualism, 378
Dual-paycheck marriage, 475
Dysmenorrhea, 121–122
Dysparenuia, 575–576

E

Eastern Orthodox Church, view of
abortion, 281
Eclampsia, 217
Ectopic pregnancy, 151, 206
Edema, 174
Edwards, Dr., 232
Ego, 130
Egocentric stage, in moral development,
61
Eidos, 641
Eiseley, Loren, 459
Ejaculation, 163
control of, 188–190
ejaculation reflex, 195, 197
female ejaculation, 186–187
nocturnal emission, 197–198
phases of
emission phase, 188, 195
propulsion phase, 188, 195
retrograde ejaculation, 188
Elderly abuse, 503
ELISA test, AIDS testing, 362
Ellis, Havelock, 16, 184
Emancipation Acts and Married
Women's Acts, 586
Embryo
amniotic fluid, 211
development of, 210
placenta, 210–211
umbilical cord, 211
Embryo adoption, 233
Emission phase, ejaculation, 188, 195
Endometriosis, 230, 310–311
symptoms of, 310
treatment of, 310–311
Ephebophilia, 542
Epidemics
historical view, 354–355
See also AIDS.
Epididymis, anatomical aspects, 161
Epididymitis, 321, 337
cause of, 321
symptoms of, 321

Episcopal Church, homosexuality as
issue, 442–443
Episiotomy, 222
Equal Employment Opportunity
Commission, 14
Equal Rights Amendment, 21, 25
Erection
female, 174
male, 174, 177–178, 182
older men, 505
Erection aids, 505–506
implanted aids, 505–506
nonsurgical aid, 505
Erikson's theory
psychosexual development, 132–134
identity crisis, 133–134
stages in, 133
Eros, 378
Erotica, versus pornography, 639–640
Erotic dreams, 386
Erotic orientation, 432
Erotic Stimulus Pathway Model, 193
Erotophilia, 135
use of contraceptives and, 244
Erotophobia, 135, 381
use of contraceptives and, 244
Escorts, 627
Estrogen, 116, 118
Estrogen replacement therapy,
menopause and, 504–505
Etiqueta, Latin sexual value, 45
Eulenspiegel Society, 538, 539
Eve Plan
feminization in brain, 90
prenatal gender differentiation,
75–76, 78, 79, 80, 81
Excitement/plateau phase, 172, 174–182
females, 174–177, 179–180
males, 177–178, 182
myotonia, 174, 178, 179
vasocongestion, 174–178, 179
Exercise, in pregnancy, 221
Exhibitionism, 418, 534–536
definition of, 534–535
development of, 531
as male activity, 535
types of, 535
Extramarital sex, 475, 477–478
gender differences, 475, 477
tolerance of, 478
women, process in, 477, 478

F

Fallopian tubes
anatomical aspects, 151
ectopic pregnancy, 206
infection of, 151

False negative results, AIDS testing,
362–363
False positive results, AIDS testing, 363
False pregnancy, 217–218
Family, domestic partners, legal
definition, 491
Fantasy, erotic, 387–389
about female anatomy, 154–155
frequency of, 389
about gay types, 157
gender differences, 389
during intercourse, 388
about male anatomy, 155
masturbation fantasies, 388
positive uses of, 389
about rape, 608
taboo subjects and, 388
Fascinating Womanhood (Andelin), 24, 59
Fathers-to-be, couvade, 217–218
Fellatio, 400
Female anatomy
breasts, 153–154
clitoris, 147, 149
erection and, 149
fallopian tubes, 151
Grafenberg spot, 153
hymen, 149–150
labia, 146–147
mons veneris, 144–146
ovaries, 151–153
Skene's glands, 153
uterus, 151
vagina, 150
vulva, 146
Female condom, 253–254
Female disorders
cystitis, 311–312
cysts, 312
endometriosis, 310–311
fibroids, 312
hernia, 312
pelvic inflammatory disease, 307–309
prolapsed uterus, 312
vaginitis, 309–310
Female impersonators, 519
Feminine Mystique, The (Freidan), 21
Feminist International Network on the
New Reproductive Technologies,
235
Feminist pornography, 640
Feminists, view of love, 408
Feminization of poverty, 503
Feminization. *See* Gender differentiation
Femme Productions, 640
Fertilization, 204, 206
infertility
artificial insemination, 230–231

Fertilization (*Continued*)
    embryo transfer, 232–233
    surrogate motherhood, 232–236
    in vitro fertilization, 231–232
    ovum in, 204, 206
    sperm in, 204
    zygote, 206
Fetal alcohol syndrome, 215
Fetal period
    gender differentiation, 82–92
        external sexual anatomy, 86
        internal sexual anatomy, 83–85
        neurological aspects, 86, 88–92
Fetishes, 530, 541–542
    development of, 541, 542
    examples of, 541
Fetus
    maternal malnutrition and, 214
    quickening, 212
    second trimester, 212–213
    stages of, 211
    third trimester, 213–214
Fibroadenomas, 315
Fibrocystic disorder, 315
Fibroids, 312
    risk factors, 312
    treatment of, 312
Fixed worldview, 55–57, 59–60
    basic concepts in, 55, 56
    popular expression of, 59–60
    sexual values in, 56
Flagyl, 343
Fletcher, John 60
Flirting
    flirtation patterns, 419
    gender differences, 90, 421
    homosexuals, 419
    initiators of, 421
    nonverbal behaviors, 422
    process of
        approach, 419
        swivel or turn, 420
        synchronization, 420
        talk, 420
        touch, 420
Flower children, 21
Follicle-stimulating hormone, 115, 116,
        117, 118
Follicular phase, menstrual cycle, 118
Foods/herbs, as aphrodisiac, 385
Foot fetish, 541
Forceps-assisted delivery, 226
Foreskin, 160
Formal values, 53
Fornication, legal aspects, 586
Frank, Barney, 450
Franklin, Benjamin, 9

Fraternal twins, 208
Free love movement, 8
Freidan, Betty, 21
Freudian theory
    homosexuality and, 446
    intimacy, 413–414
    limitations of, 131–132
    pleasure principle, 378
    view of female orgasm, 184–185
    psychosexual development
        anal stage, 131, 132
        ego, 130
        genital stage, 131
        id, 130
        latency period, 131
        Oedipus complex, 131
        oral stage, 131, 132
        phallic stage, 131, 132
        superego, 130
    view of sexuality, 15
Friday, Nancy, 387, 423, 427
Frontier era, 10, 11–12
Frotteur, 538
Fundamentalism, television programs,
        56–57
Future Shock (Toffler), 466

G

Gagnon, John, 134, 567
Gang rape, 606–607
Gay, origins of term, 434
Gender, use of term, 72
Gender chromosomes, 77
Gender development
    post-natal gender assignment, 92
    post-natal gender scripting, 92–93
    puberty, 95–96
    variations in
        androgen insensitivity syndrome,
            97
        DHT deficiency, 98–99
        Klinefelter syndrome, 96–97
        Turner syndrome, 96
Gender differences
    erotic fantasy, 389
    extramarital sex, 475, 477
    first intercourse, 471–472
    flirting, 421
    intimacy, 423, 425
    masturbation, 391–392
    moral development and, 64, 65
    puberty, 114
Gender differentiation
    Adam plan, 76, 78, 79, 80
    in different species, 74–75
    Eve Plan, 75–76, 78, 79, 80, 81

external sexual anatomy, 86
feminization in brain, 90
    defeminization in brain, 90
    masculinization axis, 91
    neural template hypothesis, 89
fetal period, 82–92
genetic gender, 77–78
gonadal gender, 79
hormonal gender, 79–82
internal sexual anatomy, 83–85
neurological aspects, 86, 88–92
Gender dysphoria
    meaning of, 516
    prenatal events in, 517
    support groups, 523
    transgenderism, 520
    transsexualism, 521–523
    transvestism, 517–520
Gender identity
    core gender identity, 72, 516
    development in childhood, 94–95
    meaning of, 72
Gender nonconformity, 447–448
Gender orientation
    biases related to
        heterosexism, 452
        homophobia, 452, 454
    biological theories of, 445
    bisexuality, 451
    gender nonconformity, 447–448
    historical view, 434–435
    homosexuality, 448–451
    Kinsey's findings, 435–436
    labels and, 432
    meaning of, 95, 516
    panerotic potential, 457–459
    psychoanalytic theories of, 445–446
    same-gender sexual experimentation,
        438
    Sexual Orientation Grid, 438–439
    situational homosexuality, 437–438
    social learning theories of, 446
    use of term, 432–433, 434
Gender reassignment, in infancy,
        99–100
Gender role
    cultural variations, 38, 100
    gender-role behavior, 433
    learning of, 93–94
    meaning of, 72–73, 516
    scripting, 134–135, 136
Genesis, 56
Genetic counseling, 219–220
Genetics, prenatal gender
        differentiation, 75–79
Genital herpes, 345–347
    course of disease, 346

incidence of, 345
medical maintenance of, 347
types of viruses in, 346
Genitals
fetal period
external sexual anatomy, 86
internal sexual anatomy, 83–85
See also Female anatomy; Male anatomy.
Genital stage, 131
Gentle Birthing method, 225
Gerontophilia, 542
Ghandi, Indira, 37
Gilligan, Carol, 423
Gilligan's moral development model, 64–65
care perspective, 64, 65
compared to justice perspective, 65
Glans, 160
Gold Rush, sex ratio imbalances, 11–12
Gonadotropin-releasing hormones, 114
Gonads, gonadal gender, 79
Gonorrhea, 338–339
risks of, 339
symptoms of, 338
treatment of, 338–339
Grafenberg spot
anatomical aspects, 153
female ejaculation and, 186
location of, 185, 187
orgasm triggered by, 185
Graham, Sylvester, 6
Great Depression, sexual attitudes, 17
Group marriage, 485–486
definition of, 8
Oneida Community, 8
polyfidelity, 488
G spot. *See* Grafenberg spot
Guilt
contraceptive use and, 245
erotophobia, 135
masturbation, 391
religious perspective, 54
sexual fantasy and, 388
sexual restrictions and, 380–381
Guilt cultures, 31–32

H

Hair, 21
Hair, attitudes about female body hair, 145–146
Harlow, Harry, 413
Harlow, Margaret, 413
Health. *See* Sexual health
Hearing impairments, 510
Hefner, Hugh, 19

Hemophilus vaginalis, 338
Hepatitis B, 345
Hermaphrodites
DHT deficiency, 98–99
Retained Mullerian Syndrome, 85
Hernia, 312
Heteroerotic behavior, 441
Heteronomous stage, in moral development, 61–62
Heterosexism, 452
High sex ratio, 493
Hijras, 38, 100
Hinduism
homosexuality, 38
marriage, 37–38
nature of religion, 35
view of sex, 35–36
westernized Hindu cultures, 38–39
women's status, 36–37
Hippocratic oath, 280
H.L. v. Matheson, 287
Home birth, 226
Home tests, pregnancy, 208–209
Homoerotic behavior, 441, 442
Homophobia, 452, 454
Homosexuality, 448–451
aging process and, 499, 501–502
biases related to
heterosexism, 452
homophobia, 452, 454
biological theories of, 445
Chinese view, 40, 42
coming out process, 456
community, importance of, 449
developmental perspective, 440–441
clinical perspective, 442
legal perspective, 442
religious perspective, 442–444
sociological perspective, 442
statistical perspective, 441
flirting and, 419
gay, origin of term, 434
gay bashing, 452, 454
gay clergy, 451
gay politicians, 450–451
gay teachers, 453
gay teens, 449–450
gender nonconformity and, 447–448
in Hinduism, 38
Islamic view, 34
issues related to
family issues, 454
legal issues, 455
social issues, 451–454
liberal attitude towards, 24
married gays, 454
normalcy aspects, personal view, 440

parenthood, 472
pornography of, 641
psychoanalytic theory of, 445–446
relationships
characteristics of, 448–449
myths about, 449
sex therapy for gays, 568–569
social learning theory of, 446
stereotypes of, 452, 453
Stonewall Bar raid, 21, 24
Homosexual sex, 401
interfemoral intercourse, 401
love play and, 401
Honeymoon cystitis, 311
Hormones
breastfeeding, 229
libido and, 199
lifelong hormonal balance, 82
ovaries and, 151–152
of placenta, 211
prenatal gender differentiation, 76, 79–82
Adam Plan, 80–81
brain, 86, 88–91
development of sexual anatomy, 83–88
Eve Plan, 80
puberty, 95, 114–117, 161–162
brain and, 114
types of hormones, 115
Human chorionic gonadotropin hormone
immunization against, 275
placenta and, 211
pregnancy tests, 208
Human chorionic somatomammotropin, placenta and, 211
Human Genome Initiative Project, 220
Human immunodeficiency virus (HIV), 355–361
geographic origin of, 356
immune system and, 358–361
particle stage, 356
provirus stage, 356
reproductive stage, 356
sero positive persons, 361
spread of, 356–358
susceptibility to, 360–361
See also AIDS.
Humanism, ethical values of, 60–61
Human life
beginning of, in abortion issue, 285–286
personhood, 285–286
social birth, 286
viability of fetus, 286
Human Life Amendment, 285

Human Life Statute, 285
Human placental lactogen, 211
Human sexuality
    as bio-psycho-cultural phenome-
        non, 4
    major aspects of, 4
Hyaline membrane disease, 213
Hybristophilia, 532
Hymen
    anatomical aspects, 149–150
    natural rupture of, 149–150
Hyperphilia, 528
Hypophilia, 528
Hypothalamus, hormone production,
        114, 198

I

Id, 130
Identical twins, 208
Identity crisis, Erikson's theory, 133–134
Imitation research model, pornography,
        637
Immune system
    divisions of, 358
    HIV and, 358–361
Incest
    definition of, 612
    father-daughter incest, 613–614
    impact on child, 614
    incidence of, 613
    legal aspects, 592
Incubus, 197
Indecent exposure, legal aspects, 590
India, 35
    sex selection and abortion, 288–289
    See also Hinduism.
Industrialization, women and, 13–14
Inexperience, sexual, 384
Infanticide, female, 41
Infantilism, 532
Infants
    nurturance and intimacy, 413–414,
        416
    sexuality in, 106
Infertility
    artificial embryonation, 233
    artificial insemination, 230–231
    causes of, 229–230
    definition of, 229
    embryo adoption, 233
    embryo transfer, 232–233
    rise in sterility, 229
    surrogate motherhood, 232–236
    in vitro fertilization, 231–232
Infibulation, 165
Informal values, 52–53

Inhibited female orgasm, 575
Inhibited male orgasm, 573–574
Inhibited sexual arousal, 573
Inhibited sexual desire, 572
Insecurity, jealousy and, 425, 427
Intercourse, 396–397
    first intercourse, 470–472
    love manuals, 396
    positions for, 396, 397
Interfemoral intercourse, 401
International Planned Parenthood/
        World Population organization,
        founding of, 11
Interracial relationships
    legal aspects, 14, 586
    slavery era, 14
Intimacy
    avoiding intimacy, rules for, 424
    definition of, 406
    development of, 412–416
        early nurturance, 413–414
    gender differences, 423, 425
    SAD syndrome and, 413
    sexual goal of, 554–555
    types of, 422–423
Intimate networks, 483
Intra-amniotic infusion, procedure in,
        296–297
Intrauterine device (IUD), 261
    complications of, 21
    types in use, 21
Intrauterine growth retardation, 214
Intuition, female, 91
In vitro fertilization, 231–232
Iran, women in, 32–33
Islam
    homosexuality, 34
    marriage, 33–34
    number of followers, 30
    as shame culture, 32
    view of sex, 30–31
    westernized Islamic cultures, 34–35
    women's status, 32–33

J

Japan, pornography in, 645
Jealousy, 425–427
    coping with, 426–427
    cross-cultural view, 425–426
    other emotions related to, 425, 427
    sibling jealousy, 425–426
Jock itch, 322
John of the Cross, 458
Johnson, Virginia, 8, 170, 567
Jorgenson, Christine, 522
Joy of Sex, The (Comfort), 24, 393

Judaism, view of abortion, 280
Juvenilism, 532

K

Kama Shastra, 35
Kama Sutra, 35, 396
Kane, Elizabeth, 233–234
Kaplan, Helen Singer, 171, 567
Kaposi's sarcoma, 358
Karezza, 190
Kegel exercises, 222, 312
Khajuraho, temple of, 35
Kiddie porn, 641
    legal aspects, 592
Kimberly Clark Company, sanitary
        napkins, 11
Kinsey, Alfred, 17–18
Kinsey reports, 17–18, 184
    on gender orientation, 435–436
Kinsey Six Scale, 435, 437
Kissing, 393–394
Klein, Fred, 438
Klinefelter syndrome, 96–97
Klismaphilia, 532
Kohlberg's moral development model,
        134
    conventional morality, 62
    criticism of, 64
    postconventional morality, 62
    preconventional morality, 62
Konarak, temple of, 35
Koop, C. Everett, 25
Kundalini, 36

L

Labels, gender orientation and, 432
Labia
    anatomical aspects, 146–147
    lubrication of, 147
    major (outer) labia, 147
    minor (inner) labia, 147
    during plateau phase, 180
Labor, 221–223
    first stage, 222
    second stage, 222
    third stage, 222–224
La Leche League, 229
Lamaze delivery, 224
Lamaze, Fernand, 224
Lanugo, 213
Laparoscopy, 265
Latency period, 131
Latin cultures
    changes in modern world, 46
    sexual values
        etiqueta, 45

machismo, 45
marianismo, 45
pronatalism, 46
view of sex, 43–45
Leboyer delivery, 225
Legal codes, 582–583
Legislation
abortion, 22
case law, 583
consenting adult laws, 21, 586, 594
interracial relationships, 21
legal codes, 582–583
legal rights of adolescents, 125–126
marriage-related
adultery, 585–586
age of majority, 585
cohabitation, 586
fornication, 586
interracial marriage, 586
oral and anal sex, 587
prenuptial contracts, 587
surrogate motherhood, 586–587
protection of minors
abortion rights, 591
contraceptives, 591
incest, 592
kiddie porn, 592
privacy issue, 593
sexual abuse, 590–591
statutory rape, 590
public protection related
contraceptives, 588
lewd behavior, 588
sexually transmitted diseases, 589
sterilization laws, 588–589
work and pregnancy, 588
reasons for sex-related laws,
583–585
regulation of sex and, 582–583
roots of sex laws, 585
sexual-assault related
indecent exposure, 590
rape, 589, 592–593
sexual harassment, 590
voyeurism, 590
victimless crimes, 594
women's rights, 14
Leisure time, modern society, 465
Lesbians, artificial insemination and,
230
Lesbian Sex (Loulan), 142
Lewd behavior, legal aspects, 588
Libido, 130, 378
Lice, pubic lice, 341–342
Licensing, prostitution, 633
Lief, Harold, 567
Life expectancy, 464

Limerance, 418–419
definition of, 418
romantic vs. lusty limerance,
418–419
Limited information, 564–565
Lingam, 35
Lo Piccolo, Joseph, 567
Love
courtly love, 407
dating, 410–412
definition of, 406
historical view of, 406–410
intimacy, 422–427
jealousy, 425–427
vs. lust, 378–380
mate selection, 416–419
romantic love, 407–408
types of, ancient Greek view, 378
Love and Intimacy (Coutts), 427
Love manuals, 396
Lovemaps, 417–418
distortions to, 418, 530–531
displacement, 531
inclusion, 531
normophilic lovemap, 417–418
scripting, 135–136
Low sex ratio, 493
Lubricants, condom use and, 252
Lubrication
vaginal
aging and, 504
excitement phase, 176–177
plateau phase, 180
Lumpectomy, breast cancer, 315
Lung disease, 508
Lust vs. love, 378–380
Luteal phase, menstrual cycle, 120
Luteinizing hormone, 115, 116, 117
Lymphogranuloma venereum, 344

M

Machismo, Latin sexual value, 45
Macho scripting, 136
Maher v. Roe, 287
Maithuna, 190
Major (outer) labia, 147
Male anatomy
epididymis, 161
penis, 158–160
penis size, myths related to, 155–157
prostate gland, 163
scrotum, 160
seminal vesicles, 162
seminiferous tubules, 161
testes, 160–162
Male contraceptive pill, 275

Male Couple's Guide to Living Together
(Marcus), 142
Male disorders
balantis, 322
cryptorchidism, 321–322
dermatoses, 322
epididymitis, 321
priapism, 322
prostatitis, 321
varicocele, 322
Male prostitution, 629–630
Male rape, 606
Male Sexuality (Zilbergeldo), 155
Male strippers, 630–631
Mammary glands
anatomical aspects, 153
in men, 154
Mammogram, 315
Man-sharing, 486–488
black community, 486–487
patriarchal cultures and, 487–488
Mao Tse-tung, 41
Mapplethorpe, Robert, 593
Marianismo, Latin sexual value, 45
Marijuana, as aphrodisiac, 385
Marital rape, 607
Marriage
bisexual marriages, 485
Chinese culture, 41–42
closed marriage, 475
dual-paycheck marriage, 475
extramarital sex, 475, 477–478
group marriage, 485
in Hinduism, 37–38
Islamic religion, 33–34
laws related to, age of majority, 585
monogamy, 474–475
open marriage, 482–483
polygamy, 486
polygyny, 486
prenuptial contracts, 480
threesomes, 484–485
Marriage brokers, 411–412
Married Love (Stopes), 15
Martyr role, 427
Marvin v. Marvin, 479–480
Masculinization. *See* Gender
differentiation
Masochism
definition of, 538
development of, 531
See also Sadomasochism.
Massage, 396
Mastectomy, breast cancer, 315
Masters, William, 18, 170, 567
Masturbation, 390–392
anti-masturbation devices, 6–7

Masturbation (*Continued*)
 definition of, 390
 Ellis' view, 16
 fantasy during, 388
 Freudian view, 15
 guilt, 391
 historical view of, 391
 infancy/childhood, 108–109
 learning of, 109
 men and, 392
 parental views of, 127
 shared masturbation, 393
 teenagers and, 392
 women and, 391–392
Mate selection
 exchange aspects, 417
 limerance and, 418–419
 lovemaps and, 417–418
 social exchange theory, 416
 stimulus/value/role theory, 416
Mead, Margaret, 31
Media
 nudity and, 21
 sexual customs and, 18, 19–20
Medical advances
 antibiotics, 10, 11
 birth control, 10, 11
Meese Commission Report, 15
 on pornography, 638
Ménage a trois, 484
Menarche, 114
Menopause, 115, 504–505
 estrogen replacement therapy, 504–505
 osteoporosis in, 504
 symptoms of, 504
 vaginal atrophy in, 504
Menses, 117, 118
Menstrual cycle
 complications of
  amenorrhea, 122
  dysmenorrhea, 121–122
  premenstrual syndrome, 120–121
  toxic shock syndrome, 122
 follicular phase, 118
 luteal phase, 120
 menstruation, 118
 ovarian cycle, 117–118
 ovulation, 117, 118, 120
 proliferative phase, 118
 secretory phase, 120
 uterine cycle, 118
Menstruation, 118
Mental retardation, 511
Mexico City Policy, 288
Middle Ages
 homoerotic behavior, 442, 444
 view of love, 407

Midlife crisis, 503
Midwives, 226
Miller v. United States, 636
Minilaparotomy, 265
Minor (inner) labia, 147
Minors
 legal protection
  abortion rights, 591
  contraceptives, 591
  incest, 592
  kiddie porn, 592
  sexual abuse, 590–591
  statutory rape, 590
 rights and abortion, 287
Miscarriage, 215–216
Missionary position, 396
Mobility
 courtship and, 10
 modern society, 464–465
Model Penal Code, 594
Monogamy, 474–475
 definition of, 8
 evolution of, 474
Mons veneris, anatomical aspects, 144–146
Moral development
 gender differences and, 64, 65
 Gilligan's moral development, 64–65
 Kohlberg's moral development, 62-63
 Piaget's moral development, 61-62
 social development, 61
Moral Majority, 24, 25, 585
Morgan, Marabel, 24
Mormons, 7–8, 486
 polygyny, 7–8
Morning after pill, 293
Mullerian ducts, 83–85
Mullerian Inhibiting Hormone
 fetal period, 80–81, 83
 prenatal period, 76
Multiple orgasms
 men, 188–190
 women, 184
Muslims. *See* Islam
Mut'a, 34
Myotonia, excitement/plateau phase, 174, 178, 179
My Secret Garden (Friday), 387
Mysophilia, 532

N

National Organization of Non-Parents (NON), 22
Natural sins, 54
Necrophilia, 532, 542

Negative sexual experiences, sexual difficulty and, 559–560
Nepiophilia, 532
Neural template hypothesis, gender differentiation, 89
Neural tube defect, 219, 220
New Right, 25
New Sex Therapy, 567
Nipple, breast, 153
Nocturnal emissions, 197–198
 Medieval view of, 197–198
 stimulus in, 197, 198
 women, 198
Nonconformity, gender nonconformity, 447–448
Nongonococcal urethritis, 337
 risks of, 337
 symptoms of, 337
Nonoxynol-9 spermicide, AIDS precaution, 366
Nonverbal behaviors
 flirting, 422
 proceptivity, 90
Normophilia, 528
Norplant, 274
Norway, sex education, 128–129
Nurturance
 Harlow experiments, 413
 intimacy and early nurturance, 413–414
Nutrition/weight gain, pregnancy, 215

O

Obscene phone calls, 537
Obscenity, legal criteria, 15
Oedipus complex, 131
Off Our Backs, 641
Oneida Community, 8, 485
 control of ejaculation, 189–190
 group marriage, 8
O'Neil, George, 23, 482
O'Neil, Nena, 23, 482
Open marriage, 482–483
Open Marriage (O'Neil and O'Neil), 23
Opportunistic infections in AIDS, 358, 361
 Kaposi's sarcoma, 358
 pneumocystic pneumonia, 358
Oral contraceptives. *See* Birth control pills
Oral sex, 398–400
 cunnilingus, 398, 400
 fellatio, 400
 legal aspects, 587
 popularity of, 398
 sixty-nine, 400

Oral stage, 131, 132
Orgasm
    pubococcygeal muscle exercise and,
        187, 191
    surrender in, 193
    variations in men
        multiorgasm, 188–190
        retrograde ejaculation, 188
        two-stage orgasm, 188
    variation in women
        A-frame orgasms, 185
        blended orgasms, 185
        female ejaculation, 186–187
        G-spot and, 185
        multiple orgasms, 184
        sequential orgasms, 184
        tenting orgasms, 185
        uterine orgasm, 185
Orgasm difficulties
    inhibited female orgasm, 575
    inhibited male orgasm, 573–574
    premature ejaculation, 573
Orgasmic platform, 180
Orgasm phase, 172, 181, 182–191
    cardopedal reflex and, 182
    females, 184–188
    length of orgasm, 182
    males, 184, 188–190
    sensation of orgasm, 182
Orthodox Judaism
    on homosexuality, 454
    worldview in, 55, 56
Osteoporosis, in menopause, 504
Otto, Herbert, 553
Otto, Roberta, 553
Our Bodies, Ourselves (Boston Women's
    Health Collective), 142
Outercourse, 250
Ovarian cycle, 117–118, 152–153
Ovaries, anatomical aspects, 151–153
Ovulation, in menstrual cycle, 117, 118,
    120
Ovum
    chromosomes of, 77–78
    fertilization and, 204, 206
    in ovarian cycle, 152–153
    production of, 152
Oxytocin, breast milk and, 229

P

Painful intercourse, dyspareunia,
    575–576
Palimony, 479–480
Panerotic potential, 457–459
    model for, 457–459
    transcendental aspects, 458–459

Pap smear, 304–306
Paraphilia, 529–530
    bondage and dominance, 538–541
    common paraphilias, 532
    definition of, 529, 536
    development of, 530–531
    ephebophilia, 542
    exhibitionism, 534–536
    fetishes, 530, 541–542
    frotteur, 538
    gerontophilia, 542
    obscene phone calls, 537
    partners of paraphilias, 542–543
    sadomasochism (S & M), 538–541
    troilism, 537
    uncommon types of, 542
    voyeurism, 536–537
Parenting
    by homosexuals, 472
    single parents, 472
Patrilineage, definition of, 33
Pedophilia, 531–534
    children vulnerable to, 532, 533
    definition of, 531
    drug treatment of, 534
    psychological profile of, 534
Peer pressure, sexual difficulty and, 562
Peggy Lee syndrome, 472
Pelvic examination, 304–306
    comfort issues, 306
    frequency of, 306
    Pap smear, 304–306
    teenage years, 306
Pelvic inflammatory disease, 230,
    307–309
    cause of, 307–308
    chlamydia and, 335
    sterility and, 336
    symptoms of, 307, 335–336
    treatment, 308–309
Penicillin
    discovery of, 11
    gonorrhea treatment, 338–339
Penis
    anatomical aspects, 158–160
    erection, 159–160, 174, 177–178, 182
    self-examination of, 318
Penis rings, 7
Penis size, myths related to, 155–157
Performance fears, sexual difficulty and,
    561
Perfumed Garden, The, 396
Perineum, 147
Permission giving, in PLISSIT model,
    563, 564
Personal ads, 411
Personhood, in abortion issue, 285–286

Phallic stage, 131, 132
Pharonic circumcision, 165
Pheromones, 144
    meaning of, 198
    sources in humans, 198–199
Philia, 378
Piaget's moral development model,
    61–62, 134
    autonomous stage, 62
    egocentric stage, 61
    heteronomous stage, 61–62
Pituitary gland, 114, 151
Placenta, 210–211
    afterbirth, 222–223
    function of, 210–211
    hormones of, 211
Planned Parenthood of Central Missouri v.
    Danforth, 287
Plateau phase, 180
    See also Excitement/plateau stage.
Play, sociosexual play, 109–111
Playboy, 19, 644
Pleasure principle, 378
PLISSIT model, 563–566
    intensive therapy, 566
    limited information, 564–565
    permission giving, 563, 564
    sensate focus exercises, 565–566
    specific suggestions in, 565
Pneumocystic pneumonia, 358
Politics, gay politicians, 450–451
Polyfidelity, 488
Polygamy, 486
    Islamic culture, 33
Polygyny, 486
    definition of, 7
Poor
    abortion issue and, 287–288
    feminization of poverty, 503
Pornography
    censorship issue, 642–647
    definition of, 635
    versus erotica, 639–640
    federal studies
        Meese Commission (1986), 638
        Surgeon General Report (1986),
            639, 647
        White House Commission (1970),
            638, 644
    feminist pornography, 640
    feminist position on, 639–640,
        646–647
    homosexual porn, 641
    kiddie porn, 534, 641
    legal aspects, 592
    obscenity, legal history of, 635–636
    romance novels as, 640–641

Pornography (*Continued*)
   sexual violence and, 644–645
   telephone sex, 641–642
   theories of
      catharsis research model, 636–637
      imitation research model, 637
Postcoital hormonal contraception,
      293–295
   DES pill, 293
   RU 486, 293, 295
Postconventional morality, in moral
      development, 62
Postpartum depression, 218
Preconventional morality, in moral
      development, 62
Preeclampsia, 217
Pregnancy
   abnormal development, 215
   breasts in, 213
   diagnostic tests
      alpha-fetoprotein tests, 220
      amniocentesis, 218–219
      chordocentesis, 219
      chorionic villi biopsy, 219
      for Tay-Sachs, 220
      ultrasonic scanning, 219
   ectopic pregnancy, 206
   embryonic period, 210–211
   exercise during, 221
   fertilization, 204, 206
   fetal development, 211–214
   genetic counseling, 219–220
   issues related to, 209
   legal aspects, 588
   medical care, 214
   nutrition/weight gain, 215
   probable signs of, 208
   problems in
      false pregnancy, 217–218
      miscarriage, 215–216
      Rh factor, 216–217
      toxemia, 217
   sex during, 220
   twins, 208
   See also Childbirth.
Pregnancy tests, 208–210
   early, importance of, 209–210
   false positive/false negative readings,
      209
   HCG tests, 208
   home tests, 208–209
Premarital sex, courtship patterns,
      history of, 8–10
Premature ejaculation, 573
Premature infant
   maternal factors in, 213
   risks of, 213

Premenstrual syndrome, 120–121
Prenatal development, gender
      dysphoria, 517
Prenatal period
   gender differentiation
      Adam plan, 76, 78, 79, 80
      Eve Plan, 75–76, 78, 79, 80, 81
      external sexual anatomy, 86
      fetal period, 82–92
      genetic gender, 77–78
      gonadal gender, 79
      hormonal gender, 79–82
      internal sexual anatomy, 83–85
      neurological aspects, 86, 88–92
Prenatal testing
   alpha-fetoprotein tests, 220
   amniocentesis, 218–219
   chordocentesis, 219
   chorionic villi biopsy, 219
   for Tay-Sachs, 220
   ultrasonic scanning, 219
Prenuptial contracts, legal aspects, 587
Prepared childbirth, 223–224
   Lamaze delivery, 224
   Leboyer delivery, 225
Prepuce, 149, 160
Presley, Elvis, 20
Priapism, 322
Privacy, 593
   evolution of, 143
   as minor's right, 591
Proceptivity, meaning of, 90
Process worldview, 55–56, 57–60
   basic concepts in, 55, 57
   popular expression of, 60
   sexual values in, 56
Prochoice movement, 283–285
   beliefs of, 283–284
   constituents of, 283, 284
Proctoscope examination, 319
Progestasert, 21
Progesterone, 116, 118
Progestin implants, 274
Progestin-only pills, 262, 263
Progestins, paraphilic treatment, 545
Prolactin, breast milk and, 229
Prolapsed uterus, 312
Proliferative phase, menstrual cycle,
      118
Pronatalism, Latin sexual value, 46
Propulsion phase, ejaculation, 188, 195
Prostate
   anatomical aspects, 163
   elderly, prostate enlargement, 505
   prostate examinations, 319
Prostatitis, 321
   cause of, 321

symptoms of, 321
   treatment of, 321
Prostitution
   bordellos, 627
   brothels, 627
   call girls, 627
   coping approaches
      criminalization, 633–634
      decriminalization, 634–635
      licensing, 633
   costs of law enforcement, 632
   customers, profile of, 631
   escorts, 627
   historical view, 624–625
   lifestyles of, 627–629
   male prostitution, 629–630
   streetwalkers, 626–627
   teenage prostitution, 629
Protestantism
   view of abortion, 281
   view of love, 407–408
   worldview in, 55, 56
Pseudocyesis, 218
Psychoanalytic theories, of gender
      orientation, 445–446
Psychogenic sexual response, 170, 173
Psychological Care of the Infant and Child
      (Watson), 112
Psychological coercion, rape and,
      600–601
Psychophysiological model of sexual
      response, 193–194
   Erotic Stimulus Pathway Model, 193
Psychosexual development
   Erikson's theory, 132–134
   flow chart of events, 74
   Freudian view, 130–132
   scripting, 134–136
Psychosexual status, use of term, 72
Puberty
   adjustment during, 123
   definition of, 114
   female cycles
      luteal phase, 120
      menstruation, 118
      ovarian cycle, 117–118
      ovulation, 117, 118, 120
      secretory phase, 120
      uterine cycle, 118
   gender development, 95
   gender differences, 114
   hormones of, 114–117, 161–162
   males, physical complications,
      122–123
   menarche, 114
   secondary sex characteristics, 124
   split brain and, 91–92

Pubic hair
   attitudes about, 144–145
   shaving of, 35, 145
Pubic lice, 341–342
Public health issues, AIDS and, 371–372
Public policies, AIDS and, 368
Public protection
   laws related to
      contraceptives, 588
      lewd behavior, 588
      sexually transmitted diseases, 589
      sterilization laws, 588–589
      work and pregnancy, 588
Pubococcygeal muscle exercise, orgasm
      and, 187, 191
Puerperal fever, 10–11
Purdah, 32–33
Puritans, 5, 10
Pyromania, erotic type, 532

Q

Quickening, 212
Qur'an, 33, 34

R

Rape
   acquaintance rape, 603
   date rape, 602–606
   definitions of, 599–600
   fantasies about, 608
   gang rape, 606–607
   historical view, 598
   legal aspects, 589, 592–593
   male rape, 606
   marital rape, 607
   motivation for rape, 601–602
   observations, making during assault,
      614
   profile of rapist, 610–611
   psychological coercion, 600–601
   rape trauma syndrome, 615–616
   reducing risk of, 608–610
   reporting rape, 615
   resisting rape, 611–612
   silent signals of, 602
   statutory rape, 590, 607–608
   stranger rape, 602
Rape Victim's Privacy Act, 589
Reality (TM), female condom, 253–254
Rectal examinations, men, 319–320
Reflex arc, 194
Reflexogenic responses, 170
   ejaculation controls, 195, 197
   erection controls, 195
Refractory phase, 191
Reich, Wilhelm, 170

Relationships
   in changing society, 464–467
   couples, 474–480
   covenants, 488
   group marriage, 485–486
   intimate networks, 483
   man-sharing, 486–488
   open marriage, 482–483
   polyfidelity, 488
   singlehood, 468–474
   swinging, 480–482
   tension and sexual difficulty, 562–563
   threesomes, 484–485
Relativist worldview. *See* Process
      worldview
Religion
   abortion, historical view, 280–281
   contraceptive use and, 245
   cross-cultural views
      Confucianism, 40–41
      Hinduism, 35–39
      Islam, 30–35
      Taoism, 40–41
   gay clergy, 451
   homosexuality as issue, 442–444
   Mormons, 7–8
   Oneida Community, 8
   Puritans, 5
   sexual values and, 53–61
      fixed worldview, 55–57, 59–60
      guilt, 54
      humanism, 60–61
      natural/unnatural sins, 54
      process worldview, 55–56, 57–60
   Shakers, 7
Renaissance, view of love, 407
Retained Mullerian Syndrome, 85
Retarded ejaculation, 573
Retifism, 532
Retirement, modern society, 465
Retrograde ejaculation, 188
Rh factor, 216–217
   prevention of, 217
Rhythm method, 263
Roaring Twenties, 17
Rock music, sexual customs and, 20, 24
Roe v. Bolton, 282
Roe v. Wade, 22, 282–283
Roman Catholicism
   view of abortion, 281
   worldview in, 55, 56
Romance novels, as pornography,
      640–641
Romantic love, 407–408
Rossetti, Dante Gabriel, 458
Roth v. United States, 635
Rousseau, Jean-Jacques, 7

Royalle, Candida, 640
RU 486 abortion pill, 25, 274, 293, 295
   administration, 293
   FDA approval and, 293, 295
Rubella, 282
   prenatal effects, 215

S

Sadomasochism (S & M), 538–541
   activities in, 538, 540
   bondage and dominance activities,
      538
   common responses in, 539
   development of, 538
   organization for, 538, 539
   profile of couple, 539
   types of interests in, 540
Safe sex, practices of, 366–367
Sagan, Carl, 459
Sager, Clifford, 466
Salpingitis, 151
Same-gender sexual experimentation,
      438
Sanger, Margaret, 11, 16
Sanitary napkins, development of, 11
Scabies, 342–343
Schlafley, Phyllis, 273
School-based health clinics, 272, 273
Scripting, 134–136
   definition of, 135
   emotional responses to sexual cues,
      135
   gender roles, 134–135, 136
   gender scripting, 92
   lovemaps, 135–136
   macho scripting, 136
Scrotum
   anatomical aspects, 160
   during excitement phase, 178
Secondary sex characteristics, puberty,
      124
Second trimester, fetal development,
      212–213
Secretory phase, menstrual cycle, 120
Self-confidence, effect on sexual
      intimacy, 381
Self-examination
   breasts, 312–314, 318–319
   penis, 318
   testicles, 318
   vaginal, 302–304
   vulval, 303
Self-image, jealousy and, 425
Semen, composition of, 162–163
Seminal vesicles, anatomical aspects,
      162

Seminiferous tubules, anatomical aspects, 161
Sensate focus exercises, 565–566
Sensuous Man, The (Comfort), 24
Sequential orgasms, women, 184
Sero positive persons, AIDS, 361
Sex appeal, survey related to, 382
Sex-change operations, 522, 523–524
Sex education
  About Your Sexuality program, 129
  AIDS crisis and, 25
  AIDS related, 371
  early views, 16
  goals for, 127
  at home, 126–127
  inadequacy, reasons for, 129, 130
  in Norway, 128–129
  Surgeon General on, 25
  Tijuana bibles, 16
Sex Education and Information Council, 127, 129
Sex flush, 182
Sexless ones, hijras, 38
Sex Lives of College Students, 398
Sex ratio imbalances
  baby boom, 13
  historical view, 11–12
Sex ratios
  high sex ratio, 493
  low sex ratio, 493
Sex research
  Freudian theory, 15
  Kinsey report, 17–18
  Masters and Johnson, 18
Sex selection, abortion issue, 288–289
Sex skin, 180
Sex therapy
  combined therapies, 567–568
  finding therapist, 569–570
  for gay persons, 568–569
  Masters & Johnson, 567
  New Sex Therapy, 567
  PLISSIT model, 563–566
  use of term, 568
Sex toys, types of, 393
Sexual abuse
  at-risk children, 532, 533, 590–591
  consequences of, 533–534
  legal aspects, 591
  pedophiles and, 534
Sexual activity, singles, decision-making about, 469
Sexual addicts, 543–545
  cycle in addiction, 543–544
Sexual adequacy, definition of, 552
Sexual assault
  legal aspects

indecent exposure, 590
  rape, 589, 592–593
  sexual harassment, 590
  voyeurism, 590
Sexual aversion, 570
Sexual behavior
  normalcy aspects
    clinical perspective, 442
    developmental perspective, 440–441
    legal perspective, 442
    personal view, 440
    religious perspective, 442–444
    sociological perspective, 442
    statistical perspective, 441
  normal pattern, normophilia, 528
  unconventional patterns
    hyperphilia, 528
    hypophilia, 528
    paraphilia, 529–530
    sexual addicts, 543–545
    treatment of, 545
Sexual Behavior in the Human Female (Kinsey), 17–18
Sexual Behavior in the Human Male (Kinsey), 17
Sexual customs
  conservative trends, 24
  courtship patterns, 8–10
  cross-cultural views
    Chinese, 39–42
    Hindu world, 35–39
    Islamic world, 30–35
    Latin cultures, 43–47
  free love movement, 8
  frontier era, 5
  interracial relationships, 14
  legal trends, 14–15
  media and arts and, 18
  medical advances and, 10–11
  1950s
    media, 19–20
    Playboy philosophy, 19
    rock music, 20
  1960s
    consulting adult laws, 21
    sexual revolution, 21
    women's rights, 21
  1970s
    alternate lifestyles, 23–24
    homosexuality, 24
    liberal trends, 22–24
  1980s
    abortion issue, 25
    AIDS crisis, 25
    liberal trends, 24–25
    media, 24
    neoconservatism, 25

post-Civil War, 13–14
  religious influences, 4–8
    Mormons, 7–8
    Oneida Community, 8
    Puritans, 5
    Shakers, 7
  sex research and, 15–18
  shifting sex ratios and, 11–13
  Victorian era, 6–7
Sexual desire
  aphrodisiacs, 385–386
  chemical/neural elements, 386
  deterents to
    communication problems, 383
    guilt, 380
    intrapsychic factors, 384–385
    lack of self-confidence, 381
    sexual inexperience, 384
  historical conceptions of, 378–380
Sexual desire conflicts, 572
Sexual difficulty
  arousal phase difficulties, inhibited sexual arousal, 573
  biological causes, 559
  carousel dynamics of, 558
  childhood experiences and, 113
  cultural context and, 556
  desire phase difficulties
    inhibited sexual desire, 572
    sexual aversion, 570
    sexual desire conflicts, 572
  dysparenuia, 575–576
  erectile difficulty, 557
  inhibited female orgasm, 575
  interpersonal causes
    ignoring personal risk, 562
    peer pressure, 562
    social pressures, 562
    tension in relationship, 562–563
  most common causes of, 571
  orgasm difficulties
    inhibited male orgasm, 573–574
    premature ejaculation, 573
  primary sexual dysfunction, 557
  psychological causes
    body image, 560
    negative learning, 560
    negative sexual experiences, 559–560
    performance fears, 561
    stress, 560
  response stage difficulties, 555–556
  secondary sexual difficulty, 557
  vaginal spasms, 576
Sexual enrichment aids, for disabled, 511–511
Sexual fantasy orientation, 432

Sexual harassment
activities constituting harassment, 618
dealing with, 618–619
definitions of, 617–618
legal aspects, 590
myths/facts about, 619
Sexual health
breast disorders, 315–317
cryptorchidism, 321–322
balanitis, 322
dermatoses, 322
priapism, 322
varicocele, 322
DES affected persons, 317
doctor, choosing, 322–323
female disorders
cystitis, 311–312
cysts, 312
endometriosis, 310–311
fibroids, 312
hernia, 312
pelvic inflammatory disease,
307–309
prolapsed uterus, 312
vaginitis, 309–310
genital tuberculosis, 317
infectious mononucleosis, 317
male disorders
epididymitis, 321
prostatitis, 321
pelvic examination, 304–306
prostate examinations, 319
rectal examinations, 319–320
self-examination
breasts, 312–314, 318–319
penis, 318
testicles, 318
vaginal, 302–304
vulval, 303
self-image and, 302
Sexual Knowledge, 42
Sexually open marriage, 482–483
Sexually transmitted diseases (STD)
asymptomatic nature of, 328–329
candidiasis, 340–341
cervicitis, 335–337
chlamydia, 335–336
condom use and, 253
diaphragm use and, 257
factors in spread of, 330–331
future view, 349
genital herpes, 345–347
gonorrhea, 338–339
hemophilus vaginalis, 338
hepatitis B, 345
historical view, 331–332
incidence of, 329

legal aspects of, 334–335, 589
lymphogranuloma venereum, 344
medical care of, 347–348
nongonococcal urethritis, 337
pubic lice, 341–342
reducing risk of, 332–334
scabies, 342–343
sharing information with partner,
348–349
as Silent Epidemic, 328–329
syphilis, 339–340
trichomonas vaginalis, 343
venereal warts, 344–345
See also AIDS.
Sexual Orientation Grid, 438–439
Sexual pleasure
shared sex
anal sex, 401
homosexual sex, 401
intercourse, 396–397
kissing, 393–394
massage, 396
oral sex, 398–400
touch, 394–396
solo sex
erotic dreams, 386
masturbation, 390–392
sex toys, 393
sexual fantasies, 387–390
Sexual preference, use of term, 434
Sexual problems
examples of, 556
nature of, 556
See also Sexual difficulty.
Sexual response
control of
ejaculation controls, 195, 197
erection controls, 195
hormones, 198, 199
nocturnal emissions, 197–198
pheromones, 198–199
desire phase, 171, 173
excitement/plateau phase, 172,
174–182
females, 174–177, 179–180
males, 177–178, 182
myotonia, 174, 178, 179
vasocongestion, 174–178, 179
Kaplan's view, 171
limitations in model of, 171
Masters and Johnson phases, 170,
171
orgasm phase, 172, 181, 182-191
females, 184–188
length of orgasm, 182
males, 184, 188–190
sensation of orgasm, 182

psychogenic sexual response, 170, 173
psychophysiological model, 193–194
Erotic Stimulus Pathway Model,
193
reflexogenic sexual response, 170
Reichian view, 170
resolution stage, 172, 182, 191, 194
Sexual revolution, 21
Sexual satisfaction, of elderly, 498
Sexual skills, 550–552
Sexual unfolding, aspects of, 550
Sexual violence, pornography and,
644–645
Shakers, 7
Shame cultures, 32
Siblings
sexual play, 111
sibling jealousy, 425–426
Silastic vaginal rings, 274
Silent Epidemic, sexually transmitted
disease as, 328
Simon, William, 134, 567
Sin
natural sins, 54
unnatural sins, 54
Singlehood, 468–474
celibacy, 470
creative singlehood, 474
divorce, 489–490
first intercourse, 470–472
research findings related to, 471
sexual activity, decision-making
about, 469
single parents, 472
statistical information, 468–469
widowhood, 490
Single parenthood, 472
as option to abortion, 289
parenthood by choice, 472
statistical information, 472, 473
Situational homosexuality, 437–438
Situation Ethics (Fletcher), 60
Sixty-nine, 400
Skene's glands, 186
anatomical aspects, 153
Slang expressions
breast, 154
ejaculation, 163
female genitals, 146, 149
penis, 159, 160
syphilis, 339
Slavery, sexual customs and, 14
Smegma, 160
Social birth, in abortion issue, 286
Social exchange theory, mate selection,
416
Socialization, sexuality and, 107–108

Social learning theories, of gender orientation, 446
Social pressures, sexual difficulty and, 562
Society
  changes related to
    contraception, 466
    leisure time, 465
    life expectancy, 464
    mobility, 464–465
    retirement, 465
    of women's status, 465–466
Society for the Second Self, 523
Somatosensory Affectional Deprivation Syndrome, 413
Spectatoring, 561
Speculum, use in self-examination, 303–304
Sperm
  chromosomes of, 77–78
  fertilization and, 204
Sperm count, low, 229, 230
Spermicidal foams, 254–255
  complications of, 255
  cost, 254
  effectiveness, 254
  noncontraceptive benefits, 255
  precautions, 255
  proper use of, 254
Spina bifida, 219
Squeal laws, 591
Starr-Weiner Report on Sex and Sexuality in the Mature Years, 498–499
Statutory rape, 590, 607–608
Stayton, William, 457–458
Steptoe, Dr., 232
Sterility
  rise in, 229
  sexually transmitted disease and, 336, 337, 339
  See also Infertility.
Sterilization
  legal aspects, 588–589
  tubal ligation, 265–266
  vasectomy, 266–267
Stern, William and Elizabeth, 234–235
Stimulus/value/role theory, mate selection, 416
Stirpiculture, 8
Stonewall Bar raid, 21, 24
Stopes, Marie, 15
Stop-Go exercise, 574
Streetwalkers, 626–627
Stress, sexual difficulty and, 560
Studds, Gerry E., 450
Succubus, 197
Suffrage movement, 14

Suicide, gay teens, 450
Superego, 130
Surgeon General
  on AIDS, 368
  on pornography, 639, 647
  on sex education, 25
Surrogate motherhood, 232–236
  artificial embryonation, 233
  controversy related to, 233–236
  embryo adoption, 233
  legal aspects, 586–587
Swinging, 480–482
  couples and, 481
  profile of swingers, 481–482
  as social activity, 481
  swing clubs, 481
Sympto-thermal method, 264–265
  effectiveness, 264–265
  noncontraceptive benefits, 265
  precautions, 265
Synchronization, in flirting, 420
Syphilis, 339–340
  historical view, 331
  slang expressions, 339
  stages of, 339–340
  treatment, 340

T

Taboos, social taboos, 583
Tantric yoga, 36
Taoism, 39
  view of sex, 40–41
Tay-Sachs disease, 220
T cells, immunity, 358
Teachers, gay teachers, 453
Teenage pregnancy, 269–274
  costs of, 273–274
  cross-cultural view, 269
  programs related to, 271
    school-based health clinics, 272, 273
  statistical information on, 269–270
Teenagers
  gay teens, 449–450
  masturbation and, 392
  teenage prostitution, 629
Telephone sex, 538, 542, 641–642
Television, sexual customs and, 19–20
Temporary marriage, 33–34
Tennov, Dorothy, 418
Tenting effect, 180
Tenting orgasms, women, 185
Teresa of Avila, 458
Testes
  anatomical aspects, 160–162
  during excitement phase, 178

  during plateau phase, 182
  self-examination of, 318
Testicular feminization, 97
Testis Determining Factor, 78
Testosterone, 116, 161
  prenatal period, 76
Test-tube baby, 22
Thalidomide, 215, 282
Theater of God, 396
Third trimester, fetal development, 213–214
Third World, abortion issue and, 288
Threesomes, 484–485
Thrush, 341
Tijuana bibles, 16
Tinea cruris, 322
Tipton, Billy, 517
Toffler, Alvin, 466, 489
Toilet training, 106
Total Sex (Otto and Otto), 553
Total Woman, The (Morgan), 24
Touch, 394–396
  importance in childhood, 112–113, 114
  kissing, 393–394
Toxemia, 217
  characteristics of, 217
Toxic shock syndrome, 122
  contraceptive sponge and, 259
  risk factors, 122
  symptoms of, 122
Traditional Indian Art of Baby Massage, The (Leboyer), 225
Transgenderism, 520
  characteristics of, 521
  use of term, 520–521
Transsexualism, 521–523
  sex-change operations, 522, 523–524
Transvestism, 517–520
  cross-cultural view, 520
  crossdressing, 518–519
  female impersonators, 519
  myths about, 518
  relationships of, 519–520
Trichomonas vaginalis, 343
  symptoms of, 343
  treatment of, 343
Troilism, 532, 537
Tubal ligation, 265–266
  complications, 266
  cost, 265
  laparoscopy, 265
  minilaparotomy, 265
  noncontraceptive benefits, 266
  precautions, 266
Tuberculosis, genital, 317
Tumescence, 174

Turner syndrome, 96
Twins, 208
  fraternal twins, 208
  identical twins, 208
Two-stage orgasm, men, 188

U

Ultrasonic scanning, 219
Umbilical cord, 211
Undescended testes
  cause of, 321
  treatment of, 322
Undinism, 532
Unnatural sins, 54
Urophilia, 532
Uterine cycle, 118
Uterine orgasm, 185
Uterus
  anatomical aspects, 151
  during plateau phase, 180
  prolapsed uterus, 312
Utopian socialists, 7, 8

V

Vacuum curettage
  development of, 282
  procedure in, 295–296
Vagina
  anatomical aspects, 150
  myths related to, 150
  self-examination of, 302–304
  and sexual arousal, 150
Vaginal atrophy, in menopause, 504
Vaginal contraceptive film, 256–257
  complications, 257
  cost, 256
  effectiveness, 256
  noncontraceptive advantages, 257
  precautions, 257
  proper use of, 256–257
Vaginal spasms, 576
Vaginal suppositories, 255
  complications, 255
  cost, 255
  effectiveness, 255
  noncontraceptive benefits, 255
  precautions, 255
  proper use of, 255
Vaginismus, 576
Vaginitis, 309–310
  causes of, 309
  prevention guidelines, 309–310
Values
  development of
    Gilligan's moral development, 64–65

Kohlberg's moral development, 62–63
    Piaget's moral development, 61–62
    social development, 61
  formal values, 53
  future view of, 64–66
  informal values, 52–53
  religion and, 53–61
    fixed worldview, 55–57, 59–60
    guilt, 54
    humanism, 60–61
    natural/unnatural sins, 54
    process worldview, 55–56, 57–60
Varicocele, 322
Vas deferens, 161
Vasectomy, 266–267
  complications, 267
  cost, 266
  noncontraceptive benefits, 267
  precautions, 267
  procedure in, 267
Vasocongestion, excitement/plateau phase, 174–178, 179
Venereal warts, 344–345
  spread of, 344–345
  treatment of, 345
Vernix caseosa, 213
Viability of fetus, in abortion issue, 286
Victimless crimes, 594
Victorian era, 6–7, 10
  anti-masturbation devices, 6–7
  antisexual values, 6
  circumcision practices, 164
  Freudian view, 15
  gender roles in, 6
  removal of clitoris, 164
  view of female orgasm, 184
  view of love, 408
Videolaseroscopy, 310
Violence
  attitudes of violence-oriented persons, 415
  early nurturance and, 413
Virginity
  hymen and, 149–150
  in Latin cultures, 45
  outercourse and, 250
Visual impairments, 509
Voyeurism, 418, 536–537
  act of, 536
  legal aspects, 590
  psychological profile of voyeur, 536
Vulva
  anatomical aspects, 146
  self-examination of, 303

W

Walker, Mary, 517
War, sexual customs and, 13–14
Warts, venereal warts, 344–345
Watson, John B., 112
Webster v. Reproductive Health Services, 25
Weight gain, in pregnancy, 214
Western Blot test, AIDS testing, 363
Whitehead, Mary Beth, 234–235
White House Commission (1970), on pornography, 638, 644
Widowhood, 490
Wise Parenthood (Stopes), 15
Withdrawal method, 268
Wolffian ducts, 83, 84
Women
  financial independence of, 465–466
  in Hinduism, 36–37
  impact of war on, 13, 14
  in Islamic culture, 32–33
  moral development, 64
Women Against Pornography, 646
Women's rights
  Constitution and, 14
  financial independence of women, 465–466
  suffrage movement, 14
  women's liberation movement, 21
Woodhull, Victoria, 8
Woodstock, 21
Worldviews
  fixed worldview, 55–57, 59–60
  humanism, 60–61
  process worldview, 55–56, 57–60
World War I, sexual customs and, 14
World War II, sexual customs and, 14

X

X-rated videotapes, 536

Y

Yeast infection. *See* Candidiasis
Yin and yang, 459
  definition of, 40
Yoga practice, control of ejaculation, 189–190
Yohimbe, as aphrodisiac, 386
Yoni, 35

Z

Zero population growth, 23
Zoophobia, 542
Zovirax, 347
Zygote, 206